Economic Growth

Second Edition

Robert J. Barro
Xavier Sala-i-Martin

The MIT Press
Cambridge, Massachusetts
London, England

This book was set in Times Roman by ICC Typesetting and was printed and bound in the United States of America.

Library of Congress Cataloging-in-Publication Data

Barro, Robert J.
Economic growth / Robert J. Barro, Xavier Sala-i-Martin—2nd ed.
p. cm.
Includes bibliographical references and index.
ISBN-13 978-0-262-02553-9
ISBN-10 0-262-02553-1
1. Economic development—Mathematical models. I. Sala-i-Martin, Xavier. II. Title.

HD75.5.B37 2003
338.9′001′51—dc22

2003059392

10 9 8 7 6

To Rachel
—Robert J. Barro

A la memòria dels meus estimats Joan Martín Pujol i Ramon Oriol Martín Montemayor
—Xavier Sala-i-Martin

Contents

Preface xv
About the Authors xvii

Introduction 1
I.1 The Importance of Growth 1
I.2 The World Income Distribution 6
I.3 Empirical Regularities about Economic Growth 12
I.4 A Brief History of Modern Growth Theory 16
I.5 Some Highlights of the Second Edition 21

1 Growth Models with Exogenous Saving Rates (the Solow–Swan Model) 23
1.1 The Basic Structure 23
1.2 The Neoclassical Model of Solow and Swan 26
1.2.1 The Neoclassical Production Function 26
1.2.2 The Fundamental Equation of the Solow–Swan Model 30
1.2.3 Markets 31
1.2.4 The Steady State 33
1.2.5 The Golden Rule of Capital Accumulation and Dynamic Inefficiency 34
1.2.6 Transitional Dynamics 37
1.2.7 Behavior of Input Prices During the Transition 40
1.2.8 Policy Experiments 41
1.2.9 An Example: Cobb–Douglas Technology 43
1.2.10 Absolute and Conditional Convergence 44
1.2.11 Convergence and the Dispersion of Per Capita Income 50
1.2.12 Technological Progress 51
1.2.13 A Quantitative Measure of the Speed of Convergence 56
1.3 Models of Endogenous Growth 61
1.3.1 Theoretical Dissatisfaction with Neoclassical Theory 61
1.3.2 The *AK* Model 63
1.3.3 Endogenous Growth with Transitional Dynamics 66
1.3.4 Constant-Elasticity-of-Substitution Production Functions 68
1.4 Other Production Functions . . . Other Growth Theories 71
1.4.1 The Leontief Production Function and the Harrod–Domar Controversy 71
1.4.2 Growth Models with Poverty Traps 74

1.5 Appendix: Proofs of Various Propositions 77
1.5.1 Proof That Each Input Is Essential for Production with a Neoclassical Production Function 77
1.5.2 Properties of the Convergence Coefficient in the Solow–Swan Model 78
1.5.3 Proof That Technological Progress Must Be Labor Augmenting 78
1.5.4 Properties of the CES Production Function 80
1.6 Problems 81

2 Growth Models with Consumer Optimization (the Ramsey Model) 85
2.1 Households 86
2.1.1 Setup of the Model 86
2.1.2 First-Order Conditions 89
2.2 Firms 94
2.3 Equilibrium 97
2.4 Alternative Environments 98
2.5 The Steady State 99
2.6 Transitional Dynamics 102
2.6.1 The Phase Diagram 102
2.6.2 The Importance of the Transversality Condition 104
2.6.3 The Shape of the Stable Arm 105
2.6.4 Behavior of the Saving Rate 106
2.6.5 The Paths of the Capital Stock and Output 110
2.6.6 Speeds of Convergence 111
2.6.7 Household Heterogeneity 118
2.7 Nonconstant Time-Preference Rates 121
2.7.1 Results under Commitment 123
2.7.2 Results without Commitment under Log Utility 124
2.7.3 Population Growth and Technological Progress 129
2.7.4 Results under Isoelastic Utility 130
2.7.5 The Degree of Commitment 132
2.8 Appendix 2A: Log-Linearization of the Ramsey Model 132
2.9 Appendix 2B: Irreversible Investment 134

2.10 Appendix 2C: Behavior of the Saving Rate 135
2.11 Appendix 2D: Proof That $\gamma_{\hat{k}}$ Declines Monotonically If the Economy Starts from $\hat{k}(0) < \hat{k}^*$ 137
2.12 Problems 139

3 Extensions of the Ramsey Growth Model 143
3.1 Government 143
3.1.1 Modifications of the Ramsey Framework 143
3.1.2 Effects of Tax Rates 146
3.1.3 Effects of Government Purchases 147
3.2 Adjustment Costs for Investment 152
3.2.1 The Behavior of Firms 152
3.2.2 Equilibrium with a Given Interest Rate 155
3.2.3 Equilibrium for a Closed Economy with a Fixed Saving Rate 159
3.3 An Open-Economy Ramsey Model 161
3.3.1 Setup of the Model 161
3.3.2 Behavior of a Small Economy's Capital Stock and Output 162
3.3.3 Behavior of a Small Economy's Consumption and Assets 163
3.3.4 The World Equilibrium 164
3.4 The World Economy with a Constraint on International Credit 165
3.4.1 Setup of a Model with Physical and Human Capital 166
3.4.2 The Closed Economy 167
3.4.3 The Open Economy 168
3.5 Variations in Preference Parameters 177
3.6 Economic Growth in a Model with Finite Horizons 179
3.6.1 Choices in a Model with Finite Horizons 179
3.6.2 The Finite-Horizon Model of a Closed Economy 183
3.6.3 The Finite-Horizon Model of an Open Economy 186
3.7 Some Conclusions 189
3.8 Appendix: Overlapping-Generations Models 190
3.8.1 Households 190
3.8.2 Firms 192
3.8.3 Equilibrium 193
3.9 Problems 200

4 One-Sector Models of Endogenous Growth 205
4.1 The *AK* Model 205
4.1.1 Behavior of Households 205
4.1.2 Behavior of Firms 206
4.1.3 Equilibrium 207
4.1.4 Transitional Dynamics 208
4.1.5 The Phase Diagram 209
4.1.6 Determinants of the Growth Rate 210
4.2 A One-Sector Model with Physical and Human Capital 211
4.3 Models with Learning by Doing and Knowledge Spillovers 212
4.3.1 Technology 212
4.3.2 Equilibrium 216
4.3.3 Pareto Nonoptimality and Policy Implications 216
4.3.4 A Cobb–Douglas Example 217
4.3.5 Scale Effects 218
4.4 Public Services and Endogenous Growth 220
4.4.1 A Public-Goods Model 220
4.4.2 A Congestion Model 223
4.5 Transitional Dynamics, Endogenous Growth 226
4.5.1 A Cobb–Douglas Example 226
4.5.2 A CES Example 230
4.6 Concluding Observations 232
4.7 Appendix: Endogenous Growth in the One-Sector Model 232
4.8 Problems 235

5 Two-Sector Models of Endogenous Growth (with Special Attention to the Role of Human Capital) 239
5.1 A One-Sector Model with Physical and Human Capital 240
5.1.1 The Basic Setup 240
5.1.2 The Constraint of Nonnegative Gross Investment 242
5.2 Different Technologies for Production and Education 247
5.2.1 The Model with Two Sectors of Production 247
5.2.2 The Uzawa–Lucas Model 251
5.2.3 The Generalized Uzawa–Lucas Model 266
5.2.4 The Model with Reversed Factor Intensities 267
5.3 Conditions for Endogenous Growth 268

5.4 Summary Observations 271
5.5 Appendix 5A: Transitional Dynamics with Inequality Restrictions on Gross Investment in the One-Sector Model 271
5.6 Appendix 5B: Solution of the Uzawa–Lucas Model 274
5.7 Appendix 5C: The Model with Reversed Factor Intensities 280
5.8 Problems 282

6 Technological Change: Models with an Expanding Variety of Products 285

6.1 A Baseline Model with a Variety of Products 285
6.1.1 The Producers of Final Output 285
6.1.2 Research Firms 289
6.1.3 Households 295
6.1.4 General Equilibrium 295
6.1.5 Determinants of the Growth Rate 297
6.1.6 Pareto Optimality 297
6.1.7 Scale Effects and the Cost of R&D 300
6.1.8 A Rising Cost of R&D 303
6.2 Erosion of Monopoly Power, Competition 305
6.3 Romer's Model of Technological Change 310
6.4 Concluding Observations 313
6.5 Problems 313

7 Technological Change: Schumpeterian Models of Quality Ladders 317

7.1 Sketch of the Model 317
7.2 The Model 319
7.2.1 The Producers of Final Output: Levels of Quality in the Production Technology 319
7.2.2 The Research Sector 321
7.2.3 Consumers 328
7.2.4 Behavior of the Aggregate Quality Index and Endogenous Growth 329
7.2.5 Scale Effects Again 331
7.3 Innovation by the Leader 333
7.3.1 Interactions Between the Leader and the Outsiders 333
7.3.2 The Leader as a Monopoly Researcher 336

7.4 Pareto Optimality 339
7.5 Summary Observations about Growth 342
7.6 Appendix 343
7.6.1 Intermediates of Various Quality Grades 343
7.6.2 The Duration of a Monopoly Position 345
7.6.3 The Market Value of Firms 346
7.6.4 Research by the Industry Leader 346
7.7 Problems 347

8 The Diffusion of Technology 349
8.1 Behavior of Innovators in the Leading Country 351
8.2 Behavior of Imitators in the Follower Country 352
8.2.1 Producers of Final Output 352
8.2.2 Imitating Firms 353
8.2.3 Consumers 357
8.2.4 Steady-State Growth 357
8.2.5 The Dynamic Path and Convergence 359
8.3 Constant (or Slowly Rising) Costs of Imitation 363
8.3.1 The Steady State 364
8.3.2 Transitional Dynamics 365
8.4 Foreign Investment and Intellectual Property Rights 368
8.5 General Implications for Growth Rates in Follower Countries 370
8.6 Switchovers of Technological Leadership, Leapfrogging 373
8.7 Welfare Considerations 376
8.8 Summary Observations about Diffusion and Growth 379
8.9 Problems 380

9 Labor Supply and Population 383
9.1 Migration in Models of Economic Growth 383
9.1.1 Migration in the Solow–Swan Model 384
9.1.2 Migration in the Ramsey Model 393
9.1.3 The Braun Model of Migration and Growth 398
9.2 Fertility Choice 407
9.2.1 An Overlapping-Generations Setup 408
9.2.2 The Model in Continuous Time 411
9.3 Labor/Leisure Choice 422

9.4 Appendix: The Form of the Utility Function with Consumption and Work Effort 427
9.5 Problems 428

10 Growth Accounting 433
10.1 Standard Primal Growth Accounting 433
10.1.1 Basic Setup 433
10.1.2 Measuring Inputs 436
10.1.3 Results from Growth Accounting 438
10.1.4 A Note on Regression-Based Estimates of TFP Growth 441
10.2 Dual Approach to Growth Accounting 442
10.3 Problems with Growth Accounting 444
10.3.1 An Increasing-Returns Model with Spillovers 445
10.3.2 Taxes 447
10.3.3 Multiple Types of Factors 449
10.4 TFP Growth and R&D 450
10.4.1 Varieties Models 451
10.4.2 Quality-Ladders Models 454
10.5 Growth Accounting Versus Sources of Growth 457

11 Empirical Analysis of Regional Data Sets 461
11.1 Two Concepts of Convergence 462
11.2 Convergence Across the U.S. States 466
11.2.1 β Convergence 466
11.2.2 Measurement Error 472
11.2.3 σ Convergence 473
11.3 Convergence Across Japanese Prefectures 474
11.3.1 β Convergence 474
11.3.2 σ Convergence Across Prefectures 478
11.4 Convergence Across European Regions 479
11.4.1 β Convergence 479
11.4.2 σ Convergence 482
11.5 Convergence Across Other Regions Around the World 482
11.6 Migration Across the U.S. States 483
11.7 Migration Across Japanese Prefectures 486
11.8 Migration Across European Regions 490

11.9 Migration and Convergence 492
11.10 β Convergence in Panel Data with Fixed Effects 495
11.11 Conclusions 496
11.12 Appendix on Regional Data Sets 497
11.12.1 Data for U.S. States 497
11.12.2 Data for European Regions 500
11.12.3 Data for Japanese Prefectures 506

12 Empirical Analysis of a Cross Section of Countries 511
12.1 Losers and Winners from 1960 to 2000 511
12.2 An Empirical Analysis of Growth Rates 515
12.2.1 Effects from State Variables 517
12.2.2 Control and Environmental Variables 518
12.3 Regression Results for Growth Rates 521
12.3.1 A Basic Regression 521
12.3.2 Tests of Stability of Coefficients 534
12.3.3 Additional Explanatory Variables 535
12.4 Summary and Conclusions about Growth 541
12.5 Robustness 541
12.5.1 Levine and Renelt (1992) 542
12.5.2 Bayesian Averaging of Classical Estimates (BACE) 543
12.5.3 Main Results in Sala-i-Martin, Doppelhofer, and Miller (2003) 547
12.5.4 Robustness Analysis 556
12.6 Appendix: Long-Term Data on GDP 559

Appendix on Mathematical Methods 567
A.1 Differential Equations 568
A.1.1 Introduction 568
A.1.2 First-Order Ordinary Differential Equations 569
A.1.3 Systems of Linear Ordinary Differential Equations 576
A.2 Static Optimization 597
A.2.1 Unconstrained Maxima 597
A.2.2 Classical Nonlinear Programming: Equality Constraints 598
A.2.3 Inequality Constraints: The Kuhn–Tucker Conditions 600
A.3 Dynamic Optimization in Continuous Time 604
A.3.1 Introduction 604

A.3.2 The Typical Problem 605
A.3.3 Heuristic Derivation of the First-Order Conditions 606
A.3.4 Transversality Conditions 609
A.3.5 The Behavior of the Hamiltonian over Time 609
A.3.6 Sufficient Conditions 610
A.3.7 Infinite Horizons 610
A.3.8 Example: The Neoclassical Growth Model 612
A.3.9 Transversality Conditions in Infinite-Horizon Problems 613
A.3.10 Summary of the Procedure to Find the First-Order Conditions 615
A.3.11 Present-Value and Current-Value Hamiltonians 616
A.3.12 Multiple Variables 617

A.4 Useful Results in Matrix Algebra: Eigenvalues, Eigenvectors, and Diagonalization of Matrices 618

A.5 Useful Results in Calculus 620
A.5.1 Implicit-Function Theorem 620
A.5.2 Taylor's Theorem 621
A.5.3 L'Hôpital's Rule 622
A.5.4 Integration by Parts 623
A.5.5 Fundamental Theorem of Calculus 624
A.5.6 Rules of Differentiation of Integrals 624

References 627
Index 641

Preface

Is there some action a government of India could take that would lead the Indian economy to grow like Indonesia's or Egypt's? If so, what, *exactly? If not, what is it about the "nature of India" that makes it so? The consequences for human welfare involved in questions like these are simply staggering: Once one starts to think about them, it is hard to think about anything else.*[1]
—Robert E. Lucas, Jr. (1988)

Economists have, in some sense, always known that growth is important. Yet, at the core of the discipline, the study of economic growth languished after the late 1960s. Then, after a lapse of two decades, this research became vigorous again in the late 1980s. The new research began with models of the determination of long-run growth, an area that is now called endogenous growth theory. Other recent research extended the older, neoclassical growth model, especially to bring out the empirical implications for convergence across economies. This book combines new results with expositions of the main research that appeared from the 1950s through the beginning of the 2000s. The discussion stresses the empirical implications of the theories and the relation of these hypotheses to data and evidence. This combination of theory and empirical work is the most exciting aspect of ongoing research on economic growth.

The introduction motivates the study, brings out some key empirical regularities in the growth process, and provides a brief history of modern growth theory. Chapters 1 and 2 deal with the neoclassical growth model, from Solow–Swan in the 1950s, to Cass–Koopmans (and recollections of Ramsey) in the 1960s, to recent refinements of the model. Chapter 3 deals with extensions to incorporate a government sector and to allow for adjustment costs in investment, as well as with the open economy and finite-horizon models of households. Chapters 4 and 5 cover the versions of endogenous growth theory that rely on forms of constant returns to reproducible factors. Chapters 6, 7, and 8 explore recent models of technological change and R&D, including expansions in the variety and quality of products and the diffusion of knowledge. Chapter 9 allows for an endogenous determination of labor supply and population, including models of migration, fertility, and labor/leisure choice. Chapter 10 works out the essentials of growth accounting and applies this framework to the endogenous growth models. Chapter 11 covers empirical analysis of regions of countries, including the U.S. states and regions of Europe and Japan. Chapter 12 deals with empirical evidence on economic growth for a broad panel of countries from 1960 to 2000.

1. These inspirational words from Lucas have probably become the most frequently quoted passage in the growth literature. Thus it is ironic (and rarely mentioned) that, even while Lucas was writing his ideas, India had already begun to grow faster than Indonesia and Egypt. The growth rates of GDP per person from 1960 to 1980 were 3.2% per year in Egypt, 3.9% in Indonesia, and 1.5% in India. In contrast, from 1980 to 2000, the growth rates of GDP per person were 1.8% per year in Egypt, 3.5% in Indonesia, and 3.6% in India. Thus, the Indian government seems to have met Lucas's challenge, whereas Egypt was faltering.

The material is written as a text at the level of first-year graduate students in economics. The widely used first edition has proven successful for graduate courses in macroeconomics, economic growth, and economic development. Most of the chapters include problems that guide the students from routine exercises through suggestive extensions of the models. The level of mathematics includes differential equations and dynamic optimization, topics that are discussed in the mathematical appendix at the end of the book. For undergraduates who are comfortable with this level of mathematics, the book works well for advanced, elective courses. The first edition has been used at this level throughout the world.

We have benefited from comments by Daron Acemoglu, Philippe Aghion, Minna S. Andersen, Marios Angeletos, Elsa V. Artadi, Abhijit Banerjee, Paulo Barelli, Gary Becker, Olivier Blanchard, Juan Braun, Francesco Caselli, Paul Cashin, Daniel Cohen, Irwin Collier, Diego Comin, Michael Connolly, Michelle Connolly, Ana Corbacho, Vivek Dehejia, Marcelo Delajara, Gernot Doppelhoffer, Paul Evans, Rosa Fernandez, Monica Fuentes-Neira, Xavier Gabaix, Oded Galor, Victor Gomes Silva, Zvi Griliches, Gene Grossman, Christian Groth, Laila Haider, Elhanan Helpman, Toshi Ichida, Dale Jorgenson, Ken Judd, Jinill Kim, Michael Kremer, Phil Lane, Stephen Lin, Norman Loayza, Greg Mankiw, Kiminori Matsuyama, Sanket Mohapatra, Casey Mulligan, Kevin M. Murphy, Marco Neuhaus, Renger van Nieuwkoop, Sylvia Noin-McDavid, Joan O'Connell, Salvador Ortigueira, Lluis Parera, Pietro Peretto, Torsten Persson, Danny Quah, Climent Quintana, Rodney Ramchandran, Jordan Rappaport, Sergio Rebelo, Joan Ribas, Paul Romer, Joan Rossello, Michael Sarel, Etsuro Shioji, Chris Sims, B. Anna Sjögren, Nancy Stokey, Gustavo Suarez, Robert Tamura, Silvana Tenreyro, Merritt Tilney, Aaron Tornell, Nuri Ucar, Jaume Ventura, Martin Weitzman, Arthur Woll, and Alwyn Young.

About the Authors

Robert J. Barro is Robert C. Waggoner Professor of Economics at Harvard University. He has a B.S. in physics from Caltech and a Ph.D. in economics from Harvard, and he previously held faculty positions at Rochester, Chicago, and Brown. He is a viewpoint columnist for *Business Week,* a senior fellow of the Hoover Institution at Stanford, and a Research Associate of the National Bureau of Economic Research. In 2003 he was president-elect of the Western Economic Association, in 1997–98 he was vice president of the American Economic Association, and in 1994–95 he was Houblon-Norman Research Fellow at the Bank of England. He is married to Rachel McCleary, with whom he codirects the Project on Religion, Economy, and Society at Harvard University.

Xavier Sala-i-Martin is a professor of economics at Columbia University and a visiting professor at the Universitat Pompeu Fabra (in Barcelona). He has a B.S. from Universitat Autònoma de Barcelona and a Ph.D. from Harvard University. He is a Research Associate of the National Bureau of Economic Research and the Center for European Policy Research. He is a columnist for *La Vanguardia* in Barcelona and a contributor to a number of shows on Channel 3 of the Catalan Television and Catalunya Radio. He is a senior economic adviser to the World Economic Forum and a member of the board of the Fundacio Catalunya Oberta. In 1992, 1995, 1998, and 1999, the students at Yale and Columbia honored him with the Distinguished Teacher Award for his classes on economic growth.

Introduction

I.1 The Importance of Growth

To think about the importance of economic growth, we begin by assessing the long-term performance of the U.S. economy. The real per capita gross domestic product (GDP) in the United States grew by a factor of 10 from $3340 in 1870 to $33,330 in 2000, all measured in 1996 dollars. This increase in per capita GDP corresponds to a growth rate of 1.8 percent per year. This performance gave the United States the second-highest level of per capita GDP in the world in 2000 (after Luxembourg, a country with a population of only about 400,000).[1]

To appreciate the consequences of apparently small differentials in growth rates when compounded over long periods of time, we can calculate where the United States would have been in 2000 if it had grown since 1870 at 0.8 percent per year, one percentage point per year below its actual rate. A growth rate of 0.8 percent per year is close to the rate experienced in the long run—from 1900 to 1987—by India (0.64 percent per year), Pakistan (0.88 percent per year), and the Philippines (0.86 percent per year). If the United States had begun in 1870 at a real per capita GDP of $3340 and had then grown at 0.8 percent per year over the next 130 years, its per capita GDP in 2000 would have been $9450, only 2.8 times the value in 1870 and 28 percent of the actual value in 2000 of $33,330. Then, instead of ranking second in the world in 2000, the United States would have ranked 45th out of 150 countries with data. To put it another way, if the growth rate had been lower by just 1 percentage point per year, the U.S. per capita GDP in 2000 would have been close to that in Mexico and Poland.

Suppose, alternatively, that the U.S. real per capita GDP had grown since 1870 at 2.8 percent per year, 1 percentage point per year greater than the actual value. This higher growth rate is close to those experienced in the long run by Japan (2.95 percent per year from 1890 to 1990) and Taiwan (2.75 percent per year from 1900 to 1987). If the United States had still begun in 1870 at a per capita GDP of $3340 and had then grown at 2.8 percent per year over the next 130 years, its per capita GDP in 2000 would have been $127,000—38 times the value in 1870 and 3.8 times the actual value in 2000 of $33,330. A per capita GDP of $127,000 is well outside the historical experience of any country and may, in fact, be infeasible (although people in 1870 probably would have thought the same about $33,330). We can say, however, that a continuation of the long-term U.S. growth rate of 1.8 percent per year implies that the United States will not attain a per capita GDP of $127,000 until 2074.

1. The long-term data on GDP come from Maddison (1991) and are discussed in chapter 12. Recent data are from Heston, Summers, and Aten (2002) and are also discussed in chapter 12.

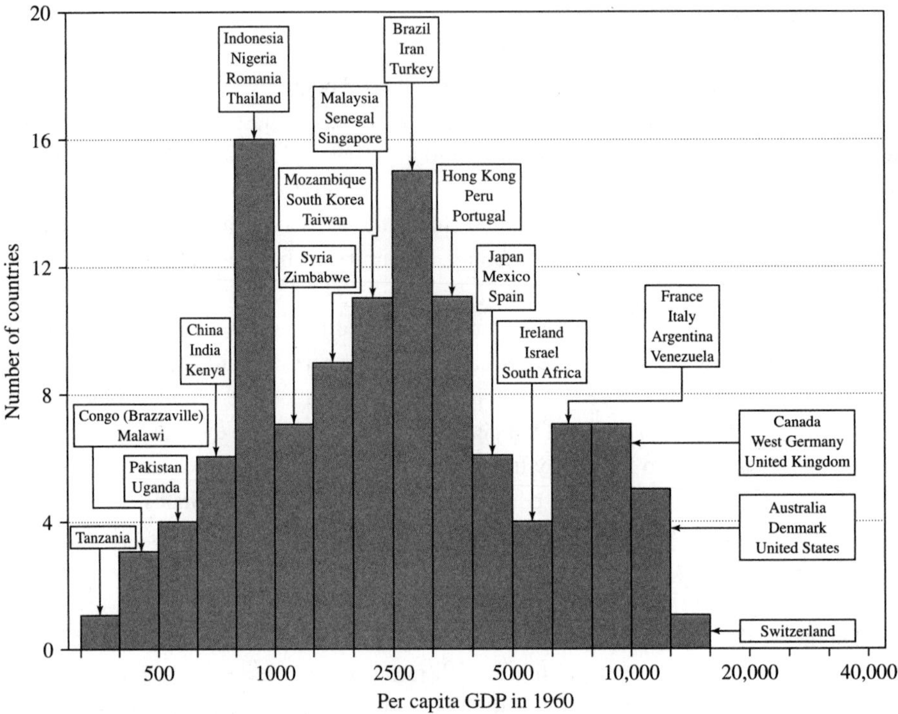

Figure I.1
Histogram for per capita GDP in 1960. The data, for 113 countries, are the purchasing-power-parity (PPP) adjusted values from Penn World Tables version 6.1, as described in Summers and Heston (1991) and Heston, Summers, and Aten (2002). Representative countries are labeled within each group.

The comparison of levels of real per capita GDP over a century involves multiples as high as 20; for example, Japan's per capita GDP in 1990 was about 20 times that in 1890. Comparisons of levels of per capita GDP across countries at a point in time exhibit even greater multiples. Figure I.1 shows a histogram for the log of real per capita GDP for 113 countries (those with the available data) in 1960. The mean value corresponds to a per capita GDP of $3390 (1996 U.S. dollars). The standard deviation of the log of real per capita GDP—a measure of the proportionate dispersion of real per capita GDP—was 0.89. This number means that a 1-standard-deviation band around the mean encompassed a range from 0.41 of the mean to 2.4 times the mean. The highest per capita GDP of $14,980 for Switzerland was 39 times the lowest value of $381 for Tanzania. The United States was second with a value of $12,270. The figure shows representative countries for each range of per capita GDP. The broad picture is that the richest countries included the OECD and

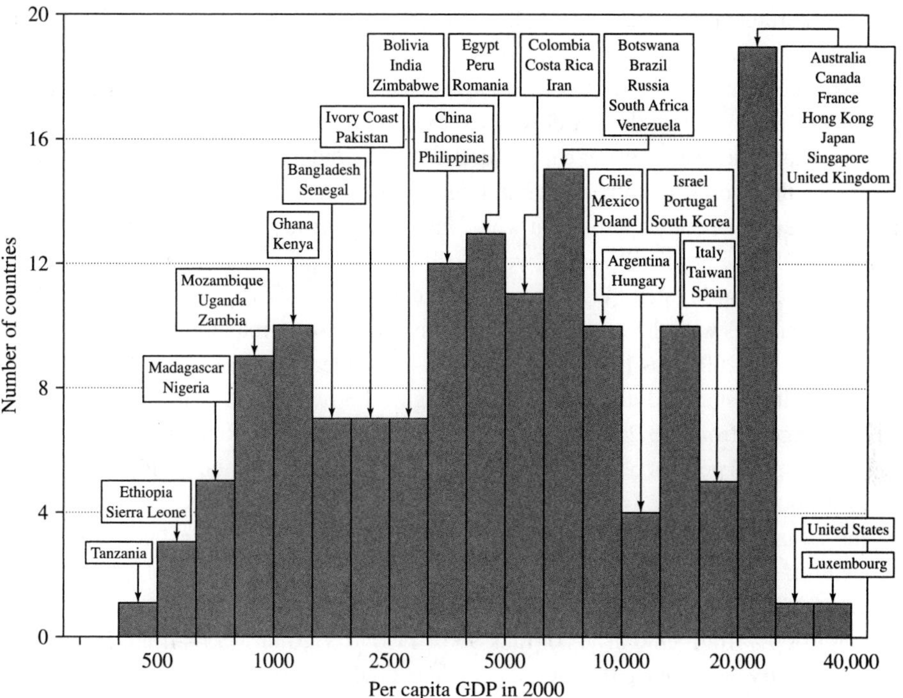

Figure I.2
Histogram for per capita GDP in 2000. The data, for 150 countries, are from the sources noted for figure I.1. Representative countries are labeled within each group.

a few places in Latin America, such as Argentina and Venezuela. Most of Latin America was in a middle range of per capita GDP. The poorer countries were a mixture of African and Asian countries, but some Asian countries were in a middle range of per capita GDP.

Figure I.2 shows a comparable histogram for 150 countries in 2000. The mean here corresponds to a per capita GDP of $8490, 2.5 times the value in 1960. The standard deviation of the log of per capita GDP in 2000 was 1.12, implying that a 1-standard-deviation band ranged from 0.33 of the mean to 3.1 times the mean. Hence, the proportionate dispersion of per capita GDP increased from 1960 to 2000. The highest value in 2000, $43,990 for Luxembourg, was 91 times the lowest value—$482 for Tanzania. (The Democratic Republic of Congo would be poorer, but the data are unavailable for 2000.) If we ignore Luxembourg because of its small size and compare Tanzania's per capita GDP with the second-highest value, $33,330 for the United States, the multiple is 69. Figure I.2 again marks out representative countries within each range of per capita GDP. The OECD countries still dominated the top group, joined by some East Asian countries. Most other Asian countries were in the middle range of per capita GDP, as were most Latin American countries. The lower range in 2000 was dominated by sub-Saharan Africa.

To appreciate the spreads in per capita GDP that prevailed in 2000, consider the situation of Tanzania, the poorest country shown in figure I.2. If Tanzania were to grow at the long-term U.S. rate of 1.8 percent per year, it would take 235 years to reach the 2000 level of U.S. per capita GDP. The required interval would still be 154 years if Tanzania were to grow at the long-term Japanese rate of 2.75 percent per year.

For 112 countries with the necessary data, the average growth rate of real per capita GDP between 1960 and 2000 was 1.8 percent per year—coincidentally the same as the long-term U.S. rate—with a standard deviation of 1.7.[2] Figure I.3 has a histogram of these growth rates; the range is from −3.2 percent per year for the Democratic Republic of Congo (the former Zaire) to 6.4 percent per year for Taiwan. (If not for missing data, the lowest-growing country would probably be Iraq.) Forty-year differences in growth rates of this magnitude have enormous consequences for standards of living. Taiwan raised its real per capita GDP by a factor of 13 from $1430 in 1960 (rank 76 out of 113 countries) to $18,730 in 2000 (rank 24 of 150), while the Democratic Republic of Congo lowered its real per capita GDP by a factor of 0.3 from $980 in 1960 (rank 93 of 113) to $320 in 1995—if not for missing data, this country would have the lowest per capita GDP in 2000.

A few other countries had growth rates from 1960 to 2000 that were nearly as high as Taiwan's; those with rates above 5 percent per year were Singapore with 6.2 percent, South Korea with 5.9 percent, Hong Kong with 5.4 percent, and Botswana with 5.1 percent. These countries increased their levels of per capita GDP by a multiple of at least 7 over 40 years. Just below came Thailand and Cyprus at 4.6 percent growth, China at 4.3 percent, Japan at 4.2 percent (with rapid growth mainly into the 1970s), and Ireland at 4.1 percent. Figure I.3 shows that a number of other OECD countries came in the next-highest growth groups, along with a few countries in Latin America (including Brazil and Chile) and more in Asia (including Indonesia, India, Pakistan, and Turkey). The United States ranked 40th in growth with a rate of 2.5 percent.

At the low end of growth, 16 countries aside from the Democratic Republic of Congo had negative growth rates of real per capita GDP from 1960 to 2000. The list (which would be substantially larger if not for missing data), starting from the bottom, is Central African Republic, Niger, Angola, Nicaragua, Mozambique, Madagascar, Nigeria, Zambia,

2. These statistics include the Democratic Republic of Congo (the former Zaire), for which the data are for 1960 to 1995.

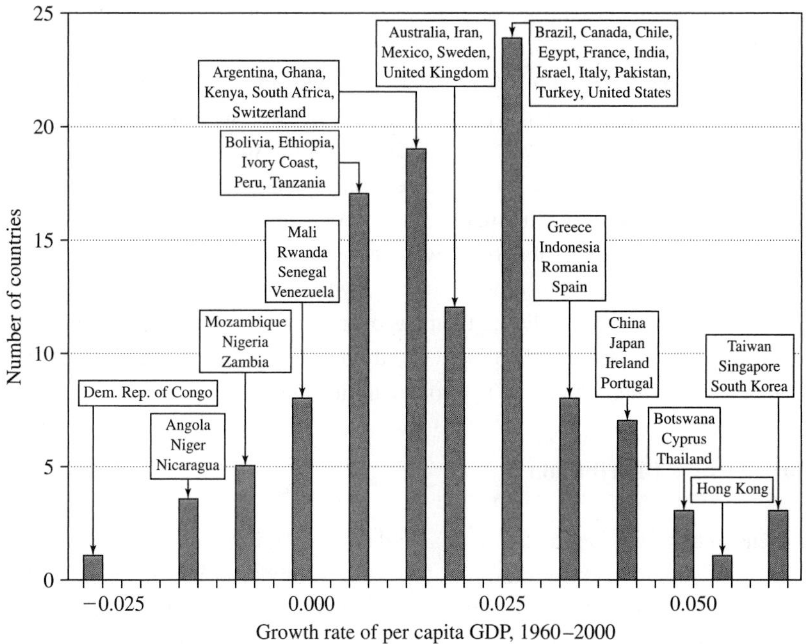

Figure I.3

Histogram for growth rate of per capita GDP from 1960 to 2000. The growth rates are computed for 112 countries from the values of per capita GDP shown for 1960 and 2000 in figures I.1 and I.2. For Democratic Republic of Congo (former Zaire), the growth rate is for 1960 to 1995. West Germany is the only country included in figure I.1 (for 1960) but excluded from figure I.3 (because of data problems caused by the reunification of Germany). Representative countries are labeled within each group.

Chad, Comoros, Venezuela, Senegal, Rwanda, Togo, Burundi, and Mali. Thus, except for Nicaragua and Venezuela, this group comprises only sub-Saharan African countries. For the 38 sub-Saharan African countries with data, the mean growth rate from 1960 to 2000 was only 0.6 percent per year. Hence, the typical country in sub-Saharan Africa increased its per capita GDP by a factor of only 1.3 over 40 years. Just above the African growth rates came a few slow-growing countries in Latin America, including Bolivia, Peru, and Argentina.

As a rough generalization for regional growth experiences, we can say that sub-Saharan Africa started relatively poor in 1960 and grew at the lowest rate, so it ended up by far the poorest area in 2000. Asia started only slightly above Africa in many cases but grew rapidly and ended up mostly in the middle. Latin America started in the mid to high range, grew somewhat below average, and therefore ended up mostly in the middle along with Asia.

Finally, the OECD countries started highest in 1960, grew in a middle range or better, and therefore ended up still the richest.

If we want to understand why countries differ dramatically in standards of living (figures I.1 and I.2), we have to understand why countries experience such sharp divergences in long-term growth rates (figure I.3). Even small differences in these growth rates, when cumulated over 40 years or more, have much greater consequences for standards of living than the kinds of short-term business fluctuations that have typically occupied most of the attention of macroeconomists. To put it another way, if we can learn about government policy options that have even small effects on long-term growth rates, we can contribute much more to improvements in standards of living than has been provided by the entire history of macroeconomic analysis of countercyclical policy and fine-tuning. Economic growth—the subject matter of this book—is the part of macroeconomics that really matters.

I.2 The World Income Distribution

Although we focus in this book on the theoretical and empirical determinants of aggregate economic growth, we should keep in mind that growth has important implications for the welfare of individuals. In fact, aggregate growth is probably the single most important factor affecting individual levels of income. Hence, understanding the determinants of aggregate economic growth is the key to understanding how to increase the standards of living of individuals in the world and, thereby, to lessen world poverty.

Figure I.4 shows the evolution of the world's per capita GDP from 1970 to 2000.[3] It is clear that the average person on the planet has been getting richer over time. But the positive average growth rate over the last three decades does not mean that the income of all citizens has increased. In particular, it does not mean that the incomes of the poorest people have grown nor that the number of people whose incomes are below a certain poverty line (say one dollar a day, as defined by the World Bank) has declined.[4] Indeed, if inequality

3. The "world" is approximated by the 126 countries (139 countries after the breakup of the Soviet Union in 1989) in Sala-i-Martin (2003a, 2003b). The individuals in these 126 countries made up about 95 percent of the world's population. World GDP per capita is estimated by adding up the data for individual countries from Heston, Summers, and Aten (2002) and then dividing by the world's population.

4. The quest for a "true" poverty line has a long tradition, but the current "one-dollar-a-day" line can be traced back to World Bank (1990). The World Bank originally defined the poverty line as one dollar a day in 1985 prices. Although the World Bank's own definition later changed to 1.08 dollars a day in 1993 dollars (notice that one 1985 dollar does not correspond to 1.08 1993 dollars), we use the original definition of one dollar a day in 1985 prices. One dollar a day (or 365 dollars a year) in 1985 prices becomes 495 dollars per year in 1996 prices, which is the base year of the Heston, Summers, and Aten (2002) data used to construct the world income distributions. Following Bhalla (2002), Sala-i-Martin (2003a) adjusts this poverty line upward by 15 percent to correct for the bias generated by the underreporting of the rich. This adjustment means that our "one-dollar-a-day" poverty line represents 570 dollars a year (or 1.5 dollars a day) in 1996 dollars.

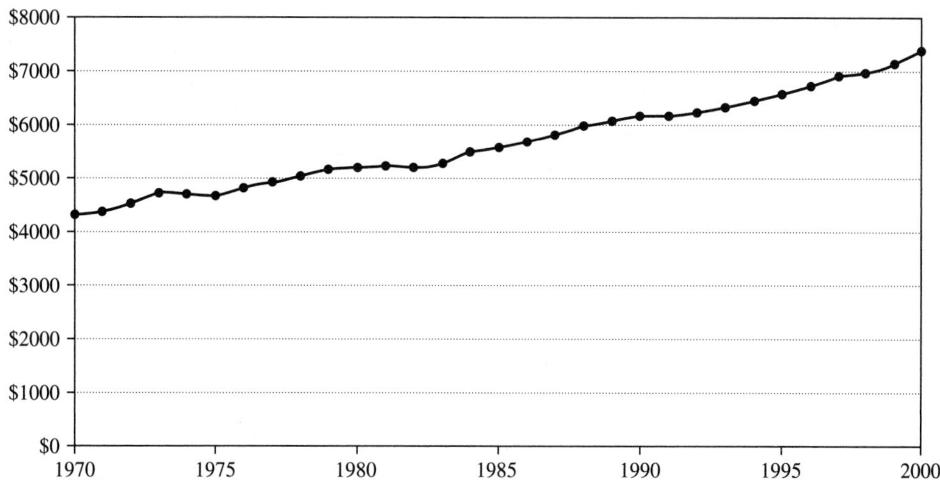

Figure I.4
World per capita GDP, 1970–2000. World per capita GDP is the sum of the GDPs for 126 countries (139 countries after the collapse of the Soviet Union) divided by population. The sample of 126 countries is the one used in Sala-i-Martin (2003a) and accounts for 95 percent of the world's population.

increased along with economic growth, it is possible for the world to have witnessed both positive per capita GDP growth and an increasing number of people below the poverty line. To assess how aggregate growth affects poverty, Sala-i-Martin (2003a) estimates the world distribution of individual income. To do so, he combines microeconomic survey and aggregate GDP data for each country, for every year between 1970 and 2000.[5] The result for 1970 is displayed in figure I.5. The horizontal axis plots the level of income (on a logarithmic scale), and the vertical axis has the number of people. The thin lines correspond to the income distributions of individual countries. Notice, for example, that China (the most populated country in the world) has a substantial fraction of the distribution below the $1/day line. The same is true for India and a large number of smaller countries. This pattern contrasts with the position of countries such as the United States, Japan, or even the USSR, which have very little of their distributions below the $1/day line. The thick line in figure I.5 is the integral of all the individual distributions. Therefore,

5. Sala-i-Martin (2003b) constructs an analogous distribution from which he estimates the number of people whose personal consumption expenditure is less than one dollar a day. The use of consumption, rather than income, accords better with the concept of "extreme poverty" used by international institutions such as the World Bank and the United Nations. However, personal consumption has the drawbacks of giving no credit to public services and saving.

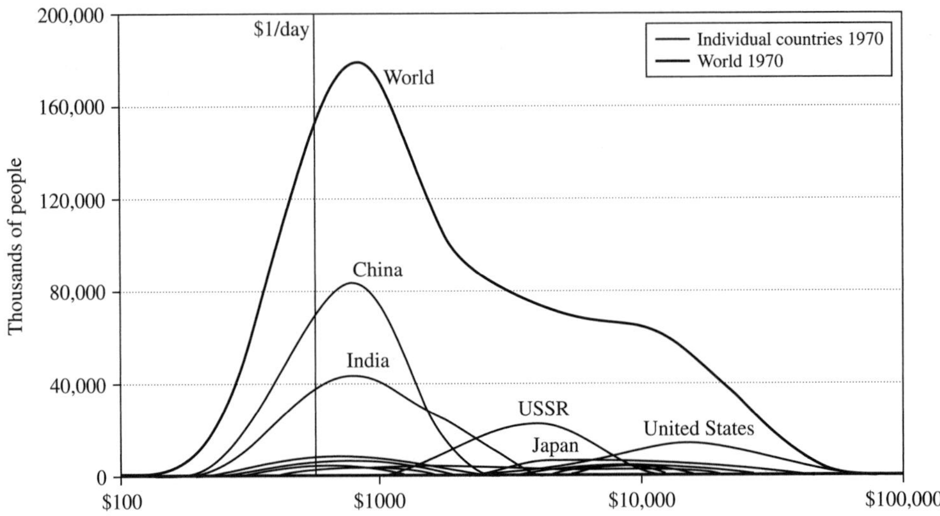

Figure I.5
The world distribution of income in 1970. The level of income is on the horizontal axis (on a logarithmic scale), and the number of people is on the vertical axis. The thin curves correspond to the income distributions of individual countries. The thick curve is the integral of individual country distributions and corresponds to the world distribution of income. The vertical line marks the poverty line (which corresponds to one dollar a day in 1985 prices). Source: Sala-i-Martin (2003a).

this line corresponds to the world distribution of income in 1970. Again, a substantial fraction of the world's citizens were poor (that is, had an income of less than $1/day) in 1970.

Figure I.6 displays the corresponding distributions for 2000. If one compares the 1970 with the 2000 distribution, one sees a number of interesting things. First, the world distribution of income has shifted to the right. This shift corresponds to the cumulated growth of per capita GDP. Second, we see that, underlying the evolution of worldwide income, there is a positive evolution of incomes in most countries in the world. Most countries increased their per capita GDP and, therefore, shifted to the right. Third, we see that the dispersion of the distributions for some countries, notably China, has increased over this period. In other words, income inequality rose within some large countries. Fourth, the increases in inequality within some countries have not been nearly enough to offset aggregate per capita growth, so that the fraction of the world's people whose incomes lie below the poverty line has declined dramatically.

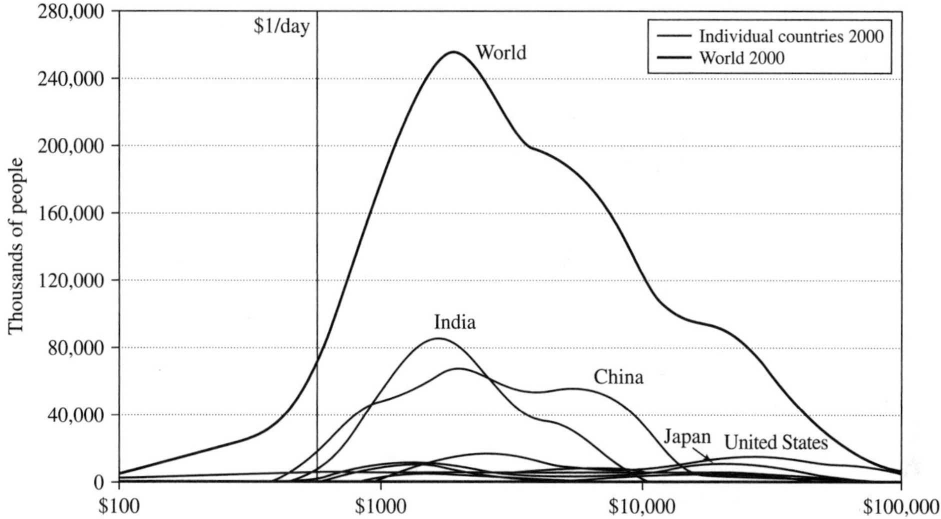

Figure I.6
The world distribution of income in 2000. The level of income is on the horizontal axis (on a logarithmic scale), and the number of people is on the vertical axis. The thin curves correspond to the income distributions of individual countries. The thick curve is the integral of individual country distributions and corresponds to the world distribution of income. The vertical line marks the poverty line (which corresponds to one dollar a day in 1985 prices). Source: Sala-i-Martin (2003a).

The exact fraction of the world's citizens that live below the poverty line can be computed from the distributions estimated by Sala-i-Martin (2003a).[6] These poverty rates, reported in figure I.7, have been cut by a factor of 3: whereas 20 percent of the world's citizens were poor in 1970, only 7 percent were poor in 2000.[7] Between 1970 and 1978, population growth more than offset the reduction in poverty rates. Indeed, Sala-i-Martin (2003a) shows that, during that period, the overall number of poor increased by 20 million people. But, since 1978, the total number of people with income below the $1/day threshold declined by more than 300 million. This achievement is all the more remarkable if we take into acount that overall population increased by more than 1.6 billion people during this period.

6. The World Bank, the United Nations, and many individual researchers define poverty in terms of consumption, rather than income. Sala-i-Martin (2003b) estimates poverty rates and head counts using consumption. The evolution of consumption poverty is similar to the one reported here for income although, obviously, the poverty rates are higher if one uses consumption instead of income and still uses the same poverty line.

7. Sala-i-Martin (2003a) reports cumulative distribution functions (CDFs) for 1970, 1980, 1990, and 2000. Using these CDFs, one can easily see that poverty rates have fallen dramatically over the last thirty years regardless of what poverty line one adopts. Thus, the conclusion that aggregate growth has reduced poverty is quite robust.

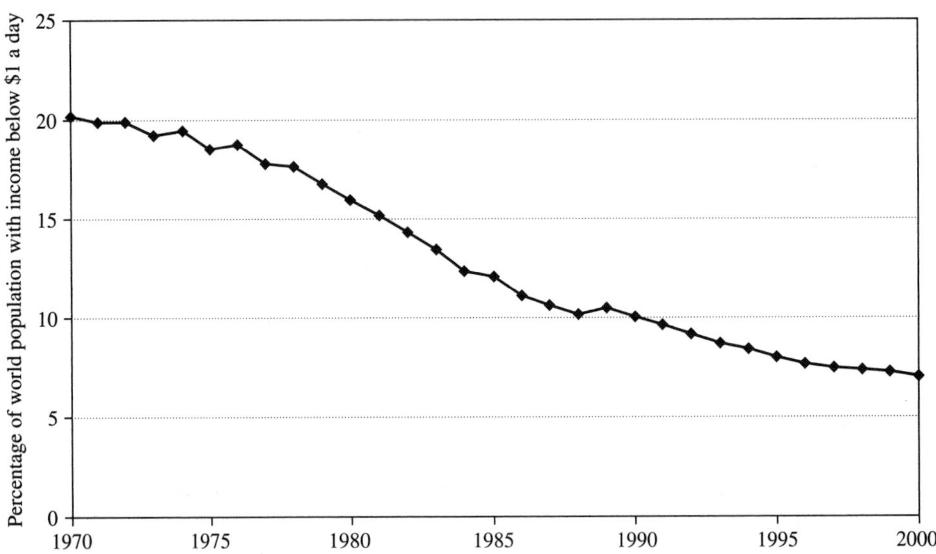

Figure I.7
World poverty rates. The graphs show the fraction of overall population with income below the poverty line. Source: Sala-i-Martin (2003a).

The clear conclusion is that economic growth led to substantial reductions in the world's poverty rates and head counts over the last thirty years. As mentioned earlier, this outcome was not inevitable: if aggregate growth had been accompanied by substantial increases in income inequality, it would have been possible for the mean of the income distribution to increase but also for the fraction of the distribution below a specified poverty threshold to also increase. Sala-i-Martin (2003a) shows that, even though this result is theoretically possible, the world did not behave this way over the last thirty years. Moreover, he also shows that world income inequality actually declined slightly between 1980 and 2000. This conclusion holds whether inequality is measured by the Gini coefficient, the Theil Index, the mean logarithmic deviation, various Atkinson indexes, the variance of log-income, or the coefficient of variation.

Sala-i-Martin (2003a) decomposes the world into regions and notes that poverty erradication has been most pronounced in the regions where growth has been the largest. Figure I.8 reports poverty rates for the poorest regions of the world: East Asia, South Asia, Latin America, Africa, the Middle East and North Africa (MENA), and Eastern Europe and Central Asia. In 1970, three of these regions had poverty rates close to or above 30 percent. Two of them (East Asia and South Asia) have experienced substantial reductions in poverty

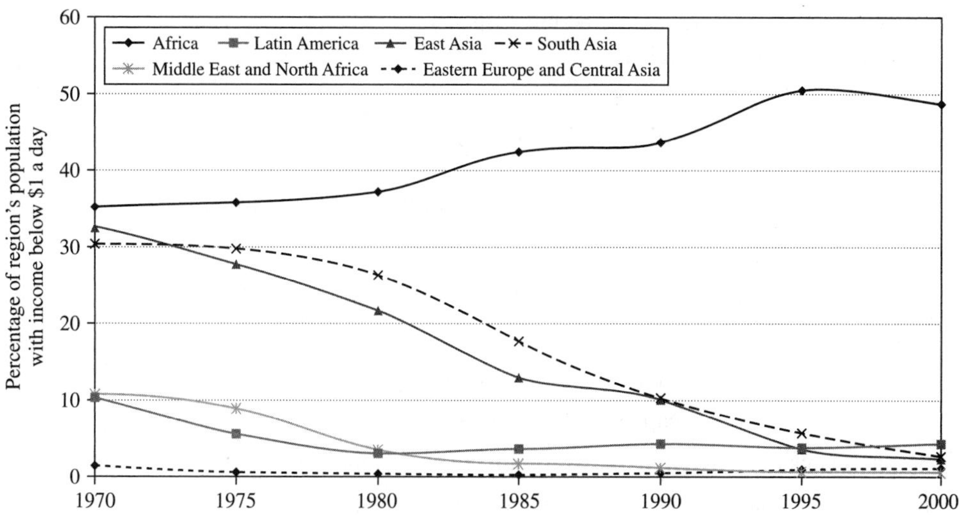

Figure I.8
Regional poverty rates. The graphs show the fraction of each region's population with income below the poverty line. The regions are the ones defined by the World Bank: East Asia, South Asia, Latin America, Africa, the Middle East and North Africa (MENA), and Eastern Europe and Central Asia. Source: Sala-i-Martin (2003a).

rates. These are the regions that also experienced large positive aggregate growth rates. The other region (Africa) has witnessed a dramatic increase in poverty rates over the last thirty years. We also know that per capita growth rates have been negative or close to zero for most countries in Africa. Figure I.8 also shows that two regions had poverty rates near 10 percent in 1970: Latin America and MENA. Both have experienced reductions in poverty rates. Latin America witnessed dramatic gains in the 1970s, when growth rates were substantial, but suffered a setback during the 1980s (the "lost decade," which featured negative growth rates). Poverty rates in Latin America stabilized during the 1990s. Poverty rates in MENA declined slightly between 1970 and 1975. The decline was very large during the high-growth decade that followed the oil shocks and then stabilized when aggregate growth stopped.

Finally, Eastern Europe and Central Asia (a region that includes the former Soviet Union) started off with very small poverty rates. The rates multiplied by a factor of 10 between 1989 and 2000. There are two reasons for the explosion of poverty rates in Eastern Europe and Central Asia. One is the huge increase in inequality that followed the collapse of the communist system. The second factor is the dismal aggregate growth performance of these countries. Notice, however, that the average levels of income for these countries remain far above the levels of Africa or even Asia. Therefore, even after the deterioration in mean income and the rise of income dispersion, poverty rates remain relatively low in Eastern Europe and Central Asia.

I.3 Empirical Regularities about Economic Growth

Kaldor (1963) listed a number of stylized facts that he thought typified the process of economic growth:

1. Per capita output grows over time, and its growth rate does not tend to diminish.
2. Physical capital per worker grows over time.
3. The rate of return to capital is nearly constant.
4. The ratio of physical capital to output is nearly constant.
5. The shares of labor and physical capital in national income are nearly constant.
6. The growth rate of output per worker differs substantially across countries.[8]

Fact 6 accords with the cross-country data that we have already discussed. Facts 1, 2, 4, and 5 seem to fit reasonably well with the long-term data for currently developed countries. For discussions of the stability of the long-run ratio of physical capital to GDP in Japan, Germany, Italy, the United Kingdom, and the United States, see Maddison (1982, chapter 3). For indications of the long-term stability of factor shares in the United States, see Denison (1974, appendix J) and Jorgenson, Gollop, and Fraumeni (1987, table 9.3). Young (1995) reports that factor shares were reasonably stable in four East Asian countries—Hong Kong, Singapore, South Korea, and Taiwan—from the early or middle 1960s through 1990. Studies of seven developed countries—Canada, France, Germany, Italy, Japan, the Netherlands, and the United Kingdom—indicate that factor shares are similar to those in the United States (Christensen, Cummings, and Jorgenson, 1980, and Dougherty, 1991). In some Latin-American countries considered by Elias (1990), the capital shares tend, however, to be higher than those in the United States.

Kaldor's claimed fact 3 on the stability of real rates of return appears to be heavily influenced by the experience of the United Kingdom; in this case, the real interest rate seems

8. Kuznets (1973, 1981) brings out other characteristics of modern economic growth. He notes the rapid rate of structural transformation, which includes shifts from agriculture to industry to services. This process involves urbanization, shifts from home work to employee status, and an increasing role for formal education. He also argues that modern growth involves an increased role for foreign commerce and that technological progress implies reduced reliance on natural resources. Finally, he discusses the growing importance of government: "The spread of modern economic growth placed greater emphasis on the importance and need for organization in national sovereign units.... The sovereign state unit was of critical importance as the formulator of the rules under which economic activity was to be carried on; as a referee ...; and as provider of infrastructure" (1981, p. 59).

to have no long-run trend (see Barro, 1987, figures 4 and 7). For the United States, however, the long-term data suggest a moderate decline of real interest rates (Barro, 1997, table 11.1). Real rates of return in some fast-growing countries, such as South Korea and Singapore, are much higher than those in the United States but have declined over time (Young, 1995). Thus it seems likely that Kaldor's hypothesis of a roughly stable real rate of return should be replaced by a tendency for returns to fall over some range as an economy develops.

We can use the data presented in chapter 12 to assess the long-run tendencies of the growth rate of real per capita GDP. Tables 12.10 and 12.11 contain figures from Angus Maddison for 31 countries over periods of roughly a century. These numbers basically exhaust the available information about growth over very long time intervals.

Table 12.10 applies to 16 currently developed countries, the major countries in Europe plus the United States, Canada, and Australia. These data show an average per capita growth rate of 1.9 percent per year over roughly a century, with a breakdown by 20-year periods as shown in table I.1. These numbers are consistent with Kaldor's proposition that the growth rate of real per capita GDP has no secular tendency to decline; in fact, the periods following World War II show growth rates well above the long-run average. The reduction in the growth rate from 3.7 percent per year in 1950–70 to 2.2 percent per year in 1970–90 corresponds to the often-discussed *productivity slowdown*. It is apparent from the table, however, that the growth rate for 1970–90 is high in relation to the long-term history.

Table 12.11 contains figures for 15 currently less-developed countries in Asia and Latin America. In this case, the average long-run growth rate from 1900 to 1987 is 1.4 percent per year, and the breakdown into four subperiods is as shown in table I.2. Again, the post–World War II period (here, 1950–87) shows growth rates well above the long-term average.

Table I.1
Long-Term Growth Rates for Currently Developed Countries

Period	Growth Rate (percent per year)	Number of Countries
1830–50	0.9	10
1850–70	1.2	11
1870–90	1.2	13
1890–10	1.5	14
1910–30	1.3	16
1930–50	1.4	16
1950–70	3.7	16
1970–90	2.2	16

Source: Table 12.10.
Note: The growth rates are simple averages for the countries with data.

Table I.2
Long-Term Growth Rates for Currently Less-Developed Countries

Period	Growth Rate (percent per year)	Number of Countries
1900–13	1.2	15
1913–50	0.4	15
1950–73	2.6	15
1973–87	2.4	15

Source: Table 12.11 in chapter 12.
Note: The growth rates are simple averages for the countries with data.

The information depicted in figures I.1–I.3 applies to the behavior of real per capita GDP for over 100 countries from 1960 to 2000. We can use these data to extend the set of stylized facts that was provided by Kaldor. One pattern in the cross-country data is that the growth rate of per capita GDP from 1960 to 2000 is essentially uncorrelated with the level of per capita GDP in 1960 (see chapter 12). In the terminology developed in chapter 1, we shall refer to a tendency for the poor to grow faster than the rich as β convergence. Thus the simple relationship between growth and the starting position for a broad cross section of countries does not reveal β convergence. This kind of convergence does appear if we limit attention to more homogeneous groups of economies, such as the U.S. states, regions of several European countries, and prefectures of Japan (see Barro and Sala-i-Martin, 1991, 1992a, and 1992b, and chapter 11). In these cases, the poorer places tend to grow faster than the richer ones. This behavior also appears in the cross-country data if we limit the sample to a relatively homogeneous collection of currently prosperous places, such as the OECD countries (see Baumol, 1986; DeLong, 1988).

We say in chapter 1 that *conditional* β convergence applies if the growth rate of per capita GDP is negatively related to the starting level of per capita GDP after holding fixed some other variables, such as initial levels of human capital, measures of government policies, the propensities to save and have children, and so on. The broad cross-country sample—that is, the data set that does not show β convergence in an absolute sense—clearly reveals β convergence in this conditional context (see Barro, 1991; Barro and Sala-i-Martin, 1992a; and Mankiw, Romer, and Weil, 1992). The rate of convergence is, however, only about 2 percent per year. Thus, it takes about 35 years for an economy to eliminate one-half of the gap between its initial per capita GDP and its long-run or target level of per capita GDP. (The target tends to grow over time.)

The results in chapter 12 show that a number of variables are significantly related to the growth rate of per capita GDP, once the starting level of per capita GDP is held constant. For example, growth depends positively on the initial quantity of human capital in the form of educational attainment and health, positively on maintenance of the rule of law and the

Table I.3
Ratios to GDP of Gross Domestic Investment and Gross National Saving (percent)

Period	Australia	Canada	France	India	Japan	Korea	United Kingdom	United States
				1. Gross Domestic Investment				
1870–89	16.5	16.0	12.8	—	—	—	9.3	19.8
1890–09	13.7	17.2	14.0	—	14.0	—	9.4	17.9
1910–29	17.4	19.8	—	6.4	16.6	5.1[a]	6.7	17.2
1930–49	13.3	13.1	—	8.4	20.5	—	8.1	12.7
1950–69	26.3	23.8	22.6	14.0	31.8	16.3[b]	17.2	18.9
1970–89	24.9	22.8	23.2	20.2	31.9	29.1	18.2	18.7
				2. Gross National Saving				
1870–89	11.2	9.1	12.8	—	—	—	13.9	19.1
1890–09	12.2	11.5	14.9	—	12.0	—	13.1	18.4
1910–29	13.6	16.0	—	6.4	17.1	2.38	9.6	18.9
1930–49	13.0	15.6	—	7.7	19.8	—	4.8	14.1
1950–69	24.0	22.3	22.8	12.2	32.1	5.9[b]	17.7	19.6
1970–89	22.9	22.1	23.4	19.4	33.7	26.2	19.4	18.5

Source: Maddison (1992).
[a]1911–29
[b]1951–69

ratio of investment to GDP, and negatively on fertility rates and the ratio of government consumption spending to GDP.

We can assess regularities in investment and saving ratios by using the long-term data in Maddison (1992). He provides long-term information for a few countries on the ratios of gross domestic investment to GDP and of gross national saving (the sum of domestic and net foreign investment) to GDP. Averages of the investment and saving ratios over 20-year intervals for the eight countries that have enough data for a long-period analysis are shown in table I.3. For an individual country, the table indicates that the time paths of domestic investment and national saving are usually similar. Domestic investment was, however, substantially higher than national saving (that is, borrowing from abroad was large) for Australia and Canada from 1870 to 1929, for Japan from 1890 to 1909, for the United Kingdom from 1930 to 1949, and for Korea from 1950 to 1969 (in fact, through the early 1980s). National saving was much higher than domestic investment (lending abroad was substantial) for the United Kingdom from 1870 to 1929 and for the United States from 1930 to 1949.

For the United States, the striking observation from the table is the stability over time of the ratios for domestic investment and national saving. The only exception is the relatively low values from 1930 to 1949, the period of the Great Depression and World War II. The United States is, however, an outlier with respect to the stability of its investment and saving ratios; the data for the other seven countries show a clear increase in these ratios over time. In particular, the ratios for 1950–89 are, in all cases, substantially greater than those from before World War II. The long-term data therefore suggest that the ratios to GDP of gross domestic investment and gross national saving tend to rise as an economy develops, at least over some range. The assumption of a constant gross saving ratio, which appears in chapter 1 in the Solow–Swan model, misses this regularity in the data.

The cross-country data also reveal some regularities with respect to fertility rates and, hence, rates of population growth. For most countries, the fertility rate tends to decline with increases in per capita GDP. For the poorest countries, however, the fertility rate may rise with per capita GDP, as Malthus (1798) predicted. Even stronger relations exist between educational attainment and fertility. Except for the most advanced countries, female schooling is negatively related with the fertility rate, whereas male schooling is positively related with the fertility rate. The net effect of these forces is that the fertility rate—and the rate of population growth—tend to fall over some range as an economy develops. The assumption of an exogenous, constant rate of population growth—another element of the Solow–Swan model—conflicts with this empirical pattern.

I.4 A Brief History of Modern Growth Theory

Classical economists, such as Adam Smith (1776), David Ricardo (1817), and Thomas Malthus (1798), and, much later, Frank Ramsey (1928), Allyn Young (1928), Frank Knight (1944), and Joseph Schumpeter (1934), provided many of the basic ingredients that appear in modern theories of economic growth. These ideas include the basic approaches of competitive behavior and equilibrium dynamics, the role of diminishing returns and its relation to the accumulation of physical and human capital, the interplay between per capita income and the growth rate of population, the effects of technological progress in the forms of increased specialization of labor and discoveries of new goods and methods of production, and the role of monopoly power as an incentive for technological advance.

Our main study begins with these building blocks already in place and focuses on the contributions in the neoclassical tradition since the late 1950s. We use the neoclassical methodology and language and rely on concepts such as aggregate capital stocks, aggregate production functions, and utility functions for representative consumers (who often have infinite horizons). We also use modern mathematical methods of dynamic optimization and differential equations. These tools, which are described in the appendix at the end of this book, are familiar today to most first-year graduate students in economics.

From a chronological viewpoint, the starting point for modern growth theory is the classic article of Ramsey (1928), a work that was several decades ahead of its time. Ramsey's treatment of household optimization over time goes far beyond its application to growth theory; it is hard now to discuss consumption theory, asset pricing, or even business-cycle theory without invoking the optimality conditions that Ramsey (and Fisher, 1930) introduced to economists. Ramsey's intertemporally separable utility function is as widely used today as the Cobb–Douglas production function. The economics profession did not, however, accept or widely use Ramsey's approach until the 1960s.

Between Ramsey and the late 1950s, Harrod (1939) and Domar (1946) attempted to integrate Keynesian analysis with elements of economic growth. They used production functions with little substitutability among the inputs to argue that the capitalist system is inherently unstable. Since they wrote during or immediately after the Great Depression, these arguments were received sympathetically by many economists. Although these contributions triggered a good deal of research at the time, very little of this analysis plays a role in today's thinking.

The next and more important contributions were those of Solow (1956) and Swan (1956). The key aspect of the Solow–Swan model is the neoclassical form of the production function, a specification that assumes constant returns to scale, diminishing returns to each input, and some positive and smooth elasticity of substitution between the inputs. This production function is combined with a constant-saving-rate rule to generate an extremely simple general-equilibrium model of the economy.

One prediction from these models, which has been exploited seriously as an empirical hypothesis only in recent years, is conditional convergence. The lower the starting level of per capita GDP, relative to the long-run or steady-state position, the faster the growth rate. This property derives from the assumption of diminishing returns to capital; economies that have less capital per worker (relative to their long-run capital per worker) tend to have higher rates of return and higher growth rates. The convergence is conditional because the steady-state levels of capital and output per worker depend, in the Solow–Swan model, on the saving rate, the growth rate of population, and the position of the production function—characteristics that might vary across economies. Recent empirical studies indicate that we should include additional sources of cross-country variation, especially differences in government policies and in initial stocks of human capital. The key point, however, is that the concept of conditional convergence—a basic property of the Solow–Swan model—has considerable explanatory power for economic growth across countries and regions.

Another prediction of the Solow–Swan model is that, in the absence of continuing improvements in technology, per capita growth must eventually cease. This prediction, which resembles those of Malthus and Ricardo, also comes from the assumption of diminishing returns to capital. We have already observed, however, that positive rates of per capita growth can persist over a century or more and that these growth rates have no clear tendency to decline.

The neoclassical growth theorists of the late 1950s and 1960s recognized this modeling deficiency and usually patched it up by assuming that technological progress occurred in an exogenous manner. This device can reconcile the theory with a positive, possibly constant per capita growth rate in the long run, while retaining the prediction of conditional convergence. The obvious shortcoming, however, is that the long-run per capita growth rate is determined entirely by an element—the rate of technological progress—that is outside of the model. (The long-run growth rate of the level of output also depends on the growth rate of population, another element that is exogenous in the standard theory.) Thus we end up with a model of growth that explains everything but long-run growth, an obviously unsatisfactory situation.

Cass (1965) and Koopmans (1965) brought Ramsey's analysis of consumer optimization back into the neoclassical growth model and thereby provided for an endogenous determination of the saving rate. This extension allows for richer transitional dynamics but tends to preserve the hypothesis of conditional convergence. The endogeneity of saving also does not eliminate the dependence of the long-run per capita growth rate on exogenous technological progress.

The equilibrium of the Cass–Koopmans version of the neoclassical growth model can be supported by a decentralized, competitive framework in which the productive factors, labor and capital, are paid their marginal products. Total income then exhausts the total product because of the assumption that the production function features constant returns to scale. Moreover, the decentralized outcomes are Pareto optimal.

The inclusion of a theory of technological change in the neoclassical framework is difficult, because the standard competitive assumptions cannot be maintained. Technological advance involves the creation of new ideas, which are partially nonrival and therefore have aspects of public goods. For a given technology—that is, for a given state of knowledge—it is reasonable to assume constant returns to scale in the standard, rival factors of production, such as labor, capital, and land. In other words, given the level of knowledge on how to produce, one would think that it is possible to replicate a firm with the same amount of labor, capital, and land and obtain twice as much output. But then, the returns to scale tend to be increasing if the nonrival ideas are included as factors of production. These increasing returns conflict with perfect competition. In particular, the compensation of nonrival old ideas in accordance with their current marginal cost of production—zero—will not provide the appropriate reward for the research effort that underlies the creation of new ideas.

Arrow (1962) and Sheshinski (1967) constructed models in which ideas were unintended by-products of production or investment, a mechanism described as learning by doing. In these models, each person's discoveries immediately spill over to the entire economy, an instantaneous diffusion process that might be technically feasible because knowledge is nonrival. Romer (1986) showed later that the competitive framework can be retained in this case to determine an equilibrium rate of technological advance, but the resulting growth rate would typically not be Pareto optimal. More generally, the competitive framework breaks down if discoveries depend in part on purposive R&D effort and if an individual's innovations spread only gradually to other producers. In this realistic setting, a decentralized theory of technological progress requires basic changes in the neoclassical growth model to incorporate an analysis of imperfect competition.[9] These additions to the theory did not come until Romer's (1987, 1990) research in the late 1980s.

The work of Cass (1965) and Koopmans (1965) completed the basic neoclassical growth model.[10] Thereafter, growth theory became excessively technical and steadily lost contact with empirical applications. In contrast, development economists, who are required to give advice to sick countries, retained an applied perspective and tended to use models that were technically unsophisticated but empirically useful. The fields of economic development and economic growth drifted apart, and the two areas became almost completely separated.

Probably because of its lack of empirical relevance, growth theory effectively died as an active research field by the early 1970s, on the eve of the rational-expectations revolution and the oil shocks. For about 15 years, macroeconomic research focused on short-term fluctuations. Major contributions included the incorporation of rational expectations into business-cycle models, improved approaches to policy evaluation, and the application of general-equilibrium methods to real business-cycle theory.

After the mid-1980s, research on economic growth experienced a boom, beginning with the work of Romer (1986) and Lucas (1988). The motivation for this research was the observation (or recollection) that the determinants of long-run economic growth are crucial issues, far more important than the mechanics of business cycles or the countercyclical effects of monetary and fiscal policies. But a recognition of the significance of long-run growth was only a first step; to go further, one had to escape the straitjacket of the neoclassical growth model, in which the long-term per capita growth rate was pegged by the rate of exogenous technological progress. Thus, in one way or another, the recent contributions determine the long-run growth rate within the model; hence, the designation *endogenous-growth* models.

The initial wave of the new research—Romer (1986), Lucas (1988), Rebelo (1991)—built on the work of Arrow (1962), Sheshinski (1967), and Uzawa (1965) and did not really introduce a theory of technological change. In these models, growth may go on indefinitely because the returns to investment in a broad class of capital goods—which includes human

9. Another approach is to assume that all of the nonrival research—a classic public good—is financed by the government through involuntary taxes; see Shell (1967).

10. However, recent research has shown how to extend the neoclassical growth model to allow for heterogeneity among households (Caselli and Ventura, 2000) and to incorporate time-inconsistent preferences (Barro, 1999).

capital—do not necessarily diminish as economies develop. (This idea goes back to Knight, 1944.) Spillovers of knowledge across producers and external benefits from human capital are parts of this process, but only because they help to avoid the tendency for diminishing returns to the accumulation of capital.

The incorporation of R&D theories and imperfect competition into the growth framework began with Romer (1987, 1990) and included significant contributions by Aghion and Howitt (1992) and Grossman and Helpman (1991, chapters 3 and 4). In these models, technological advance results from purposive R&D activity, and this activity is rewarded by some form of ex post monopoly power. If there is no tendency for the economy to run out of ideas, the growth rate can remain positive in the long run. The rate of growth and the underlying amount of inventive activity tend, however, not to be Pareto optimal because of distortions related to the creation of the new goods and methods of production. In these frameworks, the long-term growth rate depends on governmental actions, such as taxation, maintenance of law and order, provision of infrastructure services, protection of intellectual property rights, and regulations of international trade, financial markets, and other aspects of the economy. The government therefore has great potential for good or ill through its influence on the long-term rate of growth. This research program remained active through the 1990s and has been applied, for example, to understanding scale effects in the growth process (Jones, 1999), analyzing whether technological progress will be labor or capital augmenting (Acemoglu, 2002), and assessing the role of competition in the growth process (Aghion et al., 2001, 2002).

The new research also includes models of the diffusion of technology. Whereas the analysis of discovery relates to the rate of technological progress in leading-edge economies, the study of diffusion pertains to the manner in which follower economies share by imitation in these advances. Since imitation tends to be cheaper than innovation, the diffusion models predict a form of conditional convergence that resembles the predictions of the neoclassical growth model. Some recent empirical work has verified the importance of technological diffusion in the convergence process.

Another key exogenous parameter in the neoclassical growth model is the growth rate of population. A higher rate of population growth lowers the steady-state level of capital and output per worker and tends thereby to reduce the per capita growth rate for a given initial level of per capita output. The standard model does not, however, consider the effects of per capita income and wage rates on population growth—the kinds of effects stressed by Malthus—and also does not take account of the resources used up in the process of child rearing. Another line of recent research makes population growth endogenous by incorporating an analysis of fertility choice into the neoclassical model. The results are consistent, for example, with the empirical regularity that fertility rates tend to fall with per capita income over the main range of experience but may rise with per capita income for the poorest countries. Additional work related to the endogeneity of labor supply in a growth context concerns migration and labor/leisure choice.

The clearest distinction between the growth theory of the 1960s and that of the 1990s is that the recent research pays close attention to empirical implications and to the relation between theory and data. However, much of this applied perspective involved applications of empirical hypotheses from the older theory, notably the neoclassical growth model's prediction of conditional convergence. The cross-country regressions motivated by the neoclassical model surely became a fixture of research in the 1990s. An interesting recent development in this area, which we explore in chapter 12, involves assessment of the robustness of these kinds of estimates. Other empirical analyses apply more directly to the recent theories of endogenous growth, including the roles of increasing returns, R&D activity, human capital, and the diffusion of technology.

I.5 Some Highlights of the Second Edition

This second edition of *Economic Growth* includes changes throughout the book. We mention here a few of the highlights. In this introduction we already described new estimates of the distribution of income of individuals throughout the world from 1970 to 2000.

Chapter 1 has been made easier and more accessible. We added a section on markets in the Solow–Swan model. We also discussed the nature of the theoretical dissatisfaction with neoclassical theory that led to the emergence of endogenous growth models with imperfect competition.

Chapter 2 expands the treatment of the basic neoclassical growth model to allow for heterogeneity of households. There is an improved approach to ruling out "undersaving" paths and for deriving and using transversality conditions. We also include an analysis of models with nonconstant time-preference rates.

Chapter 3 has various extensions to the basic neoclassical growth model, including an expanded treatment of the government sector. The framework allows for various forms of tax rates and allows for a clear distinction between taxes on capital income and taxes on labor or consumption.

Chapters 6 and 7 discuss models of endogenous technological progress. The new material includes an analysis of the role and source of scale effects in these models. We refer in chapter 6 to Thomas Jefferson's mostly negative views on patents as a mechanism for motivating inventions. Chapter 7 has an improved analysis of models where technological advances take the form of quality improvements. We have particularly improved the treatment of the interplay between industry leaders and outsiders and, hence, of the role of outside competition in the growth process.

Chapter 8 has a model of technological diffusion. The basic model is improved, and the theoretical results are related to recent empirical findings.

Chapter 9 has an extended treatment of endogenous population growth. Chapter 10 has an improved analysis of growth accounting, including its relation to theories of endogenous technological progress. Chapter 11, which deals with regional data sets, extends the analysis of U.S. states through 2000.

In chapter 12 we include an updated treatment of cross-country growth regressions, using the new Summers–Heston data set, Penn World Tables version 6.1, which has data through 2000 (see Heston, Summers, and Aten, 2002). We also discuss in this chapter various issues about the reliability of estimates from cross-country regressions, including ways to assess the robustness of the results.

1 Growth Models with Exogenous Saving Rates (the Solow–Swan Model)

1.1 The Basic Structure

The first question we ask in this chapter is whether it is possible for an economy to enjoy positive growth rates forever by simply saving and investing in its capital stock. A look at the cross-country data from 1960 to 2000 shows that the average annual growth rate of real per capita GDP for 112 countries was 1.8 percent, and the average ratio of gross investment to GDP was 16 percent.[1] However, for 38 sub-Saharan African countries, the average growth rate was only 0.6 percent, and the average investment ratio was only 10 percent. At the other end, for nine East Asian "miracle" economies, the average growth rate was 4.9 percent, and the average investment ratio was 25 percent. These observations suggest that growth and investment rates are positively related. However, before we get too excited with this relationship, we might note that, for 23 OECD countries, the average growth rate was 2.7 percent—lower than that for the East Asian miracles—whereas the average investment ratio was 24 percent—about the same as that for East Asia. Thus, although investment propensities cannot be the whole story, it makes sense as a starting point to try to relate the growth rate of an economy to its willingness to save and invest. To this end, it will be useful to begin with a simple model in which the only possible source of per capita growth is the accumulation of physical capital.

Most of the growth models that we discuss in this book have the same basic general-equilibrium structure. First, households (or families) own the inputs and assets of the economy, including ownership rights in firms, and choose the fractions of their income to consume and save. Each household determines how many children to have, whether to join the labor force, and how much to work. Second, firms hire inputs, such as capital and labor, and use them to produce goods that they sell to households or other firms. Firms have access to a technology that allows them to transform inputs into output. Third, markets exist on which firms sell goods to households or other firms and on which households sell the inputs to firms. The quantities demanded and supplied determine the relative prices of the inputs and the produced goods.

Although this general structure applies to most growth models, it is convenient to start our analysis by using a simplified setup that excludes markets and firms. We can think of a composite unit—a household/producer like Robinson Crusoe—who owns the inputs and also manages the technology that transforms inputs into outputs. In the real world, production takes place using many different inputs to production. We summarize all of them into just three: physical capital $K(t)$, labor $L(t)$, and knowledge $T(t)$. The production

1. These data—from Penn World Tables version 6.1—are described in Summers and Heston (1991) and Heston, Summers, and Aten (2002). We discuss these data in chapter 12.

function takes the form

$$Y(t) = F[K(t), L(t), T(t)] \tag{1.1}$$

where $Y(t)$ is the flow of output produced at time t.

Capital, $K(t)$, represents the durable physical inputs, such as machines, buildings, pencils, and so on. These goods were produced sometime in the past by a production function of the form of equation (1.1). It is important to notice that these inputs cannot be used by multiple producers simultaneously. This last characteristic is known as *rivalry*—a good is *rival* if it cannot be used by several users at the same time.

The second input to the production function is labor, $L(t)$, and it represents the inputs associated with the human body. This input includes the number of workers and the amount of time they work, as well as their physical strength, skills, and health. Labor is also a *rival* input, because a worker cannot work on one activity without reducing the time available for other activities.

The third input is the level of knowledge or technology, $T(t)$. Workers and machines cannot produce anything without a *formula* or *blueprint* that shows them how to do it. This blueprint is what we call *knowledge or technology*. Technology can improve over time—for example, the same amount of capital and labor yields a larger quantity of output in 2000 than in 1900 because the technology employed in 2000 is superior. Technology can also differ across countries—for example, the same amount of capital and labor yields a larger quantity of output in Japan than in Zambia because the technology available in Japan is better. The important distinctive characteristic of knowledge is that it is a *nonrival good:* two or more producers can use the same formula at the same time.[2] Hence, two producers that each want to produce Y units of output will each have to use a different set of machines and workers, but they can use the same formula. This property of nonrivalry turns out to have important implications for the interactions between technology and economic growth.[3]

2. The concepts of *nonrivalry* and *public good* are often confused in the literature. *Public goods* are *nonrival* (they can be used by many people simultaneously) and also *nonexcludable* (it is technologically or legally impossible to prevent people from using such goods). The key characteristic of knowledge is nonrivalry. Some formulas or blueprints are nonexcludable (for example, calculus formulas on which there are no property rights), whereas others are excludable (for example, the formulas used to produce pharmaceutical products while they are protected by patents). These properties of ideas were well understood by Thomas Jefferson, who said in a letter of August 13, 1813, to Isaac McPherson: "If nature has made any one thing less susceptible than all others of exclusive property, it is the actions of the thinking power called an idea, which an individual may exclusively possess as long as he keeps it to himself; but the moment it is divulged, it forces itself into the possession of everyone, and the receiver cannot dispossess himself of it. Its peculiar character, too, is that no one possesses the less, because every other possesses the whole of it. He who receives an idea from me, receives instruction himself without lessening mine" (available on the Internet from the Thomas Jefferson Papers at the Library of Congress, lcweb2.loc.gov/ammem/mtjhtml/mtjhome.html).

3. Government policies, which depend on laws and institutions, would also affect the output of an economy. Since basic public institutions are nonrival, we can include these factors in $T(t)$ in the production function.

We assume a one-sector production technology in which output is a homogeneous good that can be consumed, $C(t)$, or invested, $I(t)$. Investment is used to create new units of physical capital, $K(t)$, or to replace old, depreciated capital. One way to think about the one-sector technology is to draw an analogy with farm animals, which can be eaten or used as inputs to produce more farm animals. The literature on economic growth has used more inventive examples—with such terms as *shmoos, putty,* or *ectoplasm*—to reflect the easy transmutation of capital goods into consumables, and vice versa.

In this chapter we imagine that the economy is closed: households cannot buy foreign goods or assets and cannot sell home goods or assets abroad. (Chapter 3 allows for an open economy.) We also start with the assumption that there are no government purchases of goods and services. (Chapter 4 deals with government purchases.) In a closed economy with no public spending, all output is devoted to consumption or gross investment,[4] so $Y(t) = C(t) + I(t)$. By subtracting $C(t)$ from both sides and realizing that output equals income, we get that, in this simple economy, the amount saved, $S(t) \equiv Y(t) - C(t)$, equals the amount invested, $I(t)$.

Let $s(\cdot)$ be the fraction of output that is saved—that is, the *saving rate*—so that $1 - s(\cdot)$ is the fraction of output that is consumed. Rational households choose the saving rate by comparing the costs and benefits of consuming today rather than tomorrow; this comparison involves preference parameters and variables that describe the state of the economy, such as the level of wealth and the interest rate. In chapter 2, where we model this decision explicitly, we find that $s(\cdot)$ is a complicated function of the state of the economy, a function for which there are typically no closed-form solutions. To facilitate the analysis in this initial chapter, we assume that $s(\cdot)$ is given exogenously. The simplest function, the one assumed by Solow (1956) and Swan (1956) in their classic articles, is a constant, $0 \leq s(\cdot) = s \leq 1$. We use this constant-saving-rate specification in this chapter because it brings out a large number of results in a clear way. Given that saving must equal investment, $S(t) = I(t)$, it follows that the *saving rate* equals the *investment rate*. In other words, the saving rate of a closed economy represents the fraction of GDP that an economy devotes to investment.

We assume that capital is a homogeneous good that depreciates at the constant rate $\delta > 0$; that is, at each point in time, a constant fraction of the capital stock wears out and, hence, can no longer be used for production. Before evaporating, however, all units of capital are assumed to be equally productive, regardless of when they were originally produced.

4. In an open economy with government spending, the condition is

$$Y(t) - r \cdot D(t) = C(t) + I(t) + G(t) + NX(t)$$

where $D(t)$ is international debt, r is the international real interest rate, $G(t)$ is public spending, and $NX(t)$ is net exports. In this chapter we assume that there is no public spending, so that $G(t) = 0$, and that the economy is closed, so that $D(t) = NX(t) = 0$.

The net increase in the stock of physical capital at a point in time equals gross investment less depreciation:

$$\dot{K}(t) = I(t) - \delta K(t) = s \cdot F[K(t), L(t), T(t)] - \delta K(t) \tag{1.2}$$

where a dot over a variable, such as $\dot{K}(t)$, denotes differentiation with respect to time, $\dot{K}(t) \equiv \partial K(t)/\partial t$ (a convention that we use throughout the book) and $0 \leq s \leq 1$. Equation (1.2) determines the dynamics of K for a given technology and labor.

The labor input, L, varies over time because of population growth, changes in participation rates, shifts in the amount of time worked by the typical worker, and improvements in the skills and quality of workers. In this chapter, we simplify by assuming that everybody works the same amount of time and that everyone has the same constant skill, which we normalize to one. Thus we identify the labor input with the total population. We analyze the accumulation of skills or human capital in chapter 5 and the choice between labor and leisure in chapter 9.

The growth of population reflects the behavior of fertility, mortality, and migration, which we study in chapter 9. In this chapter, we simplify by assuming that population grows at a constant, exogenous rate, $\dot{L}/L = n \geq 0$, without using any resources. If we normalize the number of people at time 0 to 1 and the work intensity per person also to 1, then the population and labor force at time t are equal to

$$L(t) = e^{nt} \tag{1.3}$$

To highlight the role of capital accumulation, we start with the assumption that the level of technology, $T(t)$, is a constant. This assumption will be relaxed later.

If $L(t)$ is given from equation (1.3) and technological progress is absent, then equation (1.2) determines the time paths of capital, $K(t)$, and output, $Y(t)$. Once we know how capital or GDP changes over time, the growth rates of these variables are also determined. In the next sections, we show that this behavior depends crucially on the properties of the production function, $F(\cdot)$.

1.2 The Neoclassical Model of Solow and Swan

1.2.1 The Neoclassical Production Function

The process of economic growth depends on the shape of the production function. We initially consider the neoclassical production function. We say that a production function, $F(K, L, T)$, is *neoclassical* if the following properties are satisfied:[5]

5. We ignore time subscripts to simplify notation.

1. Constant returns to scale. The function $F(\cdot)$ exhibits constant returns to scale. That is, if we multiply capital and labor by the same positive constant, λ, we get λ the amount of output:

$$F(\lambda K, \lambda L, T) = \lambda \cdot F(K, L, T) \quad \text{for all } \lambda > 0 \tag{1.4}$$

This property is also known as *homogeneity of degree one in K and L.* It is important to note that the definition of scale includes only the two rival inputs, capital and labor. In other words, we did not define constant returns to scale as $F(\lambda K, \lambda L, \lambda T) = \lambda \cdot F(K, L, T)$.

To get some intuition on why our assumption makes economic sense, we can use the following *replication argument.* Imagine that plant 1 produces Y units of output using the production function F and combining K and L units of capital and labor, respectively, and using formula T. It makes sense to assume that if we create an identical plant somewhere else (that is, if we *replicate* the plant), we should be able to produce the same amount of output. In order to replicate the plant, however, we need a new set of machines and workers, but we can use the same formula in both plants. The reason is that, while capital and labor are rival goods, the formula is a nonrival good and can be used in both plants at the same time. Hence, because technology is a nonrival input, our definition of returns to scale makes sense.

2. Positive and diminishing returns to private inputs. For all $K > 0$ and $L > 0$, $F(\cdot)$ exhibits positive and diminishing marginal products with respect to each input:

$$\begin{aligned} \frac{\partial F}{\partial K} &> 0, \qquad \frac{\partial^2 F}{\partial K^2} < 0 \\ \frac{\partial F}{\partial L} &> 0, \qquad \frac{\partial^2 F}{\partial L^2} < 0 \end{aligned} \tag{1.5}$$

Thus, the neoclassical technology assumes that, holding constant the levels of technology and labor, each additional unit of capital delivers positive additions to output, but these additions decrease as the number of machines rises. The same property is assumed for labor.

3. Inada conditions. The third defining characteristic of the neoclassical production function is that the marginal product of capital (or labor) approaches infinity as capital (or labor) goes to 0 and approaches 0 as capital (or labor) goes to infinity:

$$\begin{aligned} \lim_{K \to 0} \left(\frac{\partial F}{\partial K} \right) &= \lim_{L \to 0} \left(\frac{\partial F}{\partial L} \right) = \infty \\ \lim_{K \to \infty} \left(\frac{\partial F}{\partial K} \right) &= \lim_{L \to \infty} \left(\frac{\partial F}{\partial L} \right) = 0 \end{aligned} \tag{1.6}$$

These last properties are called *Inada conditions,* following Inada (1963).

4. Essentiality. Some economists add the assumption of *essentiality* to the definition of a neoclassical production function. An input is essential if a strictly positive amount is needed to produce a positive amount of output. We show in the appendix that the three neoclassical properties in equations (1.4)–(1.6) imply that each input is *essential* for production, that is, $F(0, L) = F(K, 0) = 0$. The three properties of the neoclassical production function also imply that output goes to infinity as either input goes to infinity, another property that is proven in the appendix.

Per Capita Variables When we say that a country is rich or poor, we tend to think in terms of output or consumption per person. In other words, we do not think that India is richer than the Netherlands, even though India produces a lot more GDP, because, once we divide by the number of citizens, the amount of income each person gets on average is a lot smaller in India than in the Netherlands. To capture this property, we construct the model in per capita terms and study primarily the dynamic behavior of the per capita quantities of GDP, consumption, and capital.

Since the definition of constant returns to scale applies to all values of λ, it also applies to $\lambda = 1/L$. Hence, output can be written as

$$Y = F(K, L, T) = L \cdot F(K/L, 1, T) = L \cdot f(k) \tag{1.7}$$

where $k \equiv K/L$ is capital per worker, $y \equiv Y/L$ is output per worker, and the function $f(k)$ is defined to equal $F(k, 1, T)$.[6] This result means that the production function can be expressed in *intensive form* (that is, in *per worker* or *per capita* form) as

$$y = f(k) \tag{1.8}$$

In other words, the production function exhibits no "scale effects": production per person is determined by the amount of physical capital each person has access to and, holding constant k, having more or fewer workers does not affect total output per person. Consequently, very large economies, such as China or India, can have less output or income per person than very small economies, such as Switzerland or the Netherlands.

We can differentiate this condition $Y = L \cdot f(k)$ with respect to K, for fixed L, and then with respect to L, for fixed K, to verify that the marginal products of the factor inputs are given by

$$\partial Y/\partial K = f'(k) \tag{1.9}$$

$$\partial Y/\partial L = f(k) - k \cdot f'(k) \tag{1.10}$$

6. Since T is assumed to be constant, it is one of the parameters implicit in the definition of $f(k)$.

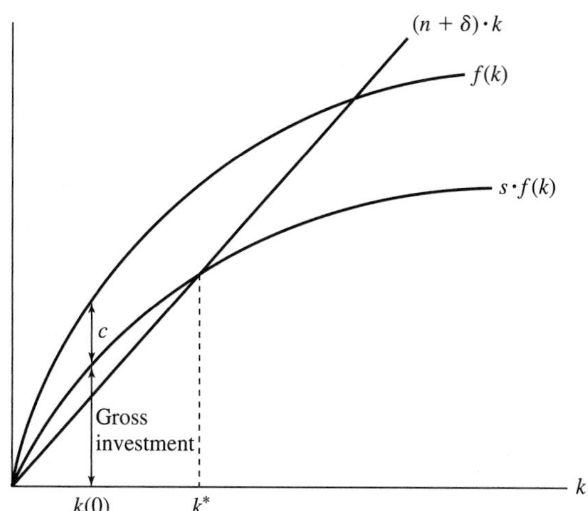

Figure 1.1
The Solow–Swan model. The curve for gross investment, $s \cdot f(k)$, is proportional to the production function, $f(k)$. Consumption per person equals the vertical distance between $f(k)$ and $s \cdot f(k)$. Effective depreciation (for k) is given by $(n + \delta) \cdot k$, a straight line from the origin. The change in k is given by the vertical distance between $s \cdot f(k)$ and $(n + \delta) \cdot k$. The steady-state level of capital, k^*, is determined at the intersection of the $s \cdot f(k)$ curve with the $(n + \delta) \cdot k$ line.

The Inada conditions imply $\lim_{k\to 0}[f'(k)] = \infty$ and $\lim_{k\to\infty}[f'(k)] = 0$. Figure 1.1 shows the neoclassical production in per capita terms: it goes through zero; it is vertical at zero, upward sloping, and concave; and its slope asymptotes to zero as k goes to infinity.

A Cobb–Douglas Example One simple production function that is often thought to provide a reasonable description of actual economies is the Cobb–Douglas function,[7]

$$Y = AK^{\alpha}L^{1-\alpha} \tag{1.11}$$

where $A > 0$ is the level of the technology and α is a constant with $0 < \alpha < 1$. The Cobb–Douglas function can be written in intensive form as

$$y = Ak^{\alpha} \tag{1.12}$$

7. Douglas is Paul H. Douglas, who was a labor economist at the University of Chicago and later a U.S. Senator from Illinois. Cobb is Charles W. Cobb, who was a mathematician at Amherst. Douglas (1972, pp. 46–47) says that he consulted with Cobb in 1927 on how to come up with a production function that fit his empirical equations for production, employment, and capital stock in U.S. manufacturing. Interestingly, Douglas says that the functional form was developed earlier by Philip Wicksteed, thus providing another example of Stigler's Law (whereby nothing is named after the person who invented it).

Note that $f'(k) = A\alpha k^{\alpha-1} > 0$, $f''(k) = -A\alpha(1-\alpha)k^{\alpha-2} < 0$, $\lim_{k\to\infty} f'(k) = 0$, and $\lim_{k\to 0} f'(k) = \infty$. Thus, the Cobb–Douglas form satisfies the properties of a neoclassical production function.

The key property of the Cobb–Douglas production function is the behavior of factor income shares. In a competitive economy, as discussed in section 1.2.3, capital and labor are each paid their marginal products; that is, the marginal product of capital equals the rental price R, and the marginal product of labor equals the wage rate w. Hence, each unit of capital is paid $R = f'(k) = \alpha Ak^{\alpha-1}$, and each unit of labor is paid $w = f(k) - k \cdot f'(k) = (1-\alpha)\cdot Ak^{\alpha}$. The capital share of income is then $Rk/f(k) = \alpha$, and the labor share is $w/f(k) = 1 - a$. Thus, in a competitive setting, the factor income shares are constant—independent of k—when the production function is Cobb–Douglas.

1.2.2 The Fundamental Equation of the Solow–Swan Model

We now analyze the dynamic behavior of the economy described by the neoclassical production function. The resulting growth model is called the Solow–Swan model, after the important contributions of Solow (1956) and Swan (1956).

The change in the capital stock over time is given by equation (1.2). If we divide both sides of this equation by L, we get

$$\dot{K}/L = s \cdot f(k) - \delta k$$

The right-hand side contains per capita variables only, but the left-hand side does not. Hence, it is not an ordinary differential equation that can be easily solved. In order to transform it into a differential equation in terms of k, we can take the derivative of $k \equiv K/L$ with respect to time to get

$$\dot{k} \equiv \frac{d(K/L)}{dt} = \dot{K}/L - nk$$

where $n = \dot{L}/L$. If we substitute this result into the expression for $\dot{K}/L$, we can rearrange terms to get

$$\dot{k} = s \cdot f(k) - (n+\delta)\cdot k \tag{1.13}$$

Equation (1.13) is the fundamental differential equation of the Solow–Swan model. This nonlinear equation depends only on k.

The term $n+\delta$ on the right-hand side of equation (1.13) can be thought of as the effective depreciation rate for the capital-labor ratio, $k \equiv K/L$. If the saving rate, s, were 0, capital per person would decline partly due to depreciation of capital at the rate δ and partly due to the increase in the number of persons at the rate n.

Figure 1.1 shows the workings of equation (1.13). The upper curve is the production function, $f(k)$. The term $(n+\delta)\cdot k$, which appears in equation (1.13), is drawn in figure 1.1 as a straight line from the origin with the positive slope $n+\delta$. The term $s\cdot f(k)$ in equation (1.13) looks like the production function except for the multiplication by the positive fraction s. Note from the figure that the $s\cdot f(k)$ curve starts from the origin [because $f(0)=0$], has a positive slope [because $f'(k)>0$], and gets flatter as k rises [because $f''(k)<0$]. The Inada conditions imply that the $s\cdot f(k)$ curve is vertical at $k=0$ and becomes flat as k goes to infinity. These properties imply that, other than the origin, the curve $s\cdot f(k)$ and the line $(n+\delta)\cdot k$ cross once and only once.

Consider an economy with the initial capital stock per person $k(0)>0$. Figure 1.1 shows that gross investment per person equals the height of the $s\cdot f(k)$ curve at this point. Consumption per person equals the vertical difference at this point between the $f(k)$ and $s\cdot f(k)$ curves.

1.2.3 Markets

In this section we show that the fundamental equation of the Solow–Swan model can be derived in a framework that explicitly incorporates markets. Instead of owning the technology and keeping the output produced with it, we assume that households own financial assets and labor. Assets deliver a rate of return $r(t)$, and labor is paid the wage rate $w(t)$. The total income received by households is, therefore, the sum of asset and labor income, $r(t)\cdot(\text{assets})+w(t)\cdot L(t)$. Households use the income that they do not consume to accumulate more assets

$$d(\text{assets})/dt=[r\cdot(\text{assets})+w\cdot L]-C \tag{1.14}$$

where, again, time subscripts have been omitted to simplify notation. Divide both sides of equation (1.14) by L, define assets per person as a, and take the derivative of a with respect to time, $\dot{a}=(1/L)\cdot d(\text{assets})/dt-na$, to get that the change in assets per person is given by

$$\dot{a}=(r\cdot a+w)-c-na \tag{1.15}$$

Firms hire labor and capital and use these two inputs with the production technology in equation (1.1) to produce output, which they sell at unit price. We think of firms as renting the services of capital from the households that own it. (None of the results would change if the firms owned the capital, and the households owned shares of stock in the firms.) Hence, the firms' costs of capital are the rental payments, which are proportional to K. This specification assumes that capital services can be increased or decreased without incurring any additional expenses, such as costs for installing machines.

Let R be the rental price for a unit of capital services, and assume again that capital stocks depreciate at the constant rate $\delta \geq 0$. The net rate of return to a household that owns a unit of capital is then $R - \delta$. Households also receive the interest rate r on funds lent to other households. In the absence of uncertainty, capital and loans are perfect substitutes as stores of value and, as a result, they must deliver the same return, so $r = R - \delta$ or, equivalently, $R = r + \delta$.

The representative firm's flow of net receipts or profit at any point in time is given by

$$\pi = F(K, L, T) - (r + \delta) \cdot K - wL \tag{1.16}$$

that is, gross receipts from the sale of output, $F(K, L, T)$, less the factor payments, which are rentals to capital, $(r + \delta) \cdot K$, and wages to workers, wL. Technology is assumed to be available for free, so no payment is needed to rent the formula used in the process of production. We assume that the firm seeks to maximize the present value of profits. Because the firm rents capital and labor services and has no adjustment costs, there are no intertemporal elements in the firm's maximization problem.[8] (The problem becomes intertemporal when we introduce adjustment costs for capital in chapter 3.)

Consider a firm of arbitrary scale, say with level of labor input L. Because the production function exhibits constant returns to scale, the profit for this firm, which is given by equation (1.16), can be written as

$$\pi = L \cdot [f(k) - (r + \delta) \cdot k - w] \tag{1.17}$$

A competitive firm, which takes r and w as given, maximizes profit for given L by setting

$$f'(k) = r + \delta \tag{1.18}$$

That is, the firm chooses the ratio of capital to labor to equate the marginal product of capital to the rental price.

The resulting level of profit is positive, zero, or negative depending on the value of w. If profit is positive, the firm could attain infinite profits by choosing an infinite scale. If profit is negative, the firm would contract its scale to zero. Therefore, in a full market equilibrium, w must be such that profit equals zero; that is, the total of the factor payments, $(r + \delta) \cdot K + wL$, equals the gross receipts in equation (1.17). In this case, the firm is indifferent about its scale.

8. In chapter 2 we show that dynamic firms would maximize the present discounted value of all future profits, which is given if r is constant by $\int_0^\infty L \cdot [f(k) - (r + \delta) \cdot k - w] \cdot e^{-rt} dt$. Because the problem does not involve any dynamic constraint, the firm maximizes static profits at all points in time. In fact, this dynamic problem is nothing but a sequence of static problems.

For profit to be zero, the wage rate has to equal the marginal product of labor corresponding to the value of k that satisfies equation (1.18):

$$[f(k) - k \cdot f'(k)] = w \tag{1.19}$$

It can be readily verified from substitution of equations (1.18) and (1.19) into equation (1.17) that the resulting level of profit equals zero for any value of L. Equivalently, if the factor prices equal the respective marginal products, the factor payments just exhaust the total output (a result that corresponds in mathematics to Euler's theorem).[9]

The model does not determine the scale of an individual, competitive firm that operates with a constant-returns-to-scale production function. The model will, however, determine the capital/labor ratio k, as well as the aggregate level of production, because the aggregate labor force is determined by equation (1.3).

The next step is to define the equilibrium of the economy. In a closed economy, the only asset in positive net supply is capital, because all the borrowing and lending must cancel within the economy. Hence, equilibrium in the asset market requires $a = k$. If we substitute this equality, as well as $r = f'(k) - \delta$ and $w = f(k) - k \cdot f'(k)$, into equation (1.15), we get

$$\dot{k} = f(k) - c - (n + \delta) \cdot k$$

Finally, if we follow Solow–Swan in making the assumption that households consume a constant fraction of their gross income, $c = (1 - s) \cdot f(k)$, we get

$$\dot{k} = s \cdot f(k) - (n + \delta) \cdot k$$

which is the same fundamental equation of the Solow–Swan model that we got in equation (1.13). Hence, introducing competitive markets into the Solow–Swan model does not change any of the main results.[10]

1.2.4 The Steady State

We now have the necessary tools to analyze the behavior of the model over time. We first consider the *long run* or *steady state,* and then we describe the *short run* or *transitional dynamics.* We define a *steady state* as a situation in which the various quantities grow at

9. Euler's theorem says that if a function $F(K, L)$ is homogeneous of degree one in K and L, then $F(K, L) = F_K \cdot K + F_L \cdot L$. This result can be proven using the equations $F(K, L) = L \cdot f(k)$, $F_K = f'(k)$, and $F_L = f(k) - k \cdot f'(k)$.

10. Note that, in the previous section and here, we assumed that each person saved a constant fraction of his or her gross income. We could have assumed instead that each person saved a constant fraction of his or her net income, $f(k) - \delta k$, which in the market setup equals $ra + w$. In this case, the fundamental equation of the Solow–Swan model would be $\dot{k} = s \cdot f(k) - (s\delta + n) \cdot k$. Again, the same equation applies to the household-producer and market setups.

constant (perhaps zero) rates.[11] In the Solow–Swan model, the steady state corresponds to $\dot{k} = 0$ in equation (1.13),[12] that is, to an intersection of the $s \cdot f(k)$ curve with the $(n+\delta) \cdot k$ line in figure 1.1.[13] The corresponding value of k is denoted k^*. (We focus here on the intersection at $k > 0$ and neglect the one at $k = 0$.) Algebraically, k^* satisfies the condition

$$s \cdot f(k^*) = (n+\delta) \cdot k^* \tag{1.20}$$

Since k is constant in the steady state, y and c are also constant at the values $y^* = f(k^*)$ and $c^* = (1-s) \cdot f(k^*)$, respectively. Hence, in the neoclassical model, the per capita quantities k, y, and c do not grow in the steady state. The constancy of the per capita magnitudes means that the levels of variables—K, Y, and C—grow in the steady state at the rate of population growth, n.

Once-and-for-all changes in the level of the technology will be represented by shifts of the production function, $f(\cdot)$. Shifts in the production function, in the saving rate s, in the rate of population growth n, and in the depreciation rate δ, all have effects on the per capita *levels* of the various quantities in the steady state. In figure 1.1, for example, a proportional upward shift of the production function or an increase in s shifts the $s \cdot f(k)$ curve upward and leads thereby to an increase in k^*. An increase in n or δ moves the $(n+\delta) \cdot k$ line upward and leads to a decrease in k^*.

It is important to note that a one-time change in the level of technology, the saving rate, the rate of population growth, and the depreciation rate do not affect the steady-state growth rates of per capita output, capital, and consumption, which are all still equal to zero. For this reason, the model as presently specified will not provide explanations of the determinants of long-run per capita growth.

1.2.5 The Golden Rule of Capital Accumulation and Dynamic Inefficiency

For a given level of A and given values of n and δ, there is a unique steady-state value $k^* > 0$ for each value of the saving rate s. Denote this relation by $k^*(s)$, with $dk^*(s)/ds > 0$. The steady-state level of per capita consumption is $c^* = (1-s) \cdot f[k^*(s)]$. We know from

11. Some economists use the expression *balanced growth path* to describe the state in which all variables grow at a constant rate and use *steady state* to describe the particular case when the growth rate is zero.

12. We can show that k must be constant in the steady state. Divide both sides of equation (1.13) by k to get $\dot{k}/k = s \cdot f(k)/k - (n+\delta)$. The left-hand side is constant, by definition, in the steady state. Since s, n, and δ are all constants, it follows that $f(k)/k$ must be constant in the steady state. The time derivative of $f(k)/k$ equals $-\{[f(k) - kf'(k)]/k\} \cdot (\dot{k}/k)$. The expression $f(k) - kf'(k)$ equals the marginal product of labor (as shown by equation [1.19]) and is positive. Therefore, as long as k is finite, $\dot{k}/k$ must equal 0 in the steady state.

13. The intersection in the range of positive k exists and is unique because $f(0) = 0$, $n+\delta < \lim_{k\to 0}[s \cdot f'(k)] = \infty$, $n+\delta > \lim_{k\to\infty}[s \cdot f'(k)] = 0$, and $f''(k) < 0$.

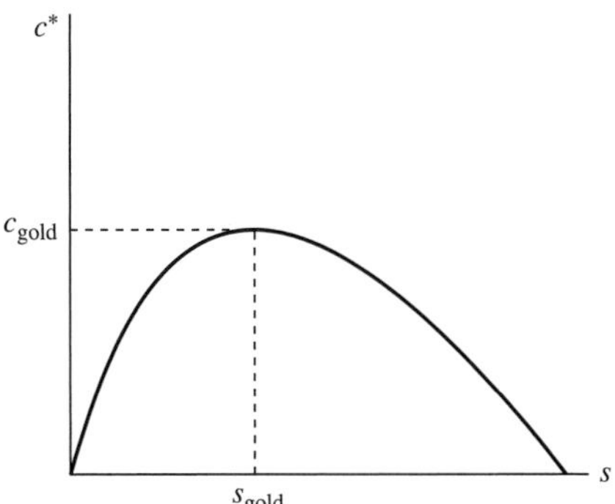

Figure 1.2
The golden rule of capital accumulation. The vertical axis shows the steady-state level of consumption per person that corresponds to each saving rate. The saving rate that maximizes steady-state consumption per person is called the golden-rule saving rate and is denoted by s_{Gold}.

equation (1.20) that $s \cdot f(k^*) = (n + \delta) \cdot k^*$; hence, we can write an expression for c^* as

$$c^*(s) = f[k^*(s)] - (n + \delta) \cdot k^*(s) \tag{1.21}$$

Figure 1.2 shows the relation between c^* and s that is implied by equation (1.21). The quantity c^* is increasing in s for low levels of s and decreasing in s for high values of s. The quantity c^* attains its maximum when the derivative vanishes, that is, when $[f'(k^*) - (n + \delta)] \cdot dk^*/ds = 0$. Since $dk^*/ds > 0$, the term in brackets must equal 0. If we denote the value of k^* that corresponds to the maximum of c^* by k_{gold}, then the condition that determines k_{gold} is

$$f'(k_{gold}) = n + \delta \tag{1.22}$$

The corresponding saving rate can be denoted as s_{gold}, and the associated level of steady-state per capita consumption is given by $c_{gold} = f(k_{gold}) - (n + \delta) \cdot k_{gold}$.

The condition in equation (1.22) is called the *golden rule of capital accumulation* (see Phelps, 1966). The source of this name is the biblical Golden Rule, which states, "Do unto others as you would have others do unto you." In economic terms, the golden-rule result can be interpreted as "If we provide the same amount of consumption to members of each current and future generation—that is, if we do not provide less to future generations than to ourselves—then the maximum amount of per capita consumption is c_{gold}."

Figure 1.3 illustrates the workings of the golden rule. The figure considers three possible saving rates, s_1, s_{gold}, and s_2, where $s_1 < s_{gold} < s_2$. Consumption per person, c, in each case equals the vertical distance between the production function, $f(k)$, and the appropriate

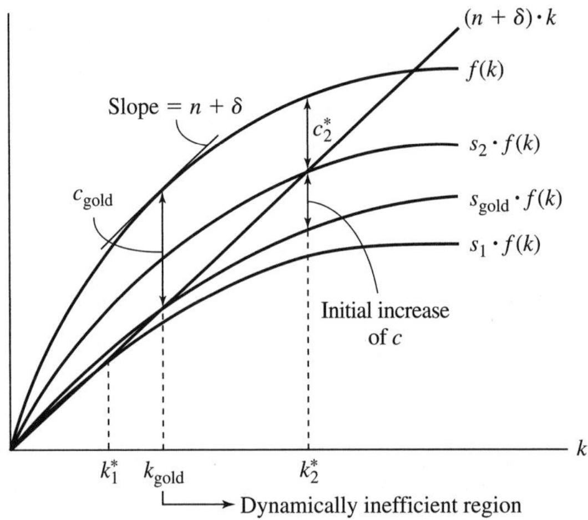

Figure 1.3
The golden rule and dynamic inefficiency. If the saving rate is above the golden rule ($s_2 > s_{gold}$ in the figure), a reduction in s increases steady-state consumption per person and also raises consumption per person along the transition. Since c increases at all points in time, a saving rate above the golden rule is dynamically inefficient. If the saving rate is below the golden rule ($s_1 < s_{gold}$ in the figure), an increase in s increases steady-state consumption per person but lowers consumption per person along the transition. The desirability of such a change depends on how households trade off current consumption against future consumption.

$s \cdot f(k)$ curve. For each s, the steady-state value k^* corresponds to the intersection between the $s \cdot f(k)$ curve and the $(n+\delta) \cdot k$ line. The steady-state per capita consumption, c^*, is maximized when $k^* = k_{gold}$ because the tangent to the production function at this point parallels the $(n+\delta) \cdot k$ line. The saving rate that yields $k^* = k_{gold}$ is the one that makes the $s \cdot f(k)$ curve cross the $(n+\delta) \cdot k$ line at the value k_{gold}. Since $s_1 < s_{gold} < s_2$, we also see in the figure that $k_1^* < k_{gold} < k_2^*$.

An important question is whether some saving rates are better than others. We will be unable to select the best saving rate (or, indeed, to determine whether a constant saving rate is desirable) until we specify a detailed objective function, as we do in the next chapter. We can, however, argue in the present context that a saving rate that exceeds s_{gold} forever is inefficient because higher quantities of per capita consumption could be obtained at all points in time by reducing the saving rate.

Consider an economy, such as the one described by the saving rate s_2 in figure 1.3, for which $s_2 > s_{gold}$, so that $k_2^* > k_{gold}^*$ and $c_2^* < c_{gold}$. Imagine that, starting from the steady state, the saving rate is reduced permanently to s_{gold}. Figure 1.3 shows that per capita consumption, c—given by the vertical distance between the $f(k)$ and $s_{gold} \cdot f(k)$ curves—initially increases by a discrete amount. Then the level of c falls monotonically during the transition[14] toward its new steady-state value, c_{gold}. Since $c_2^* < c_{gold}$, we conclude that c exceeds its previous value, c_2^*, at all transitional dates, as well as in the new steady state. Hence, when $s > s_{gold}$, the economy is oversaving in the sense that per capita consumption at all points in time could be raised by lowering the saving rate. An economy that oversaves is said to be *dynamically inefficient,* because the path of per capita consumption lies below feasible alternative paths at all points in time.

If $s < s_{gold}$—as in the case of the saving rate s_1 in figure 1.3—then the steady-state amount of per capita consumption can be increased by raising the saving rate. This rise in the saving rate would, however, reduce c currently and during part of the transition period. The outcome will therefore be viewed as good or bad depending on how households weigh today's consumption against the path of future consumption. We cannot judge the desirability of an increase in the saving rate in this situation until we make specific assumptions about how agents discount the future. We proceed along these lines in the next chapter.

1.2.6 Transitional Dynamics

The long-run growth rates in the Solow–Swan model are determined entirely by exogenous elements—in the steady state, the per capita quantities k, y, and c do not grow and the aggregate variables K, Y, and C grow at the exogenous rate of population growth n. Hence, the main substantive conclusions about the long run are that steady-state growth rates are independent of the saving rate or the level of technology. The model does, however, have more interesting implications about transitional dynamics. This transition shows how an economy's per capita income converges toward its own steady-state value and to the per capita incomes of other economies.

Division of both sides of equation (1.13) by k implies that the growth rate of k is given by

$$\gamma_k \equiv \dot{k}/k = s \cdot f(k)/k - (n + \delta) \tag{1.23}$$

where we have used the notation γ_z to represent the growth rate of variable z, notation that we will use throughout the book. Note that, at all points in time, the growth rate of the level of a variable equals the per capita growth rate plus the exogenous rate of population growth n, for example,

$$\dot{K}/K = \dot{k}/k + n$$

For subsequent purposes, we shall find it convenient to focus on the growth rate of k, as given in equation (1.23).

14. In the next subsection we analyze the transitional dynamics of the model.

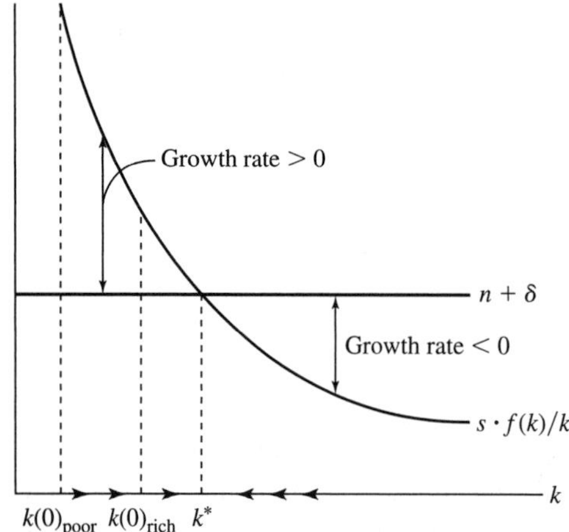

Figure 1.4
Dynamics of the Solow–Swan model. The growth rate of k is given by the vertical distance between the saving curve, $s \cdot f(k)/k$, and the effective depreciation line, $n + \delta$. If $k < k^*$, the growth rate of k is positive, and k increases toward k^*. If $k > k^*$, the growth rate is negative, and k falls toward k^*. Thus, the steady-state capital per person, k^*, is stable. Note that, along a transition from an initially low capital per person, the growth rate of k declines monotonically toward zero. The arrows on the horizontal axis indicate the direction of movement of k over time.

Equation (1.23) says that $\dot{k}/k$ equals the difference between two terms. The first term, $s \cdot f(k)/k$, we call the *saving curve* and the second term, $(n + \delta)$, the *depreciation curve*. We plot the two curves versus k in figure 1.4. The saving curve is downward sloping;[15] it asymptotes to infinity at $k = 0$ and approaches 0 as k tends to infinity.[16] The depreciation curve is a horizontal line at $n + \delta$. The vertical distance between the saving curve and the depreciation line equals the growth rate of capital per person (from equation [1.23]), and the crossing point corresponds to the steady state. Since $n + \delta > 0$ and $s \cdot f(k)/k$ falls monotonically from infinity to 0, the saving curve and the depreciation line intersect once and only once. Hence, the steady-state capital-labor ratio $k^* > 0$ exists and is unique.

Figure 1.4 shows that, to the left of the steady state, the $s \cdot f(k)/k$ curve lies above $n + \delta$. Hence, the growth rate of k is positive, and k rises over time. As k increases, $\dot{k}/k$ declines and approaches 0 as k approaches k^*. (The saving curve gets closer to the depreciation

15. The derivative of $f(k)/k$ with respect to k equals $-[f(k)/k - f'(k)]/k$. The expression in brackets equals the marginal product of labor, which is positive. Hence, the derivative is negative.

16. Note that $\lim_{k\to 0}[s \cdot f(k)/k] = 0/0$. We can apply l'Hôpital's rule to get $\lim_{k\to 0}[s \cdot f(k)/k] = \lim_{k\to 0}[s \cdot f'(k)] = \infty$, from the Inada condition. Similarly, the Inada condition $\lim_{k\to\infty}[f'(k)] = 0$ implies $\lim_{k\to\infty}[s \cdot f(k)/k] = 0$.

line as k gets closer to k^*; hence, $\dot{k}/k$ falls.) The economy tends asymptotically toward the steady state in which k—and, hence, y and c—do not change.

The reason behind the declining growth rates along the transition is the existence of diminishing returns to capital: when k is relatively low, the average product of capital, $f(k)/k$, is relatively high. By assumption, households save and invest a constant fraction, s, of this product. Hence, when k is relatively low, the gross investment per unit of capital, $s \cdot f(k)/k$, is relatively high. Capital per worker, k, effectively depreciates at the constant rate $n + \delta$. Consequently, the growth rate, $\dot{k}/k$, is also relatively high.

An analogous argument demonstrates that if the economy starts above the steady state, $k(0) > k^*$, then the growth rate of k is negative, and k falls over time. (Note from figure 1.4 that, for $k > k^*$, the $n + \delta$ line lies above the $s \cdot f(k)/k$ curve, and, hence, $\dot{k}/k < 0$.) The growth rate increases and approaches 0 as k approaches k^*. Thus, the system is globally stable: for any initial value, $k(0) > 0$, the economy converges to its unique steady state, $k^* > 0$.

We can also study the behavior of output along the transition. The growth rate of output per capita is given by

$$\dot{y}/y = f'(k) \cdot \dot{k}/f(k) = [k \cdot f'(k)/f(k)] \cdot (\dot{k}/k) \tag{1.24}$$

The expression in brackets on the far right is the *capital share,* that is, the share of the rental income on capital in total income.[17]

Equation (1.24) shows that the relation between $\dot{y}/y$ and $\dot{k}/k$ depends on the behavior of the capital share. In the Cobb–Douglas case (equation [1.11]), the capital share is the constant α, and $\dot{y}/y$ is the fraction α of $\dot{k}/k$. Hence, the behavior of $\dot{y}/y$ mimics that of $\dot{k}/k$.

More generally, we can substitute for $\dot{k}/k$ from equation (1.23) into equation (1.24) to get

$$\dot{y}/y = s \cdot f'(k) - (n + \delta) \cdot \text{Sh}(k) \tag{1.25}$$

where $\text{Sh}(k) \equiv k \cdot f'(k)/f(k)$ is the capital share. If we differentiate with respect to k and combine terms, we get

$$\partial(\dot{y}/y)/\partial k = \left[\frac{f''(k) \cdot k}{f(k)}\right] \cdot (\dot{k}/k) - \frac{(n + \delta) f'(k)}{f(k)} \cdot [1 - \text{Sh}(k)]$$

Since $0 < \text{Sh}(k) < 1$, the last term on the right-hand side is negative. If $\dot{k}/k \geq 0$, the first term

17. We showed before that, in a competitive market equilibrium, each unit of capital receives a rental equal to its marginal product, $f'(k)$. Hence, $k \cdot f'(k)$ is the income per person earned by owners of capital, and $k \cdot f'(k)/f(k)$—the term in brackets—is the share of this income in total income per person.

on the right-hand side is nonpositive, and, hence, $\partial(\dot{y}/y)/\partial k < 0$. Thus, $\dot{y}/y$ necessarily falls as k rises (and therefore as y rises) in the region in which $\dot{k}/k \geq 0$, that is, if $k \leq k^*$. If $\dot{k}/k < 0$ $(k > k^*)$, the sign of $\partial(\dot{y}/y)/\partial k$ is ambiguous for a general form of the production function, $f(k)$. However, if the economy is close to its steady state, the magnitude of $\dot{k}/k$ will be small, and $\partial(\dot{y}/y)/\partial k < 0$ will surely hold even if $k > k^*$.

In the Solow–Swan model, which assumes a constant saving rate, the level of consumption per person is given by $c = (1 - s) \cdot y$. Hence, the growth rates of consumption and income per capita are identical at all points in time, $\dot{c}/c = \dot{y}/y$. Consumption, therefore, exhibits the same dynamics as output.

1.2.7 Behavior of Input Prices During the Transition

We showed before that the Solow–Swan framework is consistent with a competitive market economy in which firms maximize profits and households choose to save a constant fraction of gross income. It is interesting to study the behavior of wages and interest rates along the transition as the capital stock increases toward the steady state. We showed that the interest rate equals the marginal product of capital minus the constant depreciation rate, $r = f'(k) - \delta$. Since the interest rate depends on the marginal product of capital, which depends on the capital stock per person, the interest rate moves during the transition as capital changes. The neoclassical production function exhibits diminishing returns to capital, $f''(k) < 0$, so the marginal product of capital declines as capital grows. It follows that the interest rate declines monotonically toward its steady-state value, given by $r^* = f'(k^*) - \delta$.

We also showed that the competitive wage rate was given by $w = f(k) - k \cdot f'(k)$. Again, the wage rate moves as capital increases. To see the behavior of the wage rate, we can take the derivative of w with respect to k to get

$$\frac{\partial w}{\partial k} = f'(k) - f'(k) - k \cdot f''(k) = -k \cdot f''(k) > 0$$

The wage rate, therefore, increases monotonically as the capital stock grows. In the steady state, the wage rate is given by $w^* = f(k^*) - k^* \cdot f'(k^*)$.

The behavior of wages and interest rates can be seen graphically in figure 1.5. The curve shown in the figure is again the production function, $f(k)$. The income per worker received by individual households is given by

$$y = w + Rk \tag{1.26}$$

where $R = r + \delta$ is the rental price of capital. Once the interest rate and the wage rate are determined, y is a linear function of k, with intercept w and slope R.

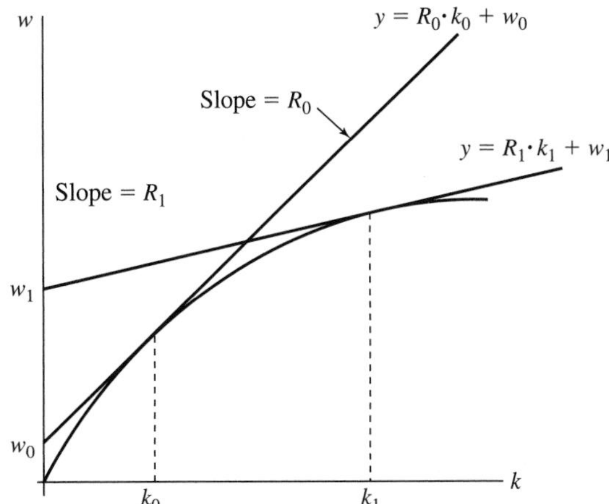

Figure 1.5
Input prices during the transition. At k_0, the straight line that is tangent to the production function has a slope that equals the rental price R_0 and an intercept that equals the wage rate w_0. As k rises toward k_1, the rental price falls toward R_1, and the wage rate rises toward w_1.

Of course, R depends on k through the marginal productivity condition, $f'(k) = R = r + \delta$. Therefore, R, the slope of the income function in equation (1.26), must equal the slope of $f(k)$ at the specified value of k. The figure shows two values, k_0 and k_1. The income functions at these two values are given by straight lines that are tangent to $f(k)$ at k_0 and k_1, respectively. As k rises during the transition, the figure shows that the slope of the tangent straight line declines from R_0 to R_1. The figure also shows that the intercept—which equals w—rises from w_0 to w_1.

1.2.8 Policy Experiments

Suppose that the economy is initially in a steady-state position with the capital per person equal to k_1^*. Imagine that the saving rate rises permanently from s_1 to a higher value s_2, possibly because households change their behavior or the government introduces some policy that raises the saving rate. Figure 1.6 shows that the $s \cdot f(k)/k$ schedule shifts to the right. Hence, the intersection with the $n + \delta$ line also shifts to the right, and the new steady-state capital stock, k_2^*, exceeds k_1^*.

How does the economy adjust from k_1^* to k_2^*? At $k = k_1^*$, the gap between the $s_1 \cdot f(k)/k$ curve and the $n + \delta$ line is positive; that is, saving is more than enough to generate an increase in k. As k increases, its growth rate falls and approaches 0 as k approaches k_2^*. The result, therefore, is that a permanent increase in the saving rate generates temporarily

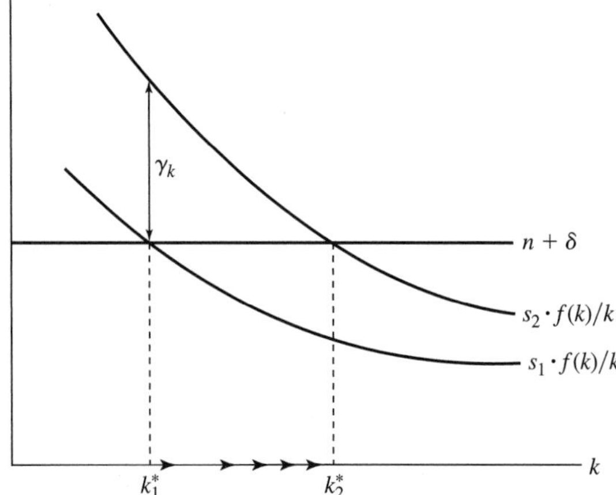

Figure 1.6
Effects from an increase in the saving rate. Starting from the steady-state capital per person k_1^*, an increase in s from s_1 to s_2 shifts the $s \cdot f(k)/k$ curve to the right. At the old steady state, investment exceeds effective depreciation, and the growth rate of k becomes positive. Capital per person rises until the economy approaches its new steady state at $k_2^* > k_1^*$.

positive per capita growth rates. In the long run, the levels of k and y are permanently higher, but the per capita growth rates return to zero.

The positive transitional growth rates may suggest that the economy could grow forever by raising the saving rate over and over again. One problem with this line of reasoning is that the saving rate is a fraction, a number between zero and one. Since people cannot save more than everything, the saving rate is bounded by one. Notice that, even if people could save all their income, the saving curve would still cross the depreciation line and, as a result, long-run per capita growth would stop.[18] The reason is that the workings of diminishing returns to capital eventually bring the economy back to the zero-growth steady state. Therefore, we can now answer the question that motivated the beginning of this chapter: "Can income per capita grow forever by simply saving and investing physical capital?" If the production function is neoclassical, the answer is "no."

We can also assess permanent changes in the growth rate of population, n. These changes could reflect shifts of household behavior or changes in government policies that influence fertility. A decrease in n shifts the depreciation line downward, so that the steady-state level of capital per worker would be larger. However, the long-run growth rate of capital per person would remain at zero.

18. Before reaching $s = 1$, the economy would reach s_{gold}, so that further increases in saving rates would put the economy in the dynamically inefficient region.

A permanent, once-and-for-all improvement in the level of the technology has similar, temporary effects on the per capita growth rates. If the production function $f(k)$ shifts upward in a proportional manner, then the saving curve shifts upward, just as in figure 1.6. Hence, $\dot{k}/k$ again becomes positive temporarily. In the long run, the permanent improvement in technology generates higher levels of k and y but no changes in the per capita growth rates. The key difference between improvements in knowledge and increases in the saving rate is that improvements in knowledge are not bounded. That is, the production function can shift over and over again because, in principle, there are no limits to human knowledge. The saving rate, however, is physically bounded by one. It follows that, if we want to generate growth in long-run per capita income and consumption within the neoclassical framework, growth must come from technological progress rather than from physical capital accumulation.

We observed before (note 3) that differences in government policies and institutions can amount to variations in the level of the technology. For example, high tax rates on capital income, failures to protect property rights, and distorting government regulations can be economically equivalent to a poorer level of technology. However, it is probably infeasible to achieve perpetual growth through an unending sequence of improvements in government policies and institutions. Therefore, in the long run, sustained growth would still depend on technological progress.

1.2.9 An Example: Cobb–Douglas Technology

We can illustrate the results for the case of a Cobb–Douglas production function (equation [1.11]). The steady-state capital-labor ratio is determined from equation (1.20) as

$$k^* = [sA/(n+\delta)]^{1/(1-\alpha)} \tag{1.27}$$

Note that, as we saw graphically for a more general production function $f(k)$, k^* rises with the saving rate s and the level of technology A, and falls with the rate of population growth n and the depreciation rate δ. The steady-state level of output per capita is given by

$$y^* = A^{1/(1-\alpha)} \cdot [s/(n+\delta)]^{\alpha/(1-\alpha)}$$

Thus y^* is a positive function of s and A, and a negative function of n and δ.

Along the transition, the growth rate of k is given from equation (1.23) by

$$\dot{k}/k = sAk^{-(1-\alpha)} - (n+\delta) \tag{1.28}$$

If $k(0) < k^*$, then $\dot{k}/k$ in equation (1.28) is positive. This growth rate declines as k rises and approaches 0 as k approaches k^*. Since equation (1.24) implies $\dot{y}/y = \alpha \cdot (\dot{k}/k)$, the behavior of $\dot{y}/y$ mimics that of $\dot{k}/k$. In particular, the lower $y(0)$, the higher $\dot{y}/y$.

A Closed-Form Solution It is interesting to notice that, when the production function is Cobb–Douglas and the saving rate is constant, it is possible to get a closed-form solution for the exact time path of k. Equation (1.28) can be written as

$$\dot{k} \cdot k^{-\alpha} + (n+\delta) \cdot k^{1-\alpha} = sA$$

If we define $v \equiv k^{1-\alpha}$, we can transform the equation to

$$\left(\frac{1}{1-\alpha}\right) \cdot \dot{v} + (n+\delta) \cdot v = sA$$

which is a first-order, linear differential equation in v. The solution to this equation is

$$v \equiv k^{1-\alpha} = \frac{sA}{(n+\delta)} + \left\{ [k(0)]^{1-\alpha} - \frac{sA}{(n+\delta)} \right\} \cdot e^{-(1-\alpha) \cdot (n+\delta) \cdot t}$$

The last term is an exponential function with exponent equal to $-(1-\alpha) \cdot (n+\delta)$. Hence, the gap between $k^{1-\alpha}$ and its steady-state value, $sA/(n+\delta)$, vanishes exactly at the constant rate $(1-\alpha) \cdot (n+\delta)$.

1.2.10 Absolute and Conditional Convergence

The fundamental equation of the Solow–Swan model (equation [1.23]) implies that the derivative of $\dot{k}/k$ with respect to k is negative:

$$\partial(\dot{k}/k)/\partial k = s \cdot [f'(k) - f(k)/k]/k < 0$$

Other things equal, smaller values of k are associated with larger values of $\dot{k}/k$. An important question arises: does this result mean that economies with lower capital per person tend to grow faster in per capita terms? In other words, does there tend to be *convergence* across economies?

To answer these questions, consider a group of closed economies (say, isolated regions or countries) that are structurally similar in the sense that they have the same values of the parameters s, n, and δ and also have the same production function $f(\cdot)$. Thus, the economies have the same steady-state values k^* and y^*. Imagine that the only difference among the economies is the initial quantity of capital per person $k(0)$. These differences in starting values could reflect past disturbances, such as wars or transitory shocks to production functions. The model then implies that the less-advanced economies—with lower values of $k(0)$ and $y(0)$—have higher growth rates of k and, in the typical case, also higher growth rates of y.[19]

19. This conclusion is unambiguous if the production function is Cobb–Douglas, if $k \leq k^*$, or if k is only a small amount above k^*.

Figure 1.4 distinguished two economies, one with the low initial value, $k(0)_{\text{poor}}$, and the other with the high initial value, $k(0)_{\text{rich}}$. Since each economy has the same underlying parameters, the dynamics of k are determined in each case by the same $s \cdot f(k)/k$ and $n+\delta$ curves. Hence, the growth rate $\dot{k}/k$ is unambiguously higher for the economy with the lower initial value, $k(0)_{\text{poor}}$. This result implies a form of convergence: regions or countries with lower starting values of the capital-labor ratio have higher per capita growth rates $\dot{k}/k$, and tend thereby to catch up or converge to those with higher capital-labor ratios.

The hypothesis that poor economies tend to grow faster per capita than rich ones—without conditioning on any other characteristics of economies—is referred to as *absolute convergence*. This hypothesis receives only mixed reviews when confronted with data on groups of economies. We can look, for example, at the growth experience of a broad cross section of countries over the period 1960 to 2000. Figure 1.7 plots the average annual growth rate of real per capita GDP against the log of real per capita GDP at the start of the period, 1960, for 114 countries. The growth rates are actually positively correlated with the initial position; that is, there is some tendency for the initially richer countries to grow faster in per capita terms. Thus, this sample rejects the hypothesis of absolute convergence.

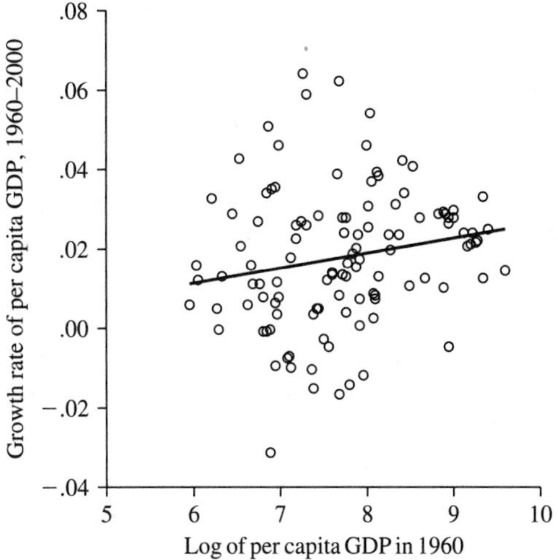

Figure 1.7
Convergence of GDP across countries: Growth rate versus initial level of real per capita GDP for 114 countries. For a sample of 114 countries, the average growth rate of GDP per capita from 1960 to 2000 (shown on the vertical axis) has little relation with the 1960 level of real per capita GDP (shown on the horizontal axis). The relation is actually slightly positive. Hence, absolute convergence does not apply for a broad cross section of countries.

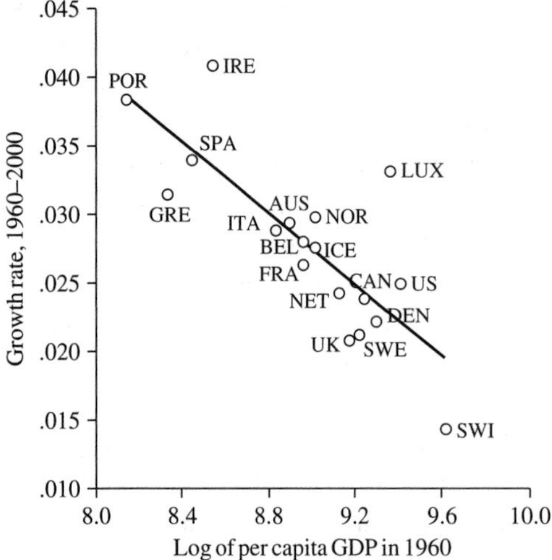

Figure 1.8
Convergence of GDP across OECD countries: Growth rate versus initial level of real per capita GDP for 18 OECD countries. If the sample is limited to 18 original OECD countries (from 1961), the average growth rate of real per capita GDP from 1960 to 2000 is negatively related to the 1960 level of real per capita GDP. Hence, absolute convergence applies for these OECD countries.

The hypothesis fares better if we examine a more homogeneous group of economies. Figure 1.8 shows the results if we limit consideration to 18 relatively advanced countries that were members of the Organization for Economic Cooperation and Development (OECD) from the start of the organization in 1961.[20] In this case, the initially poorer countries did experience significantly higher per capita growth rates.

This type of result becomes more evident if we consider an even more homogeneous group, the continental U.S. states, each viewed as a separate economy. Figure 1.9 plots the growth rate of per capita personal income for each state from 1880 to 2000 against the log of per capita personal income in 1880.[21] Absolute convergence—the initially poorer states growing faster in per capita terms—holds clearly in this diagram.

We can accommodate the theory to the empirical observations on convergence if we allow for heterogeneity across economies, in particular, if we drop the assumption that all economies have the same parameters, and therefore, the same steady-state positions. If the

20. Germany is omitted because of missing data, and Turkey is omitted because it was not an advanced economy in 1960.

21. There are 47 observations on U.S. states or territories. Oklahoma is omitted because 1880 preceded the Oklahoma land rush, and the data are consequently unavailable.

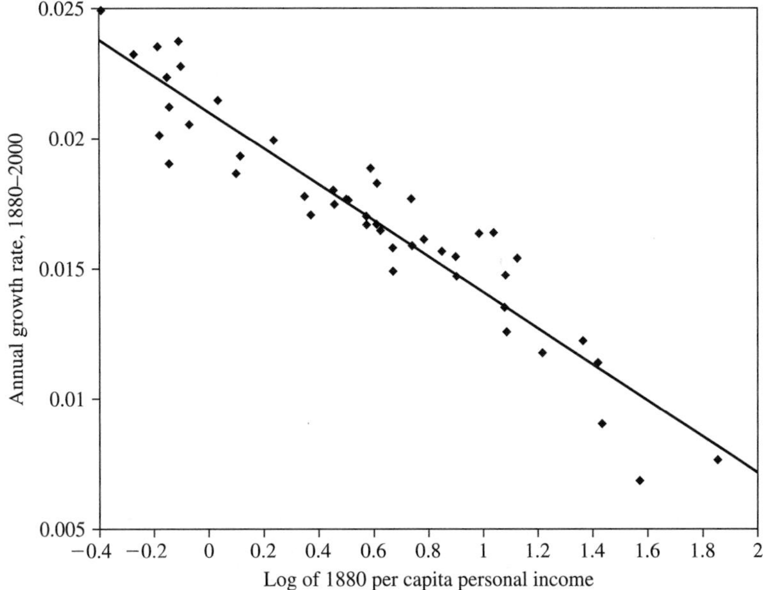

Figure 1.9
Convergence of personal income across U.S. states: 1880 personal income and income growth from 1880 to 2000. The relation between the growth rate of per capita personal income from 1880 to 2000 (shown on the vertical axis) is negatively related to the level of per capita income in 1880 (shown on the horizontal axis). Thus absolute convergence holds for the states of the United States.

steady states differ, we have to modify the analysis to consider a concept of *conditional convergence*. The main idea is that an economy grows faster the further it is from its own steady-state value.

We illustrate the concept of conditional convergence in figure 1.10 by considering two economies that differ in only two respects: first, they have different initial stocks of capital per person, $k(0)_{\text{poor}} < k(0)_{\text{rich}}$, and second, they have different saving rates, $s_{\text{poor}} \neq s_{\text{rich}}$. Our previous analysis implies that differences in saving rates generate differences in the same direction in the steady-state values of capital per person, that is, $k^*_{\text{poor}} \neq k^*_{\text{rich}}$. [In figure 1.10, these steady-state values are determined by the intersection of the $s_i \cdot f(k)/k$ curves with the common $n + \delta$ line.] We consider the case in which $s_{\text{poor}} < s_{\text{rich}}$ and, hence, $k^*_{\text{poor}} < k^*_{\text{rich}}$ because these differences likely explain why $k(0)_{\text{poor}} < k(0)_{\text{rich}}$ applies at the initial date. (It is also true empirically, as discussed in the introduction, that countries with higher levels of real per capita GDP tend to have higher saving rates.)

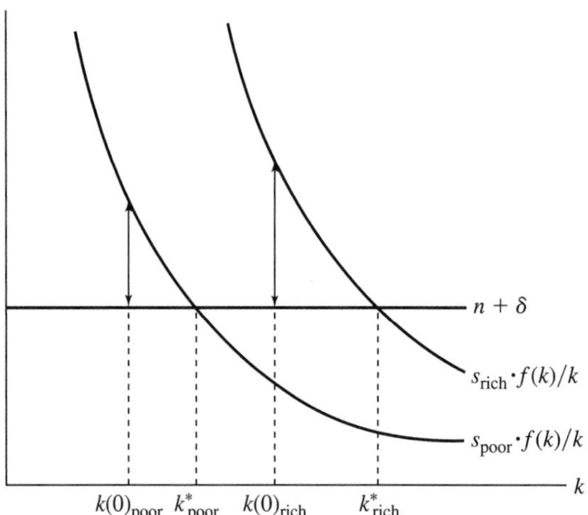

Figure 1.10
Conditional convergence. If a rich economy has a higher saving rate than a poor economy, the rich economy may be proportionately further from its steady-state position. In this case, the rich economy would be predicted to grow faster per capita than the poor economy; that is, absolute convergence would not hold.

The question is, Does the model predict that the poor economy will grow faster than the rich one? If they have the same saving rate, then the per capita growth rate—the distance between the $s \cdot f(k)/k$ curve and the $n+\delta$ line—would be higher for the poor economy, and $(\dot{k}/k)_{\text{poor}} > (\dot{k}/k)_{\text{rich}}$ would apply. However, if the rich economy has a higher saving rate, as in figure 1.10, then $(\dot{k}/k)_{\text{poor}} < (\dot{k}/k)_{\text{rich}}$ might hold, so that the rich economy grows faster. The intuition is that the low saving rate of the poor economy offsets its higher average product of capital as a determinant of economic growth. Hence, the poor economy may grow at a slower rate than the rich one.

The neoclassical model does predict that each economy converges to its own steady state and that the speed of this convergence relates inversely to the distance from the steady state. In other words, the model predicts conditional convergence in the sense that a lower starting value of real per capita income tends to generate a higher per capita growth rate, once we control for the determinants of the steady state.

Recall that the steady-state value, k^*, depends on the saving rate, s, and the level of the production function, $f(\cdot)$. We have also mentioned that government policies and institutions can be viewed as additional elements that effectively shift the position of the production function. The findings on conditional convergence suggest that we should hold constant these determinants of k^* to isolate the predicted inverse relationship between growth rates and initial positions.

Algebraically, we can illustrate the concept of conditional convergence by returning to the formula for $\dot{k}/k$ in equation (1.23). One of the determinants of $\dot{k}/k$ is the saving rate s. We can use the steady-state condition from equation (1.20) to express s as follows:

$$s = (n + \delta) \cdot k^*/f(k^*)$$

If we replace s by this expression in equation (1.23), then $\dot{k}/k$ can be expressed as

$$\dot{k}/k = (n + \delta) \cdot \left[\frac{f(k)/k}{f(k^*)/k^*} - 1\right] \tag{1.29}$$

Equation (1.29) is consistent with $\dot{k}/k = 0$ when $k = k^*$. For given k^*, the formula implies that a reduction in k, which raises the average product of capital, $f(k)/k$, increases $\dot{k}/k$. But a lower k matches up with a higher $\dot{k}/k$ only if the reduction is relative to the steady-state value, k^*. In particular, $f(k)/k$ must be high relative to the steady-state value, $f(k^*)/k^*$. Thus a poor country would not be expected to grow rapidly if its steady-state value, k^*, is as low as its current value, k.

In the case of a Cobb–Douglas technology, the saving rate can be written as

$$s = \frac{(n + \delta)}{A} \cdot k^{*(1-\alpha)}$$

which we can substitute into equation (1.23) to get

$$\dot{k}/k = (n + \delta) \cdot \left[\left(\frac{k}{k^*}\right)^{\alpha-1} - 1\right] \tag{1.30}$$

We see that the growth rate of capital, k, depends on the ratio k/k^*; that is, it depends on the distance between the current and steady-state capital-labor ratio.

The result in equation (1.29) suggests that we should look empirically at the relation between the per capita growth rate, $\dot{y}/y$, and the starting position, $y(0)$, after holding fixed variables that account for differences in the steady-state position, y^*. For a relatively homogeneous group of economies, such as the U.S. states, the differences in steady-state positions may be minor, and we would still observe the convergence pattern shown in figure 1.9. For a broad cross section of 114 countries, however, as shown in figure 1.7, the differences in steady-state positions are likely to be substantial. Moreover, the countries with low starting levels, $y(0)$, are likely to be in this position precisely because they have low steady-state values, y^*, perhaps because of chronically low saving rates or persistently bad government policies that effectively lower the level of the production function. In other words, the per capita growth rate may have little correlation with $\log[y(0)]$, as in figure 1.7, because $\log[y(0)]$ is itself uncorrelated with the gap from the steady state, $\log[y(0)/y^*]$. The perspective of conditional convergence indicates that this gap is the variable that matters for the subsequent per capita growth rate.

We show in chapter 12 that the inclusion of variables that proxy for differences in steady-state positions makes a major difference in the results for the broad cross section of countries. When these additional variables are held constant, the relation between the per capita growth rate and the log of initial real per capita GDP becomes significantly negative, as predicted by the neoclassical model. In other words, the cross-country data support the hypothesis of conditional convergence.

1.2.11 Convergence and the Dispersion of Per Capita Income

The concept of convergence considered thus far is that economies with lower levels of per capita income (expressed relative to their steady-state levels of per capita income) tend to grow faster in per capita terms. This behavior is often confused with an alternative meaning of convergence, that the dispersion of real per capita income across a group of economies or individuals tends to fall over time.[22] We show now that, even if absolute convergence holds in our sense, the dispersion of per capita income need not decline over time.

Suppose that absolute convergence holds for a group of economies $i = 1, \ldots, N$, where N is a large number. In discrete time, corresponding for example to annual data, the real per capita income for economy i can then be approximated by the process

$$\log(y_{it}) = a + (1 - b) \cdot \log(y_{i,t-1}) + u_{it} \tag{1.31}$$

where a and b are constants, with $0 < b < 1$, and u_{it} is a disturbance term. The condition $b > 0$ implies absolute convergence because the annual growth rate, $\log(y_{it}/y_{i,t-1})$, is inversely related to $\log(y_{i,t-1})$. A higher coefficient b corresponds to a greater tendency toward convergence.[23] The disturbance term picks up temporary shocks to the production function, the saving rate, and so on. We assume that u_{it} has zero mean, the same variance σ_u^2 for all economies, and is independent over time and across economies.

One measure of the dispersion or inequality of per capita income is the sample variance of the $\log(y_{it})$:

$$D_t \equiv \frac{1}{N} \cdot \sum_{i=1}^{N} [\log(y_{it}) - \mu_t]^2$$

22. See Sala-i-Martin (1990) and Barro and Sala-i-Martin (1992a) for further discussion of the two concepts of convergence.

23. The condition $b < 1$ rules out a leapfrogging or overshooting effect, whereby an economy that starts out behind another economy would be predicted systematically to get ahead of the other economy at some future date. This leapfrogging effect cannot occur in the neoclassical model but can arise in some models of technological adaptation that we discuss in chapter 8.

where μ_t is the sample mean of the $\log(y_{it})$. If there are a large number N of observations, the sample variance is close to the population variance, and we can use equation (1.31) to derive the evolution of D_t over time:

$$D_t \approx (1-b)^2 \cdot D_{t-1} + \sigma_u^2$$

This first-order difference equation for dispersion has a steady state given by

$$D^* = \sigma_u^2/[1-(1-b)^2]$$

Hence, the steady-state dispersion falls with b (the strength of the convergence effect) but rises with the variance σ_u^2 of the disturbance term. In particular, $D^* > 0$ even if $b > 0$, as long as $\sigma_u^2 > 0$.

The evolution of D_t can be expressed as

$$D_t = D^* + (1-b)^2 \cdot (D_{t-1} - D^*) = D^* + (1-b)^{2t} \cdot (D_0 - D^*) \tag{1.32}$$

where D_0 is the dispersion at time 0. Since $0 < b < 1$, D_t monotonically approaches its steady-state value, D^*, over time. Equation (1.32) implies that D_t rises or falls over time depending on whether D_0 begins below or above the steady-state value.[24] Note especially that a rising dispersion is consistent with absolute convergence ($b > 0$).

These results about convergence and dispersion are analogous to Galton's fallacy about the distribution of heights in a population (see Quah, 1993, and Hart, 1995, for discussions). The observation that heights in a family tend to regress toward the mean across generations (a property analogous to our convergence concept for per capita income) does not imply that the dispersion of heights across the full population (a measure that parallels the dispersion of per capita income across economies) tends to narrow over time.

1.2.12 Technological Progress

Classification of Inventions We have assumed thus far that the level of technology is constant over time. As a result, we found that all per capita variables were constant in the long run. This feature of the model is clearly unrealistic; in the United States, for example, the average per capita growth rate has been positive for over two centuries. In the absence of technological progress, diminishing returns would have made it impossible to maintain per capita growth for so long just by accumulating more capital per worker. The neoclassical economists of the 1950s and 1960s recognized this problem and amended the basic model

24. We could extend the model by allowing for temporary shocks to σ_u^2 or for major disturbances like wars or oil shocks that affect large subgroups of economies in a common way. In this extended model, the dispersion could depart from the deterministic path that we derived; for example, D_t could rise in some periods even if D_0 began above its steady-state value.

to allow the technology to improve over time. These improvements provided an escape from diminishing returns and thus enabled the economy to grow in per capita terms in the long run. We now explore how the model works when we allow for such technological advances.

Although some discoveries are serendipitous, most technological improvements reflect purposeful activity, such as research and development (R&D) carried out in universities and corporate or government laboratories. This research is sometimes financed by private institutions and sometimes by governmental agencies, such as the National Science Foundation. Since the amount of resources devoted to R&D depends on economic conditions, the evolution of the technology also depends on these conditions. This relation will be the subject of our analysis in chapters 6–8. At present, we consider only the simpler case in which the technology improves exogenously.

The first issue is how to introduce exogenous technological progress into the model. This progress can take various forms. Inventions may allow producers to generate the same amount of output with either relatively less capital input or relatively less labor input, cases referred to as *capital-saving* or *labor-saving* technological progress, respectively. Inventions that do not save relatively more of either input are called *neutral* or *unbiased*.

The definition of neutral technological progress depends on the precise meaning of capital saving and labor saving. Three popular definitions are due to Hicks (1932), Harrod (1942), and Solow (1969).

Hicks says that a technological innovation is neutral (Hicks neutral) if the ratio of marginal products remains unchanged for a given capital-labor ratio. This property corresponds to a renumbering of the isoquants, so that Hicks-neutral production functions can be written as

$$Y = T(t) \cdot F(K, L) \tag{1.33}$$

where $T(t)$ is the index of the state of the technology, and $\dot{T}(t) \geq 0$.

Harrod defines an innovation as neutral (Harrod neutral) if the relative input shares, $(K \cdot F_K)/(L \cdot F_L)$, remain unchanged for a given capital-output ratio. Robinson (1938) and Uzawa (1961) showed that this definition implied that the production function took the form

$$Y = F[K, L \cdot T(t)] \tag{1.34}$$

where $T(t)$ is the index of the technology, and $\dot{T}(t) \geq 0$. This form is called *labor-augmenting* technological progress because it raises output in the same way as an increase in the stock of labor. (Notice that the technology factor, $T(t)$, appears in the production function as a multiple of L.)

Finally, Solow defines an innovation as neutral (Solow neutral) if the relative input shares, $(L \cdot F_L)/(K \cdot F_K)$, remain unchanged for a given labor/output ratio. This definition can be shown to imply a production function of the form

$$Y = F[K \cdot T(t), L] \tag{1.35}$$

where $T(t)$ is the index of the technology, and $\dot{T}(t) \geq 0$. Production functions of this form are called *capital augmenting* because a technological improvement increases production in the same way as an increase in the stock of capital.

The Necessity for Technological Progress to Be Labor Augmenting Suppose that we consider only constant rates of technological progress. Then, in the neoclassical growth model with a constant rate of population growth, only labor-augmenting technological change turns out to be consistent with the existence of a steady state, that is, with constant growth rates of the various quantities in the long run. This result is proved in the appendix to this chapter (section 1.5).

If we want to consider models that possess a steady state, we have to assume that technological progress takes the labor-augmenting form. Another approach, which would be substantially more complicated, would be to deal with models that lack steady states, that is, in which the various growth rates do not approach constants in the long run. However, one reason to stick with the simpler framework that possesses a steady state is that the long-term experiences of the United States and some other developed countries indicate that per capita growth rates can be positive and trendless over long periods of time (see chapter 12). This empirical phenomenon suggests that a useful theory would predict that per capita growth rates approach constants in the long run; that is, the model would possess a steady state.

If the production function is Cobb–Douglas, $Y = AK^{\alpha}L^{1-\alpha}$ in equation (1.11), then it is clear from inspection that the form of technological progress—augmenting A, K, or L—will not matter for the results (see the appendix for discussion). Thus, in the Cobb–Douglas case, we will be safe in assuming that technological progress is labor augmenting. Recall that the key property of the Cobb–Douglas function is that, in a competitive setting, the factor-income shares are constant. Thus, if factor-income shares are reasonably stable—as seems to be true for the U.S. economy but not for some others—we may be okay in regarding the production function as approximately Cobb–Douglas and, hence, in assuming that technogical progress is labor augmenting.

Another approach, when the production function is not Cobb–Douglas, is to derive the form of technological progress from a theory of technological change. Acemoglu (2002) takes this approach, using a variant of the model of endogenous technological change that we develop in chapter 6. He finds that, under some conditions, the form of technological progress would be asymptotically labor augmenting.

The Solow–Swan Model with Labor-Augmenting Technological Progress We assume now that the production function includes labor-augmenting technological progress, as shown in equation (1.34), and that the technology term, $T(t)$, grows at the constant rate x. The condition for the change in the capital stock is

$$\dot{K} = s \cdot F[K, L \cdot T(t)] - \delta K$$

If we divide both sides of this equation by L, we can derive an expression for the change in k over time:

$$\dot{k} = s \cdot F[k, T(t)] - (n + \delta) \cdot k \tag{1.36}$$

The only difference from equation (1.13) is that output per person now depends on the level of the technology, $T(t)$.

Divide both sides of equation (1.36) by k to compute the growth rate:

$$\dot{k}/k = s \cdot F[k, T(t)]/k - (n + \delta) \tag{1.37}$$

As in equation (1.23), $\dot{k}/k$ equals the difference between two terms, where the first term is the product of s and the average product of capital, and the second term is $n + \delta$. The only difference is that now, for given k, the average product of capital, $F[k, T(t)]/k$, increases over time because of the growth in $T(t)$ at the rate x. In terms of figure 1.4, the downward-sloping curve, $s \cdot F(\cdot)/k$, shifts continually to the right, and, hence, the level of k that corresponds to the intersection between this curve and the $n + \delta$ line also shifts continually to the right. We now compute the growth rate of k in the steady state.

By definition, the steady-state growth rate, $(\dot{k}/k)^*$, is constant. Since s, n, and δ are also constants, equation (1.37) implies that the average product of capital, $F[k, T(t)]/k$, is constant in the steady state. Because of constant returns to scale, the expression for the average product equals $F[1, T(t)/k]$ and is therefore constant only if k and $T(t)$ grow at the same rate, that is, $(\dot{k}/k)^* = x$.

Output per capita is given by

$$y = F[k, T(t)] = k \cdot F[1, T(t)/k]$$

Since k and $T(t)$ grow in the steady state at the rate x, the steady-state growth rate of y equals x. Moreover, since $c = (1 - s) \cdot y$, the steady-state growth rate of c also equals x.

To analyze the transitional dynamics of the model with technological progress, it will be convenient to rewrite the system in terms of variables that remain constant in the steady state. Since k and $T(t)$ grow in the steady state at the same rate, we can work with the ratio $\hat{k} \equiv k/T(t) = K/[L \cdot T(t)]$. The variable $L \cdot T(t) \equiv \hat{L}$ is often called the *effective amount of labor*—the physical quantity of labor, L, multiplied by its efficiency, $T(t)$. (The terminology *effective labor* is appropriate because the economy operates as if its labor input were $\hat{L}$.) The variable $\hat{k}$ is then the quantity of capital per unit of effective labor.

The quantity of output per unit of effective labor, $\hat{y} \equiv Y/[L \cdot T(t)]$, is given by

$$\hat{y} = F(\hat{k}, 1) \equiv f(\hat{k}) \tag{1.38}$$

Hence, we can again write the production function in intensive form if we replace y and k by $\hat{y}$ and $\hat{k}$, respectively. If we proceed as we did before to get equations (1.13) and (1.23), but now use the condition that $A(t)$ grows at the rate x, we can derive the dynamic equation for $\hat{k}$:

$$\dot{\hat{k}}/\hat{k} = s \cdot f(\hat{k})/\hat{k} - (x + n + \delta) \tag{1.39}$$

The only difference between equations (1.39) and (1.23), aside from the hats (^), is that the last term on the right-hand side includes the parameter x. The term $x + n + \delta$ is now the effective depreciation rate for $\hat{k} \equiv K/\hat{L}$. If the saving rate, s, were zero, $\hat{k}$ would decline partly due to depreciation of K at the rate δ and partly due to growth of $\hat{L}$ at the rate $x + n$.

Following an argument similar to that of section 1.2.4, we can show that the steady-state growth rate of $\hat{k}$ is zero. The steady-state value $\hat{k}^*$ satisfies the condition

$$s \cdot f(\hat{k}^*) = (x + n + \delta) \cdot \hat{k}^* \tag{1.40}$$

The transitional dynamics of $\hat{k}$ are qualitatively similar to those of k in the previous model. In particular, we can construct a picture like figure 1.4 in which the horizontal axis involves $\hat{k}$, the downward-sloping curve is now $s \cdot f(\hat{k})/\hat{k}$, and the horizontal line is at the level $x + n + \delta$, rather than $n + \delta$. The new construction is shown in figure 1.11. We can use this figure, as we used figure 1.4 before, to assess the relation between the initial value, $\hat{k}(0)$, and the growth rate, $\dot{\hat{k}}/\hat{k}$.

In the steady state, the variables with hats—$\hat{k}$, $\hat{y}$, $\hat{c}$—are now constant. Therefore, the per capita variables—k, y, c—now grow in the steady state at the exogenous rate of technological progress, x.[25] The level variables—K, Y, C—grow accordingly in the steady state at the rate $n + x$, that is, the sum of population growth and technological change. Note that, as in the prior analysis that neglected technological progress, shifts to the saving rate or the level of the production function affect long-run levels—$\hat{k}^*$, $\hat{y}^*$, $\hat{c}^*$—but not steady-state growth rates. As before, these kinds of disturbances influence growth rates during the transition from an initial position, represented by $\hat{k}(0)$, to the steady-state value, $\hat{k}^*$.

25. We always have the condition $(1/\hat{k}) \cdot (d\hat{k}/dt) = \dot{k}/k - x$. Therefore, $(1/\hat{k}) \cdot (d\hat{k}/dt) = 0$ implies $\dot{k}/k = x$, and similarly for $\dot{y}/y$ and $\dot{c}/c$.

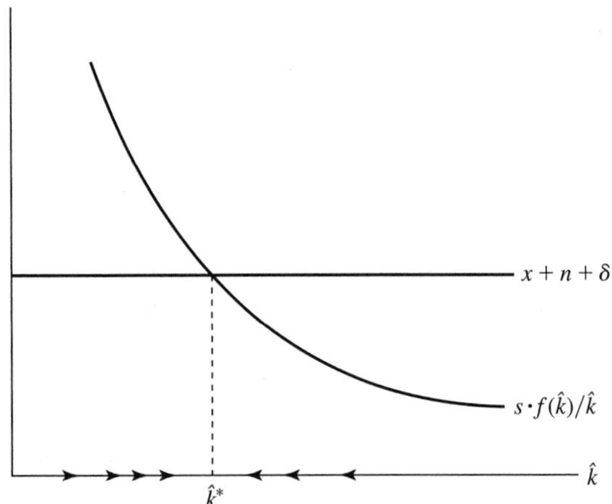

Figure 1.11
The Solow–Swan model with technological progress. The growth rate of capital per effective worker ($\hat{k} \equiv K/LT$) is given by the vertical distance between the $s \cdot f(\hat{k})/\hat{k}$ curve and the effective depreciation line, $x+n+\delta$. The economy is at a steady state when $\hat{k}$ is constant. Since T grows at the constant rate x, the steady-state growth rate of capital per person, k, also equals x.

1.2.13 A Quantitative Measure of the Speed of Convergence

It is important to know the speed of the transitional dynamics. If convergence is rapid, we can focus on steady-state behavior, because most economies would typically be close to their steady states. Conversely, if convergence is slow, economies would typically be far from their steady states, and, hence, their growth experiences would be dominated by the transitional dynamics.

We now provide a quantitative assessment of how fast the economy approaches its steady state for the case of a Cobb–Douglas production function, shown in equation (1.11). (We generalize later to a broader class of production functions.) We can use equation (1.39), with L replaced by $\hat{L}$, to determine the growth rate of $\hat{k}$ in the Cobb–Douglas case as

$$\dot{\hat{k}}/\hat{k} = sA \cdot (\hat{k})^{-(1-\alpha)} - (x+n+\delta) \tag{1.41}$$

The *speed of convergence, β*, is measured by how much the growth rate declines as the capital stock increases in a proportional sense, that is,

$$\beta \equiv -\frac{\partial(\dot{\hat{k}}/\hat{k})}{\partial \log \hat{k}} \tag{1.42}$$

Notice that we define β with a negative sign because the derivative is negative, so that β is positive.

To compute β, we have to rewrite the growth rate in equation (1.41) as a function of $\log(\hat{k})$:

$$\dot{\hat{k}}/\hat{k} = sA \cdot e^{-(1-\alpha)\cdot\log(\hat{k})} - (x+n+\delta) \tag{1.43}$$

We can take the derivative of equation (1.43) with respect to $\log(\hat{k})$ to get an expression for β:

$$\beta = (1-\alpha)\cdot sA \cdot (\hat{k})^{-(1-\alpha)} \tag{1.44}$$

Notice that the speed of convergence is not constant but, rather, declines monotonically as the capital stock increases toward its steady-state value. At the steady state, $sA \cdot (\hat{k})^{-(1-\alpha)} = (x+n+\delta)$ holds. Therefore, in the neighborhood of the steady state, the speed of convergence equals

$$\beta^* = (1-\alpha)\cdot(x+n+\delta) \tag{1.45}$$

During the transition to the steady state, the convergence rate, β, exceeds β^* but declines over time.

Another way to get the formula for β^* is to consider a log-linear approximation of equation (1.41) in the neighborhood of the steady state:

$$\dot{\hat{k}}/\hat{k} \cong -\beta^* \cdot [\log(\hat{k}/\hat{k}^*)] \tag{1.46}$$

where the coefficient β^* comes from a log-linearization of equation (1.41) around the steady state. The resulting coefficient can be shown to equal the right-hand side of equation (1.45). See the appendix at the end of this chapter (section 1.5) for the method of derivation of this log-linearization.

Before we consider further the implications of equation (1.45), we will show that it applies also to the growth rate of $\hat{y}$. For a Cobb–Douglas production function, shown in equation (1.11), we have

$$\dot{\hat{y}}/\hat{y} = \alpha \cdot (\dot{\hat{k}}/\hat{k})$$

$$\log(\hat{y}/\hat{y}^*) = \alpha \cdot \log(\hat{k}/\hat{k}^*)$$

If we substitute these formulas into equation (1.46), we get

$$\dot{\hat{y}}/\hat{y} \approx -\beta^* \cdot [\log(\hat{y}/\hat{y}^*)] \tag{1.47}$$

Hence, the convergence coefficient for $\hat{y}$ is the same as that for $\hat{k}$.

The term $\beta^* = (1-\alpha)\cdot(x+n+\delta)$ in equation (1.45) indicates how rapidly an economy's output per effective worker, $\hat{y}$, approaches its steady-state value, $\hat{y}^*$, in the neighborhood of the steady state. For example, if $\beta^* = 0.05$ per year, 5 percent of the gap between $\hat{y}$ and $\hat{y}^*$ vanishes in one year. The half-life of convergence—the time that it takes for half the initial gap to be eliminated—is thus about 14 years.[26] It would take about 28 years for three-quarters of the gap to vanish.

Consider what the theory implies quantitatively about the convergence coefficient, $\beta^* = (1-\alpha)\cdot(x+n+\delta)$, in equation (1.45). One property is that the saving rate, s, does not affect β^*. This result reflects two offsetting forces that exactly cancel in the Cobb–Douglas case. First, given $\hat{k}$, a higher saving rate leads to greater investment and, therefore, to a faster speed of convergence. Second, a higher saving rate raises the steady-state capital intensity, $\hat{k}^*$, and thereby lowers the average product of capital in the vicinity of the steady state. This effect reduces the speed of convergence. The coefficient β^* is also independent of the overall level of efficiency of the economy, A. Differences in A, like differences in s, have two offsetting effects on the convergence speed, and these effects exactly cancel in the Cobb–Douglas case.

To see the quantitative implications of the parameters that enter into equation (1.45), consider the benchmark values $x = 0.02$ per year, $n = 0.01$ per year, and $\delta = 0.05$ per year. These values appear reasonable, for example, for the U.S. economy. The long-term growth rate of real GDP, which is about 2 percent per year, corresponds in the theory to the parameter x. The rate of population growth in recent decades is about 1 percent per year, and the measured depreciation rate for the overall stock of structures and equipment is around 5 percent per year.

For given values of the parameters x, n, and δ, the coefficient β^* in equation (1.45) is determined by the capital-share parameter, α. A conventional share for the gross income accruing to a narrow concept of physical capital (structures and equipment) is about $\frac{1}{3}$ (see Denison, 1962; Maddison, 1982; and Jorgenson, Gollop, and Fraumeni, 1987). If we use $\alpha = \frac{1}{3}$, equation (1.45) implies $\beta^* = 5.6$ percent per year, which implies a half-life of 12.5 years. In other words, if the capital share is $\frac{1}{3}$, the neoclassical model predicts relatively short transitions.

26. Equation (1.47) is a differential equation in $\log[\hat{y}(t)]$ with the solution

$$\log[\hat{y}(t)] = (1 - e^{-\beta^* t})\cdot \log(\hat{y}^*) + e^{-\beta^* t}\cdot \log[\hat{y}(0)]$$

The time t for which $\log[\hat{y}(t)]$ is halfway between $\log[\hat{y}(0)]$ and $\log(\hat{y}^*)$ satisfies the condition $e^{-\beta^* t} = 1/2$. The half-life is therefore $\log(2)/\beta^* = 0.69/\beta^*$. Hence, if $\beta^* = 0.05$ per year, the half-life is 14 years.

In chapters 11 and 12 we argue that this predicted speed of convergence is much too high to accord with the empirical evidence. A convergence coefficient, β, in the range of 1.5 percent to 3.0 percent per year appears to fit better with the data. If $\beta^* = 2.0$ percent per year, the half-life is about 35 years, and the time needed to eliminate three-quarters of an initial gap from the steady-state position is about 70 years. In other words, convergence speeds that are consistent with the empirical evidence imply that the time required for substantial convergence is typically on the order of several generations.

To accord with an observed rate of convergence of about 2 percent per year, the neoclassical model requires a much higher capital-share coefficient. For example, the value $\alpha = 0.75$, together with the benchmark values for the other parameters, implies $\beta^* = 2.0$ percent per year. Although a capital share of 0.75 is too high for a narrow concept of physical capital, this share is reasonable for an expanded measure that also includes human capital.

An Extended Solow–Swan Model with Physical and Human Capital One way to increase the capital share is to add human capital to the model. Consider a Cobb–Douglas production function that uses physical capital, K, human capital, H,[27] and raw labor, L:

$$Y = AK^{\alpha}H^{\eta}[T(t)\cdot L]^{1-\alpha-\eta} \tag{1.48}$$

where $T(t)$ again grows at the exogenous rate x. Divide the production function by $T(t)\cdot L$ to get output per unit of effective labor:

$$\hat{y} = A\hat{k}^{\alpha}\hat{h}^{\eta} \tag{1.49}$$

Output can be used on a one-to-one basis for consumption or investment in either type of capital. Following Solow and Swan, we still assume that people consume a constant fraction, $1 - s$, of their gross income, so the accumulation is given by

$$\dot{\hat{k}} + \dot{\hat{h}} = sA\hat{k}^{\alpha}\hat{h}^{\eta} - (\delta + n + x)\cdot(\hat{k} + \hat{h}) \tag{1.50}$$

where we have assumed that the two capital goods depreciate at the same constant rate.

The key question is how overall savings will be allocated between physical and human capital. It is reasonable to think that households will invest in the capital good that delivers the higher return, so that the two rates of return—and, hence, the two marginal products of capital—will have to be equated if both forms of investment are taking place. Therefore,

27. Chapters 4 and 5 discuss human capital in more detail.

we have the condition[28]

$$\alpha \cdot \frac{\hat{y}}{\hat{k}} - \delta = \eta \cdot \frac{\hat{y}}{\hat{h}} - \delta \tag{1.51}$$

The equality between marginal products implies a one-to-one relationship between physical and human capital:

$$\hat{h} = \frac{\eta}{\alpha} \cdot \hat{k} \tag{1.52}$$

We can use this relation to eliminate $\hat{h}$ from equation (1.50) to get

$$\dot{\hat{k}} = s\tilde{A}\hat{k}^{\alpha+\eta} - (\delta + n + x) \cdot \hat{k} \tag{1.53}$$

where $\tilde{A} \equiv (\frac{\eta^{\eta}\alpha^{(1-\eta)}}{\alpha+\eta}) \cdot A$ is a constant. Notice that this accumulation equation is the same as equation (1.41), except that the exponent on the capital stock per worker is now the sum of the physical and human capital shares, $\alpha + \eta$, instead of α. Using a derivation analogous to that of the previous section, we therefore get an expression for the convergence coefficient in the steady state:

$$\beta^* = (1 - \alpha - \eta) \cdot (\delta + n + x) \tag{1.54}$$

Jorgenson, Gollop, and Fraumeni (1987) estimate a human-capital share of between 0.4 and 0.5. With $\eta = 0.4$ and with the benchmark parameters of the previous section, including $\alpha = \frac{1}{3}$, the predicted speed of convergence would be $\beta^* = 0.021$. Thus, with a broad concept of capital that includes human capital, the Solow–Swan model can generate the rates of convergence that have been observed empirically.

Mankiw, Romer, and Weil (1992) use a production function analogous to equation (1.48). However, instead of making the Solow–Swan assumption that the overall gross saving rate is constant and exogenous, they assume that the investment rates in the two forms of capital are each constant and exogenous. For physical capital, the growth rate is therefore

$$\dot{\hat{k}} = s_k\tilde{A}\hat{k}^{\alpha-1}\hat{h}^{\eta} - (\delta + n + x) = s_k\tilde{A} \cdot e^{-(1-\alpha)\ln\hat{k}} \cdot e^{\eta\ln\hat{h}} - (\delta + n + x) \tag{1.55}$$

28. In a market setup, profit would be $\pi = AK_t^{\alpha}H_t^{\eta}(T_tL_t)^{1-\alpha-\eta} - R_kK - R_hH - wL$, where R_k and R_h are the rental rates of physical and human capital, respectively. The first-order conditions for the firm require that the marginal products of each of the capital goods be equalized to the rental rates, $R_k = \alpha\frac{\hat{y}}{\hat{k}}$ and $R_h = \eta\frac{\hat{y}}{\hat{h}}$. In an environment without uncertainty, like the one we are considering, physical capital, human capital, and loans are perfect substitutes as stores of value and, as a result, their net returns must be the same. In other words, $r = R_k - \delta = R_h - \delta$. Optimizing firms will, therefore, rent physical and human capital up to the point where their marginal products are equal.

where s_k is an exogenous constant. Similarly, for human capital, the growth rate is

$$\dot{\hat{h}} = s_h \tilde{A} \hat{k}^{\alpha} \hat{h}^{\eta-1} - (\delta + n + x) = s_h \tilde{A} \cdot e^{\alpha \ln \hat{k}} \cdot e^{-(1-\eta) \ln \hat{h}} - (\delta + n + x) \tag{1.56}$$

where s_h is another exogenous constant. A shortcoming of this approach is that the rates of return to physical and human capital are not equated.

The growth rate of $\hat{y}$ is a weighted average of the growth rates of the two inputs:

$$\dot{\hat{y}}/\hat{y} = \alpha \cdot (\dot{\hat{k}}/\hat{k}) + \eta \cdot (\dot{\hat{h}}/\hat{h})$$

If we use equations (1.55) and (1.56) and take a two-dimensional first-order Taylor-series expansion, we get

$$\begin{aligned}
\dot{\hat{y}}/\hat{y} = \Big[&\alpha s_k \tilde{A} \cdot e^{-(1-\alpha) \ln \hat{k}^*} \cdot e^{\eta \ln \hat{h}^*} \cdot [-(1-\alpha)] \\
&+ \eta s_h \tilde{A} \cdot e^{\alpha \ln \hat{k}^*} \cdot e^{-(1-\eta) \ln \hat{h}^*} \cdot \alpha\Big] \cdot (\ln \hat{k} - \ln \hat{k}^*) \\
&+ \Big[\alpha s_k \tilde{A} \cdot e^{-(1-\alpha) \ln k^*} \cdot e^{\hat{\eta} \ln h^*} \cdot \eta \\
&+ \eta s_h \tilde{A} \cdot e^{\alpha \ln \hat{k}} \cdot e^{-(1-\eta) \ln \hat{h}^*} \cdot [-(1-\eta)]\Big] \cdot (\ln \hat{h} - \ln \hat{h}^*)
\end{aligned}$$

The steady-state conditions derived from equations (1.55) and (1.56) can be used to get

$$\begin{aligned}
\dot{\hat{y}}/\hat{y} &= -(1-\alpha-\eta) \cdot (\delta + n + x) \cdot [\alpha \cdot (\ln \hat{k} - \ln \hat{k}^*) + \eta \cdot (\ln \hat{h} - \ln \hat{h}^*)] \\
&= -\beta^* \cdot (\ln \hat{y} - \ln \hat{y}^*)
\end{aligned} \tag{1.57}$$

Therefore, in the neighborhood of the steady state, the convergence coefficient is $\beta^* = (1 - \alpha - \eta) \cdot (\delta + n + x)$, just as in equation (1.54).

1.3 Models of Endogenous Growth

1.3.1 Theoretical Dissatisfaction with Neoclassical Theory

In the mid-1980s it became increasingly clear that the standard neoclassical growth model was theoretically unsatisfactory as a tool to explore the determinants of long-run growth. We have seen that the model without technological change predicts that the economy will eventually converge to a steady state with zero per capita growth. The fundamental reason is the diminishing returns to capital. One way out of this problem was to broaden the concept of capital, notably to include human components, and then assume that diminishing returns did not apply to this broader class of capital. This approach is the one outlined in the next section and explored in detail in chapters 4 and 5. However, another view was that technological progress in the form of the generation of new ideas was the only way that an economy could escape from diminishing returns in the long run. Thus it became a priority to go beyond the treatment of technological progress as exogenous and, instead, to explain this progress within the model of growth. However, endogenous approaches to technological change encountered basic problems within the neoclassical model—the essential reason is the nonrival nature of the ideas that underlie technology.

Remember that a key characteristic of the state of technology, T, is that it is a nonrival input to the production process. Hence, the replication argument that we used before to justify the assumption of constant returns to scale suggests that the correct measure of scale is the two rival inputs, capital and labor. Hence, the concept of constant returns to scale that we used is homogeneity of degree one in K and L:

$$F(\lambda K, \lambda L, T) = \lambda \cdot F(K, L, T)$$

Recall also that Euler's theorem implies that a function that is homogeneous of degree one can be decomposed as

$$F(K, L, T) = F_K \cdot K + F_L \cdot L \tag{1.58}$$

In our analysis up to this point, we have been assuming that the same technology, T, is freely available to all firms. This availability is technically feasible because T is nonrival. However, it may be that T is at least partly excludable—for example, patent protection, secrecy, and experience might allow some producers to have access to technologies that are superior to those available to others. For the moment, we maintain the assumption that technology is nonexcludable, so that all producers have the same access. This assumption also means that a technological advance is immediately available to all producers.

We know from our previous analysis that perfectly competitive firms that take the input prices, R and w, as given end up equating the marginal products to the respective input prices, that is, $F_K = R$ and $F_L = w$. It follows from equation (1.58) that the factor payments exhaust the output, so that each firm's profit equals zero at every point in time.

Suppose that a firm has the option to pay a fixed cost, κ, to improve the technology from T to T'. Since the new technology would, by assumption, be freely available to all other producers, we know that the equilibrium values of R and w would again entail a zero flow of profit for each firm. Therefore, the firm that paid the fixed cost, κ, will end up losing money overall, because the fixed cost would not be recouped by positive profits at any future dates. It follows that the competitive, neoclassical model cannot sustain purposeful investment in technical change if technology is nonexcludable (as well as nonrival).

The obvious next step is to allow the technology to be at least partly excludable. To bring out the problems with this extension, consider the polar case of full excludability, that is, where each firm's technology is completely private. Assume, however, that there are infinitely many ways in which firms can improve knowledge from T to T' by paying the fixed cost κ—in other words, there is free entry into the business of creating formulas. Suppose that all firms begin with the technology T. Would an individual firm then have the incentive to pay κ to improve the technology to T'? In fact, the incentive appears to be enormous. At the existing input prices, R and w, a neoclassical firm with a superior technology would make a pure profit on each unit produced. Because of the assumed constant returns to scale, the firm would be motivated to hire all the capital and labor available in the economy. In this case, the firm would have lots of monopoly power and would likely no longer act as a perfect competitor in the goods and factor markets. So, the assumptions of the competitive model would break down.

A more basic problem with this result is that other firms would have perceived the same profit opportunity and would also have paid the cost κ to acquire the better technology, T'. However, when many firms improve their technology by the same amount, the competition pushes up the factor prices, R and w, so that the flow of profit is again zero. In this case, none of the firms can cover their fixed cost, κ, just as in the model in which technology was nonexcludable. Therefore, it is not an equilibrium for technological advance to occur (because all innovators make losses) and it is also not an equilibrium for this advance not to occur (because the potential profit to a single innovator is enormous).

These conceptual difficulties motivated researchers to introduce some aspects of imperfect competition to construct satisfactory models in which the level of the technology can be advanced by purposeful activity, such as R&D expenditures. This potential for endogenous technological progress and, hence, *endogenous growth,* may allow an escape from diminishing returns at the aggregate level. Models of this type were pioneered by Romer (1990) and Aghion and Howitt (1992); we consider them in chapters 6–8. For now, we deal only with models in which technology is either fixed or varying in an exogenous manner.

1.3.2 The *AK* Model

The key property of this class of endogenous-growth models is the absence of diminishing returns to capital. The simplest version of a production function without diminishing returns is the AK function:[29]

$$Y = AK \tag{1.59}$$

where A is a positive constant that reflects the level of the technology. The global absence of diminishing returns may seem unrealistic, but the idea becomes more plausible if we think of K in a broad sense to include human capital.[30] Output per capita is $y = Ak$, and the average and marginal products of capital are constant at the level $A > 0$.

29. We think that the first economist to use a production function of the AK type was von Neumann (1937).

30. Knight (1944) stressed the idea that diminishing returns might not apply to a broad concept of capital.

If we substitute $f(k)/k = A$ in equation (1.13), we get

$$\dot{k}/k = sA - (n + \delta)$$

We return here to the case of zero technological progress, $x = 0$, because we want to show that per capita growth can now occur in the long run even without exogenous technological change. For a graphical presentation, the main difference is that the downward-sloping saving curve, $s \cdot f(k)/k$, in figure 1.4 is replaced in figure 1.12 by the horizontal line at the level sA. The depreciation curve is still the same horizontal line at $n + \delta$. Hence, $\dot{k}/k$ is the vertical distance between the two lines, sA and $n + \delta$. We depict the case in which $sA > (n + \delta)$, so that $\dot{k}/k > 0$. Since the two lines are parallel, $\dot{k}/k$ is constant; in particular, it is independent of k. Therefore, k always grows at the steady-state rate, $(\dot{k}/k)^* = sA - (n + \delta)$.

Since $y = Ak$, $\dot{y}/y = \dot{k}/k$ at every point in time. In addition, since $c = (1 - s) \cdot y$, $\dot{c}/c = \dot{k}/k$ also applies. Hence, all the per capita variables in the model always grow at the same, constant rate, given by

$$\gamma^* = sA - (n + \delta) \tag{1.60}$$

Note that an economy described by the AK technology can display positive long-run per capita growth without any technological progress. Moreover, the per capita growth rate

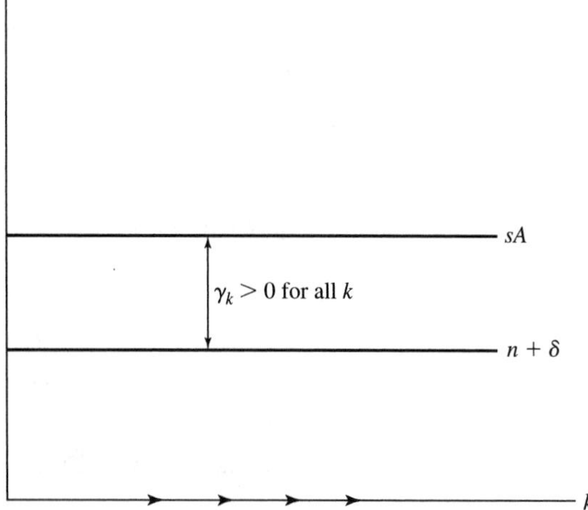

Figure 1.12
The *AK* Model. If the technology is AK, the saving curve, $s \cdot f(k)/k$, is a horizontal line at the level sA. If $sA > n + \delta$, perpetual growth of k occurs, even without technological progress.

shown in equation (1.60) depends on the behavioral parameters of the model, including s, A, and n. For example, unlike the neoclassical model, a higher saving rate, s, leads to a higher rate of long-run per capita growth, γ^*.[31] Similarly if the level of the technology, A, improves once and for all (or if the elimination of a governmental distortion effectively raises A), then the long-run growth rate is higher. Changes in the rates of depreciation, δ, and population growth, n, also have permanent effects on the per capita growth rate.

Unlike the neoclassical model, the AK formulation does not predict absolute or conditional convergence, that is, $\partial(\dot{y}/y)/\partial y = 0$ applies for all levels of y. Consider a group of economies that are structurally similar in that the parameters s, A, n, and δ are the same. The economies differ only in terms of their initial capital stocks per person, $k(0)$, and, hence, in $y(0)$ and $c(0)$. Since the model says that each economy grows at the same per capita rate, γ^*, regardless of its initial position, the prediction is that all the economies grow at the same per capita rate. This conclusion reflects the absence of diminishing returns. Another way to see this result is to observe that the AK model is just a Cobb–Douglas model with a unit capital share, $\alpha = 1$. The analysis of convergence in the previous section showed that the speed of convergence was given in equation (1.45) by $\beta^* = (1 - \alpha) \cdot (x + n + \delta)$; hence, $\alpha = 1$ implies $\beta^* = 0$. This prediction is a substantial failing of the model, because conditional convergence appears to be an empirical regularity. See chapters 11 and 12 for a detailed discussion.

We mentioned that one way to think about the absence of diminishing returns to capital in the AK production function is to consider a broad concept of capital that encompassed physical and human components. In chapters 4 and 5 we consider in more detail models that allow for these two types of capital.

Other approaches have been used to eliminate the tendency for diminishing returns in the neoclassical model. We study in chapter 4 the notion of learning by doing, which was introduced by Arrow (1962) and used by Romer (1986). In these models, the experience with production or investment contributes to productivity. Moreover, the learning by one producer may raise the productivity of others through a process of spillovers of knowledge from one producer to another. Therefore, a larger economy-wide capital stock (or a greater cumulation of the aggregate of past production) improves the level of the technology for each producer. Consequently, diminishing returns to capital may not apply in the aggregate, and increasing returns are even possible. In a situation of increasing returns, each producer's average

31. With the AK production function, we can never get the kind of inefficient oversaving that is possible in the neoclassical model. A shift at some point in time to a permanently higher s means a lower level of c at that point but a permanently higher per capita growth rate, γ^*, and, hence, higher levels of c after some future date. This change cannot be described as inefficient because it may be desirable or undesirable depending on how households discount future levels of consumption.

product of capital, $f(k)/k$, tends to rise with the economy-wide value of k. Consequently, the $s \cdot f(k)/k$ curve in figure 1.4 tends to be upward sloping, at least over some range, and the growth rate, $\dot{k}/k$, rises with k in this range. Thus these kinds of models predict at least some intervals of per capita income in which economies tend to diverge. It is unclear, however, whether these divergence intervals are present in the data.

1.3.3 Endogenous Growth with Transitional Dynamics

The AK model delivers endogenous growth by avoiding diminishing returns to capital in the long run. This particular production function also implies, however, that the marginal and average products of capital are always constant and, hence, that growth rates do not exhibit the convergence property. It is possible to retain the feature of constant returns to capital in the long run, while restoring the convergence property—an idea brought out by Jones and Manuelli (1990).[32]

Consider again the expression for the growth rate of k from equation (1.13):

$$\dot{k}/k = s \cdot f(k)/k - (n + \delta) \tag{1.61}$$

If a steady state exists, the associated growth rate, $(\dot{k}/k)^*$, is constant by definition. A positive $(\dot{k}/k)^*$ means that k grows without bound. Equation (1.13) implies that it is necessary and sufficient for $(\dot{k}/k)^*$ to be positive to have the average product of capital, $f(k)/k$, remain above $(n + \delta)/s$ as k approaches infinity. In other words, if the average product approaches some limit, then $\lim_{k\to\infty}[f(k)/k] > (n + \delta)/s$ is necessary and sufficient for endogenous, steady-state growth.

If $f(k) \to \infty$ as $k \to \infty$, then an application of l'Hôpital's rule shows that the limits as k approaches infinity of the average product, $f(k)/k$, and the marginal product, $f'(k)$, are the same. (We assume here that $\lim_{k\to\infty}[f'(k)]$ exists.) Hence, the key condition for endogenous, steady-state growth is that $f'(k)$ be bounded sufficiently far above 0:

$$\lim_{k\to\infty}[f(k)/k] = \lim_{k\to\infty}[f'(k)] > (n + \delta)/s > 0$$

This inequality violates one of the standard Inada conditions in the neoclassical model, $\lim_{k\to\infty}[f'(k)] = 0$. Economically, the violation of this condition means that the tendency for diminishing returns to capital tends to disappear. In other words, the production function can exhibit diminishing or increasing returns to k when k is low, but the marginal product of capital must be bounded from below as k becomes large. A simple example, in which the production function converges asymptotically to the AK form, is

$$Y = F(K, L) = AK + BK^{\alpha}L^{1-\alpha} \tag{1.62}$$

32. See Kurz (1968) for a related discussion.

where $A > 0$, $B > 0$, and $0 < \alpha < 1$. Note that this production function is a combination of the AK and Cobb–Douglas functions. It exhibits constant returns to scale and positive and diminishing returns to labor and capital. However, one of the Inada conditions is violated because $\lim_{K\to\infty}(F_K) = A > 0$.

We can write the function in per capita terms as

$$y = f(k) = Ak + Bk^{\alpha}$$

The average product of capital is given by

$$f(k)/k = A + Bk^{-(1-\alpha)}$$

which is decreasing in k but approaches A as k tends to infinity.

The dynamics of this model can be analyzed with the usual expression from equation (1.13):

$$\dot{k}/k = s \cdot \left[A + Bk^{-(1-\alpha)}\right] - (n + \delta) \tag{1.63}$$

Figure 1.13 shows that the saving curve is downward sloping, and the line $n + \delta$ is horizontal. The difference from figure 1.4 is that, as k goes to infinity, the saving curve in figure 1.13 approaches the positive quantity sA, rather than 0. If $sA > n + \delta$, as assumed in the figure, the steady-state growth rate, $(\dot{k}/k)^*$, is positive.

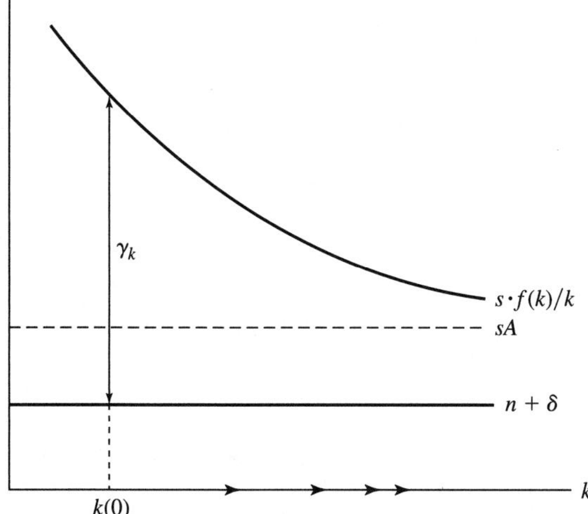

Figure 1.13
Endogenous growth with transitional dynamics. If the technology is $F(K, L) = AK + BK^{\alpha}L^{1-\alpha}$, the growth rate of k is diminishing for all k. If $sA > n+\delta$, the growth rate of k asymptotically approaches a positive constant, given by $sA - n - \delta$. Hence, endogenous growth coexists with a transition in which the growth rate diminishes as the economy develops.

This model yields endogenous, steady-state growth but also predicts conditional convergence, as in the neoclassical model. The reason is that the convergence property derives from the inverse relation between $f(k)/k$ and k, a relation that still holds in the model. Figure 1.13 shows that if two economies differ only in terms of their initial values, $k(0)$, the one with the smaller capital stock per person will grow faster in per capita terms.

1.3.4 Constant-Elasticity-of-Substitution Production Functions

Consider as another example the production function (due to Arrow et al., 1961) that has a constant elasticity of substitution (CES) between labor and capital:

$$Y = F(K, L) = A \cdot \{a \cdot (bK)^{\psi} + (1 - a) \cdot [(1 - b) \cdot L]^{\psi}\}^{1/\psi} \tag{1.64}$$

where $0 < a < 1$, $0 < b < 1$,[33] and $\psi < 1$. Note that the production function exhibits constant returns to scale for all values of ψ. The elasticity of substitution between capital and labor is $1/(1 - \psi)$ (see the appendix, section 1.5.4). As $\psi \to -\infty$, the production function approaches a fixed-proportions technology (discussed in the next section), $Y = \min[bK, (1 - b)L]$, where the elasticity of substitution is 0. As $\psi \to 0$, the production function approaches the Cobb–Douglas form, $Y = (\text{constant}) \cdot K^a L^{1-a}$, and the elasticity of substitution is 1 (see the appendix, section 1.5.4). For $\psi = 1$, the production function is linear, $Y = A \cdot [abK + (1 - a) \cdot (1 - b) \cdot L]$, so that K and L are perfect substitutes (infinite elasticity of substitution).

Divide both sides of equation (1.64) by L to get an expression for output per capita:

$$y = f(k) = A \cdot [a \cdot (bk)^{\psi} + (1 - a) \cdot (1 - b)^{\psi}]^{1/\psi}$$

The marginal and average products of capital are given, respectively, by

$$f'(k) = Aab^{\psi}[ab^{\psi} + (1 - a) \cdot (1 - b)^{\psi} \cdot k^{-\psi}]^{(1-\psi)/\psi}$$

$$f(k)/k = A[ab^{\psi} + (1 - a) \cdot (1 - b)^{\psi} \cdot k^{-\psi}]^{1/\psi}$$

Thus, $f'(k)$ and $f(k)/k$ are each positive and diminishing in k for all values of ψ.

We can study the dynamic behavior of a CES economy by returning to the expression from equation (1.13):

$$\dot{k}/k = s \cdot f(k)/k - (n + \delta) \tag{1.65}$$

33. The standard formulation does not include the terms b and $1 - b$. The implication then is that the shares of K and L in total product each approach one-half as $\psi \to -\infty$. In our formulation, the shares of K and L approach b and $1 - b$, respectively, as $\psi \to -\infty$.

If we graph versus k, then $s \cdot f(k)/k$ is a downward-sloping curve, $n + \delta$ is a horizontal line, and $\dot{k}/k$ is still represented by the vertical distance between the curve and the line. The behavior of the growth rate now depends, however, on the parameter ψ, which governs the elasticity of substitution between L and K.

Consider first the case $0 < \psi < 1$, that is, a high degree of substitution between L and K. The limits of the marginal and average products of capital in this case are

$$\lim_{k\to\infty}[f'(k)] = \lim_{k\to\infty}[f(k)/k] = Aba^{1/\psi} > 0$$
$$\lim_{k\to 0}[f'(k)] = \lim_{k\to 0}[f(k)/k] = \infty$$

Hence, the marginal and average products approach a positive constant, rather than 0, as k goes to infinity. In this sense, the CES production function with high substitution between the factors ($0 < \psi < 1$) looks like the example in equation (1.62) in which diminishing returns vanished asymptotically. We therefore anticipate that this CES model can generate endogenous, steady-state growth.

Figure 1.14 shows the results graphically. The $s \cdot f(k)/k$ curve is downward sloping, and it asymptotes to the positive constant $sAb \cdot a^{1/\psi}$. If the saving rate is high enough, so that $sAb \cdot a^{1/\psi} > n + \delta$—as assumed in the figure—then the $s \cdot f(k)/k$ curve always lies above the $n + \delta$ line. In this case, the per capita growth rate is always positive, and the model

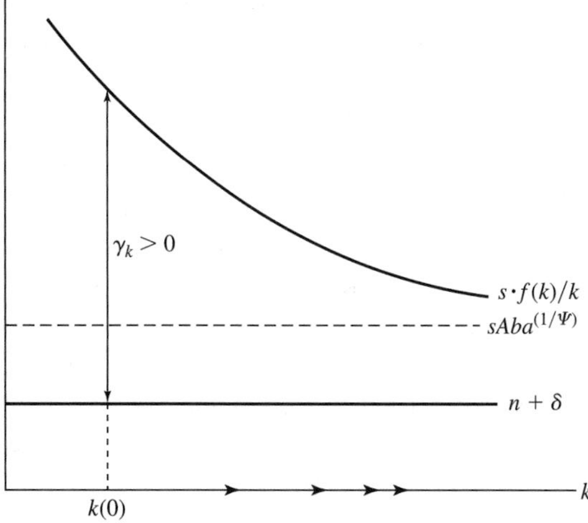

Figure 1.14
The CES model with $0 < \psi < 1$ and $sAb \cdot a^{1/\psi} > n + \delta$. If the CES technology exhibits a high elasticity of substitution ($0 < \psi < 1$), endogenous growth arises if the parameters satisfy the inequality $sAb \cdot a^{1/\psi} > n + \delta$. Along the transition, the growth rate of k diminishes.

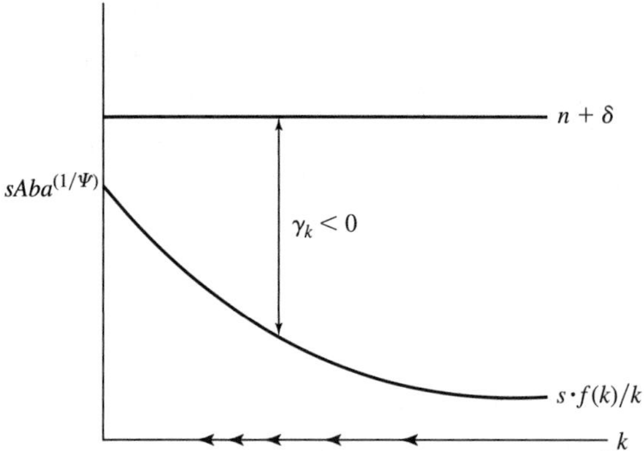

Figure 1.15
The CES model with $\psi < 0$ and $sAb \cdot a^{1/\psi} < n + \delta$. If the CES technology exhibits a low elasticity of substitution ($\psi < 0$), the growth rate of k would be negative for all levels of k if $sAb \cdot a^{1/\psi} < n + \delta$.

generates endogenous, steady-state growth at the rate

$$\gamma^* = sAb \cdot a^{1/\psi} - (n + \delta)$$

The dynamics of this model are similar to those described in figure 1.13.[34]

Assume now $\psi < 0$, that is, a low degree of substitution between L and K. The limits of the marginal and average products of capital in this case are

$$\lim_{k \to \infty} [f'(k)] = \lim_{k \to \infty} [f(k)/k] = 0$$

$$\lim_{k \to 0} [f'(k)] = \lim_{k \to 0} [f(k)/k] = Ab \cdot a^{1/\psi} < \infty$$

Since the marginal and average products approach 0 as k approaches infinity, the key Inada condition is satisfied, and the model does not generate endogenous growth. In this case, however, the violation of the Inada condition as k approaches 0 may cause problems. Suppose that the saving rate is low enough so that $sAb \cdot a^{1/\psi} < n + \delta$. In this case, the $s \cdot f(k)/k$ curve starts at a point below $n + \delta$, and it converges to 0 as k approaches infinity. Figure 1.15 shows, accordingly, that the curve never crosses the $n + \delta$ line, and, hence, no steady state exists with a positive value of k. Since the growth rate $\dot{k}/k$ is always negative, the economy shrinks over time, and k, y, and c all approach 0.[35]

34. If $0 < \psi < 1$ and $sAb \cdot a^{1/\psi} < n + \delta$, then the $s \cdot f(k)/k$ curve crosses $n + \delta$ at the steady-state value k^*, as in the standard neoclassical model of figure 1.4. Endogenous growth does not apply in this case.

35. If $\psi < 0$ and $sAb \cdot a^{1/\psi} > n + \delta$, then the $s \cdot f(k)/k$ curve again intersects the $n + \delta$ line at the steady-state value k^*.

Since the average product of capital, $f(k)/k$, is a negative function of k for all values of ψ, the growth rate $\dot{k}/k$ is also a negative function of k. The CES model therefore always exhibits the convergence property: for two economies with identical parameters and different initial values, $k(0)$, the one with the lower value of $k(0)$ has the higher value of $\dot{k}/k$. When the parameters differ across economies, the model predicts conditional convergence, as described before.

We can use the method developed earlier for the case of a Cobb–Douglas production function to derive a formula for the convergence coefficient in the neighborhood of the steady state. The result for a CES production function, which extends equation (1.45), is[36]

$$\beta^* = -(x+n+\delta) \cdot \left[1 - a \cdot \left(\frac{bsA}{x+n+\delta}\right)^{\psi}\right] \tag{1.66}$$

For the Cobb–Douglas case, where $\psi = 0$ and $a = \alpha$, equation (1.66) reduces to equation (1.45). For $\psi \neq 0$, a new result is that β^* in equation (1.66) depends on s and A. If $\psi > 0$ (high substitutability between L and K), then β^* falls with sA, and vice versa if $\psi < 0$. The coefficient β^* is independent of s and A only in the Cobb–Douglas case, where $\psi = 0$.

1.4 Other Production Functions . . . Other Growth Theories

1.4.1 The Leontief Production Function and the Harrod–Domar Controversy

A production function that was used prior to the neoclassical one is the Leontief (1941), or fixed-proportions, function,

$$Y = F(K, L) = \min(AK, BL) \tag{1.67}$$

where $A > 0$ and $B > 0$ are constants. This specification, which corresponds to $\psi \to -\infty$ in the CES form in equation (1.64), was used by Harrod (1939) and Domar (1946). With fixed proportions, if the available capital stock and labor force happen to be such that $AK = BL$, then all workers and machines are fully employed. If K and L are such that $AK > BL$, then only the quantity of capital $(B/A) \cdot L$ is used, and the remainder remains idle. Conversely, if $AK < BL$, then only the amount of labor $(A/B) \cdot K$ is used, and the remainder is unemployed. The assumption of no substitution between capital and labor led Harrod and Domar to predict that capitalist economies would have undesirable outcomes in the form of perpetual increases in unemployed workers or machines. We provide here a brief analysis of the Harrod–Domar model using the tools developed earlier in this chapter.

36. See Chua (1993) for additional discussion. The formula for β in equation (1.66) applies only for cases in which the steady-state level k^* exists. If $0 < \psi < 1$, it applies for $bsA \cdot a^{1/\psi} < x+n+\delta$. If $\psi < 0$, it applies for $bsA \cdot a^{1/\psi} > x+n+\delta$.

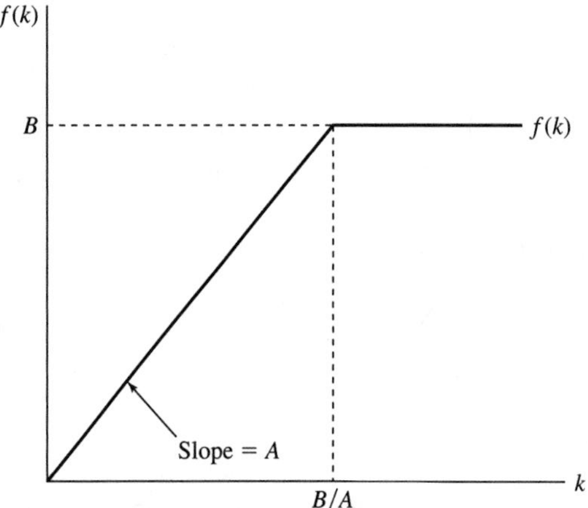

Figure 1.16
The Leontief production function in per capita terms. In per capita terms, the Leontief production function can be written as $y = \min(Ak, B)$. For $k < B/A$, output per capita is given by $y = Ak$. For $k > B/A$, output per capita is given by $y = B$.

Divide both sides of equation (1.67) by L to get output per capita:

$$y = \min(Ak, B)$$

For $k < B/A$, capital is fully employed, and $y = Ak$. Hence, figure 1.16 shows that the production function in this range is a straight line from the origin with slope A. For $k > B/A$, the quantity of capital used is constant, and Y is the constant multiple B of labor, L. Hence, output per worker, y, equals the constant B, as shown by the horizontal part of $f(k)$ in the figure. Note that, as k approaches infinity, the marginal product of capital, $f'(k)$, is zero. Hence, the key Inada condition is satisfied, and we do not expect this production function to yield endogenous steady-state growth.

We can use the expression from equation (1.13) to get

$$\dot{k}/k = s \cdot [\min(Ak, B)]/k - (n + \delta) \tag{1.68}$$

Figures 1.17*a* and 1.17*b* show that the first term, $s \cdot [\min(Ak, B)]/k$, is a horizontal line at sA for $k \leq B/A$. For $k > B/A$, this term is a downward-sloping curve that approaches zero as k goes to infinity. The second term in equation (1.68) is the usual horizontal line at $n + \delta$.

Assume first that the saving rate is low enough so that $sA < n + \delta$, as depicted in figure 1.17. The saving curve, $s \cdot f(k)/k$, then never crosses the $n + \delta$ line, so there is no

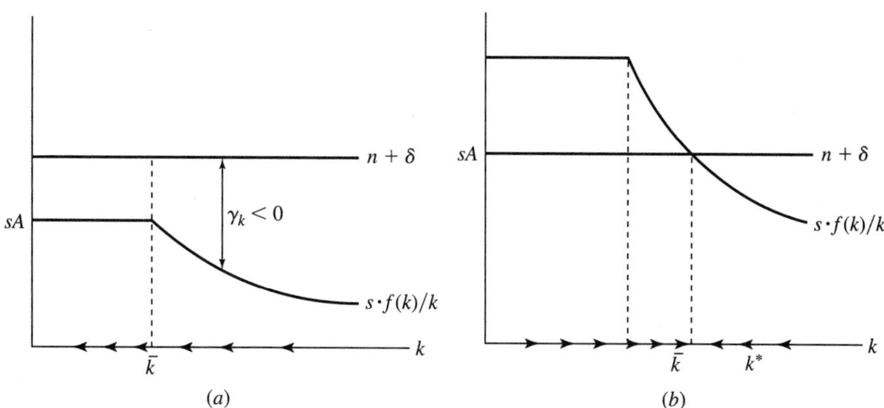

Figure 1.17
The Harrod–Domar model. In panel a, which assumes $sA < n+\delta$, the growth rate of k is negative for all k. Therefore, the economy approaches $k = 0$. In panel b, which assumes $sA > n+\delta$, the growth rate of k is positive for $k < k^*$ and negative for $k > k^*$, where k^* is the stable steady-state value. Since k^* exceeds B/A, a part of the capital stock always remains idle. Moreover, the quantity of idle capital grows steadily (along with K and L).

positive steady-state value, k^*. Moreover, the growth rate of capital, $\dot{k}/k$, is always negative, so the economy shrinks in per capita terms, and k, y, and c all approach 0. The economy therefore ends up to the left of B/A and has permanent and increasing unemployment.

Suppose now that the saving rate is high enough so that $sA > n + \delta$, as shown in figure 1.17b. Since the $s \cdot f(k)/k$ curve approaches 0 as k tends to infinity, this curve eventually crosses the $n+\delta$ line at the point $k^* > B/A$. Therefore, if the economy begins at $k(0) < k^*$, $\dot{k}/k$ equals the constant $sA - n - \delta > 0$ until k attains the value B/A. At that point, $\dot{k}/k$ falls until it reaches 0 at $k = k^*$. If the economy starts at $k(0) > k^*$, $\dot{k}/k$ is initially negative and approaches 0 as k approaches k^*.

Since $k^* > B/A$, the steady state features idle machines but no unemployed workers. Since k is constant in the steady state, the quantity K grows along with L at the rate n. Since the fraction of machines that are employed remains constant, the quantity of idle machines also grows at the rate n (yet households are nevertheless assumed to keep saving at the rate s).

The only way to reach a steady state in which all capital and labor are employed is for the parameters of the model to satisfy the condition $sA = n+\delta$. Since the four parameters that appear in this condition are all exogenous, there is no reason for the equality to hold. Hence, the conclusion from Harrod and Domar was that an economy would, in all probability, reach one of two undesirable outcomes: perpetual growth of unemployment or perpetual growth of idle machinery.

We know now that there are several implausible assumptions in the arguments of Harrod and Domar. First, the Solow–Swan model showed that Harrod and Domar's parameter A—the average product of capital—would typically depend on k, and k would adjust to satisfy the equality $s \cdot f(k)/k = n + \delta$ in the steady state. Second, the saving rate could adjust to satisfy this condition. In particular, if agents maximize utility (as we assume in the next chapter), they would not find it optimal to continue to save at the constant rate s when the marginal product of capital was zero. This adjustment of the saving rate would rule out an equilibrium with permanently idle machinery.

1.4.2 Growth Models with Poverty Traps

One theme in the literature of economic development concerns *poverty traps*.[37] We can think of a poverty trap as a stable steady state with low levels of per capita output and capital stock. This outcome is a trap because, if agents attempt to break out of it, the economy has a tendency to return to the low-level, stable steady state.

We observed that the average product of capital, $f(k)/k$, declines with k in the neoclassical model. We also noted, however, that this average product may rise with k in some models that feature increasing returns, for example, in formulations that involve learning by doing and spillovers. One way for a poverty trap to arise is for the economy to have an interval of diminishing average product of capital followed by a range of rising average product. (Poverty traps also arise in some models with nonconstant saving rates; see Galor and Ryder, 1989.)

We can get a range of increasing returns by imagining that a country has access to a traditional, as well as a modern, technology.[38] Imagine that producers can use a primitive production function, which takes the usual Cobb–Douglas form,

$$Y_A = AK^{\alpha}L^{1-\alpha} \tag{1.69}$$

The country also has access to a modern, higher productivity technology,[39]

$$Y_B = BK^{\alpha}L^{1-\alpha} \tag{1.70}$$

where $B > A$. However, in order to exploit this better technology, the country as a whole is assumed to have to pay a setup cost at every moment in time, perhaps to cover the necessary public infrastructure or legal system. We assume that this cost is proportional to

37. See especially the *big-push* model of Lewis (1954). A more modern formulation of this idea appears in Murphy, Shleifer, and Vishny (1989).

38. This section is an adaptation of Galor and Zeira (1993), who use two technologies in the context of education.

39. More generally, the capital intensity for the advanced technology would differ from that for the primitive technology. However, this extension complicates the algebra without making any substantive differences.

the labor force and given by bL, where $b > 0$. We assume further that this cost is borne by the government and financed by a tax at rate b on each worker. The results are the same whether the tax is paid by producers or workers (who are, in any event, the same persons an economy with household-producers).

In per worker terms, the first production function is

$$y_A = Ak^{\alpha} \tag{1.71}$$

The second production function, when considered net of the setup cost and in per worker terms, is

$$y_B = Bk^{\alpha} - b \tag{1.72}$$

The two production functions are drawn in figure 1.18.

If the government has decided to pay the setup cost, which equals b per worker, all producers will use the modern technology (because the tax b for each worker must be paid in any case). If the government has not paid the setup cost, all producers must use the primitive technology. A sensible government would pay the setup cost if the shift to the modern technology leads to an increase in output per worker at the existing value of k and when measured net of the setup cost. In the present setting, the shift is warranted if k exceeds a critical level, given by $\tilde{k} = [b/(B - A)]^{1/\alpha}$. Thus, the critical value of k rises with the setup cost parameter, b, and falls with the difference in the productivity parameters, $B - A$. We assume that the government pays the setup cost if $k \geq \tilde{k}$ and does not pay it if $k < \tilde{k}$.

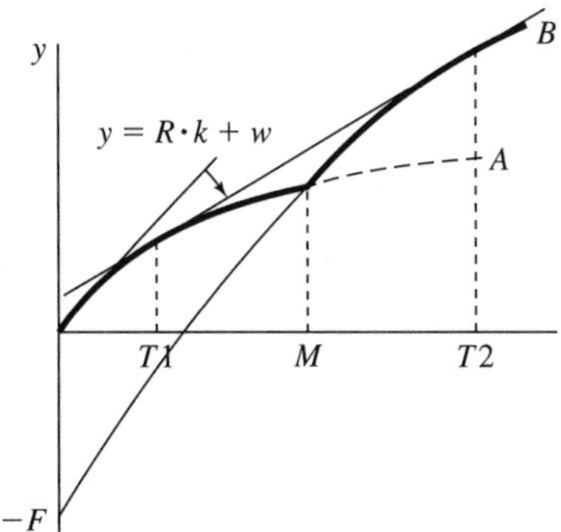

Figure 1.18
Traditional and modern production functions. The traditional production function has relatively low productivity. The modern production function exhibits higher productivity but is assumed to require a fixed cost to operate.

The growth rate of capital per worker is still given by the fundamental equation of the Solow–Swan model, equation (1.23), as

$$\dot{k}/k = s \cdot f(k)/k - (\delta + n)$$

where $f(k) = Ak^{\alpha}$ if $k < \tilde{k}$ and $f(k) = Bk^{\alpha} - b$ if $k \geq \tilde{k}$. The average product of capital, $f(k)/k$, can be measured graphically in figure 1.18 by the slope of the cord that goes from the origin to the effective production function. We can see that there is a range of $k \geq \tilde{k}$ where the average product is increasing. The saving curve therefore looks like the one depicted in figure 1.19: it has the familiar negative slope at low levels of k, is then followed by a range with a positive slope, and again has a negative slope at very high levels of k.

Figure 1.19 shows that the $s \cdot f(k)/k$ curve first crosses the $n + \delta$ line at the low steady-state value, k^*_{low}, where we assume here that $k^*_{\text{low}} < \tilde{k}$. This steady state has the properties that are familiar from the neoclassical model. In particular, $\dot{k}/k > 0$ for $k < k^*_{\text{low}}$, and $\dot{k}/k < 0$ at least in an interval of $k > k^*_{\text{low}}$. Hence, k^*_{low} is a stable steady state: it is a poverty trap in the sense described before.

The tendency for increasing returns in the middle range of k is assumed to be strong enough so that the $s \cdot f(k)/k$ curve eventually rises to cross the $n + \delta$ line again at the

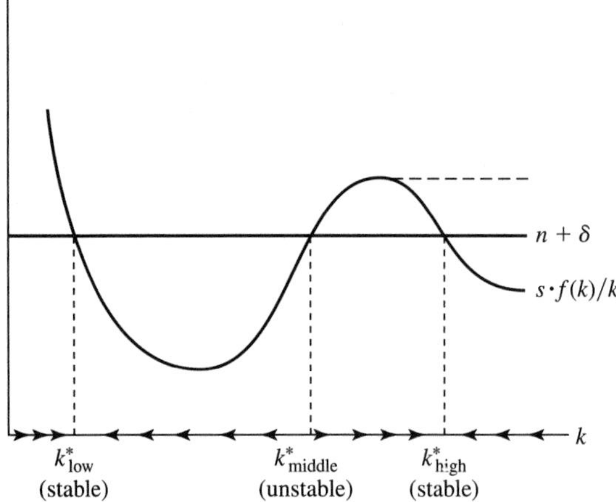

Figure 1.19
A poverty trap. The production function is assumed to exhibit diminishing returns to k when k is low, increasing returns for a middle range of k, and either constant or diminishing returns when k is high. The curve $s \cdot f(k)/k$ is therefore downward sloping for low values of k, upward sloping for an intermediate range of k, and downward sloping or horizontal for high values of k. The steady-state value k^*_{low} is stable and therefore constitutes a poverty trap for countries that begin with k between 0 and k^*_{middle}. If a country begins with $k > k^*_{\text{middle}}$, it converges to k^*_{high} if diminishing returns to k ultimately set in. If the returns to capital are constant at high values of k, as depicted by the dashed portion of the curve, the country converges to a positive long-run growth rate of k.

steady-state value k^*_{middle}. This steady state is, however, unstable, because $\dot{k}/k < 0$ applies to the left, and $\dot{k}/k > 0$ holds to the right. Thus, if the economy begins with $k^*_{\text{low}} < k(0) < k^*_{\text{middle}}$, its natural tendency is to return to the development trap at k^*_{low}, whereas if it manages somehow to get to $k(0) > k^*_{\text{middle}}$, it tends to grow further to reach still higher levels of k.

In the range where $k > k^*_{\text{middle}}$, the economy's tendency toward diminishing returns eventually brings $s \cdot f(k)/k$ down enough to equal $n + \delta$ at the steady-state value k^*_{high}. This steady state, corresponding to a high level of per capita income but to zero long-term per capita growth, is familiar from our study of the neoclassical model. The key problem for a less-developed economy at the trap level k^*_{low} is to get over the hump and thereby attain a high long-run level of per capita income.

One empirical implication of the model described by figure 1.19 is that there would exist a middle range of values of k—around k^*_{middle}—for which the growth rate, $\dot{k}/k$, is increasing in k and, hence, in y. That is, a divergence pattern should hold over this range of per capita incomes. Our reading of the evidence across countries, discussed in chapter 12, does not support this hypothesis. These results are, however, controversial—see, for example, Quah (1996).

1.5 Appendix: Proofs of Various Propositions

1.5.1 Proof That Each Input Is Essential for Production with a Neoclassical Production Function

We noted in the main body of this chapter that the neoclassical properties of the production function imply that the two inputs, K and L, are each essential for production. To verify this proposition, note first that if $Y \to \infty$ as $K \to \infty$, then

$$\lim_{K\to\infty} \frac{Y}{K} = \lim_{K\to\infty} \frac{\partial Y}{\partial K} = 0$$

where the first equality comes from l'Hôpital's rule and the second from the Inada condition. If Y remains bounded as K tends to infinity, then

$$\lim_{K\to\infty} (Y/K) = 0$$

follows immediately. We also know from constant returns to scale that, for any finite L,

$$\lim_{K\to\infty} (Y/K) = \lim_{K\to\infty} [F(1, L/K)] = F(1, 0)$$

so that $F(1, 0) = 0$. The condition of constant returns to scale then implies

$$F(K, 0) = K \cdot F(1, 0) = 0$$

for any finite K. We can show from an analogous argument that $F(0, L) = 0$ for any finite L. These results verify that each input is essential for production.

To demonstrate that output goes to infinity when either input goes to infinity, note that

$$F(K, L) = L \cdot f(k) = K \cdot [f(k)/k]$$

Therefore, for any finite K,

$$\lim_{L\to\infty} [F(K, L)] = K \cdot \lim_{k\to 0}[f(k)/k] = K \cdot \lim_{k\to 0}[f'(k)] = \infty$$

where the last equalities follow from l'Hôpital's rule (because essentiality implies $f[0] = 0$) and the Inada condition. We can show from an analogous argument that $\lim_{K\to\infty} [F(K, L)] = \infty$. Therefore, output goes to infinity when either input goes to infinity.

1.5.2 Properties of the Convergence Coefficient in the Solow–Swan Model

Equation (1.46) is a log-linearization of equation (1.41) around the steady-state position. To obtain equation (1.46), we have to rewrite equation (1.41) in terms of $\log(\hat{k})$. Note that $\dot{\hat{k}}/\hat{k}$ is the time derivative of $\log(\hat{k})$, and $(\hat{k})^{-(1-\alpha)}$ can be written as $e^{-(1-\alpha)\cdot\log(\hat{k})}$. The steady-state value of $sA(\hat{k})^{-(1-\alpha)}$ equals $x + n + \delta$. We can now take a first-order Taylor expansion of $\log(\hat{k})$ around $\log(\hat{k}^*)$ to get equation (1.46). See the appendix on mathematics at the end of the book for additional discussion. This result appears in Sala-i-Martin (1990) and Mankiw, Romer, and Weil (1992).

The true speed of convergence for $\hat{k}$ or $\hat{y}$ is not constant; it depends on the distance from the steady state. The growth rate of $\hat{y}$ can be written as

$$\dot{\hat{y}}/\hat{y} = \alpha \cdot \left[s \cdot A^{1/\alpha} \cdot (\hat{y})^{-(1-\alpha)/\alpha} - (x + n + \delta)\right]$$

If we use the condition $\hat{y}^* = A \cdot [sA/(x+n+\delta)]^{\alpha/(1-\alpha)}$, we can express the growth rate as

$$\dot{\hat{y}}/\hat{y} = \alpha \cdot (x + n + \delta) \cdot \left[(\hat{y}/\hat{y}^*)^{-(1-\alpha)/\alpha} - 1\right]$$

The convergence coefficient is

$$\beta = -d(\dot{\hat{y}}/\hat{y})]/d[\log(\hat{y})] = (1 - \alpha) \cdot (x + n + \delta) \cdot (\hat{y}/\hat{y}^*)^{-(1-\alpha)/\alpha}$$

At the steady state, $\hat{y} = \hat{y}^*$ and $\beta = (1 - \alpha) \cdot (x + n + \delta)$, as in equation (1.45). More generally, β declines as $\hat{y}/\hat{y}^*$ rises.

1.5.3 Proof That Technological Progress Must Be Labor Augmenting

We mentioned in the text that technological progress must take the labor-augmenting form shown in equation (1.34) in order for the model to have a steady state with constant growth rates. To prove this result, we start by assuming a production function that includes labor-augmenting and capital-augmenting technological progress:

$$Y = F[K \cdot B(t), L \cdot A(t)] \tag{1.73}$$

where $B(t) = A(t)$ implies that the technological progress is Hicks neutral.

We assume that $A(t) = e^{xt}$ and $B(t) = e^{zt}$, where $x \geq 0$ and $z \geq 0$ are constants. If we divide both sides of equation (1.73) by K, we can express output per unit of capital as

$$Y/K = e^{zt} \cdot \left\{ F\left[1, \frac{L \cdot A(t)}{K \cdot B(t)}\right] \right\} = e^{zt} \cdot \varphi\left[(L/K) \cdot e^{(x-z) \cdot t}\right]$$

where $\varphi(\cdot) \equiv F[1, \frac{L \cdot A(t)}{K \cdot B(t)}]$. The population, L, grows at the constant rate n. If γ_K^* is the constant growth rate of K in the steady state, the expression for Y/K can be written as

$$Y/K = e^{zt} \cdot \varphi\left[e^{(n+x-z-\gamma_K^*) \cdot t}\right] \tag{1.74}$$

Recall that the growth rate of K is given by

$$\dot{K}/K = s \cdot (Y/K) - \delta$$

In the steady state, $\dot{K}/K$ equals the constant γ_K^*, and, hence, Y/K must be constant. There are two ways to get the right-hand side of equation (1.74) to be constant. First, $z = 0$ and $\gamma_K^* = n + x$; that is, technological progress is solely labor augmenting, and the steady-state growth rate of capital equals $n + x$. In this case, the production function can be written in the form of equation (1.34).

The second way to get the right-hand side of equation (1.74) to be constant is with $z \neq 0$ and for the term $\varphi[e^{(n+x-z-\gamma_K^*)t}]$ exactly to offset the term e^{zt}. For this case to apply, the derivative of Y/K (in the proposed steady state) with respect to time must be identically zero. If we take the derivative of equation (1.74), set it to zero, and rearrange terms, we get

$$\varphi'(\chi) \cdot \chi/\varphi(\chi) = -z/(n + x - z - \gamma_K^*)$$

where $\chi \equiv e^{(n+x-z-\gamma_K^*) \cdot t}$, and the right-hand side is a constant. If we integrate out, we can write the solution as

$$\varphi(\chi) = (\text{constant}) \cdot \chi^{1-\alpha}$$

where α is a constant. This result implies that the production function can be written as

$$Y = (\text{constant}) \cdot (Ke^{zt})^{\alpha} \cdot (Le^{xt})^{1-\alpha} = (\text{constant}) \cdot K^{\alpha} \cdot (Le^{\nu t})^{1-\alpha}$$

where $\nu = [z\alpha + x \cdot (1 - \alpha)]/(1 - \alpha)$. In other words, if the rate of capital-augmenting technological progress, z, is nonzero and a steady state exists, the production function must take the Cobb–Douglas form. Moreover, if the production function is Cobb–Douglas, we can always express technological change as purely labor augmenting (at the rate ν). The conclusion, therefore, is that the existence of a steady state implies that technological progress can be written in the labor-augmenting form.

Another approach to technological progress assumes that capital goods produced later—that is, in a more recent *vintage*—are of higher quality for a given cost. If quality improves in accordance with $T(t)$, the equation for capital accumulation in this vintage model is

$$\dot{K} = s \cdot T(t) \cdot F(K, L) - \delta K \tag{1.75}$$

where K is measured in units of constant quality. This equation corresponds to Hicks-neutral technological progress given by $T(t)$ in the production function. The only difference from the standard specification is that output is $Y = F(K, L)$—not $T(t) \cdot F(K, L)$.

If we want to use a model that possesses a steady state, we would still have to assume that $F(K, L)$ was Cobb–Douglas. In that case, the main properties of the vintage model turn out to be indistinguishable from those of the model that we consider in the text in which technological progress is labor augmenting (see Phelps, 1962, and Solow, 1969, for further discussion). One difference in the vintage model is that, although K and Y grow at constant rates in the steady state, the growth rate of K (in units of constant quality) exceeds that of Y. Hence, K/Y is predicted to rise steadily in the long run.

1.5.4 Properties of the CES Production Function

The elasticity of substitution is a measure of the curvature of the isoquants. The slope of an isoquant is

$$\frac{dL}{dK}_{\text{isoquant}} = -\frac{\partial F(\cdot)/\partial K}{\partial F(\cdot)/\partial L}$$

The elasticity is given by

$$\left[\frac{\partial(\text{Slope})}{\partial(L/K)} \cdot \frac{L/K}{\text{Slope}}\right]^{-1}$$

For the CES production function shown in equation (1.64), the slope of the isoquant is

$$-(L/K)^{1-\psi} \cdot a \cdot b^{\psi}/[(1-a) \cdot (1-b)^{\psi}]$$

and the elasticity is $1/(1-\psi)$, a constant.

To compute the limit of the production function as ψ approaches 0, use equation (1.64) to get $\lim_{\psi \to 0}[\log(Y)] = \log(A) + 0/0$, which involves an indeterminate form. Apply l'Hôpital's rule to get

$$\lim_{\psi\to 0}[\log(Y)]$$
$$= \log(A) + \left[\frac{a(bK)^{\psi}\cdot \log(bK) + (1-a)\cdot[(1-b)\cdot L]^{\psi}\cdot \log[(1-b)\cdot L]}{a\cdot(bK)^{\psi} + (1-a)\cdot[(1-b)\cdot L]^{\psi}}\right]_{\psi=0}$$
$$= \log(A) + a\cdot \log(bK) + (1-a)\cdot \log[(1-b)\cdot L]$$

It follows that $Y = \tilde{A}K^{a}L^{1-a}$, where $\tilde{A} = Ab^{a}\cdot(1-b)^{1-a}$. That is, the CES production function approaches the Cobb–Douglas form as ψ tends to zero.

1.6 Problems

1.1 Convergence.

a. Explain the differences among absolute convergence, conditional convergence, and a reduction in the dispersion of real per capita income across groups.

b. Under what circumstances does absolute convergence imply a decline in the dispersion of per capita income?

1.2 Forms of technological progress. Assume that the rate of exogenous technological progress is constant.

a. Show that a steady state can coexist with technological progress only if this progress takes a labor-augmenting form. What is the intuition for this result?

b. Assume that the production function is $Y = F[B(T)\cdot K, A(t)\cdot L]$, where $B(t) = e^{zt}$ and $A(T) = e^{xt}$, with $z \geq 0$ and $x \geq 0$. Show that if $z > 0$ and a steady state exists, the production function must take the Cobb–Douglas form.

1.3 Dependence of the saving rate, population growth rate, and depreciation rate on the capital intensity. Assume that the production function satisfies the neoclassical properties.

a. Why would the saving rate, s, generally depend on k? (Provide some intuition; the precise answer will be given in chapter 2.)

b. How does the speed of convergence change if $s(k)$ is an increasing function of k? What if $s(k)$ is a decreasing function of k?

Consider now an AK technology.

c. Why would the saving rate, s, depend on k in this context?

d. How does the growth rate of k change over time depending on whether $s(k)$ is an increasing or decreasing function of k?

e. Suppose that the rate of population growth, n, depends on k. For an AK technology, what would the relation between n and k have to be in order for the model to predict convergence? Can you think of reasons why n would relate to k in this manner? (We analyze the determination of n in chapter 9.)

f. Repeat part e in terms of the depreciation rate, δ. Why might δ depend on k?

1.4 Effects of a higher saving rate. Consider this statement: "Devoting a larger share of national output to investment would help to restore rapid productivity growth and rising living standards." Under what conditions is the statement accurate?

1.5 Factor shares. For a neoclassical production function, show that each factor of production earns its marginal product. Show that if owners of capital save all their income and workers consume all their income, the economy reaches the golden rule of capital accumulation. Explain the results.

1.6 Distortions in the Solow–Swan model (based on Easterly, 1993). Assume that output is produced by the CES production function,

$$Y = \left[\left(a_F K_F^{\eta} + a_I K_I^{\eta}\right)^{\psi/\eta} + a_G K_G^{\psi}\right]^{1/\psi}$$

where Y is output; K_F is formal capital, which is subject to taxation; K_I is informal capital, which evades taxation; K_G is public capital, provided by government and used freely by all producers; $a_F, a_I, a_G > 0$; $\eta < 1$; and $\psi < 1$. Installed formal and informal capital differ in their location and form of ownership and, therefore, in their productivity.

Output can be used on a one-for-one basis for consumption or gross investment in the three types of capital. All three types of capital depreciate at the rate δ. Population is constant, and technological progress is nil.

Formal capital is subject to tax at the rate τ at the moment of its installation. Thus, the price of formal capital (in units of output) is $1 + \tau$. The price of a unit of informal capital is one. Gross investment in public capital is the fixed fraction s_G of tax revenues. Any unused tax receipts are rebated to households in a lump-sum manner. The sum of investment in the two forms of private capital is the fraction s of income net of taxes and transfers. Existing private capital can be converted on a one-to-one basis in either direction between formal and informal capital.

a. Derive the ratio of informal to formal capital used by profit-maximizing producers.

b. In the steady state, the three forms of capital grow at the same rate. What is the ratio of output to formal capital in the steady state?

c. What is the steady-state growth rate of the economy?

d. Numerical simulations show that, for reasonable parameter values, the graph of the growth rate against the tax rate, τ, initially increases rapidly, then reaches a peak, and finally decreases steadily. Explain this nonmonotonic relation between the growth rate and the tax rate.

1.7 A linear production function. Consider the production function $Y = AK + BL$, where A and B are positive constants.

a. Is this production function neoclassical? Which of the neoclassical conditions does it satisfy and which ones does it not?

b. Write output per person as a function of capital per person. What is the marginal product of k? What is the average product of k?

In what follows, we assume that population grows at the constant rate n and that capital depreciates at the constant rate δ.

c. Write down the fundamental equation of the Solow–Swan model.

d. Under what conditions does this model have a steady state with no growth of per capita capital, and under what conditions does the model display endogenous growth?

e. In the case of endogenous growth, how does the growth rate of the capital stock behave over time (that is, does it increase or decrease)? What about the growth rates of output and consumption per capita?

f. If $s = 0.4$, $A = 1$, $B = 2$, $\delta = 0.08$, and $n = 0.02$, what is the long-run growth rate of this economy? What if $B = 5$? Explain the differences.

1.8 Forms of technological progress and steady-state growth. Consider an economy with a CES production function:

$$Y = D(t) \cdot \{[B(t) \cdot K]^{\psi} + [A(t) \cdot L]^{\psi}\}^{1/\psi}$$

where ψ is a constant parameter different from zero. The terms $D(t)$, $B(t)$, and $A(t)$ represent different forms of technological progress. The growth rates of these three terms are constant, and we denote them by x_D, x_B, and x_A, respectively. Assume that population is constant, with $L = 1$, and normalize the initial levels of the three technologies to one, so that $D(0) = B(0) = A(0) = 1$. In this economy, capital accumulates according to the usual equation:

$$\dot{K} = Y - C - \delta K$$

a. Show that, in a steady state (defined as a situation in which all the variables grow at constant, perhaps different, rates), the growth rates of Y, K, and C are the same.

b. Imagine first that $x_B = x_A = 0$ and that $x_D > 0$. Show that the steady state must have $\gamma_K = 0$ (and, therefore, $\gamma_Y = \gamma_C = 0$). (Hint: Show first that $\gamma_Y = x_D + \frac{[K_0 e^{\gamma_K t}]^{\psi}}{1+[K_0 e^{\gamma_K t}]^{\psi}} \cdot \gamma_K$.)

c. Using the results in parts a and b, what is the only growth rate of $D(t)$ that is consistent with a steady state? What, therefore, is the only possible steady-state growth rate of Y?

d. Imagine now that $x_D = x_A = 0$ and that $x_B > 0$. Show that, in the steady state, $\gamma_K = -x_B$ (Hint: Show first that $\gamma_Y = (x_B + \gamma_K) \cdot \frac{[K_t \cdot B_t]^{\psi}}{1+[K_t \cdot B_t]^{\psi}}$.)

e. Using the results in parts a and d, show that the only growth rate of B consistent with a steady state is $x_B = 0$.

f. Finally, assume that $x_D = x_B = 0$ and that $x_A > 0$. Show that, in a steady state, the growth rates must satisfy $\gamma_K = \gamma_Y = \gamma_C = x_D$. (Hint: Show first that $\gamma_Y = \frac{K_t^{\psi} \cdot \gamma_K + A_t^{\psi} \cdot x_A}{K_t^{\psi} + A_t^{\psi}}$.)

g. What would be the steady-state growth rate in part f if population is not constant but, instead, grows at the rate $n > 0$?

2 Growth Models with Consumer Optimization (the Ramsey Model)

One shortcoming of the models that we analyzed in chapter 1 is that the saving rate—and, hence, the ratio of consumption to income—are exogenous and constant. By not allowing consumers to behave optimally, the analysis did not allow us to discuss how incentives affect the behavior of the economy. In particular, we could not think about how the economy reacted to changes in interest rates, tax rates, or other variables. In chapter 1 we showed that allowing for firms to behave optimally did not change any of the basic results of the Solow–Swan model. The main reason was that the overall amount of investment in the economy was still given by the saving of families, and that saving remained exogenous.

To paint a more complete picture of the process of economic growth, we need to allow for the path of consumption and, hence, the saving rate to be determined by optimizing households and firms that interact on competitive markets. We deal here with infinitely lived households that choose consumption and saving to maximize their dynastic utility, subject to an intertemporal budget constraint. This specification of consumer behavior is a key element in the Ramsey growth model, as constructed by Ramsey (1928) and refined by Cass (1965) and Koopmans (1965).

One finding will be that the saving rate is not constant in general but is instead a function of the per capita capital stock, k. Thus we modify the Solow–Swan model in two respects: first, we pin down the average level of the saving rate, and, second, we determine whether the saving rate rises or falls as the economy develops. We also learn how saving rates depend on interest rates and wealth and, in a later chapter, on tax rates and subsidies.

The average level of the saving rate is especially important for the determination of the levels of variables in the steady state. In particular, the optimizing conditions in the Ramsey model preclude the kind of inefficient oversaving that was possible in the Solow–Swan model.

The tendency for saving rates to rise or fall with economic development affects the transitional dynamics, for example, the speed of convergence to the steady state. If the saving rate rises with k, then the convergence speed is slower than that in the Solow–Swan model, and vice versa. We find, however, that even if the saving rate is rising, the convergence property still holds under fairly general conditions in the Ramsey model. That is, an economy still tends to grow faster in per capita terms when it is further from its own steady-state position.

We show that the Solow–Swan model with a constant saving rate is a special case of the Ramsey model; moreover, this case corresponds to reasonable parameter values. Thus, it was worthwhile to begin with the Solow–Swan model as a tractable approximation to the optimizing framework. We also note, however, that the empirical evidence suggests that saving rates typically rise with per capita income during the transition to the steady state. The Ramsey model is consistent with this pattern, and the model allows us to assess the implications of this saving behavior for the transitional dynamics. Moreover, the optimizing framework will be essential in later chapters when we extend the Ramsey model in various respects and consider the possible roles for government policies. Such policies will, in general, affect the incentives to save.

2.1 Households

2.1.1 Setup of the Model

The households provide labor services in exchange for wages, receive interest income on assets, purchase goods for consumption, and save by accumulating assets. The basic model assumes identical households—each has the same preference parameters, faces the same wage rate (because all workers are equally productive), begins with the same assets per person, and has the same rate of population growth. Given these assumptions, the analysis can use the usual representative-agent framework, in which the equilibrium derives from the choices of a single household. We discuss later how the results generalize when various dimensions of household heterogeneity are introduced.

Each household contains one or more adult, working members of the current generation. In making plans, these adults take account of the welfare and resources of their prospective descendants. We model this intergenerational interaction by imagining that the current generation maximizes utility and incorporates a budget constraint over an infinite horizon. That is, although individuals have finite lives, we consider an immortal extended family. This setting is appropriate if altruistic parents provide transfers to their children, who give in turn to their children, and so on. The immortal family corresponds to finite-lived individuals who are connected through a pattern of operative intergenerational transfers based on altruism.[1]

The current adults expect the size of their extended family to grow at the rate n because of the net influences of fertility and mortality. In chapter 9 we study how rational agents choose their fertility by weighing the costs and benefits of rearing children. But, at this point, we continue to simplify by treating n as exogenous and constant. We also neglect migration of persons, another topic explored in chapter 9. If we normalize the number of adults at time 0 to unity, the family size at time t—which corresponds to the adult population—is

$$L(t) = e^{nt}$$

If $C(t)$ is total consumption at time t, then $c(t) \equiv C(t)/L(t)$ is consumption per adult person.

1. See Barro (1974). We abstract from marriage, which generates interactions across family lines. See Bernheim and Bagwell (1988) for a discussion.

Each household wishes to maximize overall utility, U, as given by

$$U = \int_0^\infty u[c(t)] \cdot e^{nt} \cdot e^{-\rho t}\, dt \tag{2.1}$$

This formulation assumes that the household's utility at time 0 is a weighted sum of all future flows of utility, $u(c)$. The function $u(c)$—often called the felicity function—relates the flow of utility per person to the quantity of consumption per person, c. We assume that $u(c)$ is increasing in c and concave—$u'(c) > 0$, $u''(c) < 0$.[2] The concavity assumption generates a desire to smooth consumption over time: households prefer a relatively uniform pattern to one in which c is very low in some periods and very high in others. This desire to smooth consumption drives the household's saving behavior because they will tend to borrow when income is relatively low and save when income is relatively high. We also assume that $u(c)$ satisfies Inada conditions: $u'(c) \to \infty$ as $c \to 0$, and $u'(c) \to 0$ as $c \to \infty$.

The multiplication of $u(c)$ in equation (2.1) by family size, $L = e^{nt}$, represents the adding up of utils for all family members alive at time t. The other multiplier, $e^{-\rho t}$, involves the rate of time preference, $\rho > 0$. A positive value of ρ means that utils are valued less the later they are received.[3] We assume $\rho > n$, which implies that U in equation (2.1) is bounded if c is constant over time.

One reason for ρ to be positive is that utils far in the future correspond to consumption of later generations. Suppose that, starting from a point at which the levels of consumption per person in each generation are the same, parents prefer a unit of their own consumption to a unit of their children's consumption. This parental "selfishness" corresponds to $\rho > 0$ in equation (2.1). In a fuller specification, we would also distinguish the rate at which individuals discount their own flow of utility at different points in time (for which $\rho = 0$ might apply) from the rate that applies across generations. Equation (2.1) assumes, only for reasons of tractability, that the discount rate within a person's lifetime is the same as that across generations.

It is also plausible that parents would have diminishing marginal utility with respect to the number of children. We could model this effect by allowing the rate of time preference,

2. The results will be invariant with positive linear transformations of the utility function but not with arbitrary positive, monotonic transformations. Thus, the analysis depends on a limited form of cardinal utility. See Koopmans (1965) for a discussion.

3. Ramsey (1928) preferred to assume $\rho = 0$. He then interpreted the optimizing agent as a social planner, rather than a competitive household, who chose consumption and saving for today's generation as well as for future generations. The discounting of utility for future generations ($\rho > 0$) was, according to Ramsey, "ethically indefensible." We work out an example with $\rho = 0$ in the mathematics chapter.

ρ, to increase with the population growth rate, n.[4] Because we treat n as exogenous, this dependence of ρ on n would not materially change the analysis in this chapter. We shall, however, consider this effect in chapter 9, which allows for an endogenous determination of population growth.

Households hold assets in the form of ownership claims on capital (to be introduced later) or as loans. Negative loans represent debts. We continue to assume a closed economy, so that no assets can be traded internationally. Households can lend to and borrow from other households, but the representative household will end up holding zero net loans in equilibrium. Because the two forms of assets, capital and loans, are assumed to be perfect substitutes as stores of value, they must pay the same real rate of return, $r(t)$. We denote the household's net assets per person by $a(t)$, where $a(t)$ is measured in real terms, that is, in units of consumables.

Households are competitive in that each takes as given the interest rate, $r(t)$, and the wage rate, $w(t)$, paid per unit of labor services. We assume that each adult supplies inelastically one unit of labor services per unit of time. (Chapter 9 considers a labor/leisure choice.) In equilibrium, the labor market clears, and the household obtains the desired quantity of employment. That is, the model abstracts from "involuntary unemployment."

Since each person works one unit of labor services per unit of time, the wage income per adult person equals $w(t)$. The total income received by the aggregate of households is, therefore, the sum of labor income, $w(t) \cdot L(t)$, and asset income, $r(t) \cdot (\text{Assets})$. Households use the income that they do not consume to accumulate more assets:

$$\frac{d(\text{Assets})}{dt} = r \cdot (\text{Assets}) + wL - C \tag{2.2}$$

where we omit time subscripts whenever no ambiguity results. Since a is per capita assets, we have

$$\dot{a} = \left(\frac{1}{L}\right) \cdot \left[\frac{d(\text{Assets})}{dt}\right] - na$$

Therefore, if we divide equation (2.2) by L, we get the budget constraint in per capita terms:

$$\dot{a} = w + ra - c - na \tag{2.3}$$

4. One case common in the growth literature assumes that ρ rises one to one with n; that is, $\rho = \rho^* + n$, where ρ^* is the positive rate of time preference that applies under zero population growth. In this case, utility at time t enters into equation (2.1) as $u(c)e^{-\rho^* t}$, which depends on per capita utility, but not on the size of the family at time t. This specification is used, for example, by Sidrauski (1967) and Blanchard and Fischer (1989, chapter 2).

If each household can borrow an unlimited amount at the going interest rate, $r(t)$, it has an incentive to pursue a form of chain letter or Ponzi game. The household can borrow to finance current consumption and then use future borrowings to roll over the principal and pay all the interest. In this case, the household's debt grows forever at the rate of interest, $r(t)$. Since no principal ever gets repaid, today's added consumption is effectively free. Thus a household that can borrow in this manner would be able to finance an arbitrarily high level of consumption in perpetuity.

To rule out chain-letter possibilities, we assume that the credit market imposes a constraint on the amount of borrowing. The appropriate restriction turns out to be that the present value of assets must be asymptotically nonnegative, that is,

$$\lim_{t\to\infty}\left\{a(t)\cdot\exp\left[-\int_0^t [r(v)-n]\,dv\right]\right\}\geq 0 \tag{2.4}$$

This constraint means that, in the long run, a household's debt per person (negative values of $a[t]$) cannot grow as fast as $r(t)-n$, so that the level of debt cannot grow as fast as $r(t)$. This restriction rules out the type of chain-letter finance that we have described. We show later how the credit-market constraint expressed in equation (2.4) emerges naturally from the market equilibrium.

The household's optimization problem is to maximize U in equation (2.1), subject to the budget constraint in equation (2.3), the stock of initial assets, $a(0)$, and the limitation on borrowing in equation (2.3). The inequality restrictions, $c(t)\geq 0$, also apply. However, as $c(t)$ approaches 0, the Inada condition implies that the marginal utility of consumption becomes infinite. The inequality restrictions will therefore never bind, and we can safely ignore them.

2.1.2 First-Order Conditions

The mathematical methods for this type of dynamic optimization problem are discussed in the appendix on mathematics at the end of the book. We use these results here without further derivation. Begin with the present-value Hamiltonian,

$$J = u[c(t)]\cdot e^{-(\rho-n)t} + \nu(t)\cdot\{w(t)+[r(t)-n]\cdot a(t)-c(t)\} \tag{2.5}$$

where the expression in braces equals $\dot{a}$ from equation (2.3). The variable $\nu(t)$ is the present-value shadow price of income. It represents the value of an increment of income received at time t in units of utils at time 0.[5] Notice that this shadow price depends on time because there

5. We could deal alternatively with the shadow price $\nu e^{(\rho-n)t}$. This shadow price measures the value of an increment of income at time t in units of utils at time t. (See the discussion in the appendix on mathematics at the end of the book.)

is one of them for each "constraint," and the household faces a continuum of constraints, one for each instant. The first-order conditions for a maximum of U are

$$\frac{\partial J}{\partial c} = 0 \Longrightarrow \nu = u'(c)e^{-(\rho-n)t} \tag{2.6}$$

$$\dot{\nu} = -\partial J/\partial a \Longrightarrow \dot{\nu} = -(r-n)\cdot\nu \tag{2.7}$$

The transversality condition is

$$\lim_{t\to\infty}[\nu(t)\cdot a(t)] = 0 \tag{2.8}$$

The Euler Equation If we differentiate equation (2.6) with respect to time and substitute for ν from this equation and for $\dot{\nu}$ from equation (2.7), we get the basic condition for choosing consumption over time:

$$r = \rho - \left(\frac{du'/dt}{u'}\right) = \rho - \left[\frac{u''(c)\cdot c}{u'(c)}\right]\cdot(\dot{c}/c) \tag{2.9}$$

This equation says that households choose consumption so as to equate the rate of return, r, to the rate of time preference, ρ, plus the rate of decrease of the marginal utility of consumption, u', due to growing per capita consumption, c.

The interest rate, r, on the left-hand side of equation (2.9) is the rate of return to saving. The far right-hand side of the equation can be viewed as the rate of return to consumption. Agents prefer to consume today rather than tomorrow for two reasons. First, because households discount future utility at rate ρ, this rate is part of the rate of return to consumption today. Second, if $\dot{c}/c > 0$, c is low today relative to tomorrow. Since agents like to smooth consumption over time—because $u''(c) < 0$—they would like to even out the flow by bringing some future consumption forward to the present. The second term on the far right picks up this effect. If agents are optimizing, equation (2.9) says that they have equated the two rates of return and are therefore indifferent at the margin between consuming and saving.

Another way to view equation (2.9) is that households would select a flat consumption profile, with $\dot{c}/c = 0$, if $r = \rho$. Households would be willing to depart from this flat pattern and sacrifice some consumption today for more consumption tomorrow—that is, tolerate $\dot{c}/c > 0$—only if they are compensated by an interest rate, r, that is sufficiently above ρ. The term $[\frac{-u''(c)\cdot c}{u'(c)}]\cdot(\dot{c}/c)$ on the right-hand side of equation (2.9) gives the required amount of compensation. Note that the term in brackets is the magnitude of the elasticity of $u'(c)$ with respect to c. This elasticity, a measure of the concavity of $u(c)$, determines the amount by which r must exceed ρ. If the elasticity is larger in magnitude, the required premium of r over ρ is greater for a given value of $\dot{c}/c$.

The magnitude of the elasticity of marginal utility, $\{[-u''(c) \cdot c]/[u'(c)]\}$, is sometimes called the reciprocal of the elasticity of intertemporal substitution.[6] Equation (2.9) shows that to find a steady state in which r and $\dot{c}/c$ are constant, this elasticity must be constant asymptotically. We therefore follow the common practice of assuming the functional form

$$u(c) = \frac{c^{(1-\theta)} - 1}{(1-\theta)} \tag{2.10}$$

where $\theta > 0$, so that the elasticity of marginal utility equals the constant $-\theta$.[7] The elasticity of substitution for this utility function is the constant $\sigma = 1/\theta$. Hence, this form is called the *constant intertemporal elasticity of substitution* (CIES) utility function. The higher is θ, the more rapid is the proportionate decline in $u'(c)$ in response to increases in c and, hence, the less willing households are to accept deviations from a uniform pattern of c over time. As θ approaches 0, the utility function approaches a linear form in c; the linearity means that households are indifferent to the timing of consumption if $r = \rho$ applies.

The form of $u(c)$ in equation (2.10) implies that the optimality condition from equation (2.9) simplifies to

$$\dot{c}/c = (1/\theta) \cdot (r - \rho) \tag{2.11}$$

Therefore, the relation between r and ρ determines whether households choose a pattern of per capita consumption that rises over time, stays constant, or falls over time. A lower willingness to substitute intertemporally (a higher value of θ) implies a smaller responsiveness of $\dot{c}/c$ to the gap between r and ρ.

The Transversality Condition The transversality condition in equation (2.8) says that the value of the household's per capita assets—the quantity $a(t)$ times the shadow price

6. The elasticity of intertemporal substitution between consumption at times t_1 and t_2 is given by the reciprocal of the proportionate change in the magnitude of the slope of an indifference curve in response to a proportionate change in the ratio $c(t_1)/c(t_2)$. If we denote this elasticity by σ, we get

$$\sigma = \left[\frac{c(t_1)/c(t_2)}{-u'[c(t_1)]/u'[c(t_2)]} \cdot \frac{d\{u'[c(t_1)]/u'[c(t_2)]\}}{d[c(t_1)/c(t_2)]}\right]^{-1}$$

where $-u'[c(t_1)]/u'[c(t_2)]$ is the magnitude of the slope of the indifference curve. If we let t_2 approach t_1, we get the instantaneous elasticity,

$$\sigma = -u'(c)/[c \cdot u''(c)]$$

which is the inverse of the magnitude of the elasticity of marginal utility.

7. The inclusion of the -1 in the formula is convenient because it implies that $u(c)$ approaches $\log(c)$ as $\theta \to 1$. (This result can be proven using l'Hôpital's rule.) The term $-1/(1-\theta)$ can, however, be omitted without affecting the subsequent results, because the household's choices are invariant with respect to linear transformations of the utility function (see footnote 2).

$\nu(t)$—must approach 0 as time approaches infinity. If we think of infinity loosely as the end of the planning horizon, the intuition is that optimizing agents do not want to have any valuable assets left over at the end.[8] Utility would increase if the assets, which are effectively being wasted, were used instead to raise consumption at some dates in finite time.

The shadow price ν evolves over time in accordance with equation (2.7). Integration of this equation with respect to time yields

$$\nu(t) = \nu(0) \cdot \exp\left\{-\int_0^t [r(v) - n]\, dv\right\}$$

The term $\nu(0)$ equals $u'[c(0)]$, which is positive because $c(0)$ is finite (if U is finite), and $u'(c)$ is assumed to be positive as long as c is finite.

If we substitute the result for $\nu(t)$ into equation (2.8), the transversality condition becomes

$$\lim_{t\to\infty}\left\{a(t) \cdot \exp\left[-\int_0^t [r(v) - n]\, dv\right]\right\} = 0 \tag{2.12}$$

This equation implies that the quantity of assets per person, a, does not grow asymptotically at a rate as high as $r - n$ or, equivalently, that the level of assets does not grow at a rate as high as r. It would be suboptimal for households to accumulate positive assets forever at the rate r or higher, because utility would increase if these assets were instead consumed in finite time.

In the case of borrowing, where $a(t)$ is negative, infinite-lived households would like to violate equation (2.12) by borrowing and never making payments for principal or interest. However, equation (2.4) rules out this chain-letter finance, that is, schemes in which a household's debt grows forever at the rate r or higher. In order to borrow on this perpetual basis, households would have to find willing lenders; that is, other households that were willing to hold positive assets that grew at the rate r or higher. But we already know from the transversality condition that these other households will be unwilling to absorb assets asymptotically at such a high rate. Therefore, in equilibrium, each household will be unable to borrow in a chain-letter fashion. In other words, the inequality restriction shown in equation (2.4) is not arbitrary and would, in fact, be imposed in equilibrium by the credit market. Faced by this constraint, the best thing that optimizing households can do is to satisfy the condition shown in equation (2.12). That is, this equality holds whether $a(t)$ is positive or negative.

8. The interpretation of the transversality condition in the infinite-horizon problem as the limit of the corresponding condition for a finite-horizon problem is not always correct. See the appendix on mathematics at the end of the book.

The Consumption Function The term $\exp[-\int_0^t r(v)\,dv]$, which appears in equation (2.12), is a present-value factor that converts a unit of income at time t to an equivalent unit of income at time 0. If $r(v)$ equaled the constant r, the present-value factor would simplify to e^{-rt}. More generally we can think of an average interest rate between times 0 and t, defined by

$$\bar{r}(t) = (1/t) \cdot \int_0^t r(v)\,dv \tag{2.13}$$

The present-value factor equals $e^{-\bar{r}(t)\cdot t}$.

Equation (2.11) determines the growth rate of c. To determine the level of c—that is, the consumption function—we have to use the flow budget constraint, equation (2.3), to derive the household's intertemporal budget constraint. We can solve equation (2.3) as a first-order linear differential equation in a to get an intertemporal budget constraint that holds for any time $T \geq 0$:[9]

$$a(T) \cdot e^{-[\bar{r}(T)-n]T} + \int_0^T c(t)e^{-[\bar{r}(t)-n]t}\,dt = a(0) + \int_0^T w(t)e^{-[\bar{r}(t)-n]t}\,dt$$

where we used the definition of $\bar{r}(t)$ from equation (2.13). This intertemporal budget constraint says that the present discounted value of all income between 0 and T plus the initial available wealth have to equal the present discounted value of all future consumption plus the present value of the assets left at T. If we take the limit as $T \to \infty$, the term on the far left vanishes (from the transversality condition in equation [2.12]), and the intertemporal budget constraint becomes

$$\int_0^\infty c(t)e^{-[\bar{r}(t)-n]t}\,dt = a(0) + \int_0^\infty w(t)e^{-[\bar{r}(t)-n]t}\,dt = a(0) + \tilde{w}(0) \tag{2.14}$$

Hence, the present value of consumption equals lifetime wealth, defined as the sum of initial assets, $a(0)$, and the present value of wage income, denoted by $\tilde{w}(0)$.

If we integrate equation (2.11) between times 0 and t and use the definition of $\bar{r}(t)$ from equation (2.13), we find that consumption is given by

$$c(t) = c(0) \cdot e^{(1/\theta)\cdot[\bar{r}(t)-\rho]t}$$

9. The methods for solving first-order linear differential equations with variable coefficients are discussed in the appendix on mathematics at the end of the book.

Substitution of this result for $c(t)$ into the intertemporal budget constraint in equation (2.14) leads to the consumption function at time 0:

$$c(0) = \mu(0) \cdot [a(0) + \tilde{w}(0)] \tag{2.15}$$

where $\mu(0)$, the propensity to consume out of wealth, is determined from

$$[1/\mu(0)] = \int_0^{\infty} e^{[\bar{r}(t)\cdot(1-\theta)/\theta - \rho/\theta + n]t}\, dt \tag{2.16}$$

An increase in average interest rates, $\bar{r}(t)$, for given wealth, has two effects on the marginal propensity to consume in equation (2.16). First, higher interest rates increase the cost of current consumption relative to future consumption, an intertemporal-substitution effect that motivates households to shift consumption from the present to the future. Second, higher interest rates have an income effect that tends to raise consumption at all dates. The net effect of an increase in $\bar{r}(t)$ on $\mu(0)$ depends on which of the two forces dominates.

If $\theta < 1$, $\mu(0)$ declines with $\bar{r}(t)$ because the substitution effect dominates. The intuition is that, when θ is low, households care relatively little about consumption smoothing, and the intertemporal-substitution effect is large. Conversely, if $\theta > 1$, $\mu(0)$ rises with $\bar{r}(t)$ because the substitution effect is relatively weak. Finally, if $\theta = 1$ (log utility), the two effects exactly cancel, and $\mu(0)$ simplifies to $\rho - n$, which is independent of $\bar{r}(t)$. Recall that we assumed $\rho - n > 0$.

The effects of $\bar{r}(t)$ on $\mu(0)$ carry over to effects on $c(0)$ if we hold constant the wealth term, $a(0) + \tilde{w}(0)$. In fact, however, $\tilde{w}(0)$ falls with $\bar{r}(t)$ for a given path of $w(t)$. This third effect reinforces the substitution effect that we mentioned before.

2.2 Firms

Firms produce goods, pay wages for labor input, and make rental payments for capital input. Each firm has access to the production technology,

$$Y(t) = F[K(t), L(t), T(t)]$$

where Y is the flow of output, K is capital input (in units of commodities), L is labor input (in person-hours per year), and $T(t)$ is the level of the technology, which is assumed to grow at the constant rate $x \geq 0$. Hence, $T(t) = e^{xt}$, where we normalize the initial level of technology, $T(0)$, to 1. The function $F(\cdot)$ satisfies the neoclassical properties discussed in chapter 1. In particular, Y exhibits constant returns to scale in K and L, and each input exhibits positive and diminishing marginal product.

We showed in chapter 1 that a steady state coexists with technological progress at a constant rate only if this progress takes the labor-augmenting form

$$Y(t) = F[K(t), L(t) \cdot T(t)]$$

If we again define "effective labor" as the product of raw labor and the level of technology, $\hat{L} \equiv L \cdot T(t)$, the production function can be written as

$$Y = F(K, \hat{L}) \tag{2.17}$$

We shall find it convenient to work with variables that are constant in the steady state. In chapter 1, we showed that the steady state of the model with exogenous technical progress was such that the per capita variables grew at the rate of technological progress, x. This property will still hold in the present model. Hence, we will deal again with quantities per unit of effective labor:

$$\hat{y} \equiv Y/\hat{L} \text{ and } \hat{k} \equiv K/\hat{L}$$

The production function can then be rewritten in intensive form, as in equation (1.38),

$$\hat{y} = f(\hat{k}) \tag{2.18}$$

where $f(0) = 0$. It can be readily verified that the marginal products of the factors are given by[10]

$$\partial Y/\partial K = f'(\hat{k})$$

$$\partial Y/\partial L = [f(\hat{k}) - \hat{k} \cdot f'(\hat{k})] \cdot e^{xt} \tag{2.19}$$

The Inada conditions, discussed in chapter 1, imply $f'(\hat{k}) \to \infty$ as $\hat{k} \to 0$ and $f'(\hat{k}) \to 0$ as $\hat{k} \to \infty$.

We think of firms as renting the services of capital from the households that own the capital. (None of the results would change if the firms owned the capital, and the households owned shares of stock in the firms.) If we let $R(t)$ be the rental rate of a unit of capital, a firm's total cost for capital is RK, which is proportional to K. We assume that capital services can be increased or decreased without incurring any additional expenses, such as costs for installing machines or making other changes. We consider these kinds of adjustment costs in chapter 3.

We assume, as in chapter 1, a one-sector production model in which one unit of output can be used to generate one unit of household consumption, C, or one unit of additional

10. We can write $Y = \hat{L} \cdot f(\hat{k})$. Differentiation of Y with respect to K, holding fixed L and t, leads to $\partial Y/\partial K = f'(\hat{k})$. Differentiation of Y with respect to L, holding fixed K and t, leads to $\partial Y/\partial L = [f(\hat{k}) - \hat{k} \cdot f'(\hat{k})]e^{xt}$.

capital, K. Therefore, as long as the economy is not at a corner solution in which all current output goes into consumption or new capital, the price of K in terms of C will be fixed at unity. Because C will be nonzero in equilibrium, we have to be concerned only with the possibility that none of the output goes into new capital; in other words, that gross investment is 0. Even in this situation, the price of K in terms of C would remain at unity if capital were reversible in the sense that the existing stocks could be consumed on a one-for-one basis. With reversible capital, the economy's gross investment can be negative, and the price of K in units of C stays at unity. Although this situation may apply to farm animals, economists usually assume that investment is irreversible. In this case, the price of K in units of C is one only if the constraint of nonnegative aggregate gross investment is nonbinding in equilibrium. We maintain this assumption in the following analysis, and we deal with irreversible investment in appendix 2B (section 2.9).

Since capital stocks depreciate at the constant rate $\delta \geq 0$, the net rate of return to a household that owns a unit of capital is $R - \delta$.[11] Recall that households can also receive the interest rate r on funds lent to other households. Since capital and loans are perfect substitutes as stores of value, we must have $r = R - \delta$ or, equivalently, $R = r + \delta$.

The representative firm's flow of net receipts or profit at any point in time is given by

$$\pi = F(K, \hat{L}) - (r + \delta) \cdot K - wL \tag{2.20}$$

As in chapter 1, the problem of maximizing the present value of profit reduces here to a problem of maximizing profit in each period without regard to the outcomes in other periods. Profit can be written as

$$\pi = \hat{L} \cdot [f(\hat{k}) - (r + \delta) \cdot \hat{k} - we^{-xt}] \tag{2.21}$$

A competitive firm, which takes r and w as given, maximizes profit for given $\hat{L}$ by setting

$$f'(\hat{k}) = r + \delta \tag{2.22}$$

Also as before, in a full-market equilibrium, w equals the marginal product of labor corresponding to the value of $\hat{k}$ that satisfies equation (2.22):

$$[f(\hat{k}) - \hat{k} \cdot f'(\hat{k})]e^{xt} = w \tag{2.23}$$

This condition ensures that profit equals zero for any value of $\hat{L}$.

11. More generally, if the price of capital can change over time, the real rate of return for owners of capital equals $R/\phi - \delta + \dot{\phi}/\phi$, where ϕ is the price of capital in units of consumables. In the present case, where $\phi = 1$, the capital-gain term, $\dot{\phi}/\phi$, vanishes, and the rate of return simplifies to $R - \delta$.

2.3 Equilibrium

We began with the behavior of competitive households that faced a given interest rate, r, and wage rate, w. We then introduced competitive firms that also faced given values of r and w. We can now combine the behavior of households and firms to analyze the structure of a competitive market equilibrium.

Since the economy is closed, all debts within the economy must cancel. Hence, the assets per adult person, a, equal the capital per worker, k. The equality between k and a follows because all of the capital stock must be owned by someone in the economy; in particular, in this closed-economy model, all of the domestic capital stock must be owned by the domestic residents. If the economy were open to international capital markets, the gap between k and a would correspond to the home country's net debt to foreigners. Chapter 3 considers an open economy, in which the net foreign debt can be nonzero.

The household's flow budget constraint in equation (2.3) determines $\dot{a}$. Use $a = k$, $\hat{k} = ke^{-xt}$, and the conditions for r and w in equations (2.22) and (2.23) to get

$$\dot{\hat{k}} = f(\hat{k}) - \hat{c} - (x + n + \delta) \cdot \hat{k} \tag{2.24}$$

where $\hat{c} \equiv C/\hat{L} = ce^{-xt}$, and $\hat{k}(0)$ is given. Equation (2.24) is the resource constraint for the overall economy: the change in the capital stock equals output less consumption and depreciation, and the change in $\hat{k} \equiv K/\hat{L}$ also takes account of the growth in $\hat{L}$ at the rate $x + n$.

The differential equation (2.24) is the key relation that determines the evolution of $\hat{k}$ and, hence, $\hat{y} = f(\hat{k})$ over time. The missing element, however, is the determination of $\hat{c}$. If we knew the relation of $\hat{c}$ to $\hat{k}$ (or $\hat{y}$), or if we had another differential equation that determined the evolution of $\hat{c}$, we could study the full dynamics of the economy.

In the Solow–Swan model of chapter 1, the missing relation was provided by the assumption of a constant saving rate. This assumption implied the linear consumption function, $\hat{c} = (1 - s) \cdot f(\hat{k})$. In the present setting, the behavior of the saving rate is not so simple, but we do know from household optimization that c grows in accordance with equation (2.11). If we use the conditions $r = f'(\hat{k}) - \delta$ and $\hat{c} = ce^{-xt}$, we get

$$\dot{\hat{c}}/\hat{c} = \frac{\dot{c}}{c} - x = \frac{1}{\theta} \cdot [f'(\hat{k}) - \delta - \rho - \theta x] \tag{2.25}$$

This equation, together with equation (2.24), forms a system of two differential equations in $\hat{c}$ and $\hat{k}$. This system, together with the initial condition, $\hat{k}(0)$, and the transversality condition, determines the time paths of $\hat{c}$ and $\hat{k}$.

We can write the transversality condition in terms of $\hat{k}$ by substituting $a = k$ and $\hat{k} = ke^{-xt}$ into equation (2.12) to get

$$\lim_{t\to\infty}\left\{\hat{k}\cdot\exp\left(-\int_0^t[f'(\hat{k})-\delta-x-n]\,dv\right)\right\}=0 \tag{2.26}$$

We can interpret this result if we jump ahead to use the result that $\hat{k}$ tends asymptotically to a constant steady-state value, $\hat{k}^*$, just as in the Solow–Swan model. The transversality condition in equation (2.26) therefore requires $f'(\hat{k}^*) - \delta$, the steady-state rate of return, to exceed $x + n$, the steady-state growth rate of K.

2.4 Alternative Environments

The analysis applies thus far to a decentralized economy with competitive households and firms. We can see from the setup of the model, however, that the same equations—and, hence, the same results—would emerge under some alternative environments. First, households could perform the functions of firms by employing adult family members as workers in accordance with the production process, $f(\hat{k})$.[12] The resource constraint in equation (2.24) follows directly (total output must be allocated to consumption or gross investment, which equals net investment plus depreciation). If the households maximize the utility function in equations (2.1) and (2.10), subject to equation (2.24), then equations (2.25) and (2.26) still represent the first-order conditions. Thus, the separation of functions between households and firms is not central to the analysis.

We could also pretend that the economy was run by a benevolent *social planner,* who dictates the choices of consumption over time and who seeks to maximize the utility of the representative family. The device of the benevolent social planner will be useful in many circumstances for finding the economy's first-best outcomes. The planner is assumed to have the same form of preferences as those assumed before—in particular, the same rate of time preference, ρ, and the same utility function, $u(c)$. The planner is also constrained by the aggregate resource constraint in equation (2.24). The solution for the planner will therefore be the same as that for the decentralized economy.[13] Since a benevolent

12. This setup was considered in chapter 1.

13. The planner's problem is to choose the path of c to maximize U in equation (2.1), subject to the economy's budget constraint in equation (2.24), the initial value $\hat{k}(0)$, and the inequalities $c \geq 0$ and $\hat{k} \geq 0$. The Hamiltonian for this problem is

$$J = u(c)e^{-\rho t} + \nu\cdot[f(\hat{k}) - ce^{-xt} - (x+n+\delta)\cdot\hat{k}]$$

The usual first-order conditions lead to equation (2.25), and the transversality condition leads to equation (2.26).

social planner with dictatorial powers will attain a Pareto optimum, the results for the decentralized economy—which coincide with those of the planner—must also be Pareto optimal.

2.5 The Steady State

We now consider whether the equilibrium conditions, equations (2.24), (2.25), and (2.26), are consistent with a steady state, that is, a situation in which the various quantities grow at constant (possibly zero) rates. We show first that the steady-state growth rates of $\hat{k}$ and $\hat{c}$ must be zero, just as in the Solow–Swan model of chapter 1.

Let $(\gamma_{\hat{k}})^*$ be the steady-state growth rate of $\hat{k}$ and $(\gamma_{\hat{c}})^*$ the steady-state growth rate of $\hat{c}$. In the steady state, equation (2.25) implies

$$\hat{c} = f(\hat{k}) - (x + n + \delta) \cdot \hat{k} - \hat{k} \cdot (\gamma_{\hat{k}})^* \tag{2.27}$$

If we differentiate this condition with respect to time, we find that

$$\dot{\hat{c}} = \dot{\hat{k}} \cdot \{f'(\hat{k}) - [x + n + \delta + (\gamma_{\hat{k}})^*]\} \tag{2.28}$$

must hold in the steady state. The expression in the large braces is positive from the transversality condition shown in equation (2.26). Therefore, $(\gamma_{\hat{k}})^*$ and $(\gamma_{\hat{c}})^*$ must have the same sign.

If $(\gamma_{\hat{k}})^* > 0, \hat{k} \to \infty$ and $f'(\hat{k}) \to 0$. Equation (2.25) then implies $(\gamma_{\hat{c}}) < 0$, an outcome that contradicts the result that $(\gamma_{\hat{k}})^*$ and $(\gamma_{\hat{c}})^*$ are of the same sign. If $(\gamma_{\hat{k}})^* < 0, \hat{k} \to 0$ and $f'(\hat{k}) \to \infty$. Equation (2.25) then implies $(\gamma_{\hat{c}})^* > 0$, an outcome that again contradicts the result that $(\gamma_{\hat{k}})^*$ and $(\gamma_{\hat{c}})^*$ are of the same sign. Therefore, the only remaining possibility is $(\gamma_{\hat{k}})^* = (\gamma_{\hat{c}})^* = 0$. The result $(\gamma_{\hat{k}})^* = 0$ implies $(\gamma_{\hat{y}})^* = 0$. Thus the variables per unit of effective labor, $\hat{k}$, $\hat{c}$, and $\hat{y}$, are constant in the steady state. This behavior implies that the per capita variables, k, c, and y, grow in the steady state at the rate x, and the level variables, K, C, and Y, grow in the steady state at the rate $x + n$. These results on steady-state growth rates are the same as those in the Solow–Swan model, in which the saving rate was exogenous and constant.

The steady-state values for $\hat{c}$ and $\hat{k}$ are determined by setting the expressions in equations (2.24) and (2.25) to zero. The solid curve in figure 2.1, which corresponds to $\hat{c} = f(\hat{k}) - (x + n + \delta) \cdot \hat{k}$, shows pairs of $(\hat{k}, \hat{c})$ that satisfy $\dot{\hat{k}} = 0$ in equation (2.24). Note that the peak in the curve occurs when $f'(\hat{k}) = \delta + x + n$, so that the interest rate, $f'(\hat{k}) - \delta$, equals the steady-state growth rate of output, $x + n$. This equality between the interest rate

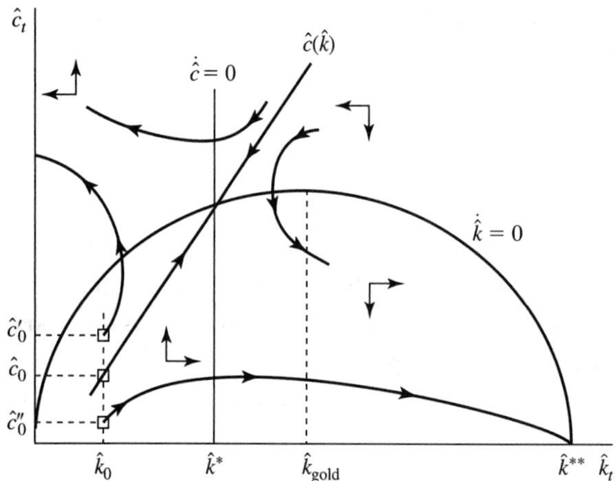

Figure 2.1
The phase diagram of the Ramsey model. The figure shows the transitional dynamics of the Ramsey model. The $\dot{\hat{c}}/\hat{c} = 0$ and $\dot{\hat{k}} = 0$ loci divide the space into four regions, and the arrows show the directions of motion in each region. The model exhibits saddle-path stability. The stable arm is an upward-sloping curve that goes through the origin and the steady state. Starting from a low level of $\hat{k}$, the optimal initial $\hat{c}$ is low. Along the transition, $\hat{c}$ and $\hat{k}$ increase toward their steady-state values.

and the growth rate corresponds to the golden-rule level of $\hat{k}$ (as described in chapter 1),[14] because it leads to a maximum of $\hat{c}$ in the steady state. We denote by $\hat{k}_{gold}$ the value of $\hat{k}$ that corresponds to the golden rule.

Equation (2.25) and the condition $\dot{\hat{c}} = 0$ imply

$$f'(\hat{k}^*) = \delta + \rho + \theta x \tag{2.29}$$

This equation says that the steady-state interest rate, $f'(\hat{k}) - \delta$, equals the effective discount rate, $\rho + \theta x$.[15] The vertical line at $\hat{k}^*$ in figure 2.1 corresponds to this condition; note that $\dot{\hat{c}}/\hat{c} = 0$ holds at this value of $\hat{k}$ independently of the value of $\hat{c}$.[16] The key to the determination of $\hat{k}^*$ in equation (2.29) is the diminishing returns to capital, which make $f'(\hat{k}^*)$ a

14. In chapter 1 we defined the golden-rule level of k as the capital stock per person that maximizes steady-state consumption per capita. It was shown that this level of capital was such that $f'(k_{gold}) = \delta + n$; see equation (1.22). When exogenous technological progress exists, the golden-rule level of $\hat{k}$ is defined as the level that maximizes steady-state consumption per effective unit of labor, $\hat{c} = f(\hat{k}) - (x + n + \delta) \cdot \hat{k}$. Notice that the maximum is achieved when $f'(\hat{k}_{gold}) = (x + n + \delta)$.

15. The θx part of the effective discount rate picks up the effect from diminishing marginal utility of consumption due to growth of c at the rate x. See equation (2.9).

16. Equation (2.25) indicates that $\dot{\hat{c}}/\hat{c} = 0$ is also satisfied if $\hat{c} = 0$, that is, along the horizontal axis in figure 2.1.

monotonically decreasing function of $\hat{k}^*$. Moreover, the Inada conditions—$f'(0)=\infty$ and $f'(\infty)=0$—ensure that equation (2.29) holds at a unique positive value of $\hat{k}^*$.

Figure 2.1 shows the determination of the steady-state values, $(\hat{k}^*, \hat{c}^*)$, at the intersection of the vertical line with the solid curve. In particular, with $\hat{k}^*$ determined from equation (2.29), the value for $\hat{c}^*$ follows from setting the expression in equation (2.24) to 0 as

$$\hat{c}^* = f(\hat{k}^*) - (x+n+\delta)\cdot\hat{k}^* \tag{2.30}$$

Note that $\hat{y}^* = f(\hat{k}^*)$ is the steady-state value of $\hat{y}$.

Consider the transversality condition in equation (2.26). Since $\hat{k}$ is constant in the steady state, this condition holds if the steady-state rate of return, $r^* = f'(\hat{k}^*) - \delta$, exceeds the steady-state growth rate, $x+n$. Equation (2.29) implies that this condition can be written as

$$\rho > n + (1-\theta)x \tag{2.31}$$

If ρ is not high enough to satisfy equation (2.31), the household's optimization problem is not well posed because infinite utility would be attained if c grew at the rate x.[17] We assume henceforth that the parameters satisfy equation (2.31).

In figure 2.1, the steady-state value, $\hat{k}^*$, was drawn to the left of $\hat{k}_{gold}$. This relation always holds if the transversality condition, equation (2.31), is satisfied. The steady-state value is determined from $f'(\hat{k}^*) = \delta+\rho+\theta x$,[18] whereas the golden-rule value comes from $f'(\hat{k}_{gold}) = \delta + x + n$. The inequality in equation (2.31) implies $\rho+\theta x > x+n$ and, hence, $f'(\hat{k}^*) > f'(\hat{k}_{gold})$. The result $\hat{k}^* < \hat{k}_{gold}$ follows from $f''(\hat{k}) < 0$.

The implication is that inefficient oversaving cannot occur in the optimizing framework, although it could arise in the Solow–Swan model with an arbitrary, constant saving rate. If the infinitely lived household were oversaving, it would realize that it was not optimizing—because it was not satisfying the transversality condition—and would therefore shift to a path that entailed less saving. Note that the optimizing household does not save enough to attain the golden-rule value, $\hat{k}_{gold}$. The reason is that the impatience reflected in the effective discount rate, $\rho+\theta x$, makes it not worthwhile to sacrifice more of current consumption to reach the maximum of $\hat{c}$ (the golden-rule value, $\hat{c}_{gold}$) in the steady state.

The steady-state growth rates do not depend on parameters that describe the production function, $f(\cdot)$, or on the preference parameters, ρ and θ, that characterize households' attitudes about consumption and saving. These parameters do have long-run effects on levels of variables.

17. The appendix on mathematics at the end of the book considers some cases in which infinite utility can be handled.

18. This condition is sometimes called the *modified golden rule*.

In figure 2.1, an increased willingness to save—represented by a reduction in ρ or θ—shifts the $\dot{\hat{c}}/\hat{c} = 0$ schedule to the right and leaves the $\dot{\hat{k}} = 0$ schedule unchanged. These shifts lead accordingly to higher values of $\hat{c}^*$ and $\hat{k}^*$ and, hence, to a higher value of $\hat{y}^*$. Similarly, a proportional upward shift of the production function or a reduction of the depreciation rate, δ, moves the $\dot{\hat{k}} = 0$ curve up and the $\dot{\hat{c}}/\hat{c} = 0$ curve to the right. These shifts generate increases in $\hat{c}^*$, $\hat{k}^*$, and $\hat{y}^*$. An increase in x raises the effective time-preference term, $\rho + \theta x$, in equation (2.29) and also lowers the value of $\hat{c}^*$ that corresponds to a given $\hat{k}^*$ in equation (2.30). In figure 2.1, these changes shift the $\dot{\hat{k}} = 0$ schedule downward and the $\dot{\hat{c}}/\hat{c} = 0$ schedule leftward and thereby reduce $\hat{c}^*$, $\hat{k}^*$, and $\hat{y}^*$. (Although $\hat{c}$ falls, utility rises because the increase in x raises the growth rate of c relative to that of $\hat{c}$.) Finally, the effect of n on $\hat{k}^*$ and $\hat{y}^*$ is nil if we hold fixed ρ. Equation (2.30) implies that $\hat{c}^*$ declines. If a higher n leads to a higher rate of time preference (for reasons discussed before), then an increase in n would reduce $\hat{k}^*$ and $\hat{y}^*$.

2.6 Transitional Dynamics

2.6.1 The Phase Diagram

The Ramsey model, like the Solow–Swan model, is most interesting for its predictions about the behavior of growth rates and other variables along the transition path from an initial factor ratio, $\hat{k}(0)$, to the steady-state ratio, $\hat{k}^*$. Equations (2.24), (2.25), and (2.26) determine the path of $\hat{k}$ and $\hat{c}$ for a given value of $\hat{k}(0)$. The phase diagram in figure 2.1 shows the nature of the dynamics.[19]

We first display the $\dot{\hat{c}} = 0$ locus. Since $\dot{\hat{c}} = \hat{c} \cdot (1/\theta) \cdot [f'(\hat{k}) - \delta - \rho - \theta x]$, there are two ways for $\dot{\hat{c}}$ to be zero: $\hat{c} = 0$, which corresponds to the horizontal axis in figure 2.1, and $f'(\hat{k}) = \delta + \rho + \theta x$, which is a vertical line at $\hat{k}^*$, the capital-labor ratio defined in equation (2.29). We note that $\hat{c}$ is rising for $\hat{k} < \hat{k}^*$ (so the arrows point upward in this region) and falling for $\hat{k} > \hat{k}^*$ (where the arrows point downward).

Recall that the solid curve in figure 2.1 shows combinations of $\hat{k}$ and $\hat{c}$ that satisfy $\dot{\hat{k}} = 0$ in equation (2.24). This equation also implies that $\hat{k}$ is falling for values of $\hat{c}$ above the solid curve (so the arrows point leftward in this region) and rising for values of $\hat{c}$ below the curve (where the arrows point rightward).

Since the $\dot{\hat{c}} = 0$ and the $\dot{\hat{k}} = 0$ loci cross three times, there are three steady states: the first one is the origin ($\hat{c} = \hat{k} = 0$), the second steady state corresponds to $\hat{k}^*$ and $\hat{c}^*$, and

19. See the appendix on mathematics for a discussion of phase diagrams.

the third one involves a positive capital stock, $\hat{k}^{**} > 0$, but zero consumption. We neglect the solution at the origin because it is uninteresting.

The second steady state is saddle-path stable. Note, in particular, that the pattern of arrows in figure 2.1 is such that the economy can converge to this steady state if it starts in two of the four quadrants in which the two schedules divide the space. The saddle-path property can also be verified by linearizing the system of dynamic equations around the steady state and noting that the determinant of the characteristic matrix is negative (see appendix 2A, section 2.8, for details). This sign for the determinant implies that the two eigenvalues have opposite signs, an indication that the system is locally saddle-path stable.

The dynamic equilibrium follows the stable saddle path shown by the solid locus with arrows. Suppose, for example, that the initial factor ratio satisfies $\hat{k}(0) < \hat{k}^*$, as shown in figure 2.1. If the initial consumption ratio is $\hat{c}(0)$, as shown, the economy follows the stable path toward the steady-state pair, $(\hat{k}^*, \hat{c}^*)$. This path satisfies all the first-order conditions, including the transversality condition, as shown in the previous section.

The two other possibilities are that the initial consumption ratio exceeds or falls short of $\hat{c}(0)$. If the ratio exceeds $\hat{c}(0)$, the initial saving rate is too low for the economy to remain on the stable path. The trajectory eventually crosses the $\dot{\hat{k}} = 0$ locus. After that crossing, $\hat{c}$ continues to rise, $\hat{k}$ starts to decline, and the path hits the vertical axis in finite time, at which point $\hat{k} = 0$.[20] The condition $f(0) = 0$ implies $\hat{y} = 0$; therefore, $\hat{c}$ must jump downward to 0 at this point. Because this jump violates the first-order condition that underlies equation (2.25), these paths—in which the initial consumption ratio exceeds $\hat{c}(0)$—are not equilibria.[21]

The final possibility is that the initial consumption ratio is below $\hat{c}(0)$. In this case, the initial saving rate is too high to remain on the saddle path, and the economy eventually crosses the $\dot{\hat{c}} = 0$ locus. After that crossing, $\hat{c}$ declines and $\hat{k}$ continues to rise. The economy converges to the point at which the $\dot{\hat{k}} = 0$ schedule intersects the horizontal axis, a point which we labeled $\hat{k}^{**}$. Note, in particular, that $\hat{k}$ rises above the golden-rule value, $\hat{k}_{gold}$, and asymptotically approaches a higher value of $\hat{k}$. Therefore, $f'(\hat{k}) - \delta$ falls below $x + n$ asymptotically, and the path violates the transversality condition given in equation (2.26). This violation of the transversality condition means that households are oversaving: utility

20. We can verify from equation (2.24) that $\dot{\hat{k}}$ becomes more and more negative in this region. Therefore, $\hat{k}$ must reach 0 in finite time.

21. This analysis applies if investment is reversible. If investment is irreversible, the constraint $\hat{c} \leq f(\hat{k})$ becomes binding before the trajectory hits the vertical axis. That is, the paths that start from points such as $\hat{c}_0'$ in figure 2.1 would eventually hit the production function, $\hat{c} = f(\hat{k})$, which lies above the locus for $\dot{\hat{k}} = 0$. Thereafter, the path would follow the production function downward toward the origin. Appendix 2B (section 2.9) shows that such paths are not equilibria.

would increase if consumption were raised at earlier dates. Accordingly, paths in which the initial consumption ratio is below $\hat{c}(0)$ are not equilibria. This result leaves the stable saddle path leading to the positive steady state, $\hat{k}^*$, as the only possibility.[22]

2.6.2 The Importance of the Transversality Condition

It is important to emphasize the role of the transversality condition in the determination of the unique equilibrium. To make this point, we consider an unrealistic variant of the Ramsey model in which everyone knows that the world will end at some known date $T > 0$. The utility function in equation (2.1) then becomes

$$U = \int_0^T u[c(t)] \cdot e^{nt} \cdot e^{-\rho t}\, dt$$

and the non-Ponzi condition is

$$a(T) \cdot \exp\left[-\int_0^T [r(v) - n]\, dv\right] \geq 0$$

The budget constraint is still given by equation (2.3). Since the only difference between this problem and that of the previous sections is the terminal date, the only optimization condition that changes is the transversality condition, which is now

$$a(T) \cdot \exp\left[-\int_0^T [r(v) - n]\, dv\right] = 0$$

Since the exponential term cannot be zero in finite time, this condition implies that the assets left at the end of the planning horizon equal zero:

$$a(T) = 0 \tag{2.32}$$

In other words, since the shadow value of assets at time T is positive, households will optimally choose to leave no assets when they "die."

The behavior of firms is the same as before, and equilibrium in the asset markets again requires $a(t) = k(t)$. Therefore, the general-equilibrium conditions are still given by equations (2.24) and (2.25), and the loci for $\dot{\hat{k}} = 0$ and $\dot{\hat{c}} = 0$ are the same as those shown

22. Similar results apply if the economy begins with $\hat{k}(0) > \hat{k}^*$ in figure 2.1. The only complication here is that, if investment is irreversible, the constraint $\hat{c} \leq f(\hat{k})$ may be binding in this region. See the discussion in appendix 2B (section 2.9).

in figure 2.1. The arrows representing the dynamics of the system are also the same as before.

Since $a(t) = k(t)$, the transversality condition from equation (2.32) can be written as

$$\hat{k}(T) = 0 \tag{2.33}$$

From the perspective of figure 2.1, this new transversality condition requires the initial choice of $\hat{c}(0)$ to be such that the capital stock equals zero at time T. In other words, optimality now requires the economy to land on the vertical axis at exactly time T. The implication is that the stable arm is no longer the equilibrium, because it is does not lead the economy toward zero capital at time T. The same is true for any initial choice of consumption below the stable arm. The new equilibrium, therefore, features an initial value $\hat{c}(0)$ that lies above the stable arm.

It is possible that $\hat{c}$ and $\hat{k}$ would both rise for awhile. In fact, if T is large, the transition path would initially be close to, but slightly above, the stable arm shown in figure 2.1. However, the economy eventually crosses the $\dot{\hat{k}} = 0$ schedule. Thereafter, $\hat{c}$ and $\hat{k}$ fall, and the economy ends up with zero capital at time T. We see, therefore, that the same system of differential equations involves one equilibrium (the stable arm) or another (the path that ends up on the vertical axis at T) depending solely on the transversality condition.

2.6.3 The Shape of the Stable Arm

The stable arm shown in figure 2.1 expresses the equilibrium $\hat{c}$ as a function of $\hat{k}$.[23] This relation is known in dynamic programming as a *policy function:* it relates the optimal value of a control variable, $\hat{c}$, to the state variable, $\hat{k}$. This policy function is an upward-sloping curve that goes through the origin and the steady-state position. Its exact shape depends on the parameters of the model.

Consider, as an example, the effect of the parameter θ on the shape of the stable arm. Suppose that the economy begins with $\hat{k}(0) < \hat{k}^*$, so that future values of $\hat{c}$ will exceed $\hat{c}(0)$. High values of θ imply that households have a strong preference for smoothing consumption over time; hence, they will try hard to shift consumption from the future to the present. Therefore, when θ is high, the stable arm will lie close to the $\dot{\hat{k}} = 0$ schedule, as shown in figure 2.2. The correspondingly low rate of investment implies that the transition would take a long time.

Conversely, if θ is low, households are more willing to postpone consumption in response to high rates of return. The stable arm in this case is flat and close to the horizontal axis for

23. The corresponding relation in the Solow–Swan model, $\hat{c} = (1 - s) \cdot f(\hat{k})$, was provided by the assumption of a constant saving rate.

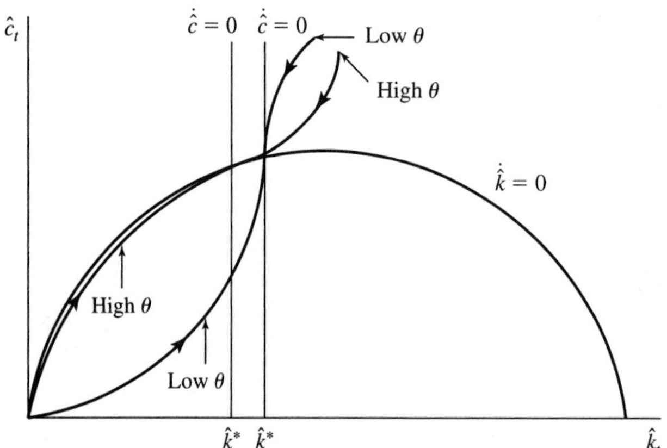

Figure 2.2
The slope of the saddle path. When θ is low, consumers do not mind large swings in consumption over time. Hence, they choose to consume relatively little when the capital stock is low (and the interest rate is high). The investment rate is high initially in this situation, and the economy approaches its steady state rapidly. In contrast, when θ is high, consumers are strongly motivated to smooth consumption over time. Hence, they initially devote most of their resources to consumption (the stable arm is close to the $\dot{\hat{k}} = 0$ schedule) and little to investment. In this case, the economy approaches its steady state slowly.

low values of $\hat{k}$ (see figure 2.2). The high levels of investment imply that the transition is relatively quick, and as $\hat{k}$ approaches $\hat{k}^*$, households increase $\hat{c}$ sharply. It is clear from the diagram that linear approximations around the steady state will not capture these dynamics accurately.

We show in appendix 2C (section 2.10) for the case of a Cobb–Douglas technology, $\hat{y} = A\hat{k}^{\alpha}$, that $\hat{c}/\hat{k}$ is rising, constant, or falling in the transition from $\hat{k}(0) < \hat{k}^*$ depending on whether the parameter θ is smaller than, equal to, or larger than the capital share, α. It follows that the stable arm is convex, linear, or concave depending on whether θ is smaller than, equal to, or larger than α. (We argue later that $\theta > \alpha$ is the plausible case.) If $\theta = \alpha$, so that $\hat{c}/\hat{k}$ is constant during the transition, the policy function has the closed-form solution $\hat{c} = (\text{constant}) \cdot \hat{k}$, where the constant turns out to be $(\delta + \rho)/\theta - (\delta + n)$.

2.6.4 Behavior of the Saving Rate

The gross saving rate, s, equals $1 - \hat{c}/f(\hat{k})$. The Solow–Swan model, discussed in chapter 1, assumed that s was constant at an arbitrary level. In the Ramsey model with optimizing consumers, s can follow a complicated path that includes rising and falling segments as the economy develops and approaches the steady state.

Heuristically, the behavior of the saving rate is ambiguous because it involves the offsetting impacts from a substitution effect and an income effect. As $\hat{k}$ rises, the decline in $f'(\hat{k})$ lowers the rate of return, r, on saving. The reduced incentive to save—an intertemporal-substitution effect—tends to lower the saving rate as the economy develops. Second, the income per effective worker in a poor economy, $f(\hat{k})$, is far below the long-run or permanent income of this economy. Since households desire to smooth consumption, they would like to consume a lot in relation to income when they are poor; that is, the saving rate would be low when $\hat{k}$ is low. As $\hat{k}$ rises, the gap between current and permanent income diminishes; hence, consumption tends to fall in relation to current income, and the saving rate tends to rise. This force—an income effect—tends to raise the saving rate as the economy develops.

The transitional behavior of the saving rate depends on whether the substitution or income effect is more important. The net effect is ambiguous in general, and the path of the saving rate during the transition can be complicated. The results simplify, however, for a Cobb–Douglas production function. Appendix 2C shows for this case that, depending on parameter values, the saving rate falls monotonically, stays constant, or rises monotonically as $\hat{k}$ rises.

We show in Appendix 2C for the Cobb–Douglas case that the steady-state saving rate, s^*, is given by

$$s^* = \alpha \cdot (x + n + \delta)/(\delta + \rho + \theta x) \tag{2.34}$$

Note that the transversality condition, which led to equation (2.31), implies $s^* < \alpha$ in equation (2.34); that is, the steady-state gross saving rate is less than the gross capital share.

We can use a phase diagram to analyze the transitional behavior of the saving rate for the case of a Cobb–Douglas production function. The methodology is interesting more generally because it provides a way to study the behavior of variables of interest, such as the saving rate, that do not enter directly into the first-order conditions of the model. The method involves transformations of the variables that appear in the first-order conditions. The dynamic relations that we used before were written in terms of the variables $\hat{c}$ and $\hat{k}$. To study the transitional behavior of the saving rate, $s = 1 - \hat{c}/\hat{y}$, we want to rewrite these relations in terms of the variables $\hat{c}/\hat{y}$ and $\hat{k}$. Then we will be able to construct a phase diagram in terms of $\hat{c}/\hat{y}$ and $\hat{k}$. The stable arm of such a phase diagram will show how $\hat{c}/\hat{y}$—and, hence, $s = 1 - \hat{c}/\hat{y}$—move as $\hat{k}$ increases.

We start by noticing that the growth rate of $\hat{c}/\hat{y}$ is given by the growth rate of $\hat{c}$ minus the growth rate of $\hat{y}$. If the production function is Cobb–Douglas, the growth rate of $\hat{y}$ is proportional to the growth rate of $\hat{k}$, that is,

$$\frac{1}{\hat{c}/\hat{y}} \cdot \frac{d(\hat{c}/\hat{y})}{dt} = (\dot{\hat{c}}/\hat{c}) - (\dot{\hat{y}}/\hat{y}) = (\dot{\hat{c}}/\hat{c}) - \alpha \cdot (\dot{\hat{k}}/\hat{k})$$

We can now use the equilibrium conditions shown in equations (2.24) and (2.25) to get

$$\frac{1}{\hat{c}/\hat{y}} \cdot \frac{d(\hat{c}/\hat{y})}{dt} = [(1/\theta) \cdot (\alpha A\hat{k}^{\alpha-1} - \delta - \rho - \theta x)] - \alpha \cdot [A\hat{k}^{\alpha-1} - (\hat{c}/\hat{y}) \cdot A\hat{k}^{\alpha-1} - (x + n + \delta)] \tag{2.35}$$

where we used the equality $\hat{c}/\hat{k} = (\hat{c}/\hat{y}) \cdot A\hat{k}^{\alpha-1}$. The growth rate of $\hat{k}$ is

$$\dot{\hat{k}}/\hat{k} = [A\hat{k}^{\alpha-1} - (\hat{c}/\hat{y}) \cdot A\hat{k}^{\alpha-1} - (x + n + \delta)] \tag{2.36}$$

Notice that equations (2.35) and (2.36) represent a system of differential equations in the variables $\hat{c}/\hat{y}$ and $\hat{k}$. Therefore, a conventional phase diagram can be drawn in terms of these two variables.

We start by setting equation (2.35) to zero to get the $\frac{d(\hat{c}/\hat{y})}{dt} = 0$ locus:

$$\hat{c}/\hat{y} = \left(1 - \frac{1}{\theta}\right) + \psi \cdot \frac{\hat{k}^{1-\alpha}}{\alpha A} \tag{2.37}$$

where $\psi \equiv [(\delta + \rho + \theta x)/\theta - \alpha \cdot (x + n + \delta)]$ is a constant. This locus is upward sloping, downward sloping, or horizontal depending on whether ψ is positive, negative, or zero. The three possibilities are depicted in figure 2.3.

Independently of the value of ψ, the arrows above the $\frac{d(\hat{c}/\hat{y})}{dt} = 0$ locus point north, and the arrows below the schedule point south.

We can find the $\dot{\hat{k}} = 0$ locus by setting equation (2.35) to zero to get

$$\hat{c}/\hat{y} = 1 - \frac{(x + n + \delta)}{A} \cdot \hat{k}^{1-\alpha} \tag{2.38}$$

which is unambiguously downward sloping.[24] Arrows point west above the schedule and east below the schedule.

The three panels of figure 2.3 show that the steady state is saddle-path stable regardless of the value of ψ. The stable arm, however, is upward-sloping when $\psi > 0$, downward-sloping when $\psi < 0$, and horizontal when $\psi = 0$. Following the reasoning of previous sections, we know that an infinite-horizon economy always finds itself on the stable arm. Thus, depending on parameter values, the consumption ratio falls monotonically, stays constant, or rises monotonically as $\hat{k}$ rises. The saving rate, therefore, behaves exactly the opposite. A high value of θ—which corresponds to a low willingness to substitute consumption intertemporally—makes it more likely that $\psi < 0$ will hold, in which case the saving rate

24. When $\psi < 0$, the $\frac{d\hat{k}}{dt} = 0$ locus is also steeper than the $\frac{d(\hat{c}/\hat{y})}{dt} = 0$ schedule.

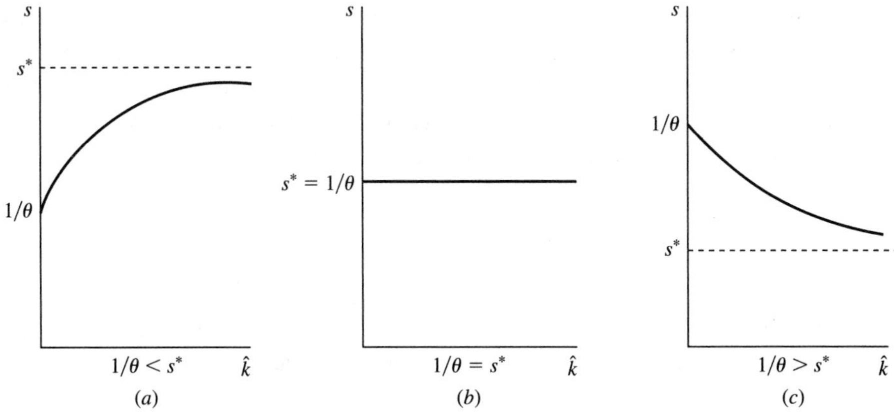

Figure 2.3
Phase diagram for the behavior of the saving rate (in the Cobb–Douglas case). In the Cobb–Douglas case, the savings rate behaves monotonically. Panel *a* shows the phase diagram for $\hat{c}/\hat{y}$ and $\hat{k}$ when the parameters are such that $(\delta + \rho + \theta x)/\theta > \alpha \cdot (x + n + \delta)$. Since the stable arm is upward sloping, the consumption ratio increases as the economy grows toward the steady state. Hence, in this case, the saving rate (one minus the consumption rate) declines monotonically during the transition. Panel *b* considers the case in which $(\delta + \rho + \theta x)/\theta < \alpha \cdot (x + n + \delta)$. The stable arm is now downward sloping and, therefore, the saving rate increases monotonically during the transition. Panel *c* considers the case $(\delta + \rho + \theta x)/\theta + \alpha \cdot (x + n + \delta)$. The stable arm is now horizonal, which means that the saving rate is constant during the transition.

is more likely to rise during the transition. This result follows because a higher θ weakens the substitution effect from the interest rate.

In the particular case where $\psi = 0$, the saving rate is constant at its steady-state value, $s^* = 1/\theta$, during the transition. For this combination of parameters, it turns out that the wealth and substitution effects cancel out, so that the saving rate remains constant as the capital stock grows toward its steady state. Thus, the constant saving rate in the Solow–Swan model is a special case of the Ramsey model. However, even in this case, there is an important difference from the Solow–Swan model. The level of s in the Ramsey model is dictated by the underlying parameters and cannot be chosen arbitrarily. In particular, an arbitrary choice of s in the Solow–Swan model may generate results that are dynamically inefficient if s leads the economy to a steady-state capital stock that is larger than the golden rule. This outcome is impossible in the Ramsey model.

In a later discussion, we use the baseline values $\rho = 0.02$ per year, $\delta = 0.05$ per year, $n = 0.01$ per year, and $x = 0.02$ per year. If we also assume a conventional capital share of $\alpha = 0.3$, the value of θ that generates a constant saving rate is 17; that is, $s^* < 1/\theta$ applies and the saving rate falls—counterfactually—as the economy develops unless θ exceeds this high value.

We noted for the Solow–Swan model that the theory cannot fit the evidence about speeds of convergence unless the capital-share coefficient, α, is much larger than 0.3. Values in the neighborhood of 0.75 accord better with the empirical evidence, and these high values of α are reasonable if we take a broad view of capital to include the human components. We show in the following section that the findings about α still apply in the Ramsey growth model, which allows the saving rate to vary over time. If we assume $\alpha = 0.75$, along with the benchmark values of the other parameters, the value of θ that generates a constant saving rate is 1.75. That is, the gross saving rate rises (or falls) as the economy develops if θ is greater (or less) than 1.75. If $\theta = 1.75$, the gross saving rate is constant at the value 0.57. We have to interpret this high value for the gross saving rate by including in gross saving the various expenditures that expand or maintain human capital; aside from expenses for education and training, this gross saving would include portions of the outlays for food, health, and so on.

Our reading of empirical evidence across countries is that the saving rate tends to rise to a moderate extent with per capita income during the transition. The Ramsey model can fit this pattern, as well as the observed speeds of convergence, if we combine the benchmark parameters with a value of α of around 0.75 and a value of θ somewhat above 2. The value of θ cannot be too much above 2 because then the steady-state saving rate, s^*, shown in equation (2.34), becomes too low. For example, the value $\theta = 10$ implies $s^* = 0.22$, which is too low for a broad concept that includes gross saving in the form of human capital.

2.6.5 The Paths of the Capital Stock and Output

The stable arm shown in figure 2.1 shows that, if $\hat{k}(0) < \hat{k}^*$, $\hat{k}$ and $\hat{c}$ rise monotonically as they approach their steady-state values. The rising path of $\hat{k}$ implies that the rate of return, r, declines monotonically from its initial position, $f'[\hat{k}(0)] - \delta$, to its steady-state value, $\rho + \theta x$. Equation (2.25) and the path of decreasing r imply that the growth rate of per capita consumption, $\dot{c}/c$, falls monotonically. That is, the lower $\hat{k}(0)$ and, hence, $\hat{y}(0)$, the higher the initial value of $\dot{c}/c$.

We would also like to relate the initial per capita growth rates of capital and output, γ_k and γ_y, to the starting ratio, $\hat{k}(0)$. In chapter 1 we referred to the negative relations between $\dot{k}/k$ and $\hat{k}(0)$ and between $\dot{y}/y$ and $\hat{y}(0)$ as convergence effects. We show in appendix 2D (section 2.11), using the consumption function from equations (2.15) and (2.16), that $\dot{k}/k$ declines monotonically as the economy develops and approaches the steady state. In other words, although the saving rate may rise during the transition, it cannot rise enough to eliminate the inverse relation between $\dot{k}/k$ and $\hat{k}$. Thus, the endogenous determination of the saving rate does not eliminate the convergence property for $\hat{k}$.

We can take logs and derivatives of the production function in equation (2.18) to derive the growth rate of output per effective worker:

$$\dot{\hat{y}}/\hat{y} = \left[\frac{\hat{k} \cdot f'(\hat{k})}{f(\hat{k})}\right] \cdot (\dot{\hat{k}}/\hat{k}) \tag{2.39}$$

that is, the growth rate of $\hat{k}$ is multiplied by the share of gross capital income in gross product. For a Cobb–Douglas production function, the share of capital income equals the constant α. Therefore, the properties of $\dot{k}/k$ carry over immediately to those of $\dot{y}/y$. This result applies more generally than in the Cobb–Douglas case unless the share of capital income rises fast enough as an economy develops to more than offset the fall in $\dot{k}/k$.

2.6.6 Speeds of Convergence

Log-Linear Approximations Around the Steady State We want now to provide a quantitative assessment of the speed of convergence in the Ramsey model. We begin with a log-linearized version of the dynamic system for $\hat{k}$ and $\hat{c}$, equations (2.24) and (2.25). This approach is an extension of the method that we used in chapter 1 for the Solow–Swan model; the only difference here is that we have to deal with a two-variable system instead of a one-variable system. The advantage of the log-linearization method is that it provides a closed-form solution for the convergence coefficient. The disadvantage is that it applies only as an approximation in the neighborhood of the steady state.

Appendix 2A examines a log-linearized version of equations (2.24) and (2.25) when expanded around the steady-state position. The results can be written as

$$\log[\hat{y}(t)] = e^{-\beta t} \cdot \log[\hat{y}(0)] + (1 - e^{-\beta t}) \cdot \log(\hat{y}^*) \tag{2.40}$$

where $\beta > 0$. Thus, for any $t \geq 0$, $\log[\hat{y}(t)]$ is a weighted average of the initial and steady-state values, $\log[\hat{y}(0)]$ and $\log(\hat{y}^*)$, with the weight on the initial value declining exponentially at the rate β. The speed of convergence, β, depends on the parameters of technology and preferences. For the case of a Cobb–Douglas technology, the formula for the convergence coefficient (which comes from the log-linearization around the steady-state position) is

$$2\beta = \left\{\zeta^2 + 4 \cdot \left(\frac{1-\alpha}{\theta}\right) \cdot (\rho + \delta + \theta x) \cdot \left[\frac{\rho + \delta + \theta x}{\alpha} - (n + x + \delta)\right]\right\}^{1/2} - \zeta \tag{2.41}$$

where $\zeta = \rho - n - (1 - \theta) \cdot x > 0$. We discuss below the way that the various parameters enter into this formula.

Equation (2.40) implies that the average growth rate of per capita output, y, over an interval from an initial time 0 to any future time $T \geq 0$ is given by

$$(1/T) \cdot \log[y(T)/y(0)] = x + \frac{(1 - e^{-\beta T})}{T} \cdot \log[\hat{y}^*/\hat{y}(0)] \tag{2.42}$$

Hold fixed, for the moment, the steady-state growth rate x, the convergence speed β, and the averaging interval T. Then equation (2.42) says that the average per capita growth rate of output depends negatively on the ratio of $\hat{y}(0)$ to $\hat{y}^*$. Thus, as in the Solow–Swan model, the effect of the initial position, $\hat{y}(0)$, is conditioned on the steady-state position, $\hat{y}^*$. In other words, the Ramsey model also predicts conditional, rather than absolute, convergence.

The coefficient that relates the growth rate of y to $\log[\hat{y}^*/\hat{y}(0)]$ in equation (2.42), $(1 - e^{-\beta T})/T$, declines with T for given β. If $\hat{y}(0) < \hat{y}^*$, so that growth rates decline over time, an increase in T means that more of the lower future growth rates are averaged with the higher near-term growth rates. Therefore, the average growth rate, which enters into equation (2.42), falls as T rises. As $T \to \infty$, the steady-state growth rate, x, dominates the average; hence, the coefficient $(1 - e^{-\beta T})/T$ approaches 0, and the average growth rate of y in equation (2.42) tends to x.

For a given T, a higher β implies a higher coefficient $(1 - e^{-\beta T})/T$. (As $T \to 0$, the coefficient approaches β.) Equation (2.41) expresses the dependence of β on the underlying parameters. Consider first the case of the Solow–Swan model in which the saving rate is constant. As noted before, this situation applies if the steady-state saving rate, s^*, shown in equation (2.34) equals $1/\theta$ or, equivalently, if the combination of parameters $\alpha \cdot (\delta + n) - (\delta + \rho)/\theta - x \cdot (1 - \alpha)$ equals 0.

Suppose that the parameters take on the baseline values that we used in chapter 1: $\delta = 0.05$ per year, $n = 0.01$ per year, and $x = 0.02$ per year. We also assume $\rho = 0.02$ per year to get a reasonable value for the steady-state interest rate, $\rho + \theta x$. As mentioned in a previous section, for these benchmark parameter values, the saving rate is constant if $\alpha = 0.3$ when $\theta = 17$ and if $\alpha = 0.75$ when $\theta = 1.75$.

With a constant saving rate, the formula for the convergence speed, β, simplifies from equation (2.41) to the result that applied in equation (1.45) for the Solow–Swan model:

$$\beta^* = (1 - \alpha) \cdot (x + n + \delta)$$

We noted in chapter 1 that a match with the empirical estimate for β of roughly 0.02 per year requires a value for α around 0.75, that is, in the range in which the broad nature of capital implies that diminishing returns to capital set in slowly. Lower values of $x + n + \delta$ reduce the required value of α, but plausible values leave α well above the value of around 0.3, which would apply to a narrow concept of physical capital.

In the case of a variable saving rate, equation (2.41) determines the full effects of the various parameters on the convergence speed. The new element concerns the tilt of the time path of the saving rate during the transition. If the saving rate falls with $\hat{k}$, the convergence speed would be higher than otherwise, and vice versa. For example, we found before that a higher value of the intertemporal-substitution parameter, θ, makes it more likely that the saving rate would rise with $\hat{k}$. Through this mechanism, a higher θ reduces the speed of convergence, β, in equation (2.41).

If the rate of time preference, ρ, increases, the level of the saving rate tends to fall (see equation [2.34]). The effect on the convergence speed depends, however, not on the level of the saving rate but on the tendency for the saving rate to rise or fall as the economy develops. A higher ρ tends to tilt downward the path of the saving rate. The effective time-preference rate is $\rho + \theta \cdot \dot{c}/c$. Because $\dot{c}/c$ is inversely related to $\hat{k}$, the impact of ρ on the effective time-preference rate is proportionately less the lower is $\hat{k}$. Therefore, the saving rate tends to decrease less the lower $\hat{k}$, and, hence, the time path of the saving rate tilts downward. A higher ρ tends accordingly to raise the magnitude of β in equation (2.41).

It turns out with a variable saving rate that the parameters δ and x tend to raise β, just as they did in the Solow–Swan model. The overall effect from the parameter n becomes ambiguous but tends to be small in the relevant range.[25]

The basic result, which holds with a variable or constant saving rate, is that, for plausible values of the other parameters, the model requires a high value of α—in the neighborhood of 0.75—to match empirical estimates of the speed of convergence, β. We can reduce the required value of α to 0.5–0.6 if we assume very high values of θ (in excess of 10) along with a value of δ close to 0. We argued before, however, that very high values of θ make the steady-state saving rate too low, and values of δ near 0 are unrealistic. In addition, as we show later, values of α that are much below 0.75 generate counterfactual predictions about the transitional behavior of the interest rate and the capital-output ratio. We discuss in chapter 3 how adjustment costs for investment can slow down the rate of convergence, but this extension does not change the main conclusions.

Numerical Solutions of the Nonlinear System We now assess the convergence properties of the model with a second approach, which uses numerical methods to solve the nonlinear system of differential equations. This approach avoids the approximation errors inherent in linearization of the model and provides accurate results for a given specification of the underlying parameters. The disadvantage is the absence of a closed-form solution. We have to generate a new set of answers for each specification of parameter values.

25. Equation (2.41) implies that the effects on β are unambiguously negative for α and positive for δ. Our numerical computations indicate that the effects of the other parameters are in the directions that we mentioned as long as the other parameters are restricted to a reasonable range.

We can use numerical methods to obtain a global solution for the nonlinear system of differential equations. In the case of a Cobb–Douglas production function, the growth rates of $\hat{k}$ and $\hat{c}$ are given from equations (2.24) and (2.25) as

$$\gamma_{\hat{k}} \equiv \dot{\hat{k}}/\hat{k} = A \cdot (\hat{k})^{\alpha-1} - (\hat{c}/\hat{k}) - (x + n + \delta) \tag{2.43}$$

$$\gamma_{\hat{c}} \equiv \dot{\hat{c}}/\hat{c} = (1/\theta) \cdot [\alpha A \cdot (\hat{k})^{\alpha-1} - (\delta + \rho + \theta x)] \tag{2.44}$$

If we specified the values of the parameters $(A, \alpha, x, n, \delta, \rho, \theta)$ and knew the relation between $\hat{c}$ and $\hat{k}$ along the path—that is, if we knew the policy function $\hat{c}(\hat{k})$—then standard numerical methods for solving differential equations would allow us to solve out for the entire time paths of $\hat{k}$ and $\hat{c}$. The appendix on mathematics shows how to use a procedure called the *time-elimination method* to derive the policy function numerically. (See also Mulligan and Sala-i-Martin, 1991). We assume now that we have already solved this part of the problem.

Once we know the policy function, we can determine the paths of all the variables that we care about, including the convergence coefficient, defined by $\beta = -\,d(\gamma_{\hat{k}})/d[\log(\hat{k})]$. (In the Cobb–Douglas case, the convergence coefficient for $\hat{y}$ is still the same as that for $\hat{k}$.) Figure 2.4 shows the relation between β and $\hat{k}/\hat{k}^*$ when we use our benchmark parameter values ($\delta = 0.05$, $x = 0.02$, $n = 0.01$, $\rho = 0.02$), $\theta = 3$, and $\alpha = 0.3$ or 0.75.[26] For either setting of α, β is a decreasing function of $\hat{k}/\hat{k}^*$; that is, the speed of convergence slows down as the economy approaches the steady state.[27] At the steady state, where $\hat{k}/\hat{k}^* = 1$, the values of β—0.082 if $\alpha = 0.3$ and 0.015 if $\alpha = 0.75$—are those implied by equation (2.41) for the log-linearization around the steady state.

If $\hat{k}/\hat{k}^* < 1$, figure 2.4 indicates that β exceeds the values implied by equation (2.41). For example, if $\hat{k}/\hat{k}^* = 0.5$, $\beta = 0.141$ if $\alpha = 0.3$ and 0.018 if $\alpha = 0.75$. If $\hat{k}/\hat{k}^* = 0.1$, $\beta = 0.474$ if $\alpha = 0.3$ and 0.026 if $\alpha = 0.75$. Thus, if we use our preferred high value for the capital-share coefficient, $\alpha = 0.75$, the convergence coefficient, β, remains between 1.5 percent and 3 percent for a broad range of $\hat{k}/\hat{k}^*$. This behavior accords with the empirical evidence discussed in chapters 11 and 12; we find there that convergence coefficients do not seem to exceed this range even for economies that are very far from their steady states. In contrast, if we assume $\alpha = 0.3$, the model incorrectly predicts extremely high rates of convergence when $\hat{k}$ is far below $\hat{k}^*$.

Since the convergence speeds rise with the distance from the steady state, the durations of the transition are shorter than those implied by the linearized model. We can use the results on the time path of $\hat{k}$ to compute the exact time that it takes to close a specified percentage

26. For a given value of $\hat{k}/\hat{k}^*$, the parameter A does not affect β in the Cobb–Douglas case.

27. This relation does not hold in general. In particular, β can rise with $\hat{k}/\hat{k}^*$ if θ is very small and α is very large, for example, if $\theta = 0.5$ and $\alpha = 0.95$.

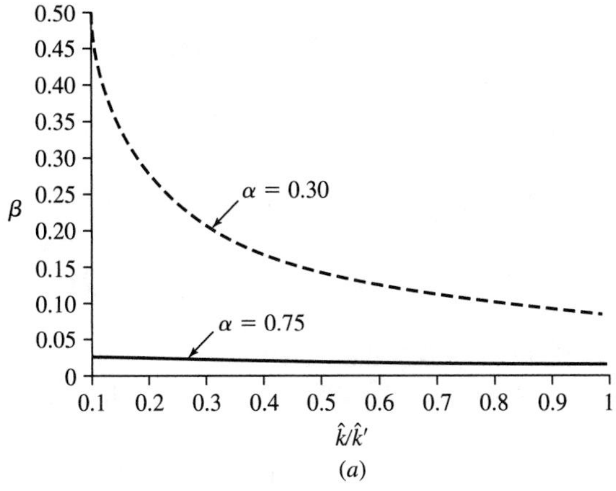

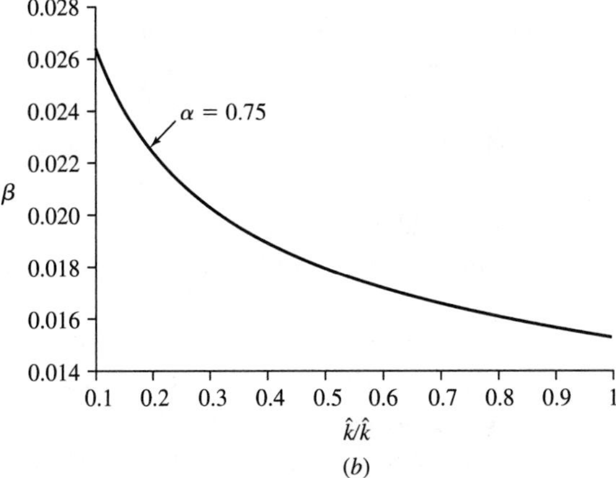

Figure 2.4
Numerical estimates of the speed of convergence in the Ramsey model. The exact speed of convergence (displayed on the vertical axis) is a decreasing function of the distance from the steady state, $\hat{k}/\hat{k}^*$ (shown on the horizontal axis). The analysis assumes a Cobb–Douglas production function, with results reported for two values of the capital share, $\alpha = 0.30$ and $\alpha = 0.75$. The change in the convergence speed during the transition is more pronounced for the smaller capital share. The value of the convergence speed, β, at the steady state ($\hat{k}/\hat{k}^* = 1$) is the value that we found analytically with a log-linear approximation around the steady state (equation [2.41]).

of the initial gap from $\hat{k}^*$. Panel a of figure 2.5 shows how the gap between $\hat{k}$ and $\hat{k}^*$ is eliminated over time if the economy begins with $\hat{k}/\hat{k}^* = 0.1$ and if $\alpha = 0.3$ or 0.75. As an example, if $\alpha = 0.75$, it takes 38 years to close 50 percent of the gap, compared with 45 years from the linear approximation.

Panel b in figure 2.5 displays the level of consumption, expressed as $\hat{c}/\hat{c}^*$; panel c the level of output, $\hat{y}/\hat{y}^*$; and panel d the level of gross investment, $\hat{\imath}/\hat{\imath}^*$. Note that for $\alpha = 0.75$, the paths of $\hat{c}/\hat{c}^*$ and $\hat{y}/\hat{y}^*$ are similar, because the gross saving rate and, hence, $\hat{c}/\hat{y}$ change only by small amounts in this case (discussed later).

Panel e shows $\gamma_{\hat{y}}$, the growth rate of $\hat{y}$. For $\alpha = 0.3$, the model has the counterfactual implication that the initial value of $\gamma_{\hat{y}}$ (corresponding to $\hat{k}/\hat{k}^* = 0.1$) is implausibly large, about 15 percent per year, which means that γ_y is about 17 percent per year. This kind of result led King and Rebelo (1993) to dismiss the transitional behavior of the Ramsey model as a reasonable approximation to actual growth experiences. We see, however, that for $\alpha = 0.75$, the model predicts more reasonably that $\gamma_{\hat{y}}$ would begin at about 3.5 percent per year, so that γ_y would be about 5.5 percent per year.

Panel f shows the gross saving rate, $s(t)$. We know from our previous analytical results for the Cobb–Douglas case, given the assumed values of the other parameters, that $s(t)$ falls monotonically when $\alpha = 0.3$ and rises monotonically when $\alpha = 0.75$. For $\alpha = 0.3$, the results are counterfactual in that the model predicts a fall in $s(t)$ from 0.28 at $\hat{k}/\hat{k}^* = 0.1$ to 0.22 at $\hat{k}/\hat{k}^* = 0.5$ and 0.18 at $\hat{k}/\hat{k}^* = 1$. The predicted levels of the saving rate are also unrealistically low for a broad concept of capital. In contrast, for $\alpha = 0.75$, the moderate rise in the saving rate as the economy develops fits well with the data. The saving rate rises in this case from 0.41 at $\hat{k}/\hat{k}^* = 0.1$ to 0.44 at $\hat{k}/\hat{k}^* = 0.5$ and 0.46 at $\hat{k}/\hat{k}^* = 1$. The predicted level of the saving rate is also reasonable if we take a broad view of capital.

Panel g displays the behavior of the interest rate, r. Note that the steady-state interest rate is $r^* = \rho + \theta x = 0.08$, and the corresponding marginal product is $f'(\hat{k}^*) = r^* + \delta = 0.13$. If we consider the initial position $\hat{k}(0)/\hat{k}^* = 0.1$, as in figure 2.5, the Cobb–Douglas production function implies

$$f'[\hat{k}(0)]/f'(\hat{k}^*) = [\hat{k}(0)/\hat{k}^*]^{\alpha-1} = (10)^{1-\alpha}$$

Hence, for $\alpha = 0.3$, we get $f'[\hat{k}(0)] = 5 \cdot f'(\hat{k}^*) = 0.55$. In other words, with a capital-share coefficient of around 0.3, the initial interest rate (at $\hat{k}[0]/\hat{k}^* = 0.1$) would take on the unrealistically high value of 60 percent. This counterfactual prediction about interest rates was another consideration that led King and Rebelo (1993) to reject the transitional dynamics of the Ramsey model. However, if we assume our preferred capital-share coefficient, $\alpha = 0.75$, we get $f'[\hat{k}(0)] = 1.8 \cdot f'(\hat{k}^*) = 0.23$, so that $r(0)$ takes on the more reasonable value of 18 percent.

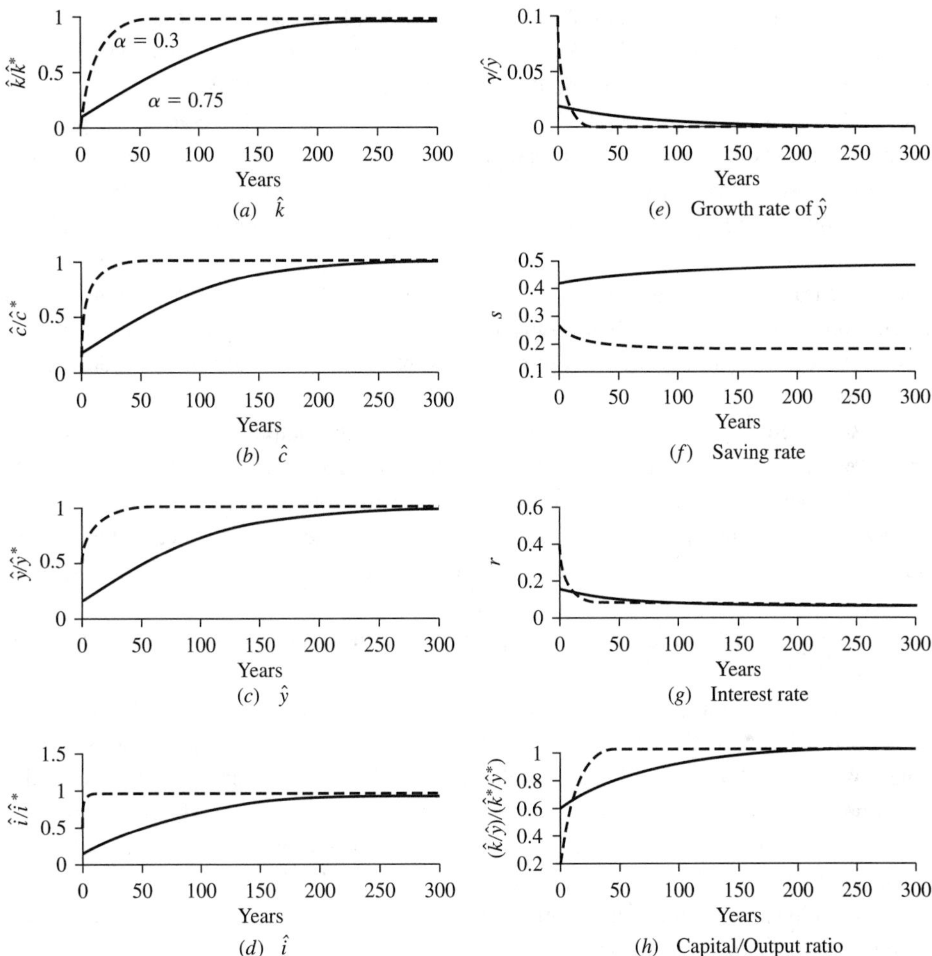

Figure 2.5
Numerical estimates of the dynamic paths in the Ramsey model. The eight panels display the exact dynamic paths of eight key variables: the values per unit of effective labor of the capital stock, consumption, output, and investment, the growth rate of output per effective worker, the saving rate, the interest rate, and the capital-output ratio. The first four variables and the last one are expressed as ratios to their steady-state values; hence, each variable approaches 1 asymptotically. The analysis assumes a Cobb–Douglas production technology, where the dotted line in each panel corresponds to $\alpha = 0.30$ and the solid line to $\alpha = 0.75$. The other parameters are reported in the text. The initial capital per effective worker is assumed in each case to be one-tenth of its steady-state value.

The final panel in figure 2.5 shows the behavior of the capital-output ratio, $(\hat{k}/\hat{y})$, expressed in relation to $(\hat{k}^*/\hat{y}^*)$. Kaldor (1963) argued that this ratio changed relatively little during the course of economic development, and Maddison (1982, chapter 3) supported this view. These observations pertain, however, to a narrow concept of physical capital, whereas our model takes a broad perspective to include human capital. The cross-country data show that places with higher real per capita GDP tend to have higher ratios of human capital in the form of educational attainment to physical capital (see Judson, 1998). This observation suggests that the ratio of human to physical capital would tend to rise during the transition to higher levels of real per capita GDP (see chapter 5 for a theoretical discussion of this behavior). If the ratio of physical capital to output remains relatively stable, the capital-output ratio for a broad measure of capital would increase during the transition.

With a Cobb–Douglas production function, the capital-output ratio is $\hat{k}/\hat{y} = (1/A) \cdot (\hat{k})^{(1-\alpha)}$. If $\alpha = 0.3$, an increase in $\hat{k}$ by a factor of 10 would raise $\hat{k}/\hat{y}$ by a factor of 5, a shift that departs significantly from the observed variations in $\hat{k}/\hat{y}$ over long periods of economic development. In contrast, if $\alpha = 0.75$, an increase in $\hat{k}$ by a factor of 10 would raise $\hat{k}/\hat{y}$ by a factor of only 1.8. For a broad concept of capital, this behavior appears reasonable.

The main lesson from the study of the time paths in figure 2.5 is that the transitional dynamics of the Ramsey model with a conventional capital-share coefficient, α, of around 0.3 does not provide a good description of various aspects of economic development. For an economy that starts far below its steady-state position, the inaccurate predictions include an excessive speed of convergence, unrealistically high growth and interest rates, a rapidly declining gross saving rate, and large increases over time in the capital-output ratio. All of these shortcomings are eliminated if we take a broad view of capital and assume a correspondingly high capital-share coefficient, α, of around 0.75. This value of α, together with plausible values of the model's other parameters, generate predictions that accord well with the growth experiences that we study in chapters 11 and 12.

2.6.7 Household Heterogeneity

Our analysis thus far has considered a single household as representing the entire economy. The consumption and saving decisions of the representative agent are supposed to capture the behavior of the average agent in a complex economy with many families. The important question is whether the behavior of this "representative" or "average" household is really equivalent to what we would get if we averaged the behavior of many heterogeneous families.

Caselli and Ventura (2000) have extended the Ramsey model to allow for various forms of household heterogeneity.[28] Following their analysis, we assume that the economy contains $\mathcal{J}$ equal-sized households, each of which is an infinitely lived dynasty. The population of each household—and, therefore, the overall population—grow at the constant rate n. Preferences of each household are still given by equations (2.1) and (2.10), with the preference parameters ρ and θ the same for each household. In this case, it is straightforward to allow for differences across households in initial assets and labor productivity.

Let $a_j(t)$ and π_j represent, respectively, the per capita assets and productivity level of the jth household. The wage rate paid to the jth household is $\pi_j w$, where w is the economy-wide average wage, π_j is constant over time, and we have normalized so that the mean value of π_j equals 1.

The flow budget constraint for each household takes the same form as equation (2.3):

$$\dot{a}_j = \pi_j \cdot w + ra_j - c_j - na_j \tag{2.45}$$

In this representation, each household could have a different value of initial assets, $a_j(0)$. The optimal growth rate of each household's per capita consumption satisfies the usual first-order condition from equation (2.9):

$$\dot{c}_j/c_j = (1/\theta) \cdot (r - \rho) \tag{2.46}$$

The household's level of per capita consumption can be found, as in the analysis of the first section of this chapter, by solving out the differential equation for c_j and using the transversality condition (of the form of equation [2.12]). The result, analogous to equation (2.15), is

$$c_j = \mu \cdot (a_j + \pi_j \tilde{w}) \tag{2.47}$$

where μ is the propensity to consume out of assets (given by equation [2.16]) and $\tilde{w}$ is the present value of the economy-wide average wage.

The economy-wide value of per capita assets is $a = (\frac{1}{\mathcal{J}}) \cdot \sum_1^{\mathcal{J}} a_j$, and the economy-wide value of per capita consumption is $c = (\frac{1}{\mathcal{J}}) \cdot \sum_1^{\mathcal{J}} c_j$. Since the population growth rate is the same for all households, aggregation is straightforward: sum equation (2.45) over the $\mathcal{J}$ households and divide by $\mathcal{J}$ to compute the economy-wide budget constraint:

$$\dot{a} = w + ra - c - na \tag{2.48}$$

This budget constraint is the same as equation (2.3).

28. Stiglitz (1969) worked out a model with household heterogeneity under a variety of nonoptimizing saving functions.

We can also aggregate the consumption function, equation (2.47), across households to get the economy-wide value of consumption per person:

$$c = \mu \cdot (a + \tilde{w}) \tag{2.49}$$

This relation is the same as equation (2.15).

Finally, we can use equations (2.48) and (2.49) to get

$$\dot{c}/c = (1/\theta) \cdot (r - \rho) \tag{2.50}$$

which is the standard economy-wide condition for consumption growth. When combined with the usual analysis of competitive firms, this description of aggregate household behavior—equations (2.48) and (2.50)—delivers the standard Ramsey model. Hence, the model with the assumed forms of heterogeneity in initial assets and worker productivity has the same macroeconomic implications as the usual, representative-agent model. In other words, if the households in the economy differ in their level of wealth or productivity, and if their preferences are CIES with identical parameters and discount rates, the average consumption, assets, income, and capital for these families behave exactly as the ones of a single representative household. Hence, the representative-agent model provides the correct description of the average variables of an economy populated with the assumed forms of heterogenous agents.

Aside from supporting the use of the representative-agent framework, the extension to include heterogeneity also allows for a study of the dynamics of inequality. Equation (2.46) implies that each household chooses the same growth rate for consumption. Therefore, relative consumption, c_j/c, does not vary over time.

The model does imply a dynamics for relative assets, a_j/a. Equations (2.45), (2.47), (2.48), and (2.49) imply that relative assets change in accordance with

$$\frac{d}{dt}\left(\frac{a_j}{a}\right) = \frac{(w - \mu\tilde{w})}{a} \cdot \left(\pi_j - \frac{a_j}{a}\right) \tag{2.51}$$

We can show that, in the steady state (where w grows at the rate x and $r = \rho + \theta x$), the relation $w = \mu\tilde{w}$ holds. Therefore, relative asset positions stay constant in the steady state. Outside of the steady state, equation (2.51) implies that the relative asset position does not change over time for a household whose relative labor productivity, π_j, is as high as its relative asset position, a_j/a. For other households, the behavior depends on the sign of $w - \mu\tilde{w}$. Imagine that $w > \mu\tilde{w}$. Roughly speaking, this condition says that the propensity to save out of (permanent) wage income is positive. In this case, equation (2.51) implies that a_j/a would rise or fall over time depending on whether relative labor productivity exceeded or fell short of the relative asset position—$\pi_j >$(or $<$) a_j/a. Thus a convergence pattern would hold, whereby relative assets moved toward relative productivity. However, the opposite pattern applies if $w < \mu\tilde{w}$. Outside of the steady state, the sign of $w - \mu\tilde{w}$ depends on the relation of interest rates to growth rates of wages and is ambiguous. Hence, the model does not have clear predictions about the way in which a_j/a will move along the transition.

Caselli and Ventura (2000) also allowed for a form of heterogeneity in household preferences. They assumed that preferences involved the felicity function $u(c + \beta_j g)$, where they interpret g as a publicly provided service. The parameter $\beta_j > 0$ indicates the value that household j attaches to the public service. The variable g could also represent the services that households get freely from the environment, for example, from staring at the sky. The main result from this extension is that the aggregation of individual behavior still corresponds to a representative-agent model, in the sense that the economy-wide average variables, a and c, evolve as they would with a single agent who had average values of initial assets, labor productivity, and preferences. In this sense, the results from the Ramsey model are robust to this extension to admit heterogeneous preferences.

2.7 Nonconstant Time-Preference Rates

Many of the basic frameworks in macroeconomics, including the neoclassical growth model that we have been analyzing, rely on the assumption that households have a constant rate of time preference, ρ. However, the rationale for this assumption is unclear.[29] Perhaps it is unclear because the reason for individuals to have positive time preference is itself unclear.

Ramsey (1928, p. 543) preferred to use a zero rate of time preference. He justified this approach in a normative context by saying "we do not discount later enjoyments in comparison with earlier ones, a practice which is ethically indefensible." Similarly, Fisher (1930, chapter 4) argued that time preference—or impatience, as he preferred to call it—reflects mainly a person's lack of foresight and self-control. One reason that economists have not embraced a zero rate of time preference is that it causes difficulties for the long-run equilibrium—in particular, the transversality condition in the model that we have analyzed requires the inequality $\rho > x \cdot (1 - \theta) + n$, which is positive if $\theta < 1 + (n/x)$. Thus most analyses have assumed that the rate of time preference is positive but constant.

29. See Koopmans (1960) and Fishburn and Rubinstein (1982) for axiomatic derivations of a constant rate of time preference.

As has been known since Strotz (1956) and the elaborations of Pollak (1968) and Goldman (1980)—and understood much earlier by Ramsey (1928)[30]—nonconstancy of the rate of time preference can create a time-consistency problem. This problem arises because the relative valuation of utility flows at different dates changes as the planning date evolves. In this context, committed choices of consumption typically differ from those chosen sequentially, taking account of the way that future consumption will be determined. Therefore, the commitment technology matters for the outcomes.

Laibson (1997a, 1997b), motivated partly by introspection and partly by experimental findings, has made compelling observations about ways in which rates of time preference vary.[31] He argues that individuals are highly impatient about consuming between today and tomorrow but are much more patient about choices advanced further in the future, for example, between 365 and 366 days from now. Hence, rates of time preference would be very high in the short run but much lower in the long run, as viewed from today's perspective. Given these insights and evidence, it is important to know whether economists can continue to rely on the standard version of the neoclassical growth model—the model analyzed in this chapter—as their workhorse framework for dynamic macroeconomics.

To assess this issue, we follow the treatment in Barro (1999) and modify the utility function from equation (2.1) to

$$U(\tau) = \int_{\tau}^{\infty} u[c(t)] \cdot e^{-[\rho\cdot(t-\tau)+\phi(t-\tau)]}\, dt \tag{2.52}$$

where τ now represents the current date and $\phi(t-\tau)$ is a function that brings in the aspects of time preference that cannot be described by the standard exponential factor, $e^{-\rho\cdot(t-\tau)}$. For convenience, we begin with a case of zero population growth, $n = 0$, so that the term $e^{n\cdot(t-\tau)}$ does not appear in equation (2.52). We assume that the felicity function takes the usual form given in equation (2.10):

$$u(c) = \frac{c^{(1-\theta)} - 1}{(1-\theta)}$$

30. In the part of his analysis that allows for time preference, Ramsey (1928, p. 439) says, "In assuming the rate of discount constant, I [mean that] the present value of an enjoyment at any future date is to be obtained by discounting it at the rate ρ.... This is the only assumption we can make, without contradicting our fundamental hypothesis that successive generations are activated by the same system of preferences. For, if we had a varying rate of discount—say a higher one for the first fifty years—our preference for enjoyments in 2000 A.D. over those in 2050 A.D. would be calculated at the lower rate, but that of the people alive in 2000 A.D. would be at the higher."

31. For discussions of the experimental evidence, see Thaler (1981), Ainslie (1992), and Loewenstein and Prelec (1992).

The new time-preference term, $\phi(t - \tau)$, is assumed, as in the case of the conventional time-preference factor, to depend only on the distance in time, $t - \tau$.[32] We can normalize to have $\phi(0) = 0$. We also assume that the function $\phi(\cdot)$ is continuous and twice differentiable. The expression $\rho + \phi'(v)$ gives the instantaneous rate of time preference at the time distance $v = t - \tau \geq 0$. The assumed properties, which follow Laibson (1997a), are $\phi'(v) \geq 0$, $\phi''(v) \leq 0$, and $\phi'(v)$ approaches zero as v tends to infinity. These properties imply that the rate of time preference, given by $\rho + \phi'(t - \tau)$, is high in the near term but roughly constant at the lower value ρ in the distant future. Consumers with these preferences are impatient about consuming right now, but they need not be shortsighted in the sense of failing to take account of long-term consequences. The analysis assumes no decision-making failures of this sort.

Except for the modification of the time-preference rate, the model is the same as before, including the specification of the production function and the behavior of firms. For convenience, we begin with the case of zero technological change, $x = 0$.

2.7.1 Results under Commitment

The first-order optimization conditions for the household's path of consumption, $c(t)$, would be straightforward if the full path of current and future consumption could be chosen in a committed manner at the present time, τ. In particular, the formula for the growth rate of consumption would be modified from equation (2.11) to

$$\dot{c}/c = (1/\theta) \cdot [r(t) - \rho - \phi'(t - \tau)] \tag{2.53}$$

for $t > \tau$. The new element is the addition of the term $\phi'(t - \tau)$ to ρ. Equation (2.53) can be viewed as coming from usual perturbation arguments, whereby consumption is lowered at some point in time and raised at another point in time—perhaps the next instant in time—with all other values of consumption held constant.

Given the assumed properties for $\phi(\cdot)$, $\rho + \phi'(t - \tau)$ would start at a high value and then decline toward ρ as $t - \tau$ tended toward infinity. Thus the steady-state rate of time preference would be ρ, and the steady state of the model would coincide with the analysis from before. The new results would involve the transition, during which time-preference rates were greater than ρ but falling over time.

One problem with this solution is that the current time, τ, is arbitrary, and, in the typical situation, the potential to commit did not suddenly arise at this time. Rather, if perpetual commitments on consumption were feasible, these commitments would likely have existed

32. The utility expression can be extended without affecting the basic results to include the chronological date, t, and a household's age and other life-cycle characteristics.

in the past, perhaps in the infinite past. In this last situation, current and all future values of consumption would have been determined earlier, and τ would be effectively minus infinity, so that $\phi'(t-\tau)$ would be zero for all $t \geq 0$. Hence, the rate of time preference would equal ρ for all $t \geq 0$, and the standard Ramsey results would apply throughout, not just in the steady state.

The more basic problem is that commitment on future choices of $c(t)$ is problematic. The next section therefore works out the solution in the absence of any commitment technology for future consumption. In this setting, the household can determine at time τ only the instantaneous flow of consumption, $c(\tau)$.

2.7.2 Results without Commitment under Log Utility

The first-order condition in equation (2.53) will not generally hold without commitment, because it is infeasible for the household to carry out the perturbations that underlie the condition. Specifically, the household cannot commit to lowering $c(\tau)$ at time τ and increasing $c(t)$ at some future date, while holding fixed consumption at all other dates. Instead, the household has to figure out how its setting of $c(\tau)$ at time τ will alter its stock of assets and how this change in assets will influence the choices of consumption at later dates.

The full solution without commitment is worked out first for log utility, where $\theta = 1$. The steady-state results for general θ are discussed in a later section. Transitional results for general θ are more complicated, but some results are sketched later.

Think of choosing $c(t)$ at time τ as the constant flow $c(\tau)$ over the short discrete interval $[\tau, \tau+\epsilon]$. The length of the interval, ϵ, will eventually approach zero and thereby generate results for continuous time. The full integral of utility flows from equation (2.52) can be broken up into two pieces:

$$U(\tau) = \int_{\tau}^{\tau+\epsilon} \log[c(t)] \cdot e^{-[\rho\cdot(t-\tau)+\phi(t-\tau)]}\, dt + \int_{\tau+\varepsilon}^{\infty} \log[c(t)] \cdot e^{-[\rho\cdot(t-\tau)+\phi(t-\tau)]}\, dt$$

$$\approx \epsilon \cdot \log[c(\tau)] + \int_{\tau+\epsilon}^{\infty} \log[c(t)] \cdot e^{-[\rho\cdot(t-\tau)+\phi(t-\tau)]}\, dt \qquad (2.54)$$

where the approximation comes from taking $e^{-[\rho\cdot(t-\tau)+\phi(t-\tau)]}$ as equal to unity over the interval $[\tau, \tau+\epsilon]$. This approximation will become exact in the equilibrium as ϵ tends to zero. Note that log utility has been assumed.[33]

The consumer can pick $c(\tau)$ and thereby the choice of saving at time τ. This selection influences $c(t)$ for $t \geq \tau+\epsilon$ by affecting the stock of assets, $k(\tau+\epsilon)$, available at time

33. Pollak (1968, section 2) works out results under log utility with a finite horizon and a zero interest rate.

$\tau + \epsilon$. (Solely for convenience, we already assume the equality between per capita assets, $a[t]$, and the per capita capital stock, $k[t]$.) To determine the optimal $c(\tau)$, the household has to know, first, the relation between $c(\tau)$ and $k(\tau + \epsilon)$ and, second, the relation between $k(\tau + \epsilon)$ and the choices of $c(t)$ for $t \geq \tau + \epsilon$.

The first part of the problem is straightforward. The household's budget constraint is

$$\dot{k}(t) = r(t) \cdot k(t) + w(t) - c(t) \tag{2.55}$$

For a given starting stock of assets, $k(\tau)$, the stock at time $\tau + \epsilon$ is determined by

$$k(\tau + \epsilon) \approx k(\tau) \cdot [1 + \epsilon \cdot r(\tau)] + \epsilon \cdot w(\tau) - \epsilon \cdot c(\tau) \tag{2.56}$$

The approximation comes from neglecting compounding over the interval $(\tau, \tau + \epsilon)$—that is, from ignoring terms of the order of ϵ^2—and from treating the variables $r(t)$ and $w(t)$ as constants over this interval. These assumptions will be satisfactory in the equilibrium when ϵ approaches zero. The important result from equation (2.56) is that

$$d[k(\tau + \epsilon)]/d[c(\tau)] \approx -\epsilon \tag{2.57}$$

Hence, more consumption today means less assets at the next moment in time.

The difficult calculation involves the link between $k(\tau + \epsilon)$ and $c(t)$ for $t \geq \tau + \epsilon$, that is, the propensities to consume out of assets. In the standard model with log utility, we know from equations (2.15) and (2.16) that—because of the cancellation of income and substitution effects related to the path of interest rates—consumption is a constant fraction of wealth:

$$c(t) = \rho \cdot [k(t) + \tilde{w}(t)]$$

where $\tilde{w}(t)$ is the present value of wages. Given this background, it is reasonable to conjecture that the income and substitution effects associated with interest rates would still cancel under log utility, even though the rate of time preference is variable and commitment is absent. However, the constant of proportionality, denoted by λ, need not equal ρ. Thus, the conjecture—which turns out to be correct—is that consumption is given by

$$c(t) = \lambda \cdot [k(t) + \tilde{w}(t)] \tag{2.58}$$

for $t \geq \tau + \epsilon$ for some constant $\lambda > 0$.[34]

34. Phelps and Pollak (1968, section 4) use an analogous conjecture to work out a Cournot–Nash equilibrium for their problem. They assume isoelastic utility and a linear technology, so that the rate of return is constant. The last property is critical, because consumption is not a constant fraction of wealth (except when $\theta = 1$) if the rate of return varies over time. The linear technology also eliminates any transitional dynamics, so that the economy is always in a position of steady-state growth.

Under the assumed conjecture, it can be verified that $c(t)$ grows at the rate $r(t) - \lambda$ for $t \geq \tau + \epsilon$. Hence, for any $t \geq \tau + \epsilon$, consumption is determined from

$$\log[c(t)] = \log[c(\tau + \epsilon)] + \int_{\tau+\epsilon}^{t} r(v)\,dv - \lambda \cdot (t - \tau - \epsilon)$$

The expression for utility from equation (2.54) can therefore be written as

$$U(\tau) \approx \epsilon \cdot \log[c(\tau)] + \log[c(\tau + \epsilon)] \cdot \int_{\tau+\epsilon}^{\infty} e^{-[\rho\cdot(t-\tau)+\phi(t-\tau)]}\,dt$$
$$+ \text{terms that are independent of } c(t) \text{ path} \tag{2.59}$$

Define the integral

$$\Omega(\epsilon) \equiv \int_{\epsilon}^{\infty} e^{-[\rho v+\phi(v)]}\,dv \tag{2.60}$$

The marginal effect of $c(\tau)$ on $U(\tau)$ can then be calculated as

$$\frac{d[U(\tau)]}{d[c(\tau)]} \approx \frac{\epsilon}{c(\tau)} + \frac{\Omega(\epsilon)}{c(\tau+\epsilon)} \cdot \frac{d[c(\tau+\epsilon)]}{d[k(\tau+\epsilon)]} \cdot \frac{d[k(\tau+\epsilon)]}{dc(\tau)}$$

The final derivative equals $-\epsilon$, from equation (2.57), and the next-to-last derivative equals λ, according to the conjectured solution in equation (2.58). Therefore, setting $d[U(\tau)]/d[c(\tau)]$ to zero implies

$$c(\tau) = \frac{c(\tau+\epsilon)}{\lambda \cdot \Omega(\epsilon)}$$

If the conjectured solution is correct, $c(\tau + \epsilon)$ must approach $c(\tau)$ as ϵ tends to zero. Otherwise, $c(t)$ would exhibit jumps at all points in time, and the conjectured answer would be wrong. The unique value of λ that delivers this correspondence follows immediately as

$$\lambda = 1/\Omega = \frac{1}{\int_0^{\infty} e^{-[\rho v+\phi(v)]}\,dv} \tag{2.61}$$

where we use the notation $\Omega \equiv \Omega(0)$.

To summarize, the solution for the household's consumption problem under log utility is that $c(t)$ be set as the fraction λ of wealth at each date, where λ is the constant shown in equation (2.61). The solution is time consistent because, if $c(t)$ is chosen in this manner at all future dates, it will be optimal for consumption to be set this way at the current date.[35]

Inspection of equation (2.61) reveals that $\lambda = \rho$ in the standard Ramsey case in which $\phi(v) = 0$ for all v. To assess the general implications of $\phi(v)$ for λ, it is convenient to rewrite equation (2.62) as

$$\lambda = \frac{\int_0^\infty e^{-[\rho v + \phi(v)]} \cdot [\rho + \phi'(v)]\, dv}{\int_0^\infty e^{-[\rho v + \phi(v)]}\, dv} \tag{2.62}$$

Since the numerator of equation (2.62) equals unity,[36] this result corresponds to equation (2.61).

The form of equation (2.62) is useful because it shows that λ is a time-invariant weighted average of the instantaneous rates of time preference, $\rho + \phi'(v)$. Since $\phi'(v) \geq 0, \phi''(v) \leq 0$, and $\phi'(v) \to 0$ as $v \to \infty$, it follows that

$$\rho \leq \lambda \leq \rho + \phi'(0) \tag{2.63}$$

That is, λ is intermediate between the long-run rate of time preference, ρ, and the short-run, instantaneous rate, $\rho + \phi'(0)$.

The determination of the effective rate of time preference can be quantified by specifying the form of $\phi(v)$. Laibson (1997a) proposes a "quasi-hyperbola" in discrete time, whereby $\phi(v) = 0$ in the current period and $e^{-\phi(v)} = \beta$ in each subsequent period, where $0 < \beta \leq 1$. (Phelps and Pollak, 1968, also use this form.) In this specification, the discount factor between today and tomorrow includes the factor $\beta \leq 1$. This factor does not enter between any two adjacent future periods. Laibson argues that β would be substantially less than one on an annual basis, perhaps between one-half and two-thirds.

This quasi-hyperbolic case can be applied to a continuous-time setting by specifying

$$\phi(v) = 0 \text{ for } 0 \leq v \leq V, \qquad e^{-\phi(v)} = \beta \text{ for } v > V \tag{2.64}$$

35. This approach derives equation (2.61) as a Cournot–Nash equilibrium but does not show that the equilibrium is unique. Uniqueness is easy to demonstrate in the associated discrete-time model with a finite horizon, as considered by Laibson (1996). In the final period, the household consumes all of its assets, and the unique solution for each earlier period can be found by working backward sequentially from the end point. This result holds as long as $u(c)$ is concave, not just for isoelastic utility. The uniqueness result also holds if the length of a period approaches zero (to get continuous time) and if the length of the horizon becomes arbitrarily large. However, Laibson (1994) uses an explicitly game-theoretic approach to demonstrate the possibility of nonuniqueness of equilibrium in the infinite-horizon case. The existence of multiple equilibria depends on punishments that sanction past departures of consumption choices from designated values, and these kinds of equilibria unravel if the horizon is finite. Our analysis of the infinite-horizon case does not consider these kinds of equilibria.

36. Use the change of variable $z = e^{-[\rho v + \phi(v)]}$.

for some $V > 0$, where $0 < \beta \leq 1$. [In this specification, $\phi'(v)$ is infinite at $v = V$ and equals zero otherwise.] Laibson's suggestion is that V is small, so that the condition $\rho V \ll 1$ would hold.

Substitution from equation (2.64) into the definition of Ω in equation (2.60) leads (when $\epsilon = 0$) to

$$\Omega = (1/\rho) \cdot [1 - (1 - \beta) \cdot e^{-\rho V}]$$

As V approaches infinity, Ω goes to $1/\rho$, which corresponds to the Ramsey case. The condition $\rho V \ll 1$ implies that the expression for Ω simplifies, as an approximation, to β/ρ, so that

$$\lambda \approx \rho/\beta \tag{2.65}$$

If β is between one-half and two-thirds, λ is between 1.5ρ and 2ρ. Hence, if ρ is 0.02 per year, the heavy near-term discounting of future utility converts the Ramsey model into one in which the effective rate of time preference, λ, is 0.03–0.04 per year.

The specification in equation (2.64) yields simple closed-form results, but the functional form implies an odd discrete jump in $e^{-\phi(v)}$ at the time V in the future. More generally, the notion from the literature on short-term impatience is that $\rho + \phi'(v)$ is high when v is small and declines, say toward ρ, as v becomes large. A simple functional form that captures this property in a smooth fashion is

$$\phi'(v) = be^{-\gamma v} \tag{2.66}$$

where $b = \phi'(0) \geq 0$ and $\gamma > 0$. The parameter γ determines the constant rate at which $\phi'(v)$ declines from $\phi'(0)$ to zero.

Integration of the expression in equation (2.66), together with the boundary condition $\phi(0) = 0$, leads to an expression for $\phi(v)$:[37]

$$\phi(v) = (b/\gamma) \cdot (1 - e^{-\gamma v}) \tag{2.67}$$

This result can be substituted into the formula in equation (2.60) to get an expression for Ω:

$$\Omega = e^{-(b/\gamma)} \cdot \int_0^{\infty} e^{[-\rho v + (b/\gamma) \cdot e^{-\gamma v}]}\, dv$$

The integral cannot be solved in closed form but can be evaluated numerically if values are specified for the parameters ρ, b, and γ.

37. The expression in equation (2.67) is similar to the "generalized hyperbola" proposed by Loewenstein and Prelec (1992, p. 580). Their expression can be written as $\phi(v) = (b/\gamma) \cdot \log(1 + \gamma v)$.

To accord with Laibson's (1997a) observations, the parameter $b = \phi'(0)$ must be around 0.50 per year, and the parameter γ must be at least 0.50 per year, so that $\phi'(v)$ gets close to zero a few years in the future. With $\rho = 0.02$, $b = 0.50$, and $\gamma = 0.50$, Ω turns out to be 19.3, so that $\lambda = 1/\Omega = 0.052$. If $b = 0.25$ and the other parameters are the same, $\Omega = 31.0$ and $\lambda = 0.032$. Thus, the more appealing functional form in equation (2.67) has implications that are similar to those of equation (2.64).

The introduction of the $\phi(\cdot)$ term in the utility function of equation (2.52) and the consequent shift to a time-inconsistent setting amount, under log utility, to an increase in the rate of time preference above ρ. Since the effective rate of time preference, λ, is constant, the dynamics and steady state of the model take exactly the same form as in the standard Ramsey framework that we analyzed before. The higher rate of time preference corresponds to a higher steady-state interest rate,

$$r^* = \lambda \tag{2.68}$$

and, thereby, to a lower steady-state capital intensity, k^*, which is determined from the condition

$$f'(k^*) = \lambda + \delta$$

Since the effective rate of time preference, λ, is constant, the model with log utility and no commitment is observationally equivalent to the conventional neoclassical growth model. That is, the equilibrium coincides with that in the standard model for a suitable choice of ρ. Since the parameter ρ cannot be observed directly, there is a problem in inferring from data whether the instantaneous rate of time preference includes the nonconstant term, $\phi'(v)$.

2.7.3 Population Growth and Technological Progress

It is straightforward to incorporate population growth in the manner of equation (2.1). The solution under log utility is similar to that from before, except that the integral Ω is now defined by

$$\Omega \equiv \int_0^\infty e^{-[(\rho-n)\cdot v+\phi(v)]}\, dv \tag{2.69}$$

The relation between the propensity to consume out of wealth, λ, and the modified Ω term is given by

$$\lambda = n + (1/\Omega) \tag{2.70}$$

and the steady-state interest rate is again $r^* = \lambda$. We leave the derivations of these results as exercises.

In the Ramsey case, where $\phi(v) = 0$ for all v, $\Omega = 1/(\rho - n)$ in equation (2.69) and $\lambda = \rho$ in equation (2.70). For Laibson's quasi-hyperbolic preferences in equation (2.64), the result is

$$\Omega \approx \beta/(\rho - n), \qquad \lambda \approx (\rho/\beta) - n \cdot (1 - \beta)/\beta \tag{2.71}$$

If $0 < \beta < 1$, an increase in n lowers λ and, therefore, reduces the steady-state interest rate, $r^* = \lambda$.

It is also straightforward to introduce exogenous, labor-augmenting technological progress at the rate $x \geq 0$. The solution for λ is still that shown in equations (2.69) and (2.70). However, since consumption per person grows in the steady state at the rate x, the condition for the steady-state interest rate is

$$r^* = \lambda + x$$

Hence, as is usual with log utility, r^* responds one-to-one to the rate of technological progress, x.

2.7.4 Results under Isoelastic Utility

In the standard analysis, where $\phi(t - \tau) = 0$ for all t, consumption is not a constant fraction of wealth unless $\theta = 1$. However, we know, for any value of θ, that the first-order condition for consumption growth at time τ is given from equation (2.11) by

$$\frac{\dot{c}}{c}(\tau) = (1/\theta) \cdot [r(\tau) - \rho] \tag{2.72}$$

A reasonable conjecture is that the form of equation (2.72) would still hold when $\phi(t - \tau) \neq 0$ but that the constant ρ would be replaced by some other constant that represented the effective rate of time preference. This conjecture is incorrect. The reason is that the effective rate of time preference at time τ involves an interaction of the path of the future values of $\phi'(t - \tau)$ with future interest rates and turns out not to be constant when interest rates are changing except when $\theta = 1$.

Although the transitional dynamics is complicated, it is straightforward to work out the characteristics of the steady state. The key point is that, in a steady state, an increase in household assets would be used to raise consumption uniformly in future periods. This property makes it easy to compute propensities to consume for future periods with respect to current assets and, therefore, makes it easy to find the first-order optimization condition for current consumption. Only the results are presented here.

In the steady state, the interest rate is given by

$$r^* = x + n + 1/\Omega \tag{2.73}$$

where the integral Ω is now defined by

$$\Omega \equiv \int_0^{\infty} e^{-\{[\rho - x\cdot(1-\theta) - n]\cdot v + \phi(v)\}}\, dv \tag{2.74}$$

Thus, if $\phi(v) = 0$, we get the standard result

$$r^* = \rho + \theta x$$

For the case of Laibson's quasi-hyperbolic utility function in equation (2.64), the result turns out to be

$$r^* \approx \frac{\rho}{\beta} - n\cdot\frac{(1-\beta)}{\beta} + x\cdot\frac{(\beta+\theta-1)}{\beta} \tag{2.75}$$

where recall that $0 < \beta < 1$. Thus, for the case considered before of log utility ($\theta = 1$), the effect of x on r^* is one-to-one. More generally, the effect of x on r^* is more or less than one-to-one depending on whether θ is greater or less than 1.

For the transitional dynamics, Barro (1999) shows that consumption growth at any date τ satisfies the condition

$$\frac{\dot{c}}{c}(\tau) = (1/\theta)\cdot[r(\tau) - \lambda(\tau)] \tag{2.76}$$

The term $\lambda(\tau)$ is the effective rate of time preference and is given by

$$\lambda(\tau) = \frac{\int_\tau^{\infty} \omega(t,\tau)\cdot[\rho + \phi'(t-\tau)]\, dt}{\int_\tau^{\infty} \omega(t,\tau)\, dt} \tag{2.77}$$

where $\omega(t,\tau) > 0$. Thus, $\lambda(\tau)$ is again a weighted average of future instantaneous rates of time preference, $\rho + \phi'(t-\tau)$. The difference from equation (2.62) is that the weighting factor, $\omega(t,\tau)$, is time varying unless $\theta = 1$.

Barro (1999) shows that, if $\theta > 1$, $\omega(t,\tau)$ declines with the average of interest rates between dates τ and t. If the economy begins with a capital intensity below its steady-state value, $r(\tau)$ starts high and then falls toward its steady-state value. The weights $\omega(t,\tau)$ are then particularly low for dates t far in the future. Since these dates are also the ones with relatively low values of $\rho + \phi'(t-\tau)$, $\lambda(\tau)$ is high initially. However, as interest rates fall, the weights, $\omega(t,\tau)$, become more even, and $\lambda(\tau)$ declines. This descending path of $\lambda(\tau)$ means that households effectively become more patient over time. However, the effects are all reversed if $\theta < 1$. The case $\theta = 1$, which we worked out before, is the intermediate one in which the weights stay constant during the transition. Hence, in this case, the effective rate of time preference does not change during the transition.

2.7.5 The Degree of Commitment

The analysis thus far considered a case of full commitment, as in equation (2.53), and ones of zero commitment, as in equation (2.76). Barro (1999) also considers intermediate cases in which commitment is possible over an interval of length T, where $0 \leq T \leq \infty$. Increases in the extent of commitment—that is, higher T—lead in the long run to a lower effective rate of time preference and, hence, to lower interest rates and higher capital intensity. However, changes in T also imply transitional effects—initially an increase in T tends to make households *less* patient because they suddenly get the ability to constrain their "future selves" to save more. Thus the analysis implies that a rise in T initially lowers the saving rate but tends, in the longer run, to raise the willingness to save.

If the parameter T can be identified with observable variables—such as the nature of legal and financial institutions or cultural characteristics that influence the extent of individual discipline—the new theoretical results might eventually have empirical application. In fact, from an empirical standpoint, the main new insights from the extended model concern the connection between the degree of commitment and variables such as interest rates and saving rates. For a given degree of commitment, the main result is that a nonconstant rate of time preference leaves intact the main implications of the neoclassical growth model.

2.8 Appendix 2A: Log-Linearization of the Ramsey Model

The system of differential equations that characterizes the Ramsey model is given from equations (2.24) and (2.25) by

$$\begin{aligned} \dot{\hat{k}} &= f(\hat{k}) - \hat{c} - (x + n + \delta) \cdot \hat{k} \\ \dot{\hat{c}}/\hat{c} &= \dot{c}/c - x = (1/\theta) \cdot [f'(\hat{k}) - \delta - \rho - \theta x] \end{aligned} \tag{2.78}$$

We now log-linearize this system for the case in which the production function is Cobb–Douglas, $f(\hat{k}) = A \cdot \hat{k}^{\alpha}$.

Start by rewriting the system from equation (2.78) in terms of the logs of $\hat{c}$ and $\hat{k}$:

$$\begin{aligned} d[\log(\hat{k})]/dt &= A \cdot e^{-(1-\alpha)\cdot\log(\hat{k})} - e^{\log(\hat{c}/\hat{k})} - (x + n + \delta) \\ d[\log(\hat{c})]/dt &= (1/\theta) \cdot [\alpha A \cdot e^{-(1-\alpha)\cdot\log(\hat{k})} - (\rho + \theta x + \delta)] \end{aligned} \tag{2.79}$$

In the steady state, where $d[\log(\hat{k})]/dt = d[\log(\hat{c})]/dt = 0$, we have

$$\begin{aligned} A \cdot e^{-(1-\alpha)\cdot\log(\hat{k}^*)} - e^{\log(\hat{c}^*/\hat{k}^*)} &= (x + n + \delta) \\ \alpha A \cdot e^{-(1-\alpha)\cdot\log(\hat{k}^*)} &= (\rho + \theta x + \delta) \end{aligned} \tag{2.80}$$

We take a first-order Taylor expansion of equation (2.79) around the steady-state values determined by equation (2.80):

$$\begin{bmatrix} d[\log(\hat{k})]/dt \\ d[\log(\hat{c})]/dt \end{bmatrix} = \begin{bmatrix} \zeta & x+n+\delta-\dfrac{(\rho+\theta x+\delta)}{\alpha} \\ -(1-\alpha)\cdot\dfrac{(\rho+\theta x+\delta)}{\theta} & 0 \end{bmatrix} \cdot \begin{bmatrix} \log(\hat{k}/\hat{k}^*) \\ \log(\hat{c}/\hat{c}^*) \end{bmatrix} \tag{2.81}$$

where $\zeta \equiv \rho - n - (1-\theta)\cdot x$. The determinant of the characteristic matrix equals

$$-[(\rho+\theta x+\delta)/\alpha - (x+n+\delta)]\cdot(\rho+\theta x+\delta)\cdot(1-\alpha)/\theta$$

Since $\rho + \theta x > x + n$ (from the transversality condition in equation [2.31]) and $\alpha < 1$, the determinant is negative. This condition implies that the two eigenvalues of the system have opposite signs, a result that implies saddle-path stability. (See the discussion in the mathematics appendix at the end of the book.)

To compute the eigenvalues, denoted by ϵ, we use the condition

$$\det\begin{bmatrix} \zeta-\epsilon & x+n+\delta-\dfrac{(\rho+\theta x+\delta)}{\alpha} \\ -(1-\alpha)\cdot\dfrac{(\rho+\theta x+\delta)}{\theta} & -\epsilon \end{bmatrix} = 0 \tag{2.82}$$

This condition corresponds to a quadratic equation in ϵ :

$$\epsilon^2 - \zeta\cdot\epsilon - [(\rho+\theta x+\delta)/\alpha - (x+n+\delta)]\cdot[(\rho+\theta x+\delta)\cdot(1-\alpha)/\theta] = 0 \tag{2.83}$$

This equation has two solutions:

$$2\epsilon = \zeta \pm \left[\zeta^2 + 4\cdot\left(\frac{1-\alpha}{\theta}\right)\cdot(\rho+\theta x+\delta)\cdot[(\rho+\theta x+\delta)/\alpha-(x+n+\delta)]\right]^{1/2} \tag{2.84}$$

where ϵ_1, the root with the positive sign, is positive, and ϵ_2, the root with the negative sign, is negative. Note that ϵ_2 corresponds to $-\beta$ in equation (2.41).

The log-linearized solution for $\log(\hat{k})$ takes the form

$$\log[\hat{k}(t)] = \log(\hat{k}^*) + \psi_1\cdot e^{\epsilon_1 t} + \psi_2\cdot e^{\epsilon_2 t} \tag{2.85}$$

where ψ_1 and ψ_2 are arbitrary constants of integration. Since $\epsilon_1 > 0$, $\psi_1 = 0$ must hold for $\log[\hat{k}(t)]$ to tend asymptotically to $\log(\hat{k}^*)$. ($\psi_1 > 0$ violates the transversality condition, and $\psi_1 < 0$ leads to $\hat{k} \to 0$, which corresponds to cases in which the system hits the vertical axis in figure 2.1.) The other constant, ψ_2, is determined from the initial condition:

$$\psi_2 = \log[\hat{k}(0)] - \log(\hat{k}^*) \tag{2.86}$$

If we substitute $\psi_1 = 0$, the value of ψ_2 from equation (2.86), and $\epsilon_2 = -\beta$ into equation (2.85), we get the time path for $\log[\hat{k}(t)]$:

$$\log[\hat{k}(t)] = (1 - e^{-\beta t}) \cdot \log(\hat{k}^*) + e^{-\beta t} \cdot \log[\hat{k}(0)] \tag{2.87}$$

Since $\log[\hat{y}(t)] = \log(A) + \alpha \cdot \log[\hat{k}(t)]$, the time path for $\log[\hat{y}(t)]$ is given by

$$\log[\hat{y}(t)] = (1 - e^{-\beta t}) \cdot \log(\hat{y}^*) + e^{-\beta t} \cdot \log[\hat{y}(0)] \tag{2.88}$$

which corresponds to equation (2.40).

2.9 Appendix 2B: Irreversible Investment

Suppose that investment is irreversible, so that $\hat{c} \le f(\hat{k})$ applies. Reconsider in this case the dynamic paths that start with $\hat{k} < \hat{k}^*$ at a position such as $\hat{c}_0'$ in figure 2.1. These paths would eventually hit the production function, $\hat{c} = f(\hat{k})$, after which the constraint from irreversible investment would become binding. Thereafter, the paths would move downward along the production function, so that $\hat{c} = f(\hat{k})$ would apply. Hence, the capital intensity would decline in accordance with $\dot{\hat{k}} = -(x + n + \delta) \cdot \hat{k}$. Therefore, $\hat{k}$ (and $\hat{c}$) would asymptotically approach zero but would not reach zero in finite time. We now argue that such paths cannot be equilibria.

When the constraint $\hat{c} \le f(\hat{k})$ is binding, so that all output goes to consumption and none to gross investment, the price of capital, denoted by ϕ, can fall below 1. The rate of return to holders of capital then satisfies (see note 11)

$$r = R/\phi - \delta + \dot{\phi}/\phi \tag{2.89}$$

Profit maximization for competitive firms still implies the condition $R = f'(\hat{k})$, which can be substituted into the formula for r.

Consumer optimization entails, as usual,

$$\dot{c}/c = (1/\theta) \cdot (r - \rho)$$

Therefore, substitution for r from equation (2.89) yields the formula for the growth rate of $\hat{c}$:

$$\dot{\hat{c}}/\hat{c} = \left(\frac{1}{\theta\phi}\right) \cdot [f'(\hat{k}) + \dot{\phi} - \phi \cdot (\delta + \rho + \theta x)] \tag{2.90}$$

The condition $\hat{c} = f(\hat{k})$, together with $\dot{\hat{k}} = -(x + n + \delta) \cdot \hat{k}$, implies another condition for the growth rate of $\hat{c}$:

$$\dot{\hat{c}}/\hat{c} = -\alpha(\hat{k}) \cdot (x + n + \delta) \tag{2.91}$$

where $\alpha(\hat{k}) \equiv \hat{k} \cdot f'(\hat{k})/f(\hat{k})$ is the capital share of income (which is a constant in the case of a Cobb–Douglas production function). Therefore, equations (2.90) and (2.91) imply a condition for $\dot{\phi}$:

$$\dot{\phi} = -f'(\hat{k}) + \phi \cdot [\delta + \rho + \theta x - \alpha(\hat{k}) \cdot \theta \cdot (x + n + \delta)] \tag{2.92}$$

Suppose that the constraint $\hat{c} \leq f(\hat{k})$ first becomes binding at some date T, where $\hat{k}(T) < \hat{k}^*$ applies. At this point, $f'(\hat{k}) - \delta > \rho + \theta x$. Therefore, when $\phi = 1$ (just at time T), equation (2.92) implies that $\dot{\phi} < 0$. Over time, the rise in R and the fall in ϕ tend to raise r in accordance with equation (2.81). Nevertheless, households are satisfied with a negative growth rate of $\hat{c}$ (equation [2.91]) because the rate of capital loss, $\dot{\phi}/\phi$, rises sufficiently in magnitude to maintain a low rate of return, r. However, equation (2.92) implies, as $\hat{k}$ decreases and $f'(\hat{k})$ rises, that $\dot{\phi}$ eventually rises in magnitude toward infinity (regardless of what happens to $\alpha[\hat{k}]$ in the range between 0 and 1). Therefore, ϕ would reach zero in finite time and then become negative. This condition violates free disposal with respect to claims on capital. Hence, paths in which the irreversibility constraint, $\hat{c} \leq f(\hat{k})$, is binding cannot exist in the region where $\hat{k} < \hat{k}^*$.

The constraint $\hat{c} \leq f(\hat{k})$ can be binding in the region where $\hat{k} > \hat{k}^*$. This possibility was noted and discussed by Arrow and Kurz (1970).

2.10 Appendix 2C: Behavior of the Saving Rate

This section provides an algebraic treatment of the transitional behavior of the saving rate. We deal here with the transition in which $\hat{k}$ and $\hat{c}$ are rising over time, and we assume a Cobb–Douglas production function, so that $f(\hat{k}) = A\hat{k}^\alpha$.

The gross saving rate, s, equals $1 - \hat{c}/f(\hat{k})$. In the steady state, $\dot{\hat{k}}$ from equation (2.24) and $\dot{\hat{c}}/\hat{c}$ from equation (2.25) are each equal to 0. If we use these conditions, together with $f(\hat{k})/\hat{k} = f'(\hat{k})/\alpha$, which holds in the Cobb–Douglas case, we find that the steady-state saving rate is

$$s^* = \alpha \cdot (x + n + \delta)/(\rho + \theta x + \delta) \tag{2.93}$$

The transversality condition in equation (2.31) implies $\rho + \theta x > x + n$ and, therefore, $s^* < \alpha$.

Since $s = 1 - \hat{c}/f(\hat{k})$, s moves in the direction opposite to the consumption ratio, $\hat{c}/f(\hat{k})$. Define $z \equiv \hat{c}/f(\hat{k})$ and differentiate the ratio to get

$$\gamma_z \equiv \dot{z}/z = \dot{\hat{c}}/\hat{c} - \frac{f'(\hat{k}) \cdot \dot{\hat{k}}}{f(\hat{k})} = \dot{\hat{c}}/\hat{c} - \alpha \cdot (\dot{\hat{k}}/\hat{k}) \tag{2.94}$$

where the last term on the right follows in the Cobb–Douglas case. Substitution from equations (2.24) and (2.25) into equation (2.94) leads to

$$\gamma_z = f'(\hat{k}) \cdot [z(t) - (\theta - 1)/\theta] + (\delta + \rho + \theta x) \cdot (s^* - 1/\theta) \tag{2.95}$$

where we used the condition $f(\hat{k})/\hat{k} = f'(\hat{k})/\alpha$, which holds in the Cobb–Douglas case.

The behavior of z depends on whether s^* is greater than, equal to, or less than $1/\theta$. Suppose first that $s^* = 1/\theta$. Then $z(t) = (\theta - 1)/\theta$ is consistent with $\gamma_z = 0$ in equation (2.95). In contrast, $z(t) > (\theta - 1)/\theta$ for some t would imply $\gamma_z > 0$ for all t, a result that is inconsistent with z approaching its steady-state value. Similarly, $z(t) < (\theta - 1)/\theta$ can be ruled out because it implies $\gamma_z < 0$ for all t. Therefore, if $s^* = 1/\theta$, z is constant at the value $(\theta - 1)/\theta$, and, hence, the saving rate, s, equals the constant $1/\theta$. By analogous reasoning, we find that $s^* > 1/\theta$ implies $z(t) < (\theta - 1)/\theta$ for all t, whereas $s^* < 1/\theta$ implies $z(t) > (\theta - 1)/\theta$ for all t.

Differentiation of equation (2.95) with respect to time implies

$$\dot{\gamma}_z = f''(\hat{k}) \cdot (\dot{\hat{k}}) \cdot [z(t) - (\theta - 1)/\theta] + f'(\hat{k}) \cdot \gamma_z \cdot z(t) \tag{2.96}$$

Suppose now that $s^* > 1/\theta$, so that $z(t) < (\theta - 1)/\theta$ holds for all t. Then $\gamma_z > 0$ for some t would imply $\dot{\gamma}_z > 0$ in equation (2.96) (because $f''(\hat{k}) < 0$, $f'(\hat{k}) > 0$, and $\dot{\hat{k}} > 0$). Therefore, $\gamma_z > 0$ would apply for all t, a result that is inconsistent with the economy's approaching a steady state. It follows if $s^* > 1/\theta$ that $\gamma_z < 0$, and, hence, $\dot{s} > 0$. By an analogous argument, $\gamma_z > 0$ and $\dot{s} < 0$ must hold if $s^* < 1/\theta$.

The results can be summarized as follows:

$s^* = 1/\theta$ implies $s(t) = 1/\theta$, a constant

$s^* > 1/\theta$ implies $s(t) > 1/\theta$ and $\dot{s}(t) > 0$

$s^* < 1/\theta$ implies $s(t) < 1/\theta$ and $\dot{s}(t) < 0$

These results are consistent with the graphical presentation in figure 2.3.

If we use the formula for s^* from equation (2.93), we find that $s^* \geq 1/\theta$ requires $\theta \geq (\rho + \theta x + \delta)/[\alpha \cdot (x + n + \delta)] > 1/\alpha$. Therefore, if $\theta \leq 1/\alpha$, the parameters must be in the range in which $\dot{s} < 0$ applies throughout. In other words, if $\theta \leq 1/\alpha$, the intertemporal-substitution effect is strong enough to ensure that the saving rate falls during the transition.

However, for our preferred value of α in the neighborhood of 0.75, this inequality requires $\theta \leq 1.33$ and is unlikely to hold.

We can analyze the behavior of the consumption/capital ratio, $\hat{c}/\hat{k}$, in a similar way. The results are as follows:

$\theta = \alpha$ implies $\hat{c}/\hat{k} = (\delta + \rho)/\theta - (\delta + n)$, a constant

$\theta < \alpha$ implies $\hat{c}/\hat{k} < (\delta + \rho)/\theta - (\delta + n)$ and $\hat{c}/\hat{k}$ rising over time

$\theta > \alpha$ implies $\hat{c}/\hat{k} > (\delta + \rho)/\theta - (\delta + n)$ and $\hat{c}/\hat{k}$ falling over time

2.11 Appendix 2D: Proof That $\gamma_{\hat{k}}$ Declines Monotonically If the Economy Starts from $\hat{k}(0) < \hat{k}^*$

We need first to prove the following: $\hat{c}(0)$ declines if $r(v)$ increases over some interval for any $v \geq 0$.[38] Equations (2.15) and (2.16) imply

$$\hat{c}(0) = \frac{\hat{k}(0) + \int_0^\infty \hat{w}(t)e^{-[\bar{r}(t)-n-x]t}\,dt}{\int_0^\infty e^{[\bar{r}(t)\cdot(1-\theta)/\theta-\rho/\theta+n]t}\,dt} \tag{2.97}$$

where $\bar{r}(t)$ is the average interest rate between times 0 and t, as defined in equation (2.13). Higher values of $r(v)$ for any $0 \leq v \leq t$ raise $\bar{r}(t)$ and thereby reduce the numerator in equation (2.97). Higher values of $r(v)$ raise the denominator if $\theta \leq 1$; therefore, the result follows at once if $\theta \leq 1$. Assume now that $\theta > 1$, so that the denominator decreases with an increase in $r(v)$. We know that $r(v)\cdot(1-\theta)/\theta - \rho/\theta + n < 0$ if $\theta > 1$ because $r(v)$ exceeds $\rho + \theta x$, the steady-state interest rate, which exceeds $x + n$ from the transversality condition. Therefore, the denominator in equation (2.97) becomes proportionately more sensitive to $r(v)$ (in the negative direction) the larger the value of θ. Accordingly, if we prove the result for $\theta \to \infty$, the result holds for all $\theta > 0$. Using $\theta \to \infty$, equation (2.97) simplifies to

$$\hat{c}(0) = \frac{\hat{k}(0) + \int_0^\infty \hat{w}(t)e^{-[\bar{r}(t)-x-n]t}\,dt}{\int_0^\infty e^{-[\bar{r}(t)-n]t}\,dt} \tag{2.98}$$

Equation (2.98) can be rewritten as

$$\hat{c}(0) = \frac{\int_0^\infty \psi(t)e^{-[\bar{r}(t)-n-x]t}\,dt}{\int_0^\infty \phi(t)e^{-[\bar{r}(t)-n-x]t}\,dt} \tag{2.99}$$

38. We are grateful to Olivier Blanchard for his help with this part of the proof.

where $\psi(t) = \hat{k}(0) \cdot [r(t) - n - x] + \hat{w}(t)$ and $\phi(t) = e^{-xt}$. The result $\dot{\phi} < 0$ follows immediately, and $\dot{\psi} > 0$ can be shown using the conditions $r(t) = f'[\hat{k}(t)] - \delta$, $\hat{w}(t) = f[\hat{k}(t)] - \hat{k}(t) \cdot f'[\hat{k}(t)]$, $\hat{k}(t) > \hat{k}(0)$, and $\dot{\hat{k}} > 0$. Therefore, an increase in $r(v)$ for $0 \le v \le t$, which raises $\bar{r}(t)$, has a proportionately larger negative effect on the numerator of equation (2.99) than on the denominator. It follows that the net effect of an increase in $r(v)$ on $\hat{c}(0)$ is negative, the result that we need.

We can use this result to get a lower bound for $\hat{c}(0)$. Since $r(0) > \bar{r}(t)$, if we substitute $r(0)$ for $\bar{r}(t)$ and $\hat{w}(0)$ for $\hat{w}(t)$ in equation (2.97), then $\hat{c}(0)$ must go down. Therefore,[39]

$$\hat{c}(0)/\hat{k}(0) > [r(0) \cdot (1-\theta)/\theta + \rho/\theta - n] \cdot \left[1 + \frac{\hat{w}(0)}{\hat{k} \cdot [r(0) - n - x]}\right] \tag{2.100}$$

We shall use this inequality later.

The growth rate of $\hat{k}$ is given from equation (2.24) as

$$\gamma_{\hat{k}} = f(\hat{k})/\hat{k} - \hat{c}/\hat{k} - (x + n + \delta) \tag{2.101}$$

where we now omit the time subscripts. Differentiation of equation (2.101) with respect to time yields

$$\dot{\gamma}_{\hat{k}} = -(\hat{w}/\hat{k}) \cdot \gamma_{\hat{k}} - d(\hat{c}/\hat{k})/dt$$

where we used the condition $\hat{w} = f(\hat{k}) - \hat{k} \cdot f'(\hat{k})$. We want to show that $\dot{\gamma}_{\hat{k}} < 0$ holds in the transition during which $\hat{k}$ and $\hat{c}$ are rising. The formulas for $\dot{\hat{c}}/\hat{c}$ in equation (2.25) and $\dot{\hat{k}}$ in equation (2.24) can be used to get

$$\dot{\gamma}_{\hat{k}} = -(\hat{w}/\hat{k}) \cdot \gamma_{\hat{k}} + (\hat{c}/\hat{k}) \cdot [\hat{w}/\hat{k} + [f'(\hat{k}) - \delta] \cdot (\theta - 1)/\theta + \rho/\theta - n - \hat{c}/\hat{k}] \tag{2.102}$$

Hence, if $\hat{c}/\hat{k} \ge \hat{w}/\hat{k} + [f'(\hat{k}) - \delta] \cdot (\theta - 1)/\theta + \rho/\theta - n$, then $\dot{\gamma}_{\hat{k}} < 0$ follows from $\gamma_{\hat{k}} > 0$, Q.E.D. Accordingly, we now assume

$$\hat{c}/\hat{k} < \hat{w}/\hat{k} + [f'(\hat{k}) - \delta] \cdot (\theta - 1)/\theta + \rho/\theta - n \tag{2.103}$$

If we replace $\hat{c}/\hat{k}$ to the left of the brackets in equation (2.102) by the right-hand side of the inequality in equation (2.103), use the formula for $\gamma_{\hat{k}}$ from equation (2.101), and replace $f(\hat{k})/\hat{k}$ by $\hat{w}/\hat{k} + f'(\hat{k})$, then we eventually get

$$\begin{aligned}\dot{\gamma}_{\hat{k}} < {} & -(\hat{w}/\hat{k}) \cdot [f'(\hat{k}) - \delta - \rho - \theta x]/\theta + [\rho/\theta - n + [f'(\hat{k}) - \delta] \cdot (\theta - 1)/\theta]^2 \\ & + [\rho/\theta - n + [f'(\hat{k}) - \delta] \cdot (\theta - 1)/\theta] \cdot (\hat{w} - \hat{c})/\hat{k}\end{aligned} \tag{2.104}$$

39. The result follows from integration of the right-hand side of equation (2.97) if $[r(0) \cdot (1-\theta)/\theta + \rho/\theta - n] > 0$. If this expression is nonpositive, the inequality in equation (2.100) holds trivially.

If $\rho/\theta - n + [f'(\hat{k}) - \delta] \cdot (\theta - 1)/\theta \leq 0$, we can use the inequality in equation (2.103) to show $\dot{\gamma}_{\hat{k}} < 0$, Q.E.D. Therefore, we now assume

$$\rho/\theta - n + [f'(\hat{k}) - \delta] \cdot (\theta - 1)/\theta > 0 \tag{2.105}$$

Given the inequality in equation (2.105), we can use the lower bound for $\hat{c}/\hat{k}$ from equation (2.100) in equation (2.104) to get, after some manipulation,

$$\dot{\gamma}_{\hat{k}} < -\frac{(\hat{w}/\hat{k}) \cdot [f'(\hat{k}) - \delta - \rho - \theta x]^2}{[f'(\hat{k}) - \delta - n - x] \cdot \theta^2} < 0 \tag{2.106}$$

where we used the condition $r = f'(\hat{k}) - \delta$. The expressions in parentheses in equation (2.106) are each positive because $f'(\hat{k}) - \delta$ exceeds $\rho + \theta x$, the steady-state interest rate, which exceeds $n + x$ from the transversality condition. Therefore, $\dot{\gamma}_{\hat{k}} < 0$ follows, Q.E.D.

2.12 Problems

2.1 Preclusion of borrowing in the Ramsey model. Consider the household optimization problem in the Ramsey model. How do the results change if consumers are not allowed to borrow, only to save?

2.2 Irreversibility of investment in the Ramsey model. Suppose that the economy begins with $\hat{k}(0) > \hat{k}^*$. How does the transition path differ depending on whether capital is reversible (convertible back into consumables on a one-to-one basis) or irreversible?

2.3 Exponential utility. Assume that infinite-horizon households maximize a utility function of the form of equation (2.1), where $u(c)$ is now given by the exponential form,

$$u(c) = -(1/\theta) \cdot e^{-\theta c}$$

where $\theta > 0$. The behavior of firms is the same as in the Ramsey model, with zero technological progress.

a. Relate θ to the concavity of the utility function and to the desire to smooth consumption over time. Compute the intertemporal elasticity of substitution. How does it relate to the level of per capita consumption, c?

b. Find the first-order conditions for a representative household with preferences given by this form of $u(c)$.

c. Combine the first-order conditions for the representative household with those of firms to describe the behavior of $\hat{c}$ and $\hat{k}$ over time. [Assume that $\hat{k}(0)$ is below its steady-state value.]

d. How does the transition depend on the parameter θ? Compare this result with the one in the model discussed in the text.

2.4 Stone–Geary preferences. Assume that the usual conditions of the Ramsey model hold, except that the representative household's instantaneous utility function is modified from equation (2.10) to the Stone–Geary form:

$$u(c) = \frac{(c - \bar{c})^{1-\theta} - 1}{1 - \theta}$$

where $\bar{c} \geq 0$ represents the subsistence level of per capita consumption.

a. What is the intertemporal elasticity of substitution for the new form of the utility function? If $\bar{c} > 0$, how does the elasticity change as c rises?

b. How does the revised formulation for utility alter the expression for consumption growth in equation (2.9)? Provide some intuition on the new result.

c. How does the modification of utility affect the steady-state values $\hat{k}^*$ and $\hat{c}^*$?

d. What kinds of changes are likely to arise for the transitional dynamics of $\hat{k}$ and $\hat{c}$ and, hence, for the rate of convergence? (This revised system requires numerical methods to generate exact results.)

2.5 End-of-the-world model. Suppose that everyone knows that the world will end deterministically at time $T > 0$. We worked out this problem in the text when we discussed the importance of the transversality condition. Go through the analysis here in the following steps:

a. How does this modification affect the transition equations for $\hat{k}$ and $\hat{c}$ in equations (2.24) and (2.25)?

b. How does the modification affect the transversality condition?

c. Use figure 2.1 to describe the new transition path for the economy.

d. As T gets larger, how does the new transition path relate to the one shown in figure 2.1? What happens as T approaches infinity?

2.6 Land in the Ramsey model. Suppose that production involves labor, L, capital, K, and land, Λ, in the form of a constant-returns, CES function:

$$Y = A \cdot [a \cdot (K^{\alpha} L^{1-\alpha})^{\psi} + (1 - a) \cdot \Lambda^{\psi}]^{1/\psi}$$

where $A > 0$, $a > 0$, $0 < \alpha < 1$, and $\psi < 1$. Technological progress is absent, and L grows at the constant rate $n > 0$. The quantity of land, Λ, is fixed. Depreciation is 0. Income now includes rent on land, as well as the payments to capital and labor.

a. Show that the competitive payments to factors again exhaust the total output.

b. Under what conditions on ψ is the level of per capita output, y, constant in the steady state? Under what conditions does y decline steadily in the long run? What do the results suggest about the role of a fixed factor like land in the growth process?

2.7 Alternative institutional environments. We worked out the Ramsey model in detail for an environment of competitive households and firms.

a. Show that the results are the same if households carry out the production directly and use family members as workers.

b. Assume that a social planner's preferences are the same as those of the representative household in the model that we worked out. Show that if the planner can dictate the choices of consumption over time, the results are the same as those in the model with competitive households and firms. What does this result imply about the Pareto optimality of the decentralized outcomes?

2.8 Money and inflation in the Ramsey model (based on Sidrauski, 1967; Brock, 1975; and Fischer, 1979). Assume that the government issues fiat money. The stock of money, M, is denoted in dollars and grows at the rate μ, which may vary over time. New money arrives as lump-sum transfers to households. Households may now hold assets in the form of claims on capital, money, and internal loans. Household utility is still given by equation (2.1), except that $u(c)$ is replaced by $u(c, m)$, where $m \equiv M/PL$ is real cash balances per person and P is the price level (dollars per unit of goods). The partial derivatives of the utility function are $u_c > 0$ and $u_m > 0$. The inflation rate is denoted by $\pi \equiv \dot{P}/P$. Population grows at the rate n. The production side of the economy is the same as in the standard Ramsey model, with no technological progress.

a. What is the representative household's budget constraint?

b. What are the first-order conditions associated with the choices of c and m?

c. Suppose that μ is constant in the long run and that m is constant in the steady state. How does a change in the long-run value of μ affect the steady-state values of c, k, and y? How does this change affect the steady-state values of π and m? How does it affect the attained utility, $u(c, m)$, in the steady state? What long-run value of μ would be optimally chosen in this model?

d. Assume now that $u(c, m)$ is a separable function of c and m. In this case, how does the path of μ affect the transition path of c, k, and y?

2.9 Fiscal policy in the Ramsey model (based on Barro, 1974, and McCallum, 1984). Consider the standard Ramsey model with infinite-horizon households, preferences given by equations (2.1) and (2.10), population growth at rate n, a neoclassical production function, and technological progress at rate x. The government now purchases goods and services in the quantity G, imposes lump-sum taxes in the amount T, and has outstanding the quantity B of government bonds. The quantities G, T, and B—which can vary over time—are all measured in units of goods, and B starts at a given value, $B(0)$. Bonds are of infinitesimal maturity, pay the interest rate r, and are viewed by individual households as perfect substitutes for claims on capital or internal loans. (Assume that the government never defaults on its debts.) The government may provide public services that relate to the path of G, but the path of G is held fixed in this problem.

a. What is the government's budget constraint?

b. What is the representative household's budget constraint?

c. Does the household still adhere to the first-order optimization condition for the growth rate of c, as described in equation (2.9)?

d. What is the transversality condition and how does it relate to the behavior of B in the long run? What does this condition mean?

e. How do differences in $B(0)$ or in the path of B and T affect the transitional dynamics and steady-state values of the variables c, k, y, and r? (If there are no effects, the model exhibits *Ricardian equivalence.*)

3 Extensions of the Ramsey Growth Model

In this chapter we extend the Ramsey model in a number of directions. We first introduce government spending and various types of taxes. Second, we introduce installation costs in the process of physical capital investment. Third, we open up the economy to allow for international borrowing and lending. Finally, we study the effects of finite lifetimes.

3.1 Government

3.1.1 Modifications of the Ramsey Framework

The Ramsey model can be modified in a straightforward way to incorporate functions of government. Suppose that the government purchases goods and services in the aggregate quantity G. We imagine, for now, that these purchases do not influence households' utility or firms' production. We allow later for these kinds of effects. The government also makes transfer payments to households in the real aggregate amount V. These transfers are lump sum, in the sense that the amount received by an individual household does not depend on the household's income or other characteristics.

The government is assumed to run a balanced budget in which it finances its total outlays, $G + V$, with various taxes. The taxes considered here are proportional levies on wage income, τ_w, private asset income, τ_a, consumption, τ_c, and firms' earnings, τ_f. Thus the government's budget constraint is

$$G + V = \tau_w wL + \tau_a r \cdot (\text{assets}) + \tau_c C + \tau_f \cdot (\text{firms' earnings}) \tag{3.1}$$

As before, w is the wage rate and r is the rate of return on assets. The variables L and C are the aggregates of labor and consumption, respectively. We consider later the definition of firms' earnings. The tax rate on asset returns, τ_a, is the same irrespective of whether the returns come from internal loans or payments from ownership of capital. We also assume that the tax rates are constant over time.

The presence of the taxes and transfers modifies the representative household's budget constraint from equation (2.2) to

$$\dot{a} = (1 - \tau_w) \cdot w + (1 - \tau_a) \cdot ra - (1 + \tau_c) \cdot c - na + v \tag{3.2}$$

where a, c, and v are the per capita amounts of assets, consumption, and transfers, respectively. We still assume that each household works a fixed amount, set at one unit per unit of time, and n is the growth rate of population and the labor force.

We can derive the household's first-order condition for consumption choice as in chapter 2. For the case of a constant intertemporal elasticity of substitution utility function, as assumed in equation (2.9),

$$u(c) = \frac{c^{1-\theta} - 1}{1 - \theta}$$

the result for the growth rate of per capita consumption is modified from equation (2.10) to[1]

$$\dot{c}/c = (1/\theta) \cdot [(1 - \tau_a) \cdot r - \rho] \tag{3.3}$$

Thus the household's decision to defer consumption depends on the after-tax rate of return, $(1 - \tau_a) \cdot r$. The tax rate on consumption, τ_c, does not appear in the first-order condition because it is constant over time. If this tax rate varied over time, it would affect the choice of when to consume and would enter accordingly into equation (3.3). The after-tax rate of return, $(1 - \tau_a) \cdot r$, also appears in the transversality condition, which is modified from equation (2.11) to

$$\lim_{t \to \infty} \left\{ a(t) \cdot \exp\left[- \int_0^t [(1 - \tau_a) \cdot r(v) - n]\, dv \right] \right\} = 0 \tag{3.4}$$

Firms still have the production function given in equation (2.16),

$$Y = F(K, \hat{L})$$

where K is capital input and $\hat{L} = Le^{xt}$ is effective labor input. Firms again pay the wage rate w for each unit of labor services, L, and the rental price $R = r + \delta$ for each unit of capital services, K, where δ is the depreciation rate on capital. We assume that the government defines firms' taxable earnings to equal output less wage payments and depreciation:[2]

$$\text{taxable earnings} = F(K, \hat{L}) - wL - \delta K \tag{3.5}$$

Firms' profit after taxes can therefore be written as

$$\text{after-tax profit} = (1 - \tau_f) \cdot [F(K, \hat{L}) - wL - \delta K] - rK \tag{3.6}$$

1. To find the Euler equation, set up the Hamiltonian, $J = e^{-(\rho - n)t} \cdot \frac{c^{1-\theta} - 1}{1 - \theta} + \nu \cdot [(1 - \tau_w) \cdot w + (1 - \tau_a) \cdot ra - (1 + \tau_c) \cdot c - na + v]$. The first-order conditions with respect to c and a are

(i) $e^{-(\rho - n)t} \cdot c^{-\theta} = \nu \cdot (1 + \tau_c)$

(ii) $-\dot{\nu} = \nu \cdot [(1 - \tau_a) \cdot r - n]$

Take logarithms and time derivatives of (i) and substitute into (ii) to get $\frac{\dot{c}}{c} = \frac{1}{\theta}[(1 - \tau_a) \cdot r - \frac{\dot{\tau}_c}{1 + \tau_c} - \rho]$. If the tax rate on consumption is constant over time, $\dot{\tau}_c$ equals zero, and the Euler equation becomes equation (3.3).

2. Note that, although depreciation is tax deductible, the real interest rate, r, part of the rental payments are not tax deductible. The situation would be different for debt finance if the interest payments were, as is customary, tax deductible for the firm.

The firm's first-order condition for choosing $\hat{k} \equiv K/\hat{L}$ to maximize after-tax profit is a modification of equation (2.21):

$$f'(\hat{k}) = \frac{r}{1-\tau_f} + \delta \tag{3.7}$$

Thus, a higher τ_f raises the required marginal product of capital, $f'(\hat{k})$, for a given r. This result follows because the rental payments on capital (aside from depreciation) are not deductible from the tax base defined in equation (3.5). It can also be verified, along the lines followed in chapter 2, that the representative firm ends up with zero after-tax profit in equation (3.6). Correspondingly, the firm equates the marginal product of labor to the wage rate:

$$w = e^{xt} \cdot [f(\hat{k}) - \hat{k} \cdot f'(\hat{k})] \tag{3.8}$$

If we use the condition for equilibrium in the asset market, $\hat{a} = \hat{k}$, along with the first-order conditions from equations (3.7) and (3.8) and the government's budget constraint from equation (3.1), then the condition for the evolution of $\hat{k}$ corresponding to equation (2.23) becomes

$$\dot{\hat{k}} = f(\hat{k}) - \hat{c} - (x + n + \delta) \cdot \hat{k} - \hat{g} \tag{3.9}$$

where $\hat{g} \equiv G/\hat{L}$. This equation still represents the resource constraint for the economy: the change in the capital stock equals output less consumption less depreciation of capital stocks less government purchases of goods and services. Notice that neither taxes nor transfers enter directly into this economy-wide resource constraint.

Equations (3.3) and (3.7) imply that the condition for the evolution of $\hat{c}$ is modified from equation (2.24) to

$$\dot{\hat{c}}/\hat{c} = \frac{1}{\theta} \cdot \{(1-\tau_a) \cdot (1-\tau_f) \cdot [f'(\hat{k}) - \delta] - \rho - \theta x\} \tag{3.10}$$

Thus the net marginal product of capital, $f'(\hat{k}) - \delta$, is attenuated for the combined effect of taxes on asset returns, τ_a, and firms' earnings, τ_f. In the model, the income on capital is effectively "double taxed"—once at the firm level at the rate τ_f when the earnings accrue to the firm and a second time at the household level at the rate τ_a when the income is received as rental payments.

The transversality condition from equation (2.25) is similarly modified to incorporate the effects of taxation:

$$\lim_{t\to\infty} \left\{\hat{k} \cdot \exp\left(-\int_0^t [(1-\tau_a) \cdot (1-\tau_f) \cdot [f'(\hat{k}) - \delta] - x - n]\, dv\right)\right\} = 0 \tag{3.11}$$

Therefore, in the steady state, where $\hat{k} = \hat{k}^*$, the net marginal product of capital, $f'(\hat{k}^*) - \delta$, must exceed $(x + n)/[(1 - \tau_a) \cdot (1 - \tau_f)]$.

3.1.2 Effects of Tax Rates

Taxes on Wages and Consumption The tax rate on wage income, τ_w, does not enter into any of the equilibrium conditions. This result follows because we assumed that households worked a fixed amount. In this case, a wage tax amounts to a lump-sum, nondistorting tax. With a labor-leisure choice, as considered in chapter 9, τ_w would no longer be equivalent to a lump-sum tax and would affect the equilibrium.

We noted before that the consumption tax rate, τ_c, does not affect the choice of consumption over time—and therefore equation (3.10)—because τ_c is constant. Otherwise, prospective changes in τ_c would affect equation (3.10) currently and in the future. For example, if the tax rate on consumption is expected to increase in the future ($\dot{\tau}_c > 0$), individuals would want to consume more now and less in the future, so consumption growth would be reduced. The opposite would be true if the tax rate on consumption were expected to decline in the future.

With a labor-leisure choice, even a constant τ_c would affect the equilibrium by influencing labor supply. However, this effect does not operate in the present setting because households are assumed to work a fixed amount. Therefore, τ_c does not affect the equilibrium and works like a lump-sum tax.

If we assume $\hat{g} = \tau_a = \tau_f = 0$, the phase diagram in $(\hat{k}, \hat{c})$ space would be exactly as shown in figure 2.1. If we assume instead that $\hat{g}$ is a positive constant, then $\dot{\hat{k}}$ is displaced downward in accordance with equation (3.9). The implied level of government purchases, G, would be financed by some combination of τ_w and τ_c, taking account of the time path of transfers, V. The precise combination of τ_w, τ_c, and V does not matter because these variables amount to lump-sum taxes or transfers in the model. The phase diagram for the model then corresponds to the solid lines shown in figure 3.1.

Taxes on Asset Income and Firms' Earnings Suppose that we continue to treat $\hat{g}$ as a positive constant but now allow for $\tau_a > 0$ or $\tau_f > 0$. By holding fixed $\hat{g}$, we are assuming that the government's budget constraint in equation (3.1) remains satisfied in each period by adjusting τ_w, τ_c, and V in some manner. Again, the precise combination of adjustments does not matter for the equilibrium.

Positive values of τ_a and τ_f affect the model only through the expression for $\dot{\hat{c}}$ in equation (3.10). Specifically, an increase in τ_a or τ_f shifts the $\dot{\hat{c}} = 0$ locus to the left, as shown by the dashed line labeled $(\dot{\hat{c}} = 0)'$ in figure 3.1. Given $\hat{g}$, an increase in τ_a or τ_f has no effect on the locus for $\dot{\hat{k}} = 0$ (see equation [3.9]).

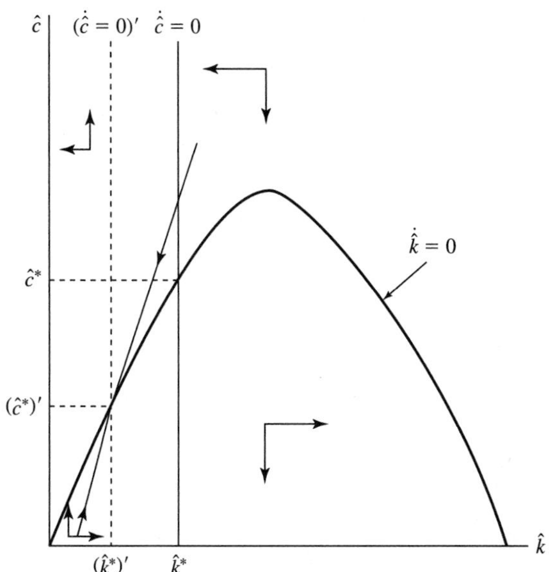

Figure 3.1
Taxes on the income from capital. The solid lines correspond to $\tau_a = \tau_f = 0$. If $\tau_a > 0$ or $\tau_f > 0$, the locus for $\dot{\hat{c}} = 0$ is shifted to the left to the dashed line denoted $(\dot{\hat{c}} = 0)'$. The locus for $\dot{\hat{k}} = 0$ is the same in both cases. Hence, $\hat{k}^*$ and $\hat{c}^*$ are lower.

As the diagram shows, the imposition of taxes on the income from capital leads to reductions in $\hat{k}^*$ and $\hat{c}^*$ in the long run. These effects arise because the taxes reduce the incentive to save. The transversality condition ensures that, after the initial increase in the tax rate at time zero, the economy will find itself on the new stable arm. Since the level of capital cannot jump at time zero, the initial level of consumption has to increase. The reason is that, initially, the increase in taxes reduces the after-tax rate of return, thereby motivating people to substitute consumption toward the present.

3.1.3 Effects of Government Purchases

Consider now the effects of a permanent and unanticipated increase in government purchases. Figure 3.2 assesses the effects by comparing a case in which $\hat{g} > 0$ with one in which $\hat{g} = 0$. The distortionary tax rates τ_a and τ_f are assumed to be the same in the two cases—that is, we are assuming that the government's purchases are financed by wage or consumption taxes or by reductions in lump-sum transfers. We are therefore considering the effects from higher government purchases that are financed by the equivalent of a

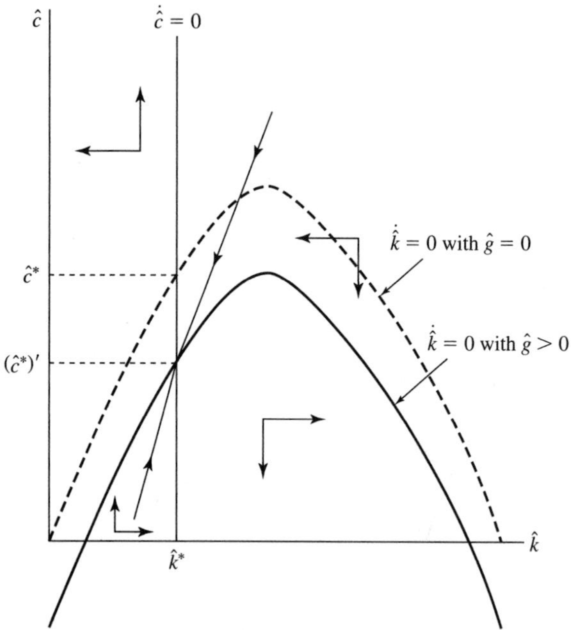

Figure 3.2
Effects of government purchases. The solid locus for $\dot{\hat{k}} = 0$ corresponds to $\hat{g} > 0$, and the higher, dashed locus corresponds to $\hat{g} = 0$. The locus for $\dot{\hat{c}} = 0$ is the same in both cases. Hence, the higher value for $\hat{g}$ corresponds to a lower value for $\hat{c}^*$.

lump-sum tax. To study the effects for government purchases financed by a distorting tax, we can combine the present discussion with the one from the previous section.

Given our assumption on financing, the locus for $\dot{\hat{c}} = 0$ is the same for the two values of $\hat{g}$. However, the locus for $\dot{\hat{k}} = 0$ is lower for the case in which $\hat{g} > 0$ than for the one in which $\hat{g} = 0$. The steady-state capital intensity, $\hat{k}^*$, is the same in the two cases, but $\hat{c}^*$ is lower when $\hat{g} > 0$. Government purchases therefore crowd out consumption one-to-one in the long run. There is no long-term effect on capital because the financing by the equivalent of a lump-sum tax means that no distortions arise. In addition, we have assumed that public expenditures have no direct effect on production.

The dynamic effects from higher government purchases are simpler if, instead of having a constant $\hat{g}$, we assume that the ratio $\lambda \equiv G/C$ is constant. The equation for $\dot{\hat{k}}$ is then modified from equation (3.9) to

$$\dot{\hat{k}} = f(\hat{k}) - (1 + \lambda) \cdot \hat{c} - (x + n + \delta) \cdot \hat{k} \tag{3.12}$$

In this case, it is clear from inspection of equations (3.10) and (3.12) that the full time paths of the variables $(1+\lambda)\cdot\hat{c}$ and $\hat{k}$ are invariant with the value of λ. Thus a higher value of λ leads to no change in the entire path of $\hat{k}$. The higher value of λ leads accordingly to a one-to-one substitution of G for C along the entire path.

Government Purchases in the Utility Function We assumed, thus far, that households received no utility from the government's services. Suppose instead that the utility of the representative household takes the form $u(c,\tilde{g})$. The specification for $\tilde{g}$ depends on the way in which public services affect households. If the government's purchases are used to provide the equivalent of private goods (such as free school lunches), then $\tilde{g}=g$ would apply. If the government's purchases are used to provide nonrival public goods, perhaps the Washington Monument, then $\tilde{g}=G$ would hold. Probably the most important example of nonrival goods would be basic ideas and knowledge generated by research and experience.

As another example, if the government's purchases are used to provide nonexcludible public goods that are subject to congestion, the services to households might take the form

$$\tilde{g}=g\cdot\Psi(G/C) \tag{3.13}$$

where $\Psi(\cdot)>0$, $\Psi'(\cdot)>0$, $\Psi(0)=0$, and $\Psi(\infty)=1$. The idea is that $\Psi(G/C)$ captures the degree of congestion of the public services. For given G/C, the services provided to each household, $\tilde{g}$, are proportional to g. However, as G falls relative to C, congestion increases, and each household receives fewer effective services for each unit of g provided. This specification might work well for services provided by highways, parks, and so on. In other cases, congestion might relate more to output, Y, or the stock of private capital, K, rather than C.

The representative household's first-order condition for c can be determined in the usual way, assuming now that $\tilde{g}$ follows an exogenous time path and that $u(c,\tilde{g})$ is the expression for household utility. The resulting first-order condition can then be derived in the usual way as

$$r\cdot(1-\tau_a)=\rho-\left(\frac{u_{cc}c}{u_c}\right)\cdot\left(\frac{\dot{c}}{c}\right)-\left(\frac{u_{c\tilde{g}}\tilde{g}}{u_c}\right)\cdot\left(\frac{d\tilde{g}/dt}{\tilde{g}}\right) \tag{3.14}$$

Thus the standard condition for $\dot{c}/c$ arises when $(\frac{u_{cc}c}{u_c})=-\theta$ and $(\frac{u_{c\tilde{g}}\tilde{g}}{u_c})=0$. In the present case, the standard condition would be modified, taking account of how $\tilde{g}$ evolves over time and the nature of the interaction term, $(\frac{u_{c\tilde{g}}\tilde{g}}{u_c})$.

Suppose that the utility function takes a form that generalizes our previous specification in which the intertemporal elasticity of substitution was constant:

$$u(c,\tilde{g})=\frac{\{[h(c,\tilde{g})]^{1-\theta}-1\}}{1-\theta} \tag{3.15}$$

where the felicity function $h(c, \tilde{g})$ satisfies $h_c > 0$ and $h_{\tilde{g}} > 0$ and is homogeneous of degree one with respect to c and $\tilde{g}$. In this case, we can show from equation (3.14) that the standard first-order condition for $\dot{c}/c$, as shown in equation (3.3), applies as long as the ratio of c to $\tilde{g}$ stays constant over time. For example, if $\tilde{g} = g$ (publicly provided private goods), then if the ratio $\lambda = g/c$ remains fixed over time, the dynamics of the system are given by equations (3.3) and (3.12). It follows that we get the same results as before when λ was constant—that is, a higher λ leaves the path of $\hat{k}$ unchanged, and the higher g crowds out c one-to-one at each point in time. The same results apply if λ is constant, and the publicly provided goods are subject to congestion in the sense of equation (3.13).

If $\tilde{g} = G$ (pure public goods), the condition for $\dot{c}/c$ shown in equation (3.3) applies if the ratio G/c is constant, which implies that $\lambda = g/c$ declines in accordance with e^{-nt}. In equation (3.12), the decline in λ over time continually shifts upward the locus for $\dot{\hat{k}} = 0$. This shifting results because the increase in population at the rate n means that the provision of a given amount of public services per person, $\tilde{g}$, becomes cheaper over time. In the steady state, the public services are effectively free (because population is infinite), and the locus for $\dot{\hat{k}} = 0$ corresponds to the solid curve shown in figure 3.2. However, these results apply only if public services are entirely nonrival. Probably there are few goods that actually fall into this category.

The Social Planner's Solution We can use the social planner's approach to assess the optimal provision of public services in the various cases. The social planner maximizes the utility function $\int_0^\infty e^{-(\rho-n)t} \cdot u(c, \tilde{g}) \cdot dt$, subject to the resource constraint (3.9). The Hamiltonian expression for the planner is, therefore,

$$J = u(c, \tilde{g}) \cdot e^{-(\rho-n)t} + \upsilon \cdot [f(\hat{k}) - \hat{c} - (x + n + \delta) \cdot \hat{k} - \hat{g}] \tag{3.16}$$

One first-order condition for this problem is

$$f'(\hat{k}) - \delta = \rho - \left(\frac{u_{cc}c}{u_c}\right) \cdot \left(\frac{\dot{c}}{c}\right) - \left(\frac{u_{c\tilde{g}}\tilde{g}}{u_c}\right) \cdot \left(\frac{d\tilde{g}/dt}{\tilde{g}}\right) \tag{3.17}$$

The decentralized solution from equation (3.14), together with the condition for firms from equation (3.7), yields equation (3.17) if $\tau_a = \tau_f = 0$, so that saving decisions are not distorted.

The other first-order condition for the social planner depends on the specification of $\tilde{g}$. If $\tilde{g} = g$, the condition is

$$u_{c}/u_{\tilde{g}} = 1 \tag{3.18}$$

The utility rate of substitution between $\tilde{g}$ and c is one because these two goods are equally costly for society to provide.

If $\tilde{g} = G$, the first-order condition for the social planner becomes

$$u_c/u_{\tilde{g}} = e^{nt} \tag{3.19}$$

In this case, the growth of population at the rate n makes public goods effectively cheaper over time. Therefore, the utility rate of substitution between $\tilde{g}$ and c rises over time at the rate n. Asymptotically, the implications are odd, because the idea of entirely nonrival public services is implausible.

If public services are subject to congestion in the form of equation (3.13), the social planner's first-order condition is

$$u_c/u_{\tilde{g}} = \Psi(g/c) + (g/c) \cdot \Psi'(g/c) \tag{3.20}$$

This result would correspond to equation (3.18) if $\Psi(g/c) = 1$ and $\Psi'(g/c) = 0$. Otherwise, the first-order condition takes account of the facts that public services are congested ($\Psi[g/c] < 1$) and that an increase in g/c relaxes the congestion ($\Psi'[g/c] > 0$).

Government Purchases in the Production Function Some public services can be modeled more naturally by including them in the production function:

$$\hat{y} = f(\hat{k}, \tilde{g}) \tag{3.21}$$

The flow of public services, $\tilde{g}$, might again be modeled as publicly provided private goods, so that $\tilde{g} = g$, or as nonrival public goods, so that $\tilde{g} = G$. We might also model the services as nonexcludible public goods that are subject to congestion, perhaps in the form

$$\tilde{g} = g \cdot \Psi(G/Y)$$

if we think of the congestion for G as being in relation to total output, Y. The results in these cases are similar to those in which public services entered directly into household utility functions. In the latter case, public services affect utility directly, whereas, in the former, public services affect output and then influence utility indirectly.

One result for publicly provided private goods or pure public goods is that the social planner would choose the level of public outlay to satisfy the condition $\partial Y/\partial G = 1$. This condition means that the output attained at the margin from an extra unit of public services just equals the cost, which equals unity. For the case of publicly provided private goods, the production function is given in the Cobb–Douglas case by

$$\hat{y} = A\hat{k}^{\alpha}\hat{g}^{\beta} \tag{3.22}$$

where $0 < \beta < 1$. The condition $\partial Y/\partial G = 1$ can then be shown to imply $G/Y = \beta$. That is, public services would constitute a constant fraction of output along the entire dynamic path.

For public goods, the production function for the Cobb–Douglas case is

$$\hat{y} = A\hat{k}^{\alpha} G^{\beta} \tag{3.23}$$

The social planner's condition $G/Y = \beta$ can be shown still to apply for this case.

Another important possibility is that public services, such as enactment and maintenance of property rights and law and order, increase the probability that individual households or firms will be able to maintain possession of the assets (capital) that they have accumulated. For households, an improvement in property rights effectively raises the rate of return on assets. In this sense, better rights work like reductions in the tax rates, τ_a and τ_f, in equation (3.10). Better property rights would, therefore, encourage capital formation.

3.2 Adjustment Costs for Investment

We mentioned in chapter 2 that the speed of convergence in the strict version of the neoclassical growth model is higher than the speed found in the data. We mentioned that one way to slow down the speed in the model was to introduce adjustment costs for investment. Adjustment costs are the costs associated with the installation of capital. This section analyzes the neoclassical growth model augmented with adjustment costs.

3.2.1 The Behavior of Firms

We assume as in chapter 2 that the production function is neoclassical:

$$Y = F(K, \hat{L}) \tag{3.24}$$

where $F(\cdot)$ satisfies the neoclassical properties (equations 1.4–1.6) and $\hat{L} = Le^{xt}$ is the effective amount of labor input. Each firm i has access to the technology shown in equation (3.24); for convenience, we omit the subscript i.

We now find it convenient to think of the firm as owning its stock of capital, K, rather than renting it from households. The households will instead have a claim on the firm's net cash flows.

The change in the firm's capital stock is given by

$$\dot{K} = I - \delta K \tag{3.25}$$

where I is gross investment. We assume that the cost in units of output for each unit of investment is 1 plus an adjustment cost, which is an increasing function of I in relation to K, that is,

$$\text{Cost of investment} = I \cdot [1 + \phi(I/K)] \tag{3.26}$$

where $\phi(0) = 0$, $\phi' > 0$, and $\phi'' \geq 0$. The assumption is that adjustment costs depend on gross investment, I, rather than net investment, $I - \delta K$.

Firms again pay the wage rate, w, for each unit of labor, L, and we neglect any adjustment costs associated with changes in L. The firm's net cash flow is given accordingly by

$$\text{Net cash flow} = F(K, \hat{L}) - wL - I \cdot [1 + \phi(I/K)] \tag{3.27}$$

The firm has a fixed number of equity shares outstanding, and the value of these shares at time 0 is determined on a stock market to be the amount $V(0)$. (If we normalize the number of shares to unity, then $V(0)$ is the price per share at time 0.) We assume that the net cash flow given in equation (3.27) is paid out as dividends to the shareowners.[3] Hence, $V(0)$ equals the present value of the net cash flows between times 0 and infinity, discounted in accordance with the market rate of return, $r(t)$. [The rate of return to holders of shares will then turn out to be $r(t)$ at each date.] The firm makes decisions to further the interests of the shareowners and seeks therefore to maximize $V(0)$.

We again define $\bar{r}(t)$ as the average interest rate between times 0 and t, as in equation (2.12):

$$\bar{r}(t) \equiv (1/t) \cdot \int_0^t r(v)\, dv$$

The firm's objective is to choose L and I at each date to maximize

$$V(0) = \int_0^\infty e^{-\bar{r}(t)\cdot t} \cdot \{F(K, \hat{L}) - wL - I \cdot [1 + \phi(I/K)]\} \cdot dt \tag{3.28}$$

subject to equation (3.25) and an initial value $K(0)$.

We can analyze this optimization problem by setting up the Hamiltonian

$$J = e^{-\bar{r}(t)\cdot t} \cdot \{F(K, \hat{L}) - wL - I \cdot [1 + \phi(I/K)] + q \cdot (I - \delta K)\} \tag{3.29}$$

where q is the shadow price associated with $\dot{K} = I - \delta K$. We set up the current-value Hamiltonian so that q has the units of goods per unit of capital at time t; that is, q represents the current-value shadow price of installed capital in units of contemporaneous output. The

3. This setup is satisfactory if we allow for negative dividends—proportionate levies on shareowners—to finance negative net cash flows. We could instead allow firms to borrow at the interest rate, $r(t)$. The results would be the same as in the text if we introduced a borrowing constraint that ruled out chain-letter debt finance. (This constraint is the same as the one already imposed on households.) We could also allow firms to fund negative net cash flows by issuing new equity shares. The results would again be the same if we expressed the firm's objective as the maximization of the price per share of the outstanding shares.

present-value shadow price is then

$$\nu = q \cdot e^{-\bar{r}(t)\cdot t}$$

The maximization entails the standard first-order conditions,

$$\partial J/\partial L = \partial J/\partial I = 0 \text{ and } \dot{\nu} = -\partial J/\partial K$$

and the transversality condition,

$$\lim_{t\to\infty} (\nu K) = 0$$

The first-order conditions can be expressed as

$$[f(\hat{k}) - \hat{k} \cdot f'(\hat{k})] \cdot e^{xt} = w \tag{3.30}$$

$$q = 1 + \phi(\hat{\imath}/\hat{k}) + (\hat{\imath}/\hat{k}) \cdot \phi'(\hat{\imath}/\hat{k}) \tag{3.31}$$

$$\dot{q} = (r + \delta) \cdot q - [f'(\hat{k}) + (\hat{\imath}/\hat{k})^2 \cdot \phi'(\hat{\imath}/\hat{k})] \tag{3.32}$$

where we have used the intensive form of the production function, $f(\cdot)$, and written capital and gross investment as quantities per unit of effective labor, $\hat{k}$ and $\hat{\imath}$, respectively.[4]

Equation (3.32) is the usual equation of the marginal product of labor to the wage rate, a result that holds because no adjustment costs are attached to changes in labor input. Equation (3.31) indicates that the shadow value of installed capital, q, exceeds unity if $\hat{\imath} > 0$ because of the adjustment costs. The relation between q and $\hat{\imath}/\hat{k}$ is monotonically increasing because $\phi'(\hat{\imath}/\hat{k}) > 0$ and $\phi''(\hat{\imath}/\hat{k}) \geq 0$.[5]

Equation (3.32) can be rewritten as

$$r = (1/q) \cdot [f'(\hat{k}) + (\hat{\imath}/\hat{k})^2 \cdot \phi'(\hat{\imath}/\hat{k})] - \delta + \dot{q}/q$$

This equation says that the market rate of return, r, is equated to the total rate of return from paying q to hold a unit of capital. This return on capital equals the marginal product, $f'(\hat{k})$, plus the marginal reduction in adjustment costs (when K rises for given I), all deflated by the cost of capital, q; less the depreciation of installed capital at rate δ; plus the rate of capital gain, $\dot{q}/q$. If adjustment costs were absent, so that $\phi(\hat{\imath}/\hat{k}) = \phi'(\hat{\imath}/\hat{k}) = 0$ and $q = 1$, equation (3.32) would reduce to the conventional result, $r = f'(\hat{k}) - \delta$.

4. For given w, r, q, and $\dot{q}$, equations (3.30)–(3.32) ensure that all firms have the same values of $\hat{k}$ and $\hat{\imath}$. The relative size of each firm, $\hat{L}_i(t)/\hat{L}(t)$, is pinned down by its initial value, $\hat{L}_i(0)/\hat{L}(0)$; in particular, changes in relative size do not occur over time because of the adjustment costs for installing capital (if we assume that these costs must be paid even when a firm sells and buys used capital).

5. This result requires only the weaker condition $2 \cdot \phi'(\hat{\imath}/\hat{k}) + (\hat{\imath}/\hat{k}) \cdot \phi''(\hat{\imath}/\hat{k}) > 0$.

The transversality condition can be expressed as

$$\lim_{t\to\infty}\left[q\hat{k}\cdot e^{-[\bar{r}(t)-n-x]\cdot t}\right]=0 \tag{3.33}$$

Thus, if q and $\hat{k}$ asymptotically approach constants (as they do), the steady-state interest rate, r^*, must, as usual, exceed the steady-state growth rate, $n+x$.

Since the relation between q and $\hat{\imath}/\hat{k}$ implied by equation (3.31) is monotonically increasing, we can invert this relation to express $\hat{\imath}/\hat{k}$ as a monotonically increasing function of q:

$$\hat{\imath}/\hat{k}=\psi(q) \tag{3.34}$$

where $\psi'(q)>0$. Relations of the form of equation (3.34) have frequently been estimated empirically.[6] These empirical studies follow the suggestion of Brainard and Tobin (1968) to use the ratio of firms' market value to the capital stock, V/K, as a proxy for q. The ratio V/K is now called *average* q, whereas the shadow price of installed capital that appears in our theoretical analysis is called *marginal* q. The two concepts of q coincide, however, in our model.

To demonstrate the correspondence between marginal and average q, use equations (3.32), (3.31), and (3.25) to get (after some manipulation)

$$d(qK)/dt=\dot{q}K+q\dot{K}=rqK-\hat{L}\cdot\{f(\hat{k})-we^{-xt}-\hat{\imath}\cdot[1+\phi(\hat{\imath}/\hat{k})]\}$$

This relation is a first-order, linear differential equation in qK and can be solved using $e^{-\bar{r}(t)\cdot t}$ as an integrating factor. If we use the transversality condition from equation (3.33) and the definition of V from equation (3.28), we get

$$qK=V$$

so that V/K (or average q) equals q (or marginal q). Hayashi (1982) shows that this result applies as long as the production function exhibits constant returns to scale and the stock market is efficient.[7]

3.2.2 Equilibrium with a Given Interest Rate

We now analyze the steady state and transitional dynamics when the interest rate, $r(t)$, is given exogenously. This setting applies to a single firm that takes as given the

6. See, for example, von Furstenberg (1977), Summers (1981), and Blanchard, Rhee, and Summers (1993). Barro (1990a) estimates in first-difference form, so that the change in the investment ratio relates to the change in firms' market value. This change in market value was then approximated by the rate of return on the stock market.

7. Two other requirements are needed for the Hayashi theorem to hold: capital goods need to be homogeneous (which we have been assuming all along) and total adjustment costs need to be homogeneous of degree one in I and K (which we are assuming since total costs are given by $I\cdot[1+\phi(I/K)]$).

economy-wide interest rate or to a small open economy that takes as given the world interest rate. This last context corresponds to an extension of the Ramsey model that we consider later in this chapter. In that extension—which neglects adjustment costs for investment—the convergence of $\hat{k}$ and $\hat{y}$ to their steady-state values turns out to be instantaneous. However, we now show that adjustment costs imply finite convergence speeds even in the presence of perfect world credit markets.

We simplify by assuming that the interest rate, r, is constant, where $r > x + n$. We also specialize to the case in which the adjustment cost is proportional to $\hat{\imath}/\hat{k}$; that is,

$$\phi(\hat{\imath}/\hat{k}) = (b/2) \cdot (\hat{\imath}/\hat{k}) \tag{3.35}$$

so that $\phi'(\hat{\imath}/\hat{k}) = (b/2) > 0$. The parameter b expresses the sensitivity of the adjustment costs to the total amount invested. Higher values of b imply more adjustment costs per unit of $\hat{\imath}/\hat{k}$. This linear specification for $\phi(\cdot)$ is not necessary for the main results but does simplify the exposition. If we substitute this form for $\phi(\cdot)$ into equation (3.31), we get a linear relation between $\hat{\imath}/\hat{k}$ and q:

$$\hat{\imath}/\hat{k} = \psi(q) = (q - 1)/b \tag{3.36}$$

Equations (3.25) and (3.36) imply that the change in $\hat{k}$ can be expressed as a function of q:

$$\dot{\hat{k}} = \hat{\imath} - (x + n + \delta) \cdot \hat{k} = [(q - 1)/b - (x + n + \delta)] \cdot \hat{k} \tag{3.37}$$

If we substitute for $\hat{\imath}/\hat{k}$ from equations (3.35) and (3.36) into equation (3.32), we can relate $\dot{q}$ to q and $\hat{k}$:

$$\dot{q} = (r + \delta) \cdot q - [f'(\hat{k}) + (q - 1)^2/2b] \tag{3.38}$$

Equations (3.37) and (3.38) form a two-dimensional system of differential equations in the state variable, $\hat{k}$, and the shadow price, q. We can use a phase diagram to analyze the steady state and transitional dynamics of this system. The phase diagram is drawn in $(\hat{k}, q)$ space in figure 3.3.

The condition $\dot{\hat{k}} = 0$ implies from equation (3.37) (if $\hat{k} \neq 0$)

$$q = q^* = 1 + b \cdot (x + n + \delta) \tag{3.39}$$

The steady-state value of q exceeds 1 because adjustment costs are borne in the steady state for the gross investment that replaces the capital that wears out at the rate δ. There is further depreciation of capital in efficiency units because $\hat{L}$ grows at the rate $x + n$. Equation (3.39) appears as the horizontal line $q = q^*$ in figure 3.3. Equation (3.37) implies $\dot{\hat{k}} > 0$ for $q > q^*$ and $\dot{\hat{k}} < 0$ for $q < q^*$, as shown by the arrows.

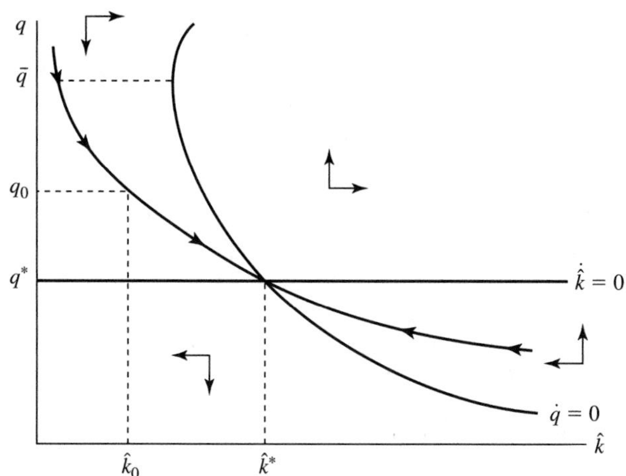

Figure 3.3
The phase diagram for the model with adjustment costs (assuming a fixed interest rate). The phase diagram is shown here in $(q, \hat{k})$ space, where q is the market value per unit of installed capital. The $\dot{\hat{k}} = 0$ locus is a horizontal line at q^*. The $\dot{q} = 0$ locus is downward sloping around the steady state. As q rises, the schedule becomes steeper, and the slope becomes positive when $q > 1 + b \cdot (r + \delta) > \overline{q}$. The stable arm is downward sloping throughout. Hence, for low values of $\hat{k}$, $q > q^*$ applies. In this case, the transition exhibits monotonic increases in $\hat{k}$ and monotonic decreases in q.

The condition $\dot{q} = 0$ leads from equation (3.38) to the condition

$$(q - 1)^2 - 2b \cdot (r + \delta) \cdot q + 2b \cdot f'(\hat{k}) = 0 \tag{3.40}$$

If we substitute $q = q^*$ from equation (3.39), then the steady-state value $\hat{k}^*$ must satisfy the condition

$$f'(\hat{k}^*) = r + \delta + b \cdot (x + n + \delta) \cdot [r + \delta - (1/2) \cdot (x + n + \delta)] \tag{3.41}$$

Since $r > x + n$, equation (3.41) shows that the presence of adjustment costs, $b > 0$, raises $f'(\hat{k}^*)$ above the value, $r + \delta$, that would otherwise apply. Consequently, $\hat{k}^*$ is reduced by adjustment costs.

The slope of the relation between q and $\hat{k}$ along the $\dot{q} = 0$ locus is given from equation (3.40) by

$$\frac{dq}{d\hat{k}} = \frac{-b \cdot f''(\hat{k})}{(q - 1) - b \cdot (r + \delta)}$$

The numerator is positive, and the denominator is negative if $q < 1 + b \cdot (r + \delta)$. This inequality must hold at the steady-state value, q^*, because $r > x + n$ (see equation [3.39]).

Therefore, the $\dot{q} = 0$ locus is downward sloping, as shown in figure 3.3, for $q \le q^*$.[8] The slope is positive if $q > 1 + b \cdot (r + \delta) > q^*$. Equation (3.39) implies $\dot{q} > 0$ for values of $\hat{k}$ to the left of the $\dot{q} = 0$ locus and $\dot{q} > 0$ for values to the right of the locus. The arrows in the figure show these movements of q.

The system described in figure 3.3 exhibits saddle-path stability. The stable arm is downward sloping, as shown by the solid line with arrows. Thus, if the economy begins at $\hat{k}(0) < \hat{k}^*$, then $q(0) > q^*$. The high market value of installed capital stimulates a great deal (but not an infinite amount) of investment; that is, $\hat{\imath}/\hat{k}$ is high when q is high in accordance with equation (3.36). The increase in $\hat{k}$ over time leads to decreases in q and, hence, to reductions in $\hat{\imath}/\hat{k}$. Eventually, q approaches q^*, $\hat{\imath}/\hat{k}$ approaches $x + n + \delta$, and $\hat{k}$ approaches $\hat{k}^*$.

The theory predicts that a poor economy [with $\hat{k}(0)$ well below $\hat{k}^*$] with access to world credit markets will have a high value of installed capital, q, and a high growth rate of the capital stock. We now quantify the implications about the speed of convergence for capital and output.

We can approximate equations (3.37) and (3.38) as a linear system in $\log(\hat{k})$ and q in the vicinity of the steady state. We assume that the production function is Cobb–Douglas, $f(\hat{k}) = A\hat{k}^{\alpha}$, and we use familiar parameter values: $\alpha = 0.75$, $x = 0.02$/year, $n = 0.01$/year, and $\delta = 0.05$/year. We also assume that the world interest rate is $r = 0.06$/year, although the results are virtually the same if r is somewhat higher, say, $r = 0.08$/year.

Given these choices for the other parameters, the convergence coefficient, β, for $\hat{k}$ and $\hat{y}$ depends on the parameter b in the adjustment-cost function in equation (3.35). To think about reasonable values of this parameter, note that at the steady state, where $(\hat{\imath}/\hat{k})^* = x + n + \delta = 0.08$/year, the cost of a unit of capital is $1 + 0.04 \cdot b$. Also, equation (3.39) implies $q^* = 1 + 0.08 \cdot b$. Thus, $b = 1$ implies that $q^* = 1.08$ and that the charge at the steady state for an incremental unit of capital is 1.04, whereas $b = 10$ implies that $q^* = 1.80$ and that the charge for extra capital is 1.40. The value $q^* = 1.80$ is high relative to the estimates of q reported by Blanchard, Rhee, and Summers (1993); their values never exceed 1.5. Thus, for physical capital, values of b as high as 10 imply unreasonably high costs of adjustment and tend thereby to generate counterfactually high values of q^*. In fact, since $q > q^*$ applies when $\hat{k} < \hat{k}^*$, the model would require b to be much less than 10 to ensure that $q > 1.5$ does not arise during the transition to the steady state.

The problem is that values of b much less than 10 imply an unrealistically high convergence coefficient, β. For the parameter values mentioned before, β falls from ∞ at $b = 0$ to 0.16 when $b = 1$, 0.11 when $b = 2$, and 0.09 when $b = 3$. The coefficient β does not fall

8. This property can be shown to hold for any adjustment-cost function $\phi(\cdot)$ that satisfies $2 \cdot \phi'(\hat{\imath}/\hat{k}) + (\hat{\imath}/\hat{k}) \cdot \phi''(\hat{\imath}/\hat{k}) > 0$.

to 0.05 until b exceeds 6 and does not fall to 0.03 until b equals 12.[9] In order to get β to fall to 0.03 at a lower value of b, we have to assume a capital-share coefficient, α, that is even greater than 0.75. For example, if $\alpha = 0.90$, β falls to 0.03 when b equals 6.

We see two possible ways out of this difficulty. One is to argue that capital includes human capital and that the adjustment costs associated with human capital are so great that b values of 10 or more—and the correspondingly high q values—are reasonable.[10] We do not know how to check this hypothesis from currently available information about the returns to human capital. The second possibility is to drop the assumption that the economy can finance all of its investment at a fixed interest rate, r. One way to do so is to return to the closed-economy frameworks of chapters 1 and 2, where r varies to equate investment demand to desired national saving. A second possibility is to allow for an open economy but to have some restrictions on the extent to which a single economy can borrow on world credit markets. We work out results in the next section for the case in which adjustment costs for investment are added to the closed-economy version of the neoclassical growth model. In a later section, we consider adjustment costs in an open economy.

3.2.3 Equilibrium for a Closed Economy with a Fixed Saving Rate

Gross investment outlays, including adjustment costs, per effective worker are

$$\hat{\imath} \cdot [1 + \phi(\hat{\imath}/\hat{k})]$$

In a closed economy, this expenditure equals gross saving per effective worker. If we assume that this saving is the constant fraction s of gross output per worker, $f(\hat{k})$, then we have

$$s \cdot f(\hat{k})/\hat{k} = (\hat{\imath}/\hat{k}) \cdot [1 + \phi(\hat{\imath}/\hat{k})]$$

If we use the linear form for $\phi(\hat{\imath}/\hat{k})$ from equation (3.35) and the corresponding expression for $\hat{\imath}/\hat{k}$ from equation (3.36), this result simplifies to

$$s \cdot f(\hat{k})/\hat{k} = \left(\frac{1}{2b}\right) \cdot (q^2 - 1) \tag{3.42}$$

If we use the Cobb–Douglas form of the production function, $f(\hat{k}) = A\hat{k}^{\alpha}$, solve out for q in terms of $\hat{k}$ from equation (3.42), and substitute the result into the expression for $\dot{\hat{k}}$ in

9. As b tends to infinity, β approaches 0.025; that is, the convergence speed does not tend to zero as the adjustment-cost parameter becomes arbitrarily large. However, as b tends to infinity, the economy is approaching a steady-state value $\hat{k}^*$ that is tending to zero.

10. Kremer and Thomson (1998) use an overlapping-generations framework in which young workers benefit from interactions with old, experienced workers in an apprentice-mentor context. Their framework effectively implies high adjustment costs for rapid increases in human capital.

equation (3.37), we get a differential equation in $\hat{k}$:

$$\dot{\hat{k}}/\hat{k} = (1/b) \cdot \{[1 + 2bsA \cdot \hat{k}^{\alpha-1}]^{1/2} - 1\} - (x + n + \delta) \tag{3.43}$$

This result generalizes the formula from equation (1.30) for the Solow–Swan model to allow for adjustment costs. The Solow–Swan result applies if $b = 0$.[11]

We can, as usual, compute the convergence coefficient β by log-linearizing equation (3.43) around the steady state. The resulting formula for β is

$$\beta = (1 - \alpha) \cdot (x + n + \delta) \cdot \left[\frac{1 + (1/2) \cdot b \cdot (x + n + \delta)}{1 + b \cdot (x + n + \delta)}\right] \tag{3.44}$$

Hence, if adjustment costs are absent ($b = 0$), the formula for β reduces to that from the Solow–Swan model, $(1 - \alpha) \cdot (x + n + \delta)$ (see equation [1.31]). If $b > 0$, equation (3.44) shows that β in the adjustment-cost model is less than that in the Solow–Swan model and is a decreasing function of b. As b tends to infinity, β tends to $(1/2) \cdot (1 - \alpha) \cdot (x + n + \delta)$, that is, to one-half the value prescribed by the Solow–Swan model.

If we use the same parameter values as before ($\alpha = 0.75$, $x = 0.02$, $n = 0.01$, $\delta = 0.05$) and consider values of the adjustment-cost coefficient, b, that are much less than 10, then the major result is that adjustment costs do not have a large impact on the speed of convergence. For example, if $b = 0$ (the Solow–Swan case), then $\beta = 0.020$/year. For $b = 2$, we get $\beta = 0.019$, and for $b = 10$, we get $\beta = 0.016$. Thus, although the presence of adjustment costs slows down convergence, the magnitude of the effect tends to be small. As we mentioned before, to get more significant effects, we have to assume adjustment-cost coefficients that are so large that the implied value of q^*—and, moreover, of transitional values of q—exceeds empirically observed values (at least for physical capital).

We can proceed in an analogous manner to allow for adjustment costs in the Ramsey model.[12] Instead of assuming a constant gross saving rate, we use the familiar condition for household optimization, $\dot{c}/c = (1/\theta) \cdot (r - \rho)$. This analysis is straightforward but cumbersome and turns out to lead to few new insights. In particular, we find that the presence of adjustment costs reduces the speed of convergence relative to that implied by the Ramsey model (equation [2.34]). But, as in the case of the Solow–Swan model, the quantitative effects are small if we assume an adjustment-cost coefficient, b, that is consistent with "reasonable" behavior of the shadow price q.

11. We can use l'Hôpital's rule to show that, as b approaches zero, the formula in equation (3.43) reduces to that shown in equation (1.30).

12. See Abel and Blanchard (1983) and problem 3.5 for analyses of this model.

3.3 An Open-Economy Ramsey Model

In the closed-economy models of chapters 1 and 2, domestic residents owned the entire stock of capital. Hence, for country i, the capital per worker, k_i, equaled the households' assets per person, a_i. We now extend the model to allow the economy to be open. We begin by modifying the Ramsey model to allow for mobility of goods across national borders and for international borrowing and lending. We find that the modification to allow for an open economy leads to some paradoxical conclusions. We then consider whether further extensions—imperfections of world credit markets, nonconstant preference parameters, finite horizons, and adjustment costs for investment—can generate more reasonable answers.

3.3.1 Setup of the Model

There are many countries in the world. For convenience, we think of one of these countries, country i, as domestic and view the others as foreign. Within any of the countries, the households and firms have the same forms of objectives and constraints as in the Ramsey model of chapter 2.

Domestic and foreign claims on capital are assumed to be perfect substitutes as stores of value; hence, each must pay the same rate of return, r. Since loans and claims on capital in any country are still assumed to be perfect substitutes as stores of value, the variable r will be the single world interest rate.

Suppose that the domestic country has assets per person a_i and capital per person k_i. If k_i exceeds a_i, the difference, $k_i - a_i$, must correspond to net claims by foreigners on the domestic economy. Conversely, if a_i exceeds k_i, $a_i - k_i$ represents net claims by domestic residents on foreign economies. If we define d_i to be the domestic country's net debt to foreigners (foreign claims on the domestic country net of domestic claims on foreign countries), then

$$d_i = k_i - a_i \tag{3.45}$$

Equivalently, domestic assets equal domestic capital less the foreign debt: $a_i = k_i - d_i$.

The current-account balance is the negative of the change in the aggregate foreign debt, $D_i = L_i d_i$, where L_i is country i's population and labor force. Therefore, if L_i grows at the rate n_i, the per capita current-account balance for country i equals $-(\dot{d}_i + n_i d_i)$.[13]

The model still contains only one physical kind of good, but foreigners can buy domestic output, and domestic residents can buy foreign output. The only function of international

13. Since D_i is the country's total foreign debt, the current-account balance equals $-\dot{D}_i$. The definition $d_i \equiv D_i/L_i$ and the condition $\dot{L}_i/L_i = n_i$ imply $-\dot{D}_i/L_i = -(\dot{d}_i + n_i d_i)$.

trade in this model is to allow domestic production to diverge from domestic expenditure on consumption and investment. In other words, we consider the intertemporal aspects of international trade but neglect the implications for patterns of specialization in production.

We continue to assume that labor is immobile; that is, domestic residents cannot work abroad (or emigrate) and foreigners cannot work in the domestic country (or immigrate). Chapter 9 allows for migration.

The budget constraint for the representative household in country i is the same as that given in equation (2.2):

$$\dot{a}_i = w_i + (r - n_i) \cdot a_i - c_i \tag{3.46}$$

The only new element is that r is the world interest rate.

We assume the same form of households' preferences as in chapter 2 (equations [2.1] and [2.9]) and we allow for each country to have its own discount rate ρ_i and elasticity of intertemporal substitution, θ_i. Since the objective and constraints are the same as in chapter 2, the first-order condition for consumption is still the one shown in equation (2.10):

$$\dot{c}_i / c_i = (1/\theta_i) \cdot (r - \rho_i)$$

or, when expressed in terms of consumption per effective worker,

$$(1/\hat{c}_i) \cdot (d\hat{c}_i/dt) = (1/\theta_i) \cdot (r - \rho_i - \theta_i x_i) \tag{3.47}$$

The transversality condition again requires $a_i(t)$ to grow asymptotically at a rate less than $r - n_i$, as in equation (2.11).

The optimization conditions for firms again entail equality between the marginal products and the factor prices (equations [2.21] and [2.22]):

$$f'(\hat{k}_i) = r + \delta_i \tag{3.48}$$

$$[f(\hat{k}_i) - \hat{k}_i \cdot f'(\hat{k}_i)] \cdot e^{x_i t} = w_i \tag{3.49}$$

If we substitute for w_i from equation (3.49) into equation (3.46) and use equation (3.48), the change in assets per effective worker can be determined as

$$d\hat{a}_i/dt = f(\hat{k}_i) - (r + \delta_i) \cdot (\hat{k}_i - \hat{a}_i) - (x_i + n_i + \delta_i) \cdot \hat{a}_i - \hat{c}_i \tag{3.50}$$

Note from equation (3.45) that $(\hat{k}_i - \hat{a}_i) = \hat{d}_i$, which equals 0 for a closed economy. Equation (3.50) extends equation (2.23) to the case in which $\hat{d}_i \neq 0$.

3.3.2 Behavior of a Small Economy's Capital Stock and Output

If country i's economy is small in relation to the world economy, the country's accumulation of assets and capital stocks has a negligible impact on the path of the world interest rate,

$r(t)$. Therefore, we can treat the path of $r(t)$ as exogenous for country i. Given this path, equations (3.48) and (3.49) determine the paths of $\hat{k}_i(t)$ and $w_i(t)$, without regard to the choices of consumption and saving by the domestic households. Given the time path for $w_i(t)$, equations (3.47) and (3.50) and the transversality condition determine the paths of $\hat{c}_i(t)$ and $\hat{a}_i(t)$. Finally, the paths of $\hat{k}_i(t)$ and $\hat{a}_i(t)$ prescribe the behavior of the net foreign debt, $\hat{d}_i(t)$, from equation (3.45).

For simplicity, we now assume that the world interest rate equals a constant r. In effect, the world economy is in the kind of steady state that we considered before for a single closed economy. If country i were a closed economy, its steady-state interest rate would be $\rho_i + \theta_i x_i$ (as in chapter 2). We assume that $r \leq \rho_i + \theta_i x_i$ applies, because if $r > \rho_i + \theta_i x_i$, the domestic economy would eventually accumulate enough assets to violate the small-country assumption that we made. We also assume $r > x_i + n_i$, that is, the world interest rate exceeds the steady-state growth rate that would apply in country i if the economy were closed. Otherwise, the present value of wages will turn out to be infinite and, hence, the attainable utility will be unbounded.

If r is constant, equation (3.48) implies that $\hat{k}_i(t)$ equals a constant, denoted $(\hat{k}_i^*)_{\text{open}}$, which satisfies the condition $f'[(\hat{k}_i^*)_{\text{open}}] = r + \delta_i$. In other words, the speed of convergence from any initial value, $\hat{k}_i(0)$, to $(\hat{k}_i^*)_{\text{open}}$ is infinite. An excess of $(\hat{k}_i^*)_{\text{open}}$ over $\hat{k}_i(0)$ causes capital to flow in from the rest of the world so fast (at an infinite rate) that the gap disappears at once. Similarly, an excess of $\hat{k}_i(0)$ over $(\hat{k}_i^*)_{\text{open}}$ induces a massive outflow of capital. This counterfactual prediction of an infinite speed of convergence for $\hat{k}_i$ is one of the problematic implications of the open-economy version of the Ramsey model.

Recall that $\hat{k}_i^*$, the steady-state value for the closed-economy model of chapter 2, satisfies the condition $f'(\hat{k}_i^*) - \delta = \rho_i + \theta_i x_i$. The condition $r \leq \rho_i + \theta_i x_i$ implies $(\hat{k}_i^*)_{\text{open}} \geq \hat{k}_i^*$; that is, the steady-state capital intensity in the open economy is at least as high as in the closed economy.

Since $\hat{k}_i(t)$ is constant, $\hat{y}_i(t)$ is constant—that is, the speed of convergence from $\hat{y}_i(0)$ to $(\hat{y}_i^*)_{\text{open}}$ is infinite—and $y_i(t)$ grows at the constant rate x_i. Equation (3.49) implies that $w_i(t)$ also grows at the rate x_i. Therefore, the wage rate per unit of effective labor, $\hat{w}_i(t) = w_i(t) \cdot e^{-x_i t}$, equals a constant, denoted $(\hat{w}_i^*)_{\text{open}}$.

3.3.3 Behavior of a Small Economy's Consumption and Assets

Equation (3.47) implies that consumption per effective worker, $\hat{c}_i(t)$, grows at the constant rate $(r - \rho_i - \theta_i x_i)/\theta_i \leq 0$. If we use the form of the consumption function that we derived in chapter 2 (equations [2.14] and [2.15]), then $\hat{c}_i(t)$ can be written as

$$\hat{c}_i = (1/\theta_i) \cdot [\rho_i - r \cdot (1 - \theta_i) - n_i\theta_i] \cdot \left[\hat{a}_i(0) + \frac{(\hat{w}_i^*)_{\text{open}}}{r - x_i - n_i}\right] \cdot e^{[(r-\rho_i-\theta_i x_i)/\theta_i]\cdot t} \tag{3.51}$$

The term in the first brackets on the right-hand side is positive from the conditions $\rho_i + \theta_i x_i \geq r$ and $r > x_i + n_i$.

If $r = \rho_i + \theta_i x_i$, then $\hat{c}_i(t)$ is constant. Otherwise—that is, if $r < \rho_i + \theta_i x_i$—$\hat{c}_i(t)$ asymptotically approaches 0. The domestic country borrows to enjoy a high level of consumption early on—because it is impatient in the sense that $\rho_i + \theta_i x_i > r$—but it pays the price later in the form of low consumption growth. Recall as a contrast that $\hat{c}_i(t)$ in a closed economy is constant asymptotically. The result that $\hat{c}_i$ tends to 0 if $r < \rho_i + \theta_i x_i$ is another problematic feature of the open-economy Ramsey model.

Equation (3.50) is a first-order linear differential equation in $\hat{a}_i(t)$. This equation, along with the formula for $\hat{c}_i(t)$ in equation (3.51) and the given initial value of assets, $\hat{a}_i(0)$, determines the time path of $\hat{a}_i(t)$ as

$$\hat{a}_i(t) = \left[\hat{a}_i(0) + \frac{(\hat{w}_i^*)_{\text{open}}}{r - x_i - n_i}\right] \cdot e^{[(r-\rho_i-\theta_i x_i)/\theta_i]\cdot t} - \frac{(\hat{w}_i^*)_{\text{open}}}{r - x_i - n_i} \tag{3.52}$$

The final term on the right-hand side is the present value of wage income (per efficiency unit of labor), where $(r - x_i - n_i) > 0$ follows from the condition $r > x_i + n_i$.

If $r = \rho_i + \theta_i x_i$, $\hat{a}_i(t)$ is constant. Otherwise—that is, if $r < \rho_i + \theta_i x_i$—the exponential term in equation (3.52), $e^{[(r-\rho_i-\theta_i x_i)/\theta_i]\cdot t}$, diminishes over time toward 0. Therefore, if $\hat{a}_i(0) > 0$, then $\hat{a}_i(t)$ eventually falls to 0, so that $\hat{d}_i(t)$ from equation (3.45) equals $(\hat{k}_i^*)_{\text{open}}$. Subsequently, $\hat{a}_i(t)$ becomes negative; that is, the domestic country becomes a debtor not only in the sense of not owning its capital stock but also of borrowing against the present value of its wage income as collateral. Asymptotically, $\hat{a}_i(t)$ approaches the final term in equation (3.52), $-[(\hat{w}_i^*)_{\text{open}}/(r - x_i - n_i)]$, so that $\hat{d}_i(t)$ approaches the positive constant $(\hat{k}_i^*)_{\text{open}} + [(\hat{w}_i^*)_{\text{open}}/(r - x_i - n_i)]$. In other words, an impatient country asymptotically mortgages all its capital and all its labor income. This counterfactual behavior of assets is yet another difficulty with the model.

3.3.4 The World Equilibrium

Suppose now that the world consists of a set of countries numbered $i = 1, \ldots, M$. We assume here that population growth, n_i, and the rate of technological progress, x_i, equal the same values, n and x, for all countries. In this case, the shares of each country's output, Y_i, in world output do not change over time.

Assume that the countries are ordered in terms of their effective rates of time preference, $\rho_i + \theta_i x$, with country 1 having the lowest value. We already showed that $\hat{c}_i(t)$ approaches 0 and $\hat{a}_i(t)$ approaches a negative number if $\rho_i + \theta_i x > r$. In contrast, if $\rho_i + \theta_i x < r$, $\hat{c}_i(t)$ and $\hat{a}_i(t)$ would rise forever, and country i's consumption would eventually exceed world output. Before this happened, the world interest rate would adjust downward; in particular, $\rho_i + \theta_i x \geq r$ must hold in the steady state for all countries. The only way to satisfy this condition and also have the world capital stock owned by someone (so that the world capital stock equals world assets) is for r to equal $\rho_1 + \theta_1 x$, the term for the most patient country. Asymptotically, country 1 owns all the wealth in the sense of the claims on capital and the present value of wage income in all countries. All other countries own a negligible amount (per unit of effective labor) in the long run.

Country 1's consumption grows asymptotically at the rate $n + x$, the same as the growth rate of world output. The ratio of country 1's consumption to world output approaches a positive constant, whereas the ratio for all other countries approaches 0.[14]

To summarize, the open-economy version of the Ramsey model generates several counterfactual results. The variables $\hat{k}_i$, $\hat{y}_i$, and $\hat{w}_i$ converge instantaneously to their steady-state values. In addition, for all but the most patient economy, $\hat{c}_i$ tends to 0, and $\hat{a}_i$ eventually becomes negative. The counterpart of these results is that net foreign claims and the current-account balance for the impatient economies become negative and large in magnitude in relation to GDP. Equivalently, the path of domestic expenditures on consumption and investment tends to evolve very differently from that of domestic production.

One way to think of some of the problematic results is in terms of the relation between the time-preference term, $\rho_i + \theta_i x$, and the interest rate, r_i, that country i faces. In the closed-economy framework of chapter 2, r_i adjusts to equal $\rho_i + \theta_i x$ in the steady state, whereas in the open-economy model, r_i is pegged at the world interest rate, r. If $r_i < \rho_i + \theta_i x$, the ratio of consumption to output asymptotically approaches 0. If $r_i > \rho_i + \theta_i x$, the ratio of consumption to output would approach infinity, but before this happens the country ends up owning all the world's wealth, and the world interest rate adjusts to equal $\rho_i + \theta_i x$. This outcome applies to the most patient country, but all other countries end up eventually in the situation in which $r_i < \rho_i + \theta_i x$, so that the ratio of consumption to output approaches 0. To avoid this result, we need some mechanism to eliminate the gap between r_i and $\rho_i + \theta_i x$ for all countries, not just for the most patient country. That is, either r_i has to differ from r, or else the effective rate of time preference, $\rho_i + \theta_i x$, has to be variable. We begin by considering a model in which r_i diverges from r.

3.4 The World Economy with a Constraint on International Credit

Our first attempt to improve the predictions of the open-economy growth model involves the introduction of a constraint on international borrowing. In the previous section, we

14. We would get similar results for a single country that comprises M family dynasties with differing values of the time-preference term, $\rho_i + \theta_i x$. Again, the most patient family ends up owning everything asymptotically. For families, this result would be tempered by imperfect inheritability of preference parameters and by marriage across dynasties. Similar considerations arise across countries, especially if we allow for migration of persons.

described an equilibrium in which an open economy eventually mortgages all its capital and labor income, and the ratio of consumption to GDP approaches zero. Cohen and Sachs (1986) observe that the economy's residents would eventually default on their debts in this kind of equilibrium. As long as the penalty for default is limited to some fraction of domestic output or of the domestic capital stock, the residents (or their government) would, at some point, prefer default to remaining on the path in which the ratio of consumption to GDP approached zero.

Since the inevitable default would presumably be foreseen by lenders, the path described before is not an equilibrium even before the time of default. In particular, the domestic residents in an impatient country would eventually reach a point at which they could not borrow the desired amount, $\hat{d}_i(t)$, at the world interest rate, r. We therefore want to reconsider the choices made by residents of an open economy when some constraints are imposed on their ability to borrow.

3.4.1 Setup of a Model with Physical and Human Capital

One tractable way to proceed is to distinguish two types of capital, one that serves well as collateral on foreign loans and another that does not serve as collateral. We can assume, for example, that human capital provides unacceptable security on loans, whereas at least some forms of physical capital are acceptable because the creditor can take possession of the object in the event of default.

We assume now that the production function involves the two kinds of capital:

$$\hat{y} = f(\hat{k}, \hat{h}) = A\hat{k}^{\alpha}\hat{h}^{\eta} \tag{3.53}$$

where $\hat{k}$ is physical capital per unit of effective labor and $\hat{h}$ is human capital per unit of effective labor.[15] We use a Cobb–Douglas form of the production function, where α is the share of physical capital, η is the share of human capital, and $0 < \alpha < 1$, $0 < \eta < 1$, and $0 < \alpha + \eta < 1$. The condition $0 < \alpha + \eta < 1$ ensures diminishing returns in the accumulation of broad capital, that is, for proportional changes in physical and human capital.

We maintain the assumption of a one-sector production technology in that units of output can now go on a one-to-one basis to consumption, additions to physical capital, or additions to human capital. (Chapter 4 deals further with this model, and chapter 5 introduces a separate education sector that produces new human capital.) The budget constraint, an

15. This analysis follows Barro, Mankiw, and Sala-i-Martin (1995). An alternative model, suggested by Cohen and Sachs (1986), sticks with one type of capital, k, but assumes that only a fraction ν, where $0 \le \nu \le 1$, of this capital serves as collateral on foreign loans. The results from this alternative framework are similar to those from the two-capital model, except that the two-capital model turns out to be simpler.

extension of equation (3.50), is

$$\begin{aligned} d\hat{a}/dt &= d\hat{k}/dt + d\hat{h}/dt - d\hat{d}/dt \\ &= A\hat{k}^{\alpha}\hat{h}^{\eta} - (r+\delta)\cdot(\hat{k}+\hat{h}-\hat{a}) - (x+n+\delta)\cdot\hat{a} - \hat{c} \end{aligned} \tag{3.54}$$

where $\hat{a} = \hat{k} + \hat{h} - \hat{d}$, and we have dropped the country subscript i for convenience. We also assume that the depreciation rate, δ, is the same for both kinds of capital.

3.4.2 The Closed Economy

If we return for the moment to a closed economy, then $d = 0$ and $a = k + h$. The results on the growth process are then the same as those worked out in chapter 2, except that we now explicitly take a broad view of capital to include physical and human components. Investors equate the marginal product of each type of capital to $r + \delta$, where r is the domestic interest rate. Given the Cobb–Douglas production function in equation (3.53), this condition implies that the ratio k/h is fixed at α/η.[16] In the steady state, the quantities of the two types of capital per unit of effective labor are constant at the values $\hat{k}^*$ and $\hat{h}^*$, respectively, where $\hat{k}^*/\hat{h}^* = \alpha/\eta$. If we start with $\hat{k}(0) < \hat{k}^*$ and $\hat{h}(0) < \hat{h}^*$, the transition involves growth of $\hat{k}$, $\hat{h}$, and $\hat{y}$. As in our previous analysis, the growth rates fall during the transition.

In the Ramsey model of chapter 2, the speed of convergence to the steady state depended on the capital share. That share equaled α in the Cobb–Douglas version of the model with one type of capital but now equals $\alpha + \eta$ in the model with two kinds of capital. Except for the substitution of $\alpha + \eta$ for α, the results are identical to those from the model that we worked out in chapter 2. In particular, the formula from equation (2.34) for the convergence coefficient, β, in the log-linearized model still applies if we replace α by $\alpha + \eta$:

$$2\beta = \left\{\zeta^2 + 4\cdot\left(\frac{1-\alpha-\eta}{\theta}\right)\cdot(\rho+\delta+\theta x)\cdot\left[\frac{\rho+\delta+\theta x}{\alpha+\eta} - (n+x+\delta)\right]\right\}^{1/2} - \zeta \tag{3.55}$$

where $\zeta = \rho - n - (1-\theta)\cdot x > 0$. If we assume, for example, that $\alpha = 0.30$ and $\eta = 0.45$, then the findings about the speed of convergence coincide with those from chapter 2 for the case in which the capital share was 0.75. If we take our usual benchmark values for the other parameters—$n = 0.01$ per year, $x = 0.02$ per year, $\delta = 0.05$ per year, and $\rho = 0.02$ per year—and use $\theta = 3$, the convergence coefficient is $\beta = 0.015$ per year.

16. The economy jumps from an arbitrary starting ratio, $k(0)/h(0)$, to α/η if we allow both kinds of investment to be reversible so that units of k can be immediately converted into units of h and vice versa. If we constrain gross investment in each kind of capital to be nonnegative, the transitional dynamics are more complicated. We explore these kinds of effects in chapter 5.

3.4.3 The Open Economy

The distinction between the two kinds of capital becomes more interesting when we allow for an open economy and introduce the credit-market constraint. We now assume that the amount of foreign debt, d, can be positive but cannot exceed the quantity of physical capital, k. Physical capital can be used as collateral on foreign loans, but human capital and raw labor cannot.

We are assuming implicitly that domestic residents own the physical capital stock but may obtain part or all of the financing for this stock by issuing bonds to foreigners. The results would be the same if we allowed for direct foreign investment, in which case the foreigners would own part of the physical capital stock rather than bonds. The important assumption is that domestic residents cannot borrow with human capital or raw labor as collateral and that foreigners cannot own domestic human capital or raw labor.

There are various ways to motivate the borrowing constraint. Physical capital is more easily repossessed than human capital and is therefore more readily financed with debt. Physical capital is also more amenable to direct foreign investment: a person can own a factory but not someone else's stream of labor income. Finally, one can abandon the terms "physical capital" and "human capital" and recognize that not all investments can be financed through perfect capital markets. The key distinction between k and h in the present context is not the physical nature of the capital but whether the cumulated goods serve as collateral for borrowing on world markets.

We still assume that the world interest rate, r, is constant. We now assume also that $r = \rho + \theta x$, the steady-state interest rate that would apply if the domestic economy were closed. That is, the home economy is neither more nor less impatient than the world as a whole. (It is straightforward to extend to the case in which $r < \rho + \theta x$.)

The initial quantity of assets per effective worker is $\hat{k}(0) + \hat{h}(0) - \hat{d}(0)$, and the key consideration is whether this quantity is greater or less than the steady-state amount of human capital, $\hat{h}^*$. If $\hat{k}(0) + \hat{h}(0) - \hat{d}(0) \geq \hat{h}^*$, the borrowing constraint is not binding, and the economy jumps to the steady state. In contrast, if $\hat{k}(0) + \hat{h}(0) - \hat{d}(0) < \hat{h}^*$, the constraint is binding—that is, $d = k$ applies—and we obtain some new results. We therefore focus on this situation.[17]

Since physical capital serves as collateral, the net return on this capital, $f_k - \delta$, where f_k is the marginal product of capital, equals the world interest rate, r, at all points in time. The formula for f_k implied by the Cobb–Douglas production function in equation (3.53)

17. If $r < \rho + \theta x$, the domestic economy must eventually become constrained on the world credit market. Hence, our analysis of a debt-constrained economy applies at some time in the future even if not at the initial date. If $r > \rho + \theta x$, the assumption of a small economy is violated eventually, and r would have to change.

therefore implies

$$\hat{k} = \alpha\hat{y}/(r+\delta) \tag{3.56}$$

Equation (3.56) ensures that the ratio of physical capital to GDP, k/y, will be constant throughout the transition to the steady state. In contrast, k/y would rise steadily during the transition for a closed economy. The rough constancy over time of k/y is one of Kaldor's (1963) stylized facts about economic development; see the discussion in the introductory chapter. The consistency of the credit-constrained open-economy model with this "fact" is therefore notable.[18]

The result for $\hat{k}$ from equation (3.56) can be combined with the production function from equation (3.53) to express $\hat{y}$ as a function of $\hat{h}$:

$$\hat{y} = \tilde{A}\hat{h}^{\epsilon} \tag{3.57}$$

where $\tilde{A} \equiv A^{1/(1-\alpha)} \cdot [\alpha/(r+\delta)]^{\alpha/(1-\alpha)}$ and $\epsilon \equiv \eta/(1-\alpha)$. The condition $0 < \alpha + \eta < 1$ implies $0 < \epsilon < \alpha + \eta < 1$. Thus the reduced-form production function in equation (3.57) expresses $\hat{y}$ as a function of $\hat{h}$ with positive and diminishing marginal product. The convergence implications of this model are therefore similar to those of the closed economy—both models involve the accumulation of a capital stock under conditions of diminishing returns.

The budget constraint from equation (3.54) can be combined with the reduced-form production function from equation (3.57), the borrowing constraint $d = k$ (which implies $a = h$), and the condition $(r+\delta) \cdot \hat{k} = \alpha\hat{y}$ from equation (3.56) to get the revised budget constraint:

$$d\hat{h}/dt = (1-\alpha) \cdot \tilde{A}\hat{h}^{\epsilon} - (\delta + n + x) \cdot \hat{h} - \hat{c} \tag{3.58}$$

Note that $\alpha\tilde{A}\hat{h}^{\epsilon}$, which subtracts from $\tilde{A}\hat{h}^{\epsilon}$ in the equation, corresponds to the flow of rental payments on physical capital, $(r+\delta)\hat{k}$ (see equation [3.56]). Since $d = k$, this term corresponds to the net factor payments to foreigners and therefore equals the difference (per unit of effective labor) between GNP and GDP. The GDP exceeds the GNP because the country is constrained on the international credit market and therefore has the positive foreign debt $d = k$.

If we use the setting in which households produce goods directly, they maximize utility (given in equations [2.1] and [2.9]), subject to the budget constraint in equation (3.58) and a given initial stock of human capital, $\hat{h}(0) > 0$. [The value $\hat{h}(0)$ equals the given amount

18. The precise constancy of k/y in the model depends on the fixity of the world interest rate, r, and on the assumption that the production function is Cobb–Douglas. This production function implies that the average product of capital, y/k, is proportional to the marginal product. Since the marginal product of capital, net of depreciation, equals the fixed world interest rate, r, the average product, y/k, must be constant.

of initial assets, which was assumed to be less than $\hat{h}^*$.] The optimizing condition for consumption over time is

$$\dot{\hat{c}}/\hat{c} = (1/\theta) \cdot [(1-\alpha) \cdot \tilde{A}\epsilon\hat{h}^{\epsilon-1} - (\delta + \rho + \theta x)] \tag{3.59}$$

where $(1-\alpha) \cdot \tilde{A}\epsilon\hat{h}^{\epsilon-1} = \tilde{A}\eta\hat{h}^{\epsilon-1} = f_h$, the marginal product of human capital. Equation (3.59) corresponds to the usual formula in equation (3.47) if we think of r in that formula as the domestic rate of return, which equals $f_h - \delta$. Equations (3.58) and (3.59) and the usual transversality condition fully describe the transitional dynamics of this model.

Because we assumed $r = \rho + \theta x$, the steady state is the same as that for the closed economy that has physical and human capital. Hence, the opportunity to borrow on the world credit market does not influence the steady state but will turn out to affect the speed of convergence.[19]

The system described by equations (3.58) and (3.59) and the transversality condition has the usual transitional dynamics. We can compare the results with those from the closed-economy model with capital goods k and h in which the total broad capital stock per worker is $k + h$ and the capital share is $\alpha + \eta$. The only differences are that equation (3.58) contains $(1-\alpha) \cdot \tilde{A}$ as a proportional constant in the production function, the capital-stock variable is h rather than $k + h$, and the exponent on the capital stock is $\epsilon \equiv \eta/(1-\alpha)$ rather than $\alpha + \eta$. Since ϵ and $\alpha + \eta$ are positive and less than 1—that is, both models feature diminishing returns—the dynamics of the models are essentially the same.

The formula for the convergence coefficient, β, coincides with that for the closed economy in equation (3.55), except that the capital-share parameter, $\alpha + \eta$, has to be replaced by $\epsilon \equiv \eta/(1-\alpha)$. (Recall that the level of the production technology does not influence the rate of convergence.) Hence, the convergence coefficient for the credit-constrained open economy is given by

$$2\beta = \left\{\zeta^2 + 4 \cdot \left(\frac{1-\epsilon}{\theta}\right) \cdot (\delta + \rho + \theta x) \cdot \left[\frac{\delta + \rho + \theta x}{\epsilon} - (\delta + n + x)\right]\right\}^{1/2} - \zeta \tag{3.60}$$

where $\zeta = \rho - n - (1-\theta) \cdot x > 0$. The coefficient determined from equation (3.60) is the same value that would arise in a closed economy that had the broad capital share ϵ, rather than $\alpha + \eta$. Since $\epsilon \equiv \eta/(1-\alpha)$, it follows that $\epsilon < \alpha + \eta$ (using the condition $\alpha + \eta < 1$). *The credit-constrained open economy therefore behaves like a closed economy with a broad capital share that is less than* $\alpha + \eta$. Recall that the rate of convergence depends inversely on the capital share (because a smaller capital share means that diminishing returns

19. If we had assumed $r < \rho + \theta x$—so that the home economy is more impatient than those of the rest of the world (see note 17)—then the availability of foreign borrowing would also affect the steady-state position. The open economy would have higher steady-state capital intensities, $\hat{h}^*$ and $\hat{k}^*$, than the closed economy.

set in more rapidly). The credit-constrained open economy therefore has a higher rate of convergence than the closed economy. Note, however, that $(\alpha + \eta) \to 1$ implies $\epsilon \to 1$ and, therefore, $\beta \to 0$ in equation (3.60). Thus, if diminishing returns to broad capital do not apply $(\alpha + \eta = 1)$, the model still does not exhibit the convergence property.[20]

We can understand why the partially open economy converges faster than the closed economy by thinking about the tendency for diminishing returns to set in as human capital, $\hat{h}$, is accumulated. For given exponents of the production function, α and η, the key issue is the transitional behavior of the ratio k/h. In the closed economy, k/h stays constant (at the value α/η), whereas in the open economy, k/h falls during the transition (see below). That is, $\hat{k}$ is relatively high at the outset in an open economy because the availability of foreign financing makes it easy to acquire physical capital quickly. The fall in k/h over time causes diminishing returns to $\hat{h}$ to set in faster than otherwise; hence, the speed of convergence is greater in the open economy than in the closed economy.

Although the credit-constrained open economy converges faster than the closed economy, the speed of convergence is finite for the open economy. If we use the values $\alpha = 0.30$ and $\eta = 0.45$, along with the benchmark values mentioned before for the other parameters, the convergence coefficient implied by equation (3.60) is 0.025, compared with 0.015 for the closed economy. The value 0.025 conforms well with empirical estimates of convergence coefficients.

Recall that an open economy with perfect capital mobility converges at an infinite rate. Therefore, our finding is that an open economy with partial capital mobility looks much more like a closed economy than a fully open economy. Although we derived this result so far only for a particular set of values for α and η, the basic finding is much more general. If we raise α/η for given $\alpha + \eta$, we increase the degree of capital mobility and thereby raise the convergence coefficient, β. For the benchmark values of the other parameters (including $\alpha + \eta = 0.75$), β rises from 0.015 at $\alpha/\eta = 0$ to 0.030 at $\alpha/\eta = 1$, 0.042 at $\alpha/\eta = 2$, and 0.053 at $\alpha/\eta = 3$. Therefore, if we use the benchmark values for the other parameters and assume that no more than half the total capital stock constitutes collateral for foreign borrowing $(\alpha/\eta \leq 1)$, the predicted convergence coefficient falls within the range 0.015 to 0.030 per year. This range accords well with empirical estimates.[21]

20. If $\alpha = 0$, so that no capital constitutes collateral, then $\epsilon = \eta$ and β from equation (3.60) corresponds to the value from equation (3.55) for a closed economy (with capital share equal to η). If $\eta = 0$, so that all capital serves as collateral, then $\epsilon = 0$ and β from equation (3.60) becomes infinite, as in the open economy with perfect capital mobility.

21. Barro, Mankiw, and Sala-i-Martin (1995) generalize the production function in equation (3.53) from a Cobb–Douglas form to a constant-elasticity-of-substitution (CES) specification. The degree of substitutability affects β—it turns out that β is higher if $\hat{k}$ and $\hat{h}$ are poorer substitutes in production. The main conclusion, however, is that β is confined to the narrow interval (0.014, 0.035) for the usual benchmark parameters if $\alpha/\eta \leq 1$. Thus the theoretical predictions accord well with the empirical estimates of β even in this more general case.

The transition to the steady state involves a monotonic increase in human capital per effective worker, $\hat{h}$, from its initial value, $\hat{h}(0)$, to its steady-state value, $\hat{h}^*$. Equation (3.57) implies that the growth rate of $\hat{y}$ is ϵ times the growth rate of $\hat{h}$, where ϵ is between 0 and 1. The ratio h/y therefore rises steadily during the transition. Recall, however, that equation (3.56) implies that the ratio k/y is constant. Therefore, $\hat{k}$ grows at the same rate as $\hat{y}$, and the ratio of human to physical capital, h/k, increases during the transition. Note that, although physical capital serves fully as collateral, $\hat{k}$ nevertheless rises gradually toward its steady-state value, $\hat{k}^*$. The reason is the constraint of domestic saving on the accumulation of human capital and the complementarity between $\hat{h}$ and $\hat{k}$ in the production function. When $\hat{h}$ is low, the schedule for the marginal product of physical capital is low; hence, $\hat{k} < \hat{k}^*$ follows even though domestic producers can finance all acquisitions of physical capital with foreign borrowing. The gradual increase of human capital impacts positively on the marginal product of physical capital and leads thereby to an expansion of $\hat{k}$.

Foreign borrowing occurs only on loans secured by physical capital, and the interest rate on these loans is pegged at the world rate, r. We can also allow for a domestic credit market, although the setting with a representative domestic agent ensures that, in equilibrium, each person will not borrow. For loans that are secured by physical capital, the shadow interest rate on the domestic market must also be r. If we assume that human capital and raw labor do not serve domestically as collateral, the shadow interest rate on the domestic market with these forms of security is infinity (or at least high enough to drive desired borrowing to zero), just as it is on the world market.

We might assume instead that human capital and raw labor serve as collateral for domestic borrowing but not for foreign borrowing. This situation would apply if the legal system enforces loan contracts based on labor income when the creditor is domestic, but not when the creditor is foreign. In this case, the shadow interest rate on domestic lending, collateralized by labor income, equals the net marginal product of human capital. This net marginal product begins at a relatively high value (corresponding to the low starting stock, $\hat{h}[0]$) and then falls gradually toward the steady-state value, r. Thus the transition features a decrease in the spread between this kind of domestic interest rate and the world rate, r. An example would be the curb market for informal lending in South Korea (see Collins and Park, 1989, p. 353). The spread between curb-market interest rates and world interest rates was 30 to 40 percentage points in the 1960s and 1970s but fell by the mid-1980s to about 15 percentage points.

Another implication of the model is that, despite the existence of international borrowing and lending, the convergence properties of gross national product and gross domestic product are the same. As noted before, the net factor income from abroad (per unit of effective labor) is $-(r+\delta)\cdot\hat{k} = -\alpha\hat{y}$. Therefore,

$$\text{GNP (per unit of effective labor)} = \hat{y} - \alpha\hat{y} = \hat{y}\cdot(1-\alpha) \tag{3.61}$$

Since GNP is proportional to GDP, which corresponds to $\hat{y}$, the convergence rates for GNP and GDP are the same. This result suggests that data sets that involve GDP are likely to generate similar rates of convergence as those that involve GNP or measures of national income. Some confirmation of this prediction comes from the study of the U.S. states by Barro and Sala-i-Martin (1991): the rates of convergence are similar for gross state product per capita and state personal income per capita.

The model implies that the gap between GDP and GNP would be large for a credit-constrained open economy: roughly 20–25 percent of GDP for the parameter values assumed before. The current-account deficit, which equals the change in physical capital, is correspondingly large. It is unusual to find developing countries that have values this high for the GDP-GNP gap and the current-account deficit.[22] We can reconcile the theory with this observation by noting, first, that many developing countries are insufficiently productive to be credit constrained and, second, that the collateral for international debt may be substantially narrower than physical capital. If the coefficient α were less than 0.3, the predicted ratios for the GDP-GNP gap and the current-account deficit would be correspondingly smaller.

The introduction of a credit constraint removes some of the counterfactual predictions from the open-economy model with perfect capital mobility; in particular, the speeds of convergence for the capital stock and output are no longer infinite. Consider, however, what happens if countries differ in their degree of impatience, as represented by the combination of preference parameters $\rho_i + \theta_i x$. With perfect capital markets, we found before that all but the most patient country followed a path in which $\hat{c}$ approached 0. In the model with a credit constraint, the prediction is instead that all but the most patient country will eventually reach a situation in which the residents are effectively constrained on the international credit market. This credit constraint implies that $\hat{c}$ approaches a positive constant, a more appealing asymptote than 0. The disturbing result, however, is that all countries except the most patient one must eventually be credit constrained. To avoid this result we have to consider models in which the effective rate of time preference, $\rho_i + \theta_i x$, is variable. A later section considers models of this type.

Adjustment Costs in the Accumulation of Human Capital One potential problem with the model outlined in this section is that the speed of convergence for the economies that are not constrained in the international credit markets should be infinite. Duczynski (2000) computes net external assets for 113 countries and 50 U.S. states and finds that 21 countries and roughly half of the U.S. states have positive values, so it is hard to argue that they

22. One counterexample is Singapore: its current-account deficit was between 10 and 20 percent of GDP throughout the 1970s (International Monetary Fund, 1991).

are borrowing constrained. The speed of convergence of these economies, however, is not infinity. This evidence suggests that the credit-constraint mechanism outlined in the previous section is not sufficient to explain the slow convergence found in the data.

A potential alternative or complementary solution is the existence of adjustment costs, which we discussed before for a closed economy. If we again distinguish between physical and human capital, we anticipate that adjustment costs would be especially important for increases in human capital through the process of education. The learning experience fundamentally takes time, and attempts to accelerate the educational process are likely to encounter rapidly diminishing rates of return. To capture these effects, we now construct a model with perfect international capital mobility in which adjustment costs affect only the accumulation of human capital.

Firms and individuals have perfect access to world financial markets, and the interest rate equals the constant r. Consumption growth is still given by

$$\dot{c}/c = (1/\theta) \cdot (r - \rho)$$

Imagine that the production function is Cobb–Douglas in physical and human capital:

$$Y = AK^{\alpha} H^{\eta} \hat{L}^{1-\alpha-\eta} \tag{3.62}$$

Assume that physical capital can be invested without installation costs and that, for every unit of human-capital investment, firms have to pay $\phi(I_h/H)$ units of output. Following the assumptions of section 3.2, $\phi(0) = 0$, $\phi'(\cdot) > 0$, and $2\phi'(\cdot) + \frac{I_h}{H} \cdot \phi''(\cdot) > 0$. Firms maximize the present discounted value of future net cash flows:

$$\max \int_0^{\infty} e^{-\bar{r}(t)\cdot t} \cdot \left\{ AK^{\alpha} H^{\eta} \hat{L}^{1-\alpha-\eta} - wL - I_k - I_h \cdot \left[1 + \phi\left(\frac{I_h}{H}\right)\right]\right\} \cdot dt \tag{3.63}$$

subject to the two accumulation constraints

$$\dot{K} = I_k - \delta K \tag{3.64}$$

and

$$\dot{H} = I_h - \delta H \tag{3.65}$$

The Hamiltonian for this program is

$$J = e^{-\bar{r}(t)t} \cdot \left\{ AK^{\alpha} H^{\eta} \hat{L}^{1-\alpha-\eta} - wL - I_k - I_h \cdot \left[1 + \phi\left(\frac{I_h}{H}\right)\right]\right\} + \upsilon_k \cdot (I_k - \delta K) + \upsilon_h \cdot (I_h - \delta H) \tag{3.66}$$

where υ_k is the shadow price associated with physical capital and υ_h is the shadow price associated with human capital. Following the analysis of section 2.3, we can define current-value shadow prices, $q_k = e^{rt} \cdot \upsilon_k$ and $q_h = e^{rt} \cdot \upsilon_h$. After finding the first-order conditions[23] and using the current-value shadow prices, we find that $q_k = 1$ at all points in time, which implies

$$\alpha \cdot (\hat{y}/\hat{k}) = r + \delta \tag{3.67}$$

In other words, the marginal product of physical capital (which is the capital good that is not subject to adjustment costs) equals the interest rate plus depreciation. This equality implies a one-to-one relation between $\hat{k}$ and $\hat{h}$, given by

$$\hat{k} = (\hat{h})^{\eta/(1-\alpha)} \cdot \left(\frac{\alpha A}{r + \delta}\right)^{1/(1-\alpha)} \tag{3.68}$$

The first-order condition with respect to I_h implies

$$q_h = 1 + \phi\left(\frac{\hat{\imath}_h}{\hat{h}}\right) + \frac{\hat{\imath}_h}{\hat{h}} \cdot \phi'\left(\frac{\hat{\imath}_h}{\hat{h}}\right) \tag{3.69}$$

where $\hat{\imath}_h = I_h/\hat{L}$ is investment in human capital per effective unit of labor. This expression can be inverted to express the human-capital investment rate as a monotonic function of the shadow price of human capital, q_h:

$$\frac{\hat{\imath}_h}{\hat{h}} = \psi(q_h) \tag{3.70}$$

with $\psi'(\cdot) > 0$. We can substitute this result into the constraint for the accumulation of human capital to get

$$\frac{d\hat{h}}{dt} = \hat{\imath}_h - (\delta + n + x) \cdot \hat{h} = \psi(q_h) \cdot \hat{h} - (\delta + n + x) \cdot \hat{h} \tag{3.71}$$

23. The first-order conditions with respect to I_k, K, I_h, and H are, respectively,

(i) $\nu_k = e^{-\bar{r}(t)t}$

(ii) $-\dot{\nu}_k = e^{-\bar{r}(t)t} \cdot \alpha \cdot (\hat{y}/\hat{k}) - \nu_k \delta$

(iii) $e^{-\bar{r}(t)t} \cdot \left(1 + \phi(\cdot) + \frac{\hat{\imath}_h}{\hat{h}} \cdot \phi'(\cdot)\right) = \nu_h$

(iv) $-\dot{\nu}_h = e^{-\bar{r}(t)t} \cdot \eta \cdot (\hat{y}/\hat{h}) - \nu_h \cdot \delta$

Notice that (i) implies $q_k = 1$ and, therefore, $\dot{q}_k = 0$. Use this result and (ii) to get $\alpha \cdot (y/k) = r + \delta$.

The first-order condition with respect to $\hat{h}$ provides a dynamic equation for q_h:

$$\dot{q}_h = (r + \delta) \cdot q_h - \eta \cdot (\hat{y}/\hat{h}) - [\psi(q_h)]^2 \cdot \phi'[\psi(q_h)] \tag{3.72}$$

Use equation (3.68) to get

$$\dot{q}_h = (r + \delta) \cdot q_h - \tilde{A} \cdot h^{-\frac{1-\alpha-\eta}{1-\alpha}} - [\psi(q_h)]^2 \cdot \phi'[\psi(q_h)] \tag{3.73}$$

where $\tilde{A}$ is a function of constants.

Equations (3.71) and (3.73) form a system of two ordinary differential equations. The phase diagram is displayed in figure 3.4. Notice that the $\frac{d\hat{h}}{dt} = 0$ locus is a horizontal line at $q_h^* = 1 + \phi(\delta + n + x) + (\delta + n + x) \cdot \phi'(\delta + n + x)$. The arrows above this locus point east, and arrows below it point west. The $\dot{q}_h$ locus is upward sloping for high values of q_h but is downward sloping when it crosses the $\frac{d\hat{h}}{dt} = 0$ line. The arrows to the left of this schedule point north. The system is saddle-path stable, and the stable arm is downward sloping. If the economy starts with too little human capital (that is, to the left of the steady state), the system does not instantaneously jump to the steady state; that is, the speed of convergence is not infinity. Instead, the economy follows the slow process of convergence along the stable arm. The reason is that a jump to the steady state would entail infinite investment in human capital in one instant. The corresponding adjustment cost would be extraordinarily large

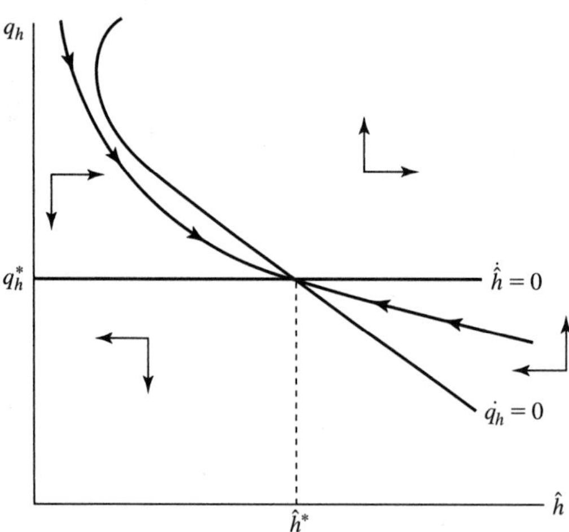

Figure 3.4
Phase Diagram for a model with physical and human capital, with adjustment costs in human capital accumulation. The phase diagram is shown in (q_h, h) space. The $\dot{h} = 0$ locus is a horizontal line at $q_h^* = 1 + \phi(\delta + n + x) + (\delta + n + x) \cdot \phi'(\delta + n + x)$. The $\dot{q}_h = 0$ locus is downward sloping around the steady state. The system is saddle-path stable and the stable arm is downward sloping.

and would therefore not be optimal. Hence, the accumulation of human capital is gradual, and the economy converges slowly to the steady state. As h increases, the stock of physical capital grows according to equation (3.68). It follows that the level of GDP also converges slowly.

Kremer and Thomson (1998) analyze an analogous model in which the production function depends on the human capital of the young and the old. They argue that these two human-capital factors are complements (think of a football team, where the human capital of the "old," the coach, is a complement to the human capital of the "young," the players). In this context, if the human capital of the first generation is small, then, even if capital is perfectly mobile, young persons will not borrow to increase their stock of human capital to the steady-state level, because the young's productivity will not be very high if the old have little human capital. Hence, the process of human-capital accumulation is gradual. The mechanism proposed by Kremer and Thompson (1998) amounts to introducing adjustment costs in the accumulation of human capital.

3.5 Variations in Preference Parameters

We now consider whether some of the disturbing implications from the open-economy Ramsey model can be eliminated if we allow the preference parameters, ρ_i and θ_i, to vary. The idea, which comes from Uzawa (1968), is that the rate of time preference and the willingness to substitute consumption over time may depend on the level of a household's wealth or consumption and may therefore change as a_i and c_i change.

Return now to the open-economy model without credit restraints. A key property of this model is that countries with high values of the time-preference term, $\rho_i + \theta_i x > r$, follow a path in which $\hat{a}_i(t)$ becomes negative and $\hat{c}_i(t)$ declines toward zero. One way to avoid this unappealing result is to assume that $\rho_i + \theta_i x$ declines as $\hat{a}_i(t)$ and $\hat{c}_i(t)$ fall. In other words, countries or individuals would have to become more patient as they become poorer.

Uzawa (1968) obtains the desired result by assuming that ρ_i is a positive function of $c_i(t)$. This mechanism is unappealing, however, because it is counterintuitive that people would raise their rates of time preference as their levels of consumption rise.[24]

We could also get the desired result by assuming that people become less willing to substitute intertemporally—that is, θ_i increases—as the level of consumption rises. The usual assumption is, however, the opposite. We showed in equation (2.8) that the effective

24. Mulligan (1993) argues that if the degree of altruism depends on the amount of time parents spend with their children, then people with high wages will be less altruistic because the opportunity cost of spending time with their children is high. It follows that rich people will have high discount rates.

time-preference term involves the negative of the elasticity of marginal utility, $-u''(c) \cdot c/u'(c)$. In the specification that we have used thus far, the magnitude of this elasticity is constant and equal to θ_i. The form of the utility function is sometimes modified, however, to exhibit a variable elasticity by allowing for a subsistence level of consumption:

$$u(c_i) = \frac{(c_i - \overline{c}_i)^{(1-\theta_i)} - 1}{(1 - \theta_i)} \tag{3.74}$$

where $\overline{c}_i > 0$ is the constant subsistence level. (This form is referred to as Stone–Geary, after Stone, 1954, and Geary, 1950–51.) Equation (3.74) implies that the magnitude of the elasticity of marginal utility is $\theta_i c_i/(c_i - \overline{c}_i)$, which equals θ_i when $\overline{c}_i = 0$ but is decreasing in c_i when $\overline{c}_i > 0$. This revised formulation of utility implies, accordingly, that the effective time-preference term declines with $c_i(t)$; that is, the term moves in the wrong direction from the perspective of resolving the difficulties in the open-economy model.

More appealing results emerge from models that assume constant parameters ρ_i and θ_i for each country (or family) but that allow for effects from finite horizons. The first models of this type, due to Samuelson (1958) and Diamond (1965), assumed that people lived a fixed number of discrete periods, such as childhood and adulthood. The period of adulthood for one generation overlapped with the period of childhood for the next; hence, the customary designation overlapping-generations (OLG) model. Individuals in these models have finite horizons—because they live for only two periods and do not, by assumption, care about the welfare of their descendants—but the economy lasts forever. Although the OLG framework captures the effects of finite horizons, one shortcoming of this framework is that the equilibrium conditions turn out to be too cumbersome to permit analytical solutions of many of the comparative-statics exercises that we would like to consider.

Blanchard (1985) retained the essence of the finite-horizon idea in a more tractable framework by assuming that people die off randomly in accordance with a Poisson process. For present purposes, the key finding in his model is that *aggregate* consumption behaves as if each individual's time-preference term were positively related to $a_i(t)$. The results come, however, from the aggregation over individuals who are heterogeneous with respect to age (and, hence, with respect to assets and consumption) and not from variations in preference parameters for individuals. To get these results, we first set up Blanchard's framework, then apply it to a closed economy, and finally use it to extend our analysis of an open economy. The appendix (section 3.8) contains an analysis of related OLG models.

3.6 Economic Growth in a Model with Finite Horizons

3.6.1 Choices in a Model with Finite Horizons

In the previous analysis, we assumed that family dynasties lasted forever so that households planned with an infinite horizon. We now want to allow for the possibility that the dynasty would terminate in finite time. This termination could reflect the death of adults who leave no descendants and therefore do not care about matters beyond their death. Alternatively, it could reflect the chance that finite-lived parents reach a position in which they are not connected to their children through a pattern of operative intergenerational transfers.

We think of "death" as the termination of a family dynasty, although this death need not correspond to anyone's literally dying. Let p be the probability of death per unit of time, so that a person (or household) born at time j is alive at time $t \geq j$ with probability $e^{-p\cdot(t-j)}$. A key assumption, which makes the aggregation tractable, is that p is invariant with age. This assumption is unrealistic if we think of the literal death of an individual but may be less troublesome in the context of the termination of a dynasty.

The probability of being dead at time t equals $1-e^{-p\cdot(t-j)}$, so that the probability density for death at time t is the derivative of this expression, $pe^{-p\cdot(t-j)}$. The expected lifetime can be calculated from this probability density as $1/p$. Thus a higher p lowers the expected lifetime and makes the finite-horizon effect more important.

We assume, as before, that population grows at the constant rate n, so that $L(t) = e^{nt}$ is the total population. The size of a cohort born at time t must then be $(p+n)\cdot e^{nt}$; that is, enough new people or households are born to replace those who die, pe^{nt}, and to provide for net growth, ne^{nt}.

The riskless interest rate on assets is again $r(t)$. We have to consider the disposition of assets for people or households who die. In the infinite-life model, these assets implicitly go to descendants in the form of intergenerational transfers. These transfers are motivated by altruistic linkages that are strong enough to keep people away from the corner solution of zero transfers. But the whole idea of "dying" in the finite-horizon model is that these linkages are not operative. We could assume that the assets go as unintended bequests to children or as unintended transfers to society as a whole. But if people are really unconcerned with events that occur after their deaths—which is the central idea in finite-horizon models—then they could do better by using markets for annuities. Also, if we allow people to die in debt without descendants to assume the debt, then lenders would require a rate of interest above r to cover the possibility that the borrower will die.

We follow Yaari (1965) and Blanchard (1985) by assuming that all loans are secured by life insurance. If a person lives, he or she pays the interest rate r plus the life insurance premium on the loan. If the person dies in debt, the life insurance pays off the loan. Because the probability of death per unit of time is p, the necessary premium is p. That is, the total rate paid on loans is $r + p$ if someone lives. From the perspective of a life-insurance company, the premium at rate p just covers the expected payouts on policies for borrowers who die. Similarly, lenders can hold annuities that pay $r + p$ if the person lives and zero if the person dies. From the standpoint of an annuity company, the extra payout at rate p just balances the expected proceeds from the people who die. From the perspective of individuals with finite horizons, the rate of return on annuities (conditional on survival) of $r + p$ is more attractive than the riskless rate of return, r. Therefore, all assets would be held in the form of annuities.[25]

Since life insurance and annuity markets are fully exploited by a large population, the total of assets released by people who die, $p \cdot a(t)$, coincides with the extra return (above the riskless rate r) for the people who live. Insurance and annuity companies therefore break even, and we have accounted fully for the disposition of assets at death. It also follows that the relevant rate of return for surviving individuals—whether lenders or borrowers—is $r + p$, rather than r.

Let $c(j, v)$ be the consumption and $a(j, v)$ the assets at time v for a person born at time $j \leq v$. We assume that productivity is independent of age, so that the wage rate, $w(v)$, is the same for all $j \leq v$. Starting from the current time t, the household maximizes expected utility, given by

$$E_t U = E_t \left[\int_t^{\infty} \log[c(j, v)] \cdot e^{-\rho(v-t)} \, dv \right] \tag{3.75}$$

where we have assumed $u(c) = \log(c)$, which corresponds to $\theta = 1$ in equation (2.9). Although log utility is convenient, we can readily generalize the steady-state results to cases in which $\theta \neq 1$. (The transitional analysis is feasible, but cumbersome, if $\theta \neq 1$.)

The formulation in equation (3.75) differs from that in equation (2.1) of the Ramsey model by the omission of the population term, e^{nt}, as a multiple on per capita utility. The assumption in this finite-horizon model is that people give no weight to their descendants in the utility function or in the budget constraint, which we will consider in the next paragraph. Since $e^{-p(v-t)}$ is the probability of being alive at time v, conditioned on being alive at the

25. Economists sometimes dismiss this possibility by arguing that annuities are quantitatively not important in the real world, although private pensions and government pensions through social security are common. The limited use of annuities may, in any case, be an indication that the infinite-horizon model, which assumes altruistic linkages across generations, is a satisfactory framework. In this model, the demand for annuities is small, and the observed quantity of annuities would also be small.

earlier time t, the expected utility becomes

$$E_t U = \int_t^{\infty} \log[c(j, v)] \cdot e^{-(\rho+p)\cdot(v-t)}\, dv \qquad (3.76)$$

Thus $\rho + p$ is the effective rate of time preference in the context of an uncertain lifetime.

The flow budget constraint for the household is now

$$da(j, v)/dv = [r(v) + p] \cdot a(j, v) + w(v) - c(j, v) \qquad (3.77)$$

Each household maximizes expected utility in equation (3.76), subject to equation (3.77) and to the amount of initial assets, $a(j, j)$. The first-order condition for consumption is the same as that found before (equation [2.10] with $\theta = 1$):

$$\frac{dc(j, t)/dt}{c(j, t)} = r - \rho \qquad (3.78)$$

Note that the probability of death, p, cancels out because it impacts equally on the effective time-preference rate, $\rho + p$, and the rate of return, $r + p$.

The transversality condition is now

$$\lim_{v\to\infty} \left[e^{-[\bar{r}(t,v)+p]\cdot(v-t)} \cdot a(j, v)\right] = 0 \qquad (3.79)$$

where $\bar{r}(t, v)$ is the "average" interest rate between times t and v (see equation [2.12], which refers to the period between 0 and t). Equations (3.77) and (3.79) imply that the household's lifetime budget constraint is

$$\int_t^{\infty} c(j, v) \cdot e^{-[\bar{r}(t,v)+p]\cdot(v-t)}\, dv = a(j, t) + \tilde{w}(t) \qquad (3.80)$$

where $\tilde{w}(t) = \int_t^{\infty} w(v) \cdot e^{-[\bar{r}(t,v)+p]\cdot(v-t)}\, dv$ is the present value of wage income. Equation (3.80) corresponds to equation (2.13) in the infinite-horizon model.

We can also use equations (3.78) and (3.80) to determine consumption as a function of "wealth":

$$c(j, t) = (\rho + p) \cdot [a(j, t) + \tilde{w}(t)] \qquad (3.81)$$

which corresponds to equations (2.14) and (2.15) (with $\theta = 1$) in the infinite-horizon model. The simplification from log utility is that the marginal propensity to consume out of wealth is the constant $\rho + p$.

The aggregate variables, $C(t)$, $A(t)$, and $\tilde{W}(t)$, come from addition across the cohorts, indexed by the time of birth, $j \le t$. Each cohort is weighted by its size, which equals the initial size, $(p+n) \cdot e^{nj}$, multiplied by the fraction, $e^{-p\cdot(t-j)}$, who remain alive at time $t \geq j$.[26] Therefore, aggregate consumption and assets are given by

$$C(t) = \int_{-\infty}^{t} c(j,t) \cdot (p+n) \cdot e^{nj} e^{-p(t-j)}\, dj \tag{3.82}$$

$$A(t) = \int_{-\infty}^{t} a(j,t) \cdot (p+n) \cdot e^{nj} e^{-p(t-j)}\, dj \tag{3.83}$$

Since wage rates are independent of age, the aggregate of the present value of wage income is

$$\tilde{W}(t) = \tilde{w}(t) \cdot e^{nt} = e^{nt} \cdot \int_{t}^{\infty} w(v) \cdot e^{-[\bar{r}(t,v)+p]\cdot(v-t)}\, dv \tag{3.84}$$

Since the propensity to consume out of wealth in equation (3.81) is $\rho + p$, which is independent of age, j, the aggregate relationship is the same as the individual one:

$$C(t) = (\rho + p) \cdot [A(t) + \tilde{W}(t)] \tag{3.85}$$

We want to use equation (3.82) to compute the aggregate analogue to equation (3.78), which determines the change over time in individual consumption. The change over time in aggregate consumption, $\dot{C}$, depends on the change over time in aggregate wealth, $\dot{A} + d\tilde{W}/dt$.

We can calculate $\dot{A}$ by differentiating equation (3.83) with respect to t. The result is

$$\dot{A} = r(t) \cdot A(t) + w(t) \cdot e^{nt} - C(t) \tag{3.86}$$

where $w(t) \cdot e^{nt}$ is aggregate wages paid at time t. The derivation of equation (3.86) uses the individual budget constraint in equation (3.77) and the condition $a(j, j) = 0$, that is, individuals are born with zero assets. Note that the aggregate equation corresponds to the individual one in equation (3.77), except that the rate of return on total assets is r, whereas that on individual assets (for someone who survives) is $r + p$.

We can also compute the change in $\tilde{W}$ by differentiating equation (3.84) with respect to t. The result is

$$d\tilde{W}/dt = [r(t) + p + n] \cdot \tilde{W}(t) - w(t) \cdot e^{nt} \tag{3.87}$$

The term on the far right equals aggregate wages, which are effectively the dividend paid on the asset stock $\tilde{W}(t)$. The first term on the right reflects the discounting of individual

26. We are assuming that the age structure of the population is always at its steady-state distribution. However, in the present context, the age structure does not matter because the probability of dying, p, and the wage rate, w, are independent of age.

wages at the rate $r(t) + p$ (because wages vanish when a person dies) and the growth of population at the rate n.

We can use equations (3.81)–(3.87) to determine the change over time in aggregate consumption, $\dot{C}$. The result, expressed in terms of the growth rate of per capita consumption, is[27]

$$\dot{c}/c = r(t) - \rho - (p + n) \cdot (\rho + p) \cdot a(t)/c(t) \tag{3.88}$$

Note that $c(t)$ refers to aggregate consumption divided by aggregate population and not to the consumption of a surviving individual. The evolution of a surviving individual's consumption, $c(j, t)$, is given by equation (3.78).

The key new element in equation (3.88) is the term on the far right, $(p + n) \cdot (\rho + p) \cdot a(t)/c(t)$. Since $\rho + p$ is the propensity to consume out of wealth, $(\rho + p) \cdot a(t)$ is the consumption per person associated with $a(t)$. New people enter the economy at the rate $p + n$. Because these new people arrive with zero assets, the inflow of these people lowers the average consumption per person by the amount $(p + n) \cdot (\rho + p) \cdot a(t)$. Finally, the division by $c(t)$ gives the contribution of this term to the reduction in the growth rate of consumption per person, $\dot{c}/c$.

Note from the discussion that the crucial feature is the arrival of new persons (with zero assets) and not the departure of old persons. Thus, as Weil (1989) points out, the main results go through with infinite lifetimes ($p = 0$) if new people are born ($n > 0$). It is, however, crucial that the old people not care about the new ones in the manner of the altruistic linkages assumed in the infinite-horizon framework of chapter 2. Thus, we can think of the new persons as unloved children and immigrants (as in Weil, 1989). We deal explicitly with immigrants in chapter 9.

3.6.2 The Finite-Horizon Model of a Closed Economy

We consider again the model with one type of capital, k. For a closed economy, $\hat{a} = \hat{k}$, $f'(\hat{k}) = r + \delta$, and $\hat{w} = f(\hat{k}) - \hat{k} \cdot f'(\hat{k})$. The formula that determines $\dot{\hat{k}}$ is then the same as that in the infinite-horizon model (equation [2.23]):

$$\dot{\hat{k}} = f(\hat{k}) - \hat{c} - (x + n + \delta) \cdot \hat{k} \tag{3.89}$$

Equation (3.88) and the conditions $\hat{a} = \hat{k}$ and $r = f'(\hat{k}) - \delta$ imply

$$\dot{\hat{c}}/\hat{c} = f'(\hat{k}) - (\delta + \rho + x) - (p + n) \cdot (\rho + p) \cdot \hat{k}/\hat{c} \tag{3.90}$$

27. For $\theta \neq 1$, this result turns out to generalize when $r(t)$ equals the constant r to

$$\dot{c}/c = (1/\theta) \cdot (r - \rho) - (1/\theta) \cdot [\rho + \theta p - (1 - \theta) \cdot r] \cdot (p + n) \cdot a(t)/c(t)$$

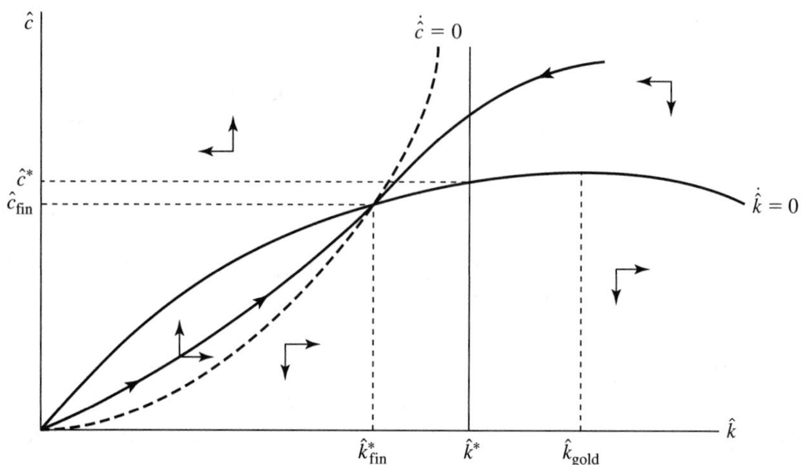

Figure 3.5
Dynamics in a finite-horizon closed economy. The $\dot{\hat{k}} = 0$ locus displays the usual inverse U shape. The $\dot{\hat{c}} = 0$ locus goes through the origin, slopes upward, and asymptotes vertically at $\hat{k} = \hat{k}^*$. The shape of the stable arm and, therefore, the transitional dynamics of the model are similar to those of the Ramsey model.

Figure 3.5 shows the phase diagram for $\hat{k}$ and $\hat{c}$. The concave solid curve, which corresponds to $\dot{\hat{k}} = 0$, is the same as the curve for the infinite-horizon model in figure 2.1. The solid vertical line at $\hat{k}^*$, where $f'(\hat{k}^*) = \delta + \rho + x$, is the steady-state value in the infinite-horizon model (if $\theta = 1$). The term that involves $\hat{k}/\hat{c}$ in equation (3.90) effectively adds to the time-preference rate, ρ, if $p + n > 0$. The dashed curve in figure 3.5, which shows the locus for $\dot{\hat{c}} = 0$, therefore lies everywhere to the left of the vertical line. As the ratio of $\hat{c}$ to $\hat{k}$ rises along the dashed curve, the size of the term that involves $\hat{k}/\hat{c}$ diminishes toward 0; therefore, the dashed curve asymptotically approaches the vertical line.

The steady-state values for the finite-horizon model of a closed economy, determined at the intersection of the solid and dashed curves, are denoted $\hat{k}^*_{\text{fin}}$ and $\hat{c}^*_{\text{fin}}$ in figure 3.5. The important observation is that the higher effective rate of time preference leads to a higher marginal product of capital and therefore to a lower ratio of capital to effective labor, that is, $\hat{k}^*_{\text{fin}} < \hat{k}^*$. Correspondingly, the steady-state interest rate is higher than that for the infinite-horizon economy, $r^*_{\text{fin}} > r^* = \rho + x$,[28] and consumption per effective worker is lower, $\hat{c}^*_{\text{fin}} < \hat{c}^*$.

28. We can use the formula in note 27 to show that this result still holds if $\theta \neq 1$, in which case $r^* = \rho + \theta x$. It is also possible to show that $r^*_{\text{fin}} < \rho + \theta x + p + n$.

The transition from an initial ratio, $\hat{k}(0)$, to $\hat{k}^*_{\text{fin}}$ is similar to that in the infinite-horizon model. If $\hat{k}(0) < \hat{k}^*_{\text{fin}}$, $\hat{k}$ rises monotonically along the solid curve marked by the arrows in figure 3.5. The dynamics of the other variables—$\hat{c}$, r, and the growth rates of $\hat{k}$, $\hat{y}$, and $\hat{c}$—is also similar to that in the infinite-horizon model.

Since $\hat{k}^*_{\text{fin}} < \hat{k}^*$, it follows that $\hat{k}^*_{\text{fin}} < \hat{k}_{\text{gold}}$—see figure 3.5.[29] Hence, the asymptotic behavior of $\hat{k}$ in the finite-horizon model of a closed economy does not exhibit the kind of inefficient oversaving that can arise in the Solow–Swan model with an arbitrary saving rate. Diamond (1965) showed that oversaving can arise in a two-period overlapping-generations model of a closed economy. As our results (based on Blanchard, 1985) have shown, the feature of the Diamond model that generates the possibility of oversaving is not the finite horizons of individuals. Rather, the key difference from the model that we have just analyzed is the assumed life-cycle pattern of wage incomes. In the Diamond version of the OLG model, wages are positive in the first (working) period and zero in the second (retirement) period. Thus the model assumes that wage income declines sharply over the life cycle, whereas the finite-horizon model that we have been considering assumes that wage income is invariant with age. A declining pattern of wage income with respect to age motivates additional saving; inefficient oversaving can emerge if this effect is very strong.

We can extend the finite-horizon model that we analyzed before to allow for a decline in labor productivity over the life cycle. (See Blanchard, 1985, for an analysis of this situation.) If labor productivity and, hence, wage rates decline with age at the rate ω, equation (3.90) is modified to[30]

$$\dot{\hat{c}}/\hat{c} = f'(\hat{k}) - (\delta + \rho + x - \omega) - (p + n + \omega) \cdot (\rho + p) \cdot \hat{k}(t)/\hat{c}(t) \tag{3.91}$$

The direct effect of ω in equation (3.91) subtracts from ρ and thereby effectively lowers the rate of time preference. Because of this encouragement to saving, $\hat{k}^*_{\text{fin}} > \hat{k}^*$ applies if ω is high enough. Moreover, for a still higher value of ω, the steady state exhibits inefficient oversaving: $\hat{k}^*_{\text{fin}} > \hat{k}_{\text{gold}}$.

Although inefficient oversaving is possible in the finite-horizon economy if wage income declines over the life cycle—that is, for sufficiently high ω—it is unclear in practice that we should even treat ω as positive. If we begin at the time of an individual's first job—say, age 18 or 21—then wage income *rises* substantially with age (and experience) for about 25 years

29. We used the condition $\rho > n$ to ensure $\hat{k}^* < \hat{k}_{\text{gold}}$ in the infinite-horizon model. We are still assuming that $\rho > n$ holds in the finite-horizon case.

30. We are again assuming that the age structure of the population corresponds to its steady-state distribution. In the present context, changes in the age distribution would matter because they would affect the distribution of labor productivities and wage rates. For a given distribution of ages and, hence, labor productivities, the aggregate quantity of effective labor input will be proportional to $e^{(n+x)t}$, just as in our other models. Thus, $\hat{k}$ can be measured as $Ke^{-(n+x)t}$.

and is relatively flat for the next 20–25 years (see Murphy and Welch, 1990, p. 207). Wage income then declines dramatically for the roughly 10–15-year span of retirement. Thus, the two-period overlapping-generations model ignores the interval of rising wage incomes and also errs in assuming that the retirement period is as long as the working span. Each of the errors works in the direction of overstating the life-cycle incentive to save.

To get a complete picture, we also have to decide how to treat the first 18–21 years of life that correspond to childhood and schooling. If we treat children as independent households, these 18–21 years feature wage incomes that are sharply below the lifetime average. The shortfall of current from expected future wage income impacts negatively on the aggregate desire to save; presumably, this effect would show up as children borrowing from their parents to finance consumption.

We can reasonably argue that minor children should not be treated as separate households.[31] But then the period of low wage income for children up to age 18 or 21 translates, for given parental wage income, into low per capita wage income of the family when the family contains dependent children. Therefore, the low level of children's wage income motivates parents to save less than otherwise during an interval of parental ages that corresponds typically to middle age. Thus this effect combines with the influence of rising wage income of adults during much of their working span to offset the positive effect on saving from the existence of the retirement period.

The upshot of this discussion is that $\omega \approx 0$—a flat profile of the family's per capita wage income—may not be a bad first approximation for the purpose of analyzing the aggregate willingness to save. In that case, the analysis rules out the possibility of oversaving in the finite-horizon model of a closed economy.

3.6.3 The Finite-Horizon Model of an Open Economy

Consider now the finite-horizon model of an open economy with one type of capital, k, and no constraint on borrowing. We omit the country subscript i for convenience. If the world interest rate, $r(t)$, equals the constant r, then the ratio of capital to effective labor in the domestic country equals the constant $(\hat{k}^*)_{\text{open}}$, where $f'[(\hat{k}^*)_{\text{open}}] = r + \delta$. Hence, this model still implies an infinite speed of convergence for $\hat{k}$ and $\hat{y}$. The behavior of $\hat{c}$ and $\hat{a}$ will, however, be more reasonable than before.

Equation (3.50) gives the change in assets:

$$\begin{aligned}\dot{\hat{a}} &= f[(\hat{k}^*)_{\text{open}}] - (r+\delta)\cdot[(\hat{k}^*)_{\text{open}} - \hat{a}] - (x+n+\delta)\cdot\hat{a} - \hat{c} \\ &= (\hat{w}^*)_{\text{open}} + (r-x-n)\cdot\hat{a} - \hat{c} \qquad (3.92)\end{aligned}$$

31. This argument is, however, more compelling in the infinite-horizon model in which parents' altruistic motives lead them to provide for their children's consumption. In the finite-horizon model, in which parents apparently do not care about their children, the rationale for parental support of minor children is harder to understand.

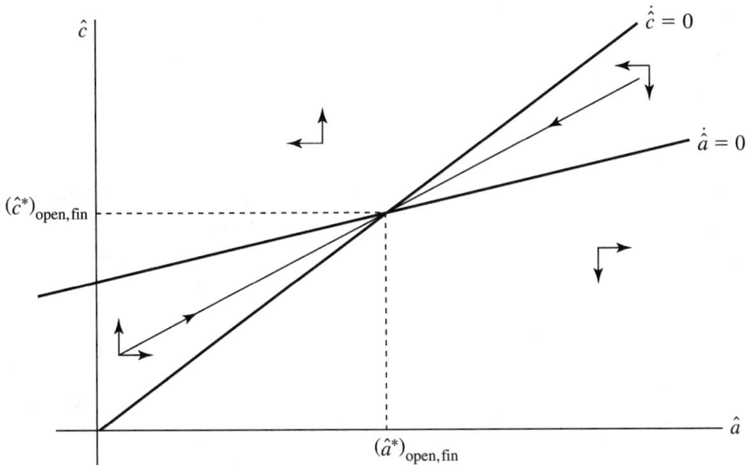

Figure 3.6
The phase diagram for a finite-horizon open economy (for a fixed interest rate). The diagram considers a small open economy that faces a fixed interest rate, given on world capital markets. The two loci are straight lines in this case, and the model exhibits saddle-path stability. If the economy starts with a low level of assets per effective person, the transition features monotonically increasing levels of consumption and assets per effective person.

where we used the condition $f[(\hat{k}^*)_{\text{open}}] = (\hat{w}^*)_{\text{open}} + (r + \delta) \cdot (\hat{k}^*)_{\text{open}}$. The behavior of household consumption from equation (3.88) implies

$$\dot{\hat{c}}/\hat{c} = r - \rho - x - (p + n) \cdot (\rho + p) \cdot \hat{a}/\hat{c} \tag{3.93}$$

Figure 3.6 shows the phase diagram for $(\hat{a}, \hat{c})$ that is implied by equations (3.92) and (3.93). Note that this diagram applies for a constant r; that is, we consider the dynamics for a small open economy when the world economy is in a steady state. The line for $\dot{\hat{a}} = 0$, from equation (3.92), has a positive intercept (equal to $[\hat{w}^*]_{\text{open}}$) and a positive slope of $r - x - n$. The line for $\dot{\hat{c}} = 0$, from equation (3.93), goes through the origin, and the sign of the slope equals the sign of $r - \rho - x$. This last term is positive in the finite-horizon model of a closed economy that we considered in the previous section. Now this term will be positive for any country that ends up holding positive assets in the steady state. Figure 3.6 shows the $\dot{\hat{c}} = 0$ line with a positive slope that exceeds the slope of the $\dot{\hat{a}} = 0$ line.[32]

Figure 3.6 shows the steady-state values for $\hat{c}$ and $\hat{a}$ in the finite-horizon open economy. In contrast with the infinite-horizon model, these steady-state values are positive and finite.

32. If the slope of the $d\hat{c}/dt = 0$ locus is positive, but not greater than the slope of the $d\hat{a}/dt = 0$ locus, we can show that $\hat{c}$ rises forever. This outcome is inconsistent with the fixed world interest rate, r.

This outcome is consistent with $\dot{\hat{c}} = 0$ in equation (3.93) because the ratio $\hat{a}/\hat{c}$ adjusts so that the overall time-preference term, $\rho + x + (p + n) \cdot (\rho + p) \cdot \hat{a}/\hat{c}$, equals r. In other words, the key property is that the effective time-preference rate is an increasing function of $\hat{a}/\hat{c}$.

A higher value of ρ steepens the slope of the $\dot{\hat{c}} = 0$ locus in figure 3.6 (see equation [3.93]). That is, the locus pivots around the origin in a counterclockwise manner. The figure then implies that less-patient countries—with higher values of ρ—have lower steady-state values of $\hat{a}$ and $\hat{c}$. We can also verify from the figure that the steady-state values of $\hat{a}$ and $\hat{c}$ decline with increases in x, p, and n. (They also decline with θ if $\theta \neq 1$ is allowed.)

The steady-state value of $\hat{a}$ is positive for a range of parameter values; that is, the debt, $\hat{d}$, remains below the capital stock, $\hat{k}$. However, a sufficiently high value of ρ (or of x or θ) makes the slope of the $\dot{\hat{c}} = 0$ locus negative, so that the steady-state value for $\hat{a}$ becomes negative. In other words, $\hat{d} > \hat{k}$ applies for sufficiently impatient economies. In these situations, borrowers use a part of the present value of wage income as collateral.

For a given r and a given array of parameter values for countries $i = 1, \ldots, M$, we can determine the corresponding array of $\hat{a}_i$ from figure 3.6. We can also determine the array of $\hat{k}_i$ from the condition $f'(\hat{k}_i) = r + \delta_i$. In a full steady-state equilibrium, the world interest rate, r, is the value that equates the sum of the $\hat{a}_i$ (weighted by each country's effective labor force) to the sum of the $\hat{k}_i$ (similarly weighted).

The finite-horizon framework is attractive because economies with different underlying parameters can share a common capital market without the implication that $\hat{c}_i$ tends to zero for all but the most patient country. The model implies, however, that convergence rates of $\hat{k}_i$ and $\hat{y}_i$ would be infinite. To avoid this conclusion, we can combine the finite-horizon model with the analysis of credit constraints that we considered in a previous section. The results follow readily if we identify $\hat{k}_i$ with broad capital, $\hat{k}_i + \hat{h}_i$, in the model with a credit constraint.

For given $(\hat{k}_i^*)_{\text{open}}$, the countries that have high steady-state values of $\hat{a}_i$ in figure 3.6 end up unconstrained on the credit market, whereas those with low values (and surely those with negative values) of $\hat{a}_i$ end up constrained. Thus the countries with relatively high values of ρ_i, x_i, p_i, n_i, and θ_i tend to be credit constrained. In addition to the impatient countries—with high values of ρ_i and θ_i—the candidates for credit constraints therefore include those that grow rapidly in the steady state (high x_i and n_i) and those with high mortality rates (high p_i).

The finite-horizon model of an open economy with credit constraints implies that $\hat{c}_i$ and $\hat{a}_i$ remain positive in all countries. Also, only some of the countries are credit constrained in the steady state. For these constrained countries, the convergence speeds for $\hat{k}_i$ and $\hat{y}_i$ in the neighborhood of the steady state are finite, as shown in the previous section. For the unconstrained countries, however, the convergence speeds for $\hat{k}_i$ and $\hat{y}_i$ are still infinite. To avoid this result, we can reintroduce the adjustment costs for investment that we considered before.

3.7 Some Conclusions

We began with an extension of the Ramsey model to incorporate taxation and public expenditure. Taxation of capital income tended to depress capital formation, and government purchases of goods and services tended to drive out private consumption.

We then introduced adjustment costs for investment, costs that we thought would be especially important for the accumulation of human capital. These costs imply finite speeds of convergence for capital and output even if world capital markets are perfect and horizons are infinite. We argue, however, that adjustment costs cannot by themselves explain the slow speeds of convergence that are observed empirically, because the implied values of Brainard and Tobin's q would be counterfactually high. Moreover, the adjustment-cost model does not eliminate the puzzling behavior of consumption and assets that arises in open-economy settings.

We then began the seemingly straightforward task of extending the Ramsey model to an open economy by allowing for international borrowing and lending. This extension led, however, to some counterfactual results: convergence speeds for capital stock and output were infinite and, except for the most patient country, consumption (per unit of effective labor) tended to zero and assets became negative. The most patient country asymptotically owned everything and consumed nearly all of the world's output.

We considered several modifications of the Ramsey model to eliminate these paradoxical findings. With imperfect international credit markets, the infinite speeds of convergence for capital and output would not apply to countries that were effectively constrained in their ability to borrow. Moreover, assets remained positive, and consumption per unit of effective labor did not tend to zero in these countries. The particular model that we considered had, however, the counterfactual implication that all but the most patient country would eventually become credit constrained.

We continued our analysis with a model where individuals had finite horizons and where new individuals came into the economy. The accumulation of assets effectively raised a country's rate of time preference. (Preference parameters were constant for individuals; the result derived from the aggregation over persons who differed with respect to levels of assets and consumption.) Therefore, even without credit-market constraints, the variation in the effective rate of time preference motivated the most patient country not to accumulate all the world's wealth. Similarly, the relatively impatient countries did not tend to zero consumption per effective worker.

When we combined the finite-horizon framework with the model of imperfect credit markets, we found that the long-run equilibrium featured a range of countries that were not effectively constrained in their ability to borrow and another range of countries that were effectively constrained. The results are attractive in that many countries—with different preference parameters—were not constrained on the international credit market. In addition, the constrained countries exhibited finite speeds of convergence for capital stocks and output. One remaining problem, however, is that these speeds of convergence were still infinite for the unconstrained countries. This last, counterfactual prediction can be eliminated if we reintroduce adjustment costs for investment, especially in human capital.

We cannot argue at this stage that economists have settled on a fully satisfactory way to apply the Ramsey model to an open economy. The various pieces of analysis that we have gone through in this chapter do, however, get us closer to such a model. In particular, the combination of these pieces can account simultaneously for the observed slow convergence of capital stocks and output, while avoiding counterfactual implications about the behavior of consumption and assets.

3.8 Appendix: Overlapping-Generations Models

In the main text of this chapter we considered the model of finite-horizon households that was developed by Blanchard (1985). His model is basically a tractable version of overlapping-generations (OLG) models, which were originated by Samuelson (1958) and Diamond (1965). This appendix describes the structure of OLG models and works out some implications of these models.

3.8.1 Households

The most popular OLG framework assumes that each person lives for only two periods. People work in the first period, when they are young, retire in the second period, when they are old, and then die off. To relate this setup to the real world, we have to think of a period as representing a generation, say, 30 years. Since people consume in both periods of life, they have to pay for consumption in the second period by saving in the first period (if we do not allow for transfers from the government or from members of other generations).

We shall refer to the cohort that is born at time t as generation t. Members of this generation are young in period t and old in period $t + 1$. Therefore, during period t, the young of generation t overlap with the old of generation $t - 1$. At each point in time, members of only two generations are alive. The main justification for considering only two periods is that it simplifies the aggregation of consumption and other variables.[33]

Each person maximizes lifetime utility, which depends on consumption in the two periods of life. We make the crucial assumption that people do not care about events after their death; specifically, they are not altruistic toward their children and, therefore, do not provide bequests or other transfers to members of the next generation. We assume that the form of the lifetime utility function is a discrete-time analogue to the one assumed in the Ramsey model:

$$U_t = \frac{c_{1t}^{1-\theta} - 1}{1-\theta} + \left(\frac{1}{1+\rho}\right) \cdot \left(\frac{c_{2t+1}^{1-\theta} - 1}{1-\theta}\right) \tag{3.94}$$

where $\theta > 0$, $\rho > 0$, c_{1t} is consumption of generation t when young (that is, in period t), and c_{2t+1} is consumption of generation t when old (that is, in period $t+1$).

Consider the lifetime of an individual born at time t. Since members of previous generations do not care about this person, we assume that he is born with no assets. He supplies one unit of labor inelastically while young and receives the wage income w_t. He does not work when old. If s_t denotes the amount saved in period t, the budget constraint for period t is

$$c_{1t} + s_t = w_t \tag{3.95}$$

In period $t+1$, the individual consumes the previous savings plus the accrued interest:

$$c_{2t+1} = (1 + r_{t+1}) \cdot s_t \tag{3.96}$$

where r_{t+1} is the interest rate on one-period loans between periods t and $t+1$. Equation (3.96) incorporates the notion that, because individuals do not care about their descendants, they choose to end up with zero assets when they die. If we allow for borrowing, $s_t < 0$, we have to assume that the credit market imposes the constraint that people cannot die in debt.

Each individual treats w_t and r_{t+1} as given and chooses c_{1t} and s_t (and, hence, c_{2t+1}) to maximize utility from equation (3.94), subject to equations (3.95) and (3.96). We can use equations (3.95) and (3.96) to substitute out for c_{1t} and c_{2t+1} in the utility function in

33. In the Blanchard (1985) model, discussed in the text, the aggregate consumption function is simple because individuals of all ages have the same propensity to consume out of wealth. Aggregate consumption is therefore a simple function of aggregate wealth. In the OLG model, individuals of different generations have different propensities to consume and different levels of wealth. Aggregation is simple, however, because only two generations are alive at each point in time.

equation (3.94) and then compute the first-order condition with respect to s, $\partial U/\partial s_t = 0$, to get

$$(s_t)^{-\theta} \cdot (1 + r_{t+1})^{1-\theta} = (1 + \rho) \cdot (w_t - s_t)^{-\theta} \tag{3.97}$$

If we use equations (3.95) and (3.96), equation (3.97) implies

$$c_{2t+1}/c_{1t} = [(1 + r_{t+1})/(1 + \rho)]^{1/\theta} \tag{3.98}$$

This expression is the discrete-time counterpart of the usual relation from the Ramsey model, $(1/c) \cdot (dc/dt) = (1/\theta) \cdot (r - \rho)$ from equation (2.24).

Equation (3.97) implies that the saving rate can be written as

$$s_t = w_t/\psi_{t+1} \tag{3.99}$$

where $\psi_{t+1} \equiv [1 + (1 + \rho)^{1/\theta} \cdot (1 + r_{t+1})^{-(1-\theta)/\theta}] > 1$. The dependence of s_t on w_t and r_{t+1} can be described by

$$s_w \equiv \partial s_t/\partial w_t = 1/\psi_{t+1}$$

$$s_r \equiv \partial s_t/\partial r_{t+1} = \left(\frac{1-\theta}{\theta}\right) \cdot \left[\frac{1+\rho}{1 + r_{t+1}}\right]^{1/\theta} \cdot s_t/\psi_{t+1}$$

Note that $0 < s_w < 1$, and $s_r > 0$ if $\theta < 1$, $s_r < 0$ if $\theta > 1$, and $s_r = 0$ if $\theta = 1$.

3.8.2 Firms

Firms have the usual neoclassical production function,

$$y_t = f(k_t) \tag{3.100}$$

where $y_t \equiv Y_t/L_t$ and $k_t \equiv K_t/L_t$ are output and capital per worker. (We simplify by neglecting technological progress—that is, $x = 0$—because it does not affect the main points of this analysis.) Since each young person works one unit of time, the variable L_t is the total number of young people in the economy. Note that we assume that the capital stock in period t is productive in the same period; that is, there is no lag in the production and use of capital. The standard maximization of profit by competitive firms leads, as in chapter 2, to the equation of net marginal products to factor prices:

$$w_t = f(k_t) - k_t \cdot f'(k_t) \tag{3.101}$$

$$r_t = f'(k_t) - \delta \tag{3.102}$$

where δ is the depreciation rate.

3.8.3 Equilibrium

We assume a closed economy, so that households' assets—all owned at the start of a period by members of the old generation—equal the capital stock. Aggregate net investment equals total income minus total consumption:

$$K_{t+1} - K_t = w_t L_t + r_t K_t - c_{1t} L_t - c_{2t} L_{t-1} \tag{3.103}$$

where L_{t-1} is the number of people born at time $t-1$, all of whom are old at time t. If we substitute for w_t and r_t from equations (3.101) and (3.102) into equation (3.103), we get the economy's resource constraint:

$$K_{t+1} - K_t = F(K_t, L_t) - C_t - \delta K_t \tag{3.104}$$

where $C_t = c_{1t} L_t + c_{2t} L_{t-1}$ is aggregate consumption, that is, the sum of consumption by the young, $c_{1t} L_t$, and the old, $c_{2t} L_{t-1}$.

If we substitute out for c_{1t} and c_{2t} in equation (3.103) from equations (3.95) and (3.96), we get[34]

$$K_{t+1} = s_t L_t \tag{3.105}$$

that is, the savings of the young equal the next period's capital stock. This result holds because the old want to end up with no assets when they die (because they do not care about their descendants); hence, they sell all their capital stock to the young of the next generation. All of the capital owned by the old plus any net increase in capital must therefore be purchased by the young with their savings.

Note that the savings of period t become capital in period $t+1$. If we think of a period as 30 years, equation (3.105) says that the output that is not consumed becomes productive 30 years later. This unrealistic lag structure is an unfortunate by-product of overlapping-generations models with only two periods of life. The structure also means that we have to interpret the various rates—such as r_t and δ—as quantities per generation. For example, an interest rate of 6 percent per year corresponds to a value for r_t of 5.0, and a depreciation rate of 5 percent per year corresponds to a value for δ of 0.78.

34. Substitution from equations (3.95) and (3.96) into equation (3.103) yields the difference equation

$$K_{t+1} = s_t L_t + (1 + r_t) \cdot (K_t - s_{t-1} L_{t-1})$$

We have to get the economy started off somehow, for example, with an initial capital stock, K_1, that is owned by the L_0 persons who are old in period 1. These old people consume the amount $c_{21} L_0 = (1 + r_1) \cdot K_1$. This condition, in conjunction with equations (3.95) and (3.103), implies $K_2 = s_1 L_1$. The difference equation shown then implies $K_{t+1} = s_t L_t$ for all $t \geq 2$.

Assume a constant rate of population growth, so that $L_{t+1}/L_t = 1 + n$. (A population growth rate of 1 percent per year corresponds to a value for n of 0.35.) We can express equation (3.105) in per capita terms as

$$k_{t+1} \equiv K_{t+1}/L_{t+1} = s_t/(1+n)$$

Substitution for s_t from equation (3.99) into this result implies

$$k_{t+1} \cdot (1+n) = w_t/\psi_{t+1} \tag{3.106}$$

If we replace ψ_{t+1} by the expression that appears below equation (3.99), we get

$$k_{t+1} \cdot (1+n) \cdot \left\{1 + (1+\rho)^{1/\theta} \cdot [1 + r(k_{t+1})]^{(\theta-1)/\theta}\right\} = w(k_t) \tag{3.107}$$

where $r(k_{t+1})$ is given in equation (3.102), and $w(k_t)$ is given in equation (3.101).

Equation (3.107) is a nonlinear difference equation in k_t; for every value of k_t, the equation implicitly determines the equilibrium value of k_{t+1}.[35] Therefore, for a given initial value of k_t, equation (3.107) will prescribe the future path of capital stocks.

Equation (3.107) can be solved in closed form only for special cases of the production and utility functions. For example, if utility is logarithmic ($\theta = 1$), the expression in braces on the left-hand side of equation (3.107) becomes $2 + \rho$. The difference equation then simplifies to

$$k_{t+1} = [f(k_t) - k_t \cdot f'(k_t)]/[(1+n) \cdot (2+\rho)] \tag{3.108}$$

The Steady State To compute the steady-state capital intensity, let $k_{t+1} = k_t = k^*$ in equation (3.107) to get

$$(1+n) \cdot \left\{1 + (1+\rho)^{1/\theta} \cdot [1 + f'(k^*) - \delta]^{(\theta-1)/\theta}\right\} = f(k^*)/k^* - f'(k^*) \tag{3.109}$$

We can see the nature of the determination of k^* by specializing to a Cobb–Douglas production function, $f(k_t) = Ak_t^\alpha$. Equation (3.109) simplifies in this case to

$$(1+n) \cdot \left\{1 + (1+\rho)^{1/\theta} \cdot [1 + \alpha A \cdot (k^*)^{\alpha-1} - \delta]^{(\theta-1)/\theta}\right\} = (1-\alpha) \cdot A \cdot (k^*)^{\alpha-1} \tag{3.110}$$

If we define z^* to be the gross average product of capital—that is, $z^* \equiv A \cdot (k^*)^{\alpha-1}$—then equation (3.110) can be rewritten as

$$(1+n) \cdot \left\{1 + (1+\rho)^{1/\theta} \cdot [1 + \alpha z^* - \delta]^{(\theta-1)/\theta}\right\} = (1-\alpha) \cdot z^* \tag{3.111}$$

35. This equilibrium value may or may not be unique; see the next subsection.

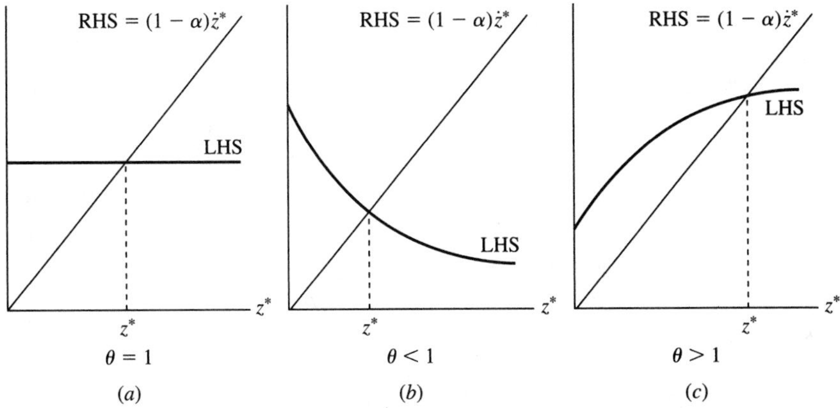

Figure 3.7
Determination of the steady state in the OLG model. Equation (3.111) determines the steady-state gross average product of capital, z^*, in the overlapping-generations model with a Cobb–Douglas technology. In the figure, the straight line from the origin shows the right-hand side of the equation. The three panels plot the left-hand side of the equation for $\theta = 1$, $\theta < 1$, and $\theta > 1$. In each case, the steady state exists and is unique.

We determine z^* graphically in figure 3.7 by plotting the two sides of equation (3.111) as functions of z^*. The right-hand side (RHS) of the equation is a straight line through the origin with slope $1 - \alpha$. The shape of the left-hand side (LHS) depends on whether θ is equal to, less than, or greater than 1. These three cases are depicted in the three panels of the figure.

If utility is logarithmic, so that $\theta = 1$, the left-hand side of equation (3.111) is a horizontal line at $(1+n)\cdot(2+\rho) > 0$, as shown in panel *a* of figure 3.7. This line crosses the $(1-\alpha)\cdot z^*$ line at a positive z^*, given by $(1+n)\cdot(2+\rho)/(1-\alpha)$; hence, the steady-state capital stock exists and is unique. The solution for the steady-state capital intensity in this case is

$$k^* = \left[\frac{A\cdot(1-\alpha)}{(1+n)\cdot(2+\rho)}\right]^{1/(1-\alpha)} \tag{3.112}$$

Panel *b* of figure 3.7 applies when $\theta < 1$. The left-hand side of equation (3.111) is an inverse function of z^*. This function has a positive intercept, and it asymptotes to $1+n$ as z^* goes to infinity. The intersection with the right-hand side, the straight line $(1-\alpha)\cdot z^*$, therefore occurs at a unique, positive z^*. Hence, the steady-state capital stock exists and is unique.

Panel *c* of figure 3.7 applies if $\theta > 1$. The left-hand side of equation (3.111) is an increasing function of z^*. The intercept is positive, and the slope diminishes monotonically toward 0 as z^* approaches infinity. The intersection with the right-hand side, the straight line $(1-\alpha)\cdot z^*$, therefore again occurs at a unique, positive z^*.

The Golden Rule and Dynamic Efficiency Consider now whether the overlapping-generations economy can generate the type of oversaving that may appear in the Solow–Swan model of chapter 1. Recall that oversaving could arise in the Solow–Swan model only because it assumes an arbitrary saving rate; oversaving cannot arise in the Ramsey model of chapter 2, in which infinite-lived households choose saving optimally. The surprising result in the OLG model is that oversaving can occur even though households choose saving optimally. This possibility exists because households have a finite horizon, corresponding to the two-period length of life, whereas the economy goes on forever.

To assess the possibility of oversaving, we first compute the capital intensity that yields a maximum of steady-state consumption per capita. At a point in time, aggregate consumption is $C_t \equiv c_{1t} \cdot L_t + c_{2t} \cdot L_{t-1}$. Since total population equals $L_t + L_{t-1}$, consumption per capita equals $C_t/(L_t + L_{t-1})$. Since $L_{t-1} = L_t/(1+n)$, this expression for consumption per capita is the multiple $(1+n)/(2+n)$ of consumption per worker, $c_t \equiv C_t/L_t$. Hence, maximization of consumption per capita is equivalent to maximization of consumption per worker.

To find the steady-state level of consumption per worker, we can divide both sides of equation (3.111) by L_t to get

$$k_{t+1} \cdot (1+n) - k_t = f(k_t) - c_t - \delta k_t \tag{3.113}$$

In a steady state, $k_{t+1} = k_t = k^*$, and the steady-state consumption per worker, c^*, is given by

$$c^* = f(k^*) - (n+\delta) \cdot k^* \tag{3.114}$$

The maximization of c^* therefore occurs at the value $k^* = k_g$ that satisfies $f'(k_g) = n + \delta$, that is, at the golden-rule value described in chapter 1. It is easy to show that, even for simple functional forms for utility and production, the economy's steady-state value k^* may end up in the dynamically inefficient region where $k^* > k_g$.

Consider the case of log utility ($\theta = 1$) and Cobb–Douglas technology. Equation (3.112) implies that the steady-state capital intensity is given in this case by $k^* = [\{A \cdot (1-\alpha)\}/\{(1+n) \cdot (2+\rho)\}]^{1/(1-\alpha)}$. In contrast, the golden-rule value is $k_{\text{gold}} = [\alpha A/(n+\delta)]^{1/(1-\alpha)}$. The condition for the steady-state capital intensity to exceed the golden-rule value (and, hence, for the economy to be in the dynamically inefficient region) is therefore

$$\frac{1-\alpha}{(1+n) \cdot (2+\rho)} > \frac{\alpha}{n+\delta} \tag{3.115}$$

Thus oversaving is more likely to occur if the rates of time preference, ρ, and population growth, n, are small; if the depreciation rate, δ, is large; and if the capital share, α, is small.

Oversaving cannot occur if α is close to 1 (because wages are then close to 0, and young people have little capacity to save).

If we consider conventional parameter values, such as $n = 0.35$, $\rho = 0.82$, and $\delta = 0.78$ (which correspond to respective annual rates of 0.01, 0.02, and 0.05), then the condition in equation (3.115) becomes $\alpha < 0.32$. That is, inefficient oversaving occurs only if the capital share is one-third or less. We have argued before that a much higher capital share is reasonable if human capital is included. For example, if $\alpha = 0.75$, oversaving does not arise with reasonable parameter values in this OLG framework.

Dynamics The dynamics of the OLG economy come from equation (3.107). Consider first the case of log utility ($\theta = 1$), as shown in equation (3.108). If we also assume a Cobb–Douglas production function, $f(k) = Ak^{\alpha}$, equation (3.108) becomes

$$k_{t+1} = (1-\alpha) \cdot Ak_t^{\alpha}/[(1+n) \cdot (2+\rho)] \equiv \Omega(k_t) \tag{3.116}$$

Figure 3.8 shows the relation between k_{t+1} and k_t, which we denote by $\Omega(k_t)$. The slope of $\Omega(k_t)$ is infinite at $k_t = 0$ and diminishes toward 0 as k_t approaches infinity. The function $\Omega(k_t)$ crosses the 45-degree line at the steady-state value, k^*. In this case, the capital stock monotonically approaches its unique steady-state value as time evolves. In other words, the

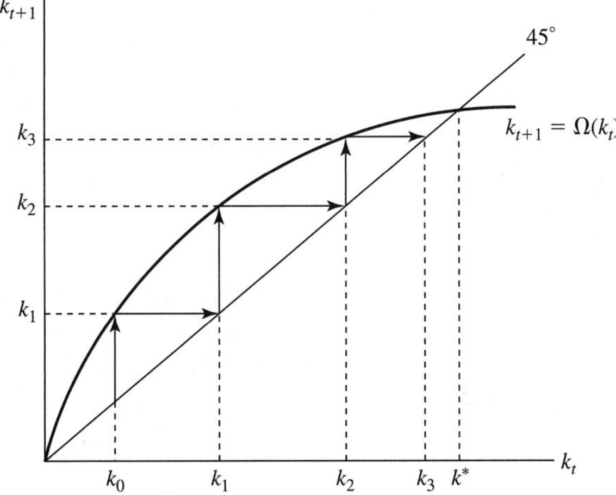

Figure 3.8
Dynamics in the OLG model. Equation (3.116) prescribes the dynamics in the overlapping-generations model for the case of logarithmic utility and Cobb–Douglas technology. The function $\Omega(k_t)$, given in equation (3.116) and shown in the figure, determines the value of k_{t+1} that corresponds to each value of k_t. If the economy begins at k_0, it follows the sequence $k_1, k_2, \ldots$ shown in the figure.

steady state is stable. The reason is that the curve $\Omega(k_t)$ is always upward sloping, and it crosses the 45-degree line from above.

For general production and utility functions, the dynamics of the OLG economy can be complicated. It is possible to generate examples in which the $\Omega(k_t)$ curve is downward sloping when it crosses the 45-degree line. In these cases, the economy may display cycles.[36] The stability of the steady state is also not guaranteed.

Altruism, Bequests, and Infinite Horizons The key assumption in the OLG model is that individuals have finite horizons in the sense that they do not care about their descendants. We now assume instead that people value their children's happiness (see Barro, 1974). If the altruistic linkage from parents to children is strong enough to generate intergenerational transfers—that is, if the typical person does not end up at a corner solution in which these transfers are zero—the finite-horizon effect turns out to vanish. In particular, if intergenerational altruism is strong, we return effectively to the Ramsey model of chapter 2, in which horizons are infinite.

One way to allow for altruistic linkages across generations is to assume that a person born at time t derives utility from lifetime consumption and also from the prospective utility of children. For example, we could have

$$U_t = \frac{c_{1t}^{1-\theta} - 1}{1-\theta} + \left(\frac{1}{1+\rho}\right) \cdot \left(\frac{c_{2t+1}^{1-\theta} - 1}{1-\theta}\right) + \left(\frac{1+n}{(1+\rho)\cdot(1+\phi)}\right) \cdot U_{t+1} \tag{3.117}$$

The first two terms on the right-hand side coincide with those from equation (3.94) and represent the utility derived from consumption over the two periods of life. The term on the far right-hand side involves the prospective utility, U_{t+1}, of each immediate descendant. This utility will depend on the descendant's consumption in two periods of life and on the utility of descendants in the subsequent generation.

The term U_{t+1} in equation (3.117) is multiplied by the number of descendants, $1+n$, and is discounted by two terms. The first discount, $1+\rho$, applies because the prospective utility arises one generation later and is, in this respect, comparable to own consumption when old, c_{2t+1}. The second discount, $1+\phi$, arises because people may not count the anticipated utility of their children—derived in part from their children's prospective consumption—in the same way as their own consumption. Specifically, if $\phi > 0$, parents are selfish in the

36. The potential for cycles depends, however, on the discrete-time setup. For an individual family, this discreteness may be reasonable because it represents the length of a generation. At the aggregate level, however, the discreteness would be smoothed out by the adding up across families who differ in their positions in the life cycle. If the aggregated model involves a single state variable—such as the aggregate capital stock—cycles would no longer materialize.

sense that, if parent's consumption when old equals a child's consumption when young, the parent prefers an additional unit of own old-age consumption to an added unit of a child's young-period consumption.

If we use equation (3.117) repeatedly to substitute out for U_{t+1}, U_{t+2}, and so on, utility can be written as a forward, weighted sum of each generation's consumption when young and old

$$U_t = \sum_{i=0}^{\infty} \left(\frac{1+n}{(1+\rho)\cdot(1+\phi)} \right)^i \cdot \left[\frac{c_{1t+i}^{1-\theta} - 1}{1-\theta} + \left(\frac{1}{1+\rho} \right) \cdot \left(\frac{c_{2t+1+i}^{1-\theta} - 1}{1-\theta} \right) \right] \tag{3.118}$$

In order for utility to be bounded when c_{1t+i} and c_{2t+i} are constant over time, we have to impose the condition $1+n < (1+\rho)\cdot(1+\phi)$.

Let b_t be the intergenerational transfer received by each descendant born at time t. The amount transferred by each old person in period t is then $(1+n)\cdot b_t$. The budget constraints for the two periods of life are revised accordingly from equations (3.95) and (3.96) to

$$c_{1t} + s_t = w_t + b_t \tag{3.119}$$

$$c_{2t+1} + (1+n)\cdot b_{t+1} = (1+r_{t+1})\cdot s_t \tag{3.120}$$

Note that we have set up the transfers so that they occur while the older generation is still alive and are therefore available to fund the young-period consumption of the next generation. One new element is that people have two sources of income when young: wage income and the transfers provided by their parents (if $b_t > 0$). People also have two ways to spend their resources when old: consumption and transfers to children.

A young person of generation t maximizes utility in equation (3.118), subject to a given transfer b_t and to the constraints imposed by equations (3.119) and (3.120) on each generation. We assume that the constraint $b_{t+i} \geq 0$ applies for all $i \geq 0$; that is, parents cannot require their children to provide transfers. If the restriction $b_{t+i} \geq 0$ is not binding for all $i \geq 0$, the problem is straightforward; we deal here only with this case. (See Weil, 1987, and Kimball, 1987, for discussions of these restrictions and for an analysis of reverse transfers from children to parents.)

The specification of the utility function in equation (3.118) implies that the form of the optimum problem does not change as old generations die and new ones are born. That is, the relative weighting on consumption in various periods does not change as new generations arrive. We can therefore pretend that the members of generation t can commit at time t to the choices that will be made by their descendants.

An easy way to get the first-order conditions is to use equations (3.119) and (3.120) to substitute out for c_{1t}, c_{2t+1}, c_{1t+1}, and so on, in equation (3.118) and then maximize over s_t

and b_{t+1}. The resulting conditions can be expressed as

$$\frac{c_{2t+1}}{c_{1t}} = \left(\frac{1+r_{t+1}}{1+\rho}\right)^{1/\theta} \tag{3.121}$$

$$\frac{c_{2t}}{c_{1t}} = (1+\phi)^{1/\theta} \tag{3.122}$$

Equation (3.121) prescribes the allocation of consumption over a person's lifetime and has the same form as equation (3.98). Equation (3.122) relates parental consumption at time t to children's consumption at time t. These consumption levels differ only if the selfishness parameter, ϕ, is nonzero. In particular, if $\phi > 0$, children consume less when they are young than parents consume when they are old.

Equations (3.121) and (3.122) can be combined to compute the evolution over time of consumption per worker, c_t:[37]

$$\frac{c_{t+1}}{c_t} = \frac{c_{1t+1}}{c_{1t}} = \frac{c_{2t+1}}{c_{2t}} = \left(\frac{1+r_{t+1}}{(1+\phi)\cdot(1+\rho)}\right)^{1/\theta} \tag{3.123}$$

This result is the discrete-time counterpart to the standard solution for the change in c_t over time in the Ramsey model. The only difference is that the discount factor combines pure time preference, ρ, and the selfishness parameter, ϕ. The pure time effect can now be 0—that is, $\rho = 0$ is satisfactory—and the discount then reflects only the selfishness of parents ($\phi > 0$).

Equation (3.123) can be combined with the economy's budget constraint in equation (3.113) to determine the dynamics of k_t and c_t. An inspection of this system shows, however, that it is the discrete-time analogue of the Ramsey model. Since the dynamic equations for k_t and c_t are the same as those in the Ramsey model—except for the shift to discrete time—the results are also the same. In particular, the steady state and dynamics are well behaved, and the equilibrium cannot be dynamically inefficient. Thus, if altruism is strong enough to ensure an interior solution for intergenerational transfers, the OLG structure and finite lifetimes do not provide new insights about the evolution of the economy.

3.9 Problems

3.1 Time-varying consumption tax rates. Start with a situation in which the government does not tax capital income or purchase goods and services—$\tau_a = \tau_f = G = 0$—and the

37. The results for c_{1t} and c_{2t} in equation (3.123) follow from equations (3.121) and (3.122). The result for c_t holds because $c_t = [(1+n)c_{1t} + c_{2t}]/(1+n)$, and the ratio of c_{2t} to c_{1t} is the constant shown in equation (3.129).

consumption tax rate, τ_c, is constant. Suppose that the government switches to a rising path of τ_c, while maintaining $\tau_a = \tau_f = G = 0$. How does this change affect the households' first-order condition for consumption growth? How does it affect the equilibrium for the economy? Is the shift to a time-varying consumption tax rate a good idea?

3.2 Public services in the production function. Suppose that the production function is

$$\hat{y} = f(\hat{k}, \tilde{g})$$

where $\tilde{g}$ is the flow of public services. Analyze the effects of the path of $\tilde{g}$ on the economy for the following cases:

a. $\tilde{g} = \hat{g}$ and G/Y is constant over time.

b. $\tilde{g} = G$ and G/Y is constant over time.

3.3 International specialization and diversification (based on Ventura, 1997). Each small economy can produce two intermediate goods, X_1 and X_2, and a final good, Y, which can be used for consumption and investment. The production functions are

$$X_1 = (K_1)^{\alpha_1}(L_1)^{1-\alpha_1} \tag{1}$$

$$X_2 = (K_2)^{\alpha_2}(L_2)^{1-\alpha_2} \tag{2}$$

$$Y = (X_1)^{\alpha_3}(X_2)^{1-\alpha_3} \tag{3}$$

where $\alpha_1, \alpha_2, \alpha_3 > 0$; K_1 and L_1 are the quantities of domestic capital and labor employed in the sector that produces X_1; K_2 and L_2 are the quantities employed in the sector that produces X_2; $K_1 + K_2 = K$; and $L_1 + L_2 = L$. The final output Y can be used, as usual, for C or for expansion of K. Total labor, L, is constant. Intermediate goods are tradable on world markets at the constant price p (in units of X_1 per unit of X_2). Final goods, Y, and units of C and K are not tradable internationally. There is no world credit market, so each country's sale or purchase of X_1 must equal its purchase or sale of X_2. In equation (3), the quantities of X_1 and X_2 used to produce Y are the amounts produced domestically (from equations [1] and [2]) plus the net quantity bought from abroad.

a. For what range of $k \equiv K/L$ will the domestic economy be in the "diversification range" in which it produces both types of intermediate goods? Derive expressions for the rental rate on capital, R, and the wage rate, w, when k is in the diversification range. (Note that, in the absence of factor mobility, factor-price equalization is achieved through the mobility of goods.)

b. Assume that k increases but not by enough to move the economy outside of the diversification range. Why does the increase in k not lead to diminishing returns? (Note: the results are an application of the Rybczinski, 1955, theorem.)

c. Suppose that infinite-horizon consumers solve the usual Ramsey optimization problem. Derive the laws of motion for c and k, assuming that p is constant.

d. Suppose that the world consists of a large number of small countries, identical except for their values of $k(0)$. Furthermore, assume that all countries fall in the diversification range. Derive the world equilibrium path for p and obtain the laws of motion for the world's c and k. How do the results relate to those from part (c)?

3.4 International credit constraints (based on Cohen and Sachs, 1986). Imagine that the domestic country, country i, can borrow on world credit markets at the constant real interest rate, r. The country can, however, borrow only up to a fraction $\lambda \geq 0$ of its capital stock, so that

$$d_i \leq \lambda k_i \tag{1}$$

Since $d_i = k_i - a_i$ (equation [3.1]), equation (1) implies

$$a_i \geq (1 - \lambda) \cdot k_i \tag{2}$$

Assume that the domestic economy has the usual infinite-horizon consumers with $\rho_i + \theta_i x_i > r$. The country also starts with sufficient assets, $a_i(0)$, so that equation (2) is not binding initially.

a. What are the first-order optimization conditions if equation (2) is not binding? Relate these conditions to those discussed in section 3.4.3.

b. Argue that equation (2) becomes binding in finite time. Then use equation (3.50) to find an expression for $\dot{\hat{k}}$ when equation (2) is binding. What is the expression for $\dot{\hat{c}}/\hat{c}$ when equation (2) is binding? Provide economic intuition for this result for situations in which $\lambda = 1$, $\lambda = 0$, and $0 < \lambda < 1$.

c. What is the steady-state value of $\hat{k}$, and how does this value depend on λ and r?

d. How does the parameter λ affect the transitional dynamics?

3.5 Adjustment costs in the Ramsey model (based on Abel and Blanchard, 1983). Consider the model of adjustment costs worked out in this chapter. Assume that consumers have the usual Ramsey preferences. But, instead of assuming a constant interest rate, consider the equilibrium for a closed economy.

a. Find an expression for $\dot{q}$ as a function of q, i/k, $\dot{c}/c$, and k.

b. Use a phase diagram to work out the dynamics of i/k and k. (Note: It is easier to work with i/k than with q.)

3.6 End-of-the-world model II. Suppose that the Ramsey model is the same as the one described in chapter 2, except that utility is logarithmic ($\theta = 1$) and everyone thinks that the world will end with probability $p \geq 0$ per unit of time. That is, if the world exists at time t, the probability that it will still exist at the future date T is $e^{-p\cdot(T-t)}$.

a. What are the transition equations for $\hat{k}$ and $\hat{c}$? How do these equations relate to equations (2.23) and (2.24) from chapter 2 and to equations (3.89) and (3.90) from the Blanchard (1985) model?

b. Use a modification of figure 2.1 to describe the transition path for the economy.

c. As p gets smaller, how does the transition path relate to the one shown in figure 2.1? What happens as p approaches 0?

3.7 Fiscal policy in a finite-horizon model. Reconsider problem 2.9 in the context of the Blanchard (1985) model of a closed economy, as described in this chapter. Assume that $n = x = G = 0$, and begin with the case in which B is constant at the value $B(0)$.

a. How do differences in $B(0)$ affect the economy's transition path and steady state?

b. Suppose that B follows some path but eventually approaches a constant. How does the path of B affect the economy's transition path and steady state?

4 One-Sector Models of Endogenous Growth

In the Ramsey model, as in the Solow–Swan model, the steady-state per capita growth rate equals the rate of technological progress, x, which is assumed to be exogenous. Thus, although these models provide interesting frameworks for studying transitional dynamics, they are not helpful for understanding the sources of long-term growth of income per capita.

We mentioned in chapter 1 that one way to construct a theory of endogenous growth is to eliminate the long-run tendency for capital to experience diminishing returns. We discussed as a simple example the *AK* model, in which the returns to capital are always constant, and we considered technologies in which the returns to capital diminished but asymptotically approached a positive constant.

We begin our analysis in this chapter by combining the *AK* technology with optimizing behavior of households and firms. This framework generates endogenous growth, and the outcomes are Pareto optimal as in the Ramsey model. One difficulty, however, is that this kind of model is inconsistent with the empirical evidence on convergence.

One interpretation of the *AK* model is that capital should be viewed broadly to include physical and human capital. In section 4.2 we work out a simple model with human capital that makes this interpretation explicit.

We noted in chapter 1 that a constant-returns production function at the aggregate level can reflect learning by doing and spillovers of knowledge. This kind of technology may support endogenous growth, but the outcomes tend not to be Pareto optimal because the spillovers constitute a form of externality. Hence, these models may have implications for desirable government policy. We also examine models with governmentally provided public goods and show that they have analogous implications for growth and government policy.

At the end of the chapter, we analyze transitional dynamics in models with optimizing agents when the technology features returns to capital that diminish but asymptotically approach a positive constant. These models can combine the endogenous-growth features of *AK* models with the convergence behavior found in the Ramsey model. Thus the empirical evidence on convergence may be consistent with these kinds of endogenous-growth models.

4.1 The *AK* Model

4.1.1 Behavior of Households

We use the setup from chapter 2 in which infinite-lived households maximize utility, as given by

$$U = \int_0^\infty e^{-(\rho-n)t} \cdot \left[\frac{c^{(1-\theta)} - 1}{(1-\theta)}\right] dt \tag{4.1}$$

subject to the constraint

$$\dot{a} = (r - n) \cdot a + w - c \tag{4.2}$$

where a is assets per person, r is the interest rate, w is the wage rate, and n is the growth rate of population. We again impose the constraint that rules out chain-letter debt finance:

$$\lim_{t\to\infty} \left\{ a(t) \cdot \exp\left[-\int_0^t [r(v) - n]\, dv \right] \right\} \geq 0 \tag{4.3}$$

The conditions for optimization are again

$$\dot{c}/c = (1/\theta) \cdot (r - \rho) \tag{4.4}$$

and the transversality condition,

$$\lim_{t\to\infty} \left\{ a(t) \cdot \exp\left[-\int_0^t [r(v) - n]\, dv \right] \right\} = 0 \tag{4.5}$$

4.1.2 Behavior of Firms

The only departure from chapter 2 is that firms have the linear production function,

$$y = f(k) = Ak \tag{4.6}$$

where $A > 0$. Equation (4.6) differs from the neoclassical production function in that the marginal product of capital is not diminishing ($f'' = 0$), and the Inada conditions are violated, in particular, $f'(k) = A$ as k goes to zero or infinity. The chapter appendix (section 4.7) shows more generally that the violation of the Inada condition $\lim_{k\to\infty}[f'(k)] = 0$ is the key element that underlies endogenous growth.

We noted in chapter 1 that the global absence of diminishing returns to capital in equation (4.6) may seem unrealistic, but the idea becomes more plausible if we construe capital, K, broadly to encompass human capital, knowledge, public infrastructure, and so on. Subsequent sections of this chapter explore these interpretations in more detail.

The conditions for profit maximization again require the marginal product of capital to equal the rental price, $R = r + \delta$. The only difference here is that the marginal product of capital is the constant A; hence,

$$r = A - \delta \tag{4.7}$$

Since the marginal product of labor is zero, the wage rate, w, is zero. (We can think of this zero wage rate as applying to raw labor, which has not been augmented by human capital.)

4.1.3 Equilibrium

We assume, as in chapter 2, that the economy is closed, so that $a = k$ holds. If we substitute $a = k$, $r = A - \delta$, and $w = 0$ into equations (4.2), (4.4), and (4.5), we get

$$\dot{k} = (A - \delta - n) \cdot k - c \tag{4.8}$$

$$\dot{c}/c = (1/\theta) \cdot (A - \delta - \rho) \tag{4.9}$$

$$\lim_{t \to \infty} \left\{ k(t) \cdot e^{-(A-\delta-n) \cdot t} \right\} = 0 \tag{4.10}$$

The striking aspect of equation (4.9) is that consumption growth does not depend on the stock of capital per person, k. In other words, if the level of consumption per capita at time 0 is $c(0)$, consumption per capita at time t is given by

$$c(t) = c(0) \cdot e^{(1/\theta) \cdot (A-\delta-\rho) \cdot t} \tag{4.11}$$

where the initial level of consumption, $c(0)$, remains to be determined.

We assume that the production function is sufficiently productive to ensure growth in c, but not so productive as to yield unbounded utility:

$$A > \rho + \delta > (A - \delta) \cdot (1 - \theta) + \theta n + \delta \tag{4.12}$$

The first part of this condition implies $\dot{c}/c > 0$. The second part, which is analogous to $\rho + \theta x > x + n$ in the model of chapter 2, ensures that the attainable utility is bounded[1] and that the transversality condition holds.

To compute the growth rate of capital and output per worker, divide equation (4.8) by k to get

$$c/k = (A - \delta - n) - \dot{k}/k$$

In the steady state (where, by definition, all variables grow at constant rates), the growth rate of capital per person is constant. Therefore, the right-hand side of the expression for c/k is constant. Consequently, c/k is constant, and the growth rate of capital per person (and, hence, the growth rate of output per person, y) equals the growth rate of consumption

1. To verify this result, substitute for $c(t)$ from equation (4.11) into the utility function to get

$$U = [1/(1-\theta)] \cdot \int_0^\infty e^{-(\rho-n) \cdot t} \cdot \left[c(0)^{1-\theta} \cdot e^{[(1-\theta)/\theta] \cdot (A-\delta-\rho) \cdot t} - 1 \right] dt$$

This integral converges to infinity unless $\rho - n > [(1-\theta)/\theta] \cdot (A - \delta - \rho)$. Add δ to both sides and rearrange this expression to get the second inequality in equation (4.12). An alternative way to write this expression is $(A - \delta - n) > \gamma$, where γ is the growth rate of per capita consumption, given by equation (4.9). The appendix on mathematics considers some cases in which unbounded utility can be handled.

per capita, which is given by equation (4.9). Note that this argument works only at the steady state: in principle, the growth rate of capital outside the steady state might not be constant. If that were the case, the ratio c/k would not be constant. Having said this, however, we now show that, in fact, consumption and capital (and, therefore, output) grow at the same rate at all times. In other words, the model has no transitional dynamics.

4.1.4 Transitional Dynamics

To compute the growth rate of capital outside of the steady state, we start by substituting for $c(t)$ from equation (4.11) into equation (4.8) to get

$$\dot{k} = (A - \delta - n) \cdot k - c(0) \cdot e^{(1/\theta)\cdot(A-\delta-\rho)\cdot t}$$

which is a first-order, linear differential equation in k. The general solution of this equation is[2]

$$k(t) = (\text{constant}) \cdot e^{(A-\delta-n)\cdot t} + [c(0)/\varphi] \cdot e^{(1/\theta)\cdot(A-\delta-\rho)\cdot t} \tag{4.13}$$

where

$$\varphi \equiv (A - \delta) \cdot (\theta - 1)/\theta + \rho/\theta - n \tag{4.14}$$

Note that an alternative way to write this combination of parameters is $\varphi \equiv (A-\delta-n)-\gamma$, where γ is the constant growth rate of per capita consumption, given by equation (4.9). Condition (4.12) implies $\varphi > 0$.

If we substitute for $k(t)$ from equation (4.13) into the transversality condition in equation (4.10), we get

$$\lim_{t\to\infty} \{\text{constant} + [c(0)/\varphi] \cdot e^{-\varphi t}\} = 0$$

Since $c(0)$ is finite and $\varphi > 0$, the second term inside the square brackets converges toward zero. Hence, the transversality condition requires the constant to be zero. Equations (4.11) and (4.13) therefore imply[3]

$$c(t) = \varphi \cdot k(t) \tag{4.15}$$

$$\dot{k}/k = \dot{c}/c = (1/\theta) \cdot (A - \delta - \rho) \tag{4.16}$$

Since $y = Ak$, it also follows that $\dot{y}/y = \dot{k}/k = \dot{c}/c$. Thus the model has no transitional dynamics: the variables $k(t)$, $c(t)$, and $y(t)$ begin at the values $k(0)$, $c(0) = \varphi \cdot k(0)$, and

2. See the appendix on mathematics for a discussion of this kind of first-order, linear differential equation.

3. Note that this model yields a closed-form policy function for c.

$y(0) = A \cdot k(0)$, respectively, and all three variables then grow at the constant rate $(1/\theta) \cdot (A - \delta - \rho)$.

In the *AK* model, changes in the underlying parameters can affect levels and growth rates of variables. For example, a permanent increase in the rate of population growth, n, does not affect the per capita growth rates shown in equation (4.16), but it reduces the level of per capita consumption (see equations [4.14] and [4.15]). Changes in A, ρ, and θ affect the levels and growth rates of c and k.

The gross saving rate is given by

$$s = (\dot{K} + \delta K)/Y = (1/A) \cdot (\dot{k}/k + n + \delta) = \left[\frac{A - \rho + \theta n + (\theta - 1) \cdot \delta}{\theta A}\right] \tag{4.17}$$

where $\dot{k}/k = (1/\theta) \cdot (A - \delta - \rho)$. Thus the gross saving rate is constant and, aside from n, depends on the same parameters that influence the per capita growth rate.

4.1.5 The Phase Diagram

We can analyze the dynamic behavior of the economy by constructing a phase diagram in k and c. Note that, because $A > \rho + \delta$, consumption growth is always positive—therefore, a $\dot{c} = 0$ schedule does not exist. Thus the arrows in the phase diagram displayed in figure 4.1 point north. We can use equation (4.8) to find that the $\dot{k} = 0$ schedule is a straight line

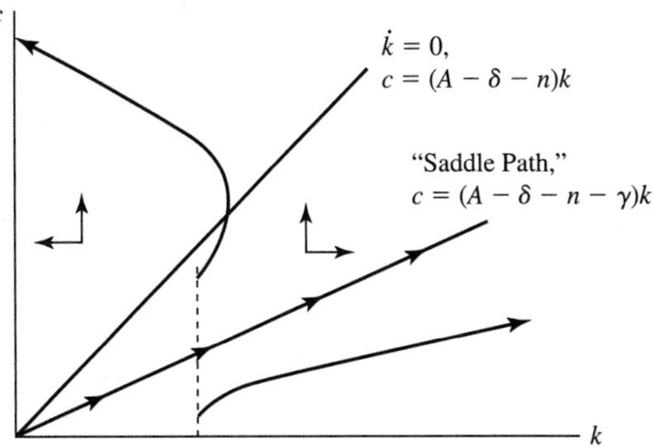

Figure 4.1
Phase diagram for the AK model. The $\dot{k} = 0$ schedule is a straight line through the origin with slope $A - \delta - n > 0$. The arrows to the right of this line point east, and the opposite is true to the left. Because $A > \rho + \delta$, consumption growth is always positive, so the $\dot{c} = 0$ schedule does not exist and arrows always point north. Equation (4.15) suggests that the saddle path is another straight line with slope $\varphi = (A - \delta - n) - \gamma$, which is smaller than the slope of the $\dot{k} = 0$ schedule. The transversality condition and the Euler equation ensure that the economy is always on the saddle path so that the ratio of consumption to capital is always constant.

through the origin with slope $A - \delta - n$. The arrows to the right of this line point east, and the opposite holds to the left. Equation (4.15) suggests that the path that the economy takes (the "saddle path") is another straight line with slope φ. Notice that, since $\varphi = (A - \delta - n) - \gamma$, the slope of the stable arm is smaller than the slope of the $\dot{k} = 0$ schedule. Given $k(0)$, if initial consumption is chosen above the saddle path, the economy will crash into the vertical axis. This outcome violates the Euler equation (an analogous argument was discussed in chapter 2 for the neoclassical model). If the initial consumption is chosen below the saddle path, c and k grow without bound. Along this path, the capital stock k grows faster than c, and the transversality condition is violated. The only choice that satisfies all first-order conditions (including transversality) is the saddle path, which entails a constant value of c/k.

4.1.6 Determinants of the Growth Rate

A striking difference between the *AK* model and the neoclassical growth model of chapter 2 concerns the determination of the long-run per capita growth rate. In the *AK* model, the long-run growth rate (which equals the short-run growth rate) depends in equation (4.16) on the parameters that determine the willingness to save and the productivity of capital. Lower values of ρ and θ, which raise the willingness to save, imply a higher per capita growth rate in equation (4.16) and a higher saving rate in equation (4.17). An improvement in the level of technology, A, which raises the marginal and average products of capital, also raises the growth rate and alters the saving rate. In a later section of this chapter, we show that changes in various kinds of government policies amount to shifts in A; that is, we can generalize the interpretation of the parameter A to go beyond literal differences in the level of the production function.

In contrast to the effects on long-run growth in the *AK* model, the Ramsey model of chapter 2 implies that the long-run per capita growth rate is pegged at the value x, the exogenous rate of technological change. A greater willingness to save or an improvement in the level of technology shows up in the long run as higher levels of capital and output per effective worker but in no change in the per capita growth rate.

The different results reflect the workings of diminishing returns to capital in the neoclassical model, and the absence of these diminishing returns in the *AK* model. Quantitatively, the extent of the difference depends on how rapidly diminishing returns set in, a characteristic that determines how quickly economies converge to the steady state in the neoclassical model. If diminishing returns set in slowly, the convergence period is long. In this case, shifts in the willingness to save or the level of technology affect the growth rate for a long time in the neoclassical model, even if not forever. Thus, the distinction between the neoclassical and *AK* models is substantial if convergence is rapid, but becomes less serious if—as seems to be the case—convergence occurs slowly. If convergence is extremely slow, the growth effects that appear in the *AK* model provide a satisfactory approximation to the effects on the growth rate over a long interval in the neoclassical model.

We showed in chapter 2 that the outcomes in the Ramsey model were Pareto optimal. We demonstrated this result by showing that the outcomes coincided with those that would be generated by a hypothetical social planner who had the same form of objective function as the representative household. It is straightforward to follow the same procedure here to prove that the equilibrium in the AK model is Pareto optimal.[4] This result makes sense because the elimination of diminishing returns in the production function—that is, the replacement of the neoclassical production function by the AK form—does not introduce any sources of market failure into the model.

4.2 A One-Sector Model with Physical and Human Capital

We mentioned before that one interpretation of the AK model is that capital should be viewed broadly to include physical and human components. We now work out a simple model with human capital that makes this interpretation explicit.

Assume that the inputs to the production function are physical and human capital, K and H:

$$Y = F(K, H) \tag{4.18}$$

where $F(\cdot)$ exhibits the standard neoclassical properties, including constant returns to scale in K and H. This production function is similar to one used in chapter 3, except that we previously assumed a Cobb–Douglas form with diminishing returns to scale in K and H. We can use the condition of constant returns to scale to write the production function in an intensive form:

$$Y = K \cdot f(H/K) \tag{4.19}$$

where $f'(H/K) > 0$.

Output can be used on a one-for-one basis for consumption, for investment in physical capital, or for investment in human capital. Hence, we assume that the one-sector technology applies to the production of human capital—that is, to education—as well as to the production of consumables and physical capital. (We introduce a separate education sector in chapter 5.) The stocks of physical and human capital depreciate at the rates δ_K and δ_H, respectively. We assume that population, L, is constant, so that changes in H reflect only the net investment in human capital.

Let R_K and R_H be the rental prices paid by competitive firms for the use of the two types of capital. In the absence of barriers to entry, competition among firms will drive

4. The planner chooses the path of c to maximize U in equation (4.1), subject to equation (4.8), $c(t) \geq 0$, and the given initial value $k(0)$.

profits down to zero. Profit maximization and this zero-profit condition then imply (as in the discussion of chapter 2) that the marginal product of each input equals its rental price:

$$\partial Y/\partial K = f(H/K) - (H/K) \cdot f'(H/K) = R_K \tag{4.20}$$

$$\partial Y/\partial H = f'(H/K) = R_H$$

Since the two types of capital are perfectly substitutable with each other and with consumables on the production side, the price of each type of capital would be fixed at unity.[5] Hence, the rates of return to owners of capital are $R_K - \delta_K$ and $R_H - \delta_H$, respectively, and each rate of return must be equal in equilibrium to the interest rate, r. If we use equation (4.20) and rearrange terms, this equalization of rates of return implies

$$f(H/K) - f'(H/K) \cdot (1 + H/K) = \delta_K - \delta_H \tag{4.21}$$

This condition determines a unique, constant value of H/K.[6]

If we define $A \equiv f(H/K)$, a constant, then equation (4.19) implies $Y = AK$. Thus this model with two types of capital is essentially the same as the AK model that we analyzed in the previous section. We know from that analysis that the equilibrium features constant and equal growth rates of C, K, and Y. (These growth rates equal the per capita growth rates because L is constant.) Since H/K is fixed, H grows at the same rate as the other variables.

The main conclusion from this simple case is that we can think of K as a proxy for a composite of capital goods that includes physical and human components. If we regard constant returns to the two kinds of capital as plausible, then the AK model may be a satisfactory representation of this broader model. We consider in chapter 5 some additional effects that arise when we drop the assumptions of the one-sector model and assume instead that the production function for education differs from that for goods.

4.3 Models with Learning by Doing and Knowledge Spillovers

4.3.1 Technology

The key to endogenous growth in the AK model is the absence of diminishing returns to the factors that can be accumulated. A number of authors—including Frankel (1962),

5. This result applies if the constraint of nonnegative gross investment in each type of capital is nonbinding or if units of old capital can, unrealistically, be consumed or converted into the other type of capital. We take explicit account of these kinds of constraints in chapter 5.

6. The expression on the left-hand side of equation (4.21) can be shown readily to be monotonically increasing in H/K. Moreover, this expression ranges from $-\infty$ to $+\infty$ as H/K goes from 0 to ∞. It follows that the solution for H/K exists and is unique.

Griliches (1979), Romer (1986), and Lucas (1988)—have constructed models of endogenous growth in which spillover effects play a central role. For reasons probably related to timing, the Romer analysis has exerted the greatest influence.[7] He used Arrow's (1962) setup to eliminate the tendency for diminishing returns to capital accumulation by assuming that knowledge creation was a side product of investment. A firm that increases its physical capital learns simultaneously how to produce more efficiently. This positive effect of experience on productivity is called learning by doing or, in this case, learning by investing.

We can illustrate the possibilities by considering a neoclassical production function with labor-augmenting technology for firm i,

$$Y_i = F(K_i, A_i L_i) \tag{4.22}$$

where L_i and K_i are the conventional inputs, and A_i is the index of knowledge available to the firm. The function $F(\cdot)$ satisfies the neoclassical properties that we detailed in chapter 1 (equations [1.5a]–[1.5c]): positive and diminishing marginal products of each input, constant returns to scale, and the Inada conditions. Technology is assumed to be labor augmenting so that a steady state exists when A_i grows at a constant rate. Unlike chapter 2, however, we do not assume here that A_i grows exogenously at the rate x. Furthermore, for reasons that will become apparent later, we assume that the aggregate labor force, L, is constant.

We follow Arrow (1962), Sheshinski (1967), and Romer (1986) and make two assumptions about productivity growth. First, learning by doing works through each firm's net investment. Specifically, an increase in a firm's capital stock leads to a parallel increase in its stock of knowledge, A_i. This process reflects Arrow's idea that knowledge and productivity gains come from investment and production, a formulation that was inspired by the empirical observation of large positive effects of experience on productivity in airframe manufacturing, shipbuilding, and other areas (see Wright, 1936; Searle, 1946; Asher, 1956; and Rapping, 1965). This idea is supported more broadly by Schmookler's (1966) evidence that patents—a proxy for learning—closely follow investment in physical capital.

The second key assumption is that each firm's knowledge is a public good that any other firm can access at zero cost. In other words, once discovered, a piece of knowledge spills over instantly across the whole economy. This assumption implies that the change in each firm's technology term, $\dot{A}_i$, corresponds to the economy's overall learning and is therefore proportional to the change in the aggregate capital stock, $\dot{K}$.

7. Cannon (2000) says in this respect: "Frankel (1962) anticipates ideas in use in the modern literature and deserves wider recognition. Why the paper was ignored at the time remains a bit of a puzzle and perhaps serves as a demonstration of the role of chance in the research and growth processes."

If we combine the assumptions of learning by doing and knowledge spillovers, we can replace A_i by K in equation (4.22) and write the production function for firm i as[8]

$$Y_i = F(K_i, KL_i) \tag{4.23}$$

If K and L_i are constant, each firm faces diminishing returns to K_i as in the neoclassical model of chapter 2. However, if each producer expands K_i, then K rises accordingly and provides a spillover benefit that raises the productivity of all firms. Moreover, equation (4.23) is homogeneous of degree one in K_i and K for given L_i; that is, there are constant returns to capital at the social level—when K_i and K expand together for fixed L. This constancy of the social returns to capital will yield endogenous growth.

The essence of the Romer analysis leading up to equation (4.23) appeared in the Frankel (1962) paper, which assumed that an economy-wide productivity factor (which he called the "development modifier") equaled the sum of the capital stocks employed by each firm. However, Frankel did not detail the nature of the spillover process; in particular, he did not focus on the role of knowledge.

In the Griliches (1979) version of equation (4.23), K_i represents firm i's specific knowledge capital, whereas K (modeled again as the sum of the K_i) is the aggregate level of knowledge in an industry. The only substantive difference from Romer (1986) is that Griliches focused on R&D investments as relevant to the expansion of knowledge, whereas Romer looked at overall net investment.

In the Lucas (1988) story, knowledge is thought to be created and transmitted through human capital. Therefore, K_i refers to a firm's employment of human capital and K to the aggregate level of human capital in an industry or country. In this case, the spillover effects involve interactions with smart people. One important issue, discussed later, is whether the spillovers involve the total or average level of human capital.

On one level, the spillover assumption is natural because knowledge has a nonrival character: if one firm uses an idea, it does not prevent others from using it. On another level, firms have incentives to maintain secrecy over their discoveries as well as formal patent protection for inventions. Knowledge about productivity improvements would therefore leak out only gradually, and innovators would retain competitive advantages for some time. In fact, in a decentralized setup, this individual advantage is essential to motivate investments, such as Griliches's (1979) outlays on R&D, that are specifically directed at making discoveries. The type of interaction among firms that arises in this setup cannot, however, be adequately described by standard models of perfect competition, and we postpone a consideration of alternative approaches until chapters 6 and 7. In this section, we make the extreme assumption that all discoveries are unintended by-products of investment and that

8. We neglect any baseline knowledge that producers have when no capital has ever been produced.

these discoveries immediately become common knowledge. This specification allows us to retain the framework of perfect competition, although the outcomes will turn out not to be Pareto optimal.

The assumption here is that the spillovers of knowledge operate at the level of the overall economy. Alternative assumptions are that the spillovers apply to an industry, to a limited geographical area, within a particular political jurisdiction, and so on. The extent to which these spillovers apply will be crucial for the model's empirical implementation.

A firm's profit can be written as

$$L_i \cdot [F(k_i, K) - (r + \delta) \cdot k_i - w] \tag{4.24}$$

where $r + \delta$ is the rental price of capital and w is the wage rate. We assume, as usual, that each competitive firm takes these factor prices as given. We now also make the parallel assumption that each firm is small enough to neglect its own contribution to the aggregate capital stock and, therefore, treats K as given. Profit maximization and the zero-profit condition (as detailed in chapter 2) then imply

$$\partial y_i/\partial k_i = F_1(k_i, K) = r + \delta \tag{4.25}$$

$$\partial Y_i/\partial L_i = F(k_i, K) - k_i \cdot F_1(k_i, K) = w$$

where $F_1(\cdot)$—the partial derivative of $F(k_i, K)$ with respect to its first argument, k_i—is the *private* marginal product of capital. In particular, this marginal product neglects the contribution of k_i to K and, hence, to aggregate knowledge.

In equilibrium, all firms make the same choices, so that $k_i = k$ and $K = kL$ apply. Since $F(k_i, K)$ is homogeneous of degree one in k_i and K, we can write the average product of capital as

$$F(k_i, K)/k_i = f(K/k_i) = f(L) \tag{4.26}$$

where $f(L)$—the function for the average product of capital—satisfies $f'(L) > 0$ and $f''(L) < 0$. Note that this average product is invariant with k, because the learning-by-doing and spillover effects eliminate the tendency for diminishing returns. The average product is, however, increasing in the size of the labor force, L. This last property is unusual and leads to scale effects that we discuss later.

The private marginal product of capital can be expressed from equation (4.26) as

$$F_1(k_i, K) = f(L) - L \cdot f'(L) \tag{4.27}$$

Hence, the private marginal product of capital is less than the average product, $f(L)$, and is invariant with k. Equation (4.27) implies also that the private marginal product of capital is increasing in L (because $f''(L) < 0$).

4.3.2 Equilibrium

We still assume a closed economy in which infinite-lived households maximize utility in the usual way. Therefore, the budget constraint is given by equation (4.2), the growth rate of per capita consumption by equation (4.4), and the transversality condition by equation (4.5). If we use the condition $r = F_1(k_i, K) - \delta$ and the form for the private marginal product of capital from equation (4.27), then equation (4.4) can be rewritten as

$$\dot{c}/c = (1/\theta) \cdot [f(L) - L \cdot f'(L) - \delta - \rho] \tag{4.28}$$

As in the *AK* model, this growth rate is constant (as long as L is constant). We assume that the parameters are such that the growth rate is positive but not large enough to yield infinite utility:

$$f(L) - L \cdot f'(L) > \rho + \delta > (1 - \theta) \cdot [f(L) - L \cdot f'(L) - \delta - \rho]/\theta + \delta \tag{4.29}$$

This condition corresponds to equation (4.12) in the *AK* model.

If we substitute $a = k$ and the first-order conditions from equation (4.25) into the budget constraint of equation (4.2), we get the accumulation equation for k:

$$\dot{k} = f(L) \cdot k - c - \delta k \tag{4.30}$$

If we use this equation along with the transversality condition, we can show that the model has no transitional dynamics: the variables k and y always grow at the rate shown for $\dot{c}/c$ in equation (4.28). Since the analysis is essentially the same as that for the *AK* model, we leave this demonstration as an exercise.

4.3.3 Pareto Nonoptimality and Policy Implications

To see whether the outcomes are Pareto optimal, we can follow our usual practice of comparing the decentralized solution with the results from the social planner's problem. The planner maximizes the utility shown in equation (4.1) (with n assumed here to be zero), subject to the accumulation constraint in equation (4.30). The key aspect of this optimization is that, unlike an individual producer, the planner recognizes that each firm's increase in its capital stock adds to the aggregate capital stock and, hence, contributes to the productivity of all other firms in the economy. In other words, the social planner *internalizes* the spillovers of knowledge across the firms.

To find the optimal choices of c and k, set up the Hamiltonian,

$$J = e^{-\rho t} \cdot (c^{1-\theta} - 1)/(1 - \theta) + \nu \cdot [f(L) \cdot k - c - \delta k]$$

The optimization involves the standard first-order conditions, $J_c = 0$ and $\dot{\nu} = -J_k$, and the transversality condition, $\lim_{t\to\infty} \nu k = 0$. We can manipulate the first-order conditions in the usual way to derive the condition for the growth rate of c:

$$\dot{c}/c \text{ (planner)} = (1/\theta) \cdot [f(L) - \delta - \rho] \tag{4.31}$$

The social planner sets the growth rate of consumption in accordance with the average product of capital, $f(L)$, whereas the decentralized solution shown in equation (4.28) relates the growth rate to the private marginal product of capital, $f(L) - L \cdot f'(L)$. Since this private marginal product falls short of the average product, growth is too low in the decentralized equilibrium.

In the present model, the learning-by-doing and spillover effects exactly offset the diminishing returns that face an individual producer. Hence, the returns are constant at the social level, and the social marginal product of capital equals the average product, $f(L)$. Since the social planner internalizes the spillovers, this social marginal product appears as a determinant of the growth rate in equation (4.31). The decentralized solution in equation (4.28) dictates a lower growth rate because the individual producers do not internalize the spillovers; that is, they base decisions on the private marginal product, $f(L) - L \cdot f'(L)$, which falls short of the social marginal product.

The social optimum can be attained in a decentralized economy by subsidizing purchases of capital goods (an investment-tax credit). Alternatively, the government can generate the optimum by subsidizing production. These subsidies work in the model because they raise the private rate of return to investment and thereby tend to eliminate the excess of social over private returns. Of course, to avoid other distortions, the subsidies on capital or production would have to be financed with a lump-sum tax. These kinds of taxes are normally difficult to find, but in the current model—which contains no labor/leisure choice—a consumption tax at a constant rate would amount to a lump-sum tax. This kind of tax was explored in chapter 3.

4.3.4 A Cobb–Douglas Example

If the production function in equation (4.23) takes the Cobb–Douglas form, output for firm i is given by

$$Y_i = A \cdot (K_i)^{\alpha} \cdot (KL_i)^{1-\alpha} \tag{4.32}$$

where $0 < \alpha < 1$. If we substitute $y_i = Y_i/L_i$, $k_i = K_i/L_i$, and $k = K/L$, and then set $y_i = y$ and $k_i = k$, the average product of capital is

$$y/k = f(L) = AL^{1-\alpha} \tag{4.33}$$

which is a special case of equation (4.26). Note that equation (4.33) satisfies the general properties that y/k is invariant with k and increasing in L.

We can determine the private marginal product of capital by differentiating equation (4.32) with respect to K_i, while holding fixed K and L. If we then substitute $k_i = k$, the result is

$$\partial Y_i/\partial K_i = A\alpha L^{1-\alpha} \tag{4.34}$$

a special case of equation (4.27). In accordance with the general properties discussed before, the private marginal product of capital in equation (4.34) is invariant with k, increasing in L, and less than the average product shown in equation (4.33) (because $0 < \alpha < 1$).

If we substitute from equation (4.34) into equation (4.28), we find that the decentralized growth rate is given by[9]

$$\dot{c}/c = (1/\theta) \cdot (A\alpha L^{1-\alpha} - \delta - \rho) \tag{4.35}$$

Substitution from equation (4.33) into equation (4.31) gives the social planner's growth rate as

$$\dot{c}/c \text{ (planner)} = (1/\theta) \cdot (AL^{1-\alpha} - \delta - \rho) \tag{4.36}$$

Since $\alpha < 1$, the decentralized growth rate is lower than the planner's growth rate.

The social optimum can be attained in the decentralized economy by introducing an investment-tax credit at the rate $1 - \alpha$ and financing it with a lump-sum tax. If buyers of capital pay only the fraction α of the cost, the private return on capital corresponds to the social return. We can then show that the decentralized choices coincide with those of the social planner. Alternatively, the government could generate the same outcome by subsidizing production at the rate $(1 - \alpha)/\alpha$.

4.3.5 Scale Effects

The model implies a scale effect in that an expansion of the aggregate labor force, L, raises the per capita growth rate for the decentralized economy in equation (4.28) and for the social planner in equation (4.31). These results reflect, respectively, the positive effect of L on the private marginal product of capital, $f(L) - L \cdot f'(L)$, in equation (4.27) and on the average product, $f(L)$, in equation (4.26). Moreover, if the labor force grows over time, the per capita growth rates would increase over time.[10]

9. We assume that the parameters allow for positive growth and bounded utility; hence,

$$A\alpha L^{1-\alpha} > \rho + \delta > (1 - \theta) \cdot (A\alpha L^{1-\alpha} - \delta - \rho)/\theta + \delta$$

a result that specializes equation (8.23).

10. This result follows at once for $\dot{c}/c$, but $\dot{k}/k$ and $\dot{y}/y$ would not correspond to $\dot{c}/c$ in an environment of growing L. Also, if L rises enough, the condition for bounded utility in equation (8.23) must eventually be violated if $\theta < 1$.

If we can identify L with the aggregate labor force of a country, the prediction is that countries with more workers tend to grow faster in per capita terms. The empirical results discussed in chapter 12 for a large number of countries in the post–World War II period indicate that the growth rate of per capita GDP bears little relation to the country's level of population. (These results apply when the initial level of per capita GDP, the average person's education, and some other variables are held constant.) Thus these findings do not support a scale effect in country size.

It is possible that the scale variable for spillovers, L, does not relate closely to aggregates measured at the country level. The relevant scale can, for example, be larger than the size of the domestic economy if producers benefit from knowledge accumulated in other countries. Kremer (1993) argues that the correct scale variable might be world population, and he provides some evidence from the long-run history that world population is positively correlated with productivity growth. Alternatively, if the free transmission of ideas is limited to close neighbors (either geographically or in terms of industry), the appropriate scale may be smaller than the home economy. These caveats blur the empirical implications of the spillovers model and make difficult the testing of this model with macroeconomic data.

We derived the scale effect from a model that assumed learning by doing and spillovers of knowledge. These elements generate a scale effect on growth rates because they imply constant returns to K and increasing returns to K and L at the social level. A similar scale effect would result if this pattern of factor returns prevailed for other reasons. The learning-by-doing/spillovers model is special, however, in that it also implies constant returns to scale in the factors, K_i and L_i, that are chosen by an individual firm. If increasing returns applied at the level of a firm, the model would be inconsistent with perfect competition, because firms would have an incentive to grow arbitrarily large in order to benefit from the scale economy. We avoided this outcome by assuming that a firm's technology depended on the aggregate capital stock, K, and that each firm neglected its own contribution to this aggregate. This specification allows us to maintain the assumption of perfect competition, but it also implies that the competitive equilibrium is not Pareto optimal.

One way to eliminate the scale effect is to argue that the term A_i in equation (4.22) depends on the economy's average capital per worker, K/L, rather than the aggregate capital stock, K. This alternative specification was used by Frankel (1962) in his main analysis but without much discussion. Lucas (1988) also uses this specification, because he assumes that the learning and spillovers involve human capital and that each producer benefits from the *average* level of human capital in the economy, rather than the *aggregate*. Thus, instead of thinking about the accumulated knowledge or experience of other producers, we have to think here about the benefit from interacting (freely) with the average person, who possesses the average level of skills and knowledge. The Lucas formulation might arise if we thought that the presence of stupid people makes it difficult to identify and use the good ideas provided by smart people.

To analyze this model, we can let $A_i = K/L$ in equation (4.22) and then proceed as before. The only difference in the results is that the average product of capital and the private marginal product of capital no longer depend on L. For example, in the Cobb–Douglas case, the average product in equation (4.33) becomes A rather than $AL^{1-\alpha}$, and the private marginal product in equation (4.34) becomes $A\alpha$ rather than $A\alpha L^{1-\alpha}$. Since the formal analysis is the same as before, we leave the proof of these results as an exercise.

4.4 Public Services and Endogenous Growth

In the *AK* model, anything that changes the level of the baseline technology, A, affects the long-run per capita growth rate. In the model with learning by doing and knowledge spillovers, the nonrivalry of ideas could eliminate the tendency for diminishing returns to capital accumulation and, thereby, generate the *AK* form. We show in this section that the government's public services are another possible source of the *AK* form. In this case, the government's choices about public services determine the coefficient A and thereby affect the economy's long-run growth rate.

4.4.1 A Public-Goods Model

We extend here the model from chapter 3 in which the government's purchases of goods and services, G, enter into the production function as pure public goods. If the production function takes the Cobb–Douglas form, the specification for firm i is (following Barro, 1990b)

$$Y_i = AL_i^{1-\alpha} \cdot K_i^{\alpha} \cdot G^{1-\alpha} \tag{4.37}$$

where $0 < \alpha < 1$. This equation implies that production for each firm exhibits constant returns to scale in the private inputs, L_i and K_i. We assume that the aggregate labor force, L, is constant. For fixed G, the economy will face diminishing returns to the accumulation of aggregate capital, K, as in the Ramsey model of chapter 2. If, however, G rises along with K, equation (4.37) implies that diminishing returns will not arise; that is, the production function specifies constant returns in K_i and G for fixed L_i. For this reason, the economy is capable of endogenous growth, as in the *AK* model studied earlier in this chapter. Note also that the form of the production function implies that the public services are complementary with the private inputs in the sense that an increase in G raises the marginal products of L_i and K_i.

If the exponent on G in equation (4.37) were less than $1 - \alpha$, diminishing returns to K_i and G would apply, and these diminishing returns would rule out endogenous growth.

Conversely, if the exponent were greater than $1 - \alpha$, growth rates would tend to rise over time. We are therefore focusing on the special case in which the exponent on G exactly equals $1 - \alpha$, so that the constant returns to K_i and G imply that the economy is capable of endogenous growth. This setting parallels the production function for the learning-by-doing/spillovers model in equation (4.23), except that the aggregate capital stock, K, has been replaced by the quantity of public goods, G.

Suppose that the government finances its purchases of goods and services with lump-sum taxes (which, in the absence of a labor-leisure choice, could be tax rates on consumption or labor income as discussed in chapter 3). For given G, each profit-maximizing firm equates the marginal product of capital to the rental price, $r + \delta$. Hence, equation (4.37) implies

$$\alpha A \cdot k_i^{-(1-\alpha)} \cdot G^{1-\alpha} = r + \delta \tag{4.38}$$

Therefore, each firm chooses the same capital-labor ratio, $k_i = k$. The production function from equation (4.37) can therefore be aggregated to get

$$Y = ALk^{\alpha}G^{1-\alpha} \tag{4.39}$$

Equation (4.39) implies

$$G = (G/Y)^{1/\alpha}(AL)^{1/\alpha} \cdot k \tag{4.40}$$

We assume now that the government chooses a constant ratio of its purchases to GDP, G/Y. If we use equation (4.40) to substitute for G in equation (4.38), we get

$$r + \delta = \alpha A^{1/\alpha} \cdot (G/Y)^{(1-\alpha)/\alpha} \cdot L^{(1-\alpha)/\alpha} \tag{4.41}$$

If G/Y and L are constant, the marginal product of capital is invariant with k and, hence, constant over time. The level of the marginal product is increasing in L, so the model predicts scale effects. These results parallel the findings from the model with learning by doing and spillovers (see equation [4.27]).

The constant marginal product of capital in equation (4.41) plays the same role in the growth process that the constant A played in the AK model. There are no transitional dynamics, and the growth rates of c, k, and y all equal the same constant. We can determine this common growth rate from the expression for consumption growth in equation (4.4):[11]

$$\dot{c}/c = (1/\theta) \cdot [\alpha A^{1/\alpha} \cdot (G/Y)^{(1-\alpha)/\alpha} \cdot L^{(1-\alpha)/\alpha} - \delta - \rho] \tag{4.42}$$

11. As in the AK and spillover models, we require some inequality conditions for the growth rate to be positive and for utility to be bounded. The former condition is $\partial Y_i/\partial K_i - \delta > \rho$, and the latter condition—which corresponds to the transversality condition—is $[(\theta - 1)/\theta] \cdot (\partial Y_i/\partial K_i - \delta) + \rho/\theta > 0$. The value for $\partial Y_i/\partial K_i$ is given by the right-hand side of equation (4.41).

The growth rate is increasing in G/Y because we assumed that public outlays, G, were financed by a nondistorting tax.

We could have assumed instead that G was financed partly by a distorting tax—in the present model, these could be the taxes on capital income, τ_a and τ_f, that we considered in chapter 3. In this case, the expression for the net marginal product of capital in equation (4.42), $\alpha A^{1/\alpha} \cdot (G/Y)^{(1-\alpha)/\alpha} \cdot L^{(1-\alpha)/\alpha} - \delta$, would be multiplied by $(1-\tau_a) \cdot (1-\tau_f)$ to get the after-tax marginal product of capital. Then, if τ_a and τ_f tended to rise with G/Y, the direct positive effect of G/Y on the growth rate in equation (4.42) would be offset by a negative effect from the higher tax rates. The relation between the growth rate and G/Y is then likely to be nonmonotonic—first rising and subsequently falling when the tax-rate effect became dominant. The detailed results depend on the way in which τ_a and τ_f relate to G/Y. We leave this analysis as an exercise.

We now return to the case of lump-sum taxes, as assumed in equation (4.42). We can, as usual, determine the optimal outcomes in the model by figuring out the choices of a benevolent social planner who seeks to maximize the utility attained by the representative household. The maximization entails the natural efficiency condition $\partial Y/\partial G = 1$.[12] The particular functional form of the production function [equation (4.39)] implies that this condition corresponds to

$$G/Y = 1 - \alpha \tag{4.43}$$

Therefore, the optimal ratio of government purchases to GDP is, in fact, constant in this model.

If G/Y is determined from equation (4.43), the decentralized growth-rate solution from equation (4.42) is also the one that a social planner would choose.[13] This optimality of the decentralized result applies because of the assumption that G is financed by lump-sum taxes. Substitution from equation (4.43) into the condition for the growth rate in equation (4.42) therefore yields

$$\dot{c}/c \text{ (Social planner)} = (1/\theta) \cdot \left[\alpha A^{1/\alpha} \cdot (1-\alpha)^{(1-\alpha)/\alpha} \cdot L^{(1-\alpha)/\alpha} - \delta - \rho\right] \tag{4.44}$$

12. The planner would choose c, k, and G so as to maximize $\int_0^\infty e^{-\rho t} \cdot \frac{c^{1-\theta}-1}{1-\theta} \cdot dt$, subject to $\dot{k} = Ak^\alpha G^{1-\alpha} - c - \delta k - G/L$. The Hamiltonian is $J = e^{-\rho t} \cdot \frac{c^{1-\theta}-1}{1-\theta} + \nu \cdot (Ak^\alpha G^{1-\alpha} - c - \delta k - G/L)$. The first-order conditions are

(i) $e^{-\rho t} \cdot c^{-\theta} = \nu$

(ii) $A \cdot (1-\alpha) \cdot k^\alpha G^{-\alpha} = 1/L$

(iii) $-\dot{\nu} = \nu \cdot (A\alpha k^{\alpha-1} G^{1-\alpha} - \delta)$

plus the usual transversality condition. Notice that (ii) is equivalent to $\partial Y/\partial G = 1$.

13. Take logarithms and derivatives of the first-order condition (i) from the previous note, substitute the result into (iii), and use (ii) to get equation (4.44).

An increase in scale, represented by L, raises the marginal product of capital in equation (4.41) and raises the growth rate correspondingly in equation (4.44). Therefore, the public-goods model predicts scale effects that resemble those in the model with learning by doing and spillovers (see equations [4.35] and [4.36]). In the present context, the economy benefits from a greater scale because the governmental services are assumed to be nonrival and can therefore be spread costlessly over additional users. A continuing expansion of L, resulting from population growth, would imply rising per capita growth rates. Thus, as in the learning-by-doing/spillovers model, we had to assume zero population growth to study steady states.

As mentioned before, the cross-country data indicate that the growth rate of per capita GDP bears little relation to country size, as measured by population. (Countries are a natural unit of observation here if we think that the benefits from the government's public goods extend only over the government's political jurisdiction.) The failure to detect more important scale effects likely means that most of the government's services do not have the nonrival character that is assumed in the model. We therefore now consider an alternative setting in which the government's services are subject to congestion. We shall show that this model has very different implications for scale effects and for desirable public finance.

4.4.2 A Congestion Model

As mentioned in chapter 3, many governmental activities, such as highways, water systems, police and fire services, and courts, are subject to congestion. For a given quantity of aggregate services, G, the quantity available to an individual declines as other users congest the facilities. For governmental activities that serve as an input to private production, we model this congestion (as in Barro and Sala-i-Martin, 1992c) by writing the production function for the ith producer as

$$Y_i = AK_i \cdot f(G/Y) \tag{4.45}$$

where $f' > 0$ and $f'' < 0$. The production process is AK modified by the term that involves public services: an increase in G *relative* to aggregate output, Y, expands Y_i for given K_i. Because of congestion, an increase in Y for given G lowers the public services available to each producer and therefore reduces Y_i. The formulation assumes that G has to rise in relation to total output, Y, in order to expand the public services available to each user. We could have assumed alternatively that G had to rise in relation to aggregate private capital, K, in order to raise the quantity of services. The results would be essentially the same under this specification.

For given G and Y, a firm's production exhibits constant returns with respect to the private input K_i. If G grows at the same rate as Y, G/Y remains fixed, and the constant returns in K_i imply that the economy will generate endogenous growth, as in the AK model.

The condition for the marginal product of capital is modified from equation (4.41) to

$$r + \delta = A \cdot f(G/Y) \tag{4.46}$$

Note that, unlike the public-goods model, the marginal product and, hence, the rate of return, do not depend on the scale variable, L. The growth rates of c, k, and y all equal the same constant, given from equation (4.4) by

$$\dot{c}/c = (1/\theta) \cdot [A \cdot f(G/Y) - \delta - \rho] \tag{4.47}$$

This growth rate is increasing in G/Y and independent of L. The independence from L means that the puzzling scale effects do not appear in this model.

We can again work through the social planner's problem to assess the Pareto optimality of the decentralized outcomes. The planner would maximize the usual utility function, subject to the resource constraint (expressed in per capita terms),

$$\dot{k} = Ak \cdot f(G/Y) - c - \delta k - G/L \tag{4.48}$$

where we assume that the rate of population growth is zero. The Hamiltonian for this program is

$$J = e^{-\rho t} \cdot \frac{c^{1-\theta} - 1}{1 - \theta} + \upsilon \cdot [Ak \cdot f(G/Y) - c - \delta k - G/L] \tag{4.49}$$

Before we take derivatives with respect to c, k, and G, notice that the derivative of the production function with respect to k and G is a bit complicated. The reason is that aggregate output appears inside the expression for aggregate output. Hence, when we take the derivative of y with respect to k, we need to take into account that Y depends on Y through the term $f(G/Y)$. One way to solve the problem is to write the derivative with respect to k as

$$\frac{\partial y}{\partial k} = A \cdot f(G/Y) + Ak \cdot f'(G/Y) \cdot \left(\frac{-G/L}{y^2}\right) \cdot \frac{\partial y}{\partial k} \tag{4.50}$$

and then factor out $\frac{\partial y}{\partial k}$ to get, after rearranging terms,

$$\frac{\partial y}{\partial k} = \frac{A \cdot f(G/Y)}{1 + (G/Y) \cdot \frac{f'(G/Y)}{f(G/Y)}} \tag{4.51}$$

Similarly, the derivative of y with respect to G is

$$\frac{\partial y}{\partial G} = L \cdot \frac{\frac{f'(G/Y)}{f(G/Y)}}{1 + (G/Y) \cdot \frac{f'(G/Y)}{f(G/Y)}} \tag{4.52}$$

We are now ready to compute the first-order conditions for the planner. The FOC with respect to consumption delivers the usual consumption growth equation $\frac{\dot{c}}{c} = \frac{1}{\theta}(-\frac{\dot{\upsilon}}{\upsilon} - \rho)$. The FOC with respect to G requires that $\partial Y / \partial G = 1$. It is not surprising that the social planner satisfies this last condition: efficiency entails using G as an input up to the point where its marginal product equals its marginal unit, which is fixed at unity. Using equation (4.52), the efficiency condition can be written as

$$\frac{f'(G/Y)}{f(G/Y)} = \frac{1}{1 - (G/Y)} \tag{4.53}$$

Let $(G/Y)^*$ represent the ratio that satisfies this condition. The FOC with respect to capital requires

$$-\dot{\upsilon} = \upsilon \cdot \left(\frac{\partial y}{\partial k} - \delta\right) \tag{4.54}$$

Substituting equations (4.54), (4.51), and (4.52) into the consumption growth equation, we find that the social planner's growth rate is given by

$$\dot{c}/c \text{ (Social planner)} = (1/\theta) \cdot \{[1 - (G/Y)^*] \cdot A \cdot f[(G/Y)^*] - \delta - \rho\} \tag{4.55}$$

Thus a new result is that the social planner's growth rate would not correspond to the decentralized growth rate, given from equation (4.47), even when $G/Y = (G/Y)^*$. The reason is that the decentralized result reflects lump-sum taxation, and lump-sum taxes are inappropriate when the public services are subject to congestion. The intuition for equation (4.55) is as follows. An individual producer's decision to expand capital, K_i, and hence, output, Y_i, contributes to total output, Y, and thereby increases congestion for a given aggregate of public services, G. With a lump-sum tax, the individual producer neglects these adverse external effects and therefore has too great an incentive to expand K_i and Y_i. To internalize the distortion, a producer who raises Y_i has to provide enough additional resources to maintain the public services available to others, that is, to keep G/Y constant. The required compensation is G/Y times the addition to Y. That is why the term $[1 - (G/Y)^*]$ multiplies the gross marginal product of capital, $A \cdot f[(G/Y)^*]$, in equation (4.55). Interestingly, the decentralized solution would correspond to the social planner's result if output were taxed proportionately at the rate $(G/Y)^*$. This tax rate—effectively a user fee for the publicly provided services—would lower the after-tax marginal product of capital to $[1 - (G/Y)^*] \cdot A \cdot f[(G/Y)^*]$, which is the expression that appears in equation (4.55).

4.5 Transitional Dynamics, Endogenous Growth

The models considered thus far in this chapter lack any transitional dynamics. In particular, the prediction is that per capita growth rates would be independent of the initial levels of k and y. Thus these models are inconsistent with the empirical evidence on convergence, as discussed in chapters 11 and 12.

We showed in chapter 1, in models that assume a constant saving rate, that it is possible to construct an endogenous growth model that exhibits transitional dynamics in which the convergence property holds. These results follow if we modify the technology to reintroduce diminishing returns to capital but also assume that capital's marginal product is bounded from below as the capital stock tends to infinity (so that the Inada condition at infinity is violated). We show in this section how this kind of technology can be combined with the type of household optimization that applies in the Ramsey model.

The technologies that we consider here take the form considered by Jones and Manuelli (1990),

$$Y = F(K, L) = AK + \Omega(K, L) \tag{4.56}$$

where $\Omega(K, L)$ satisfies the properties of a neoclassical production function: positive and diminishing marginal products, constant returns to scale, and the Inada conditions (equations [1.5a]–[1.5c]). Production functions of the form of equation (4.56) are not neoclassical only because they violate one of the Inada conditions, $\lim_{K\to\infty}[\partial Y/\partial K] = A > 0$. The AK part of the production function will deliver endogenous growth, whereas the $\Omega(K, L)$ part will generate the convergence behavior. To keep the dynamic analysis manageable, we limit the discussion to some specific functional forms for $\Omega(K, L)$.

4.5.1 A Cobb–Douglas Example

We begin with the production function that we considered in chapter 1 (equation [1.35]):

$$Y = F(K, L) = AK + BK^{\alpha}L^{1-\alpha}$$

where $A > 0$, $B > 0$, and $0 < \alpha < 1$.[14] We can rewrite this function in per capita terms as

$$y = f(k) = Ak + Bk^{\alpha} \tag{4.57}$$

Note that $\lim_{k\to\infty}[f'(k)] = A > 0$.

14. All the results that we discuss in this section go through if L is replaced by $\hat{L}$, where $\hat{L} = Le^{xt}$. That is, we can allow for exogenous technological progress in the part of the production function that is subject to diminishing returns. If the parameter A grew steadily over time, the model would not have a steady state.

The dynamic equations for k and c are the usual ones derived for the Ramsey model in chapter 2 (equations [2.23] and [2.24] with $x = 0$):

$$\dot{k}/k = f(k)/k - c/k - (n+\delta) = A + B \cdot k^{\alpha-1} - c/k - (n+\delta) \tag{4.58}$$

$$\dot{c}/c = (1/\theta) \cdot [f'(k) - \delta - \rho] = (1/\theta) \cdot [A + B\alpha \cdot k^{\alpha-1} - \delta - \rho] \tag{4.59}$$

If the model generates endogenous growth—that is, $(\dot{k}/k)^* > 0$—then $k \to \infty$ as $t \to \infty$, and the terms involving $k^{\alpha-1}$ asymptotically become negligible. Therefore, the steady state looks exactly like the *AK* model, and the steady-state growth rates of c, k, and y are all given (from equation [4.16]) by

$$\gamma^* = (1/\theta) \cdot (A - \delta - \rho) \tag{4.60}$$

We assume $A > \delta + \rho$, so that $\gamma^* > 0$.[15] (If $A \leq \delta + \rho$, then $\gamma^* = 0$, just as in the standard Ramsey model discussed in chapter 2.)

We could try to follow the approach from figure 2.1 by constructing a phase diagram in (k, c) space. This method does not work, however, because k and c grow forever if $\gamma^* > 0$. A procedure that does work involves a transformation to variables that are constant in the steady state. We choose to study the evolution of the average product of capital, denoted by $z \equiv f(k)/k$, and the ratio of consumption to the capital stock, denoted by $\chi \equiv c/k$. Note that z is a *statelike variable* in that, like k, its value at a point in time is dictated by past investments and the evolution of L. Thus, if investment is finite and L has no jumps, z and k cannot jump at a point in time. In contrast, χ is a *controllike variable* in that, like c, its value can jump at a point in time. (Such jumps will, however, not be optimal in the equilibria that we focus on.) Unlike k and c, the two new variables, z and χ, approach constants in the steady state.

We can use equations (4.58) and (4.59) to derive a dynamic system in terms of the transformed variables, z and χ. The results can be written, after a fair amount of algebra, in the form

$$\dot{z} = -(1-\alpha) \cdot (z - A) \cdot (z - \chi - n - \delta) \tag{4.61}$$

$$\dot{\chi} = \chi \cdot \left[(\chi - \varphi) - \frac{(\theta - \alpha)}{\theta} \cdot (z - A) \right] \tag{4.62}$$

where $\varphi \equiv (A - \delta) \cdot (\theta - 1)/\theta + \rho/\theta - n$. We require $\varphi > 0$ to satisfy the transversality condition. This condition also ensures that utility is finite when c grows at the rate γ^* shown

15. We also continue to assume $\rho > n$, so that $A > \delta + \rho$ implies $A > \delta + n$. If the last inequality did not hold, utility would be unbounded if c were constant over time.

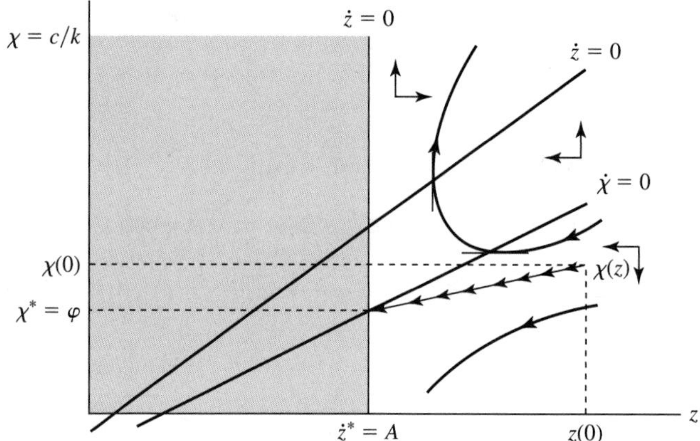

Figure 4.2
Transitional dynamics in an endogenous growth model (when $F[K, L] = AK + BK^{\alpha}L^{1-\alpha}$). The phase diagram is shown in (z, χ) space, where $z \equiv f(k)/k$ is the gross average product of capital and $\chi \equiv c/k$. The $\dot{\chi} = 0$ locus is a line with a slope that is less than one and is positive, as shown, if $\theta > \alpha$. There are two conditions that satisfy $\dot{z} = 0$. One is a vertical line at $z = A$, and the other is an upward-sloping line with unit slope. This line must cross the vertical line at A at a value of χ that exceeds χ^*. Since $z \equiv f(k)/k = A + Bk^{\alpha-1} > A$, the only steady state is the point at which the $\dot{\chi} = 0$ schedule intersects the vertical line $z = A$. Since $z > z^*$ applies initially, z and χ decline monotonically during the transition. (Note that the result on the path of χ depends on the assumption $\theta > \alpha$.)

in equation (4.60). It is clear from equations (4.61) and (4.62) that $\dot{z} = \dot{\chi} = 0$ is consistent with $z = A$ and $\chi = \varphi$, which turn out to be the steady-state values of z and χ. (Note that $z = A$ means that, asymptotically, the AK part of the production function dominates the $BK^{\alpha}L^{1-\alpha}$ part.)

Figure 4.2 shows the phase diagram in (z, χ) space. Equation (4.62) implies that the $\dot{\chi} = 0$ locus is (aside from $\chi = 0$) the straight line $\chi = \varphi - A \cdot (\theta - \alpha)/\theta + z \cdot (\theta - \alpha)/\theta$. The slope is less than 1 and is positive, as shown, if $\theta > \alpha$. If $\theta < \alpha$, the line would have a negative slope. This case requires an unrealistically high degree of intertemporal substitution in that θ would have to be significantly below unity.

Equation (4.61) implies that $\dot{z} = 0$ if $z = A$ or if $\chi = z - n - \delta$. The former condition corresponds to the vertical line at A in figure 4.2. The latter condition is shown by the straight line with slope 1 and negative intercept. Note that the slope of this $\dot{z} = 0$ line must be steeper than that of the $\dot{\chi} = 0$ line, which has slope less than 1. (The inequality $A > \rho + \delta$ implies that the $\dot{z} = 0$ line intersects the vertical line at A at a value of χ that exceeds φ, as shown in the figure.)

Because $z = A + B \cdot k^{\alpha-1} > A$, the portions of figure 4.2 in which $z < A$ are irrelevant. We can therefore confine the analysis to the region in which $z \geq A$. Note from the figure that the $\dot{z} = 0$ and $\dot{\chi} = 0$ lines intersect in this region only at $z^* = A$ and $\chi^* = \varphi$, which are the steady-state values.

We now consider the transitional dynamics, starting from an initial position $z(0) > A$. The figure shows the stable arm that corresponds to the appropriately chosen initial value $\chi(0)$. Along this arm, the average product of capital, z, and the ratio of consumption to capital, χ, each decline monotonically.[16] The monotonic decline in z corresponds to the monotonic increase in k. The monotonic fall in χ depends on the assumption $\theta > \alpha$.[17] If we had assumed $\theta < \alpha$, then χ would have risen monotonically during the transition. (If $\theta = \alpha$, then $\chi = \varphi$, the steady-state value, throughout the transition.)

Capital's share of product is given by

$$k \cdot f'(k)/f(k) = (Ak + \alpha Bk^{\alpha})/(Ak + Bk^{\alpha})$$

which equals α if $A = 0$ and equals 1 if $B = 0$. If $A > 0$ and $B > 0$, capital's share rises toward one and labor's share falls toward zero as k increases without bound. This implication of the model would conflict with the data if we interpreted capital in the narrow sense of plant and equipment but is more reasonable if we add human capital. In this case, the implication is that the share of raw labor in total product falls toward zero as the economy develops.

The most important aspect of the extended model is that it restores a transitional dynamics during which the average and marginal products of capital decline gradually toward the steady-state value, A. The falling productivity of capital tends to generate a decline over time in per capita growth rates; that is, the model again exhibits the convergence property that applies in the Ramsey model.

Appendix 2C showed that the growth rate of capital per person, $\dot{k}/k$, declines monotonically during the transition of the Ramsey model.[18] The proof relied on the diminishing marginal product of capital, $f''(k) < 0$, but not on the Inada condition, $\lim_{k\to\infty}[f'(k)] = 0$. Therefore, the convergence property of declining growth rates of capital per person applies immediately to the present model in which the production function is given by equation (4.57) or, more generally, by equation (4.56). This framework features the long-run growth properties of the *AK* model, together with the convergence behavior exhibited by the Ramsey model.

16. We can rule out the unstable paths from the usual arguments. The paths that approach $\chi = 0$ and $z = A$ violate the transversality condition. Those that involve $\chi \to \infty$ and $z \to \infty$ entail running out of capital in finite time and therefore lead eventually to a discrete downward jump to zero consumption.

17. Appendix 2B noted that c/k fell monotonically in the Ramsey model with a Cobb–Douglas technology if $\theta > \alpha$. This result still holds if the production function is modified to $f(k) = Ak + Bk^{\alpha}$, the case presently being considered.

18. This result applies in the Ramsey model if the economy begins at $k(0) < k^*$. In the present case, k^* is effectively infinite, so that this inequality is never a constraint.

4.5.2 A CES Example

We now demonstrate that we can get similar results for endogenous growth and transitional dynamics if the production function takes a constant-elasticity-of-substitution (CES) form. We showed in chapter 1 that endogenous growth is feasible with a CES production function if the elasticity of substitution between the factors K and L is high. Specifically, we now assume that the technology is

$$Y = F(K, L) = B \cdot \{a \cdot (bK)^{\psi} + (1-a) \cdot [(1-b) \cdot L]^{\psi}\}^{1/\psi} \tag{4.63}$$

where $0 < a < 1$, $0 < b < 1$, and $0 < \psi < 1$, so that the elasticity of substitution, $1/(1-\psi)$, is greater than 1.

The production function can be written in terms of per capita quantities as

$$y = f(k) = B \cdot [a \cdot (bk)^{\psi} + (1-a) \cdot (1-b)^{\psi}]^{1/\psi} \tag{4.64}$$

We showed in chapter 1 that the marginal and average products of capital are positive and diminishing and have the following limits:

$$\lim_{k\to\infty} [f'(k)] = \lim_{k\to\infty} [f(k)/k] = Bba^{1/\psi}$$

$$\lim_{k\to 0} [f'(k)] = \lim_{k\to 0} [f(k)/k] = \infty$$

In particular, since $f'(k)$ approaches a positive constant as k goes to infinity, the key Inada condition is violated, and the model may generate endogenous growth.

To make the analysis parallel with that in the previous section, we define the parameter A as

$$A \equiv Bba^{1/\psi} \tag{4.65}$$

With this definition, the CES production function (with $0 < \psi < 1$) is a special case of equation (4.56). If we define $\Omega(K, L) \equiv F(K, L) - AK$, where $F(K, L)$ is the CES function in equation (4.63) and A is given by equation (4.65), then the function $\Omega(K, L)$ satisfies all of the neoclassical properties (equations [1.5a]–[1.5c]), including the Inada conditions.

Since A is the limiting value of $f'(k)$, the previous analysis suggests that, to generate endogenous growth, the parameters of the model have to satisfy the condition $A > \delta + \rho$. This inequality will tend to hold when the level of technology, B, is high, when the elasticity of substitution (reflected in ψ) is high, and when the parameters a and b are large (the larger the values of a and b are, the more important capital is in the production process).

The dynamic equations for k and c are again the ones derived for the Ramsey model in chapter 2 (equations [2.23] and [2.24] with $x = 0$):

$$\dot{k}/k = f(k)/k - c/k - (n + \delta)$$

$$\dot{c}/c = (1/\theta) \cdot [f'(k) - \delta - \rho]$$

If we define $z \equiv f(k)/k$ and $\chi \equiv c/k$, as in the previous section, the dynamic equations for z and χ can be shown to be

$$\begin{aligned} \dot{z}/z &= [(z/A)^{-\psi} - 1] \cdot (z - \chi - n - \delta) \\ \dot{\chi}/\chi &= (A/\theta) \cdot [(z/A)^{-\psi} - 1] - (z - A) + (\chi - \varphi) \end{aligned} \tag{4.66}$$

where $\varphi \equiv (A - \delta) \cdot (\theta - 1)/\theta + \rho/\theta - n > 0$, as before. The analysis again applies in the region in which $z \geq A$, because $f(k)/k$ can never fall below A. The steady-state position is again at $z^* = A$ and $\chi^* = \varphi$.

To analyze the dynamics of the model, we construct a phase diagram in (z, χ) space in figure 4.3. There are two lines (other than $z = 0$) that make $\dot{z} = 0$: a vertical line at $z = A$ and an upward-sloping line with unit slope and intercept $-(n + \delta)$. The two lines cross at $z = A$ and $\chi = A - \delta - n$.

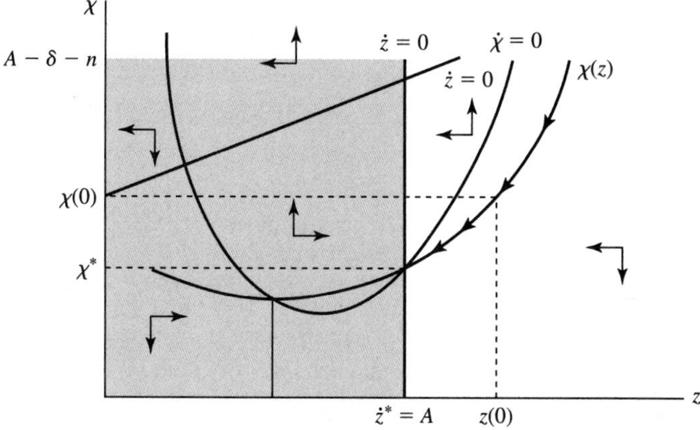

Figure 4.3
Transitional dynamics in an endogenous growth model when the production function is CES (with $0 < \psi < 1$). The phase diagram is shown in (z, χ) space, as in figure 4.2. We assume $\theta > 1 - \psi$. The $\dot{\chi} = 0$ locus then displays a U shape with a minimum to the left of A. The two $\dot{z} = 0$ loci cross at $\chi = A - \delta - n$. The $\dot{\chi} = 0$ locus intersects the $z = A$ line below $A - \delta - n$. The steady state is given accordingly by the intersection of the $\dot{\chi} = 0$ locus with the vertical line $z = A$. Since the economy begins with $z > z^*$, the transition features monotonically decreasing values of z and χ. (Note: The result on the path of χ depends on the assumption $\theta > 1 - \psi$.)

The $\dot{\chi} = 0$ schedule is given (other than by $\chi = 0$) by the curve $\chi = \varphi + (z - A) - (A/\theta) \cdot [(z/A)^{1-\psi} - 1]$. This curve is downward sloping for low values of z and reaches a minimum at $z = A \cdot [(1 - \psi)/\theta]^{1/\psi}$. This minimum occurs to the left of A, as shown, if $\theta > 1 - \psi$. Since $0 < \psi < 1$, this condition must hold if $\theta \geq 1$. (We leave the case in which $\theta \leq 1 - \psi$ as an exercise.) As z goes to infinity, the slope of the $\dot{\chi} = 0$ schedule approaches 1. This curve crosses the vertical line $z = A$ below the point $A - \delta - n$ (if $A > \rho + \delta > n + \delta$, as we assume).

Figure 4.3 shows the stable saddle path beginning from a value $z(0) > A$. The variables z and χ decline monotonically during the transition, just as in the model discussed in the previous section. This transition again exhibits the convergence property, whereby $\dot{k}/k$ declines as k rises (and z approaches A).

4.6 Concluding Observations

This chapter shows that endogenous growth may arise if the returns to capital do not fall in the long run below some positive, baseline value. The long-run growth rate then depends on the level of the technology and the willingness to save. In some models, the effects from the level of technology can be generalized to include the extent of spillovers across producers, scale effects, and the influences of public services.

The simplest kinds of endogenous-growth models—which look like the *AK* model—are inconsistent with empirical observations on convergence. However, extended versions of endogenous-growth models combine the convergence behavior of the neoclassical growth model with the long-run growth properties of the *AK* model. These theories accord better with the empirical evidence on convergence.

4.7 Appendix: Endogenous Growth in the One-Sector Model

In this chapter, we studied several models that could generate endogenous growth. The key property of these examples was that diminishing returns were not present, at least asymptotically, in the sense that the average and marginal products of capital had positive lower bounds. In particular, the Inada condition $\lim_{k \to \infty}[f'(k)] = 0$ was violated. We now discuss more generally the role of this condition in one-sector models of endogenous growth.

Consider a model without exogenous technological progress in which the dynamic equations are those from the Ramsey model of chapter 2 (equations [2.23] and [2.24]):

$$\gamma_k \equiv \dot{k}/k = f(k)/k - c/k - (n + \delta) \tag{4.67}$$

$$\gamma_c \equiv \dot{c}/c = (1/\theta) \cdot [f'(k) - \delta - \rho] \tag{4.68}$$

If $f'(k)$ and γ_k asymptotically approach finite limits, the transversality condition from equation (2.25) can be expressed as

$$\lim_{t\to\infty} [f'(k) - \delta] > \lim_{t\to\infty} (\gamma_k + n) \tag{4.69}$$

that is, the asymptotic rate of return on capital, given on the left-hand side, exceeds the asymptotic growth rate of the capital stock, given on the right-hand side.

We define a steady state, as usual, as a situation in which the growth rates of the various quantities, K, Y, and C, are constant. In the steady states that we studied in chapter 2, the growth rates of the quantities per unit of effective labor, such as $\gamma_{\hat{k}}$ and $\gamma_{\hat{c}}$, were 0, so that the per capita growth rates, γ_k and γ_c, equaled x, and the growth rates of levels, γ_K and γ_C, equaled $n + x$. Since we now assume $x = 0$, the per capita growth rates would be 0 in the steady states considered in chapter 2. Hence, we want to consider what modifications of the technology will allow for steady states in which the per capita growth rates are positive constants, rather than 0, when $x = 0$.

Imagine that the steady-state per capita growth is positive, so that

$$\lim_{t\to\infty} (\gamma_k) \equiv \gamma_k^* > 0$$

Since k then grows in the long run at a positive rate, $\lim_{t\to\infty}(k) = \infty$; that is, k rises without bound. The transversality condition in equation (4.69) then requires

$$\lim_{k\to\infty} [f'(k)] > \gamma_k^* + n + \delta > n + \delta > 0 \tag{4.70}$$

Note that the limit on the left-hand side of expression (4.70) refers to $k \to \infty$, a situation that applies as $t \to \infty$ if k grows in the long run at a constant, positive rate.

The standard Inada condition, $\lim_{k\to\infty}[f'(k)] = 0$, rules out the inequality in expression (4.70): it is for that reason that endogenous growth does not apply with a neoclassical production function. The model may, however, be able to generate positive long-term growth of k if capital's marginal product has a positive lower bound. We denote this asymptotic marginal product by $A > 0$, that is, we now assume

$$\lim_{k\to\infty} [f'(k)] = A > 0 \tag{4.71}$$

The inequality in expression (4.70) implies that $A > 0$ is not a sufficient condition to generate growth of k in the steady state. A necessary condition for γ_k^* to be positive is

$$A > n + \delta \tag{4.72}$$

Hence, the asymptotic rate of return to capital, $A - \delta$, must exceed the growth rate, n, of the capital stock that would obtain if k were constant in the steady state (as in the Ramsey model with $x = 0$).

If $\gamma_k^* > 0$, so that $\lim_{t\to\infty}(k) = \infty$ and, hence, $\lim_{t\to\infty}[f'(k)] = A$, equation (4.68) implies

$$(\gamma_c)^* = (1/\theta) \cdot (A - \delta - \rho) \tag{4.73}$$

Therefore, $\gamma_c^* > 0$ requires

$$A > \delta + \rho \tag{4.74}$$

We showed in chapter 2 that, when $x = 0$, the transversality condition required $\rho > n$. If this last inequality still holds—as we assume—then the inequality in expression (4.74) implies the inequality in expression (4.72). If the inequality in expression (4.74) fails to hold, the analysis of chapter 2 still goes through—including the result $\gamma_k^* = 0$—even though the technology could physically support perpetual growth of k. The asymptotic rate of return on capital, $A - \delta$, is too low in this case for $\gamma_k^* > 0$ to be optimal. We assume, henceforth, that the inequality in expression (4.74) is satisfied.

We now want to show that $\gamma_k^* = \gamma_c^*$. Equation (4.67) implies

$$\gamma_k^* = \lim_{k\to\infty} [f(k)/k] - \lim_{k\to\infty} (c/k) - (n + \delta)$$

We know from l'Hôpital's rule (if $f[k]$ tends to infinity as k tends to infinity) that $\lim_{k\to\infty}[f(k)/k] = \lim_{k\to\infty}[f'(k)] = A$. Therefore,

$$\gamma_k^* = A - n - \delta - \lim_{k\to\infty} (c/k) \tag{4.75}$$

If $\gamma_c^* > \gamma_k^*$, then $\lim_{k\to\infty}(c/k) = \infty$, which is obviously inconsistent with $\gamma_k^* > 0$ in equation (4.75). If $\gamma_c^* < \gamma_k^*$, then $\lim_{k\to\infty}(c/k) = 0$, which implies $\gamma_k^* = A - n - \delta$. This result implies $A - \delta = \gamma_k^* + n$, a violation of the transversality condition given in expression (4.69). We can therefore rule out $\gamma_c^* < \gamma_k^*$.

The only remaining possibility is

$$\gamma_k^* = \gamma_c^* = (1/\theta) \cdot (A - \delta - \rho) \tag{4.76}$$

where we used the formula for γ_c^* from equation (4.73). This solution works if it satisfies the transversality condition shown in expression (4.69), that is, if $A - \delta$ exceeds $\gamma_k^* + n$. The formula for γ_k^* in equation (4.76) implies that the transversality condition can be written as

$$\varphi \equiv (A - \delta) \cdot (\theta - 1)/\theta + \rho/\theta - n > 0 \tag{4.77}$$

This condition corresponds to expression (4.12). Equations (4.75)–(4.77) then imply

$$\lim_{k\to\infty} (c/k) = \varphi > 0 \tag{4.78}$$

If we interpret A as the asymptotic value of $f'(k)$, then the conditions derived in this appendix are satisfied by all the models that we discussed in this chapter. In particular, the steady-state per capita growth rate is given in equation (4.76), and the steady-state level of c/k is given in equation (4.78).

4.8 Problems

4.1 The *AK* model as the limit of the neoclassical model. Consider the neoclassical growth model discussed in chapter 2. Imagine that the production function is Cobb–Douglas, $\hat{y} = A\hat{k}^{\alpha}$.

a. How does an increase in α affect the transition equations for $\hat{k}$ and $\hat{c}$ in equations (2.23) and (2.24)? How, therefore, does the increase in α affect the loci for $\dot{\hat{c}} = 0$ and $\dot{\hat{k}} = 0$ in figure 2.1? How does it affect the steady-state values, $\hat{k}^*$ and $\hat{c}^*$?

b. What happens, for example, to $\hat{k}^*$ as α approaches 1? How does this result relate to the *AK* model that was discussed in this chapter?

4.2 Oversaving in the *AK* model (based on Saint-Paul, 1992). We know from chapter 1 that an economy oversaves if it approaches a steady state in which the rate of return, r, is smaller than the growth rate. Suppose that the technology is $Y = AK$, and the ratio c/k approaches the constant $(c/k)^*$ in the steady state.

a. Use equation (4.8) to determine the steady-state growth rate of K (and, hence, of Y and C). Can this steady-state growth rate exceed the interest rate, r, given in equation (4.7)? Is it possible to get oversaving if the economy approaches a steady state and the technology is $Y = AK$?

b. Suppose that we combine the *AK* technology with the model of finite-horizon consumers of Blanchard (1985), as described in section 3.7. Is it possible to get oversaving in this model? What if we combine the *AK* technology with an overlapping-generations model, as described in the appendix to chapter 3?

4.3 Transitional dynamics. Show that in the model of learning by doing with knowledge spillovers presented in section 4.3 there is no transitional dynamics. That is, output and capital always grow at the constant consumption growth rate given in equation (4.28).

4.4 Spillovers from average capital per worker. In the model presented in section 4.3, assume that the firm's productivity parameter, A_i, depends on the economy's average capital per worker, K/L, rather than on the aggregate capital stock, K. The production function is assumed to be Cobb–Douglas:

$$Y_i = A \cdot (K_i)^{\alpha} \cdot [(K/L) \cdot L_i]^{1-\alpha}$$

Derive the growth rates for the decentralized economy and for the social planner. Comment on how the scale effect discussed in section 4.3 does not appear with this new specification.

4.5 Distorting taxes in the public-goods model. Suppose, in the model of section 4.4.1, that public expenditures, G, are financed by a tax on household asset income at the rate τ_a. How does this change affect the relation between the growth rate and G/Y, that is, how does equation (4.42) change?

4.6 Congestion of public services (based on Barro and Sala-i-Martin, 1992c). In the congestion model discussed in section 4.4.2, suppose that output for firm i is given by

$$Y_i = AK_i \cdot f(G/K)$$

that is, the congestion of public services involves G in relation to K, rather than Y. How do the results change under this revised specification of congestion? Consider, in particular, the growth rates that arise in the decentralized economy and in the social planner's solution.

4.7 Adjustment costs with an *AK* technology (based on Barro and Sala-i-Martin, 1992c). Imagine that firms face an AK technology, but that investment requires adjustment costs as described in section 3.3. The unit adjustment-cost function is $\phi(i/k) = (b/2)\cdot(i/k)$, so that the total cost of purchasing and investment for 1 unit of capital is $1 + (b/2) \cdot (i/k)$. Producers maximize the present value of cash flows,

$$\int_0^{\infty} \{AK - I \cdot [1 + (b/2) \cdot (I/K)]\} \cdot e^{-rt} \cdot dt$$

where $r = A - \delta$. The maximization is subject to the constraint $\dot{K} = I - \delta K$.

a. Set up the Hamiltonian and work out the first-order conditions for the representative firm. Find the relation between the interest rate and the growth rate of capital. Is this relation monotonic? Explain.

b. Assume that consumers solve the usual infinite-horizon Ramsey problem, so that the growth rate of consumption relates positively to the interest rate. Suppose that the growth rate of consumption equals the growth rate of the capital stock. Does this condition pin down the growth rate? If not, can one of the solutions be ruled out from the transversality condition?

c. Show that the growth rate of consumption equals the growth rate of the capital stock. What does this finding imply about the model's transitional dynamics? Explain.

4.8 Growth in a model with spillovers (based on Romer, 1986). Assume that the production function for firm i is

$$Y_i = AK_i^{\alpha} \cdot L_i^{1-\alpha} \cdot K^{\lambda}$$

where $0 < \alpha < 1$, $0 < \lambda < 1$, and K is the aggregate stock of capital.

a. Show that if $\lambda < 1 - \alpha$ and L is constant, the model has transitional dynamics similar to those of the Ramsey model. What is the steady-state growth rate of Y, K, and C in this case?

b. If $\lambda < 1 - \alpha$ and L grows at the rate $n > 0$, what is the steady-state growth rate of Y, K, and C?

c. Show that if $\lambda = 1 - \alpha$ and L is constant, the steady state and transitional dynamics are like those of the AK model.

d. What happens if $\lambda = 1 - \alpha$ and L grows at the rate $n > 0$?

5 Two-Sector Models of Endogenous Growth (with Special Attention to the Role of Human Capital)

Long-term per capita growth without exogenous technological progress can be achieved if the returns to capital are constant asymptotically. This was one of the lessons we learned in chapter 4. In that chapter we argued that this absence of diminishing returns might apply if we took a broad view of capital to include human, as well as physical, components. This chapter deals explicitly with models that distinguish between physical and human capital. More generally, the structure can be applied to various types of capital, including the kinds of accumulated knowledge that we shall study in chapters 6 and 7.

We begin with a framework, similar to the one that we used to study an open economy in chapter 3, in which physical and human capital are produced by identical production functions. In this setting, the output from the usual one-sector technology can be used on a one-for-one basis for consumption, investment in physical capital, and investment in human capital. New results arise, however, when we allow for the constraint that gross investment in physical and human capital must each be nonnegative. This constraint introduces effects on the growth process due to imbalances between the levels of physical and human capital: the growth rate of output is higher the larger the magnitude of the gap between the ratio of physical to human capital and the steady-state value of this ratio.

We next allow for the possibility that physical and human capital are produced by different technologies. Specifically, we focus on the empirically relevant case in which education—the production of new human capital—is relatively intensive in human capital as an input. This property holds, for example, in the model developed by Uzawa (1965) and used by Lucas (1988), in which existing human capital is the only input in the education sector. This modification of the production structure creates an asymmetry in the effect from imbalances between physical and human capital on the growth rate. The source of the asymmetry derives from the positive effect of the ratio of physical to human capital on the real wage rate (per unit of human capital) and, hence, on the opportunity cost of human capital devoted to education. In this setting, the growth rate for a broad concept of output still increases with the magnitude of the imbalance between physical and human capital if human capital is relatively abundant but tends to fall with the magnitude of the imbalance if human capital is relatively scarce.

The presence of human capital may relax the constraint of diminishing returns to a broad concept of capital and can lead thereby to long-term per capita growth in the absence of exogenous technological progress. Hence, the production of human capital may be an alternative to improvements in technology as a mechanism to generate long-term growth. We should emphasize, however, some respects in which the accumulation of human capital differs from the creation of knowledge in the form of technological progress. If we think of human capital as the skills embodied in a worker, then the use of these skills in one activity precludes their use in another activity; hence, human capital is a rival good. Since people have property rights in their own skills, as well as in their raw labor, human capital is also an excludable good. In contrast, ideas or knowledge may be nonrival—in that they can be spread freely over activities of arbitrary scale—and may in some circumstances be nonexcludable. This distinction means that theories of technological progress—the subject of chapters 6–8—differ in fundamental respects from the models of the accumulation of human capital that we consider in this chapter.

5.1 A One-Sector Model with Physical and Human Capital

5.1.1 The Basic Setup

We start with a Cobb–Douglas production function that exhibits constant returns to physical and human capital, K and H:

$$Y = AK^{\alpha}H^{1-\alpha} \tag{5.1}$$

where $0 \leq \alpha \leq 1$. We can think of human capital, H, as the number of workers, L, multiplied by the human capital of the typical worker, h. The assumption here is that the quantity of workers, L, and the quality of workers, h, are perfect substitutes in production in the sense that only the combination Lh matters for output. This specification means that a fixed number of bodies, L, will not be a source of diminishing returns because a doubling of K and h, for fixed L, leads to a doubling of Y. We assume, only for convenience, that the total labor force, L, is fixed and, hence, that H grows only because of improvements in the average quality, h. We also omit any technological progress (that is, we assume that A is constant).

Output can be used for consumption or investment in physical or human capital. We assume that the stocks of physical and human capital depreciate at the same rate, δ. The depreciation of human capital includes losses from skill deterioration and mortality, net of benefits from experience. (Different depreciation rates for physical and human capital can be introduced, but this generalization complicates the algebra without providing much additional insight.)

The economy's resource constraint is

$$Y = AK^{\alpha}H^{1-\alpha} = C + I_K + I_H \tag{5.2}$$

where I_K and I_H are gross investment in physical and human capital, respectively. The changes in the two capital stocks are given by

$$\dot{K} = I_K - \delta K, \qquad \dot{H} = I_H - \delta H \tag{5.3}$$

We showed in chapter 2 that we could deal equivalently with a model of distinct households and firms or with a setup in which households carry out production directly. This equivalence also holds in the present setup. We use here the formulation in which the households are the producers of goods. If we neglect population growth, households maximize the usual utility function

$$U = \int_0^{\infty} u[c(t)] \cdot e^{-\rho t}\, dt \tag{5.4}$$

subject to the two constraints in equation (5.3) and subject to the economy-wide resource constraint equation (5.2). The Hamiltonian expression is

$$J = u(C) \cdot e^{-\rho t} + \nu \cdot (I_K - \delta K) + \mu \cdot (I_H - \delta H) + \omega \cdot (AK^{\alpha} H^{1-\alpha} - C - I_K - I_H) \tag{5.5}$$

where ν and μ are shadow prices associated with $\dot{K}$ and $\dot{H}$, respectively, and ω is the Lagrange multiplier associated with equation (5.2).[1] We use the usual utility function, $u(C) = (C^{1-\theta} - 1)/(1 - \theta)$.

The first-order conditions can be obtained in the usual manner by setting the derivatives of J with respect to C, I_K, and I_H to 0, equating $\dot{\nu}$ and $\dot{\mu}$ to $\partial J/\partial K$ and $\partial J/\partial H$, respectively, and allowing for the budget constraint in equation (5.2).[2] If we simplify these conditions, we obtain the familiar result for the growth rate of consumption:

$$\dot{C}/C = (1/\theta) \cdot [A\alpha \cdot (K/H)^{-(1-\alpha)} - \delta - \rho] \tag{5.6}$$

where $A\alpha \cdot (K/H)^{-(1-\alpha)} - \delta$ is the net marginal product of physical capital.

The second condition is that the net marginal product of physical capital equal the net marginal product of human capital:

$$A\alpha \cdot (K/H)^{-(1-\alpha)} - \delta = A \cdot (1 - \alpha) \cdot (K/H)^{\alpha} - \delta$$

This condition implies that the ratio of the two capital stocks is given by[3]

$$K/H = \alpha/(1 - \alpha) \tag{5.7}$$

1. We could equivalently write the Hamiltonian as

$$J = u(C)e^{-\rho t} + \nu \cdot (AK^{\alpha} H^{1-\alpha} - C - \delta K - I_H) + \mu \cdot (I_H - \delta H)$$

This formulation implicitly imposes the condition

$$I_K = AK^{\alpha} H^{1-\alpha} - C - I_H$$

which involves the Lagrange multiplier ω in equation (5.5).

2. We neglect, for the moment, the inequality restrictions $I_K \geq 0$ and $I_H \geq 0$.

3. The equality between net marginal products still holds if the depreciation rates on the two kinds of capital differ. This condition again determines K/H, but the solution cannot be written, in general, as a closed-form expression in terms of the underlying parameters.

This result for K/H implies that the net rate of return to physical and human capital is given by[4]

$$r^* = A\alpha^\alpha \cdot (1-\alpha)^{(1-\alpha)} - \delta \tag{5.8}$$

This rate of return is constant because the production function in equation (5.1) exhibits constant returns with respect to broad capital, K and H. Therefore, diminishing returns do not apply when K/H stays constant (equation [5.7]), that is, when K and H grow at the same rate.

If K/H is constant, equation (5.6) implies that $\dot{C}/C$ is constant and equal to

$$\gamma^* = (1/\theta) \cdot \left[A\alpha^\alpha \cdot (1-\alpha)^{(1-\alpha)} - \delta - \rho\right] \tag{5.9}$$

where we substituted for K/H from equation (5.7). We assume that the parameters are such that $\gamma^* > 0$.

To see how this model relates to some previous analysis, we can substitute from equation (5.7) into the production function from equation (5.1) to get

$$Y = AK \cdot \left(\frac{1-\alpha}{\alpha}\right)^{(1-\alpha)}$$

Thus the model is equivalent to the AK model that we studied in chapter 4. We can use the method of analysis from that chapter to show that, if the transversality condition holds, the growth rates of Y, K, and H must equal the growth rate of C.[5] That is, all quantities grow at the constant rate γ^* shown in equation (5.9).

The results for r^* and γ^* in equations (5.8) and (5.9) are essentially the same as those obtained from the AK model developed in chapter 4. That is, we have thus far made no meaningful distinction between a model with two types of capital, K and H, and a model with a single form of broad capital.

5.1.2 The Constraint of Nonnegative Gross Investment

Suppose that the economy begins with the two capital stocks $K(0)$ and $H(0)$. If the ratio $K(0)/H(0)$ deviates from the value $\alpha/(1-\alpha)$ prescribed by equation (5.7), the solution that we just found dictates discrete adjustments in the two stocks to attain the value $\alpha/(1-\alpha)$ instantaneously. This adjustment features an increase in one stock and a corresponding decrease in the other stock, so that the sum, $K + H$, does not change instantaneously.

4. The rate of return, r, would apply on a competitive credit market if we introduced such a market into the model.

5. The transversality condition is $r^* > \gamma^*$. Equations (5.8) and (5.9) imply that this condition can be expressed as $\rho > (1-\theta) \cdot [A\alpha^\alpha \cdot (1-\alpha)^{(1-\alpha)} - \delta]$.

The difficulty with this solution is that it depends on the possibility of an infinite positive rate of investment in one form of capital and an infinite negative rate of investment in the other form. We must, in other words, assume that investments are reversible, so that old units of physical capital can be converted into human capital and vice versa. This assumption is not very realistic. One would imagine that, even though investors can decide, ex ante, whether to invest in human or physical capital, once the decision is made, it is irreversible. Mathematically, these irreversibility constraints would take the form of inequality restrictions: $I_K \geq 0$ and $I_H \geq 0$. In other words, one cannot disinvest human or physical capital. One can choose not to invest at all in each form of capital; that is, one can set $I_K = 0$, which would entail a continuous decline in K at the rate $\dot{K}/K = -\delta$, but one cannot actually disinvest K. Notice that, in the previous solution, if $K(0)/H(0)$ differs from $\alpha/(1-\alpha)$, the discrete shift in the composition of capital at time zero requires negative gross investment (at an infinite rate) in one of the stocks so that one of the irreversibility constraints is necessarily violated. We therefore now reconsider the solution to the model in the presence of these inequality restrictions. The discussion in the text omits some details, which appear in appendix 5A, section 5.5.

If $K(0)/H(0) < \alpha/(1-\alpha)$—that is, if H is initially abundant relative to K—the previous solution dictates a decrease in H and an increase in K at time zero. The desire to lower H by a discrete amount implies that the inequality $I_H \geq 0$ will be binding at time zero (and for a finite interval thereafter). When this restriction is binding, the household chooses $I_H = 0$; hence, the growth rate of H is given by $\dot{H}/H = -\delta$, and H follows the path

$$H(t) = H(0) \cdot e^{-\delta t}, \quad \text{for } t = 0, \ldots \tag{5.10}$$

The agents realize that they have too much H in relation to K, but since it is infeasible to have negative gross investment in H, they allow H to depreciate at the exogenously given rate δ.

If $I_H = 0$, the household's optimization problem can be written in terms of the simplified Hamiltonian expression,

$$J = u(C) \cdot e^{-\rho t} + \nu \cdot (AK^{\alpha} H^{1-\alpha} - C - \delta K) \tag{5.11}$$

where ν multiplies the expression for $\dot{K}$ (when $I_H = 0$).[6] This setup is equivalent to the standard neoclassical growth model in which households choose consumption and investment in a single form of capital, K, subject to exogenous technological progress that augments the quantity of the other input, here H. In the standard model, the other input, effective

6. We could equivalently write the Hamiltonian expression in a form that sets $I_H = 0$ in the last term on the right-hand side of equation (5.5):

$$J = u(C) \cdot e^{-\rho t} + \nu \cdot (I_K - \delta K) + \omega \cdot (AK^{\alpha} H^{1-\alpha} - C - I_K)$$

Equation (5.11) has already imposed the condition $I_K = AK^{\alpha} H^{1-\alpha} - C$.

labor, grows at the rate x (with zero population growth), whereas in the present setting, the other input, H, grows at the rate $-\delta$.

The crucial difference from the standard neoclassical growth model is that K/H rises over time and reaches the value $\alpha/(1-\alpha)$ shown in equation (5.7) in finite time. At this point, the net marginal products of physical and human capital are equal, and, hence, the constraint of nonnegative gross investment in human capital becomes nonbinding. The two capital stocks then grow forever at the common rate γ^* shown in equation (5.9). We have already assumed that the parameters are such that $\gamma^* > 0$. Hence, the dynamics of the neoclassical growth model apply during the transition, but the long-run growth rate is positive (even without exogenous technological progress), because of the absence of diminishing returns to broad capital.

Some details of the transitional dynamics are contained in the appendix. We provide here a heuristic treatment. We know that the growth rates of K, H, and Y equal $\gamma^* > 0$ in the steady state, where $K/H = \alpha/(1-\alpha)$. Prior to that time, $K/H < \alpha/(1-\alpha)$, and $I_H = 0$. We have shown in this situation that the dynamics of K and Y accord with the usual pattern from the neoclassical growth model (with a Cobb–Douglas technology). Hence, the analysis from chapter 2 implies that the solution exhibits the convergence property in the sense that the growth rates, $\gamma_K \equiv \dot{K}/K$ and $\gamma_Y \equiv \dot{Y}/Y$, decline monotonically over time. Since the two growth rates fall monotonically toward $\gamma^* > 0$, they must be positive, but declining, during the transition. Thus, K/H rises monotonically over time, partly because H is falling (at the rate δ) and partly because K is rising (at a rate that decreases toward γ^*). The increase in K/H implies that the net marginal product of physical capital—and, hence, the rate of return—declines monotonically.[7] This declining path of the rate of return corresponds in the usual way to a falling path of γ_C.

The results imply that the growth rate of output, γ_Y, is inversely related to the ratio K/H as long as this ratio is below its steady-state value, $\alpha/(1-\alpha)$. The relation between γ_Y and K/H can be described as an *imbalance effect*. The greater the imbalance—that is, the further K/H is below its steady-state value—the higher the growth rate.

One reason for K/H to be low would be a war that destroyed a great deal of physical capital but left human capital relatively intact. The situations of Japan and Germany after World War II are examples. The theory predicts that output would grow at a high rate—well above the steady-state value, γ^*—in this situation.

7. The increase in K/H implies that the net marginal product of H rises over time. This net marginal product is, however, below that for physical capital. Hence, gross investment in H remains at its minimal value, 0. If we could observe a market price for existing units of H, we would find that this price is below the replacement cost, 1, but rises toward 1 as K/H approaches $\alpha/(1-\alpha)$. The total rate of return from holding H—from capital gains and "dividends"—would then equal the net marginal product of K at each point in time. Thus the net marginal product of K equals the single rate of return that would be observed on a credit market.

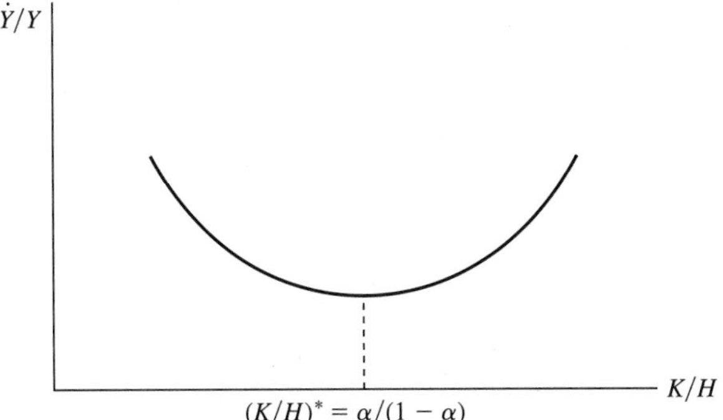

Figure 5.1
The imbalance effect in the one-sector model. The growth rate of output depends on the ratio of the two capital stocks, K/H. The minimal growth rate corresponds to the steady-state ratio, $(K/H)^* = \alpha/(1-\alpha)$. On either side of the steady state, the growth rate rises symmetrically with the magnitude of the gap between K/H and $(K/H)^*$.

The results are analogous if the economy begins instead with a relative abundance of physical capital, $K(0)/H(0) > \alpha/(1-\alpha)$. This situation could arise from an epidemic, such as the Black Death in medieval Europe, that killed people but did not destroy physical capital. In this case, the constraint $I_K \geq 0$ is binding. Hence, $I_K = 0$, and K grows at the rate $-\delta$. The choices of C and H are then governed by the conditions from the usual neoclassical growth model, except that the investment to be chosen involves H, rather than K. In particular, γ_H and γ_Y decline monotonically toward the steady-state value, γ^*. The decline in K (at rate δ) and the rise in H (at a rate that diminishes toward γ^*) imply that K/H falls over time. The decrease in K/H lowers the net marginal product of H and thereby reduces the rate of return and the growth rate of consumption.[8]

The results imply that K/H and γ_Y are positively related in the region in which $K/H > \alpha/(1-\alpha)$. Thus there is again an imbalance effect—the greater the imbalance, in the sense of the excess of K/H from its steady-state value, the higher the growth rate.

Figure 5.1 plots the growth rate, γ_Y, against K/H. The minimal growth rate, γ^*, corresponds to the steady-state ratio, $\alpha/(1-\alpha)$. On either side of the steady state, γ_Y rises with the magnitude of the gap between K/H and its steady-state value.

8. The behavior of rates of return is analogous to the case in which H is relatively abundant. The decrease in K/H implies that the net marginal product of K rises. This net marginal product is, however, below that for human capital, and gross investment in K remains at its minimal value, 0. The market price for existing units of K is below the replacement cost, 1, but rises toward 1 as K/H approaches $\alpha/(1-\alpha)$. The total rate of return from holding K—from capital gains and dividends—equals the net marginal product of H at each point in time. Thus this net marginal product equals the single rate of return that would be observed on a credit market.

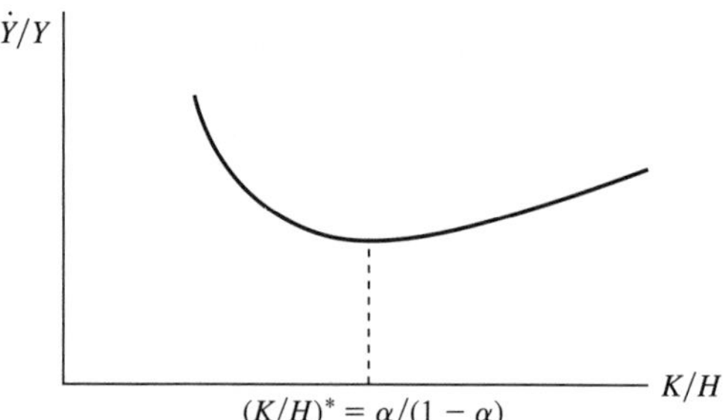

Figure 5.2
The imbalance effect with adjustment costs for human capital. We assume here that the adjustment costs for changing human capital are greater than those for changing physical capital. In this case, the sensitivity of the growth rate to K/H is larger in magnitude in the region in which $K/H < (K/H)^*$ (physical capital is relatively scarce) than in the region in which $K/H > (K/H)^*$ (human capital is relatively scarce).

In the theory, a shortfall of physical capital—the situation in which K but not H is destroyed during a war—need not have a larger effect on the growth rate than a corresponding shortfall of human capital—caused, for example, by an epidemic that eliminated H but not K. There is little empirical evidence about the effects on growth from a sudden decline in human capital, but Hirshleifer's (1987, chapters 1 and 2) discussion of the Black Death suggests that growth was not rapid in this situation. Thus it may be that empirically an increase in K/H above its steady-state value has only a small positive effect, or possibly even a negative effect, on the growth rate.

One extension of the theory that would lead to asymmetric effects from K/H below or above its steady-state value is the type of adjustment cost for capital accumulation that we explored in chapter 3. It is plausible that these adjustment costs would be much greater for H than for K; presumably, the educational process cannot be greatly accelerated without encountering a significant falloff in the rate of return from investment. In this case, a relative abundance of H would lead to substantial investment in K and, accordingly, to a high growth rate of output. However, a corresponding relative abundance of K would have a much smaller effect on investment in H and, hence, on the growth rate of output. Figure 5.2 shows a case in which the minimal growth rate still occurs when K/H equals its steady-state value, $\alpha/(1-\alpha)$,[9] but the slope in the region in which $K/H < \alpha/(1-\alpha)$ is much steeper in magnitude than that in the region in which $K/H > \alpha/(1-\alpha)$. This model

9. Some specifications of adjustment costs would affect the steady-state ratio of K to H, whereas others would not. See the discussion in chapter 3.

predicts that an economy would recover much faster from a war that destroyed mainly K than from an epidemic that destroyed mainly H.

Another implication of adjustment costs for investment is that positive gross investment in both types of capital can occur when K/H deviates from its steady-state value, $\alpha/(1-\alpha)$. This outcome applies if the rates of return from each type of investment are high at low rates of investment and low at high rates of investment. The potential for positive gross investment outside of the steady state in both kinds of capital also arises in models in which the technology for producing goods, C and $\dot{K}$, differs from the technology for education, $\dot{H}$. We explore this idea in the next section.

5.2 Different Technologies for Production and Education

5.2.1 The Model with Two Sectors of Production

We have assumed, thus far, that physical goods and education are generated by the same production functions. This specification neglects a key aspect of education; it relies heavily on educated people as an input. We should, therefore, modify the model to reflect the property that the production of human capital is relatively intensive in human capital. This change in specification modifies some of the conclusions about the effects on growth from imbalances between physical and human capital.

We follow Rebelo (1991) and use a setup with two Cobb–Douglas production functions:[10]

$$Y = C + \dot{K} + \delta K = A \cdot (vK)^{\alpha} \cdot (uH)^{1-\alpha} \tag{5.12}$$

$$\dot{H} + \delta H = B \cdot [(1-v) \cdot K]^{\eta} \cdot [(1-u) \cdot H]^{1-\eta} \tag{5.13}$$

where Y is the output of goods (consumables and gross investment in physical capital); $A, B > 0$ are technological parameters; α $(0 \leq \alpha \leq 1)$ and η $(0 \leq \eta \leq 1)$ are the shares of physical capital in the outputs of each sector; and v $(0 \leq v \leq 1)$ and u $(0 \leq u \leq 1)$ are the fractions of physical and human capital, respectively, used in production. The corresponding fractions of physical and human capital used in education—that is, to generate human capital—are $1-v$ and $1-u$.

Equation (5.12) indicates that consumables, C, and investment in physical capital, $I_K = \dot{K} + \delta K$, are still perfect substitutes on the supply side. In other words, C and I_K come

10. Bond, Wang, and Yip (1996) and Mino (1996) analyze this model with general forms of neoclassical production functions.

from a single output stream for goods.[11] If $\eta \neq \alpha$, equation (5.13) implies that human capital is generated from a technology that differs from that for goods. (If $\eta = \alpha$, the model is equivalent to the one-sector production setup that we considered in the previous section; see note 13, below.) As already mentioned, we consider the empirically relevant case to be the one in which $\eta < \alpha$, that is, the education sector is relatively intensive in human capital, and the goods sector is relatively intensive in physical capital.[12] In fact, it is this feature of the model that may make it reasonable to identify "H" with human capital in the real world.

The forms of equations (5.12) and (5.13) imply that the two production activities each exhibit constant returns to scale in the quantities of the two capital inputs. For this reason, the model will display endogenous steady-state growth of the type that we found in chapter 4 in a one-sector model. In the steady state, v and u are constant, and C, K, H, and Y grow at the common rate γ^*.

Measured output can be broadened to include gross investment in human capital, $\dot{H} + \delta H$, multiplied by an appropriate shadow price of human capital. (We discuss this shadow price later.) This broader measure of output will also grow at the rate γ^* in the steady state. Gross output as defined in the standard national accounts falls somewhere between the narrow and broad concepts, because this measured output includes a fraction of the gross investment in human capital. For example, gross product includes teacher salaries but neglects the value of time forgone by students and also omits part of the value of time expended in on-the-job training. Kendrick (1976, tables A-1 and B-2) made a rough estimate for the United States that one-half of gross investment in human capital was included in measured output.

We can embed the technologies shown in equations (5.12) and (5.13) into the standard model of household optimization that we considered before. The Hamiltonian expression can be written as[13]

$$\begin{aligned} J = {} & u(C) \cdot e^{-\rho t} + \nu \cdot [A \cdot (vK)^{\alpha} \cdot (uH)^{1-\alpha} - \delta K - C] \\ & + \mu \cdot \{B \cdot [(1-v) \cdot K]^{\eta} \cdot [(1-u) \cdot H]^{1-\eta} - \delta H\} \end{aligned} \tag{5.14}$$

where ν multiplies the expression for $\dot{K}$, and μ multiplies the expression for $\dot{H}$. If the inequality restrictions of nonnegative gross investment are not binding, the solution satisfies

11. We could go further to allow for different factor intensities in the production of consumables and capital goods (the two-sector model used by Uzawa, 1964, and Srinivasan, 1964) or in the production of different types of final products (Ventura, 1997).

12. We can interpret K and H more generally as two different types of capital goods, not necessarily physical and human capital. The assumption that the production of H is relatively intensive in H is more or less plausible depending on how H is interpreted.

13. We can equivalently have ν multiply $I_K - \delta K$ and μ multiply $I_H - \delta H$ and then introduce two Lagrange multipliers to correspond to the two equality constraints, $A \cdot (vK)^{\alpha} \cdot (uH)^{1-\alpha} = C + I_K$ and $B \cdot [(1-v) \cdot K]^{\eta} \cdot [(1-u) \cdot H]^{1-\eta} = I_H$. The formulation in equation (5.14) already imposes these equality constraints.

the usual first-order conditions, which come from setting the derivatives of J with respect to C, v, and u to 0 and from the conditions $\dot{\nu} = -\partial J/\partial K$ and $\dot{\mu} = -\partial J/\partial H$.

If we manipulate the first-order conditions, we get a familiar-looking expression for the growth rate of consumption:

$$\dot{C}/C = (1/\theta) \cdot \left[A\alpha \cdot (vK/uH)^{-(1-\alpha)} - \delta - \rho\right] \tag{5.15}$$

The term $A\alpha \cdot (vK/uH)^{-(1-\alpha)} - \delta$, the net marginal product of physical capital in the production of goods, equals the rate of return, r, in this model.

Physical capital must receive the same rate of return when allocated to either sector of production, and the same condition holds for human capital. These conditions lead to the following relation between v and u:

$$\left(\frac{\eta}{1-\eta}\right) \cdot \left(\frac{v}{1-v}\right) = \left(\frac{\alpha}{1-\alpha}\right) \cdot \left(\frac{u}{1-u}\right) \tag{5.16}$$

Equation (5.16) implies that v and u are positively related, with $v = 1$ when $u = 1$, and $v = 0$ when $u = 0$.[14] In other words, for given values of α and η, an expansion of goods production occurs via a simultaneous increase in the fraction of the two inputs, K and H, allocated to the goods sector.

Let $p \equiv \mu/\nu$ be the shadow price of human capital in units of goods. Equation (5.16) and the condition that the rates of return to K and H be equalized leads to a formula for p:[15]

$$p \equiv \mu/\nu = (A/B) \cdot (\alpha/\eta)^{\eta} \cdot [(1-\alpha)/(1-\eta)]^{1-\eta} \cdot (vK/uH)^{\alpha-\eta} \tag{5.17}$$

14. If $\alpha = \eta$, equation (5.16) implies $v = u$. If we substitute this result into equations (5.12) and (5.13), the production functions become

$$Y = AuK^{\alpha}H^{1-\alpha}$$

$$\dot{H} + \delta H = B \cdot (1-u) \cdot K^{\alpha}H^{1-\alpha}$$

Broad output, Q, can be defined as

$$Q = Y + (A/B) \cdot (\dot{H} + \delta H) = AK^{\alpha}H^{1-\alpha}$$

where A/B is the constant price of H in units of Y; we can, in fact, define the units of H so that $A/B = 1$. With this definition, the economy's budget constraint is

$$Q = C + \dot{K} + \delta K + \dot{H} + \delta H$$

The model is then equivalent to the one-sector version analyzed earlier in this chapter.

15. Although p is the appropriate shadow price, it is not the unique market equilibrium price if we allow for a market for human capital in the model. The reason is that, in this model, human capital and goods cannot be transformed into each other, so the equilibrium is a corner solution. Quah (2002) shows that the equilibrium price range turns out to be $(0, \mu/\nu]$. We thank Danny Quah for pointing this fact out to us.

The shadow price p equals the ratio of the marginal product of H in the goods sector (the wage rate) to its marginal product in the education sector. Equation (5.17) shows that this price depends only on the ratio of K employed in the goods sector, vK, to H employed in the goods sector, uH.

The formula for p enables us to calculate the broader concept of gross output that we mentioned before:

$$Q = Y + pB \cdot [(1-v) \cdot K]^{\eta} \cdot [(1-u) \cdot H]^{1-\eta} \tag{5.18}$$

Note that broad output, Q, is the sum of narrow output, Y, and the value in units of goods of the gross investment in human capital, $pB \cdot [(1-v) \cdot K]^{\eta} \cdot [(1-u) \cdot H]^{1-\eta}$.

We can use equation (5.17) along with the first-order conditions for $\dot{\mu}$ and $\dot{\nu}$ to derive an expression for the growth rate of p. The result, after a significant amount of algebra, is

$$\dot{p}/p = A\phi^{\alpha/(\eta-\alpha)} \cdot \left[\alpha\phi^{1/(\alpha-\eta)} \cdot p^{(1-\alpha)/(\eta-\alpha)} - (1-\alpha) \cdot p^{\eta/(\alpha-\eta)}\right] \tag{5.19}$$

where $\phi \equiv (A/B) \cdot (\alpha/\eta)^{\eta} \cdot [(1-\alpha)/(1-\eta)]^{1-\eta}$. The key finding here is that the growth rate of p depends only on p and not on any other variables.

If $\alpha \neq \eta$, equation (5.17) determines a one-to-one relation between p and vK/uH. Equation (5.19), therefore, implies that the growth rate of the ratio vK/uH depends only on the value of the ratio and not on any other variables.

The equation for the growth rate of vK/uH (derived from equations [5.17] and [5.19]), the condition for $\dot{C}/C$ in equation (5.15), the relation between u and v from equation (5.16), and the conditions for $\dot{K}$ and $\dot{H}$ from the budget constraints determine the behavior over time of u, v, C, K, and H. The variable v can be eliminated using equation (5.16). Since the production functions in equations (5.1) and (5.13) exhibit constant returns to scale, the absolute levels of K, H, and C will not influence the dynamics, and the system can be written in terms of ratios of these variables. Thus it is possible to express the model in terms of the variables u, C/K, and K/H. The steady state of this system involves constant values of u, C/K, and K/H. Hence, the growth rates of C, K, and H—as well as of Y and Q—are equal in the steady state.

The form of equation (5.17) has immediate implications for the nature of the dynamics. This relation is a differential equation in the single variable p. The equation can be readily shown to be stable ($\partial[\dot{p}/p]/\partial[p] < 0$) if $\alpha > \eta$ and unstable ($\partial[\dot{p}/p]/\partial[p] > 0$) if $\alpha < \eta$. (If $\alpha = \eta$, the model is equivalent to the one-sector setup; see note 13.) Thus, if $\alpha > \eta$—the case that we regard as empirically relevant—p converges monotonically to its steady-state value.

Since equation (5.17) relates p one-to-one to vK/uH, the monotonic convergence of p when $\alpha > \eta$ implies that vK/uH also converges monotonically to its steady-state value. The ratio vK/uH determines the marginal product of physical capital in the production of goods. Therefore, r—equal to the net marginal product of physical capital in the production of goods—and $\dot{C}/C$—determined in equation (5.15)—also converge monotonically to their steady-state values.

The rest of the model turns out to be difficult to analyze for the general situation in which $\alpha > \eta \geq 0$. Therefore, we begin with the special case in which $\eta = 0$, because it allows for a complete analytical description of the transitional dynamics. We then provide some results for the more general case, where $\alpha > \eta > 0$. Finally, we address the case $\alpha < \eta$, although we regard this configuration of parameters as implausible.

5.2.2 The Uzawa–Lucas Model

The Basic Framework We now specialize to the model studied by Uzawa (1965) and Lucas (1988) in which the production of human capital involves no physical capital; that is, $\eta = 0$ in equation (5.13). This setting is the extreme case in which the education sector is relatively intensive in human capital ($\eta \leq \alpha$). Thus, by comparing the Uzawa–Lucas model with the one-sector framework—in which the relative intensities of physical and human capital are the same in each sector—we can bring out the main implications from the assumption about relative factor intensities. Appendix 5B (section 5.6) contains the details of the Uzawa–Lucas model. We provide here a sketch of the results, starting with the case in which the nonnegativity constraints on gross investment in K and H are not binding.

The specification $\eta = 0$ implies $v = 1$; that is, since K is not productive in the education sector, all of it is used in the goods sector. The production functions from equations (5.1) and (5.13), therefore, simplify to[16]

$$Y = C + \dot{K} + \delta K = AK^{\alpha} \cdot (uH)^{1-\alpha} \tag{5.20}$$

$$\dot{H} + \delta H = B \cdot (1 - u) \cdot H \tag{5.21}$$

We shall find it useful, as in chapter 4, to express the system in terms of variables that will be constant in the steady state. A specification that facilitates the dynamic analysis uses the ratios $\omega \equiv K/H$ and $\chi \equiv C/K$. If we use these definitions along with equations (5.20) and (5.21), we get expressions for the growth rates of K and H:

$$\dot{K}/K = A \cdot u^{(1-\alpha)} \omega^{-(1-\alpha)} - \chi - \delta \tag{5.22}$$

$$\dot{H}/H = B \cdot (1 - u) - \delta \tag{5.23}$$

Hence, the growth rate of ω is given by

$$\dot{\omega}/\omega = \dot{K}/K - \dot{H}/H = A \cdot u^{(1-\alpha)} \omega^{-(1-\alpha)} - B \cdot (1 - u) - \chi \tag{5.24}$$

16. Arnold (1997) generalizes the model by replacing equation (5.20) with a general form of neoclassical production function.

The first-order conditions can be used to show that the growth rate of consumption is given by the familiar formula, $\dot{C}/C = (1/\theta) \cdot (r - \rho)$, where r equals the net marginal product of physical capital in the production of goods, $\alpha Au^{1-\alpha}\omega^{-(1-\alpha)} - \delta$. Therefore, the growth rate of consumption is given by

$$\dot{C}/C = \frac{1}{\theta} \cdot \left[\alpha Au^{1-\alpha}\omega^{-(1-\alpha)} - \delta - \rho\right] \tag{5.25}$$

The growth rate of χ follows from equations (5.25) and (5.22) as

$$\dot{\chi}/\chi = \dot{C}/C - \dot{K}/K = \left(\frac{\alpha - \theta}{\theta}\right) \cdot Au^{1-\alpha}\omega^{-(1-\alpha)} + \chi - \frac{1}{\theta} \cdot [\delta \cdot (1 - \theta) + \rho] \tag{5.26}$$

Finally, appendix 5B shows that equations (5.19) and (5.17) imply that the growth rate of u is given by

$$\dot{u}/u = \frac{B \cdot (1 - \alpha)}{\alpha} + Bu - \chi \tag{5.27}$$

Steady-State Analysis Appendix 5B shows that the variables u, ω, and χ are constant in a steady state. If we define the combination of parameters

$$\varphi \equiv \frac{\rho + \delta \cdot (1 - \theta)}{B\theta} \tag{5.28}$$

then the steady-state values, which correspond to $\dot{u} = \dot{\omega} = \dot{\chi} = 0$, are given by

$$\omega^* = (\alpha A/B)^{1/(1-\alpha)} \cdot \left[\varphi + \frac{\theta - 1}{\theta}\right]$$

$$\chi^* = B \cdot \left(\varphi + 1/\alpha - \frac{1}{\theta}\right) \tag{5.29}$$

$$u^* = \varphi + \frac{\theta - 1}{\theta}$$

The rate of return and the common growth rate of C, K, H, Y, and Q are given in this steady state by

$$r^* = B - \delta \tag{5.30}$$

$$\gamma^* = \left(\frac{1}{\theta}\right) \cdot (B - \delta - \rho) \tag{5.31}$$

The usual transversality condition, $r^* > \gamma^*$, ensures that the values of ω^*, χ^*, and u^* shown in equation (5.29) are all positive. The condition $u^* < 1$ holds if $\gamma^* > 0$ in equation (5.30).

Transitional Dynamics The dynamic system for ω, χ, and u consists of equations (5.24), (5.26), and (5.27). We shall find it convenient to work with a transformed system that replaces ω by the gross average product of physical capital in the production of goods, denoted by z:[17]

$$z \equiv Au^{1-\alpha}\omega^{-(1-\alpha)} \tag{5.32}$$

The gross *marginal* product of physical capital equals αz, and the rate of return is $r = \alpha z - \delta$. Although the variable z is a combination of a state variable, ω, and a control variable, u, we show later that, in the equilibrium, z relates in a simple way to ω. In particular, we can determine the initial value $z(0)$ from the initial value $\omega(0)$.

The system given by equations (5.24), (5.26), and (5.27) can be rewritten in terms of z, χ, and u as

$$\dot{z}/z = -(1-\alpha)\cdot(z - z^*) \tag{5.33}$$

$$\dot{\chi}/\chi = \left(\frac{\alpha-\theta}{\theta}\right)\cdot(z - z^*) + (\chi - \chi^*) \tag{5.34}$$

$$\dot{u}/u = B\cdot(u - u^*) - (\chi - \chi^*) \tag{5.35}$$

where z^* is the steady-state value of z. Equation (5.29) and the definition of z in equation (5.32) imply that this steady-state value is given by

$$z^* = B/\alpha \tag{5.36}$$

Dynamics of the average product of physical capital, the rate of return, and the wage rate. Equation (5.33) is a one-variable differential equation, which determines the time path of z, the gross average product of physical capital. This equation can be solved in closed form to get

$$\left(\frac{z - z^*}{z}\right) = \left[\frac{z(0) - z^*}{z(0)}\right]\cdot e^{-(1-\alpha)\cdot z^* t} \tag{5.37}$$

where $z(0)$ is the initial value of z. This equation shows that z adjusts monotonically from its initial value, $z(0)$, to its steady-state value, z^*. Figure 5.3 provides a graphical representation of this stability property.

17. We could also work with the ratio vK/uH, which equals $(A\alpha/z)^{1/(1-\alpha)}$.

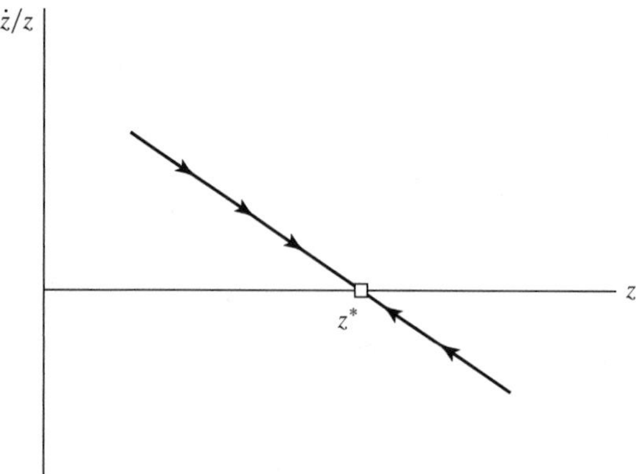

Figure 5.3
Stability of z, the gross average product of capital. Equation (5.33) from the Uzawa–Lucas model is a linear differential equation in z. When $z < z^*$, the growth rate of z is positive, and z increases toward its steady-state value. The opposite pattern applies when $z > z^*$. Hence, the steady-state value, z^*, is stable.

Since the rate of return is $r = \alpha z - \delta$, the behavior of z determines the behavior of r. In particular, if $z(0) < z^*, r(0) < r^*$, and r rises monotonically over time toward its steady-state value. These properties are all reversed if $z(0) > z^*$.

The wage rate, w, equals the marginal product of the human capital, uH, employed in the production of goods. The production function from equation (5.20) and the definition of z in equation (5.32) imply that this marginal product can be written as

$$w = A \cdot (1-\alpha) \cdot u^{-\alpha}\omega^{\alpha} = A^{1/(1-\alpha)} \cdot (1-\alpha) \cdot z^{-\alpha/(1-\alpha)} \tag{5.38}$$

Hence, if $z(0) < z^*$, $w(0) > w^*$, and w falls monotonically over time toward its steady-state value. These properties are reversed if $z(0) > z^*$.

Dynamics of $\chi \equiv C/K$. The evolution of χ depends on the combination of parameters $\alpha - \theta$, which appears as a determinant of $\dot{\chi}/\chi$ in equation (5.34). Since $\alpha \leq 1$ and we usually assume $\theta > 1$, the inequality $\alpha < \theta$ is likely to hold in practice. Thus we assume $\alpha < \theta$ in the main analysis.

We can treat equations (5.33) and (5.34) as a two-dimensional system in z and χ and construct the usual type of phase diagram in (z, χ) space. (Note that the variable u does not appear in these equations.) The vertical line at z^* on the right side of figure 5.4 corresponds to $\dot{z} = 0$ in equation (5.33). This equation also implies that z declines when $z > z^*$ and rises when $z < z^*$. Thus, the $\dot{z} = 0$ locus is stable, as shown in the figure.

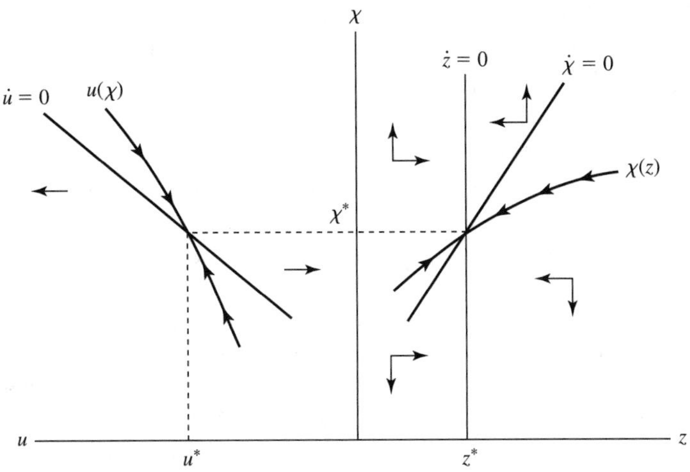

Figure 5.4
Dynamics of z, χ, and u in the Uzawa–Lucas model (when $\alpha < \theta$). The right side uses (z, χ) space to show the $\dot{z} = 0$ locus, the $\dot{\chi} = 0$ locus, and the dynamics of z and χ. The stable arm, $\chi(z)$, is upward sloping. The left side uses (u, χ) space to show the $\dot{u} = 0$ locus and the dynamics of u and χ. (Movements to the left correspond to higher values of u in this panel.) The stable arm, $u(\chi)$, is upward sloping. If $z(0) > z^*$, then $\chi(0) > \chi^*$ (from the right side) and $u(0) > u^*$ (from the left side). During the transition, z, χ, and u fall monotonically. (Note: the results on χ and u depend on the assumption $\alpha < \theta$.)

Equation (5.34) implies that the $\dot{\chi} = 0$ locus satisfies the condition

$$\chi = \chi^* + \left(\frac{\theta - \alpha}{\theta}\right) \cdot (z - z^*) \tag{5.39}$$

Since $\theta > \alpha$, this locus is linear and positively sloped, as shown on the right side of figure 5.4. Moreover, the slope is less than 1, a property that we shall use later. Equation (5.34) implies that χ rises for points that lie above the $\dot{\chi} = 0$ locus and falls otherwise. That is, this locus is unstable, as shown in the figure.

The configuration of the two loci in the right side of figure 5.4 implies that the stable, saddle path, denoted by $\chi(z)$, is upward sloping as shown. Thus, if $z(0) > z^*$, then $\chi(0) > \chi^*$, and z and χ decline monotonically over time toward their steady-state values. Conversely, if $z(0) < z^*$, then $\chi(0) < \chi^*$, and z and χ rise monotonically toward their steady-state values.

Dynamics of u, the fraction of human capital used in production. To ascertain the dynamics of u, use equation (5.35) to determine the $\dot{u} = 0$ locus as

$$u = u^* + (\chi - \chi^*)/B \tag{5.40}$$

This locus is linear and upward sloping in (u, χ) space, as shown on the left side of figure 5.4. (Movements to the left correspond to higher values of u.) The stable, saddle path for u is denoted by $u(\chi)$ in the figure. Note that, if $z(0) > z^*$, so that $\chi(0) > \chi^*$, then $u(0) > u^*$. (It can be verified from the figure that $u(0) \leq u^*$ or $u(0)$ lying to the left of the $\dot{u} = 0$ locus would cause u to diverge over time from u^*.)

To sum up, we have shown that, if $\alpha < \theta$, then $z(0) > z^*$ implies $\chi(0) > \chi^*$ and $u(0) > u^*$, with z, χ, and u all decreasing monotonically toward their steady-state values. Conversely, if $z(0) < z^*$, then $\chi(0) < \chi^*$ and $u(0) < u^*$, with z, χ, and u all increasing monotonically toward their steady-state values.

Dynamics when $\alpha \geq \theta$. We can use the same approach to deal with cases in which $\alpha \geq \theta$. Since we do not regard these cases as empirically relevant, we just indicate the results and leave the derivations as exercises. If $\alpha > \theta$, the results for χ and u are the reverse of those found before. For example, if $z(0) > z^*$, then $\chi(0) < \chi^*$ and $u(0) < u^*$. The monotonic fall in z over time is then associated with monotonic increases in χ and u.

If $\alpha = \theta$, then $\chi(0) = \chi^*$ and $u(0) = u^*$. That is, in this knife-edge case, the variables χ and u remain fixed at their steady-state values throughout the transition from $z(0)$ to z^*.

The relation between z, the gross average product of physical capital, and the state variable $\omega \equiv K/H$. Return now to the case in which $\alpha < \theta$. To finish the dynamic analysis, we have to relate the behavior of z—and, hence, of χ and u—to the behavior of the state variable ω. In particular, we want to make use of the initial condition that ω begins at $\omega(0)$.

Appendix 5B shows that $z(0)$ and $\omega(0)$ are inversely related, with $z(0) \gtreqless z^*$ as $\omega(0) \lesseqgtr \omega^*$. In other words, the gross average product of physical capital, z, is high initially if ω, the ratio of K to H, is low initially, and vice versa.

As an example, if ω starts above its steady-state value—a situation in which human capital is scarce relative to physical capital—then z, the average product of physical capital, and r, the rate of return, start at low values and then rise monotonically toward their steady-state positions. We also know in this situation that the wage rate, w, starts above its steady-state value and then declines, whereas χ and u start below their steady-state values and then increase. The behavior of u means that relatively little human capital is allocated initially to the production of goods and relatively more is allocated to education. Over time, the allocation shifts toward production and away from education. These results are all reversed if ω begins below its steady-state value.

Policy functions for χ and u. We can summarize the results for χ and u in terms of policy functions. Figure 5.5 shows that the choices of χ and u are each downward-sloping functions

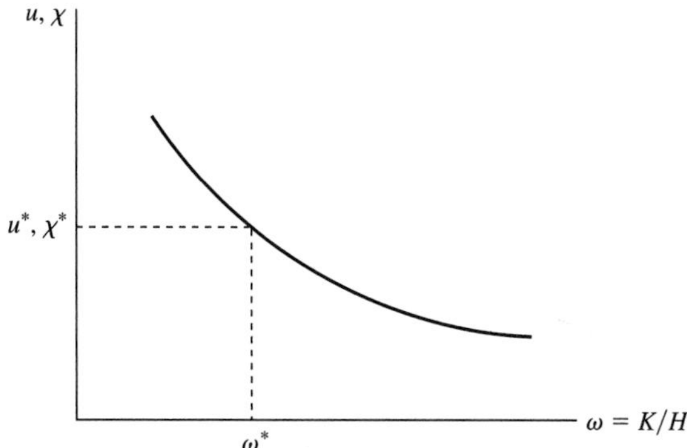

Figure 5.5
Policy functions for u and χ (when $\alpha < \theta$). The policy functions relate the optimal values of the control variables, u and $\chi \equiv C/K$, to the state variable, $\omega \equiv K/H$. When $\alpha < \theta$, the policy functions are each downward sloping. (The figure shows one curve only for convenience.) If $\alpha = \theta$, the policy functions would be flat, and if $\alpha > \theta$, the functions would be upward sloping.

of ω.[18] (We draw a single curve here for both variables only for convenience.) Thus, if we think again of a country that starts with a relative scarcity of human capital—$\omega > \omega^*$—then ω falls over time, while χ and u rise. Thus the country initially allocates relatively little of its resources to consumption ($\chi \equiv C/K$ is low), but it spends a lot of time on education ($1 - u$ is high).

Transitional behavior of growth rates. We consider now how the dynamics of ω, z, χ, and u relate to the transitional behavior of growth rates. We consider, in particular, whether imbalances between K and H—that is, excesses or shortfalls of ω from ω^*—lead to higher or lower growth rates of the various quantities in the model.

The growth rate of consumption. If the economy begins with relatively low physical capital, $\omega < \omega^*$, the interest rate, r, declines monotonically toward its steady-state value, $B - \delta$. This fall in r implies a decline in $\dot{C}/C$. Conversely, if $\omega > \omega^*$, then r and $\dot{C}/C$ rise steadily during the transition. If we graph $\dot{C}/C$ versus ω, we determine a downward-sloping curve, as shown in the upper panel of figure 5.6.

Recall that, in the one-sector model with inequality constraints on gross investment, the relation between $\dot{C}/C$ and ω was described by a U-shaped curve of the form shown in figure 5.1. Imbalances between K and H in either direction led, therefore, to a higher growth rate of consumption. In contrast, in the range of the Uzawa–Lucas model in which

18. Figure 5.5 applies if $\alpha < \theta$. The policy functions are positively sloped if $\alpha > \theta$ and flat if $\alpha = \theta$.

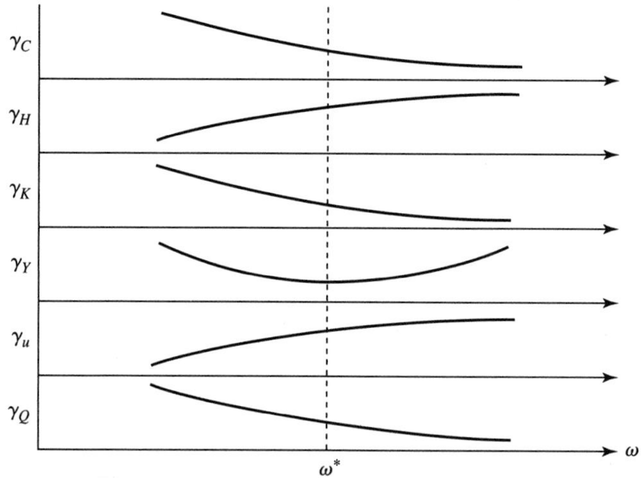

Figure 5.6
Patterns for growth rates in the Uzawa–Lucas model. The figure shows the behavior of the growth rates of consumption, human capital, physical capital, goods output (Y), the fraction of capital devoted to goods production (u), and broad output (Q). These variables are all related to $\omega \equiv K/H$. (Note: the minimal value of $\dot{Y}/Y$ can occur to the right or left of the steady-state value, ω^*.)

inequality constraints on gross investment in K and H are not binding, an imbalance that involves a shortfall of K ($\omega < \omega^*$) implies a higher value of $\dot{C}/C$, whereas an imbalance that involves a shortfall of H ($\omega > \omega^*$) implies a lower value of $\dot{C}/C$.

The growth rates of human and physical capital. The transitional behavior of the growth rates of other variables is more complicated. Appendix 5B demonstrates that we can manipulate the formulas for $\dot{z}/z$, $\dot{\chi}/\chi$, and $\dot{u}/u$ from equations (5.33)–(5.35) and use the condition for $\dot{C}/C$ from equation (5.25) to get expressions for the growth rates of H and K:

$$\dot{H}/H = \gamma^* - B \cdot (u - u^*) \tag{5.41}$$

$$\dot{K}/K = \gamma^* + (z - z^*) - (\chi - \chi^*) \tag{5.42}$$

where γ^* is the steady-state growth rate, $(1/\theta) \cdot (B - \delta - \rho)$, given in equation (5.30).

If $\alpha < \theta$, as we have been assuming, figure 5.5 shows that $u - u^*$ is monotonically declining in ω. Hence, equation (5.41) implies that $\dot{H}/H$ is monotonically increasing in ω. A rise in the relative quantity of physical capital increases the growth rate of human capital. This property is shown in the second panel of figure 5.6.

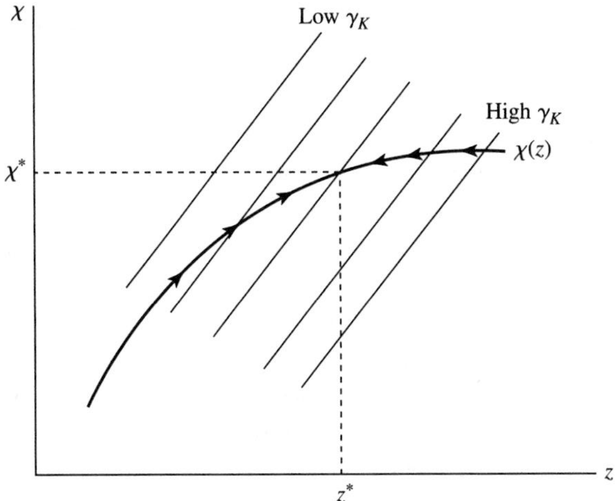

Figure 5.7
Determination of the growth rate of physical capital. In the vicinity of the steady state, the isogrowth lines are steeper than the saddle path, $\chi(z)$. The isogrowth lines that lie farther to the right correspond to higher values of $\dot{K}/K$. Therefore, $\dot{K}/K$ is positively related to z in the vicinity of the steady state. The inverse relation between z and ω implies that $\dot{K}/K$ is inversely related to ω.

Recall that $z - z^*$—the deviation of the average product of capital from its steady-state value—is monotonically decreasing in ω. This effect tends to make $\dot{K}/K$ fall with ω in accordance with equation (5.42). Figure 5.5 shows, however, that $\chi - \chi^*$ is monotonically decreasing in ω, and this effect offsets the tendency for $\dot{K}/K$ to decline.[19]

Figure 5.7 provides a graphical approach to the determination of $\dot{K}/K$. We begin by reproducing the saddle path, denoted $\chi(z)$, from the right side of figure 5.4. Note that this curve is positively sloped but flatter than the $\dot{\chi}=0$ locus, at least in the neighborhood of the steady state. Recall also from equation (5.39) that the slope of the $\dot{\chi}=0$ locus is positive but less than 1. Therefore, the slope of the $\chi(z)$ curve must also be less than 1 in the neighborhood of the steady state.

We can use equation (5.42) to construct isogrowth lines, that is, loci for z and χ that correspond to constant values of $\dot{K}/K$. The equation implies that these loci are linear with slope 1. Figure 5.7 shows several isogrowth lines, where those further to the right—with higher values of z—correspond to higher values of $\dot{K}/K$. We know also that the slope of these lines exceeds the slope of the $\chi(z)$ curve, at least in the neighborhood of the steady state [because, in this region, the $\chi(z)$ curve has slope less than 1].

19. If $\alpha \geq \theta$, $\chi - \chi^*$ is either monotonically increasing in z or constant. It follows unambiguously in this case that $\dot{K}/K$ is monotonically decreasing in ω.

Figure 5.7 shows that $\dot{K}/K$ is positively related to z in the vicinity of the steady state. Hence, $\dot{K}/K$ is negatively related to ω in this region. In other words, if $\omega(0) < \omega^*$, then, as ω rises over time, the fall in $z - z^*$ dominates the fall in $\chi - \chi^*$ in terms of the effects on $\dot{K}/K$ in equation (5.42).

We have found through numerical simulations that the inverse relation between $\dot{K}/K$ and ω holds for a broad range of ω around its steady-state position (see Mulligan and Sala-i-Martin, 1993). That is, the fall in $z - z^*$ dominates the fall in $\chi - \chi^*$ for a wide array of parameter values that we have considered.[20] Thus the model implies that a higher ratio of physical to human capital, ω, is associated with a lower growth rate of physical capital, $\dot{K}/K$. We show this property in the third panel of figure 5.6.

The growth rate of Y, the output of goods. The quantity of goods produced (in the form of consumables and physical capital) is given from equation (5.20) by $Y = AK^{\alpha} \cdot (uH)^{1-\alpha}$. We can, therefore, use the expressions for $\dot{H}/H$ and $\dot{K}/K$ from equations (5.41) and (5.42), along with the formula for $\dot{u}/u$ from equation (5.35), to determine the growth rate of Y:

$$\dot{Y}/Y = \gamma^* + \alpha \cdot (z - z^*) - (\chi - \chi^*) \tag{5.43}$$

We can analyze $\dot{Y}/Y$ by a procedure that parallels our treatment of $\dot{K}/K$. Equation (5.43) implies that isogrowth lines for $\dot{Y}/Y$ in (z, χ) space are linear with slope $\alpha < 1$. Several of these lines appear in figure 5.8; note that lines further to the right are associated with higher growth rates. The difference from the previous case is that the isogrowth lines are not necessarily steeper than the $\chi(z)$ curve in the neighborhood of the steady state. Thus the relation of $\dot{Y}/Y$ to z is ambiguous in the vicinity of the steady state. We conclude that $\dot{Y}/Y$ may either rise or fall with ω.[21]

Our numerical results verify these findings and show that the relation between $\dot{Y}/Y$ and ω tends to be U-shaped, as depicted by the fourth panel of figure 5.6. The minimum of $\dot{Y}/Y$ can occur either to the left or right of the steady state; that is, $\dot{Y}/Y$ can be either rising or falling with ω in the neighborhood of the steady state.

Suppose, for example, that we fix α at 0.5, use our standard values for some parameters that we have considered before ($\rho = 0.02$, $n = 0.01$, $\delta = 0.05$), and set $B = 0.11$ to get a steady-state rate of return, $B - \delta$, of 0.06. (The steady-state growth rate, $[1/\theta] \cdot [B - \delta - \rho]$, then equals 0.02 if $\theta = 2$.) For this specification of parameters, the minimum of $\dot{Y}/Y$ occurs

20. We find numerically that the inverse relation between $\dot{K}/K$ and ω may reverse at very high values of ω. However, for very high (or very low) values of ω, the inequality constraints on gross investment become binding (see section 2.2.4). If we examine only the range of ω for which these constraints are not operative, our numerical results indicate that $\dot{K}/K$ is decreasing in ω for all parameter values that we have considered.

21. If $\alpha \geq \theta$, $\chi - \chi^*$ is either increasing in ω or constant. Hence, $\dot{Y}/Y$ is then unambiguously decreasing in ω.

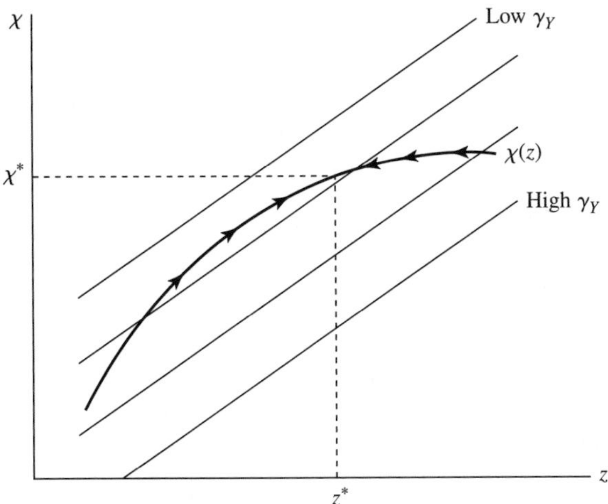

Figure 5.8
Determination of the growth rate of goods output. In the vicinity of the steady state, the isogrowth lines could be steeper or flatter than the saddle path, $\chi(z)$. The growth rate $\dot{Y}/Y$ is therefore ambiguously related to z and ω. Note that the $\chi(z)$ curve comes from the right side of figure 5.4 and applies when $\alpha < \theta$.

at the steady-state value of ω if $\theta = 3.5$, to the left of the steady state if $\theta > 3.5$, and to the right of the steady state if $\theta < 3.5$. (Note that, if the minimum of $\dot{Y}/Y$ occurs to the left of the steady state, $\dot{Y}/Y$ is increasing with z in the vicinity of the steady state, and vice versa.) Thus the imbalance effect can be symmetric, with higher growth rates of output emerging if either K or H is in relatively short supply, or asymmetric, with growth rates rising with one type of imbalance and falling with the other type in the neighborhood of the steady state.

The growth rate of broad output, Q. Broad output, Q, is defined in equation (5.18) (recall that $\eta = 0$ now applies). If we use the formula for μ/ν from equation (5.17) and the expressions for $\dot{Y}/Y$ from equation (5.43), $\dot{H}/H$ from equation (5.41), and $\dot{u}/u$ from equation (5.35), the growth rate of Q can be computed as

$$\dot{Q}/Q = \dot{Y}/Y - (\dot{u}/u) \cdot \left(\frac{1-\alpha}{1-\alpha+\alpha u}\right) \tag{5.44}$$

We have already discussed the determination of $\dot{Y}/Y$. Therefore, to analyze $\dot{Q}/Q$, we have to study the behavior of $\dot{u}/u$.

Equation (5.35) implies that isogrowth lines for $\dot{u}/u$ are linear with slope equal to that of the $\dot{u} = 0$ locus, which appears on the left side of figure 5.4. Figure 5.9 shows several of these isogrowth lines; those farther to the left (for higher values of u) correspond to higher

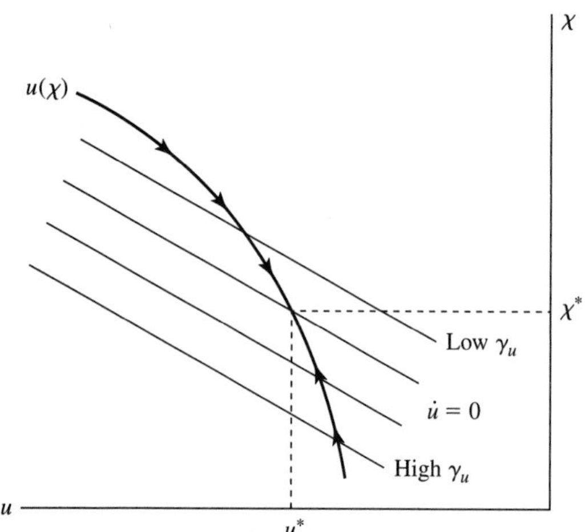

Figure 5.9
Determination of $\dot{u}/u$. In the vicinity of the steady state, the isogrowth lines are flatter than the saddle path, $\chi(u)$. The isogrowth lines that lie farther to the upper right correspond to lower values of $\dot{u}/u$. Therefore, $\dot{u}/u$ is negatively related to χ—and, hence, to z—around the steady state. The inverse relation between z and ω implies that $\dot{u}/u$ is positively related to ω.

values of $\dot{u}/u$. If $z(0) > z^*$, corresponding to $\omega(0) < \omega^*$, then $u(0) > u^*$ and $\chi(0) > \chi^*$. The economy, therefore, moves downward along the $u(\chi)$ curve shown in figure 5.9 toward lower values of u and χ. The figure also shows that $\dot{u}/u$ goes up; that is, as z increases, $\dot{u}/u$ rises from a negative value toward its steady-state value of 0. We show this behavior in the fifth panel of figure 5.6.

Return now to the formula for $\dot{Q}/Q$ in equation (5.44). As ω rises, $\dot{u}/u$ increases (as we just showed) and u declines. Therefore, the term on the far right of the equation tends to generate an inverse relation between $\dot{Q}/Q$ and ω.

The formula for $\dot{Q}/Q$ also contains $\dot{Y}/Y$, which tends to be U-shaped versus ω (see figure 5.6), with the minimum occurring to the left or the right of the steady state. Our numerical results show, however, that $\dot{Q}/Q$ is downward sloping versus ω for a broad range of ω.[22] That is, the new term on the far right of equation (5.44) is strong enough to eliminate the U shape for the parameter values that we have considered. The bottom panel of figure 5.6, therefore, shows $\dot{Q}/Q$ as a monotonically decreasing function of ω.

22. As mentioned in note 20, very low or very high values of ω cause the inequality constraints on gross investment to become operative. If we examine only the range of ω for which these constraints are not binding, our numerical results indicate that $\dot{Q}/Q$, like $\dot{K}/K$, is decreasing in ω for all parameter values that we have considered.

Summary of dynamics in the Uzawa–Lucas model. The Uzawa–Lucas model provides a perspective on the effects of imbalances between K and H that differs from that in the one-sector model. In the one-sector model, larger imbalances between K and H in either direction raised the growth rates of output and consumption. Note that, in the one-sector model, output includes consumables plus both forms of capital. Therefore, we should compare the growth rate of output in the one-sector context with the growth rate of broad output in the Uzawa–Lucas model.

In the Uzawa–Lucas model, $\dot{C}/C$ is always inversely related to ω, and $\dot{Q}/Q$ tends to be inversely related to ω (see figure 5.6). Hence, these growth rates tend to rise with the amount of the imbalance between human and physical capital if human capital is abundant relative to physical capital ($\omega < \omega^*$), but they tend to fall with the amount of the imbalance if human capital is relatively scarce ($\omega > \omega^*$). The model predicts, accordingly, that an economy would recover faster in response to a war that destroyed mainly physical capital than to an epidemic that destroyed mainly human capital.

The underlying source of the new results is the assumption that the education sector is relatively intensive in human capital. If $\omega > \omega^*$, for example, the marginal product of human capital in the goods sector is high, and growth would be expected to occur mainly because of the high growth rate of human capital. The high level of ω implies, however, a high wage rate and therefore a high cost of operation for the sector, education, that is relatively intensive in human capital. In other words, this effect motivates people to allocate human capital to production of goods, rather than to education, the sector that produces the relatively scarce factor, H. This effect tends accordingly to retard the economy's growth rate when ω rises above ω^*.

Behavior of the saving rate. We discussed in chapter 2 the behavior of the gross saving rate in the one-sector Ramsey model. If the production function was Cobb–Douglas, the saving rate fell monotonically, stayed constant, or rose monotonically during the transition depending on whether a particular combination of parameters was positive, zero, or negative (see appendix 2B). We also noted that, if we assumed a high capital share of approximately 0.75, corresponding to a broad notion of capital, then reasonable parameter values were consistent with a roughly constant gross saving rate.

A similar analysis can be applied to the Uzawa–Lucas model with a Cobb–Douglas form of the production function for goods. Suppose that we define gross saving to be the portion of the output of goods, Y, that is not consumed. That is, we take narrow definitions that exclude the production of human capital from output and saving. We can then show (following a procedure analogous to that in appendix 2B) that the transitional behavior of the saving rate is determined as follows:

$$\Psi = -B \cdot (1-\alpha)/\alpha + \delta - (\rho+\delta)/\theta > 0 \implies ds/d\omega > 0 \tag{5.45}$$

$$\Psi = -B \cdot (1-\alpha)/\alpha + \delta - (\rho+\delta)/\theta = 0 \implies s = 1 - \alpha \cdot (\theta-1)/\theta$$

$$\Psi = -B \cdot (1-\alpha)/\alpha + \delta - (\rho+\delta)/\theta < 0 \implies ds/d\omega < 0$$

The condition for a constant saving rate, $\Psi = 0$, is now difficult to satisfy. First, equation (5.45) implies that $\alpha\delta > B \cdot (1-\alpha)$ must hold to get $\Psi = 0$. For the parameter values that we assumed before, $\delta = 0.05$ and $B = 0.11$, this condition implies $\alpha > 0.69$. Since α is supposed to refer now only to physical capital, this inequality is unlikely to be satisfied. Second, the transversality condition for the model—the steady-state rate of return, $B-\delta$, exceeds the steady-state growth rate, $(1/\theta) \cdot (B-\delta-\rho)$—can be used to show that Ψ can equal 0 only if $(1/\theta) + (1/\alpha) < 2$. This condition requires, in particular, $\theta > 1/\alpha$. Thus, if a low value of α worked in the first inequality, then a constant saving rate would require a high value of θ.

If the saving rate were constant during the transition, then its value, $s = 1 - \alpha(\theta-1)/\theta$, would be very high unless α is close to 1 and θ is high. For example, if $\alpha = 0.5$ and $\theta = 2$, then $s = 0.75$. Since saving corresponds here only to the part of goods output that goes into physical capital—and does not include investment in human capital—this high value of s is unrealistic.

Reasonable values of the parameters, including a value of α well below 1, correspond to $\Psi < 0$ and, hence, $ds/d\omega < 0$ in equation (5.45). Consider a less-developed country that starts with a relative scarcity of human capital, so that $\omega > \omega^*$. The model predicts that this country's gross saving rate (defined as the fraction of goods output that is not consumed) would start out low and then rise as the economy approaches its steady state.

Inequality Restrictions on Gross Investment In the one-sector model that we analyzed in the first part of this chapter, one of the inequality constraints for nonnegative gross investment was binding if the initial value of $\omega \equiv K/H$ departed from its steady-state value. In particular, $\omega < \omega^*$ implied that gross investment in human capital was set to zero, whereas $\omega > \omega^*$ implied that gross investment in physical capital was set to zero. In the Uzawa–Lucas model, the inequality constraints are not binding for a range of ω around its steady-state value, and the dynamics that we have considered thus far applies in this range. However, if ω starts sufficiently below or above its steady-state value, an inequality restriction on gross investment becomes operative.

If $\alpha < \theta$, as we assume, then u and ω are inversely related, as shown in figure 5.5. If ω is far enough below ω^*, the restriction $u \leq 1$ binds; that is, if K is sufficiently in short supply relative to H, gross investment in H is set to zero. In this case, H grows at the constant rate

$-\delta$, and the situation parallels the usual one-sector growth model in which output can be used for either C or K. We know that the growth rates of C, K, and Y are inversely related to ω in this range. Hence, in figure 5.6, the downward-sloping curves for $\dot{C}/C$ and $\dot{K}/K$ and the downward-sloping portion of the curve for $\dot{Y}/Y$ apply even when ω is low enough for the restriction $u \leq 1$ to bind.

We can determine numerically how far ω has to fall below ω^* for the inequality constraint $u \leq 1$, and, hence, $\dot{H} + \delta H \geq 0$, to become operative. For the parameter values mentioned before, including $\alpha = 0.5$ and $\theta = 2$, ω has to decline to 5 percent of ω^* to make the restriction bind. Similar conclusions apply if we allow the parameters to depart somewhat from our preferred values.[23] Thus the results indicate that we can satisfactorily neglect the restriction $u \leq 1$ for a wide range of ω below ω^*.

A sufficient increase in ω above ω^* causes the restriction $\dot{K} + \delta K \geq 0$ to bind. That is, if K is sufficiently abundant relative to H, gross investment in K is set to zero.[24] In this case, K grows at the constant rate $-\delta$, and all of the output is used for consumption. The household's only decision here is the allocation of H between production (u) and education ($1 - u$). This framework amounts to a two-sector model in which consumables are produced by one technology and capital (H) with another technology. The only difference from standard two-sector models of this type (such as Uzawa, 1964, and Srinivasan, 1964) is that the consumables sector involves diminishing returns, whereas the capital-goods (H) sector features constant returns.

Appendix 5B shows that the growth rates of C and Y are constant in the Uzawa–Lucas model when the restriction $\dot{K} + \delta K \geq 0$ is operative. That is, if ω is high enough for the constraint of nonnegative physical investment to bind, then $\dot{C}/C$ and $\dot{Y}/Y$, as well as $\dot{K}/K$, are invariant with ω. In figure 5.6, the graphs of $\dot{C}/C$, $\dot{Y}/Y$, and $\dot{K}/K$, therefore, become horizontal for high enough ω.

The behavior of the other growth rates depends on the dynamics of u. In particular, even if $\alpha < \theta$, the policy function for u need not be downward sloping versus ω (as it was in figure 5.5) when the restriction $\dot{K} + \delta K \geq 0$ is operative. If u were inversely related to ω in the restricted range, $\dot{H}/H$ and $\dot{Q}/Q$ would rise with ω in this range. In contrast, if u were positively related to ω, $\dot{H}/H$ and $\dot{Q}/Q$ would fall with ω. This last outcome turns out to hold unambiguously if $\theta \leq 1$, but either result can apply if $\theta > 1$.

We have found numerically how high ω has to be for the constraint of nonnegative physical investment to bind. For the parameter values mentioned before, ω has to be almost

23. If $\alpha \geq \theta$, the constraint $u \leq 1$ never binds.

24. If $\alpha < \theta$, u declines with ω as shown in figure 5.5. A sufficient increase in ω would cause the inequality $u \geq 0$ to bind. However, the restriction $C \geq 0$ never binds because $u'(c) \to \infty$ as $c \to 0$. Therefore, as ω increases, the inequality $\dot{K} + \delta K \geq 0$ becomes operative before the inequality $u \geq 0$. We also find numerically that the restriction $\dot{K} + \delta K \geq 0$ becomes binding for high enough ω even if $\alpha \geq \theta$.

five times ω^* for the constraint to become operative. Similar conclusions apply if we allow the parameters to differ somewhat from our preferred values. Hence, the results indicate that we can satisfactorily neglect the restriction $\dot{K} + \delta K \geq 0$ for a wide range of ω above ω^*.

For reasonable parameter values, the range of ω over which the inequality constraints do not bind—from 5 percent of ω^* to 5 times ω^* for our favored parameter values—appears to be wide relative to the ranges of the K/H ratio that are likely to prevail empirically. Therefore, it seems reasonable to focus on the empirical implications that derive from interior solutions to the model, that is, from the graphs shown in figures 5.5 and 5.6.

5.2.3 The Generalized Uzawa–Lucas Model

The generalized form of the Uzawa–Lucas model maintains the assumption that education is relatively intensive in human capital, $\eta < \alpha$, but allows for the presence of physical capital in the education sector, $\eta > 0$. We already observed from equations (5.17) and (5.19) for the case $\eta < \alpha$ that vK/uH—the ratio of physical capital employed in production to human capital employed in production—converges monotonically to its steady-state value. This result implies that the rate of return, r, and the growth rate of consumption, $\dot{C}/C$, converge monotonically to their steady-state values. Thus these results are the same as those for the Uzawa-Lucas case, where $\eta = 0$.

The difference from before is that we cannot simplify the dynamic system to a two-dimensional setup and, therefore, cannot construct phase diagrams of the form presented in figure 5.4. Moreover, we cannot demonstrate, in general, that the policy functions for χ and u are monotonically related to ω[25] or that the growth rates of K, H, Y, and Q behave qualitatively as they did before.[26]

We have carried out simulations in which α is set at 0.4 and the parameter η is varied between 0 and 0.4. We assume familiar values for the other parameters; a representative case is $\delta = 0.05$, $\rho = 0.02$, $n = 0.01$, and $\theta = 3$. For $\eta = 0$, we set $B = 0.13$, so that the steady-state interest rate is 0.08 and the steady-state per capita growth rate is 0.02. The patterns for the various growth rates when $\eta = 0$ then correspond to those shown in figure 5.6. As we raise η, we adjust B so as to maintain the steady-state interest and growth rates.[27]

As η approaches α, the simulations show that the policy functions for u and χ continue to be monotonically and inversely related to ω, as shown in figure 5.5 for the case in which

25. We have found from simulations that u can be nonmonotonically related to $\omega \equiv K/H$ but only for strange values of the underlying parameters. We have also found cases with odd parameter values in which the policy function for χ can slope in the direction opposite to that for u—a result that cannot hold when $\eta = 0$.

26. Bond, Wang, and Yip (1996) and Mino (1996) demonstrate local stability for the more general case in which the production functions satisfy the neoclassical properties.

27. We normalize to set $A = 1$ throughout.

$\eta = 0$ (see, however, note 25). We find also that the qualitative behavior of the various growth rates remains as shown in figure 5.6, except that higher values of η tend to make the $\dot{Y}/Y$ curve slope upward in the vicinity of the steady state. Thus these numerical results suggest that, if we assume "reasonable" values of the underlying parameters, the main qualitative conclusions from the Uzawa–Lucas model are likely to be preserved when we drop the unrealistic assumption that the education sector has no inputs of physical capital ($\eta = 0$). In particular, our previous discussion of the effects from imbalances between K and H is likely to remain valid.

Another difference in the generalized model is that the range in which the inequality restrictions $u \leq 1$ and $\dot{K} + \delta K \geq 0$ are not binding narrows as η rises toward α. This result makes sense because we know from our previous analysis of the one-sector model that this range compresses to zero when $\eta = \alpha$. If we make the reasonable assumption that η is much less than α—even if η is now positive—then we still find that there exists a broad range of values of ω around the steady state for which the inequality constraints are not binding.

5.2.4 The Model with Reversed Factor Intensities

We have dealt, thus far, with environments in which the education sector is relatively intensive in human capital, that is, $\alpha > \eta \geq 0$. This section considers briefly the implications of reversed factor intensities, $\alpha < \eta$. We spend little time on this case because the assumption that education is relatively intensive in physical capital is implausible. (If we were to interpret K and H not as physical and human capital, but in some alternative way, then the reversed factor intensities might apply.)

We observed before that the condition $\alpha < \eta$ implies that equation (5.19) is an unstable differential equation in the variable $p \equiv \mu/\nu$. (This equation applies as long as inequality restrictions on gross investment are not operative.) Hence, any departure of p from its steady-state value would be magnified over time. This unstable behavior would then be transmitted to the ratio vK/uH (from equation [5.17]). Recall that this ratio determines the marginal product of physical capital in the production of goods and, therefore, determines r and $\dot{C}/C$. The unstable behavior of vK/uH would be transmitted, accordingly, to r and $\dot{C}/C$. Since these explosive outcomes will conflict with household optimization, we focus on the case in which p equals its steady-state value at all points in time.[28]

The constancy of p implies that the ratio vK/uH is constant (from equation [5.17]). Hence, r and $\dot{C}/C$ are also constant throughout the transition to the steady state.

28. Bond, Wang, and Yip (1996) and Mino (1996) provide analogous results for the more general case in which the production functions satisfy the usual neoclassical properties.

Appendix 5C (section 5.7) shows that the growth rate of broad output, $\dot{Q}/Q$, is also constant and equal to $\dot{C}/C$. Thus we get the surprising result that the growth rates of C and Q do not vary as the state variable $\omega \equiv K/H$ changes (in the range in which inequality restrictions are not binding). In other words, the imbalance effect does not operate on these growth rates when the factor intensities are reversed.

The constancy of vK/uH, $\dot{C}/C$, and $\dot{Q}/Q$ makes it easy to assess the dynamics of the variables u, χ, $\dot{H}/H$, and $\dot{K}/K$. Appendix 5C shows that each of these variables adjusts monotonically toward its steady-state value as the state variable, ω, adjusts toward its steady-state value. The slopes of the variables in relation to ω are all unambiguous and are negative for u and χ, positive for $\dot{H}/H$, and negative for $\dot{K}/K$.

5.3 Conditions for Endogenous Growth

We have worked, thus far, with models in which constant returns to scale apply in the sectors for goods and education; that is, we assumed production functions of the forms of equations (5.1) and (5.13). (The Uzawa–Lucas model, expressed in equations [5.20] and [5.21], is the special case in which the education sector uses only human capital as an input, that is, $\eta = 0$.) These production functions imply that diminishing returns do not arise when physical and human capital grow at the same rate. Thus, in the steady state, rates of return remain constant, and the economy can grow at a constant rate. Following Mulligan and Sala-i-Martin (1993), we now consider whether more general specifications of the production functions are consistent with positive growth in the steady state, that is, with endogenous growth.

We modify equations (5.1) and (5.13) to

$$Y = C + \dot{K} + \delta K = A \cdot (vK)^{\alpha_1} \cdot (uH)^{\alpha_2} \tag{5.46}$$

$$\dot{H} + \delta H = B \cdot [(1-v) \cdot K]^{\eta_1} \cdot [(1-u) \cdot H]^{\eta_2} \tag{5.47}$$

Thus we retain Cobb–Douglas forms of the production functions, but we allow the sums $\alpha_1 + \alpha_2$ and $\eta_1 + \eta_2$ to depart from unity, so that constant returns to scale need not apply.

If a sector exhibits diminishing returns, say $\alpha_1 + \alpha_2 < 1$, we can remain within the usual competitive framework if we add to the production function a factor such as raw labor or land that is in fixed aggregate supply. If this factor has an exponent of $1 - \alpha_1 - \alpha_2$, constant returns again apply at the level of an individual producer. The important consideration is that diminishing returns, $\alpha_1 + \alpha_2 < 1$, apply to the factors that can be accumulated.

The model can also have increasing returns, say $\alpha_1 + \alpha_2 > 1$, within a competitive setup if we introduce the types of spillover effects that we considered in chapter 4. For example, for the production of Y, an individual firm's inputs of K and H could have exponents α_1 and $1 - \alpha_1$, respectively, so that constant returns apply for an individual firm. The economy's aggregate of H could then appear as an additional input in the production function (as in Lucas, 1988) with an exponent of $\alpha_1 + \alpha_2 - 1$, where $\alpha_2 > 1 - \alpha_1$. The key consideration here is that increasing returns, $\alpha_1 + \alpha_2 > 1$, apply to the factors that can be accumulated by the overall economy.[29]

Suppose that we look for a steady state in which u and v are constant, and C, Y, K, and H grow at constant, but not necessarily equal, rates. (Unless u or v approaches 0, we cannot allow u and v to grow at constant rates because of the constraints $0 \leq v \leq 1$ and $0 \leq u \leq 1$.) If we divide equation (5.47) by H and then take logs and derivatives with respect to time, we get

$$\eta_1 \gamma_K^* + (\eta_2 - 1) \cdot \gamma_H^* = 0 \tag{5.48}$$

where γ^* denotes the steady-state growth rate of the variable indicated by the subscript.

If we divide equation (5.46) by K and then take logs and derivatives, we get

$$\left(\frac{C/K}{C/K + \gamma_K^* + \delta}\right) \cdot (\gamma_C^* - \gamma_K^*) = (\alpha_1 - 1) \cdot \gamma_K^* + \alpha_2 \gamma_H^* \tag{5.49}$$

We can show that $\gamma_C^* = \gamma_K^*$ from the arguments that we used in chapter 4. (If $\gamma_C^* > \gamma_K^*$, then γ_K^*, as computed from equation [5.46], tends to $-\infty$. If $\gamma_C^* < \gamma_K^*$, then $\gamma_K^* = r$, the net marginal product of K in the goods sector. This equality violates the transversality condition.) Equation (5.49) then simplifies to

$$(\alpha_1 - 1) \cdot \gamma_K^* + \alpha_2 \gamma_H^* = 0 \tag{5.50}$$

We can use the condition $\gamma_Y^* = \alpha_1 \gamma_K^* + \alpha_2 \gamma_H^*$ implied by equation (5.46), along with equation (5.50), to show that $\gamma_Y^* = \gamma_K^*$. Thus, the variables C, K, and Y must all grow at the same rate in the steady state.

29. We observed in chapter 4 that the presence of these kinds of spillovers implies that the competitive outcomes will generally not be Pareto optimal. Thus these models tend to have roles for government intervention, basically to subsidize the activities with positive spillovers. In extreme situations, in which the spillovers are very large, multiple equilibria are possible, and the equilibria can typically be ranked by the Pareto criterion. Suppose, as an example, that an individual's return to education depends positively on the average education level of the population. Then, in one kind of equilibrium, everyone gets education, because when most people are educated, the remaining people find it advantageous also to be educated. In another kind of equilibrium, no one receives education, because when most people are not educated, the remaining people find it desirable not to be educated. We have not explored the class of models with multiple equilibria because the amount of spillovers required to generate this multiplicity seems to be unrealistically large. Moreover, from a positive standpoint, models that do not select among the possible equilibria are incomplete. For analyses of these types of models—and for more favorable appraisals of them—see Krugman (1991), Matsuyama (1991), Benhabib and Farmer (1996), Boldrin and Rustichini (1994), Chamley (1992), and Xie (1992).

Equations (5.48) and (5.50) form a system of two linear homogeneous equations with two unknowns, γ_K^* and γ_H^*. This system has a solution other than $\gamma_K^* = \gamma_H^* = 0$ only if the determinant of the characteristic matrix of the coefficients is zero. This condition requires the parameters to satisfy

$$\alpha_2\eta_1 = (1-\eta_2)\cdot(1-\alpha_1) \tag{5.51}$$

Equation (5.51) is the key condition that must hold if the model is to deliver endogenous growth at positive, constant rates.

One example that satisfies equation (5.51) is the case that we have already considered of constant returns in each sector: $\alpha_1+\alpha_2 = 1$ and $\eta_1+\eta_2 = 1$. In this situation, $\gamma_H^* = \gamma_K^*$, so that the ratio K/H is constant in the steady state. Equation (5.51) can, however, be satisfied in other ways.

If $\eta_1 = 0$ and $\eta_2 = 1$—the case assumed by Uzawa (1965) and Lucas (1988)—equation (5.51) holds for any values of α_1 and α_2. Thus, if education is linear in H, all variables can grow in the steady state even if the production of goods involves diminishing returns to scale, $\alpha_1+\alpha_2 < 1$. Lucas highlighted a spillover benefit from aggregate human capital that led to the condition $\alpha_1+\alpha_2 > 1$. Our results show that this condition is consistent with, but not essential for, endogenous growth. If $\eta_1 = 0$ and $\eta_2 = 1$, as Lucas also assumed, this model can generate endogenous growth even if no human-capital spillovers are present.

Equation (5.50) implies, if $\alpha_1 \neq 1$,

$$\gamma_K^* = \left(\frac{\alpha_2}{1-\alpha_1}\right)\cdot\gamma_H^*$$

Hence, $\gamma_K^* \lesseqgtr \gamma_H^*$ as $\alpha_1+\alpha_2 \lesseqgtr 1$. Thus, although all quantities can grow at constant rates when $\eta_1 = 0$ and $\eta_2 = 1$, the ratios K/H, Y/H, and C/H do not approach constant values unless $\alpha_1+\alpha_2 = 1$.

For another example, assume that $\alpha_i, \eta_i > 0$ for $i = 1, 2$. If $\alpha_1+\alpha_2 < 1$, then equation (5.51) can be satisfied if $\eta_1+\eta_2 > 1$. Analogously, $\alpha_1+\alpha_2 > 1$ can be paired with $\eta_1+\eta_2 < 1$. In other words, diminishing returns to scale in one sector can be offset by the appropriate degree of increasing returns in the other sector. If $\alpha_1+\alpha_2 < 1$, then $\gamma_K^* < \gamma_H^*$, and vice versa.

Finally, equation (5.51) is also satisfied if $\alpha_1 = 1$ and $\alpha_2 = 0$. This specification corresponds to the AK model studied in chapter 4. In this specification, human capital serves no purpose; it does not help to produce goods and also does not appear in the utility function. Hence, optimizing agents would not accumulate any H, and all of K would be allocated to the production of goods ($v = 1$ in equations [5.46] and [5.47]).

If we want endogenous growth and also want K and H to grow at the same rate in the steady state, equation (5.51) can be satisfied only if each sector exhibits constant returns to scale, $\alpha_1 + \alpha_2 = 1$ and $\eta_1 + \eta_2 = 1$, that is, the specification in equations (5.1) and (5.13). Since the alternative in which K/H rises or falls forever seems implausible, we assumed in the main discussion in this chapter that constant returns held in each sector.

5.4 Summary Observations

We extended the AK model from chapter 4 to allow for two sectors, one that produced consumables, C, and physical capital, K, and another that created human capital, H. If the sectors have the same factor intensities, the main new results about growth come from the restriction that gross investment in each type of capital good must be nonnegative. This restriction generates an imbalance effect, whereby the growth rate of output rises with the magnitude of the gap between the ratio K/H and its steady-state value.

The assumption of equal factor intensities neglects a key aspect of education; it relies heavily on educated people as an input. Therefore, we modified the structure to specify that the production of human capital is relatively intensive in human capital. This change in specification alters the conclusions about the imbalance effect. The growth rate of output (defined broadly to include the production of new human capital) tends to rise with the extent of the imbalance if human capital is relatively abundant but to decline with the extent of the imbalance if human capital is relatively scarce. These results imply that an economy would recover rapidly in reaction to a war that destroyed primarily physical capital but would rebound only slowly from an epidemic that eliminated mainly human capital.

5.5 Appendix 5A: Transitional Dynamics with Inequality Restrictions on Gross Investment in the One-Sector Model

Suppose that $K(0)/H(0) > \alpha/(1-\alpha)$. Recall that, in this case, the household wants to reduce K and raise H by discrete amounts, so that the inequality restriction $I_K \geq 0$ will be binding. Hence, $I_K = 0$ and $\dot{K}/K = -\delta$. In this situation, the household's problem amounts to maximizing utility, subject to this path for K and to the constraint $\dot{H} = Y - C - \delta H$. The Hamiltonian for this problem is

$$J = u(C) \cdot e^{-\rho t} + \nu \cdot [AK^{\alpha}H^{1-\alpha} - \delta H - C] \tag{5.52}$$

where $u(C) = (C^{1-\theta} - 1)/(1-\theta)$. The first-order conditions, $\partial J/\partial C = 0$ and $\dot{\nu} = -\partial J/\partial H$, lead in the usual way to the condition for the growth rate of consumption:

$$\dot{C}/C = (1/\theta) \cdot [A \cdot (1-\alpha) \cdot (K/H)^{\alpha} - \delta - \rho] \tag{5.53}$$

where $A \cdot (1-\alpha) \cdot (K/H)^{\alpha} - \delta$ is the net marginal product of H. This condition and the budget constraint,

$$\dot{H} = AK^{\alpha}H^{1-\alpha} - \delta H - C$$

along with $K(t) = K(0) \cdot e^{-\delta t}$, determine the paths of C, H, and K.

We can proceed, as in chapter 4, by defining two variables, $\omega \equiv K/H$ and $\chi \equiv C/K$, that will be constant in the steady state. The conditions for $\dot{C}$ and $\dot{H}$ can be used to get the transition equations for ω and χ:

$$\dot{\omega}/\omega = -A\omega^{\alpha} + \chi\omega \tag{5.54}$$

$$\dot{\chi}/\chi = (1/\theta) \cdot [A \cdot (1-\alpha) \cdot \omega^{\alpha} - \rho] + \delta \cdot (\theta - 1)/\theta \tag{5.55}$$

Figure 5.10 shows the phase diagram in (ω, χ) space. The condition $\dot{\omega} = 0$ implies $\chi = A\omega^{-(1-\alpha)}$, the downward-sloping curve in the figure. A value of χ above (below) the curve corresponds to $\dot{\omega} > 0$ ($\dot{\omega} < 0$). These directions of motion are shown by the arrows in the figure.

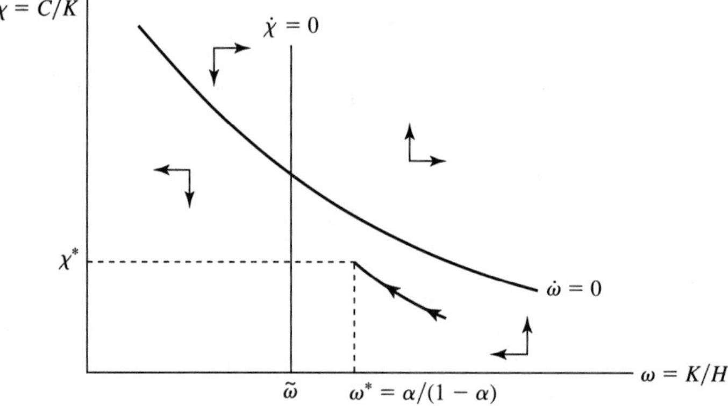

Figure 5.10
Phase diagram for the one-sector model when $\omega > \omega^*$. The dynamics shown in this figure applies when $\omega \equiv K/H > \omega^* = \alpha/(1-\alpha)$. When $\omega > \omega^*$, the economy moves along a path where $\chi \equiv C/K$ rises monotonically and ω falls monotonically. The economy reaches ω^* in finite time (before it reaches $\tilde{\omega}$), just when χ attains the value χ^*. At this point the inequality constraint that gross investment in K cannot be negative is no longer binding. The variables K and H then grow together at a constant, positive rate.

The condition $\dot{\chi} = 0$ requires

$$\omega = \left[\frac{\rho + \delta \cdot (1 - \theta)}{A \cdot (1 - \alpha)}\right]^{1/\alpha} \equiv \tilde{\omega} \tag{5.56}$$

We assume $\rho + \delta \cdot (1 - \theta) \geq 0$, so that $\tilde{\omega}$ is well defined and nonnegative, but this condition is not required for the analysis. A value of ω above (below) $\tilde{\omega}$ corresponds to $\dot{\chi} > 0$ ($\dot{\chi} < 0$), as shown by the arrows in the figure. [If $\rho + \delta \cdot (1 - \theta) < 0$, then $\dot{\chi} > 0$ applies for all $\chi \geq 0$.])

The figure shows $\tilde{\omega} < \omega^* = \alpha/(1 - \alpha)$, the ratio of K to H that applies in equation (5.7) in the absence of effective inequality constraints on both types of gross investment. The formula for $\tilde{\omega}$ implies that the condition $\tilde{\omega} < \omega^*$ corresponds to $\rho + \delta < A\alpha^{\alpha} \cdot (1 - \alpha)^{1-\alpha}$, a result that holds from the assumption $\gamma^* > 0$ in equation (5.9). The figure also shows the value χ^*, which applies to the model without effective inequality constraints. The value for χ^* in this model turns out to be

$$\chi^* = \left(\frac{\theta - 1}{\theta}\right) \cdot \left[A \cdot \left(\frac{1 - \alpha}{\alpha}\right)^{1-\alpha} - \frac{\delta}{\alpha}\right] + \frac{\rho}{\theta\alpha} \tag{5.57}$$

The dynamics shown in figure 5.10 is relevant for $\omega > \omega^*$, the condition that causes $I_K \geq 0$ to be a binding constraint. The figure shows that, in this region, χ rises monotonically and ω falls monotonically. Eventually, ω attains the value ω^*, and the constraint $I_K \geq 0$ no longer binds. From that point on, ω remains at ω^*, and K and H grow together at the rate γ^* shown in equation (5.9). This rate applies to the model in which the inequality constraints on both types of investment are not binding. The position of the dynamic path is determined so that χ attains the value χ^* shown in equation (5.57) just when ω reaches ω^*. Thereby, the level of consumption does not jump when the constraint of nonnegative gross investment in physical capital becomes nonbinding.[30]

The results are analogous if $K(0)/H(0) < \alpha/(1 - \alpha)$. The condition $I_H \geq 0$ is then binding, and $\dot{H}/H = -\delta$. The transition equations for ω and χ are

$$\dot{\omega}/\omega = A\omega^{-(1-\alpha)} - \chi \tag{5.58}$$

$$\dot{\chi}/\chi = -A \cdot \left(\frac{\theta - \alpha}{\theta}\right) \cdot \omega^{-(1-\alpha)} + \chi + \delta \cdot (\theta - 1)/\theta - \rho/\theta \tag{5.59}$$

Figure 5.11 shows the phase diagram for the case in which $\alpha < \theta$. The condition $\dot{\omega} = 0$ corresponds to $\chi = \omega^{-(1-\alpha)}$. The condition $\dot{\chi} = 0$ corresponds to

$$\chi = A \cdot \left(\frac{\theta - \alpha}{\theta}\right) \cdot \omega^{-(1-\alpha)} - \delta \cdot (\theta - 1)/\theta + \rho/\theta \tag{5.60}$$

30. We are grateful to Kiminori Matsuyama for providing this solution.

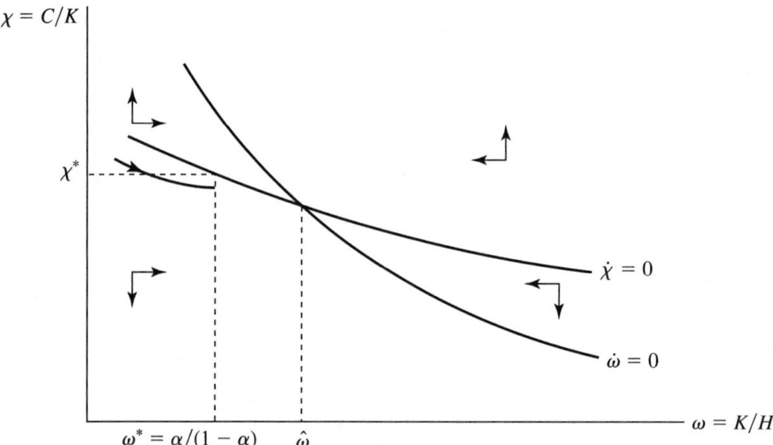

Figure 5.11
Phase diagram for the one-sector model when $\omega < \omega^*$. The dynamics shown in this figure applies when $\omega \equiv K/H < \omega^* = \alpha/(1-\alpha)$. When $\omega < \omega^*$, the economy moves along a path where $\chi \equiv C/K$ falls monotonically (if $\alpha < \theta$, as assumed for this case) and ω rises monotonically. The economy reaches ω^* in finite time (before it reaches $\hat{\omega}$), just when χ attains the value χ^*. At this point, the inequality constraint that gross investment in H cannot be negative is no longer binding. The variables K and H then grow together at a constant, positive rate.

The $\dot{\chi} = 0$ locus slopes downward, as shown, if $\alpha < \theta$. This locus must be less negatively sloped than the $\dot{\omega} = 0$ locus (but the $\dot{\chi} = 0$ locus would be positively sloped if $\alpha > \theta$). The $\dot{\omega} = 0$ and $\dot{\chi} = 0$ loci intersect at the value $\hat{\omega}$, which can be shown (from the condition $\gamma^* > 0$) to exceed $\omega^* = \alpha/(1-\alpha)$.

The dynamics shown in figure 5.11 applies if $\omega < \omega^*$. The figure shows that, in this region, χ declines monotonically and ω rises monotonically. (If $\alpha > \theta$, χ rises monotonically, and, if $\alpha = \theta$, χ remains constant.) The position of the dynamic path is again determined so that χ attains the value χ^* shown in equation (5.57) just when ω reaches ω^*.

5.6 Appendix 5B: Solution of the Uzawa–Lucas Model

The Hamiltonian expression for this model is given by

$$J = u(C) \cdot e^{-\rho t} + \nu \cdot [AK^{\alpha} \cdot (uH)^{1-\alpha} - C - \delta K] + \mu \cdot [B \cdot (1-u) \cdot H - \delta H] \quad (5.61)$$

The term in the first set of brackets equals $\dot{K}$, and the term in the second set of brackets equals $\dot{H}$. If we define $\omega \equiv K/H$ and $\chi \equiv C/K$, the growth rates of K and H are given by

$$\dot{K}/K = Au^{1-\alpha}\omega^{-(1-\alpha)} - \chi - \delta \tag{5.62}$$

$$\dot{H}/H = B \cdot (1-u) - \delta \tag{5.63}$$

The growth rate of ω is, therefore, given by

$$\dot{\omega}/\omega = \dot{K}/K - \dot{H}/H = Au^{1-\alpha}\omega^{-(1-\alpha)} - \chi - B \cdot (1-u) \tag{5.64}$$

The first-order conditions, $\partial J/\partial C = 0$ and $\partial J/\partial u = 0$, lead respectively to

$$u'(C) = \nu e^{\rho t} \tag{5.65}$$

$$\mu/\nu = (A/B) \cdot (1-\alpha) \cdot u^{-\alpha}\omega^{\alpha} \tag{5.66}$$

The condition $\dot{\nu} = -\partial J/\partial K$ implies

$$\dot{\nu}/\nu = -A\alpha u^{1-\alpha}\omega^{-(1-\alpha)} + \delta \tag{5.67}$$

The condition $\dot{\mu} = -\partial J/\partial H$ implies

$$\dot{\mu}/\mu = -(\nu/\mu) \cdot A \cdot (1-\alpha) \cdot u^{1-\alpha}\omega^{\alpha} - B \cdot (1-u) + \delta$$

If we substitute for ν/μ from equation (5.66) and simplify, the result is

$$\dot{\mu}/\mu = -B + \delta \tag{5.68}$$

We can differentiate equation (5.65) with respect to time and use $u(C) = (C^{1-\theta} - 1)/(1-\theta)$ and the expression for $\dot{\nu}/\nu$ in equation (5.67) to get the usual equation for consumption growth:

$$\dot{C}/C = (1/\theta) \cdot \left[A\alpha u^{1-\alpha}\omega^{-(1-\alpha)} - \delta - \rho\right] \tag{5.69}$$

This result corresponds to equation (5.25). The growth rate of χ can then be determined from equations (5.69) and (5.62) to get the formula given in equation (5.26):

$$\dot{\chi}/\chi = \dot{C}/C - \dot{K}/K = \left(\frac{\alpha-\theta}{\theta}\right) \cdot Au^{1-\alpha}\omega^{-(1-\alpha)} + \chi - (1/\theta) \cdot [\delta \cdot (1-\theta) + \rho] \tag{5.70}$$

If we differentiate equation (5.66) with respect to time and use the formulas for $\dot{\nu}/\nu$ from equation (5.67), $\dot{\mu}/\mu$ from equation (5.68), and $\dot{\omega}/\omega$ from equation (5.64), we get, after simplifying,

$$\dot{u}/u = B \cdot (1-\alpha)/\alpha + Bu - \chi \tag{5.71}$$

This result appears in equation (5.27). Equations (5.64), (5.70), and (5.71) form a system of three differential equations in the variables ω, χ, and u, where the state variable ω begins at some value $\omega(0)$.

The steady state of this system can be found readily by setting the three time derivatives to zero. If we define the combination of parameters as in the text,

$$\varphi \equiv \frac{\rho + \delta \cdot (1 - \theta)}{B\theta}$$

the results are

$$\begin{aligned} \omega^* &= (\alpha A/B)^{1/(1-\alpha)} \cdot [\varphi + (\theta - 1)/\theta] \\ \chi^* &= B \cdot (\varphi + 1/\alpha - 1/\theta) \\ u^* &= \varphi + (\theta - 1)/\theta \end{aligned} \tag{5.72}$$

These values are given in equation (5.29). The steady-state rate of return, which equals the net marginal product of K in the goods sector and the net marginal product of H in the education sector, is

$$r^* = B - \delta$$

The corresponding steady-state growth rate of Y, C, K, and H is

$$\gamma^* = (1/\theta) \cdot (B - \delta - \rho)$$

The values for r^* and γ^* are shown in equation (5.30).

Define z to be the gross average product of physical capital:

$$z \equiv Au^{1-\alpha}\omega^{-(1-\alpha)}$$

The steady-state value of z can be determined from equation (5.72) to be $z^* = B/\alpha$. The system of three differential equations, as expressed in equations (5.64), (5.70), and (5.71), can then be rewritten as

$$\dot{\omega}/\omega = (z - z^*) - (\chi - \chi^*) + B \cdot (u - u^*) \tag{5.73}$$

$$\dot{\chi}/\chi = \left(\frac{\alpha - \theta}{\theta}\right) \cdot (z - z^*) + (\chi - \chi^*) \tag{5.74}$$

$$\dot{u}/u = B \cdot (u - u^*) - (\chi - \chi^*) \tag{5.75}$$

The definition of z implies

$$\dot{z}/z = (1-\alpha)\cdot(\dot{u}/u - \dot{\omega}/\omega) = -(1-\alpha)\cdot(z - z^*) \tag{5.76}$$

The results for $\dot{z}/z$, $\dot{\chi}/\chi$, and $\dot{u}/u$ are in equations (5.33)–(5.35).

Equation (5.76) can be integrated to get equation (5.37):

$$\frac{z - z^*}{z} = \left[\frac{z(0) - z^*}{z(0)}\right]\cdot e^{-(1-\alpha)\cdot z^* t}$$

where $z(0)$ is the initial value of z. This equation can be rewritten to solve for z as

$$z = z^*\cdot z(0)/\left\{z^*\cdot e^{-(1-\alpha)\cdot z^* t} + z(0)\cdot\left[1 - e^{-(1-\alpha)\cdot z^* t}\right]\right\} \tag{5.77}$$

Equation (5.77) implies $z \to z^*$ as $t \to \infty$. If $z(0) > z^*$, then $\dot{z} < 0$ and $z > z^*$ for all t, whereas if $z(0) < z^*$, then $\dot{z} > 0$ and $z < z^*$ for all t.

We now look for the characteristics of the stable path of χ and u, that is, the path along which χ approaches χ^* and u approaches u^*. Assume $z(0) > z^*$, so that $z - z^*$ declines monotonically over time. Equation (5.74) can then be written as

$$\dot{\chi}/\chi = (\chi - \chi^*) + \left(\frac{\alpha - \theta}{\theta}\right)\cdot\Omega(t) \tag{5.78}$$

where $\Omega(t) = z - z^*$ is a monotonically decreasing function of time. If $\alpha < \theta$, the term on the right of equation (5.78) is negative but declining in magnitude over time. If $\chi \le \chi^*$ for some finite t, the equation implies $\dot{\chi} < 0$ for all subsequent t. Since the magnitude of $\dot{\chi}$ asymptotically exceeds some finite lower bound, χ would diverge from χ^* and reach zero in finite time. The stable path, therefore, features $\chi > \chi^*$ for all t. If $\dot{\chi} \ge 0$ for some t, then equation (5.78) implies $\dot{\chi} > 0$ for all subsequent t (because the negative term on the right decreases in size over time). Hence, χ would diverge from χ^* and approach infinity. The stable path, therefore, involves $\dot{\chi} < 0$ for all t.

The conclusions are analogous if we assume $\alpha > \theta$ or begin with $z(0) < z^*$. The columns for $\chi - \chi^*$ and $\dot{\chi}$ in table 5.1 summarize the results.

Equation (5.75) determines the behavior of u, given the behavior of χ. Suppose, for example, that $z(0) > z^*$ and $\alpha < \theta$, so that $\chi > \chi^*$ and $\dot{\chi} < 0$. If $u \le u^*$ for some t, then equation (5.75) implies $\dot{u} < 0$ for all subsequent t. Therefore, u diverges from u^* and approaches 0. The stable path, therefore, features $u > u^*$ for all t. If $\dot{u} \ge 0$ for some t, then $\dot{u} > 0$ for all subsequent t, because the term $-(\chi - \chi^*)$ in equation (5.75) is negative and decreasing in size over time. Therefore, $\dot{u} < 0$ holds for all t. The behavior of $u - u^*$ and $\dot{u}$ are shown for the various sign combinations of $z(0) - z^*$ and $\alpha - \theta$ in table 5.1.

Table 5.1
Transitional Behavior of χ and u

$z(0) - z^*$	$\alpha - \theta$	$\chi - \chi^*$	χ	$u - u^*$	u
>0	<0	>0	<0	>0	<0
>0	>0	<0	>0	<0	>0
=0	—	=0	=0	=0	=0
<0	<0	<0	>0	<0	>0
—	=0	=0	=0	=0	=0

We want to show now how the starting value $z(0) - z^*$ relates to the starting value of the state variable, ω. If we use equation (5.74) to substitute for $\chi - \chi^*$ in the formula for $\dot{\omega}/\omega$ in equation (5.73), we get

$$\dot{\omega}/\omega = (\alpha/\theta) \cdot (z - z^*) - \gamma_\chi + B \cdot (u - u^*) \tag{5.79}$$

Suppose $\alpha \leq \theta$ and $z(0) > z^*$. In this case, the conditions $z - z^* > 0$, $\dot{\chi} \leq 0$, and $u - u^* \geq 0$ imply $\dot{\omega}/\omega > 0$ in equation (5.79). Hence, the system can be on the stable path only if $\omega(0) < \omega^*$. Moreover, ω then rises monotonically from $\omega(0)$ toward ω^* (because $\dot{\omega}/\omega > 0$). Hence, the monotonic decline in z corresponds to a monotonic rise in ω. This result implies that a lower starting value of the state variable, $\omega(0)$, is associated with a higher initial value $z(0)$. By similar reasoning, $z(0) < z^*$ corresponds to $\omega(0) > \omega^*$, and $z(0) = z^*$ to $\omega(0) = \omega^*$.

To deal with the case in which $\alpha > \theta$, substitute for $u - u^*$ from equation (5.75) into equation (5.73) to get

$$\dot{\omega}/\omega = (z - z^*) + \dot{u}/u \tag{5.80}$$

We can use this equation when $\alpha > \theta$ to show that $z(0) > z^*$ $(z[0] < z^*)$ corresponds to $\omega(0) < \omega^*$ $(\omega[0] > \omega^*)$.

We conclude that $z(0) \gtreqless z^*$ corresponds to $\omega(0) \lesseqgtr \omega*$ for all configurations of α and θ. Moreover, a smaller $\omega(0)$ matches up with a higher $z(0)$. Thus z is high or low initially depending only on whether physical capital is scarce or abundant relative to human capital. We can use this result along with the findings in table 5.1 to draw policy functions for χ and u as functions of ω. These results appear in figure 5.5.

The rate of return, r, equals the net marginal product of physical capital in the production of goods, which equals $\alpha z - \delta$. Therefore, r moves together with z and inversely with ω. Equation (5.69) implies that the growth rate of C is given by

$$\dot{C}/C = (1/\theta) \cdot (\alpha z - \delta - \rho) \tag{5.81}$$

Since $\dot{C}/C$ moves directly with z, it moves inversely with ω.

The growth rate of K is given by

$$\dot{K}/K = \dot{C}/C - \dot{\chi}/\chi = (1/\theta) \cdot (\alpha z - \delta - \rho) - \dot{\chi}/\chi$$

where we substituted for $\dot{C}/C$ from equation (5.81). If we substitute for $\dot{\chi}/\chi$ from equation (5.79) and use the formulas $z^* = B/\alpha$ and $\gamma^* = (1/\theta) \cdot (B - \delta - \rho)$, we get

$$\dot{K}/K = \gamma^* + (z - z^*) - (\chi - \chi^*) \tag{5.82}$$

the formula that appears in equation (5.42).

The growth rate of H is given by

$$\dot{H}/H = \dot{K}/K - \dot{\omega}/\omega$$

If we substitute for $\dot{K}/K$ from equation (5.82) and for $\dot{\omega}/\omega$ from equation (5.80) and use equation (5.75) to substitute for $\dot{u}/u$, we can simplify to get

$$\dot{H}/H = \gamma^* - B \cdot (u - u^*) \tag{5.83}$$

the formula that appears in equation (5.41).

Since $Y = AK^{\alpha} \cdot (uH)^{1-\alpha}$, the growth rate of output is given by

$$\dot{Y}/Y = \alpha \cdot \dot{K}/K + (1 - \alpha) \cdot (\dot{u}/u + \dot{H}/H)$$

If we substitute for $\dot{K}/K$ from equation (5.82), for $\dot{u}/u$ from equation (5.75), and for $\dot{H}/H$ from equation (5.83), we get

$$\dot{Y}/Y = \gamma^* + \alpha \cdot (z - z^*) - (\chi - \chi^*) \tag{5.84}$$

the formula that appears in equation (5.43).

Broad output is given by

$$Q = Y + (\mu/\nu) \cdot B \cdot (1 - u) \cdot H = AK^{\alpha} \cdot (uH)^{1-\alpha} + (\mu/\nu) \cdot B \cdot (1 - u) \cdot H$$

where μ/ν, the shadow price of human capital in units of goods, is given in equation (5.66). If we substitute out for μ/ν, we get

$$Q = Y \cdot (1 - \alpha + \alpha u)/u$$

Hence, the growth rate of broad output is given by

$$\dot{Q}/Q = \dot{Y}/Y - \dot{u}/u \cdot (1 - \alpha)/(1 - \alpha + \alpha u) \tag{5.85}$$

the formula given in equation (5.44).

For alternative treatments of the Uzawa–Lucas model, see Faig (1995) and Caballe and Santos (1993).

5.7 Appendix 5C: The Model with Reversed Factor Intensities

We consider here the production structure from equations (5.1) and (5.13) with the condition $\alpha < \eta$. Let $p \equiv \mu/\nu$ be the value of H in units of goods. We noted in the text that equation (5.19) is an unstable differential equation in p and that p always equals its steady-state value, which is given by

$$p = p^* = \psi^{1/(\alpha-\eta)} \cdot \left(\frac{\alpha}{1-\alpha}\right)^{(\alpha-\eta)/(1-\alpha+\eta)} \tag{5.86}$$

where

$$\psi \equiv \left(\frac{A}{B}\right) \cdot \left(\frac{\alpha}{\eta}\right)^{\eta} \cdot \left(\frac{1-\alpha}{1-\eta}\right)^{1-\eta}$$

Equation (5.17) implies, accordingly, that vK/uH always equals its steady-state value,

$$\frac{vK}{uH} = \left(\frac{vK}{uH}\right)^* = \left[\psi \cdot \left(\frac{\alpha}{1-\alpha}\right)\right]^{1/(1-\alpha+\eta)} \tag{5.87}$$

The rate of return and the growth rate of consumption are then constants, given by

$$r = r^* = \alpha A \cdot \left[\left(\frac{vK}{uH}\right)^*\right]^{\alpha-1} - \delta \tag{5.88}$$

$$\dot{C}/C = \gamma^* = (1/\theta) \cdot (r^* - \rho) \tag{5.89}$$

We now show that full wealth, $K + pH$, and full output, $Q \equiv Y + p \cdot (\dot{H} + \delta H)$, always grow at the rate γ^*, that is, at the same rate as C. The analysis of consumer optimization from chapter 2 applies if we think of households as earning the rate of return r on their full wealth, $K + pH$. (The wage rate on raw labor is zero in this setting.) Equations (2.14) and (2.15) showed that consumption is a multiple of full wealth; moreover, the multiple is constant here because r is constant. Consequently, $K + pH$ grows at the same rate, γ^*, as C.

The Hamiltonian expression from equation (5.14) can be written as

$$J = u(C) \cdot e^{-\rho t} + \nu \cdot (Q - C) - \nu\delta \cdot (K + pH) \tag{5.90}$$

where

$$u(C) = \frac{C^{1-\theta} - 1}{1-\theta}$$

We can verify from the first-order conditions for optimization that $\dot{J} = -\rho \cdot u(C) \cdot e^{-\rho t}$. If we differentiate the right-hand side of equation (5.90) with respect to time, use the first-order condition $\nu = C^{-\theta} e^{-\rho t}$, and simplify, we get

$$(\dot{\nu}/\nu - \delta) \cdot [C + \delta \cdot (K + pH)] + \delta Q = (\dot{\nu}/\nu) \cdot Q + \dot{Q}$$

If we use $\dot{\nu}/\nu = -(\rho + \theta \cdot \dot{C}/C)$ and rearrange terms, we get a formula for the growth rate of Q:

$$\dot{Q}/Q = (\delta + \rho + \theta \gamma_C) \cdot \left\{1 - \left(\frac{1}{Q}\right) \cdot [C + \delta \cdot (K + pH)]\right\} \tag{5.91}$$

Since $\dot{C}/C$ is constant and $K + pH$ is a constant, positive multiple of C, equation (5.91) expresses $\dot{Q}/Q$ as a negative, linear function of C/Q.

One solution to equation (5.91) is $\dot{Q}/Q = \dot{C}/C = \gamma^*$, so that C/Q is the constant $(C/Q)^*$. Alternatively, if $C/Q < (C/Q)^*$, then equation (5.91) implies $\dot{Q}/Q > \gamma^*$ and $C/Q \to 0$, whereas $C/Q > (C/Q)^*$ implies $\dot{Q}/Q < \gamma^*$ and $C/Q \to \infty$. Therefore, the stable path features $\dot{Q}/Q = \gamma^*$ at all times.

If we use the relation between u and v from equation (5.16), then equation (5.87) allows us to write u as a function of $\omega \equiv K/H$:

$$u = \frac{\eta \cdot (1 - \alpha)}{(\eta - \alpha)} - \left[\frac{\alpha \cdot (1 - \eta)}{(vK/uH)^* \cdot (\eta - \alpha)}\right] \cdot \omega \tag{5.92}$$

Hence, the policy function for u is a closed-form, linear, negative function of ω. Since the intercept exceeds 1, equation (5.92) determines a range of ω for which the indicated value of u is in the interior, $u \in (0, 1)$. The form of the equation implies that the width of this range diminishes to 0 as $\beta - \alpha$ approaches 0.

We can use the relation $v = (vK/uH)^* \cdot (u/\omega)$ along with equation (5.92) to derive a formula for v:

$$v = -\frac{\alpha \cdot (1 - \beta)}{\beta - \alpha} + \left[\frac{\beta \cdot (1 - \alpha)}{\beta - \alpha}\right] \cdot \left[\left(\frac{vK}{uH}\right)^*\right] \cdot \left(\frac{1}{\omega}\right) \tag{5.93}$$

Hence, v is a positive, linear function of $1/\omega$ and, therefore, a decreasing function of ω. We can also verify that the solution for v is in the interior; that is, $v \in (0, 1)$, when $u \in (0, 1)$. (This result follows readily from equation [5.16].)

Equations (5.13) and (5.16) imply that the growth rate of H is given by

$$\dot{H}/H = B \cdot \left[\frac{\eta \cdot (1 - \alpha)}{\alpha \cdot (1 - \eta)}\right]^{\eta} \cdot \left[\left(\frac{vK}{uH}\right)^*\right]^{\eta} \cdot (1 - u) - \delta$$

If we substitute for u from equation (5.92), we get

$$\dot{H}/H = -a_1 + a_2 \cdot \omega \tag{5.94}$$

where $a_1 > 0$, $a_2 > 0$ are constants. Thus $\dot{H}/H$ is a positive, linear function of ω.

Since full wealth, $K + pH$, grows at the constant rate γ^*, we have

$$\gamma^* = \left(\frac{\omega}{\omega + p}\right) \cdot (\dot{K}/K) + \left(\frac{p}{\omega + p}\right) \cdot (\dot{H}/H)$$

Hence, the growth rate of K is given by

$$\dot{K}/K = \gamma^* + (\gamma^* - \gamma_H) \cdot (p/\omega)$$

If we substitute for $\dot{H}/H$ from equation (5.94), we get

$$\dot{K}/K = \gamma^* - a_2 \cdot p + p \cdot (\gamma^* + a_1)/\omega \tag{5.95}$$

Thus $\dot{K}/K$ is a positive, linear function of $1/\omega$ and, therefore, an inverse function of ω. We can also use equation (5.95) to determine a range of ω for which the inequality restriction $\dot{K}/K + \delta \geq 0$ is not binding.

To ascertain the dynamics of $\chi \equiv C/K$, note that the condition $Y = C + \dot{K} + \delta K$ implies

$$\chi = Av \cdot \left[\left(\frac{vK}{uH}\right)^*\right]^{\alpha - 1} - \delta - \dot{K}/K$$

If we substitute for v from equation (5.93) and for $\dot{K}/K$ from equation (5.95), we get

$$\chi = \text{constant} + \left\{A \cdot \left[\frac{\eta \cdot (1 - \alpha)}{\eta - \alpha}\right] \cdot \left[\left(\frac{vK}{uH}\right)^*\right]^{\alpha} - p \cdot (\gamma^* + a_1)\right\} \cdot \left(\frac{1}{\omega}\right) \tag{5.96}$$

where $-a_1$ is the constant term in the expression for $\dot{H}/H$ in equation (5.94). If we substitute for a_1 and use the expression for p from equation (5.86), we can use the transversality condition—$r^* > \gamma^*$ in equations (5.88) and (5.89)—to show that the term in the braces in equation (5.96) is positive. Hence, χ is a positive, linear function of $1/\omega$ and, therefore, a negative function of ω.

5.8 Problems

5.1 A CES production function with physical and human capital. Consider the CES production function in terms of physical capital, K, and human capital, H:

$$Y = A \cdot \{a \cdot (bK)^{\psi} + (1 - a) \cdot [(1 - b) \cdot H]^{\psi}\}^{1/\psi}$$

where $0 < a < 1, 0 < b < 1, \psi < 1$. Output can be used on a one-for-one basis for consumption and for investment in K and H. The depreciation rate for each type of capital is δ. Households have the usual infinite-horizon preferences, as in the Ramsey model. Assume initially that there are no irreversibility constraints on K and H, so that gross investment in either form of capital can be negative.

a. Set up the Hamiltonian and find the first-order conditions.

b. What is the optimal relation between K and H? Substitute this relation into the given production function to get a relation between Y and K. What does this "reduced-form" production function look like?

c. What is the steady-state value of the ratio of physical to human capital, $(K/H)^*$?

d. Describe the behavior of the economy over time if the initial condition is such that $K(0)/H(0) < (K/H)^*$. What are the instantaneous rates of investment in each type of capital at time 0?

e. Suppose that the inequality restrictions $I_K \geq 0$ and $I_H \geq 0$ apply. How do these constraints affect the dynamics if the economy begins with $K(0)/H(0) < (K/H)^*$?

5.2 Adjustment costs for human and physical capital. Consider the model from section 5.1 in which consumables and physical and human capital are produced by the same technology. Imagine, however, that there are adjustment costs for changes in the two types of capital. The unit adjustment costs, analogous to the formulation discussed in section 3.3, are $(b_K/2) \cdot (I_K/K)$ for K and $(b_H/2) \cdot (I_H/H)$ for H. Assume that the depreciation rates for each types of capital are 0.

a. Discuss the parameters b_K and b_H. Which one would likely be larger?

b. Suppose that $b_K = b_H$. Discuss the short-run dynamics if the economy begins with $K(0)/H(0) < (K/H)^*$. What if $K(0)/H(0) > (K/H)^*$?

c. Suppose now that $b_K < b_H$. Redo part b, and comment on the main differences in the results.

5.3 Externalities in human capital (based on Lucas, 1988). The production function for the ith producer of goods is

$$Y_i = A \cdot (K_i)^\alpha \cdot (H_i)^\lambda \cdot H^\epsilon$$

where $0 < \alpha < 1, 0 < \lambda < 1, 0 \leq \epsilon < 1$. The variables K_i and H_i are the inputs of physical and human capital used by firm i to produce goods, Y_i. The variable H is the economy's average level of human capital; the parameter ϵ represents the strength of the external effect from average human capital to each firm's productivity. Output from the goods sector can be used as consumables, C, or as gross investment in physical capital, I_K. Physical capital depreciates at the rate δ. The production function for human capital is

$$(I_H)_j = BH_j$$

where H_j is the human capital employed by the jth producer of human capital. Human capital also depreciates at the rate δ. Households have the usual infinite-horizon preferences, as in the Ramsey model, with rate of time preference ρ and intertemporal-substitution parameter θ. Consider, first, a competitive equilibrium in which producers of Y and H act as perfect competitors.

a. What is the steady-state growth rate of C, Y, and K? How does the answer depend on the size of the human-capital externality, that is, the parameter ϵ?

b. What is the steady-state growth rate of H? Under what circumstances does H grow at the same rate as K in the steady state?

c. How would the social planner's solution differ from the competitive one?

6 Technological Change: Models with an Expanding Variety of Products

In chapters 4 and 5 we studied models of endogenous growth in which diminishing returns to a broad concept of capital did not apply, at least asymptotically. This absence of diminishing returns meant that long-term per capita growth was feasible in the absence of technological progress. A different view is that the mere accumulation of capital—even a broad concept that includes human capital—cannot sustain growth in the long run, because this accumulation must eventually encounter a significant decline in the rate of return. This view implies that we have to look to technological progress—continuing advances in methods of production and types and qualities of products—to escape from diminishing returns in the long run.

The exogenous rate of technological progress, x, determined the steady-state per capita growth rate in the Solow–Swan and Ramsey models in chapters 1 and 2. In this and the next chapter, we describe recent theoretical advances that endogenize this process of technological improvement; that is, these models effectively explain the origin of the parameter x. These theories therefore determine how government policies and other factors influence an economy's long-term per capita growth rate.

This chapter considers models in which technological progress shows up as an expansion of the number of varieties of products. We think of a change in this number as a basic innovation, akin to opening up a new industry. Of course, the identification of the state of technology with the number of varieties of products should be viewed as a metaphor; it selects one aspect of technical advance and thereby provides a tractable framework to study long-term growth.

The next chapter uses another metaphor in which progress shows up as quality improvements for an array of existing kinds of products. These quality enhancements represent the more or less continuous process of upgrading that occurs within an established industry. Thus the approach in the next chapter should be viewed as complementary with the analysis of variety in this chapter.

6.1 A Baseline Model with a Variety of Products

There are three types of agents in this model. First, producers of final output hire labor and intermediate inputs and combine them to produce final output, which is sold at unit price. Second, R&D firms devote resources to invent new products. Once a product has been invented, the innovating R&D firm obtains a perpetual patent, which allows the firm to sell the good at whatever price it chooses. This price is chosen to maximize profits. Third, households maximize utility, subject to the usual budget constraint.

6.1.1 The Producers of Final Output

The producers of final output have access to a production technology that combines labor with a number of intermediate inputs to produce final goods, which are then sold in the market at unit price. We follow Spence (1976), Dixit and Stiglitz (1977), Ethier (1982), and Romer (1987, 1990) by writing the production function for firm i as

$$Y_i = AL_i^{1-\alpha} \cdot \sum_{j=1}^{N} (X_{ij})^{\alpha} \tag{6.1}$$

where $0 < \alpha < 1$, Y_i is output, L_i is labor input, X_{ij} is the employment of the jth type of specialized intermediate good, and N is the number of varieties of intermediates.[1] The parameter A is an overall measure of productivity or efficiency. This formulation considers the variety of intermediate goods as an element of the production function. We could, as an alternative, model utility as a function of a variety of consumer goods. This alternative, pursued by Grossman and Helpman (1991, chapter 4), yields similar results.

The production function in equation (6.1) specifies diminishing marginal productivity of each input, L_i and X_{ij}, and constant returns to scale in all inputs together. The additively separable form for the $(X_{ij})^{\alpha}$ means that the marginal product of intermediate good j is independent of the quantity employed of intermediate good j'.[2] In this sense, a new type of product is neither a direct substitute for nor a direct complement with the types that already exist. We think that this specification is reasonable on average for breakthrough innovations, the kinds of changes that we wish to model in this chapter. In a particular case, a new product j may substitute for an existing good j' (that is, reduce the marginal product of $X_{j'}$) or complement the good (raise the marginal product of $X_{j'}$). But the independence of marginal products may hold in the average situation. This assumption of independence is important because it implies that discoveries of new types of goods do not tend to make any existing types obsolete.

In contrast, for the quality improvements studied in the next chapter, a reasonable specification is that a good of superior quality is a close substitute for a good of lesser quality. This assumption means that the goods of lesser quality tend to become obsolete when the new and better kinds are introduced.

1. The basic approach to the benefits from variety comes from Spence (1976), although he dealt with consumer preferences and wrote utility as an integral over the various types (his equation [45]), rather than a sum. Dixit and Stiglitz (1977) refined Spence's analysis and used a form analogous to equation (6.1) to express consumer preferences over a variety of goods. Ethier (1982) applied this representation to inputs of production. Romer (1987, 1990) used Ethier's model with a variety of productive inputs in the context of technological change and economic growth.

2. An alternative to equation (6.1) is

$$Y_i = AL_i^{1-\alpha} \cdot \left[\sum_{j=1}^{N} (X_{ij})^{\sigma} \right]^{\alpha/\sigma}$$

where $o < \sigma < 1$. In this case, the parameter σ, which can differ from α, governs the monopoly power possessed by the owner of the rights to intermediate j. The case considered in the text corresponds to $\alpha = \sigma$.

Equation (6.1) implies that the marginal product of each intermediate good, $\partial Y_i/\partial X_{ij}$, is infinite at $X_{ij} = 0$ and then diminishes as X_{ij} rises. If N types of goods are available at finite prices at the current time, the firm will be motivated to use all N types.

It is important to notice that technological progress takes the form of expansions in N, the number of specialized intermediate goods available, rather than increases in A, the productivity parameter. To see the effect from an increase in N, suppose that the intermediate goods can be measured in a common physical unit and that all are employed in the same quantity, $X_{ij} = X_i$ (which turns out to hold in equilibrium). The quantity of output is then given from equation (6.1) by

$$Y_i = AL_i^{1-\alpha}NX_i^{\alpha} = AL_i^{1-\alpha} \cdot (NX_i)^{\alpha} \cdot N^{1-\alpha} \tag{6.2}$$

For given N, equation (6.2) implies that production exhibits constant returns to scale in L_i and NX_i, the total quantity of intermediate inputs. For given quantities of L_i and NX_i, Y_i increases with N in accordance with the term $N^{1-\alpha}$. This effect, which captures a form of technological progress, reflects the benefit from spreading a given total of intermediates, NX_i, over a wider range, N. The benefit arises because of the diminishing returns to each of the X_{ij} individually.

For fixed L_i, equation (6.2) implies that an expansion of intermediates, NX_i, encounters diminishing returns if it occurs through an increase in X_i (that is, in all of the X_{ij}) for given N. Diminishing returns do not arise, however, if the increase in NX_i takes the form of a rise in N for given X_i. Thus technological change in the form of continuing increases in N avoids the tendency for diminishing returns. This property of the production function provides the basis for endogenous growth.

We shall find it convenient to think of the number of varieties, N, as continuous rather than discrete. This assumption is unrealistic if we view N as literally the number of kinds of intermediate goods employed, although the error would be small if N is large. More generally, N should be viewed as a tractable proxy for the technological complexity of the typical firm's production process or, alternatively, for the average degree of specialization of the factors employed by the typical firm. This broader notion of N would be continuous rather than discrete.[3]

3. We could justify the continuous nature of N formally by shifting from the sum over a discrete number of types in equation (6.1) to an integral over a continuum of types:

$$Y_i = AL_i^{1-\alpha} \cdot \int_0^N [X_i(j)]^{\alpha} dj$$

where j is the continuous index of type, and N is the range of types available. We would get essentially the same results if we used this formulation instead of equation (6.1).

The final goods, Y_i, produced by all firms are physically identical. The aggregate of the outputs of all firms, which we call Y, can be used in a perfectly substitutable manner for various purposes. Specifically, this output can be used for consumption, production of intermediates, X_j, and later for the R&D needed to invent new types of intermediates (that is, to expand N). All prices are measured in units of the homogeneous flow of goods, Y.

We could model the X_{ij} as service flows from durable goods. Firms would then rent the underlying capital goods, K_{ij}; and the total quantity of capital rented by firm i, $K_i = \sum_{j=1}^{N} K_{ij}$, would look like the capital input in our previous models.[4] If we took this approach, we would end up with a model with two state variables: the aggregate quantity of capital, K, and the number of varieties of goods, N. The model would then be formally similar to those studied in chapter 5.

We shall find it more convenient to assume that the X_{ij} represent purchases of nondurable goods and services. This model and the one with durable intermediates turn out to yield similar insights about the determinants of technological change and long-run economic growth. The model with nondurable inputs is simpler, because it involves only a single state variable, the number of products, N.

The profit for a producer of final goods is

$$Y_i - wL_i - \sum_{j=1}^{N} P_j X_{ij}$$

where w is the wage rate, and P_j is the price of intermediate j. These producers are competitive and therefore take w and the prices P_j as given. Hence, we get the usual equations between factor prices and marginal products, and the resulting profit is zero.

The production function in equation (6.1) implies that the marginal product of the jth intermediate good is given by

$$\partial Y_i / \partial X_{ij} = A\alpha L_i^{1-\alpha} X_{ij}^{\alpha-1} \tag{6.3}$$

The equation of this marginal product to P_j therefore implies

$$X_{ij} = L_i \cdot (A\alpha / P_j)^{1/(1-\alpha)} \tag{6.4}$$

This result determines the quantity of the jth input demanded, X_{ij}, as a function of the price, P_j. The price elasticity of demand for each type of intermediate is the constant $-1/(1-\alpha)$.

4. Acemoglu (2002) extends the varieties framework by assuming that one set of intermediates augments labor, L, and another set augments capital, K. Researchers can then choose whether to devote their R&D efforts to labor-augmenting or capital-augmenting innovations. He shows that technological progress may be asymptotically labor augmenting if the elasticity of substitution between labor and capital is less than one.

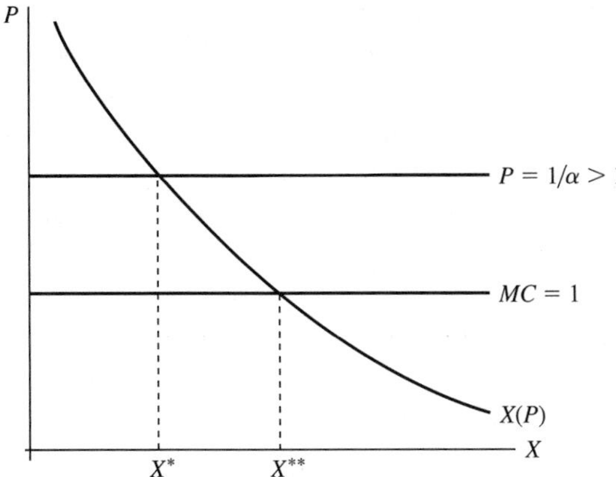

Figure 6.1
The demand for intermediate inputs. The demand for intermediate inputs is a constant-elasticity downward-sloping function. When price equals marginal cost, firms demand the quantity X^{**}. For prices above marginal cost, the quantity demanded is less than X^{**}.

The demand function is depicted in figure 6.1. The equality between w and the marginal product of labor implies

$$w = (1 - \alpha) \cdot (Y_i/L_i) \tag{6.5}$$

6.1.2 Research Firms

At a point in time, the technology exists to produce N varieties of intermediate goods. An expansion of the number N requires a technological advance in the sense of an invention that permits the production of the new kind of intermediate good. We assume that this advance requires purposive effort in the form of R&D.

R&D firms face a two-stage decision process. First, they decide whether to devote resources to invent a new design. Firms expend these resources if the net present value of future expected profits is at least as large as the R&D expenditures, which are paid up front. In the second stage, the inventors determine the optimal price at which to sell their newly invented goods to the producers of final output. This price determines the flow of profit at each date and, thereby, the present value of profit that was considered in the first stage.

We proceed by solving the model backward. First, we derive the optimal price, assuming that a new design has already been invented. Second, we calculate the present value of profits and compare it with the R&D cost. If the present value is as large as the R&D cost, the firm will undertake the R&D expenditures. Finally, we look at the equilibrium when there is free entry into the R&D business.

Stage 2: Optimal Price, Once the Good Has Been Invented In order to motivate research, successful innovators have to be compensated in some manner. The basic problem is that the creation of a new idea or design, say for intermediate good j, is costly but could then be used in a nonrival way by all potential producers of good j. That is, one producer's use of the design would not affect the output that could be generated for given inputs by other producers who use the design. It would be efficient, ex post, to make the existing discoveries freely available to all producers, but this practice fails to provide the ex ante incentives for further inventions. A trade-off arises, as in the usual analysis of patents, between restrictions on the use of existing ideas—that is, some kind of excludability—and the rewards to inventive activity.

Remarkably, these issues about rivalry and excludability were well understood almost 200 years ago by Thomas Jefferson, the third U.S. president and author of the Declaration of Independence, who also served for a time on the U.S. patent board. Jefferson said in his letter of August 13, 1813, to Isaac McPherson:[5]

> If nature has made any one thing less susceptible than all others of exclusive property, it is the actions of the thinking power called an idea, which an individual may exclusively possess as long as he keeps it to himself; but the moment it is divulged, it forces itself into the possession of everyone, and the receiver cannot dispossess himself of it. Its peculiar character, too, is that no one possesses the less, because every other possesses the whole of it. He who receives an idea from me, receives instruction himself without lessening mine ... inventions that cannot in nature be a subject of property, society may give an exclusive right to the profits arising from them as an encouragement to man to pursue ideas which may produce utility, but this may or may not be done, according to the will and convenience of the society, without claim or complaint from anybody. Accordingly, it is a fact, as far as I am informed, that England was, until we copied her, the only country on earth which ever, in a general law, gave a legal right to the exclusive use of an idea. In some other countries, it is sometimes done, in a great case, and by a special and personal act, but generally speaking other nations have thought that these monopolies produce more embarrassment than advantage to society. And it may be observed that the nations which refuse monopolies of inventions are as fruitful as England in new and useful devices.

Thus, although Jefferson understood the possible gains from patents as spurs to inventions, he came down in the end against a regime that tried to maintain these monopoly rights in ideas.

Notwithstanding Jefferson's viewpoint, we consider an institutional setup in which the inventor of good j retains a perpetual monopoly right over the production and sale of the good, X_j, that uses his or her design.[6] The flow of monopoly rentals will then provide

5. The letter is available on the Internet from the *Thomas Jefferson Papers* at the Library of Congress (lcweb2.loc.gov/ammem/mtjhtml/mtjhome.html).

6. We assume for convenience that the inventor of the jth design is also the producer of the jth intermediate good. We would get the same results if we assumed instead that the inventor charged a royalty for the use of the design by competitive producers of goods.

the incentive for invention. The monopoly rights could be enforced through explicit patent protection or through secrecy. It would, in either case, be realistic to assume that the inventor's monopoly position lasted only for a finite time or eroded gradually over time. We consider this extension later in this chapter.

The present value of the returns from discovering the jth intermediate good is given by

$$V(t) = \int_t^{\infty} \pi_j(v) \cdot e^{-\bar{r}(t,v)\cdot(v-t)}\, dv \tag{6.6}$$

where $\pi_j(v)$ is the profit flow at date v, and $\bar{r}(t, v) \equiv [1/(v-t)] \cdot \int_t^v r(\omega)\, d\omega$ is the average interest rate between times t and v. If the interest rate equals a constant, r—which turns out to be true in the equilibrium—then the present-value factor simplifies to $e^{-r\cdot(v-t)}$.

The producer's revenue at each date equals the price, $P_j(v)$, times the amount of goods sold. The flow of profit equals revenue less production costs. We assume that, once invented, an intermediate good of type j costs one unit of Y to produce. In effect, the inventor of good j sticks a distinctive label on the homogenous flow of final product and, thereby, converts this product into the jth type of intermediate good. Formally, we are assuming that the marginal and average cost of production is a constant, normalized to 1. Hence, the profit flow is given by

$$\pi_j(v) = [P_j(v) - 1] \cdot X_j(v) \tag{6.7}$$

where

$$X_j(v) = \sum_i X_{ij}(v) = [A\alpha/P_j(v)]^{1/(1-\alpha)} \cdot \sum_i L_i = L \cdot [A\alpha/P_j(v)]^{1/(1-\alpha)} \tag{6.8}$$

is the aggregate of the quantity demanded over the producers i from equation (6.4). The quantity L is the aggregate of labor input and is assumed to be constant.

Since there are no state variables on the production side and no intertemporal elements in the demand function, the producer of X_j selects P_j at each date to maximize the flow of monopoly profit at that date.[7] The maximization problem follows from equations (6.7) and (6.8) as

$$\max_{P_j(v)} \pi_j(v) = [P_j(v) - 1] \cdot L \cdot [A\alpha/P_j(v)]^{1/(1-\alpha)} \tag{6.9}$$

7. We could derive this result from our familiar dynamic analysis by setting up the Hamiltonian and finding the usual first-order condition with respect to P. Since P is a control variable, the FOC would dictate setting the derivative of the profit to zero, just as if the model were static.

The solution for the monopoly price is[8]

$$P_j(v) = P = 1/\alpha > 1 \tag{6.10}$$

Hence, the price P_j is constant over time and the same for all intermediate goods j. The monopoly price is the markup $1/\alpha$ on the marginal cost of production, 1. The price is the same for all goods j because the cost of production is the same for all goods, and each good enters symmetrically into the production function in equation (6.1).

If we substitute for P_j from equation (6.10) into equation (6.4), we can determine the aggregate quantity produced of each intermediate good:

$$X_j = A^{1/(1-\alpha)}\alpha^{2/(1-\alpha)}L \tag{6.11}$$

which is also constant over time and across j. It is important to notice that, because price exceeds marginal cost, the quantity X_j is smaller than it would be if intermediates were priced at marginal cost (see figure 6.1). The quantity X_j is the same for all goods and at all points in time (if L is constant). The aggregate quantity of intermediates, denoted by X, is given by

$$X = NX_j = A^{1/(1-\alpha)}\alpha^{2/(1-\alpha)}LN \tag{6.12}$$

The level of aggregate output is determined from equations (6.2) and (6.12) as

$$Y = AL^{1-\alpha}X^{\alpha}N^{1-\alpha} = A^{1/(1-\alpha)}\alpha^{2\alpha/(1-\alpha)}LN \tag{6.13}$$

If we substitute for P_j and X_j from equations (6.10) and (6.11) into equation (6.9), we get a formula for the profit flow:

$$\pi_j(v) = \pi = LA^{1/(1-\alpha)} \cdot \left(\frac{1-\alpha}{\alpha}\right) \cdot \alpha^{2/(1-\alpha)} \tag{6.14}$$

which is, again, constant over time and across goods. Finally, we can substitute the optimal values of P_j and X_j into equation (6.6) to get that the inventor's net present value of profit at time t is given by

$$V(t) = LA^{1/(1-\alpha)} \cdot \left(\frac{1-\alpha}{\alpha}\right) \cdot \alpha^{2/(1-\alpha)} \cdot \int_t^{\infty} e^{-\bar{r}(t,v)\cdot(v-t)}\, dv \tag{6.15}$$

Stage 1: The Decision to Enter the R&D Business We now know that, once a good has been invented, the institutional setup will allow the inventor to collect the present value

8. This result implies that the factor share for intermediate inputs, which is α, equals the reciprocal of the markup ratio. However, this restriction no longer applies if one assumes the generalized form of production function given in note 2. In that case, the monopoly price turns out to be $P_j = P = 1/\sigma$.

$V(t)$ shown in equation (6.15). A researcher will find R&D investment attractive if this present value is at least as large as the R&D cost. Hence, the R&D investment depends on the nature of the R&D costs. A realistic description of the research process would include uncertainty about the quantity of resources required to generate an invention and about the success of the invention. We simplify the analysis, however, by assuming that it takes a deterministic amount of effort to generate a successful new product. (Chapter 7 considers a model in which the research process is subject to uncertainty.)

The deterministic framework for the invention of new products ultimately generates a smooth path for aggregate economic growth. Randomness in the discovery of new products would eliminate the smoothness at the aggregate level and thereby induces variations of the growth rate around a long-term trend. These variations would look like the fluctuations that occur in real business-cycle models. (See, for example, Kydland and Prescott, 1982, and McCallum, 1989.) Since we are primarily interested here in the determinants of the long-term growth trend, we assume a deterministic R&D process in which the cyclical elements are absent.

We assume in this first model that the cost to create a new type of product is η units of Y. This specification means that we are applying the assumptions of the usual one-sector production model to the use of output for R&D.[9] In general, one would imagine that the cost of creating a new variety depends on the number of varieties previously invented, as described by the function $\eta(N)$. The tendency to run out of new ideas suggests that the cost would rise with N, so that $\eta'(N) > 0$. But if the concepts already discovered make it easier to come up with new ideas, the cost could fall with N, so that $\eta'(N) < 0$ would apply.[10] We assume here that these effects cancel, so that the cost of inventing a new good does not change over time; that is,

$$\text{R\&D cost} = \eta\text{, a constant} \tag{6.16}$$

This specification turns out to be consistent with a constant growth rate of aggregate output. However, the specification does create some puzzles with regard to scale effects, which we discuss later. A firm decides to devote resources to R&D if $V(t) \geq \eta$.

The Free-Entry Condition We assume that there is free entry into the business of being an inventor, so that anyone can pay the R&D cost η to secure the net present value, $V(t)$, shown in equation (6.15). If $V(t) > \eta$, an infinite amount of resources would be channeled

9. Rivera-Batiz and Romer (1991) use this specification in the framework that they describe as the lab-equipment model of R&D.

10. The assumption that the cost of inventing a new product declines is equivalent to the assumption that the cost is constant but that new products are more productive per unit than the old ones. Chapter 7 considers a model in which the new goods are more productive than the old goods.

into R&D at time t;[11] hence, $V(t) > \eta$ cannot hold in equilibrium. If $V(t) < \eta$, no resources would be devoted at time t to R&D, and, therefore, the number of goods, N, would not change over time.[12] We focus the main discussion on equilibria with positive R&D and, hence, growing N at all points in time. In these cases,

$$V(t) = \eta \tag{6.17}$$

holds for all t.

If we differentiate the free-entry condition in equation (6.17) with respect to time, using the formula for $V(t)$ from equation (6.15) and taking account of the condition $\bar{r}(t, v) \equiv [1/(v-t)] \cdot \int_t^v r(\omega)\, d\omega$,[13] we get

$$r(t) = \frac{\pi}{V(t)} + \frac{\dot{V}(t)}{V(t)} \tag{6.18}$$

where π is the constant profit flow given by equation (6.9). Equation (6.18) says that the rate of return to bonds, $r(t)$, equals the rate of return to investing in R&D. The R&D rate of return equals the profit rate, $\pi/V(t)$, plus the rate of capital gain or loss derived from the change in the value of the research firm, $\dot{V}(t)/V(t)$. Since η is constant, the free-entry condition in equation (6.17) implies $\dot{V}(t) = 0$. It follows from equation (6.18) that the interest rate is constant and equal to $r(t) = r = \pi/\eta$. Substituting for π from equation (6.9), we get

$$r = (L/\eta) \cdot A^{1/(1-\alpha)} \cdot \left(\frac{1-\alpha}{\alpha}\right) \cdot \alpha^{2/(1-\alpha)} \tag{6.19}$$

The underlying technology and market structure peg the rate of return at the value shown in equation (6.19) (assuming that the underlying growth rate of N is positive). The situation therefore parallels the one in the AK model of chapter 4, in which the technology and incentives to invest pegged the rate of return at the value $A - \delta$.

The intermediate good that is about to be discovered generates a present value of monopoly profits that just covers the R&D cost, η. That is, $V(t) = \eta$ in equation (6.15). Since old and new products receive the same flow of monopoly profits, the present value of the profits for each existing intermediate good must also equal η. Hence, η is the market

11. The investment would be infinite if there are no limitations on borrowing at the interest rate $r(t)$, where this debt could be collateralized by the value of the investment.

12. The number of inventions, N, is not reversible. That is, it is impossible to forget some of the existing designs and thereby get a rebate on the R&D expenditures that went into the discovery of those designs. If N were reversible in this sense, $V(t) = \eta$ would have to hold at all points in time.

13. We use here Leibniz's rule for differentiation of a definite integral. See the discussion in the mathematical appendix.

value of a firm that possesses the blueprint to produce one of the intermediate goods, and the aggregate market value of firms is ηN. (Recall that firms own no capital, because there are no durable goods in the model.)

6.1.3 Households

Households still maximize utility over an infinite horizon:

$$U = \int_0^\infty \left(\frac{c^{1-\theta} - 1}{1-\theta}\right) \cdot e^{-\rho t}\, dt \tag{6.20}$$

where the rate of population growth, n, is 0 in the present model. Households earn the rate of return r on assets and receive the wage rate w on the fixed aggregate quantity L of labor. The households' aggregate budget constraint is, as usual,

$$d(\text{assets})/dt = wL + r \cdot (\text{assets}) - C \tag{6.21}$$

Households satisfy the familiar Euler equation,[14]

$$\dot{C}/C = (1/\theta) \cdot (r - \rho) \tag{6.22}$$

The usual transversality condition implies that r must exceed the long-run growth rate of output, Y.

6.1.4 General Equilibrium

In a closed economy, the total of households' assets equals the market value of firms,

$$\text{assets} = \eta N$$

Since η is constant, the change in assets must be

$$d(\text{assets})/dt = \eta \dot{N}$$

The wage rate is given from equation (6.5) by

$$w = (1 - \alpha) \cdot (Y/L)$$

After some manipulation, the interest rate, given by equation (6.19), can be written as

$$r = \frac{1}{\eta} \cdot (1 - \alpha) \cdot \alpha \cdot (Y/N)$$

14. Since population, L, is constant, the growth rate of consumption equals the growth rate of per capita consumption.

Hence, aggregate income, $wL + r \cdot \text{assets}$, equals $Y - \alpha^2 Y$. It follows that the households' budget constraint in equation (6.21) becomes

$$\eta \dot{N} = Y - C - X \tag{6.23}$$

where we used the condition $X = \alpha^2 Y$ from equations (6.12) and (6.13). Equation (6.23) is the economy-wide resource constraint. This condition states that, at every point in time, GDP, Y, must be allocated to consumption, C, the production of intermediates, X, and the creation of $\dot{N}$ new goods, each of which costs η.

Substitution for r from equation (6.19) into equation (6.22) leads to the growth rate:

$$\gamma = (1/\theta) \cdot \left[(L/\eta) \cdot A^{1/(1-\alpha)} \cdot \left(\frac{1-\alpha}{\alpha} \right) \cdot \alpha^{2/(1-\alpha)} - \rho \right] \tag{6.24}$$

This growth rate applies to the number of designs, N, and output, Y, as well as consumption, C. The present model, like the AK model, exhibits no transitional dynamics, and the three variables grow at the same, constant rate.[15]

Equation (6.24) is valid only if the underlying parameters lead to $\gamma \geq 0$ in the equation. If $\gamma < 0$ were indicated, potential inventors would have insufficient incentive to expend resources on R&D and, hence, N would stay constant over time. The growth rate, γ, would then equal zero. We assume, henceforth, that $\gamma \geq 0$ applies in equation (6.24).

The number of varieties of goods, N, starts at some value $N(0)$ and then grows at the constant rate γ shown in equation (6.24). The solution for output in equation (6.13) indicates that, for fixed L, Y is proportional to N. It follows that Y and N grow at the same constant rate.

The level of consumption, C, must satisfy the economy's budget constraint in equation (6.23), which can be rewritten as

$$C = Y - \eta \gamma N - X$$

where $\eta \gamma N = \eta \dot{N}$ is the amount of resources devoted to R&D. If we substitute for Y from equation (6.13), γ from equation (6.24), and X from equation (6.12), we can simplify to get

$$C = (N/\theta) \cdot \left\{ LA^{1/(1-\alpha)} \cdot (1-\alpha) \cdot \alpha^{2\alpha/(1-\alpha)} \cdot [\theta - \alpha \cdot (1-\theta)] + \eta\rho \right\} \tag{6.25}$$

Equation (6.25) verifies that, for fixed L, C and N grow at the same rate, γ, shown in equation (6.24).[16]

15. We demonstrate here that an equilibrium exists with no transitional dynamics. A proof that no other equilibria are possible can be constructed along the lines followed in chapter 4. We leave this proof as an exercise.

16. The transversality condition is $r > \gamma$. (Recall that population growth, n, equals zero.) Since $\gamma = (1/\theta) \cdot (r - \rho)$, the transversality condition can be written as $r \cdot (1-\theta) < \rho$. Substitution for r from equation (6.19) leads to the inequality $LA^{1/(1-\alpha)} \cdot (1-\alpha) \cdot \alpha^{2\alpha/(1-\alpha)} \alpha \cdot (1-\theta) < \eta\rho$. This condition guarantees that the expression for the level of C in equation (6.25) is positive.

6.1.5 Determinants of the Growth Rate

Consider the determinants of the growth rate, γ, shown in equation (6.24). The households' preference parameters, ρ and θ, and the level of the production technology, A, enter essentially in the same way as they did in the *AK* model, which we considered in chapter 4. A greater willingness to save—lower ρ and θ—and a better technology—higher A—raise the growth rate.

A new effect involves the cost of inventing a new product, η. A decrease in η raises the rate of return, r, in equation (6.19) and therefore raises the growth rate, γ, in equation (6.24).

The model contains a scale effect in that a larger labor endowment, L, raises the growth rate, γ, in equation (6.24). This effect is similar to those that arose in chapter 4 in the model of learning by doing with spillovers and in the model of public goods. As in these earlier models, the economy would not tend toward a steady state with a constant per capita growth rate if we allowed for growth in population, L, at a positive rate. The present model has a scale effect because a new product, which costs η to invent, can be used in a nonrival manner across the entire economy. The larger the economy—represented by L—the lower the cost of an invention per unit of L (or Y). Therefore, as with a decrease in η, an increase in L raises γ.

We already observed in chapter 4 that scale effects are not supported empirically if we identify scale with the size of a country's population or economic activity. Countries may, however, not be the proper unit for measuring scale in the present context. The scale that matters in the model has two aspects: first, it involves the total of production over which a new idea can be used in a nonrival manner, and, second, it measures the scope of the inventor's property rights. If ideas flow readily across borders, countries would not define the proper units in the first context. (We consider the diffusion of technology in chapter 8.) Countries may also be inappropriate in the second context if patent protection applies internationally or if a monopoly position can be sustained at least partially in foreign countries by secrecy.

If the world operated as a single unit with respect to the flow of ideas and the maintenance of property rights, L would be identified with world population or an aggregate of world economic activity. The model would then predict a positive relation between world per capita growth and the levels of world population or the aggregate of world output. Kremer (1993) argues that this hypothesis may be correct over very long periods of time. However, the usual view is that the predicted scale effect is counterfactual; therefore, many economists have sought to modify the framework to eliminate this prediction. For a summary of this literature, see Jones (1999).

6.1.6 Pareto Optimality

The Social Planner's Problem We now demonstrate that the outcomes in the decentralized economy are not Pareto optimal. We can, as usual, assess Pareto optimality by comparing the previous results—specifically, the growth rate γ shown in equation (6.24)—with the results from the parallel problem for a hypothetical social planner.

The social planner seeks to maximize the utility of the representative household, as given in equation (6.20). The planner is constrained only by the economy's budget constraint:

$$Y = AL^{1-\alpha}N^{1-\alpha}X^{\alpha} = C + \eta\dot{N} + X \tag{6.26}$$

We have used the same production function as in equation (6.1), but we have already imposed the condition that the quantity of intermediates is the same for all firms i and intermediate products j. We can readily show by optimizing with respect to each of the X_{ij} that the planner satisfies these conditions for efficient production. The right-hand side of equation (6.26) comprises the three possible uses of output: consumption, R&D, and intermediate goods.

The Hamiltonian expression for the social planner's problem can be written as

$$J = u(c) \cdot e^{-\rho t} + \nu \cdot (1/\eta) \cdot (AL^{1-\alpha}N^{1-\alpha}X^{\alpha} - Lc - X) \tag{6.27}$$

where the shadow price ν applies to $\dot{N}$, and we substituted the condition $C = Lc$. The control variables are c and X, and the state variable is N.

The contrast with the decentralized solution involves the determination of X, the quantity of intermediates, and γ, the growth rate of N. The usual optimization conditions for the social planner lead to the formulas for X and γ:

$$X \text{ (social planner)} = A^{1/(1-\alpha)}\alpha^{1/(1-\alpha)}LN \tag{6.28}$$

$$\gamma \text{ (social planner)} = (1/\theta) \cdot \left[(L/\eta) \cdot A^{1/(1-\alpha)} \cdot \left(\frac{1-\alpha}{\alpha}\right) \cdot \alpha^{1/(1-\alpha)} - \rho\right] \tag{6.29}$$

The choice of X in equation (6.28) implies that the level of output is

$$Y \text{ (social planner)} = A^{1/(1-\alpha)}\alpha^{\alpha/(1-\alpha)}LN \tag{6.30}$$

In comparison with the social planner's choice in equation (6.28), the decentralized solution for X in equation (6.11) is multiplied by $\alpha^{1/(1-\alpha)} < 1$. Hence, the decentralized economy allocates fewer resources than the social planner to intermediates and, therefore, ends up with a lower level of output (equation [6.13] versus equation [6.30]).

In figure 6.1, the quantity of intermediates that the planner would like produced is X^{**}, which is the amount that would be demanded if price were equated to marginal cost. In the decentralized economy, where intermediates are priced at the monopoly value, $1/\alpha$, the quantity demanded is the smaller amount X^*, also shown in the figure. The gap between X^{**} and X^* generates a static efficiency loss from monopoly.

In the decentralized solution for the growth rate, equation (6.24), the first term inside the large brackets is the multiple $\alpha^{1/(1-\alpha)} < 1$ of the corresponding term for the social planner in equation (6.29). Recall that this term in equation (6.24) corresponded to the private rate of return, r, as given in equation (6.19). Thus the decentralized economy has a lower growth rate than the planned economy, and the lower growth rate corresponds to a shortfall of the private rate of return from the rate of return implicitly used by the social planner. This social rate of return is the first term inside the brackets in equation (6.29):

$$r \text{ (social planner)} = (L/\eta) \cdot A^{1/(1-\alpha)} \cdot \left(\frac{1-\alpha}{\alpha}\right) \cdot \alpha^{1/(1-\alpha)} \tag{6.31}$$

In the model of learning by doing with spillovers in chapter 4, the private rate of return fell short of the social rate of return because of the uncompensated benefits that one producer conveyed to others. The model with inventions of new products and monopoly rights in these inventions generates a gap between social and private returns from a different source. The underlying distortion is the monopoly pricing of intermediates: the price P in equation (6.10) is the multiple $1/\alpha$ of the marginal cost of production, 1. The government could induce the private sector to attain the social optimum in a decentralized setting if it could engineer a tax-subsidy policy—a form of "industrial policy"—that induced marginal-cost pricing without eliminating the appropriate incentive for inventors to create new types of products. We now consider some of these possibilities.

Subsidies to Purchases of Intermediate Goods Suppose that the economy is decentralized, but the government uses a lump-sum tax to finance a subsidy on the purchase of all varieties of intermediate goods. If the subsidy is at the rate $1-\alpha$, the producers of Y would pay only αP for each unit of X. The demand, X_{ij} in equation (6.4), rises accordingly by the factor $(1/\alpha)^{1/(1-\alpha)}$. The equilibrium price P is still the multiple $1/\alpha$ of marginal cost, 1, but the equilibrium quantity, X in equation (6.11), is multiplied by the factor $(1/\alpha)^{1/(1-\alpha)}$ and thereby coincides with the social planner's choice in equation (6.28). This result follows because the user price of X, net of the public subsidy, equals 1.

The expansion of the quantity of intermediates, X, provides a static and a dynamic gain in efficiency. In a static context, with fixed N, the monopoly pricing implies that the marginal product of X exceeds its cost of production, 1, and, therefore, that the economy fails to maximize the goods available for consumption. If more output were allocated to X, the expansion of Y on a more than one-for-one basis means that consumption could rise. The government's subsidy to purchases of X allows the economy to secure this static gain.

The higher level of X also has a dynamic effect that involves the incentive to expand N over time. The increase in the quantity of intermediates raises the flow of monopoly profit in equation (6.6) by the factor $(1/\alpha)^{1/(1-\alpha)}$. This increase in profit raises the rate of return, r, in equation (6.19) by the same factor; hence, the private rate of return coincides with the social rate of return, given in equation (6.31).[17] It follows that the decentralized growth rate equals the social planner's growth rate, shown in equation (6.29). Thus the public subsidy provides a dynamic gain in that N now grows at the efficient rate. In more general models a first-best solution cannot be attained just with a subsidy on the purchases of intermediate goods. For example, in a model considered later in which the inventor's monopoly position is temporary, a subsidy to research would also be required.

Subsidies to Final Product The government could also induce the private economy to attain the social optimum if it stimulated the demand for intermediates by subsidizing production. The required subsidy rate on output, Y_i, is $(1-\alpha)/\alpha$, so that producers receive $1/\alpha$ units of revenue for each unit of goods produced.

Subsidies to Research One policy that seems natural but that fails to achieve the social optimum in this model is a subsidy to research and development. If the government absorbs part of the cost of R&D, a potential inventor lowers the net cost of research, η, accordingly in equation (6.19). This change can raise the privately chosen values of r and γ to equal the social planner's values. The problem is that the quantity of intermediates, X in equation (6.11), is still wrong from a social perspective because of monopoly pricing. Thus, although the economy grows at the "right" rate, it fails to achieve static efficiency, because it allocates insufficient resources to intermediates for given N.

Although various governmental tax-subsidy policies can work in the model to improve allocations, the successful execution of any of these industrial policies would be difficult. The government not only has to subsidize the right things—basically the demands for the goods that are monopoly priced—but then has to finance the scheme with a nondistorting tax. If the tax were levied on output, the scheme would be self-defeating. Moreover, in a more realistic model, the required subsidy would have to vary across factors of production or final products; in other words, the government would have to pick winners in an omniscient and benevolent manner. Section 6.2 illustrates this problem by allowing for a distinction between monopolized and competitive goods.

6.1.7 Scale Effects and the Cost of R&D

One way to alter the predictions about scale effects is to change the specification for the cost of R&D. The key assumption was that the invention of a new variety required a fixed amount η of output, Y. This assumption means that $\dot{N}$ is the constant multiple $1/\eta$ of R&D

17. The exact coincidence depends on the constant price elasticity of the demand for intermediates. This property stemmed from the form of the production function in equation (6.1).

outlays. Hence, the growth rate of N is given by

$$\dot{N}/N = (1/\eta) \cdot \left(\frac{\text{R\&D}}{N}\right) \tag{6.32}$$

Equation (6.13) implies that Y/L is proportional to N. Hence, equation (6.32) implies a positive relation between the rate of productivity growth, $\dot{N}/N$, and the ratio of R&D to Y/L. It follows that a common secular trend in the variables R&D, Y, and L would generate a corresponding trend in productivity growth. This implication has been criticized empirically by Jones (1995, 1999), based on time-series behavior in the most advanced countries, because the rate of productivity growth has been relatively stable despite upward trends in the levels of R&D, Y, and L.

An alternative specification that fits the data better is for $\dot{N}/N$ to be positively related to the ratio of R&D to Y. Then the absence of a trend in productivity growth would correspond to the lack of a trend in the ratio of R&D outlays to GDP. The R&D ratio has, in fact, changed little in the United States since 1970—the ratio went from 2.6 percent in 1970 to 2.5 percent in 1996. In the United Kingdom, the share fell slightly from 2.0 percent in 1972 to 1.8 percent in 1997. Other major OECD countries experienced a moderate increase in the R&D ratio over some periods—the share in Japan went from 1.7 percent in 1970 to 2.8 percent in 1997; in Germany, from 2.1 percent in 1970 to 2.3 percent in 1998; in France from 1.9 percent in 1970 to 2.2 percent in 1997; in Italy from 0.8 percent in 1970 to 1.4 percent in 1996; and in Canada, from 1.2 percent in 1970 to 1.7 percent in 1998.[18]

The data refer to expenditures on formal R&D, but the concept of research that matters in the theory is much broader. If the fraction of true outlays on R&D in the measured data tends to rise as countries develop, as seems plausible, then the true ratios may not have risen in some of the OECD countries. Thus the stability of ratios of R&D to GDP may be a reasonable approximation to the behavior in advanced countries. It would then also be satisfactory as a first-order approximation to assume that productivity growth, $\dot{N}/N$, had a fixed positive relation with the ratio of R&D to GDP.

In the theoretical model, the corresponding assumption is that the cost of inventing a new variety of intermediate is proportional to the extra output that would be created by the new variety. Since output, Y, is proportional to N in equation (6.13), an equivalent assumption is that the R&D cost is proportional to Y/N. Since equation (6.13) implies

$$Y/N = A^{1/(1-\alpha)}\alpha^{2\alpha/(1-\alpha)}L$$

18. These data are from World Bank, *World Development Indicators 2002*, and the National Science Foundation at http://www.nsf.gov.

the new specification amounts to replacing η in the original model by the term $\eta A^{1/(1-\alpha)}\alpha^{2\alpha/(1-\alpha)}L$. Since the new term is still constant, the form of the results from before goes through immediately. Hence, the rate of return and the growth rate simplify from equations (6.19) and (6.24) to

$$r = \frac{\alpha \cdot (1-\alpha)}{\eta} \tag{6.33}$$

and

$$\gamma = (1/\theta) \cdot \left[\frac{\alpha \cdot (1-\alpha)}{\eta} - \rho\right] \tag{6.34}$$

The main new element is that the rate of return and the growth rate no longer rise with L or A. Hence, the economy is still capable of endogenous growth, but scale effects are no longer present.

The revised specification also admits growth in population without predicting rising growth rates for output. If $L(t)$ grows at the constant rate n, the present value of the monopoly rights over a variety of intermediates is modified from equation (6.15) to

$$V(t) = A^{1/(1-\alpha)} \cdot \left(\frac{1-\alpha}{\alpha}\right) \cdot \alpha^{2/(1-\alpha)} \cdot L(t) \cdot \left(\frac{1}{r-n}\right)$$

where we assumed, as turns out to be correct, that r is constant over time. The new feature is that $V(t)$ increases with n, because a higher n implies higher levels of future demands for intermediate goods.

The free-entry condition is now

$$\eta A^{1/(1-\alpha)}\alpha^{2\alpha/(1-\alpha)}L(t) = A^{1/(1-\alpha)} \cdot \left(\frac{1-\alpha}{\alpha}\right) \cdot \alpha^{2/(1-\alpha)} \cdot L(t) \cdot \left(\frac{1}{r-n}\right)$$

where the left-hand side is the cost of innovation (which is proportional to $L[t]$), and the right-hand side is $V(t)$. Simplification of the free-entry condition leads to an expression for the equilibrium rate of return:

$$r = n + \frac{\alpha \cdot (1-\alpha)}{\eta} \tag{6.35}$$

The growth rate is, as usual, $\gamma = (1/\theta) \cdot (r - \rho)$. Therefore, r and γ would be invariant with the level of L but increasing in n.

6.1.8 A Rising Cost of R&D

We consider now a case in which the cost of R&D is an increasing function of the number of ideas previously invented, that is, $\eta = \eta(N)$, where $\eta'(N) > 0$. This case is plausible if we think of the main effect from a rising N as the using up of the given total number of potential ideas. We consider a simple functional form with a constant elasticity:

$$\eta(N) = \phi N^{\sigma} \tag{6.36}$$

where $\sigma > 0$ and $\phi > 0$ are exogenous constants.

Note first that the pricing strategy followed once a good has been invented is independent of the shape of the R&D cost. Therefore, the optimal price is still the monopoly value, $P = 1/\alpha$, the quantity of each intermediate is again given by equation (6.11), and the profit flow is still given by equation (6.14). As before, the free-entry condition entails

$$V(t) = \eta(N)$$

The key difference from before is that, as N increases and, hence, $\eta(N)$ rises, the present value, $V(t)$, must rise correspondingly. Since $\dot{V}(t)$ is no longer zero, equation (6.18) implies that the interest rate is not constant. Instead, we have

$$r(t) = \frac{\pi}{\phi N^{\sigma}} + \sigma \cdot \left(\frac{\dot{N}}{N}\right) \tag{6.37}$$

The last term, which depends on $\dot{N}/N$, represents the growth rate of the value of a firm that possesses the monopoly rights over the use of an existing intermediate good. This value is rising over time because the cost of innovation is rising and because the existing intermediate goods are just as good as the new ones.[19]

If we substitute for $r(t)$ from equation (6.37) into equation (6.22), we get

$$\frac{\dot{C}}{C} = \frac{1}{\theta} \cdot \left(\frac{\pi}{\phi N^{\sigma}} + \sigma \cdot \frac{\dot{N}}{N} - \rho\right) \tag{6.38}$$

Hence, the growth rate of consumption is no longer constant but rather tends to decline with N and to increase with $\dot{N}/N$. To solve the model, we need an expression for $\dot{N}/N$. If we substitute the formula for the R&D cost from equation (6.36) into the resource constraint,

19. The result applies when the free-entry condition always holds with equality. In this case, new innovations continue to be made even though the cost of innovation is rising.

which is still given by equation (6.23), we get

$$\frac{\dot{N}}{N} = \frac{\psi_1}{\phi} \cdot N^{-\sigma} - \frac{C}{\phi} \cdot N^{-(1+\sigma)} \tag{6.39}$$

where $\psi_1 \equiv (1-\alpha^2) \cdot A^{1/(1-\alpha)} \alpha^{2\alpha/(1-\alpha)} L > 0$ is a constant for a fixed L.

We can solve the model graphically by constructing a phase diagram in (C, N) space. The $\dot{N} = 0$ schedule is a straight line from the origin, $C = \psi_1 N$. To the north of this schedule, arrows point west, as shown in figure 6.2.

We can substitute from equation (6.39) into equation (6.38) to get an expression for $\dot{C}/C$ as a function of N and C:

$$\frac{\dot{C}}{C} = \frac{1}{\theta} \cdot \left\{ \left(\frac{\pi}{\phi}\right) \cdot N^{-\sigma} + \sigma \cdot \left[\left(\frac{\psi_1}{\phi}\right) \cdot N^{-\sigma} - \frac{C}{\phi} \cdot N^{-(1+\sigma)} \right] - \rho \right\} \tag{6.40}$$

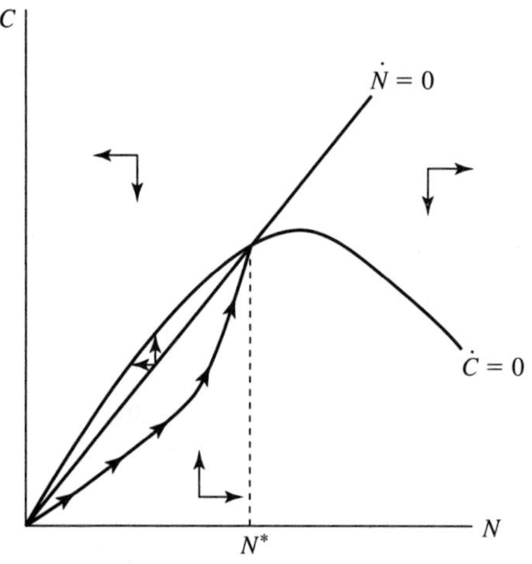

Figure 6.2
Phase diagram for the model with increasing R&D costs. The $\dot{N} = 0$ schedule is a straight line from the origin, $C = \psi_1 N$. To the north of this schedule, arrows point west. The $\dot{C} = 0$ schedule is given by

$$C = \left(\frac{\pi}{\sigma} + \psi_1\right) \cdot N - \frac{\rho\phi}{\sigma} \cdot N^{(1+\sigma)}$$

which is a hump-shaped curve with a maximum at

$$N^{max} = \left(\frac{\pi + \sigma\psi_1}{\rho\phi \cdot (1+\sigma)}\right)^{1/\sigma}$$

Arrows above this curve point south, and the opposite is true below the curve. Notice that $N^* < N^{max}$, so that the the steady state is to the left of the maximum of the $\dot{C} = 0$ schedule. The steady state displays saddle-path stability, and the economy converges along an upward-sloping path, which entails growing consumption and numbers of varieties.

The corresponding $\dot{C} = 0$ schedule is given by

$$C = \left(\frac{\pi}{\sigma} + \psi_1\right) \cdot N - \frac{\rho\phi}{\sigma} \cdot N^{(1+\sigma)} \tag{6.41}$$

This equation defines a hump-shaped curve with a maximum at

$$N^{\max} = \left(\frac{\pi + \sigma\psi_1}{\rho\phi \cdot (1+\sigma)}\right)^{1/\sigma}$$

Arrows to the north of this curve point south, as displayed in figure 6.2. The steady-state value of N, which is determined in the figure by the intersection of the two loci, is given by

$$N^* = \left(\frac{\pi}{\rho\phi}\right)^{1/\sigma} = \left(\frac{LA^{1/(1-\alpha)} \cdot \left(\frac{1-\alpha}{\alpha}\right) \cdot \alpha^{2/(1-\alpha)}}{\rho\phi}\right)^{1/\sigma} \tag{6.42}$$

Notice that $N^* < N^{\max}$, so that the steady state is to the left of the maximum of the $\dot{C} = 0$ schedule.

The steady state displays saddle-path stability, and the economy converges along an upward-sloping path, which entails growing consumption and numbers of varieties.[20] In the long run, however, the number of ideas is constant, as long as L is constant. If L grows at the constant rate n, N will also grow at this rate in the steady state. Hence, the model has no scale effects on the steady-state growth rate. (The model does have a scale effect in the sense that a higher level of L corresponds to a higher level of N and, therefore, higher levels of y and c.) Note that the long-run growth rate is also invariant with saving parameters, ρ and θ, and the cost parameter for R&D, η. The only element that influences the steady-state growth rate is n, the rate of population growth.[21]

6.2 Erosion of Monopoly Power, Competition

We have been assuming that the inventor of an intermediate good retains a perpetual monopoly over its use. More realistically, this position would erode over time as competitors

20. We rule out paths that lie above the stable arm in a similar way that we ruled out such paths in the model with irreversible investment in chapter 2. (The irreversibility arises here because it is impossible to forget ideas that have been invented, so that $\dot{N} \geq 0$ must apply.) Along these paths, the price of a patent would become negative in finite time, and this outcome would violate the free-disposal assumption. See appendix 2B in chapter 2 for a more detailed discussion.

21. In some other models in this literature, a nonzero long-term growth rate of per capita output depends on a nonzero growth rate of population, but the two growth rates are not necessarily equal. See Jones (1995), Segerstrom (1998), and Peretto (1998).

learned about the new product (or new technique) and imitated it or created close substitutes. Monopoly power might also diminish over time because patent protection was only temporary.

A tractable way to model the gradual erosion of monopoly power is to assume that goods transform from monopolized to competitive with a probability that is generated from a Poisson process.[22] That is, if intermediate good j is currently monopolized, this good becomes competitive in the next instant dT with probability $p \cdot dT$, where $p \geq 0$. Thus, if a good is invented at time t and is initially monopolized, the probability of it still being monopolized at the future date $v \geq t$ is $e^{-p\cdot(v-t)}$. (The parameter p works like the death probability that we used in the finite-horizon model of chapter 3.)

A monopolized intermediate good sells as before at the monopoly price $1/\alpha$. The quantity demanded of each monopolized intermediate, now denoted by X^m, is still given by equation (6.11):

$$X^m = LA^{1/(1-\alpha)}\alpha^{2/(1-\alpha)} \tag{6.43}$$

In a monopolized state, the flow of profit is

$$\pi^m = \left(\frac{1-\alpha}{\alpha}\right) \cdot X^m \tag{6.44}$$

whereas, in a competitive state, the flow of profit is 0. The expected present value from the discovery of an (initially monopolized) intermediate good at time t is therefore a modification of equation (6.6) to include the probability term $e^{-p\cdot(v-t)}$:

$$E[V(t)] = \int_t^\infty \pi^m \cdot e^{-[p+\bar{r}(t,v)]\cdot(v-t)}\, dv \tag{6.45}$$

We assume that potential inventors care only about this expectation.[23]

If we take the derivative of equation (6.45) with respect to time, we get an expression analogous to equation (6.18):

$$r(t) = \frac{\pi^m}{E[V(t)]} + \frac{dE[V(t)]/dt}{E[V(t)]} - p \tag{6.46}$$

The first term on the right-hand side is the profit rate, $\pi^m/E[V(t)]$. The second term is the rate of capital gain, assuming that the monopoly position remains in place. The last

22. See Judd (1985) for a discussion of an analogous model.

23. This result is consistent with individual risk aversion because the risks are purely idiosyncratic, and the ownership of firms would be diversified.

term, $-p$, accounts for the probability per unit of time of losing the monopoly position. When this loss occurs, the amount of the loss is $E[V(t)]$, the full value of the firm, because the loss of the monopoly position implies that the present value of all future profits drops to zero. Since the loss occurs with probability p per unit of time, the effect on the rate of return is given by $-p \cdot E[V(t)]/E[V(t)] = -p$.

We return now to the environment in which the R&D cost is the constant η. The free-entry condition with positive R&D entails $E[V(t)] = \eta$, so that $dE[V(t)]/dt = 0$. Substitution of these results into equation (6.46) yields

$$r(t) = \frac{\pi^m}{\eta} - p$$

Since the right-hand side of this expression is constant, it follows that $r(t)$ equals the constant r. Substitution for π^m from equation (6.46) leads to

$$r = (L/\eta) \cdot A^{1/(1-\alpha)} \cdot \left(\frac{1-\alpha}{\alpha}\right) \cdot \alpha^{2/(1-\alpha)} - p \tag{6.47}$$

The result in equation (6.47) modifies equation (6.19) only by the subtraction of the parameter p on the right-hand side. Therefore, the temporary nature of the monopoly position lowers r from its previous value by the amount p. Recall also that the rate of return shown in equation (6.19) was already below the social rate of return given in equation (6.31). Consequently, the temporary nature of an innovator's monopoly position creates an even larger gap between the social and private rates of return. The reason is that, from a social perspective, the gain from a discovery is permanent, whereas, from a private standpoint, the reward is now temporary.

The constant rate of return determined in equation (6.47) implies, as usual, a constant growth rate of consumption:[24]

$$\dot{c}/c = (1/\theta) \cdot \left[(L/\eta) \cdot A^{1/(1-\alpha)} \cdot \left(\frac{1-\alpha}{\alpha}\right) \cdot \alpha^{2/(1-\alpha)} - p - \rho\right] \tag{6.48}$$

The growth rate of the number of intermediates, N, and the level of output, Y, no longer generally equal $\dot{c}/c$. To study these other growth rates, we have to analyze the breakdown of N into monopolized and competitive parts.

Let N^c be the number of intermediates that have become competitive, so that $N - N^c$ is the number that remain monopolized. The quantity produced of each monopolized intermediate is the amount X^m shown in equation (6.43). For each competitive good, which is priced at

24. If equation (6.48) indicates $\dot{c}/c < 0$, then a corner solution applies with $\dot{c}/c = \dot{N}/N = \dot{y}/y = 0$.

marginal cost, 1, the quantity produced follows from equation (6.4) as

$$X^c = LA^{1/(1-\alpha)}\alpha^{1/(1-\alpha)} > X^m \tag{6.49}$$

The level of aggregate output can be computed from equations (6.1), (6.43), and (6.49) as

$$Y = A^{1/(1-\alpha)}\alpha^{2\alpha/(1-\alpha)}LN \cdot \left[1 + (N^c/N) \cdot \left(\alpha^{-\alpha/(1-\alpha)} - 1\right)\right] \tag{6.50}$$

Hence, for given N, Y exceeds the quantity shown in equation (6.13) if $N^c > 0$ (because $0 < \alpha < 1$). Moreover, Y rises with N^c/N for given N; this effect represents the static gain from shifting from monopoly to competition in the provision of the existing intermediate goods.

Since each monopolized good becomes competitive with probability p per unit of time, the change in N^c over time can be approximated if $N - N^c$ is large by

$$\dot{N}^c \approx p \cdot (N - N^c) \tag{6.51}$$

Finally, the model is closed by using the economy's budget constraint to determine the level of C:

$$C = Y - \eta\dot{N} - N^c X^c - (N - N^c) \cdot X^m \tag{6.52}$$

That is, consumption equals output, Y, less R&D spending, $\eta\dot{N}$, less production of competitive intermediates, $N^c X^c$, less production of monopolized intermediates, $(N - N^c) \cdot X^m$.

The model contains two state variables, N and N^c, and features a transitional dynamics in which the ratio N^c/N approaches its steady-state value, $(N^c/N)^*$. In this respect, the model resembles the two-sector framework discussed in chapter 5 in which the ratio of the two types of capital goods, K/H, adjusted gradually toward $(K/H)^*$. In the present context, the transitional analysis is cumbersome, and we limit attention to the characteristics of the steady state.

In the steady state, N, N^c, Y, and C all grow at the rate shown in equation (6.48), which we now denote by γ^*. Equation (6.51) implies accordingly

$$(N^c/N)^* = \frac{p}{\gamma^* + p} \tag{6.53}$$

Thus the competitive fraction rises with the rate, p, at which goods become competitive and falls with the rate, γ^*, at which new (monopolized) intermediates are discovered.

If we substitute for N^c/N from equation (6.53) into equation (6.50), we can determine a formula for output that applies along the steady-state path:

$$Y^* = A^{1/(1-\alpha)}\alpha^{2\alpha/(1-\alpha)}LN \cdot \left[1 + \left(\frac{p}{\gamma^* + p}\right) \cdot \left(\alpha^{-\alpha/(1-\alpha)} - 1\right)\right] \tag{6.54}$$

(Note that Y^* grows at the same rate as N.) If $p=0$, so that $(N^c/N)^*=0$ (see equation [6.53]), the expression for Y^* is the same as that shown in equation (6.13) for the pure monopoly model. If $p\rightarrow\infty$—so that intermediate goods become competitive instantly and, hence, $(N^c/N)^*=1$—the formula for Y^* approaches the social planner's expression in equation (6.30). The difficulty, however, is that $p\rightarrow\infty$ also implies $\gamma^*=0$.[25] In other words, if p had always been infinite, nothing would ever have been invented, and N would equal the endowed value, $N(0)$, which predates any purposive R&D activity.

In the pure monopoly model, we showed that the social optimum can be attained if the government uses a lump-sum tax to finance a subsidy at the rate $1-\alpha$ on purchases of intermediate goods. In the present context, this subsidy has to be limited to purchases of the monopolized intermediates. The selection of which goods to subsidize is feasible in the model—because goods can be observed to be either completely monopolized or completely competitive—but would be a challenge in practice.

In any event, a subsidy at the rate $1-\alpha$ on the monopolized intermediates does not attain the social optimum because the term p still leaves a gap between the social rate of return (equation [6.31]) and the private rate of return (equation [6.47] with $\alpha^{2/(1-\alpha)}$ replaced by $\alpha^{1/(1-\alpha)}$). To reach the social optimum, the government would also have to subsidize research spending to raise the private rate of return on R&D by the amount p. In other words, two policy instruments are now required—one to encourage production of the monopolized intermediates and another to stimulate R&D.

The government can also affect the parameter p directly by attempting to curb monopoly power, for example, through antitrust enforcement or limitations on patent protection. An increase in p involves the usual trade-off that appears in models of optimal patent policy—the static gain from increased competition versus the dynamic loss from too low a rate of growth of new products (see, for example, Reinganum, 1989).[26] This analysis is difficult because it encounters time-consistency problems: the government would like to eliminate all existing monopoly power—make the N existing products available at a competitive price—but then promise protection of property rights over future inventions. Such promises tend, of course, not to be credible. One possible way to proceed is to assume that the government commits itself not to change the probability p for existing products but can choose this probability for goods that are yet to be invented.

25. A large value of p implies $r<0$ in equation (6.47) and $\dot{c}/c<0$ in equation (6.48). The equilibrium is then the corner solution in which inventors spend zero on R&D (because they cannot spend a negative amount), so that N stays constant and $\gamma^*=0$.

26. In the present setting, a reduced rate of innovation constitutes a social loss. In other contexts, such as the model considered in chapter 7, a reduced rate of innovation may be desirable.

6.3 Romer's Model of Technological Change

Romer's (1990) paper provided the first formal application of the varieties structure to the modeling of endogenous growth. His specification is that the discovery of a new type of good requires η units of labor, rather than final product.[27] Therefore, an increase in N—which raises output and the marginal product of labor—raises the real wage rate and, therefore, increases the goods cost of R&D. From this perspective, the Romer model is similar to the one explored in section 6.1.8 in which the R&D cost rose with N. We already know for this model that, if L is constant, as Romer assumed, growth would eventually cease, and N would be constant in the steady state. Hence, per capita output, Y/L, would also be constant in the long run.

Romer's (1990) model generates endogenous growth because of another difference in specification. He assumes that the cost of inventing a new product declines as society accumulates more ideas, represented by the number of products, N.[28] More specifically, suppose that the fraction λ of labor is used in production, and the fraction $1 - \lambda$ is used in R&D. Then Romer's assumption is that the change in N depends on the amount of R&D labor, $(1 - \lambda) \cdot L$, divided by η/N, so that

$$\dot{N}/N = (1 - \lambda) \cdot L/\eta \tag{6.55}$$

Jones (1995, 1999) has criticized this type of specification because it implies a positive relation between the rate of technological change, $\dot{N}/N$, and the absolute quantity of labor engaged in R&D, $(1-\lambda) \cdot L$. Jones argues that data for the United States and other advanced countries conflict with this setup, because the number of scientists and engineers engaged in R&D has increased substantially over time, whereas the rate of productivity growth has not risen secularly. For example, in the United States, the number of R&D scientists and engineers rose from 544,000 in 1970 to 960,000 in 1991. Even larger proportionate increases applied to other major OECD countries—the number in Japan increased from 172,000 in 1970 to 511,000 in 1992, in Germany from 82,000 in 1970 to 176,000 in 1989, in France from 58,000 in 1970 to 129,000 in 1991, and in the United Kingdom from 77,000 in 1972 to 123,000 in 1992.[29] We already noted that this type of criticism does not apply to models that assume a fixed positive relation between productivity growth and the share of GDP devoted to R&D.

27. Romer (1990) treated the intermediate goods as infinite-lived durables, rather than nondurables, but this difference does not affect the main results.

28. Grossman and Helpman (1991, chapter 3) make an analogous assumption.

29. These data are from the National Science Foundation at www.nsf.gov.

If we proceed with Romer's specification of the innovation process from equation (6.55), despite Jones's reasonable objections, the implication is that the cost of invention is proportional to w/N. Since w is proportional to N (from equations [6.5] and [6.13]), the end result is that the cost of inventing a new product remains constant over time in units of goods. Thus this specification will be consistent with a constant steady-state growth rate of N and Y/L.

Although the growth rate is constant in equilibrium, the determination of this growth rate in a decentralized economy involves a new type of externality: an individual's decision to conduct R&D and, hence, to expand N reduces the required amount of labor needed for subsequent inventions. Current research, therefore, has a positive spillover on the productivity of future research. The failure of the decentralized economy to compensate researchers for this spillover benefit constitutes another form of distortion. Consequently, a policymaker who seeks to guide the decentralized economy to a Pareto optimal solution has to worry about this spillover effect in addition to the monopoly pricing of intermediate goods.

The free-entry condition is modified in the Romer model to

$$r = \alpha\lambda L/\eta \tag{6.56}$$

Hence, equation (6.55) and the usual first-order condition, $\dot{c}/c = (1/\theta) \cdot (r - \rho)$, imply

$$(1 - \lambda) \cdot L/\eta = (1/\theta) \cdot (\alpha\lambda L/\eta - \rho) \tag{6.57}$$

We can use this condition to solve for λ and, hence, for r and γ, the growth rate of N:

$$\begin{aligned} \lambda &= \frac{(\theta L + \eta\rho)}{L \cdot (\theta + \alpha)} \\ r &= \frac{\alpha \cdot (\theta L + \eta\rho)}{\eta \cdot (\theta + \alpha)} \\ \gamma &= \frac{(\alpha L - \eta\rho)}{\eta \cdot (\theta + \alpha)} \end{aligned} \tag{6.58}$$

The result for the growth rate, γ, is in many respects similar to that obtained in equation (6.24) for the decentralized economy when the R&D cost was fixed in terms of goods, rather than labor. The similarities are, first, γ is higher if households are more willing to save (lower ρ or θ); second, γ is higher if η, the cost of R&D, is lower; and, third, there is a scale effect in that γ is higher if L is higher.

One difference in the results is that γ in equation (6.58) is independent of the productivity parameter, A, that appears in the production function for goods (equation [6.1]). This result follows from the assumption that the research sector uses no intermediate goods as inputs.

If intermediates entered as productive inputs in this sector (even if less intensively than in the goods sector), an increase in A would raise γ.

To clarify the distortions in the Romer model, we can consider the social planner's problem. The social planner seeks to maximize the representative household's utility, subject to the constraints

$$Y = A \cdot (\lambda L)^{(1-\alpha)} N^{1-\alpha} X^{\alpha} = C + X$$

$$\dot{N}/N = (1 - \lambda) \cdot L/\eta$$

The control variables are C, X, and λ, and the state variable is N. If we invoke the usual optimization conditions, we find that the solutions are

$$\begin{aligned} \gamma \text{ (social planner)} &= (1/\theta) \cdot (L/\eta - \rho) \\ \lambda \text{ (social planner)} &= (1/\theta) \cdot (L - \rho\eta)/L \end{aligned} \tag{6.59}$$

The choice of γ in equation (6.59) corresponds to an implicit social rate of return of L/η.

The social planner's growth rate in equation (6.59) exceeds the decentralized growth rate in equation (6.58). The gap between the growth rates reflects the excess of the social planner's choice of labor devoted to research, $(1 - \lambda) \cdot L$, over the privately determined value. The improper allocation of labor between production and research reflects the underlying distortions: monopoly pricing and research spillovers. To clarify the nature of these distortions, we can consider policies that would cause the decentralized outcomes to coincide with the Pareto-optimal choices made by the social planner.

A policymaker can again neutralize the direct effect of monopoly pricing by using a lump-sum tax to subsidize the purchase of intermediate goods at the rate $1-\alpha$. This subsidy raises the decentralized values of the rate of return and the growth rate above the values shown in equation (6.58). However, the growth rate remains below the social planner's value, because the research spillovers have yet to be internalized.

The elimination of the remaining distortion requires another form of subsidy, one that applies directly to research. The required rate of subsidy on R&D spending turns out to be $(1/\theta) \cdot [1 - (\rho\eta/L)]$. This subsidy provides a sufficient incentive for research so that the decentralized growth rate coincides with the social planner's choice shown in equation (6.59). Equivalently, the private rate of return becomes $r = L/\eta$, which is the rate implicitly used by the social planner in the determination of γ.

The call for a subsidy to research because of positive spillovers is analogous to the argument for a subsidy on purchases of capital goods or output in the model with positive spillovers in production in chapter 4. A successful subsidy policy is again difficult to implement in practice because it requires the government to identify promising areas of research that have substantial spillover benefits, and it assumes that the necessary public finance will not have distorting influences that outweigh the benefits from the internalization of the spillovers. The next chapter brings out another potential drawback from research subsidies: the private benefit from innovation can be too high because it includes the transfer of rents from an existing monopolist to the innovator. This kind of effect can also arise in models in which competitive researchers race to discover a new product or process (see Reinganum, 1989, for a survey).

6.4 Concluding Observations

We modeled technological progress as an expansion of the variety of intermediate goods used by producers. Researchers are motivated by the prospect of monopoly profits to expend resources to discover new types of goods. In the main setting that we considered—production exhibits constant returns to the number of types of goods, and the cost structure entails a fixed outlay of goods for each invention—the economy is capable of generating endogenous growth. The rate of growth depends on various characteristics of preferences and technology, including the willingness to save, the level of the production function, the cost of R&D, and the scale of the economy (measured by the quantity of a fixed factor, such as raw labor or human capital). Some alternative specifications of the R&D technology can preserve most of the growth implications while eliminating the apparently counterfactual scale effects.

The resulting growth rate—and the related choices about the quantities of intermediate goods to use in production—are generally not Pareto optimal. We discussed possibilities for improving on outcomes by means of tax and subsidy schemes. Although these possibilities exist in the model, these kinds of industrial policies would be difficult to implement in more realistic situations.

The equilibrium growth rate in the model corresponds to the exogenous rate of technological change, x, in the Solow–Swan and Ramsey models of chapters 1 and 2. Thus, the analysis endogenizes the parameter x and, therefore, fills a significant gap in the theories. For example, if the diffusion of ideas from one country to another is rapid, the model explains why the technology in all countries would improve over time. Therefore, the model can explain why the long-term growth rate of the world's real per capita GDP would be positive.

6.5 Problems

6.1 Transitional dynamics in the varieties model. We showed in the model of section 6.1 that an equilibrium exists in which N, Y, and C grow at the same constant rate, and the rate of return, r, is constant.

a. Show that there are no other equilibria; that is, the model has no transitional dynamics. (Hint: consider the analysis of a related situation in chapter 4.)

b. Suppose that the growth rate shown in equation (6.24) is negative. What is the equilibrium in this case? What condition on the underlying parameters leads to this situation?

6.2 An alternative production function with varieties. Suppose that, instead of equation (6.1), the production function is

$$Y_i = AL_i^{1-\alpha} \cdot \left[\sum_{j=1}^{N} (X_{ij})^{\sigma} \right]^{\alpha/\sigma}$$

where $0 < \sigma < 1$. The parameter σ, rather than α, will now determine the elasticity of demand for each type of intermediate.

a. How are monopolized intermediates priced, and what is the quantity of each intermediate, X_j?

b. What is the free-entry condition for R&D, and how is the rate of return determined?

c. What are the growth rates of N, X_j, and total output, Y, in the steady state?

6.3 Policy implications of the varieties model. Consider the first model of varieties of producer intermediates, for which the economy's equilibrium growth rate is given in equation (6.24).

a. Show that the government can ensure a first-best equilibrium if it uses a lump-sum tax to finance the appropriate subsidy of the intermediate goods. What rate of subsidy is required? In a richer model, why would it be difficult to carry out the required form of policy?

b. Can the government ensure a first-best solution if it relies solely on a subsidy to R&D (financed again by a lump-sum tax)? Explain the answer. What modifications to the model would make it important for the government to subsidize research?

6.4 Intermediate inputs as durables (based on Barro and Sala-i-Martin, 1992). Suppose that the intermediate inputs, X_{ij}, are infinite-lived durable goods. New units of these durables can be formed from one unit of final output. The inventor of the jth type of intermediate good charges the rental price R_j, and the competitive producers of final goods treat R_j as given.

a. How is R_j determined?

b. In the steady state, what is the quantity, X_j, of each type of intermediate good?

c. What is the steady-state growth rate of the economy? How does this answer differ from the one discussed in the text for the case in which the intermediate inputs were perishable goods?

d. If the intermediate goods are durables, what kinds of dynamic effects arise in the transition to the steady state?

6.5 The duration of monopoly positions. Consider the model of section 6.2, in which the monopolized intermediate goods became competitive with the probability p per unit of time.

a. How do differences in p affect the steady-state properties of the model?

b. What kinds of policy interventions by the government would lead to a first-best outcome in this model? In particular, is it possible to reach the first best solely by subsidizing purchases of the monopolized intermediate goods?

c. If the government can influence p through various instruments (such as antitrust enforcement and patent protection), what are the model's implications about desirable policies?

6.6 Scale effects

a. Why does the varieties model of technological change from section 6.1 exhibit a scale effect in the sense that the growth rate rises with the aggregate quantity of labor, L? Is it reasonable to identify L empirically with a country's population?

b. What happens in this model if population, L, grows at a constant positive rate?

c. What types of modifications to the model would eliminate the scale effects?

7 Technological Change: Schumpeterian Models of Quality Ladders

The last chapter modeled technological progress as an increase in the number of types of products, N. In this chapter, we allow for improvements in the quality or productivity of each type. This approach has come to be known as the Schumpeterian approach to endogenous growth. We can think of increases in N as basic innovations that amount to dramatically new kinds of goods or methods of production. In contrast, increases in the quality of the existing products involve a continuing series of improvements and refinements of goods and techniques. Thus the analysis of this chapter complements the discussion in chapter 6.

Figure 7.1 shows the basic setup. Intermediate goods come in N varieties, arrayed along the horizontal axis. In chapter 6, N could increase over time, but now we treat it as fixed. The leading-edge quality of each type of intermediate good is currently at the level shown on the vertical axis. We specify later the precise meaning of the ladder numbers indicated on this axis. Since the process of quality improvement turns out to occur at different rates (and in a random manner), the figure shows that the levels currently attained vary in an irregular way across the sectors.

For the analysis of basic innovation in chapter 6, we assumed that the new types of intermediate inputs did not interact directly with the old ones. (We used the Spence, 1976/Dixit–Stiglitz, 1977, functional form in which these inputs entered in an additively separable manner.) Therefore, the introduction of a new kind of good did not make any old goods obsolete.

An important aspect of the Schumpeterian model is that, when a product or technique is improved, the new good or method tends to displace the old one. Thus it is natural to model different quality grades for a good of a given type as close substitutes. We make the extreme assumption that the different qualities of a particular type of intermediate input are perfect substitutes; hence, the discovery of a higher grade turns out to drive out the lower grades completely. For this reason, successful researchers along the quality dimension tend to eliminate or "destroy" the monopoly rentals of their predecessors, a process labeled as "creative destruction" by Schumpeter (1934) and Aghion and Howitt (1992). On the normative side, the process of creative destruction implies a "business-stealing" effect that leads firms to perform more research than is socially optimal. Consequently, the growth rate in a decentralized economy may be too high.

7.1 Sketch of the Model

Before we get into the technical details, we provide a sketch of the structure of the model that we shall develop to analyze improvements in quality. There are three sectors in this economy: producers of final output, R&D firms, and consumers. Producers of final output

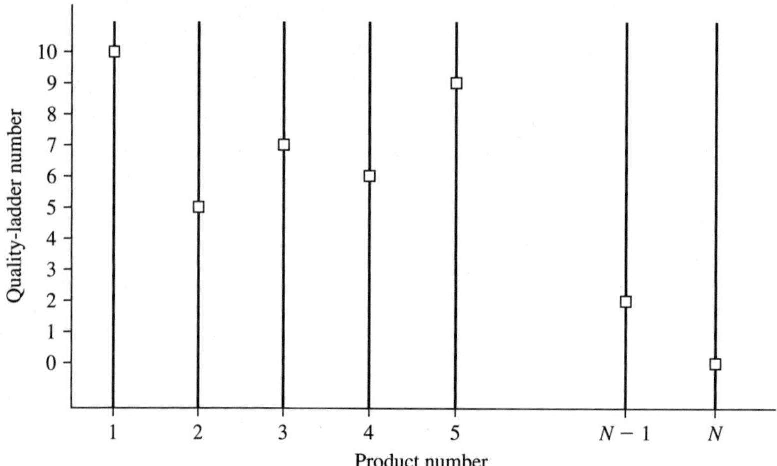

Figure 7.1
Quality ladders and product varieties. The horizontal axis shows the number of types of products, and the vertical axis shows the quality rung currently attained in each sector.

demand intermediates from research firms, and they, again, use N varieties of intermediate inputs, but N is now constant. Each type of intermediate good has a quality ladder along which improvements can occur. At each point in time, the knowledge exists to produce an array of qualities of each type of intermediate good. We consider, however, a type of equilibrium in which only the leading-edge quality is actually produced in each sector and used by final-goods producers to generate output.

Researchers invest resources to improve the quality of existing intermediate inputs. A successful researcher retains exclusive rights over the use of his improved intermediate good so he can sell the intermediates at the monopoly price to the producers of final output. The researcher who has a monopoly over the use of the latest technology receives a flow of profit. We begin with a model in which the latest innovator is a different person from the previous innovator, so that a research success terminates the predecessor's flow of profit. Therefore, in considering how many resources to devote to research, entrepreneurs consider the size of the profit flow and its likely duration. This duration is random, because it depends on the uncertain outcomes from the research efforts of competitors.

The temporary nature of an inventor's monopoly position brings in two considerations that differentiate the present model from the one with perpetual monopoly rights in chapter 6. First, the shorter the expected duration of the monopoly, the smaller the anticipated payoff from R&D; this is a distortion because the advances are permanent from a social perspective. (This force also appears in chapter 6 for the model in which the intermediate goods became competitive over time.) Second, part of the reward from successful research is the creative-destruction or business-stealing effect that involves the transfer of profits from the incumbent innovator to the newcomer. Since this transfer has no social value, this second force constitutes an excessive incentive for R&D. We show that the second element is larger than the first, because the two effects are basically the same, except that the second element comes earlier in time so it is not discounted so heavily. Hence, the net effect is an increase in the private return from research relative to the social return.

In a later section we assume that the industry leader has a first-mover advantage in R&D, as well as lower costs of carrying out research. In this case, the leader tends to carry out all the research. However, if the cost advantage is small, the probability of research success is determined by the threat of potential entry, basically in the same way as in the initial model. If the cost advantage is larger, the industry leader can ignore the outsiders and act as a monopolistic researcher.

7.2 The Model

7.2.1 The Producers of Final Output: Levels of Quality in the Production Technology

We modify the production function for firm i from equation (6.1) to

$$Y_i = AL_i^{1-\alpha} \cdot \sum_{j=1}^{N} (\tilde{X}_{ij})^{\alpha} \tag{7.1}$$

where, as before, L_i is labor input and $0 < \alpha < 1$. The new element is that $\tilde{X}_{ij}$ is the *quality-adjusted* amount employed of the jth type of intermediate good.

The potential grades of each intermediate good are arrayed along a quality ladder with rungs spaced proportionately at interval $q > 1$.[1] We normalize so that each good begins—when first invented—at quality 1. The subsequent rungs are at the levels q, q^2, and so on. Thus, if κ_j improvements in quality have occurred in sector j, the available grades in the sector are $1, q, q^2, \ldots, (q)^{\kappa_j}$. Increases in the quality of goods available in a sector—that is, rises in κ_j—result from the successful application of research effort, to be described later. These improvements must occur sequentially, one rung at a time.

Figure 7.2 shows a possible path for the evolution of the leading-edge quality in sector j. The best quality available equals 1 at time t_0, rises to q (rung 1) at time t_1, to q^2 (rung 2) at time t_2, to q^k (rung k) at time t_k, and so on. Thus $t_{k+1} - t_k$ is the interval over which the

1. This setup follows the models of Aghion and Howitt (1992) and Grossman and Helpman (1991, chapter 4).

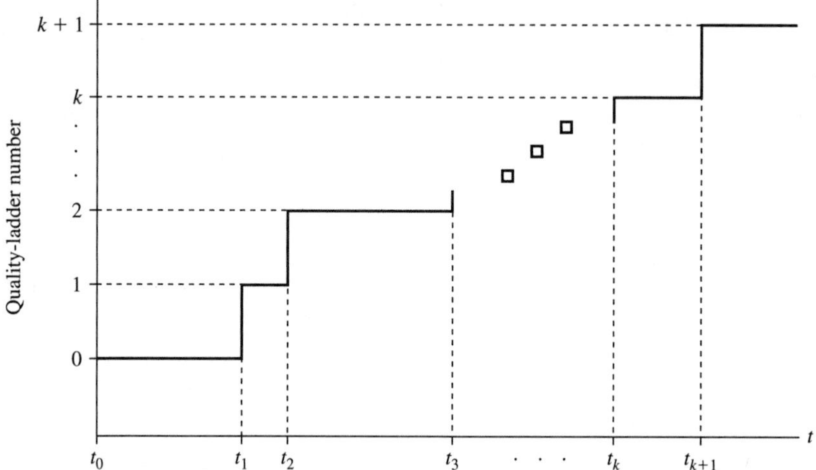

Figure 7.2
A quality ladder in a single sector. Over time, the quality-ladder position in a single sector either stays constant or jumps discretely to the next rung. The timing of the jumps is stochastic because it depends on the uncertain outcomes from research effort.

best quality is q^k. The figure shows intervals of differing length for each k; these lengths are random and depend on the successes that researchers have in coming up with new ideas.

The intermediate good is nondurable and entails a unit marginal cost of production (in terms of output, Y). That is, the cost of production is the same for all qualities q^k, where $k = 0, \ldots, \kappa_j$. Thus the latest innovator has an efficiency advantage over the prior innovators in the sector but will eventually be at a disadvantage relative to future innovators. We assume here that each innovator is a different person.

The researcher responsible for each quality improvement in sector j retains a monopoly right to produce the jth intermediate good at that quality level. In particular, if the quality rungs $k = 1, \ldots, \kappa_j$ have been reached, the kth innovator is the sole source of intermediate goods with the quality level q^k.[2]

We assume in the main analysis that only the highest grade of intermediates that is currently available in each sector will actually be produced and used.[3] Hence, in sector j,

2. Since this model does not consider the initial discovery of a type of product, we have to assume that goods of quality 1 (rung 0) can be produced by anyone. The treatment of these lowest quality goods will not be an issue if substantial quality improvements have already occurred in each sector.

3. This assumption turns out to amount to the condition $\alpha q \geq 1$. The general nature of the results would be the same if $\alpha q < 1$, in which case we could analyze an equilibrium with limit pricing, rather than monopoly pricing. The appendix (section 7.6) considers this issue in detail.

the intermediate good will be of quality q^{κ_j}. If X_{ij} is the physical quantity of this intermediate employed by firm i, the quality-adjusted amount of this input is given by

$$\tilde{X}_{ij} = q^{\kappa_j} X_{ij} \tag{7.2}$$

Hence, the production function from equation (7.1) becomes

$$Y_i = AL_i^{1-\alpha} \cdot \sum_{j=1}^{N} (q^{\kappa_j} X_{ij})^{\alpha} \tag{7.3}$$

In chapter 6, quality improvements were not considered, and $\kappa_j = 0$ applied in each sector. Therefore, technological advances arose in equation (7.3) only from increases in N. Since N is now fixed, we are assuming implicitly that all the existing types of intermediate goods were discovered sometime in the (distant) past. But we allow κ_j to evolve over time in each sector in response to the R&D effort aimed at quality improvement in that sector.

Equation (7.3) implies that the marginal product of intermediate j is

$$\partial Y_i / \partial X_{ij} = A\alpha L_i^{1-\alpha} q^{\alpha\kappa_j} X_{ij}^{\alpha-1} \tag{7.4}$$

Each firm seeks to maximize profit,

$$Y_i - w \cdot L_i - \sum_{j=1}^{N} P_j X_{ij} \tag{7.5}$$

where P_j is the price of good j. The first-order conditions require the equations of marginal products to prices, so that

$$A\alpha L_i^{1-\alpha} q^{\alpha\kappa_j} X_{ij}^{\alpha-1} = P_j$$

Rearrangement of this expression and summation across all firms i yields the aggregate demand function for good j:

$$X_j = L \cdot [A\alpha q^{\alpha\kappa_j} / P_j]^{1/(1-\alpha)} \tag{7.6}$$

This demand function corresponds to those derived in chapter 6 if $\kappa_j = 0$ (see, for example, equation [6.4]). In particular, the demand elasticity is still the constant $-1/(1-\alpha)$. As in chapter 6, we assume that the aggregate labor force, L, is constant.

7.2.2 The Research Sector

R&D firms face the same kind of two-stage decision process faced by the research firms discussed in chapter 6. First, they must decide whether to engage in research and, if so, they must decide how much to invest in R&D. In the second stage, the successful researchers determine the price at which to sell their previously invented goods to the producers of final output. We again proceed by solving the model backward; that is, we start by deriving the optimal price for a good that has already been invented. Subsequently, we discuss the first stage.

Stage 2: Pricing, Profits, and Production after a Good Has Been Invented Innovation in a sector takes the form of an improvement in quality by the multiple q. The κ_jth innovator in sector j raises the quality from q^{κ_j-1} to q^{κ_j}. This innovator will obtain a flow of monopoly profit given by

$$\pi(\kappa_j) = (P_j - 1) \cdot X_j \tag{7.7}$$

where X_j is given by equation (7.6) and 1 is the marginal cost of production. Firms choose prices to maximize the present discounted value of all future profits. Since there are no dynamic constraints, this problem is equivalent to maximizing profit period by period. The optimal price P_j is given by the same markup formula as in equation (6.7):

$$P_j = 1/\alpha \tag{7.8}$$

Hence, the monopoly price is again constant over time and across sectors.[4]

The aggregate quantity produced of intermediate good j can be determined from equations (7.6) and (7.8) as

$$X_j = LA^{1/(1-\alpha)}\alpha^{2/(1-\alpha)} \cdot q^{\kappa_j\alpha/(1-\alpha)} \tag{7.9}$$

Since $\kappa_j = 0$ in the model of chapter 6, this quantity was constant over time and across sectors (see equation [6.8]). The evolution of κ_j over time in each sector and the divergences of the κ_j across the sectors will lead now to variations in X_j over time and across sectors.

Since the innovator will be able to price in accordance with equation (7.8) and sell the quantity of intermediate goods given by equation (7.9), the flow of profit is given from substitution into equation (7.7) by

$$\pi(\kappa_j) = \bar{\pi} \cdot q^{\kappa_j\alpha/(1-\alpha)} \tag{7.10}$$

where

$$\bar{\pi} \equiv A^{1/(1-\alpha)} \cdot \left(\frac{1-\alpha}{\alpha}\right) \cdot \alpha^{2/(1-\alpha)} L \tag{7.11}$$

4. The monopoly price applies because the demand function in equation (7.6) assumes that lower grades of intermediates of type j do not provide any effective competition for the leading-edge type. See the appendix (section 7.6). Aghion, Harris, Howitt, and Vickers (2001) consider a setting in which goods of different quality are imperfect substitutes and, therefore, can coexist in the market.

is constant over time as long as population, L, is constant. We think of $\bar{\pi}$ as the basic profit flow, which corresponds to $\kappa_j = 0$. The profit $\bar{\pi}$ is the same as the profit in chapter 6 (equation [6.13]), because the quality level did not change in that setting. For given $\bar{\pi}$, $\pi(\kappa_j)$ shown in equation (7.10) is an increasing function of κ_j. Thus the profit received by inventors of higher quality products will be larger. Moreover, since, in equilibrium, q^{κ_j} will increase over time, profits will also increase over time.

One of the key differences between this model and the one in chapter 6 is that, although the monopoly right over an invention is perpetual, the value of this right will fall to zero when a new quality improvement is made by a competitor. (Recall that the innovators are assumed to be different persons.) In other words, if we let t_{κ_j} be the moment when the κ_jth quality improvement is made and t_{κ_j+1} the time of the next improvement by a competitor, the flow of profit shown in equation (7.10) applies only from time t_{κ_j} to t_{κ_j+1}. It is important to note that t_{κ_j+1} is determined by the research effort chosen by competitors and is, therefore, endogenous. The interval over which the κ_jth innovation is in the forefront is

$$T(\kappa_j) = t_{\kappa_j+1} - t_{\kappa_j}$$

The present value of all the profits that the inventor of rung κ_j will get, evaluated at time t_{κ_j}, is given by

$$V(\kappa_j) = \int_{t_{\kappa_j}}^{t_{\kappa_j+1}} \pi(\kappa_j) \cdot e^{-\bar{r}(v,t_{\kappa_j})\cdot(v-t_{\kappa_j})}\, dv \tag{7.12}$$

where, as usual, $\bar{r}(v, t_{\kappa_j}) \equiv [1/(v - t_{\kappa_j})] \cdot \int_{t_{\kappa_j}}^{v} r(\omega)\, d\omega$ is the average interest rate between times t_{k_j} and v. Notice that, if the interest rate, r, is constant over time, as will be true in equilibrium, this present value simplifies to

$$V(\kappa_j) = \pi(\kappa_j) \cdot \left[1 - e^{-r\cdot T(\kappa_j)}\right]/r \tag{7.13}$$

This present value, which represents the prize for the κ_jth innovation, depends positively on the profit flow, $\pi(\kappa_j)$, and the duration of the monopoly for the inventor of rung j, $T(\kappa_j)$. Since we know $\pi(\kappa_j)$, we have to determine the duration, $T(\kappa_j)$, to determine $V(\kappa_j)$.

If we substitute L_i for L in equation (7.9), we determine the quantity X_{ij} of intermediate j used by firm i. If we then use equation (7.3) and aggregate over the firms i, we get an expression for aggregate output:

$$Y = A^{1/(1-\alpha)}\alpha^{2\alpha/(1-\alpha)}L \cdot \sum_{j=1}^{N} q^{\kappa_j\alpha/(1-\alpha)} \tag{7.14}$$

Since L and N are constants, the key to growth of aggregate output in this model is expansions of the quality-ladder positions, κ_j, in the various sectors.

We can define an aggregate quality index,

$$Q \equiv \sum_{j=1}^{N} q^{\kappa_j \alpha/(1-\alpha)} \tag{7.15}$$

so that

$$Y = A^{1/(1-\alpha)} \alpha^{2\alpha/(1-\alpha)} L Q \tag{7.16}$$

The index Q is a combination of the various κ_j's, and increases in the κ_j's affect aggregate output to the extent that they raise Q. We also note from aggregation of equation (7.9) across the sectors that the total quantity of intermediates produced, denoted by X, is proportional to Q:

$$X = A^{1/(1-\alpha)} \alpha^{2/(1-\alpha)} L Q \tag{7.17}$$

The randomness of innovations implies that progress will occur unevenly in an individual sector; usually nothing happens, but on rare occasions productivity jumps by a discrete amount. We assume, however, that individual sectors are small and that the probabilities of research success across sectors are independent. The law of large numbers then implies that the jumpiness in microeconomic outcomes will not be transmitted to the macroeconomic variables: the adding up across a large number, N, of independent sectors will lead to a smooth path for the aggregate quality index, Q, shown in equation (7.15), and, therefore, for aggregate economic growth. Thus, as in chapter 6, the analysis abstracts from the aggregate fluctuations that are the focus of real business-cycle models. We now consider the determinants of changes in the κ_j's.

Stage 1: Innovation

The duration of monopoly profit. Denote by $p(\kappa_j)$ the probability per unit of time of a successful innovation in sector j when the top-of-the-line quality is κ_j. In other words, $p(\kappa_j)$ is the probability per unit of time that an outside researcher will raise the quality in sector j from κ_j to $\kappa_j + 1$. This probability depends on research efforts, as detailed subsequently. For the moment, however, we take $p(\kappa_j)$ to be a given number so that the probability of the incumbent losing his monopoly position is generated from a Poisson process, analogous to the model in chapter 6 in which an innovator's monopoly position was temporary.

The incumbent's present value of profits, $V(\kappa_j)$ in equation (7.13), is a random variable because the terminal date, t_{κ_j+1}, arrives with probability $p(\kappa_j)$ per unit of time. The expectation of $V(\kappa_j)$ is given by

$$E[V(\kappa_j)] = \pi(\kappa_j)/[r + p(\kappa_j)] \tag{7.18}$$

The derivation of equation (7.18) is in the appendix (section 7.6.2), but its interpretation is intuitive.[5] If we rewrite equation (7.18) as

$$r = \frac{\pi(\kappa_j) - p(\kappa_j) \cdot E[V(\kappa_j)]}{E[V(\kappa_j)]}$$

then the equation says that the market rate of return equals the rate of return to R&D. The key point is that the return to R&D on the right-hand side includes the incumbent's expected capital loss, $p(\kappa_j) \cdot E[V(\kappa_j)]$, generated by the possibility of the next innovation in sector j. Equation (7.18) indicates that the probability of losing one's monopoly position, $p(\kappa_j)$, combines with r to get an effective discount rate, $r + p(\kappa_j)$. Note that an increase in $p(\kappa_j)$ reduces $E[V(\kappa_j)]$. Substitution for $\pi(\kappa_j)$ from equation (7.10) into equation (7.18) leads to

$$E[V(\kappa_j)] = \bar{\pi} \cdot q^{\kappa_j \alpha/(1-\alpha)}/[r + p(\kappa_j)] \tag{7.19}$$

where $\bar{\pi}$ is defined in equation (7.11).

The R&D technology. We now have to consider how the probability $p(\kappa_j)$ depends on R&D effort in sector j. Let $Z(\kappa_j)$ be the aggregate flow of resources expended by potential innovators in sector j when the highest rung available is κ_j. We assume that $p(\kappa_j)$ depends only on the total R&D expenditure, $Z(\kappa_j)$, and not on the distribution of this expenditure across researchers. We also assume that a larger outlay, $Z(\kappa_j)$, leads to a larger probability of success, $p(\kappa_j)$. A plausible assumption is that the marginal effect of $Z(\kappa_j)$ on $p(\kappa_j)$ would diminish with $Z(\kappa_j)$. That is, R&D investment would encounter diminishing returns at a point in time. However, because it substantially simplifies the analysis and also preserves most of the conclusions, we assume in the main analysis that the probability of success is proportional to the R&D outlays, $Z(\kappa_j)$.[6]

The probability of innovation likely depends, for given $Z(\kappa_j)$, also on κ_j. If innovations become increasingly difficult, the probability of success would depend negatively on κ_j. In contrast, if earlier innovations make subsequent inventions easier, the probability of success

5. The result also corresponds to equation (6.18) in chapter 6.

6. The linearity in $Z(\kappa_j)$ means that the marginal contribution of R&D effort to the probability of success equals the average contribution. That is, the research process is *not* being modeled as a congestible resource, like a fishing pond, in which an individual's likelihood of success declines with the aggregate level of investment. The model, therefore, will not have the property of some patent-race formulations in which—for congestion reasons—the overall level of research tends to be too high from a social perspective (see Reinganum, 1989, for a survey of these models).

would depend positively on κ_j. In any event, we assume that the probability of research success is given by the relation

$$p(\kappa_j) = Z(\kappa_j) \cdot \phi(\kappa_j) \tag{7.20}$$

where the function $\phi(\kappa_j)$ captures the effect of the current technology position, κ_j.

Equation (7.19) shows the expected reward from making the κ_jth innovation. Note that the uncertainty that underlies $E[V(\kappa_j)]$ involves the duration of the monopoly position, that is, the randomness of the time of success of the $(\kappa_j + 1)$th innovator. We have yet to consider the additional uncertainty that innovators face, ex ante, because of the randomness of the success of their own research efforts.

Determination of R&D Effort: The Free Entry Condition In sector j, the total R&D expenditure of $Z(\kappa_j)$ results in the success probability per unit of time $p(\kappa_j)$, given by equation (7.20). If a firm succeeds, it obtains the equivalent of a patent with the expected value given by equation (7.19). We assume that potential innovators care only about this expected value and not about the randomness of the return. This assumption can be satisfactory even if individuals are risk averse because each R&D project is small and has purely idiosyncratic uncertainty.[7]

R&D investments will be attractive, so that $Z(\kappa_j) > 0$, only if the expected return per unit of time, $p(\kappa_j) \cdot E[V(\kappa_j + 1)]$, is at least as large as the cost, $Z(\kappa_j)$. Moreover, if there is free entry into the research business, as we assume, the net expected return per unit of time must be zero, that is,

$$p(\kappa_j) \cdot E[V(\kappa_j + 1)] - Z(\kappa_j) = 0 \tag{7.21}$$

If we substitute for $p(\kappa_j)$ from equation (7.20), the condition becomes

$$Z(\kappa_j) \cdot \{\phi(\kappa_j) \cdot E[V(\kappa_j + 1)] - 1\} = 0 \tag{7.22}$$

Since we are considering a sector in which R&D outlays are positive, $Z(\kappa_j) > 0$, the term inside the large brackets in equation (7.22) must be zero:

$$\phi(\kappa_j) \cdot E[V(\kappa_j + 1)] - 1 = 0 \tag{7.23}$$

Hence, after substitution for $E[V(\kappa_j + 1)]$ from equation (7.19), the free-entry condition becomes

$$r + p(\kappa_j + 1) = \phi(\kappa_j) \cdot \bar{\pi} \cdot q^{(\kappa_j+1)\cdot\alpha/(1-\alpha)} \tag{7.24}$$

7. We have to assume that research projects are carried out by syndicates that are large enough to diversify the risk. The syndicates cannot be so large, however, that they would internalize the distortions that are present in the model.

The rest of the analysis depends on the form of the function $\phi(\kappa_j)$, that is, on how the probability of success in equation (7.20) varies with the quality-ladder position.

The simplest specification for $\phi(\kappa_j)$ is one in which successes become more difficult exactly in relation to the output that would be produced at the newly attained ladder position, $\kappa_j + 1$. That is,

$$\phi(\kappa_j) = (1/\zeta) \cdot q^{-(\kappa_j+1)\cdot\alpha/(1-\alpha)} \tag{7.25}$$

where $\zeta > 0$ is a parameter that represents the cost of doing research. Equation (7.25) implies that the cost of R&D rises in proportion (and, hence, the probability of success falls in proportion) to the prospective output level, which is proportional to the term $q^{(\kappa_j+1)\cdot\alpha/(1-\alpha)}$. If we substitute for $\phi(\kappa_j)$ from equation (7.25) into equation (7.24), we get

$$r + p(\kappa_j + 1) = \frac{\bar{\pi}}{\zeta} \tag{7.26}$$

Equation (7.26) implies that the probability of research success per unit of time is the same in each sector, independent of the quality-ladder position, and is given by

$$p = \frac{\bar{\pi}}{\zeta} - r \tag{7.27}$$

If r is constant over time, p is also constant.

The amount of resources devoted to R&D in sector j follows from equations (7.20), (7.25), and (7.27) as

$$Z(\kappa_j) = q^{(\kappa_j+1)\cdot\alpha/(1-\alpha)} \cdot (\bar{\pi} - r\zeta) \tag{7.28}$$

Hence, more advanced sectors—with higher κ_j—have more R&D effort devoted to them. The probability of success is, however, the same for all sectors, because equations (7.20) and (7.25) imply that $p(\kappa_j)$ depends on $Z(\kappa_j)$ divided by $q^{(\kappa_j+1)\cdot\alpha/(1-\alpha)}$.

The aggregate of R&D spending, denoted by Z, is given from equation (7.28) by

$$Z \equiv \sum_{j=1}^{N} Z(\kappa_j) = q^{\alpha/(1-\alpha)} Q \cdot (\bar{\pi} - r\zeta) \tag{7.29}$$

where Q is the aggregate quality index, as defined in equation (7.15). Hence, Z is proportional to Q for given r.

The results are different if we change equation (7.25) to make a different assumption about how $\phi(\kappa_j)$ relates to κ_j. One possibility is that, instead of falling with κ_j as $q^{-(\kappa_j+1)\cdot\alpha/(1-\alpha)}$, $\phi(\kappa_j)$ is less sensitive to κ_j. This case can be illustrated by assuming that $\phi(\kappa_j) = 1/\zeta$, a constant. The free-entry condition in equation (7.24) then implies (for any sector in which $Z[\kappa_j] > 0$) that $p(\kappa_j + 1)$ is an increasing function of κ_j. In this case, more advanced sectors will have higher expected growth rates than less advanced sectors. This result will ultimately determine a rising growth rate for the overall economy.

Alternatively, we might have assumed that $\phi(\kappa_j)$ was more negatively related to κ_j than the function $q^{-(\kappa_j+1)\cdot\alpha/(1-\alpha)}$. In this case, the free-entry condition in equation (7.24) implies (for any sector in which $Z[\kappa_j] > 0$) that $p(\kappa_j + 1)$ is a decreasing function of κ_j. This result will lead to a falling growth rate for the overall economy.

The case that we have focused on, where $\phi(\kappa_j)$ is given by equation (7.25), is, therefore, the specification that corresponds to the AK formulations that we have used in chapter 6 and elsewhere. With this specification, the expected growth rate of each sector will be the same, and the growth rate of the overall economy will end up being constant. Our subsequent analysis focuses on this case.

7.2.3 Consumers

To close the model, we include the consumption-smoothing households that we have used throughout the book (as described in chapter 2). The key equation is for consumption growth:

$$\dot{C}/C = (1/\theta) \cdot (r - \rho) \tag{7.30}$$

where C is aggregate consumption. (This equation holds because L is constant.)

The resource constraint for the economy says that aggregate output equals aggregate consumption, C, plus total resources expended on intermediates, X, plus total expenditure on R&D, Z, that is,

$$Y = C + X + Z \tag{7.31}$$

Equations (7.16), (7.17), and (7.29), imply that Y, X, and Z are linear functions of Q. It follows that C, too, is a linear function of Q. Therefore, the growth rates of all of these quantities will equal the growth rate of Q:

$$\dot{C}/C = \dot{X}/X = \dot{Z}/Z = \dot{Y}/Y = \dot{Q}/Q = \gamma$$

We could substitute the interest rate from equation (7.27) into the formula for the growth rate of consumption from equation (7.30) to find that the growth rate is given by

$$\gamma = \dot{C}/C = (1/\theta) \cdot \left(\frac{\bar{\pi}}{\zeta} - p - \rho\right)$$

However, this expression does not provide the final solution to the model because the probability of R&D success, p, is endogenous. To get the final solution for growth, we have to explain the behavior of the quality index, Q.

7.2.4 Behavior of the Aggregate Quality Index and Endogenous Growth

Recall the definition of Q from equation (7.15):

$$Q \equiv \sum_{j=1}^{N} q^{\kappa_j \alpha/(1-\alpha)}$$

In sector j, the term $q^{\kappa_j \alpha/(1-\alpha)}$ does not change if no innovation occurs but rises to $q^{(\kappa_j+1)\cdot\alpha/(1-\alpha)}$ in the case of a research success. The probability per unit of time of a success is the value p shown in equation (7.27). Since p is the same for all sectors, the expected change in Q per unit of time is given by

$$\begin{aligned} E(\Delta Q) &= \sum_{j=1}^{N} p \cdot \left[q^{(\kappa_j+1)\cdot\alpha/(1-\alpha)} - q^{\kappa_j \alpha/(1-\alpha)}\right] \\ &= p \cdot \left[q^{\alpha/(1-\alpha)} - 1\right] \cdot \sum_{j=1}^{N} q^{\kappa_j \alpha/(1-\alpha)} = p \cdot \left[q^{\alpha/(1-\alpha)} - 1\right] \cdot Q \end{aligned} \tag{7.32}$$

The expected proportionate change in Q per unit of time is, therefore, given by

$$E\left(\frac{\Delta Q}{Q}\right) = p \cdot \left[q^{\alpha/(1-\alpha)} - 1\right] \tag{7.33}$$

If the number of sectors, N, is large, the law of large numbers implies that the average growth rate of Q measured over any finite interval of time will be close to the expression shown on the right-hand side of equation (7.33). We assume, in particular, that N is large enough to treat Q as differentiable, with $\dot{Q}/Q$ nonstochastic and equal to the right-hand side of equation (7.33). If we substitute for p from equation (7.27), we get the growth rate of Q:

$$\dot{Q}/Q = \left(\frac{\bar{\pi}}{\zeta} - r\right) \cdot \left[q^{\alpha/(1-\alpha)} - 1\right] \tag{7.34}$$

Equation (7.34) shows that the growth rate of Q is a negative function of the interest rate, r. The intercept is $(\bar{\pi}/\zeta) \cdot [q^{\alpha/(1-\alpha)} - 1]$, and the slope is $-[q^{\alpha/(1-\alpha)} - 1]$. This function is

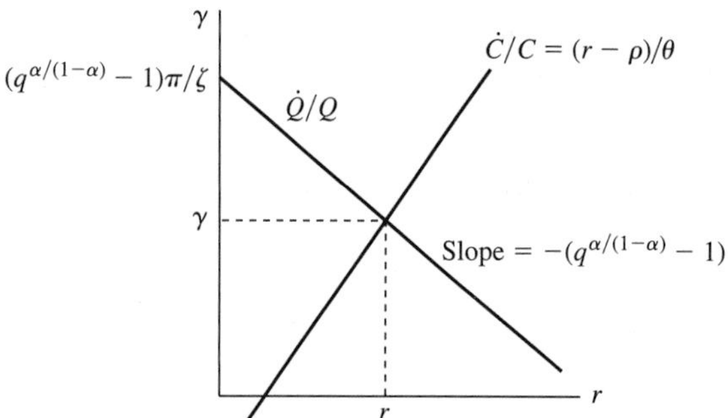

Figure 7.3
Determination of the interest and growth rates. The interest rate and the growth rate of the model are determined by the intersection of the $\dot{Q}/Q$ and $\dot{C}/C$ schedules. Equation (7.34) shows that the growth rate of Q is a negative function of the interest rate, r. The intercept is $(\bar{\pi}/\zeta) \cdot [q^{\alpha/(1-\alpha)} - 1]$, and the slope is $-[q^{\alpha/(1-\alpha)} - 1]$. The formula for consumption growth in equation (7.30) provides a positive relation between the growth rate and r.

displayed in figure 7.3. As mentioned before, C and Q grow at the same, constant rate, which we denoted by γ. The formula for consumption growth in equation (7.30) therefore provides another relation between the growth rate and r. The intersection of these two lines defines the equilibrium where $\dot{Q}/Q = \dot{C}/C$.

Equation (7.11) shows that the basic profit flow, $\bar{\pi}$, rises if the production function parameter A rises or the size of the population, L, increases. These changes shift the $\dot{Q}/Q$ line upward in a parallel fashion. Therefore, the growth rate of the economy rises. A reduction in ζ, which is the parameter that governs the cost of R&D, has the same kind of effect. An increase in q (the step size between innovations) has two effects: the intercept of the $\dot{Q}/Q$ schedule increases, but the slope becomes more negative. However, it is clear from equation (7.34) that a rise in q raises the growth rate for a given value of r, as long as $(\frac{\bar{\pi}}{\zeta} - r) > 0$, which must hold in an equilibrium with positive growth. Therefore, the net effect from an increase in q is to raise the growth rate.

Algebraically, we can substitute from equation (7.30) into equation (7.34) to get

$$r = \frac{\rho + \theta \cdot \left[q^{\alpha/(1-\alpha)} - 1\right] \cdot (\bar{\pi}/\zeta)}{1 + \theta \cdot \left[q^{\alpha/(1-\alpha)} - 1\right]} \tag{7.35}$$

$$\gamma = \frac{\left[q^{\alpha/(1-\alpha)} - 1\right] \cdot [(\bar{\pi}/\zeta) - \rho]}{1 + \theta \cdot \left[q^{\alpha/(1-\alpha)} - 1\right]} \tag{7.36}$$

where $\bar{\pi} = A^{1/(1-\alpha)} \cdot \left(\frac{1-\alpha}{\alpha}\right) \cdot \alpha^{2/(1-\alpha)} L$. We assume that the parameters are such that γ is positive (so that the free-entry condition in equation [7.26] holds with equality), and $r > \gamma$

applies (to satisfy the transversality condition).[8] Equation (7.33) implies that the equilibrium value of p is the expression for γ in equation (7.36) divided by $[q^{\alpha/(1-\alpha)} - 1]$:

$$p = \frac{(\bar{\pi}/\zeta) - \rho}{1 + \theta \cdot \left[q^{\alpha/(1-\alpha)} - 1\right]} \tag{7.37}$$

The results are like those from the varieties model of chapter 6 in that no transitional dynamics exists.[9] The single state variable is now the aggregate quality index, Q. Given an initial value, $Q(0)$, the variables Q, Y, X, Z, and C all grow at the constant rate γ shown in equation (7.36). The interest rate, r, is the constant value shown in equation (7.35).

The realized growth in each sector depends on the random outcomes of research efforts. In particular, the relative quality positions of the sectors and, hence, the relative amounts spent on intermediate goods and R&D evolve in a random fashion. At a point in time, the realized quality positions across the sectors will, therefore, exhibit an irregular pattern, as suggested by figure 7.2.

Notice that, as we showed graphically, the algebra implies that the growth rate is a decreasing function of the parameters of the utility function (ρ and θ) and of the cost of research, represented by the parameter ζ. The growth rate is an increasing function of $\bar{\pi}$ and q.[10]

7.2.5 Scale Effects Again

The growth rate increases with the size of the population, L, because the basic profit flow, $\bar{\pi}$, rises with L in equation (7.11). A similar scale effect emerged in chapter 6, and we discussed there how this effect could be eliminated if the economy's scale also affected the cost of R&D in a particular way.

In the present model, the key relation is the one for the probability of research success in equation (7.20):

$$p(\kappa_j) = Z(\kappa_j) \cdot \phi(\kappa_j)$$

We focused on a specification for $\phi(\kappa_j)$ in equation (7.25) in which successes became more difficult in relation to the output that would be produced at the newly attained ladder

8. Equations (7.35) and (7.36) imply that the condition for $r > \gamma$ is $\rho > (1 - \theta) \cdot [1 - q^{-\alpha/(1-\alpha)}] \cdot (\bar{\pi}/\zeta)$. The condition for $\gamma > 0$ in equation (7.36) is $\rho < \bar{\pi}/\zeta$.

9. We have shown here and in the appendix only that an equilibrium exists with no transitional dynamics. A proof that no other equilibria are possible can be constructed from the transversality condition, along the lines followed in chapter 4.

10. If the cost of research is specified as an increasing function of q, we can use the model to determine q.

position, $\kappa_j + 1$, that is,

$$\phi(\kappa_j) = (1/\zeta) \cdot q^{-(\kappa_j+1)\cdot\alpha/(1-\alpha)}$$

This specification means that research successes are more difficult in more advanced sectors, where the innovations contribute more to output. However, changes in the economy-wide scale of output were assumed not to affect $\phi(\kappa_j)$ and, hence, $p(\kappa_j)$.

An alternative assumption is that $\phi(\kappa_j)$ varies inversely with the absolute level of output attributable to intermediate j when the next quality level, $\kappa_j + 1$, is attained. This output level is given from equation (7.14) by

$$Y(\kappa_j + 1) = A^{1/(1-\alpha)}\alpha^{2\alpha/(1-\alpha)}L \cdot q^{(\kappa_j+1)\cdot\alpha/(1-\alpha)}$$

Hence, instead of equation (7.25), we could assume

$$\phi(\kappa_j) = \frac{1}{\zeta \cdot Y(\kappa_j + 1)} = \frac{1}{\zeta A^{1/(1-\alpha)}\alpha^{2\alpha/(1-\alpha)}L \cdot q^{(\kappa_j+1)\cdot\alpha/(1-\alpha)}} \tag{7.38}$$

where $\zeta > 0$ is again a parameter that measures the cost of research. The new element, relative to equation (7.25), is the inverse relation between $\phi(\kappa_j)$ and the term $A^{1/(1-\alpha)}\alpha^{2\alpha/(1-\alpha)}L$.

If we follow the same steps as before to solve the model, we end up with a new expression for the growth rate:

$$\gamma = \frac{\left[q^{\alpha/(1-\alpha)} - 1\right] \cdot \{[\alpha \cdot (1-\alpha)/\zeta] - \rho\}}{1 + \theta \cdot \left[q^{\alpha/(1-\alpha)} - 1\right]} \tag{7.39}$$

This expression is independent of scale, as represented by L. The quantity L does not influence growth because the probability of research success, $p(\kappa_j)$, depends through equations (7.20) and (7.38) on R&D expenditure in sector j, $Z(\kappa_j)$, expressed *relative* to the size of the sector, as measured by its prospective contribution to output, $Y(\kappa_j + 1)$. Since L ends up affecting $Z(\kappa_j)$ and $Y(\kappa_j + 1)$ in the same proportion, the probability p ends up independent of L. Since the growth rate is determined by p in equation (7.33), the solution for γ in equation (7.39) does not involve L. By similar reasoning, γ is independent of the level of the production technology, as represented by the parameter A in equation (7.1).

These results are similar to those in section 6.1.7 for the case in which the cost of inventing a new variety of product rose with the ratio of output to the number of intermediates, Y/N. Some models in the literature, including Young (1998), Aghion and Howitt (1998, chapter 12), and Dinopoulos and Thompson (1998), eliminate scale effects in basically similar ways. These models assume, in one way or another, that an increase in scale effectively dilutes the effect of research outlays, $Z(\kappa_j)$, on the probability of success, $p(\kappa_j)$.

7.3 Innovation by the Leader

7.3.1 Interactions Between the Leader and the Outsiders

Thus far we have assumed that all R&D effort is carried out by outsiders. Suppose now that we also allow for R&D by the sector leader. Let $Z^o(\kappa_j)$ be the total R&D expenditure by outsiders and $Z^\ell(\kappa_j)$ the amount expended by the leader, so that $Z(\kappa_j) = Z^o(\kappa_j) + Z^\ell(\kappa_j)$. If the outsiders and the leader are equally good at conducting research (which we assume, for now), the probabilities of R&D success per unit of time for the outsiders and the leader are given, respectively, by

$$\begin{aligned} p^o(\kappa_j) &= Z^o(\kappa_j) \cdot \phi(\kappa_j) \\ p^\ell(\kappa_j) &= Z^\ell(\kappa_j) \cdot \phi(\kappa_j) \end{aligned} \tag{7.40}$$

The total probability of an R&D success per unit of time is $p(\kappa_j) = p^o(\kappa_j) + p^\ell(\kappa_j)$.

The net return from R&D for outsiders is

$$p^o(\kappa_j) \cdot E[V(\kappa_j + 1)] - Z^o(\kappa_j) = Z^o(\kappa_j) \cdot \{\phi(\kappa_j) \cdot E[V(\kappa_j + 1)] - 1\} \tag{7.41}$$

The net return for the leader is

$$\begin{aligned} & p^\ell(\kappa_j) \cdot E[V(\kappa_j + 1)] - Z^\ell(\kappa_j) - p(\kappa_j) \cdot E[V(\kappa_j)] \\ & \quad = Z^\ell(\kappa_j) \cdot \{\phi(\kappa_j) \cdot E[V(\kappa_j + 1)] - 1\} - Z(\kappa_j) \cdot \phi(\kappa_j) \cdot E[V(\kappa_j)] \end{aligned} \tag{7.42}$$

Note that an R&D success by the outsiders or the leader results in the leader's loss of the existing present value, $EV(\kappa_j)$.

If outsiders are carrying out any research, so that $Z^o(\kappa_j) > 0$, the free-entry condition from equation (7.23) must hold. This condition implies that the net return from R&D for outsiders shown in equation (7.41) must be zero. But this condition implies that the first term in the expression for the leader's net return in equation (7.42) is also zero. Hence, the leader's net return associated with R&D is negative if $Z(\kappa_j) > 0$. More importantly, if the leader takes the outsiders' R&D outlays, $Z^o(\kappa_j)$, as given, an increase in the leader's R&D effort, $Z^\ell(\kappa_j)$, raises the total R&D effort, $Z(\kappa_j)$, and, therefore, lowers the leader's net return from R&D. Hence, if the outsiders are undertaking a given, positive amount of R&D, the leader's best response is to set $Z^\ell(\kappa_j) = 0$. This result shows that the equilibrium worked out before—where the leader was assumed to do no research—is a Cournot–Nash equilibrium.[11]

11. See Aghion and Howitt (1992) for this argument.

These results predict a continual leapfrogging of leadership positions within an industry. The incumbent is replaced at the time of the next quality improvement by an outside competitor, who is subsequently replaced by another outsider, and so on. These predictions conflict with patterns in the real world, where most improvements in the quality of existing products seem to be made by industry leaders. Therefore, it is important to see whether modifications of the model can make the model more realistic in this respect.

In a Cournot–Nash equilibrium, the leader takes as given the research effort of outsiders, $Z^o(\kappa_j)$, and each outsider takes as given the research efforts of other outsiders and of the leader, $Z^\ell(\kappa_j)$ (which happened to be nil in equilibrium). Since the leader is entrenched in production and can make various types of visible investments, it may not be reasonable to maintain the Cournot–Nash assumption, whereby the leader takes as given the actions of the outsiders. Rather, it may be more reasonable to make the Stackelberg assumption, whereby the leader can move first and effectively commit to a specified level of R&D outlay, $Z^\ell(\kappa_j)$. In this case, outsiders would choose $Z^o(\kappa_j)$ for given $Z^\ell(\kappa_j)$, but the leader would select $Z^\ell(\kappa_j)$ taking account of the implied reaction function for $Z^o(\kappa_j)$.

The determination of $Z^o(\kappa_j)$ for given $Z^\ell(\kappa_j)$ is equivalent to the analysis that we already carried out. The free-entry condition has to hold (if $Z^o(\kappa_j) > 0$), so that the net return from outsiders' R&D in equation (7.41) is zero. Moreover, the overall probability of research success, $p(\kappa_j)$, and the corresponding total of R&D outlay, $Z(\kappa_j)$, are determined as before.[12] Therefore, when choosing $Z^\ell(\kappa_j)$ to maximize the net return shown in equation (7.42), the leader takes as given the term farthest to the right (because $Z[\kappa_j]$ is given). The free-entry condition for outsiders also implies that the first term on the right-hand side of equation (7.42) is zero. Therefore, as long as $Z^o(\kappa_j) > 0$, the leader is now indifferent about his choice of $Z^\ell(\kappa_j)$. Hence, there is an indeterminacy about how the total of research is divided between the leader and the outsiders. However, a sufficiently high value of $Z^\ell(\kappa_j)$ would cause $Z^o(\kappa_j)$ to fall to zero. Beyond that point, the leader's net return would fall with further increases in $Z^\ell(\kappa_j)$. Hence, the leader would not go beyond this value of $Z^\ell(\kappa_j)$. Note that, in this solution, the leader does all the research, but the equilibrium values of $Z(\kappa_j)$ and $p(\kappa_j)$ are determined just as they were in the previous model. That is, the potential for outsider R&D defines the equilibrium.

The indeterminacy of the research allocation disappears if we modify the model to allow the industry leader to have a cost advantage in research. This modification seems reasonable because the leader would typically have the best information about the current technology

12. This conclusion follows readily from the first-order conditions for outsiders' choices of $Z^o(\kappa_j)$ if $p(\kappa_j)$ is a concave, rather than linear, function of $Z(\kappa_j)$.

and may also possess other advantages that lower the cost of R&D.[13] Moreover, if agents have different costs of carrying out research, the one with the lowest cost will tend to become the industry leader.

To analyze this situation, replace the term $\phi(\kappa_j)$ in the two probability functions of equation (7.40) by $\phi^o(\kappa_j)$ and $\phi^\ell(\kappa_j)$, respectively, where $\phi^o(\kappa_j) < \phi^\ell(\kappa_j)$. If outsiders are still conducting research, so that $Z^o(\kappa_j) > 0$, the free-entry condition follows from a modification of equation (7.41) as[14]

$$Z^o(\kappa_j) \cdot \{\phi^o(\kappa_j) \cdot E[V(\kappa_j + 1)] - 1\} = 0 \tag{7.43}$$

The leader's net return is now given from a modification of equation (7.42) by

$$Z^\ell(\kappa_j) \cdot \{\phi^\ell(\kappa_j) \cdot E[V(\kappa_j + 1)] - 1\} - p(\kappa_j) \cdot E[V(\kappa_j)] \tag{7.44}$$

The behavior of outsiders will still fix the value of $p(\kappa_j)$ on the right-hand side. However, the free-entry condition in equation (7.43), together with the condition $\phi^o(\kappa_j) < \phi^\ell(\kappa_j)$, implies that the term multiplying $Z^\ell(\kappa_j)$ is positive, rather than zero. Therefore, the leader is now motivated to raise $Z^\ell(\kappa_j)$ at least until outsiders are driven out of the research business. That is, it is now unambiguous that the leader would carry out all the research.[15]

Suppose now that the leader chooses the level of $Z^\ell(\kappa_j)$ that is just high enough to deter research by the outsiders. At that point, a further increase in $Z^\ell(\kappa_j)$ would raise $Z(\kappa_j)$ one-for-one and, thereby, raise $p(\kappa_j)$ on the right-hand side of equation (7.44). If the leader's cost advantage is small, the net effect on the leader's return would still be negative. Hence, the leader would not be motivated to select a higher value of $Z^\ell(\kappa_j)$. Thus, although the leader unambiguously carries out all the research, the probability of research success, $p(\kappa_j)$, is still determined by the potential for the outside competition.

If the leader's cost advantage in research is large enough, he would want to expand $Z^\ell(\kappa_j)$ beyond the point at which outsiders were driven out of the research business. In this case, the leader effectively acts as an R&D monopolist and determines the probability of research

13. Current technological leaders—companies or countries—are less likely to have a cost advantage for the discovery of entirely new products, as considered in chapter 6. See Brezis, Krugman, and Tsiddon (1993) for this argument.

14. The assumption here is that, once an outsider obtains an R&D success, he becomes just like the previous insider with respect to the costs of doing R&D. Therefore, $E[V(\kappa_{j+1})]$ is the same for everyone.

15. We could get an equilibrium in which multiple agents carry out research if we drop the assumption that the probability of research success depends only on the aggregate of R&D outlays, $Z(\kappa_j)$. If individual probabilities of success, $p_i(\kappa_j)$, depend through a concave function on individual R&D spending, $Z_i(\kappa_j)$, outsiders and the leader would tend to participate simultaneously in the research business.

success without regard to the potential outside competition.[16] The next section considers this case.

7.3.2 The Leader as a Monopoly Researcher

We assume now that the leader's cost advantage in research is sufficient for him to ignore the potential competition from outsiders. Suppose that the probability of research success is again determined by the forms of equations (7.20) and (7.25):

$$p(\kappa_j) = \frac{Z(\kappa_j)}{\zeta_\ell \cdot q^{(\kappa_j+1)\cdot\alpha/(1-\alpha)}} \tag{7.45}$$

where ζ_ℓ is the R&D cost parameter for the leader. For convenience, we omit the ℓ superscripts for p and Z. We now have to compute the leader's expected present value of net revenues, $E[V(\kappa_j)]$.

The flow of monopoly profit when the leading-edge position is κ_j is still given by equation (7.10):

$$\pi(\kappa_j) = \bar{\pi} \cdot q^{\kappa_j \alpha/(1-\alpha)} \tag{7.46}$$

where $\bar{\pi} = A^{1/(1-\alpha)} \cdot (\frac{1-\alpha}{\alpha}) \cdot \alpha^{2/(1-\alpha)} L$. The calculation of $E[V(\kappa_j)]$ can be broken down into two parts. The first part is the present value of net earnings, $\pi(\kappa_j) - Z(\kappa_j)$, up to the time of the next quality improvement. These earnings accrue, as before, over an interval of random length, $T(\kappa_j)$. The expected present value of this flow has the same form as equation (7.18):

$$E[V(\kappa_j)] \text{ (first part)} = [\pi(\kappa_j) - Z(\kappa_j)]/[r + p(\kappa_j)]$$

The second part of the expectation covers the period after the time of the next quality improvement, $T(\kappa_j)$. The expected present value starting from that date is $E[V(\kappa_j + 1)]$, discounted by the factor $\exp[-r \cdot T(\kappa_j)]$. The appendix (section 7.6.4) shows that the

16. The critical value of the differential in research parameters can be found by setting the derivative of equation (7.44) with respect to $Z^\ell(\kappa_j)$ to zero. In this computation, $Z^o(\kappa_j) = 0$ and $dp(\kappa_j)/dZ^\ell(\kappa_j) = \phi^\ell(\kappa_j)$ apply. The values of $E[V(\kappa_j + 1)]$ and $E[V(\kappa_j)]$ are the ones determined by the free-entry condition for outsiders and are given by $E[V(\kappa_j + 1)] = 1/\phi^o(\kappa_j)$ and $E[V(\kappa_j)] = q^{-\alpha/(1-\alpha)}/\phi^o(\kappa_j)$. Putting these elements together, we find that the critical value of $\phi^\ell(\kappa_j)$ is given by

$$\phi^\ell(\kappa_j) = \frac{\phi^o(\kappa_j)}{1 - q^{-\alpha/(1-\alpha)}}$$

If $\phi^\ell(\kappa_j)$ is at least as large as this value, the leader ignores the competition and acts as a monopolist in the determination of R&D effort.

expectation of this second part is

$$E[V(\kappa_j)] \text{ (second part)} = p(\kappa_j) \cdot E[V(\kappa_j + 1)]/[r + p(\kappa_j)]$$

If we combine the two parts, we get

$$E[V(\kappa_j)] = \frac{\pi(\kappa_j) - Z(\kappa_j) + p(\kappa_j) \cdot E[V(\kappa_j + 1)]}{r + p(\kappa_j)} \tag{7.47}$$

The expression $E[V(\kappa_j)]$ will be the market value of a firm that is currently at quality level κ_j and has monopoly power over future innovative activity in sector j.

We can gain economic intuition for the last expression by rewriting it as

$$r = \frac{\pi(\kappa_j) - Z(\kappa_j) + p(\kappa_j) \cdot \{E[V(\kappa_j + 1)] - E[V(\kappa_j)]\}}{E[V(\kappa_j)]} \tag{7.48}$$

Equation (7.48) is a familiar arbitrage condition. It says that the rate of return on bonds, r, equals the rate of return to ownership of the sector leading firm. The first part of the return to firm ownership is the profit net of R&D spending, $\pi(\kappa_j) - Z(\kappa_j)$. The second part is the product of the success probability, $p(\kappa_j)$, and the capital gain that results from success, $E[V(\kappa_j + 1)] - E[V(\kappa_j)]$. The rate of return to firm ownership is the sum of these two parts divided by the current value of the firm, $E[V(\kappa_j)]$.

We can use equation (7.45) to substitute out for $Z(\kappa_j)$ in equation (7.47). The result is

$$E[V(\kappa_j)] = \frac{\pi(\kappa_j) - p(\kappa_j) \cdot \zeta_\ell \cdot q^{(\kappa_j+1)\cdot\alpha/(1-\alpha)} + p(\kappa_j) \cdot E[V(\kappa_j + 1)]}{r + p(\kappa_j)}$$

Thus $E[V(\kappa_j)]$ depends on $p(\kappa_j)$ and some other terms, including $E[V(\kappa_j + 1)]$, that are independent of $p(\kappa_j)$. Since there is no "entry" in this model, we cannot use the free-entry condition as we did before. In a way, however, the monopolist decides his own "entry" optimally by choosing $p(\kappa_j)$ (by selecting the R&D effort, $Z[\kappa_j]$) to maximize $E[V(\kappa_j)]$. If we set the derivative of $E[V(\kappa_j)]$ with respect to $p(\kappa_j)$ to zero to get the first-order condition, the result can be written as

$$\begin{aligned} E[V(\kappa_j + 1)] - E[V(\kappa_j)] &= \zeta_\ell \cdot q^{(\kappa_j+1)\cdot\alpha/(1-\alpha)} \\ &= Z(\kappa_j)/p(\kappa_j) \end{aligned} \tag{7.49}$$

where the last equality uses equation (7.45).

The result in equation (7.49) differs from the one in equation (7.21) in two respects. First, $Z(\kappa_j)/p(\kappa_j)$ is now equated to the increment in present value, $E[V(\kappa_j + 1)] - E[V(\kappa_j)]$, rather than to the full present value, $E[V(\kappa_j + 1)]$, because the leader does not value the expropriation of his own monopoly profit. Second, the term $E[V(\kappa_j)]$ is calculated differently from before because it considers the leadership position to be permanent, rather than temporary.

To see this last property, substitute $E[V(\kappa_j + 1)] = E[V(\kappa_j)] + Z(\kappa_j)/p(\kappa_j)$ from equation (7.49) into equation (7.47) to get

$$E[V(\kappa_j)] = \pi(\kappa_j)/r \tag{7.50}$$

The term on the right-hand side is the present value yielded by a (hypothetical) permanent stream of profit of size $\pi(\kappa_j)$. Since the stream is permanent, the discount rate is r, rather than $r + p(\kappa_j)$.

If we substitute from equation (7.50) into equation (7.49) and use equation (7.46) to substitute out for $\pi(\kappa_j)$, we get a condition for r. The resulting value, denoted r_ℓ, is the equilibrium rate of return for an environment in which research in each sector is carried out by the industry leader:[17]

$$r_\ell = \frac{\bar{\pi}}{\zeta_\ell} \cdot \left[1 - q^{-\alpha/(1-\alpha)}\right] \tag{7.51}$$

The corresponding growth rate of Q and the other quantities is given, as usual, from

$$\gamma_\ell = \frac{1}{\theta} \cdot (r_\ell - \rho) \tag{7.52}$$

Recall that the rate of return in the previous model satisfies the condition (from equation [7.27])

$$r = \frac{\bar{\pi}}{\zeta} - p \tag{7.53}$$

where ζ is the R&D cost parameter for outsiders. This expression includes p on the right-hand side, although we could substitute the equilibrium value for p from equation (7.37). The result for r_ℓ in equation (7.51) differs from the solution for r in equation (7.53) in three ways. First, $\zeta_\ell < \zeta$ tends to make $r_\ell > r$. Second, r falls with p in equation (7.53), because the private return to an innovation is temporary. This force tends to make $r_\ell > r$. Finally, equation (7.51) includes the term $[1 - q^{-\alpha/(1-\alpha)}] < 1$, because the leader weighs only the increment in present value from a research success. This term tends to make $r_\ell < r$.

17. If $r < r_\ell$, where r_ℓ is given in equation (7.51), the derivative of $E[V(\kappa_j)]$ with respect to $p(\kappa_j)$ is positive, so that the leader would like to carry out an infinite amount of research. If $r > r_\ell$, the derivative is negative, so that no research is carried out, and the economy does not grow. Therefore, an equilibrium with positive growth requires $r = r_\ell$.

7.4 Pareto Optimality

We can assess the Pareto optimality of the decentralized equilibria by comparing them with the solution to the social planner's problem. The social planner seeks to maximize the usual expression for the representative household's utility,

$$U = \int_0^\infty \left(\frac{c^{1-\theta} - 1}{1-\theta}\right) \cdot e^{-\rho t}\, dt$$

subject to the economy's resource constraint,

$$Y = AL^{1-\alpha} \cdot \sum_{j=1}^{N} (q^{\kappa_j} X_j)^\alpha = C + \sum_{j=1}^{N} [X_j + Z(\kappa_j)] = C + X + Z \tag{7.54}$$

The first part of the equation says that total output depends on the quality levels, κ_j, and the quantities employed, X_j, of the leading-edge intermediates in each sector. The next part of the equation indicates that output can be used for consumption C, intermediates X, and R&D effort Z.

The planner's problem is also constrained by the R&D technology. The probability $p(\kappa_j)$ is assumed again to be given from equation (7.45) by

$$p(\kappa_j) = \frac{Z(\kappa_j)}{\zeta_\ell \cdot q^{(\kappa_j+1)\alpha/(1-\alpha)}}$$

We enter the leader's research cost, ζ_ℓ, which we assume is no larger than the cost for outsiders, because the social planner would assign the research activity to the lowest-cost researcher.

It is convenient first to work out the planner's choice of intermediate quantities (a static problem) and then use the result to write out a simplified Hamiltonian expression. It is straightforward to show that the first-order condition for maximizing U with respect to the choice of X_j implies

$$X_j \text{ (social planner)} = LA^{1/(1-\alpha)}\alpha^{1/(1-\alpha)}q^{\kappa_j\alpha/(1-\alpha)} \tag{7.55}$$

Recall from equation (7.9) that the choice in a decentralized economy is

$$X_j = LA^{1/(1-\alpha)}\alpha^{2/(1-\alpha)}q^{\kappa_j\alpha/(1-\alpha)}$$

The social planner's choice of X_j relates to the decentralized choice in the usual manner: monopoly pricing implies that the privately chosen quantity is smaller than the socially chosen amount (by the multiple $\alpha^{1/(1-\alpha)} < 1$).

Substitution for X_j from equation (7.55) into equation (7.54) gives an expression for aggregate output:

$$Y \text{ (social planner)} = A^{1/(1-\alpha)} \alpha^{\alpha/(1-\alpha)} LQ \tag{7.56}$$

where $Q = \sum_{j=1}^{N} q^{\kappa_j \alpha/(1-\alpha)}$ is the same aggregate quality index that we defined in equation (7.15) for the decentralized economy. In contrast, the level of output for a decentralized economy is given from equation (7.16) by

$$Y = A^{1/(1-\alpha)} \alpha^{2\alpha/(1-\alpha)} LQ$$

Therefore, for given Q, the social planner's level of output exceeds the decentralized value. This result reflects the decentralized economy's failure to achieve static efficiency by choosing a high enough quantity of intermediate goods, X_j, in each sector.

Equation (7.56) implies that the social planner's growth rate of Y equals the growth rate of Q. The expected change in Q per unit of time is given by

$$E(\Delta Q) = \sum_{j=1}^{N} p(\kappa_j) \cdot \left[q^{(\kappa_j+1)\cdot \alpha/(1-\alpha)} - q^{\kappa_j \alpha/(1-\alpha)}\right]$$

Substitution for $p(\kappa_j)$ from equation (7.45) leads to

$$E(\Delta Q) = \frac{Z \cdot \left[1 - q^{-\alpha/(1-\alpha)}\right]}{\zeta_\ell} \tag{7.57}$$

Thus the expected change in Q—and, hence, in Y—depends only on aggregate R&D spending, Z, and not on the manner in which this spending is spread across the sectors. (This result reflects the assumption that the sectoral returns to R&D do not diminish with the current flow of R&D investment.) We again assume that the number of sectors is large enough so that we can treat Q as differentiable; hence, we use equation (7.57) to represent the actual change, $\dot{Q}$, in the quality index.

We can use the results to write the social planner's Hamiltonian expression as

$$J = \left(\frac{c^{1-\theta} - 1}{1-\theta}\right) \cdot e^{-\rho t} + \nu \cdot \left[LA^{1/(1-\alpha)} \cdot \left(\frac{1-\alpha}{\alpha}\right) \cdot \alpha^{1/(1-\alpha)} Q - Z - cL\right] + \mu \cdot \frac{Z \cdot \left[1 - q^{-\alpha/(1-\alpha)}\right]}{\zeta_\ell} \tag{7.58}$$

The Lagrange multiplier ν applies to the resource constraint, $Y = C + X + Z$. This constraint comes from equation (7.54) after substitution for Y from equation (7.56) and X from equation (7.55). The shadow price μ attaches to the expression for $\dot{Q}$ from equation (7.57).

We can now use our familiar methods to derive the dynamic-optimization conditions for the choices of c and Z in equation (7.58). The first-order conditions and the transition equation for Q lead to the social planner's growth rate:

$$\gamma \text{ (social planner)} = (1/\theta) \cdot \left\{ \frac{1}{\zeta_\ell} \cdot LA^{1/(1-\alpha)} \cdot \left(\frac{1-\alpha}{\alpha}\right) \cdot \alpha^{1/(1-\alpha)} \cdot \left[1 - q^{-\alpha/(1-\alpha)}\right] - \rho \right\} \tag{7.59}$$

The implicit social rate of return, which corresponds to the expression in the square brackets that precedes the term $-\rho$, is, therefore,

$$r \text{ (social planner)} = \frac{1}{\zeta_\ell} \cdot LA^{1/(1-\alpha)} \cdot \left(\frac{1-\alpha}{\alpha}\right) \cdot \alpha^{1/(1-\alpha)} \cdot \left[1 - q^{-\alpha/(1-\alpha)}\right] \tag{7.60}$$

The social planner's growth rate and rate of return in equations (7.59) and (7.60) exceed the values γ_ℓ and r_ℓ for the monopolist in equations (7.52) and (7.51). This distortion reflects, as usual, the impact of the monopoly pricing of the intermediate goods. The appropriate subsidy on the purchases of intermediate goods could eliminate this distortion in the manner familiar from chapter 6.

The rate of return r_ℓ prevails in the decentralized economy if industry leaders have a sufficient cost advantage in research (see note 16). Otherwise, the threat of potential competition determines the rate of return to equal the value r shown in equation (7.35). The relation of r to the social rate of return in equation (7.60) is ambiguous. Monopoly pricing tends, as already noted, to make the private rate of return fall short of the social planner's value.[18] The other forces reflect the incompleteness of property rights over research successes under competition. First, r in equation (7.35) is too high from a social perspective because it includes the expropriation of the predecessor's monopoly profit. But, second, r is too low in a social context because it views the benefits from an innovation as temporary. The net effect of these two forces is unambiguous because they are essentially the same, except that they differ in sign and one comes earlier than the other. The extraction of the monopoly profit is the amount taken from one's predecessor. The treatment of an innovation as temporary is equivalent to ignoring the rents that will be taken by one's followers. The terms are the same in magnitude, except for two considerations: the latter term is higher because of growth of the economy at the rate γ, but it is smaller in present value because of discounting at the rate r. The relation $r > \gamma$—the transversality condition—implies that the first term dominates. Hence, the net effect from incomplete property rights is to make r

18. Another effect is that r depends on the outsiders' R&D cost parameter, ζ. If $\zeta > \zeta_\ell$, r also falls below the social rate of return on this account.

excessive. Thus it is possible, with the threat of competition, that the rate of return and growth rate in the decentralized economy would exceed the socially optimal values. Moreover, it is clear in this case that the competitively driven rate of return and growth rate would exceed the values determined by a monopolistic industry leader (that is, $r > r_\ell$ must hold because r_ℓ is always less than the social rate of return). Thus, competition can spur R&D and growth and may do so in an excessive manner.[19]

The distortions associated with research competition could be eliminated if a scheme were implemented—in the spirit of Coase (1960)—effectively to endow industry leaders with property rights over their monopoly profits. This scheme would require innovators to compensate their immediate predecessor for the loss of rental income. An innovator in sector j then raises the cost of innovation to include the required compensation to the current leader but also raises the prospective reward to include the anticipated compensation from the next innovator. The first part of the scheme causes the innovator to count only the net change in the flow of monopoly rentals as a contribution; that is, the incentive to seek the existing rents is eliminated. The second part motivates the innovator to view his or her contribution as lasting forever, rather than just until the next innovation. As usual, however, the successful implementation of this kind of policy becomes problematic in a richer model—for example, in contexts where quality improvements are hard for a policymaker to evaluate.

The internalization just described occurs automatically in the model where leaders have a monopoly position in research. It is for that reason that the monopoly setting generates the social optimum if a subsidy policy is implemented to eliminate the static distortion from monopoly pricing.

7.5 Summary Observations about Growth

The quality improvements studied in this chapter represent ongoing refinements of products and techniques, whereas the expansions of variety considered in the previous chapter describe basic innovations. From a modeling standpoint, one distinction between the two kinds of technological progress is that goods of higher quality are close substitutes for those of lesser quality, so that quality enhancements tend to make the old goods obsolete. In contrast, we assumed that the new varieties were not direct substitutes or complements

19. Aghion et al. (2002) consider the relation between competition and growth in the framework of Aghion, Harris, Howitt, and Vickers (2001). In that setting, multiple firms with different productivity levels can produce simultaneously at a point in time because their outputs are imperfect substitutes. Then R&D investment involves partly an effort to escape competition and partly an effort to catch up. The result is an inverse U-shape relation, where R&D and growth first rise and later decline with the extent of competition.

for the existing types; therefore, innovation did not tend to drive out the old varieties in chapter 6. One consequence of this distinction is that, in a decentralized economy, the R&D effort aimed at quality improvements may be too high because of the incentive to seek the monopoly rents of incumbents.

Another difference in specification is that the costs of quality improvements for industry leaders tend to be smaller than those for outsiders. Hence, we argued that the leaders would tend, in equilibrium, to carry out most or all of the research that underlies the regular process of product refinement. In contrast, insiders are unlikely to have a cost advantage in breakthrough research, basically because there are no insiders for this activity. Therefore, dramatically new innovations are less likely to come from existing industry leaders.

7.6 Appendix

7.6.1 Intermediates of Various Quality Grades

In the text, we assumed that only the best available quality grade, κ_j, of intermediate j would be produced and used. We also assumed that this grade would be priced at the monopoly level. We now reexamine these assumptions.

Suppose that the quality grades available for intermediate j are numbered from $k = 0, \ldots, \kappa_j$. Let X_{ijk} be the quantity used by the ith firm of the jth type of intermediate good of quality rung k. The rung k corresponds to quality q^k, so that $k = 0$ refers to quality 1, $k = 1$ to quality q, and so on. Thus the total quality-adjusted input of type j used by firm i is given by

$$\tilde{X}_{ij} = \sum_{k=0}^{\kappa_j} (q^k X_{ijk}) \tag{7.61}$$

The assumption in equation (7.61) is that the quality grades within a sector are perfect substitutes as inputs to production. The overall input from a sector, $\tilde{X}_{ij}$, is therefore the quality-weighted sum of the amounts used of each grade, $q^k X_{ijk}$.

The researcher responsible for each quality improvement in sector j retains a monopoly right to produce the jth intermediate good at that quality level. In particular, if the quality rungs $k = 1, \ldots, \kappa_j$ have been reached, the kth innovator is the sole source of intermediate goods with the quality level q^k. We know from the text that, if only the leading-edge quality is produced and if the potential providers of the lower quality grades can be ignored, then the intermediate would be priced at the monopoly level, $P = 1/\alpha$.

Suppose now that goods from quality rungs below κ_j are also available for production in sector j. Consider, in particular, the next lowest grade, $\kappa_j - 1$. If the leading-edge producer charges the monopoly price, $1/\alpha$, and if this price is high enough, then the producer of the next lowest grade will be able to make positive profits by producing.

Recall from equation (7.61) that the different quality grades are perfect substitutes but are weighted by their respective grades. Thus each unit of the leading-edge good is equivalent to $q > 1$ units of the next best good. It follows that if the highest grade is priced at P, a good of the next lowest grade could be sold, at most, at the price $(1/q) \cdot P$. A good that is one grade lower could be sold, at most, at the price $(1/q^2) \cdot P$, and so on. If $(1/q) \cdot P$ is less than the unit marginal cost of production, the next best grade (and, moreover, all of the lower quality grades) cannot survive. Thus, if the leading-edge producer prices at the monopoly level, $1/\alpha$, then the next best producer could price at most at $1/(\alpha q)$, the one below that at $1/(\alpha q^2)$, and so on. If $1/(\alpha q)$ is less than one, the next best producer (and all lower quality producers) cannot compete against the leader's monopoly price. Therefore, the condition $\alpha q > 1$ implies that monopoly pricing will prevail. This inequality will hold if q, the spacing between quality improvements, is large enough; the lower grades are then immediately driven out of the market even though the leading good is priced at the monopoly level. In this case, the results that we derived in the text are valid.

If $\alpha q \leq 1$, we can follow Grossman and Helpman (1991, chapter 4) by assuming that the providers of intermediate goods of a given type engage in Bertrand price competition. In this case, the quality leader employs a limit-pricing strategy; that is, the leader sets a price that is sufficiently below the monopoly price so as to make it just barely unprofitable for the next best quality to be produced.[20] This limit price is given by

$$\text{Limit pricing} \Longrightarrow P = q \tag{7.62}$$

If the leader prices at $q - \epsilon$, where ϵ is an arbitrarily small positive amount, the producer of the next best quality can charge, at most, $1 - \epsilon/q$, a price that results in negative profit. The lower quality goods are therefore again driven out of the market. If $\alpha q \leq 1$—the condition for limit pricing to prevail—the limit price, q, is no larger than the monopoly price, $1/\alpha$.

The total quantity produced (of the highest quality) when limit pricing applies is given from equation (7.6) by

$$\text{Limit pricing} \Longrightarrow X_j = LA^{1/(1-\alpha)} \cdot (\alpha/q)^{1/(1-\alpha)} \cdot (q)^{\kappa_j \alpha/(1-\alpha)} \tag{7.63}$$

20. Grossman and Helpman (1991, chapter 4) effectively assume $\alpha = 0$, so that the magnitude of the elasticity of demand is 1, and the monopoly price, $1/\alpha$, would be infinite. Since the inequality $\alpha q \leq 1$ must hold in this situation, monopoly pricing cannot apply in their model.

A comparison with equation (7.9) shows that, if $\alpha q \leq 1$, the quantity produced under limit pricing is at least as large as the amount that would have been produced under monopoly.

The monopoly formulas in equations (7.8) and (7.9) apply if $\alpha q \geq 1$, and the limit-pricing formulas in equations (7.62) and (7.63) hold if $\alpha q \leq 1$. Either way, price is a fixed markup on the marginal cost of production, and only the best available quality of each type of intermediate good is actually produced in each sector and used by final-goods producers. We implicitly assumed in the main discussion that $\alpha q \geq 1$, so that the monopoly formulas in equations (7.8) and (7.9) applied. However, the general nature of the results would be the same if $\alpha q < 1$, so that limit pricing prevailed.[21]

7.6.2 The Duration of a Monopoly Position

To work out a researcher's prize for success, $E[V(\kappa_j)]$, we needed the probability density function for the duration, $T(\kappa_j)$, of the monopoly position. Define $G(\tau)$ to be the cumulative probability density function for $T(\kappa_j)$, that is, the probability that $T(\kappa_j) \leq \tau$. The change in $G(\tau)$ with respect to τ represents the probability per unit of time that the monopoly position ends because of the occurrence of the next innovation at time τ. In order for an innovation to happen at τ, it must not have occurred earlier, an outcome that has probability $1 - G(\tau)$. Then, conditional on a discovery not having happened yet, the probability of one occurring is $p(\kappa_j)$ per unit of time. Hence, the derivative of $G(\tau)$ with respect to τ is

$$G'(\tau) = [1 - G(\tau)] \cdot p(\kappa_j) \tag{7.64}$$

Since $p(\kappa_j)$ is constant over time, we can readily solve the differential equation (7.64). If we use the boundary condition $G(0) = 0$, the result is

$$G(\tau) = 1 - \exp[-p(\kappa_j) \cdot \tau]$$

The probability density function can then be found from differentiation of the cumulative density:

$$g(\tau) = G'(\tau) = p(\kappa_j) \cdot \exp[-p(\kappa_j) \cdot \tau] \tag{7.65}$$

Equation (7.13) shows the present value of profit, $V(\kappa_j)$, as a function of the duration, $T(\kappa_j)$:

$$V(\kappa_j) = \pi(\kappa_j) \cdot \{1 - \exp[-r \cdot T(\kappa_j)]\}/r$$

21. Limit pricing applies, in any case, only if successive innovators are different persons. In the analysis where the industry leader does all the innovating, the limit-pricing results would not be relevant.

where $\pi(\kappa_j)$ is the flow of monopoly profit. Equation (7.65) gives the probability density for $T(\kappa_j)$. The expected present value of profit is, therefore,

$$E[V(\kappa_j)] = [\pi(\kappa_j)/r] \cdot p(\kappa_j) \cdot \int_0^\infty (1 - e^{-r\tau}) \cdot \exp[-p(\kappa_j) \cdot \tau] \cdot d\tau$$

The integral can be evaluated to get

$$E[V(\kappa_j)] = \pi(\kappa_j)/[r + p(\kappa_j)] \tag{7.66}$$

which is the expression given in equation (7.18).

7.6.3 The Market Value of Firms

Wealth in this model corresponds, as in chapter 6, to the market value of firms. Since goods below leading-edge quality are not produced, the only firm with market value in each sector is the one that possesses the rights over the latest (κ_jth) innovation. The market value of this innovation, $E[V(\kappa_j)]$, is given from equation (7.19) by

$$E[V(\kappa_j)] = \bar{\pi} \cdot q^{\kappa_j \alpha/(1-\alpha)}/[r + p(\kappa_j)]$$

If we substitute for $r + p$ from equation (7.26), the formula becomes

$$E[V(\kappa_j)] = \zeta \cdot q^{\kappa_j \alpha/(1-\alpha)} \tag{7.67}$$

Note that the more advanced a sector—the higher κ_j—the greater the market value of the leading-edge firm.

The aggregate market value of firms, denoted by V, is the sum of equation (7.67) over the N sectors:

$$V = \zeta \cdot \sum_{j=1}^{N} q^{\kappa_j \alpha/(1-\alpha)} = \zeta Q \tag{7.68}$$

The total market value of firms is, therefore, a constant multiple of Q.

7.6.4 Research by the Industry Leader

Up to date $T(\kappa_j)$, the industry leader receives the net revenue of $\pi(\kappa_j) - Z(\kappa_j)$. The probability density function for $T(\kappa_j)$ is again given by equation (7.65). Therefore, the expected present value of the net revenue flow up to date $T(\kappa_j)$ corresponds to equation (7.66) with $\pi(\kappa_j)$ replaced by $\pi(\kappa_j) - Z(\kappa_j)$. Hence, as in the text,

$$E[V(\kappa_j)] \text{ (first part)} = [\pi(\kappa_j) - Z(\kappa_j)]/[r + p(\kappa_j)] \tag{7.69}$$

The present value of net revenues from date $T(\kappa_j)$ onward is $\exp[-r \cdot T(\kappa_j)] \cdot E[V(\kappa_j + 1)]$. Using the density function for $T(\kappa_j)$ from equation (7.65), we get

$$E[V(\kappa_j)] \text{ (second part)} = E[V(\kappa_j + 1)] \cdot p(\kappa_j) \cdot \int_0^{\infty} \exp\{-[r + p(\kappa_j)] \cdot \tau\} \cdot d\tau$$

Evaluation of the integral yields the expression in the text:

$$E[V(\kappa_j)] \text{ (second part)} = p(\kappa_j) \cdot E[V(\kappa_j + 1)]/[r + p(\kappa_j)] \tag{7.70}$$

7.7 Problems

7.1 The step size between innovations. Suppose that the cost of research is a function, $Z(q)$, of the step size, q, between innovations. (We continue to assume that q is known with certainty.) Assume that the function $Z(\cdot)$ satisfies $Z' > 0$ and $Z'' > 0$.

a. What value of q will be determined in equilibrium—say, in the model in which the leader's cost advantage in R&D is sufficiently great to neglect the potential research of outsiders?

b. Under what conditions is the previous answer consistent with the assumption that the leader can neglect the potential research by outsiders?

7.2 Monopoly rights in research. Suppose that the government maintains the monopoly position of industry leaders by precluding research by outsiders. Under what conditions will such a policy be welfare enhancing? What problems would arise in practice in the pursuit of this kind of policy?

7.3 The industry leader as the exclusive researcher. Assume that the industry leader's cost parameter for research in quality improvements, ζ_ℓ, is less than that for outsiders, ζ.

a. Under what conditions will the leader carry out all of the research on quality improvements in equilibrium? Would the results be different for breakthrough research, rather than quality refinements?

b. Under what conditions will the equilibrium research intensity on quality improvements be independent of the outsiders' potential to carry out research? Describe the nature of the interaction for the case in which the outsiders' potential research matters for the equilibrium. Is there a sense in which more competition raises the economy's growth rate?

7.4 Alternative relations between the probability of research success and the research intensity. Suppose that the dependence of the probability of research success, $p(\kappa_j)$, on the total R&D effort in sector j, $Z(\kappa_j)$, is modified from equation (7.20) to

$$p(\kappa_j) = [Z(\kappa_j) \cdot \phi(\kappa_j)]^{\epsilon}$$

where $0 < \epsilon < 1$. Each researcher's probability of success per unit of time is $p(\kappa_j)$ multiplied by the researcher's share of the total R&D effort in sector j.

a. What is the free-entry condition for R&D in sector j? How does the condition differ from the one obtained before when $\epsilon = 1$?

b. What new kind of distortion arises if $\epsilon < 1$? (Hint: Consider the analogy of a fishing pond that has free entry and is subject to congestion.)

c. What happens if $\epsilon > 1$?

d. Discuss how equilibrium research intensities in each sector are determined for a setting in which $0 < \epsilon < 1$.

8 The Diffusion of Technology

In the Solow–Swan model of chapter 1, the tendency for convergence across economies derived from the diminishing returns to capital. The higher rate of return on capital in poor economies—or at least in economies that were further below their own steady-state positions—generated a faster rate of per capita growth. We showed in the Ramsey model of chapter 2 how this tendency would be modified by the behavior of the saving rate. The convergence rate was faster or slower depending on whether poor economies tended to save a higher or lower fraction of their incomes. Then we found in chapter 3 that the international mobility of capital among open economies tended to speed up the process of convergence.

In the models developed in chapters 4 and 5, economies could sustain positive per capita growth in the steady state if the returns to a broad concept of capital, which includes human capital, were constant. If the returns to broad capital diminish for awhile, but are roughly constant asymptotically, economies exhibit convergence behavior but also feature endogenous growth in the long run. (We discussed in chapter 1 some specifications that had this character.) We also examined in chapter 5 how imbalances between physical and human capital affected the transitional dynamics. Economies that began with a high ratio of human to physical capital would grow especially fast. Thus the endogenous growth theories that rely on constant long-run returns to broad capital are consistent with a rich transitional dynamics, which can include convergence-type behavior.

In the models of chapters 6 and 7, long-term growth arose if R&D investments—the source of technological progress in these models—exhibited constant returns. We have not yet discussed whether these theories are consistent with the empirical evidence on convergence. In a multieconomy setting, the key issue is how rapidly the discoveries made in leading economies diffuse to follower economies. We shall find in this chapter that the diffusion of technology gives us another reason to predict a pattern of convergence across economies.

In this chapter we study technological diffusion in the context of the model of variety of intermediate products from chapter 6.[1] We would, however, get similar results if we examined the type of quality improvements that we introduced in chapter 7.[2] The main idea is that follower countries tend to catch up to the leaders because imitation and implementation of discoveries are cheaper than innovation. This mechanism tends to generate convergence even if diminishing returns to capital or to R&D do not apply.

We begin with the spread of technology from a leading economy, called country 1, to a follower economy, called country 2. We use the setup from chapter 6 in which the level of

1. The previous theoretical research on technological diffusion that we build on includes Nelson and Phelps (1966), Krugman (1979), Jovanovic and Lach (1991), Grossman and Helpman (1991, chapters 11 and 12), and Segerstrom (1991).

2. For a development along this line, see Connolly (1999).

technology corresponds to the number of varieties of intermediate products that have been discovered by the technological leader. Researchers in country 1 expend effort to invent these products, and they are initially used to produce final goods in country 1. The inventor of a new variety of product in country 1 is the monopolistic provider of this good for use in country 1.

Country 2 does not invent intermediate goods but instead imitates or adapts the products that have been discovered in country 1. The use of one of these products in country 2 requires some effort for adaptation to a different environment. We think of this effort as a cost of imitation. This cost is similar to the R&D outlay considered in chapter 6, except that the cost of imitation is typically less than the cost of invention. The agent who incurs the cost of imitation is assumed to become the monopoly provider of the intermediate good for use in country 2. We assume that imitators pay no fees to foreign inventors; hence, agents in country 1 do not receive any compensation for the use of their innovations in country 2. A later section considers a different setup in which the adaptation of a technology to country 2 involves foreign investment by an agent from country 1.

Final goods produced in the two countries are identical and tradable across borders. However, final-goods producers in country 2 can use a particular variety of intermediate good only if someone has first expended resources to adapt the good to this environment. We assume that there is no global capital market; hence, trade is balanced between the two countries at every point in time. Thus, in effect, the economies are closed except for the transfer of technology through imitation.

Some success stories of economic development involve the absorption of technological expertise from abroad in ways that correspond roughly to our theoretical setup. Young (1989, chapter 6) argues that many entrepreneurs in Hong Kong learned businesses as production workers, serving effectively as apprentices to foreign managers. The locals subsequently used this knowledge to establish their own enterprises. In Singapore entry into several leading-edge industries, such as electronics and financial services, depended on substantial foreign investment and expertise. This foreign involvement was actively encouraged by the Singaporean government (Young, 1992). Foreign investments in China from Hong Kong and in Mexico from the United States have been important in facilitating the flow of knowledge about advanced manufacturing techniques (Romer, 1993). In Mauritius the dramatic growth of garment manufacturing entailed the importation of foreign entrepreneurs, who trained and supervised the local workers. These foreigners, principally from Hong Kong, were attracted by an export processing zone that featured a number of favorable government policies, including low taxes and guaranteed low wages (see Gulhati and Nallari, 1990; Bowman, 1991; and Romer, 1992).

8.1 Behavior of Innovators in the Leading Country

The discussion presented in this section follows Barro and Sala-i-Martin (1997). The model for the innovator in country 1 is the same as that worked out in the first part of chapter 6. We provide a quick summary of the model here. If N_1 intermediate goods have been discovered, the quantity Y_1 of final goods produced by firms in country 1 is given by

$$Y_1 = A_1 L_1^{1-\alpha} \cdot \sum_{j=1}^{N_1} (X_{1j})^{\alpha} \tag{8.1}$$

where $0 < \alpha < 1$, A_1 is a productivity parameter, L_1 is the quantity of labor input, and X_{1j} is the quantity of nondurable input of type j. We assume that population and, hence, the aggregate labor input, L_1, are constant. The parameter A_1 represents the level of the technology in country 1, but it can also represent various aspects of government policy—such as taxation, provision of public services, and maintenance of property rights—that influence productivity in country 1.

The cost of production of each intermediate input, X_{1j}, is unity, and each good is sold, as in chapter 6, at the monopoly price, $P = 1/\alpha > 1$. The equation of the marginal product of X_{1j} to the price determines the quantity of each type used in country 1:

$$X_{1j} = X_1 = (A_1)^{1/(1-\alpha)} \alpha^{2/(1-\alpha)} L_1 \tag{8.2}$$

Substitution from equation (8.2) into equation (8.1) implies that the level of output per worker in country 1 is

$$y_1 \equiv Y_1/L_1 = (A_1)^{1/(1-\alpha)} \alpha^{2\alpha/(1-\alpha)} N_1 \tag{8.3}$$

Hence, output per worker, y_1, increases with the productivity parameter, A_1, and the number of products, N_1. The wage rate, w_1, equals a firm's marginal product of labor and is the multiple $1 - \alpha$ of y_1.

Equation (8.2) implies that the flow of monopoly profit from sales of the jth intermediate good in country 1 is

$$\pi_{1j} = \pi_1 = \left(\frac{1-\alpha}{\alpha}\right) \cdot (A_1)^{1/(1-\alpha)} \alpha^{2/(1-\alpha)} L_1 \tag{8.4}$$

The present discounted value of all future profits is the value of the R&D firm, V_1. The nonarbitrage condition requires that the rate of return to purchasing an R&D firm be the same as the rate of return to bonds. The instantaneous rate of return from buying the firm is the profit rate plus the capital gains that accrue from changes in the value of the firm:

$$r_1 = \frac{\pi_1 + \dot{V}_1}{V_1} \tag{8.5}$$

Equation (8.5) corresponds to equation (6.18) in chapter 6. The cost of inventing a new product in country 1 is a fixed amount of goods, which we denote by η_1. We assume that a positive amount of innovation occurs in the equilibrium in country 1 and, hence, that the equilibrium growth rate is positive. In this case, the free-entry condition equates the value of the firm, V_1, to η_1. Since η_1 is a constant, the value of the firm must be constant over time. Hence, $\dot{V}_1 = 0$ and $r_1 = \pi_1/\eta_1$, so the interest rate in country 1 is constant in equilibrium. Equation (8.4) implies that this interest rate is given by

$$r_1 = \pi_1/\eta_1 = (L_1/\eta_1) \cdot \left(\frac{1-\alpha}{\alpha}\right) \cdot (A_1)^{1/(1-\alpha)} \alpha^{2/(1-\alpha)} \tag{8.6}$$

The usual consumer-optimization condition implies that the growth rate of consumption, C_1, is given by

$$\gamma_1 = \dot{C}_1/C_1 = (1/\theta) \cdot (r_1 - \rho) \tag{8.7}$$

The preference parameters, ρ and θ, are assumed to be the same in all countries. If we substitute for r_1 from equation (8.6), the growth rate is

$$\gamma_1 = (1/\theta) \cdot \left[(L_1/\eta_1) \cdot \left(\frac{1-\alpha}{\alpha}\right) \cdot (A_1)^{1/(1-\alpha)} \cdot \alpha^{2/(1-\alpha)} - \rho\right] \tag{8.8}$$

As in chapter 6, country 1 is always in a steady state with the quantities N_1, Y_1, and C_1 all growing at the constant rate γ_1.

8.2 Behavior of Imitators in the Follower Country

8.2.1 Producers of Final Output

The form of the production function, equation (8.1), is the same in country 2 as in country 1:

$$Y_2 = A_2 L_2^{1-\alpha} \cdot \sum_{j=1}^{N_2} (X_{2j})^{\alpha} \tag{8.9}$$

where N_2 is the number of intermediate products available for use in country 2. Since we think of country 1 as the technological leader and country 2 as the follower, we assume

$N_2(0) < N_1(0)$. We further assume that the N_2 products available in country 2 are a subset of the N_1 goods known in country 1.[3] In the initial setting, country 2 will also not make any new discoveries and will just imitate the intermediate goods known by country 1.

The productivity parameter, A_2, and the aggregate labor input, L_2, may differ from the corresponding parameters for country 1. Differences between A_2 and A_1 could, as already mentioned, reflect differences in government policies. The total labor input represents the scale over which an intermediate good can be utilized in production. Thus the gap between L_2 and L_1 reflects the differences in scale of the two economies. The producers of final output in country 2 choose labor and intermediate inputs so as to maximize profits, taking prices as given. The first-order conditions deliver the usual input demand function for intermediate j as a decreasing function of the price P_{2j}:

$$X_{2j} = L_2 \cdot (A_2 \cdot \alpha)^{1/(1-\alpha)} \cdot (P_{2j})^{-\alpha/(1-\alpha)} \tag{8.10}$$

8.2.2 Imitating Firms

The Cost of Imitation Following the analysis of chapter 6, we assume that the cost of innovation in country 2, η_2, is a constant (which need not equal η_1). This assumption means that discoveries of new types of products do not encounter diminishing returns in either country. As mentioned in chapter 6, this assumption can be rationalized from the idea that the number of potential inventions is unbounded.

The copying and adaptation of one of country 1's intermediates for use in country 2 is assumed to entail a lump-sum outlay, denoted by $\nu_2(t)$. Imitation differs from innovation in that the number of goods that can be copied at a point in time is limited to the finite number that have been discovered elsewhere. Specifically, in the present model, country 2 can select for imitation only from the uncopied subset of the N_1 goods that are known in country 1. As N_2 increases relative to N_1, the cost of imitation is likely to rise. This property would hold, for example, if the products known in country 1 varied in terms of how costly they were to adapt to the environment of country 2. The goods that were easier to imitate would then be copied first, and the cost ν_2 that applied at the margin would increase with the number already imitated. We capture this property here by assuming that ν_2 is an increasing function of N_2/N_1:

$$\nu_2 = \nu_2(N_2/N_1) \tag{8.11}$$

3. We do not explain how country 2 learned to produce its first type of good. The problem is that equation (8.9) implies that country 2 produces nothing if it lacks access to any type of intermediate product. The same difficulty arises for country 1's initial innovation and for the discoveries of products in the model of chapter 6. Given the form of the production function, we have to assume that people always knew how to produce at least one type of intermediate good.

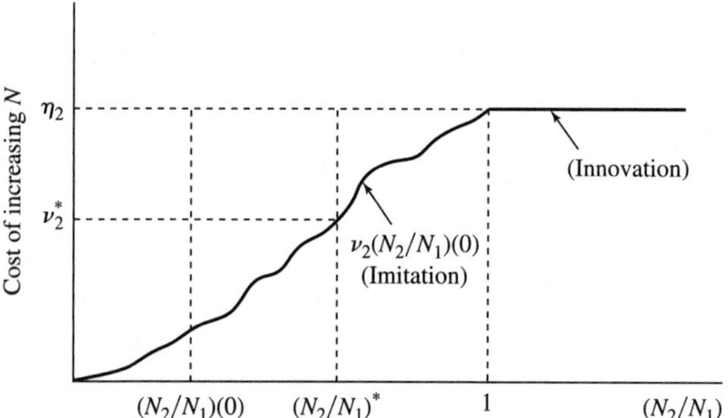

Figure 8.1
Cost of technological change in country 2. The cost of imitation in country 2, ν_2, is an increasing function of N_2/N_1 and is assumed to approach the cost of innovation, η_2, as N_2/N_1 approaches 1. The steady-state value of the imitation cost, ν_2^*, is assumed to be less than η_2.

where $\nu_2' > 0$. We also assume $\nu_2[N_2(0)/N_1(0)] < \eta_2$, so that imitation is initially cheaper than innovation for country 2.

If $N_2/N_1 < 1$, that is, if not all the intermediates of country 1 have been copied by country 2, the imitation cost, ν_2, tends to be less than η_2 because copying is typically cheaper than discovery. But ν_2 can exceed η_2 when $N_2/N_1 < 1$ if the remaining pool of uncopied inventions comprises goods that are difficult to adapt to country 2. In other words, it would be cheaper in some circumstances for a technological follower to start from scratch and invent something new rather than adapt one of the leader's goods. Figure 8.1 shows, however, a simpler case in which $\nu_2(N_2/N_1) < \eta_2$ applies when $N_2/N_1 < 1$. The main results hold if $\nu_2(N_2/N_1) > \eta_2$ applies for a range of values where $N_2/N_1 < 1$. The figure also shows $\nu_2(N_2/N_1)$ approaching η_2 as N_2/N_1 approaches 1. We modify this assumption in a later section.

A crucial assumption in the model is that the costs of imitation are nontrivial; that is, innovations cannot be transferred to other locations at negligible cost. Mansfield, Schwartz, and Wagner (1981, pp. 908–909) studied the cost of imitation in the United States for 48 product innovations that were made in the chemical, drug, electronics, and machinery industries. They found that the cost of imitation averaged 65 percent of the cost of innovation. The ratio of costs varied substantially, however, across the products; only half of the ratios were between 40 percent and 90 percent.

Griliches (1957) found in U.S. regional data that the time at which hybrid corn was introduced and the rate at which this innovation spread depended on measures of the cost of absorption and the eventual profitability of the new technology. The date of introduction tended to be sooner the more similar an area's preferred hybrids were to those developed initially in the corn belt (the location to which most of the early research on hybrid corn was directed). The rate of absorption was faster the greater the market size and the larger the potential improvement in crop yields.

Teece (1977) examined the cost of technology transfer across countries for multinational firms. For 26 cases in chemicals, petroleum refining, and machinery, he found that the cost averaged 19 percent of total project expenditures. He also found that the transfer cost declined with measures of experience with the technology being transferred but did not depend on the level of economic development in the recipient country. In contrast, Nelson and Phelps (1966) conjectured that the cost ν_2 would be lower the more abundant human capital was in the receiving location. In any case, one clear conclusion from the results of Mansfield, Schwartz, and Wagner (1981) and Teece (1977) is that the transfer cost, ν_2, would typically be significant.

Optimal Pricing, Once the Good Has Been Copied If an agent in country 2 pays $\nu_2(t)$ at time t to imitate the jth variety of intermediate good from country 1, we assume that this agent obtains a perpetual monopoly over the use of intermediate j in country 2.[4] Hence, the treatment of imitation in country 2 parallels the setup for innovation in country 1. The imitator of intermediate good j chooses the price P_{2j} to maximize profit subject to the demand function given by equation (8.10). The marginal cost of producing an intermediate input is assumed to be 1, the same as in country 1. The monopoly price of each intermediate in country 2 is a constant markup over marginal cost, $P_{2j} = P_2 = 1/\alpha > 1$, which is the same as that in country 1 and is independent of j. Substitution of the monopoly price into the demand function of equation (8.10) leads to the quantity of intermediates sold:

$$X_{2j} = X_2 = (A_2)^{1/(1-\alpha)}\alpha^{2/(1-\alpha)}L_2 \tag{8.12}$$

Once the amount of each input is known, we can get the formulas for output per worker, y_2, and flow of profit, π_{2j}:

$$y_2 \equiv Y_2/L_2 = (A_2)^{1/(1-\alpha)}\alpha^{2\alpha/(1-\alpha)}N_2 \tag{8.13}$$

$$\pi_{2j} = \pi_2 = \left(\frac{1-\alpha}{\alpha}\right) \cdot (A_2)^{1/(1-\alpha)}\alpha^{2/(1-\alpha)}L_2 \tag{8.14}$$

4. Producers in country 2 are assumed to be unable to circumvent the local monopoly by importing intermediate j from country 1. Even if this good could be purchased from abroad at a price below the monopoly level, the idea is that producers must make the lump-sum outlay ν_2 to learn how to use the good effectively in the context of country 2.

Note that these formulas parallel the expressions for country 1 in equations (8.2)–(8.4). The wage rate, w_2, is the multiple $1-\alpha$ of y_2.

Equations (8.13) and (8.3) imply that the ratio of the per-worker products for the two countries is given by

$$y_2/y_1 = (A_2/A_1)^{1/(1-\alpha)} \cdot (N_2/N_1) \tag{8.15}$$

Thus the ratio depends positively on the relative values of the productivity parameters, A_2/A_1, and on the relative value of the number of known varieties of intermediates, N_2/N_1.

The ratio for the profit flows is given by

$$\pi_2/\pi_1 = (A_2/A_1)^{1/(1-\alpha)} \cdot (L_2/L_1) \tag{8.16}$$

This ratio also increases with A_2/A_1. The positive effect from L_2/L_1 is a scale benefit. The relevant scale variable is the total of complementary factor input, L_i, that the intermediates work with in country i.

The Free-Entry Condition The present value of profits from imitation of intermediate j in country 2 is

$$V_2(t) = \pi_2 \cdot \int_t^\infty e^{-\int_t^s r_2(v)\cdot dv} \cdot ds \tag{8.17}$$

where $r_2(v)$ is the rate of return in country 2 at time t. A gap in rates of return between the two countries, $r_2(v) \neq r_1$, is possible because international lending is ruled out.[5] If there is free entry into the imitation business in country 2 and the equilibrium amount of resources devoted to imitation is nonzero at each point in time, $V_2(t)$ must equal the cost of imitation, $\nu(t)$, at each point in time:

$$V_2(t) = \nu_2(N_2/N_1) \tag{8.18}$$

Substitution of the formula for $V_2(t)$ from equation (8.17) and differentiation of both sides of equation (8.18) with respect to t yields the familiar nonarbitrage condition:

$$r_2 = \frac{\pi_2 + \dot{\nu}_2}{\nu_2} \tag{8.19}$$

Hence, if ν_2 were constant, r_2 would be constant and equal to π_2/ν_2, the ratio of the profit flow to the lump-sum cost of obtaining this profit. This result would parallel the one for r_1 in

5. If international lending were permitted, all current investment would flow to the R&D activity that offered the highest rate of return. Investments in more than one kind of R&D could coexist if the model were modified to include an inverse relation between the rate of return and the quantity of each type of R&D investment.

equation (8.6). However, if ν_2 varies over time, r_2 includes the capital-gain term, $\dot{\nu}_2/\nu_2$. With free entry, the monopoly right over an intermediate good must equal the cost of obtaining it, ν_2. If ν_2 is rising (because N_2/N_1 is increasing in equation [8.18]), the expanding value of the monopoly right implies a capital gain at the rate $\dot{\nu}_2/\nu_2$. This gain adds to the "dividend" term, π_2/ν_2, to get the full rate of return in equation (8.19). This result is analogous to the one in section 6.8, where we allowed the cost of R&D to be a function of the number of goods previously discovered.

8.2.3 Consumers

The model can be closed with the usual Ramsey consumers. Their Euler equation implies that the rate of return, r_2, determines the growth rate of consumption in country 2 in the usual way:

$$\dot{C}_2/C_2 = (1/\theta) \cdot (r_2 - \rho) \tag{8.20}$$

Note the assumption that the preference parameters, ρ and θ, are the same in country 2 as in country 1.

8.2.4 Steady-State Growth

In the steady state, N_2 grows at the same rate, γ_1, as N_1. The ratio N_2/N_1 therefore equals a constant, denoted $(N_2/N_1)^*$. The formula for the imitation cost in equation (8.11) then implies that ν_2 is also constant in the steady state. Assume, for now, that the parameters are such that the follower never catches up completely, so that $0 < (N_2/N_1)^* < 1$. The subsequent analysis relates this inequality to the parameters A_i, L_i, and η_i.

In the steady state, the growth rates of Y_2 and C_2 equal the growth rate of N_2, which equals γ_1. Therefore, the steady-state growth rate of all quantities in country 2, denoted by γ_2^*, equals γ_1.

Since C_2 and C_1 grow in the long run at the same rate, γ_1, and since the preference parameters, ρ and θ, are the same in the two countries, equations (8.6), (8.7), and (8.20) imply that the rates of return in the two countries are the same:

$$r_2^* = r_1 = \pi_1/\eta_1 \tag{8.21}$$

where π_1 is given in equation (8.4). The adjustment of N_2/N_1 to the value $(N_2/N_1)^*$—which ensures $\gamma_2^* = \gamma_1$—implies $r_2^* = r_1$. Thus, in the long run, the process of technological diffusion equalizes the rates of return, even though the two countries do not share a common capital market.

Since $r_2^* = r_1$, equations (8.19) and (8.5) imply

$$\pi_2/\nu_2^* = \pi_1/\eta_1$$

where ν_2^* is the steady-state value of ν_2. (Note that, in the steady state, the capital-gain term, $\dot{\nu}_2/\nu_2$, equals zero because ν_2^* is constant.) The formula for the ratio of profit flows in equation (8.16) therefore implies

$$\nu_2^* = \eta_1 \cdot (\pi_2/\pi_1) = \eta_1 \cdot (A_2/A_1)^{1/(1-\alpha)} \cdot L_2/L_1 \tag{8.22}$$

The assumption, thus far, is that country 2 never chooses to innovate. This behavior is optimal for agents in country 2 if $\nu_2(t) < \eta_2$ applies along the entire path. Since ν_2 is an increasing function of N_2/N_1, the required condition (if N_2/N_1 starts below its steady-state value) is $\nu_2^* < \eta_2$, which implies from equation (8.22)

$$(A_2/A_1)^{1/(1-\alpha)} \cdot (L_2/L_1) \cdot (\eta_1/\eta_2) < 1 \tag{8.23}$$

In other words, country 2 has to be intrinsically inferior to country 1 in terms of the indicated combination of productivity parameters, A_2/A_1, labor endowments, L_2/L_1,[6] and costs of innovating, η_1/η_2. If the inequality in equation (8.23) holds, country 2 never has an incentive to innovate (because $\nu_2[t] < \eta_2$ applies throughout). Moreover, country 1 can never imitate, because there never exists a pool of foreign goods to copy. Thus the equilibrium is the one already described in which country 1 is the perpetual leader and country 2 is the perpetual follower. We discuss in a later section the results when the inequality does not hold.

Since $(N_2/N_1)^* < 1$, equation (8.15) implies that the steady-state ratio of per-worker products, $(y_2/y_1)^*$, is less than one if $A_2 \leq A_1$. (Note that $A_2 > A_1$ can be consistent with the inequality in equation [8.23] if $L_2 < L_1$ or $\eta_2 > \eta_1$.) Thus the follower country's per-worker output is likely to fall short of the leader's value even in the steady state. The potential to imitate does not generally provide a strong enough force to equalize the levels of per-worker product in the long run.

Consumption, C_2, grows in the steady state at the constant rate γ_1. The level of this consumption path can be determined from country 2's budget constraint: C_2 equals output, Y_2 (from equation [8.13]), less the goods devoted to production of intermediates, N_2X_2 (where X_2 is given in equation [8.12]), less the resources expended on imitation. Along the steady-state path, the last amount is $\nu_2^*\dot{N}_2 = \nu_2^*\gamma_1 N_2$, where ν_2^* is given in equation (8.22). The formula for C_2 and the parallel result for C_1 can be manipulated to verify that the steady-state ratio of per capita consumptions, $(c_2/c_1)^*$, equals the steady-state ratio of per-worker products, $(y_2/y_1)^*$. Therefore, if $A_2 \leq A_1$, $(c_2/c_1)^* < 1$; that is, the follower country also tends to lag behind in the long run in terms of per capita consumption.

6. Scale, represented by L_i, is a positive element because the costs of innovating or imitating are assumed to be lump sum, rather than dependent on the extent of economic activity in a country. The results would be different if the costs depended on scale, as in some models considered in chapter 6.

8.2.5 The Dynamic Path and Convergence

The dynamic behavior for country 2 is not as simple as that for country 1. (Remember that the growth rate of country 1 is constant at all points in time.) The reason is that the growth rate of consumption, given by equation (8.20), is a linear function of the rate of return, r_2. Equation (8.19) implies that this rate of return equals $(\pi_2 + \dot{\nu}_2)/\nu_2$, which involves the rate of change of the cost of imitation, ν_2. We know that the profit flow, π_2, is constant. But ν_2 depends on the ratio N_2/N_1. If, along the transition path, the growth rate of N_2 differs from that of N_1, the ratio N_2/N_1 will display transitional dynamics and, therefore, so will the rate of return, r_2, and the growth rate of consumption.

In this section we study the dynamic behavior of country 2 outside the steady state. This behavior can be studied by considering differential equations for the variables C_2 and N_2. (Since Y_2 is proportional to N_2, from equation [8.13], the dynamics of Y_2 are the same as those of N_2.) We know that, in the steady state, N_2 and C_2 grow at a constant rate. Following our analysis from chapter 4, if we want to draw a phase diagram that displays the qualitative behavior of the economy, it will be convenient to work with controllike and statelike variables that remain constant in the steady state. Since N_2 and N_1 grow at the same constant rate, the ratio N_2/N_1 will remain constant in the long run. Hence, we use this ratio as a statelike variable. To simplify notation, define $\hat{N} \equiv N_2/N_1$. We also know that, in the steady state, C_2 and N_2 grow at the same rate; hence, the ratio C_2/N_2 is constant. Thus this ratio is a good controllike variable. We use the letter $\chi_2 \equiv C_2/N_2$ to describe this ratio. Since Y_2 is proportional to N_2 (equation [8.13]), χ_2 is proportional to the consumption-output ratio, C_2/Y_2.

We now describe the dynamic analysis for the variables χ_2 and $\hat{N}$. For tractability, we assume a constant-elasticity form of the cost function from equation (8.11):

$$\nu_2 = \eta_2 \cdot \hat{N}^{\sigma} \tag{8.24}$$

for $\hat{N} < 1$, where $\sigma > 0$. Note that ν_2 approaches η_2 as $\hat{N}$ approaches 1, the property assumed in figure 8.1. Equations (8.22) and (8.24) imply that the steady-state ratio of N_2 to N_1 is given by

$$\hat{N}^* = \left[(A_2/A_1)^{1/(1-\alpha)} \cdot (L_2/L_1) \cdot (\eta_1/\eta_2)\right]^{1/\sigma} \tag{8.25}$$

The parameters are assumed to satisfy the inequality in equation (8.23), so that $\hat{N}^* < 1$, as shown in figure 8.1.

The growth rate of χ_2 is given by

$$\frac{\dot{\chi}_2}{\chi_2} = \frac{\dot{C}_2}{C_2} - \frac{\dot{N}_2}{N_2}$$

We now compute the growth rates of C_2 and N_2.

The growth rate of consumption for country 2 is given by equation (8.20). Substitute the expressions for the rate of return, r_2, from equation (8.19) and the cost of imitation, ν_2, from equation (8.24) to get

$$\frac{\dot{C}_2}{C_2} = (1/\theta) \cdot \left[\pi_2/\nu_2 + \sigma \cdot \frac{\dot{\hat{N}}}{\hat{N}} - \rho \right] \tag{8.26}$$

It follows that, to determine the growth rate of C_2, we have to know the growth rate of $\hat{N}$, which is the the difference between the growth rates of N_2 and N_1:

$$\frac{\dot{\hat{N}}}{\hat{N}} = \frac{\dot{N}_2}{N_2} - \frac{\dot{N}_1}{N_1}$$

The change in N_2 is determined by the budget constraint: $Y_2 = C_2 + N_2 X_2 + \nu_2 \dot{N}_2$. In other words, total output, Y_2 (equation [8.13]), equals total consumption, C_2, plus the resources devoted to the production of intermediates, $N_2 X_2$ (where X_2 is given in equation [8.12] and where the marginal cost of producing one unit of intermediates is one), plus the resources devoted to imitation (which equals the cost per good imitated, ν_2, times the quantity of new products imitated over the next instant, $\dot{N}_2$). Rearranging the resource constraint and using equations (8.13) and (8.12), we get

$$\dot{N}_2 = (1/\nu_2) \cdot [\pi_2 \cdot (1+\alpha)/\alpha \cdot N_2 - C_2] \tag{8.27}$$

We can now divide both sides of the equation by N_2 to compute the growth rate of N_2 and use equation (8.24) for the imitation cost, ν_2, to get

$$\frac{\dot{N}_2}{N_2} = \frac{1}{\eta_2 \cdot \hat{N}^\sigma} \cdot [\pi_2 \cdot (1+\alpha)/\alpha - \chi_2] \tag{8.28}$$

We are now ready to compute the growth rates of $\hat{N}$ and χ_2. Subtract γ_1 from equation (8.28) to get the growth rate of $\hat{N}$:

$$\frac{\dot{\hat{N}}}{\hat{N}} = \frac{1}{\eta_2 \cdot \hat{N}^\sigma} \cdot [\pi_2 \cdot (1+\alpha)/\alpha - \chi_2] - \gamma_1 \tag{8.29}$$

Substitution for $\dot{\hat{N}}/\hat{N}$ from equation (8.29) into equation (8.26) yields an expression for the growth rate of C_2. We can subtract $\dot{N}_2/N_2$ from equation (8.28) to get the growth rate of χ_2:

$$\frac{\dot{\chi}_2}{\chi_2} = \frac{1}{\theta\eta_2 \cdot \hat{N}^\sigma} \cdot \{\pi_2 + (\theta - \sigma) \cdot [\chi_2 - \pi_2 \cdot (1+\alpha)/\alpha]\} - \frac{1}{\theta} \cdot (\sigma\gamma_1 + \rho) \tag{8.30}$$

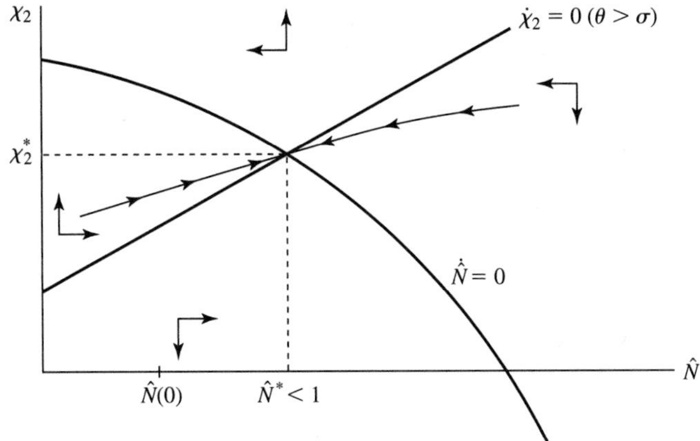

Figure 8.2
Phase diagram for country 2 when $\theta > \sigma$. The locus for $\dot{\hat{N}} = 0$ is downward sloping and stable. The locus for $\dot{\chi}_2 = 0$ is upward sloping and unstable if $\theta > \sigma$.

Equations (8.29) and (8.30) form a system of autonomous differential equations in the variables $\hat{N}$ and χ_2. The steady state of this system has already been discussed in the previous section. The dynamics can be described by means of a standard two-dimensional phase diagram in $(\hat{N}, \chi_2)$ space.

The locus for $\dot{\hat{N}} = 0$ is given by

$$\chi_2 = [\pi_2 \cdot (1 + \alpha)/\alpha] - \eta_2 \cdot \gamma_1 \cdot \hat{N}^\sigma$$

This locus is downward sloping in $(\hat{N}, \chi_2)$ space, as shown in figures 8.2 and 8.3. Equation (8.29) implies that the $\dot{\hat{N}} = 0$ locus is stable; that is, an increase in $\hat{N}$ reduces $\dot{\hat{N}}$ in the neighborhood of the locus.

The $\dot{\chi}_2 = 0$ schedule is given by

$$\chi_2 = \pi_2 \cdot (1 + \alpha)/\alpha - \pi_2/(\theta - \sigma) + (\sigma\gamma_1 + \rho) \cdot \eta_2 \cdot \hat{N}^\sigma/(\theta - \sigma)$$

Note that the slope of this locus depends on the sign of $\theta - \sigma$. If $\theta > \sigma$, the locus is upward sloping, as shown in figure 8.2. This locus is unstable; that is, an increase in χ_2 raises $\dot{\chi}_2$.

The directions of motion are shown by arrows for the four regions in figure 8.2. The only path that avoids unstable behavior of $\hat{N}$ and χ_2 is the stable, saddle path, shown by the dashed arrows. The unstable paths can be ruled out as equilibria by arguments analogous to those used for the neoclassical growth model in chapter 2. If country 2 begins with $\hat{N}(0) < \hat{N}^*$, $\hat{N}$ and χ_2 each rise monotonically during the transition toward their steady-state values.

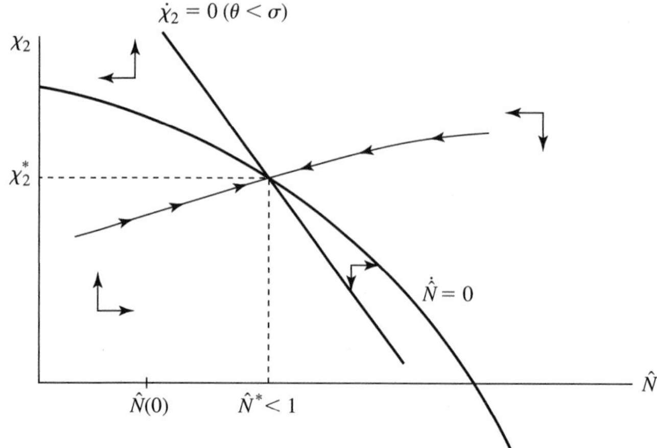

Figure 8.3
Phase diagram for country 2 when $\theta < \sigma$. The locus for $\dot{\hat{N}} = 0$ is again downward sloping and stable. The locus for $\dot{\chi}_2 = 0$ is downward sloping and stable if $\theta < \sigma$.

Figure 8.3 deals with the case in which $\theta < \sigma$. Equation (8.30) implies that the $\dot{\chi}_2 = 0$ locus is now downward sloping and stable. (We can show that the slope of this locus is always steeper in magnitude than that of the $\dot{\hat{N}} = 0$ locus.) The key finding is that the stable, saddle path is again upward sloping; that is, $\hat{N}$ and χ_2 still rise monotonically during the transition from $\hat{N}(0)$ to $\hat{N}^*$.[7]

Since χ_2 and $\hat{N}$ always rise monotonically toward their steady-state values, equation (8.29) implies that the growth rate of $\hat{N}$ falls monotonically toward its steady-state value, 0. (The monotonic rise of $\hat{N}$ implies a monotonic increase in ν_2.) Thus, during the transition, N_2 grows faster than N_1—imitation is proportionately greater than innovation—but the growth rate of N_2 falls steadily toward that of N_1. In the steady state, the rates of imitation and innovation occur at the same rate, γ_1, and $\hat{N} \equiv N_2/N_1$ remains constant.

The follower's growth rate slows down during the transition because the imitation cost, ν_2, steadily increases. This increase in ν_2 represents a form of diminishing returns, in this case to imitation. In the standard neoclassical growth model, the diminishing returns to capital accumulation played an analogous role.

The monotonic increase of $\hat{N}$ and monotonic decline of $\dot{\hat{N}}/\hat{N}$ imply a monotonic decline in the growth rate of consumption in country 2, $\dot{C}_2/C_2$, in accordance with equation (8.26).

7. If $\theta = \sigma$, the $\dot{\chi}_2 = 0$ locus is vertical. The stable saddle path is again upward sloping in this case.

Equation (8.20) therefore implies that r_2 is monotonically decreasing; it falls steadily toward its steady-state value, r_1.

Since country 2's per-worker product, y_2, is proportional to N_2 (equation [8.13]), the growth rate of y_2 exceeds γ_1 during the transition but falls gradually toward γ_1. Thus the model exhibits the familiar convergence pattern in which the follower country's per-worker output grows faster than the leader's, but the differential in the growth rates diminishes the more the follower catches up.

As mentioned before, the follower's per-worker output, y_2, is likely to fall short of the leader's, y_1, in the steady state; that is, $(y_2/y_1)^* < 1$. Equations (8.15) and (8.25) imply that $(y_2/y_1)^*$ is an increasing function of A_2/A_1 and L_2/L_1 and a decreasing function of η_2/η_1.

8.3 Constant (or Slowly Rising) Costs of Imitation

The type of equilibrium discussed thus far depends on the assumption that the imitation cost, ν_2, rises to a sufficient degree as $\hat{N}$ increases. Specifically, in figure 8.1, the condition is that ν_2 rise above ν_2^* for $\hat{N} \equiv N_2/N_1 < 1$. (The property that ν_2 approaches η_2 as N_2/N_1 approaches 1 is not critical.) Figure 8.4 deals with an alternative case in which ν_2 is constant and low, so that $\nu_2 < \nu_2^*$. The analysis would be similar if ν_2 were instead slowly rising, so that ν_2 approached (from the left) a value below ν_2^* as N_2/N_1 approached 1.

Intuitively, if ν_2 is small (namely, below ν_2^*), the imitation process will be carried on at a sufficient pace to eventually exhaust all the available products discovered in country 1. That is, $\hat{N} = 1$ will be reached at some finite date T. At this point, there will be an excess

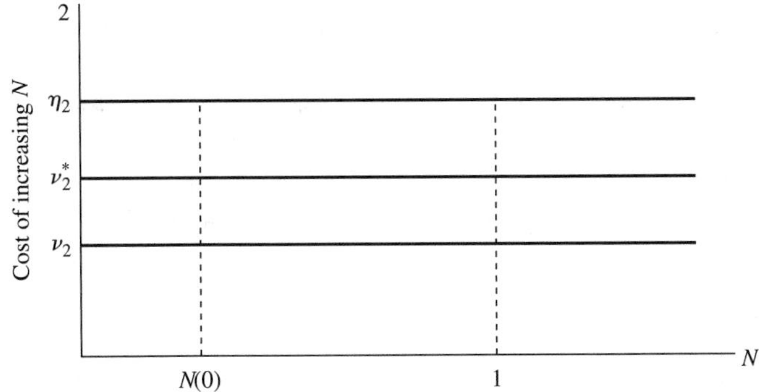

Figure 8.4
Low and constant cost of imitation in country 2. The cost, ν_2, of imitation in country 2 is constant and lower than the steady-state value, ν_2^*, which is again less than the innovation cost, η_2.

supply of persons willing to pay ν_2 to copy one of country 1's discoveries, which continue to flow in at the rate γ_1. Somehow, this excess supply has to be resolved in the equilibrium. Moreover, for $t < T$, where $\hat{N} < 1$, agents in country 2 realize that a state of excess supply will arise later, and their previous choices of rates of imitation must be consistent with this expectation.

8.3.1 The Steady State

It is easiest to begin at the end; that is, when $t > T$, so that $\hat{N} = 1$ has already been attained. In this case, the natural conjecture from the previous analysis is that country 2 would be in a steady state in which N_2 grows at the rate γ_1, the growth rate of N_1, so that $\hat{N} = 1$ applies forever. In this situation, the goods discovered in country 1 are immediately copied for use in country 2.[8] Also, C_2 grows at the rate γ_1, so that $\chi_2 \equiv C_2/N_2$ remains fixed over time.

Suppose, however, that r_2 equaled π_2/ν_2, the value implied by equation (8.19) when ν_2 is constant. In this case, $r_2 > r_1$ would apply. This result follows from the expression for ν_2^* in equation (8.22), using also the expression for r_1 from equation (8.6) and the condition $\nu_2 < \nu_2^*$ in figure 8.4. But $r_2 > r_1$ implies that C_2 would grow faster than γ_1, the growth rate of C_1, so that country 2 would not be in a steady state. The problem is that making copies at the low cost ν_2 is too good a deal to be consistent with the growth of C_2 and N_2 at the steady-state rate, γ_1. If the rate of return were π_2/ν_2, agents in country 2 would want to devote enough resources to copying so that N_2 would grow at a rate faster than γ_1. But, since new goods are discovered only at the rate γ_1, there is insufficient copyable material available to support imitation at this fast a rate. Somehow the rate of return in country 2 must be bid down to r_1 to support the allocations that arise in the steady state.

If $N_2 = N_1$ and imitators in country 2 expend the flow of resources $\nu_2\gamma_1 N_1$, N_2 would grow along with N_1 at the constant rate γ_1. However, if each individual in country 2 thinks that he can copy a good just by paying ν_2, the amount spent on copying would exceed $\nu_2\gamma_1 N_1$; that is, there would be excess demand for goods to be copied. We suppose in this excess-demand situation that the monopoly rights to the copied goods in country 2 are allocated in a random manner. Specifically, we assume that each person's probability of obtaining the property right is proportional to the amount spent on copying effort. In equilibrium, the total flow of

8. If we had assumed that imitation takes time, as well as goods, the imitation would occur with a lag, and a gap between country 1 and country 2 could persist forever. Jovanovic and Lach (1991) construct a model that includes a time lag for imitation. Mansfield, Schwartz, and Wagner (1981, p. 909) find in their sample of 48 innovations that the ratio of the time required for imitation to that for innovation averaged 70 percent. The lag with which advances become known in an industry appears to be brief. For example, Mansfield (1985) reports that 70 percent of product innovations are familiar to rival companies within a year. Caballero and Jaffe (1993) reach similar conclusions from their use of patent citation data (references in patent documents to previous patents upon which the current discovery builds) to measure the time required for ideas to influence other researchers. They find that the diffusion is rapid with a mean lag between one and two years.

resources expended by potential imitators would then be $\nu_2^* \gamma_1 N_1$, where $\nu_2^* > \nu_2$ is the cost per good that drives the expected rate of return down to r_1 (see equations [8.21] and [8.22] and figure 8.4).[9] This bidding up of the effective cost of copying to ν_2^* deters any further entry of potential imitators. The same type of result would arise if we used a richer model in which potential imitators raced or competed against each other to obtain the property rights over the use of an intermediate good in country 2.

In the steady state, the effective cost of copying is $\nu_2^* > \nu_2$, and the expected rate of return to imitation in country 2 is r_1. This rate of return is consistent with growth of C_2 and N_2 at the steady-state rate, γ_1. The steady-state solution is therefore the same as that shown in figure 8.1, except that $(N_2/N_1)^* = 1$ applies. (We continue to assume that $\eta_2 > \nu_2^*$, as shown in figure 8.4; that is, the inequality in equation [8.23] holds, and agents in country 2 have no incentive to innovate.)

8.3.2 Transitional Dynamics

Consider now the situation when $t < T$, so that $N_2 < N_1$, and the copyable products are in plentiful supply. The rate of return in country 2 must then be

$$r_2 = \pi_2/\nu_2 \tag{8.31}$$

which is constant. The growth rate of consumption is therefore also constant and given by

$$\dot{C}_2/C_2 = (1/\theta) \cdot (\pi_2/\nu_2 - \rho) \tag{8.32}$$

This result corresponds to equation (8.26) with σ set to 0.[10]

The formula for $\dot{\hat{N}}/\hat{N}$ is the same as equation (8.29) and that for $\dot{\chi}_2/\chi_2$ is the same as equation (8.30) with σ set to zero:

$$\dot{\hat{N}}/\hat{N} = (1/\nu_2) \cdot [\pi_2 \cdot (1+\alpha)/\alpha - \chi_2] - \gamma_1 \tag{8.33}$$

$$\dot{\chi}_2/\chi_2 = (1/\theta) \cdot (\pi_2/\nu_2) \cdot [1 - \theta \cdot (1+\alpha)/\alpha] - \rho/\theta + \chi_2/\nu_2 \tag{8.34}$$

where, again, $\chi_2 \equiv C_2/N_2$.

Equations (8.33) and (8.34) can be used, as before, to construct a phase diagram in $(\hat{N}, \chi_2)$ space. Figure 8.5 shows the resulting diagram. Note that each locus is now a horizontal line. We can show readily (if $r_2 = \pi_2/\nu_2 > r_1$) that the $\dot{\hat{N}} = 0$ locus lies above the $\dot{\chi}_2 = 0$ locus, as shown in the figure. We also have that $\hat{N}$ is falling for values above the $\dot{\hat{N}} = 0$ locus and rising for values below it, whereas χ_2 is rising for values above the $\dot{\chi}_2 = 0$ locus and falling

9. This result holds if the risk involved in imitation is diversifiable, so that potential imitators consider only the expectation of the return.

10. In equation (8.24), $\sigma = 0$ implies that ν_2 is independent of N_2/N_1. However, in the present case, $\nu_2 < \eta_2$ also applies.

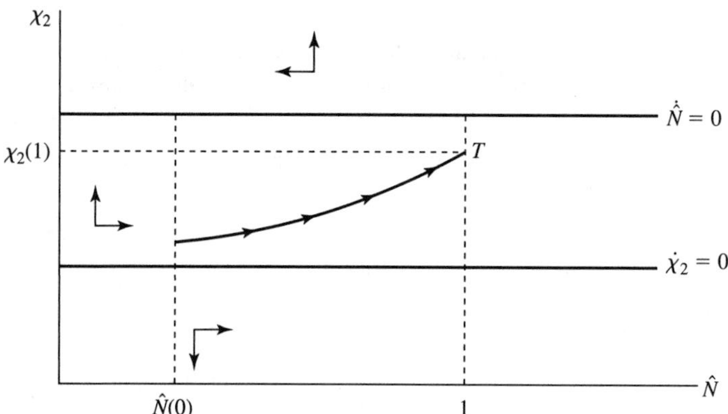

Figure 8.5
Phase diagram for country 2 when ν_2 is constant. The locus for $\dot{\hat{N}} = 0$ is a horizontal line and lies above the locus for $\dot{\chi}_2 = 0$, which is also a horizontal line. The stable, saddle path lies between the two loci and is upward sloping.

for values below it. These patterns imply that the stable, saddle path begins between the two horizontal loci and is then upward sloping. We have drawn the path so that it remains below the $\dot{\hat{N}} = 0$ locus when $\hat{N}$ reaches 1, a configuration that is implied by the subsequent analysis.

Figure 8.5 implies a transition in which $\hat{N}$ and χ_2 increase monotonically. The rise in $\hat{N}$ means that $\dot{N}_2/N_2$ exceeds γ_1 along the path. The expansion of χ_2 implies from equation (8.29) that $\dot{N}_2/N_2$ declines steadily. Thus the solution accords with the one in section 8.2.5 in the sense of predicting that the follower grows faster (in terms of number of known products and output) than the leader, but the gap in the growth rates diminishes as the follower catches up. One difference from the previous analysis is that $\dot{C}_2/C_2$ is now constant at a value that exceeds γ_1 (see equation [8.32]).

The tricky part of the solution concerns the behavior just at time T, when $\hat{N}$ reaches 1. Just after this date, imitations effectively cost $\nu_2^* > \nu_2$, and the rate of return is r_1. Just before this date, imitations cost ν_2, and the rate of return (from equation [8.31]) is $\pi_2/\nu_2 > r_1$. Anyone who pays ν_2 to imitate a good just before date T will, in the next instant, experience a sharp capital gain corresponding to the increase in the shadow price of an imitated product from ν_2 to ν_2^*. In fact, in this model, the rate of return to copying a good is infinite for an instant of time at date T. This curious behavior for the rate of return supports the equilibrium for quantities when the cost of copying is small and constant.[11]

11. If we had introduced durable capital goods into the model, the path of $r(t)$ would correspond at each date to the net marginal product of capital and would never be infinite. Hence, the result that $r(t)$ can be infinite for an instant of time depends on the assumption that all inputs are nondurables.

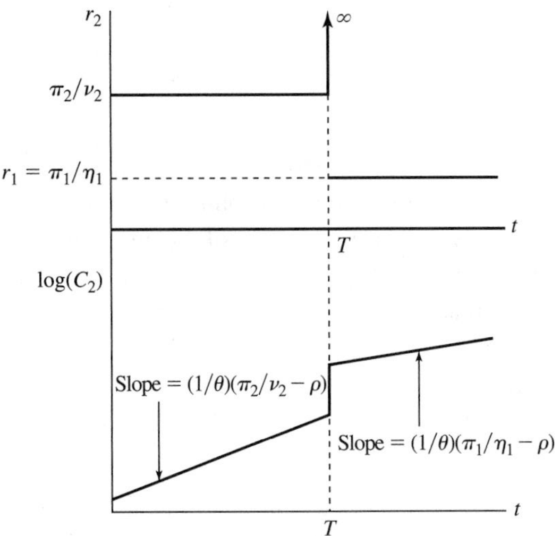

Figure 8.6
Time paths of r_2 and $\log(C_2)$ when ν_2 is small and constant. The rate of return, r_2, is constant up to date T and constant at a lower level just after date T. The rate of return is infinite just at date T. Correspondingly, $\log(C_2)$ has a constant slope up to date T, has a constant flatter slope after date T, and jumps upward at date T.

Figure 8.6 shows the full path of the equilibrium for country 2's rate of return, r_2, and log of consumption, $\log(C_2)$. To the left of date T, the rate of return is constant at π_2/ν_2, and the slope of $\log(C_2)$ is the associated constant, $(1/\theta) \cdot (\pi_2/\nu_2 - \rho)$. To the right of date T, the rate of return is constant at the lower value, $r_1 = \pi_1/\eta_1$, and the slope of $\log(C_2)$ is the correspondingly smaller value, $(1/\theta) \cdot (\pi_1/\eta_1 - \rho)$. At time T, the infinite rate of return (for an instant of time) supports a jump in the level of $\log(C_2)$. This jump is consistent with country 2's overall resource constraint, because the amount expended on imitation jumps downward at the same time by an equal amount.[12] Note that there is no jump at time T (or any other time) in the level of total output.

Suppose now that ν_2 were slowly rising, rather than constant, but that the value of ν_2 at $\hat{N} = 1$ remained below ν_2^*. In this case, the behavior at time T would still involve an infinite

12. The change in the resources devoted to imitation involves two offsetting effects. First, the resource use falls because the growth rate of N_2 declines by a discrete amount. Second, the resource use rises because each unit now costs $\nu_2^* > \nu_2$. In the equilibrium (which involves an infinite rate of return at date T and, hence, an upward jump in consumption), the net effect must be a reduction in resource use for imitation. Also, the stable, shadow path shown in figure 8.5 must remain below the $\dot{\hat{N}} = 0$ locus at date T to be consistent with the downward jump in $\dot{\hat{N}}$ and the upward jump in χ_2 at date T. (The loci for $\dot{\hat{N}} = 0$ and $\dot{\chi}_2 = 0$ shift after date T—downward and upward, respectively—because ν_2 is replaced in the equations by the higher value ν_2^*.)

rate of return and a jump in the level of consumption. The main new results are that r_2 will fall steadily for $t < T$, and the growth rate of C_2 will therefore also decline in this range. Hence, the constancy of $\dot{C}_2/C_2$ in the period before date T holds only if ν_2 does not vary at all.

The bottom line is that cases of constant or slowly rising imitation costs agree qualitatively with the model from the previous section in the predictions about the follower's growth rates. In each case, a lower value of N_2/N_1 implies a higher growth rate of N_2 and, hence, of Y_2. This property extends also to the growth rate of C_2, except for the case in which the imitation cost, ν_2, does not rise at all until N_2 reaches N_1 at date T.

8.4 Foreign Investment and Intellectual Property Rights

We now consider some aspects of foreign investment and intellectual property rights in the process of technological diffusion. In the previous analysis an innovator in country 1 paid the cost η_1 to obtain the monopoly right over the use of an intermediate good in country 1. The innovator obtained no property rights over the use of the intermediate good in country 2. We now assume instead that innovators from country 1 have perpetual monopoly rights over the use of their intermediate goods in both countries. This situation would apply if countries fully respected the intellectual property rights of foreigners, a major topic of ongoing international negotiations in world trade. These intellectual property rights make it infeasible for agents in country 2 to imitate products without paying a fee to the inventor.

We assume that the cost of adapting a variety of intermediate good from country 1 to country 2 is the constant ν_2. We now think of this cost as an outlay made by the inventor of the variety of intermediate good in country 1.[13] We assume that $\nu_2 < \nu_2^*$, as given in equation (8.22), so that $\gamma_2 > \gamma_1$ and $r_2 > r_1$ would apply in the previous model when $N_2/N_1 < 1$. That is, the cost of adaptation to country 2 is low enough so that country 2 will tend to grow faster than country 1. We also assume that entrepreneurs in country 2 do not find it worthwhile to innovate. Hence, all the innovations and adaptations stem from the efforts of entrepreneurs from country 1.

Suppose that country 2 was previously closed to foreign investment and had not experienced much imitation of country 1's inventions. We also assume that country 2 had not invented much on its own, perhaps because of relatively low values of the parameters A_2 and L_2 or a relatively high innovation cost, η_2. If country 2 were suddenly opened up to foreign investment, the number N_1 of known products from country 1 would greatly exceed the number N_2 available in country 2. The rate of return to foreign investment by country 1

13. The cost estimates provided by Teece (1977), which we discussed earlier, apply directly to this situation.

in country 2—that is, adaptation of products for use in country 2—is given by $r_2 = \pi_2/\nu_2$, as shown in equation (8.31). The rate r_2 exceeds the rate $r_1 = \pi_1/\eta_1$ for innovation, as given in equation (8.6). (This result follows from the assumption $\nu_2 < \nu_2^*$ in equation [8.22].) Since the model assumes no diminishing returns to adaptation or innovation, researchers from country 1 would initially devote all their R&D outlays to foreign investment in country 2. (This allocation of R&D investment did not arise before, although $r_2 > r_1$, because of the absence of a global capital market.)

The backlog of unadapted products is eventually eliminated—that is, N_2 reaches N_1—and the rate of return r_2 from pure adaptation becomes unavailable. The researchers from country 1 are then motivated to direct R&D expenditures to the discovery of new products, that is, to expand N_1. However, the rate of return to innovation now exceeds the value for r_1 shown in equation (8.6) because an entrepreneur knows that a successful product can also be adapted at the cost ν_2 for use under conditions of monopoly in country 2. If the inequality $\nu_2 < \nu_2^*$ holds, as already assumed, this adaptation is immediately worthwhile.

The total flow of monopoly profits from the discovery of a new product in country 1 and the simultaneous adaptation of this product to country 2 is now the sum of the flows shown in equations (8.4) and (8.14):

$$\tilde{\pi} = \pi_1 + \pi_2 = \left(\frac{1-\alpha}{\alpha}\right) \cdot \alpha^{2/(1-\alpha)} \cdot \left[(A_1)^{1/(1-\alpha)} \cdot L_1 + (A_2)^{1/(1-\alpha)} \cdot L_2\right] \tag{8.35}$$

The assumption underlying equation (8.35) is that the intermediate inputs used to produce goods in country 1 operate through the technology in equation (8.1)—with productivity parameter A_1—whereas those used to produce goods in country 2 operate through the technology in equation (8.9)—with productivity parameter A_2. In other words, foreign investment makes country 1's intermediate inputs more readily available to country 2 but is assumed not to affect the productivity parameter that governs the production process in country 2. This assumption is appropriate, for example, if the parameter A_2 represents local government policies—such as taxation, provision of public services, and maintenance of property rights—that apply to all producers that operate in country 2.

An innovator in country 1 now pays the total cost $\eta_1 + \nu_2$ to secure the flow of monopoly profit $\tilde{\pi}$ shown in equation (8.35). Accordingly, the free-entry condition implies that the rate of return in country 1 is given by

$$\tilde{r}_1 = \tilde{\pi}/(\eta_1 + \nu_2) = \left(\frac{1-\alpha}{\alpha}\right) \cdot \alpha^{2/(1-\alpha)} \cdot \left[\frac{(A_1)^{1/(1-\alpha)} \cdot L_1 + (A_2)^{1/(1-\alpha)} \cdot L_2}{\eta_1 + \nu_2}\right] \tag{8.36}$$

The inequality $\nu_2 < \nu_2^*$ in equation (8.22) implies that $\tilde{r}_1$ exceeds the value for r_1 shown in equation (8.6).[14]

The constant rate of return in equation (8.36) corresponds to a steady state in which the various quantities—N_1, Y_1, C_1, N_2, Y_2, and C_2—all grow at a constant rate given by $\tilde{\gamma}_1 = (1/\theta) \cdot (\tilde{r}_1 - \rho)$. This steady state features a simultaneous flow of new products, N_1, and adapted versions of these products, $N_2 = N_1$. Since $\tilde{r}_1$ is higher than before, $\tilde{\gamma}_1$ exceeds the value γ_1 shown in equation (8.8) for the model with no foreign investment. We discuss some welfare implications of foreign investment and intellectual property rights later in this chapter.

8.5 General Implications for Growth Rates in Follower Countries

The various models considered imply that the growth rate of output per worker in country 2 can be written in the form

$$\dot{y}_2/y_2 = \gamma_1 + G[y_2/y_1, (y_2/y_1)^*] \tag{8.37}$$

where the partial derivatives of the function G satisfy $G_1 < 0$ and $G_2 > 0$. The function also satisfies the condition $G(\cdot, \cdot) = 0$ when $y_2/y_1 = (y_2/y_1)^*$. Growth rates do not necessarily exhibit absolute convergence, in the sense described in chapter 1, because the growth rate of the rich leader is not necessarily lower than the growth rate of the poorer follower—that is, $\dot{y}_2/y_2 < \gamma_1$ can apply when $y_2/y_1 < 1$. If the steady-state level of income for the poor relative to the rich, $(y_2/y_1)^*$, is small—for example, because A_2/A_1 is low—the growth rate of the follower, $\dot{y}_2/y_2$, can be below the growth rate of the leader, γ_1, even when the follower is poorer than the leader ($y_2 < y_1$). Country 2's growth rate, $\dot{y}_2/y_2$, exceeds γ_1 if $y_2/y_1 < (y_2/y_1)^*$.

The results exhibit conditional convergence, in the sense that the growth rate of the follower, $\dot{y}_2/y_2$, declines as y_2/y_1 rises for a given value of $(y_2/y_1)^*$. Also, for given y_2/y_1, $\dot{y}_2/y_2$ rises with $(y_2/y_1)^*$. In other words, the growth rate of the follower is an increasing function of the distance to its steady state. For example, if the government of country 2 adopts policies that are more favorable to production and investment—perhaps in the form of lower tax rates on capital income or more effective enforcement of property rights—the change in policy amounts to an increase in A_2. In this case, $(y_2/y_1)^*$ increases, and the growth rate, $\dot{y}_2/y_2$, rises on impact.

14. The condition $\nu_2 < \nu_2^*$ also implies $\tilde{r}_1 < r_2 = \pi_2/\nu_2$. Therefore, as we implicitly assumed before, entrepreneurs in country 1 would first adapt the entire pool of existing products to country 2 and then switch subsequently to discovery of new products.

In the neoclassical growth model with labor-augmenting technological progress, as described in chapter 2, the formula for the growth rate of per capita output in a closed economy looked similar to equation (8.37). The differences are that γ_1 is replaced by the rate of exogenous technical change, denoted by x; y_2/y_1 is replaced by $\hat{y}$, the country's output per *effective* worker (a concept that takes account of the growth at rate x because of technological progress); and $(y_2/y_1)^*$ is replaced by $(\hat{y})^*$, the steady-state level of output per effective worker. Thus the growth formula in the standard model can be written as

$$\dot{y}/y = x + H[\hat{y}, (\hat{y})^*] \tag{8.38}$$

where the partial derivatives of the function H satisfy $H_1 < 0$, $H_2 > 0$, and $H(\cdot, \cdot) = 0$ when $\hat{y} = (\hat{y})^*$. The value $(\hat{y})^*$ depends on elements included in the parameter A, such as government policies, and on the willingness to save. Higher values of A raise $(\hat{y})^*$, whereas higher values of the preference parameters, ρ and θ, reduce $(\hat{y})^*$.

One distinction between the two classes of models is that the intercept in equation (8.37) is γ_1, the growth rate of the leading economy (or economies), whereas that in equation (8.38) is x, the constant rate of exogenous technological progress. Operationally, γ_1 might be identified with the average growth rate of output per worker in a set of advanced countries.[15] The parameter x would not be directly observable and might vary over time or across countries.

If all followers have the same leaders—because the costs of imitation, ν_i, are the same in all cases—and if the rates of exogenous technical change are the same for all countries at a given point in time, both models imply that the intercept is the same for all countries. In a single cross section, equation (8.37) would constrain the intercept to equal the observable value γ_1, whereas equation (8.38) would not impose this constraint. Thus the diffusion model would amount to a restricted version of the neoclassical growth model, and this restriction would be testable empirically.

In a panel setting, equation (8.37) would allow the intercept to vary over time but only in line with the observable changes in γ_1. Equation (8.38) would fix the intercept, but only if we retain the version of the neoclassical growth model in which the rate of technological progress, x, is constant (as well as the same for all countries). If the rate of technical change is exogenous, but not necessarily constant, equation (8.38) would allow the intercept to vary over time in an unconstrained manner. In this case, the diffusion model would again amount to a constrained version of the neoclassical growth model, and the constraint would be testable empirically.

15. Followers are influenced by the growth of N_1, not by the growth of the leader's output per worker, y_1, although the two growth rates coincide in the present model. Direct measures of N_1 and N_2 would not generally be available, although patents or cumulated R&D spending would be possibilities.

With respect to the terms $G(\cdot)$ and $H(\cdot)$, the key aspect of equation (8.37) is that the growth rate depends on a country's characteristics expressed *relative* to those in the leading economy (or economies), whereas equation (8.38) involves the absolute levels of these characteristics. Suppose, for example, that the growth rate, γ_1, in the United States—the representation of the technological leader—is 2 percent per year. Equation (8.37) says that, for given γ_1, the growth rate of a typical follower, say Mexico, depends on the quality of its political and economic institutions (determinants of the parameter A_2) expressed relative to those in the United States. Equation (8.38) says that the characteristics of Mexican institutions matter for Mexican growth, but it is not necessary to condition these characteristics on the comparable attributes of the United States.

If all countries have the same leader, then, in a single cross section, the leader's characteristics merge into the overall intercept. However, in a panel context, changes in the leader's characteristics—in particular, changes that affect γ_1—would shift the intercept over time in an observable manner. Empirical identification is facilitated if the costs of imitation vary in an observable way across country pairs or over time. In Jaumotte (1999) this idea is implemented by arguing that imitation costs would be lower the higher is the volume of trade between a follower country and the relevant set of leaders.[16] The idea is that imports by a follower country from leading countries facilitate the absorption of superior technologies from the leaders.

Jaumotte (1999) used a sample of 63 developing countries over the period 1960–94 to represent the follower group, analogous to our country 2. The leaders, which parallel our country 1, were the OECD countries plus Israel. She used a growth-accounting approach, which we discuss in chapter 10, to estimate the time paths of N_i for each country in the two groups. Basically, she filtered out the contribution from a country's observed growth of inputs—physical capital, human capital (measured by education), and raw labor—from the observed growth of output and identified the residual with N_i. She assumed that the cost of adaptation, ν_2, depended positively on N_2/N_1, as in equation (8.24), but also that the cost depended negatively on a follower country's ratio of imports from the group of leaders to the country's GDP.

Jaumotte (1999, table 2) found that a follower country's growth rate of technology, measured by the constructed $\dot{N}_2/N_2$, depended negatively on N_2 and positively on N_1. Moreover, the results were consistent with the hypothesis that only the ratio of N_2 to N_1 mattered for $\dot{N}_2/N_2$. She also found that a larger trade share made $\dot{N}_2/N_2$ more sensitive to N_2/N_1. Within the model this effect would arise if more trade lowers the cost of technological

16. Chua (1993) and Easterly and Levine (1997) examined the idea that a country's growth depends on developments in other countries. However, these studies focus on influences from physically adjacent locations, rather than on locations that are linked through international trade.

imitation. Thus these empirical results provide some support for the analysis of technological diffusion in this chapter.

Caselli and Coleman (2001) obtained a direct measure of technological diffusion by considering countries' imports of high-tech equipment, mostly computers. Especially for the many countries that do not have significant exports of computers, this measure is a good proxy for investment in computers. Then the idea is that accumulation of computers tends to go along with expanded use of advanced technologies.

Caselli and Coleman (2001, table 2) found, consistent with Jaumotte (1999), that their measure of technological diffusion was spurred by increased imports of manufacturing products from OECD countries. Another result, consistent with the theory of Nelson and Phelps (1966) mentioned before, was that a greater quantity of human capital in a country raised the rate of technological diffusion. An interpretation of this result is that greater availability of human capital reduces a country's costs of adopting sophisticated techniques or, equivalently, raises the return to this adoption. The human-capital measures that had the most explanatory power in their framework were the average years of school attainment at secondary and higher levels. This pattern makes sense because these advanced levels of education are likely to be especially important for the use of new and sophisticated technologies. Caselli and Coleman also found that their measure of technological diffusion was encouraged by better enforcement of property rights and by a reduced level of output originating in agriculture.

8.6 Switchovers of Technological Leadership, Leapfrogging

Consider again the situation in which innovators possess intellectual property rights only in their home countries. We have considered thus far the case in which $(A_2/A_1)^{1/(1-\alpha)} \cdot (L_2/L_1) \cdot (\eta_1/\eta_2) < 1$, as shown in equation (8.23), so that country 2 is intrinsically inferior to country 1 in terms of the underlying parameters. This inequality guarantees in figures 8.1 and 8.4 that ν_2^* lies below η_2 on the vertical axis. For this reason, agents in country 2 never wish to innovate.

Suppose now that the inequality is reversed,

$$(A_2/A_1)^{1/(1-\alpha)} \cdot (L_2/L_1) \cdot (\eta_1/\eta_2) > 1 \tag{8.39}$$

so that country 2 is intrinsically superior to country 1. Since $N_2(0) < N_1(0)$ still applies, country 2 again begins in a technologically inferior state. This situation could arise, for example, if country 2 had been inferior to country 1 for a long time but a recent improvement in government policy—represented by an increase in A_2—made country 2 intrinsically superior.

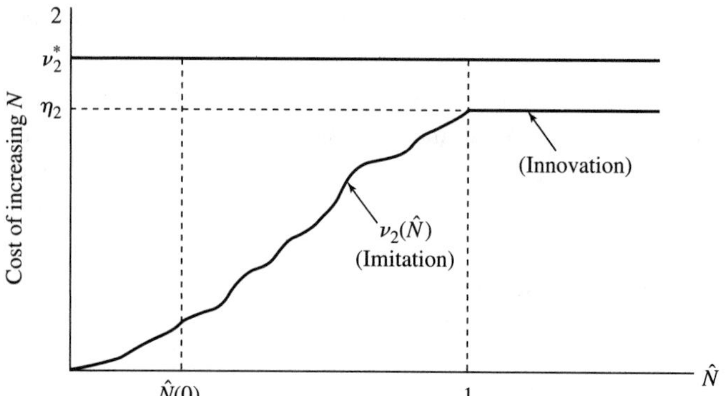

Figure 8.7
Cost of technological change in country 2 when $\nu_2^* > \eta_2$. The cost of imitation in country 2, ν_2, is again an increasing function of N_2/N_1 and approaches the cost of innovation, η_2, as N_2/N_1 approaches 1. The steady-state value of the imitation cost, ν_2^*, is now assumed to exceed η_2.

Return now to the case shown in figure 8.1 in which ν_2 rises with N_2/N_1 and approaches η_2 as N_2/N_1 approaches 1. The inequality in equation (8.39) implies, however, that the value ν_2^* given in equation (8.22) now exceeds η_2. Thus, figure 8.7 shows that N_2/N_1 reaches unity and, correspondingly, ν_2 reaches η_2 at a point where the cost of increasing N_2 is still below ν_2^*. This result means that agents in country 2 find it advantageous to raise N_2/N_1 above unity by innovating at the cost η_2. Thus, once all of country 1's discoveries have been copied, country 2 switches to innovation.

The inventions in country 2 create a pool of products that can be imitated by country 1. Since the cost of copying is lower than η_1, agents in country 1 now find imitation preferable to invention. Country 1's role shifts accordingly from leader to follower.[17] Note that country 1's welfare will be enhanced by the presence of the technologically superior country 2.[18]

The initial model applies after the switchover, except that the roles are reversed. Country 2 is now the permanent technological leader, and country 1 is the permanent follower.

17. In the specification where $\nu_2(N_2/N_1)$ approaches η_2 as N_2/N_1 approaches 1 (as in figures 8.1 and 8.7), country 1 switches all at once from leader to follower, and country 2 moves all at once from follower to leader. The switchover involves a transition with mixing of innovation and imitation within a country if $\nu_2(N_2/N_1)$ rises above η_2 before N_2/N_1 reaches 1 and if an analogous cost function for imitation applies to country 1. In this revised formulation, country 2 would switch at some point from pure imitation to a mixture of imitation and innovation. Then, after a finite stock of country 2's discoveries were built up, the cost of imitation by country 1 would become low enough so that country 1 would shift to a mixture of imitation and innovation. Eventually, country 2 would move completely out of imitation, and country 1 would move fully out of innovation.

18. Since final product is physically homogeneous, the rise in productivity in country 2 does not generate an adverse relative-price effect for country 1.

Country 2's rate of return, r_2, and growth rate, γ_2 (of N_2, Y_2, and C_2), are constant after the switchover. The values of r_2 and γ_2 are given, respectively, by equations (8.6) and (8.8) if the subscripts in the formulas are changed from 1 to 2. The steady-state ratio of numbers of products, $(N_2/N_1)^*$, is still given by equation (8.25) but now exceeds unity.

Figures 8.2 and 8.3 describe the postswitchover dynamics for country 1 if $\hat{N}$ now equals N_1/N_2 and χ_1 replaces χ_2. The only difference from before is that $\hat{N}$ starts at unity, a value to the right of $\hat{N}^*$. The dynamic path therefore features steadily declining values of $\hat{N}$ and $\chi_1 \equiv C_1/N_1$. The steady fall in $\hat{N}$ means that country 2 continues to grow faster than country 1 during the postswitchover transition. As $\hat{N}$ falls, the cost, ν_1, for imitation in country 1 declines, and the rate of return and growth rates in country 1 *increase*. In the steady state, country 1's rate of return reaches r_2, a constant, and its growth rate (of N_1, Y_1, and C_1) reaches γ_2, also a constant.[19]

The switch of technological leadership can occur only once in the model if the underlying parameters A_i, L_i, and η_i do not change. The switch occurs at some point if the country that starts with the relatively small number of known products, N_i, is intrinsically superior in the sense of the inequality in equation (8.39). Thus the present framework differs from models of leapfrogging, as explored by Brezis, Krugman, and Tsiddon (1993), Jovanovic and Nyarko (1996), and Ohyama and Jones (1995). In those settings, the changes in technological leadership reflect the effects of backwardness on the willingness to explore and adopt radically new ideas. In the present model, the countries that start out behind have a benefit from low costs of imitation but have no advantages with respect to the discovery or implementation of leading-edge technologies.

In practice, the parameters A_i, L_i, and η_i would change over time; for example, because of shifts in government policies. These movements would occasionally create changes in the positions of technological leadership. (These changes would be lagged substantially from the shifts in the underlying parameters.) However, since backwardness does not enhance the discovery or implementation of new technologies and since the leaders are selected for the favorable values of their underlying parameters, there would be no tendency for leapfrogging in the sense that a particular follower is likely eventually to surpass a particular leader.[20] In contrast, the probability that a leader would be overtaken eventually by *some* follower would likely be high.

19. The final possibility is that $(A_2/A_1)^{1/(1-\alpha)} \cdot (L_2/L_1) \cdot (\eta_1/\eta_2) = 1$. In this case, the equilibrium can be of the first type (where country 1 is the permanent leader and country 2 the permanent follower) or of the second type (where the leadership positions are reversed). There could also be a mixture of invention and imitation in the two places. In the steady state, agents in both countries are indifferent between innovation and imitation.

20. An interesting, unresolved empirical question is whether leapfrogging applies in this sense to professional sports teams. One force that goes in this direction is the new-player draft; teams typically get to pick in inverse relation to their past performance.

These results seem consistent with the broad patterns of change in world technological leadership that are highlighted by Brezis, Krugman, and Tsiddon (1993). They argue that Great Britain overtook the Netherlands as leader in the 1700s, the United States (and, in some respects, Germany) overtook Great Britain by the late 1800s, and Japan surpassed the United States in some sectors by the 1980s.[21] More recently, the United States may have resumed the position of technological leadership in many high-tech fields. The striking aspect of this pattern is not that changes in technological leadership occur but rather that the positions at the top persist for so long. In particular, most countries have never been technological leaders. The empirical evidence therefore does not suggest any great benefits from backwardness, per se, in the discovery and use of the newest technologies.

8.7 Welfare Considerations

Consider the model described in figure 8.1 in which country 1 is always the technological leader, country 2 is always the follower, and the cost of imitation is increasing in N_2/N_1. One source of distortion in this model involves the monopoly pricing of the intermediates that have already been discovered in country 1 or imitated in country 2. This element is familiar from the model of chapter 6. From a static perspective, the distortion reflects the excess of the price paid for each intermediate, $1/\alpha$, over the marginal cost of production, 1. This wedge can be eliminated by using a lump-sum tax in each country to subsidize purchases of intermediates at the rate $(1-\alpha)/\alpha$. Each user of an intermediate then faces a net price of one, the marginal cost of production.

Another distortion in the model is that agents in country 1 have insufficient incentive to innovate because they do not take account of the benefit to country 2 from an increase in the pool of copyable ideas. This effect would be internalized if each innovator in country 1 retained the international property rights over the use of his or her idea. The framework with intellectual property rights and foreign investment that we considered before provides one way to achieve this internalization. The guarantee of worldwide property rights over innovations motivates researchers to consider the global benefits of their R&D.[22]

21. In premodern times, the dominant technological leader was China. See Temple (1986). For a discussion in the context of recent theories of endogenous growth, see Young (1993).

22. In the model, foreign investment also gets around the capital-market imperfection that allowed for a divergence between the rates of return, r_1 and r_2, that prevailed in the two countries. In effect, the property rights over the use of designs in another country provide the collateral for foreign investment. The implicit assumption in the original model was that households from country 1 were unwilling to loan funds to investors in country 2, even though the rate of return r_2 that these investors would be willing to pay exceeded the rate of return r_1 available to savers in country 1.

Another distortion arises because agents in country 2 do not consider that the imitation of one of country 1's ideas raises the cost that will apply to future imitations. To isolate this effect, suppose that N_1 grows at the given rate γ_1 and that the effect from monopoly pricing in country 2 has been neutralized by a subsidy at the rate $(1-\alpha)/\alpha$ on the use of intermediates. This subsidy, financed by a lump-sum tax, implies that the net price of intermediates to users is one, the marginal cost of production. We can then compare the outcomes of a decentralized solution with those that would be determined by a social planner in country 2. (A social planner in country 1 would not be relevant here, because we are assuming that the growth rate γ_1 is given and that the distortion from monopoly pricing in country 1 has been neutralized by the subsidy and tax scheme.)

The social planner seeks to maximize the utility of the representative consumer in country 2, subject to the production function in equation (8.9); the specification of the cost of copying ν_2, assumed to be given by equation (8.24); and the growth rate of N_1 at the given rate γ_1. The optimal quantity of each intermediate, X_2, maximizes output, Y_2, net of the outlay on intermediates, and is given by

$$X_2 = L_2 A_2^{1/(1-\alpha)} \alpha^{1/(1-\alpha)} \tag{8.40}$$

The usual conditions for dynamic optimization lead to the following expressions for the growth rates of N_2 and C_2:

$$\dot{N}_2/N_2 = (1/\nu_2) \cdot (\Psi - \chi_2) \tag{8.41}$$

$$\dot{C}_2/C_2 = (1/\theta) \cdot (\Psi/\nu_2 - \rho - \sigma\gamma_1) \tag{8.42}$$

where $\chi_2 \equiv C_2/N_2$, and the new parameter Ψ is defined as

$$\Psi \equiv (1-\alpha) \cdot L_2 A_2^{1/(1-\alpha)} \alpha^{\alpha/(1-\alpha)} \tag{8.43}$$

In a decentralized situation in which purchases of intermediates are subsidized at the rate $(1-\alpha)/\alpha$, Ψ turns out to equal the profit flow, π_2. (This amount exceeds the value for π_2 shown in equation [8.14].)

For the decentralized setting, the subsidy on purchases of intermediates implies that X_2 equals the social planner's choice shown in equation (8.40). Since the values of X_2 are equal, the decentralized path for N_2 would coincide with the planner's path if the choices of χ_2 were the same. That is, the formula that determines $\dot{N}_2/N_2$ in the decentralized case would be the same as equation (8.41). Therefore, differences in results arise only because of differences in the choices of consumption.

The growth rate of consumption in the decentralized solution turns out to be

$$\dot{C}_2/C_2 = (1/\theta) \cdot [\Psi/\nu_2 - \rho - \sigma\gamma_1 + (\sigma/\nu_2) \cdot (\Psi - \chi_2)] \tag{8.44}$$

This expression differs from the social planner's result in equation (8.42) only by the term that involves $\Psi - \chi_2$. It is possible to show that $\Psi > \chi_2$ applies in the steady state. Moreover, since χ_2 can be shown to be monotonically increasing during the transition (from the type of phase-diagram analysis used before), $\Psi - \chi_2$ must be positive throughout. It follows that the decentralized choice of $\dot{C}_2/C_2$ is greater than the social planner's selection for any given value of N_2/N_1 (and, hence, ν_2). In other words, the decentralized solution involves lower levels of χ_2 and higher growth rates of C_2. Equation (8.41) then implies that the decentralized choice of $\dot{N}_2/N_2$ is greater than the social planner's choice at each value of N_2/N_1. This result implies that the steady-state value of N_2/N_1 in the decentralized solution exceeds the steady-state value chosen by the social planner.[23]

The growth rate of N_2 is too high in the decentralized solution because the allocation of resources to imitation (and, hence, growth) is analogous to increased fishing in a congestible pond. Specifically, an agent that expends $\nu_2(N_2/N_1)$ to raise N_2 does not consider that this action will raise the cost faced by future imitators of products. Viewed alternatively, private agents count the capital gain, $\dot{\nu}_2/\nu_2$, as part of their return to imitation, whereas this term does not enter into the social return. This kind of distortion would not arise if potential imitators in country 2 were somehow assigned well-defined property rights at the outset to the goods that each could copy from country 1. Alternatively, the distortion would not arise if the inventors in country 1 possessed these rights of adaptation to country 2.

We can make analogous welfare comparisons for the case discussed in section 8.3 in which ν_2 is low and constant. In the steady state, the social planner's and decentralized solutions each feature $N_2/N_1 = 1$ with N_2 and C_2 growing at the rate γ_1. However, in the decentralized case, the competition among potential copiers drives the effective cost of imitation up to $\nu_2^* > \nu_2$. This waste of resources implies that the steady-state level of $\chi_2 \equiv C_2/N_2$ is lower than in the social planner's setting. (This result holds even if the decentralized solution involves the appropriate subsidy for the use of intermediates in country 2.)

Recall that, when $N_2 = N_1$ was attained at time T in the decentralized case, C_2 jumped upward, and the resources devoted to copying jumped downward correspondingly. We can show that the solution for the social planner in country 2 entails no such jumps. The growth rate of C_2 falls discretely at time T, but the level of C_2—and, hence, the amount of resources spent on copying—do not jump.

For $t < T$, we can show that the decentralized choice for $\dot{N}_2/N_2$ exceeds the social planner's value. (This result holds if the decentralized solution involves the appropriate subsidy on the use of intermediates in country 2.) The values for $\dot{C}_2/C_2$ are the same

23. The parameters are assumed to be such that N_2/N_1 remains below unity in the steady state.

(and constant) in the two environments, but the decentralized path features lower levels of $\chi_2 \equiv C_2/N_2$ and correspondingly higher levels of resources devoted to copying, $\nu_2\dot{N}_2$.

Again, the problem is the excessive incentive to secure property rights in country 2. In the model with smoothly rising costs of copying, $\nu_2(N_2/N_1)$, this incentive is communicated by a stream of capital gains to holders of monopoly rights in country 2. In the model with constant ν_2, the inducement comes from the prospect of an infinite rate of capital gain for an instant at time T. Either way, the capital gains motivate imitation at too fast a rate.[24]

8.8 Summary Observations about Diffusion and Growth

The diffusion of technology from leading economies to followers involves costs of imitation and adaptation. We assumed that these costs were lower than those for innovation when little copying had occurred but rose as the pool of uncopied ideas contracted. This cost structure implies a form of diminishing returns to imitation and thereby tends to generate a pattern of convergence. Follower countries tend to grow faster the greater the gap from the leaders. This process is, however, conditional, in that the growth rate depends, for a given technological gap, on government policies and other variables that influence the rate of return to imitation in a follower economy.

In the steady state, the leading and following countries grow at the same rate. Thus equalization of growth rates occurs in the long run even if countries differ in costs of R&D, levels of productivity, and the willingness to save. If the countries have the same preferences about saving (that is, equal parameters ρ_i and θ_i), the equalization of growth rates implies that rates of return are also the same in the steady state. Hence, even without a global capital market, the diffusion of technology can equate the rates of return across countries in the long run.

In some cases, technological diffusion involves imitation by local entrepreneurs of products or ideas developed elsewhere. This process is costly, but often escapes any fees paid to the inventor of the good or method of production. In other cases, the diffusion occurs by means of foreign investment. The honoring of intellectual property rights across international borders helps to provide the proper incentive for discoveries of new goods and techniques in the leading economies. For this reason, the institution of these rights tends to raise the long-term growth rate in leading *and* following economies.

24. In an alternative setting, the cost ν_2 is independent of N_2/N_1 but inversely related to the time since the invention was made in country 1. The idea is that quicker adaptations are more costly. In this environment, the distortion would involve agents in country 2 imitating too soon and thereby bearing socially excessive costs of imitation. Again, the problem stems from the incentive to secure property rights in country 2.

8.9 Problems

8.1 Pareto optimality in the leader-follower model. Consider the leader-follower model described in sections 8.1 and 8.2.

a. Discuss the distortions that lead to Pareto nonoptimal outcomes. How do the distortions differ from those present in the one-country varieties model of chapter 6?

b. What policies could be implemented to ensure Pareto optimality?

c. Suppose that the leading country has a decentralized equilibrium with no government intervention. Would it ever be optimal for the government of the follower country to subsidize innovation in the leading country?

8.2 Rates of return in the leader-follower model. Consider again the leader-follower model from sections 8.1 and 8.2.

a. Are the rates of return constant in the two countries? Which rate of return is higher?

b. What happens if the leader and follower countries share a common, perfect credit market?

8.3 Convergence in the leader-follower model

a. In the model of sections 8.1 and 8.2, discuss whether the two countries converge to the same levels of per capita output and wage rate. Discuss whether they converge to a common growth rate of per capita output.

b. Is it possible for the country with an initially lower level of per capita output to become the country with the higher level of per capita output? Is it possible to get another switch later on in the relative levels of per capita output?

c. Can the countries switch roles at some point in terms of innovation and imitation?

d. What are the implications of the model for absolute and relative convergence?

8.4 Different theories of convergence. Contrast the results on convergence from the diffusion theories with those from the Ramsey model. Is it feasible to distinguish the theories empirically? If so, how?

8.5 Foreign investment

a. Discuss the role of foreign investment in the context of the diffusion models.

b. Does the potential for foreign investment in the imitating economy, country 2, benefit the agents of the innovating economy, country 1?

c. Does the potential for foreign investment benefit the agents of the imitating economy, country 2? Would country 2 always want to respect the intellectual property rights of entrepreneurs from country 1?

8.6 Leapfrogging

a. Discuss the concept of leapfrogging and demonstrate how it differs from absolute convergence.

b. Does the Ramsey model of chapter 2 (augmented to allow for random shocks to the technology) preclude leapfrogging? Is this model inconsistent with the observation that an economy that is initially lagging in technological sophistication becomes the leader at a later date?

8.7 Innovation and technology transfer (based on Krugman, 1979). Consider a two-country world (North and South) with M types of consumer goods. These goods cannot be stored but can be traded across countries. Each country has L consumer-workers with instantaneous utility functions given by

$$U = \left(\sum_{i=1}^{M} (c_i)^\theta \right)^{1/\theta}$$

where $0 < \theta < 1$ and c_i is the amount of good i consumed. There are two kinds of goods, old ones and new ones. At a point in time, M_o of the M goods are old, and $M_n = M - M_o$ are new. The technology for producing old goods is common property, so that they can be produced in the North or the South. The technology for producing new goods is freely accessible in the North but is unavailable in the South. It takes one unit of labor to produce one unit of any good, and all goods are produced under conditions of perfect competition.

Normalize the price of each old good to 1, and let P_n be the price of each new good. (Note that the price of all old goods must be the same, and the price of all new goods must be the same.) Let w_N and w_S be the wage rates in the North and South, respectively. Define τ to be the terms of trade for the North, that is, the ratio of the prices of goods produced in the North to those produced in the South.

a. How does τ depend on w_N and w_S? How does y, the ratio of the North's per capita income to the South's per capita income, depend on w_N and w_S?

b. Let $\sigma \equiv M_n/M_o$. Derive the pattern of specialization in the world economy as a function of σ. Use this result to relate w_N, w_S, τ, and y to σ.

c. Let $\dot{M} = iM$ describe the rate of innovation in the North, where i is exogenous. Let $\dot{M}_o = tM_n$ describe the rate of technological transfer, where t is exogenous. Find the steady-state value of σ and its law of motion. How does the world pattern of specialization change over time? What happens to y over time?

d. Define the set of initial conditions under which convergence applies, that is, $\dot{y} < 0$. In this model, is convergence equivalent to the long-run equalization of incomes, that is, $y^* = 1$?

8.8 Technology choice and overtaking (based on Ohyama and Jones, 1993). Consider a two-country world with a single, nonstorable good. Each country has L consumer-workers with linear preferences and rate of time preference $\rho > 0$. There is a traditional technology, characterized by

$$q_i^T = A_i \cdot (1 - \theta_i)$$

for $i = 1, 2$, where $1 - \theta_i$ is the share of the labor force used in the traditional technology in country i. Country 1 is the current technological leader, in the sense that $A_1 > A_2$.

At time 0, a new technology appears with the following characteristics:

$$q_i^N = B_i \theta_i$$

$$B_i = B + \lambda \cdot \int_0^t q_i^N \cdot d\tau$$

where B is a constant with $0 < B < A_i$, and λ is another constant with $0 < \lambda < \rho$. The new technology is less productive initially ($B < A_i$) but exhibits learning by doing ($\lambda > 0$).

a. Assume that the technologies are mutually exclusive within a country, so that θ_i must equal 0 or 1. Under what conditions will the new technology be adopted and by which country? Is it possible to observe leapfrogging? If so, calculate the time T that it takes for country 2 to overtake country 1.

b. Assume now that the technologies can be operated simultaneously within each country, so that $0 \leq \theta_i \leq 1$. At time 0, each country chooses a value for θ_i and is then constrained to maintain it forever. Will we ever observe partial adoption? Discuss whether leapfrogging is possible and, if so, characterize T.

c. Assume now that there are one-time costs of switching from the traditional to the new technology, and these costs are given by $c(\theta_i) = c\theta_i/(1 - \theta_i)$, where $c > 0$ is a constant. Under what conditions will we observe partial adoption? Discuss whether leapfrogging is possible and, if so, characterize T.

d. (*difficult*) Finally, assume that θ_i can be set at different values at each point in time. Assume again that there are no costs of switching from the old to the new technology. Describe the dynamics of θ_i and output. Discuss whether leapfrogging is possible and, if so, characterize T. Redo the analysis for the case in which the one-time cost of switching is $c(\theta_i)$.

9 Labor Supply and Population

In previous chapters, we assumed that population and the labor force grew together at the exogenous rate n. We now endogenize population and labor force participation in three different ways. First, we consider the possibility of immigration and emigration in response to economic opportunities. This process alters population and the labor force for given fertility and mortality. Second, we introduce choices about fertility, another channel that allows for an endogenous determination of population and the labor force. Finally, we allow for variations in work effort. That is, we relax the equality between labor force and population.

9.1 Migration in Models of Economic Growth

The migration of persons is one mechanism for change in an economy's population and labor supply. This migration or labor mobility is analogous to the capital mobility that we explored in chapter 3. The difference is that, whereas capital tends to move from places with low rates of return to those with high rates of return, labor tends to move from economies with low wage rates or other unfavorable characteristics to those with high wage rates or other favorable elements. We found before that capital mobility tends to speed up an economy's convergence toward its steady-state position, and we shall find that labor mobility typically works in a similar way.

Migration differs in some ways from natural population growth, that is, differences between births and deaths. First, in the case of migration, gains in population for the destination economy represent corresponding losses for the source economy. Thus we have to consider immigration and emigration as two sides of a single process.

Second, unlike newly born persons, migrants come with accumulated human capital. Since the movement of a person entails the movement of this human capital, labor mobility or migration implies some degree of capital mobility. Newborns also differ from migrants in that the residents of an economy tend to care about the newborns—that is, about their children—but not about the migrants. This difference in linkages with the existing population implies differences in the way that population growth interacts with saving behavior and, hence, with rates of economic growth.

A convenient starting point for the study of migration and growth is the Solow–Swan model, which assumes a closed economy and an exogenous, constant saving rate. The extension to incorporate migration means that economies are opened to some extent; that is, the migration process implies some degree of mobility of raw labor and human capital. Although the analysis allows for feedback from economic growth to wage rates to the rate of migration, the underlying optimization problem for migrants is not considered at this point. That is, the first model just postulates a functional form for a migration function.

We next extend the analysis to the Ramsey framework in which saving behavior reflects household optimization. This extension assumes that the representative household determines the path of consumption without regard to the welfare of immigrants. This model continues to use a postulated form for the migration function.

Finally, we present a model that allows for capital mobility and assumes that migration rates are determined by household optimization. In this setting, we can analyze how changes in the costs or benefits associated with moving affect the dynamic paths of migration and growth.

9.1.1 Migration in the Solow–Swan Model

The Model with Migration This section introduces migration into the Solow–Swan model of a closed economy. Thus we allow for mobility of persons but assume that the economy is closed with respect to foreign goods and assets; that is, we make the unrealistic assumption that people are more mobile than physical capital. Although this assumption is extreme, the analysis does bring out some effects of migration on the growth process. A later section allows for capital mobility.

Let $M(t)$, which can be positive or negative, be the flow of migrants into the domestic economy and $\kappa(t)$ the quantity of capital that each migrant brings along. Since we assume that capital cannot move by itself, the quantity of capital that each migrant carries brings in a degree of capital mobility.

Migrants typically do not carry much physical capital (machines and buildings) but possess significant amounts of human capital. We find it convenient here not to distinguish among the different forms of capital (as we did in chapters 4 and 5) and to deal instead with a single broad concept of capital that encompasses physical and human forms. Therefore, κ is the quantity of this broad capital that accompanies each migrant.[1]

The domestic population and labor force, $L(t)$, grow due to fertility net of mortality at the constant, exogenous rate n. The overall growth rate of the domestic population is therefore

$$\dot{L}/L = n + M/L = n + m \tag{9.1}$$

where $m \equiv M/L$ is the net migration rate. We have omitted time subscripts for convenience.

The change in the domestic capital stock is given by

$$\dot{K} = s \cdot F(K, \hat{L}) - \delta K + \kappa M \tag{9.2}$$

where s is the constant gross saving rate. The new element is that κM—the capital brought

1. In this model the migrants cannot maintain any financial claims on foreign-source income. People who move relinquish or consume all capital that they cannot carry with them. We also do not consider remittances by migrants to family members who remain in the source country.

in by immigrants or taken out by emigrants—contributes to $\dot{K}$. The growth rate of capital per effective worker, $\hat{k}$, can be determined from equations (9.1) and (9.2) as

$$\dot{\hat{k}}/\hat{k} = s \cdot f(\hat{k})/\hat{k} - (x + n + \delta) - m \cdot [1 - (\hat{\kappa}/\hat{k})] \tag{9.3}$$

where $\hat{\kappa} \equiv \kappa e^{-xt}$ is the capital per "effective immigrant," that is, immigrants augmented by the technology factor e^{xt}. (We assume here that the rate of exogenous technical progress, x, is the same in the foreign and domestic economies.) Recall that $x + n + \delta$ is the effective depreciation rate for capital in models without migration, that is, the rate of decline in $\hat{k}$ due to growth of effective labor at the rate $x + n$ and to depreciation of the capital stock at the rate δ. (See, for example, equation [1.30] in the Solow–Swan model.) This effective depreciation rate is now augmented by a migration term, $m \cdot [1 - (\hat{\kappa}/\hat{k})]$. The overall term would therefore be the same as in previous models if $m = 0$ or if $\hat{\kappa} = \hat{k}$ at all points in time.

Since migrants bring little physical capital, $\hat{\kappa} < \hat{k}$ would apply unless the human capital per migrant were substantially greater than that per worker in the domestic economy.[2] If $\hat{\kappa} < \hat{k}$, the migration term, $m \cdot [1 - (\hat{\kappa}/\hat{k})]$, adds to the effective depreciation rate if $m > 0$ and subtracts from it if $m < 0$. If migrants come with no capital, $\hat{\kappa} = 0$, the migration rate, m, adds one-to-one to the natural population growth rate, n, in equation (9.3). If we think of n as corresponding to the birth of children, this result makes sense because we treat children as beginning life with no human capital.[3]

If $m > 0$, the quantity $\hat{\kappa}$ is the capital per effective worker brought by each immigrant. This quantity would be related to the total capital per effective worker that prevails in the immigrant's place of origin. Given the conditions in the origin country—which determine $\hat{\kappa}$—the quantity $\hat{\kappa}/\hat{k}$ would decline as $\hat{k}$ rises in the destination country.[4] Moreover, if we assume that the typical foreign country is close to its steady-state position, we can treat $\hat{\kappa}$ as roughly constant over time.

If $m < 0$, $\hat{\kappa}$ represents the capital per effective worker of each emigrant.[5] In this case, $\hat{\kappa}/\hat{k}$ is likely to be roughly constant; that is, $\hat{\kappa}/\hat{k}$ would not change as $\hat{k}$ rises.

The Migration Function In a later section we work out a model in which the migration rate responds positively to the present value of domestic wage rates, compared to the present

2. If $m > 0$, we have to compare the capital of immigrants with that of persons in the receiving economy. If $m < 0$, the comparison is between emigrants and persons in the sending economy.

3. In contrast, death implies the loss of a person's human capital. We have, however, simplified the analysis by treating the depreciation of physical and human capital as the constant multiple δ of the existing stocks of capital.

4. We neglect the possibility that a change in $\hat{k}$ alters the selection of immigrants with respect to their capital $\hat{\kappa}$.

5. We assume that immigration and emigration do not occur simultaneously, so that net and gross migration coincide. More generally, heterogeneity in human capital or other variables would cause gross flows to exceed net flows.

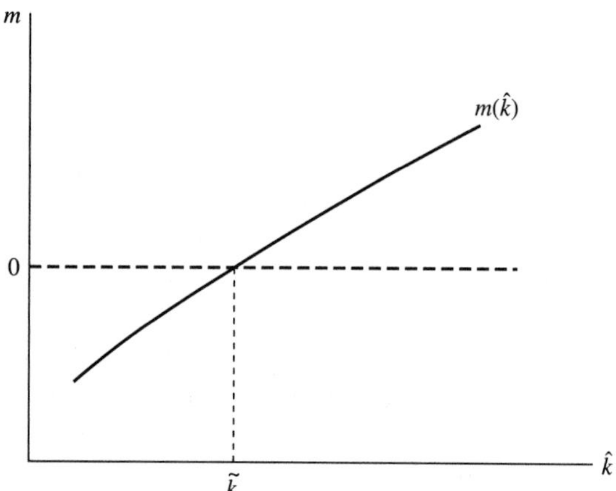

Figure 9.1
The migration rate. For given conditions in other economies, a higher value of $\hat{k}$ raises the domestic wage rate and tends accordingly to increase the net migration rate, m. The value $\tilde{k}$ is the quantity of capital per effective worker that yields a zero net migration rate.

value in other economies. For given conditions elsewhere, a higher value of $\hat{k}$ raises the domestic wage rate and tends accordingly to increase the migration rate, m.[6]

In the present setting, we postulate a positive relation between m and $\hat{k}$, as shown in figure 9.1. The assumption is that conditions that affect wage rates per unit of effective labor in other economies do not change as $\hat{k}$ changes. We also hold constant any domestic or foreign amenities that enter into households' utility functions. Note that the value denoted $\tilde{k}$ in the figure corresponds to zero net migration.

An experiment that we would like to consider is a shift of the migration function, $m(\hat{k})$. The migration theory that we use later relates these shifts to changes in the costs or benefits associated with moving. For example, a reduction of wage rates or a worsening of amenities in foreign countries makes migration to the domestic country more attractive and, therefore, shifts the function $m(\hat{k})$ upward. The slope of the function depends, among other things, on the relation between the cost of moving (for the marginal migrant) and the volume of migration. If this cost increases rapidly with the number of migrants, then a change in $\hat{k}$ has only a small effect on migration; that is, the curve $m(\hat{k})$ is relatively flat.

Define the overall migration term that appears on the right-hand side of equation (9.3) as

$$\xi(\hat{k}) \equiv m(\hat{k}) \cdot [1 - (\hat{\kappa}/\hat{k})] \tag{9.4}$$

6. With no capital mobility, however, a higher $\hat{k}$ also reduces the domestic rate of return on capital, including the human capital that the migrants bring with them. We assume that the effect from the higher wage rate is dominant.

so that the growth rate of $\hat{k}$ is given by

$$(1/\hat{k}) \cdot \dot{\hat{k}} = s \cdot f(\hat{k})/\hat{k} - [x + n + \delta + \xi(\hat{k})] \quad (9.5)$$

The effective depreciation rate, $x + n + \delta + \xi(\hat{k})$, includes the term $\xi(\hat{k})$ on a one-to-one basis. The $m(\hat{k})$ part of $\xi(\hat{k})$ in equation (9.4) adds to the growth rate of effective labor and thereby to $x + n$. The $-m(\hat{k}) \cdot (\hat{\kappa}/\hat{k})$ part of $\xi(\hat{k})$ is the negative of the effect of the migrants' human capital on the growth rate of the domestic capital stock. This inflow of human capital subtracts from the effective depreciation rate.

If $m(\hat{k}) > 0$, we argued that we could treat $\hat{\kappa}$ as independent of $\hat{k}$. In this case, the effect of $\hat{k}$ on $\xi(\hat{k})$ is given from equation (9.4) by

$$\xi'(\hat{k}) = m'(\hat{k}) \cdot [1 - (\hat{\kappa}/\hat{k})] + m(\hat{k}) \cdot \hat{\kappa}/(\hat{k})^2$$

Thus, $\xi'(\hat{k}) > 0$ follows from $m'(\hat{k}) > 0$, $\hat{\kappa} < \hat{k}$, and $m(\hat{k}) > 0$.

If $m(\hat{k}) < 0$, we argued that we could treat $\hat{\kappa}/\hat{k}$ as constant. In this case, $\xi'(\hat{k}) > 0$ follows from equation (9.4) because of $m'(\hat{k}) > 0$ and $\hat{\kappa} < \hat{k}$. Thus we assume that $\xi'(\hat{k}) > 0$ holds whether the migration rate is positive or negative. It follows that a higher $\hat{k}$ raises the effective depreciation term, $x + n + \delta + \xi(\hat{k})$, in equation (9.5). In contrast, this term was independent of $\hat{k}$ in earlier models.

The Steady State Figure 9.2 is our standard form of a growth diagram. The $s \cdot f(\hat{k})/\hat{k}$ curve is downward sloping as usual because of the diminishing average product of capital. The horizontal line at $x + n + \delta$ has now been replaced by the upward-sloping curve, $x+n+\delta+\xi(\hat{k})$. If $\hat{k} = \tilde{k}$, then $m(\hat{k}) = 0$ (see figure 9.1) and $\xi(\hat{k}) = 0$ (see equation [9.4]). Therefore, the height of the effective-depreciation curve at $\tilde{k}$ is $x + n + \delta$. If $\hat{k} > \tilde{k}$, then $m(\hat{k}) > 0$, and the effective-depreciation curve lies above $x + n + \delta$. Conversely, if $\hat{k} < \tilde{k}$, then the curve lies below $x + n + \delta$. We have drawn the curves in figure 9.2 so that the intersection occurs at a point $\hat{k}^*$ that exceeds $\tilde{k}$.

The steady state corresponds to the intersection of the $s \cdot f(\hat{k})/\hat{k}$ and $x + n + \delta + \xi(\hat{k})$ curves at the point $\hat{k}^*$. Given the way that we drew the curves, so that $\hat{k}^* > \tilde{k}$, $m^* > 0$ and the domestic economy is a recipient of migrants in the steady state. That is, the economy remains in the steady state as a perpetual receiver of migrants (or would persist as a sender of migrants if $\hat{k}^* < \tilde{k}$).[7]

We can use figure 9.2 to assess the effects of changes in various parameters on the steady-state values. For example, an increase in s or a permanent improvement of the production

7. The migration theory that we consider in a later section assumes that a higher level of population congests some fixed factor, such as land. This congestion implies that the steady-state migration rate is zero for each economy (if the natural population growth rate, n, is also zero in each economy in the steady state).

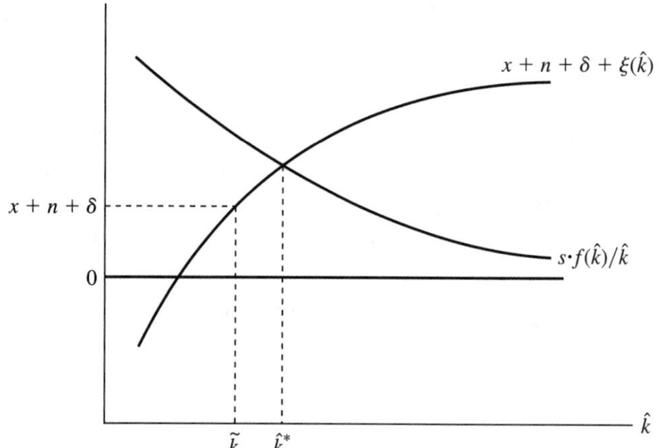

Figure 9.2
The Solow–Swan model with migration. The positive response of net migration to the wage rate implies that the rate of population growth is a positive function of $\hat{k}$. Hence, the effective depreciation term in the Solow–Swan model becomes upward sloping. The steady state is determined by the intersection of the saving curve, $s \cdot f(\hat{k})/\hat{k}$, with the effective depreciation curve, $x + n + \delta + \xi(\hat{k})$. For any value of $\hat{k}$, the growth rate of $\hat{k}$ is given by the vertical distance between these two curves.

function shifts the $s \cdot f(\hat{k})/\hat{k}$ curve upward and leads thereby to increases in $\hat{k}^*$ and m^*. The higher value of m^* arises because the shift raises the steady-state wage rate per unit of effective labor and thereby makes the domestic economy more attractive to foreigners.

If conditions worsen in other economies, the migration function, $m(\hat{k})$, would shift upward in figure 9.1. This change shifts the curve for effective depreciation, $x + n + \delta + \xi(\hat{k})$, in figure 9.2 in a similar manner (see the expression for $\xi[\hat{k}]$ in equation [9.4]). Hence, $\hat{k}^*$ falls and m^* rises. Thus an expansion of the supply of immigrants lowers the steady-state capital intensity in the domestic economy. This result follows because the immigrants come with relatively little capital.

Transitional Dynamics and Convergence To assess the speed of convergence implied by equation (9.5), we follow our usual practice and assume a Cobb–Douglas production function, $f(\hat{k}) = A\hat{k}^{\alpha}$. We also approximate the $\xi(\hat{k})$ function from equation (9.4) in a log-linear form:

$$\xi(\hat{k}) \equiv m(\hat{k}) \cdot [1 - (\hat{\kappa}/\hat{k})] \approx b \cdot [\log(\hat{k}/\hat{k}_{\text{world}})] \tag{9.6}$$

where $b \geq 0$ and $\hat{k}_{\text{world}}$ represents the capital intensity in other economies. Equation (9.6) implies that $\xi(\hat{k}) = 0$ if the domestic economy has the same capital intensity as the rest of the world—because the incentive to migrate would then be nil (if we neglect differences in amenities or in forms of production functions). We treat $\hat{k}_{\text{world}}$ as a constant; that is, we assume that the world is (on average) in the steady state.

The key element for the convergence analysis will be the size of the parameter b. To see what this parameter represents, differentiate equation (9.6) with respect to $\log(\hat{k})$ to get[8]

$$b = \partial\xi(\hat{k})/\partial[\log(\hat{k})] = [1 - (\hat{\kappa}/\hat{k})] \cdot \partial m(\hat{k})/\partial[\log(\hat{k})] \tag{9.7}$$

This equation shows that, if $\hat{\kappa} < \hat{k}$, b depends positively on the sensitivity of migration to $\log(\hat{k})$. We noted before that, if the cost of moving (for the marginal migrant) increases rapidly with the number of migrants, the function $m(\hat{k})$ in figure 9.1 will be relatively flat. In this case, the coefficient b will be small. For a limiting case in which the cost of moving rises extremely rapidly with m, b is close to 0, $\xi(\hat{k})$ is therefore near 0, and the effective-depreciation term in equation (9.5) is approximately $x + n + \delta$, as in our earlier models.

For a given sensitivity of migration to $\log(\hat{k})$, the coefficient b declines if $\hat{\kappa}/\hat{k}$ rises. In particular, if $\hat{\kappa} = \hat{k}$, then $b = 0$, and the effective depreciation term is again $x + n + \delta$.

If we log-linearize the differential equation (9.5) around its steady-state position, we can compute the speed of convergence to the steady state as

$$\beta = (1 - \alpha) \cdot (x + n + \delta) + b + b \cdot (1 - \alpha) \cdot \log(\hat{k}^*/\hat{k}_{\text{world}}) \tag{9.8}$$

This formula reduces to the Solow–Swan value (equation [1.33]) if $b = 0$.

If we consider the typical economy, for which $\hat{k}^* = \hat{k}_{\text{world}}$, and assume $b > 0$, equation (9.8) shows that the potential for migration raises the convergence coefficient, β, above the Solow–Swan value by the amount b. To assess the size of b, we use some empirical results on the determinants of migration.

Barro and Sala-i-Martin (1991) and Braun (1993) used data from the U.S. states, the regions of Japan, and five European countries (France, Germany, Italy, Spain, and the United Kingdom) to estimate the sensitivity of within-country migration to differentials in per capita income. The regression coefficient for the net migration rate on the log of initial per capita income or product averaged 0.012 per year.

The sensitivity of international migration to income differentials tends to be smaller than that for regions within a country. For example, Hatton and Williamson (1994) examine the behavior of migration from 11 European countries to the United States from 1850 to 1913. Their regression coefficients, based on responses of immigration to proportional differentials in wage rates, averaged 0.008 per year.

8. For $m < 0$, we hold fixed $\hat{\kappa}/\hat{k}$ to get equation (9.7). For $m > 0$, if we hold fixed $\hat{\kappa}$, the equation would have the additional term $m(\hat{k}) \cdot (\hat{\kappa}/\hat{k})$ on the right-hand side. Equation (9.7) is then an approximation that is satisfactory when $m(\hat{k})$ is relatively small.

To relate these results to the coefficient b, we can use the Cobb–Douglas relation, $\log(\hat{y}) = \log(A) + \alpha \cdot \log(\hat{k})$, along with equation (9.7), to get

$$b = \alpha \cdot [1 - (\hat{\kappa}/\hat{k})] \cdot \partial m/\partial[\log(\hat{y})] \tag{9.9}$$

The empirical estimates mentioned before suggest that $\partial m/\partial[\log(\hat{y})]$ is about 0.012 per year for regions of countries and about 0.008 per year across countries. We have argued (in chapters 1 and 2) that a coefficient α of around 0.75 is reasonable for a broad concept of capital. Therefore, we have to specify the ratio $\hat{\kappa}/\hat{k}$ to pin down the coefficient b in equation (9.9).

Dolado, Goria, and Ichino (1994, table 2) examine the composition of immigration for 1960–87 to nine developed countries—Australia, Belgium, Canada, Germany, the Netherlands, Sweden, Switzerland, the United Kingdom, and the United States. They observe that the educational attainment of immigrants averaged about 80 percent of that of natives, assuming that the schooling of immigrants did not differ systematically from the average schooling in their countries of origin. Chiswick (1978, table 1) finds for U.S. census data in 1970 that the school attainment of foreign-born men was 91 percent of that of natives. Borjas (1992, table 1.4) reports from U.S. census data that the schooling of foreign-born men rose from 79 percent of natives in 1940 to 82 percent in 1950, 87 percent in 1960, 94 percent in 1970, and 93 percent in 1980.

For international immigration, we take 80 percent as a typical value for the ratio of immigrants' to natives' human capital. If immigrants carry no physical capital and if the ratio of human to total capital in the domestic economy is 5/8—the value that we specified in chapter 5—then $\hat{\kappa}/\hat{k}$ is 0.5 (0.8 times 5/8).

For migration within a country, the ratio of immigrants' to natives' human capital is likely to be higher than that for international migration. For example, Borjas, Bronars, and Trejo (1992) find for young U.S. males in 1986 that immigrants to a state averaged 3 percent more years of education than the average of natives of the state.[9] If we assume that this ratio is 100 percent, $\hat{\kappa}/\hat{k}$ is 0.62.

In the context of regions of a country, we use $\hat{\kappa}/\hat{k} = 0.62$ and $\partial m/\partial[\log(\hat{y})] = 0.012$ per year. If we assume $\alpha = 0.75$, we find that b is around 0.003 per year. In the international context, we use $\hat{\kappa}/\hat{k} = 0.5$ and $\partial m/\partial[\log(\hat{y})] = 0.008$ per year. If we assume $\alpha = 0.75$, we get that b is again around 0.003 per year. The results are similar in the two contexts because the higher value of $\partial m/\partial[\log(\hat{y})]$ in the regional setting is offset by the higher value of $\hat{\kappa}/\hat{k}$.

For the other parameter values that we have assumed previously ($x = 0.02$, $n = 0.01$, $\delta = 0.05$), the Solow–Swan value for β when $\alpha = 0.75$ is 0.020. The value for β implied

9. This information comes from a supplementary table that was provided to us by Steve Trejo.

by equation (9.8) is higher than the Solow–Swan value by the amount b; that is, β would be around 0.023 in the cross-region and international contexts. Therefore, the inclusion of migration suggests, first, that there is a small increase—by roughly 10 percent—in the convergence speed and, second, that convergence coefficients estimated across regions within countries would not differ greatly from those estimated across countries. This prediction accords with the findings of Barro and Sala-i-Martin (1992a), who report that estimated (conditional) convergence rates across regions of countries are only slightly higher than those across countries.

A lower value of $\hat{\kappa}/\hat{k}$ raises b in equation (9.9) and thereby increases the convergence coefficient, β. The predictions about convergence would therefore differ for an economy that is receiving migrants, $m > 0$, from one that is sending migrants, $m < 0$. Since the receivers tend to have higher capital intensities than the senders, the value of $\hat{\kappa}/\hat{k}$ tends to be lower for the receivers. Hence, the propensity to migrate raises the speed at which destination economies approach their steady states relative to the speed for source economies. It is even possible, as we will discuss, that migration would lower the speed of convergence for the sending economies.

The potential to migrate raises the speed of convergence because we assumed $b > 0$. If the migration rate responds positively to income—that is, if $\partial m/\partial[\log(\hat{y})] > 0$—then the coefficient b in equation (9.9) would be negative if $\hat{\kappa}/\hat{k} > 1$. This case could arise if migrants possess human capital that is substantially greater than the average in their home economies.

For destination economies, where $m > 0$, the condition $\hat{\kappa}/\hat{k} \geq 1$ seems implausible. The immigrants would not only have to possess more human capital than the average person in the receiving location, but this gap in human capital would also have to more than offset the immigrants' failure to carry significant amounts of nonhuman capital. This condition is unlikely to be satisfied because, as already noted, immigrants tend to have less human capital than the residents of the receiving economy.

For source economies, where $m < 0$, the condition $\hat{\kappa}/\hat{k} \geq 1$ is conceivable but still unlikely. For migration across regions of a country, the usual view—expressed, for example, by Greenwood (1975)—is that more educated persons are more likely to migrate. Borjas, Bronars, and Trejo (1992, tables 2 and 4) quantify this effect for young men in the United States in 1986. Their figures imply that migrants averaged 2 percent more years of schooling than the average of native persons from their states of origin. This small excess of human capital would, however, be offset by the migrants' failure to carry physical capital (if we continue to assume that physical capital is not perfectly mobile across the U.S. states).

Hatton and Williamson (1994) observe that European emigrants from 1850 to 1913 were typically unskilled, so that $\hat{\kappa}/\hat{k} < 1$ would hold even for human capital for the sending countries in these cases. For poorer countries, it is plausible that persons with relatively high human capital would be more inclined to migrate, a phenomenon often described as a *brain drain*. This situation is especially likely to apply to the return of settlers from crumbling empires, as in the case of the British from India, the French from Algeria, and the Portuguese from Mozambique. In some cases, this force may be great enough to more than offset the migrants' failure to carry much nonhuman capital. Thus the potential to migrate would, in these cases, slow down the speed of convergence for economies that are senders of immigrants.

A new result when $b > 0$ is that β in equation (9.8) increases with $\hat{k}^*$ for given values of the other parameters. The reason is that a higher $\hat{k}^*$ implies a higher steady-state migration rate, m^*, and, hence, a faster speed of convergence in the neighborhood of the steady state. Recall, for example, that a permanent improvement in the production function or an increase in the domestic economy's saving rate, s, raises $\hat{k}^*$. We find now that these changes also increase the speed of convergence, β. In contrast, β was invariant with the level of the production function or the saving rate in the Solow–Swan model.

If we assume perfect labor mobility—that is, let the cost of migration approach 0—then $\partial m/\partial[\log(\hat{y})]$ becomes infinite. Therefore, if $\hat{\kappa} < \hat{k}$, the coefficient b would become infinite in equation (9.9). Equation (9.8) implies accordingly that β becomes infinite; that is, perfect labor mobility generates an infinite speed of convergence. This result corresponds to the effect of perfect capital mobility, as studied in chapter 3.

Finally, consider the effect of the capital-share coefficient, α, on the speed of convergence. The usual result is that an increase in α implies a smaller tendency of capital to experience diminishing returns. The convergence speed therefore declines and tends to 0 as α tends to 1; that is, the convergence property does not appear in the AK model, which we studied in chapter 4.

The form for the convergence coefficient, β, in equation (9.8) exhibits this standard inverse relation between β and α for a given coefficient b. (We assume here that $\hat{k}^* = \hat{k}_{\text{world}}$, so that the last term on the right-hand side of equation [9.8] is zero.) Equation (9.9) shows how the coefficient b is determined. For a given value of $\partial m/\partial[\log(\hat{y})]$, b increases with α, an effect that would offset the inverse relation between β and α. However, we also have to consider the effect of α on $\partial m/\partial[\log(\hat{y})]$.

In the Cobb–Douglas case, the wage rate per unit of effective labor is $\hat{w} = (1 - \alpha) \cdot A\hat{k}^{\alpha}$, which is proportional to $\hat{y}$. As α rises, the share of income represented by wages (on raw labor) declines. We therefore anticipate that $\partial m/\partial[\log(\hat{y})]$ would also decline, because the benefit from moving raw labor from one place to another becomes smaller. Thus it is unclear, on net, whether b rises or falls with α. However, as α approaches 1, $\hat{w}$ approaches 0, and $\partial m/\partial[\log(\hat{y})]$ would tend to 0 (because the benefit from moving raw labor becomes nil). This result means that b approaches 0 as α approaches 1 and, hence, that the coefficient β in equation (9.8) also tends to 0 as α approaches 1. Thus, even with migration, the model does not exhibit the convergence property if diminishing returns to capital are absent.

9.1.2 Migration in the Ramsey Model

In chapter 2 we used the Ramsey framework of household optimization to extend the Solow–Swan model to the context of a variable saving rate. We now apply the Ramsey formulation to the version of the Solow–Swan model that includes migration. The new results involve the interaction between migration and the choices of saving rates. These results concern the transitional behavior of saving and, hence, the speed of convergence, and also involve the level of the saving rate and, hence, some characteristics of the steady state.

Setup of the Ramsey Model with Migration The framework that we use is a modification of Weil's (1989) extension of the Blanchard (1985) model and is formally similar to the study of finite-horizon households that we carried out in chapter 3. We now assume, however, that the domestic residents consist of immortal families, as in the Ramsey model; that is, $p = 0$ in the context of the Blanchard model. The size of each family grows at the constant, exogenous rate n.

Migrants again enter the economy at the rate $m(t)$, and each migrant comes with the quantity of capital $\kappa(t)$, presumably mainly in the form of human capital.[10] A key assumption is that, unlike the children of the existing residents, no one cares about the immigrants. That is, their consumption does not appear as an argument in the utility functions of the residents.[11]

Let $L(t)$ be the total domestic population at time t, given by

$$L(t) = L(0) \cdot e^{nt} \cdot \exp\left[\int_0^t m(v)\, dv\right] \tag{9.10}$$

The $L(0)$ inhabitants at time 0 represent identical "natives," who arrived all at once in the manner of the Oklahoma land rush of the 1890s.[12] The population at later dates then consists partly of descendants of natives and partly of immigrants and their descendants. We normalize, henceforth, by setting $L(0) = 1$.

Immigrant households are indexed by their vintage $j \geq 0$ of arrival in the country. For native families, we set $j = 0-$; that is, these families arrived in the country sometime before time 0.

10. As before, migrants cannot maintain any financial claims on foreign-source income.

11. The analysis works also for emigration, $m(t) < 0$, if the domestic residents do not care about the people who leave. For example, if migration takes the form of the departure of an entire extended family, it is natural to assume that the remaining families do not care about those who left. The problem is more complicated if family members migrate to other places and then send home remittances or receive funding from those who remain in the domestic economy.

12. We have to get the domestic population started off in some manner. For dates $t > 0$ that are far in the future, the precise way that things begin does not matter much. For further discussion, see Braun (1993).

Optimization Conditions and Aggregation of the Results Households of each vintage j maximize utility, as given at time t by

$$U(j,t) = \int_t^\infty \left\{\log[c(j,v)] \cdot e^{-(\rho-n)\cdot(v-t)}\right\} dv \tag{9.11}$$

where $c(j, v)$ is the consumption per person for households of vintage j at time v. We assume log utility, as in chapter 3, to simplify the aggregation over immigrants of differing vintages.

The analysis in chapter 2 implies that each household's maximization of utility, subject to its budget constraint, dictates the following conditions:

$$[1/c(j,t)] \cdot \dot{c}(j,t) = r(t) - \rho \tag{9.12}$$

$$\dot{a}(j,t) = [r(t) - n] \cdot a(j,t) + w(t) - c(j,t) \tag{9.13}$$

$$c(j,t) = (\rho - n) \cdot [a(j,t) + \tilde{w}(t)] \tag{9.14}$$

where $a(j, t)$ is assets per person, $w(t)$ is the wage rate (the same for all persons), and $\tilde{w}(t)$ is the per capita present value of future wages, as given by

$$\tilde{w}(t) = \int_t^\infty w(v) \cdot e^{n(v-t)} \cdot e^{-\bar{r}(v,t)\cdot(v-t)} \cdot dv \tag{9.15}$$

where $\bar{r}(v, t) \equiv [1/(v - t)] \cdot \int_t^v r(v)\, dv$ is the average interest rate between times t and v. We also have the usual transversality condition, which requires the present value of assets to tend asymptotically to 0.

The method for studying aggregate consumption and assets is essentially the same as that used for the finite-horizon economy in chapter 3; therefore, we provide only a sketch of the analysis. Aggregate consumption at time t is found by summing (integrating) over the vintages j for $0 \le j \le t$ of immigrants:

$$\begin{aligned} C(t) &= \int_0^t \left[c(j,t) \cdot m(j) \cdot L(j) \cdot e^{n(t-j)}\right] dj + e^{nt} \cdot c(0-,t) \\ &= e^{nt} \cdot \int_0^t \left\{c(j,t) \cdot m(j) \cdot \exp\left[\int_0^j m(v)\, dv\right]\right\} dj + e^{nt} \cdot c(0-,t) \end{aligned} \tag{9.16}$$

where $m(j) \cdot L(j)$ is the initial size of immigrant vintage j, we used the formula for $L(j)$ from equation (9.10), and the final term represents the consumption of native families. The result for aggregate assets is similar:

$$A(t) = e^{nt} \cdot \int_0^t \left\{ a(j,t) \cdot m(j) \cdot \exp\left[\int_0^j m(v)\, dv \right] \right\} dj + e^{nt} \cdot a(0-, t) \tag{9.17}$$

The aggregate of the present value of wage income is given from equation (9.15) by

$$\tilde{W}(t) = L(t) \cdot \tilde{w}(t) = e^{nt} \cdot \exp\left[\int_0^t m(v)\, dv \right] \cdot \int_t^\infty w(v) e^{n(v-t)} \cdot e^{-\bar{r}(v,t)\cdot(v-t)} \cdot dv \tag{9.18}$$

The changes over time in $A(t)$ and $\tilde{W}(t)$ come from differentiation of equations (9.17) and (9.18) as

$$\begin{aligned} \dot{A}(t) &= \kappa(t) \cdot m(t) \cdot L(t) + r(t) \cdot A(t) - C(t) \\ &\quad + w(t) \cdot e^{nt} \cdot \left\{ 1 + \int_0^t m(j) \cdot \exp\left[\int_0^j m(v)\, dv \right] \right\} \end{aligned} \tag{9.19}$$

$$\dot{\tilde{W}} = [r(t) + m(t)] \cdot \tilde{W}(t) - w(t) \cdot L(t) \tag{9.20}$$

To get equation (9.19) we used the individual family's budget constraint in equation (9.13) and the condition $a(t,t) = \kappa(t)$; that is, immigrant families arrive with per capita assets $\kappa(t)$.

Equation (9.14) implies $\dot{C}(t) = (\rho - n) \cdot [\dot{A}(t) + d\tilde{W}/dt]$. If we use equations (9.19) and (9.20) and the condition $A(t) = K(t)$, we eventually get an expression for the growth rate of per capita consumption:

$$\dot{c}/c = r(t) - \rho - m(t) \cdot (\rho - n) \cdot [k(t) - \kappa(t)]/c(t) \tag{9.21}$$

where $c(t) \equiv C(t)/L(t)$. This relation reduces to the standard Ramsey result under log utility if $m(t) = 0$ or $\kappa(t) = k(t)$. If $m(t) > 0$ and $\kappa(t) < k(t)$, the inflow of migrants reduces per capita consumption in accordance with the last term on the right-hand side of equation (9.21). In this sense, a higher flow of migrants, $m(t)$, works like an increase in ρ. This effect is analogous to the inflow of children in the Blanchard (1985) model (the term $p + n$ in equation [3.32]) because, as Weil (1989) pointed out, immigrants are just like Blanchard's unloved children.

Steady State and Dynamics of the Model As in the Ramsey model, the dynamics can be expressed as a system of differential equations in $\hat{k}$ and $\hat{c}$. The equation for the growth rate of $\hat{k}$, analogous to equation (9.3) in the Solow–Swan context, is

$$\dot{\hat{k}}/\hat{k} = f(\hat{k})/\hat{k} - \hat{c}/\hat{k} - (x + n + \delta) - m \cdot [1 - (\hat{\kappa}/\hat{k})] \tag{9.22}$$

The equation for the growth rate of $\hat{c}$ comes from equation (9.21):

$$\dot{\hat{c}}/\hat{c} = f'(\hat{k}) - (x + \rho + \delta) - m \cdot (\rho - n) \cdot (\hat{k} - \hat{\kappa})/\hat{c} \tag{9.23}$$

We again use the specification for migration that we assumed in equation (9.6) for the Solow–Swan model:

$$m \cdot [1 - (\hat{\kappa}/\hat{k})] = b \cdot [\log(\hat{k}/\hat{k}_{\text{world}})]$$

where $\hat{k}_{\text{world}}$ is constant. If we substitute this form for migration into equations (9.22) and (9.23), we can use our usual methods to work out a phase diagram in $(\hat{k}, \hat{c})$ space and use this diagram to analyze the steady state and transitional dynamics.

Equations (9.23) and (9.6) imply that, if $\hat{c} \neq 0$, then the $\dot{\hat{c}} = 0$ locus is given by

$$f'(\hat{k}) = \delta + \rho + x + \frac{(\rho - n) \cdot b \cdot \log(\hat{k}/\hat{k}_{\text{world}})}{\hat{c}/\hat{k}} \tag{9.24}$$

This condition differs from the standard one in chapter 2 by the inclusion of the last term on the right-hand side. Let $\hat{k}^*$ be the steady-state value for the model that excludes migration, that is, the value that satisfies $f'(\hat{k}^*) = \delta + \rho + x$. Then the form of the $\dot{\hat{c}} = 0$ locus depends on the relation between $\hat{k}^*$ and $\hat{k}_{\text{world}}$. If $\hat{k}^* = \hat{k}_{\text{world}}$, as would be true for the typical economy, the locus is a vertical line at $\hat{k}^*$, as shown in panel *a* of figure 9.3. The locus

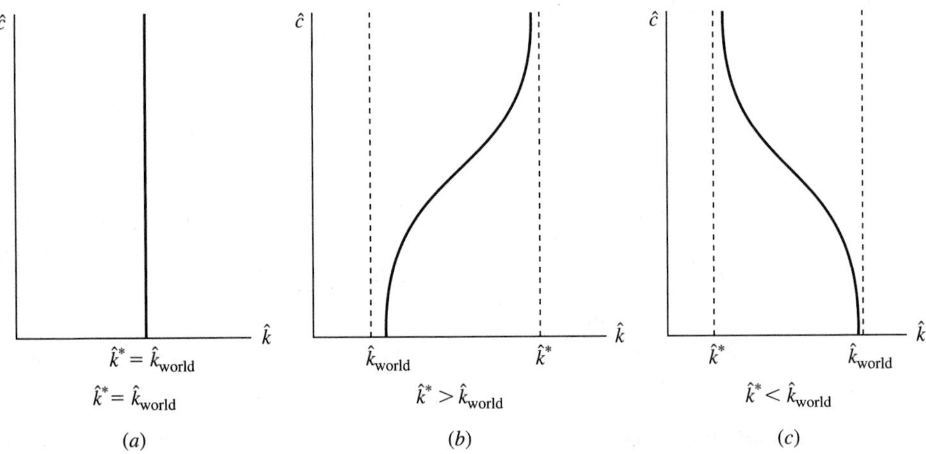

Figure 9.3
The shape of the $\dot{\hat{c}} = 0$ locus in the Ramsey model with migration. The shape of the $\dot{\hat{c}} = 0$ locus depends on the relation between $\hat{k}^*$ and $\hat{k}_{\text{world}}$. If $\hat{k}^* = \hat{k}_{\text{world}}$, the locus is vertical, as shown in panel (*a*). If $\hat{k}^* > \hat{k}_{\text{world}}$, the locus is upward sloping (*b*), and if $\hat{k}^* < \hat{k}_{\text{world}}$, the locus is downward sloping (*c*).

therefore coincides in this case with the standard one from the model without migration (see figure 2.1).

If the domestic economy would be attractive to immigrants in the no-migration steady state—that is, if $\hat{k}^* > \hat{k}_{\text{world}}$—the locus looks as shown in panel *b* of figure 9.3. In particular, $\hat{k}_{\text{world}} < \hat{k} < \hat{k}^*$, $\hat{c}$ approaches 0 as $\hat{k}$ tends to $\hat{k}_{\text{world}}$, and $\hat{c}$ approaches infinity as $\hat{k}$ tends to $\hat{k}^*$. Finally, if $\hat{k}^* < \hat{k}_{\text{world}}$, the locus looks as shown in panel *c* of the figure, with $\hat{k}^* < \hat{k} < \hat{k}_{\text{world}}$.

Equations (9.22) and (9.6) imply that the $\dot{\hat{k}} = 0$ locus is determined by

$$\hat{c} = f(\hat{k}) - (x + n + \delta) \cdot \hat{k} - b \cdot \log(\hat{k}/\hat{k}_{\text{world}}) \cdot \hat{k} \tag{9.25}$$

This condition also differs from the standard one in chapter 2 by the inclusion of the last term on the right-hand side. If $\hat{k} < \hat{k}_{\text{world}}$, $\hat{c}$ is higher than before for a given value of $\hat{k}$, whereas if $\hat{k} > \hat{k}_{\text{world}}$, $\hat{c}$ is lower than before. Otherwise, the shape of the locus, shown in figure 9.4, is similar to the standard one, shown in figure 2.1.

Figure 9.4 uses the vertical $\dot{\hat{c}} = 0$ locus from panel *a* of figure 9.3, the case that corresponds to $\hat{k}^* = \hat{k}_{\text{world}}$. The steady-state value of $\hat{k}$, denoted by $(\hat{k}^*)_{\text{mig}}$, then equals $\hat{k}^*$. This result follows because $(\hat{k}^*)_{\text{mig}} = \hat{k}_{\text{world}}$ implies $m^* = 0$ (from equation [9.6]). Thus, for the typical economy, the steady-state capital intensity is unaffected by the potential for migration, and the steady-state migration rate is 0.

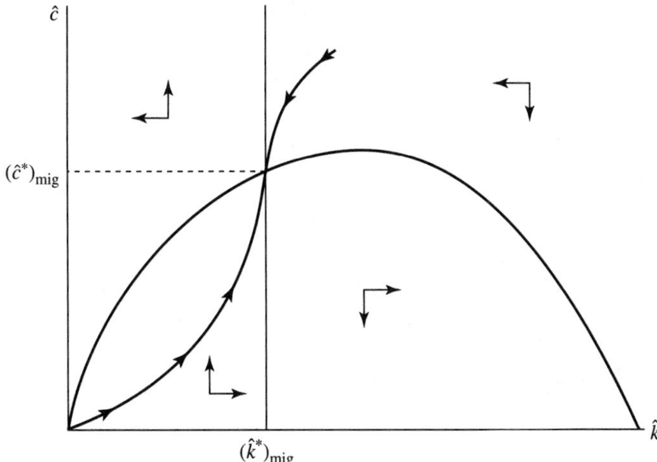

Figure 9.4
The phase diagram for the Ramsey model with migration. This diagram considers the case in which $\hat{k}^* = \hat{k}_{\text{world}}$, so that the $\dot{\hat{c}} = 0$ locus is vertical, as shown in panel *a* of figure 9.3. The $\dot{\hat{k}} = 0$ locus has the usual inverse U shape. The steady-state $\hat{k}^*$ exhibits zero net migration because we assumed $\hat{k}^* = \hat{k}_{\text{world}}$. The model exhibits the usual saddle-path stability. If the economy begins at a low value of $\hat{k}$, $\hat{k}$ and $\hat{c}$ rise monotonically during the transition. Net migration is negative throughout this transition but asymptotically approaches the steady-state value of zero.

If $\hat{k}^* > \hat{k}_{\text{world}}$, as in panel *b* of figure 9.3, the $\dot{\hat{k}} = 0$ locus intersects the $\dot{\hat{c}} = 0$ locus at a point where $\hat{k}_{\text{world}} < (\hat{k}^*)_{\text{mig}} < \hat{k}^*$ and $m^* > 0$. Thus, if the domestic economy would be attractive to immigrants in its no-migration steady state, the opening up to migration leads to a steady state with positive immigration and, consequently, a reduced capital intensity (because migrants bring relatively little capital with them). These conclusions are reversed if $\hat{k}^* < \hat{k}_{\text{world}}$, as in panel *c* of figure 9.3. In this case, $\hat{k}^* < (\hat{k}^*)_{\text{mig}} < \hat{k}_{\text{world}}$ and $m^* < 0$.

The model is saddle-path stable, as usual, and the phase diagram in figure 9.4 can be used to show the directions of motion. To assess the implications for the speed of convergence, we follow our usual procedure and use a Cobb–Douglas production function, $f(\hat{k}) = A\hat{k}^\alpha$. We can substitute this functional form into equations (9.22) and (9.23) and then log-linearize the system around its steady-state position. Since this procedure is familiar, we leave the details as an exercise and just note that the convergence coefficient turns out to be given by

$$2\beta = \left\{\zeta^2 + 4b\cdot(\rho - n) + 4(1-\alpha)(\rho+\delta+x)\cdot\left[\frac{\rho+\delta+x}{\alpha} - (n+x+\delta)\right]\right\}^{1/2} - \zeta \tag{9.26}$$

where $\zeta = \rho - n - b$. The result from the standard Ramsey model of chapter 2 (equation [2.34]) corresponds to equation (9.26) if $b = 0$ (and $\theta = 1$).

We can readily verify from equation (9.26) that β rises with b. That is, as in the Solow–Swan model, a greater propensity to migrate raises the convergence speed (if $\hat{\kappa} < \hat{k}$). To assess this effect quantitatively, we use our usual parameter values, $\alpha = 0.75$, $x = 0.02$, $n = 0.01$, $\delta = 0.05$, and $\rho = 0.02$. For these values, the convergence coefficient, β, implied by equation (9.26) would be 0.025 if $b = 0$. (This relatively high value of β applies because log utility—$\theta = 1$—implies a higher intertemporal elasticity of substitution than we usually assume.) We mentioned before that estimates of migration propensities and of the ratio $\hat{\kappa}/\hat{k}$ suggest that b would be around 0.003 in the context of regions of a country or in an international setting. Equation (9.26) implies that these values of b raise β from 0.025 in the model without migration to 0.027. This minor effect of migration on the convergence speed is similar to that found in the Solow–Swan model.

9.1.3 The Braun Model of Migration and Growth

The theories of migration and growth considered thus far have two major shortcomings. First, the flows of migrants are determined by a postulated migration function and not by households' optimizing choices of whether to move. Second, the only capital mobility in the models derives from the migrants' carrying of human capital.

Braun (1993) works out several models in which migration reflects optimizing decisions and in which varying degrees of capital mobility are assumed. A key simplifying assumption in his analysis is the existence of a perfect world credit market, which offers the same real interest rate to residents of all economies. In this case, the choice of whether to migrate depends only on comparisons across economies of paths of wage rates (and of amenities).

Braun makes some alternative assumptions about the mobility of physical capital. In one model, physical capital is perfectly mobile across economies, and, in another model, the changes in an economy's stock of capital entail adjustment costs of the type that we studied in chapter 3. To bring out the main ideas in a tractable setting, we work out the case in which physical capital is perfectly mobile, and we consider the situation of a small economy that faces a given, constant world real interest rate.

If we use our usual constant-returns-to-scale production functions and assume that the levels of the technology are the same in all countries, labor would never move if the migration of people is costly and the movements of capital are free. In contrast, if the levels of technology differ, people (and capital) tend to flow toward the better places. In fact, if natural population growth rates are zero, the cost function for migration that we specify later implies that only the economy with the best technology would remain populated in the long run. The introduction of adjustment costs for investment does not invalidate this conclusion, because workers and capital still flow continually toward the best location.

To avoid this result, we introduce a form of diminishing returns to scale in each economy. In particular, we adopt Braun's (1993) assumption that an increase in an economy's population congests a natural resource, such as land.[13] This effect leads to a steady-state distribution of the world's population and implies that no location ever gets depopulated.

Setup of the Model The domestic economy and all other economies have access to a Cobb–Douglas production function,

$$Y = AK^{\alpha}\hat{L}^{1-\alpha} \cdot (R/L)^{\lambda} \tag{9.27}$$

where $\hat{L} \equiv Le^{xt}$ is the effective labor input and $x \geq 0$ is the rate of exogenous, labor-augmenting technological progress in all economies. The new element in equation (9.27) is the input R, a constant that represents a natural resource to which residents of the domestic economy have free access. This good is, however, subject to congestion in that the per capita magnitude, R/L, enters into the production function. We assume $0 < \lambda < 1 - \alpha$, so that the overall returns to K and L are diminishing for fixed R, but the social marginal product of L is positive.

We could treat R in equation (9.27) as private land, although, in that case, immigrants would share in the use of the land only by paying a rental fee. We could alternatively view

13. An alternative assumption is that a location initially features increasing returns to scale, L, and only eventually exhibits diminishing returns due to congestion.

R as a governmentally provided service that was provided to residents in fixed aggregate supply and at no user charge. The incentives to migrate would also be affected by taxation. For example, a head tax or a fee for immigration would reduce the incentive for foreigners to come. We study an environment in which immigrants share automatically in the use of R and where taxes and fees are not levied.

A competitive individual producer views R/L as given (because the L in this term represents the aggregate population of the economy) and chooses the inputs, K and L, subject to a usual constant-returns production function. The factor prices will therefore equal the respective private marginal products, and the factor payments will exhaust the total domestic product. The wage rate equals the private marginal product of labor and is given from equation (9.27) by

$$w = (1 - \alpha) \cdot A\hat{k}^{\alpha} \cdot (R/L)^{\lambda} \cdot e^{xt} \tag{9.28}$$

where $\hat{k} \equiv K/\hat{L}$.

The rental price of capital is $r + \delta$, where r is the world real interest rate. We treat r as a constant, with $r > x$; that is, the world economy is in a steady state in which the transversality condition is satisfied.[14] Producers in the domestic economy equate the private marginal product of capital, determined from equation (9.27), to the rental price:

$$\alpha A\hat{k}^{\alpha-1} \cdot (R/L)^{\lambda} = r + \delta$$

This condition determines the capital intensity in the domestic economy as

$$\hat{k} = \left[\frac{\alpha A \cdot (R/L)^{\lambda}}{r + \delta}\right]^{1/(1-\alpha)} \tag{9.29}$$

If we substitute for $\hat{k}$ from equation (9.29) into equation (9.28), the formula for the domestic wage rate becomes

$$w = \left[\frac{(1-\alpha) \cdot A^{1/(1-\alpha)}\alpha^{\alpha/(1-\alpha)} \cdot (R/L)^{\lambda/(1-\alpha)}}{(r+\delta)^{\alpha/(1-\alpha)}}\right] \cdot e^{xt} \tag{9.30}$$

Hence, the domestic wage rate is high relative to that offered elsewhere if the domestic economy has a relatively large per capita quantity of natural resources, R/L, and a relatively high level of technology, A. Recall also that some forms of government policies can be represented by the parameter A.

14. We simplify by assuming that the world's population growth rate is zero.

The Decision to Migrate Since we assume perfect capital mobility and neglect any differences in amenities that enter into utility functions, people will evaluate locations solely on the basis of wage rates. Suppose that we think of the world economy as offering the single wage rate, w_{world}. The benefit from a permanent move at time t from the world to the domestic economy is the present value of the wage differential:

$$B(t) \equiv \int_t^{\infty} [w(v) - w_{\text{world}}] \cdot e^{-r \cdot (v-t)}\, dv \tag{9.31}$$

If we define $\hat{B}(t) \equiv B(t) \cdot e^{-xt}$, the time derivative of $\hat{B}(t)$ is given from equation (9.31) by

$$\dot{\hat{B}} = -[\hat{w}(t) - \hat{w}_{\text{world}}] + (r - x) \cdot \hat{B}(t) \tag{9.32}$$

where $\hat{w}(t) \equiv w(t) \cdot e^{-xt}$ and $\hat{w}_{\text{world}} \equiv w_{\text{world}} \cdot e^{-xt}$. Since we are assuming that the world economy is in a steady state, $\hat{w}_{\text{world}}$ is constant.

We assume, without loss of generality, that $\hat{w}(t) \geq \hat{w}_{\text{world}}$. This condition turns out to imply $\hat{w}(v) \geq \hat{w}_{\text{world}}$ and, hence, $\hat{B}(v) \geq 0$ for all $v \geq t$. Any migration that occurs will therefore always be in the direction toward the domestic economy. The situation is reversed if $\hat{w}(t) \leq \hat{w}_{\text{world}}$.

We simplify by assuming that the natural rate of population growth in the domestic economy is zero. Then, if $M(t) \geq 0$ denotes the flow of migrants at time t from the world to the domestic economy, the growth rate of the domestic population is

$$\dot{L}/L = M(t)/L(t) \tag{9.33}$$

The key matter now is to specify the costs of migration. The cost incurred by each migrant is assumed to be an increasing function of $M(t)/L(t)$. This specification is reasonable if, for example, the expenses for finding a job or a house increase with the number of new searchers in relation to the population of the receiving location.[15] The cost is assumed to take the form of a quantity of work time forgone, so that, for a given value of $M(t)/L(t)$, the cost in units of output is proportional to the world wage rate, w_{world}, that the migrants would have earned in their original locations. Hence, the amount paid by each migrant takes the form

$$\text{Cost of moving} = \eta[M(t)/L(t)] \cdot w_{\text{world}} \tag{9.34}$$

15. The key property is that the cost of moving for the marginal mover rises with the number of movers. This relation would also hold if there were heterogeneity with respect to moving costs. The persons with lower costs would move sooner, and the cost of moving would therefore rise at the margin with the number of movers (although, in this case, with the cumulated number, rather than the current flow).

where we assume $\eta' > 0$ and $\eta'' \geq 0$. We also simplify the analysis by assuming $\eta(0) = 0$; that is, we ignore any fixed expenses associated with transportation and related outlays and assume accordingly that the cost per migrant goes to 0 as the flow of migrants goes to 0 (see Braun, 1993, for further discussion).

As people move to the domestic economy, R/L falls, and w declines accordingly in equation (9.30). If enough people have moved to equate w to w_{world}, the incentive to migrate would vanish. (If the domestic technology parameter, A, is the same as the world parameter, then the equality in wage rates arises when the domestic value of R/L equals the world value of R/L.) At the point of equal wage rates, the domestic economy is in a steady state in which migration is zero; population, L, is constant; and the capital intensity, $\hat{k}$, is also constant. The condition $\eta(0) = 0$ implies that the system actually approaches this steady state, because if $w > w_{\text{world}}$, $B > 0$, and people would be motivated to move at zero cost. Thus more people migrate, and the domestic population changes as long as $w > w_{\text{world}}$. (If we had assumed $\eta(0) > 0$, then a positive gap between domestic and world wage rates could persist in the steady state.)

Since the world economy is not depopulated in the steady state,[16] we know that some of the world's inhabitants will never move to the domestic economy; that is, some of these people do not exercise the option to migrate. If people are identical and if they all optimize, then some of them can end up in equilibrium with a zero net benefit from migration only if they all end up with a zero net benefit. Hence, the equilibrium entails enough migration at each date so that the benefits and costs of moving are equated:

$$B(t) = \eta[M(t)/L(t)] \cdot w_{\text{world}} \tag{9.35}$$

for all t. This equation still holds if we replace $B(t)$ by $\hat{B}(t)$ on the left and w_{world} by the constant $\hat{w}_{\text{world}}$ on the right.

We can compute the flow of migrants at each date and therefore the growth rate of the domestic population by inverting equation (9.35):

$$\dot{L}/L = M(t)/L(t) = \psi(\hat{B}/\hat{w}_{\text{world}}) \tag{9.36}$$

where the function ψ is the inverse of the function η in equation (9.34). Since $\eta' > 0$ and $\eta'' \geq 0$, the function η is one-to-one, and the inverse function ψ is well defined and one-to-one. The function ψ satisfies the conditions $\psi' > 0$ and $\psi'' \leq 0$. The assumption $\eta(0) = 0$ implies $\psi(0) = 0$.

16. This condition holds because a large decrease in world population would significantly raise the world value of R/L and thereby increase w_{world}. The form for the wage rate in equation (9.28), which also applies for the world, implies that the equality between w and w_{world} must occur before population reaches zero in the domestic or the world economy.

In our discussions of the Solow–Swan and Ramsey models, we postulated a migration function in figure 9.1 in which the migration rate, $m = M/L$, varied positively with $\hat{w}$ and, hence, with $\hat{k}$. We noted that this function assumed that conditions elsewhere, represented now by $\hat{w}_{\text{world}}$, were held constant. The main difference between the postulated function and the present one is that the former relation involved only the current wage rate per unit of effective labor, $\hat{w}$, whereas the latter relation involves the entire path of effective wage rates as they enter into the benefit expression, $\hat{B}$.

The Dynamic System, the Steady State, and the Transitional Dynamics The dynamic system for L and $\hat{B}$ is given by equations (9.32) and (9.36), where $\hat{w}$ varies inversely with L in accordance with equation (9.30):

$$\hat{w} = \left[\frac{(1-\alpha)\cdot A^{1/(1-\alpha)}\alpha^{\alpha/(1-\alpha)}\cdot (R/L)^{\lambda/(1-\alpha)}}{(r+\delta)^{\alpha/(1-\alpha)}}\right] \tag{9.37}$$

Figure 9.5 uses equations (9.32) and (9.36) to construct a phase diagram in $(L, \hat{B})$ space. Equation (9.36) and the properties of the ψ function, including $\psi(0) = 0$, imply that $\dot{L} = 0$ corresponds (if $L \neq 0$) to $\hat{B} = 0$. The equation also implies (because $\psi' > 0$) that $\dot{L} > 0$ if $\hat{B} > 0$ and $\dot{L} < 0$ if $\hat{B} < 0$.

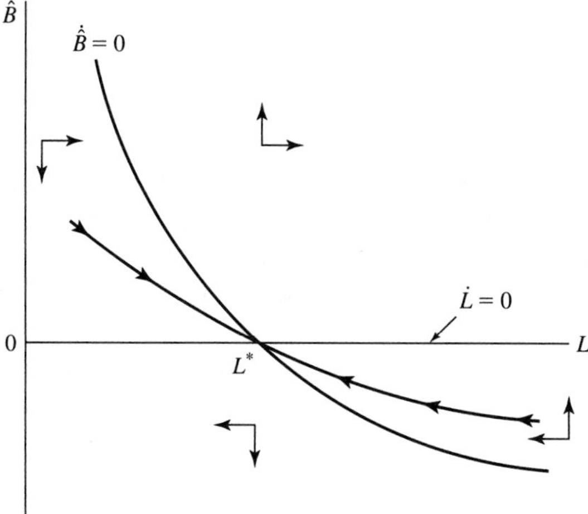

Figure 9.5
The phase diagram when migration is a choice variable. The dynamics of the model can be expressed in terms of the present value of the benefits from moving, $\hat{B}$, and the domestic population, L. The system is saddle-path stable, and the stable arm is downward sloping. Thus a low initial population is associated with high benefits from net migration toward the domestic economy and, consequently, with a high net migration rate, m. As population increases, the net benefit from migration diminishes. In the steady state, the net benefit, $\hat{B}$, is zero, and population, L, is constant.

Equation (9.32) implies that $\dot{\hat{B}} = 0$ corresponds to a positive, linear relation between $\hat{B}$ and $\hat{w}$. Since $\hat{w}$ is inversely related to L in equation (9.37), the relation between $\hat{B}$ and L is also inverse, as shown in figure 9.5. Since $r > x$, values of $\hat{B}$ above the curve imply $\dot{\hat{B}} > 0$, and values below the curve imply $\dot{\hat{B}} < 0$.

The figure shows that the steady state involves $L = L^*$, a constant, and $\hat{B}^* = 0$. Equation (9.32) therefore implies $\hat{w}^* = \hat{w}_{\text{world}}$, and equation (9.37) determines the value L^* that satisfies this equality. In particular, L^* rises with A (for the domestic economy) and increases equiproportionately with R (for the domestic economy).

The system is saddle-path stable, and figure 9.5 shows the directions of motion. If the domestic economy starts with $L < L^*$, then $\hat{B} > 0$, and L rises over time. The resulting decline in $\hat{w}$ leads to a fall in $\hat{B}$ and, hence, to a decrease in the migration rate. Over time, the migration rate falls steadily and approaches zero as L tends to L^*.

We can determine the speed of convergence to the steady state in the usual way by linearizing in the neighborhood of the steady state. In this case, the system is described by equations (9.32) and (9.36), and the linearization is in terms of $\hat{B}$ and $\log(L/L^*)$. The migration rate, which equals the growth rate of L, is given by

$$M/L = \dot{L}/L \approx \beta \cdot \log(L^*/L) \tag{9.38}$$

where the convergence coefficient, β, is given by

$$2\beta = \left[(r-x)^2 + \frac{4\lambda \cdot \psi'(0)}{1-\alpha}\right]^{1/2} - (r-x) \tag{9.39}$$

Equation (9.39) shows that the key determinant of the convergence speed is $\psi'(0)$, the sensitivity of the migration rate in the vicinity of the steady state to the relative benefit from moving, $\hat{B}/\hat{w}_{\text{world}}$ (see equation [9.36]). The greater this sensitivity, the faster the speed of convergence. Recall that the function ψ is the inverse of the function η, which relates the cost of moving to the migration rate in equation (9.34). The slope $\psi'(0)$ is the reciprocal of $\eta'(0)$; therefore, the more rapidly migration costs rise with the volume of migration, the smaller is the responsiveness of the migration rate to the relative benefit, $\hat{B}/\hat{w}$, and, hence, the slower is the speed of convergence.

The convergence speed for L is also the convergence speed for $\hat{y}$. To see this point, use the production function from equation (9.27) and the expression for $\hat{k}$ in equation (9.29) to derive a formula for $\hat{y}$:

$$\hat{y} = \left[\frac{A^{1/(1-\alpha)}\alpha^{\alpha/(1-\alpha)} \cdot (R/L)^{\lambda/(1-\alpha)}}{(r+\delta)^{\alpha/(1-\alpha)}}\right] \tag{9.40}$$

This formula is the same as that for $\hat{w}$ in equation (9.37), except for the multiple $1-\alpha$ in the expression for $\hat{w}$. The result for $\hat{y}$ implies

$$\log(\hat{y}/\hat{y}^*) = [\lambda/(1-\alpha)] \cdot \log(L^*/L) \tag{9.41}$$

that is, $\hat{y}$ is above its steady-state value when L is below its steady-state value, and vice versa. Equation (9.40) also implies that the growth rate of $\hat{y}$ is given by

$$\dot{\hat{y}}/\hat{y} = -[\lambda/(1-\alpha)] \cdot (\dot{L}/L) \tag{9.42}$$

We can use equation (9.42) along with equations (9.38) and (9.41) to get a familiar-looking convergence equation for $\hat{y}$:

$$\dot{\hat{y}}/\hat{y} = -\beta \cdot \log(\hat{y}/\hat{y}^*) \tag{9.43}$$

Thus the growth rate of $\hat{y}$ is inversely related to the level of $\hat{y}$, and the speed of convergence, β, is given by equation (9.39).

Recall that we discussed earlier some empirical findings on net migration rates. These findings relate the migration rate to differentials in per capita income or product. We can write equation (9.38) in this form if we use equation (9.41) to transform from $\log(L^*/L)$ to $\log(\hat{y}/\hat{y}^*)$:

$$M/L = \dot{L}/L \approx \left[\frac{\beta \cdot (1-\alpha)}{\lambda}\right] \cdot \log(\hat{y}/\hat{y}^*) \tag{9.44}$$

We can look at equations (9.43) and (9.44) as a system of two equations that involve the growth rate of output and the migration rate. Suppose that we examine a group of economies for which we can assume that the parameters α and λ are the same. Then, places with a higher $\psi'(0)$ have a higher value of β. Therefore, these places have a larger responsiveness of the migration rate to differentials in per capita product in equation (9.44) *and* a faster speed of convergence for per capita output in accordance with equation (9.43).

Braun (1993) tested the hypothesis that a higher migration-rate sensitivity tended to go along with a higher speed of convergence for per capita product or income. He used information on within-country migration and convergence for the U.S. states, regions of five European countries (France, Germany, Italy, Spain, and the United Kingdom), and Japan. That is, he effectively compared seven estimates of migration-rate sensitivities with the corresponding seven estimates of convergence coefficients for per capita output or income. Although the number of data points is small, the results provided some support for the underlying theory, because the places with greater migration-rate sensitivities tended also to have higher convergence rates. See chapter 11 for a discussion of this evidence.

Dynamics of the World Economy In the previous analysis we assumed that the world economy was in a steady state with a constant wage rate per unit of effective labor, $\hat{w}_{\text{world}}$, and an associated constant capital intensity, which we can denote by $\hat{k}_{\text{world}}$. We described a dynamic process for migration whereby the domestic economy's effective wage rate, $\hat{w}$, approached the constant world value, $\hat{w}_{\text{world}}$. If the domestic economy has the same level of technology, A, as the world, then $\hat{k}$ tends toward the constant $\hat{k}_{\text{world}}$.

More generally, we could allow for a transitional dynamics in which $\hat{k}_{\text{world}}$ approached its steady-state value, $(\hat{k}_{\text{world}})^*$. Then, for economy i, the changes over time in $\hat{k}_i$ can be broken into two parts: first, the adjustment of $\hat{k}_i$ toward $\hat{k}_{\text{world}}$ and, second, the adjustment of $\hat{k}_{\text{world}}$ toward $(\hat{k}_{\text{world}})^*$.

Braun (1993) works out an analysis of this type in which the world consists of only two regions, $i = 1, 2$. Migration is possible between the regions at the cost specified in equation (9.34). For the world economy—that is, for the aggregate of the two regions—the evolution of the capital stock and consumption per effective worker, $\hat{k}_{\text{world}}$ and $\hat{c}_{\text{world}}$, are similar to that in the Ramsey model of chapter 2. This process implies a gradual adjustment of $\hat{k}_{\text{world}}$ to its steady-state value, $(\hat{k}_{\text{world}})^*$, and the speed of convergence depends on the same parameters that mattered in the Ramsey setting.

At the same time, people migrate toward the region with a higher wage rate, and this movement tends to reduce per capita output in the high-wage region and raise per capita output in the low-wage region. The speed of this process involves the convergence coefficient given in equation (9.39).

The growth rate of each region's output per effective worker can be approximated by

$$\frac{\dot{\hat{y}}_i}{\hat{y}_i} = -\beta \cdot \log(\hat{y}_i/\hat{y}_{\text{world}}) - \mu \cdot \log[\hat{y}_{\text{world}}/(\hat{y}_{\text{world}})^*] \tag{9.45}$$

where β is given in equation (9.39), and μ is determined by a Ramsey model of the world economy. Equation (9.45) combines a cross-sectional effect that involves the elimination of differences across economies with a time-series effect that involves the adjustment of the world economy to its steady-state position. If we consider a cross section of data for a single time period, the relative growth rates would depend inversely on the initial relative positions, $\hat{y}_i/\hat{y}_{\text{world}}$, and would involve the coefficient β. In contrast, if we examine time-series data on the world variable $\hat{y}_{\text{world}}$, the growth rate would vary negatively with $\hat{y}_{\text{world}}/(\hat{y}_{\text{world}})^*$ and would involve the coefficient μ. In a panel setting, the growth rate for each economy depends on $\hat{y}_i/\hat{y}_{\text{world}}$ and $\hat{y}_{\text{world}}/(\hat{y}_{\text{world}})^*$ and involves both coefficients, β and μ.

Imperfect Capital Mobility In the present setting, an economy's speed of convergence toward the world economy involves the coefficient β in equation (9.39), which reflects only the gradual migration of persons. If we assume less than complete capital mobility, the forces that influenced convergence in some of our previous models would also affect β. For example, we would get these additional effects on convergence if investment entails adjustment costs or if capital markets are imperfect.

It is straightforward to allow for adjustment costs for investment if we retain the framework of perfect capital markets (see Braun, 1993). These adjustment costs can be introduced in the way discussed in chapter 3. The main new finding is that the convergence coefficient, β, is higher if the sensitivity of the adjustment cost to the quantity of investment is smaller.

The analysis is more complicated if credit markets are imperfect. The rate of return then differs across the economies, and the decision to migrate would be based on this difference along with the gap in wage rates. We also have to keep track of ownership of assets in various places, and the behavior of consumption is correspondingly more complicated. The results that we obtained before in the settings of the Solow–Swan and Ramsey models apply when capital flows are entirely absent, except for the human capital carried by migrants.

9.2 Fertility Choice

For Malthus (1798), the effects of economic factors on fertility and mortality were a central element in the theory of economic development. Few scholars have generated more controversy than Malthus, whose main theory states that population is controlled by the availability of food. Malthus's insight was based on the assumptions that food is necessary for the subsistence of humans and that the power of population growth is far greater than the power of the earth to produce food. Malthus's theory was based on the idea that, since the Neolithic agricultural revolution around 8000 B.C., the economy was overwhelmingly agricultural. The law of diminishing returns to land led Malthus to conclude that an expansion in the number of people would force society to use less productive land, which would not generate enough food to support the larger population. Food shortages then force families to postpone marriage and fertility, and the rate of population growth self-corrects. In the words of Malthus:

We will suppose the means of subsistence in any country just equal to the easy support of its inhabitants. The constant effort towards population, which is found to act even in the most vicious societies, increases the number of people before the means of subsistence are increased. The food, therefore, which before supported eleven million, must now be divided among eleven million and a half. The poor consequently must live much worse, and many of them be reduced to severe distress.... During this season of distress, the discouragements to marriage and the difficulty of rearing a family are so great that the progress of population is retarded.[17]

17. See Malthus (1798, p. 161, n. 19).

The problem for Malthus was that, at the same time he was writing his book, a new revolution was taking place in England: the industrial revolution. Perhaps for the first time in history, standards of living for a substantial number of citizens increased substantially. But, contrary to Malthus's preductions, rising prosperity did not lead inevitably to increased population growth. In fact, the empirical evidence for recent years indicates that, except for very poor countries or households, increases in per capita income tend to reduce fertility. Although empirical studies have not confirmed Malthus's specific predictions, these studies have typically found important linkages from economic variables—such as per capita income, wage rates, levels of female and male education, and urbanization—to fertility and mortality (see Wahl, 1985; Behrman, 1990; Schultz, 1989; and Barro and Lee, 1994). Thus the empirical findings firmly reject the notion that the natural growth rate of population is exogenous with respect to economic growth.

Despite this evidence, most modern theories of economic growth have assumed that the rate of population growth is an exogenous constant. For example, in our presentations of the Solow–Swan and Ramsey models in chapters 1 and 2, different settings for the rate of population growth, n, mattered for the growth process, but we did not consider feedback from the growth process to the rate of population growth. We have allowed in this chapter for endogenous responses of population through migration but have not yet considered variations in the natural growth rate of population.

In this section, we construct a growth model in which economic development influences family choices about the number of children and, hence, the fertility rate.[18] We want, in particular, to design a model that mimics some of the major empirical findings, especially a negative relation between fertility and per capita income, except at very low levels of per capita income.

9.2.1 An Overlapping-Generations Setup

We begin with the approach of Becker and Barro (1988) and Barro and Becker (1989), in which parents and children are linked through altruism. Parental decisions about numbers of children are made jointly with choices about consumption and intergenerational transfers. Children are costly to produce and raise, but the addition to utility—as viewed by the parents—may be sufficient to justify these costs. If the marginal utility attached to children diminishes with their number, or if the cost of rearing an additional child increases with the number, the model determines the fertility rate from a standard first-order condition. The choice of the quantity of children also interacts with the determination of their quality,

18. We do not attempt to explain why the industrial revolution occurred. Lucas (2002), Galor and Weil (2000), Hansen and Prescott (2002), and Jones (2001) provide models in which a demographic transition and the industrial revolution occur as endogenous responses to changing economic environments.

as represented in the model by the amounts of consumption and capital stock allocated to each person.

Becker and Barro (1988) use an overlapping-generations (OLG) framework in which people live for two periods, childhood and adulthood. (See the appendix to chapter 3 for a discussion of OLG frameworks.) Marriage is not considered, and a single adult of generation i has n_i children. The utility function takes the form

$$U_i = u(c_i, n_i) + \Upsilon(n_i) \cdot n_i U_{i+1} \tag{9.46}$$

where the subscript i is the period in which a person is an adult, U_i is the adult's utility, c_i is consumption per adult person during adulthood, and n_i is the number of children per adult. The term $u(c_i, n_i)$ represents the utils generated during adulthood from consumption and the presence of children. (This formulation does not distinguish the consumption of children during their childhood from that of their parents.)

The last term on the right-hand side of equation (9.46) represents the utils that adults obtain by considering the prospective happiness of their children when the children become adults. The term U_{i+1} is the utility that each child will attain as an adult. This utility is also determined by equation (9.46), with all variables updated by one period. We assume that children are identical and are treated equally by parents, so that all attain the same utility, U_{i+1}. (This egalitarian treatment will apply if everyone has the same utility function, $u[\cdot]$, and if this utility is a concave function of the resources provided to each child.)

The function $\Upsilon(n_i)$ in equation (9.46) represents the degree of altruism that parents attach to each child's utility; hence, $\Upsilon(n_i)$ multiplies the "aggregate" utility attained by the next generation, $n_i U_{i+1}$. The assumed properties are $\Upsilon(n_i) > 0$ (parents value their children's happiness), $\Upsilon'(n_i) < 0$ (a form of diminishing marginal utility of children), and $\Upsilon(1) < 1$. The last property implies that, if the number of children per adult equals one, parents are selfish in the sense that they value a unit of $u(c_i, 1)$ more than a unit of $u(c_{i+1}, 1)$.[19]

Becker and Barro (1988) assume that the altruism function takes a constant-elasticity form,

$$\Upsilon(n_i) = \Upsilon n_i^{-\epsilon} \tag{9.47}$$

where $\epsilon > 0$ and $0 < \Upsilon < 1$. The parameter Υ represents the degree of altruism between parents and children that applies when $n_i = 1$. The notion of parents liking children is captured by $\Upsilon > 0$, and the idea of parental selfishness is reflected in $\Upsilon < 1$. The condition $\epsilon > 0$ yields diminishing marginal utility in the number of children in the sense that $\Upsilon(n_i)$ declines with n_i.

19. In terms of the discussion of altruism in the appendix to chapter 3, the term Υ combines pure time preference (the term that involves ρ) with the attitude toward children. We can think of the pure rate of time preference, ρ, as zero in the present context.

If we use equations (9.46) and (9.47), we can write U_i as a forward, weighted sum of the $u(c_j, n_j)$ for each generation starting with the ith:

$$U_i = \sum_{j=i}^{\infty} \Upsilon^{j-i} \cdot N_j^{1-\epsilon} \cdot u(c_j, n_j) \tag{9.48}$$

where N_j is the number of adult descendants in generation j. This number equals 1 when $j = i$ (that is, when we start from the perspective of a single adult) and equals the product of the various n_j for $j > i$:

$$N_i = 1; \quad N_j = \prod_{k=i}^{j-1} n_k, \quad \text{for } j = i+1, i+2, \ldots \tag{9.49}$$

In previous settings, we assumed a functional form for $u(c)$ that implied a constant elasticity of marginal utility, $u'(c)$, with respect to c. We now make the parallel assumption that the functional form for $u(c_j, n_j)$ implies constant elasticities of marginal utility with respect to c_j and n_j:

$$u(c_j, n_j) = [c_j \cdot (n_j)^{\phi}]^{1-\theta}/(1-\theta) \tag{9.50}$$

where $\phi > 0$ and $\theta > 0$. We also assume $\phi \cdot (1-\theta) < 1$ to get diminishing marginal utility with respect to n_j. If we define

$$\psi \equiv (1-\epsilon)/(1-\theta)$$

where we assume $\psi > 0$,[20] and substitute the form for $u(c_j, n_j)$ from equation (9.50) into equation (9.48), we get

$$U_i = \sum_{j=i}^{\infty} \Upsilon^{j-i} \cdot \{[(N_j)^{\psi} \cdot c_j \cdot (n_j)^{\phi}]^{1-\theta} - 1\}/(1-\theta) \tag{9.51}$$

Note that the condition $\epsilon > 0$ implies $\psi \cdot (1-\theta) < 1$. We added the term –1 inside the large brackets, so that, as θ tends to 1, the expression inside the integral approaches the log-utility form:

$$U_i = \sum_{j=i}^{\infty} \Upsilon^{j-i} \cdot [\psi \cdot \log(N_j) + \log(c_j) + \phi \cdot \log(n_j)] \tag{9.52}$$

20. The condition $\psi > 0$ implies $\epsilon < 1$ if $\theta < 1$, as in the case considered by Becker and Barro (1988). The present formulation also allows $\epsilon > 1$ if $\theta > 1$. If $\theta = 1$, $\epsilon = 1$ must hold for ψ to be finite.

If we let θ approach 1, we can derive equation (9.52) from equation (9.51) by using l'Hôpital's rule.

We can complete the model as in Becker and Barro (1988) by specifying a cost for having and raising children and by introducing an intergenerational budget constraint. This constraint relates a parent's intergenerational transfer to each child to the parent's initial assets, the amounts of wage and asset income, and the expenditures on child rearing and consumption. The adults in each generation then choose consumption and fertility to maximize U_i in equation (9.51), subject to the intertemporal budget constraint. The analysis is straightforward if the solutions for intergenerational transfers are interior, that is, if parents always opt for positive transfers. We then do not have to consider that the environment likely precludes negative transfers in the sense of debts left for children. We do not carry out the details of this analysis here, because we prefer to work instead with a continuous-time version of the model.

9.2.2 The Model in Continuous Time

The overlapping-generations setup is useful for a study of fertility choice because the length of the period has an important meaning. It represents the average spread in age between parents and children, that is, the length of a generation. For aggregate purposes, however, we would have to add up across families who, at a given point in time, have children of varying ages. In this setup, the restriction to an integer number of children would be important at the family level, but this restriction would be smoothed out in the aggregation across heterogeneous families.

These considerations suggest that it would not be useful to work out an individual family's choice problem in a discrete-time setup and then apply the findings directly to the behavior of economy-wide variables. The results that we would get from the underlying discreteness in time—which may include a potential to cycle around the steady state—would reflect the failure to add up appropriately across households. Thus we either have to carry out the aggregation explicitly or else use as an approximation a continuous-time representation for the behavior of the typical household. The continuous-time approach lacks realism at the level of a family—for example, it neglects integer restrictions on the number of children—but may nevertheless be satisfactory for a study of economy-wide variables.

We now use the results from the previous section to modify the continuous-time model of infinite-lived households that we introduced in the Ramsey model in chapter 2. The infinite horizon is natural here because it represents the altruistic linkage from parents to children to the children's children and so on. The rate of time preference, $\rho > 0$, in the Ramsey formulation corresponds to the degree of intergenerational altruism, $\Upsilon < 1$, in the overlapping-generations model. Two new elements are that time preference also depends on the number of children and that child rearing uses up resources.

Births and Deaths In the discrete-period model, a new generation of finite size is born each period, and each person lives for two periods, childhood and adulthood. In the continuous-time formulation, we instead treat births and deaths as continuous flows.

Let $n \geq 0$ be a family's birth rate, treated as a choice variable at every point in time, and $d > 0$ the mortality rate. For reasons of tractability, we do not allow d to depend on a family's age structure. We also do not allow d to depend on family or public expenditures on medical care, sanitation, and so on, although these influences on the mortality rate would be an important extension of the model. The size of the family, N, changes continuously in accordance with

$$\dot{N} = (n - d) \cdot N \tag{9.53}$$

The variable N will now be an additional state variable for households.

The Utility Function We use the formulation of household utility from the discrete-time model in equation (9.51) to modify the standard continuous-time representation from equation (2.1) to

$$U = \int_0^\infty \frac{e^{-\rho t}}{1-\theta} \cdot \{[N^\psi c \cdot (n-d)^\phi]^{1-\theta} - 1\} \cdot dt \tag{9.54}$$

The term $e^{-\rho t}$ corresponds to the altruism factor, Υ^{j-i}, in equation (9.51). Equation (9.54) includes the net growth rate of population, $n - d$, rather than the gross fertility rate, n. If we think of d as representing infant mortality, then $n - d$ refers to surviving children, the variable that would plausibly appear in the utility function.[21] Note that the stock of people N enters the utility function. It turns out that this fact implies a great deal of difficulty when it comes to solving the model. Jones (2001) uses a simpler specification of utility that is independent of the stock of population, a specification that delivers a more tractable mathematical solution.

Child-Rearing Costs The birth and rearing of each child costs an amount η. We think of η as expended entirely at the time of birth, although a more realistic model would recognize that these expenditures arise over a long period of child development. We attempt to get around this shortcoming by thinking of η as a large single outlay that represents the present value of expenditures for each child. Since nN is the number of births per unit of time, ηnN is the total of expenditures on child rearing, and ηn is the amount expended per capita.

21. The model is not rich enough for the mortality rate to depend on age. However, the household's choices would not be affected if we entered a factor like $d^{-\iota}$, where $\iota > 0$, multiplicatively with $N^\psi \cdot c \cdot (n-d)^\phi$ in equation (9.54). This factor could perhaps capture the disutility associated with adult mortality.

A key issue is the relation of the cost η to other variables, such as the value of parents' time and measures of child quality, which correspond in the model to consumption and capital stock per person, c and k.[22] If η represents only purchases of market goods and services, the cost of rearing a child declines relative to per capita income as the economy grows. In this case, the fertility rate, n, tends—counterfactually—to rise as the economy develops.

Becker (1991) and others argue that child rearing is intensive in parental time, especially in the mother's time in societies in which women are the primary providers of child care.[23] In other words, the productivity advances that apply to market goods and services because of capital accumulation and technological progress are not thought to apply very much to the raising of children. In this case, the cost η tends to rise with parents' wage rates or with other measures of the opportunity costs of parental time. Greater educational attainment of adults (especially of women) tends in this case to raise η. More generally, η increases with the per capita quantities of human and physical capital, represented by the variable k in the model.

To introduce a linkage between η and parents' wage rates, we would have to allow for alternative uses of parental time, for example, for choices between time spent producing goods and time spent raising children. This extension leads to technical complexity in the form of nonlinearities. Since the main idea involves a positive relation between η and k, we proceed instead by postulating a linear relation,

$$\eta = b_0 + bk \tag{9.55}$$

where $b_0 \geq 0$ and $b \geq 0$. The b_0 term represents the goods cost of child rearing, and the bk term represents the cost that increases with the capital intensity.

The specification in equation (9.55) turns out to be especially simple if we assume $b_0 = 0$, because the per capita child-rearing cost, $\eta n = bnk$, then combines with the term nk that has appeared all along as a negative term in the household's budget constraint (see equation [2.23]). We discuss later some results for specifications that include the goods cost, b_0.

22. We treat the child-rearing cost as proportional to the number of children. The setup cost for a family to have its first child suggests that there might be a range in which the cost per child diminishes with the number of children. Eventually, however, the costs would increase more than linearly with the number, because the bearing of more children implies that the spacing between births gets inconveniently short or that the parents are very old when they have children.

23. See Galor and Weil (1996) for an emphasis on this element in the context of growth models. Becker, Murphy, and Tamura (1990) also stress the linkage between human capital and the costs of child rearing.

The Family's Budget Constraint We assume that each family member receives the same wage rate, w. (More realistically, we could allow a dependence of w on age, so that children would not start immediately to earn wages.) The family's assets earn the rate of return r.

Let c and k be the family's per capita consumption and assets, respectively. (We have, for convenience, already imposed the closed-economy condition that per capita assets, a, equals k.) The budget constraint can then be expressed as

$$\dot{k} = w + (r - n + d) \cdot k - bnk - c \tag{9.56}$$

where we used the form for the child-rearing cost, η, from equation (9.55) with b_0 set to zero. We assume, as usual, that each household takes as given the path of the wage rate, w, and the rate of return, r.[24] The change from the standard formulation is the inclusion of the per capita outlay on child rearing, bnk.

Optimization Conditions The household's optimization problem is to choose the path of the control variables c and n to maximize U in equation (9.54). This maximization problem is subject to the initial assets $k(0)$; the transition equations for the two state variables, N and k, given by equations (9.53) and (9.56); the inequalities $c \geq 0$ and $n \geq 0$ (which will never bind because of the form of the utility function in equation [9.54]); and the usual restriction that rules out chain-letter behavior for debt (if we allow $k < 0$).

We can set up the Hamiltonian expression,

$$\begin{aligned} J = {} & \frac{e^{-\rho t}}{1-\theta} \cdot \{[N^{\psi} c \cdot (n-d)^{\phi}]^{1-\theta} - 1\} \\ & + \nu \cdot [w + (r+d) \cdot k - (1+b) \cdot nk - c] + \mu \cdot (n-d) \cdot N \end{aligned} \tag{9.57}$$

where ν and μ are the shadow prices associated with the two state variables, k and N. Since the restrictions $c \geq 0$ and $n \geq 0$ will never bind (because the marginal utilities approach infinity as c and n tend to 0 and $d \geq 0$), the household satisfies the usual first-order conditions obtained from setting $\partial J/\partial c = \partial J/\partial n = 0$, $\dot{\nu} = -\partial J/\partial k$, and $\dot{\mu} = -\partial J/\partial N$.[25] The results simplify considerably under log utility, $\theta = 1$, and we concentrate on this case.

24. We assume, however, that the child-rearing cost, η, depends on the household's own assets, k, rather than on the economy-wide capital per person. The analysis is somewhat different if η depends only on economy-wide variables, perhaps through a relation between η and the wage rate.

25. The one possible problem is that children may be so cheap to produce that it would be attractive to borrow enough to make n arbitrarily large. This difficulty does not arise if the cost parameter b is big enough to ensure that the variable Ω—defined later to equal $(1+b) \cdot k/c - \phi/(n-d)$—is always positive.

The conditions $\partial J/\partial c = 0$ and $\dot{\nu} = -\partial J/\partial k$ can be manipulated in the usual way to get an expression for the growth rate of c:[26]

$$\dot{c}/c = (1/\theta) \cdot \{r - \rho - (n-d) \cdot [1 - \psi \cdot (1-\theta)] - nb + \phi \cdot (1-\theta) \cdot \dot{n}/(n-d)\}$$

This result simplifies in the case of log utility, $\theta = 1$, to

$$\dot{c}/c = r - \rho - (n-d) - bn \tag{9.58}$$

When $\theta = 1$, the rate of population growth, $n - d$, effectively adds to the time-preference rate, ρ (see note 26 for a comparison with the standard Ramsey model). In addition, the term bn subtracts from r because a higher k raises child-rearing costs, given by bnk.

We shall find it useful to define a new variable Ω as follows:

$$\Omega \equiv (1+b) \cdot k/c - \phi/(n-d)$$

We can then use the conditions $\partial J/\partial c = \partial J/\partial n = 0$ to get

$$\mu = e^{-\rho t} \cdot N^{\psi(1-\theta)-1} \cdot c^{1-\theta} \cdot (n-d)^{\phi(1-\theta)} \cdot \Omega$$

If we differentiate this expression for μ with respect to time and use the condition $\dot{\mu} = -\partial J/\partial N$ to substitute out for $\dot{\mu}$, we eventually get

$$\dot{\Omega} = -\psi + (\Omega/\theta) \cdot \{\rho - (1-\theta) \cdot [r - (1-\psi) \cdot (n-d) - nb + \phi \cdot \dot{n}/(n-d)]\}$$

If $\theta = 1$, this differential equation simplifies to

$$\dot{\Omega} = -\psi + \Omega\rho$$

which is unstable. Therefore, if $\Omega(0)$ departs from its steady-state value, ψ/ρ, Ω moves over time toward $\pm\infty$. Since these unstable paths violate the transversality condition associated

26. In the standard Ramsey analysis considered in chapter 2, n is an exogenous constant and $b = 0$, so that the growth rate of c is given by

$$\dot{c}/c = (1/\theta) \cdot \{r - \rho - (n-d) \cdot [1 - \psi \cdot (1-\theta)]\}$$

The standard analysis also assumes that $\psi \cdot (1-\theta)$, which equals $1 - \epsilon$, is unity, so that the formula becomes

$$\dot{c}/c = (1/\theta) \cdot (r - \rho)$$

The specification $\psi \cdot (1-\theta) = 1$ (or, equivalently, $\epsilon = 0$) implies, however, that the marginal contribution of N to the flow of utility (for given c and n) is negative if $\theta > 1$ and becomes of unbounded magnitude as θ approaches 1. For that reason, Becker and Barro (1988) and Barro and Becker (1989) dealt only with the case $\theta < 1$. We assume here that ψ is positive and finite, in which case the marginal contribution of N to the flow of utility is also positive and finite.

with N,[27] optimizing behavior dictates that Ω equal ψ/ρ at every point in time. The definition of Ω then implies that the fertility rate always satisfies the condition

$$n = d + \frac{\phi\rho \cdot (c/k)}{\rho \cdot (1+b) - \psi \cdot (c/k)} \tag{9.59}$$

Equation (9.59) indicates that the fertility rate, n, varies one-to-one with the mortality rate, d, for given values of the parameters ϕ, ψ, b, and ρ, and for a given value of the variable c/k. Higher values of ϕ and ψ raise the marginal utility associated respectively with n and N (see equation [9.54]) and thereby raise n. A higher value of b increases the cost of child rearing and tends accordingly to reduce n. A higher value of ρ deters investment (in N) and therefore tends to lower n.

The variable c/k expresses the ratio of the income effect on the demand for children, represented by c, to the cost of children, which depends linearly on k through the term $(1+b) \cdot nk$ in the budget constraint shown in equation (9.56). Hence, an increase in c/k goes along with a rise in n. This result means that n moves in the same direction as c/k during the transition to the steady state.

Transitional Dynamics and the Steady State The dynamic model consists of the expressions for $\dot{k}$ and $\dot{c}/c$ in equations (9.56) and (9.58) and the relation for n in equation (9.59). The equations for $\dot{k}$ and $\dot{c}/c$ involve w and r, which are determined in the usual way by the production function. We assume, as usual, that labor input, L, and population, N, coincide; that labor-augmenting technological progress occurs at the constant rate $x \geq 0$; and that the production function has the Cobb–Douglas form,

$$\hat{y} = A\hat{k}^{\alpha}$$

where $0 < \alpha < 1$, $\hat{k} \equiv K/\hat{L}$, and $\hat{y} \equiv Y/\hat{L}$. If capital depreciates at the constant rate δ, the profit-maximizing behavior of competitive firms implies the usual formulas,

$$r = \alpha A\hat{k}^{\alpha-1} - \delta, \; w = (1-\alpha) \cdot A\hat{k}^{\alpha} \cdot e^{xt} \tag{9.60}$$

27. The differential equation for Ω has the general solution,

$$\Omega = \psi/\rho + [\Omega(0) - \psi/\rho] \cdot e^{\rho t}$$

The condition for μ simplifies when $\theta = 1$ to $\mu N = \Omega e^{-\rho t}$. Substitution of the solution for Ω into this expression for μN leads to

$$\mu N = e^{-\rho t} \cdot (\psi/\rho) + \Omega(0) - \psi/\rho$$

Therefore, the transversality condition associated with N—$\lim_{t\to\infty}(\mu N) = 0$—is satisfied only if $\Omega(0) = \psi/\rho$. In this case, $\dot{\Omega} = 0$ for all t, and Ω always equals its steady-state value, ψ/ρ.

It is convenient to express the system in terms of the transformed variables

$\chi \equiv c/k$ and $z \equiv A\hat{k}^{\alpha-1}$

where z is the gross average product of capital. Equations (9.56) and (9.58) can then be used along with equation (9.60) to get the transition equation for χ:

$$\dot{\chi}/\chi = -\rho - (1-\alpha)\cdot z + \chi \tag{9.61}$$

If we substitute for n from equation (9.59) and use equations (9.56) and (9.60), we get the transition equation for z:

$$\dot{z}/z = -(1-\alpha)\cdot\left[z - \delta - bd - x - \chi - \frac{\phi\rho\chi\cdot(1+b)}{\rho\cdot(1+b)-\psi\chi}\right] \tag{9.62}$$

Figure 9.6 uses equations (9.61) and (9.62) to construct a phase diagram in (z, χ) space. The curves shown correspond to a particular specification of the underlying parameters:

$\alpha = 0.75, \delta = 0.05, \rho = 0.02, x = 0.02$

$d = 0.01, b = 1, \psi = 0.2, \phi = 0.2$

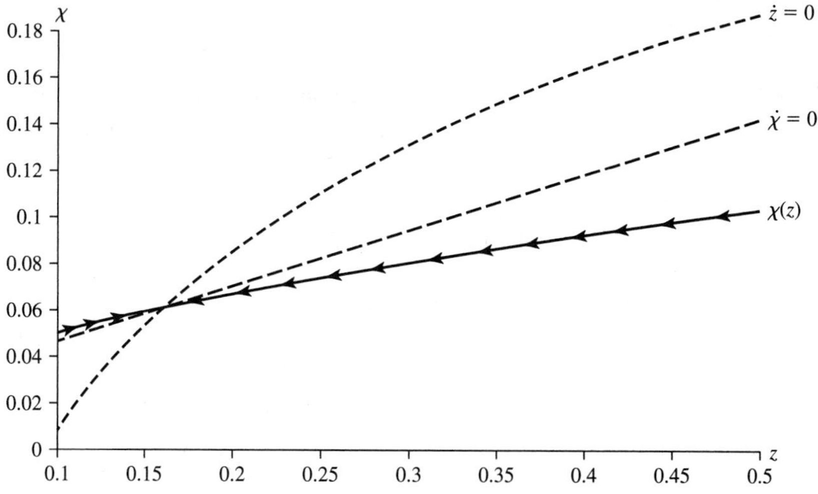

Figure 9.6
Phase diagram for the fertility model in (z, χ) space. The fertility model exhibits saddle-path stability. In (z, χ) space, the stable arm is upward sloping. Therefore, if the economy begins with a high gross average product of capital, z, then z and $\chi \equiv c/k$ decline monotonically during the transition.

The first row contains values that are familiar from previous discussions. In the second row, we assume a mortality rate, d, of 0.01 per year. The settings for b, ψ, and ϕ are more arbitrary, and we will discuss the dependence of the answers on variations in these parameters. In any event, the general appearance of the phase diagram is not very sensitive to these choices.

The locus for $\dot{\chi} = 0$ from equation (9.61) is a positively sloped straight line with intercept ρ. This locus is unstable, that is, $\dot{\chi}/\chi$ rises with χ for a given z.

Equation (9.62) implies that the $\dot{z} = 0$ locus is positively sloped and stable, that is, $\dot{z}/z$ declines with z for a given χ. The relation between χ and z along this locus is the solution to a quadratic equation, which has two real, positive roots for a range of "reasonable" parameters. The larger root turns out always to lie above the $\dot{\chi} = 0$ locus. The locus for $\dot{z} = 0$ shown in figure 9.6 corresponds to the smaller root.

The intersection of the two loci determines the steady-state values, z^* and χ^*. Once these values are known, we can use equation (9.59) to compute n^*. The steady-state interest rate can be calculated from the relation

$$r^* = \alpha z^* - \delta$$

Figure 9.6 shows that the stable, saddle path is positively sloped in (z, χ) space. Therefore, if the economy begins with $z(0) > z^*$ (that is, $\hat{k}[0] < \hat{k}^*$), z and χ fall monotonically toward their steady-state positions.

Equation (9.59) implies that n is positively related to $\chi \equiv c/k$ along the transition path. Therefore, the declining path of χ in figure 9.6 corresponds to a declining path of n. Figure 9.7 shows the relation between n and z during the transition. (Once we know the relation between χ and z from figure 9.6, we can use the relation between n and χ from equation [9.59] to determine n as a function of z.) As z decreases, n falls monotonically toward its steady-state value. That is, with a given mortality rate, d, the fertility rate declines steadily as the economy develops.

The result that fertility falls as per capita product rises accords with empirical findings for countries. The one exception in the data is that fertility and per capita GDP seem to be positively related at extremely low levels of per capita GDP. That is, the relation for very poor countries appears to be consistent with Malthus's theory. This initially rising segment of the relation between fertility and per capita product tends to appear in the theory if we introduce a goods cost of child rearing along with the cost that rises linearly with k. The goods cost introduces a force—an income effect—that generates a positive relation between fertility and per capita product. Moreover, since the goods cost is relatively more important in poor countries, the net positive relation between fertility and per capita product tends to appear only at low levels of per capita product.

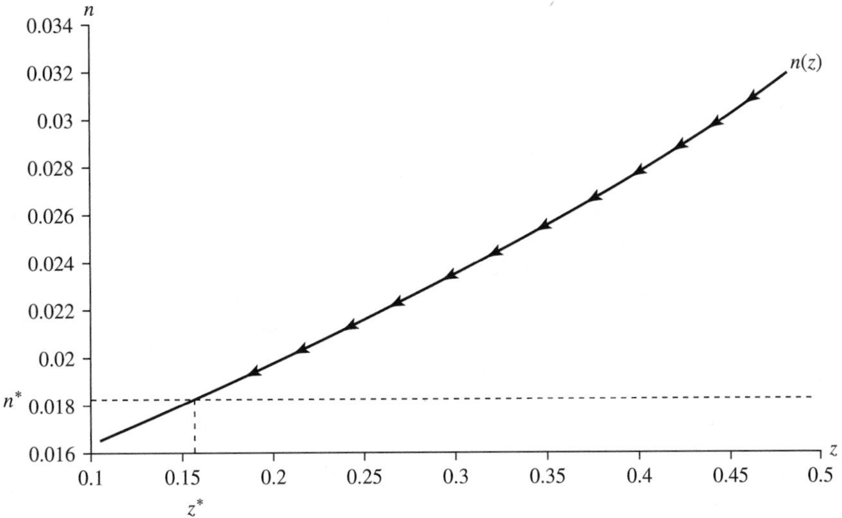

Figure 9.7
Transitional behavior of the fertility rate. If the economy begins with a high gross average product of capital, z, then, as z declines—along the saddle path shown in figure 9.6—the fertility rate, n, falls toward its steady-state value. Quantitatively, for the assumed parameter values, if z begins at 0.3 (corresponding to a rate of return of 0.25), n starts at 0.023 and falls gradually toward its steady-state value of 0.018.

We can allow for a goods cost of child rearing by letting the intercept b_0 in equation (9.55) be nonzero. Although our analytical procedure does not go through when the expression for the child-rearing cost contains a positive intercept, we can use numerical methods to work out the dynamics of this revised model. Specifically, we provide detailed results for the case $b_0 = 50$. If we maintain the parameter values, including $b = 1$, that we used to construct figures 9.6 and 9.7, a value $b_0 = 50$ means, when $n = 0.02$ and $\hat{k}$ is one-tenth of $\hat{k}^*$, that the goods cost of raising a child is about one-sixteenth of total output (if the parameter A in the production function is set to equal 1).

We find numerically that the specification $\eta = 50 + bk$ leads to the phase diagram in (z, χ) space shown in figure 9.8.[28] The associated relation between n and z appears in figure 9.9. The interesting feature of figure 9.9, in comparison with figure 9.7, is that n now rises as z falls for very high values of z (that is, for very low values of $\hat{k}$). Thus the extended model can be consistent with the observation that fertility rises with per capita product for very poor countries but falls with per capita product in the main range of experience.

28. These results assume that the goods cost, which starts at 50, rises at the rate $x = 0.02$ per year along with exogenous technological progress.

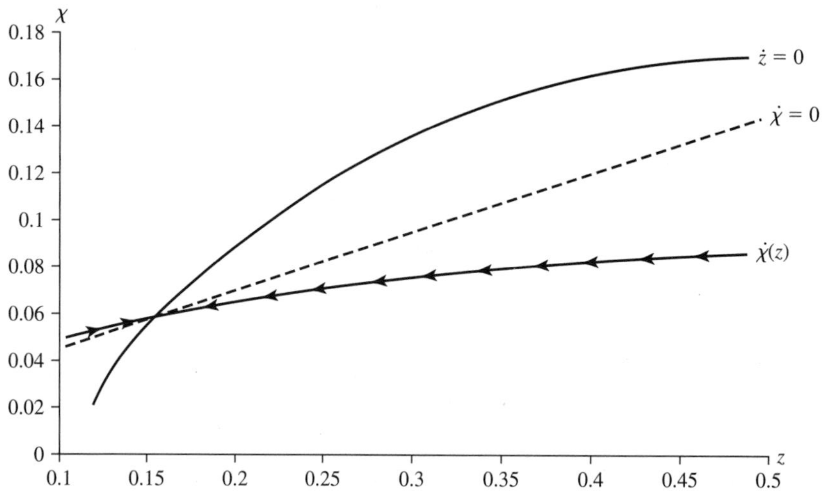

Figure 9.8
Phase diagram in (z, χ) space with a goods cost of child rearing. This figure modifies figure 9.6 to include a goods cost of child rearing. If the economy begins with a high gross average product of capital, z, then z and $\chi \equiv c/k$ still decline monotonically during the transition.

Table 9.1 returns to the specification with $b_0 = 0$ to show how the steady-state values n^* and r^* depend on the settings of the parameters ϕ, ψ, d, and b. For the baseline parameters, the results are $n^* = 0.018$ and $r^* = 0.067$. Increases in ϕ or ψ raise the benefit from children and thereby increase n^*. For example, n^* rises to 0.030 if ϕ or ψ increase to 0.4. The value n^* falls to 0.014 if ϕ declines to 0.1 and to 0.017 if ψ decreases to 0.1. Since $\dot{c}/c = x$ in the steady state, we can use equation (9.58) to think about the relation between n^* and r^*. For given values of ρ, b, and d, r^* moves by the factor $1 + b$ in the same direction as n^*. Therefore, table 9.1 shows that an increase in ϕ or ψ leads to a rise in r^*.

For a given c/k, equation (9.59) shows that n moves one-to-one with the mortality rate, d. Because an increase in d turns out to raise $(c/k)^*$, the full effect of d on n^* is slightly greater than one-to-one. For example, if d increases from 0.01 to 0.02, table 9.1 shows that n^* rises from 0.0183 to 0.0291. Since the change in the rate of population growth, $n^* - d$, is small, equation (9.58) implies that r^* still moves in the same direction as n^*, roughly by the factor b. The table shows accordingly that a rise in d leads to an increase in r^*.

An increase in the cost parameter b leads to a decline in n^*. For example, table 9.1 shows that if b rises to 2, n^* decreases to 0.015, whereas if b falls to 0.5, n^* increases to 0.023. Since a rise in b is accompanied by a reduction of n^*, equation (9.58) suggests that the effect on r^* would be ambiguous. In the range considered in the table, the net effect of b on r^* turns out to be positive.

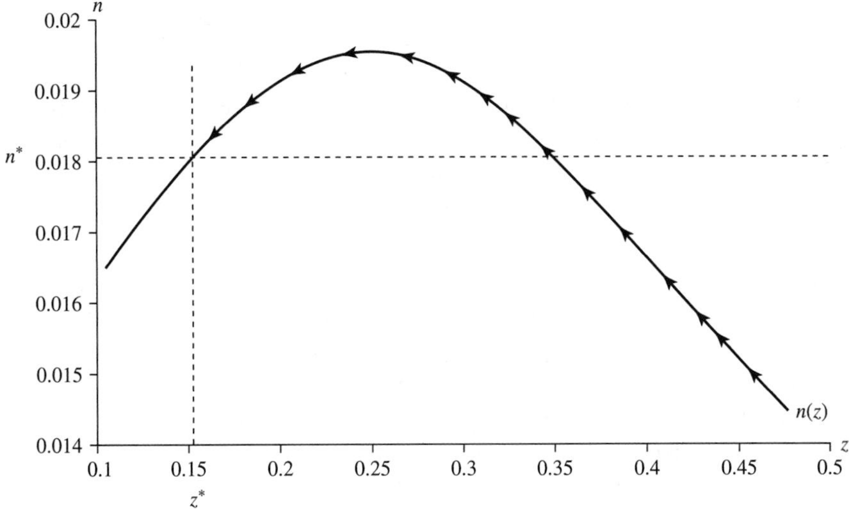

Figure 9.9
Transitional behavior of the fertility rate with a goods cost of child rearing. This figure modifies figure 9.7 to include a goods cost of child rearing. If the economy starts with a high gross average product of capital, z, then, as z declines along the saddle path shown in figure 9.8, the fertility rate can now adjust in a nonmonotonic fashion. In contrast with figure 9.7, the fertility rate can rise for a while and then decline later to approach its steady-state value. This behavior corresponds to the tendency of fertility rates to rise with per capita income for the poorest countries but to fall with per capita income in the main range of experience.

Table 9.1
Effects of Parameter Variations on n^* and r^*

Parameter Specification	n^*	r^*
Baseline	0.0183	0.067
$\phi = 0.4$	0.0300	0.090
$\phi = 0.1$	0.0139	0.058
$\psi = 0.4$	0.0300	0.090
$\psi = 0.1$	0.0168	0.064
$d = 0.02$	0.0291	0.078
$d = 0$	0.0076	0.055
$b = 0.5$	0.0226	0.064
$b = 2$	0.0152	0.076

Note: The baseline specification is $\alpha = 0.75$, $\delta = 0.05$, $\rho = 0.02$, $x = 0.02$, $d = 0.01$, $b = 1$, $\psi = 0.2$, $\phi = 0.2$. The table shows the effect on the steady-state values n^* and r^* when the designated parameter is changed to the value indicated while all other parameters remain at their baseline settings.

9.3 Labor/Leisure Choice

We have assumed, thus far, a fixed relation between labor supply and population; that is, we have neglected changes in labor-force participation or in work hours and effort. In this section we let labor supply vary for a given population by allowing for a labor/leisure choice. The changes in labor supply in this model represent some combination of variations in labor-force participation, work hours, and work effort, but the analysis does not distinguish these different components of labor supply.

We carry out the analysis within the Ramsey framework by introducing leisure as an additional argument of the utility function. We use a specification of preferences that allows for transitional variations in labor supply but guarantees that the fraction of time devoted to work effort approaches a constant in the steady state. The model, therefore, allows us to study the transitional behavior of work effort and also to consider how changes in various parameters affect the steady-state quantity of work effort.

Population, denoted by $N(t)$, now has to be distinguished from labor input, $L(t)$. We return to the setting in which $N(t)$ grows exogenously at the constant rate n, but $L(t)$ can now vary for given $N(t)$. Define $\ell(t)$ to be the typical person's intensity of work effort at time t, so that

$$L(t) \equiv \ell(t) \cdot N(t) \tag{9.63}$$

If $\ell(t)$ is the fraction of time spent working, it can be measured with available data and would have a natural upper bound of 100 percent. In contrast, if $\ell(t)$ allows for variations in work effort, it would not be readily measurable and would not have an obvious upper bound.

We now modify the formulation of household utility from equation (2.1) to include a disutility of work effort:

$$U = \int_0^\infty u[c(t), \ell(t)]e^{-(\rho-n)t}\, dt \tag{9.64}$$

where the partial derivatives satisfy the usual concavity conditions, including $u_c > 0$, $u_\ell < 0$, $u_{cc} < 0$, and $u_{\ell\ell} \leq 0$.[29] If the wage rate, w, is the amount paid per unit of labor input, the

29. This formulation assumes that work effort, ℓ, enters negatively into a utility function. Another approach, due to Becker (1965), assumes that time not spent at market work is used for home production. The important distinguishing feature of this alternative approach is that the productivity of home work is affected by capital accumulation and technological progress. The allocation of time between market and home work then depends on relative productivity trends and on the evolution of relative demands for market- and home-produced goods. See Greenwood and Hercowitz (1991) and Benhabib, Rogerson, and Wright (1991) for the use of this approach in dynamic contexts.

household's budget constraint is modified from equation (2.2) to

$$\dot{a} = w\ell + (r - n) \cdot a - c \tag{9.65}$$

We can proceed as usual by setting up the Hamiltonian expression,

$$J = u(c, \ell) \cdot e^{-(\rho - n)t} + \nu \cdot [w\ell + (r - n) \cdot a - c]$$

The maximization problem is the same as that in chapter 2, except that u_c, the marginal utility of consumption, may depend on ℓ, and we have to add a new first-order condition, $\partial J / \partial \ell = 0$.

The first-order condition that corresponds to equation (2.7) from the Ramsey model is

$$r = \rho - \left[\frac{u_{cc} \cdot c}{u_c}\right] \cdot (\dot{c}/c) - \left[\frac{u_{c\ell} \cdot \ell}{u_c}\right] \cdot (\dot{\ell}/\ell) \tag{9.66}$$

Note that we get the original formula from chapter 2 if $u_{c\ell} = 0$. If $u_{c\ell} > 0$, a higher value of $\dot{\ell}/\ell$ effectively subtracts from the rate of time preference, ρ, because households prefer to consume a lot in the future when ℓ will be high, that is, when they have little leisure. This effect is reversed in the introspectively more plausible case in which consumption and leisure are complements in the sense that $u_{c\ell} < 0$.

The new first-order condition, which reflects the substitution between consumption and leisure at a point in time, is

$$-u_\ell / u_c = w \tag{9.67}$$

We would like equation (9.67) to be consistent with the empirical regularity that hours worked per worker—which we take as a rough proxy for ℓ—typically decline at early stages of economic development but tend eventually to level off (see the discussion in Barro, 1997, chapter 2). In particular, we would like the model to have a steady state in which ℓ is constant.

In the steady state of the Ramsey model, w and c grow at the same rate, x. Therefore, we want to use a form of the utility function for which equation (9.67) implies that ℓ is constant, at least asymptotically, when w and c grow at the same rate. We also want to retain the property that the model has a steady state in which c grows at a constant rate. The appendix 9A (section 9.4) shows that these conditions require the utility function asymptotically to take the form

$$u(c, \ell) = \frac{c^{1-\theta} \cdot \exp[(1 - \theta) \cdot \omega(\ell)] - 1}{1 - \theta} \tag{9.68}$$

where $\theta > 0$, $\omega'(\ell) < 0$, and $\omega''(\ell) \leq 0$.[30] This formulation corresponds to the one used by King, Plosser, and Rebelo (1988a) and Rebelo (1991).[31] The sign of $u_{c\ell}$ depends on the magnitude of θ: $u_{c\ell} \lesseqgtr 0$ as $\theta \lesseqgtr 1$. The standard isoelastic function used in equation (2.8) is the special case in which $\omega(\ell) = 0$. This specification is, however, inconsistent with the choice of a finite amount of work effort.

If we use equation (9.68) to compute u_ℓ and u_c, the first-order condition in equation (9.67) implies

$$-\omega'(\ell) = w/c \tag{9.69}$$

The algebra for the rest of the model turns out to be cumbersome for general θ, but we can bring out the main results by considering the special case in which $\theta = 1$. The application of l'Hôpital's rule to equation (9.68) shows that the limit of $u(c, \ell)$ as θ approaches 1 is

$$u(c, \ell) = \log(c) + \omega(\ell) \tag{9.70}$$

That is, if utility is logarithmic in c, the function is separable between c and ℓ, so that $u_{c\ell} = 0$. If the utility function takes the form of equation (9.70), the first-order condition in equation (9.66) reduces to the familiar expression for the growth rate of c:

$$\dot{c}/c = r - \rho \tag{9.71}$$

We now define the variables per unit of effective labor to include the effect from variable work effort, ℓ; that is,

$$\hat{k} \equiv K/(\ell N e^{xt})$$

$$\hat{c} \equiv C/(\ell N e^{xt})$$

If we assume a closed economy and introduce firms in the usual way, equation (9.71) and the conditions $r = f'(\hat{k}) - \delta$ and $a = k$ imply

$$\dot{\hat{c}}/\hat{c} = f'(\hat{k}) - (\delta + \rho + x) - \dot{\ell}/\ell \tag{9.72}$$

$$\dot{\hat{k}}/\hat{k} = f(\hat{k})/\hat{k} - (x + n + \delta) - \hat{c}/\hat{k} - \dot{\ell}/\ell \tag{9.73}$$

These results differ from the standard ones (equations [2.23] and [2.24]) only because $\dot{\ell}/\ell$

30. These properties imply $u_c > 0$, $u_\ell < 0$, and $u_{cc} < 0$. The condition $u_{\ell\ell} \leq 0$ requires $\omega''(\ell) + (1 - \theta) \cdot [\omega'(\ell)]^2 \leq 0$, an inequality that must hold if $\theta \geq 1$.

31. Rebelo (1991, p. 513) shows that another alternative is to specify utility as $u(c, \ell k)$, where $u(\cdot)$ is homogeneous of some positive degree, and k should now be thought of as human capital per person. The term ℓk can then be viewed as forgone leisure time, adjusted for a person's quality, as in the formulation used by Becker (1965) and Heckman (1976).

adds to the growth rate of effective labor input. Since $\dot{\ell}/\ell = 0$ in the steady state, the formulas for $\hat{k}^*$ and $\hat{c}^*$ are the same as those in the Ramsey model.

We now assume that the production function is Cobb–Douglas, $f(\hat{k}) = A\hat{k}^\alpha$, and that the disutility of work takes a constant-elasticity form:

$$\omega(\ell) = -\zeta \cdot \ell^{1+\sigma}$$

where $\zeta > 0$ and $\sigma \geq 0$. Since the wage rate is given in the Cobb–Douglas case by $w = (1-\alpha) \cdot A\hat{k}^\alpha \cdot e^{xt}$, equation (9.69) becomes

$$\zeta \cdot (1+\sigma) \cdot \ell^{1+\sigma} = (1-\alpha) \cdot A\hat{k}^\alpha / \hat{c} \tag{9.74}$$

(Note that the replacement of c by $\hat{c}$ on the right-hand side brings in the additional factor of ℓ on the left-hand side.) Since $\hat{y}$ is proportional to $\hat{k}^\alpha$, equation (9.74) implies that a high value of ℓ—little leisure—goes along with a low value of c/y. [This relation holds for a general form of $\omega(\ell)$ if $\omega'(\ell) > 0$ and $\omega''(\ell) \geq 0$.] Equation (9.74) implies that the growth rate of ℓ is given by

$$\dot{\ell}/\ell = \left(\frac{\alpha}{1+\sigma}\right) \cdot (\dot{\hat{k}}/\hat{k}) - \left(\frac{1}{1+\sigma}\right) \cdot (\dot{\hat{c}}/\hat{c}) \tag{9.75}$$

If we use the Cobb–Douglas forms for $f'(\hat{k})$ and $f(\hat{k})$ and the expression for $\dot{\ell}/\ell$ from equation (9.75), then equations (9.72) and (9.73) lead, after some algebra, to the dynamic system for $\hat{k}$ and $\hat{c}$:

$$\dot{\hat{k}}/\hat{k} = A\hat{k}^{\alpha-1} - \left(\frac{1}{\alpha+\sigma}\right) \cdot [\sigma \cdot (\hat{c}/\hat{k}) + (1+\sigma) \cdot (x+\delta) + \rho + \sigma n] \tag{9.76}$$

$$\dot{\hat{c}}/\hat{c} = \alpha A\hat{k}^{\alpha-1} + \left(\frac{1}{\alpha+\sigma}\right) \cdot [\alpha \cdot (\hat{c}/\hat{k}) - (1+\sigma) \cdot (x+\delta) - (1+\alpha+\sigma) \cdot \rho + \alpha n] \tag{9.77}$$

These results reduce to the standard formulas shown in equations (2.36) and (2.37) if $\theta = 1$ (to get the log-utility specification that we have assumed here) and σ approaches infinity. An infinite σ deters any variation in ℓ over time and therefore reproduces the results from the model with fixed labor supply.

We already mentioned that the steady-state values of $\hat{k}$ and $\hat{c}$ are the same as those in the Ramsey model, a result that can be verified by setting equations (9.76) and (9.77) to zero. These steady-state values can be expressed as

$$r^* = \alpha A \cdot (\hat{k}^*)^{\alpha-1} - \delta = \rho + x$$

$$\hat{c}^*/\hat{k}^* = (\rho + \delta + x)/\alpha - (n + x + \delta)$$

We can substitute these values into equation (9.74) to determine the steady-state level of work effort, ℓ^*:

$$\ell^* = \left\{ \left[\frac{1-\alpha}{\zeta \cdot (1+\sigma)} \right] \cdot \left[\frac{\rho + \delta + x}{\rho + \delta + x - \alpha \cdot (n + x + \delta)} \right] \right\}^{1/(1+\sigma)} \tag{9.78}$$

The transitional dynamics of $\hat{k}$ and $\hat{c}$ implied by equations (9.76) and (9.77) can be analyzed, as usual, with a phase diagram in $(\hat{k}, \hat{c})$ space. The system is again saddle-path stable, and we leave the construction of the phase diagram as an exercise.

If we log-linearize equations (9.76) and (9.77) around the steady state in the usual manner, the formula for the speed of convergence to the steady state turns out to be

$$2\beta = \rho - n - \left\{ (\rho - n)^2 + \left[\frac{4 \cdot (1-\alpha) \cdot (1+\sigma)}{\alpha + \sigma} \right] \cdot (\rho + \delta + \theta x) \cdot \left[\frac{\rho + \delta + x}{\alpha} - (n + x + \delta) \right] \right\}^{1/2} \tag{9.79}$$

This formula reduces to the standard Ramsey result (equation [2.34] with $\theta = 1$) if we let σ approach infinity.

If we use our familiar parameter values ($\alpha = 0.75, x = 0.02, n = 0.01, \delta = 0.05, \rho = 0.02$), then the value of β implied by equation (9.79) is 0.030 if $\sigma = 0$. As σ rises above 0, β declines and approaches the Ramsey value—which is 0.025 with the assumed parameter values—as σ tends to infinity. Thus the inclusion of a labor/leisure choice raises the speed of convergence but only to a moderate extent.

The reason that the convergence coefficient is somewhat higher with variable labor supply is that ℓ declines monotonically during the transition to the steady state; that is, in this model, poor people (who expect to be richer later) work harder than rich people. We can prove this result by substituting for $\dot{\hat{k}}/\hat{k}$ and $\dot{\hat{c}}/\hat{c}$ from equations (9.76) and (9.77) into the formula for $\dot{\ell}/\ell$ in equation (9.75) to get (after simplifying)

$$\dot{\ell}/\ell = \left(\frac{\alpha}{\alpha + \sigma} \right) \cdot (\chi^* - \chi)$$

where $\chi \equiv \hat{c}/\hat{k}$. It is possible to use the method developed in appendix 2B to show that, if $\hat{k}(0) < \hat{k}^*$, χ falls monotonically during the transition and, hence, $\chi > \chi^*$ applies throughout. (We leave this demonstration as an exercise.) This result implies $\dot{\ell}/\ell < 0$, that is, ℓ falls monotonically from its initial value, $\ell(0)$, to the steady-state value, ℓ^*. The model, therefore, accords with the empirical observation that work effort declines during early stages of economic development.

9.4 Appendix: The Form of the Utility Function with Consumption and Work Effort

We study here the required form of the utility function, $u(c, \ell)$, in the model with a labor/leisure choice. We want the economy to have a steady state in which $\dot{c}/c$ and ℓ are constants. Equation (9.66) implies accordingly that the elasticity of the marginal utility of consumption must be constant (just as in the Ramsey model):

$$\frac{u_{cc} \cdot c}{u_c} = -\theta, \text{ a constant} \tag{9.80}$$

The first-order condition in equation (9.67) can be written as

$$\frac{w}{c} = \frac{-u_\ell}{c \cdot u_c}$$

We are looking for a steady state in which w and c grow at the same rate, so that w/c is constant. Therefore, if we take logs of the right-hand side and differentiate with respect to time, in the steady state,

$$(u_{\ell c} \cdot \dot{c} + u_{\ell\ell} \cdot \dot{\ell})/u_\ell - (u_{cc} \cdot \dot{c} + u_{c\ell} \cdot \dot{\ell})/u_c - \dot{c}/c = 0$$

Since $\dot{\ell} = 0$ and $\dot{c}/c$ is generally nonzero, this condition can be rewritten as

$$\frac{c \cdot u_{\ell c}}{u_\ell} = 1 + \frac{c \cdot u_{cc}}{u_c} = 1 - \theta \tag{9.81}$$

Rewrite equation (9.81) as

$$\frac{1}{u_\ell} \cdot \frac{\partial(u_\ell)}{\partial c} = \frac{1-\theta}{c}$$

and integrate with respect to c to get

$$\log(u_\ell) = (1-\theta) \cdot \log(c) + (\text{function of } \ell)$$

Integration of this result with respect to ℓ yields

$$u(c, \ell) = c^{1-\theta} \cdot \varphi(\ell) + \psi(c) \tag{9.82}$$

where φ and ψ are, as yet, arbitrary functions.

Equations (9.80) and (9.82) imply

$$\frac{u_{cc} \cdot c}{u_c} = \frac{-\theta \cdot (1-\theta) \cdot c^{-\theta} \cdot \varphi(\ell) + c \cdot \psi''(c)}{(1-\theta) \cdot c^{-\theta} \cdot \varphi(\ell) + \psi'(c)} = -\theta$$

and the function $\psi(c)$ must be consistent with this equation. Therefore, $\psi(c)$ must satisfy

$$c \cdot \psi''(c) = -\theta \cdot \psi'(c)$$

If we integrate this condition twice, we get, aside from multiplicative and additive constants,

$$\psi(c) = c^{1-\theta} \quad \text{if } \theta \neq 1$$

$$\psi(c) = \log(c) \quad \text{if } \theta = 1$$

We can substitute the result for $\psi(c)$ into equation (9.82) to get the required form of $u(c, \ell)$. One way to write the result, as in equation (9.68), is

$$u(c, \ell) = \frac{c^{1-\theta} \cdot \exp[(1-\theta) \cdot \omega(\ell)] - 1}{1-\theta} \tag{9.83}$$

In this form, $\theta > 0$ and $\omega'(\ell) < 0$ guarantee $u_c > 0$, $u_\ell < 0$, and $u_{cc} < 0$. The condition $u_{\ell\ell} \leq 0$ requires $\omega''(\ell) + (1-\theta) \cdot [\omega'(\ell)]^2 \leq 0$, which must hold if $\omega''(\ell) \leq 0$ and $\theta \geq 1$. An application of l'Hôpital's rule shows that the function in equation (9.83) approaches $\log(c) + \omega(\ell)$ as θ approaches 1.

9.5 Problems

9.1 Migration in neoclassical growth models

a. Under what circumstances does the potential for migration raise the speed of convergence in the Solow–Swan model? What about in the Ramsey model? What are the sources of the effects on convergence?

b. Might a government of a country that is receiving immigrants find it desirable to restrict the number that come? Might the government wish to charge a fee for immigration? Would the fee tend to vary with the immigrant's quantity of human capital?

c. Redo part b for the case of a country that is sending emigrants.

9.2 A model of rural-urban migration (based on Mas-Colell and Razin, 1973). Consider an economy with two productive sectors. The rural or agricultural sector, denoted A, produces output only for consumption. The urban or industrial sector, denoted I, produces output for consumption and investment. The production functions are Cobb–Douglas:

$$Y_A = (K_A)^\alpha \cdot (L_A)^{1-\alpha}; \; Y_I = (K_I)^\lambda \cdot (L_I)^{1-\lambda}$$

where $0 < \alpha < 1$, $0 < \lambda < 1$. There is no technological progress.

Each person inelastically supplies 1 unit of labor, and total population, $L = L_A + L_I$, grows at the constant rate $n \geq 0$. The natural rates of population growth are the same in the rural and urban areas. Capital, $K = K_A + K_I$, can move costlessly across sectors. People can move across sectors at some cost. The rate of migration to the urban sector is assumed to be positively related to the wage-rate differential:

$$\dot{\mu}/\mu = b \cdot (w_I - w_A)/w_A$$

where $b > 0$ and μ is the proportion of the population employed in the urban sector.

People save a constant fraction s of income and spend the fraction η of income on industrial products for consumption purposes. Capital does not depreciate. The price of the industrial good in units of the agricultural good is denoted by p.

a. Derive the formulas at each point in time for the capital rental rate R, the wage rates w_A and w_I, and the relative price of industrial output p. What is the fraction of total capital employed in the urban sector?

b. Construct a phase diagram in (k, μ) space, where $k \equiv K/L$. What are the steady-state levels, k^* and μ^*? Is the steady state stable?

c. Suppose that the economy begins with $\mu < \mu^*$. Show that the migration rate into the urban sector decreases as the economy moves toward its steady state. Characterize the behavior of the relative price, p, and the growth rate of capital along the transition path. Does the model exhibit a convergence property?

9.3 Growth in an optimizing model of migration (based on Braun, 1993). Consider Braun's model of migration, which we presented in section 9.1.3. Toward the end of that section, we mentioned an extension to allow for the dynamics of the world economy. Assume that the framework of section 9.1.3 applies, including the production function in equation (9.27), except that the world now consists of only two economies, country 1 and country 2. The natural resources in each country, R_1 and R_2, are fixed. The populations of each country are denoted by L_1 and L_2, where $L = L_1 + L_2$ is world population. Natural population growth rates are 0 in each economy, and the initial conditions are such that the flow of migrants is from country 2 to country 1. The cost of moving from country 2 to country 1 is still given by equation (9.34), except that w_{world} is replaced by w_2. The moving cost for each migrant again approaches 0 as the number of migrants goes to 0. Capital is perfectly mobile across the economies. The total capital stock, $K = K_1 + K_2$, is allocated across the economies to equalize the net marginal products of capital at each point in time. The world rate of return, r—which can now vary over time—equals the net marginal product of capital. Assume for simplicity that technological progress and depreciation are absent. Consumers in each country have Ramsey preferences with infinite horizons, as assumed in chapter 2.

a. Work out the dynamic system in terms of the variables k, L_2, B, and c, where B is the present value of the benefit from a permanent move from country 2 to country 1 (an analogue to equation [9.31]) and $c \equiv C/L$ is the world's average consumption per person. Note that the state variables for the system are k and L_2; for given L, the variable L_2 determines the allocation of population between the two countries. (Hint: people who start in country 1 never move, and the path of consumption, c_1, is the same for each person. For people who start in country 2, the path of consumption, c_2, must be the same regardless of when they move to country 1 or whether they ever move. These considerations, along with the standard Ramsey formula for consumption growth, determine the behavior of c in relation to the rate of return, r.)

b. What are the steady-state values of k, L_2, and B?

c. Consider a log-linear approximation of the dynamic system in the neighborhood of the steady state.

(i) Observe that, close to the steady state, a small change in L_2 has a negligible effect on wage rates in the two countries, world output, and the rate of return. Use these facts to break the four-dimensional system into two separate parts: one that applies to the world variables, k and c, and another that applies to the migration variables, L_2 and B.

(ii) Find the speed of convergence, β, for the world variables and relate the answer to the solution of the Ramsey model from chapter 2.

(iii) Find the speed of convergence, μ, for L_2. Show how the convergence speed for per capita output in one country, y_1, depends on β and μ (see equation [9.45]).

9.4 Endogenous mortality. Consider the model of fertility choice in section 9.2.2. Suppose that the mortality rate, d, can be influenced by family or public expenditures on health.

a. Assume that d depends on the household's current flow of expenditures on health. Determine the optimal path of these expenditures. How does d evolve as the economy develops? What are the implications for the behavior of the fertility rate, n, and the capital intensity, k?

b. Assume now that d depends on public health expenditures per capita. Suppose that the ratio of this spending to total output is the constant g and that this spending is financed by a lump-sum tax. How do the paths of the fertility rate, n, and the capital intensity, k, depend on the choice of g? What is the government's optimal choice of g? Would it be preferable to allow g to vary over time?

9.5 Transitional dynamics with a labor/leisure choice. In section 9.3 we worked out the dynamic conditions for a model with a labor/leisure choice. For the case of log utility and a Cobb–Douglas production function, the equations for the growth rates of $\hat{k}$ and $\hat{c}$ are given in equations (9.76) and (9.77). Equation (9.74) relates the choice of work effort, ℓ, to the variables $\hat{k}$ and $\hat{c}$.

a. Construct the phase diagram in $(\hat{k}, \hat{c})$ space.

b. If $\hat{k}(0) < \hat{k}^*$, describe the transition paths for $\hat{k}$, $\hat{c}$, and ℓ.

c. Verify that the speed of convergence, β, in the neighborhood of the steady state is given by equation (9.79). Why is the speed of convergence higher than that in the standard Ramsey model (equation [2.34])?

10 Growth Accounting

Growth accounting is an empirical methodology that allows for the breakdown of observed growth of GDP into components associated with changes in factor inputs and in production technologies. Given the impossibility of measuring technological progress directly, the growth rate of technology is measured "indirectly" as the growth rate in GDP that cannot be accounted for by the growth of the observable inputs, that is, as "residual growth." Usually, the accounting exercise is viewed as a first step in the analysis of fundamental determinants of economic growth because it does not attempt to explain the forces that drive the growth rates of each of the inputs or factor shares. The final step involves the relations of factor growth rates, factor shares, and technological change (the residual) to elements such as government policies, household preferences, natural resources, initial levels of physical and human capital, and so on. The growth-accounting exercise can be particularly useful if the fundamental determinants that matter for factor growth rates are substantially independent from those that matter for technological change.

The basics of growth accounting were presented in Solow (1957), Kendrick (1961), Denison (1962), and Jorgenson and Griliches (1967). Griliches (1997, part 1) provides an overview of this intellectual history, with stress on the development of the Solow residual.

10.1 Standard Primal Growth Accounting

10.1.1 Basic Setup

The analysis starts from a standard production function, which we can write as

$$Y = F(T, K, L) \tag{10.1}$$

where T is the level of technology, K is the capital stock, and L is the quantity of labor. Capital and labor can be disaggregated among types or qualities as in Jorgenson and Griliches (1967). The production function makes clear that GDP can grow only if there is growth in productive inputs, including the level of technology.

The growth rate of output can be partitioned into components associated with factor accumulation and technological progress. Taking logarithms of equation (10.1) and derivatives with respect to time we get

$$\dot{Y}/Y = g + \left(\frac{F_K K}{Y}\right) \cdot (\dot{K}/K) + \left(\frac{F_L L}{Y}\right) \cdot (\dot{L}/L) \tag{10.2}$$

where F_K, F_L are the factor (social) marginal products and g—the growth due to technological change—is given by

$$g \equiv \left(\frac{F_T T}{Y}\right) \cdot (\dot{T}/T) \tag{10.3}$$

Equation (10.2) says that the growth rate of GDP can be decomposed into the growth rate of the three inputs: capital, labor, and technology. In particular, it says that the decomposition is a weighted average of the growth rates of the three inputs, where the weights are given by the relative contributions of each of the factors to GDP. (These contributions, in turn, are the social marginal products times the amount of input divided by GDP.) This formulation includes Hicks-neutral and labor-augmenting technological progress as special cases. If the technology factor appears in a Hicks-neutral way, so that $F(T, K, L) = T \cdot \tilde{F}(K, L)$, then $F_T T = Y$ and $g = \dot{T}/T$. If the technology factor appears in labor-augmenting form, so that $F(T, K, L) = \tilde{F}(K, TL)$, then $F_T T = F_L L$ and $g = (\frac{F_L L}{Y}) \cdot (\dot{T}/T)$.

We argue in the next section that the growth rates of Y, K, and L can be computed empirically (although not without difficulty!). Imagine for now that we are able to compute the social marginal products, F_K and F_L (and we argue next that, under some circumstances, these can be approximated by factor prices). The part of equation (10.2) that cannot be measured directly is g. However, if all other components of equation (10.2) can be estimated empirically, we can compute g from the others. Specifically, the contribution of technological progress to growth, g, can be calculated from equation (10.2) as a "residual" or difference between the actual growth rate of GDP and the part of the growth rate that can be "accounted for" by the growth rate of capital and labor:

$$g = \dot{Y}/Y - \left(\frac{F_K K}{Y}\right) \cdot (\dot{K}/K) - \left(\frac{F_L L}{Y}\right) \cdot (\dot{L}/L) \tag{10.4}$$

Notice that, to estimate g empirically, we need to know the social marginal products, F_K and F_L, but these values would typically not be measurable directly. In practice, researchers typically assume that the social marginal products can be measured by observed factor prices. If the factors are paid their social marginal products, so that $F_K = R$ (the rental price of capital) and $F_L = w$ (the wage rate), then $F_L L = wL$, which is the total amount of wages paid in the economy (the wage bill). Hence, $\frac{F_L L}{Y} = \frac{wL}{Y}$ is the fraction of GDP used to pay wages, a fraction known as the *labor share,* which we denote by s_L. Similarly, the ratio $\frac{F_K K}{Y} = \frac{RK}{Y}$ is the fraction of GDP used to rent capital, a fraction known as the *capital share,* which we denote by s_K. Using this notation, the estimation of the rate of technological progress can be rewritten as

$$\hat{g} = \dot{Y}/Y - s_K \cdot (\dot{K}/K) - s_L \cdot (\dot{L}/L) \tag{10.5}$$

In the Cobb–Douglas case, the factor shares would be constant over time (and would correspond to the exponents in the production function). However, the present analysis is more general in that the shares are allowed to vary over time.

The value $\hat{g}$ is often described as an estimate of total factor productivity (TFP) growth. This formulation was first presented by Solow (1957), so the value $\hat{g}$ is also sometimes called the *Solow residual*. Since the method just described relies on the growth rates of the quantities of inputs, the label *primal* is sometimes attached to *TFP growth* or to *Solow residual*. This labeling distinguishes this approach from a price-based method (which will be described in the next section), which is labeled as *dual*.

If all the income associated with the gross domestic product, Y, is attributed to capital and labor, then the condition $s_K + s_L = 1$—or $Y = RK + wL$—must hold.[1] In this case, the computation of the residual simplifies to

$$\hat{g} = \dot{Y}/Y - s_K \cdot (\dot{K}/K) - (1 - s_K) \cdot (\dot{L}/L) \tag{10.6}$$

Equation (10.6) can also be rewritten in per capita terms as

$$\hat{g} = \dot{y}/y - s_K \cdot (\dot{k}/k) \tag{10.7}$$

where $y \equiv Y/L$ and $k \equiv K/L$ are quantities per unit of labor.

Although the continuous-time formulation in equation (10.6) is useful conceptually, it has to be modified empirically to implement on discrete-time data. Thörnqvist (1936) dealt with this problem by measuring the growth rate between two points in time, t and $t + 1$, by logarithmic differences and by using as weights the arithmetic averages of the factor shares at times t and $t + 1$. With this approach, the TFP growth rate is approximated in the Hicks-neutral case by

$$\begin{aligned} \log[T(t+1)/T(t)] \approx \log[Y(t+1)/Y(t)] &- \bar{s}_K(t) \cdot \log[K(t+1)/K(t)] \\ &- [1 - \bar{s}_K(t)] \cdot \log[L(t+1)/L(t)] \end{aligned} \tag{10.8}$$

where $\bar{s}_K(t) \equiv [s_K(t) + s_K(t+1)]/2$ is the average share of capital for periods t and $t + 1$.[2] If Hicks neutrality does not hold, equation (10.8) can still be used to approximate the contribution of technological progress to growth.

1. The equation of output, Y, to total factor income is consistent with equality between the factor prices and marginal products if the production function, $F(\cdot)$, exhibits constant returns to scale in K and L—as is true for a neoclassical production function—so that $Y = F_K K + F_L L$ holds. In an international context, some net factor income may accrue to foreign-owned factors, and $RK + wL$ would include this net factor income.

2. Equation (10.8) is only an approximation if the production function takes a general neoclassical form. Diewert (1976) showed, however, that the equation holds exactly if the production function has the translog specification:

$$\begin{aligned} \log(Y) = \alpha_0 &+ \alpha_L \cdot \log(L) + \alpha_K \cdot \log(K) + \alpha_t t + (\beta_{KK}/2) \cdot (\log[K])^2 \\ &+ (\beta_{LL}/2) \cdot (\log[L])^2 + (\beta_{tt}/2) \cdot t^2 + \beta_{KL} \cdot \log(K) \cdot \log(L) \\ &+ \beta_{Kt} \cdot \log(K) \cdot t + \beta_{Lt} \cdot \log(L) \cdot t \end{aligned}$$

where the α's and β's are constants. To ensure constant returns to scale, the parameters must satisfy the restriction

$$\beta_{KK} + \beta_{KL} = \beta_{LL} + \beta_{KL} = \beta_{Kt} + \beta_{Lt} = 0$$

We leave the proof of Diewert's proposition as an exercise.

10.1.2 Measuring Inputs

Capital The practical implementation of the ideas sketched in the previous section requires measuring the growth rate of inputs as well as the shares of capital and labor. Ideally, we would use the flow of services from physical capital as a measure of capital input. For example, we would calculate the amount of "machine hours" used in the production process during period t. Since the available data do not usually permit this measurement, the typical procedure calculates the quantity of physical capital of a particular type and then assumes that the flow of services is proportional to the stock. Sometimes attempts are made to distinguish the outstanding stock of capital from the portion that is currently utilized in production.

Measures of the stock of physical capital come from cumulations of figures on gross physical investment along with estimates of depreciation of existing stocks. This approach, termed the *perpetual-inventory method,* considers that the capital stock available in period $t+1$, $K(t+1)$, is the sum of the capital stock left over from period t—which is the capital from the previous period minus depreciation, $K(t) - \delta \cdot K(t)$—plus the capital purchased during the period or investment, $I(t)$:

$$K(t+1) = K(t) + I(t) - \delta \cdot K(t) \tag{10.9}$$

where δ is the constant depreciation rate.[3] If data on $I(t)$ are available and δ is known (often an unrealistic assumption), the only other ingredient required to implement equation (10.9) is the initial stock of capital, $K(0)$. One way to measure $K(0)$ is to obtain a direct estimate of the stock of capital outstanding in a benchmark year. Another procedure is to make a rough guess about $K(0)$ and then use equation (10.9) to calculate $K(t)$ in subsequent years. The estimated stocks of capital during the first few years are sensitive to the initial guess about $K(0)$ and are, therefore, unreliable. However, as $K(0)$ is depreciated away, the estimated stocks become progressively more accurate. With this method, it is necessary to have data on $I(t)$ that substantially predate the interval over which the constructed series on $K(t)$ is to be used.

Labor The labor input can increase if the number of hours worked in a given period increases or if the quality of the workers increases. When measuring changes in hours, it is important to take into account changing labor-force participation rates, as well as the rates of unemployment and hours worked per worker.

3. This approach assumes that the contribution of each machine to the overall value of the capital stock equals the machine's replacement cost. In the language of section 3.6, this formulation neglects adjustment costs for investment and assumes, therefore, $q = 1$.

Qualities of Inputs Early applications of the growth-accounting methodology used a weighted sum of the growth rate of capital and the growth rate of hours worked. The weights equaled the shares of each input in total income and were often assumed to be constant over time. The subtraction of the weighted sum of input growth rates from the growth rate of aggregate output then yielded an estimate of the TFP growth rate. These studies, such as Solow (1957) and Denison (1962, 1967), usually found large residuals. In other words, a substantial fraction of the growth rate of aggregate output was not accounted for by the growth rates of measured inputs, and, consequently, a substantial role was assigned to technological progress.

Jorgenson and Griliches (1967) showed that a substantial fraction of the Solow residual could be explained by changes in the quality of inputs. For example, improvements in the quality of the labor force reflect increases in average years of schooling and better health. For given quantities of capital and worker hours, improvements in the quality of labor raise output. But if labor input is measured only by worker hours, the unmeasured quality improvements show up as TFP growth. Unmeasured improvements in the quality of capital have similar effects.

To take improvements in the quality of labor into account, worker hours can be disaggregated into many different categories based on schooling, experience, gender, and so on (see Jorgenson, Gollop, and Fraumeni, 1987, for a detailed discussion and implementation of this approach). Each category is weighed in accordance with its observed average wage rate, the usual proxy for the marginal product of labor. For example, if persons with college education have higher wage rates (and are presumably more productive) than persons with high school education, then an extra worker with a college education accounts for more output expansion than would an extra worker with a high school education.

In this approach, the overall labor input is the weighted sum over all categories, where the weights are the relative wage rates. For a given total of worker hours, the quality of the labor force improves—and, hence, the measured labor input increases—if workers shift toward the categories that pay higher wage rates. For example, if the fraction of the labor force that is college educated increases and the fraction with no schooling declines, then the total labor input rises even if the aggregate amount of worker hours does not change.

The allowance for quality change in the capital stock also requires a disaggregation into many components. The aggregate measure of capital input is the weighted sum over all types, where the weights are the relative rental rates.[4] To compute the rental rates, the usual assumption is that all investments yield the same rate of return. Under perfect foresight, the

4. Feenstra and Markusen (1995) extend this procedure to allow for the introduction of new types of capital goods. In chapter 6, recall that technological progress took the form of increases in the number of product varieties.

rental rate of capital is given by the arbitrage condition,

$$R_i(t) = [1 + r(t)] \cdot P_i(t) - (1 - \delta_i) \cdot P_i(t + 1) \tag{10.10}$$

where $R_i(t)$ is the rental rate on the capital good, $P_i(t)$ is the price of the capital good, δ_i is the depreciation rate, and $r(t)$ is the economy-wide real interest rate. The hope is to define categories of capital goods that are homogeneous with respect to $P_i(t)$ and δ_i. In practice, however, new varieties of a given category of goods tend to have higher quality than old ones. The usual failure to take this quality change fully into account leads to an underestimate of the growth of the capital stock (and also to an understatement of the flow of current output).

Equation (10.10) shows that, for given $P_i(t)$, the source of variation in rental rates is the rate of depreciation, δ_i. Other things equal, short-lived capital has a higher rental rate than long-lived capital. In this sense, a shift from long-lived to short-lived capital looks like an improvement in the "quality" of capital.

10.1.3 Results from Growth Accounting

Table 10.1 reports growth-accounting relationships for a number of countries over different time periods. The results come from four different studies, all of which adjust for changes in the quality of inputs by using the methodology of Jorgenson and Griliches (1967). In the table, the growth rate of real GDP is decomposed into contributions from the growth rates of capital and labor and a residual for TFP growth.

Panel A of table 10.1, from Christensen, Cummings, and Jorgenson (1980), covers Canada, France, Germany, Italy, Japan, the Netherlands, the United Kingdom, and the United States for the period 1947–73. The annual growth rates of TFP for these countries were substantial, ranging from 1.4 percent for the United States to 4.0 percent for Japan. TFP growth accounts for more than one-third of the overall growth rate of real GDP in all of the countries.

Panel B of the table, from Jorgenson and Yip (2001), reports the decomposition of growth into the same three categories for the same OECD countries, except for the Netherlands, for a more recent period, 1960–95. One observation is that the TFP growth rates are much smaller than those found for 1947–73. The TFP growth rates in the later period range from 0.6 percent for Canada and 0.8 percent for the United States to 1.5 percent for Italy and 2.6 percent for Japan. This reduction in the worldwide growth rate of productivity is known as the *productivity slowdown*. Although the TFP growth rate is lower for all the countries in the later period, the share of overall growth accounted for by TFP change remains high in some countries because the growth accounted for by changes in factor inputs also declined. For example, in Germany, Italy, and Japan, TFP growth still accounts for over 40 percent of overall growth

Table 10.1
Growth Accounting for a Sample of Countries

Country	(1) Growth Rate of GDP	(2) Contribution from Capital	(3) Contribution from Labor	(4) TFP Growth Rate
		Panel A: OECD Countries, 1947–73		
Canada	0.0517	0.0254	0.0088	0.0175
($\alpha = 0.44$)		(49%)	(17%)	(34%)
France[a]	0.0542	0.0225	0.0021	0.0296
($\alpha = 0.40$)		(42%)	(4%)	(54%)
Germany[b]	0.0661	0.0269	0.0018	0.0374
($\alpha = 0.39$)		(41%)	(3%)	(56%)
Italy[b]	0.0527	0.0180	0.0011	0.0337
($\alpha = 0.39$)		(34%)	(2%)	(64%)
Japan[b]	0.0951	0.0328	0.0221	0.0402
($\alpha = 0.39$)		(35%)	(23%)	(42%)
Netherlands[c]	0.0536	0.0247	0.0042	0.0248
($\alpha = 0.45$)		(46%)	(8%)	(46%)
U.K.[d]	0.0373	0.0176	0.0003	0.0193
($\alpha = 0.38$)		(47%)	(1%)	(52%)
U.S.	0.0402	0.0171	0.0095	0.0135
($\alpha = 0.40$)		(43%)	(24%)	(34%)
		Panel B: OECD Countries, 1960–95		
Canada	0.0369	0.0186	0.0123	0.0057
($\alpha = 0.42$)		(51%)	(33%)	(16%)
France	0.0358	0.0180	0.0033	0.0130
($\alpha = 0.41$)		(53%)	(10%)	(38%)
Germany	0.0312	0.0177	0.0014	0.0132
($\alpha = 0.39$)		(56%)	(4%)	(42%)
Italy	0.0357	0.0182	0.0035	0.0153
($\alpha = 0.34$)		(51%)	(9%)	(42%)
Japan	0.0566	0.0178	0.0125	0.0265
($\alpha = 0.43$)		(31%)	(22%)	(47%)
U.K.	0.0221	0.0124	0.0017	0.0080
($\alpha = 0.37$)		(56%)	(8%)	(36%)
U.S.	0.0318	0.0117	0.0127	0.0076
($\alpha = 0.39$)		(37%)	(40%)	(24%)

Table continued

Table 10.1
(Continued)

Country	(1) Growth Rate of GDP	(2) Contribution from Capital	(3) Contribution from Labor	(4) TFP Growth Rate
		Panel C: Latin American Countries, 1940–90		
Argentina	0.0279	0.0128	0.0097	0.0054
($\alpha = 0.54$)		(46%)	(35%)	(19%)
Brazil	0.0558	0.0294	0.0150	0.0114
($\alpha = 0.45$)		(53%)	(27%)	(20%)
Chile	0.0362	0.0120	0.0103	0.0138
($\alpha = 0.52$)		(33%)	(28%)	(38%)
Colombia	0.0454	0.0219	0.0152	0.0084
($\alpha = 0.63$)		(48%)	(33%)	(19%)
Mexico	0.0522	0.0259	0.0150	0.0113
($\alpha = 0.69$)		(50%)	(29%)	(22%)
Peru	0.0323	0.0252	0.0134	−0.0062
($\alpha = 0.66$)		(78%)	(41%)	(−19%)
Venezuela	0.0443	0.0254	0.0179	0.0011
($\alpha = 0.55$)		(57%)	(40%)	(2%)
		Panel D: East Asian Countries, 1966–90		
Hong Kong[e]	0.073	0.030	0.020	0.023
($\alpha = 0.37$)		(41%)	(28%)	(32%)
Singapore	0.087	0.056	0.029	0.002
($\alpha = 0.49$)		(65%)	(33%)	(2%)
South Korea	0.103	0.041	0.045	0.017
($\alpha = 0.30$)		(40%)	(44%)	(16%)
Taiwan	0.094	0.032	0.036	0.026
($\alpha = 0.26$)		(34%)	(39%)	(28%)

Sources: Panel A estimates for OECD countries are from Christenson, Cummings, and Jorgenson (1980). Panel B estimates for OECD countries are from Jorgenson and Yip (2001, tables 3, 5, 7, 10). Panel C estimates for Latin American countries are from Elias (1990), updated with unpublished notes from Victor Elias. (For this source only, the calculations assumed that the capital share, α, was constant over time.) Panel D estimates for East Asian countries are from Young (1995, tables V–VIII).

The average value of the capital share, α, is shown in parentheses below the name of each country. Column 1 reports the annualized growth rate of real GDP. Column 2 is the product of the capital share, α, and the growth rate of quality-adjusted capital input. The number in parentheses is the percentage of the GDP growth rate that is explained by the growth of capital input. Column 3 is the product of the labor share, $1 - \alpha$, and the growth rate of quality-adjusted labor input. The number in parentheses is the percentage of the GDP growth rate that is explained by the growth of labor input. Column 4 shows the growth rate of total factor productivity (TFP). The number in parentheses is the percentage of the GDP growth rate that is explained by TFP growth.

[a] 1950–73
[b] 1952–73
[c] 1951–73
[d] 1955–73
[e] 1966–91

for 1960–95. Column 3 of panels A and B shows that the growth rate of labor input is virtually nil for France, Germany, Italy, and the United Kingdom for the entire period from 1947 to 1995.

Panel C of table 10.1 reports analogous decompositions of real GDP growth for seven Latin American countries. The basic results come from Elias (1990) and they have been updated with unpublished notes from Victor Elias. The estimates of TFP growth for these countries from 1940 to 1990 ranged between −0.6 percent per year for Peru to 1.4 percent for Chile.[5]

Finally, panel D of the table shows the decomposition of the aggregate growth rate for four fast-growing East Asian countries. The results, from Young (1995), are for Hong Kong, Singapore, South Korea, and Taiwan for the period 1966–90. Despite the enormous growth rates in aggregate GDP, the estimates of TFP growth for these countries ranged from only 0.2 percent for Singapore to 2.6 percent for Taiwan. The reason is that the growth rates of physical capital and labor were also very large in these countries and, therefore, account for a substantial fraction of the overall growth rate.

Many economists were surprised by the low TFP growth estimates for these East Asian countries. After seeing these results, some economists concluded that the growth of the East Asian Miracles was nothing miraculous because, unlike miracles, which, by definition, cannot be explained, the growth performance of these countries could be explained easily within the simple framework of factor accumulation. In later sections, however, we will reexamine the empirical results and the conclusions about East Asian growth.

10.1.4 A Note on Regression-Based Estimates of TFP Growth

An important point about the TFP growth estimates displayed in table 10.1 is that they represent a direct implementation of equations of the form of equations (10.6) and (10.8)—extended to include multiple types of capital and labor—and do not involve econometric estimation. The estimated Solow residual, $\hat{g}$, is computed at each date by using time-series data on Y, K, L, s_K, and s_L. In practice, researchers report an average of the computed $\hat{g}$ values for designated time periods.

An alternative approach would be to regress the growth rate of output, $\dot{Y}/Y$, on the growth rates of inputs, $\dot{K}/K$ and $\dot{L}/L$, in the form of equation (10.2). (This approach would be implemented by making suitable adjustments to use discrete-period data.) The intercept then measures g, and the coefficients on the factor growth rates measure $(\frac{F_K K}{Y})$ and $(\frac{F_L L}{Y})$,

5. The estimated TFP growth rates in Latin America are particularly low—typically negative—from 1980 to 1990. The negative values are hard to understand as technical regress in the sense of literal forgetting of technology, but they may represent declining efficiency of market organization due to policy or other changes.

respectively. The main advantage of this approach is that it dispenses with the assumption that the factor social marginal products coincide with the observable factor prices, that is, $F_K = R$ and $F_L = w$.

The disadvantages of the regression approach are several:

• The variables $\dot{K}/K$ and $\dot{L}/L$ cannot usually be regarded as exogenous with respect to variations in g—in particular, the factor growth rates would receive credit for correlated variations in unobservable technological change.

• If $\dot{K}/K$ and $\dot{L}/L$ (computed as averages over discrete periods) are measured with error, then standard estimates of the coefficients of these variables would deliver inconsistent estimates of $(\frac{F_K K}{Y})$ and $(\frac{F_L L}{Y})$, respectively. This problem is likely to be especially serious for the growth rate of capital input, where the measured capital stock is unlikely to correspond well to the stock currently utilized in production. This problem often leads to low estimates of the contribution of capital accumulation to economic growth when high-frequency data are employed.

• The regression framework has to be extended from its usual form to allow for time variations in factor shares and the TFP growth rate.

Given the drawbacks from the regression method, the usually preferred approach to TFP estimation is the noneconometric one exemplified by the studies shown in table 10.1.

10.2 Dual Approach to Growth Accounting

Hsieh (2002) exploited a dual approach to growth accounting, whereby the Solow residual is computed from growth rates of factor prices, rather than factor quantities. This idea goes back at least to Jorgenson and Griliches (1967).

The dual approach can be derived readily from the equality between output and factor incomes:

$$Y = RK + wL \tag{10.11}$$

Taking logarithms and differentiating both sides of equation (10.11) with respect to time leads to

$$\dot{Y}/Y = s_K \cdot (\dot{R}/R + \dot{K}/K) + s_L \cdot (\dot{w}/w + \dot{L}/L)$$

where s_K and s_L are again the factor income shares. If the terms involving the growth rates of factor quantities are placed on the left-hand side of the equation, then the estimated TFP growth rate is given by

$$\hat{g} = \dot{Y}/Y - s_K \cdot (\dot{K}/K) - s_L \cdot (\dot{L}/L) = s_K \cdot \dot{R}/R + s_L \cdot \dot{w}/w \tag{10.12}$$

Hence, the primal estimate of the TFP growth rate in the middle of the equation—based on filtering $\dot{Y}/Y$ for the share-weighted growth in factor quantities—equals the share-weighted growth of factor prices on the right-hand side of the equation. Note that this estimate of TFP growth uses the same factor-income shares, s_K and s_L, as the primal estimate but considers changes in factor prices, rather than quantities. It is for this reason that it is called the dual or price-based estimate of TFP growth.[6]

The intuition for the dual estimate on the right-hand side of equation (10.12) is that rising factor prices (for factors of given quality) can be sustained only if output is increasing for given inputs. Therefore, the appropriately weighted average of the growth of the factor prices measures the extent of TFP growth.

It is important to recognize that the derivation of equation (10.12) uses only the condition $Y = RK + wL$. No assumptions were made about the relations of factor prices to social marginal products or about the form of the production function. If $Y = RK + wL$ holds, then the primal and dual estimates of TFP growth inevitably coincide. In some cases—notably when factor prices deviate from social marginal products—the estimated value $\hat{g}$ from equation (10.12) would deviate from the true value, g. However, the error, $g - \hat{g}$, from the dual approach will be the same as that from the primal approach.[7]

Hsieh (2002) used the dual approach—the right-hand side of equation (10.12)—to redo Young's (1995) estimates of TFP growth for the four East Asian countries included in table 10.1. Hsieh's procedure uses an array of quality categories for L and K. The results, shown along with primal estimates that are similar to Young's findings, are in table 10.2. The most striking conclusion is that the estimate for Singapore changes from the primal estimate of around zero to a dual estimate of 2.2 percent per year. The estimate for Taiwan is also revised upward substantially, but those for Hong Kong and South Korea change little. Hsieh also observed that dual estimates for the United States were similar to primal estimates.

6. This derivation was suggested by Susanto Basu. The approach was used earlier by Jorgenson and Griliches (1967, pp. 251–253), who also extend equation (10.12) to allow for changes over time in the relative prices of multiple outputs. In this case, $\dot{Y}/Y$ becomes a share-weighted average of output growth rates, and the right-hand side of the dual-accounting expression subtracts off the share-weighted average of the growth rates of the output prices. This last term is zero in the present context, which features a fixed relative price of a single form of output.

7. This equivalence does not generally hold if the factor-income shares, s_K and s_L, are replaced by the marginal-product weights, $(\frac{F_K K}{Y})$ and $(\frac{F_L L}{Y})$. If these marginal-product weights are used, then the primal estimate $\hat{g}$ calculated from equation (10.4) correctly measures the TFP growth rate, g. The corresponding dual estimate is

$$\left(\frac{F_K K}{Y}\right) \cdot (\dot{R}/R) + \left(\frac{F_L L}{Y}\right) \cdot (\dot{w}/w)$$

It is possible to show that this estimate equals the primal one if the ratios of the factor prices to social marginal products—R/F_K and w/F_L—do not vary over time. (It is not necessary for these ratios to equal unity.) However, the practical significance of these results is unclear, because F_K and F_L would not generally be observable.

Table 10.2
Primal and Dual Estimates of TFP Growth Rates

Country	Primal Estimate	Dual Estimate
Hong Kong, 1966–91	0.023	0.027
Singapore, 1972–90	−0.007	0.022
South Korea, 1966–90	0.017	0.015
Taiwan, 1966–90	0.021	0.037

Notes: These estimates are from Hsieh (2002, table 1). The primal estimates are computed from data on growth rates of quantities of factor inputs, using factor income shares as weights. The dual estimates are computed from data on growth rates of prices of factor inputs, using the same factor income shares as weights. The lack of coincidence for the primal and dual estimates of TFP growth rates reflects the use of different data, as described in the text.

If the condition $Y = RK + wL$ holds, then the discrepancy between the primal and dual estimates of TFP growth has to reflect the use of different data in the two calculations. Hsieh's discussion brings out the general nature of this data discrepancy for Singapore. The Singaporean national accounts show remarkable growth of K over time. Given the behavior of Y and wL, the rental price, R, should have suffered a correspondingly sharp decline. However, direct estimates of returns on capital in Singapore—based on observed returns on financial markets—are relatively stable over time. Put another way, if the path of R implied by the observed rates of return is accurate—and if information on Y and wL is also viewed as reasonable—then the implied path of K exhibits much more moderate growth than that indicated by the national-accounts data. Hsieh argues that the official statistics have, in fact, substantially overstated the growth of the capital stock and, hence, that the reduced estimates of capital growth implied by the observed R values are reasonable.

Hsieh's dual estimate of TFP growth for Singapore—2.2 percent per year—is a weighted average of the robust wage-rate growth (for given labor quality) and a small amount of rental-price growth. We should notice, however, that Hsieh could just as well have computed a primal estimate of TFP growth based on the time series for K that is implied by the observed and presumed accurate time series for R. (With multiple types of capital, K_j, this calculation would be applied to each type, given the estimated values of the rental prices, R_j.) Since $Y = RK + wL$ holds here by construction, the primal estimate would coincide with the dual estimate. Thus it is not actually necessary ever to do the dual computation.

10.3 Problems with Growth Accounting

A key assumption in growth-accounting exercises is that factor prices coincide with social marginal products. If this assumption is violated, then the estimated value $\hat{g}$ calculated from equation (10.6) deviates from the true contribution, g, of technical change to economic growth. The next sections illustrate these problems for models with increasing returns and spillovers, for environments with various kinds of taxes, and for settings with different types of factors.

10.3.1 An Increasing-Returns Model with Spillovers

We discussed in chapter 3 how a number of authors—including Griliches (1979), Romer (1986), and Lucas (1988)—have constructed models of economic growth with increasing returns and spillovers. Romer's analysis is a generalization of Arrow's (1962) learning-by-doing model, in which the efficiency of production rises with cumulated experience. In the version of the Romer model discussed in chapter 4, the output, Y_i, of firm i depended not only on the standard private inputs, K_i and L_i, but also on the economy-wide capital stock, K. The idea is that producers learned by investing (a specific form of "doing") to produce more efficiently. Moreover, this knowledge spilled over immediately from one firm to others so that each firm's productivity depended on the aggregate of learning, as reflected in the overall capital stock.

These ideas can be represented with a Cobb–Douglas production function as

$$Y_i = AK_i^{\alpha} K^{\beta} L_i^{1-\alpha} \tag{10.13}$$

where $0 < \alpha < 1$ and $\beta \geq 0$. For given K, this production function exhibits constant returns to scale in the private inputs, K_i and L_i. If $\beta > 0$, the spillover effect is present and positive.

In the Griliches (1979) version of the production function in equation (10.13), K_i represents firm i's specific knowledge capital, whereas K (modeled as the sum of the K_i) is the aggregate level of knowledge in an industry. Hence, the spillovers again represent the diffusion of knowledge across firms. In the Lucas (1988) version, K_i is the firm's employment of human capital, and K is the aggregate (or possibly average) level of human capital in an industry or country. In this case, the spillovers involve benefits from interactions with smart people.

Returning to the Romer interpretation of equation (10.13), each firm behaves competitively, taking as given the economy-wide factor prices, R and w, and the aggregate capital stock, K. Hence, private marginal products are equated to the factor prices, thereby yielding

$$R = \alpha Y_i / K_i \quad \text{and} \quad w = (1 - \alpha) \cdot Y_i / L_i \tag{10.14}$$

The factor-income shares are, therefore, given, as usual, by

$$s_k = \alpha \quad \text{and} \quad s_L = 1 - \alpha \tag{10.15}$$

In equilibrium, each firm adopts the same capital-labor ratio, k_i, but the scale of each firm is indeterminate. The production function from equation (10.13) can be rewritten as

$$Y_i = Ak_i^{\alpha} k^{\beta} L_i L^{\beta}$$

where $k \equiv K/L$. The equilibrium condition $k_i = k$ then implies

$$Y_i = Ak^{\alpha+\beta} L_i L^{\beta}$$

which can be aggregated across firms to get

$$Y = Ak^{\alpha+\beta} L^{1+\beta}$$

Finally, the condition $k \equiv K/L$ leads to the economy-wide production function,

$$Y = AK^{\alpha+\beta} L^{1-\alpha} \tag{10.16}$$

This expression relates aggregate output, Y, to the aggregate inputs, K and L. If $\beta > 0$, increasing returns to scale apply economy wide.

The right-hand side of equation (10.16) shows that the correct way to do the growth accounting with aggregate data is to compute

$$\hat{g} = \dot{T}/T = \dot{Y}/Y - (\alpha + \beta) \cdot (\dot{K}/K) - (1 - \alpha) \cdot (\dot{L}/L) \tag{10.17}$$

Hence, $s_L = 1 - \alpha$ is the correct weight for $\dot{L}/L$, but the coefficient $s_K = \alpha$ understates by $\beta \geq 0$ the contribution of $\dot{K}/K$. This understatement arises because—with the assumed investment-based spillovers of knowledge—the social marginal product of capital, $(\alpha + \beta) \cdot Y/K$, exceeds the private marginal product, $\alpha Y/K$. (This private marginal product does equal the factor price, R.) Note also that the weights on the factor-input growth rates in equation (10.17) sum to $1 + \beta$, which exceeds one if $\beta > 0$ because of the underlying increasing returns to scale. The increasing returns arise because ideas about how to produce more efficiently are fundamentally nonrival and spill over freely and instantaneously across firms.

The interpretation of K—the factor that receives a weight above its income share in the growth accounting of equation (10.17)—depends on the underlying model. Griliches (1979) identifies K with knowledge-creating activities, such as R&D. Romer (1986) stresses physical capital itself. Lucas (1988) emphasizes human capital in the form of education. It is, of course, also possible to have spillover effects that are negative, such as traffic congestion and environmental damage.

Implementation of the results from equation (10.17) is difficult because the proper weights on the factor growth rates cannot be inferred from income shares; specifically, no direct estimates are available for the coefficient β. If one instead computes the standard Solow residual within this model, then one gets

$$g(\text{Solow}) = \dot{T}/T + \beta \cdot (\dot{K}/K) = \dot{Y}/Y - \alpha \cdot (\dot{K}/K) - (1-\alpha) \cdot (\dot{L}/L) \tag{10.18}$$

Thus the standard calculation includes the growth effect from spillovers and increasing returns—$\beta \cdot (\dot{K}/K)$—along with the rate of exogenous technological progress, $\dot{T}/T$, in the Solow residual.

It seems that the separation of the spillovers/increasing returns effect from exogenous technological progress requires a regression approach. In this approach, the usual Solow residual, $g(\text{Solow})$, calculated from equation (10.18) could be regressed on the factor growth rate, $\dot{K}/K$, that was thought to carry the spillover effects. This method does, however, encounter the usual econometric problems with respect to simultaneity.

10.3.2 Taxes

In most cases, taxes do not disturb the TFP calculations. Suppose, for example, that firms' net revenues are taxed, wage and rental payments are tax-deductible expenses for firms, and wage and rental incomes are taxed at the household level. In this case, competitive firms equate the marginal product of labor, F_L, to the wage, w, and the marginal product of capital, F_K, to the rental price, R. The condition $Y = RK + wL$ also holds (with firms' net revenue and taxes equal to zero in equilibrium). Therefore, the formula for $\hat{g}$ in equation (10.6) remains valid.

Suppose, instead, that firms acquire capital through equity finance, that wages and depreciation, δK, are tax deductible for firms, and that r is the required (gross-of-personal-tax) rate of return on equity. A competitive firm still equates the marginal product of labor to the wage rate, w. The firm also equates the after-tax net marginal product of capital, $(1-\tau) \cdot (F_K - \delta)$, to r, where τ is the marginal tax rate on the firm's earnings. Therefore, the marginal product of capital is given by

$$F_K = \frac{r}{1-\tau} + \delta$$

The growth-accounting formula in equation (10.4) implies, after substitution for F_K and F_L,

$$g = \dot{Y}/Y - \left[\frac{r}{(1-\tau)} \cdot \frac{K}{Y} + \frac{\delta K}{Y}\right] \cdot (\dot{K}/K) - s_L \cdot (\dot{L}/L) \tag{10.19}$$

If taxes on firms' earnings are proportional, so that τ is the average, as well as the marginal, tax rate, then $rK/(1-\tau)$ is equal in equilibrium to firms' earnings (net of depreciation but gross of the earnings tax). Hence, the bracketed term in equation (10.19) equals s_K, the income share of capital, if capital income is measured by firms' earnings (gross of earnings taxes) plus depreciation. The usual formula for the TFP growth rate in equation (10.6) therefore remains valid.

For a tax on output or sales, competitive firms satisfy $F_L = w/(1-\tau)$ and $F_K = R/(1-\tau)$, where R is again the rental price of capital and τ is the marginal tax rate on output. The growth-accounting formula in equation (10.4) therefore implies, after substitution for F_K and F_L,

$$g = \dot{Y}/Y - \left[\frac{R}{(1-\tau)} \cdot \frac{K}{Y}\right] \cdot (\dot{K}/K) - \left[\frac{w}{(1-\tau)} \cdot \frac{L}{Y}\right] \cdot (\dot{L}/L) \tag{10.20}$$

If the tax on output is proportional, so that marginal and average tax rates coincide, the total revenue collected is τY. Output, Y, equals factor incomes plus the amount collected by the indirect tax:

$$Y = RK + wL + \tau Y$$

so that the total factor income, $RK + wL$, equals $(1-\tau) \cdot Y$. Hence, the bracketed terms on the right-hand side of equation (10.20) equal s_K and s_L, respectively. (Note that these shares are expressed in relation to factor income, rather than gross domestic product.) It follows that the usual formula for the TFP growth rate given in equation (10.6) still holds.[8]

The standard growth-accounting formula works, for example, with a proportionate value-added tax that attaches the same tax rate to value added by capital and labor inputs. However, the usual formula would be inaccurate if different tax rates applied to the value added by each factor. If firms pay the tax rate τ_K on RK and the rate τ_L on wL, then the growth-accounting formula in equation (10.4) leads to

$$g = \dot{Y}/Y - \left(\frac{1+\tau_K}{1+\tau}\right) \cdot s_K \cdot (\dot{K}/K) - \left(\frac{1+\tau_L}{1+\tau}\right) \cdot s_L \cdot (\dot{L}/L) \tag{10.21}$$

where τ is the average of the tax rates, as given by

$$\tau = s_K\tau_K + s_L\tau_L$$

If, for example, $\tau_K > \tau_L$, equation (10.21) indicates that the weight on $\dot{K}/K$ should be raised relative to that on $\dot{L}/L$ to compute g accurately.

8. The analysis is more complicated if firms are subject to nonproportional tax schedules (with respect to output or earnings). If marginal tax rates on firms are increasing, there is effectively a penalty on large firms. Hence, in the present setup with constant returns to scale, firms would be of infinitesimal size in equilibrium. Nonproportional tax schedules can be admitted in models in which the establishment of a firm requires a fixed cost or in which span-of-control or other considerations eventually create diminishing returns to firm size.

10.3.3 Multiple Types of Factors

Suppose now that the production function is

$$Y = F(A, K_1, K_2, L_1, L_2) \tag{10.22}$$

One interpretation of equation (10.22) is that K_1 and K_2 represent different types or qualities of capital goods, whereas L_1 and L_2 represent different types or qualities of labor. Then the usual growth-accounting exercise goes through in the manner of Jorgenson and Griliches (1967) if each type of factor is weighted by its income share. That is, $\dot{K}_1/K_1$ is weighted by R_1K_1/Y, and so on. The usual Solow residual generated from this procedure accurately measures the contribution of technological progress to growth, g, as long as all factors are paid their social marginal products.

Problems arise if the factor categories cannot be distinguished in the data, for example, if $\dot{K}_1/K_1$ and $\dot{K}_2/K_2$ are each associated with the overall capital share, $(R_1K_1 + R_2K_2)/Y$. One source of this kind of problem is that newer, and typically better, types of capital goods might be aggregated with the older types. Similarly, different categories of labor may be aggregated in the data.

Another interpretation of equation (10.22) is that K_1 and L_1 represent factor employments in sector 1—say, urban manufacturing—whereas K_2 and L_2 represent employments in sector 2—say, rural agriculture. Changes may occur over time in sectoral composition, for example, as a shift from agriculture to industry. Such shifts cause no trouble for the growth accounting if the various growth rates of factor quantities—distinguished by their sector of location—are weighted by their income shares. However, errors occur if capital or labor is aggregated across sectors and if the growth of these aggregates is weighted by overall income shares of capital or labor, respectively.

To illustrate, suppose that the TFP growth rate is incorrectly estimated as

$$\tilde{g} = \dot{Y}/Y - \left(\frac{R_1K_1 + R_2K_2}{Y}\right) \cdot (\dot{K}/K) - \left(\frac{w_1L_1 + w_2L_2}{Y}\right) \cdot (\dot{L}/L) \tag{10.23}$$

where $K = K_1 + K_2$ and $L = L_1 + L_2$. This estimate compares with the appropriate formula,

$$\begin{aligned} \hat{g} = \dot{Y}/Y &- \left(\frac{R_1K_1}{Y}\right) \cdot (\dot{K}_1/K_1) - \left(\frac{R_2K_2}{Y}\right) \cdot (\dot{K}_2/K_2) \\ &- \left(\frac{w_1L_1}{Y}\right) \cdot (\dot{L}_1/L_1) - \left(\frac{w_2L_2}{Y}\right) \cdot (\dot{L}_2/L_2) \end{aligned} \tag{10.24}$$

Equation (10.24) correctly estimates the contribution to growth from exogenous technological progress—that is, $\hat{g} = g$—if all factors are paid their social marginal products.

The expression for $\tilde{g}$ in equation (10.23) can be shown from algebraic manipulation to relate to true TFP growth, as estimated by equation (10.24), in accordance with

$$\tilde{g} - \hat{g} = \left(\frac{K_1}{K}\right) \cdot \left(\frac{K_2}{K}\right) \cdot \frac{K}{Y} \cdot (R_1 - R_2) \cdot \left(\frac{\dot{K}_1}{K_1} - \frac{\dot{K}_2}{K_2}\right) + \left(\frac{L_1}{L}\right) \cdot \left(\frac{L_2}{L}\right) \cdot \frac{L}{Y} \cdot (w_1 - w_2) \cdot \left(\frac{\dot{L}_1}{L_1} - \frac{\dot{L}_2}{L_2}\right) \tag{10.25}$$

Hence, if $R_1 \neq R_2$ and $\dot{K}_1/K_1 \neq \dot{K}_2/K_2$ or if $w_1 \neq w_2$ and $\dot{L}_1/L_1 \neq \dot{L}_2/L_2$, then $\tilde{g} \neq \hat{g}$. Specifically, if $R_1 > R_2$, then $\dot{K}_1/K_1 > \dot{K}_2/K_2$ leads to $\tilde{g} > \hat{g}$ and similarly for labor.

With the interpretation of the factor types as quality classes, the result is that measured TFP growth overstates true TFP growth if the composition of factors is shifting over time toward types of higher quality (and such shifts are not allowed for in the estimation). This problem is the one emphasized and resolved subject to data limitations by Jorgenson and Griliches (1967).

One sectoral interpretation of the results involves the migration of labor from rural to urban areas. The urban wage rate, w_1, may exceed the rural wage rate, w_2, for various reasons, including minimum-wage legislation and requirements of union membership for the city jobs. In this case, a shift of labor from the rural to the urban sector represents a gain in economy-wide productivity. The term involving labor in equation (10.25) reflects the economic growth generated by this change in the sectoral composition of labor, for a given growth rate of aggregate labor, $\dot{L}/L$. This type of growth effect, applied to movements of labor from low-productivity agriculture to high-productivity industry, was discussed by Kuznets (1961, p. 61), who derived an expression analogous to equation (10.25).

From the perspective of growth accounting, the terms that involve sectoral shifts should appear somewhere in the calculations. If the changes in labor quantities in each sector are weighted by labor-income shares for each type of labor, then the growth contribution from the sectoral changes appears in the part accounted for by changes in factor quantities in equation (10.24). If the weighting is done instead in the manner of equation (10.23), then the contribution appears in the estimated TFP growth rate.

10.4 TFP Growth and R&D

Growth accounting is often viewed as a first step in explaining the TFP growth rate, g, as estimated in equation (10.6). For example, the research program summarized by Griliches (1973) focuses on R&D spending as a determinant of the TFP growth rate.[9] The theories of

9. Earlier contributors to this literature include Terleckyj (1958), Minasian (1962), Griliches (1964), and Mansfield (1965).

endogenous growth that we examined in chapters 6 and 7 have implications for the modeling of the relationship between technological change and R&D outlays. The following sections explore these relationships for models that involve increases in the number of types of products and improvements in the quality of existing products.

10.4.1 Varieties Models

In the product-varieties framework from chapter 6, the aggregate production function is given from equation (6.13) by

$$Y = TL^{1-\alpha}N^{1-\alpha}X^{\alpha} \tag{10.26}$$

where T is an exogenous technology factor, L is aggregate labor input, N is the number of varieties of intermediate products that are currently known and used, X is the aggregate quantity employed of intermediate inputs, and $0 < \alpha < 1$. Technological progress occurs through the R&D outlays that raise N over time. Hence, the variable N represents the current state of the endogenously determined technology. In this model, the leading technology—that is, the one that employs all N varieties that have been discovered—is used by all producers. Therefore, this specification fits best for general-purpose technologies (David, 1991; Bresnahan and Trajtenberg, 1995), which have broad application in the economy.

Competitive producers of output, Y, equated the marginal product of labor to the wage rate, so that

$$w = (1-\alpha)\cdot(Y/L)$$

Hence, the share of labor income is, as usual,

$$s_L = wL/Y = 1-\alpha \tag{10.27}$$

Competitive producers of final goods equated the marginal product of each type of intermediate input to the price of intermediates, which equaled the monopoly value, $1/\alpha$. This condition can be expressed as

$$1/\alpha = \alpha\cdot(Y/X)$$

Therefore, the share of income expended on the N intermediates is

$$s_X = (1/\alpha)\cdot(X/Y) = \alpha \tag{10.28}$$

The growth rate of output can be computed from equation (10.26) as

$$\dot{Y}/Y = \dot{T}/T + (1-\alpha)\cdot(\dot{N}/N) + s_L\cdot(\dot{L}/L) + s_X\cdot(\dot{X}/X) \tag{10.29}$$

where the formulas for s_L and s_X from equations (10.27) and (10.28) were used. The baseline model in chapter 6 assumed $\dot{T}/T = \dot{L}/L = 0$. However, equation (10.29) is valid when T and L are changing as long as the marginal products of labor and each of the intermediate inputs are equated to their factor prices. Therefore, the usual approach for computing the TFP growth rate yields, in this model,

$$\hat{g} = \dot{Y}/Y - s_L \cdot (\dot{L}/L) - s_X \cdot (\dot{X}/X) = \dot{T}/T + (1-\alpha) \cdot (\dot{N}/N) \tag{10.30}$$

Hence, despite the monopoly pricing of the intermediate inputs, the Solow residual correctly measures the sum of the contributions to productivity growth from exogenous technological change, $\dot{T}/T$, and endogenous expansion of varieties, $\dot{N}/N$.

Note from equation (10.30) that the endogenous-growth part of the Solow residual reflects only the fraction $1-\alpha$ of the growth rate of the number of varieties, $\dot{N}/N$. The remaining part, $\alpha \cdot (\dot{N}/N)$, is picked up as part of the term $s_X \cdot (\dot{X}/X) = \alpha \cdot (\dot{X}/X)$ on the left-hand side of equation (10.30). For a fixed quantity of intermediates of each type, the discovery of new types of products at the rate $\dot{N}/N$ induces an increase in the aggregate of intermediates at the same rate. The contribution of this expansion of intermediates to growth—which involves the coefficient α, the income share of payments to intermediates—is attributed to growth of factor inputs, rather than to the underlying technological progress. In effect, part of the technological advance from discoveries of new types of intermediate goods is embodied in the intermediates that use the new technology.

In the baseline model of chapter 6, $\dot{N}$ was proportional to the amount of output devoted to R&D, that is, $\dot{N} = (1/\eta)\cdot$ (R&D), where η was the amount of R&D required to achieve a unit increase in N. Hence, the growth rate of N was given by

$$\dot{N}/N = (\text{R\&D})/\eta N = (\text{R\&D})/(\text{market value of past R\&D}) \tag{10.31}$$

Note that ηN is the product of the number of inventions, N, and the reproduction cost, η, of each invention. Hence, ηN is the market value of firms, which corresponds to the market value of their past R&D outlays. The measured TFP growth rate in equation (10.30) therefore satisfies

$$\hat{g} = \dot{T}/T + (1-\alpha) \cdot (\text{R\&D})/(\text{market value of past R\&D}) \tag{10.32}$$

In the varieties model, the chosen quantity X is proportional to L, so that the value Y/L computed from equation (10.26) is proportional to N. Since the denominator of the final term on the right-hand side of equation (10.32) equals ηN, this final term ends up proportional to the ratio of R&D to per worker output, Y/L. Thus, $\hat{g}$ in equation (10.32) can be expressed as a linear function of the ratio (R&D)/(Y/L). This result is similar to specifications used by Griliches (1973) and Coe and Helpman (1995), among others, except that R&D outlays enter in the baseline varieties model in relation to per worker output, Y/L, rather that the level of output, Y. The source of the difference is that the model features a scale benefit from increases in L. In the alternative specification of chapter 6, where the scale effect from L was eliminated, $\hat{g}$ would depend on the ratio of R&D to output, as in the usual empirical specifications.

The empirical methodology described in Griliches (1973) accords well with the general setting of the varieties model. The Griliches approach begins by applying the usual growth-accounting analysis to compute a residual. This method corresponds to the calculation of $\hat{g}$ in accordance with equation (10.30). The main difference from the theoretical model is that the intermediate inputs X include service flows from an array of capital goods; that is, the intermediate inputs are not treated exclusively as nondurables. Griliches then uses a regression approach to assess the effect of an R&D variable on the computed TFP growth rate. For example, the TFP growth rate could be regressed on R&D expenditures (typically expressed as a ratio to output or sales), a trend term (to pick up exogenous technical progress), and random influences. The regression coefficient on the R&D variable would provide an estimate of the social rate of return to R&D.

The Griliches methodology has been implemented in a number of studies for firms and industries in the United States, including Griliches and Lichtenberg (1984) and Griliches (1988). A major problem in this research is the poor quality of the data on R&D. Nevertheless, the studies tend to show high social rates of return to R&D, typically in a range of 20 to 40 percent per year.

Coe and Helpman (1995) applied the approach to aggregate data for 22 OECD countries. They report remarkably high rates of return to R&D within a country—around 100 percent per year. Their estimates are even higher—about 130 percent per year—if spillover benefits across countries are included.

One drawback of the Griliches methodology, which we already discussed generally for regression approaches to growth accounting, is that the estimation can be confounded by reverse-causation problems. In this case, the difficulty is that R&D spending would respond to exogenous changes in productivity growth—the variable $\dot{T}/T$ in equation (10.32)—so that the estimated coefficient on the R&D variable would proxy partly for exogenous technological progress. This problem may explain the high estimates of rates of return to R&D in the studies that we mentioned before. For example, in the Coe and Helpman (1995) analysis, the large regression coefficient on a country's R&D variable may reflect the positive response of R&D spending to growth opportunities, rather than the effect of R&D on productivity growth. This potential for reverse causation also exists in the U.S. studies of firms and industries.

In principle, the simultaneity problem could be solved by using instrumental variables. However, satisfactory instruments may not be available. Possible instrumental variables include measures of government policies toward R&D, including research subsidies, legal provisions such as the patent system, and the tax treatment of R&D expenditures.

The varieties model suggests a possible way to extend the usual growth-accounting procedure to assess the contribution from R&D. An extended Solow residual could be computed that subtracts from the growth rate of output, $\dot{Y}/Y$, not only the contributions from the growth of factor inputs, $s_L \cdot (\dot{L}/L) + s_X \cdot (\dot{X}/X)$, as in equation (10.30), but also the term

$$(1-\alpha) \cdot (\text{R\&D})/(\text{market value of past R\&D})$$

which appears in equation (10.32). However, this computation entails knowledge not only of the labor share, $1-\alpha$, and the current flow of R&D spending, but also the cumulated stock or capitalized value of past R&D outlays.

10.4.2 Quality-Ladders Models

The other prominent model of technological change in the endogenous-growth literature is the quality-ladders formulation, which we discussed in chapter 7. In this framework, technological progress consists of improvements in the quality of intermediate inputs (or, equivalently, reductions in the cost of providing inputs of given quality). The number of varieties of products is usually assumed to be fixed in this setting, although changes in this number could also be included.

The model worked out in chapter 7 (equations [7.15] and [7.16]) implies that the aggregate production function can be written as

$$Y = TL^{1-\alpha}X^{\alpha}Q^{1-\alpha} \tag{10.33}$$

where T is the exogenous level of technology, L is aggregate labor input, $0 < \alpha < 1$, and X is the aggregate quantity employed of intermediate inputs. The variable $Q \equiv \sum_{j=1}^{N} q^{\kappa_j \alpha/(1-\alpha)}$ is the aggregate quality index, where N is the fixed number of varieties of intermediates, $q > 1$ is the proportionate spacing between rungs on the quality ladder in each sector, and κ_j is the highest quality-ladder position currently achieved in sector j. Each type of intermediate good is priced at the monopoly level, $1/\alpha > 1$. Technological progress occurs through R&D outlays that allow movements up each sector's quality ladder, one step at a time.

The key element of the quality-ladders framework is that different quality grades of intermediate inputs within a given sector were modeled as perfect substitutes. Higher ranked inputs were simply better than lower ranked ones. For this reason, lower quality intermediates of type j (at the rungs $\kappa_j - 1, \kappa_j - 2, \ldots$) were driven out of the market in equilibrium. This technological obsolescence—or creative destruction—distinguishes the quality-ladders model from the varieties framework. In that framework—explored in the previous section—no technological obsolescence occurred, and new varieties of products worked alongside the old ones to produce goods.

Equation (10.33) implies that the standard growth-accounting approach would yield in the quality-ladders model

$$\hat{g} = \dot{Y}/Y - s_L \cdot (\dot{L}/L) - s_X \cdot (\dot{X}/X) = \dot{T}/T + (1-\alpha) \cdot (\dot{Q}/Q) \tag{10.34}$$

where, as in the varieties model, $s_L = wL/Y$ and $s_X = (1/\alpha) \cdot (X/Y)$.[10] Therefore, in this model, the Solow residual measures the sum of exogenous technological progress, $\dot{T}/T$, and the growth rate of overall quality, $\dot{Q}/Q$, weighted by the labor share, $1-\alpha$. This result is similar to equation (10.30) from the varieties model, except that the measure of technological change is $\dot{Q}/Q$, rather than $\dot{N}/N$. Again, a portion of the contribution from technological change (the part $\alpha \cdot \dot{Q}/Q$) is embodied in the growth of inputs, $\dot{X}/X$, and only the remainder appears in the Solow residual.

Some new results arise from the relation of $\dot{Q}/Q$ to R&D expenditures. In the version of the quality-ladders model explored in chapter 7, the growth rate of Q can be expressed as[11]

$$\dot{Q}/Q = \left[1 - q^{-\alpha/(1-\alpha)}\right] \cdot (\text{R\&D})/(\text{market value of past R\&D}) \tag{10.35}$$

The main difference from the expression for $\dot{N}/N$ in equation (10.31) is the presence of the constant in front, $[1 - q^{-\alpha/(1-\alpha)}]$, which is between zero and one. This term is less than one because of the obsolescence of the old types of intermediates in the sectors that experience quality enhancements. The constant is higher the larger is q, which represents the ratio of the productivity of a newly discovered grade of intermediate input to the productivity of the next lowest grade. If q is higher, then creative destruction is more creation

10. We have assumed $\dot{N} = 0$ to derive equation (10.34). The underlying model also assumed that L and T were constant over time. However, equation (10.34) is valid even when L and T are changing.

11. Equation (7.33) implies

$$\dot{Q}/Q = p \cdot \left[q^{\alpha/(1-\alpha)} - 1\right]$$

where p is the probability per unit time of research success in each sector. (In the equilibrium considered in chapter 7, the probability of research success, p, is the same in each sector.) The probability is given from equations (7.19) and (7.21) by

$$p = \frac{Z(\kappa_j)}{q^{\alpha/(1-\alpha)} \cdot E[V(\kappa_j)]}$$

where $Z(\kappa_j)$ is the current flow of R&D expenditure in sector j and $E[V(\kappa_j)]$ is the market value of the leading-edge firm in sector j. Since only the leading-edge firm in a sector has positive market value, the term $E[V(\kappa_j)]$ corresponds to the market value of past R&D in the sector. It follows that the proportionate constant in equation (10.35) is $1 - q^{-\alpha/(1-\alpha)}$, which is between zero and one.

than destruction, and, hence, the contribution of the current R&D flow to the overall quality index, Q, is attenuated to a lesser extent.

The quality index, Q, can be viewed as a measure of the R&D capital stock. However, it is incorrect in this model to follow the common practice by which this stock is constructed. In the usual perpetual-inventory approach, the change in the R&D capital stock equals current R&D spending—the counterpart to gross investment—less depreciation on the existing R&D capital stock. The last term, often modeled as a constant fraction of the existing stock, is thought to correspond to obsolescence of old technologies. In the quality-ladders framework, the correct procedure is to discount current R&D expenditure by the factor $[1 - q^{-\alpha/(1-\alpha)}] < 1$ to allow for the contemporaneous obsolescence of lower quality intermediate inputs. Then this discounted R&D spending enters one-to-one as the net investment flow that changes the R&D capital stock (that is, the quality index, Q). The depreciation rate on this stock is zero, because no technological forgetting occurs in the model.

The growth-accounting formula can be written from equations (10.34) and (10.35) as

$$\hat{g} = \dot{T}/T + (1-\alpha) \cdot \left[1 - q^{-\alpha/(1-\alpha)}\right] \cdot (\text{R\&D})/(\text{market value of past R\&D}) \tag{10.36}$$

This result parallels equation (10.32), except for the presence of the coefficient $[1 - q^{-\alpha/(1-\alpha)}] < 1$. Thus, in the quality-ladders model, the contribution of the R&D variable to TFP growth is less than one-to-one partly because of the multiplication by the labor share, $1-\alpha$, and partly because of the multiplication by the obsolescence coefficient, $[1 - q^{-\alpha/(1-\alpha)}]$. Since the parameter q would not be directly observable, a nonregression approach to assessing the growth effects from R&D seems not to be feasible within the quality-ladders framework.

In the basic quality-ladders model, the market value of past R&D is proportional to per worker output, Y/L.[12] Hence, the TFP growth rate can be expressed from equation (10.36) as a linear function of the ratio (R&D)$/(Y/L)$, which is the R&D variable that also arose in the basic version of the varieties model. Also as before, this variable becomes the one typically used in empirical studies, (R&D)$/Y$, if the specification of R&D costs is changed to eliminate the scale effect in the model.

The impact of R&D on the TFP growth rate in equation (10.36) can be assessed empirically from a regression approach. In principle, the results could be used to estimate the obsolescence coefficient, $[1 - q^{-\alpha/(1-\alpha)}]$. However, this approach again involves problems of simultaneity and would require satisfactory instruments for the R&D variable.

12. See equations (7.68) and (7.16).

10.5 Growth Accounting Versus Sources of Growth

Growth accounting is often used inappropriately to pinpoint the ultimate sources of growth, whereas, in fact, it is only an accounting decomposition. To see this point, consider a neoclassical economy in the steady state. Assume that the production function is Cobb–Douglas with exogenous, labor-augmenting technological progress at the rate x:

$$Y = AK^{\alpha} \cdot (Le^{xt})^{1-\alpha}$$

Assume, for simplicity, that the aggregate labor force, L, is constant.

We found in chapters 1 and 2 that the steady-state growth rate of output and the capital stock will also be x. Hence, if we use the growth-accounting decomposition described in this chapter, we get

$$\dot{Y}/Y = \alpha \cdot (\dot{K}/K) + (1-\alpha) \cdot x$$

where $\dot{Y}/Y = \dot{K}/K = x$. Since we attribute αx of the steady-state growth rate, x, of output to the growth of capital, we compute a TFP growth rate of $(1-\alpha) \cdot x$. Hence, we assign only the fraction $1-\alpha$ of the growth rate of output to technological progress, whereas, in fact, no growth would have occurred without this progress.

A reasonable view for this model is that the ultimate source of growth is entirely technological because, without such progress, no growth of GDP would have occurred. Nevertheless, the growth-accounting decomposition gets the accounting right in the sense that technological progress triggered an additional accumulation of capital which, in turn, generated a larger growth of GDP than would have occurred had the capital stock remained constant. To the extent that capital is endogenous and responds to technological progress, all the growth in GDP can be attributed to technology. In this sense, the allocation of only the part $(1-\alpha) \cdot x$ of the growth rate of GDP to technological progress is misleading. However, it is also true that, if the capital stock had not grown in response to the technological progress, GDP would have grown at the rate $(1-\alpha) \cdot x$, rather than x.

It is easy to illustrate the point with a picture. Figure 10.1 graphs a production function in per capita terms. Suppose that the economy starts in a steady state with the constant capital stock k^* and the constant GDP per person y^*. Imagine that the technology improves so that the production function shifts upward proportionately. If the capital stock did not increase, GDP would go up from y^* to $y^{*\prime}$. Thus, $y^{*\prime} - y^*$ is the increase in GDP that can be attributed directly to the improvement in technology. The capital stock, however, increases in response to the improvement in technology (as was shown in chapters 1 and 2). Let the new steady-state capital stock be k^{**} and the new steady-state GDP level be $y^{**} > y^{*\prime}$. Notice that $y^{**} - y^{*\prime}$ is the increase in GDP that can be attributed to the endogenous increase

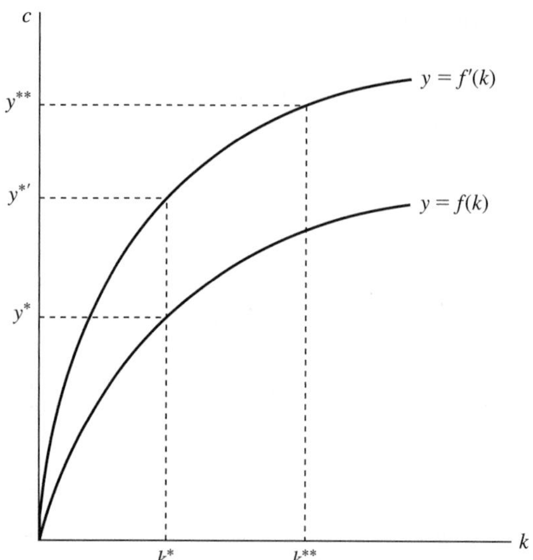

Figure 10.1
The economy's reaction to technological progress. This figure graphs two production functions in per capita terms. Suppose that the economy starts in a steady state with the constant capital stock k^* and the constant GDP per person y^*. Imagine that the technology improves so that the production function shifts upward proportionately. If the capital stock did not increase, GDP would go up from y^* to $y^{*\prime}$. Thus, $y^{*\prime} - y^*$ is the increase in GDP that can be attributed directly to the improvement in technology. The capital stock, however, increases in response to the improvement in technology. The new steady-state capital stock k^{**} and the new steady-state GDP level is y^{**}. The difference $y^{**} - y^*$ is the increase in GDP that can be attributed to the endogenous increase in capital. The growth-accounting exercise correctly indicates that the increase of output from y^* to $y^{*\prime}$ can be attributed to technological progress, whereas the increase from $y^{*\prime}$ to y^{**} can be attributed to the subsequent response of the capital stock. However, the example should make clear that the only ultimate source of growth is technological progress in the sense that, without it, GDP would not have increased.

in capital. The growth-accounting exercise correctly indicates that the increase of output from y^* to $y^{*\prime}$ can be attributed to technological progress, whereas the increase from $y^{*\prime}$ to y^{**} can be attributed to the subsequent response of the capital stock. However, the example should make clear that the only ultimate source of growth is technological progress in the sense that, without it, GDP would not have increased.

The TFP growth rate, $(1 - \alpha) \cdot x$, is the answer to the question, What would the growth rate of output have been if technological progress occurred at the rate x and the capital stock (and labor input) had been constant? Similarly, the growth rate αx is the answer to the question, What would the growth rate of output have been if the capital stock grew as it did (at the rate x) and technological progress had been nil? These answers follow logically, given the premises, but do not correspond well to economic causation. If technological progress is truly exogenous, then the reasonable economic statement for the steady state of the neoclassical growth model is that different rates of technological change show up one-to-one in the long run as differences in growth rates of output.

If we want to attribute to technology both the direct increase in GDP and the increase in GDP that results from the endogenous response of capital, we would have to divide the measured $\hat{g}$ by $(1-\alpha)$. In other words, we have[13]

$$x = \frac{\hat{g}}{1-\alpha} \tag{10.37}$$

As an illustration, table 10.3 displays the corrections for the four East Asian Miracle countries that appear in table 10.2. Column 1 displays the growth rate of aggregate GDP. Column 2 shows the estimated growth rate of TFP from the last column of table 10.2. In parentheses, we show the fraction of the aggregate growth that can be accounted for by technology. Column 3 computes the growth rate of GDP for which technological progress is ultimately responsible (directly and indirectly) by using the correction suggested in equation (10.37). Notice that the fraction of total GDP growth for which technological progress is responsible is 59 percent for Hong Kong, 49 percent for Singapore, and 53 percent for Taiwan (up from 37 percent, 25 percent, and 39 percent, respectively). Only South Korea's growth rate remains largely explained by exogenous factor accumulation (TFP growth is responsible for only 20 percent of GDP growth). Thus, even though the estimates of TFP growth are small, it is possible that technological progress is responsible for more than half of the growth of GDP.

The problem is magnified when we recognize that human capital would also respond endogenously to exogenous improvements in technology. Correction for this additional factor would deliver a formula similar to equation (10.37), except that the relevant capital share would be the sum of the shares of physical and human capital. As discussed elsewhere in this book, this share is not known, but the evidence on the speed of convergence suggests that it may be close to 0.7. Column 4 of table 10.3 uses this number for the share of broad capital to show the growth of GDP for which technological progress is ultimately responsible when physical and human capital both respond. Technological progress is now responsible for all of the growth rate of GDP in Hong Kong and Taiwan. (Technological change is responsible for more than 100 percent of the growth rate because the responses of human and physical capital to the exogenous improvements in technology should have been larger than they actually were.) Technology also explains 84 percent of the growth rate for Singapore and 49 percent for South Korea.

13. This calculation assumes that all of the response in capital occurs within the period of observation.

Table 10.3
TFP Growth Adjusted for Endogenous Responses of Capital

Country	(1) GDP Growth Rate	(2) TFP Growth Rate	(3) TFP Growth Adjusted for Physical Capital	(4) TFP Growth Adjusted for Broad Capital
Hong Kong	0.073	0.027	0.043	0.090
		(37%)	(59%)	(123%)
Singapore	0.087	0.022	0.043	0.073
		(25%)	(49%)	(84%)
South Korea	0.103	0.015	0.021	0.050
		(14%)	(20%)	(49%)
Taiwan	0.094	0.037	0.050	0.123
		(39%)	(53%)	(131%)

Notes: Column 1 shows the growth rate of GDP as given in table 10.1, panel D. Column 2 shows the TFP growth rate indicated for the dual column in table 10.2. Column 3 adjusts for responses of physical capital by multiplying the TFP growth rate by $1/(1-\alpha)$, where α is the capital share shown in table 10.1, panel D. Column 4 adjusts for responses of physical and human capital by multiplying the TFP growth rate by $1/0.3$, that is, by assuming a broad capital share of $\alpha = 0.7$. The numbers in parentheses show the percentages of the growth rate of GDP accounted for by each measure of TFP growth.

The corrections made in this section surely overstate the importance of technological progress because they assume that all of the endogenous responses of capital occur within the period of observation. The calculations are not meant to offer a realistic way of adjusting the TFP estimates to make causality statements about ultimate sources of growth but, rather, to warn the reader that such claims should be avoided. A small positive number for $\hat{g}$ is, in principle, consistent with a situation in which technological progress is ultimately responsible for a small part of GDP growth, but it is also consistent with a situation in which it is ultimately responsible for the entirety of GDP growth. Thus the same accounting decomposition is consistent with two entirely different visions of growth.

Growth accounting may be able to provide a mechanical decomposition of the growth of output into growth of an array of inputs and growth of total factor productivity. Successful accounting of this sort is likely to be useful and may stimulate the development of useful economic theories of growth. Growth accounting does not, however, constitute a theory of growth because it does not attempt to explain how the changes in inputs and the improvements in total factor productivity relate to elements—such as aspects of preferences, technology, and government policies—that can reasonably be viewed as fundamentals.

11 Empirical Analysis of Regional Data Sets

A key property of the neoclassical growth model is its prediction of conditional convergence, a concept that applies when the growth rate of an economy is positively related to the distance between this economy's level of income and its own steady state. Conditional convergence should not be confused with absolute convergence, a concept that applies when poor economies tend to grow faster than rich ones (and, therefore, the poor tend to "catch up"). It is possible that two economies converge in the conditional sense (the growth rate of each economy declines as it approaches its own steady state) but not in the absolute sense (the rich economy can grow faster than the poor one if the former is further below its own steady state). The two concepts are identical if a group of economies tend to converge to the same steady state. We found in chapters 1 and 2 that neoclassical economies with similar tastes and technologies converge to the same steady state. Therefore, in this case, the neoclassical growth model predicts absolute convergence; that is, poor economies tend to grow faster than rich ones. Thus one way to test the convergence hypothesis is to check whether economies with similar tastes and technologies—economies that are likely to converge to the same steady state—converge in an absolute sense.

In this chapter, we test the convergence predictions of the neoclassical growth model by looking at the behavior of regions within countries. Although differences in technology, preferences, and institutions exist across regions, these differences are likely to be smaller than those across countries. Firms and households of different regions within a single country tend to have access to similar technologies and have roughly similar tastes and cultures. Furthermore, the regions share a common central government and therefore have similar institutional setups and legal systems. This relative homogeneity means that regions are more likely to converge to similar steady states. Hence, absolute convergence is more likely to apply across regions within countries than across countries.

It can be argued that using regions to test the convergence hypothesis is incorrect because inputs tend to be more mobile across regions than across countries. Legal, cultural, linguistic, and institutional barriers to factor movements tend to be smaller across regions within a country than across countries. Hence, the assumption of a closed economy—a standard condition of the neoclassical growth model—is likely to be violated for regional data sets. However, we found in chapter 3 that the dynamic properties of economies that are open to capital movements can be similar to those of closed economies if a fraction of the capital stock—which includes human capital—is not mobile or cannot be used as collateral in interregional or international credit transactions. The speed of convergence is increased by the existence of capital mobility but remains within a fairly narrow range for reasonable values of the fraction of capital that is mobile. Another result is that a technology without diminishing returns to capital—that is, some version of the AK technology—implies a zero convergence speed whether the economy is open or closed.

We also found in chapter 9 that the allowance for migration in neoclassical growth models tends to accelerate the process of convergence. The change is, again, a quantitative modification to the speed of convergence. The main point, therefore, is that although regions within a country are relatively open to flows of capital and persons, the neoclassical growth model still provides a useful framework for the empirical analysis.

11.1 Two Concepts of Convergence

Two concepts of convergence appear in discussions of economic growth across countries or regions. In one view (Barro, 1984, chapter 12; Baumol, 1986; DeLong, 1988; Barro, 1991a; Barro and Sala-i-Martin, 1991, 1992a, 1992b), convergence applies if a poor economy tends to grow faster than a rich one, so that the poor country tends to catch up to the rich one in terms of levels of per capita income or product. This property corresponds to our concept of *β convergence*.[1] The second concept (Easterlin, 1960a; Borts and Stein, 1964, chapter 2; Streissler, 1979; Barro, 1984, chapter 12; Baumol, 1986; Dowrick and Nguyen, 1989; Barro and Sala-i-Martin, 1991, 1992a, 1992b) concerns cross-sectional dispersion. In this context, convergence occurs if the dispersion—measured, for example, by the standard deviation of the logarithm of per capita income or product across a group of countries or regions—declines over time. We call this process *σ convergence*. Convergence of the first kind (poor countries tending to grow faster than rich ones) tends to generate convergence of the second kind (reduced dispersion of per capita income or product), but this process is offset by new disturbances that tend to increase dispersion.

To make the relation between the two concepts more precise, we consider a version of the growth equation predicted by the neoclassical growth model of chapter 2. Equation (2.35) relates the growth rate of income per capita for economy i between two points in time to the initial level of income. We apply equation (2.35) here to discrete periods of unit length (say years), and we also augment it to include a random disturbance:

$$\log(y_{it}/y_{i,t-1}) = a_{it} - (1 - e^{-\beta}) \cdot \log(y_{i,t-1}) + u_{it} \tag{11.1}$$

where the subscript t denotes the year, and the subscript i denotes the country or region. The theory implies that the intercept, a_{it}, equals $x_i + (1 - e^{-\beta}) \cdot [\log(\hat{y}_i^*) + x_i \cdot (t-1)]$, where $\hat{y}_i^*$ is the steady-state level of $\hat{y}_i$ and x_i is the rate of technological progress. We assume that the random variable u_{it} has 0 mean, variance σ_{ut}^2, and is distributed independently of $\log(y_{i,t-1})$, u_{jt} for $j \neq i$, and lagged disturbances.

1. This phenomenon is sometimes described as "regression toward the mean."

We can think of the random disturbance as reflecting unexpected changes in production conditions or preferences. We begin by treating the coefficient a_{it} as the same for all economies so that $a_{it} = a_t$. This specification means that the steady-state value, $\hat{y}_i^*$, and the rate of exogenous technological progress, x_i, are the same for all economies. This assumption is more reasonable for regional data sets than for international data sets; it is plausible that different regions within a country are more similar than different countries with respect to technology and preferences.

If the intercept a_{it} is the same in all places and $\beta > 0$, equation (11.1) implies that poor economies tend to grow faster than rich ones. The neoclassical growth models of chapters 1 and 2 made this prediction. The *AK* model discussed in chapter 4 predicts, in contrast, a 0 value for β and, consequently, no convergence of this type. The same conclusion holds for various endogenous growth models (chapters 6 and 7) that incorporate a linearity in the production function.[2]

Since the coefficient on $\log(y_{i,t-1})$ in equation (11.1) is less than 1, the convergence is not strong enough to eliminate the serial correlation in $\log(y_{it})$. Put alternatively, in the absence of random shocks, convergence to the steady state is direct and involves no oscillations or overshooting. Therefore, for a pair of economies, the one that starts out behind is predicted to remain behind at any future date.

Let σ_t^2 be the cross-economy variance of $\log(y_{it})$ at time t. Equation (11.1) and the assumed properties of u_{it} imply that σ_t^2 evolves over time in accordance with the first-order difference equation[3]

$$\sigma_t^2 = e^{-2\beta} \cdot \sigma_{t-1}^2 + \sigma_{ut}^2 \tag{11.2}$$

where we have assumed that the cross section is large enough so that the sample variance of $\log(y_{it})$ corresponds to the population variance.

If the variance of the disturbance, σ_{ut}^2, is constant over time ($\sigma_{ut}^2 = \sigma_u^2$ for all t), the solution of the first-order difference equation (11.2) is

$$\sigma_t^2 = \frac{\sigma_u^2}{1 - e^{-2\beta}} + \left(\sigma_0^2 - \frac{\sigma_u^2}{1 - e^{-2\beta}}\right) \cdot e^{-2\beta t} \tag{11.3}$$

where σ_0^2 is the variance of $\log(y_{i0})$. (It can be readily verified that the solution in equation [11.3] satisfies equation [11.2].) Equation (11.3) implies that σ_t^2 monotonically approaches its steady-state value, $\sigma^2 = \sigma_u^2/(1 - e^{-2\beta})$, which rises with σ_u^2 but declines with

2. We showed, however, in chapter 4 that β convergence would apply if the technology were asymptotically *AK* but featured diminishing returns to capital for finite K.

3. To derive equation (11.2), add $\log(y_{i,t-1})$ to both sides of equation (11.1), compute the variance, and use the condition that the covariance between u_{it} and $\log(y_{i,t-1})$ is 0.

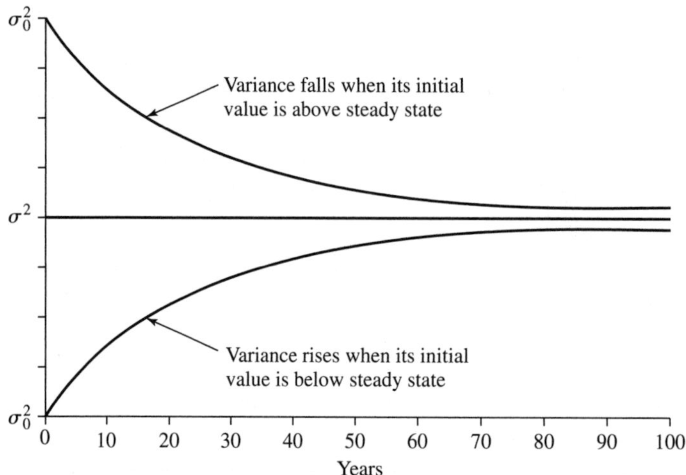

Figure 11.1
Theoretical behavior of dispersion. The figure shows the dispersion of per capita product, measured as the variance of the log of per capita product across economies. Although β convergence is assumed to apply, the dispersion may fall, rise, or remain constant, depending on whether it starts above, below, or at its steady-state value, σ^2. The figure assumes $\beta = 0.02$ per year.

the convergence coefficient, β. Over time, σ_t^2 falls (or rises) if the initial value σ_0^2 is greater than (or less than) the steady-state value, σ^2. Thus a positive coefficient β (β convergence) does not imply a falling σ_t^2 (σ convergence). To put it another way, β convergence is a necessary but not a sufficient condition for σ convergence.

Figure 11.1 shows the time pattern of σ_t^2 with σ_0^2 above or below σ^2. The convergence coefficient used, $\beta = 0.02$ per year, corresponds to the estimates that we report in a later section. With this value of β, the cross-sectional variance is predicted to fall or rise over time at a slow rate. In particular, if σ_0^2 departs substantially from the steady-state value, σ^2, then it takes about 100 years for σ_t^2 to get close to σ^2.

The cross-sectional dispersion of $\log(y_{it})$ is sensitive to shocks that have a common influence on subgroups of countries or regions. These kinds of disturbances violate the condition that u_{it} in equation (11.1) is independent of u_{jt} for $i \neq j$. To the extent that these shocks tend to benefit or hurt regions with high or low income (that is, to the extent that the shocks are correlated with the explanatory variable), the omission of such shocks from the regressions will tend to bias the estimates of β.

Examples are shocks that generate changes in the terms of trade for commodities. For the United States, an example is the sharp drop in the relative prices of agricultural goods during the 1920s. This disturbance had an adverse effect on the incomes of agricultural regions relative to the incomes of industrial regions. We can think also of the two oil price increases of the 1970s and the price decline of the 1980s. These shocks had effects in the same direction on the incomes of oil-producing regions relative to other regions. Another example for the United States is the Civil War. This shock had a strong adverse impact on the incomes of southern states relative to the incomes of northern states.

Formally, let S_t be a random variable that represents an economy-wide disturbance for period t. For example, S_t could reflect the relative price of oil as determined on world markets. Then equation (11.1) can be modified to

$$\log(y_{it}/y_{i,t-1}) = a_{it} - (1 - e^{-\beta}) \cdot \log(y_{i,t-1}) + \varphi_i S_t + u_{it} \tag{11.4}$$

where φ_i measures the effect of the aggregate disturbance on the growth rate in region i. If a positive value of S_t signifies an increase in the relative price of oil, then φ_i would be positive for countries or regions that produce a lot of oil.[4] The coefficient φ_i would tend to be negative for economies that produce goods, such as automobiles, that use oil as an input. We think of the coefficient φ_i as distributed cross sectionally with mean $\bar{\varphi}$ and variance σ_φ^2.

If $\log(y_{i,t-1})$ and φ_i are uncorrelated, estimates of β in equation (11.4) would be consistent when the shock is omitted from the regression. If $\log(y_{i,t-1})$ and φ_i are positively correlated, the coefficient estimated by OLS on $\log(y_{i,t-1})$ in equation (11.4) would be positively or negatively biased as S_t is positive or negative. As an example, if oil producers have relatively high per capita income, an increase in oil prices will benefit the relatively rich states. Consequently, an OLS regression of growth on initial income will underestimate the true convergence coefficient. In the empirical analysis of the next sections, we hold constant proxies for S_t as an attempt to obtain consistent estimates of the convergence coefficients.

Equation (11.4) implies that the variance of the log of per capita income evolves as

$$\sigma_t^2 = e^{-2\beta} \cdot \sigma_{t-1}^2 + \sigma_{ut}^2 + S_t^2 \cdot \sigma_\varphi^2 + 2S_t \cdot e^{-\beta} \cdot \text{cov}[\log(y_{i,t-1}), \varphi_i] \tag{11.5}$$

where the variances and covariances are conditioned on the current and past realizations of the aggregate shocks, $S_t, S_{t-1}, \ldots$. If $\text{cov}[\log(y_{i,t-1}), \varphi_i]$ equals 0—that is, if the shock is uncorrelated with initial income—equation (11.5) corresponds to equation (11.2), except that realizations of S_t effectively move σ_{ut}^2 around over time. A temporarily large value of S_t raises σ_t^2 above the long-run value σ^2 that corresponds to a typical value of S_t. Therefore, in the absence of a new shock, σ_t^2 returns gradually toward σ^2, as shown in figure 11.1.

4. More precisely, this shock would have a positive effect on the real income derived from the countries or regions that produce a lot of oil. This income may be owned by "foreigners" and appear as part of the net factor payments from "abroad," the term that differentiates GNP from GDP. For example, a substantial fraction of the capital inputs of Wyoming is owned by residents of other states. A positive oil shock will increase Wyoming's nominal GDP (and raise the real value of this GDP when deflated by a national price index) but not necessarily raise its GNP or personal income. For the U.S. states, this distinction is important in a few cases, notably for oil producers.

11.2 Convergence Across the U.S. States

11.2.1 β Convergence

We now use the data on per capita income for the U.S. states to estimate the speed of convergence, β.[5] (The definitions and sources of the data are in the appendix, section 11.12.) Suppose, for the moment, that we have observations at only two points in time, 0 and T. Then equation (2.35) implies that the average growth rate of per capita income for economy i over the interval from 0 to T is given by

$$(1/T) \cdot \log(y_{iT}/y_{i0}) = x - [(1 - e^{-\beta T})/T] \cdot \log(y_{i0}) + [(1 - e^{-\beta T})/T] \cdot \log(\hat{y}_i^*) + u_{i0,T} \tag{11.6}$$

where $u_{i0,T}$ represents the effect of the error terms, u_{it}, between dates 0 and T; $\hat{y}_i^*$ is the steady-state level of income; and x is the rate of technological progress, which we assume is the same for all economies.

The coefficient on initial income in equation (11.6) is $(1 - e^{-\beta T})/T$, an expression that declines with the length of the interval, T, for a given β. That is, if we estimate a linear relation between the growth rate of income and the log of initial income, the coefficient is predicted to be smaller the longer the time span over which the growth rate is averaged. The reason is that the growth rate declines as income increases (if $y_{i0} < \hat{y}_i^*$). Hence, if we compute the growth rate over a longer time span, it combines more of the smaller future growth rates with the initially larger growth rates. Hence, as the interval increases, the effect of the initial position on the average growth rate declines. The coefficient $(1 - e^{-\beta T}/T)$ approaches 0 as T approaches infinity, and it tends to β as T approaches 0.

Notice that equation (11.6) includes the term $[(1 - e^{-\beta T})/T] \cdot \log(\hat{y}_i^*)$ as an explanatory variable. That is, the growth rate of economy i depends on its initial level of income, y_{i0}, but it also depends on the steady-state level of income. This is why we use the concept of conditional rather than absolute convergence: the growth rate of an economy depends negatively on its initial level of income, after we "condition" on the steady state.

5. Barro and Sala-i-Martin (1992a) also use the data on gross state product (GSP), reported by the Bureau of Economic Analysis. GSP is analogous to GDP in that it assigns the product to the state in which it has been produced. In contrast, income (like GNP) assigns the product to the state in which the owners of the inputs reside. This distinction is potentially important if the economies are open and people tend to own capital in other states, or if there is a lot of interstate commuting (people live in one state and work in another). Barro and Sala-i-Martin (1992a) show that, in practice, the distinction turns out not to be that important; the estimates of the speed of convergence for GSP are similar to those for personal income. Since GSP data are available only starting in 1963, we limit attention in this chapter to the results that use the income data.

The usefulness of using regional data can be seen as follows: imagine that, instead of estimating the multivariate equation (11.6), we estimate the univariate regression

$$(1/T)\cdot\log(y_{iT}/y_{i0}) = a - [(1 - e^{-\beta T})/T]\cdot\log(y_{i0}) + w_{i0,T} \tag{11.7}$$

Notice that, in equation (11.7), the term $[(1-e^{-\beta T})/T]\cdot\log(\hat{y}_i^*)$ is no longer an explanatory variable. If the term that multiplies initial income in equation (11.7) turns out to be negative, we will conclude that poor economies tend to grow faster than rich economies so that "absolute convergence" applies. It is for this reason that regressions like equation (11.7) have been used in the literature to test the absolute convergence hypothesis. The question is whether the failure to find a negative coefficient is reason to reject the neoclassical growth model. Remember that the neoclassical model predicts a multivariate relation such as equation (11.6). Suppose that, instead of equation (11.6), we estimate equation (11.7). If we analyze data sets in which the various economies converge to different steady states, that is $\hat{y}_i^* \neq \hat{y}_j^*$ for all i and j, then the univariate regression equation (11.7) is misspecified and the excluded term is incorporated into the error term: $w_{i0,T} = u_{i0,T} + [(1-e^{-\beta T})/T]\cdot\log(\hat{y}_i^*)$. If the steady-state level of income, $\hat{y}_i^*$, is correlated with the explanatory variable y_{i0}, the error term is correlated with the right-hand-side variable, and the univariate regression equation (11.7) will provide biased estimates of β. In particular, if currently richer economies tend to converge to a higher steady-state level of income (that is, if $\hat{y}_i^*$ and y_{i0} are positively correlated), the estimate of β in equation (11.7) is biased toward zero. In other words, researchers could find no relation between growth and the initial level of income, even though conditional convergence holds. Under these circumstances, the only way to get consistent estimates of β is to get measures of $\hat{y}_i^*$ and include them in the regression.

Imagine now that we have a data set in which the various economies converge to different steady states, but that there is no correlation between the initial and the steady-state level of income. Although the univariate regression is still misspecified, the error term (which again includes the missing variable, $\hat{y}_i^*$) is not correlated with the explanatory variable. Hence, the usual estimation of equation (11.7) can provide a consistent estimate of β. Finally, if we analyze a data set in which all economies have the same steady state, that is, if $\hat{y}_i^* = \hat{y}_j^*$ for all i and j, the term $[(1-e^{-\beta T})/T]\cdot\log(\hat{y}_i^*)$ is incorporated into the constant term, and the usual estimation of equation (11.7) will again provide a consistent estimate of β.

In sum, there are two ways to estimate the speed of convergence, β. The first is to use general data sets (that is, data sets for which there is no guarantee that the initial level of income is uncorrelated with the steady-state level of income) and find proxies for the steady-state level of income. The second is to use data sets in which the various economies tend to converge to similar steady states or that, at least, the steady states are unrelated to the initial level of income. This second context is the one in which regional data sets play an important role. Although differences in technology, preferences, and institutions exist across regions, these differences are likely to be smaller than those across countries. Firms and households of different regions within a single country tend to have access to similar technologies and have roughly similar tastes and cultures. Furthermore, the regions share a common central government and therefore have similar institutional setups and legal systems. This relative homogeneity means that absolute convergence is more likely to apply across regions within countries than across countries.

Table 11.1 shows nonlinear least-squares estimates in the form of equation (11.7) for 47 or 48 U.S. states or territories for various time periods. The rows of table 11.1 correspond to the different time periods. For example, the first row applies to the 120-year period between 1880 and 2000. The first column of the table refers to the equation with only one explanatory variable, the logarithm of income per capita at the beginning of the period. Column two adds four regional dummies, corresponding to the four main census regions: Northeast, South, Midwest, and West. Finally, column three includes sectoral variables that are meant to capture the aggregate shocks discussed in the previous section. We already argued that the inclusion of these auxiliary variables would help to obtain accurate estimates of β.

Each cell contains the estimate of β, the standard error of this estimate (in parentheses), the R^2, and the standard error of the regression (in brackets). All equations have been estimated with constant terms, which are not reported in table 11.1.

The point estimate of β for the long sample, 1880–2000, is 0.0172 (s.e. = 0.0024).[6] The high R^2, 0.92, can be appreciated from figure 11.2, which provides a scatter plot of the average growth rate of income per capita between 1880 and 2000 against the log of income per capita in 1880.

The second column of the first row presents the estimated speed of convergence when the four regional dummies are incorporated. The estimated β coefficient is 0.0160 (0.0034). The similarity between this estimate and the previous one suggests that the speed at which average incomes converge across the census regions is not substantially different from the speed at which average incomes converge for the states within each of the regions. We can check this result by computing the average income for each of the four regions. The growth rate of a region's average income between 1880 and 2000 is plotted against the log of the region's average income in 1880 in figure 11.3. The negative relation is clear (the correlation coefficient is −0.97). The estimated speed of convergence implied by this relation is 2.1 percent per year, about the same as the within-region rate shown in column 2.

The next ten rows of table 11.1 divide the sample into subperiods. The first two are twenty years long (1880 to 1900 and 1920 to 1940), because income data for 1890 and 1910 are unavailable. The remaining eight subperiods are ten years long.

6. This regression includes 47 states or territories. Data for the Oklahoma territory are unavailable for 1880.

Table 11.1
Regressions for Personal Income Across U.S. States

	(1) Basic Equation		(2) Equations with Regional Dummies		(3) Equations with Structural Variables and Regional Dummies	
Period	$\hat{\beta}$	$R^2[\hat{\sigma}]$	$\hat{\beta}$	$R^2[\hat{\sigma}]$	$\hat{\beta}$	$R^2[\hat{\sigma}]$
1880–2000	0.0172 (0.0024)	0.92 [0.0012]	0.0160 (0.0034)	0.95 [0.0010]	—	—
1880–1900	0.0101 (0.0022)	0.36 [0.0068]	0.0224 (0.0043)	0.62 [0.0054]	0.0268 (0.0051)	0.65 [0.0053]
1900–20	0.0218 (0.0031)	0.62 [0.0065]	0.0209 (0.0065)	0.67 [0.0062]	0.0270 (0.0077)	0.71 [0.0060]
1920–30	−0.0149 (0.0051)	0.14 [0.0132]	−0.0128 (0.0078)	0.43 [0.0111]	0.0209 (0.0119)	0.64 [0.0089]
1930–40	0.0129 (0.0033)	0.28 [0.0079]	0.0072 (0.0052)	0.34 [0.0078]	0.0147 (0.0083)	0.37 [0.0078]
1940–50	0.0502 (0.0058)	0.73 [0.0087]	0.0512 (0.0062)	0.88 [0.0059]	0.0304 (0.0065)	0.91 [0.0052]
1950–60	0.0193 (0.0039)	0.40 [0.0051]	0.0191 (0.0056)	0.52 [0.0047]	0.0305 (0.0053)	0.74 [0.0035]
1960–70	0.0286 (0.0039)	0.61 [0.0040]	0.0181 (0.0046)	0.73 [0.0034]	0.0196 (0.0061)	0.74 [0.0035]
1970–80	0.0186 (0.0049)	0.27 [0.0044]	0.0079 (0.0055)	0.44 [0.0040]	0.0057 (0.0068)	0.46 [0.0040]
1980–90	0.0036 (0.0085)	0.01 [0.0077]	0.0095 (0.0074)	0.57 [0.0052]	0.0029 (0.0070)	0.69 [0.0045]
1990–2000	0.0016 (0.0035)	0.01 [0.0035]	−0.0005 (0.0045)	0.07 [0.0035]	0.0029 (0.0050)	0.14 [0.0034]
Joint, 9 subperiods	0.0150 (0.0015)	— —	0.0164 (0.0021)	— —	0.0212 (0.0023)	— —

Note: The regressions use nonlinear least squares to estimate equations of the form

$$(1/T) \cdot \log(y_{it}/y_{i,t-T}) = a - [\log(y_{i,t-T})] \cdot [(1 - e^{-\beta T})/T] + \text{other variables}$$

where $y_{i,t-T}$ is per capita income in state i at the beginning of the period divided by the overall CPI, T is the length of the interval, and the other variables are regional dummies and structural measures (see the description in the text). See the appendix (section 11.12) for a discussion of the data on the U.S. states. The samples that begin in 1880 have 47 observations. The others have 48 observations. Each column contains the estimate of β, the standard error of this estimate (in parentheses), the R^2 of the regression, and the standard error of the equation (in brackets). The estimated coefficients for constants, regional dummies, and structural variables are not reported. The likelihood-ratio statistic refers to a test of the equality of the coefficients of the log of initial income over the nine subperiods. The p value comes from a χ^2 distribution with eight degrees of freedom.

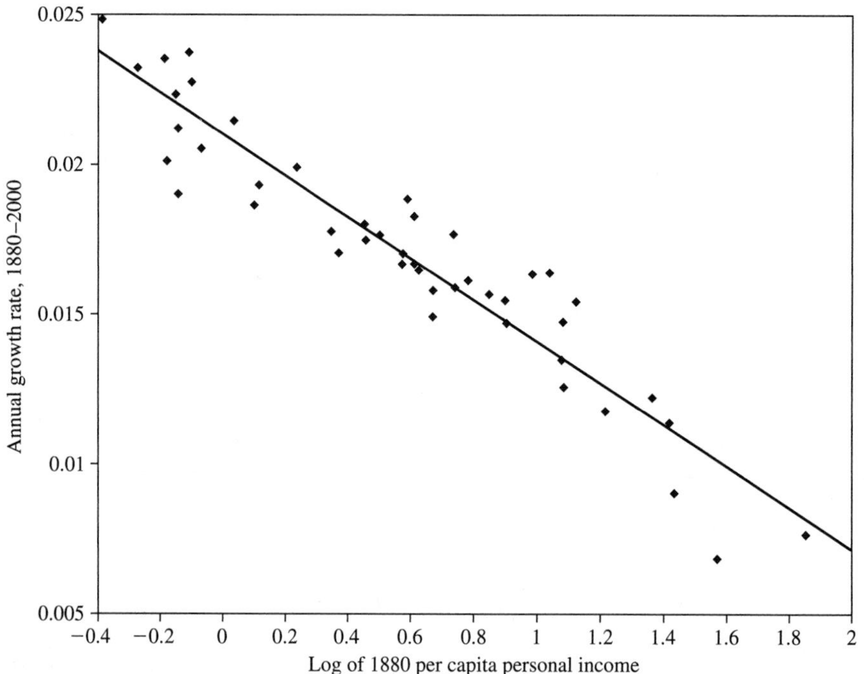

Figure 11.2
Convergence of personal income across U.S. states: 1880 personal income and 1880–2000 income growth. The average growth rate of state per capita income for 1880–2000, shown on the vertical axis, is negatively related to the log of per capita income in 1880, shown on the horizontal axis. Thus, absolute β convergence exists for the U.S. states.

The estimated β coefficient is significantly positive—indicating β convergence—for seven of the ten subperiods. The coefficient has the wrong sign ($\beta < 0$) for only one of the subperiods, 1920–30, a time of large declines in the relative price of agricultural commodities. A likely explanation for this result is that agricultural states tended to be poor states, and the agricultural states suffered the most from the fall in agricultural prices. The estimated coefficient is insignificant for the two most recent subperiods, the 1980s and the 1990s. If we constrain the β coefficients to be the same for all subperiods, the joint estimate for the basic equation is 0.0150 (0.0015).

Column 2 of Table 11.1 adds regional dummies, where the coefficients of these dummies are allowed to differ for each period. These regional variables capture effects that are common to all states within a region in a given period. The estimated β coefficient for the 1920s still has the wrong sign, as does the the coefficient for the 1990s, although they

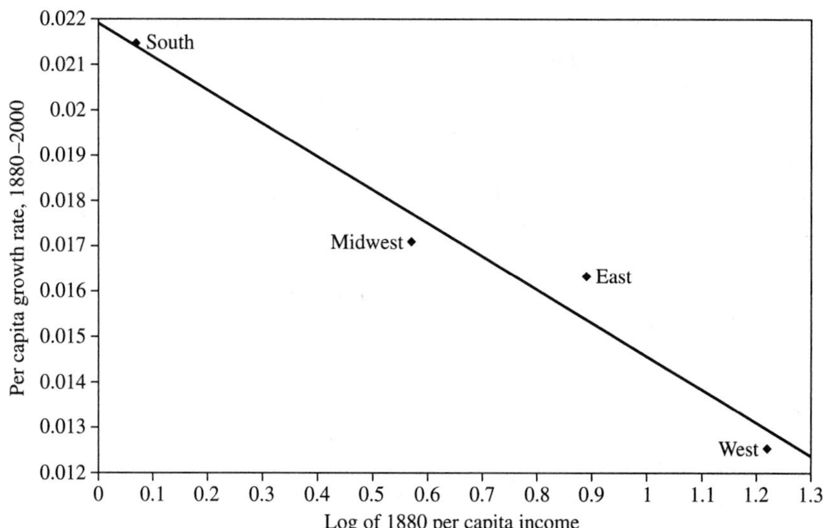

Figure 11.3
Convergence of personal income across U.S. regions: 1880 income and 1880–2000 income growth. The negative relation between income growth and initial income, shown for the U.S. states in figure 11.2, applies in figure 11.3 to averages over the four main census regions.

are both estimated with substantial error. Hence, even within regions, poor states tended to grow slower than rich states during the 1920s. The joint estimate for the nine subperiods is now 0.0164 (0.0021), similar to that for the basic regression.

Aggregate shocks that affect groups of states differentially, such as shifts in the relative prices of agricultural products or oil, might explain the instability of the estimated coefficients. Following Barro and Sala-i-Martin (1991, 1992a, 1992b), the third column of table 11.1 adds an additional variable to the regression as an attempt to hold these aggregate shocks constant. The variable, denoted by S_{it} (for structure), is calculated as

$$S_{it} = \sum_{j=1}^{9} \omega_{ij,t-T} \cdot [\log(y_{jt}/y_{j,t-T})/T] \tag{11.8}$$

where $\omega_{ij,t-T}$ is the weight of sector j in state i's personal income at time $t - T$ and y_{jt} is the national average of personal income per worker in sector j at time t. The nine sectors used are agriculture, mining, construction, manufacturing, trade, finance and real estate, transportation, services, and government. We think of S_{it} as a proxy for the effects reflected in the term $\varphi_i S_t$ in equation (11.4).

The structural variable reveals how much a state would grow if each of its sectors grew at the national average rate. For example, suppose that economy i specializes in the production of cars and that the aggregate car sector does not grow over the period between $t-T$ and t. The low value of S_{it} for this region indicates that it should not grow very fast because the car industry has suffered from the shock.

Note from equation (11.8) that S_{it} depends on the contemporaneous growth rates of national averages and on lagged values of state i's sectoral shares. For this reason, the variable can be reasonably treated as exogenous to the current growth experience of state i.

Because of lack of data, we can include the structural variable only for the periods after 1929. For the periods before 1929, we obtain a rough measure of S_{it} by using the share of agriculture in the state's total income.

Column three includes structural variables, as well as regional dummies, in the growth regressions. (The coefficients on the regional and structural variables are allowed to differ for each period.) One contrast with the previous results is that the estimated β coefficient for the 1920s becomes positive and close to 0.02. The coefficients for the 1980s and 1990s are also positive but their size continues to be small. The joint estimate of β for the nine subperiods is 0.0212 (0.0023).

The main conclusion is that the U.S. states tend to converge at a speed of about 2 percent per year. Averages for the four census regions converge at a rate that is similar to that for states within regions. If we hold constant measures of structural shocks, we cannot reject the hypothesis that the speed of convergence is stable over time, although the estimates for the last two decades are insignificantly different from zero.

11.2.2 Measurement Error

The existence of temporary measurement error in income tends to introduce an upward bias in the estimate of β; that is, the elimination of measurement error over time can generate the appearance of convergence.[7] One reason for measurement error is that each state's nominal income is deflated by a national price index, because accurate indexes do not exist at the state level.

One way to handle measurement error is to use earlier lags of the log of income as instruments in the regressions. If measurement error is temporary (and the error term is not serially correlated), the earlier lags of the log of income would be satisfactory instruments for the log of income at the start of each period. If we reestimate column 1 of table 11.1 with the previous lag of the log of income used as an instrument, we get a joint estimate

7. The same property holds for short-term business fluctuations. We may want to design a model in which these temporary fluctuations of output are distinguished from the kinds of transitional dynamics that appear in growth models.

of β of 0.0176 (0.0019). This panel uses nine subperiods starting in 1900 because the observation for 1880–1900 is lost. The OLS estimate of β for the same nine subperiods is 0.0165 (0.0018). Hence, the use of instruments generates a minor change in the estimate of β, which suggests that measurement error does not explain the significantly negative relation between growth and the initial level of income.

When we estimate the subperiods separately, we again find only a small difference between the instrumental-variable (IV) and OLS estimates. The largest change applies to 1950–60, for which the IV estimate is 0.0139 (0.0040), compared with the OLS value of 0.0193 (0.0039).

The results for columns 2 and 3 of table 11.1 are similar. Our conclusion is that measurement error is unlikely to be a key element in the results.

11.2.3 σ Convergence

Figure 11.4 shows the cross-sectional standard deviation for the log of per capita personal income net of transfers for 47 or 48 U.S. states or territories from 1880 to 2000. The dispersion declined from 0.54 in 1880 to 0.33 in 1920 but then rose to 0.40 in 1930. This

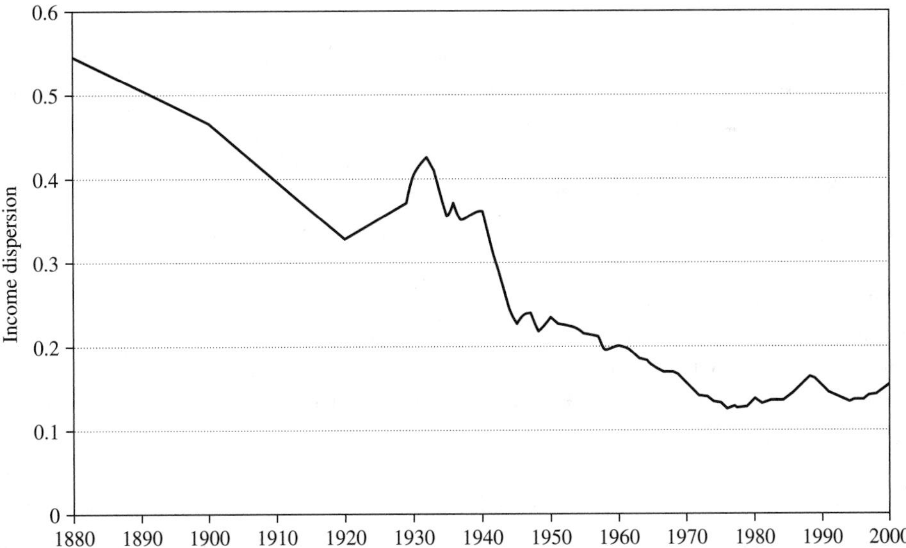

Figure 11.4
Dispersion of personal income across U.S. states, 1880–2000. The figure shows the cross-sectional standard deviation of the log of per capita personal income for 47 or 48 U.S. states or territories from 1880 to 2000. This measure of dispersion declined from 1880 to 1920, rose in the 1920s, fell from 1930 to the mid-1970s, rose through 1988, declined again through 1992, and then remained fairly flat.

rise reflects the adverse shock to agriculture during the 1920s; the agricultural states were relatively poor in 1920 and suffered a further reduction in income with the fall in agricultural prices.

After reaching a peak in 1932, the dispersion fell to 0.36 in 1940, 0.24 in 1950, 0.20 in 1960, and 0.16 in 1970. The long-run decline stopped in the mid-1970s, with a low point of 0.14 in 1976. After that, σ_t rose to a peak of 0.16 in 1988. Dispersion fell to 0.14 in the early 1990s, then remained relatively flat.

11.3 Convergence Across Japanese Prefectures

11.3.1 β Convergence

Barro and Sala-i-Martin (1992b) analyze the pattern of β convergence for per capita income across 47 Japanese prefectures (see the appendix, section 11.12, for the sources and definitions). Table 11.2 reports nonlinear estimates of the convergence coefficient, β, for the period 1930–90. The setup of table 11.2 parallels that of table 11.1.

The first row of table 11.2 pertains to regressions for the whole period, 1930–90. The basic equation in column 1 includes only the log of initial income as a regressor. The estimated β coefficient is 0.0279 (0.0033), with an R^2 of 0.92. The good fit can be appreciated in figure 11.5. The strong negative correlation between the growth rate from 1930 to 1990 and the log of per capita income in 1930 confirms the existence of β convergence across the Japanese prefectures.

The estimated β coefficient is essentially the same in column 2, which incorporates dummies for the seven Japanese districts as explanatory variables. This finding suggests that the speed of convergence for prefectures within districts is similar to that across districts. This idea can be checked by running a regression that uses the seven data points for the growth and level of the average per capita income of districts. The negative relation between the growth rate from 1930 to 1990 and the log of per capita income in 1930 is displayed in figure 11.6. The β coefficient estimated from these observations (not reported in the table) is 0.0261 (0.0079). Hence, we confirm that the speed of convergence across districts is about the same as that within districts.

The second and third rows of table 11.2 break the full sample into two long subperiods, 1930–55 and 1955–90. For the basic equation, the speed of convergence for the first subperiod is larger than that for the second, 0.0358 (0.0035) versus 0.0191 (0.0035). The same relation holds for the second column, which adds the district dummies as explanatory variables. (Different coefficients on the dummies are estimated for the two subperiods.) Hence, we conclude that the speed of convergence after 1955 was substantially slower than that between 1930 and 1955. The lack of sectoral data for the early period does not, how-

Table 11.2
Regressions for Personal Income Across Japanese Prefectures

	(1) Basic Equation		(2) Equations with District Dummies		(3) Equations with Structural Variables and District Dummies	
Period	$\hat{\beta}$	$R^2[\hat{\sigma}]$	$\hat{\beta}$	$R^2[\hat{\sigma}]$	$\hat{\beta}$	$R^2[\hat{\sigma}]$
1930–90	0.0279 (0.0033)	0.92 [0.0019]	0.0276 (0.0024)	0.97 [0.0012]	—	—
1930–55	0.0358 (0.0035)	0.86 [0.0045]	0.0380 (0.0037)	0.90 [0.0038]	—	—
1955–90	0.0191 (0.0035)	0.59 [0.0027]	0.0222 (0.0035)	0.81 [0.0020]	—	—
1955–60	−0.0152 (0.0079)	0.07 [0.0133]	−0.0023 (0.0082)	0.44 [0.0111]	0.0047 (0.0118)	0.46 [0.0112]
1960–65	0.0296 (0.0072)	0.30 [0.0108]	0.0360 (0.0079)	0.55 [0.0093]	0.0414 (0.0096)	0.56 [0.0093]
1965–70	−0.0010 (0.0062)	0.00 [0.0097]	0.0127 (0.0067)	0.47 [0.0076]	0.0382 (0.0091)	0.62 [0.0065]
1970–75	0.0967 (0.0100)	0.78 [0.0095]	0.0625 (0.0092)	0.87 [0.0078]	0.0661 (0.0118)	0.87 [0.0079]
1975–80	0.0338 (0.0100)	0.23 [0.0087]	0.0455 (0.0119)	0.37 [0.0085]	0.0469 (0.0145)	0.37 [0.0086]
1980–85	−0.0115 (0.0077)	0.04 [0.0075]	0.0076 (0.0089)	0.37 [0.0066]	0.0102 (0.0094)	0.37 [0.0067]
1985–90	0.0007 (0.0067)	0.00 [0.0067]	0.0086 (0.0082)	0.28 [0.0061]	0.0085 (0.0085)	0.28 [0.0062]
Joint, 7 subperiods	0.0125	—	0.0232	—	0.0312	—
Likelihood-ratio	(0.0032)	—	(0.0034)	—	(0.0040)	—
statistic	94.6		40.6		26.4	
(p value)	(0.000)		(0.000)		(0.002)	

Note: See the appendix (section 11.12) for a discussion of the data on Japanese prefectures, and see the note to table 11.1 for the form of the regressions. The variable $y_{i,t-T}$ is per capita income in prefecture i at the beginning of the period divided by the overall CPI. All samples have 47 observations. The likelihood-ratio statistic refers to a test of the equality of the coefficients of the log of initial income over the seven subperiods. The p value comes from a χ^2 distribution with six degrees of freedom.

ever, allow us to investigate the cause of this difference. We therefore restrict the rest of the analysis to the post-1955 period.

The next seven rows of table 11.2 break the sample into five-year subperiods starting in 1955. For three of the subperiods, the sign of the estimated β coefficient in the basic equation is opposite to the one expected. The speed of convergence is positive and significant for the periods 1960–65, 1970–75, and 1975–80. The joint estimate for the seven subperiods

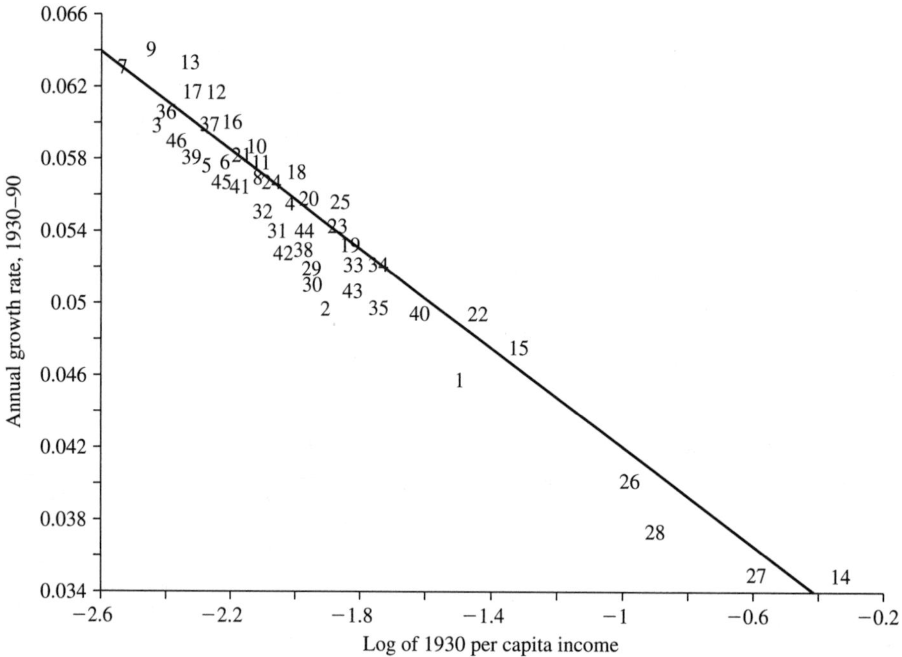

Figure 11.5
Convergence of personal income across Japanese prefectures: 1930 income and 1930–90 income growth. The growth rate of prefectural per capita income for 1930–90, shown on the vertical axis, is negatively related to the log of per capita income in 1930, shown on the horizontal axis. Thus absolute β convergence exists for the Japanese prefectures. The numbers shown identify each prefecture; see table 11.10.

is 0.0125 (0.0032). A test for the equality of coefficients over time is strongly rejected; the p value is 0.000.

The results with district dummies in column 2 allow for different coefficients on the dummies in each subperiod. In this case, only the estimated β coefficient for 1955–60 has the wrong sign, and it is not significant. The joint estimate is 0.0232 (0.0034). However, we still reject the equality of coefficients; the p value is again 0.000.

Column 3 adds a measure of the structural variable, S_{it}, defined in equation (11.8). This variable is analogous to the one constructed for the U.S. states. The coefficients on the structural variable are allowed to differ for each subperiod. In contrast with the previous two columns, none of the subperiods has the wrong sign when the sectoral variable is included. The joint estimate for the seven subperiods is 0.0312 (0.0040). We still reject the hypothesis of coefficient stability over time: the p value is now 0.002.

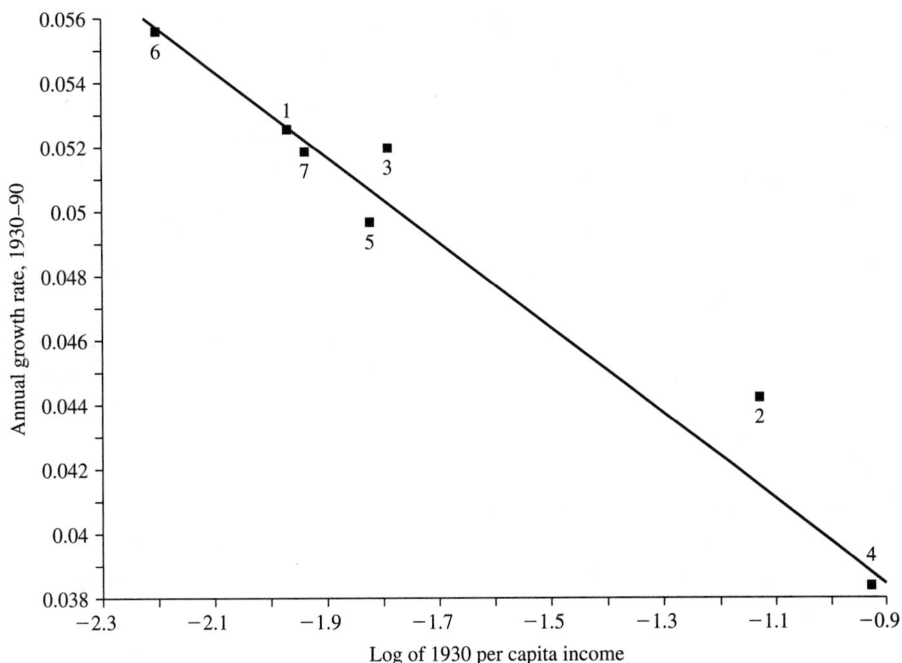

Figure 11.6
Convergence of personal income across Japanese districts: 1930 income and 1930–90 income growth. The negative relation between income growth and initial income, shown for Japanese prefectures in figure 11.5, applies also in figure 11.6 to averages for the seven major districts.

One source of instability in the estimated β coefficients is that Tokyo is an outlier in the 1980s: Tokyo was by far the richest prefecture in its district in 1980 and had the largest growth rate from 1980 to 1990, an outcome not captured by the structural variable that we have included. If we add a dummy for Tokyo for the 1980s, we get estimated β coefficients of 0.0218 (0.0112) for 1980–85 and 0.0203 (0.0096) for 1985–90. With this dummy included, the test of equality of coefficients now rejects with a p value of 0.010.

Another source of instability is the period 1970–75, for which the estimated β coefficient of 0.0661 (0.0118) is substantially higher than the others. A likely explanation for this high estimated value of β is that the oil shock of 1973 had an especially adverse impact on the richer industrial areas. The structural variable is supposed to hold constant this type of shock, but the construct that we have been able to measure does not seem to capture this effect.

As with the U.S. states, we reestimated the equations for Japanese prefectures with earlier lags of income used as instruments. The conclusion again is that the estimates are not materially affected. For example, in column 3 of table 11.2, the joint estimate of β falls from 0.0312 (0.0040) to 0.0282 (0.0042) when the instruments are used.

11.3.2 σ Convergence Across Prefectures

We want now to assess the extent to which there has been σ convergence across prefectures in Japan. We calculate the unweighted cross-sectional standard deviation for the log of per capita income, σ_t, for the 47 prefectures from 1930 to 1990. Figure 11.7 shows that the dispersion of personal income increased from 0.47 in 1930 to 0.63 in 1940. One explanation of this phenomenon is the explosion of military spending during the period. The average growth rates for districts 1 (Hokkaido–Tohoku) and 7 (Kyushu), which are mainly agricultural, were -2.4 percent and -1.7 percent per year, respectively. In contrast, the industrial regions of Tokyo, Osaka, and Aichi grew at 3.7, 3.1, and 1.7 percent per year, respectively.

The cross-prefectural dispersion decreased dramatically after World War II: it fell to 0.29 in 1950, 0.25 in 1960, 0.23 in 1970, and hit a minimum of 0.12 in 1978. The dispersion then increased slightly: σ_t rose to 0.13 in 1980, 0.14 in 1985, and 0.15 in 1987, but has been relatively stable since 1987. Thus the pattern is similar to that for the U.S. states.

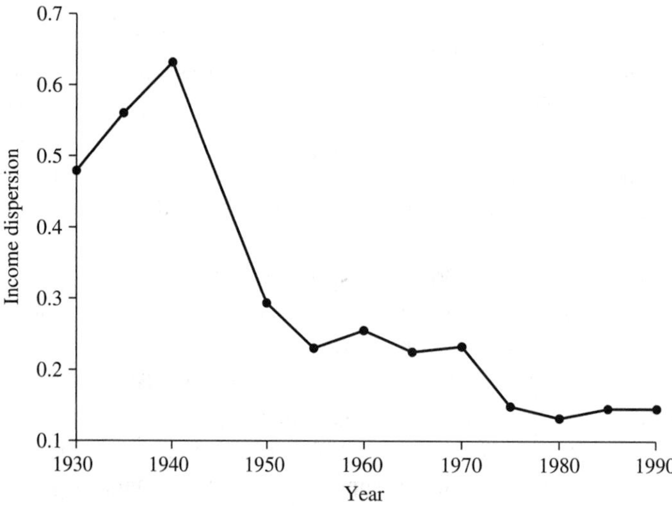

Figure 11.7
Dispersion of personal income across Japanese prefectures, 1930–90. The figure shows the cross-sectional standard deviation of the log of per capita personal income for 47 Japanese prefectures from 1930 to 1990. This measure of dispersion fell from the end of World War II until 1980.

11.4 Convergence Across European Regions

11.4.1 β Convergence

Barro and Sala-i-Martin (1991) analyzed convergence for 90 regions in eight European countries: 11 in Germany, 11 in the United Kingdom, 20 in Italy, 21 in France, 4 in the Netherlands, 3 in Belgium, 3 in Denmark, and 17 in Spain. The data, described in the appendix (section 11.12), correspond to GDP per capita for the first seven countries and to income per capita for Spain.

Table 11.3 shows the estimates of β in the form of equation (11.6) for the period 1950–90. The regressions include country dummies for each period to proxy for differences in the steady-state values of x_i and $\hat{y}_i^*$ in equation (11.6) and for countrywide fixed effects in the error terms. The country dummies, which are not reported in table 11.3, have substantial explanatory power. The first four rows of column 1 show the results for four decades. The estimates of β are reasonably stable over time; they range from 0.010 (0.004) for the 1980s to 0.023 (0.009) for the 1960s. The joint estimate for the four decades is 0.019 (0.002). The

Table 11.3
Convergence Across European Regions

	(1) Equations with Country Dummies		(2) Equations with Sectoral Shares and Country Dummies	
Period	$\hat{\beta}$	$R^2[\hat{\sigma}]$	$\hat{\beta}$	$R^2[\hat{\sigma}]$
1950–60	0.018 (0.006)	0.83 [0.0099]	0.034 (0.009)	0.84 [0.0094]
1960–70	0.023 (0.009)	0.97 [0.0065]	0.020 (0.006)	0.97 [0.0064]
1970–80	0.020 (0.009)	0.99 [0.0079]	0.022 (0.007)	0.99 [0.0077]
1980–90	0.010 (0.004)	0.97 [0.0066]	0.007 (0.005)	0.97 [0.0064]
Joint, 4 subperiods	0.019 (0.002)	— —	0.018 (0.003)	— —
Likelihood-ratio statistic (p value)	4.9 (0.179)		8.6 (0.034)	

Note: See the appendix (section 11.12) for a discussion of the data on European regions, and see the note to table 11.1 for the form of the regressions. The variable $y_{i,t-T}$ is an index of the per capita GDP (income for Spain) in region i at the beginning of the interval. All samples have 90 observations. The likelihood-ratio statistic refers to a test of the equality of the coefficients of the log of initial per capita GDP or income over the four subperiods. The p value comes from a χ^2 distribution with three degrees of freedom.

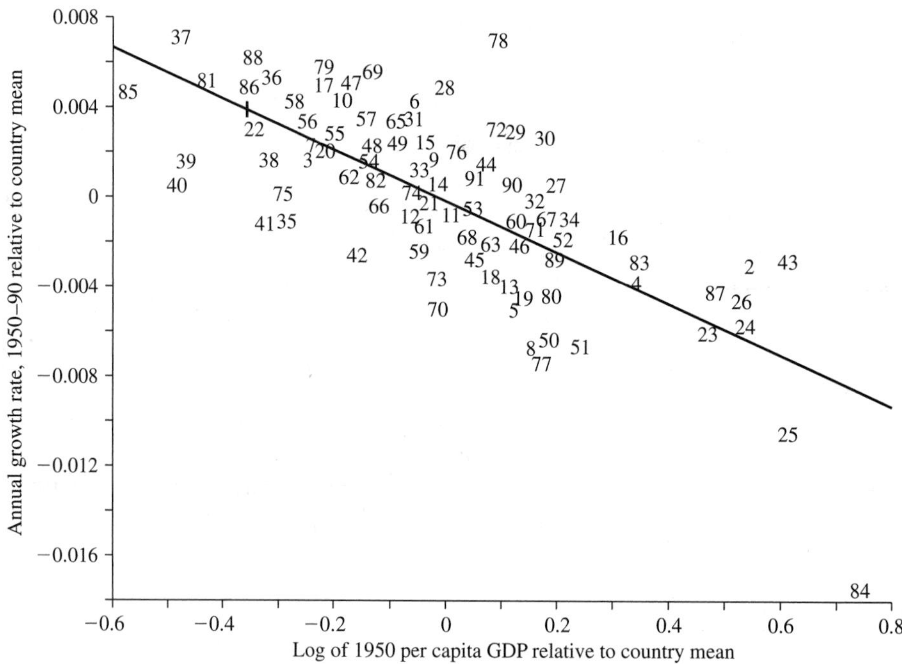

Figure 11.8
Growth rate from 1950 to 1990 versus 1950 per capita GDP for 90 regions in Europe. The growth rate of a region's per capita GDP for 1950–90, shown on the vertical axis, is negatively related to the log of per capita GDP in 1950, shown on the horizontal axis. The growth rate and level of per capita GDP are measured relative to the country means. Hence, this figure shows that absolute β convergence exists for the regions within Germany, the United Kingdom, Italy, France, the Netherlands, Belgium, Denmark, and Spain. The numbers shown identify the regions; see table 11.9.

hypothesis of constant β over time cannot be rejected at conventional levels of significance; the p value is 0.18.

Figure 11.8 shows for the 90 regions the relation of the growth rate of per capita GDP (income for Spain) from 1950 to 1990 (1955 to 1987 for Spain) to the log of per capita GDP or income at the start of the period. The variables are measured relative to the means of the respective countries. The figure shows the negative relation that is familiar from the U.S. states and Japanese prefectures. The correlation between the growth rate and the log of initial per capita GDP or income in figure 11.8 is −0.72. Since the underlying numbers are expressed relative to own-country means, the relation in figure 11.8 pertains to β convergence within countries, rather than between countries. The graph therefore corresponds to the estimates that include country dummies in column 1 of table 11.3.

Column 2 adds the share of agriculture and industry in total employment or GDP at the start of each subperiod.[8] These share variables are as close as we can come with our present data for the European regions to measuring the structural variable, S_{it}, that appears in equation (11.8). The results allow for period-specific coefficients for the sectoral shares.

The joint estimate of β for the four subperiods is now 0.018 (0.003). The test of the hypothesis of stability of β across periods yields a p value of 0.034. Thus, in contrast to our findings for the United States and Japan, the inclusion of the share variables makes the β coefficients appear less stable over time. Probably, a better measure of structural composition would yield more satisfactory results.

We have also estimated the joint system for Europe with individual β coefficients for the five large countries (Germany, the United Kingdom, Italy, France, and Spain). This system corresponds to the four-period regression shown in column 2 of table 11.3, except that the coefficient β is allowed to vary over the countries (but not over the subperiods). This system contains country dummies (with different coefficients for each subperiod) and share variables (with coefficients that vary over the subperiods but not across the countries). The resulting estimates of β are as follows: Germany (11 regions), 0.0224 (0.0067); United Kingdom (11 regions), 0.0277 (0.0104); Italy (20 regions), 0.0155 (0.0037); France (21 regions), 0.0121 (0.0061); and Spain (17 regions), 0.0182 (0.0048). Note that the individual point estimates are all close to 2 percent per year; they range from 1.2 percent per year for France to 2.8 percent per year for the United Kingdom.

A test for equality of the β coefficients across the five countries yields a p value of 0.55. Hence, we cannot reject the hypothesis that the speed of regional convergence within the five European countries is the same.

We also reestimated the European equations with earlier lags of per capita GDP or income used as instruments. This procedure necessitated the elimination of the first subperiod; hence, we include only the three decades from 1960 to 1990. The use of instruments had little impact on the results that included only country dummies, corresponding to column 1 of table 11.3. The joint estimate of β goes from 0.0187 (0.0022) in the OLS case (with only three subperiods included) to 0.0165 (0.0023). If the agricultural and industrial share variables are added, however, the joint estimate of β goes from 0.0153 (0.0034) to 0.0073 (0.0038). We think that the sharp drop in the estimated β coefficient in this case reflects inadequacies in the share variables as measures of structural shifts.

8. The share figures for the first three subperiods are based on employment. The values for 1980–90 are based on GDP.

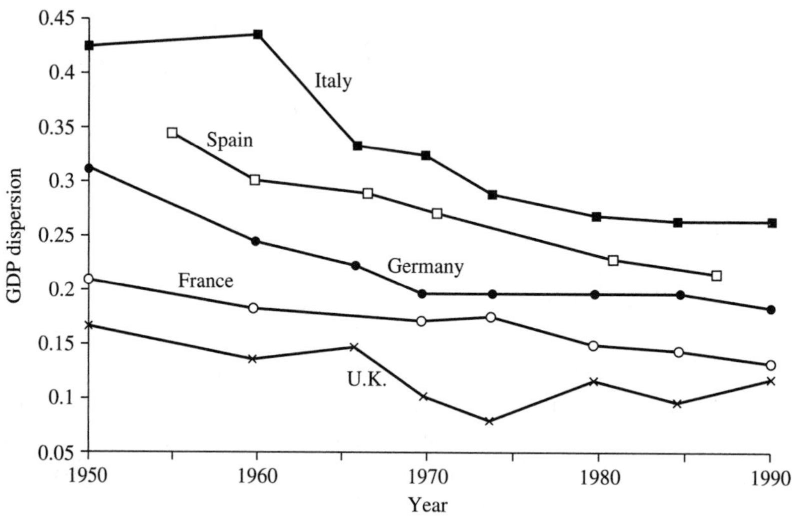

Figure 11.9
Dispersion of per capita GDP within five European countries. The figure shows the cross-sectional standard deviation of the log of per capita GDP from 1950 to 1990 for 11 regions in Germany, 11 in the United Kingdom, 20 in Italy, 21 in France, and 17 in Spain. This measure of dispersion fell in most cases since 1950 but has been roughly stable in Germany and the United Kingdom since 1970.

11.4.2 σ Convergence

Figure 11.9 shows the behavior of σ_t for the regions within the five large countries: Germany, the United Kingdom, Italy, France, and Spain. The countries are always ranked in descending order of dispersion as Italy, Spain, Germany, France, and the United Kingdom. The overall pattern shows declines in σ_t over time for each country, although little net change occurs since 1970 for Germany and the United Kingdom. The rise in σ_t from 1974 to 1980 for the United Kingdom—the only oil producer in the European sample—likely reflects the effect of oil shocks. In 1990 the values of σ_t are 0.27 for Italy, 0.22 for Spain (for 1987), 0.19 for Germany, 0.14 for France, and 0.12 for the United Kingdom.

11.5 Convergence Across Other Regions Around the World

Many researchers have recently studied the patterns of convergence across regions in various countries around the world. Coulombe and Lee (1993) find that the speed of convergence across regions in Canada is not too different from the 2 percent per year we found for the U.S. states, Japanese prefectures, and European regions. Persson (1997) finds similar results for 24 Swedish counties for the period 1911–93. Cashin and Sahay (1995) find strong evidence of absolute convergence across Indian states between 1961 and 1991. Other regional studies in the recent literature include O'Leary (2000) for Ireland; Petrakos and Saratsis (2000) for Greece; Hossain (2000) for Bangladesh; Utrera and Koroch (1998) for Argentina; Magalhaes, Hewings, and Azzoni (2000) for Brazil; Cashin (1995) for Australasia; Yao and Weeks (2000) for China; Cashin and Loayza (1995) for South Pacific countries; Gezici and Hewings (2001) for Turkey; and Sanchez-Robles and Villaverde (2001) for Spain.

11.6 Migration Across the U.S. States

This section considers the empirical determinants of net migration among the U.S. states. The analysis in section 9.1.3 suggests that m_{it}, the annual rate of net migration into region i between years $t - T$ and t, can be described by a function of the form

$$m_{it} = f(y_{i,t-T}, \theta_i, \pi_{i,t-T}; \text{variables that depend on } t \text{ but not } i) \tag{11.9}$$

where $y_{i,t-T}$ is per capita income at the beginning of the period, θ_i is a vector of fixed amenities (such as climate and geography), and $\pi_{i,t-T}$ is the population density in region i at the beginning of the period.[9] The set of variables that depends on t but not on i includes any elements that influence per capita incomes and population densities in other economies. Also included are effects like technological progress in heating and air conditioning—these changes alter people's attitudes about weather and population density.

Per capita income—a proxy for wage rates—would have a positive effect on migration, whereas population density would have a negative effect. The functional form that we implement empirically is

$$m_{it} = a + b \cdot \log(y_{i,t-T}) + c_1\theta_i + c_2\pi_{i,t-T} + c_3 \cdot (\pi_{i,t-T})^2 + v_{it} \tag{11.10}$$

where v_{it} is an error term, $b > 0$, and the form allows for a quadratic in population density, $\pi_{i,t-T}$. The marginal effect of $\pi_{i,t-T}$ on m_{it} is negative if $c_2 + 2c_3 < 0$.

Although there is an extensive literature about variables to include as amenities, θ_i, the present analysis includes only the log of average heating-degree days, denoted $\log(\text{heat}_i)$, which is a disamenity so that $c_1 < 0$. The variable $\log(\text{heat}_i)$ has a good deal of explanatory power for net migration across the U.S. states. We considered alternative measures of the weather, but they did not fit as well. It would be useful to include migration for retirement, a mechanism that likely explains outliers such as Florida. However, these kinds of

9. Some amenities, such as government policies with respect to tax rates and regulations, would vary over time. We do not deal with these types of variables in the present analysis.

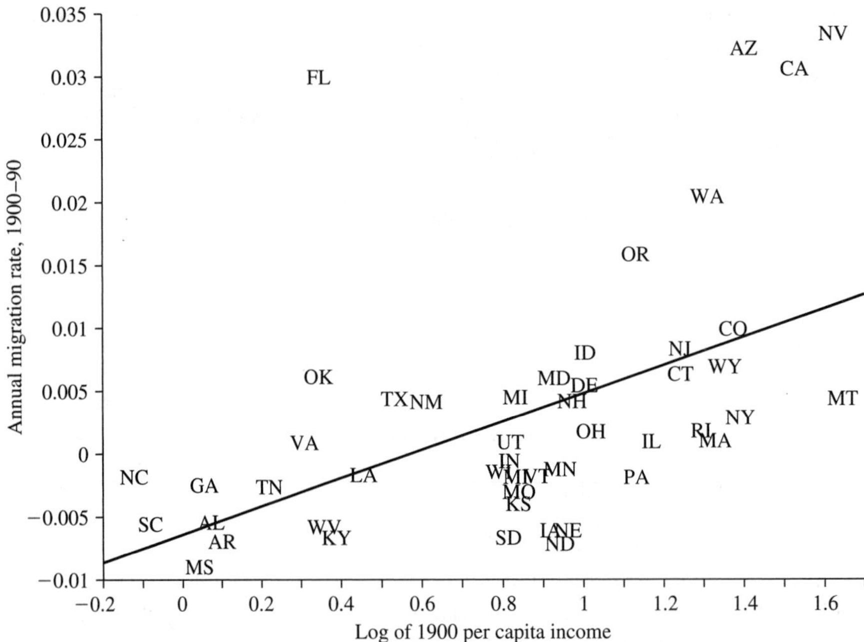

Figure 11.10
Migration and initial state income, 1900–90. The average net migration rate for 48 U.S. states or territories from 1900 to 1990, shown on the vertical axis, is positively related to the log of initial per capita income, shown on the horizontal axis. Florida, Arizona, California, and Nevada have notably higher net migration rates than the values predicted by their initial levels of income.

modifications probably would not change the basic findings that we now present about the relation between net migration and state per capita income.

The data on net migration for the U.S. states start in 1900 and are available for every census year except 1910 and 1930—see Barro and Sala-i-Martin (1991). We calculate the 10-year annual migration rates into a state by dividing the number of net migrants between dates $t - T$ and t by the state's population at date $t - T$.

Figure 11.10 shows the simple long-term relation between the migration rate and the log of initial income per capita.[10] The horizontal axis plots the log of state per capita income in 1900. The positive association is evident (correlation $= 0.51$). The main outlier is Florida, which has a lower than average initial income per capita and a very high net migration rate of 3 percent per year.

10. The variable on the vertical axis is the average annual in-migration rate for each state from 1900 to 1987. The variable is the average for each subperiod weighted by the length of the interval.

Table 11.4
Regressions for Net Migration into U.S. States, 1900–89

Period	Log of Per Capita Income	Heating Degree Days	Population Density	Square of Population Density	$R^2[\hat{\sigma}]$
1900–20	0.0335 (0.0075)	−0.0066 (0.0037)	−0.0433 (0.0079)	0.0307 (0.0095)	0.70 [0.0111]
1920–30	0.0363 (0.0078)	−0.0124 (0.0027)	−0.0433 (0.0079)	0.0307 (0.0095)	0.61 [0.0079]
1930–40	0.0191 (0.0037)	−0.0048 (0.0014)	−0.0433 (0.0079)	0.0307 (0.0095)	0.71 [0.0041]
1940–50	0.0261 (0.0055)	−0.0135 (0.0022)	−0.0433 (0.0079)	0.0307 (0.0095)	0.82 [0.0065]
1950–60	0.0438 (0.0086)	−0.0205 (0.0031)	−0.0433 (0.0079)	0.0307 (0.0095)	0.70 [0.0091]
1960–70	0.0435 (0.0083)	−0.0056 (0.0025)	−0.0433 (0.0079)	0.0307 (0.0095)	0.70 [0.0069]
1970–80	0.0240 (0.0091)	−0.0077 (0.0024)	−0.0433 (0.0079)	0.0307 (0.0095)	0.73 [0.0072]
1980–89	0.0163 (0.0061)	−0.0066 (0.0019)	−0.0433 (0.0079)	0.0307 (0.0095)	0.72 [0.0053]
Joint, 8 subperiods	0.0260 (0.0023)	individual coefficients	−0.0427 (0.0079)	0.0300 (0.0097)	— —

Note: The likelihood-ratio statistic for a test of the equality of the income coefficients over the eight subperiods is 17.1, with a p value of 0.017 (from a χ^2 distribution with seven degrees of freedom). The regressions use iterative, weighted least squares and take the form

$$m_{it} = a_t + b_t \cdot \log(y_{i,t-T}) + c_{1t} \cdot \text{Heat}_i + c_2 \cdot \pi_{i,t-T} + c_3 \cdot \pi_{i,t-T}^2 + c_{4t} \cdot \text{Region}_i + c_{5t} \cdot S_{it}$$

where m_{it} is the net flow of migrants into state i between years $t-T$ and t, expressed as a ratio to the population at $t-T$; Heat$_i$ is heating degree days; $\pi_{i,t-T}$ is population density (thousands of persons per square mile); Region$_i$ is a set of dummies for the four main census regions; and S_{it} is the structural variable described in the text. The estimates of a_t, c_{4t}, and c_{5t} are not shown. The data are discussed in the appendix (section 11.12). All samples have 48 observations. Standard errors are in parentheses.

Table 11.4 shows regression results in the form of equation (11.10) for net migration into U.S. states. The results reported are for eight subperiods starting with 1900–20. The regressions include period-specific coefficients for $\log(y_{i,t-T})$ and for the log of heating-degree days. (The hypothesis of stability over the subperiods in the coefficients of log[heat$_i$] is rejected at the 5 percent level, although the estimated coefficients on $\log[y_{i,t-T}]$ change little if only a single coefficient is estimated for the heat variable.) Since the hypothesis that the coefficients for the population-density variables are stable over time is accepted at the 5 percent level, we estimate equation (11.10) with one coefficient for the density and one for the square of the density. The regressions also include period-specific coefficients for regional dummies and structural-share variables. (The estimated coefficients for the regional and structural variables are sometimes significant but play a minor role overall.)

The estimated coefficients for $\log(\text{heat}_i)$ in table 11.4 are all negative and most are significantly different from 0; other things equal, people prefer warmer states. The jointly estimated coefficients for density are −0.043 (0.008) on the linear term and 0.030 (0.010) on the squared term. These point estimates imply that the marginal effect of population density on migration is negative for all states, except for the three with the highest densities: New Jersey, Rhode Island since 1960, and Massachusetts since 1970.

The coefficient on the log of initial per capita income is significantly positive for all subperiods. The joint estimate is 0.0260 (0.0023). The estimated response of migration to the log of initial level is, however, not stable over time: the p value for the rejection of this hypothesis is 0.017. The main sources of instability are the unusually large coefficients on income in the 1950s and 1960s; the coefficients in these two subperiods are 0.0438 (0.0086) and 0.0435 (0.0083), respectively.

Although highly significant, the jointly estimated coefficient on initial income, 0.026, is small in an economic sense. The coefficient means that, other things equal, a 10 percent differential in income per capita raises net in-migration only by enough to raise the area's rate of population growth by 0.26 percent per year. Our previous results suggest that differences in per capita income tend themselves to vanish at a slow speed, roughly 2 percent per year. The combination of the results for migration with those for income convergence suggests that net migration rates would be highly persistent over time. The data confirm this idea: the correlation between the average migration rate for 1900–40 with that for 1940–89 is 0.70.

11.7 Migration Across Japanese Prefectures

Before we analyze migration across Japanese prefectures and implement equation (11.10) for Japan, we should mention that there is a substantial difference between the typical Japanese prefecture and the typical U.S. state in terms of area. The average size of a Japanese prefecture is 6394 square kilometers,[11] roughly half the size of Connecticut. The largest prefecture, Hokkaido, is 83,520 km^2, or roughly the size of South Carolina. The second largest prefecture, Iwate, has an area of 15,277 km^2, a bit larger than Connecticut and a bit smaller than New Jersey. In comparison, the average U.S. state has an area of 163,031 km^2, and the area of the largest state in the continental United States, Texas, is

11. This figure excludes Hokkaido, which is about five times as large as any of the other prefectures. The average size including Hokkaido is 8036 km^2, two-thirds the size of Connecticut.

691,030 km^2. California, with an area of 411,049 km^2, is slightly larger than all of Japan (377,682 km^2).

The contrast in size means that Japanese prefectures resemble metropolitan areas more than states, so that daytime commuting across prefectures can be significant. Urban economists, such as Henderson (1988), think that people like to live in cities for two reasons. First, there are demand or consumption externalities. That is, cities provide amenities, such as theaters and museums, features that can be supplied only if there is a sufficient scale of demand. Second, there are production externalities, which tend to generate high wages in big cities. An offsetting force is that people want to live away from crowded cities because they tend to be associated with crime, less friendly neighborhoods, and (in equilibrium) high land and housing prices (see Roback, 1982). Thus the decision to migrate to a city involves a trade-off. This trade-off can be avoided if people live in a suburb and commute to the central city. People are especially willing to pay high commuting costs when densities in the central city are extremely high.

To deal with these issues empirically, we would like to have a measure of the density of the neighboring prefectures. Conceptually, we could construct such a measure by weighting the neighbors' densities by their distance in some way. In practice, however, we observe that there are two main areas in Japan that have an abnormally high population density, Tokyo and Osaka. In 1990, Tokyo's density was 5470 people/km^2 and Osaka's was 4674 people/km^2, compared to an average for the other prefectures of 624 people/km^2.[12] Hence, the problems that we have mentioned are likely to arise in these two regions only. We can confirm this idea by considering the ratio of daytime to nighttime population, a measure of the extent of commuting.[13] A ratio smaller than one indicates that there are people who live in that prefecture but work in another, and a ratio larger than one indicates the opposite. The ratio is close to one for all prefectures except for the ones around Tokyo and Osaka: Tokyo's ratio is 1.184 and Osaka's is 1.053. The ratios for the Tokyo region are 0.872 for Saitama, 0.876 for Chiba, and 0.910 for Kanagawa. For the Osaka region, the ratios are 0.955 for Hyogo, 0.871 for Nara, and 0.986 for Wakayama.[14]

We constructed a variable called *neighbor's density* by assigning the prefectures of the Tokyo area (Tokyo and its immediate neighbors, Saitama, Chiba, and Kanagawa) and the Osaka area (Osaka and its immediate neighbors, Hyogo, Nara, and Wakayama) the average density of their immediate neighbors. For other prefectures, the variable equals its

12. In comparison, the U.S. state with the largest density in 1990 was New Jersey with 390 people/km^2.

13. The source of these data is the Statistics Bureau, Management and Coordination Agency.

14. There seems to be some commuting across prefectures in the areas surrounding Kyoto and Aichi, but the magnitudes are much smaller: Aichi's ratio is 1.016 (and its neighboring prefecture, Gifu, has a ratio of 0.977) and Kyoto's is 1.011.

own population density. We expect to find a positive relation between migration and this neighbor variable and a negative relation between migration and own density. This relation would indicate that people do not like to live in dense areas (they have to pay the congestion costs) but like to be close to these areas (so that they get the benefits of a big city).

The functional form that we estimate is

$$m_{it} = a + b \cdot \log(y_{i,t-T}) + c_1\theta_i + c_2\pi_{i,t-T} + c_3\pi^{ne}_{i,t-T} + v_{it} \tag{11.11}$$

where v_{it} is an error term, and $\pi^{ne}_{i,t-T}$ is the population density of the surrounding prefectures. To calculate the amenity (weather) variable, we squared the difference between the maximum and average temperatures, added the square of the difference between the minimum and average temperatures, and then took the square root. Hence, this variable measures extreme temperature. A variable similar to the one used for the United States (heating degree days) was unavailable. We experimented with other weather variables, such as maximum and minimum temperatures and average snowfall over the year. These alternative variables did not fit as well.

Figure 11.11 shows the relation between the average annual migration rate for 1955–87 and the log of income per capita in 1955. The clear positive association (simple correlation of 0.58) suggests that net migration reacts positively to income differentials. An interesting point is that the three outliers at the top of the figure are Chiba, Saitama, and Kanagawa, the prefectures surrounding Tokyo.

Table 11.5 shows the results of estimating migration equations of the form of equation (11.10). The first row refers to the average migration rate for the whole period, 1955–90. The coefficient on the log of initial income per capita is 0.0126 (0.0061). As expected, net migration is negatively associated with own density (−0.0049 [0.0022]) and positively associated with neighbor's density (0.0190 [0.0034]). The extreme temperature variable is insignificant.

The next seven rows in table 11.5 show results for the 5-year subperiods beginning with 1955–60. The estimated coefficient on initial income is significantly positive for all subperiods, except for 1975–80, for which the coefficient is positive, but insignificant. The joint estimate is 0.0188 (0.0019), which implies that, other things equal, a 10 percent increase in a prefecture's per capita income raises net in-migration by enough to raise that prefecture's rate of population growth by 0.19 percentage points per year. This result is close to that found for the U.S. states. A test of the stability of the income coefficients over time is rejected with a p value of 0.006.

The own-density variable is significantly negative, except for the first subperiod, and the neighbors' density variable is positive for all subperiods (significantly so for four of the seven subperiods). The extreme weather variable is negative, but only marginally significant.

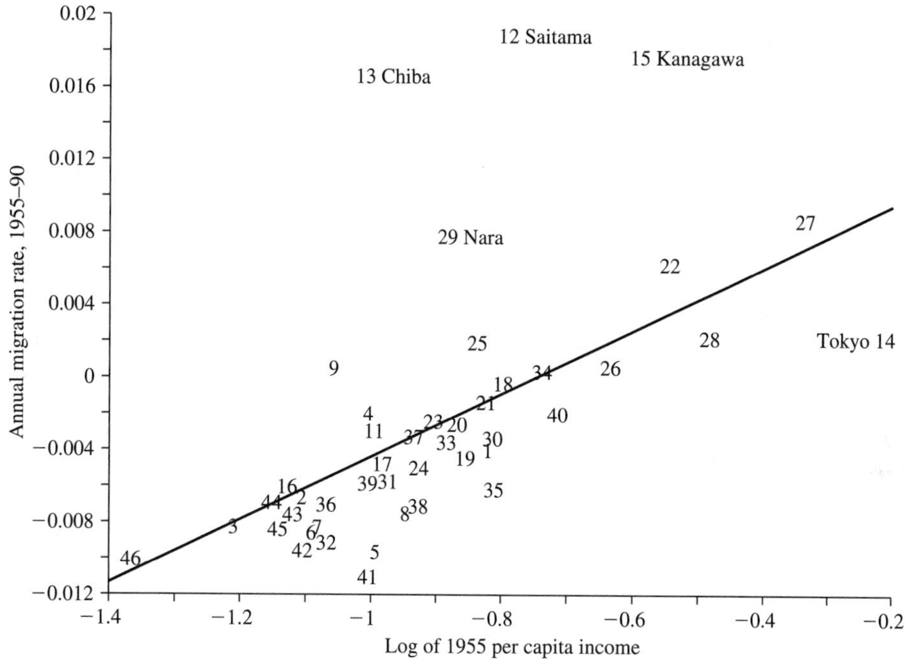

Figure 11.11
Migration and initial prefectural income, 1955–90. The average net migration rate for 47 Japanese prefectures from 1955 to 1990, shown on the vertical axis, is positively related to the log of 1955 per capita income, shown on the horizontal axis. The three prefectures surrounding Tokyo—Chiba, Saitama, and Kanagawa—had substantially higher net migration rates than the values predicted by their initial levels of income.

Thus weather does not seem to play an important role in the process of internal migration in Japan.

To summarize, some main findings are that the rate of net in-migration to a prefecture is negatively related to own density and positively related to the density of neighbors. Holding other things constant, migration is positively associated with initial per capita income. A notable result is the similarity of the coefficients on income for the United States and Japan, 0.026 from the joint estimation for the U.S. states and 0.019 from the joint estimation for Japanese prefectures.

Recall that differences in per capita income tend to dissipate at a slow rate, something like 2.5 to 3 percent per year for the Japanese prefectures. Putting this result together with those for migration, the implication is that net migration rates would be highly persistent over time. The data confirm this idea: the correlation between the average migration rate for 1955–70 with that for 1970–90 is 0.60.

Table 11.5
Regressions for Net Migration into Japanese Prefectures, 1955–90

Period	Log of Per Capita Income	Extreme Temperature	Own Population Density	Neighbors' Population Density	$R^2[\hat{\sigma}]$
1955–90	0.0126	0.00014	−0.0049	0.0190	0.62
	(0.0061)	(0.00062)	(0.0022)	(0.0034)	[0.0061]
1955–60	0.0216	−0.00014	0.0060	0.0025	0.85
	(0.0036)	(0.00012)	(0.0013)	(0.0019)	[0.0038]
1960–65	0.0317	−0.00014	−0.0019	0.0147	0.74
	(0.0058)	(0.00012)	(0.0020)	(0.0031)	[0.0071]
1965–70	0.0344	−0.00014	−0.0065	0.0142	0.71
	(0.0070)	(0.00012)	(0.0017)	(0.0025)	[0.0066]
1970–75	0.0194	−0.00014	−0.0064	0.0114	0.53
	(0.0060)	(0.00012)	(0.0015)	(0.0023)	[0.0070]
1975–80	0.0060	−0.00014	−0.0037	0.0052	0.32
	(0.0067)	(0.00012)	(0.0011)	(0.0014)	[0.0043]
1980–85	0.0101	−0.00014	−0.0023	0.0037	0.39
	(0.0044)	(0.00012)	(0.0006)	(0.0086)	[0.0030]
1985–90	0.0148	−0.00014	−0.0026	0.0046	0.56
	(0.0040)	(0.00012)	(0.0006)	(0.0084)	[0.0029]
Joint, 7	0.0188	−0.00040	individual	individual	—
subperiods	(0.0019)	(0.00015)	coefficients	coefficients	—

Note: The likelihood-ratio statistic for the hypothesis that the income coefficients are the same is 18.0, with a p value of 0.006. The regressions use iterative, weighted least squares to estimate equations of the form

$$m_{it} = a_t + b \cdot \log(y_{i,t-T}) + c_1 \cdot \text{Temp}_i + c_{2t} \cdot \pi_{i,t-T} + c_{3t} \cdot \pi^{ne}_{i,t-T} + c_{4t} \cdot \text{District}_i + c_{5t} \cdot S_{it}$$

where m_{it} is the net flow of migrants into prefecture i between years $t - T$ and t, expressed as a ratio to the population at time $t - T$; Temp_i is a measure of extreme temperature, calculated as deviations of maximum and minimum temperatures from the average temperature; $\pi_{i,t-T}$ is population density (thousands of persons per square kilometer); $\pi^{ne}_{i,t-T}$ is the population density of the neighboring prefectures (see the text); District_i is a set of dummy variables for the district; and S_{it} is the structural variable described in the text. All samples have 47 observations. (See the note to table 11.4 for additional information.)

11.8 Migration Across European Regions

We now estimate the sensitivity of the net migration rate to income across the regions of the five large European countries: Germany, the United Kingdom, Italy, France, and Spain. The dependent variable is the average net migration rate for each of the four decades starting in 1950. We are missing observations for the United Kingdom in the 1950s and 1980s and for France in the 1980s.

We estimate a system of regressions similar to those for the United States and Japan. The explanatory variables are the logarithm of per capita GDP or income at the beginning of the decade, population density at the beginning of the decade, sectoral variables (shares in employment or GDP of agriculture and industry at the start of each decade), a temperature variable, and country dummies. We estimate a system of equations for the five countries, with the density and temperature variables restricted to have the same coefficients over time and across countries but with the coefficients of the other variables allowed to vary over time and across countries.

Table 11.6 reports the estimated coefficients on the log of initial per capita GDP or income. The first column contains the estimates for the 1950s, the second for the 1960s, and so on. The last column restricts the coefficients to be the same over the decades. The first row is for Germany, the second for the United Kingdom, the third for Italy, the fourth for France, and the fifth for Spain. The last row restricts the coefficients to be the same for the five countries.

Table 11.6
Regressions for Net Migration into European Regions, 1950–90, Coefficients on the Log of Per Capita GDP

	1950s	1960s	1970s	1980s	Total
Germany	0.0311 (0.0121)	0.0074 (0.0088)	0.0040 (0.0038)	0.0024 (0.0086)	0.0076 (0.0014)
United Kingdom	—	0.0049 (0.0011)	−0.0069 (0.0013)	—	−0.0041 (0.0023)
Italy	0.0182 (0.0041)	0.0208 (0.0027)	0.0089 (0.0020)	0.0309 (0.0106)	0.0117 (0.0018)
France	0.0090 (0.0056)	−0.0008 (0.0095)	0.0097 (0.0041)	—	0.0100 (0.0036)
Spain	0.0126 (0.0068)	0.0135 (0.0112)	0.0117 (0.0063)	0.0031 (0.0070)	0.0034 (0.0021)
Overall	0.0107 (0.0038)	0.0072 (0.0040)	0.0046 (0.0024)	0.0141 (0.0070)	0.0064 (0.0021)

Note: The regressions take the form

$$m_{ijt} = a_{jt} + b_{jt} \cdot \log(y_{ij,t-T}) + c_1 \cdot \text{Temp}_{ij} + c_2 \cdot \pi_{ij,t-T} + c_3 \cdot (\text{Country dummy}) + c_{4jt} \cdot \text{AG}_{ij,t-T} + c_{5jt} \cdot \text{IN}_{ij,t-T}$$

where m_{ijt} is the net flow of migrants into region i of country j between years $t-T$ and t, expressed as a ratio to the population at time $t-T$; Temp_{ij} is the average maximum temperature; $\pi_{ij,t-T}$ is population density (thousands of persons per square kilometer); $\text{AG}_{ij,t-T}$ is the share of employment or GDP (for the 1980s) in agriculture; and $\text{IN}_{ij,t-T}$ is the corresponding share in industry. All estimation is by the iterative, seemingly unrelated procedure. The table reports only the estimates of the coefficients b_{jt}. The numbers in the first five rows and first four columns apply when each country has a different coefficient for each period. The last column restricts the coefficients to be the same over time for each country. The last row restricts the coefficients to be the same across countries for each decade. The number in the intersection of the last row and column applies when all countries and time periods have a single coefficient.

In contrast with the results for the United States and Japan, the coefficients on the log of per capita GDP or income are not precisely estimated for the European countries. For Germany, the estimated coefficient for the 1950s is positive and significant, 0.031 (0.012), whereas those for the other three decades are insignificant. The estimated income coefficients for Italy are significantly positive, but many of those for the United Kingdom, France, and Spain are insignificant.

If we restrict the coefficients to be the same over time but allow them to vary across countries, the estimated values are 0.0076 (0.0014) for Germany, −0.0041 (0.0023) for the United Kingdom, 0.0117 (0.0018) for Italy, 0.0100 (0.0036) for France, and 0.0034 (0.0021) for Spain. If we restrict the coefficients to be the same across countries but allow them to vary over time, the estimated values are 0.0107 (0.0038) for the 1950s, 0.0072 (0.0040) for the 1960s, 0.0046 (0.0024) for the 1970s, and 0.0141 (0.0070) for the 1980s. Finally, if we restrict the coefficients to be the same across countries *and* over time, we get the estimate 0.0064 (0.0021). Although this estimate is significantly positive, the size of the coefficient is much smaller than the comparable values for the United States (0.026) and Japan (0.019). The main finding, therefore, is that the migration rate for European regions is positively related to per capita GDP or income, but the magnitude of the relation is weak, and the coefficients cannot be estimated with great precision.

11.9 Migration and Convergence

We found in chapter 9 that the migration of workers with low human capital from poor to rich economies tended to speed up the convergence of per capita income and product. The convergence coefficients estimated in growth regressions would include this effect from migration. In this section we attempt to estimate the effect of migration on convergence by including the net migration rate as an explanatory variable in the growth regressions. If migration is an important source of convergence—and if we can treat the migration rate as exogenous with respect to the error term in the growth equation—the estimated convergence coefficient, β, should become smaller when migration is held constant.

We enter the contemporaneous net migration rate in growth regressions in table 11.7. The first row reports the estimated speed of convergence, β, for the U.S. states. The sample period, 1920–90, is divided into seven ten-year subperiods. The regression includes period-specific coefficients for constant terms, dummies for the four major census regions, and the structural variable discussed before. The coefficient on the log of initial per capita income is constrained to be the same for each subperiod. This setup parallels the joint estimation shown in table 11.1, column 3, except for the elimination of the two early subperiods.

Column 1 of the table reports the estimate of β when the migration rate is not included in

Table 11.7
Migration and Convergence

	(1) Migration Excluded	(2) Migration Included (OLS)		(3) Migration Included (IV)	
	β	β	Migration	β	Migration
United States, 1920–90	0.0196 (0.0025)	0.0231 (0.0028)	0.0931 (0.0305)	0.0174 (0.0033)	−0.006 (0.048)
Japan, 1955–90	0.0312 (0.0040)	0.0340 (0.0044)	0.0907 (0.0041)	0.0311 (0.0042)	−0.108 (0.112)
Germany, 1950–90	0.0243 (0.0088)	0.0240 (0.0091)	−0.014 (0.235)	0.0181 (0.0093)	−0.542 (0.429)
United Kingdom, 1960–80[a]	0.0176 (0.0132)	0.0220 (0.0203)	0.116 (0.395)	0.0261 (0.0267)	0.222 (0.570)
Italy, 1950–90	0.0206 (0.0058)	0.0244 (0.0070)	0.166 (0.156)	0.0180 (0.0098)	−0.121 (0.370)
France, 1950–80[b]	0.0224 (0.0265)	0.0172 (0.0063)	−0.038 (0.126)	0.0177 (0.0065)	−0.084 (0.178)
Spain, 1950–90	0.0245 (0.0102)	0.0295 (0.0096)	−0.124 (0.102)	0.0268 (0.0119)	−0.068 (0.203)

Note: The regressions for the growth rates of per capita income or GDP are analogous to the joint estimations shown in table 11.1, column 3, for the U.S. states; table 11.2, column 3, for the Japanese prefectures; and table 11.3, column 2, for the European regions (except that the five large European countries are treated separately here). The β coefficients refer to the log of initial per capita income or GDP, and the migration coefficients refer to the net migration rate. In column 1 the migration rate is not included as a regressor. In column 2 the migration rate is added, and the estimation is by OLS. In column 3 instrumental estimation is used. The instruments are the regressors included in the migration equations, as reported in table 11.4 for the United States, table 11.5 for Japan, and table 11.6 for Europe.
[a]Two subperiods.
[b]Three subperiods.

the regressions. The speed of convergence is 0.0196 (0.0025), close to the familiar 2 percent per year. Column 2 adds the net migration rate as a regressor. (The coefficient on this variable is constrained to be the same for each subperiod.) The estimated coefficient on the migration rate is positive and significant, 0.093 (0.030), and the estimate of β, 0.0231 (0.0028), is actually somewhat higher than that shown in column 1. Thus, contrary to expectations, the estimate of β does not diminish when the net migration rate is held constant.

The results are likely influenced by the endogeneity of the net migration rate. Specifically, states with more favorable growth prospects (owing to factors not held constant by the included explanatory variables) are likely to have higher per capita growth rates *and* higher net migration rates. We attempt to isolate exogenous shifts in migration by using as instruments the explanatory variables used to explain the net migration rate in table 11.4. These variables include population density and the log of heating degree days. (The assumption is that these determinants of migration do not enter directly into the growth equation.) The results, contained in column 3 of table 11.7, show an insignificant coefficient on the migration rate, −0.006 (0.048), and an estimated β coefficient, 0.0174 (0.0033), that is slightly lower than that in column 1. These results suggest that migration does not account for a large part of β convergence for the U.S. states.

The second row of table 11.7 applies the same procedure to Japan. The first column reports the joint estimate of β over seven five-year periods when the migration rate is excluded as a regressor. The estimate of β, 0.0312 (0.0040), is the same as that in column 3 of table 11.2. When the migration rate is added in column 2 of table 11.7, the estimated coefficient on migration is positive and similar to that found for the United States, 0.0907 (0.0041), and the estimate of β increases to 0.0340 (0.0044). In column 3, which includes instruments for migration, the estimated coefficient on migration is insignificant, −0.11 (0.11), and the estimate of β, 0.0311 (0.0042), is essentially the same as that in column 1. Hence, as for the U.S. states, migration does not appear to be a major element in β convergence for the Japanese prefectures.

The last five rows of table 11.7 apply an analogous procedure to the five large European countries. The main findings are similar to those for the United States and Japan in that the estimated β coefficients do not change a great deal when migration rates are held constant. One surprising result is that the net migration rates are insignificant in the OLS regressions for the European regions, whereas the usual endogeneity story suggests positive coefficients. It may be that the regional net migration rates are not well measured for the European countries, a possibility that would also account for the difficulties in the estimated migration equations in these cases.

A second prediction from the migration theory in chapter 9 is that economies with higher sensitivity of net migration to per capita income will have higher convergence coefficients, β. To check this possibility, we plot in figure 11.12 the estimated β coefficients against the estimated coefficients of the log of per capita GDP or income from the migration equations. The figure has seven data points, corresponding to the United States, Japan, Germany, the United Kingdom, Italy, France, and Spain. The figure shows a weak positive relation between the two coefficients; the correlation is 0.27.[15] The imprecision with which the coefficients in the migration equations are estimated for the European countries suggests that this relation should be interpreted with caution. See Braun (1993) for further discussion of this approach.

15. The β coefficients for France and the United Kingdom are those estimated over the same subperiods for which the migration data are available. The β coefficient estimated over the full sample is lower for France and higher for the United Kingdom. If we use these alternative estimates of β, the correlation with the coefficient from the migration equations is slightly higher, 0.32.

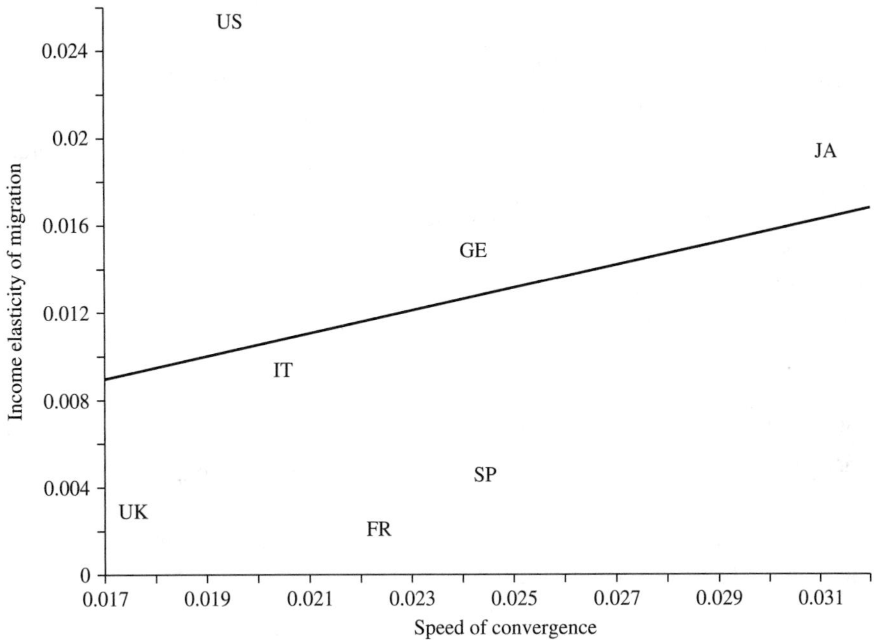

Figure 11.12
Income Coefficient of Migration and Speed of Convergence. The vertical axis shows the estimated coefficient on the log of per capita income or GDP from migration regressions. The horizontal axis has the estimated β convergence coefficient from growth regressions. The seven data points—for the United States, Japan, Germany, the United Kingdom, Italy, France, and Spain—exhibit a positive relation, as predicted by the theory of migration and growth.

11.10 β Convergence in Panel Data with Fixed Effects

Following Islam (1995), a number of researchers have attempted to estimate the speed of convergence using panel data sets and variants of fixed-effects estimation. Caselli, Esquivel, and Laffort (1996), for example, use panel data for a cross section of countries, while Canova and Marcet (1995) use regional data. One claimed advantage of panel data over cross sections is that one does not need to hold constant the steady state because it can be implicitly estimated using fixed effects. The main result is that estimates of the speed of convergence from panel data with fixed effects tend to be much larger than the 2 percent-per-year number estimated from cross sections or panels without fixed effects. Speeds of convergence in the range of 12 to 20 percent per year are not uncommon in this literature.

One potential problem with the fixed-effects approach is that, in order to work, one needs to include many time-series observations. This procedure can be carried out only by shortening the time periods within which the growth rate is computed. In other words, the dependent variable tends to be the yearly growth rate or the growth rate over two to five years. The problem with such short time spans is that the growth rates tend to capture short-term adjustments around the trend rather than long-term convergence. In particular, the existence of business cycles tends to bias upward the estimates of speeds of convergence. In this context, Shioji (1997) provides evidence that, once one corrects for the measurement error introduced by business cycles, the estimated speed of convergence from panels with fixed effects is still close to 2 percent per year.

11.11 Conclusions

We studied the behavior of the U.S. states since 1880, the prefectures of Japan since 1930, and the regions of eight European countries since 1950. The results indicate that absolute β convergence is the norm for these regional economies. That is, poor regions of these countries tend to grow faster per capita than rich ones. The convergence is absolute because it applies when no explanatory variables other than the initial level of per capita product or income are held constant.

We can interpret the results as consistent with the neoclassical growth model described in chapters 1 and 2 if regions within a country have roughly similar tastes, technologies, and political institutions. This relative homogeneity generates similar steady-state positions. The observed convergence effect is, however, also consistent with the models of technological diffusion described in chapter 8.

One surprising result is the similarity of the speed of β convergence across data sets. The estimates of β are around 2–3 percent per year in the various contexts. This slow speed of convergence implies that it takes 25–35 years to eliminate one-half of an initial gap in per capita incomes. This behavior deviates from the quantitative predictions of the neoclassical growth model if the capital share is close to one-third. The empirical evidence is, however, consistent with the theory if the capital share is around three-quarters.

The analysis of migration indicates that the rate of net migration tends to respond positively to the initial level of per capita product or income, once a set of other explanatory variables is held constant. This relation is clear for the U.S. states and the Japanese prefectures but is weaker for the regions of five large European countries. We also check whether the presence of β convergence in the regional data can be explained by the behavior of net migration. The evidence here is not definitive but suggests that migration plays only a minor role in the convergence story.

11.12 Appendix on Regional Data Sets

We describe data for the U.S. states, regions of eight European countries (Germany, the United Kingdom, Italy, France, the Netherlands, Belgium, Denmark, and Spain), and prefectures of Japan. Data for regions of other countries, such as Argentina, Brazil, China, India, Mexico, and the USSR, are also available. Additional information is available by city and county; see, for example, Ades and Glaeser (1995).

11.12.1 Data for U.S. States

Table 11.8 shows a sampling of the data for the U.S. states (shown on the U.S. map in figure 11.13). Figures on nominal personal income and nominal per capita personal income are available by state since 1929 from the U.S. Commerce Department (Bureau of Economic Analysis, 2002; updates appear in issues of *U.S. Survey of Current Business*). The concept of personal income used in these regional accounts corresponds to that employed in the national accounts. The numbers are reported annually, but values prior to 1965 are based on interpolations of estimates constructed at approximately five-year intervals. Data are reported with and without transfer payments. Figures on gross state product are available annually since 1963 (from issues of *U.S. Survey of Current Business*).

Reliable data on price levels are unavailable by state, although some information exists for cities. We have computed real income by dividing the nominal figures on personal income by the national values of the consumer price index (1982–84 = 1.0). (We used the figures from *Citibase* for all items except shelter since 1947. Before 1947, we used the overall index from U.S. Department of Commerce, 1975, series E135.) As long as the same index is used at each date for each state, the particular index chosen does not affect the relative levels and growth rates across the states.

Earlier income figures are reported by Easterlin (1960a, 1960b) for 1920 (48 states), 1900 (48 states or territories), 1880 (47 states or territories, with Oklahoma excluded), and 1840 (29 states or territories). These data are exclusive of transfer payments, and the figures for 1840 do not cover all components of personal income. Estimates of the consumer price index for all items (U.S. Department of Commerce, 1975, series E135) are used to deflate these earlier values.

For the census years since 1930, labor earnings (including those from self-employment) can be broken down into nine sectors: agriculture; mining; construction; total manufacturing; transportation and public utilities; wholesale and retail trade; finance, insurance, and real estate; services; and government and government enterprises. For periods before 1930, information is available on the fraction of income originating in agriculture.

Table 11.8
Data for U.S. States

State		Real Per Capita Income, 1900 ($1000s, 1982–84 base)	Real Per Capita Income, 2000 ($1000s, 1982–84 base)	Growth Rate of Real Per Capita Income	Population, 1900 (millions)	Population, 1990 (millions)	Growth Rate of Population, 1900–90	Net Migrants, 1900–89 (millions)
AL	Alabama	1.00	12.95	0.0256	1.829	4.046	0.0088	−1.32
AZ	Arizona	3.69	13.79	0.0132	0.093	3.681	0.0409	2.03
AR	Arkansas	1.03	12.11	0.0246	1.312	2.353	0.0065	−1.14
CA	California	4.20	17.78	0.0144	1.403	29.956	0.0340	16.59
CO	Colorado	3.66	17.90	0.0159	0.529	3.302	0.0203	1.11
CT	Connecticut	3.19	22.55	0.0196	0.908	3.290	0.0143	0.76
DE	Delaware	2.52	17.15	0.0192	0.185	0.669	0.0143	0.18
FL	Florida	1.29	15.36	0.0248	0.529	13.044	0.0356	9.37
GA	Georgia	0.98	15.33	0.0275	2.222	6.504	0.0120	−0.28
ID	Idaho	2.54	13.04	0.0164	0.154	1.011	0.0209	0.04
IL	Illinois	2.99	17.57	0.0177	4.822	11.443	0.0096	−0.17
IN	Indiana	2.09	14.81	0.0196	2.516	5.554	0.0088	−0.30
IA	Iowa	2.33	14.55	0.0183	2.232	2.780	0.0024	−1.41
KS	Kansas	2.15	15.12	0.0195	1.470	2.480	0.0058	−0.65
KY	Kentucky	1.38	13.27	0.0226	2.147	3.690	0.0060	−1.54
LA	Louisiana	1.47	12.71	0.0216	1.382	4.211	0.0124	−0.52
ME	Maine	2.16	14.02	0.0187	0.694	1.231	0.0064	−0.11
MD	Maryland	2.34	18.55	0.0207	1.188	4.802	0.0155	1.26
MA	Massachusetts	3.49	20.81	0.0179	2.850	6.020	0.0083	0.14
MI	Michigan	2.13	16.04	0.0202	2.421	9.314	0.0150	0.62
MN	Minnesota	2.38	17.61	0.0200	1.737	4.390	0.0103	−0.34
MS	Mississippi	0.97	11.51	0.0247	1.551	2.574	0.0056	−1.62
MO	Missouri	2.16	15.00	0.0194	3.107	5.127	0.0056	−0.83
MT	Montana	4.77	12.44	0.0096	0.226	0.799	0.0140	−0.07
NE	Nebraska	2.43	15.26	0.0184	1.066	1.580	0.0044	−0.71
NV	Nevada	4.54	16.31	0.0128	0.035	1.224	0.0395	0.79

NH	New Hampshire	2.46	18.23	0.0200	0.412	1.111	0.0110	0.31
NJ	New Jersey	3.19	20.48	0.0186	1.884	7.735	0.0157	2.20
NM	New Mexico	1.70	12.08	0.0196	0.180	1.520	0.0237	0.16
NY	New York	3.71	19.04	0.0164	7.269	18.002	0.0101	1.13
NC	North Carolina	0.82	14.81	0.0289	1.894	6.653	0.0140	−0.30
ND	North Dakota	2.40	13.67	0.0174	0.312	0.637	0.0079	−0.49
OH	Ohio	2.55	15.40	0.0180	4.158	10.859	0.0107	0.14
OK	Oklahoma	1.31	13.01	0.0230	0.670	3.146	0.0172	−0.19
OR	Oregon	2.85	15.26	0.0168	0.395	2.861	0.0220	1.27
PA	Pennsylvania	2.88	16.30	0.0173	6.302	11.893	0.0071	−1.99
RI	Rhode Island	3.36	16.09	0.0157	0.429	1.005	0.0095	0.05
SC	South Carolina	0.86	13.22	0.0273	1.340	3.498	0.0107	−0.75
SD	South Dakota	2.11	14.34	0.0192	0.381	0.696	0.0067	−0.43
TN	Tennessee	1.16	14.28	0.0251	2.021	4.887	0.0098	−0.46
TX	Texas	1.58	15.30	0.0227	3.049	17.055	0.0191	3.33
UT	Utah	2.11	12.89	0.0181	0.272	1.729	0.0206	0.06
VT	Vermont	2.19	14.85	0.0191	0.344	0.565	0.0055	−0.05
VA	Virginia	1.27	17.14	0.0260	1.854	6.213	0.0134	0.61
WA	Washington	3.40	17.18	0.0162	0.496	4.909	0.0255	2.16
WV	West Virginia	1.35	12.01	0.0219	0.959	1.790	0.0069	−1.10
WI	Wisconsin	2.05	15.49	0.0202	2.058	4.906	0.0097	−0.33
WY	Wyoming	3.57	15.14	0.0144	0.089	0.452	0.0181	0.03

Notes: The two-letter abbreviation (zip code) for each of the 48 states is shown before the state name.
The U.S. Census regional classifications are as follows:
Northeast: ME, NH, VT, MA, RI, CT, NY, NJ, PA.
South: DE, MD, VA, WV, NC, SC, GA, FL, KY, TN, AL, MS, AR, LA, OK, TX.
Midwest: MN, IA, MO, ND, SD, NE, KS, OH, IN, IL, MI, WI.
West: MT, ID, WY, CO, NM, AZ, UT, NV, WA, OR, CA.

Figure 11.13
Map of the U.S. states.

Population density is the ratio of population to total area (land plus water); the data on area are in U.S. Department of Commerce, Bureau of the Census (1990). Net migration flows can be computed from census figures by taking the change in population over a period, subtracting the number of births, and adding the number of deaths.

11.12.2 Data for European Regions

Table 11.9 has a sampling of the data for regions of European countries (shown on the map in figure 11.14). We have data on GDP, population, and related variables for regions of eight European countries—Germany (11 regions), the United Kingdom (11), Italy (20), France (21), the Netherlands (4), Belgium (3), Denmark (3), and Spain (17).

For the countries other than Spain, the data on GDP and population for 1950, 1960, and 1970 are from Molle, Van Holst, and Smits (1980). Figures for 1966 (missing France and Denmark), 1970 (missing Denmark), 1974, 1980, 1985, and 1990 (missing Denmark) are from *Eurostat*. For Spain, data on regional income and GDP are provided for various years from 1955 to 1987 by the Banco de Bilbao (various issues). The figures on population are from INE, *Anuario Estatistico de España* (various issues). The data applied originally to 50 provinces and have been aggregated to 17 regions.

Table 11.9
Data for European Regions

Region	Real Per Capita GDP, 1950 Proportionate Deviation from Country Mean[a]	Real Per Capita GDP, 1990 Proportionate Deviation from Country Mean[b]	Growth Rate of Real Per Capita GDP Deviation from Country Mean[c]	Population, 1950[d] (millions)	Population, 1990[e] (millions)	Growth Rate of Population[f]	Net Migrants, Various Periods[g] (millions)
Germany							
1. Schleswig-Holstein	−0.36	−0.20	0.0039	2.595	2.615	0.0002	0.31
2. Hamburg	0.54	0.42	−0.0029	1.606	1.641	0.0005	0.13
3. Niedersachsen	−0.25	−0.18	0.0019	6.797	7.342	0.0019	0.21
4. Bremen	0.34	0.20	−0.0034	0.559	0.679	0.0049	0.10
5. Nordrhein Westfalia	0.12	−0.08	−0.0049	13.207	17.248	0.0067	2.05
6. Hessen	−0.06	0.12	0.0044	4.324	5.718	0.0070	1.19
7. Rheinland-Pfalz	−0.25	−0.15	0.0023	3.005	3.735	0.0054	0.25
8. Saarland	0.17	−0.10	−0.0067	0.955	1.071	0.0029	0.00
9. Baden-Württemberg	−0.03	0.02	0.0014	6.430	9.729	0.0104	1.78
10. Bayern	−0.19	−0.01	0.0045	9.185	11.337	0.0053	1.52
11. Berlin (West)	−0.02	−0.04	−0.0005	2.147	2.118	−0.0003	0.26
United Kingdom							
12. North	−0.07	−0.07	−0.0008	3.133	3.075	−0.0005	−0.24
13. Yorkshire-Humberside	0.11	−0.01	−0.0039	4.494	4.952	0.0024	−0.16
14. East Midlands	−0.02	0.04	0.0005	2.909	4.019	0.0081	0.21
15. East Anglia	−0.04	0.10	0.0027	1.381	2.059	0.0100	0.34
16. South-East	0.30	0.27	−0.0016	15.174	17.458	0.0035	−0.45
17. South-West	−0.22	0.03	0.0056	3.238	4.667	0.0091	0.66
18. North-West	0.08	−0.02	−0.0034	6.424	6.389	−0.0001	−0.48
19. West Midlands	0.14	−0.01	−0.0045	4.422	5.219	0.0041	−0.20
20. Wales	−0.24	−0.10	0.0025	2.584	2.881	0.0027	0.08
21. Scotland	−0.03	0.00	−0.0002	5.096	5.102	0.0000	−0.45
22. Northern Ireland	−0.35	−0.22	0.0031	1.371	1.589	0.0037	−0.20
Italy							
23. Piemonte	0.47	0.23	−0.0066	3.504	4.357	0.0054	0.87
24. Valle d'Aosta	0.53	0.31	−0.0057	0.095	0.116	0.0050	0.02
25. Liguria	0.61	0.18	−0.0106	1.555	1.723	0.0026	0.30
26. Lombardia	0.52	0.34	−0.0045	6.433	8.928	0.0082	1.25

Table continued

Table 11.9
(Continued)

Region	Real Per Capita GDP, 1950 Proportionate Deviation from Country Mean[a]	Real Per Capita GDP, 1990 Proportionate Deviation from Country Mean[b]	Growth Rate of Real Per Capita GDP Deviation from Country Mean[c]	Population, 1950[d] (millions)	Population, 1990[e] (millions)	Growth Rate of Population[f]	Net Migrants, Various Periods[g] (millions)
27. Trentino–Alto Adige	0.19	0.22	0.0007	0.735	0.889	0.0048	−0.03
28. Veneto	−0.01	0.19	0.0050	3.841	4.392	0.0034	−0.35
29. Fruili-Venezia-Giulia	0.12	0.24	0.0030	1.200	1.202	0.0000	−0.58
30. Emilia-Romagna	0.17	0.28	0.0027	3.509	3.925	0.0028	0.19
31. Marche	−0.06	0.08	0.0036	1.352	1.433	0.0015	−0.13
32. Toscana	0.16	0.13	−0.0006	3.152	3.562	0.0031	0.29
33. Umbria	−0.04	0.03	0.0016	0.806	0.822	0.0005	−0.07
34. Lazio	0.21	0.17	−0.0008	3.322	5.181	0.0111	0.62
35. Campania	−0.29	−0.33	−0.0011	4.276	5.831	0.0078	−0.88
36. Abruzzi	−0.32	−0.10	0.0054	1.238	1.269	0.0006	−0.27
37. Molise	−0.49	−0.20	0.0071	0.398	0.336	−0.0042	−0.14
38. Puglia	−0.33	−0.26	0.0017	3.181	4.076	0.0062	−0.77
39. Basilicata	−0.47	−0.41	0.0016	0.617	0.624	0.0003	−0.25
40. Calabria	−0.48	−0.46	0.0005	1.987	2.153	0.0020	−0.79
41. Sicilia	−0.32	−0.37	−0.0012	4.422	5.185	0.0040	−1.08
42. Sardegna	−0.16	−0.27	−0.0027	1.259	1.661	0.0069	−0.23
France							
43. Region Parisienne	0.61	0.50	−0.0026	7.009	10.227	0.0094	1.02
44. Champagne-Ardenne	0.05	0.11	0.0015	1.110	1.341	0.0047	−0.06
45. Picarde	0.05	−0.05	−0.0026	1.355	1.804	0.0072	0.04
46. Haute Normandie	0.13	0.05	−0.0020	1.232	1.731	0.0085	0.03
47. Centre	−0.18	0.02	0.0049	1.758	2.363	0.0074	0.30
48. Basse Normandie	−0.14	−0.04	0.0024	1.145	1.385	0.0048	−0.10
49. Bourgogne	−0.11	−0.01	0.0025	1.376	1.602	0.0038	0.10
50. Nord–Pas de Calais	0.17	−0.09	−0.0067	3.309	3.945	0.0044	−0.39
51. Lorraine	0.24	−0.03	−0.0067	1.874	2.293	0.0050	−0.22
52. Alsace	0.19	0.14	−0.0014	1.196	1.619	0.0075	0.15
53. Franche-Comte	0.05	0.03	−0.0005	0.841	1.092	0.0065	0.02
54. Pays de la Loire	−0.11	−0.03	0.0020	2.293	3.048	0.0071	0.03

55.	Bretagne	−0.20	−0.08	0.0030	2.358	2.784	0.0042	0.03
56.	Poitou-Charente	−0.25	−0.11	0.0035	1.379	1.588	0.0035	−0.03
57.	Aquitaine	−0.15	0.00	0.0036	2.206	2.787	0.0058	0.35
58.	Midi-Pyrénées	−0.27	−0.10	0.0043	1.982	2.423	0.0050	0.29
59.	Limousin	−0.05	−0.14	−0.0023	0.760	0.719	−0.0014	0.04
60.	Rhône-Alpes	0.12	0.09	−0.0009	3.580	5.338	0.0100	0.77
61.	Auvergne	−0.06	−0.09	−0.0009	1.261	1.314	0.0010	0.03
62.	Languedoc-Roussillon	−0.18	−0.14	0.0008	1.453	2.119	0.0094	0.48
63/64.	Provence–Alpes–Côtes d'Azur–Corse	0.08	−0.01	−0.0021	2.533	4.499	0.0144	1.52
Netherlands								
65.	Noord	−0.10	0.04	0.0035	1.215	1.596	0.0068	—
66.	Oost	−0.12	−0.13	−0.0003	1.788	3.050	0.0134	—
67.	West	0.18	0.12	−0.0015	5.155	6.996	0.0076	—
68.	Zuid	0.04	−0.03	−0.0016	2.007	3.306	0.0125	—
Belgium								
69.	Vlaanderen	−0.14	0.09	0.0057	3.963	4.486	0.0030	—
70.	Wallonie	−0.01	−0.21	−0.0049	2.841	3.251	0.0034	—
71.	Brabant	0.15	0.12	−0.0008	1.849	2.248	0.0049	—
Denmark								
72.	Sjalland-Lolland-Falster-Bornholm	0.08	0.19	0.0031	1.984	1.718	−0.0040	—
73.	Fyn	−0.02	−0.14	−0.0034	0.396	0.586	0.0109	—
74.	Jylland	−0.06	−0.05	0.0003	1.902	2.817	0.0109	—

Table continued

Table 11.9
(Continued)

Region	Real Per Capita GDP, 1950 Proportionate Deviation from Country Mean[a]	Real Per Capita GDP, 1990 Proportionate Deviation from Country Mean[b]	Growth Rate of Real Per Capita GDP Deviation from Country Mean[c]	Population, 1950[d] (millions)	Population, 1990[e] (millions)	Growth Rate of Population[f]	Net Migrants, Various Periods[g] (millions)
Spain							
75. Andalucia	−0.29	−0.29	0.0002	5.621	6.920	0.0053	−1.67
76. Aragon	0.01	0.08	0.0022	1.095	1.213	0.0026	−0.12
77. Asturias	0.17	−0.06	−0.0074	0.893	1.126	0.0059	−0.02
78. Balears	0.08	0.34	0.0080	0.423	0.682	0.0122	0.12
79. Canaries	−0.22	−0.03	0.0059	0.800	1.485	0.0158	0.02
80. Cantabria	0.18	0.05	−0.0043	0.406	0.527	0.0067	−0.04
81. Castilla–La Mancha	−0.43	−0.26	0.0052	2.028	1.714	−0.0043	−0.91
82. Castilla-Leon	−0.13	−0.11	0.0007	2.864	2.626	−0.0022	−0.97
83. Catalunya	0.34	0.25	−0.0029	3.271	6.008	0.0156	1.42
84. Euskadi (Basque)	0.74	0.11	−0.0197	1.075	2.129	0.0175	0.43
85. Extremadura	−0.58	−0.43	0.0047	1.366	1.129	−0.0049	−0.70
86. Galicia	−0.36	−0.20	0.0050	2.604	2.804	0.0019	−0.41
87. Madrid	0.48	0.34	−0.0042	1.956	4.876	0.0234	1.40
88. Murcia	−0.35	−0.15	0.0062	0.759	1.027	0.0078	−0.16
89. Navarra	0.19	0.13	−0.0019	0.384	0.521	0.0078	0.00
90. La Rioja	0.11	0.14	0.0008	0.230	0.260	0.0032	−0.03
91. Valencia	0.05	0.10	0.0014	2.316	3.787	0.0126	0.54

[a] Difference of logarithm of per capita GDP in 1950 from country mean in 1950. Values for Spain are for 1955.
[b] Difference of logarithm of per capita GDP in 1990 from country mean in 1990. Values for Denmark are for 1985 and for Spain are for 1987.
[c] Difference of annual growth rate of per capita GDP from 1950 to 1990 from country mean growth rate. Values for Denmark are for 1950–85 and for Spain are for 1955–87.
[d] Values for Spain are for 1951.
[e] Values for Denmark are for 1986.
[f] Annual growth rate of population from 1950 to 1990. Values for Denmark are for 1950–86 and for Spain are for 1951–90.
[g] Time periods are 1954–88 for Germany, 1961–85 for the United Kingdom, 1951–87 for Italy, 1954–82 for France, and 1951–87 for Spain.
Note: The numbers for the regions correspond to those used for the map in figure 11.4.

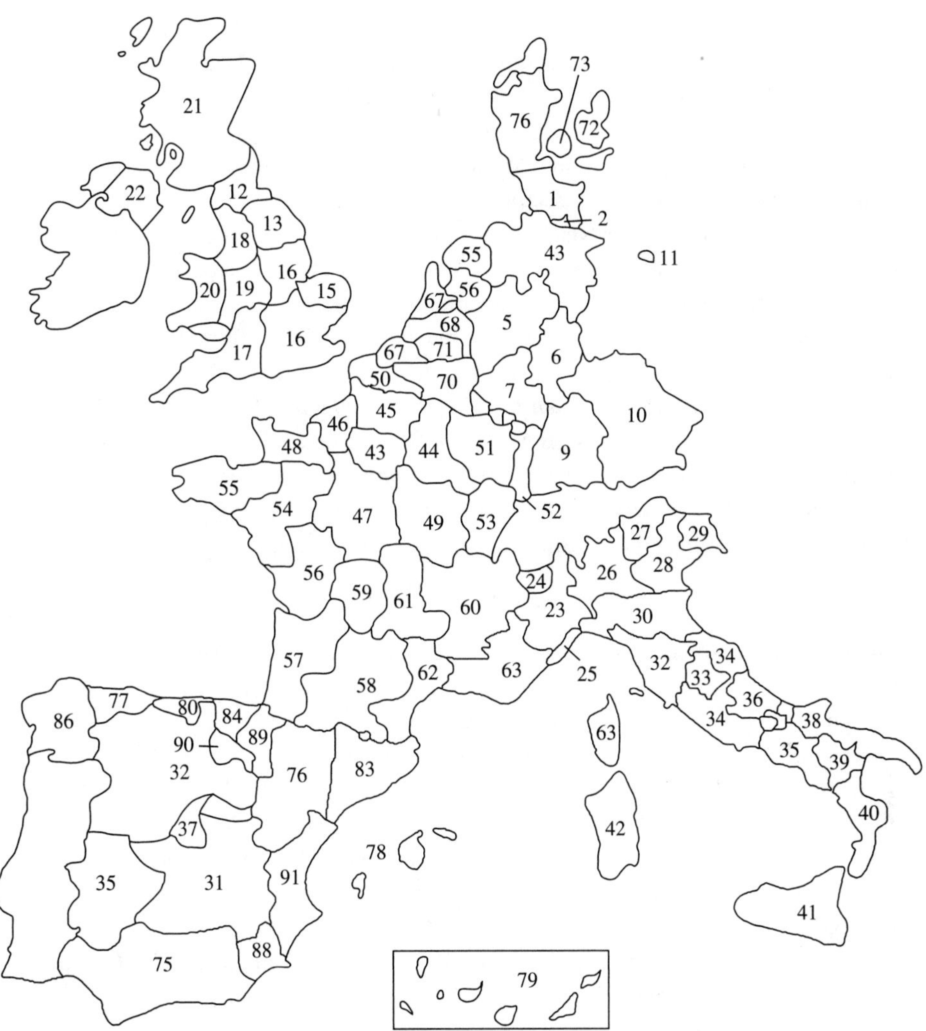

Figure 11.14
Map of European regions.

We do not have regional price data. In addition, the figures on GDP are sometimes provided in an index form that are not comparable across countries. We have therefore focused on regional GDP figures that are expressed as deviations from means for the respective countries.

For the countries other than Spain, Molle, Van Holst, and Smits (1980) provide a breakdown of employment into three sectors—agriculture, industry, and services—for 1950, 1960, and 1970. For the other years, *Eurostat* provides a division of GDP into the same three sectors. For Spain, the breakdown of GDP into these three components for the various years is available from Banco de Bilbao (various issues).

Net migration flows are computed for the five larger countries from information on population, births, and deaths. The national sources are as follows: Germany: Statistischen Bundesamtes, *Statistisches Jahrbuch für die Bundesrepublik Deutschland,* various years. United Kingdom: *Population Trends 51,* Spring 1988. France: INSEE, *Statistiques et Indicateurs des Regions Francaises,* 1978; INSEE, *Donnes de Demographie Regionale 1982,* 1986. Italy: ISTAT, *Sommario Storice di Statistiche Sulla Populazzione: Anni 1951–1987,* 1990. Spain: INE, *Anuario Estatistico de España,* various issues.

11.12.3 Data for Japanese Prefectures

Data for Japanese prefectures are in table 11.10 (a prefectural map is shown in figure 11.15). The figures on income are collected since 1955 by the Economic Planning Agency (EPA) of Japan. The accounts are constructed in accordance with the "1983 standardized system of prefectural accounts," so that all figures are comparable. The aggregate of the income figures from the 47 prefectures coincides theoretically with Japan's national income. The data are collected annually and published in the *Annual Report on Prefectural Accounts*. For 1930, we obtained income data by prefecture from *National Economy Studies Association*. We do not have price data by prefecture and therefore use national price indexes to deflate each region's income.

Data on population are from the Statistics Bureau at the Management and Coordination Agency. The principal source of these figures is the quinquennial population census taken by the Statistics Bureau.

Migration data are collected by the Statistics Bureau. These figures are derived from the *Basic Resident Registers* and the *Statistical Survey on Legal Migrants*. These data exclude persons without Japanese nationality.

Table 11.10
Data for Japanese Prefectures

Prefecture	Real Per Capita Income, 1955[a] (million yen, 1985 base)	Real Per Capita Income, 1990 (million yen, 1985 base)	Growth Rate of Real Per Capita Income[b]	Population, 1955 (millions)	Population, 1990 (millions)	Growth Rate of Population	Net Migrants, 1955–90[c] (millions)
1. Hokkaido	0.441	2.396	0.0484	4.784	5.644	0.0030	−0.76
2. Aomori	0.326	2.045	0.0525	1.391	1.483	0.0012	−0.36
3. Iwate	0.298	2.093	0.0557	1.437	1.417	−0.0003	−0.41
4. Miyagi	0.367	2.453	0.0543	1.748	2.249	0.0046	−0.11
5. Akita	0.371	2.137	0.0500	1.362	1.227	−0.0019	−0.44
6. Yamagata	0.337	2.206	0.0537	1.370	1.258	−0.0016	−0.38
7. Fukushima	0.339	2.413	0.0561	2.120	2.104	−0.0001	−0.57
8. Niigata	0.388	2.398	0.0520	2.501	2.475	−0.0002	−0.63
9. Ibaraki	0.348	2.648	0.0580	2.099	2.845	0.0055	0.09
10. Tochigi	0.518	2.788	0.0561	1.571	1.935	0.0038	−0.13
11. Gumma	0.369	2.640	0.0562	1.624	1.966	0.0035	−0.15
12. Saitama	0.460	2.825	0.0519	2.279	6.405	0.0188	2.41
13. Chiba	0.368	2.880	0.0588	2.225	5.555	0.0166	1.93
14. Tokyo	0.811	4.238	0.0472	8.016	11.855	0.0071	0.10
15. Kanagawa	0.564	2.960	0.0474	2.901	7.980	0.0184	2.58
16. Yamanashi	0.321	2.557	0.0593	0.819	0.853	0.0007	−0.16
17. Nagano	0.374	2.633	0.0558	2.050	2.157	0.0009	−0.33
18. Shizuoka	0.452	2.883	0.0530	2.638	3.671	0.0060	−0.02
19. Toyama	0.426	2.616	0.0518	1.028	1.120	0.0016	−0.16
20. Ishikawa	0.412	2.608	0.0527	0.964	1.165	0.0034	−0.09
21. Gifu	0.441	2.551	0.0502	1.599	2.067	0.0047	−0.07
22. Aichi	0.579	2.971	0.0467	3.779	6.690	0.0104	0.86
23. Mie	0.406	2.621	0.0533	1.505	1.793	0.0032	−0.11
24. Fukui	0.395	2.429	0.0519	0.758	0.824	0.0015	−0.13
25. Shiga	0.434	2.794	0.0532	0.857	1.222	0.0065	0.09
26. Kyoto	0.531	2.664	0.0461	1.928	2.603	0.0054	0.02
27. Osaka	0.709	3.190	0.0430	4.586	8.735	0.0117	1.27

Table continued

Table 11.10
(Continued)

Prefecture	Real Per Capita Income, 1955[a] (million yen, 1985 base)	Real Per Capita Income, 1990 (million yen, 1985 base)	Growth Rate of Real Per Capita Income[b]	Population, 1955 (millions)	Population, 1990 (millions)	Growth Rate of Population	Net Migrants, 1955–90[c] (millions)
28. Hyogo	0.618	2.668	0.0418	3.660	5.405	0.0071	0.29
29. Nara	0.418	2.190	0.0473	0.777	1.375	0.0104	0.30
30. Wakayama	0.438	2.109	0.0449	1.012	1.074	0.0011	−0.15
31. Tottori	0.373	2.193	0.0506	0.615	0.616	0.0000	−0.12
32. Shimane	0.336	2.121	0.0527	0.931	0.781	−0.0032	−0.26
33. Okayama	0.413	2.555	0.0521	1.716	1.926	0.0021	−0.16
34. Hiroshima	0.478	2.678	0.0492	2.180	2.850	0.0049	0.00
35. Yamaguchi	0.445	2.299	0.0469	1.619	1.573	−0.0005	−0.34
36. Tokushima	0.344	2.297	0.0542	0.898	0.832	−0.0014	−0.20
37. Kagawa	0.394	2.524	0.0531	0.951	1.023	0.0013	−0.11
38. Ehime	0.397	2.157	0.0483	1.563	1.515	−0.0006	−0.37
39. Kochi	0.367	2.025	0.0484	0.917	0.825	−0.0019	−0.18
40. Fukuoka	0.490	2.502	0.0466	3.867	4.811	0.0040	−0.28
41. Saga	0.368	2.131	0.0502	0.982	0.878	−0.0020	−0.34
42. Nagasaki	0.369	2.027	0.0487	1.795	1.563	−0.0025	−0.65
43. Kumamoto	0.326	2.294	0.0558	1.898	1.840	−0.0006	−0.47
44. Oita	0.316	2.218	0.0556	1.298	1.237	−0.0009	−0.30
45. Miyazaki	0.317	2.078	0.0537	1.155	1.169	0.0002	−0.28
46. Kagoshima	0.255	2.019	0.0591	2.084	1.798	−0.0027	−0.68
47. Okinawa	0.282	1.880	0.0542	0.801	1.222	0.0077	−0.01

[a] Value for Tochigi is for 1960.
[b] Value for Tochigi is for 1960–90.
[c] Value for Okinawa is for 1965–90.

Notes: The numbers for the prefectures correspond to those used for the map in figure 11.15. The district classifications are as follows: District 1 (Hokkaido-Tohoku), prefectures 1–8. District 2 (Kanto-Koshin), prefectures 9–17. District 3 (Chubu), prefectures 18–24. District 4 (Kinki), prefectures 25–30. District 5 (Chugoku), prefectures 31–35. District 6 (Shikoku), prefectures 36–39. District 7 (Kyushu), prefectures 40–47.

Figure 11.15
Map of Japanese prefectures.

12 Empirical Analysis of a Cross Section of Countries

Growth rates vary enormously across countries over long periods of time. Figure 12.1 (which repeats figure I.3 from the Introduction) illustrates these divergences in the form of a histogram for the growth rate of real per capita GDP for 112 countries with available data from 1960 to 2000.[1] The mean value for the growth rate is 1.8 percent per year, with a standard deviation of 1.7. The lowest decile comprises 11 countries with growth rates below −0.5 percent per year, and the highest decile consists of the 11 with growth rates above 3.9 percent per year. For quintiles, the poorest performing 22 places have growth rates below 0.4 percent per year, and the best performing 22 have growth rates above 3.0 percent per year.

The difference between per capita growth at −1.3 percent per year—the average for the lowest decile—and growth at 5.0 percent per year—the average for the highest decile—is that real per capita GDP falls by 41 percent over 40 years in the former case and rises by a factor of more than 7 in the latter. Even more extreme, the two slowest growing countries, the Democratic Republic of Congo (the former Zaire) and Central African Republic, fell from levels of real per capita GDP in 1960 of $980 and $2180 (1996 U.S. dollars), respectively, to levels of $320 and $1120 in 2000 (1995 for the former Zaire). From 1960 to 2000, the two fastest growing countries, Taiwan and Singapore, rose from $1430 and $2160, respectively, to $18,700 and $26,100. Thus, although the Central African Republic was 50 percent richer than Taiwan in 1960, Taiwan was richer by an amazing factor of 17 in 2000. Over 40 years, the observed variations in growth rates have made dramatic differences in the average living standards of a country's residents.

12.1 Losers and Winners from 1960 to 2000

Table 12.1 applies to loser countries, the 20 with the lowest per capita growth rates from 1960 to 2000. The countries are arranged in ascending order of growth rates, as shown in column 2. This group contains an astonishing 18 countries in sub-Saharan Africa and two in Latin America (Nicaragua and Venezuela). The table also shows per capita growth rates over the three ten-year subperiods, 1965–75, 1975–85, and 1985–95. The fitted values shown for these periods will be discussed later.

Table 12.2 provides a parallel treatment of winners, that is, the 20 countries with the highest per capita growth rates. These countries are arranged in descending order of growth

1. The GDP data are the purchasing-power adjusted values from version 6.1 of the Penn-World Tables, as described in Summers and Heston (1991) and Heston, Summers, and Aten (2002). For 11 countries with missing data for 2000, the growth rates for 1995–2000 were computed from World Bank figures. For Taiwan, the growth rate for 1995–2000 came from national sources. For the Democratic Republic of Congo (former Zaire), the growth rate is for 1960–95.

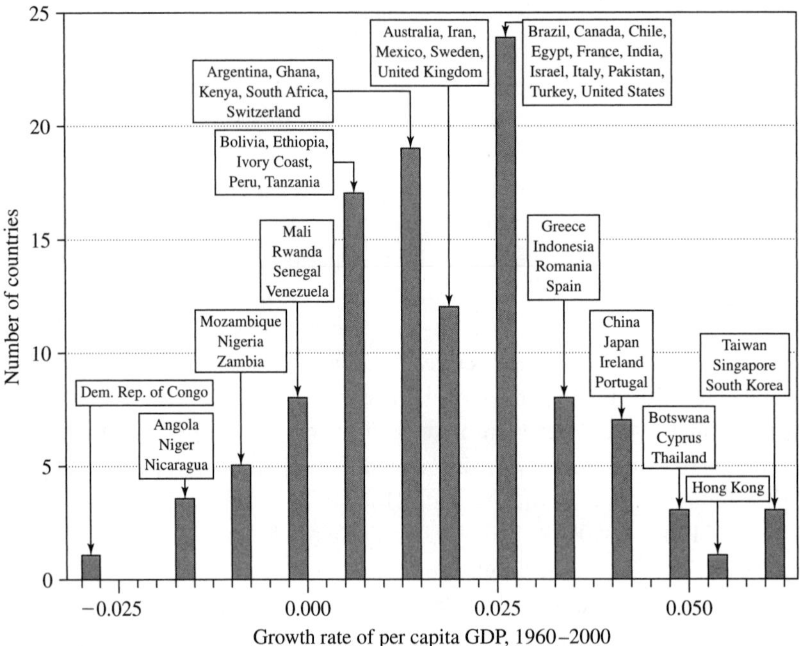

Figure 12.1
Histogram for growth rate of per capita GDP from 1960 to 2000. The growth rates are computed for 112 countries from the values of per capita GDP shown for 1960 and 2000 in figures I.1 and I.2. For Democratic Republic of Congo (former Zaire), the growth rate is for 1960 to 1995. The data are from Penn-World Tables version 6.1, as described in Summers and Heston (1991) and Heston, Summers, and Aten (2002). The GDP values are chain weighted and in 1996 U.S. dollars. For the 112 countries, the mean growth rate is 0.018 per year, and the standard deviation is 0.017. The highest growth rate is 0.064 and the lowest is −0.032. Representative countries are labeled within each group.

rates, as shown in column 2. The winners include nine economies in East Asia (Taiwan, Singapore, South Korea, Hong Kong, Thailand, China, Japan, Malaysia, and Indonesia), four in western Europe (Ireland, Portugal, Spain, and Luxembourg), and two in sub-Saharan Africa (Botswana and Congo-Brazzaville). Also included are Cyprus, Barbados, Romania, and two islands off of Africa, Cape Verde and Mauritius.

The main regressions for per capita growth rates that we will discuss apply to the three ten-year periods 1965–75, 1975–85, and 1985–95. This econometric analysis can be viewed, in part, as a determination of which characteristics make it likely that a country will end up in the losers or winners lists shown in tables 12.1 and 12.2. The fitted values indicated for the three ten-year periods (for countries that have the necessary data to be

Table 12.1
Details of 20 Slowest Growing Countries

Country	Growth 1960–2000[a]	Growth 1965–75	Fitted 1965–75	Growth 1975–85	Fitted 1975–85	Growth 1985–95	Fitted 1985–95	Growth 1995–2000[b]
Congo (Kinshasa)	−0.032	0.001	0.005	−0.040	−0.003	−0.069	−0.026	—
Central African Republic	−0.017	−0.012	—	−0.019	—	−0.035	—	0.004
Niger	−0.015	−0.041	−0.015	−0.026	−0.067	−0.008	−0.004	0.012
Angola	−0.014	−0.032	—	−0.011	—	−0.040	—	0.021
Nicaragua	−0.012	0.012	0.003	−0.037	−0.009	−0.050	−0.024	−0.006
Mozambique	−0.011	0.004	—	−0.081	—	0.003	−0.001	0.051
Madagascar	−0.010	0.004	—	−0.021	—	−0.015	—	0.004
Nigeria	−0.009	0.000	—	−0.004	—	−0.010	—	−0.054
Zambia	−0.008	−0.008	0.021	−0.021	0.007	−0.029	−0.003	0.018
Chad	−0.007	−0.012	—	−0.004	—	−0.014	—	0.003
Comoros	−0.005	0.007	—	−0.005	—	−0.031	—	−0.011
Venezuela	−0.005	−0.019	0.014	−0.019	0.006	0.004	0.004	−0.020
Senegal	−0.003	−0.008	−0.005	−0.006	−0.003	−0.002	0.005	0.021
Rwanda	−0.001	0.015	—	0.023	—	−0.037	—	0.038
Togo	−0.001	0.004	−0.005	0.011	0.000	−0.039	0.004	−0.002
Burundi	−0.001	0.024	—	−0.004	—	−0.007	—	−0.056
Mali	0.000	0.008	0.014	0.002	0.000	−0.006	0.011	0.036
Guinea	0.001	−0.016	—	−0.006	—	0.015	—	0.015
Equatorial Guinea	0.002	0.015	—	−0.084	—	−0.041	—	0.229
Benin	0.003	−0.013	—	0.018	—	−0.009	—	0.026

Notes: The data, from Penn-World Tables version 6.1, are described in Summers and Heston (1991) and Heston, Summers, and Aten (2002). The fitted values come from the regression system shown in column 2 of table 12.3.
[a]For Congo (Kinshasa), the growth rate is for 1960–95.
[b]For countries for which the Penn-World Tables version 6.1 data are unavailable for 1995–2000, the values are from World Bank (Central African Republic and Angola).

Table 12.2
Details of 20 Fastest Growing Countries

Country	Growth 1960–2000	Growth 1965–75	Fitted 1965–75	Growth 1975–85	Fitted 1975–85	Growth 1985–95	Fitted 1985–95	Growth 1995–2000[a]
Taiwan	0.064	0.069	0.056	0.065	0.050	0.068	0.041	0.047
Singapore	0.062	0.094	—	0.054	0.074	0.052	0.062	0.028
South Korea	0.059	0.071	0.052	0.059	0.048	0.072	0.052	0.032
Hong Kong	0.054	0.048	0.062	0.062	0.052	0.053	0.041	0.008
Botswana	0.051	0.082	—	0.062	0.027	0.036	0.007	0.043
Thailand	0.046	0.043	0.046	0.045	0.042	0.073	0.051	0.003
Cyprus	0.046	0.012	0.043	0.075	0.036	0.052	0.015	0.029
China	0.043	0.017	—	0.049	0.055	0.065	0.044	0.057
Japan	0.042	0.065	0.055	0.030	0.033	0.027	0.030	0.012
Ireland	0.041	0.035	0.027	0.025	0.012	0.046	0.012	0.085
Barbados	0.039	0.064	—	0.023	—	0.028	—	0.036
Malaysia	0.039	0.036	0.031	0.042	0.041	0.047	0.037	0.026
Portugal	0.038	0.049	0.054	0.021	0.026	0.035	0.015	0.040
Mauritius	0.037	0.010	—	0.038	—	0.050	—	0.041
Romania	0.035	0.072	—	0.063	—	−0.020	—	−0.020
Cape Verde	0.035	0.022	—	0.076	—	0.023	—	0.048
Spain	0.034	0.047	0.047	0.005	0.024	0.033	0.021	0.020
Indonesia	0.034	0.046	0.018	0.047	0.025	0.047	0.014	0.000
Luxembourg	0.033	0.022	—	0.021	—	0.054	—	0.049
Congo (Brazzaville)	0.032	0.041	0.029	0.059	0.018	−0.021	−0.017	0.005

Notes: The data, from Penn-World Tables version 6.1, are described in Summers and Heston (1991) and Heston, Summers, and Aten (2002). The fitted values come from the regression system shown in column 2 of table 12.3.
[a]For countries for which the Penn-World Tables version 6.1 data are unavailable for 1995–2000, the values are from World Bank (Singapore, Botswana, and Cyprus) or national sources (Taiwan).

included in the statistical analysis) show how much of the growth rates can be explained by the regressions.

The correlations of growth rates across the 10-year periods are positive but not very strong—0.43 for growth between 1975–85 and 1965–75 and 0.42 for the comparison between 1985–95 and 1975–85. Therefore, although there is persistence over time in which countries are slow or fast growers, there are also substantial changes over time in these groupings. If one examines 5-year intervals, the correlations are weaker. For example, for the seven intervals from 1960–65 to 1995–2000, the average correlation of one period's growth rate with the previous one is only 0.17. The lower correlation applies because five-year intervals tend to be sensitive to temporary factors associated with "business cycles." The last five-year period is noteworthy for being virtually unrelated to the history—the correlation of growth rates in 1995–2000 with those in 1990–95 is only 0.05.

12.2 An Empirical Analysis of Growth Rates

This section considers the empirical determinants of growth; that is, the regression results that underlie the fitted values shown in tables 12.1 and 12.2. The sample of 87 countries (constituting 241 observations for countries at 10-year intervals), listed in the appendix in table 12.8, covers a broad range of experience from developing to developed countries. The included countries were determined by the availability of data.

An interesting empirical question is whether poor economies tend to "catch up," that is, tend to grow faster than rich economies. This is the concept of absolute convergence described in chapters 1 and 2. Figure 12.2 shows that this proposition fares badly in terms of the cross-country data: for the 112 countries with the necessary data, the growth rate from 1960 to 2000 is virtually unrelated to the log of per capita GDP in 1960. (The correlation is actually somewhat positive, 0.19.) Some researchers have used this lack of correlation between growth and the initial level of income as evidence against the neoclassical growth models of Solow–Swan and Ramsey. In chapters 1, 2, and 11, however, we showed that the lack of absolute convergence across economies is perfectly consistent with neoclassical theory if the different economies in the data set tend to converge to different steady states. In other words, the neoclassical model predicts conditional rather than absolute convergence: holding constant variables that proxy for the steady state, the theory predicts a negative *partial* correlation between growth and the initial level of income. We have to examine the relation between the growth rate and the starting position after holding constant some variables that distinguish the countries.

We use an empirical framework that relates the real per capita growth rate to two kinds of variables: first, initial levels of state variables, such as the stock of physical capital and

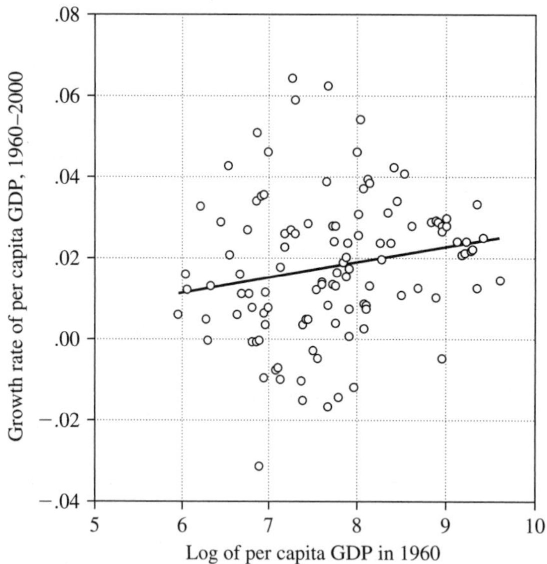

Figure 12.2
Growth rate versus GDP (simple relation). These data are for the 112 countries described in figure 12.1. The log of per capita GDP in 1960 is on the horizontal axis, and the growth rate of per capita GDP from 1960 to 2000 is on the vertical. The correlation between the two is weakly positive: 0.19. Thus there is no evidence from the broad cross-country sample of absolute convergence.

the stock of human capital in the forms of educational attainment and health; and second, control or environmental variables (some of which are chosen by governments and some by private agents), such as the ratio of government consumption to GDP, the ratio of domestic investment to GDP, the extent of international openness, movements in the terms of trade, the fertility rate, indicators of macroeconomic stability, measures of maintenance of the rule of law and democracy, and so on.

One of the state variables that we use is school attainment at various levels, as constructed by Barro and Lee (2001). We use standard UN numbers on life expectancy at various ages to represent the level of health. Life expectancy at age one turns out to have the most explanatory power. The available data on physical capital seem unreliable, especially for developing countries and even relative to the measures of human capital, because they depend on arbitrary assumptions about depreciation and also rely on inaccurate measures of benchmark stocks and investment flows. As an alternative to using the limited data that are available on physical capital, we assume that, for given values of schooling and health, a higher level of initial real per capita GDP reflects a greater stock of physical capital per person (or a larger quantity of natural resources).

We can write a function for a country's per capita growth rate in period t, Dy_t, as

$$Dy_t = F(y_{t-1}, h_{t-1}, \ldots) \tag{12.1}$$

where y_{t-1} is initial per capita GDP and h_{t-1} is initial human capital per person (based on measures of educational attainment and health). The omitted variables, denoted by $\ldots$, comprise an array of control and environmental influences. These variables would include preferences for saving and fertility, government policies with respect to spending and market distortions, and so on.

12.2.1 Effects from State Variables

The Solow–Swan and Ramsey models predict that, for given values of the environmental and control variables, an equiproportionate increase in y_{t-1} and h_{t-1} would reduce Dy_t in equation (12.1). That is, because of diminishing returns to reproducible factors, a richer economy—with higher levels of y and h—tends to grow at a slower rate. The environmental and control variables determine the steady-state level of output per "effective" worker in these models. A change in any of these variables, such as the saving rate or a government policy instrument or the growth rate of population, affects the growth rate for given values of the state variables. For example, a higher saving rate tends to increase Dy_t in equation (12.1) for given values of y_{t-1} and h_{t-1}.

The model with human and physical capital in chapter 5 predicts some influences on growth from imbalances between physical and human capital. In particular, for given y_{t-1}, a higher value of h_{t-1} in equation (12.1) tends to raise the growth rate. This situation applies, for example, in the aftermath of a war that destroys primarily physical capital. Thus, although the influence of y_{t-1} on Dy_t in equation (12.1) would be negative, the effect of h_{t-1} tends to be positive.

Empirically, we enter the initial level of per capita GDP into the growth equation in the form $\log(y_{t-1})$ so that the coefficient on this variable represents the rate of convergence, that is, the responsiveness of the growth rate, Dy_t, to a proportional change in y_{t-1}.[2] In the regressions, the variable h_{t-1} is represented by average years of school attainment and life expectancy.

2. This identification would be exact if the length of the observation interval for the data were negligible. Suppose that the data are observed at interval T, convergence occurs continuously at the rate β, and all right-hand-side variables other than $\log(y)$ do not change over time. In this case, equation (2.42) from chapter 2 implies that the coefficient on $\log(y_{t-T})$ in a regression for the average growth rate, $(1/T)\cdot\log(y_t/y_{t-T})$, is $-(1-e^{-\beta T})/T$. This expression tends to β as T tends to 0 and tends to 0 as T approaches infinity.

12.2.2 Control and Environmental Variables

In the basic regression that we will consider, the control and environmental variables are a measure of international openness,[3] the ratio of government consumption to GDP,[4] a subjective indicator of maintenance of the rule of law, a subjective indicator of democracy (electoral rights), the log of the total fertility rate, the ratio of real gross domestic investment to real GDP, and the inflation rate. The system also includes the contemporaneous growth rate of the terms of trade, interacted with the extent of international openness (the ratio of exports plus imports to GDP). We take account of the likely endogeneity of the explanatory variables by using lagged values as instruments. These lagged variables may be satisfactory because the error term in the equation for the per capita growth rate turns out to display little serial correlation.[5]

In the neoclassical growth models of Solow–Swan and Ramsey, the effects of the control and environmental variables on the growth rate correspond to their influences on the steady-state position. For example, an exogenously higher value of the rule of law indicator raises the steady-state level of output per effective worker. The growth rate, Dy_t, tends accordingly to increase for given values of the state variables. Similarly, a higher ratio of (nonproductive) government consumption to GDP tends to depress the steady-state level of output per effective worker and thereby reduce the growth rate for given values of the state variables.

In neoclassical growth models, a change in a control or environmental variable affects the steady-state level of output per effective worker, but not the long-term per capita growth rate. The long-run or steady-state growth rate is given by the rate of exogenous technological progress. In contrast, in the endogenous-growth models of chapters 6 and 7, variables that affect R&D intensity also influence long-term growth rates. However, even in the Solow–Swan and Ramsey models, if the adjustment to the new steady-state position takes a long time—as seems to be true empirically—then the growth effect of a variable such as the rule-of-law indicator or the government consumption ratio lasts for a long time.

The measures of educational attainment that we use in the main analysis are based on years of schooling and do not adjust for variations in school quality. A measure of quality, based on internationally comparable test scores, turns out to have much more explanatory

3. This variable is the ratio of exports plus imports to GDP, filtered for the usual relation of this ratio to country size as represented by the logs of population and area.

4. The variable used in the main analysis nets out from the standard measure of government consumption the outlays on defense and education.

5. Instead of including lagged inflation, the system includes dummy variables for whether the country is a former colony of Spain or Portugal or a former colony of another country other than Britain or France. These colonial dummies turn out to have substantial explanatory power for inflation.

power for growth. However, this test-score measure is unavailable for much of the sample and is, therefore, excluded from the basic system.

Health capital is proxied in the basic system by the reciprocal of life expectancy at age one. If the probability of dying were independent of age, then this reciprocal would give the probability per year of dying. We also consider later measures of infant mortality (up to age 1) and child mortality (for ages 1–5), as well as incidence of a specific disease, malaria.

We assume that the government consumption variable measures expenditures that do not directly affect productivity but that entail distortions of private decisions. These distortions can reflect the governmental activities themselves and also involve the adverse effects from the associated public finance.[6] A higher value of the government consumption ratio leads to a lower steady-state level of output per effective worker and, hence, to a lower growth rate for given values of the state variables.

The fertility rate is an important influence on population growth, which has a negative effect on the steady-state ratio of capital to effective worker in the neoclassical growth model. Hence, we anticipate a negative effect of the fertility rate on economic growth. Higher fertility also reflects greater resources devoted to child rearing, as in the model developed in chapter 9. This channel provides another reason why higher fertility would be expected to reduce growth.

The effect of the saving rate in the neoclassical growth model is measured empirically by the ratio of real investment to real GDP. Recall that we attempt to isolate the effect of the saving rate on growth, rather than the reverse, by using lagged values—in this case, the lagged investment ratio—as instruments.

We assume that an improvement in the rule of law, as gauged by the subjective indicator provided by an international consulting firm (Political Risk Services), implies enhanced property rights and, therefore, an incentive for higher investment and growth. More broadly, the idea is that well-functioning political and legal institutions help to sustain growth. Some historical analyses attempt to relate current institutional characteristics, such as maintenance of the rule of law, to practices of colonial powers long ago. Acemoglu, Johnson, and Robinson (2002) argue that European colonists were more likely to invest in institutions in regions that were previously poor or empty, notably present-day Canada and the United States, because they lacked the potential for exploitation of mineral wealth and indigenous populations. Acemoglu, Johnson, and Robinson (2001) stress that the adverse mortality experience of settlers in parts of Latin America and Africa may have limited institutional investments in those colonies. Woodberry (2002) argues that the establishment of quality

6. We would hold constant the tax effects directly, but the available data on public finance are inadequate for this purpose. See Easterly and Rebelo (1993) for attempts to measure the relevant marginal tax rates.

schooling by missionaries in some colonies may have had a long-lasting influence on political institutions. These analyses suggest instrumental variables—from the long-term history—that can be used to get more reliable estimates of the effects of current variables, such as the rule-of-law indicator.

We also include another subjective indicator (from Freedom House) of the extent of democracy in the sense of electoral rights. Theoretically, the effect of democracy on growth is ambiguous. Negative effects arise in political models that stress the incentive of electoral majorities to use their political power to transfer resources away from rich minority groups. Democracy may also be productive as a mechanism for government to commit itself not to confiscate the capital accumulated by the private sector. The empirical analysis allows for a linear and squared term in democracy, thereby allowing for the possibility that the sign of the net effect would depend on the extent of democracy.

The explanatory variables also include a measure of the extent of international openness—the ratio of exports plus imports to GDP. Openness is well known to vary by country size—larger countries tend to be less open because internal trade offers a large market that can substitute effectively for international trade. The explanatory variable used in the analysis of growth filters out the normal relationship (estimated in another regression system) of international openness to the logs of population and area. This filtered variable reflects especially the influences of government policies, such as tariffs and trade restrictions, on international trade.

We include also the growth rate over each decade of the terms of trade, measured by the ratio of export prices to import prices. This ratio appears as a product with the extent of openness, measured by exports plus imports over GDP. This terms-of-trade variable measures the effect of changes in international prices on the income position of domestic residents. This real income position would rise because of higher export prices and fall with higher import prices. We view the terms of trade as determined on world markets and, hence, exogenously to the behavior of an individual country. Since an improvement in the terms of trade raises a country's real income, we would predict an increase in domestic consumption. An effect on production, GDP, depends, however, on a response of allocations or effort to the shift in relative prices. If an increase in the relative price of the goods that a country produces tends to generate more output, that is, a positive response of supply, then the effect of this variable on the growth rate would be positive. One effect of this type is that an increase in the relative price of oil—an import for most countries—would reduce the production of goods that use oil as an input.

Finally, the basic system includes the average inflation rate as a measure of macroeconomic stability. Alternative measures can also be considered, including fiscal variables.

12.3 Regression Results for Growth Rates

12.3.1 A Basic Regression

Table 12.3 contains regression results for the growth rate of real per capita GDP. For the basic system shown in column 2, 72 countries are included for 1965–75, 86 countries for 1975–85, and 83 countries for 1985–95. Table 12.9 in the appendix shows the means and standard deviations for the variables that are included in the various regressions.

The estimation uses instrumental variables, as already discussed, and allows the error terms to be correlated across the time periods and to have different variances for each period. The error terms are assumed to be independent across countries, and the error variances are not allowed to vary across countries. The system includes separate dummies for the different time periods. Hence, the analysis does not explain why the world's average growth rate changes over time. The following discussion of results refers to the system shown in column 2 of table 12.3.

Initial Per Capita GDP The variable log(GDP) is an observation of the log of real per capita GDP for 1965 in the 1965–75 regression, for 1975 in the 1975–85 regression, and for 1985 in the 1985–95 equation. Earlier values—for 1960, 1970, and 1980, respectively—are included in the list of instruments. This instrumental procedure lessens the tendency to overestimate the convergence rate because of temporary measurement error in GDP. (For example, if log[GDP] in 1965 were low due to temporary measurement error, then the growth rate from 1965 to 1975 would tend to be high because the observation for 1975 would tend not to include the same measurement error.)

The estimated coefficient on log(GDP), −0.025 (s.e. = 0.003), shows the conditional convergence that has been reported in various studies, such as Barro (1991) and Mankiw, Romer, and Weil (1992). The convergence is conditional in that it predicts higher growth in response to lower starting GDP per person only if the other explanatory variables (some of which are highly correlated with GDP per person) are held constant. The magnitude of the estimated coefficient implies that convergence occurs at the rate of about 2.5 percent per year.[7] According to this coefficient, a one-standard-deviation decline in the log of per capita GDP (1.03 in 1985) would raise the growth rate on impact by 0.026. This effect is very large in comparison with the other effects that we are about to describe—that is, conditional convergence can have important influences on growth rates.

7. This result uses the formula from note 2. The result is correct, however, only if the other right-hand-side variables do not change as per capita GDP varies.

Table 12.3
Basic Cross-Country Growth Regressions

(1) Explanatory Variable	(2) Coefficient	(3) Coefficient for Low-Income Sample	(4) Coefficient for High-Income Sample	(5) p Value[a]	(6) Coefficient with Data at 5-Year Intervals
Log of per capita GDP	−0.0248 (0.0029)	−0.0207 (0.0052)	−0.0318 (0.0049)	0.12	−0.0237 (0.0029)
Male upper-level schooling	0.0036 (0.0016)	0.0056 (0.0045)	0.0020 (0.0016)	0.44	0.0023 (0.0015)
1/(life expectancy at age 1)	−5.04 (0.86)	−5.13 (1.18)	−1.28 (1.44)	0.040	−4.91 (0.90)
Log of total fertility rate	−0.0118 (0.0050)	−0.0209 (0.0120)	−0.0211 (0.0054)	0.99	−0.0160 (0.0048)
Government consumption ratio	−0.062 (0.023)	−0.102 (0.031)	−0.000 (0.031)	0.021	−0.066 (0.021)
Rule of law	0.0185 (0.0059)	0.0237 (0.0099)	0.0223 (0.0063)	0.90	0.0174 (0.0062)
Democracy	0.079 (0.028)	0.044 (0.049)	0.105 (0.038)	0.32[b]	0.032 (0.017)
Democracy squared	−0.074 (0.025)	−0.054 (0.052)	−0.080 (0.031)	0.67	−0.028 (0.016)
Openness ratio	0.0054 (0.0048)	0.0169 (0.0113)	0.0061 (0.0046)	0.38	0.0094 (0.0043)
Change in terms of trade	0.130 (0.053)	0.181 (0.076)	0.036 (0.070)	0.16	0.029 (0.021)
Investment ratio	0.083 (0.024)	0.109 (0.035)	0.077 (0.027)	0.46	0.058 (0.022)
Inflation rate	−0.019 (0.010)	−0.019 (0.012)	−0.019 (0.009)	0.99	−0.031 (0.007)
Constant	0.296 (0.034)	0.294 (0.052)	0.295 (0.052)	0.99[c]	0.306 (0.035)
Dummy, 1975–85	−0.0078 (0.0026)	−0.0078 (0.0038)	−0.0066 (0.0032)	0.81	[d]
Dummy, 1985–95	−0.0128 (0.0034)	−0.0194 (0.0051)	−0.0052 (0.0040)	0.031	
Number of observations	72, 86, 83	26, 38, 33	46, 48, 50		72, 79, 86, 84 79, 80, 60
R-squared	.60, .49, .51	.78, .53, .65	.56, .56, .40		.40, .26, .27, .31, .46, .19, .04

Notes: Estimation is by three-stage least squares. In column 2 the dependent variables are the growth rates of per capita GDP for 1965–75, 1975–85, and 1985–95. Instruments are the values in 1960, 1970, and 1980 of the log of per capita GDP, the life-expectancy variable, and the fertility variable; averages for 1960–64, 1970–74, and 1980–84 of the government consumption variable and the investment ratio; values in 1965, 1975, and 1985 of the schooling variable and the democracy variables; the openness and terms-of-trade variables (growth rates over 1965–75, 1975–85, and 1985–95, interacted with the corresponding averages of the ratio of exports plus imports to GDP); and dummies for Spanish or Portuguese colonies and other colonies (aside from Britain and France). The variances of the error terms are allowed to be correlated over the time periods and to have different variances for each period. Columns 3 and 4 separate the samples into countries with levels of per capita GDP below and above the median (for 1960, 1970, and 1980). Column 6 uses equations for economic growth for seven five-year periods, 1965–70, . . . , 1995–2000.

[a] The p values refer to the hypothesis that the coefficients are the same for the two income groups.

[b] The p value for democracy and democracy-squared jointly is 0.022.

[c] The p value for the constant and two time dummies jointly is 0.10.

[d] The time dummies at the 5-year intervals are −0.0014 (0.0040) for 1970–75, −0.0000 (0.0040) for 1975–80, −0.0180 (0.0040) for 1980–85, −0.0112 (0.0037) for 1985–90, −0.0184 (0.0045) for 1990–95, and −0.0165 (0.0042) for 1995–2000.

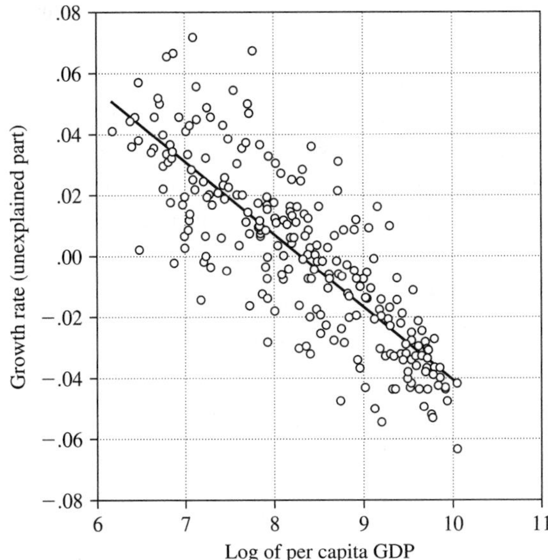

Figure 12.3
Growth rate versus GDP (partial relation). The log of per capita GDP for 1965, 1975, and 1985 is shown on the horizontal axis. The vertical axis plots the corresponding growth rate of real per capita GDP from 1965 to 1975, 1975 to 1985, and 1985 to 1995. These growth rates are filtered for the estimated effect of the explanatory variables other than the log of per capita GDP that are shown in column 2 of table 12.3. The filtered values were then normalized to have zero mean. Thus the diagram shows the partial relation between the growth rate of per capita GDP and the log of per capita GDP.

Figure 12.3 provides a graphical description of the partial relation between the growth rate and the level of per capita GDP. The horizontal axis shows the values of the log of per capita GDP at the start of each of the three ten-year periods: 1965, 1975, and 1985. The vertical axis refers to the subsequent ten-year growth rate of per capita GDP—for 1965–75, 1975–85, and 1985–95. These growth rates have been filtered for the estimated effects of the explanatory variables other than the log of per capita GDP that are included in the system of column 2, table 12.3. (The average value has also been normalized to have zero mean.) Thus, conceptually, the figure shows the estimated effect of the log of per capita GDP on subsequent growth when all the other explanatory variable are held constant. The graph suggests that the estimated relationship is not driven by obvious outlier observations and does not have any clear departures from linearity. An analogous construction will be used for each of the explanatory variables.

Educational Attainment The school-attainment variable that tends to be significantly related to subsequent growth is the average years of male secondary and higher schooling (referred to as upper-level schooling), observed at the start of each period, 1965, 1975, and 1985. Since these variables are predetermined, they enter as their own instruments in the regressions. Attainment of females and for both sexes at the primary level turn out not to be significantly related to growth rates, as discussed later. The estimated coefficient, 0.0036 (0.0016), means that a one-standard-deviation increase in male upper-level schooling (by 1.3 years, the value for 1985 shown in table 12.9) raises the growth rate on impact by 0.005. Figure 12.4 depicts the partial relationship between economic growth and the school-attainment variable.

Life Expectancy The life-expectancy variable—the reciprocal of life expectancy at age one—applies to 1960, 1970, and 1980, respectively, for the three growth equations. These values would correspond to the mortality rate per year if mortality were (counterfactually) independent of age. The reciprocal of life expectancy at age one has slightly more explanatory power than variables based on life expectancy at birth or at age 5. (The reciprocals

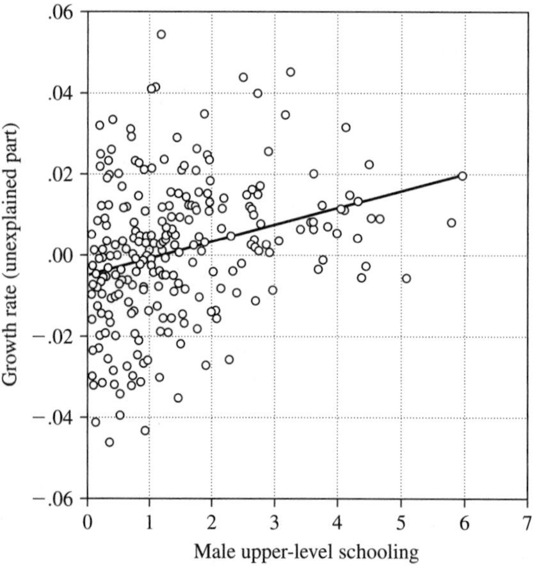

Figure 12.4
Growth rate versus schooling (partial relation). The diagram shows the partial relation between the growth rate of per capita GDP and the average years of school attainment of males at the upper level (higher schooling plus secondary schooling). The variable on the horizontal axis is measured in 1965, 1975, and 1985. See the description of figure 12.3 for the general procedure.

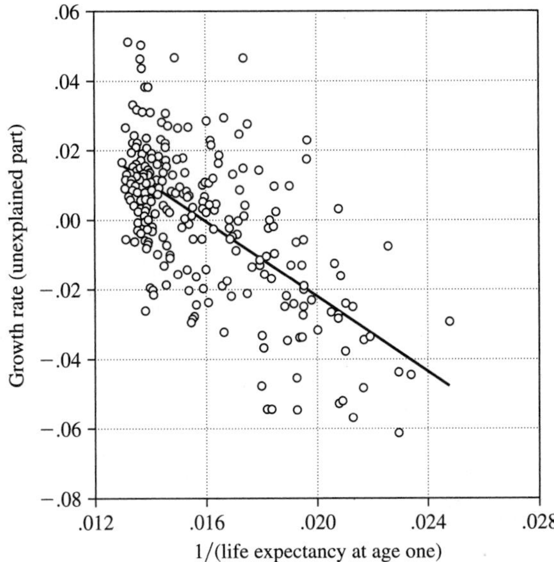

Figure 12.5
Growth rate versus life expectancy (partial relation). The diagram shows the partial relation between the growth rate of per capita GDP and the reciprocal of life expectancy at age one. The variable on the horizontal axis is measured in 1960, 1970, and 1980. See the description of figure 12.3 for the general procedure.

of life expectancy at age 1 also appear in the instrument lists.) The estimated coefficient of −5.0 (s.e. = 0.9) is highly significant and indicates that better health predicts higher economic growth. A one-standard error reduction in the reciprocal of life expectancy at age 1 (0.0022 in 1980) is estimated to raise the growth rate on impact by 0.011. Figure 12.5 shows graphically the partial relation between growth and this health indicator.

Fertility Rate The fertility rate (total lifetime live births for the typical woman over her expected lifetime) enters as a log at the dates 1960, 1970, and 1980. These variables also appear in the instrument lists. The estimated coefficient is negative and significant: −0.012 (s.e. = 0.005). A one-standard-deviation decline in the log of the fertility rate (by 0.53 in 1980) is estimated to raise the growth rate on impact by 0.006. The partial relation appears in figure 12.6.

Government Consumption Ratio The ratio of real government consumption to real GDP[8] was adjusted by subtracting the estimated ratio to real GDP of real spending on defense

8. These data are from Penn-World Tables version 6.1, as described in Summers and Heston (1991).

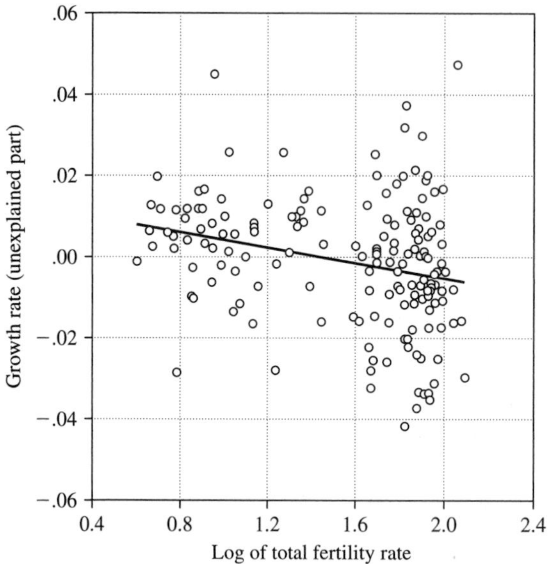

Figure 12.6
Growth rate versus fertility rate (partial relation). The diagram shows the partial relation between the growth rate of per capita GDP and the log of the total fertility rate. The variable on the horizontal axis is measured in 1960, 1970, and 1980. See the description of figure 12.3 for the general procedure.

and noncapital real expenditures on education. The elimination of expenditures for defense and education—categories of spending that are included in standard measures of government consumption—was made because these items are not properly viewed as consumption. In particular, they are likely to have direct effects on productivity or the security of property rights. The growth equation for 1965–75 includes as a regressor the average of the adjusted government consumption ratio for 1965–74 and includes the adjusted ratio for 1960–64 in the list of instruments. The analogous timing applies to the growth equations for the other two ten-year periods.

The estimated coefficient of the government consumption ratio is negative and significant: −0.062 (0.023). This estimate implies that a reduction in the ratio by 0.059 (its standard deviation in 1985–94) would raise the growth rate on impact by 0.004. The partial relation is shown in figure 12.7.

Rule of Law The rule-of-law variable comes from a subjective measure provided in *International Country Risk Guide* by the international consulting company Political Risk Services. This variable was first proposed by Knack and Keefer (1995). The underly-

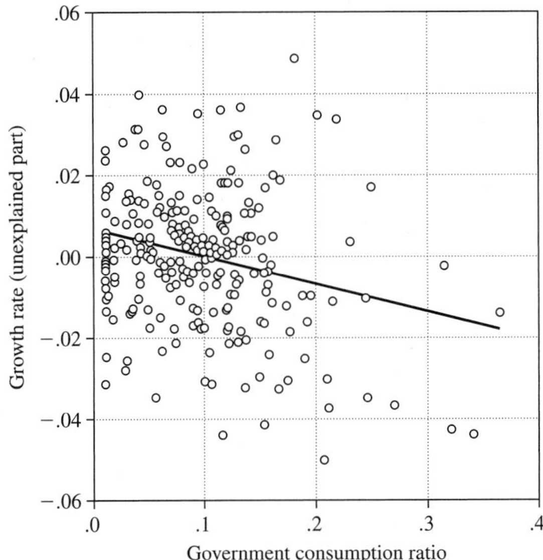

Figure 12.7
Growth rate versus government consumption (partial relation). The diagram shows the partial relation between the growth rate of per capita GDP and the ratio of government consumption to GDP. The ratio involves the standard measure of government consumption less the estimated real outlays on defense and education. The variable on the horizontal axis is the average for 1965–74, 1975–84, and 1985–94. See the description of figure 12.3 for the general procedure.

ing data are tabulated in seven categories, which have been adjusted here to a zero-to-one scale, with one representing the most favorable environment for maintenance of the rule of law. These data start only in 1982. The estimation shown in table 12.3 uses the earliest value available (usually for 1982 but sometimes for 1985) in the growth equations for 1965–75 and 1975–85. (This procedure may be satisfactory because the rule-of-law variable exhibits substantial persistence over time.) The third equation uses the average of the rule of law for 1985–94 as a regressor and enters the value for 1985 in the instrument list. The estimated coefficient is positive and significant: 0.0185 (0.0059). This estimate means that an increase in the rule of law by one standard deviation (0.26 for 1985–94) would raise the growth rate on impact by 0.005. The partial relation with growth is shown in figure 12.8. (Note that many of the rule-of-law observations apply to one of seven categories. The averaging for 1985–94 generates the intermediate values.)

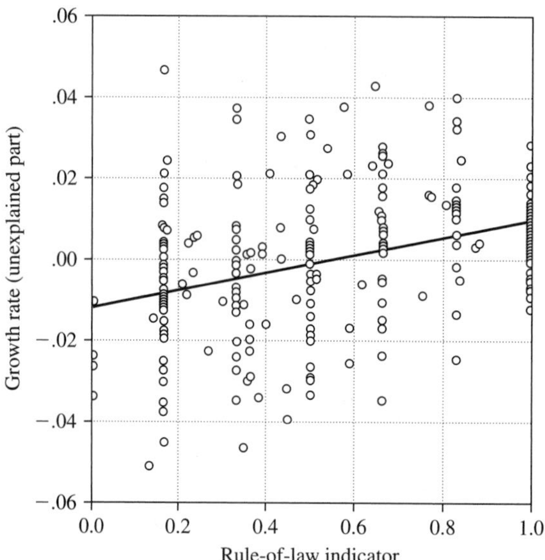

Figure 12.8
Growth rate versus rule of law (partial relation). The diagram shows the partial relation between the growth rate of per capita GDP and the Political Risk Services indicator for maintenance of the rule of law. The variable on the horizontal axis associated with growth in 1965–75 and 1975–85 applies to 1982 or 1985. The value associated with growth in 1985–95 is the average for 1985–94. See the description of figure 12.3 for the general procedure.

Democracy The democracy variable comes from a subjective measure provided by Freedom House.[9] The variable used refers to electoral rights—an alternative measure that applies to civil liberties is considered later. The underlying data are tabulated in seven categories, which have been adjusted here to a zero-to-one scale, with one indicating a full representative democracy and zero a complete totalitarian system. These data begin in 1972, but information from another source (Bollen, 1990) was used to generate data for 1960 and 1965. The systems include also the square of democracy to allow for a nonlinear effect on economic growth. The first growth equation includes as regressors the average of democracy and the average of its square over the period 1965–74. The instrument list includes the level and squared value in 1965 (or sometimes 1960). The other two growth equations use as regressors the average values for 1975–84 and 1985–94, respectively, and include the values at the start of each period in the instrument lists.

9. For an earlier discussion, see Gastil (1987).

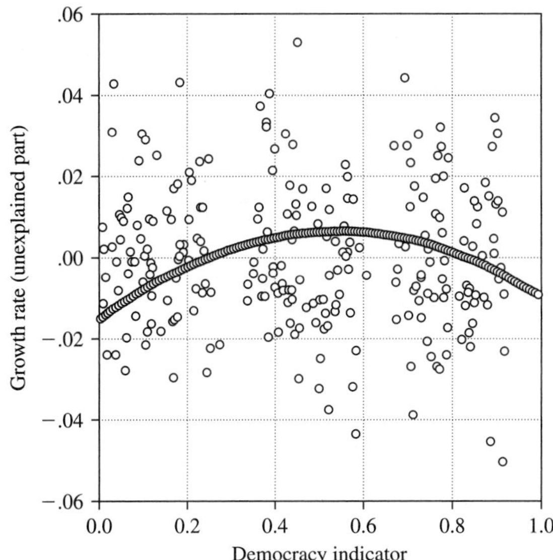

Figure 12.9
Growth rate versus democracy (partial relation). The diagram shows the partial relation between the growth rate of per capita GDP and the Freedom House indicator for democracy (electoral rights). The variable on the horizontal axis is the average for 1965–74, 1975–84, and 1985–94. The solid curve is the fitted relation implied by the estimated coefficients on the linear and squared terms for democracy. See the description of figure 12.3 for the general procedure.

The results indicate that the linear and squared term in democracy are each statistically significant: 0.079 (0.028) and −0.074 (0.025), respectively. The p value for joint significance is 0.011. These estimates imply that, starting from a fully totalitarian system (where the democracy variable takes on the value zero), increases in democracy tend to stimulate growth. However, the positive influence attenuates as democracy rises and reaches zero when the indicator takes on a midrange value of 0.53. (Note that the mean of the democracy variable for 1985–94 is 0.64.) Therefore, democratization appears to enhance growth for countries that are not very democratic but to retard growth for countries that have already achieved a substantial amount of democracy. This nonlinear relation is shown by the diagram in figure 12.9. The solid line indicates the fitted value implied by the linear and squared terms in democracy.

International Openness The degree of international openness is measured by the ratio of exports plus imports to GDP. This measure is highly sensitive to country size, as large countries tend to rely relatively more on domestic trade. To take account of this relation, the

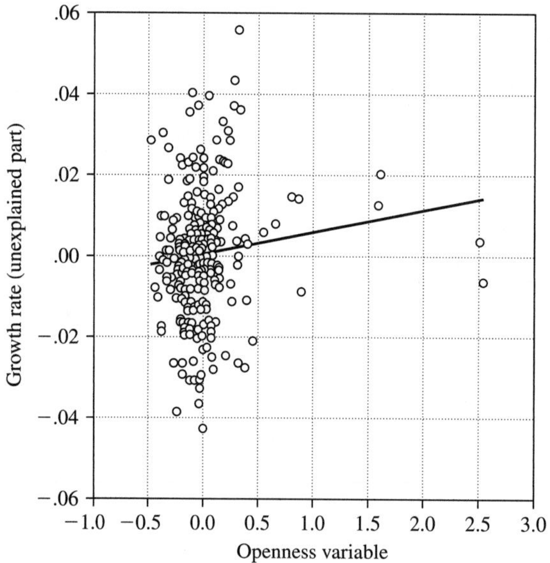

Figure 12.10
Growth rate versus openness (partial relation). The diagram shows the partial relation between the growth rate of per capita GDP and the openness ratio. This variable is the ratio of exports plus imports to GDP, filtered for the usual relation of this ratio to the logs of population and area. The variable on the horizontal axis is the average for 1965–74, 1975–84, and 1985–94. See the description of figure 12.3 for the general procedure.

ratio of exports plus imports to GDP was filtered for its relation in a regression context to the logs of population and area. We consider later whether country size has itself a relation to economic growth.

The openness variable enters into each growth equation as an average for the corresponding ten-year period (1965–74 and so on). In the basic system, these variables also appear in the respective instrument lists. This specification is appropriate if the trade ratio is (largely) exogenous to economic growth. The estimated coefficient on the openness variable is positive but not statistically significant, 0.0054 (0.0048). Hence, there is only weak statistical evidence that greater international openness stimulates economic growth. The point estimate implies that a one-standard-deviation increase in the openness ratio (0.39 in 1985–94) would raise the growth rate on impact by 0.002. The partial relation between growth and the openness variable is shown graphically in figure 12.10.

The Terms of Trade This variable is measured by the growth rate of the terms of trade (export prices relative to import prices) over each ten-year period (1965–75 and so on),

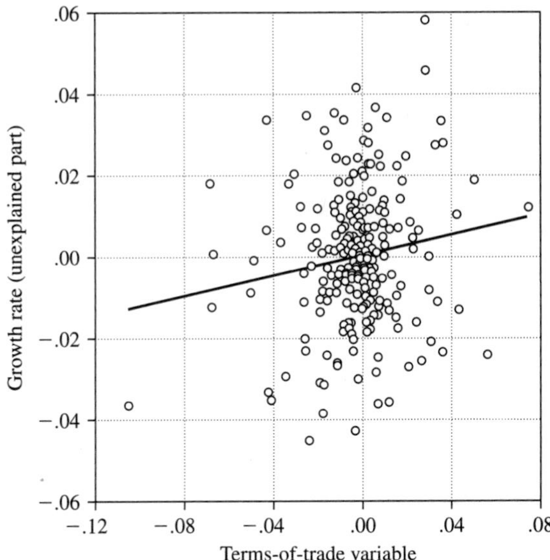

Figure 12.11
Growth rate versus terms of trade (partial relation). The diagram shows the partial relation between the growth rate of per capita GDP and the terms-of-trade variable. This variable is the growth rate of the terms of trade (export prices relative to import prices) multiplied by the average ratio of exports plus imports to GDP. The growth rate of the terms of trade is for 1965–75, 1975–85, and 1985–95. The ratios of exports plus imports to GDP are averages for 1965–74, 1975–84, and 1985–94. See the description of figure 12.3 for the general procedure.

multiplied by the average ratio of exports plus imports to GDP for the period (1965–74 and so on). These variables also appear in the instrument lists. The idea here is that movements in the terms of trade depend primarily on world conditions and would, therefore, be largely exogenous with respect to contemporaneous economic growth for an individual country.[10] The estimated coefficient is positive and significant: 0.130 (0.053). Hence, changes in the terms of trade do matter for growth over ten-year periods. The results imply that a one-standard-deviation increase in the variable (by 0.017 in 1985–95) would raise the growth rate on impact by 0.002. Figure 12.11 shows the partial relation between growth and the terms-of-trade variable.

Investment Ratio The ratio of real gross domestic investment (private plus public) to real GDP enters into the regressions as averages for each of the ten-year periods (1965–74 and

10. The results are virtually the same if the instrument list includes the growth rate of the terms of trade interacted with the lagged ratio of exports plus imports to GDP, rather than the contemporaneous ratio.

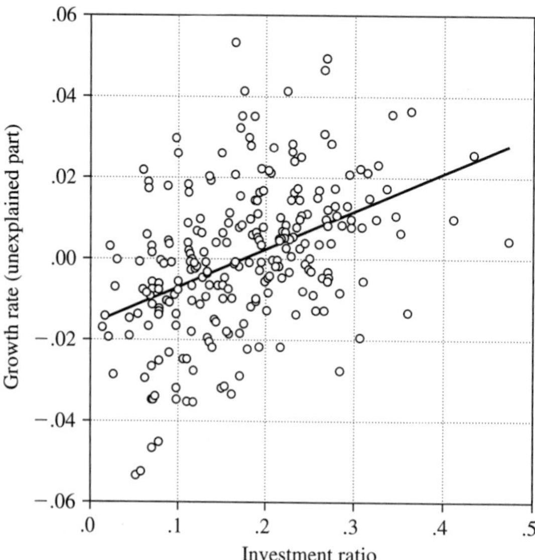

Figure 12.12
Growth rate versus investment (partial relation). The diagram shows the partial relation between the growth rate of per capita GDP and the ratio of investment to GDP. The variable on the horizontal axis is the average for 1965–74, 1975–84, and 1985–94. See the description of figure 12.3 for the general procedure.

so on).[11] The corresponding instrument is the average value of the ratio over the preceding five years (1960–64, 1970–74, and 1980–84). The estimated coefficient is positive and statistically significant, 0.083 (0.024). This point estimate implies that a one-standard-deviation increase in the investment ratio (by 0.081 in 1985–94) would raise the growth rate on impact by 0.007. The partial relation with growth is depicted graphically in figure 12.12.

Inflation Rate The inflation variable is the average rate of retail price inflation over each of the ten-year periods (1965–75 and so on). A cross-country analysis of inflation suggested as instruments dummies for prior colonial status. In particular, former colonies of Spain and Portugal and of other countries aside from Britain and France had substantial explanatory power for inflation. The results shown in table 12.3 apply when the instrument lists include these two colony dummies—former colony of Spain or Portugal and former colony of another country aside from Britain and France—but neither contemporaneous nor

11. The data are from Penn-World Tables version 6.1, as described in Summers and Heston (1991).

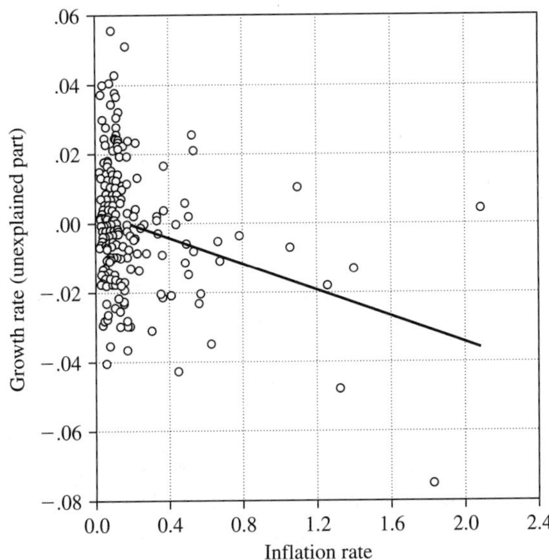

Figure 12.13
Growth rate versus inflation (partial relation). The diagram shows the partial relation between the growth rate of per capita GDP and the average rate of retail price inflation. The variable on the horizontal axis is for 1965–75, 1975–85, and 1985–95. See the description of figure 12.3 for the general procedure.

lagged inflation itself. The estimated coefficient, −0.019 (0.010), is negative and marginally statistically significant. This coefficient implies that a one-standard-deviation increase in the inflation rate (0.38 in 1985–95) lowers the growth rate on impact by 0.007. However, the coefficient also implies that the moderate variations of inflation experienced by most countries—say, changes on the order of 0.05 per year—affect growth rates by less than 0.001. Figure 12.13 shows graphically the partial relation between growth and inflation. This diagram makes clear that the main force driving the estimated relationship is the behavior at high rates of inflation—notably at rates above 20–30 percent per year.

The point estimate of the coefficient on the inflation rate is similar, −0.018 (0.005), if contemporaneous inflation appears instead of the colony dummies in the instrument lists. However, the estimated coefficient is close to zero, 0.003 (0.009), if the instrument lists contain lagged inflation (for 1960–65, 1970–75, and 1980–85), rather that contemporaneous inflation. This result is surprising because lagged inflation does have substantial explanatory power for inflation.

Constant Terms The regressions include an overall constant term and separate time dummies for the two later periods, 1975–85 and 1985–95. These two time dummies are significantly negative: −0.0078 (0.0026) and −0.0128 (0.0034), respectively. Hence, the world's rate of economic growth seems to have declined from 1965 to 1995.[12]

12.3.2 Tests of Stability of Coefficients

Columns 3 and 4 of table 12.3 show results when countries with per capita GDP below the median for each period are separated from those above the median. The division was based on values of per capita GDP in 1960, 1970, and 1980. Since the median was calculated for all countries with GDP data, it turns out that far more than half of the countries in the regression sample are in the portion with per capita GDP above the median. (Higher income countries are more likely to have data on the other variables needed for inclusion in the regression sample.)

A joint test for equality of all coefficients across the two income groups is rejected with a very low p value. However, when considering variables individually, the results show considerable stability across the low and high income groups. In particular, for the p values shown in column 5 of table 12.3, the only values that are less than 0.05 are for the life-expectancy variable, the government consumption ratio, and the dummy for the 1985–95 period. Notably, the low-income countries exhibit more sensitivity of growth to life expectancy and government consumption than do the high-income countries. Also, the decline in the growth rate from 1965–75 to 1985–95 applies mainly to the low-income group. Despite these exceptions, the most striking finding about the results in columns 3–5 of the table is the extent to which similar coefficients are found for poor and rich countries.

Column 6 of table 12.3 shows the coefficient estimates when the data are employed at five-year intervals, instead of the ten-year periods used before. In the five-year case, there are seven equations, where the dependent variables are the rates of growth of per capita GDP from 1965–70 to 1995–2000. In most cases, the coefficients shown for the five-year specification in column 6 are similar to those from the ten-year estimation, which are in column 2. The main exceptions are for the terms-of-trade variable (which has a smaller coefficient in the five-year sample), the openness variable (which is larger and now statistically significant in the five-year setting), and the democracy variable (for which the magnitudes of the two coefficients are smaller in the five-year case). The fits of the equations in the five-year setting, as gauged by R-squared values, are notably poorer than those for the ten-year setting. This pattern suggests that growth outcomes over intervals as short as five years are influenced considerably by short-term and temporary forces ("business

12. The mean growth rate for each decade also depends on the mean values of the regressors. For the 70 countries included in the regressions for all three ten-year periods, the average growth rates were 0.0255 for 1965–75, 0.0162 for 1975–85, and 0.0138 for 1985–95.

Table 12.4
Stability of Coefficients over Time in Cross-Country Growth Regressions

	Coefficients by Time Period			
(1) Explanatory Variable	(2) 1965–75	(3) 1975–85	(4) 1985–95	(5) *p* value[a]
Log of per capita GDP	−0.0222 (0.0041)	−0.0231 (0.0064)	−0.0338 (0.0061)	0.25
Male upper-level schooling	0.0038 (0.0026)	0.0070 (0.0028)	0.0022 (0.0029)	0.13
1/(life expectancy at age 1)	−5.48 (1.48)	−3.74 (1.59)	−7.94 (1.86)	0.13
Log of total fertility rate	0.0008 (0.0079)	−0.0143 (0.0104)	−0.0307 (0.0101)	0.052
Government consumption ratio	−0.060 (0.035)	−0.017 (0.035)	−0.099 (0.059)	0.35
Rule of law	0.0262 (0.0087)	0.0191 (0.0117)	0.0079 (0.0173)	0.64
Democracy	0.129 (0.070)	0.111 (0.055)	0.120 (0.053)	0.98
Democracy squared	−0.127 (0.058)	−0.109 (0.051)	−0.097 (0.048)	0.93
Openness ratio	−0.0005 (0.0123)	0.0043 (0.0095)	0.0028 (0.0079)	0.95
Change in terms of trade	0.063 (0.094)	0.225 (0.110)	−0.120 (0.133)	0.16
Investment ratio	0.117 (0.037)	0.068 (0.050)	0.095 (0.056)	0.73
Inflation rate	0.061 (0.031)	−0.046 (0.032)	−0.018 (0.014)	0.033
Constant	0.239 (0.056)	0.252 (0.062)	0.428 (0.068)	0.046
Number of observations	72	86	83	
R-squared	0.55	0.48	0.57	

Notes: Columns 2–4 provide estimates of the regression system from column 2 of table 12.3 when the coefficients are allowed to vary across the three time periods, 1965–75, 1975–85, and 1985–95.
[a]The *p* values refer to the hypothesis that the coefficients are the same for all three time periods.

cycles"), which were not considered in the theories of long-term economic growth. One notable finding is the poor fit for the final five-year period, 1995–2000. In this case, the R-squared value is only 0.04. One reason for this result is that several previous growth champions in East Asia did poorly in 1995–2000 because of the Asian financial crisis.

Table 12.4 allows for an array of different coefficients over the three ten-year time periods. (In the initial estimation, only the constant terms differed across the periods.) A joint test for equality of all coefficients across the time periods would be rejected with a low p value. However, when the variables are considered individually, the only p values of 0.05 or less are for the inflation rate and the fertility rate—see column 5 of table 12.4. Overall, the striking finding from table 12.4 is the extent of stability of the estimated coefficients over time.

12.3.3 Additional Explanatory Variables

The empirical literature on the determinants of economic growth has become very large and has suggested numerous additional explanatory variables. Table 12.5 shows the estimated coefficients of some of these candidate variables when added one at a time to the basic regression shown in column 2 of table 12.3.

Table 12.5
Additional Explanatory Variables in Cross-Country Growth Regressions

(1) New Explanatory Variable	(2) Coefficient	(3) Additional New Variable	(4) Coefficient	(5) p Value[a]
Log of population	0.0004 (0.0009)			
Log of per capita GDP squared	−0.0035 (0.0020)			
Female upper-level schooling	−0.0034 (0.0041)			
Male primary schooling	−0.0011 (0.0025)	Female primary schooling	0.0007 (0.0024)	0.90
Male college schooling[b]	0.0105 (0.0093)	Male secondary schooling	0.0024 (0.0020)	0.075
Student test scores[c]	0.121 (0.024)			
Infant mortality rate	−0.001 (0.057)			
1/(life expectancy at birth)	−0.97 (2.52)			
1/(life expectancy at age 5)	0.90 (2.00)			
Malaria incidence	0.0019 (0.0045)			
Official corruption	0.0093 (0.0068)			
Quality of bureaucracy	0.0076 (0.0088)			
Civil liberties[d]	−0.045 (0.081)	Civil liberties squared	0.003 (0.070)	0.36
Sub-Saharan Africa dummy[e]	−0.0080 (0.0051)	Latin America dummy	0.0031 (0.0039)	0.011
East Asia dummy	0.0100 (0.0047)	OECD dummy	0.0004 (0.0054)	
Population share < 15	−0.070 (0.070)	Population share > 64	−0.080 (0.110)	0.61
Government spending on education	−0.057 (0.068)	Government spending on defense	0.064 (0.028)	0.069
Log of black-market premium	−0.0122 (0.0058)			
Private financial system credit	−0.0041 (0.0065)			
Financial system deposits	−0.002 (0.011)			
British legal structure dummy	−0.0018 (0.0044)	French legal structure dummy	0.0047 (0.0045)	0.10
Absolute latitude (degrees ÷ 100)	0.066 (0.027)	Latitude squared	−0.085 (0.044)	0.036
Landlocked dummy	−0.0088 (0.0032)			
Ethnic fractionalization	−0.0080 (0.0059)			
Linguistic fractionalization	−0.0084 (0.0050)			
Religious fractionalization	−0.0088 (0.0058)			
British colony dummy[f]	−0.0064 (0.0043)	French colony dummy	0.0003 (0.0053)	0.39
Spanish/Portuguese colony dummy	−0.0019 (0.0053)	Other colony dummy	−0.0055 (0.0075)	

Notes: Each new explanatory variable or group of new variables is added to the system shown in column 2 of table 12.3.
[a] p value is for the test of the hypothesis that the coefficients of the new explanatory variables are jointly zero.
[b] Upper-level male schooling is omitted. The p value for equality of college and secondary variables is 0.44.
[c] Numbers of observations for this sample are 39, 45, and 44.
[d] This system is only for the two periods 1975–85 and 1985–95.
[e] The four regional dummy variables are entered together.
[f] The four colony dummies are entered together.

The first variable, the log of population, is intended to see whether the scale of a country matters for its growth outcomes. This variable is entered for 1960, 1970, and 1980, and appears also in the instrument lists. The estimated coefficient is insignificant, 0.0004 (0.0009). Hence, there is no indication that country size matters for economic growth.

The square of the log of per capita GDP was entered to see whether the rate of convergence depended on the level of per capita GDP. This new variable enters with the same timing as the linear term in log of per capita GDP. If the coefficient on the square variable were negative, the rate of convergence would be increasing with per capita GDP. The result is a negative and statistically significant coefficient, −0.0035 (0.0020). This result conflicts with the theory, in which increases in per capita GDP (moving toward the steady state) were predicted to slow down the rate of convergence.

We considered a number of alternative measures of years of education, all of which enter with the same timing as the male upper-level schooling variable. Female upper-level schooling has a negative but statistically insignificant coefficient, −0.0034 (0.0041). Schooling at the primary level for males or females also has statistically insignificant coefficients: −0.0011 (0.0025) and 0.0007 (0.0024), respectively. Hence, the main relation between growth and years of schooling involves the male upper-level component, the variable included in column 2 of table 12.3. A separation of this male variable into college and high-school components generates two positive coefficients, 0.0105 (0.0093) and 0.0024 (0.0020), that are insignificantly different from each other (p value for equality is 0.46).

All these schooling variables refer to the quantity of education, as measured by years of schooling, rather than the quality. A possible measure of quality is the outcome on internationally comparable examinations. Of course, these test scores may reflect inputs other than formal education, for example, the influences of family members. In any event, the main problem here is that the data are available only for a subset of the countries and time periods from the original regression sample. Because of the limited data, we constructed a single cross section of test scores and used the same value for each country for the three time periods considered for growth. (Thus the underlying test scores apply at different points in time in each equation, and some of the data refer to scores that postdate the measured rates of economic growth.) The estimated coefficient of the test-scores variable is positive and highly significant, 0.121 (0.024). Another result in this specification is that the estimated coefficient of male upper-level schooling becomes insignificant, 0.0013 (0.0015). Thus the overall indication is that the quality of education is far more important for economic outcomes than the years of schooling . Unfortunately, the limited amount of international data on test scores makes it difficult to go further with this analysis.

Another set of results refers to alternative measures of health. Recall that we previously included the reciprocal of life expectancy at age 1. (This measure has more explanatory power than life expectancy at age 1 or the log of this life expectancy.) With this variable held fixed, the infant mortality rate (for 1960, 1970, and 1980) is insignificant, −0.001 (0.057). Also insignificant are the reciprocal of life expectancy at birth (−0.97, s.e. = 2.52) or at age 5 (0.90, s.e. = 2.00). (These variables also enter for 1960, 1970, and 1980.) Gallup and Sachs (1998) have generated numerous measures of the effects of specific diseases. We did not find important relations with growth, once the basic life expectancy variable was considered. As an example, the variable for the incidence of malaria in 1966 was insignificant, 0.0019 (0.0045).

Alternatives to the rule-of-law indicator have also been proposed in the literature. With our rule-of-law measure (and the other explanatory variables, including democracy) held constant, an indicator from Political Risk Services of the extent of official corruption was positive but insignificant, 0.0067 (0.0071).[13] (Note that, for this indicator, a higher value means a "better" system with less official corruption.) Also insignificant was an indicator from Political Risk Services for the quality of the bureaucracy, 0.0054 (0.0091). The corruption and bureaucratic quality indicators were entered with the same timing as the rule-of-law variable, which we discussed before.

The democracy variable included in column 2 of table 12.3 is the Freedom House indicator of electoral rights. Because of the high degree of correlation, it turns out to be impossible to distinguish this measure empirically from the other Freedom House indicator, which refers to civil liberties. The linear and squared term in civil liberties are insignificant if added to the system (p value = 0.53).[14] However, the linear and squared terms in electoral rights are also jointly insignificant when the civil liberties variables are already included (p value = 0.12).

The discussion earlier in this chapter indicated how the group of slowest growing countries was dominated by sub-Saharan Africa, whereas the fastest growing group was dominated by East Asia. A natural question is whether the low and high growth outcomes by region continue to apply after holding constant the explanatory variables included in the basic regression system shown in column 2 of table 12.3. That is, the question is whether the included explanatory variables already measure the growth consequences of being located in a particular region. The regional dummy variables shown in table 12.5 have estimated coefficients of −0.007 (0.005) for sub-Saharan Africa, 0.006 (0.004) for Latin America, 0.009 (0.005) for East Asia, and −0.001 (0.006) for the OECD.[15] Thus only the East Asian dummy is significant at usual critical levels. The main observation here is that most of the consequences of an economy being included in any of these

13. For a discussion of corruption, see Mauro (1995).

14. This system covers only the two ten-year periods for growth, 1975–85 and 1985–95, because independent measures of electoral rights and civil liberties were unavailable before 1972. The timing for the civil liberties variable is the same as that discussed before for the electoral rights indicator.

15. The OECD countries are those other than Turkey that have been members since the 1960s.

regions is already held constant by the explanatory variables included in the basic regression system.

A reasonable expectation is that productivity would depend on age structure—notably, output per person would be expected to be higher if a larger fraction of the population is in the prime age category of 15–65 and less in the categories of under 15 and over 65. However, the two population share variables (for under 15 and over 65) are jointly insignificant if added to the regression system—the p value for the two jointly is 0.78. (These age structure variables are observed in 1960, 1970, and 1980.)

The basic system includes as a measure of government spending the standard definition of government consumption less the outlays on defense and education. If these last two components of government spending are entered separately (each as estimated ratios of real spending to real GDP), the estimated coefficients are 0.009 (0.074) for education and 0.033 (0.028) for defense. The timing of these variables is the same as that discussed before for the government consumption ratio. These two variables are jointly insignificant (p value is 0.4).[16]

The black-market premium on the foreign exchange is sometimes entered into growth equations as a proxy for a class of market distortions. However, this indicator can also proxy more generally for macroeconomic instability, in particular, for instability that relates to the balance of payments. The estimated coefficient on the log of one plus the black-market premium is negative and marginally significant: −0.010 (0.006). (This variable enters as averages for 1965–74, 1975–84, and 1985–92. The instrument lists include values for 1960–64, 1970–74, and 1980–84.) Hence, there is an indication that this distortion measure has inverse predictive power for economic growth.

Other analyses, such as King and Levine (1993) and Greenwood and Jovanovic (1990), have stressed the special role of the domestic financial system as an engine of growth. We consider here two proxies for this financial development. One is the ratio of private financial system credit to GDP and the other is a measure of financial system deposits (the M3 aggregate less the transactions-related M1 aggregate, again as a ratio to GDP). These variables are measured at the beginning of each ten-year period: 1965, 1975, and 1985. Of course, the development of the financial system is endogenous with respect to general economic development. Thus these financial proxies would be expected to matter only to the extent that they take on values that are unusual for an economy's level of development—as measured empirically by per capita GDP and some of the other explanatory variables. In any event, the estimated coefficients of the financial proxies are

16. Since the variable included in table 12.3 is based on standard government consumption less outlays on education and defense, we can also test whether the standard government consumption measure is the appropriate one to enter into the growth systems. This hypothesis is rejected with a p value of 0.022.

insignificantly different from zero: −0.005 (0.007) for the credit measure and 0.000 (0.011) for the deposit measure.

The line of research exemplified by La Porta et al. (1998) stresses the role of legal structures. In particular, this literature argues that the British common-law tradition is superior as a basis for economic development to the French statute-law system. The data consist of dummy variables for five types of legal traditions: British, French, Scandinavian, German, and socialist. Dummy variables for British and French legal structure turn out to have little explanatory power for growth: the coefficient on the British variable is 0.0027 (0.0045) and that on the French variable is 0.0095 (0.0046). The two variables are jointly significant, with a p value of 0.04—but, contrary to the basic hypothesis, the French system seems to be somewhat more favorable for growth than the British one (or other systems). Note, however, that these legal structure variables are entered into the basic system of table 12.3, column 2, which already holds constant measures of the rule of law and democracy.

Geographical elements have been stressed in the research by Gallup and Sachs (1998). One commonly used indicator is the absolute value of degrees latitude. The idea is that places too close to the equator have bad climate from the standpoint of excessive heat and humidity. Since too great a departure from the equator would signify excessive cold, we also include the square of latitude in the system. The result is that the linear term (0.065, s.e. = 0.028) and squared term (−0.101, s.e. = 0.047) are jointly marginally significant, with a p value of 0.07. The point estimates imply that the optimal (absolute) latitude from the standpoint of growth promotion is 32 degrees.

Another geographical factor, landlocked status, is likely to be important from the standpoint of encouraging trade and other communication with the rest of the world. (Note, however, that international openness is already held constant in the basic regression system.) A dummy for land-locked status turns out to be significantly negative: −0.0110 (0.0033).

Various measures of ethnic, linguistic, and religious fractionalization have been argued to matter for political decision making and conflict and, hence, for economic growth. A standard measure of fractionalization is one minus the Herfindahl index for membership shares (in ethnic, linguistic, or religious groups). This measure gives the probability that two randomly chosen persons in a country will come from different groups. The three measures of fractionalization considered in table 12.5 each have negative but statistically insignificant coefficients in the growth equations.[17]

Finally, colonial heritage has been argued to be important for growth. Sometimes these influences are thought to derive from inherited legal or monetary institutions—therefore, it is important to note the explanatory variables that are already included in column 2 of

17. The indices for ethnicity and language come from Alesina et al. (2003) and apply to the late 1990s. The value for religion was computed from Barrett's (1982) data on religious affiliation among ten major groups in 1970.

table 12.3. In any event, dummies for four colonial categories (British, French, Spanish or Portuguese, and other) are jointly insignificant for growth, with a p value of 0.39.[18]

12.4 Summary and Conclusions about Growth

Differences in per capita growth rates across countries are large and relate systematically to a set of quantifiable explanatory variables. One element of this set is a net convergence term, the positive effect on growth when the initial level of real per capita GDP is low relative to the starting amount of human capital in the forms of educational attainment and life expectancy and relative to explanatory variables that capture policies and national characteristics. There is also evidence that countries with higher initial human capital converge faster to their steady-state positions.

The empirical findings on conditional convergence are consistent with the neoclassical growth model of chapters 1 and 2 and with the imbalance effect for physical and human capital that was described in chapter 5. This convergence effect also appears in models of technological diffusion, as described in chapter 8.

For given values of per capita GDP and human capital, growth depends positively on the rule of law and international openness and negatively on the ratio of government consumption to GDP and the rate of inflation. Growth increases with favorable movements in the terms of trade and declines with increases in the fertility rate. The relation between growth and the investment ratio is positive but weak when the variables already mentioned are held constant and if the lagged investment ratio is used as an instrument.

12.5 Robustness

A central question for empirical economics in general and for economic growth in particular is which explanatory variables to include and which to exclude. The problem is that variables are significantly correlated with growth depending on which other variables are held constant. Specifically, which variables should be included in the growth regressions? Although we have dealt thus far with panels of three ten-year periods or seven five-year periods, we describe the problem and some possible solutions in the framework of a single cross-sectional regression. The reason is that we follow closely the analysis of Sala-i-Martin (1997a, 1997b) and Sala-i-Martin, Doppelhoffer, and Miller (2003).

18. The system in table 12.3, column 2, included in the instrument lists the dummies for Spanish or Portuguese and other colonies and excluded measures of inflation. The present system adds the other two colony dummies and also includes the lagged inflation rate.

Our starting point is a cross-country regression of the form

$$\gamma = \alpha + \beta_1 x_1 + \beta_2 x_2 + \cdots + \beta_n x_n + \epsilon \tag{12.2}$$

where γ is the vector of rates of economic growth, and $x_1, \ldots, x_n$ are vectors of potential explanatory variables. The question we consider is which variables x_j should be included in the regression. One problem is that economic theories are not precise enough to pinpoint the exact determinants of growth. For example, throughout the book, we have explored a number of growth theories, each of which suggests a different set of potential regressors. A second, perhaps more important, problem is that the theories tend not be mutually inconsistent: it is reasonable that physical capital accumulation matters for growth and, at the same time, that human capital, technological progress, and government polices matter as well.

Notice that we cannot include all potential variables in one regression and "let the data speak," because the number of potential variables is larger than the number of countries in the world, rendering the all-inclusive regression computationally impossible. The methodology usually used by empirical growth analysts consists of simply "trying" the variables that are thought to be potentially important determinants of growth.[19] However, as soon as one starts running regressions combining the various variables, one finds that x_1 is significant when the regression includes x_2 and x_3 but becomes insignificant when x_4 is included. Since one does not know a priori the "true" variables to include, one is left with the question, Which variables are "truly" correlated with growth?

12.5.1 Levine and Renelt (1992)

An initial answer to this question was given by Levine and Renelt (1992). They applied a modified version of Leamer's (1983, 1985) extreme-bounds analysis to identify "robust" empirical relations for economic growth. In brief, the extreme-bounds test works as follows. Imagine that we have a pool of potential K variables and are interested in knowing whether variable z is "robust." We would estimate regressions of the form:

$$\gamma = \alpha_j + \beta_{zj} z + \beta_{zj} x_j + \epsilon \tag{12.3}$$

where x_j is a vector of variables taken from the pool of the K variables available.[20] One needs to estimate this regression for all possible x_j combinations. For each model, j, one finds

19. The typical economic growth paper first presents a theory, followed by an empirical section in which it is shown that the variable that captures the phenomenon highlighted by the theory is correlated with growth when a number of other variables are held constant. The typical paper then proceeds to show that the central variable remains significant even when changes are made in the set of explanatory variables.

20. Following Leamer (1983, 1985), Levine and Renelt also include some "fixed" variables that appear in all regressions and are not tested. The researcher is supposed to know that these variables belong in the regression for sure. Since we do not know whether there are any variables that belong in the true model for sure, we ignore the fixed variables in our description of Levine and Renelt (1992).

an estimate, $\hat{\beta}_{zj}$, and the corresponding standard deviation, $\hat{\sigma}_{zj}$. The lower extreme bound is defined to be the lowest value of $\hat{\beta}_{zj} - 2\hat{\sigma}_{zj}$ over all possible models j, and the upper extreme bound is defined to be the largest value of $\hat{\beta}_{zj} + 2\hat{\sigma}_{zj}$. The extreme-bounds test for variable z says that if the lower extreme bound is negative and the upper extreme bound is positive, then variable z is fragile. The test is then repeated for all variables in the data set.

Notice that, if $\hat{\beta}_{zj}$ is not significantly different from zero for a single one of the millions of possible regressions, the extreme-bounds test says that this variable is not robust. The reason is that we say that $\hat{\beta}_{zj}$ is not "significant" when the interval $[\hat{\beta}_{zj} - 2\hat{\sigma}_{zj}, \hat{\beta}_{zj} + 2\hat{\sigma}_{zj}]$ includes zero. Thus every regression carries a "veto power" (independent of how poorly the regression actually fits) in the sense that, if the coefficient β_{zj} for that particular regression happens not to be significant, then variable z will be labeled nonrobust regardless of what the other millions of regressions that include z as an explanatory variable say. The main result in the Levine and Renelt (1992) analysis is that *all* variables are, not surprisingly, found to be "fragile."

12.5.2 Bayesian Averaging of Classical Estimates (BACE)

The fact that any single regression carries a veto power to render a variable nonrobust led Sala-i-Martin (1997a, 1997b) to argue that this test was too strong to be meaningful.[21] He proposed to depart from this "extreme" test and, instead of assigning a label of "fragile" or "not fragile" to a particular variable, he assigned a "level of confidence" to each variable. To this end, he constructed weighted averages of all the estimates of $\hat{\beta}_{zj}$ and its corresponding standard deviations, $\hat{\sigma}_{zj}$, using weights proportional to the likelihoods of each of the models. In other words, the $\hat{\beta}_{zj}$ that come from models that fit well tend to have larger weights in the weighted average of OLS coefficients. To measure significance, Sala-i-Martin calculated a likelihood-weighted sum of normal cumulative distribution functions. He finds that Levine and Renelt's pessimistic conclusion is not warranted and that a number of variables are significantly correlated with growth. In order to maintain comparability, Sala-i-Martin (1997a, 1997b) followed Levine and Renelt in assuming that there is a set of "fixed regressors" that belongs in all models, and he restricts all the regressions to have seven explanatory variables. One of the shortcomings of this approach is that the statistical properties of these weighted averages are not well understood, since he did not derive them from a statistical theory.

Sala-i-Martin, Doppelhoffer, and Miller (2003) (SDM from now on) show that Sala-i-Martin's approach is a particular case of Bayesian model averaging, a method that we

21. For other criticisms of the extreme bounds test, see Durlauf and Quah (1999) and Temple (1999). Granger and Uhlig (1990) have proposed what they call the reasonable extreme bounds, and Doppelhoffer (2000) applies this bound to economic growth regressions.

discuss next. A natural way to think about model uncertainty is to admit that we do not know which model is "true" and, instead, attach probabilities to different possible models. While intuitively appealing, this approach requires a departure from the classical framework in which conditioning on a model is essential. This approach has recently come to be known as Bayesian model averaging. The procedure accords with standard Bayesian reasoning: the idea dates back at least to Jeffreys (1961) and was extended by Leamer (1978).

The fully Bayesian approach has been applied to various problems by a number of authors. Examples include Raftery, Madigan, and Hoeting (1997) and York et al. (1995). A pure Bayesian approach requires specification of the prior distributions of all of the relevant parameters conditional on each possible model. Under ideal conditions, elicitation of prior parameters is difficult and is indeed one of the major reasons for Bayesian approaches remaining relatively unpopular. When the number of possible regressors is K, the number of possible linear models is 2^K, so with K large, fully specifying priors is infeasible. Thus authors implementing the fully Bayesian approach have used priors that are essentially arbitrary. This technique makes the ultimate estimates dependent on arbitrarily chosen prior parameters in a manner that is difficult to interpret. In existing applications of this approach, the impact of these prior parameters has been neither examined nor explained.

SDM (2003) use the Bayesian approach to averaging across models, while following the classical spirit. They propose a model-averaging technique, which they call Bayesian averaging of classical estimates, or BACE, to determine the "importance" of variables in cross-country growth regressions. They show that the weighting method can be derived as a limiting case of a standard Bayesian analysis as the prior information becomes "dominated" by the data. BACE combines the averaging of estimates across models, which is a Bayesian concept, with classical OLS estimation, which comes from the assumption of diffuse priors.

A full derivation of the BACE methodology is in SDM (2003). Here we report the main findings. Let model M_j be a statistical growth model with a particular set of explanatory variables. Bayes's rule and basic probability theory suggest that the posterior distribution of the parameters is the weighted average of all the possible conditional posterior densities with the weights given by the posterior probabilities of each of the possible models:

$$g(\beta \mid y) = \sum_{j=1}^{2^K} P(M_j \mid y) \cdot g(\beta \mid y, M_j) \tag{12.4}$$

where $g(\beta \mid y)$ is the posterior distribution of β (conditional on the data set), $g(\beta \mid y, M_j)$ is the distribution of β conditional on the data and on model M_j, and $P(M_j \mid y)$ is the posterior probability of model j conditional on the data. If we have K potential explanatory variables, there are 2^K possible models. If the researcher has diffuse priors (that is, if we are incapable or unwilling to specify priors) and we assume that the priors get dominated by the data,[22] then the posterior probability of the jth model can be written as

$$P(M_j \mid y) = P(M_j) \cdot \omega(j) \tag{12.5}$$

where

$$\omega(j) = \frac{T^{-k_j/2} \cdot SSE_j^{-T/2}}{\sum_{i=1}^{2^K} P(M_i) T^{-k_i/2} \cdot SSE_i^{-T/2}}$$

SSE_j is the sum of the squares of residuals for model j, T is the number of observations, and k_j is the size (that is, the number of regressors) of model j. In other words, the weights assigned to each model in equation (12.4) are the product of the prior we have for model j, $P(M_j)$, times a measure of the goodness of fit for model j relative to the goodness of fit of all possible models. Notice that the weights in equation (12.5) are corrected by the degrees of freedom (larger models get penalized) in the spirit of the Schwarz (1978) model selection criterion.

The only remaining issue is to decide what is the prior probability that we attach to model j. In other words, before we see the data, what probability do we attach to each of the possible 2^K models.

One common approach to this problem in the statistical literature has been to think of each model as having an equal probability. This is one way to confess ignorance: before we analyze the data, we don't know which model is more likely, so we assume that they are all equally likely. While this approach is sensible for some applications, in our case it is not for at least two reasons. First, since we have a large number of potential regressors, this prior has the odd and troubling implication that the expected size (the expected number of regressors) is large. In particular, since we are going to use a data set with 67 variables, assuming that all models are equally likely means that we expect the number of explanatory variables of the cross-country regression to be 33.5 on average. The second undesirable implication is that the expected size of the model depends on the data set used. If we use a data set with 32 variables and we assume that all models are equally likely, we implicitly assume that the expected size of the model is 16. If, instead, we had a data set with 100 potential regressors, we would be assuming that the expected size is 50. Since we do not believe that the size of the regression that "explains" growth should depend on the data set that we happen to use, we need to modify our priors about each of the models.

SDM (2003) specify the model prior probabilities by assuming that each variable has a prior probability $\bar{k}/K$ of entering each particular regression, where $\bar{k}$ is the prior mean

22. See SDM (2003).

model size and K is the total number of potential regressors.[23] The implied prior $P(M_j)$ for a model of size k_j is, therefore,

$$P(M_j) = \left(\frac{\bar{k}}{K}\right)^{k_j}\left(1 - \frac{\bar{k}}{K}\right)^{K-k_j} \tag{12.6}$$

Notice that the "equal probability for each possible model" is the special case in which $\bar{k} = K/2$. One of the beauties of this approach is that the only parameter that the researcher needs to specify ex ante is the "expected models size," $\bar{k}$. And since we only need to specify one parameter, it is very easy to perform robustness tests by changing this single prior parameter.

Equations (12.4), (12.5), and (12.6) describe the posterior distribution of β. Once this distribution is determined, we can find its mean, its variance, and other moments. For example, taking expectations with respect to β across equation (12.4), we have

$$E(\beta \mid y) = \sum_{j=1}^{2^K} P(M_i \mid y) \cdot \hat{\beta}_j \tag{12.7}$$

where $\hat{\beta}_j = E(\beta \mid y, M_j)$ is the OLS estimate of β with the regressors in model j. In Bayesian terms, $\hat{\beta}_j$ is the posterior mean conditional on model j. Note that any variable excluded from a particular model has a slope coefficient with degenerate posterior distribution at zero. In words, the expected value of β is the weighted average of OLS estimates, where the weights are proportional to a measure of goodness of fit and the prior model size.[24]

The posterior variance of β is given by

$$\mathrm{var}(\beta \mid y) = \sum_{j=1}^{2^K} P(M_i \mid y) \cdot \mathrm{var}(\beta \mid y, M_j) + \sum_{j=1}^{2^K} P(M_i \mid y) \cdot \left(\hat{\beta}_j - \sum_{j=1}^{2^K} P(M_i \mid y) \cdot \hat{\beta}_j\right)^2 \tag{12.8}$$

23. In most applications the prior probability of including a particular variable is not, for most researchers, independent of the probability of including any other variable. For example, in a growth regression if a variable proxying political instability is included, such as a count of revolutions, many researchers would think it less likely that another measure, such as the number of assassinations, would be included as well. While this sort of interdependence can be readily incorporated into the BACE framework, SDM (2003) do not pursue this avenue.

24. Note that the weighted average of OLS coefficients, where the weights are proportial to a measure of goodness of fit, is similar to the one postulated by Sala-i-Martin (1997a, 1997b). This is exactly true when all the regressions have the same size.

Inspection of equation (12.8) demonstrates that the posterior variance incorporates both the estimated variances in individual models and the variance in estimates of the β's across different models.

While posterior means and variances are of interest, there are other ways to summarize the large amount of information supplied by the full posterior distribution. In particular, an interesting statistic is the posterior probability that a particular variable is in the regression (i.e., has a nonzero coefficient). SDM (2003) call this the *posterior inclusion probability* for the variable—it is calculated as the sum of the posterior model probabilities for all the models that include the variable. The posterior mean and variance *conditional* on the inclusion of the variable can also be estimated. The true (unconditional) posterior mean is computed according to equation (12.7), while the posterior standard deviation is the square root of the variance formula in equation (12.8). The true posterior mean is a weighted average of the OLS estimates for all regressions, including regressions in which the variable does not appear and thus has a coefficient of zero. Hence, the conditional posterior mean can be computed by dividing the unconditional mean by the posterior inclusion probability.[25]

12.5.3 Main Results in Sala-i-Martin, Doppelhofer, and Miller (2003)

SDM (2003) apply BACE to a set of 67 variables. The variables were selected using the following criteria. (1) Use variables that are available as closely as possible to the beginning of the sample, 1960. This restriction means that some interesting variables in the literature (such as the measures of the rule of law and corruption considered earlier) are excluded from the analysis. (2) Use variables that allow for a "balanced" data set. By balanced, we mean an equal number of observations for all regressions. With these restrictions, the total size of the data set becomes 68 variables (including the dependent variable, the growth rate of GDP per capita between 1960 and 1996) for 88 countries.

Column 1 of table 12.6 reports the fraction of regressions that are significant at the 95 percent level for each explanatory variable, when we combine each variable with all possible combinations of the remaining 67 variables. Notice that all variables are insignificant for a subset of the models. Hence, the Levine and Renelt (1992) extreme-bounds test would label all of them as nonrobust.

Figure 12.14 shows the posterior densities (approximated by histograms) of the coefficient estimates for four selected variables (the investment price, the initial level of GDP per capita, primary schooling, and the number of years an economy has been "open").[26] Note that, in figure 12.14, each distribution consists of two parts: first, a continuous part that is the

25. Similarly, the unconditional variance can be computed from the conditional variance as follows:

$\sigma^2_{\text{uncond}} = [\sigma^2_{\text{cond}} + \beta^2_{\text{cond}}] \cdot (\text{Posterior inclusion probablity}) - \beta^2_{\text{uncond}}$

26. See SDM (2003) for results on the remaining variables.

Table 12.6
Baseline Estimation for All 67 Variables

Rank	Variable	Fraction of Regressions with $\lvert t \text{ stat} \rvert > 2$ (1)	Posterior Inclusion Probability (2)	Posterior Mean Conditional on Inclusion (3)	Posterior s.d. Conditional on Inclusion (4)	Posterior Unconditional Mean (3)′	Posterior Unconditional s.d. (4)′	Sign Certainty Probability (5)
1	East asian	0.99	0.823	0.021805	0.006118	0.017935	0.010010	0.999
2	Primary schooling 1960	0.96	0.796	0.026852	0.007977	0.021386	0.012945	0.999
3	Investment price	0.99	0.774	−0.000084	0.000025	−0.000065	0.000041	0.999
4	GDP 1960 (log)	0.30	0.685	−0.008538	0.002888	−0.005845	0.004631	0.999
5	Fraction of tropical area (or people)	0.59	0.563	−0.014757	0.004227	−0.008312	0.007977	0.997
6	Population density in coastal areas 1960s	0.85	0.428	0.000009	0.000003	0.000004	0.000005	0.996
7	Malaria prevalence in 1960s	0.84	0.252	−0.015702	0.006177	−0.003956	0.007489	0.990
8	Life expectancy in 1960	0.79	0.209	0.000808	0.000354	0.000168	0.000366	0.986
9	Fraction Confucian	0.97	0.206	0.054429	0.022426	0.011239	0.024275	0.988
10	African dummy	0.90	0.154	−0.014706	0.006866	−0.002260	0.005948	0.980
11	Latin American dummy	0.30	0.149	−0.012758	0.005834	−0.001905	0.005075	0.969
12	Fraction GDP in mining	0.07	0.124	0.038823	0.019255	0.004818	0.014487	0.978
13	Spanish colony	0.24	0.123	−0.010720	0.005041	−0.001320	0.003942	0.972
14	Years open	0.98	0.119	0.012209	0.006287	0.001457	0.004514	0.977
15	Fraction Muslim	0.11	0.114	0.012629	0.006257	0.001446	0.004545	0.973
16	Fraction Buddhist	0.90	0.108	0.021667	0.010722	0.002348	0.007604	0.974
17	Ethnolinguistic fractionalization	0.52	0.105	−0.011281	0.005835	−0.001181	0.003936	0.974
18	Government consumption share 1960s	0.77	0.104	−0.044171	0.025383	−0.004586	0.015761	0.975
19	Population density 1960	0.01	0.086	0.000013	0.000007	0.000001	0.000004	0.965
20	Real exchange rate distortions	0.92	0.082	−0.000079	0.000043	−0.000006	0.000025	0.966
21	Fraction speaking foreign language	0.43	0.080	0.007006	0.003960	0.000559	0.002204	0.962

22	(Imports + exports)/GDP	0.67	0.076	0.008858	0.005210	0.000674	0.002754	0.949
23	Political rights	0.35	0.066	−0.001847	0.001202	−0.000121	0.000551	0.939
24	Government share of GDP	0.58	0.063	−0.034874	0.029379	−0.002205	0.011253	0.935
25	Higher education in 1960	0.10	0.061	−0.069693	0.041833	−0.004282	0.019688	0.946
26	Fraction population in tropics	0.85	0.058	−0.010741	0.006754	−0.000622	0.002990	0.940
27	Primary exports in 1970	0.75	0.053	−0.011343	0.007520	−0.000604	0.003082	0.926
28	Public investment share	0.00	0.048	−0.061540	0.042950	−0.002964	0.016201	0.922
29	Fraction protestants	0.29	0.046	−0.011872	0.009288	−0.000544	0.003180	0.909
30	Fraction Hindus	0.07	0.045	0.017558	0.012575	0.000790	0.004512	0.915
31	Fraction population less than 15	0.24	0.041	0.044962	0.041100	0.001850	0.012216	0.871
32	Air distance to big cities	0.18	0.039	−0.000001	0.000001	0.000000	0.000000	0.888
33	Gov C share deflated with GDP prices	0.05	0.036	−0.033647	0.027365	−0.001195	0.008087	0.893
34	Absolute latitude	0.37	0.033	0.000136	0.000233	0.000004	0.000049	0.737
35	Fraction Catholic	0.16	0.033	−0.008415	0.008478	−0.000278	0.002155	0.837
36	Fertility rates in 1960s	0.46	0.031	−0.007525	0.010113	−0.000232	0.002199	0.767
37	European dummy	0.19	0.030	−0.002278	0.010487	−0.000068	0.001858	0.544
38	Outward orientation	0.01	0.030	−0.003296	0.002727	−0.000098	0.000730	0.886
39	Colony dummy	0.44	0.029	−0.005010	0.004721	−0.000147	0.001169	0.858
40	Civil liberties	0.15	0.029	−0.007192	0.007122	−0.000207	0.001705	0.846
41	Revolutions and coups	0.07	0.029	−0.007065	0.006089	−0.000202	0.001565	0.877
42	British colony dummy	0.09	0.027	0.003654	0.003626	0.000097	0.000835	0.844
43	Hydrocarbon deposits in 1993	0.01	0.025	0.000307	0.000418	0.000008	0.000081	0.773
44	Fraction population over 65	0.20	0.022	0.019382	0.119469	0.000435	0.018127	0.566
45	Defense spending share	0.26	0.021	0.045336	0.076813	0.000967	0.012992	0.737
46	Population in 1960	0.07	0.021	0.000000	0.000000	0.000000	0.000000	0.806

Table continued

Table 12.6
(Continued)

Rank	Variable	Fraction of Regressions with $\|t \text{ stat}\| > 2$ (1)	Posterior Inclusion Probability (2)	Posterior Mean Conditional on Inclusion (3)	Posterior s.d. Conditional on Inclusion (4)	Posterior Unconditional Mean (3)′	Posterior Unconditional s.d. (4)′	Sign Certainty Probability (5)
47	Terms of trade growth in 1960s	0.00	0.021	0.032627	0.046650	0.000693	0.008265	0.752
48	Public educ. spend. /GDP in 1960s	0.11	0.021	0.129517	0.172847	0.002698	0.031056	0.777
49	Landlocked country dummy	0.04	0.021	−0.002080	0.004206	−0.000043	0.000671	0.701
50	Religion measure	0.18	0.020	−0.004737	0.007232	−0.000097	0.001233	0.751
51	Size of economy	0.18	0.020	−0.000520	0.001443	−0.000011	0.000218	0.661
52	Socialist dummy	0.00	0.020	0.003983	0.004966	0.000081	0.000903	0.788
53	English-speaking population	0.07	0.020	−0.003669	0.007137	−0.000073	0.001132	0.686
54	Average inflation 1960–90	0.01	0.020	−0.000073	0.000097	−0.000001	0.000017	0.784
55	Oil-producing country dummy	0.00	0.019	0.004845	0.007088	0.000094	0.001193	0.751
56	Population growth rate 1960–90	0.21	0.019	0.020837	0.307794	0.000401	0.042787	0.533
57	Timing of independence	0.11	0.019	0.001143	0.002051	0.000022	0.000324	0.716
58	Fraction land area near navigable water	0.35	0.019	−0.002598	0.005864	−0.000048	0.000875	0.657
59	Square of inflation 1960–90	0.00	0.018	−0.000001	0.000001	0.000000	0.000000	0.736
60	Fraction spent in war 1960–90	0.00	0.016	−0.001415	0.009226	−0.000022	0.001176	0.555
61	Land area	0.01	0.016	0.000000	0.000000	0.000000	0.000000	0.577
62	Tropical climate zone	0.16	0.016	−0.002069	0.006593	−0.000032	0.000864	0.616
63	Terms of trade ranking	0.23	0.016	−0.003730	0.009625	−0.000058	0.001288	0.647
64	Capitalism	0.06	0.015	−0.000231	0.001080	−0.000003	0.000136	0.589
65	Fraction Orthodox	0.00	0.015	0.005689	0.013576	0.000086	0.001804	0.660
66	War participation 1960–90	0.02	0.015	−0.000734	0.002983	−0.000011	0.000377	0.593
67	Interior density	0.00	0.015	−0.000001	0.000016	0.000000	0.000002	0.532

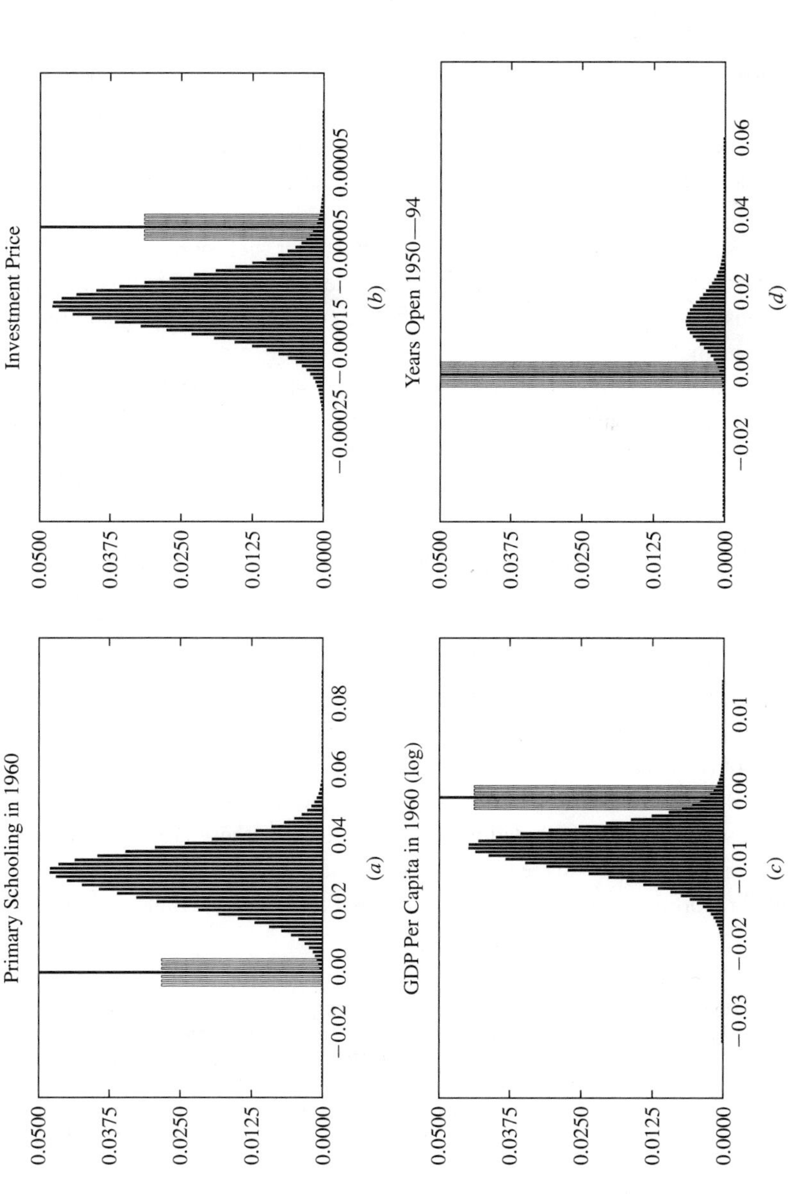

Figure 12.14
Posterior densities. This figure shows the posterior densities (approximated by histograms) of the coefficient estimates for four selected variables. Panels (a), (b), (c), and (d) refer to primary schooling, the investment price, the initial level of GDP per capita GDP, and the number of years an economy has been "open." Each distribution consists of two parts: first, a continuous part that is the posterior density conditional on inclusion in the model and, second, a discrete mass at zero representing the probability that the variable does not belong in the model (one minus the posterior inclusion probability).

posterior density conditional on inclusion in the model, and second, a discrete mass at zero representing the probability that the variable does not belong in the model (one minus the posterior inclusion probability).

Baseline Estimation This section presents the baseline estimation results with a prior expected model size $\bar{k} = 7$. The choice of the baseline model size is motivated by the fact that most empirical growth studies include a moderate number of explanatory variables. The posterior model size for the baseline estimation is 7.46, which is very close to the prior model size. In the next section, we check the robustness of our results to changes in the prior mean model size. The results are based on approximately 89 million randomly drawn regressions.[27]

Table 12.6 shows the results: column 2 reports the posterior inclusion probability of a variable in the growth regression. Variables are sorted in descending order of this posterior probability. The posterior inclusion probability is the sum of the posterior probabilities of all of the regressions that include that variable. The goodness-of-fit measure is adjusted to penalize highly parameterized models in the fashion of the Schwarz model selection criterion. Thus variables with high inclusion probabilities are variables that have high marginal contribution to the goodness-of-fit of the regression model.

We can divide the variables according to whether seeing the data causes us to increase or decrease our inclusion probability relative to the prior probability. Since our expected model size is 7, the prior inclusion probability for each variable is $7/67 = 0.104$. There are 18 variables for which the posterior inclusion probability increases relative to the prior probability after we have estimated all the regressions (these variables are shaded in table 12.6). For these variables, our belief that they belong in the regression is strengthened once we see the data. We could label these variables as "strong" or "robust." The remaining 49 variables have little or no support for inclusion: seeing the data further reduces our already modest initial assessment of their inclusion probability.

Columns 3 and 4 show the posterior mean and standard deviation of the distributions, conditional on the variable being included in the model. That is, these are the means and standard deviation of the "hump-shaped" part of the distribution shown in figure 12.14. Columns 3′ and 4′ report the corresponding unconditional means and variances.[28]

27. The total number of possible regression models equals 2^{67}, which is approximately equal to 1.48×10^{20} models. However, convergence of the estimates is attained relatively quickly; after 33 million draws the maximum change of coefficient estimates normalized by the standard deviation of the regressors relative to the dependent variable is smaller than 10^{-3} per 10,000, and after 89 million draws, the maximum change is smaller than 10^{-6}. See SDM (2003) for details on sampling and other technical issues.

28. Remember that the unconditional mean is equal to the conditional mean times the posterior probability of inclusion and that the relation between the unconditional and conditional variances is given by the formula in note 25.

From the posterior density, we can also estimate the posterior probability, conditional on inclusion, that a coefficient has the same sign as its posterior mean. This "sign certainty probability," reported in column 5 is another measure of the significance of the variables. This is the posterior probability on the same side of zero as the posterior mean of the coefficient, conditional on the variable's inclusion. As noted earlier, for each individual regression, the posterior density is equal to the classical sampling distribution of the coefficient. In classical terms, a coefficient would be 5 percent significant in a two-sided test if 97.5 percent of the probability in the sampling distribution were on the same side of zero as the coefficient estimate. So if, for example, it just happened that a coefficient were exactly 5 percent significant in every single regression, its sign certainty probability would be 97.5 percent. Applying a 0.975 cutoff to this quantity identifies a set of 13 variables, all of which are also in the group of 18 "strong" variables for which the posterior inclusion probability is larger than the prior inclusion probability. The remaining five have very large sign certainty probabilities (between 0.970 and 0.975). Note that there is in principle no reason why a variable could not have a very high posterior inclusion probability and still have a low sign certainty probability. It just happens that in our data set there are no such variables.[29]

Another interesting statistic is the posterior mean model size. For the baseline estimation, the prior model size was seven, and the posterior mean model size is 7.46. This number is, of course, sensitive to the specification of the prior mean model size, as we will discuss subsequently.

We are now ready to analyze the variables that are "strongly" related to growth.

Variables Strongly or Robustly Related to Growth Not surprisingly, the top variable is the dummy for East Asian countries, which is positively related with economic growth. This finding, of course, reflects the exceptional growth performance of East Asian countries between 1960 and the mid-1990s.[30] The sign certainty probability in column 5 shows that the probability mass of the density to the left of zero equals to 0.9992. Notice that the fraction of regressions for which the East Asian dummy has a t statistic greater than 2 in absolute value is 99 percent.

The second variable is a measure of human capital: the primary schooling enrollment rate in 1960. This variable is positively related to growth and the inclusion probability is 0.80. The posterior distribution of the coefficient estimates is shown in the first panel of figure 12.14. Since the inclusion probability is relatively high, the mass at zero (which shows

29. This result would occur if, for example, a variable contributed a great deal to the fit of the model but switched signs in the presence of another important variable. Notice that the BACE weights in equation (12.5) penalize the inclusion of additional variables that are strongly correlated with other included regressors and do not explain more of the variation of the dependent variable.

30. Notice that the dummy is present despite the robust positive relationship between the fraction of population Confucian (which is ranked ninth in the table).

one minus the inclusion probability) is relatively small. Conditional on being included in the model, a 10 percentage point increase of the primary school enrollment rate is associated with a 0.27 percentage point increase of the growth rate. This can be contrasted with the average sample growth rate of 1.82 percent between 1960 and 1996. The sign certainty probability for this variable is also 0.999, and the fraction of regressions with a t statistic larger than 2 is 96 percent.

The third variable is the average price of investment goods between 1960 and 1964. Its inclusion probability is 0.77. This variable is depicted graphically in the second panel of figure 12.14. The posterior mean coefficient is very precisely estimated to be negative, which indicates that a relative high price of investment goods at the beginning of the sample is strongly and negatively related to subsequent income growth.[31] The sign certainty probability in column 5 shows that the probability mass of the density to the left of zero equals 0.99. This result can also be seen in figure 12.14, where almost all of the continuous density lies below zero.

The next variable is the initial level of per capita GDP, a measure of conditional convergence. The inclusion probability is 0.69. The third panel in figure 12.14 shows the posterior distribution of the coefficient estimates for initial income. Conditional on inclusion, the posterior mean coefficient is -0.009 (with a standard deviation of 0.003). In other words, the coefficient associated with conditional convergence is very precisely estimated, although the mean coefficient is somewhat smaller than the convergence coefficient predicted by the neoclassical models described in chapters 1 and 2 or from the technological diffusion models described in chapter 8. The sign certainty probability in column 5 is 0.999. The fraction of regressions in which the coefficient for initial income has a t statistic greater than 2 in absolute value is only 30 percent, so that an extreme-bounds test very easily labels the variable as not robust.

The next variables reflect the poor economic performance of tropical countries: the proportion of a country's area in the tropics and the index of malaria prevalence both have a negative relation with growth. Another geographical variable that performs well is the density of the population in coastal areas, which has a positive relationship with growth, suggesting that areas that are densely populated and are close to the sea have experienced higher growth rates.

Life expectancy in 1960, which reflects nutrition, health care, and literacy rates, is positively related to growth: countries with high life expectancy in 1960 tended to grow faster over the following four decades. The inclusion probability for this variable is 0.21.

31. Once the relative price of investment goods is included among the pool of explanatory variables, the share of investment in GDP in 1961 becomes insignificant and has the "wrong sign," while the other results are unaffected. The estimation results including investment share are available from the authors upon request.

Dummies for sub-Saharan Africa and Latin America are negatively related to income growth. The posterior means conditional on inclusion are both negative, implying that Latin American and sub-Saharan African countries had income per capita growth rates between 1960 and 1996 that were 1.47 and 1.28 percentage points respectively below the level that would be predicted by the countries' other characteristics. For comparison, the sample average growth rate is 1.82. The African dummy is significant in 90 percent of the regressions, and the sign certainty probability is 98 percent. Although the Latin American dummy is only significant in 33 percent of the regressions, its sign certainty is almost as high as the African: 97 percent.

The fraction of GDP in mining has a positive relationship with growth and inclusion probability of 0.12. This variable captures the success of countries with a large endowment of natural resources. Many economists expect that the large rents associated with more political instability or rent-seeking would lower economic growth. However, our study shows that economies with a larger mining sector tend to perform better.

Former Spanish colonies tend to grow less, whereas the number of years an economy has been open has a positive sign. The fractions of the population Muslim and Buddhist each have a positive association with growth. The index of ethnolinguistic fractionalization is negatively related to growth and it also appears to be robust.

Finally, the share of government consumption in GDP is robustly estimated, and its sign is negative. Perhaps the real surprise is the negative coefficient of the public investment share. Table 12.6 shows that this variable is not robust when the prior model size is $\bar{k} = 7$. However, we will see later that this is one of the variables that become important in larger models, and the sign remains negative.

Variables Marginally Related to Growth There are three variables that have posterior probabilities somewhat lower than their prior probabilities but nonetheless are fairly precisely estimated if they are included in the growth regression (that is, their sign certainty probability is larger than 95 percent). These variables are the overall density in 1960 (which is positively related to growth), real exchange rate distortions (negative), and the fraction of population speaking a foreign language (positive).

Variables Not Robustly Related to Growth The remaining 46 variables show little evidence of robust partial correlation with growth. They neither contribute importantly to the goodness-of-fit of growth regressions, as measured by their posterior inclusion probabilities, nor have estimates that are robust across different sets of conditioning variables. It is interesting to notice that some political variables such as the number of revolutions and coups or the index of political rights are not robustly related to economic growth. Similarly, the degree of capitalism measure or a socialism dummy have no strong relationship with growth.[32] Some macroeconomic variables, such as the inflation rate, also do not appear to be strongly related to growth. Other surprisingly weak variables are the spending in public education, measures of higher education, geographical measures such as latitude, and various proxies for "scale effects," such as the total population, aggregate GDP, or the total area of a country.

12.5.4 Robustness Analysis

Until now we have concentrated on results derived for a prior model size $\bar{k} = 7$. As discussed earlier, while we feel that this is a reasonable expected model size, it is in some sense arbitrary. We need to explore the effects of the prior on our conclusions. Table 12.7 performs precisely this task, reporting the posterior inclusion probabilities and conditional posterior means, respectively, for $\bar{k}$ equal to 5, 9, 11, 16, and 22. Note that each $\bar{k}$ has a corresponding value of the prior probability of inclusion, which is reported in the first row of the table. Thus, to see whether a variable improves its probability of inclusion relative to the prior, we need to compare the posterior probability to the corresponding prior probability. The variables that are important in the baseline case of $\bar{k} = 7$ and are not important for other prior model sizes are shaded in table 12.7. Variables that are not important for $\bar{k} = 7$ but become important with other sizes are both shaded and their cells are bordered.

"Strong" Variables That Become "Weak" Note that most of the strongest variables show little sensitivity to the choice of prior model size, either in terms of their inclusion probabilities or their coefficient estimates. Some of the important variables seem to improve substantially with the prior model size. For example, for the fraction of GDP in mining, the posterior inclusion probability rises from 7 percent with $\bar{k} = 5$ to 66 percent with $\bar{k} = 22$. This result suggests that mining is a variable that requires other conditioning variables in order to display its full importance. The fraction of Confucians and the sub-Saharan Africa dummy also do better with more conditioning variables and have stable coefficient estimates.

Although most of the strong variables remain strong, five of them tend to lose power as we increase the prior model size. That is, for larger models, the posterior probability declines to levels below the prior size. These variables are the index of malaria prevalence, the former Spanish colony, the number of years an economy has been open, the index of ethnolinguistic fractionalization, and the government consumption share. These findings suggest that these variables could be acting as catchalls for various other effects. For example, the openness index captures various aspects of the openness of a country to trade (tariff and nontariff barriers, black market premium, degree of socialism, and monopolization of exports by the

32. We should point out that neither the former Soviet Union nor most of the rest of socialist East European countries are included in the data set, mainly because of missing data.

Table 12.7
Posterior Inclusion Probabilities with Different Prior Model Sizes

Rank	Variable	kbar5	kbar7	kbar9	kbar11	kbar16	kbar22	kbar28
	Prior inclusion probability	0.075	0.104	0.134	0.164	0.239	0.328	0.418
1	East Asian	0.891	0.823	0.757	0.711	0.585	0.481	0.455
2	Primary schooling 1960	0.709	0.796	0.826	0.862	0.890	0.924	0.950
3	Investment price	0.635	0.774	0.840	0.891	0.936	0.968	0.985
4	GDP 1960 (log)	0.526	0.685	0.788	0.843	0.920	0.960	0.978
5	Fraction of tropical area (or people)	0.536	0.563	0.548	0.542	0.462	0.399	0.388
6	Population density coastal 1960s	0.350	0.428	0.463	0.473	0.433	0.389	0.352
7	Malaria prevalence in 1960s	0.339	0.252	0.203	0.176	0.145	0.131	0.138
8	Life expectancy in 1960	0.176	0.209	0.262	0.278	0.368	0.440	0.467
9	Fraction confucian	0.140	0.206	0.272	0.333	0.501	0.671	0.777
10	African dummy	0.095	0.154	0.223	0.272	0.406	0.519	0.565
11	Latin American dummy	0.101	0.149	0.205	0.240	0.340	0.413	0.429
12	Fraction GDP in mining	0.072	0.124	0.209	0.275	0.478	0.659	0.761
13	Spanish colony	0.130	0.123	0.119	0.116	0.124	0.148	0.182
14	Years open	0.090	0.119	0.124	0.132	0.145	0.155	0.177
15	Fraction Muslim	0.078	0.114	0.150	0.178	0.267	0.366	0.450
16	Fraction Buddhist	0.073	0.108	0.152	0.190	0.320	0.465	0.563
17	Ethnolinguistic fractionalization	0.080	0.105	0.131	0.140	0.155	0.160	0.184
18	Government consumption share 1960s	0.090	0.104	0.135	0.147	0.213	0.262	0.297
19	Population density 1960	0.043	0.086	0.137	0.175	0.257	0.295	0.316
20	Real exchange rate distortions	0.059	0.082	0.117	0.134	0.205	0.263	0.319
21	Fraction speaking foreign language	0.052	0.080	0.110	0.149	0.247	0.374	0.478
22	(Imports + exports)/GDP	0.063	0.076	0.085	0.099	0.131	0.181	0.240
23	Political rights	0.042	0.066	0.082	0.095	0.114	0.130	0.154
24	Government share of GDP	0.044	0.063	0.087	0.112	0.186	0.252	0.291
25	Higher education in 1960	0.059	0.061	0.066	0.070	0.079	0.103	0.131
26	Fraction population in tropics	0.047	0.058	0.061	0.074	0.099	0.132	0.157
27	Primary exports in 1970	0.047	0.053	0.065	0.072	0.104	0.137	0.162
28	Public investment share	0.023	0.048	0.096	0.151	0.321	0.525	0.669
29	Fraction Protestants	0.035	0.046	0.055	0.061	0.083	0.120	0.156
30	Fraction Hindus	0.028	0.045	0.059	0.077	0.126	0.179	0.227
31	Fraction population less than 15	0.035	0.041	0.045	0.050	0.067	0.093	0.123
32	Air distance to big cities	0.024	0.039	0.054	0.072	0.097	0.115	0.141
33	Gov C share deflated with GDP price	0.021	0.036	0.056	0.075	0.137	0.225	0.310
34	Absolute latitude	0.029	0.033	0.040	0.042	0.059	0.086	0.115
35	Fraction Catholic	0.019	0.033	0.042	0.056	0.104	0.163	0.223
36	Fertility rates in 1960s	0.020	0.031	0.043	0.063	0.108	0.170	0.232
37	European dummy	0.020	0.030	0.043	0.049	0.094	0.148	0.201
38	Outward orientation	0.019	0.030	0.043	0.054	0.085	0.134	0.178
39	Colony dummy	0.022	0.029	0.039	0.049	0.075	0.105	0.146
40	Civil liberties	0.021	0.029	0.037	0.044	0.069	0.106	0.155
41	Revolutions and coups	0.019	0.029	0.038	0.056	0.106	0.188	0.282
42	British colony dummy	0.022	0.027	0.034	0.041	0.057	0.085	0.119

Table continued

Table 12.7
(Continued)

Rank	Variable	kbar5	kbar7	kbar9	kbar11	kbar16	kbar22	kbar28
43	Hydrocarbon deposits in 1993	0.015	0.025	0.035	0.048	0.089	0.143	0.196
44	Fraction population over 65	0.020	0.022	0.029	0.038	0.069	0.119	0.169
45	Defense spending share	0.016	0.021	0.027	0.033	0.049	0.073	0.102
46	Population in 1960	0.016	0.021	0.040	0.041	0.063	0.092	0.118
47	Terms of trade growth in 1960s	0.015	0.021	0.026	0.033	0.051	0.068	0.104
48	Public education spending/GDP in 1960s	0.014	0.021	0.027	0.037	0.063	0.102	0.141
49	Landlocked country dummy	0.012	0.021	0.029	0.033	0.055	0.080	0.109
50	Religion measure	0.012	0.020	0.025	0.037	0.048	0.068	0.092
51	Size of economy	0.016	0.020	0.026	0.033	0.051	0.076	0.104
52	Socialist dummy	0.012	0.020	0.024	0.032	0.054	0.091	0.144
53	English-speaking population	0.015	0.020	0.025	0.028	0.043	0.063	0.087
54	Average inflation 1960–90	0.015	0.020	0.024	0.030	0.043	0.064	0.100
55	Oil-producing country dummy	0.012	0.019	0.025	0.033	0.050	0.071	0.095
56	Population growth rate 1960–90	0.014	0.019	0.023	0.029	0.046	0.074	0.098
57	Timing of independence	0.014	0.019	0.024	0.031	0.048	0.076	0.099
58	Fraction land area near navigable water	0.013	0.019	0.024	0.031	0.055	0.092	0.142
59	Square of inflation 1960–90	0.013	0.018	0.022	0.027	0.041	0.063	0.105
60	Fraction spent in war 1960–90	0.010	0.016	0.019	0.024	0.039	0.060	0.087
61	Land area	0.010	0.016	0.022	0.026	0.043	0.071	0.103
62	Tropical climate zone	0.012	0.016	0.020	0.028	0.042	0.067	0.100
63	Terms of trade ranking	0.011	0.016	0.019	0.026	0.039	0.063	0.086
64	Capitalism	0.010	0.015	0.020	0.026	0.047	0.084	0.128
65	Fraction Othodox	0.011	0.015	0.020	0.025	0.036	0.059	0.083
66	War participation 1960–90	0.010	0.015	0.019	0.025	0.040	0.060	0.089
67	Interior density	0.010	0.015	0.019	0.023	0.039	0.062	0.085

government). The other 13 variables that were robust in the baseline model also appear to be robust to different prior specifications.

"Weak" Variables That Become "Strong" At the other end of the scale, most of the 46 variables that showed little partial correlation in the baseline estimation are not helped by alternative priors. Their posterior inclusion probabilities rise as $\bar{k}$ increases, a result which is hardly surprising as their prior inclusion probabilities are rising. But their posterior inclusion probabilities remain below the prior so we are forced to think of them as "weak."

There are three variables that are weak in the baseline study but become "strong" with some prior model sizes. These are the population density, the fraction of population that speaks a foreign language (a measure of international social capital and openness), and the public investment share. As mentioned before, the public investment share is particularly interesting because it becomes strong for larger prior model sizes, but the sign of the correlation is negative. That is, a larger public investment share tends to be associated with lower grow rates.

Our interpretation of these results is that our baseline results are robust to alternative prior size specifications. This robustness applies also to the "sign certainty probabilities," which are not reported here.

Nonlinearities The literature has identified some variables that may affect growth in a highly nonlinear way: for example, it has been argued that inflation has important negative effects on growth but only for very high levels of inflation. To test this hypothesis, we include the average inflation rate in the 1960s, 1970s, and 1980s, and its square as separate regressors. The BACE procedure allows such variables to enter individually, and the data would assign larger weight to well-fitting models if there were a nonlinear relationship. The posterior inclusion probabilities for inflation and its square are very low, and the conditional coefficient estimates are not different from zero.

12.6 Appendix: Long-Term Data on GDP

Maddison (1991) and subsequent unpublished updates describe long-term data on real GDP and population for 16 developed countries. His estimates try to adjust for changes in

Table 12.8
Countries Included in Growth Sample (Table 12.3, column 2)

Algeria	El Salvador	Kenya	South Africa
Argentina	Finland	Malawi	South Korea
Australia	France	Malaysia	Spain
Austria	Gambia	Mali	Sri Lanka
Bangladesh	Ghana	Mexico	Sweden
Belgium	Greece	Mozambique	Switzerland
Bolivia	Guatemala	Netherlands	Syria
Botswana	Guyana	New Zealand	Taiwan
Brazil	Haiti	Nicaragua	Thailand
Cameroon	Hong Kong	Niger	Togo
Canada	Honduras	Norway	Trinidad
Chile	Hungary	Pakistan	Tunisia
China	Iceland	Panama	Turkey
Colombia	India	Papua New Guinea	Uganda
Congo (Brazzaville)	Indonesia	Paraguay	Uruguay
Congo (Kinshasa)	Iran	Peru	United Kingdom
Costa Rica	Ireland	Philippines	United States
Cyprus	Israel	Poland	Venezuela
Denmark	Italy	Portugal	West Germany
Dominican Republic	Jamaica	Senegal	Zambia
Ecuador	Japan	Sierra Leone	Zimbabwe
Egypt	Jordan	Singapore	

Table 12.9
Means and Standard Deviations for Variables in Basic Growth System

	1965–75 Regression	1975–85 Regression	1985–95 Regression
Growth rate	0.026 (0.020)	0.016 (0.024)	0.014 (0.026)
Log of per capita GDP	8.15 (0.94)	8.32 (0.97)	8.45 (1.03)
Male upper-level schooling	1.04 (0.96)	1.39 (1.15)	1.91 (1.34)
1/(life expectancy at age 1)	0.0165 (0.0027)	0.0159 (0.0024)	0.0152 (0.0022)
Log of total fertility rate	1.58 (0.41)	1.50 (0.46)	1.31 (0.53)
Government consumption ratio	0.093 (0.061)	0.104 (0.070)	0.091 (0.059)
Rule-of-law indicator	0.56 (0.33)	0.55 (0.33)	0.58 (0.26)
Democracy indicator	0.60 (0.32)	0.56 (0.33)	0.64 (0.32)
Square of democracy	0.49 (0.37)	0.44 (0.38)	0.52 (0.37)
Openness ratio	−0.02 (0.18)	−0.01 (0.35)	0.00 (0.39)
Terms-of-trade variable	−0.004 (0.020)	0.000 (0.021)	−0.003 (0.017)
Investment ratio	0.185 (0.092)	0.179 (0.078)	0.178 (0.081)
Inflation rate	0.100 (0.110)	0.180 (0.209)	0.231 (0.375)
Number of observations	72	86	83

Note: The entries give the means and standard deviations (in parentheses) of the variables that enter into the panel regression in table 12.3, column 2. The statistics apply only to the samples used for each subperiod.

national boundaries. Data are available annually through 1990 from starting dates between 1870 and 1900. The real GDP numbers are expressed in 1985 U.S. dollars. The conversion from domestic real GDP values was based on Eurostat/OECD benchmark studies for 1985. These studies follow the methodology of the UN's International Comparison Project (ICP), which is analogous to the procedure used by Summers and Heston (1991) and Heston, Summers, and Aten (2002) for more recent data.

The figures on real per capita GDP begin in 1870 for 13 countries (Australia, Austria, Belgium, Canada, Denmark, Finland, France, Germany, Italy, Norway, Sweden, the United Kingdom, and the United States), in 1885 for Japan, in 1889 for Switzerland, and in 1900 for the Netherlands. Data for selected years beginning in 1820 are provided in Maddison (1991, table A.5) for the 16 countries except Canada, which starts in 1850. This source also provides data for the United Kingdom in 1700 and 1780 and for the Netherlands in 1700.

Table 12.10 shows data at 20-year intervals starting in 1870 for GDP per capita in 1985 U.S. dollars, the corresponding ratio to the U.S. GDP per capita, and the level of population. The table also indicates the annual growth rate over each period for real per capita GDP and population.

Maddison (1989) provides long-term data for some additional countries. Data on real GDP indexes are presented in his tables B-4 and B-5 for selected years from 1900 and annually for 1950–87 for nine Asian countries (Bangladesh, China, India, Indonesia, Pakistan, Philippines, South Korea, Taiwan, and Thailand) and six Latin American countries (Argentina, Brazil, Chile, Colombia, Mexico, and Peru). Population figures are in his tables C-3 and

Table 12.10
Long-Term Data for 16 Currently Developed Countries

	GDP Per Capita (1985 $US)	Ratio to U.S. GDP Per Capita	Growth Rate GDP Per Capita	Population (1000s)	Growth Rate Population
Australia					
1870	3143	1.40	—	1620	—
1890	3949	1.27	0.0114	3107	0.0326
1910	4615	1.02	0.0078	4375	0.0171
1930	3963	0.70	−0.0076	6469	0.0196
1950	5970	0.69	0.0205	8177	0.0117
1970	9747	0.76	0.0245	12,507	0.0212
1990	13,514	0.74	0.0163	17,806	0.0177
Austria					
1870	1442	0.64	—	4520	—
1890	1892	0.61	0.0136	5394	0.0088
1910	2547	0.56	0.0149	6614	0.0102
1930	2776	0.49	0.0043	6684	0.0005
1950	2869	0.33	0.0016	6935	0.0018
1970	7547	0.59	0.0484	7467	0.0037
1990	12,976	0.71	0.0271	7718	0.0017
Belgium					
1870	2009	0.90	—	5096	—
1890	2654	0.86	0.0139	6096	0.0090
1910	3146	0.69	0.0085	7498	0.0104
1930	3855	0.68	0.0102	8076	0.0037
1950	4229	0.49	0.0046	8640	0.0034
1970	8235	0.64	0.0333	9638	0.0055
1990	13,320	0.73	0.0240	9967	0.0017
Canada					
1870	1330	0.59	—	3736	—
1890	1846	0.60	0.0164	4918	0.0137
1910	3179	0.70	0.0272	7188	0.0190
1930	3955	0.70	0.0109	10,488	0.0189
1950	6112	0.71	0.0218	13,737	0.0135
1970	10,200	0.80	0.0256	21,324	0.0220
1990	17,070	0.93	0.0257	26,620	0.0111
Denmark					
1870	1543	0.69	—	1888	—
1890	1944	0.63	0.0116	2294	0.0097
1910	2856	0.63	0.0192	2882	0.0114
1930	4114	0.73	0.0182	3542	0.0103
1950	5227	0.61	0.0120	4269	0.0093
1970	9575	0.75	0.0303	4929	0.0072
1990	14,086	0.77	0.0193	5140	0.0021
Finland					
1870	933	0.42	—	1754	—
1890	1130	0.36	0.0096	2364	0.0149
1910	1560	0.34	0.0161	2929	0.0107
1930	2181	0.39	0.0168	3449	0.0082
1950	3481	0.40	0.0234	4009	0.0075
1970	7838	0.61	0.0406	4606	0.0069
1990	14,012	0.77	0.0290	4986	0.0040

Table continued

Table 12.10
(Continued)

	GDP Per Capita (1985 $US)	Ratio to U.S. GDP Per Capita	Growth Rate GDP Per Capita	Population (1000s)	Growth Rate Population
France					
1870	1582	0.70	—	38,440	—
1890	1955	0.63	0.0106	40,107	0.0021
1910	2406	0.53	0.0104	41,398	0.0016
1930	3591	0.64	0.0200	41,610	0.0003
1950	4176	0.49	0.0075	41,836	0.0003
1970	9245	0.72	0.0397	50,772	0.0097
1990	14,245	0.78	0.0216	56,420	0.0053
Germany (West)					
1870	1223	0.55	—	24,870	—
1890	1624	0.52	0.0142	30,014	0.0094
1910	2256	0.50	0.0164	39,356	0.0135
1930	2714	0.48	0.0092	44,026	0.0056
1950	3542	0.41	0.0133	49,983	0.0063
1970	9257	0.72	0.0480	60,651	0.0097
1990	14,288	0.78	0.0217	63,232	0.0021
Italy					
1870	1216	0.54	—	27,888	—
1890	1352	0.44	0.0053	31,702	0.0064
1910	1891	0.42	0.0168	36,572	0.0071
1930	2366	0.42	0.0112	40,791	0.0055
1950	2840	0.33	0.0091	47,105	0.0072
1970	7884	0.62	0.0511	53,661	0.0065
1990	13,215	0.72	0.0258	57,647	0.0036
Japan					
1890	842	0.27	—	40,077	—
1910	1084	0.24	0.0126	49,518	0.0106
1930	1539	0.27	0.0175	64,203	0.0130
1950	1620	0.19	0.0026	83,563	0.0132
1970	8168	0.64	0.0809	104,334	0.0111
1990	16,144	0.88	0.0341	123,540	0.0084
Netherlands					
1910	2965	0.65	—	5902	—
1930	4400	0.78	0.0197	7884	0.0145
1950	4708	0.55	0.0034	10,114	0.0125
1970	9392	0.73	0.0345	13,194	0.0133
1990	13,078	0.72	0.0166	14,947	0.0062
Norway					
1870	1190	0.53	—	1735	—
1890	1477	0.48	0.0108	1997	0.0070
1910	1875	0.41	0.0119	2384	0.0089
1930	3086	0.55	0.0249	2807	0.0082
1950	4541	0.53	0.0193	3265	0.0076
1970	8335	0.65	0.0304	3879	0.0086
1990	15,418	0.84	0.0308	4241	0.0045

Table 12.10
(Continued)

	GDP Per Capita (1985 $US)	Ratio to U.S. GDP Per Capita	Growth Rate GDP Per Capita	Population (1000s)	Growth Rate Population
Sweden					
1870	1401	0.62	—	4164	—
1890	1757	0.57	0.0112	4780	0.0069
1910	2509	0.55	0.0178	5449	0.0065
1930	3315	0.59	0.0139	6131	0.0059
1950	5673	0.66	0.0269	7015	0.0067
1970	10,707	0.84	0.0318	8043	0.0068
1990	14,804	0.81	0.0162	8559	0.0031
Switzerland					
1910	2979	0.66	—	3735	—
1930	4511	0.80	0.0207	4051	0.0041
1950	6546	0.76	0.0186	4694	0.0074
1970	12,208	0.95	0.0312	6267	0.0145
1990	15,650	0.86	0.0124	6796	0.0041
United Kingdom					
1870	2693	1.20	—	29,312	—
1890	3383	1.09	0.0114	35,000	0.0089
1910	3891	0.86	0.0070	41,938	0.0090
1930	4287	0.76	0.0048	45,866	0.0045
1950	5651	0.66	0.0138	50,363	0.0047
1970	8994	0.70	0.0232	55,632	0.0050
1990	13,589	0.74	0.0206	57,411	0.0016
United States					
1870	2244	1.0	—	40,061	—
1890	3101	1.0	0.0162	63,302	0.0229
1910	4538	1.0	0.0190	92,767	0.0191
1930	5642	1.0	0.0109	123,668	0.0144
1950	8605	1.0	0.0211	152,271	0.0104
1970	12,815	1.0	0.0199	205,052	0.0149
1990	18,258	1.0	0.0177	251,394	0.0102

Note: These data are from Maddison (1991) and updates.

C-4, and values of real GDP per capita are expressed in terms of 1980 international dollars in his table A-1. Numbers are also provided for the Soviet Union, although post-1990 experience suggested that these data were highly inaccurate.

Table 12.11 presents the figures for the nine Asian and six Latin American countries for 1900, 1913, 1950, 1973, and 1987. The table shows real per capita GDP in 1980 international dollars, the ratio of these values to the U.S. real per capita GDP, and the level of population. Also shown are the annual growth rates for each period of real per capita GDP and population.

Table 12.11
Long-Term Data for 15 Currently Less-Developed Countries

	GDP Per Capita (1985 $US)	Ratio to U.S. GDP Per Capita	Growth Rate GDP Per Capita	Population (1000s)	Growth Rate Population
Bangladesh					
1900	349	0.12	—	29,012	—
1913	371	0.10	0.0047	31,786	0.0070
1950	331	0.05	−0.0031	43,135	0.0083
1973	281	0.03	−0.0071	74,368	0.0237
1987	375	0.03	0.0206	102,961	0.0232
China					
1900	401	0.14	—	400,000	—
1913	415	0.11	0.0026	430,000	0.0056
1950	338	0.05	−0.0055	546,815	0.0065
1973	774	0.07	0.0360	881,940	0.0208
1987	1748	0.13	0.0582	1,069,608	0.0138
India					
1900	378	0.13	—	234,655	—
1913	399	0.11	0.0042	251,826	0.0054
1950	359	0.05	−0.0029	359,943	0.0097
1973	513	0.05	0.0155	579,000	0.0207
1987	662	0.05	0.0182	787,930	0.0220
Indonesia					
1900	499	0.17	—	40,209	—
1913	529	0.14	0.0045	48,150	0.0139
1950	484	0.07	−0.0024	72,747	0.0112
1973	786	0.07	0.0211	124,189	0.0233
1987	1200	0.09	0.0302	170,744	0.0227
Pakistan					
1900	413	0.14	—	19,759	—
1913	438	0.12	0.0045	20,007	0.0010
1950	390	0.06	−0.0031	37,646	0.0171
1973	579	0.05	0.0172	67,900	0.0256
1987	885	0.07	0.0303	101,611	0.0288
Philippines					
1900	718	0.25	—	7324	—
1913	985	0.26	0.0243	9384	0.0191
1950	898	0.13	−0.0025	20,062	0.0205
1973	1400	0.13	0.0193	39,701	0.0297
1987	1519	0.11	0.0058	57,011	0.0258
South Korea					
1900	549	0.19	—	8772	—
1913	610	0.16	0.0081	10,277	0.0122
1950	564	0.08	−0.0021	20,557	0.0187
1973	1790	0.16	0.0502	34,103	0.0220
1987	4143	0.31	0.0599	42,512	0.0157
Taiwan					
1900	434	0.15	—	2858	—
1913	453	0.12	0.0033	3469	0.0149
1950	526	0.08	0.0040	7882	0.0222
1973	2087	0.19	0.0599	15,427	0.0292
1987	4744	0.35	0.0587	19,551	0.0169

Table 12.11
(Continued)

	GDP Per Capita (1985 $US)	Ratio to U.S. GDP Per Capita	Growth Rate GDP Per Capita	Population (1000s)	Growth Rate Population
Thailand					
1900	626	0.22	—	7320	—
1913	652	0.17	0.0031	8690	0.0132
1950	653	0.10	0.0000	19,442	0.0218
1973	1343	0.12	0.0314	39,303	0.0306
1987	2294	0.17	0.0382	53,377	0.0219
Argentina					
1900	1284	0.44	—	4693	—
1913	1770	0.47	0.0247	7653	0.0376
1950	2324	0.35	0.0074	17,150	0.0218
1973	3713	0.34	0.0204	25,195	0.0167
1987	3302	0.24	−0.0084	31,500	0.0160
Brazil					
1900	436	0.15	—	17,984	—
1913	521	0.14	0.0137	23,660	0.0211
1950	1073	0.16	0.0195	51,941	0.0213
1973	2504	0.23	0.0368	99,836	0.0284
1987	3417	0.25	0.0222	140,692	0.0245
Chile					
1900	956	0.33	—	2974	—
1913	1255	0.33	0.0209	3491	0.0123
1950	2350	0.35	0.0170	6091	0.0150
1973	3309	0.30	0.0149	9899	0.0211
1987	3393	0.25	0.0018	12,485	0.0166
Colombia					
1900	610	0.21	—	3998	—
1913	801	0.21	0.0210	5195	0.0201
1950	1395	0.21	0.0150	11,597	0.0217
1973	2318	0.21	0.0221	22,571	0.0290
1987	3027	0.22	0.0191	29,496	0.0191
Mexico					
1900	649	0.22	—	13,607	—
1913	822	0.22	0.0182	14,971	0.0073
1950	1169	0.17	0.0095	27,376	0.0163
1973	2349	0.21	0.0303	56,481	0.0315
1987	2667	0.20	0.0091	81,163	0.0259
Peru					
1900	624	0.21	—	3791	—
1913	819	0.22	0.0209	4507	0.0133
1950	1349	0.20	0.0135	7630	0.0142
1973	2357	0.21	0.0243	14,350	0.0275
1987	2380	0.18	0.0007	20,756	0.0264

Note: These data are from Maddison (1989).

Maddison (1992) describes long-term data on saving rates and investment ratios for 11 countries: Australia, Canada, France, Germany, Japan, the Netherlands, the United Kingdom, the United States, India, South Korea, and Taiwan. These data begin in 1820 for France; 1870 for Australia, Canada, the United Kingdom, and the United States; and later years for the other countries. Intermediate years are missing for some of the countries. The table in the introduction shows data over 20-year intervals for the eight countries for which a long-term picture can be constructed.

Appendix on Mathematical Methods

Contents

A.1 Differential Equations
- A.1.1 Introduction
- A.1.2 First-Order Ordinary Differential Equations
  - Graphical Solutions
    - Constructing the Diagram
    - Stability
  - Analytical Solutions
    - Linear, First-Order Differential Equations with Constant Coefficients
    - Linear, First-Order Differential Equations with Variable Coefficients
- A.1.3 Systems of Linear Ordinary Differential Equations
  - Phase Diagrams
    - Diagonal Systems
    - A Nondiagonal Example
    - A Nonlinear Example
  - Analytical Solutions of Linear, Homogeneous Systems
  - The Relation Between the Graphical and Analytical Solutions
  - Stability
  - Analytical Solutions of Linear, Nonhomogeneous Systems
  - Linearization of Nonlinear Systems
  - The Time-Elimination Method for Nonlinear Systems

A.2 Static Optimization
- A.2.1 Unconstrained Maxima
- A.2.2 Classical Nonlinear Programming: Equality Constraints
- A.2.3 Inequality Constraints: The Kuhn–Tucker Conditions

A.3 Dynamic Optimization in Continuous Time
- A.3.1 Introduction
- A.3.2 The Typical Problem
- A.3.3 Heuristic Derivation of the First-Order Conditions
- A.3.4 Transversality Conditions
- A.3.5 The Behavior of the Hamiltonian over Time

A.3.6 Sufficient Conditions
A.3.7 Infinite Horizons
A.3.8 Example: The Neoclassical Growth Model
A.3.9 Transversality Conditions in Infinite-Horizon Problems
A.3.10 Summary of the Procedure to Find the First-Order Conditions
A.3.11 Present-Value and Current-Value Hamiltonians
A.3.12 Multiple Variables
A.4 Useful Results in Matrix Algebra: Eigenvalues, Eigenvectors, and Diagonalization of Matrices
A.5 Useful Results in Calculus
A.5.1 Implicit Function Theorem
A.5.2 Taylor's Theorem
A.5.3 L'Hôpital's Rule
A.5.4 Integration by Parts
A.5.5 Fundamental Theorem of Calculus
A.5.6 Rules of Differentiation of Integrals
Differentiation with Respect to the Variable of Integration
Leibniz's Rule for Differentiation of Definite Integrals

This appendix discusses the main mathematical methods used in the text. We consider differential equations, static optimization, dynamic optimization, some results in matrix theory, and a few results from calculus.

A.1 Differential Equations

A.1.1 Introduction

A differential equation is an equation that involves derivatives of variables. If there is only one independent variable, it is called an *ordinary differential equation* (ODE). The *order* of the ODE is that of the highest derivative; that is, if the highest derivative is an ODE of order n, it is an nth-order ODE. When the functional form of the equation is linear, it is a *linear ODE*. Most of the differential equations that we encounter in the book involve derivatives of functions with respect to *time*.

An example of a differential equation is

$$a_1 \cdot \dot{y}(t) + a_2 \cdot y(t) + x(t) = 0 \tag{A.1}$$

where the dot on top of $y(t)$ represents the derivative of $y(t)$ with respect to time, $\dot{y}(t) \equiv dy(t)/dt$, a_1 and a_2 are constants, and $x(t)$ is a known function of time. The function $x(t)$ is sometimes called the *forcing function*. Equation (A.1) is a first-order linear ODE with constant coefficients. If $x(t) = a_3$, a constant, the equation is called *autonomous*. (An equation is autonomous when it depends on time only through the variable $y[t]$.) If $x(t) = 0$, the equation is called *homogeneous*.

A second-order, linear ODE with constant coefficients takes the form,

$$a_1 \cdot \ddot{y}(t) + a_2 \cdot \dot{y}(t) + a_3 \cdot y(t) + x(t) = 0 \tag{A.2}$$

where a_1, a_2, and a_3 are constants and $\ddot{y}(t) \equiv d^2y(t)/dt^2$. The equation

$$a_1 \cdot \dot{y}(t) + a_2(t) \cdot y(t) + x(t) = 0 \tag{A.3}$$

where $a_2(t)$ is a known function of time, is a first-order, linear ODE with *variable coefficients*. The equation

$$\log[\dot{y}(t)] + 1/y(t) = 0 \tag{A.4}$$

is a *nonlinear first-order ODE.*

The goal when solving a differential equation is to find the behavior of $y(t)$. The first solution method that we use is *graphical*, a technique that can be used for nonlinear, as well as linear, differential equations. The disadvantage is that it can be used only for autonomous equations. The second method is *analytical*. In some circumstances, we will be able to find an exact formula for $y(t)$, even when the equation is not autonomous. The drawback of the analytical approach is that it can be used only with a limited set of functional forms. One of them, however, is the linear function in equation (A.1). When we encounter nonlinear differential equations, we will often approximate the solution by linearizing the equation by means of a Taylor-series expansion. (See section A.6.2.)

A third method for solving differential equations relies on numerical analysis. Most modern mathematical computer packages contain subroutines that solve differential equations numerically. Matlab, for example, has the subroutines ODE23 and ODE45, and Mathematica has the command NDSOLVE.

A.1.2 First-Order Ordinary Differential Equations

Graphical Solutions

CONSTRUCTING THE DIAGRAM Consider an autonomous ordinary differential equation of the form,

$$\dot{y}(t) = f[y(t)] \tag{A.5}$$

where $f(\cdot)$ is a known function. Equation (A.5) is autonomous because the function $f(\cdot)$ does not depend on time independently of y. The function $f(\cdot)$ may or may not be linear.

To solve equation (A.5) graphically, we plot $f(\cdot)$ as a function of y in figure A.1. The horizontal axis shows the value of y, and the vertical axis has $f(\cdot)$ and $\dot{y}$. Positive values of $f(\cdot)$ correspond to positive values of $\dot{y}$, in accordance with equation (A.5). Since $\dot{y}$ is the derivative of y with respect to time, positive values of $\dot{y}$ correspond to increasing values of y. To reflect this relation, we draw arrows pointing east (increasing y) when $f(\cdot)$ lies above

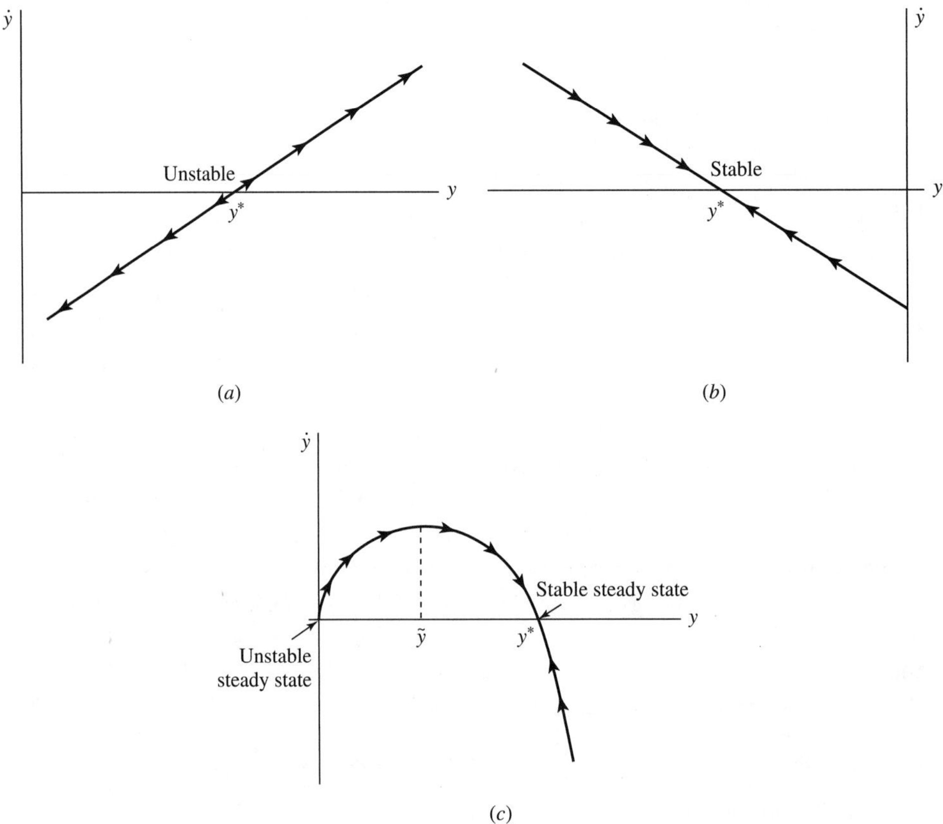

Figure A.1
(a) **Linear ODE.** If the coefficient a in equation (A.6) is positive, then the differential equation for y is unstable.
(b) **Linear ODE.** If the coefficient a in equation (A.6) is negative, then the differential equation for y is stable.
(c) **Nonlinear ODE.** In equation (A.7), the slope of $f(\bullet)$ with respect to y is initially positive and is subsequently negative. The steady state at 0 is unstable, whereas that at y^* is stable.

the horizontal axis and pointing west (decreasing y) when $f(\cdot)$ lies below the horizontal axis. The arrows reveal the direction in which y moves over time and therefore provide a qualitative solution to the differential equation.

Sometimes the differential equation is expressed in terms of the difference of two functions, for example,

$$\dot{y}(t) = f[y(t)] - g[y(t)]$$

Instead of graphing $f(\cdot) - g(\cdot)$, we can graph $f(\cdot)$ and $g(\cdot)$ separately. The rate of change of $y(t)$, $\dot{y}(t)$, is given in this case by the vertical distance between $f(\cdot)$ and $g(\cdot)$. For values of y where $f(\cdot)$ lies above $g(\cdot)$, $\dot{y}(t)$ is positive and therefore $y(t)$ is increasing over time. The opposite is true when $f(\cdot)$ lies below $g(\cdot)$. The steady state is given by the point(s) at which the curves $f(\cdot)$ and $g(\cdot)$ cross.

As an example, consider a linear form for $f(\cdot)$:

$$\dot{y}(t) = f[y(t)] = a \cdot y(t) - x \tag{A.6}$$

where a and x are constants, with $a > 0$. The graph of $f(\cdot)$ is a straight line with positive slope. This line, depicted in figure A.1a, intercepts the vertical axis at $\dot{y} = -x$ and crosses the horizontal axis at $y^* = x/a$. For values of y above y^*, the function lies above the horizontal axis. Thus, $\dot{y}$ is positive and y is increasing. Hence, to the right of y^*, we draw arrows pointing northeast (see figure A.1a). The opposite conditions apply to the left of y^*, and we draw arrows pointing southwest.

If the initial value, $y(0)$, equals y^*, equation (A.6) implies that $\dot{y}$ equals 0, so that y does not change over time. It follows that $y(t)$ remains forever at y^*. The value y^* is called the *steady-state* value of y.

If $y(0) > y^*$, then $\dot{y} > 0$, so that y grows over time. Conversely, if $y(0) < y^*$, then $\dot{y} < 0$, so that y decreases over time. The qualitative dynamics of $y(t)$ are fully determined in figure A.1a: once the initial value, $y(0)$, is specified, the arrows show how y moves as time evolves. An interesting point is that unless $y(0) = y^*$, the dynamics of the equation when $a > 0$ move y away from the steady state. This behavior applies for initial values below and above y^*. In this case, we say that the differential equation is *unstable*.

Imagine now that $a < 0$. The graph of $f(\cdot)$ is then a downward-sloping straight line, depicted in figure A.1b, which intercepts the vertical axis at $\dot{y} = -x$ and the horizontal axis at $y^* = -x/a$. To the left of y^*, $\dot{y}$ is positive, so that y increases over time. Correspondingly, the arrows in the figure point southeast. The opposite relation applies to the right of y^*. Note that, regardless of the initial value, $y(0)$, the dynamics of the equation brings $y(t)$ back to the steady state, y^*. In this case, we say that equation (A.6) is *stable*.

This graphical approach can be used to analyze the dynamics of more complicated nonlinear functions. Consider, for example, the differential equation

$$\dot{y}(t) = f[y(t)] = s \cdot [y(t)]^{\alpha} - \delta \cdot y(t) \tag{A.7}$$

where s, δ, and α are positive constants and $\alpha < 1$. Chapter 1 shows that the fundamental equation of the Solow–Swan growth model takes the form of equation (A.7), where $y(t)$ is the capital stock. Under this interpretation, equation (A.7) says that the net increase in the capital stock equals the difference between total saving and total depreciation. Total saving is assumed to be the constant fraction, s, of output, y^{α}, and total depreciation is proportional to the existing capital stock.

Since only nonnegative values of the capital stock are economically meaningful, we look only at the first quadrant in figure A.1c. For low values of y, the function $f(\cdot)$ is upward sloping. It reaches a maximum when $s\alpha\tilde{y}^{\alpha-1} = \delta$, and it becomes downward sloping for higher values of y. The function $f(\cdot)$ crosses the horizontal axis at two points, $y = 0$ and $y = y^* = (\delta/s)^{1/(\alpha-1)}$.

To the right of y^*, $\dot{y}$ is negative, so that y is falling. Hence, we draw arrows pointing west. To the left of y^*, $\dot{y}$ is positive, so that y is rising, and we draw arrows pointing east. It follows that the equation has two steady states. The first one is y^* and is stable in that, for any positive initial value, $y(0)$, the dynamics of the equation moves $y(t)$ toward y^*. The second steady state, 0, is unstable: if $y(0) > 0$, the dynamics moves $y(t)$ away from 0.

STABILITY The preceding discussion suggests that if $f(\cdot)$ slopes upward at the steady-state value, y^*, the steady state is unstable. That is, if $y(0) \neq y^*$, $y(t)$ moves away from y^*. The reason is simple: if $f(\cdot)$ is upward sloping when $f(y^*) = 0$, then, for $y > y^*$, $f(y) > 0$. Hence, $\dot{y} > 0$ and y increases over time. On the other hand, for $y < y^*$, $f(y) < 0$, $\dot{y} < 0$, and y decreases over time. The conclusion is that y increases when it is already too large and falls when it is already too small, an indication of instability.

Conversely, if $f(\cdot)$ is downward sloping at the steady-state value, y^*, the equation is stable. In this case, if $y(0) \neq y^*$, $y(t)$ approaches y^* over time.

To summarize, if we are interested in the stability of the differential equation in the neighborhood of a steady state, all we have to do is compute the derivative of $f(\cdot)$ and evaluate it at the steady-state value, y^*:

$$\begin{aligned} &\text{If } \partial\dot{y}/\partial y|_{y^*} > 0,\ y \text{ is locally unstable} \\ &\text{If } \partial\dot{y}/\partial y|_{y^*} < 0,\ y \text{ is locally stable} \end{aligned} \tag{A.8}$$

Although nonlinear differential equations may have more than one steady state, the local stability properties of each of these steady states will still be determined by the condition in equation (A.8).

Analytical Solutions The solution to some equations is almost immediate because the equation can be integrated. For instance, the solution to $\dot{y}(t) = a$ is obviously $y(t) = b + at$, where b is an arbitrary constant.

Equations that involve polynomial functions of time are equally easy to solve, for example,

$$\dot{y}(t) = a_0 + a_1 t + a_2 \cdot t^2 + \cdots + a_n \cdot t^n$$

has the solution

$$y(t) = b + a_0 t + a_1 \cdot (t^2/2) + \cdots + a_n \cdot [t^{n+1}/(n+1)]$$

In general, the functional forms that we work with will not be this simple. We now derive the general solution for linear, first-order ODEs.

LINEAR, FIRST-ORDER DIFFERENTIAL EQUATIONS WITH CONSTANT COEFFICIENTS The general form of the linear, first-order ODE with constant coefficients is

$$\dot{y}(t) + a \cdot y(t) + x(t) = 0 \tag{A.9}$$

where a is a constant and $x(t)$ is a known function of time. The easiest way to solve this equation is to carry out the following steps.

First, put all the terms involving y and its derivatives on one side of the equation and the rest on the other side:

$$\dot{y}(t) + a \cdot y(t) = -x(t)$$

Second, multiply both sides of the equation by e^{at} and integrate:

$$\int e^{at} \cdot [\dot{y}(t) + a \cdot y(t)] \cdot dt = -\int e^{at} \cdot x(t) \cdot dt \tag{A.10}$$

The term e^{at} is called the *integrating factor*. The reason for multiplying by the integrating factor is that the term inside the left-hand side integral becomes the derivative of $e^{at} \cdot y(t)$ with respect to time:

$$e^{at} \cdot [\dot{y}(t) + a \cdot y(t)] = (d/dt)[e^{at} \cdot y(t) + b_0]$$

where b_0 is an arbitrary constant. Note that the integral on the left-hand side of equation (A.10) is the integral of the derivative of some function and therefore equals the function itself (see section A.5.5). Hence, the term on the left-hand side of equation (A.10) equals $e^{at} \cdot y(t) + b_0$.

Third, compute the integral on the right-hand side of equation (A.10), making sure to add another constant term b_1. Note that this integral is a function of t. Call the result $\text{INT}(t) + b_1$. Since $x(t)$ is a known function of time, $\text{INT}(t)$ is also a known function of time.

Fourth, multiply both sides by e^{-at} to get $y(t)$:

$$y(t) = -e^{-at} \cdot \text{INT}(t) + be^{-at} \tag{A.11}$$

where $b = b_1 - b_0$ is an arbitrary constant. Equation (A.11) is the general solution to the ODE in equation (A.9).

Consider, as an example, the differential equation

$$\dot{y}(t) - y(t) - 1 = 0 \tag{A.12}$$

In this example, the forcing function $x(t)$ is a constant, -1. To solve this equation, we follow the steps outlined previously. First, put all the terms involving $y(t)$ and its derivatives on the left-hand side of the equation and all the other terms on the right-hand side. Then multiply both sides by e^{-t} and integrate:

$$\int e^{-t}[\dot{y}(t) - y(t)] \cdot dt = \int e^{-t}\, dt \tag{A.13}$$

The term inside the integral on the left-hand side is the derivative of $e^{-t} \cdot y(t) + b_0$ with respect to time. Hence, the integral on the left-hand side equals $e^{-t} \cdot y(t) + b_0$. The right-hand side equals $-e^{-t} + b_1$. Hence, the solution to equation (A.12) is

$$y(t) = -1 + be^{t} \tag{A.14}$$

where $b = b_1 - b_0$ is an arbitrary constant. We can verify that equation (A.14) satisfies equation (A.12) by taking derivatives with respect to time to get $\dot{y}(t) = be^{t} = y(t) + 1$.

The result in equation (A.11) is the *general solution* to equation (A.9); to get a *particular* or *exact solution,* we have to specify the arbitrary constant of integration, b. To pin down which of the infinitely many possible paths applies, we need to know a value of $y(t)$ for at least one point in time. This *boundary condition* will determine the unique solution to the differential equation.

Figure A.2 shows an array of solutions to the ODE in the example of equation (A.12). To choose among them, imagine that we know that $y(t) = 0$ when $t = 0$. This type of boundary condition is called an *initial condition* because it pins down the path by specifying the value of $y(t)$ at the initial date. In our example, we can substitute $t = 0$ and $y(0) = 0$ in equation (A.14) to find that $y(0) = -1 + be^{0} = 0$, which implies $b = 1$. We can therefore plug $b = 1$ into equation (A.14) to get the particular solution,

$$y(t) = -1 + e^{t} \tag{A.15}$$

This equation, which determines a unique value of y at each point in time, corresponds to the time path labeled A in figure A.2.

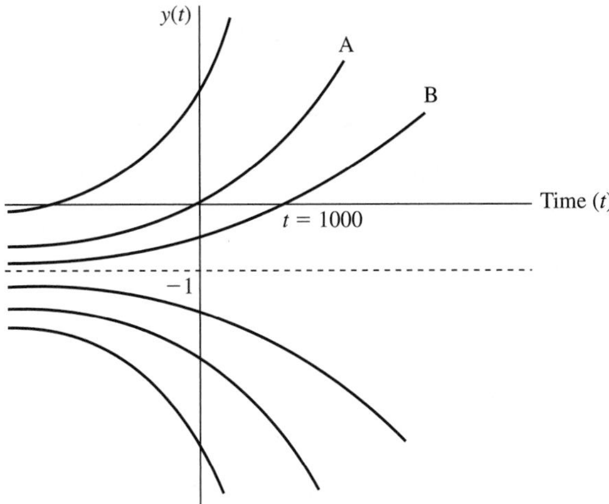

Figure A.2
Solutions to a differential equation. The figure shows an array of solutions to the differential equation (A.12).

Instead of knowing the initial value of the function, we may know the value at some terminal date; that is, we could have a *terminal condition*.[1] As an example, suppose that the terminal date is $t_1 = 1000$, and the value of $y(t)$ at that time is 0. Thus, $y(1000) = -1 + b \cdot e^{1000} = 0$. The solution, $b = e^{-1000}$, implies

$$y(t) = -1 + (e^{-1000}) \cdot e^t \tag{A.16}$$

This result corresponds to path B in figure A.2.

LINEAR, FIRST-ORDER DIFFERENTIAL EQUATIONS WITH VARIABLE COEFFICIENTS Consider now the differential equation

$$\dot{y}(t) + a(t) \cdot y(t) + x(t) = 0 \tag{A.17}$$

where $a(t)$ is a known function of time but is no longer a constant. We can follow the same steps as before. The difference is that the integrating factor is now $e^{\int_0^t a(\tau)d\tau}$, so that the left-hand side becomes the derivative of $y(t) \cdot e^{\int_0^t a(\tau)d\tau}$.[2] Again, when we integrate the derivative of a function, we get back the original function. Using this information, we

1. When we deal with growth models with infinite horizons, we may know the limiting value of a variable as time tends to infinity. This information will provide us with a terminal condition.

2. The lower limit of integration can be an arbitrary constant. Leibniz's rule for differentiation of definite integrals says that $d[\int_0^t f(\tau)\, d\tau]/dt = f(t)$. Note that we are taking the derivative with respect to the upper limit of integration. See section A.6.6.

find that the solution to the ODE is

$$y(t) = -e^{-\int_0^t a(\tau)d\tau} \cdot \int e^{\int_0^t a(\tau)d\tau} \cdot x(t) \cdot dt + b \cdot e^{-\int_0^t a(\tau)d\tau} \tag{A.18}$$

where b is an arbitrary constant of integration. To find the particular or exact solution, we again have to make use of a boundary condition.

A.1.3 Systems of Linear Ordinary Differential Equations

We now study a system of linear, first-order ODEs of the form

$$\dot{y}_1(t) = a_{11}y_1(t) + \cdots + a_{1n}y_n(t) + x_1(t)$$

$$\ldots$$

$$\dot{y}_n(t) = a_{n1}y_1(t) + \cdots + a_{nn}y_n(t) + x_n(t)$$

In matrix notation, the system is

$$\dot{y}(t) = A \cdot y(t) + x(t) \tag{A.19}$$

where $y(t)$ is a column vector of n functions of time, $\begin{bmatrix} y_1(t) \\ \cdots \\ y_n(t) \end{bmatrix}$, $\dot{y}(t)$ is the column vector of the n corresponding derivatives, A is an $n \times n$ square matrix of constant coefficients, and $x(t)$ is a vector of n functions.

We consider three procedures for solving this system of differential equations. The first one is a graphical device called a *phase diagram,* similar to the one that we used for a single differential equation. The advantage of a phase diagram is that it is simple and provides a qualitative solution. Furthermore, this technique works for nonlinear, as well as linear, systems. The drawbacks of phase diagrams are that they work only for 2×2 systems and only for autonomous equations with steady states.

The second procedure is *analytical.* The advantages of the analytical approach are that it gives quantitative answers and can be used in larger systems. The disadvantage is that it works, in general, only for linear equations. Later in this section, however, we use linear approximations to nonlinear systems.

The third procedure is *numerical.* Later in this section, we describe the time-elimination method for solving nonlinear systems numerically.

Phase Diagrams

DIAGONAL SYSTEMS Start with the simple case in which A is a 2×2 *diagonal* matrix and the equations are homogeneous; that is, the components of the vector $x(t)$ are 0. The system

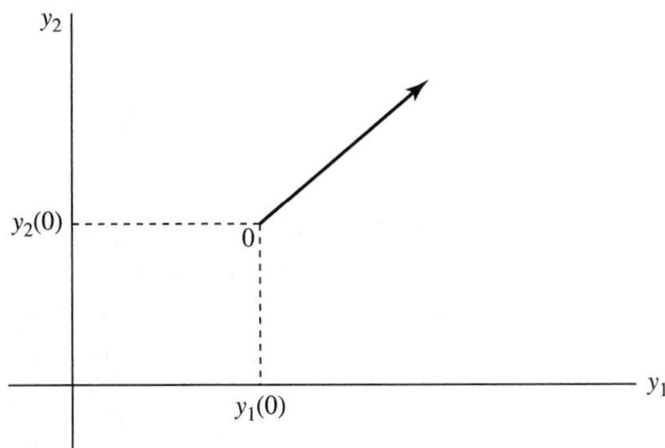

Figure A.3
Directions of motion. The figure shows the directions of motion for y_1 and y_2 in the diagonal system given in equation (A.20).

can then be rewritten as

$$\begin{aligned} \dot{y}_1(t) &= a_{11} \cdot y_1(t) \\ \dot{y}_2(t) &= a_{22} \cdot y_2(t) \end{aligned} \tag{A.20}$$

where a_{11} and a_{22} are real numbers.

A phase diagram is a graphical tool, similar to the one used in the previous section, which allows us to visualize the dynamics of the system. In figure A.3, y_1 is on the horizontal axis, and y_2 is on the vertical axis. Each point in the space represents the position of the system (y_1, y_2) at a given moment in time. Imagine that, at time 0, we are at the point labeled "0" in the figure; that is, y_1 equals $y_1(0)$ and y_2 equals $y_2(0)$. If we want to see what the position of the economy will be at the "next instant," we could have a third dimension to represent time. More conveniently, we can represent the dynamics with arrows that point in the direction of motion, just as in section A.1.2. For instance, an arrow that points northeast at point "0" signifies that the variables y_1 and y_2 are each growing over time. If the arrow points north, y_2 grows and y_1 is stationary, and so on.

The object of a phase diagram is to translate the dynamics implied by the two differential equations into a system of arrows that describe the qualitative behavior of the economy over time. As a simple example, consider the diagonal system that we studied before. The dynamics depend on the signs of the two diagonal elements of A. We now consider three cases.

Case 1, $a_{11} > 0$ and $a_{22} > 0$ To construct the phase diagram, follow the following steps:

1. Start in figure A.4a by plotting the locus of points for which $\dot{y}_1$ equals 0, called the $\dot{y}_1 = 0$ *schedule*. In this case, the locus corresponds to the points for which $y_1(t) = 0$; that is, the vertical axis.

2. Analyze the dynamics of y_1 in each of the two regions generated by the $\dot{y}_1 = 0$ schedule. For positive y_1 (that is, to the right of the $\dot{y}_1 = 0$ schedule), $\dot{y}_1$ is positive because $a_{11} > 0$ and $y_1 > 0$. Hence, the arrows point east. The opposite is true to the left of the vertical axis because in that region, $\dot{y}_1$ is given by the product of a positive number, $a_{11} > 0$, and a negative number, $y_1 < 0$. Therefore, the arrows point west.

3. Repeat the procedure for $\dot{y}_2$. In the present example, the $\dot{y}_2 = 0$ schedule is the horizontal axis shown in figure A.4b. For positive y_2, $\dot{y}_2$ is the product of two positive numbers and is therefore positive. Hence, y_2 is increasing and, correspondingly, the arrows point north. Similarly, the arrows point south for negative y_2.

4. Join the two pictures in figure A.4c. The two schedules divide the space into four regions. (In this simple case, the regions correspond to the four quadrants, a result that is not general.) In the first quadrant, one arrow points east and the other points north. We combine the two into an arrow that points northeast. This construction means that, if the economy is in this region, y_1 and y_2 are increasing. The combined arrows for the second, third, and fourth quadrants point northwest, southwest, and southeast, respectively. Along the vertical axis, the arrows point north for positive y_2 and south for negative y_2. On the horizontal axis, the arrows point east for positive y_1 and west for negative y_1. Finally, at the origin, $\dot{y}_1$ and $\dot{y}_2$ are 0. Hence, if the economy happens to be at the origin, it remains there forever. This point is the *steady state*. It is *unstable* in that if the initial position deviates from the origin by a small amount in any direction, the dynamics of the system (the arrows) take it away from the steady state.

5. Use the boundary conditions to see which one of the many paths depicted in the picture constitutes the exact solution. Imagine, for example, that, at time zero, the value of y_1 is 1 and the value of y_2 is 2. (In this case, the two boundary conditions are initial conditions, but, in other cases that we consider, we may have one initial condition and one terminal condition or two terminal conditions.) The initial conditions imply that the system starts at point "0" in figure A.4c. The subsequent behavior of y_1 and y_2 is given by the path going through "0," as depicted in figure A.4c.

Case 2, $a_{11} < 0$ and $a_{22} < 0$ Arguments similar to those of the previous section imply that the $\dot{y}_1 = 0$ schedule is again the vertical axis, and the $\dot{y}_2 = 0$ schedule is again the horizontal axis. We follow the same steps as before to find in figure A.5 that the arrows point southwest in the first quadrant, southeast in the second, northeast in the third, and northwest in the

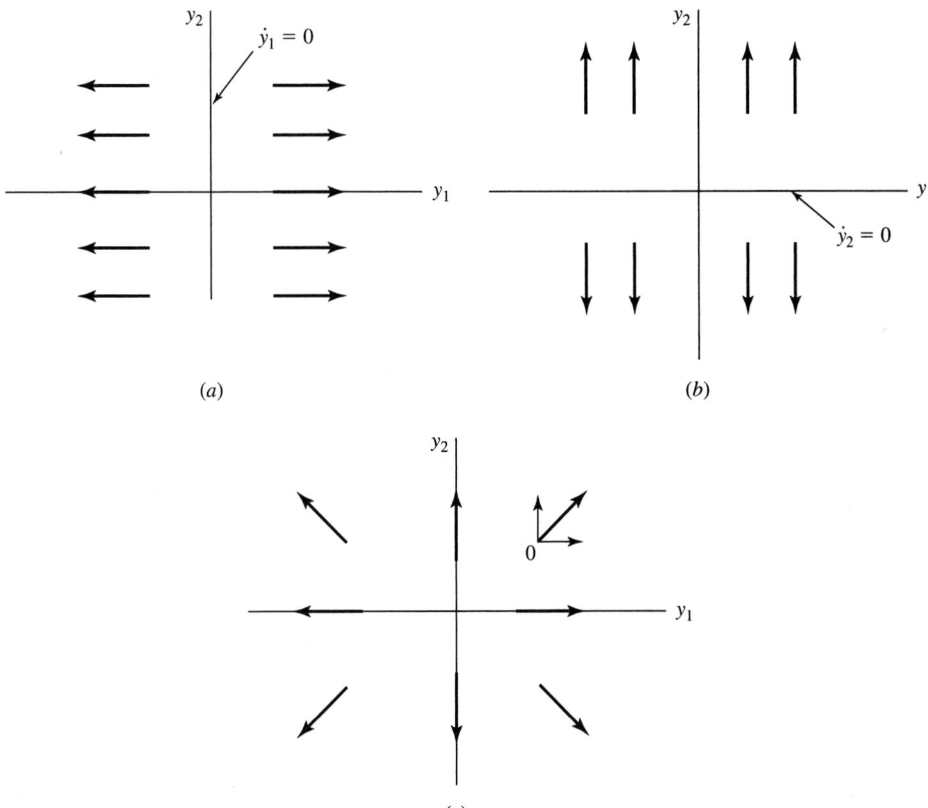

Figure A.4
(*a*) **The $\dot{y}_1 = 0$ locus.** The figure shows the $\dot{y}_1 = 0$ schedule (the vertical axis in this example) for the system in equation (A.20) when $a_{11} > 0$. The arrows show the direction of motion for y_1. (*b*) **The $\dot{y}_2 = 0$ locus.** The figure shows the $\dot{y}_2 = 0$ schedule (the horizontal axis in this example) for the system in equation (A.20) when $a_{22} > 0$. The arrows show the direction of motion for y_2. (*c*) **The phase diagram in an unstable case.** The results from figures A.4(a) and A.4(b) are joined to generate a simple phase diagram. The arrows show the directions of motion for y_1 and y_2 when $a_{11} > 0$ and $a_{22} > 0$. This system is unstable.

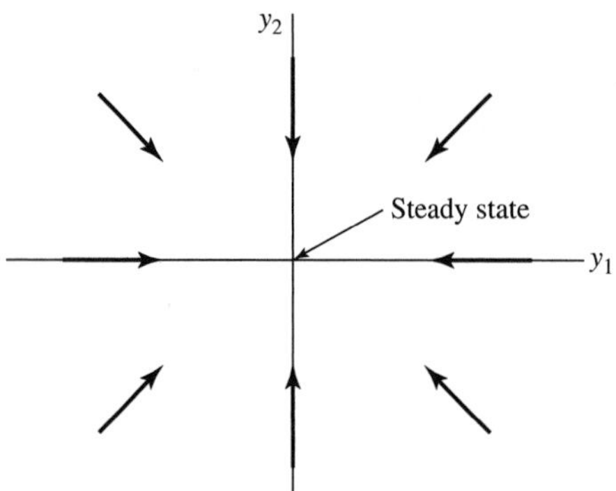

Figure A.5
The phase diagram in a stable case. In this example, $a_{11} < 0$ and $a_{22} < 0$ apply in equation (A.20). This system is stable.

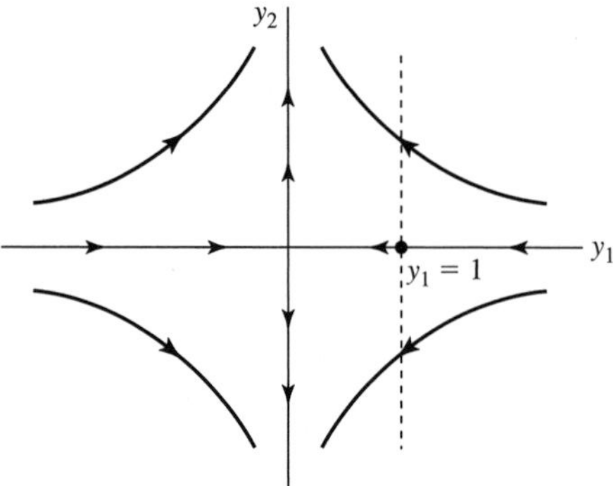

Figure A.6
The phase diagram in a case of saddle-path stability. In this example, $a_{11} < 0$ and $a_{22} > 0$ apply in equation (A.20). This system is saddle-path stable.

fourth. The steady state is the origin and, unlike the previous case, this position is *stable*. For any initial values of y_1 and y_2, the dynamics of the system takes it back to the steady state.

Case 3, $a_{11} < 0$ and $a_{22} > 0$ As in the previous cases, the $\dot{y}_1 = 0$ schedule is the vertical axis, and the $\dot{y}_2 = 0$ schedule is the horizontal axis. The dynamics in this third case, shown in figure A.6, is, however, more complicated than before. The arrows point northwest in the first quadrant, northeast in the second, southeast in the third, and southwest in the fourth. The arrows point toward the origin along the horizontal axis and away from it along the vertical axis. The origin is, again, the steady state.

The new element is that the system is neither stable nor unstable. If the system starts at the steady state, it remains there. If it starts along the horizontal axis, the dynamics of the system takes it back to the steady state. But if the system starts at any point off the horizontal axis, no matter how close to it, the dynamics takes it away from the steady state. The system explodes in the sense that y_2 approaches infinity as t tends to infinity.

This case is called *saddle-path stable*. The reason for this name is the analogy with a marble left on top of a saddle. There is one point on the saddle where, if left there, the marble does not move. This point corresponds to the steady state. There is a trajectory on the saddle with the property that if the marble is left at any point on that trajectory, it rolls toward the steady state. But if the marble is left at any other point, the marble falls to the ground.

Two results about the dynamic paths shown in figure A.6 are worth highlighting. First, none of the paths cross each other. Second, there are only two paths going through the steady state, one is the saddle path that we just mentioned, and the other is the unstable path that corresponds to the vertical axis. These paths are called the *stable arm* and the *unstable arm,* respectively. All two-dimensional systems of ODEs that exhibit saddle-path stability have one stable arm and one unstable arm, each going through the steady state.

Figure A.6 shows the dynamics of the economy for all possible points. The particular path followed depends on two boundary conditions, which have to be specified. As an example, suppose that the initial condition is $y_1(0)=1$, and the terminal condition is $\lim_{t\to\infty}[y_2(t)]=0$. The initial condition says that the economy starts anywhere on the vertical line $y_1=1$ (see figure A.6). Among all the possible points on this line, only the one on the horizontal axis has the property that y_2 approaches 0 as time goes to infinity. Hence, the terminal condition ensures that the starting point for this economy is $y_2(0)=0$, right on the stable arm.

By symmetry, the case in which $a_{11}>0$ and $a_{22}<0$ also displays saddle-path stability. The only difference is that now the horizontal axis is unstable, whereas the vertical axis is stable.

The key lesson in this section is that if the matrix associated with the system of ODEs is diagonal, its stability properties depend on the signs of the coefficients. If both are positive, the system is unstable. If both are negative, the system is stable. If they have opposite signs, the system is saddle-path stable.

A NONDIAGONAL EXAMPLE When the system of ODEs is nondiagonal, we follow the same steps to construct the phase diagram. As an example, consider the case

$$\begin{aligned}\dot{y}_1(t) &= 0.06\cdot y_1(t) - y_2(t) + 1.4\\ \dot{y}_2(t) &= -0.004\cdot y_1(t) + 0.04\end{aligned} \tag{A.21}$$

with the boundary conditions $y_1(0)=1$ and $\lim_{t\to\infty}[e^{-0.06t}\cdot y_1(t)]=0$.

The $\dot{y}_1 = 0$ locus is the upward-sloping line $y_2 = 1.4 + 0.06 \cdot y_1$. If we start at a point on the $\dot{y}_1 = 0$ schedule and increase y_1 a bit, the right-hand side of the expression for $\dot{y}_1$ in equation (A.21) increases. Hence, $\dot{y}_1$ becomes positive and y_1 is increasing in that region. The arrows in this region therefore point east. A symmetric argument implies that the arrows point west for points to the left of the $\dot{y}_1 = 0$ schedule.

The $\dot{y}_2 = 0$ locus is given by $y_1 = 10$, a vertical line; that is, this locus is independent of y_2. The expression for $\dot{y}_2$ in equation (A.21) implies that if y_1 rises, $\dot{y}_2$ decreases. Hence, to the right of the $\dot{y}_2 = 0$ locus, $\dot{y}_2$ is negative, and the arrows point south. The reverse is true to the left of the locus.

The two loci divide the space into four regions, labeled 1 through 4 in figure A.7a. The steady state is the point at which the two loci cross, a condition that corresponds in this case to $y_1^* = 10$ and $y_2^* = 2$. In region 1, the combined arrows point southwest; in region 2, northwest; in region 3, northeast; and in region 4, southeast.

To assess the stability properties of the system, we can ask the following question: From how many of the four regions do the arrows allow the system to move toward the steady state? If the answer is two, the system is saddle-path stable, and the saddle path is located in these two regions.

Figure A.7a shows that the system can move toward the steady state if and only if it starts in regions 1 and 3. Therefore, the system is saddle-path stable. The saddle path, located in regions 1 and 3, goes through the steady state. If the system starts on this path, it converges to the steady state. If it starts slightly above the saddle path in region 3—say, at point x_0 in figure A.7a—it follows the arrows northeast for a while. The path eventually crosses the $\dot{y}_1 = 0$ locus, and the system then moves northwest, away from the steady state. We can also show readily that the system diverges from the steady state if it starts below the stable arm in region 3. In fact, the system diverges from the steady state if it begins at any point that is not on the stable arm.

The exact path along which the system evolves depends on the boundary conditions. This example specifies one initial and one terminal condition. The initial condition says that the system starts somewhere on the vertical line $y_1 = 1$. The terminal condition says that the product of y_1 and a term that goes to 0 at a rate of 0.06 per year goes to 0 as t goes to infinity. If the system ends up in the steady state, y_1 will be constant, so that the product of a constant and a term that approaches zero will be zero. Hence, the terminal condition will be satisfied if y_1 approaches a constant in the long run. If the system does not end up in the steady state, y_1 will increase or decrease at an ever-increasing rate. (The arrows move the economy away from the $\dot{y}_1 = 0$ axis, and y_1 grows in magnitude at an increasing rate.) Since the product of a factor that decreases at rate of 0.06 per year and a factor whose absolute value grows at ever-increasing rates is not 0, the terminal condition requires the system to end up at the steady state. It follows that, because $y_1(0)$ is not at the steady state,

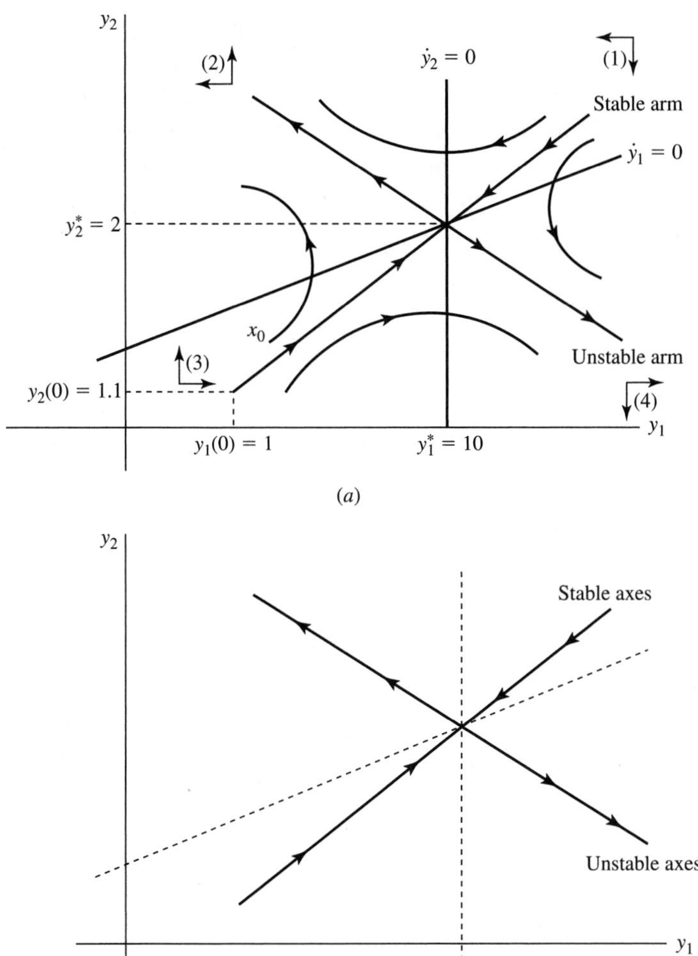

Figure A.7
(*a*) **The phase diagram in a nonlinear example with saddle-path stability.** The figure shows the phase diagram for the system in equation (A.21). This system is saddle-path stable. (*b*) **The stable arm and the unstable arm.** This figure is generated by erasing the $y_1 = 0$ and $y_2 = 0$ schedules and the normal axes in figure A.7a. We are left with the stable arm and the unstable arm.

the corresponding value $y_2(0)$ must be the one that puts the system on the stable arm, as shown in figure A.7a.

Suppose that we erase the normal axes and the $\dot{y}_1 = 0$ and $\dot{y}_2 = 0$ schedules, as shown in figure A.7b. We are then left with the stable arm (with arrows pointing toward the steady state) and the unstable arm (with arrows pointing away from the steady state). These two lines divide the space into four regions with the corresponding dynamics as represented by the arrows. Note the similarity between figure A.7b and figure A.6. We can, in fact, think of figure A.7b as a distorted version of figure A.6. This perspective will allow us to interpret the analytical solution to these systems.

A NONLINEAR EXAMPLE We conclude this section on phase diagrams with a nonlinear example. Consider the following system:

$$\dot{k}(t) = k(t)^{0.3} - c(t) \tag{A.22}$$

$$\dot{c}(t) = c(t) \cdot [0.3 \cdot k(t)^{-0.7} - 0.06] \tag{A.23}$$

with boundary conditions $k(0) = 1$ and $\lim_{t\to\infty}[e^{-0.06t} \cdot k(t)] = 0$. The main difference between this system and the ones already considered is that the functional forms are now nonlinear. However, to construct a phase diagram for nonlinear systems, we follow exactly the same steps as before.

The $\dot{k} = 0$ locus is given from equation (A.22) by $c = k^{0.3}$. If we put k on the horizontal axis and c on the vertical, this locus is an upward-sloping and concave curve, as shown in figure A.8. Consider a point slightly to the right of the $\dot{k} = 0$ locus; that is, with slightly higher k and the same c. Equation (A.22) implies that the new point has a larger right-hand side; hence, $\dot{k}$ must be positive. Therefore, k rises to the right of the $\dot{k} = 0$ schedule and the arrows point east. A symmetric argument shows that the arrows point west to the left of the $\dot{k} = 0$ schedule.

The $\dot{c} = 0$ schedule is given from equation (A.23) by $k = 10$, a vertical line (see figure A.8). Consider a point to the right of the $\dot{c} = 0$ locus; that is, with the same c and higher k. Equation (A.23) implies $\dot{c} < 0$; hence, the arrows point south. By a similar argument, the arrows to the left of the $\dot{c} = 0$ schedule point north.

We can now combine the dynamics for k and c. The steady state is the point at which the $\dot{k} = 0$ and $\dot{c} = 0$ loci cross, a condition that corresponds to $k^* = 10$ and $c^* = 2$. Figure A.8 shows that the arrows are such that the system approaches the steady state only from regions 1 and 3. We conclude that the system is saddle-path stable. The stable arm in this case is *not* a linear function. It is still true, however, that the stable arm runs between regions 1 and 3 and goes through the steady state. The unstable arm moves between regions 2 and 4.

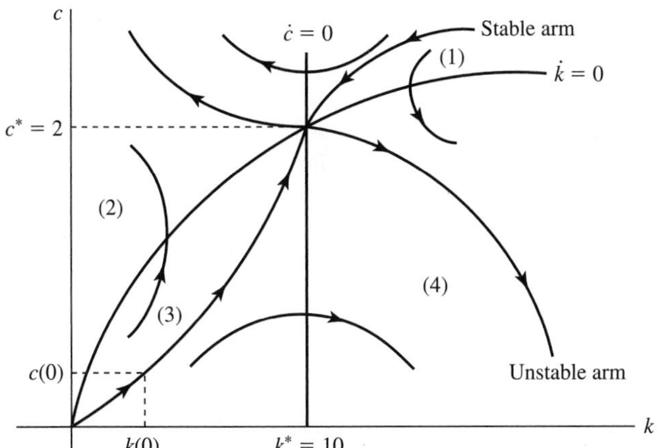

Figure A.8
The phase diagram for a nonlinear model. The figure shows the phase diagram for the system in equations (A.22) and (A.23). This system is saddle-path stable.

We can again use the boundary conditions to select the path that the system will follow. In this example, the boundary conditions ensure that the system begins on the stable arm and therefore approaches its steady state over time.

Analytical Solutions of Linear, Homogeneous Systems We now consider the analytical solution to systems of linear ODEs. We start with the homogeneous case because the solution to the general case is intensive in notation. The $x(t)$ vector in equation (A.19) is then set to 0, so the system becomes

$$\dot{y}(t) = A \cdot y(t) \tag{A.24}$$

where $y(t)$ is an $n \times 1$ column vector of functions of time, $y_i(t)$, A is an $n \times n$ matrix of constant coefficients, and $\dot{y}(t)$ is the vector of time derivatives corresponding to $y(t)$.

Imagine that there is an $n \times n$ matrix V with the property that if we premultiply A by V^{-1} and postmultiply by V, we get a diagonal $n \times n$ matrix:

$$V^{-1}AV = D \tag{A.25}$$

where D is a square matrix in which all the off-diagonal elements are 0. Section A.5 shows that V and D may exist: they are, respectively, the matrix of eigenvectors and the diagonal matrix of eigenvalues associated with A.[3]

3. A sufficient condition for the matrix A to be diagonalizable is for all the eigenvalues to be different. In this case, the eigenvectors are linearly independent, so that $\det(V) \neq 0$ and V^{-1} exists.

We can define the variables $z(t)$ as

$$z(t) = V^{-1} \cdot y(t)$$

Since V^{-1} is a matrix of constants, $\dot{z}(t) = V^{-1} \cdot \dot{y}(t)$. We can therefore rewrite the system from equation (A.24) in terms of the transformed $z(t)$ variables:

$$\dot{z}(t) = V^{-1} \cdot \dot{y}(t) = V^{-1}A \cdot y(t) = V^{-1}AVV^{-1} \cdot y(t) = D \cdot z(t) \tag{A.26}$$

This system consists of n one-dimensional differential equations:

$$\begin{aligned} \dot{z}_1(t) &= \alpha_1 \cdot z_1(t) \\ \dot{z}_2(t) &= \alpha_2 \cdot z_2(t) \\ &\cdots \\ \dot{z}_n(t) &= \alpha_n \cdot z_n(t) \end{aligned} \tag{A.27}$$

We showed in section A.2.2 that the solution for each of these differential equations takes the form $z_i(t) = b_i \cdot e^{\alpha_i t}$, where each b_i is an arbitrary constant of integration that is determined by the boundary conditions (see equation [A.11]). We can express this result in matrix notation as

$$z(t) = Eb \tag{A.28}$$

where E is a diagonal matrix with $e^{\alpha_i t}$ in the ith diagonal term, and b is a column vector of the constants b_i.

We can transform the solution for the z variables back to the y variables by using the relation $y = Vz$. The solution for y is

$$y = VEb$$

or, in nonmatrix notation,

$$y_i(t) = v_{i1}e^{\alpha_1 t} \cdot b_1 + v_{i2}e^{\alpha_2 t} \cdot b_2 + \cdots + v_{in}e^{\alpha_n t} \cdot b_n \tag{A.29}$$

In summary, the general method to solve a system of equations of the form of equation (A.24) is as follows:

1. Find the eigenvalues of the matrix A and call them $\alpha_1, \ldots, \alpha_n$.
2. Find the corresponding eigenvectors and arrange them as columns in a matrix V.
3. The solution takes the form of equation (A.29).
4. Use the boundary conditions to determine the arbitrary constants of integration (b_i).

The Relation Between the Graphical and Analytical Solutions We now relate the graphical and analytical approaches to each other. Remember that when we constructed the phase diagram, we suggested that if we erase the axes and the $\dot{y}_i = 0$ loci and look at the remaining picture in figure A.7b, we get a distorted version of the picture in figure A.6, for which the matrix A was diagonal. We saw also that the analytical solution involved a diagonal matrix of eigenvalues. The similarities in the two approaches are no coincidence: when we diagonalize a matrix we implicitly find a set of axes (or vector basis) on which the linear application represented by A can be expressed as a diagonal matrix (see section A.5). The new axes are the eigenvectors, and the elements in the corresponding diagonal matrix are the eigenvalues.

The graphical solution to the system of equations is basically the same thing. The stable and unstable arms correspond to the two eigenvectors. If we think of these two arms as a new set of axes—that is, if we erase the old axes and the $\dot{y}_i = 0$ schedules—then the old matrix A can be represented by the diagonal eigenvalue matrix. The phase diagram for the nondiagonal case looks accordingly like a distorted version of the diagonal one.

Stability Recall that the stability properties of the diagonal examples depend on the signs of the diagonal elements. Not surprisingly, therefore, the stability properties of the nondiagonal system depend on the signs of its eigenvalues. Several possibilities arise:

1. The two eigenvalues are *real* and *positive*. In this case, the system is unstable.

2. The two eigenvalues are *real* and *negative*. In this case the system is stable.

3. The two eigenvalues are *real* with *opposite signs*. In this case, the system is saddle-path stable. Furthermore, when the system is saddle-path stable, *the stable arm corresponds to the eigenvector associated with the negative eigenvalue*.[4] Similarly, the unstable arm corresponds to the eigenvector associated with the positive eigenvalue. The intuition is again that the axes associated with the diagonal matrix are given by the eigenvectors. As we saw in the examples, when the system is diagonal, the axis associated with the negative component of the diagonal matrix is the stable arm, and the axis associated with the positive component is the unstable arm.

4. The two eigenvalues are *complex* with *negative real parts*. The system converges in this case to the steady state in an oscillating manner (figure A.9a).

5. The two eigenvalues are *complex* with *positive real parts*. The system is unstable and oscillating, as depicted in figure A.9b.

4. Throughout the book we will use interchangeably the terms eigenvector associated with negative eigenvalue and negative eigenvector.

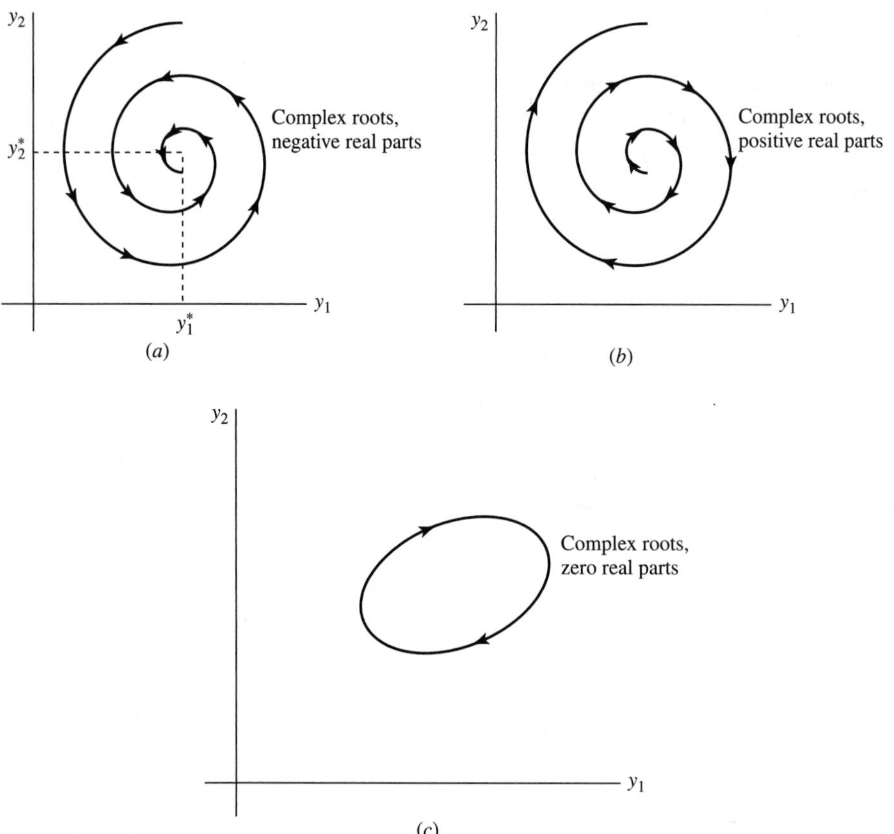

Figure A.9
(*a*) **Stable, oscillating dynamics.** If the two eigenvalues are complex with negative real parts, then the system converges to the steady state in an oscillating manner. (*b*) **Unstable, oscillating dynamics.** If the two eigenvalues are complex with positive real parts, then the system diverges from the steady state in an oscillating manner. (*c*) **Oscillating dynamics.** If the two eigenvalues are complex with 0 real parts, then the trajectories are ellipses around the steady state. This system neither converges nor diverges.

6. The two eigenvalues are *complex* with *zero real parts*. The trajectories are then ellipses around the steady state, as shown in figure A.9c.

7. The two eigenvalues are *equal*. In this case, the matrix of eigenvectors cannot be inverted, and the analytical solution outlined earlier in this section cannot be applied. The solution in this case takes the form

$$y_i(t) = (b_{i1} + b_{i2} \cdot t) \cdot e^{\alpha t}$$

where b_{i1} and b_{i2} are functions of the constants of integration and the coefficients in A, and α is the unique eigenvalue. The solution is stable if $\alpha < 0$ and unstable if $\alpha > 0$.

We should mention that, in nonlinear systems, there is one more type of equilibrium called a *limit cycle*. A stable limit cycle is one toward which trajectories converge, and an unstable limit cycle is one from which trajectories diverge.

The stability properties of systems with higher dimensions are similar. If all eigenvalues are positive, the system is unstable. If all the eigenvalues are negative, the system is stable. If the eigenvalues have different signs, the system is saddle-path stable. Since, as argued before, the stable arm corresponds to the eigenvector(s) associated with the negative eigenvalue(s), the dimension of the stable arm is the number of negative eigenvalues. For instance, in a 3×3 system with one negative eigenvalue, the stable arm is a line going through the steady state and corresponding to the negative eigenvector. If there are two negative eigenvalues, the stable manifold is a plane going through the steady state. This plane is generated by the two negative eigenvalues. In an $n \times n$ system, the stable arm (sometimes called the *stable manifold*) is a hyperplane generated by the associated eigenvectors, with dimension equal to the number of negative eigenvalues.

Analytical Solutions of Linear, Nonhomogeneous Systems Consider now the nonhomogeneous system of differential equations,

$$\dot{y}(t) = A \cdot y(t) + x(t) \tag{A.30}$$

where $y(t)$ is an $n \times 1$ vector of functions of time, $\dot{y}(t)$ is the corresponding vector of time derivatives, A is an $n \times n$ matrix of constants, and $x(t)$ is an $n \times 1$ vector of known functions of time, where these functions can be constants. The procedure to find the solutions to equation (A.30) parallels the one that we used for the homogeneous case. Begin again with the matrix V, composed of the eigenvectors of A, such that $V^{-1}AV$ generates a diagonal matrix D, which contains the eigenvalues of A. Transform the system by premultiplying all terms by V^{-1} and then define $z \equiv V^{-1}y$ to get

$$\dot{z} = V^{-1}\dot{y} = V^{-1} \cdot (Ay + x) = V^{-1}AVV^{-1}y + V^{-1}x = Dz + V^{-1}x$$

This matrix equation defines a system of n linear differential equations of the form

$$\dot{z}_i(t) = \alpha_i \cdot z_i(t) + V_i^{-1} \cdot x(t)$$

where V_i^{-1} is the ith row of V^{-1}. As we saw in section A.2.2, the solution to each of these linear ODEs with fixed coefficients takes the form of equation (A.11):

$$z_i(t) = e^{\alpha_i t} \cdot \int e^{-\alpha_i \tau} \cdot V_i^{-1} \cdot x(\tau) \cdot d\tau + e^{\alpha_i t} \cdot b_i$$

for $i = 1, \ldots, n$, where b_i is again an arbitrary constant of integration. We can write these solutions in matrix notation as

$$z = E\hat{X} + Eb \tag{A.31}$$

where, again, E is a diagonal matrix of terms $e^{\alpha_i t}$, $\hat{X}$ is a column vector with integrals of the form

$$\int e^{-\alpha_i \tau} \cdot V_i^{-1} \cdot x(\tau) \cdot d\tau$$

as each of its elements, and b is a column vector of arbitrary constants. Once the time path of z is known, we can find the time path of y by premultiplying z by V.

As an example, consider the system of ODEs in equation (A.21). In matrix notation, this system can be written as

$$\begin{bmatrix} \dot{y}_1(t) \\ \dot{y}_2(t) \end{bmatrix} = \begin{bmatrix} 0.06 & -1 \\ -0.004 & 0 \end{bmatrix} \bullet \begin{bmatrix} y_1(t) \\ y_2(t) \end{bmatrix} + \begin{bmatrix} 1.4 \\ 0.04 \end{bmatrix} \tag{A.32}$$

with the boundary conditions $y_1(0) = 1$ and

$$\lim_{t \to \infty} [e^{-0.06 \cdot t} \cdot y_1(t)] = 0$$

In this example, x is a vector of constants. In section A.5 we show how to find the eigenvalues and eigenvectors associated with a matrix A. We find that the diagonal matrix of eigenvalues, D, and the matrix of eigenvectors, V, are given by

$$D = \begin{bmatrix} 0.1 & 0 \\ 0 & -0.4 \end{bmatrix}, \qquad V = \begin{bmatrix} 1 & 1 \\ -0.04 & 0.1 \end{bmatrix}$$

where

$$V^{-1} = \begin{bmatrix} 0.1/0.14 & -1/0.14 \\ 0.04/0.14 & 1/0.14 \end{bmatrix}$$

Define $\begin{matrix} z_1 \\ z_2 \end{matrix} = V^{-1} \bullet \begin{matrix} y_1 \\ y_2 \end{matrix}$. The system in terms of the new variables can be written as

$$\dot{z}_1 = 0.1 \cdot z_1 + 10/14$$

$$\dot{z}_2 = -0.04 \cdot z_2 + 9.6/14$$

a system of two differential equations that we know how to solve (see section A.2.2):

$$z_1(t) = -100/14 + b_1 e^{0.1 \cdot t}$$

$$z_2(t) = 240/14 + b_2 e^{-0.04 \cdot t}$$

where b_1 and b_2 are constants of integration, which have to be pinned down by the boundary conditions. We can transform the solution for z_1 and z_2 into a solution for y_1 and y_2 by premultiplying z by V to get

$$y_1(t) = 10 + b_1 e^{0.1 \cdot t} + b_2 e^{-0.04 \cdot t} \tag{A.33}$$

$$y_2(t) = 2 - 0.04 \cdot b_1 e^{0.1 \cdot t} + 0.1 \cdot b_2 e^{-0.04 \cdot t} \tag{A.34}$$

We now need to determine the values of the constants, b_1 and b_2. The initial condition $y_1(0) = 1$ implies $b_1 + b_2 = -9$. We can multiply both sides of equation (A.33) by $e^{-0.06 \cdot t}$, take limits as t goes to infinity, and use the terminal condition, $\lim_{t \to \infty} [e^{-0.06t} \cdot y_1(t)] = 0$, to get

$$\lim_{t \to \infty} [e^{-0.06 \cdot t} \cdot y_1(t)] = \lim_{t \to \infty} [10 \cdot e^{-0.06 \cdot t} + b_1 e^{0.04 \cdot t} + b_2 e^{-0.1 \cdot t}] = 0$$

The first and third terms in the middle expression go to 0 as t goes to infinity, but the second term approaches infinity unless b_1 equals 0. Hence, the condition for the whole expression to equal 0 is $b_1 = 0$, which implies $b_2 = -9$. The exact solution to the system of ODEs is therefore

$$y_1(t) = 10 - 9 \cdot e^{-0.04 \cdot t}$$

$$y_2(t) = 2 - 0.9 \cdot e^{-0.04 \cdot t}$$

Note that $y_1(t)$ equals 1 at $t = 0$, increases over time, and asymptotes to its steady-state value, $y_1^* = 10$ (see figure A.10a). The variable y_2 equals 1.1 at $t = 0$, increases over time, and asymptotes to its steady-state value, $y_2^* = 2$ (see figure A.10b). In other words, the boundary conditions select the initial value of y_2 that causes the system to end up at its steady state. In terms of figure A.7a, the value $y_2(0)$ is chosen so as to put the system on the stable arm. At the initial point, $[\begin{smallmatrix} y_1(0) \\ y_2(0) \end{smallmatrix}] = [\begin{smallmatrix} 1 \\ 1.1 \end{smallmatrix}]$, the vector going toward the steady state is $[\begin{smallmatrix} 9 \\ 0.9 \end{smallmatrix}]$ or, by normalizing the first element to unity, $[\begin{smallmatrix} 1 \\ 0.1 \end{smallmatrix}]$, the negative eigenvector. Hence, as noted before,

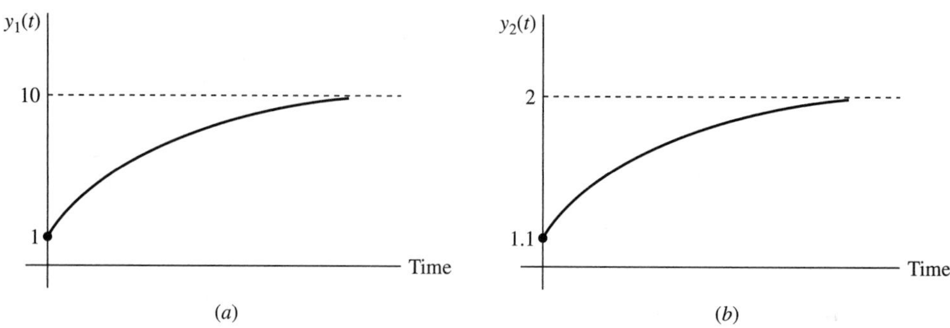

Figure A.10
(*a*) **Solution for $y_1(t)$.** The figure shows the solution for $y_1(t)$ in the system in equation (A.32). (*b*) **Solution for $y_2(t)$.** The figure shows the solution for $y_2(t)$ in the system in equation (A.32).

the stable arm goes through the steady state and corresponds to the eigenvector associated with the negative eigenvalue.

Linearization of Nonlinear Systems Many of the systems of ODEs that we encounter in the book are nonlinear. In this case, we can use the phase-diagram techniques that we discussed before, or alternatively, we can approximate the equations linearly by means of Taylor-series expansions.

Consider the following system of ODEs:

$$\begin{aligned} \dot{y}_1(t) &= f^1[y_1(t), \ldots, y_n(t)] \\ \dot{y}_2(t) &= f^2[y_1(t), \ldots, y_n(t)] \\ &\ldots \\ \dot{y}_n(t) &= f^n[y_1(t), \ldots, y_n(t)] \end{aligned} \tag{A.35}$$

where the functions $f^1(\bullet), f^2(\bullet), \ldots, f^n(\bullet)$ are nonlinear. We can use a Taylor-series expansion to study the system's dynamics in the neighborhood of its steady state. (Taylor's theorem is in section A.6.2.) The first-order expansion can be written as

$$\begin{aligned} \dot{y}_1(t) &= f^1(\bullet) + (f^1)_{y_1}(\bullet) \cdot (y_1 - y_1^*) + \cdots + (f^1)_{y_n}(\bullet) \cdot (y_n - y_n^*) + R_1 \\ &\ldots \\ \dot{y}_n(t) &= f^n(\bullet) + (f^n)_{y_1}(\bullet) \cdot (y_1 - y_1^*) + \cdots + (f^n)_{y_n}(\bullet) \cdot (y_n - y_n^*) + R_n \end{aligned} \tag{A.36}$$

where $f^1(\bullet), \ldots, f^n(\bullet)$ are the values of the functions $f^1(\bullet), \ldots, f^n(\bullet)$ at the steady state, and $(f^1)_{y_i}(\bullet), \ldots, (f^n)_{y_i}(\bullet)$ are the partial derivatives with respect to y_i at the steady state. The terms R_i are the Taylor residuals. If the system is close to its steady state, these residuals are small and can be neglected. The convenience of linearizing around the steady state is that, by definition of a steady state, the first element in each of the equations—$f^1(\bullet), \ldots, f^n(\bullet)$—is 0; that is, the steady-state value of $\dot{y}_i$ is zero for all i.

The linearized system in equation (A.36) can be written in matrix notation as

$$\dot{y} = A \cdot (y - y^*) \tag{A.37}$$

where A is an $n \times n$ matrix of constants corresponding to the first partial derivatives evaluated at the steady state. This linear system is similar to those analyzed in previous sections.

Consider the example of the system of nonlinear equations that we have already studied graphically,

$$\dot{k} = k^{0.3} - c \tag{A.22}$$

$$\dot{c} = c \cdot (0.3 \cdot k^{-0.7} - 0.06) \tag{A.23}$$

with the boundary conditions $k(0) = 1$ and $\lim_{t\to\infty}[e^{-0.06t} \cdot k(t)] = 0$. The steady-state values are $k^* = 10$ and $c^* = 2$. We can linearize this system as follows:

$$\begin{aligned} \dot{k} &= 0.3 \cdot (k^*)^{-0.7} \cdot (k - k^*) - (c - c^*) = 0.06 \cdot k - c + 1.4 \\ \dot{c} &= c^* \cdot [0.3 \cdot (-0.7) \cdot (k^*)^{-1.7}] \cdot (k - k^*) - 0 \cdot (c - c^*) = -0.008 \cdot k + 0.08 \end{aligned} \tag{A.38}$$

We know how to solve this linear system; in fact, we have already solved it! If we relabel k and c as y_1 and y_2, respectively, then it coincides with the system in equation (A.32).

As a graphical intuition, consider the phase diagram that we constructed for the nonlinear system defined by equations (A.22) and (A.23), as depicted in figure A.8. The loci in this figure are nonlinear. Around the steady state, however, the $\dot{c} = 0$ locus is vertical, and the $\dot{k} = 0$ locus is upward sloping. We can approximate these two loci with a vertical line and an upward-sloping line going through the same steady state. When the system is close to its steady state, this approximation is good. The approximation deteriorates as we move away from the steady state because the $\dot{k} = 0$ schedule is strictly concave. The dynamics of the nonlinear system is similar to that of the linear system in the vicinity of the steady state. In fact, at the steady state, the nonlinear stable arm corresponds to the negative eigenvector of the linearized system. Qualitatively, we see by comparing figures A.7a and A.8 that the two systems have similar dynamic properties.

The Time-Elimination Method for Nonlinear Systems In section A.2.3 we saw that one way to get a qualitative solution to a system of nonlinear differential equations was to use a phase diagram. The problem with this graphical approach is that it does not allow us to evaluate the model quantitatively. Later in that section we worked out an analytical solution to a linearized version of the system. The problem with this approach is that the quantification is local, valid only as an approximation in the neighborhood of the steady state. This section describes a method to find global numerical solutions to a system of ODEs. This method provides accurate results for a given configuration of parameters.

Consider again the system of nonlinear equations defined by equations (A.22) and (A.23):

$$\dot{k}(t) = k(t)^{0.3} - c(t) \tag{A.22}$$

$$\dot{c}(t) = c(t) \cdot [0.3 \cdot k(t)^{-0.7} - 0.06] \tag{A.23}$$

with the boundary conditions $k(0) = 1$ and $\lim_{t\to\infty}[e^{-0.06t} \cdot k(t)] = 0$. The phase diagram for this system is in figure A.8. If we knew the initial values, $c(0)$ and $k(0)$, then standard numerical methods for solving differential equations would allow us to solve out for the entire paths of c and k by integrating equations (A.22) and (A.23) with respect to time.[5]

The problem is that $c(0)$ is unknown. Instead, we are given the transversality condition, a restriction that forces the initial value of c to be on the stable arm. The challenge is to express this condition in terms of the required value of $c(0)$. The usual solution involves a method called *shooting*. Start with a guess about $c(0)$ and then work out the time paths implied by the differential equations (A.22) and (A.23). Then check whether the time paths approach the steady state and therefore satisfy the transversality condition. If the paths miss—as is almost sure to be true on the first try—then the system eventually diverges from the steady state. In this case, adjust the guess accordingly; reduce the conjectured value of $c(0)$ if the prior guess is too high, and vice versa. An approximation to the correct $c(0)$ can be found by iterating many times in this manner.

Mulligan and Sala-i-Martin (1991) worked out a much more efficient numerical technique called the *time-elimination method*. The key to this method is to eliminate time from the equations, just as we do when we construct a phase diagram. Recall that the stable arm shown in figure A.8 expresses c as a function of k. In dynamic programming this function is sometimes called the *policy function*. Imagine for a moment that we had a closed-form solution to this policy function, $c = c(k)$. In this case, we could use equation (A.22) to express $\dot{k}$ as a function of k: $\dot{k} = k^{0.3} - c(k)$. Since we know $k(0)$, we could use standard numerical methods to solve this first-order differential equation in k. Once we knew the path for k, we could determine the path for c (since we know the policy function, $c[k]$).

The time-elimination method provides a numerical technique for working out the policy function, $c = c(k)$. The trick is to note that the slope of this function is given by the

5. When the boundary conditions of a problem take the form of a set of values for all the variables at a single point in time, we call it an *initial-value problem*. For instance, the present problem would be an initial-value problem if we replaced the transversality condition, $\lim_{t\to\infty}[e^{-0.06t} \cdot k(t)] = 0$, with some value for $c(0)$. In contrast, for a *boundary-value problem,* the boundary conditions apply at different points in time. The present system is a *boundary-value problem* because we are given an initial condition, $k(0) = 1$, which applies at $t = 0$, and a terminal condition, $\lim_{t\to\infty}[e^{-0.06t} \cdot k(t)] = 0$, which applies at $t = \infty$. Initial-value problems are much easier to solve numerically.

ratio of $\dot{c}$ to $\dot{k}$:

$$dc/dk = c'(k) = \dot{c}/\dot{k} = \frac{c(k) \cdot [0.3 \cdot k^{-0.7} - 0.06]}{k^{0.3} - c(k)} \tag{A.39}$$

where we used the formulas for $\dot{k}$ and $\dot{c}$ from equations (A.22) and (A.23). Time does not appear in equation (A.39); hence, the name time-elimination method.

Note that equation (A.39) is a differential equation in c, where the derivative, dc/dk, is with respect to k rather than t. To solve this equation numerically by standard methods, we need one boundary condition; that is, we have to know one point, (c, k), that lies on the stable arm. Although we do not know the initial pair, $[c(0), k(0)]$, we know that the policy function goes through the steady state, (c^*, k^*). We can therefore start from this point and then solve equation (A.39) numerically to determine the rest of the policy function.[6] Note that, by eliminating time, we transformed a difficult *boundary-value problem* into a much easier *initial-value problem.*

Before we implement this method, there is one more problem that must be addressed. The slope of the policy function at the steady state is

$$c'(k^*) = (\dot{c})^*/(\dot{k})^* = 0/0$$

which is an indeterminate form. There are two ways to solve this problem. The first one uses l'Hôpital's rule for evaluating indeterminate forms (see section A.6.3). In this example, the application of l'Hôpital's rule yields

$$c'(k^*) = [c^* \cdot (-0.21) \cdot (k^*)^{-1.7}]/[0.3 \cdot (k^*)^{-0.7} - c'(k^*)]$$

which implies a quadratic equation in $c'(k)$:

$$[c'(k^*)]^2 - [0.3 \cdot (k^*)^{-0.7}] \cdot c'(k^*) - 0.21 \cdot c^* \cdot (k^*)^{-1.7} = 0$$

This equation has two solutions for $c'(k^*)$:

$$c'(k^*) = [0.3 \cdot (k^*)^{-0.7} - \{[0.3 \cdot (k^*)^{-0.7}]^2 + 4 \cdot (0.21) \cdot c^* \cdot (k^*)^{-1.7}\}^{1/2}]/2 \tag{A.40}$$

$$c'(k^*) = [0.3 \cdot (k^*)^{-0.7} + \{[0.3 \cdot (k^*)^{-0.7}]^2 + 4 \cdot (0.21) \cdot c^* \cdot (k^*)^{-1.7}\}^{1/2}]/2 \tag{A.41}$$

There are two solutions because there are two trajectories that go through the steady state: the stable arm and the unstable arm. The phase diagram in figure A.8 suggests that the stable arm

6. We might have considered starting from the steady state and going backward in time to solve the original system of two differential equations numerically. This idea does not work, however, because $\dot{k}$ and $\dot{c}$ are 0 at the steady state. Therefore, if we start at the steady state, we do not know how to move backward in time; that is, we cannot tell from where we came.

is upward sloping and the unstable arm is downward sloping. Since the slope of the stable arm at the steady state is positive, it must be given by the solution in equation (A.41).

The second way to compute the steady-state is to realize that, at the steady state, the policy function corresponds to the negative eigenvector. In other words, the slope of the negative eigenvector coincides with the steady-state slope of the policy function. Hence, we can use this value as the initial slope and then use equation (A.39) to compute the whole policy function. The advantage of the eigenvalue method over the l'Hôpital's rule method is that it does not require prior qualitative information about the sign of the steady-state slope.

The time-elimination method can be readily extended to systems of three differential equations with two controls and one state variable (see Mulligan and Sala-i-Martin, 1991, 1993). Consider a nonlinear system of equations,

$$\begin{aligned}\dot{c}(t) &= c[c(t), u(t), k(t)]\\ \dot{u}(t) &= u[c(t), u(t), k(t)]\\ \dot{k}(t) &= k[c(t), u(t), k(t)]\end{aligned} \tag{A.42}$$

where $c(t)$ and $u(t)$ are control variables, and $k(t)$ is the state variable. Imagine that we are given the initial value $k(0)$ and two transversality conditions (which apply at $t = \infty$). Suppose that the steady-state values are c^*, u^*, and k^*. Again, if we knew $c(0)$ and $u(0)$, we could find the solution to equation (A.42) by integrating with respect to time. The problem, however, is that $c(0)$ and $u(0)$ are unknown.

Imagine for the moment that we had closed-form expressions for $c(k)$ and $u(k)$, the policy functions for the problem. In this case we could plug these two functions into the $\dot{k}$ equation to get a single differential equation in k. Since we know $k(0)$, the whole time path for $k(t)$ could be found by integrating this differential equation with respect to time. Once we knew the path for k, we could determine the paths for c and u by plugging $k(t)$ into the two functions $c(k)$ and $u(k)$.

The time-elimination method provides a simple way to find $c(k)$ and $u(k)$ numerically. Use the chain rule of calculus to eliminate time from equation (A.42) to get the slopes of $c(k)$ and $u(k)$ as follows:

$$\begin{aligned}dc/dk &= c'(k) = \dot{c}/\dot{k} = \frac{c[c(k), u(k), k]}{k[c(k), u(k), k]}\\ du/dk &= u'(k) = \dot{u}/\dot{k} = \frac{u[c(k), u(k), k]}{k[c(k), u(k), k]}\end{aligned} \tag{A.43}$$

We can solve this system numerically by using the steady state, (c^*, u^*, k^*), as the initial condition. The steady-state slopes can be found by using l'Hôpital's rule or by computing the slope of the eigenvector associated with the negative eigenvalue.

A.2 Static Optimization

A.2.1 Unconstrained Maxima

Consider a univariate real function $u(\bullet)$. We say that a function $u(x)$ has a local maximum at $\bar{\bar{x}}$ if for all x in the neighborhood of $\bar{\bar{x}}$ (that is, for all x in the interval $[\bar{\bar{x}} - \epsilon, \bar{\bar{x}} + \epsilon]$, where ϵ is some positive number), $u(\bar{\bar{x}}) \geq u(x)$. We say that $u(x)$ has an absolute maximum[7] at $\bar{\bar{x}}$ if for all x in the domain of u, $u(\bar{\bar{x}}) \geq u(x)$.

Let $u(x)$ be twice continuously differentiable in the closed interval $[a, b]$ and let $\bar{\bar{x}}$ in the interior of $[a, b]$ be a local maximum. A *necessary condition* for $\bar{\bar{x}}$ to be an *interior local maximum* is for the first derivative of $u(\bullet)$ evaluated at $\bar{\bar{x}}$ to be 0, $u'(\bar{\bar{x}}) = 0$, and for the second derivative to be nonpositive, $u''(\bar{\bar{x}}) \leq 0$. If $u'(\bar{\bar{x}}) = 0$ and $u''(\bar{\bar{x}}) \leq 0$, then $\bar{\bar{x}}$ is an interior local maximum. That is, if the objective function is strictly concave (a negative second derivative), the necessary condition $u'(\bar{\bar{x}}) = 0$ is also a *sufficient condition.*

For practical purposes, if we want to find the maximum of a function in some interval, we compute the first derivative of that function and find the values of x that satisfy the equation $u'(\bar{\bar{x}}) = 0$. This condition gives us some candidate points, often called *critical points.* We then compute the second derivative of $u(\bullet)$ and evaluate it at the critical points. If it is negative, the critical point is a local maximum. We then compare the value $u(\bar{\bar{x}})$ with the value of the function at each of the corners a and b. The absolute maximum of $u(\bullet)$ in the interval $[a, b]$ occurs at one of the $\bar{\bar{x}}$, a, or b, depending on which has the largest image.

The multidimensional case is similar to the unidimensional case that we just described. Consider a function $u : R^n \rightarrow R$, twice continuously differentiable. A necessary condition for $u(x)$ to have an interior local maximum at $\bar{\bar{x}}$ (where x is now an n-dimensional vector, $x \equiv [x_1, \ldots, x_n]$) is for all the partial derivatives to vanish when evaluated at $\bar{\bar{x}}$. In other words, just as in the unidimensional case, functions are "flat at the top."

These necessary conditions are not sufficient, however, because local minima and saddle points also satisfy them. As a parallel to the unidimensional case, a sufficient condition is for the function u to be strictly concave at the critical point.[8]

7. A function $u(\bullet)$ achieves a minimum at point $\bar{\bar{x}}$ if $-u(\bullet)$ achieves a maximum at that point. Hence, to analyze minima of the function $u(\bullet)$, we can analyze maxima of $-u(\bullet)$.

8. One way to check strict concavity is to determine the definiteness of the Hessian, the matrix of second derivatives: if the Hessian is negative definite, the function u is strictly concave. A matrix is *negative definite* if and only if all its eigenvalues are negative. A matrix is *negative semidefinite* if and only if all its eigenvalues are nonpositive. A matrix is *positive definite* if and only if all its eigenvalues are positive. A matrix is *positive semidefinite* if and only if all its eigenvalues are nonnegative. A matrix is not definite if its eigenvalues do not all have the same signs. As we argued in a previous section, if we want to know the signs of the eigenvalues, we do not necessarily have to calculate them. For instance, in the 2×2 case, if the determinant of a matrix is negative, the eigenvalues must have opposite signs, because the determinant of the matrix equals the product of its eigenvalues.

A.2.2 Classical Nonlinear Programming: Equality Constraints

Suppose that we want to find the maximum of the function $u : R^n \to R$, subject to the constraint that the chosen point lie along a plane generated by the restriction $g(x) = a$, where $g : R^n \to R$, and x is an n-dimensional vector, $x \equiv (x_1, \ldots, x_n)$. That is, the problem is

$$\max_{x_1,\ldots,x_n} [u(x_1, \ldots, x_n)], \quad \text{subject to } g(x_1, \ldots, x_n) = a \tag{A.44}$$

We assume that $u(\bullet)$ and $g(\bullet)$ are twice continuously differentiable. One easy way to solve this problem is to realize that the restriction describes an implicit function for x_1: $x_1 = \tilde{x}_1(x_2, \ldots, x_n)$. (We assume here that the restriction uniquely determines x_1 for given values of $x_2, \ldots, x_n$.) We can plug the result for x_1 into $u(x)$ to get an unconstrained function of $(x_2, \ldots, x_n)$:

$$u[\tilde{x}_1(x_2, \ldots, x_n), (x_2, \ldots, x_n)] \equiv \tilde{u}(x_2, \ldots, x_n) \tag{A.45}$$

As just mentioned, the necessary condition for an unconstrained maximum of a function is for all the partial derivatives to vanish. When taking partial derivatives of $u(\bullet)$ with respect to each of the arguments x_i, $i = 2, \ldots, n$, we have to realize that $u(\bullet)$ depends on x_i directly and also indirectly through the dependence of x_1 on x_i. Hence, the necessary condition for a constrained maximum is

$$\partial\tilde{u}(\bullet)/\partial x_i = [\partial u(\bullet)/\partial x_1] \cdot \partial\tilde{x}_1/\partial x_i + \partial u(\bullet)/\partial x_i = 0 \tag{A.46}$$

for $i = 2, \ldots, n$. We can calculate the partial derivatives $\partial\tilde{x}_1/\partial x_i$ from the implicit function theorem (section A.6.1), $\partial\tilde{x}_1/\partial x_i = -[\partial g(\bullet)/\partial x_i]/[\partial g(\bullet)/\partial x_1]$. By plugging this expression into equation (A.46) we get

$$\frac{\partial g(\bullet)/\partial x_i}{\partial g(\bullet)/\partial x_1} = \frac{\partial u(\bullet)/\partial x_i}{\partial u(\bullet)/\partial x_1} \tag{A.47}$$

Another way to satisfy these conditions is for each of the partial derivatives of g with respect to x_i to be proportional to the partial derivative of u with respect to x_i, where the constant of proportionality μ is the same for all i. This set of conditions can be written in matrix notation as

$$Du(\bar{\bar{x}}) = \mu \cdot Dg(\bar{\bar{x}}) \tag{A.48}$$

where $\bar{\bar{x}}$ is an n-dimensional vector, and Dg and Du are the vectors of partial derivatives of g and u with respect to each of their arguments ($Dg \equiv [\partial g(\bullet)/\partial x_1, \ldots, \partial g(\bullet)/\partial x_n]$, and analogously for Du). The vectors Dg and Du are called the *gradients* of g and u,

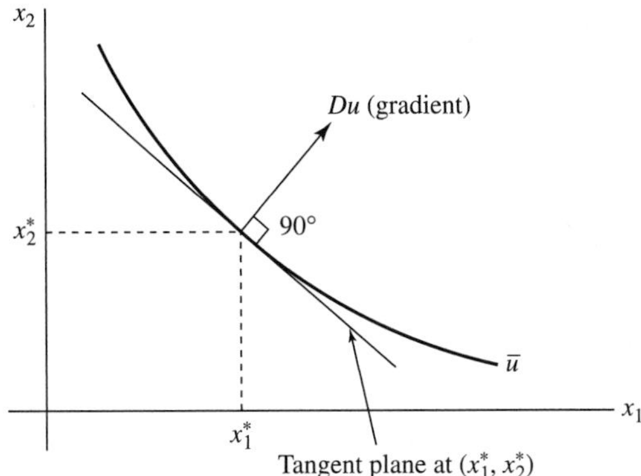

Figure A.11
Solution to a maximization problem subject to equality constraints. The figure illustrates the solution from equation (A.48), which involves a Lagrange multiplier, μ.

respectively. The gradient of a function $u(\bullet)$ evaluated at a point $\overline{\overline{x}}$ is a vector perpendicular to the tangent line of the function at that point (see figure A.11). Equation (A.48) says that a necessary condition for $\overline{\overline{x}}$ to be a maximum of the constrained problem is for the gradient of the restriction to be proportional to the gradient of the objective function at that point. The factor of proportionality is often called the *Lagrange multiplier,* μ. If we think of $u(\bullet)$ as a utility function and $g(\bullet) = a$ as a budget constraint (total spending, $g[\bullet]$, equals total income, a), then equation (A.48) is the familiar equality between marginal rates of substitution and marginal rates of transformation (or relative prices).

A convenient device for the derivation of these first-order conditions is the *Lagrangian,* which adds to the objective function a constant μ times the constraint:

$$L(\bullet) = u(x_1, \ldots, x_n) + \mu \cdot [a - g(x_1, \ldots, x_n)] \tag{A.49}$$

The first-order conditions in equation (A.48) are found by taking derivatives of the Lagrangian with respect to each of its arguments. Note that the derivative with respect to the Lagrange multiplier, μ, recovers the constraint.

To give an economic interpretation to the Lagrange multiplier, consider the change in utility, $u(\bullet)$, when income, a, changes. The total change in utility is given by

$$du(\bullet)/da = \sum_{i=1}^{n} [\partial u(\bullet)/\partial x_i] \cdot \partial \overline{\overline{x}}_i/\partial a$$

where $\partial \overline{\overline{x}}_i/\partial a$ is the change in the optimal quantity of good x_i when the constraint is relaxed by the amount ∂a. We can use the first-order conditions in equation (A.48) to rewrite this expression as

$$du(\bullet)/da = \sum_{i=1}^{n} \mu \cdot [\partial g(\bullet)/\partial x_i] \cdot \partial \overline{\overline{x}}_i/\partial a \tag{A.50}$$

If we totally differentiate the budget constraint with respect to a, we get

$$dg(\bullet)/da = \sum_{i=1}^{n} [\partial g(\bullet)/\partial x_i] \cdot \partial \overline{\overline{x}}_i/\partial a = 1$$

Substitution of this result into equation (A.50) implies

$$du(\bullet)/da = \mu \tag{A.51}$$

In other words, the Lagrange multiplier, μ, represents the extra utility that the agent gets when the constraint is relaxed by one unit. The Lagrange multiplier is therefore often referred to as the *shadow price* or *shadow value of the constraint.* This interpretation is important and will be used throughout the book.

A.2.3 Inequality Constraints: The Kuhn–Tucker Conditions

Imagine now that an agent faces m inequality restrictions of the form

$$g_i(x_1, \ldots, x_n) \leq a_i \quad \text{for } i = 1, \ldots, m$$

All the functions $g_i(\bullet)$ are assumed to be twice continuously differentiable, and each a_i is constant. The problem can be written as

$$\begin{aligned} &\max_{x_1,\ldots,x_n} [u(x_1, \ldots, x_n)], \quad \text{subject to} \\ &\quad g_1(x_1, \ldots, x_n) \leq a_1 \\ &\quad \ldots \\ &\quad g_m(x_1, \ldots, x_n) \leq a_m \end{aligned} \tag{A.52}$$

Most economic constraints take the form shown in equation (A.52). For example, a budget constraint does not require an agent to spend all of his income but says that he cannot spend more than his income.

An easy way to solve the problem in equation (A.52) is to use the Kuhn–Tucker (1951) theorem. The theorem says that if $\overline{\overline{x}} = (\overline{\overline{x}}_1, \ldots, \overline{\overline{x}}_n)$ is a solution to problem (A.52),[9] then

9. An additional condition is that the "constraint qualification" be satisfied. This condition requires the gradients of the constraints to be linearly independent.

there exists a set of m Lagrange multipliers such that

$$\begin{aligned}
&(a)\ \ Du(\bullet) = \sum_{i=1}^{m} \mu_i \cdot [Dg_i(\bullet)] \\
&(b)\ \ g_i(\bullet) \leq a_i,\ \mu_i \geq 0 \\
&(c)\ \ \mu_i \cdot [a_i - g_i(\bullet)] = 0
\end{aligned} \tag{A.53}$$

Condition (a) in equation (A.53) says that the gradient of the objective function must be a linear combination of the gradients of the restrictions. The weights in this linear combination are the Lagrange multipliers. In the particular case when there is only one restriction, $m = 1$, this condition is equivalent to equation (A.48). Condition (b) in equation (A.53) says that for $\overline{\overline{x}}$ to be an optimum, the constraints have to be satisfied and the shadow prices must be nonnegative. That is, $Du(\bullet)$ must lie on the cone generated by the $Dg_i(\bullet)$.

Condition (c) in equation (A.53) is often called the *complementary-slackness condition.* It says that the product of the shadow price and the constraint is 0. This condition means that if the constraint $g_i(\bullet) - a_i$ is not binding (if it is not satisfied with strict equality), the shadow price must be 0. That is, $Dg_i(\bullet)$ receives no weight in the linear combination that generates $Du(\bullet)$. In contrast, if the price is strictly positive, the constraint associated with it must be binding.[10]

Consider the example in figure A.12. There are two constraints, $g_1(\bullet) \leq a_1$ and $g_2(\bullet) \leq a_2$. The first constraint restricts the set of points in the space to lie between the curve labeled g_1 and the origin. Similarly, the second constraint restricts to the space between the curve labeled g_2 and the origin. The objective function can be represented by a set of indifference curves labeled u_i, which increase in the northeast direction. The gradients of the two constraints (which point in the direction perpendicular to the tangent at that particular point) are labeled Dg_1 and Dg_2. Condition (a) says that if $\overline{\overline{x}}$ is to be an optimum, the gradient of $u(\bullet)$ must be a linear combination of the two gradients Dg_1 and Dg_2. Condition (b) says that the linear combination must involve nonnegative weights. Graphically, these conditions mean that the gradient of u must lie on the cone described by the gradients of the two constraints.

To understand the meaning of the complementary-slackness condition, imagine that the preferences for a pair of goods take the form of a bell (figure A.13a). The indifference curves are circles around a point that yields maximum utility. (This point would correspond to a level of satiation beyond which agents would not like to go, no matter what the prices are.) Suppose that the budget constraint lies to the left of this satiation point (see figure A.13b).

10. In economic terms, the complementary-slackness condition says that if a constraint is not binding (that is, if it is unimportant) and we relax it by one unit, the attained utility does not change.

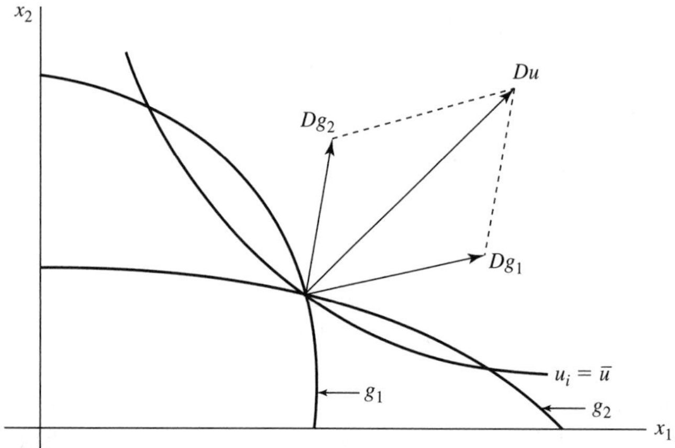

Figure A.12
Solution to a maximization problem subject to inequality constraints. The figure illustrates the solution to a maximization problem of the form of equation (A.53) with two inequality constraints.

The agent would like to consume more of both goods, but the budget constraint does not permit him or her to do so. Hence, the constraint is binding. The Kuhn–Tucker theorem says that the gradient of the objective function at the optimum is proportional to the gradient of the constraint. Since the gradient is perpendicular to the function, this condition means that the maximum occurs at the tangency point.

Consider now what happens when the satiation point is fully inside the budget set (figure A.13c). The individual clearly achieves maximum utility by remaining inside the budget set. In other words, since the constraint is not binding, the agent behaves as if he were not constrained. The Kuhn–Tucker theorem says that, at the optimum, the gradient of the objective function is proportional to the gradient of the constraint. The complementary-slackness condition says that when the constraint is not binding, the factor of proportionality is 0. Hence, the gradient of the objective function must equal 0, the condition for an unconstrained maximum. To summarize, the complementary-slackness condition says that if a constraint is not binding, it will not affect the optimal choice.

The Kuhn–Tucker conditions can be read another way by writing the Lagrangian function as

$$L(x_1, \ldots, x_n; \mu_1, \ldots, \mu_m) = u(x_1, \ldots, x_n) + \sum_{i=1}^{m} \mu_i \cdot [a_i - g_i(x_1, \ldots, x_n)] \qquad \text{(A.54)}$$

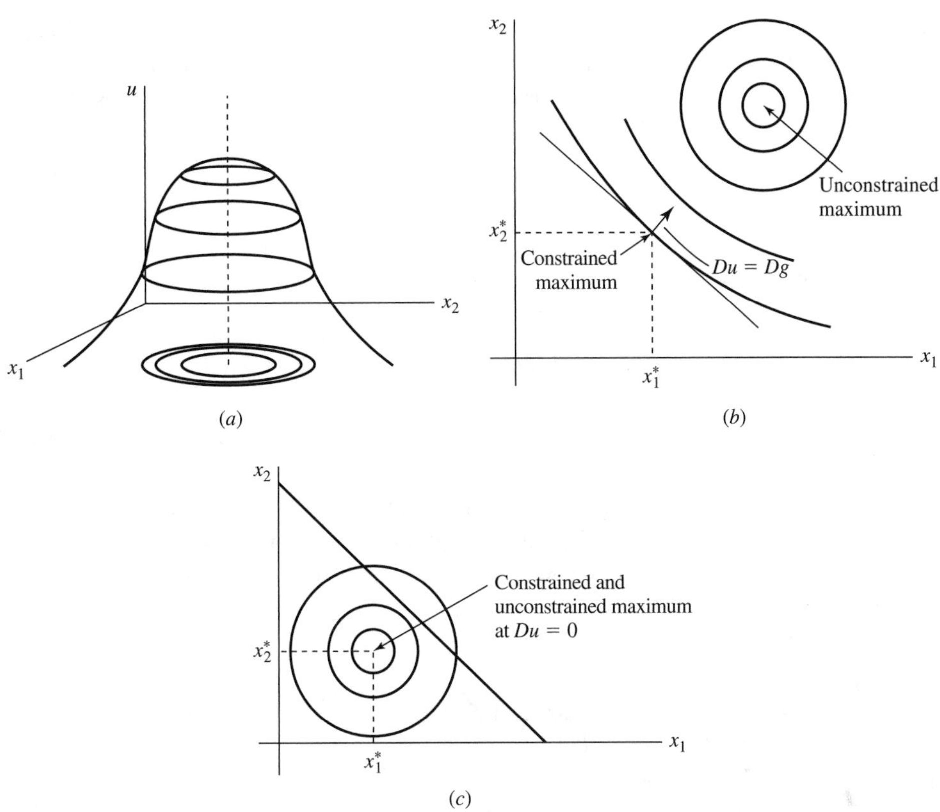

Figure A.13
(*a*) **Preferences over two goods.** The indifference curves for x_1 and x_2 are assumed to take the form of a bell. (*b*) **Maximizing utility subject to a binding inequality constraint.** In this example, the budget constraint for x_1 and x_2 is binding. (*c*) **Maximizing utility subject to a nonbinding inequality constraint.** In this example, the budget constraint for x_1 and x_2 is not binding.

Condition (*a*) in equation (A.53) says that a necessary condition for the vector $\overline{\overline{x}}$ to be a maximum of the constrained problem is for it to be a maximum of the associated Lagrangian. Conditions (*b*) and (*c*) in equation (A.53) say that, at the optimum, the Lagrangian has a minimum with respect to the vector $\mu \equiv (\mu_1, \ldots, \mu_m)$. (Condition [*b*] says that the two components in [*c*] are nonnegative; hence, the product of the two is minimized at 0.) Taken together, conditions (*a*)–(*c*) in equation (A.53) say that a necessary condition for $\overline{\overline{x}}$ to be an optimum is for the Lagrangian to have a saddle point at $(\overline{\overline{x}}, \mu)$; that is, a maximum with respect to x and a minimum with respect to μ.

Conditions (a)–(c) in equation (A.53) are the set of necessary conditions from the Kuhn–Tucker theorem; if a point is to be an optimum, it must satisfy them. If the objective function $u(\bullet)$ is concave and the constraints form a convex set, the necessary conditions are also sufficient.[11]

A.3 Dynamic Optimization in Continuous Time

A.3.1 Introduction

Mathematicians have long worried about dynamic problems. It is commonly thought that the first person to solve one of these problems was Bernoulli in 1696. Euler and Lagrange also worked with dynamic problems. Most applications of their theoretical findings were in physics, especially as related to Hamilton's principle or the principle of least action. Economists have been interested in dynamic problems since at least the work of Hotelling and Ramsey in the 1920s. It was not until the 1960s, however, that dynamic mathematical techniques were widely introduced into economics, mainly in the work of the neoclassical growth theorists. These techniques are now part of the toolbox of most modern economists.

The methodology that classical mathematicians used to solve dynamic problems is known as the *calculus of variations.* This approach has since been generalized in two ways. First, Richard Bellman, an American mathematician, developed the method of *dynamic programming* in the 1950s. This method is especially suited to discrete-time problems and is particularly useful for stochastic models. Second, also in the 1950s, a team of Russian mathematicians led by L. Pontryagin developed the *maximum principle of optimal control.* (The first English translation of this work did not appear, however, until 1962.)

In this chapter, we demonstrate how to use Pontryagin's technique. The maximum principle is a generalization of the classical calculus of variations in that it provides solutions to problems in which one or more of the constraints involve the derivatives of some of the state variables. This type of constraint is central to the theory of economic growth.

Our goal in this section is not to prove the maximum principle but, rather, to provide a heuristic derivation along with a description of the procedure that we follow to use the solutions. This approach will provide us with a set of tools that will allow us to solve the various dynamic models that will be encountered in the book.[12]

11. A slightly less restrictive set of sufficient conditions is given by Arrow and Enthoven (1961): they require the objective function to be quasi-concave, that is, to exhibit convex upper-level sets.

12. A full proof of the maximum principle is in Pontryagin et al. (1962).

A.3.2 The Typical Problem

The typical problem that we want to solve takes the following form. The agent chooses or controls a number of variables, called *control variables,*[13] so as to maximize an objective function subject to some constraints. These constraints are dynamic in that they describe the evolution of the state of the economy, as represented by a set of *state variables,* over time. The problem is given by

$$\max_{c(t)} V(0) = \int_0^T v[k(t), c(t), t] \cdot dt, \quad \text{subject to}$$

$$(a)\ \dot{k}(t) = g[k(t), c(t), t] \tag{A.55}$$

$$(b)\ k(0) = k_0 > 0$$

$$(c)\ k(T) \cdot e^{-\bar{r}(T) \cdot T} \geq 0$$

where $V(0)$ is the value of the objective function as seen from the initial moment 0, $\bar{r}(t)$ is an average discount rate that applies between dates 0 and t, and T is the terminal planning date, which could be finite or infinite. We discuss the difference between a finite and an infinite horizon in section A.4.7.

The variable $k(t)$—which appears with an overdot in part (a) of equation (A.55)—is the *state variable,* and the variable $c(t)$ is the *control variable*. Each of these variables is a function of time. The objective function in equation (A.55) is the integral of instantaneous felicity functions, $v(\bullet)$,[14] over the interval from 0 to T. These felicity functions depend on the state and control variables, $k(t)$ and $c(t)$, and on time, t.

The accumulation constraint in part (a) of equation (A.55) is a differential equation in $k(t)$; this constraint shows how the choice of the control variable, $c(t)$, translates into a pattern of movement for the state variable, $k(t)$. The expression for $\dot{k}(t)$ is called the *transition equation* or *equation of motion*. Although we have only one transition equation, there is a continuum of constraints, one for every point in time between 0 and T.[15]

The initial condition in part (b) of equation (A.55) says that the state variable, $k(t)$, begins at a given value, k_0. The final constraint, in part (c) of equation (A.55), says that the chosen

13. Pontryagin et al. (1962) call these control variables *steering variables*.

14. Examples of felicity functions are utility functions of consumers, profit functions of firms, and objective functions of governments. To fix ideas, in this chapter we identify them with utility functions.

15. This accumulation equation could be cast as an inequality restriction, $\dot{k} \leq g(\bullet)$. Typically, individuals will not find it optimal to satisfy this restriction with strict inequality because it will be advantageous to increase $c(t)$ to raise the current flow of utility or to increase $k(t)$ to raise the future flows of utility. We therefore leave the restriction as an equality.

value of the state variable at the end of the planning horizon, $k(T)$, discounted at the rate $\bar{r}(T)$, must be nonnegative. For finite values of T, this constraint implies $k(T) \geq 0$, as long as the discount rate $\bar{r}(T)$ is positive and finite. If $k(t)$ represents a person's net assets and T the person's lifetime, the constraint in part (c) of equation (A.55) precludes dying in debt. If the planning horizon is infinite, the condition says that net assets can be negative and grow forever in magnitude, as long as the rate of growth is less than $\bar{r}(t)$. This constraint rules out chain letters or Ponzi schemes for debt.

An economic example of a dynamic problem of this kind is a growth model in which $v(\bullet)$ is an instantaneous utility function that depends on the level of consumption and is discounted by a time-preference factor,

$$v(k, c, t) = e^{-\rho t} \cdot u[c(t)] \tag{A.56}$$

In this example, $v(\bullet)$ does not depend on the capital stock, $k(t)$, and depends directly on time only through the discount factor, $e^{-\rho t}$. The constraint describes the accumulation of the variable $k(t)$. If we think of $k(t)$ as physical capital, an example of such a constraint is

$$\dot{k} = g[k(t), c(t), t] = f[k(t), t] - c(t) - \delta \cdot k(t) \tag{A.57}$$

where δ is the fraction of the capital stock that depreciates at every instant. Equation (A.57) says that the increase in the capital stock (net investment) equals total saving minus depreciation. Total saving, in turn, equals the difference between output, $f(\bullet)$, and consumption, $c(t)$. The dependence of production on t, for given $k(t)$, could reflect the state of technology or knowledge at a given point in time.

A.3.3 Heuristic Derivation of the First-Order Conditions

A formal proof of the maximum principle is outside the scope of this book; we will instead provide a heuristic derivation. Readers who are interested only in the procedure for finding the first-order conditions, and not in the derivation, can skip sections A.4.3–A.4.9 and go directly to section A.4.10.

The starting point is the static method for solving nonlinear optimization problems, the Kuhn–Tucker Theorem. This theorem, described in section A.3.3, suggests the construction of a Lagrangian of the form,

$$L = \int_0^T v[k(t), c(t), t] \cdot dt + \int_0^T \{\mu(t) \cdot (g[k(t), c(t), t] - \dot{k}(t))\} \cdot dt + \nu \cdot k(T) \cdot e^{\bar{r}(T) \cdot T} \tag{A.58}$$

where $\mu(t)$ is the Lagrange multiplier associated with the constraint in part (a) of equation (A.55), and ν is the multiplier associated with the constraint in part (c) of equation (A.55).[16] Since there is a continuum of constraints from part (a), one for each instant t between 0 and T, there is a corresponding continuum of Lagrange multipliers, $\mu(t)$. The $\mu(t)$ are called *costate variables* or *dynamic Lagrange multipliers*. Following the parallel with the static case, these costate variables can be interpreted as shadow prices: $\mu(t)$ is the price or value of an extra unit of capital stock at time t in units of utility at time 0. Since each of the constraints, $g(\bullet) - \dot{k}$, equals 0, each of the products, $\mu(t) \cdot [g(\bullet) - \dot{k}]$, also equals 0. It follows that the "sum" of all of the constraints equals 0:

$$\int_0^T \{\mu(t) \cdot (g[k(t), c(t), t] - \dot{k}(t))\} \cdot dt = 0$$

This expression appears in the middle of equation (A.58).

To find the set of first-order necessary conditions in a static problem, we would maximize L with respect to $c(t)$ and $k(t)$ for all t between 0 and T. The problem with this procedure is that we do not know how to take the derivative of $\dot{k}$ with respect to k. To avoid this problem, we can rewrite the Lagrangian by integrating the term $\mu(t) \cdot \dot{k}(t)$ by parts to get[17]

$$L = \int_0^T (v[k(t), c(t), t] + \mu(t) \cdot g[k(t), c(t), t])\, dt$$

$$+ \int_0^T \dot{\mu}(t) k(t)\, dt + \mu(0)k_0 - \mu(T)k(T) + \nu k(T)e^{-\bar{r}(T)T} \tag{A.59}$$

The expression inside the first integral is called the *Hamiltonian* function,

$$H(k, c, t, \mu) \equiv v(k, c, t) + \mu \cdot g(k, c, t) \tag{A.60}$$

The Hamiltonian function has an economic interpretation (see Dorfman, 1969). At an instant in time, the agent consumes $c(t)$ and owns a stock of capital $k(t)$. These two variables affect utility through two channels. First, the direct contribution of consumption, and perhaps capital, to utility, is captured by the term $v(\bullet)$ in equation (A.60). Second, the choice of consumption affects the change in the capital stock in accordance with the transition equation for $\dot{k}$ in part (a) of equation (A.55). The value of this change in the capital stock

16. We would also have the constraints $c(t) \geq 0$, but commonly assumed forms of the utility function imply that these constraints will not be binding. We therefore ignore these inequality restrictions in the present discussion.

17. To integrate $\int_0^T (\dot{k}) \cdot \mu\, dt$ by parts, start with $(d/dt)(\mu k) = \dot{\mu}k + \dot{k}\mu$. Integrate both sides of this expression between 0 and T and note that $\int_0^T (d/dt)(k\mu) \cdot dt = k(T) \cdot \mu(T) - k(0) \cdot \mu(0)$. From this expression, subtract the integral of $k\dot{\mu}$ to get $\int_0^T (\dot{k}) \cdot \mu\, dt = k(T) \cdot \mu(T) - k(0) \cdot \mu(0) - \int_0^T (\dot{\mu}) \cdot k\, dt$, which is the expression used to compute equation (A.59). See sections A.6.4 and A.6.5 for further discussion.

is the term $\mu \cdot g(\bullet)$ in equation (A.60). Hence, for a given value of the shadow price, μ, the Hamiltonian captures the total contribution to utility from the choice of $c(t)$.

Rewrite the Lagrangian from equation (A.59) as

$$L = \int_0^T \{H[k(t), c(t), t] + \dot{\mu}(t) \cdot k(t)\} \cdot dt + \mu(0) \cdot k_0 - \mu(T) \cdot k(T) + \nu \cdot k(T) \cdot e^{-\bar{r}(T) \cdot T} \tag{A.61}$$

Let $\overline{\overline{c}}(t)$ and $\overline{\overline{k}}(t)$ be the optimal time paths for the control and state variables, respectively. If we perturb the optimal path $\overline{\overline{c}}(t)$ by an arbitrary perturbation function, $p_1(t)$, we can generate a neighboring path for the control variable,

$$c(t) = \overline{\overline{c}}(t) + \epsilon \cdot p_1(t)$$

When $c(t)$ is thus perturbed, there must be a corresponding perturbation to $k(t)$ and $k(T)$ so as to satisfy the budget constraint:

$$k(t) = \overline{\overline{k}}(t) + \epsilon \cdot p_2(t)$$

$$k(T) = \overline{\overline{k}}(T) + \epsilon \cdot dk(T)$$

If the initial paths are optimal, then $\partial L/\partial\epsilon$ should equal 0. Before we compute such a derivative, it will be convenient to rewrite the Lagrangian in terms of ϵ:

$$\overline{\overline{L}}(\cdot, \epsilon) = \int_0^T \{H[k(\bullet, \epsilon); c(\bullet, \epsilon)] + \dot{\mu}(\bullet) \cdot k(\bullet, \epsilon)\} \cdot dt$$
$$+ \mu(0) \cdot k_0 - \mu(T) \cdot k(T, \epsilon) + \nu \cdot k(T, \epsilon) \cdot e^{-\bar{r}(T) \cdot T}$$

We can now take the derivative of the Lagrangian with respect to ϵ and set it to 0:

$$\partial\overline{\overline{L}}/\partial\epsilon = \int_0^T [\partial H/\partial\epsilon + \dot{\mu} \cdot \partial k/\partial\epsilon] \cdot dt + [\nu e^{-\bar{r}(T)T} - \mu(T)] \cdot \partial k(T, \epsilon)/\partial\epsilon = 0$$

The chain rule of calculus implies $\partial H/\partial\epsilon = [\partial H/\partial c] \cdot p_1(t) + [\partial H/\partial k] \cdot p_2(t)$ and $\partial k(T, \epsilon)/\partial\epsilon = dk(T)$. Use these formulas and rearrange terms in the expression for $\partial\overline{\overline{L}}/\partial\epsilon$ to get

$$\partial L/\partial\epsilon = \int_0^T \{[\partial H/\partial c] \cdot p_1(t) + [\partial H/\partial k + \dot{\mu}] \cdot p_2(t)\} \cdot dt$$
$$+ [\nu \cdot e^{-\bar{r}(T)T} - \mu(T)] \cdot dk(T) = 0 \tag{A.62}$$

Equation (A.62) can hold for all perturbation paths, described by $p_1(t)$, $p_2(t)$, and $dk(T)$, only if each of the components in the equation vanishes, that is,

$$\partial H/\partial c = 0 \tag{A.63}$$

$$\partial H/\partial k + \dot{\mu} = 0 \tag{A.64}$$

$$\nu \cdot e^{-\bar{r}(T)\cdot T} = \mu(T) \tag{A.65}$$

The first-order condition with respect to the control variable in equation (A.63) says that if $\bar{\bar{c}}(t)$ and $\bar{\bar{k}}(t)$ are a solution to the dynamic problem, the derivative of the Hamiltonian with respect to the control c equals 0 for all t. This result is called the *maximum principle*. Equation (A.64) says that the partial derivative of the Hamiltonian with respect to the state variable equals the negative of the derivative of the multiplier, $-\dot{\mu}$. This result and the transition equation in part (a) of equation (A.55) are often called the Euler equations. Finally, equation (A.65) says that the costate variable at the terminal date, μ, equals ν, the static Lagrange multiplier associated with the nonnegativity constraint on k at the terminal date, discounted at the rate $\bar{r}(T)$.

A.3.4 Transversality Conditions

Section A.3.3 showed that the Kuhn–Tucker necessary first-order conditions include a complementary-slackness condition associated with the inequality constraints. In the static problem, these conditions say that if a restriction is not binding, the shadow price associated with it is 0. In the present dynamic problem, there is an inequality constraint that says that the stock of capital left at the end of the planning period, discounted at the rate $\bar{r}(T)$, cannot be negative, $k(T)\cdot e^{-\bar{r}(T)\cdot T} \geq 0$. The condition associated with this constraint requires $\nu \cdot k(T) \cdot e^{-\bar{r}(T)\cdot T} = 0$, with $\nu \geq 0$. Equation (A.65) implies that we can rewrite this complementary-slackness condition as

$$\mu(T) \cdot k(T) = 0 \tag{A.66}$$

This boundary condition is often called the *transversality condition*. It says that if the quantity of capital left is positive, $k(T) > 0$, its price must be 0, $\mu(T) = 0$. Alternatively, if capital at the terminal date has a positive value, $\mu(T) > 0$, the agent must leave no capital, $k(T) = 0$. We discuss later the meaning of equation (A.66) when T is infinite.

A.3.5 The Behavior of the Hamiltonian over Time

To see how the optimal value of the Hamiltonian behaves over time, take the total derivative of H with respect to t to get

$$dH(k, c, \mu, t)/dt = [\partial H/\partial k] \cdot \dot{k} + [\partial H/\partial c \cdot \dot{c}] + [\partial H/\partial \mu] \cdot \dot{\mu} + \partial H/\partial t \tag{A.67}$$

The first-order condition in equation (A.63) implies that, at the optimum, $\partial H/\partial c = 0$; hence, the second term on the right-hand side of equation (A.67) equals 0. Equation (A.64) requires $\partial H/\partial k = -\dot{\mu}$. Since $\partial H/\partial \mu = g = \dot{k}$, the first and third terms on the right-hand side of equation (A.67) cancel. Hence, at the optimum, the total derivative of the Hamiltonian with respect to time equals the partial derivative, $\partial H/\partial t$. If the problem is autonomous—that is, if neither the objective function nor the constraints depend directly on time—then the derivative of the Hamiltonian with respect to time is 0. In other words, the Hamiltonian associated with autonomous problems is constant at all points in time. These results on the behavior of the Hamiltonian will be used later in this appendix.

A.3.6 Sufficient Conditions

In a static, nonlinear maximization problem, the Kuhn–Tucker necessary conditions are also sufficient when the objective function is concave and the restrictions generate a convex set. Mangasarian (1966) extends this result to dynamic problems and shows that if the functions $v(\bullet)$ and $g(\bullet)$ in equation (A.55) are both concave in k and c, then the necessary conditions are also sufficient. This sufficiency result is easy to use but is somewhat restrictive.

More general sufficiency conditions are given by Arrow and Kurz (1970). Define $H^0(k, \mu, t)$ to be the maximum of $H(k, c, \mu, t)$ with respect to c, given k, μ, and t. The Arrow–Kurz theorem says that if $H^0(k, \mu, t)$ is concave in k, for given μ and t, then the necessary conditions are also sufficient. Concavity of $v(\bullet)$ and $g(\bullet)$ is sufficient, but not necessary, for the Arrow–Kurz condition to be satisfied. The disadvantage of this more general result is that checking the properties of a derived function, such as H^0, tends to be harder than checking the properties of $v(\bullet)$ and $g(\bullet)$.

A.3.7 Infinite Horizons

Most of the growth models that we discuss in the book involve economic agents with infinite planning horizons. The typical problem takes the form

$$\max_{c(t)} V(0) = \int_0^\infty v[k(t), c(t), t] \cdot dt, \quad \text{subject to}$$

$$\begin{aligned} &(a)\ \dot{k}(t) = g[k(t), c(t), t] \\ &(b)\ k(t) = k_0 \\ &(c)\ \lim_{t\to\infty} [k(t) \cdot e^{-\bar{r}(t)\cdot t}] \geq 0 \end{aligned} \tag{A.68}$$

The only difference between equation (A.68) and equation (A.55) is that the planning horizon—the number on top of the integral—in equation (A.68) is infinity, rather than

$T < \infty$. The first-order conditions for the infinite-horizon problem are the same as those for the finite horizon case, equations (A.63) and (A.64). The key difference is that the transversality condition, shown in equation (A.66), applies not to a finite T, but to the limit as T tends to infinity. In other words, the transversality condition is now

$$\lim_{t\to\infty} [\mu(t) \cdot k(t)] = 0 \tag{A.69}$$

The intuitive explanation for the new condition is that the value of the capital stock must be asymptotically 0; otherwise, something valuable would be left over. If the quantity $k(t)$ remains positive asymptotically, then the price, $\mu(t)$, must approach 0 asymptotically. If $k(t)$ grows forever at a positive rate—as occurs in some of the models that we study in this book—then the price $\mu(t)$ must approach 0 at a faster rate so that the product, $\mu(t) \cdot k(t)$, goes to 0.

Although equation (A.69) has intuitive appeal as the limiting version of equation (A.66), there is disagreement over the conditions under which equation (A.69) is actually a necessary condition for the infinite-horizon problem in equation (A.68). Recall that the only argument we gave for its validity was the analogue to the transversality condition in the finite-horizon case. Some researchers have found counterexamples in which equation (A.69) is not a necessary condition for optimization. In section A.4.9 we discuss one of these examples.

One transversality condition that always applies was found by Michel (1982). He argues that the transversality condition requires the value of the Hamiltonian to approach 0 as t goes to infinity:

$$\lim_{t\to\infty} [H(t)] = 0 \tag{A.70}$$

We can derive this transversality condition if we follow Michel and think of the infinite-horizon case as a setting in which the agent chooses the terminal date, T. If we perturb the terminal date T in equation (A.61) by $\epsilon \cdot dT$, we find that the limit of integration now depends on ϵ. When we take derivatives of the Lagrangian with respect to ϵ, we find that one of the terms in equation (A.62) is $H(T) \cdot dT$. This term comes from taking the derivative of the limit of integration, $T(\epsilon)$, with respect to ϵ. As with all the terms in equation (A.62), this one will have to be 0 at the optimum. If the terminal date is fixed, so that $dT = 0$, then $H(T)$ can take on any value. But if the terminal date is variable, so that dT is nonzero, then $H(T)$ must vanish. If we take the limit as T goes to infinity, we get the transversality condition in equation (A.70). This condition is redundant in most of the models that we study in the book because it will be satisfied whenever equation (A.69) is satisfied. Thus, in most cases, we can use equation (A.69) and ignore equation (A.70).

A.3.8 Example: The Neoclassical Growth Model

We consider here the example of the neoclassical growth model with a Cobb–Douglas production function. (See chapter 2 for more details.) Assume that economic agents choose the path of consumption, $c(t)$, and capital, $k(t)$, so as to maximize the objective function,

$$U(0) = \int_0^\infty e^{-\rho t} \cdot \log[c(t)] \cdot dt$$

$$\begin{aligned} &(a)\;\; \dot{k}(t) = [k(t)^\alpha - c(t) - \delta \cdot k(t)] \\ &(b)\;\; k(0) = 1 \\ &(c)\;\; \lim_{t\to\infty} [k(t) \cdot e^{-\bar{r}(t)\cdot t}] \geq 0 \end{aligned} \qquad \text{(A.71)}$$

where α is a constant with $0 < \alpha < 1$. We normalize the initial capital $k(0)$ to unity. The interest rate, $r(t)$, equals the net marginal product of capital, $\alpha \cdot k(t)^{\alpha-1} - \delta$, and the average interest rate, $\bar{r}(t)$, equals $(1/t) \cdot \int_0^t r(v) \cdot dv$.

The agent can be thought of as a household-producer who wants to maximize utility, represented as the present discounted value of a stream of instantaneous felicities. Each of these felicities depends on the instantaneous flow of consumption. The felicity function is assumed in equation (A.71) to be logarithmic. The discount rate is $\rho > 0$. The agent has access to the technology (the Cobb–Douglas form described in chapter 1) that transforms capital into output according to $y(t) = [k(t)]^\alpha$. The accumulation constraint in part (a) of equation (A.71) says that total output has to be divided between consumption, $c(t)$, depreciation, $\delta \cdot k(t)$, and capital accumulation, $\dot{k}(t)$. The initial condition in part (b) of equation (A.71) says that the capital stock at time 0 is 1. The restriction in part (c) of equation (A.71) says that the capital stock left over at the "end of the planning horizon," when discounted at the average interest rate, $\bar{r}(t)$, is nonnegative. (If $k[t]$ represents household assets, this condition precludes chain-letter policies in which debt accumulates forever at a rate at least as high as the interest rate.)

To solve the optimization problem, set up the Hamiltonian,

$$H(c, k, t, \mu) = e^{-\rho t} \cdot \log(c) + \mu \cdot (k^\alpha - c - \delta k) \qquad \text{(A.72)}$$

Equations (A.63) and (A.64) imply that the first-order conditions are

$$H_c = e^{-\rho t} \cdot (1/c) - \mu = 0 \qquad \text{(A.73)}$$

$$H_k = \mu \cdot (\alpha k^{\alpha-1} - \delta) = -\dot{\mu} \qquad \text{(A.74)}$$

and equation (A.69) implies that the transversality condition is

$$\lim_{t\to\infty} [\mu(t) \cdot k(t)] = 0 \qquad \text{(A.75)}$$

Equation (A.74) and the transition relation in part (*a*) of equation (A.71) form a system of ODEs in which $\dot{\mu}$ and $\dot{k}$ depend on μ, k, and c. Equation (A.73) relates μ to c, so that we can eliminate one of these two variables from the system. If we eliminate μ and take logs and time derivatives of equation (A.73), we get

$$-\rho - \dot{c}/c = \dot{\mu}/\mu$$

We can substitute this result into equation (A.74) to eliminate $\dot{\mu}/\mu$ to get

$$\dot{c}/c = (\alpha k^{\alpha-1} - \rho - \delta) \tag{A.76}$$

This condition says that consumption accumulates at a rate equal to the difference between the net marginal product of capital, $\alpha k^{\alpha-1} - \delta$, and the discount rate, ρ.

Part (*a*) of equation (A.71) and equation (A.76) form a system of nonlinear ODEs in k and c. In the steady state, the term $\alpha k^{\alpha-1}$ equals $\rho + \delta$, which determines the steady-state capital stock as $k^* = [(\rho + \delta)/\alpha]^{-1/(1-\alpha)}$. Part (*a*) of equation (A.71) then determines the steady-state level of consumption as $c^* = (k^*)^\alpha - \delta k^*$. Equation (A.74) implies that, as t goes to infinity, $\dot{\mu}/\mu$ tends to $-\rho$, so that $\mu(t)$ tends to $\mu(0) \cdot e^{-\rho t}$. The transversality condition in equation (A.75) can therefore be expressed as

$$\lim_{t \to \infty} [e^{-\rho t} \cdot k(t)] = 0 \tag{A.77}$$

Equation (A.77) provides a terminal condition, which, together with the initial condition $k(0) = 1$, yields the exact solution to the system of ODEs.

If we set $\rho = 0.06$, $\delta = 0$, and $\alpha = 0.3$, this system corresponds to the nonlinear system that we studied in section A.2.3 with equations (A.22) and (A.23) and linearized later in that section with equation (A.38). We know from before that this system exhibits saddle-path stability, and the initial and terminal conditions ensure that the economy starts exactly on the stable arm. We use more complicated versions of this model in the text.

Finally, we can verify that the preceding conditions imply that the steady-state value of the Hamiltonian is 0, as implied by equation (A.70):

$$\begin{aligned}
\lim_{t \to \infty} [H(t)] &= \lim_{t \to \infty} \{e^{-\rho t} \cdot \log[c(t)]\} + \lim_{t \to \infty} \{\mu(t) \cdot [k(t)^\alpha - c(t) - \delta \cdot k(t)]\} \\
&= \log(c^*) \cdot \lim_{t \to \infty} (e^{-\rho t}) + 0 \cdot \lim_{t \to \infty} [\mu(t)] = 0 + 0 = 0
\end{aligned}$$

Hence, although equation (A.70) is a necessary condition for optimization, it is already implied by the other conditions.

A.3.9 Transversality Conditions in Infinite-Horizon Problems

The transversality condition in equation (A.75) is not universally accepted as a necessary condition for the infinite-horizon problem. Halkin (1974) provides an example in which the optimum does not satisfy the transversality condition.[18] An even more famous counterexample is the neoclassical growth model of Ramsey (1928). The difference between the original Ramsey model and the one described in the last section is that Ramsey assumed no discounting. His version of the model is

$$U(0) = \int_0^{\infty} \log[c(t)] \cdot dt$$

$$(a)\ \dot{k}(t) = [k(t)^{\alpha} - c(t) - \delta \cdot k(t)]$$

$$(b)\ k(0) = 1 \tag{A.78}$$

$$(c)\ \lim_{t\to\infty} [k(t)] \geq 0$$

The main difference from before, equation (A.71), is that ρ has now been set to 0. An immediate problem with equation (A.78) is that, if $c(t)$ asymptotically approaches a constant (as in the previous problem), then utility is not bounded. To solve this problem, Ramsey rewrote the integrand as the deviation from a "bliss point." This revised specification will result in bounded utility if the deviation from the bliss point approaches 0 at a fast enough rate.

We found in the previous section that steady-state consumption converged to a constant, given by $c^* = (k^*)^{\alpha} - \delta k^*$, where k^* satisfied $\alpha \cdot (k^*)^{\alpha-1} = (\rho + \delta)$. We therefore begin with the conjecture that steady-state consumption in the present model will be $\tilde{c} = \tilde{k}^{\alpha} - \delta \tilde{k}$, where $\tilde{k}$ satisfies $\alpha \tilde{k}^{\alpha-1} = \delta$. The corresponding Ramseylike objective function is

$$U(0) = \int_0^{\infty} (\log[c(t)] - \log[\tilde{c}]) \cdot dt \tag{A.79}$$

To solve the problem of maximizing $U(0)$, as given in equation (A.79), set up the Hamiltonian,

$$H(c, k, \mu) = [\log(c) - \log(\tilde{c})] + \mu \cdot (k^{\alpha} - c - \delta k) \tag{A.80}$$

The first-order conditions are

$$H_c = 1/c - \mu = 0 \tag{A.81}$$

$$H_k = \mu \cdot (\alpha k^{\alpha-1} - \delta) = -\dot{\mu} \tag{A.82}$$

which correspond to equations (A.73) and (A.74).

18. This example was first presented in Arrow and Kurz (1970, p. 46). They mention, however, that the idea came from Halkin, who published the result later in *Econometrica*.

If c tends to $\tilde{c}$ as t approaches infinity, equation (A.81) implies

$$\lim_{t\to\infty}[\mu(t)] = 1/\tilde{c} > 0 \tag{A.83}$$

Since $\lim_{t\to\infty}[k(t)] = \tilde{k} > 0$, it follows that $\lim_{t\to\infty}[\mu(t) \cdot k(t)] \neq 0$; hence, the usual transversality condition in equation (A.75) is violated.

The literature has a number of examples of this sort in which the standard transversality condition is not a necessary condition for optimization. Pitchford (1977) observes that all known cases involve no time discounting. Weitzman (1973) shows that, for discrete-time problems, a transversality condition analogous to equation (A.75) is necessary when there is time discounting and the objective function converges. Benveniste and Scheinkman (1982) show that this result holds also in continuous time.

All the models discussed in this book feature time discounting and an objective function that converges. We therefore assume that the transversality condition in equation (A.75) is a necessary condition for optimization in our infinite-horizon problems.

A.3.10 Summary of the Procedure to Find the First-Order Conditions

Instead of going through the whole derivation every time we encounter a dynamic problem, we shall use the following cookbook procedure.

Step one: Construct a Hamiltonian function by adding to the felicity function, $v(\bullet)$, a Lagrange multiplier times the right-hand side of the transition equation:

$$H = v(k, c, t) + \mu(t) \cdot g(k, c, t) \tag{A.84}$$

Step two: Take the derivative of the Hamiltonian with respect to the control variable and set it to 0:

$$\partial H/\partial c = \partial v/\partial c + \mu \cdot \partial g/\partial c = 0 \tag{A.85}$$

Step three: Take the derivative of the Hamiltonian with respect to the state variable (the variable that appears with an overdot in the transition equation) and set it to equal the negative of the derivative of the multiplier with respect to time:

$$\partial H/\partial k \equiv \partial v/\partial k + \mu \cdot \partial g/\partial k = -\dot{\mu} \tag{A.86}$$

Step four (transversality condition):

Case 1: Finite horizons. Set the product of the shadow price and the capital stock at the end of the planning horizon to 0:

$$\mu(T) \cdot k(T) = 0 \tag{A.87}$$

Case 2: Infinite horizons with discounting. The transversality condition is

$$\lim_{t\to\infty} [\mu(t) \cdot k(t)] = 0 \tag{A.88}$$

Case 3: Infinite horizons without discounting. The Ramsey counterexample shows that equation (A.88) need not apply. In this case, we use Michel's condition,

$$\lim_{t\to\infty} [H(t)] = 0 \tag{A.89}$$

If we combine equations (A.85) and (A.86) with the transition equation from part (a) of equation (A.55), we can form a system of two differential equations in the variables μ and k. Alternatively, we can use equation (A.85) to transform the ODE for $\dot{\mu}$ into an ODE for $\dot{c}$. For the system to be determinate, we need two boundary conditions. One initial condition is given by the starting value of the state variable, $k(0)$. One terminal condition is given by the transversality condition, equation (A.87), (A.88), or (A.89), depending on the nature of the problem.

A.3.11 Present-Value and Current-Value Hamiltonians

Most of the models that we deal with in this book have an objective function of the form,

$$\int_0^T v[k(t), c(t), t] \cdot dt = \int_0^T e^{-\rho t} \cdot u[k(t), c(t)] \cdot dt \tag{A.90}$$

where ρ is a constant discount rate, and $e^{-\rho t}$ is a discount factor. Once the discount factor is taken into account, the instantaneous felicity function does not depend directly on time. If the constraints are the ones assumed before, we can solve the problem by constructing the Hamiltonian,

$$H = e^{-\rho t} \cdot u(k, c) + \mu \cdot g(k, c, t)$$

In this formulation, the shadow price $\mu(t)$ represents the value of the capital stock at time t in units of time-zero utils.

It is sometimes convenient to restructure the problem in terms of current-value prices; that is, prices of the capital stock at time t in units of time-t utils. To accomplish this restructuring, rewrite the Hamiltonian as

$$H = e^{-\rho t} \cdot [u(k, c) + q(t) \cdot g(k, c, t)]$$

where $q(t) \equiv \mu(t) \cdot e^{\rho t}$. The variable $q(t)$ is the *current-value shadow price*. Define $\hat{H} \equiv He^{\rho t}$ to be the *current-value Hamiltonian:*

$$\hat{H} \equiv u(k, c) + q(t) \cdot g(k, c, t) \tag{A.91}$$

The first-order conditions are still $H_c = 0$ and $H_k = -\dot{\mu}$. They can be expressed, however, in terms of the current-value Hamiltonian and current-value prices as

$$\hat{H}_c = 0 \tag{A.92}$$

$$\hat{H}_k = \rho q - \dot{q} \tag{A.93}$$

The transversality condition, $\mu(T) \cdot k(T) = 0$, can be expressed as

$$q(T) \cdot e^{-\rho T} \cdot k(T) = 0 \tag{A.94}$$

An interesting point about equation (A.93) is that it looks like an asset-pricing formula: q is the price of capital in terms of current utility, $\hat{H}_k$ is the dividend received by the agent (the marginal contribution of capital to utility), $\dot{q}$ is the capital gain (the change in the price of the asset), and ρ is the rate of return on an alternative asset (consumption). Equation (A.93) says that, at the optimum, the agent is indifferent between the two types of investments because the overall rate of return to capital, $(\hat{H}_k + \dot{q})/q$, equals the return to consumption, ρ.

A.3.12 Multiple Variables

Consider a more general dynamic problem with n control and m state variables. Choose $c_1(t), c_2(t), \ldots, c_n(t)$ to maximize

$$\int_0^T u[k_1(t), \ldots, k_m(t); c_1(t), \ldots, c_n(t); t] \cdot dt, \quad \text{subject to}$$

$$\begin{aligned} \dot{k}_1(t) &= g^1[k_1(t), \ldots, k_m(t), c_1(t), \ldots, c_n(t), t] \\ \dot{k}_2(t) &= g^2[k_1(t), \ldots, k_m(t), c_1(t), \ldots, c_n(t), t] \\ &\cdots \\ \dot{k}_m(t) &= g^m[k_1(t), \ldots, k_m(t), c_1(t), \ldots, c_n(t), t] \end{aligned} \tag{A.95}$$

$$k_1(0) > 0, \ldots, k_m(0) > 0, \quad \text{given}$$

$$k_1(T) \geq 0, \ldots, k_m(T) \geq 0, \quad \text{free}$$

The solution is similar to that for one control variable and one state variable, as analyzed before. The Hamiltonian is

$$H = u[k_1(t), \ldots, k_m(t); c_1(t), \ldots, c_n(t); t] + \sum_{i=1}^{m} \mu_i \cdot g^i(\bullet) \tag{A.96}$$

The first-order necessary conditions for a maximum are

$$\partial H/\partial c_i(t) = 0, \qquad i = 1, \ldots, n \tag{A.97}$$

$$\partial H/\partial k_i(t) = -\dot{\mu}_i, \qquad i = 1, \ldots, m \tag{A.98}$$

and the transversality conditions are

$$\mu_i(T) \cdot k_i(T) = 0, \qquad i = 1, \ldots, m \tag{A.99}$$

A.4 Useful Results in Matrix Algebra: Eigenvalues, Eigenvectors, and Diagonalization of Matrices

Given an n-dimensional square matrix A, can we find the values of a scalar α and the corresponding nonzero column vectors v, such that

$$(A - \alpha I) \cdot v = 0 \tag{A.100}$$

where I is the n-dimensional identity matrix? Note that equation (A.100) forms a system of n homogeneous linear equations (that is, the constant term is 0 for all equations). If we want nontrivial solutions, so that $v \neq 0$, then the determinant of $(A - \alpha I)$ must vanish:

$$\det(A - \alpha I) = 0 \tag{A.101}$$

Equation (A.101) defines a polynomial equation of nth degree in α and is called the *characteristic equation*. Typically, there will be n solutions to this equation. These solutions are called *characteristic roots* or *eigenvalues*.

By construction and rearrangement of equation (A.101), each eigenvalue, α_i, is associated with a vector v_i (determined up to a scalar multiple) that satisfies

$$Av_i = v_i\alpha_i, \qquad i = 1, \ldots, n \tag{A.102}$$

The vector v_i is called the *characteristic vector* or *eigenvector*. For every α_i, equation (A.102) determines an $n \times 1$ column vector (A is $n \times n$, v_i is $n \times 1$, and α_i is 1×1). We can arrange these column vectors into an $n \times n$ matrix V to get

$$AV = VD \tag{A.103}$$

where V is the $n \times n$ matrix of eigenvectors, and D is an $n \times n$ diagonal matrix with the eigenvalues as diagonal elements.

If $\det(V) \neq 0$, a condition that holds if the eigenvectors are linearly independent, V can be inverted and equation (A.103) can be rewritten as

$$V^{-1}AV = D \tag{A.104}$$

In other words, if we premultiply A by the inverse of V and postmultiply it by V, we get a diagonal matrix with the eigenvalues as diagonal elements. This procedure is called *diagonalization* of the matrix A. This result is useful for solving systems of differential equations.

Intuitively, when we diagonalize a matrix, we find a set of axes (a *vector basis*) for which the linear application represented by A can be expressed as a diagonal matrix. The new axes correspond to the eigenvectors. The linear application in these transformed axes is given by the diagonal matrix of eigenvalues.

We can state two useful results. First, if all the eigenvalues are different, then the matrix of eigenvectors is nonsingular; that is, $\det(V) \neq 0$. In this case, V^{-1} exists and, hence, the matrix A can be diagonalized.

A second interesting theorem states that the determinant and trace (the sum of the elements on the main diagonal) of the diagonal matrix equal, respectively, the determinant and trace of the original matrix. This result will be useful in situations in which we want to know the signs of the eigenvalues. Suppose, for example, that A is a 2×2 matrix and we want to know whether its two eigenvalues have the same sign. If the determinant of A is negative, the determinant of D will be negative. But, since D is diagonal, its determinant is just the product of the two eigenvalues. Hence, the two eigenvalues must have opposite signs.

As an example, consider the eigenvalues, eigenvectors, and diagonal matrix associated with $A = \begin{bmatrix} 0.06 & -1 \\ -0.004 & 0 \end{bmatrix}$. Start by constructing the system of equations

$$(A - \alpha I) \cdot v = \begin{bmatrix} 0.06 - \alpha & -1 \\ -0.004 & 0 - \alpha \end{bmatrix} \cdot \begin{bmatrix} v_1 \\ v_2 \end{bmatrix} = 0 \tag{A.105}$$

To get a nontrivial solution, where $v \neq 0$, we must have

$$\begin{bmatrix} 0.06 - \alpha & -1 \\ -0.004 & 0 - \alpha \end{bmatrix} = 0$$

This equality determines the characteristic equation $\alpha^2 - 0.06 \cdot \alpha - 0.004 = 0$, which is satisfied for two values of α: $\alpha_1 = 0.1$ and $\alpha_2 = -0.04$. The diagonal matrix associated with A is therefore

$$D = \begin{bmatrix} 0.1 & 0 \\ 0 & -0.04 \end{bmatrix}$$

To find the eigenvector associated with the positive eigenvalue, $\alpha_1 = 0.1$, substitute α_1 into equation (A.105):

$$\begin{bmatrix} 0.06 - 0.1 & -1 \\ -0.004 & -0.1 \end{bmatrix} \cdot \begin{bmatrix} v_1 \\ v_2 \end{bmatrix} = 0$$

This equation imposes two conditions on the relation between v_{11} and v_{21}: $-0.04 \cdot v_{11} - v_{21} = 0$ and $-0.004 \cdot v_{11} - 0.1 \cdot v_{21} = 0$. The second condition is linearly dependent on the first and can be ignored. The resulting solution for v_{11} and v_{21} will therefore be unique only up to an arbitrary scalar multiple of each value. If we normalize v_{11} to 1, we get $v_{21} = -0.04$. The first eigenvector is therefore $\left[\begin{smallmatrix}1\\-0.004\end{smallmatrix}\right]$.

If we repeat the procedure for $\alpha_2 = -0.04$, we find a relation between v_{12} and v_{22}: $01 \cdot v_{12} - v_{22} = 0$. If we normalize v_{12} to 1, we get $v_{22} = 0.1$, and the second eigenvector is $\left[\begin{smallmatrix}1\\0.1\end{smallmatrix}\right]$. The two eigenvectors are linearly independent, and the matrix of normalized eigenvectors is

$$V = \begin{bmatrix} 1 & 1 \\ -0.04 & 0.1 \end{bmatrix}$$

We can now check that, indeed, $V^{-1}AV = D$ by calculating the inverse of V:

$$V^{-1} = \begin{bmatrix} 0.1/0.14 & -1/0.14 \\ 0.04/0.14 & 1/0.14 \end{bmatrix}$$

It is then easy to verify that $V^{-1}AV$ is the diagonal matrix D shown earlier.

A.5 Useful Results in Calculus

A.5.1 Implicit-Function Theorem

Let $f(x_1, x_2)$ be a bivariate function in the real space. Assume that $f(\bullet)$ is twice continuously differentiable. Let $\phi(x_1, x_2) = 0$ be an equation that involves x_1 and x_2 only through $f(x_1, x_2)$ and that implicitly defines x_2 as a function of x_1: $x_2 = \tilde{x}_2(x_1)$. An example is $\phi(x_1, x_2) = f(x_1, x_2) - a = 0$, where a is a constant. The implicit-function theorem says that the slope of the implicit function, $\tilde{x}_2(x_1)$, is

$$\frac{d\tilde{x}_2}{dx_1} = -\frac{\partial f(x_1, x_2)/\partial x_1}{\partial f(x_1, x_2)/\partial x_2} \tag{A.106}$$

This result holds whether or not an explicit or closed-form solution exists for $\tilde{x}_2(x_1)$.

As an example, consider the function $f(x_1, x_2) = 3x_1^2 - x_2$ and the equation $\phi(x_1, x_2) = 3x_1^2 - x_2 - 1 = 0$. In this case, we can find an explicit function $\tilde{x}_2(x_1) = 3x_1^2 - 1$. If we apply the implicit-function theorem from equation (A.106), we get

$$d\tilde{x}_2/dx_1 = -(6x_1)/(-1) = 6x_1$$

In this example, we do not need the implicit-function theorem to compute $d\tilde{x}_2/dx_1$, because we can differentiate $\tilde{x}_2(x_1) = 3x_1^2 - 1$ directly to get $6x_1$. The theorem is useful, however, when no closed-form solution exists for $\tilde{x}_2(x_1)$.

As another example, consider $f(x_1, x_2) = \log(x_1) + 3 \cdot (x_1)^2 \cdot x_2 + e^{x_2}$ and the equation $\phi(x_1, x_2) = \log(x_1) + 3.(x_1)^2 \cdot x_2 + e^{x_2} - 17 = 0$, which implicitly defines x_2 as a function of x_1. An explicit function $\tilde{x}_2(x_1)$ cannot be found. We can, however, compute the derivative of this function by using the implicit-function theorem,

$$d\tilde{x}_2/dx_1 = -[(1/x_1) + 6x_1x_2]/[3 \cdot (x_1)^2 + e^{x_2}]$$

A multivariate version of the implicit-function theorem is also available. Let $f(x_1, \ldots, x_n)$ be an n-variate function in the real space. Assume that $f(\bullet)$ is twice continuously differentiable. Let $\phi(x_1, \ldots, x_n) = 0$ be an equation that involves $x_1, \ldots, x_n$ only through $f(x_1, \ldots, x_n)$ and that implicitly defines x_n as a function of $x_1, x_2, \ldots, x_{n-1}$: $x_n = \tilde{x}_n(x_1, \ldots, x_{n-1})$. The implicit-function theorem gives the derivatives of the implicit function $\tilde{x}_n(x_1, \ldots, x_{n-1})$ as

$$\frac{\partial \tilde{x}_n}{\partial x_i} = -\frac{\partial f(\bullet)/\partial x_i}{\partial f(\bullet)/\partial x_n}, \quad i = 1, \ldots, n-1 \tag{A.107}$$

A.5.2 Taylor's Theorem

Let $f(x)$ be a univariate function in the real space. Taylor's theorem says that we can approximate this function around the point x^* with a polynomial of degree n as follows:

$$\begin{aligned} f(x) = {} & f(x^*) + (df/dx)|_{x^*} \cdot (x - x^*) + (d^2 f/dx^2)|_{x^*} \cdot (x - x^*)^2 \cdot (1/2!) \\ & + (d^3 f/dx^3)|_{x^*} \cdot (x - x^*)^3 \cdot (1/3!) + \cdots \\ & + (d^n f/dx^n)|_{x^*} \cdot (x - x^*)^n \cdot (1/n!) + R_n \end{aligned} \tag{A.108}$$

where $(d^n f/dx^n)|_{x^*}$ is the nth derivative of f with respect to x evaluated at the point x^*, $n!$ is n factorial $[n \cdot (n-1) \cdot \cdots \cdot 2 \cdot 1]$, and R_n is a residual. The expression in equation (A.108), with R_n omitted, is the *Taylor-Series expansion* of $f(x)$ around x^*. The presence of the residual R_n in the equation indicates that the Taylor expansion is not an exact formula for $f(x)$. The content of the theorem is that it describes conditions under which the approximation gets better as n increases.

We can check on the accuracy of the Taylor formula—that is, the size of R_n—by computing the approximation to a polynomial. If the formula is useful, it should reproduce the exact polynomial. For example, if we use a polynomial of degree 3 to approximate x^3

around 1, we get

$$\begin{aligned} x^3 &= 1^3 + (3 \cdot 1^2) \cdot (x-1) + (6 \cdot 1) \cdot (x-1)^2/2 + 6 \cdot (x-1)^3/6 + R_3 \\ &= 1 + (3x - 3) + 3 \cdot (x^2 - 2x + 1) + (x^3 - 3x^2 + 3x - 1) + R_3 \\ &= x^3 \end{aligned}$$

The residual, R_3, is 0 in this case.

As another example, we can use a polynomial of order 4 to approximate the nonlinear function e^x around 0:

$$\begin{aligned} e^x &= e^0 + e^0 \cdot x + e^0 \cdot (x^2/2) + e^0 \cdot (x^3/6) + e^0 \cdot (x^4/24) + R_4 \\ &= 1 + x + x^2/2 + x^3/6 + x^4/24 + R_4 \end{aligned}$$

The approximation (the formula with R_n omitted) gets better as the value of n increases.

If we use a polynomial of order 1 to approximate a function around a point x^*, we say that we *linearize* the function around x^*. We can also *log-linearize* a function $f(x)$ by using a first-order Taylor expansion of $\log(x)$ around $\log(x^*)$. Log-linearizations are used frequently in this book and are often useful for empirical analyses.

The two-dimensional version of Taylor's theorem is as follows. Let $f(x_1, x_2)$ be a twice continuously differentiable real function. We can approximate $f(x_1, x_2)$ around the point (x_1^*, x_2^*) with a second-order expansion as follows:

$$\begin{aligned} f(x_1, x_2) = f(x_1^*, x_2^*) &+ f_{x_1}(\bullet) \cdot (x_1 - x_1^*) + f_{x_2}(\bullet) \cdot (x_2 - x_2^*) \\ &+ (1/2) \cdot [f_{x_1 x_2}(\bullet) \cdot (x_1 - x_1^*)^2 + 2 \cdot f_{x_1 x_2}(\bullet) \cdot (x_1 - x_1^*) \cdot (x_2 - x_2^*) \\ &+ f_{x_2 x_2}(\bullet) \cdot (x_2 - x_2^*)^2] + R_2 \end{aligned} \tag{A.109}$$

where $f_{x_i}(\bullet)$ is the partial derivative of $f(\bullet)$ with respect to x_i evaluated at (x_1^*, x_2^*), and $f_{x_i x_j}(\bullet)$ is the second partial derivative of $f(\bullet)$ with respect to x_i and x_j evaluated at (x_1^*, x_2^*). The linear approximation of $f(\bullet)$ around (x_1^*, x_2^*) is given by the first three terms of the right-hand side of equation (A.109).

A.5.3 L'Hôpital's Rule

Let $f(x)$ and $g(x)$ be two real functions twice continuously differentiable. Suppose that the limits of both functions as x approaches x^* are 0; that is,

$$\lim_{x \to x^*} [f(x)] = \lim_{x \to x^*} [g(x)] = 0$$

Imagine that we are interested in the limit of the ratio, $f(x)/g(x)$, as x approaches x^*. In this case, the ratio takes on the indeterminate form $0/0$ as x tends to x^*. L'Hôpital's rule is

$$\lim_{x\to x^*}\left(\frac{f(x)}{g(x)}\right) = \lim_{x\to x^*}\left(\frac{f'(x)}{g'(x)}\right) \tag{A.110}$$

provided that the limit on the right-hand side exists. If the right-hand side still equals $0/0$, we can apply l'Hôpital's rule again, until we get a result that is hopefully not an indeterminate form. L'Hôpital's rule applies to the indeterminate form $0/0$ and also works for the indeterminate form ∞/∞. The rule does not apply, however, if $f(x)/g(x)$ tends to infinity as x approaches x^*.

As an example, consider $f(x)=2x$ and $g(x)=x$. The limit of the ratio $f(x)/g(x)$ as x tends to 0 is

$$\lim_{x\to x^*}\left(\frac{f(x)}{g(x)}\right) = \frac{0}{0} = \lim_{x\to x^*}\left(\frac{f'(x)}{g'(x)}\right) = \frac{2}{1} = 2$$

A.5.4 Integration by Parts

To integrate a function by parts, note that the formula for the derivative of a product of two functions of time, $v_1(t)$ and $v_2(t)$, implies

$$d[v_1v_2] = v_2 \cdot dv_1 + v_1 \cdot dv_2$$

where $dv_1 = v_1'(t)\cdot dt$ and $dv_2 = v_2'(t)\cdot dt$. Take the integral of both sides of the above equation to get

$$v_1v_2 = \int v_2 \cdot dv_1 + \int v_1 \cdot dv_2$$

Rearrange to get the formula for integration by parts:

$$\int v_2 \cdot dv_1 = v_1v_2 - \int v_1 \cdot dv_2 \tag{A.111}$$

As an example, compute the integral $\int te^t\, dt$. Define $v_1 = t$ and $dv_2 = e^t\, dv$. By integrating dv_2 we get $v_2 = e^t$. Take the derivative of v_1 to get $dv_1 = 1$. Use the formula for integration by parts in equation (A.111) to get

$$\int te^t dt = te^t - \int e^t dt = e^t \cdot (t-1)$$

A.5.5 Fundamental Theorem of Calculus

Let $f(t)$ be continuous in $a \leq t \leq b$. If $F(t) = \int f(t) \cdot dt$ is the indefinite integral of $f(t)$, so that $F'(t) = f(t)$, the definite integral is

$$\int_a^b f(t)\,dt = \int_a^b F'(t)\,dt = F(b) - F(a) \tag{A.112}$$

An interpretation of a definite integral is that it represents the area below the function $f(t)$ and between the points a and b (see figure A.14).

A.5.6 Rules of Differentiation of Integrals

Differentiation with Respect to the Variable of Integration The condition $F'(t) = f(t)$ implies that the derivative of an indefinite integral with respect to the variable of integration, t, is the function $f(t)$ itself:

$$\frac{\partial}{\partial t}\left(\int f(t)\,dt\right) = \frac{\partial}{\partial t}[F(t)] = F'(t) = f(t) \tag{A.113}$$

Leibniz's Rule for Differentiation of Definite Integrals Let $F(a, b, c)$ be the function describing the definite integral of $f(c, t)$, where a and b are, respectively, the lower and upper limits of integration, and c is a parameter of the function $f(\bullet)$:

$$F(a, b, c) = \int_a^b f(c, t) \cdot dt \tag{A.114}$$

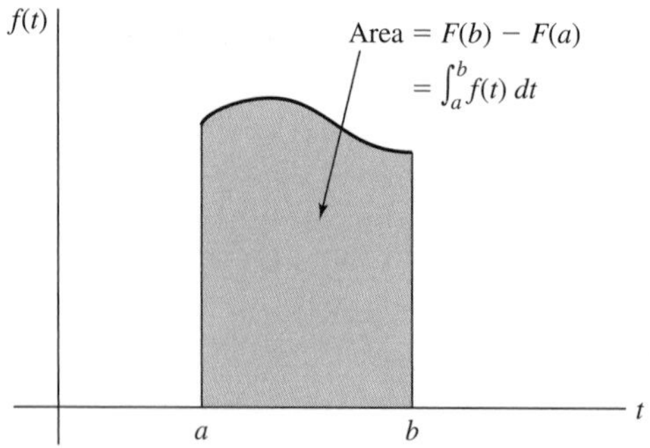

Figure A.14
The definite integral. The definite integral corresponds to the area under a curve between the limits of integration.

We assume that $f(c,t)$ has a continuous partial derivative with respect to c, $f_c(\bullet) \equiv \partial f(\bullet)/\partial c$. The derivative of $F(\bullet)$ with respect to c is

$$\frac{\partial F(\bullet)}{\partial c} = \int_a^b f_c(c,t)\,dt \tag{A.115}$$

The derivatives of $F(\bullet)$ with respect to the limits of integration are

$$\frac{\partial F(\bullet)}{\partial b} = \frac{\partial}{\partial b}\left\{\int_a^b f_c(c,t)\,dt\right\} = f(c,t)\mid_{t=b} = f(c,b) \tag{A.116}$$

$$\frac{\partial F(\bullet)}{\partial a} = \frac{\partial}{\partial a}\left\{\int_a^b f_c(c,t)\,dt\right\} = -f(c,t)\mid_{t=a} = -f(c,a) \tag{A.117}$$

We can combine equations (A.115)–(A.117) to get Leibniz's rule of integration. Suppose that a and b are functions of c:

$$F(c) = \int_{a(c)}^{b(c)} f(c,t)\cdot dt \tag{A.118}$$

Leibniz's rule is

$$\frac{dF(c)}{dc} = \int_{a(c)}^{b(c)} f_c(c,t)\cdot dt + f(c,b[c])\cdot b'(c) - f(c,a[c])\cdot a'(c) \tag{A.119}$$

References

Abel, Andrew, and Olivier Blanchard (1983). "An Intertemporal Equilibrium Model of Saving and Investment." *Econometrica,* 51, May, 675–692.

Acemoglu, Daron (2002). "Labor- and Capital-Augmenting Technical Change." Unpublished, MIT, November.

Acemoglu, Daron, Simon Johnson, and James A. Robinson (2001). "The Colonial Origins of Comparative Development: An Empirical Investigation." *American Economic Review,* 91, December, 1369–1401.

Acemoglu, Daron, Simon Johnson, and James A. Robinson (2002). "Reversal of Fortune: Geography and Institutions in the Making of the Modern World Income Distribution." *Quarterly Journal of Economics,* 117, November, 1231–1294.

Ades, Alberto F., and Edward L. Glaeser (1995). "Trade and Circuses: Explaining Urban Giants." *Quarterly Journal of Economics,* 110, February, 195–227.

Aghion, Philippe, Nicholas Bloom, Richard Blundell, Rachel Griffith, and Peter Howitt (2002). "Competition and Innovation: An Inverted U Relationship." National Bureau of Economic Research, working paper 9269, October.

Aghion, Philippe, Christopher Harris, Peter Howitt, and John Vickers (2001). "Competition, Imitation, and Growth with Step-by-Step Innovation." *Review of Economic Studies,* 68, July, 467–492.

Aghion, Philippe, and Peter Howitt (1992). "A Model of Growth Through Creative Destruction." *Econometrica,* 60, March, 323–351.

Aghion, Philippe, and Peter Howitt (1998). *Endogenous Growth Theory,* Cambridge MA: MIT Press.

Ainslie, George W. (1992). *Picoeconomics.* Cambridge: Cambridge University Press.

Alesina, Alberto, Arnaud Devleeschauwer, William Easterly, Sergio Kurlat, and Romain Wacziarg (2003). "Fractionalization." Unpublished, Harvard University, January.

Arnold, Lutz (1997). "Stability of the Steady-State Equilibrium in the Uzawa–Lucas Model: A Simple Proof." *Zeitschrift für Wirtschafts- und Sozialwissenschaften,* 117, January, 197–207.

Arrow, Kenneth J. (1962). "The Economic Implications of Learning by Doing." *Review of Economic Studies,* 29, June, 155–173.

Arrow, Kenneth J., Hollis B. Chenery, Bagicha S. Minhas, and Robert M. Solow (1961). "Capital-Labor Substitution and Economic Efficiency." *Review of Economics and Statistics,* 43, August, 225–250.

Arrow, Kenneth J., and Alain C. Enthoven (1961). "Quasiconcave Programming." *Econometrica,* 29, October, 779–800.

Arrow, Kenneth J., and Mordecai Kurz (1970). "Optimal Growth with Irreversible Investment in a Ramsey Model." *Econometrica,* 38, March, 331–344.

Asher, H. (1956). *Cost-Quantity Relationships in the Airframe Industry,* R-291. Santa Monica, CA: Rand Corporation.

Banco de Bilbao (various issues). *Renta Nacional de España y su Distribucion Provincial.* Bilbao, Banco de Bilbao-Vizcaya.

Barrett, David B. (1982). *World Christian Encyclopedia,* 1st ed. Oxford: Oxford University Press.

Barro, Robert J. (1974). "Are Government Bonds Net Wealth?" *Journal of Political Economy,* 81, December, 1095–1117.

Barro, Robert J. (1984). *Macroeconomics,* 1st ed. New York: Wiley.

Barro, Robert J. (1987). "Government Spending, Interest Rates, Prices, and Budget Deficits in the United Kingdom, 1701–1918." *Journal of Monetary Economics,* 20, September, 221–247.

Barro, Robert J. (1990a). "The Stock Market and Investment." *Review of Financial Studies,* 3, 115–130.

Barro, Robert J. (1990b). "Government Spending in a Simple Model of Endogenous Growth." *Journal of Political Economy,* 98, October, part II, S103–S125.

Barro, Robert J. (1991). "Economic Growth in a Cross Section of Countries." *Quarterly Journal of Economics,* 106, May, 407–443.

Barro, Robert J. (1997). *Macroeconomics,* 5th ed. Cambridge, MA: MIT Press.

Barro, Robert J. (1999). "Laibson Meets Ramsey in the Neoclassical Growth Model." *Quarterly Journal of Economics,* 114, November, 1125–1152.

Barro, Robert J., and Gary S. Becker (1989). "Fertility Choice in a Model of Economic Growth." *Econometrica,* 57, March, 481–501.

Barro, Robert J., and Jong-Wha Lee (1994). "Sources of Economic Growth." *Carnegie-Rochester Conference Series on Public Policy.*

Barro, Robert J., and Jong-Wha Lee (2001). "International Data on Educational Attainment: Updates and Implications." *Oxford Economic Papers,* 53, July, 541–563.

Barro, Robert J., N. Gregory Mankiw, and Xavier Sala-i-Martin (1995). "Capital Mobility in Neoclassical Models of Growth." *American Economic Review,* 85, March, 103–115.

Barro, Robert J., and Xavier Sala-i-Martin (1991). "Convergence across States and Regions." *Brookings Papers on Economic Activity,* no. 1, 107–182.

Barro, Robert J., and Xavier Sala-i-Martin (1992a). "Convergence." *Journal of Political Economy,* 100, April, 223–251.

Barro, Robert J., and Xavier Sala-i-Martin (1992b). "Regional Growth and Migration: A Japan–United States Comparison." *Journal of the Japanese and International Economies,* 6, December, 312–346.

Barro, Robert J., and Xavier Sala-i-Martin (1992c). "Public Finance in Models of Economic Growth." *Review of Economic Studies,* 59, October, 645–661.

Barro, Robert, and Xavier Sala-i-Martin (1997). "Technological diffusion, convergence, and growth." *Journal of Economic Growth,* 2, March, 1–26.

Baumol, William J. (1986). "Productivity Growth, Convergence, and Welfare: What the Long-Run Data Show." *American Economic Review,* 76, December, 1072–1085.

Becker, Gary S. (1965). "A Theory of the Allocation of Time." *Economic Journal,* 75, September, 493–517.

Becker, Gary S. (1991). "The Demand for Children," chapter 5 in *A Treatise on the Family.* Cambridge, MA: Harvard University Press.

Becker, Gary S., and Robert J. Barro (1988). "A Reformulation of the Economic Theory of Fertility." *Quarterly Journal of Economics,* 103, February, 1–25.

Becker, Gary S., Kevin M. Murphy, and Robert Tamura (1990). "Human Capital, Fertility, and Economic Growth." *Journal of Political Economy,* 98, October, part II, S12–S37.

Behrman, Jere R. (1990). "Women's Schooling and Nonmarket Productivity: A Survey and a Reappraisal." Unpublished, University of Pennsylvania.

Benhabib, Jess, and Roger E. A. Farmer (1996). "Indeterminacy and Sector-Specific Externalities." *Journal of Monetary Economics,* 37, 397–419.

Benhabib, Jess, Richard Rogerson, and Randall Wright (1991). "Homework in Macroeconomics: Household Production and Aggregate Fluctuations." *Journal of Political Economy,* 99, December, 1166–1187.

Benveniste, Lawrence M., and Jose A. Scheinkman (1982). "Duality Theory for Dynamic Optimization Models of Economics: The Continuous Time Case." *Journal of Economic Theory,* 27, June, 1–19.

Bernheim, B. Douglas, and Kyle Bagwell (1988). "Is Everything Neutral?" *Journal of Political Economy,* 96, April, 308–338.

Bhalla, Surjit S. (2002). *Imagine There's No Country: Poverty, Inequality and Growth in the Era of Globalization.* Washington, DC: Institute for International Economics.

Blanchard, Olivier (1985). "Debt, Deficits, and Finite Horizons." *Journal of Political Economy,* 93, April, 223–247.

Blanchard, Olivier, and Stanley Fischer (1989). *Lectures on Macroeconomics.* Cambridge, MA: MIT Press.

Blanchard, Olivier, Changyong Rhee, and Lawrence H. Summers (1993). "The Stock Market, Profit, and Investment." *Quarterly Journal of Economics,* 108, February, 115–136.

Boldrin, Michele, and Aldo Rustichini (1994). "Growth and Indeterminacy in Dynamic Models with Externalities." *Econometrica,* 62, March, 323–343.

Bollen, Kenneth A. (1990). "Political Democracy: Conceptual and Measurement Traps." *Studies in Comparative International Development,* Spring, 7–24.

Bond, Eric, Ping Wang, and C. K. Yip (1996). "A General Two-Sector Model of Endogenous Growth with Human and Physical Capital: Balanced Growth and Transitional Dynamics." *Journal of Economic Theory,* 68, 149–173.

Borjas, George J. (1992). "Ethnic Capital and Intergenerational Mobility." *Quarterly Journal of Economics,* 107, February, 123–150.

Borjas, George J., Stephen G. Bronars, and Stephen J. Trejo (1992). "Self-Selection and Internal Migration in the United States." *Journal of Urban Economics,* 32, September, 159–185.

Borts, George H., and Jerome L. Stein (1964). *Economic Growth in a Free Market,* New York, Columbia University Press.

Bowman, Larry W. (1991). *Mauritius: Democracy and Development in the Indian Ocean,* Boulder, CO: Westview.

Brainard, William C., and James Tobin (1968). "Pitfalls in Financial Model Building." *American Economic Review,* 58, May, 99–122.

Braun, Juan (1993). *Essays on Economic Growth and Migration.* Ph.D. dissertation, Harvard University.

Bresnahan, Tim, and Manuel Trajtenberg (1995). "General Purpose Technologies—Engines of Growth?" *Journal of Econometrics,* 65, 1, 83–108.

Brezis, Elise, Paul Krugman, and Daniel Tsiddon (1993). "Leapfrogging in International Competition: A Theory of Cycles in National Technological Leadership." *American Economic Review,* 83, December, 1211–1219.

Brock, William A. (1975). "A Simple Perfect Foresight Monetary Model." *Journal of Monetary Economics,* 1, April, 133–150.

Caballe, Jordi, and Manuel S. Santos (1993). "On Endogenous Growth with Physical and Human Capital." *Journal of Political Economy,* 101, December, 1042–1067.

Caballero, Ricardo J., and Adam B. Jaffe (1993). "How High are the Giants' Shoulders: An Empirical Assessment of Knowledge Spillovers and Creative Destruction in a Model of Economic Growth." In *NBER Macroeconomics Annual, 1993,* 15–74. Cambridge, MA: MIT Press.

Cannon, Edmund S. (2000). "Economies of Scale and Constant Returns to Capital: A Neglected Early Contribution to the Theory of Economic Growth." *American Economic Review,* 90, March, 292–295.

Canova, Fabio, and Albert Marcet (1995). "The Poor Stay Poor: Non-Convergence across Countries and Regions." Unpublished, Universitat Pompeu Fabra.

Caselli, Francesco, and Wilbur John Coleman (2001). "Cross-Country Technology Diffusion: The Case of Computers." National Bureau of Economic Research, working paper 8130, February.

Caselli, Francesco, Gerardo Esquivel, and Fernando Lefort (1996). "Reopening the Convergence Debate: A New Look at Cross-Country Growth Empirics." *Journal of Economic Growth,* 1996.

Caselli, Francesco, and Jaume Ventura (2000). "A Representative Consumer Theory of Distribution." *American Economic Review,* 90, September, 909–926.

Cashin, Paul (1995). "Economic Growth and Convergence across Seven Colonies of Australasia: 1861–1991." *The Economic Record,* 71, 213 June, 132–144.

Cashin, Paul, and Norman Loayza (1995). "Paradise Lost? Growth, Convergence and Migration in the South Pacific." IMF working paper no. 95/28, International Monetary Fund.

Cashin, Paul, and Ratna Sahay (1995). "Internal Migration, Center-State Grants and Economic Growth in the States of India." IMF working paper.

Cass, David (1965). "Optimum Growth in an Aggregative Model of Capital Accumulation." *Review of Economic Studies,* 32, July, 233–240.

Chamley, Christophe (1992). "The Last Shall Be First: Efficient Constraints on Foreign Borrowing in a Model of Endogenous Growth." *Journal of Economic Theory,* 58, December, 335–354.

Chiswick, Barry R. (1978). "The Effect of Americanization on the Earnings of Foreign-Born Men." *Journal of Political Economy,* 86, October, 897–921.

Christensen, Laurits R., Dianne Cummings, and Dale W. Jorgenson (1980). "Economic Growth, 1947–1973: An International Comparison." In John W. Kendrick and Beatrice Vaccara, eds., *New Developments in Productivity Measurement and Analysis,* NBER Conference Report. Chicago: University of Chicago Press.

Chua, Hak B. (1993). "Regional Spillovers and Economic Growth," Ph.D. Dissertation, Harvard University.

Coase, Ronald W. (1960). "The Problem of Social Cost." *Journal of Law and Economics,* 3, October, 1–44.

Coe, David T., and Elhanan Helpman (1995). "International R&D Spillovers." *European Economic Review,* 39, 859–887.

Cohen, Daniel, and Jeffrey Sachs (1986). "Growth and External Debt under Risk of Debt Repudiation." *European Economic Review,* 30, June, 526–560.

Collins, Susan M., and Won Am Park (1989). "External Debt and Macroeconomic Performance in South Korea." In Jeffrey D. Sachs, ed., *Developing Country Debt and the World Economy,* 121–140. Chicago: University of Chicago Press.

Connolly, Michelle (1999). "North-South Technological Diffusion: A New Case for Dynamic Gains from Trade." Unpublished, Duke University, September.

Coulombe, Serge, and Frank C. Lee (1993). "Regional Economic Disparities in Canada." Unpublished, University of Ottawa, July.

David, Paul A. (1991). "Computer and Dynamo: The Modern Productivity Paradox in a Not-Too-Distant Mirror." In *Technology and Productivity: The Challenge for Economic Policy.* Paris: OECD.

DeLong, J. Bradford (1988). "Productivity Growth, Convergence, and Welfare: Comment." *American Economic Review,* 78, December, 1138–1154.

Denison, Edward F. (1962). "Sources of Growth in the United States and the Alternatives Before Us." Supplement Paper 13. New York: Committee for Economic Development.

Denison, Edward F. (1967). *Why Growth Rates Differ.* Washington, DC: Brookings Institution.

Denison, Edward F. (1974). *Accounting for United States Economic Growth, 1929–1969.* Washington, DC: Brookings Institution.

Diamond, Peter (1965). "National Debt in a Neoclassical Growth Model." *American Economic Review,* 55, December, 1126–1150.

Diewert, W. Erwin (1976). "Exact and Superlative Index Numbers." *Journal of Econometrics,* 4, May, 115–146.

Dinopoulos, Elias, and Peter Thompson (1998). "Schumpeterian Growth Without Scale Effects." *Journal of Economic Growth,* 3, December, 313–335.

Dixit, Avinash K., and Joseph E. Stiglitz (1977). "Monopolistic Competition and Optimum Product Diversity." *American Economic Review,* 67, June, 297–308.

Dolado, Juan, Alessandra Goria, and Andrea Ichino (1994). "Immigration, Human Capital, and Growth in the Host Country: Evidence from Pooled Country Data." *Journal of Population Economics,* 7, June, 193–215.

Domar, Evsey D. (1946). "Capital Expansion, Rate of Growth, and Employment." *Econometrica,* 14, April, 137–147.

Doppelhofer, Gernot (2000). "Three Essays on the Determinants of Economic Growth." Unpublished Ph.D. dissertation, Columbia University.

Dorfman, Robert (1969). "An Economic Interpretation of Optimal Control Theory." *American Economic Review,* 59, December, 817–831.

Dougherty, Christopher (1991). "A Comparison of Productivity and Economic Growth in the G-7 Countries." Ph.D. dissertation, Harvard University.

Douglas, Paul H. (1972). *In the Fullness of Time: The Memoirs of Paul H. Douglas,* New York, Harcourt Brace Jovanovich.

Dowrick, Steve, and Duc Tho Nguyen (1989). "OECD Comparative Economic Growth, 1950–85: Catch-Up and Convergence." *American Economic Review,* 79, December, 1010–1030.

Duczynsti, Petr (2001). "Capital Mobility in Neoclassical Models of Growth." *American Economic Review,* 90, June, 687–694.

Durlauf, Steven N., and Danny T. Quah (1999). "The New Empirics of Economic Growth." In *Handbook of Macroeconomics,* vol. 1, ed. John B. Taylor and Michael Woodford. Amsterdam: North Holland.

Easterlin, Richard A. (1960a). "Regional Growth of Income: Long-Run Tendencies." In Simon Kuznets, Ann Ratner Miller, and Richard A. Easterlin, eds., *Population Redistribution and Economic Growth, United States, 1870–1950. II: Analyses of Economic Change.* Philadelphia: American Philosophical Society.

Easterlin, Richard A. (1960b). "Interregional Differences in Per Capita Income, Population, and Total Income, 1840–1950." In *Trends in the American Economy in the Nineteenth Century.* Princeton, NJ: Princeton University Press.

Easterly, William (1993). "How Much Do Distortions Affect Growth?" *Journal of Monetary Economics,* 32, November, 187–212.

Easterly, W., and Ross Levine (1997). "Africa's Growth Tragedy: Politics and Ethnic Divisions." *Quarterly Journal of Economics,* 112(4), 1203–1250.

Easterly, William, and Sergio Rebelo (1993). "Fiscal Policy and Economic Growth: An Empirical Investigation." *Journal of Monetary Economics,* 32, December, 417–458.

Elias, Victor J. (1990). *Sources of Growth: A Study of Seven Latin American Economies.* San Francisco: ICS Press.

Ethier, Wilfred J. (1982). "National and International Returns to Scale in the Modern Theory of International Trade." *American Economic Review,* 72, June, 389–405.

Faig, Miguel (1995). "A Simple Economy with Human Capital Accumulation: Transitional Dynamics, Technology Shocks, and Fiscal Policies." *Journal of Macroeconomics,* 17, summer, 421–446.

Feenstra, Robert C., and James R. Markusen (1995). "Accounting for Growth with New Intermediate Inputs." *International Economic Review,* 35, May, 429–447.

Fischer, Stanley (1979). "Anticipations and the Nonneutrality of Money." *Journal of Political Economy,* 87, April, 225–252.

Fishburn, Peter C., and Ariel Rubinstein (1982). "Time Preference." *International Economic Review,* 23, October, 677–693.

Fisher, I. (1930). *The Theory of Interest.* New York: Macmillan.

Frankel, Marvin (1962). "The Production Function in Allocation and Growth: A Synthesis." *American Economic Review,* 52, December, 995–1022.

Galor, Oded, and Harl E. Ryder (1989). "Existence, Uniqueness, and Stability of Equilibrium in an Overlapping-Generations Model with Productive Capital." *Journal of Economic Theory,* 49, December, 360–375.

Galor, Oded, and David N. Weil (1996). "The Gender Gap, Fertility, and Growth." *American Economic Review,* 86, June, 374–387.

Galor, Oded, and David N. Weil (2000). "Population, Technology, and Growth: From Malthusian Stagnation to the Demographic Transition and Beyond." *American Economic Review,* 90, September, 806–828.

Galor, Oded, and Joseph Zeira (1993). "Income Distribution and Macroeconomics." *Review of Economic Studies,* 60, January, 35–52.

Gallup, John L., and Jeffrey D. Sachs (1998). "Geography and Economic Development." National Bureau of Economic Research, working paper no. 6849, December.

Gastil, Raymond D. (1987). *Freedom in the World.* Westport, CT: Greenwood Press.

Geary, Robert C. (1950–51). "A Note on 'A Constant Utility Index of the Cost of Living.' " *Review of Economic Studies,* 18, 1, 65–66.

Gezici, Ferhan, and Geoffrey Hewings (2001). "Regional Convergence and the Economic Performance of Peripheral Areas in Turkey." Mimeograph, University of Illinois at Urbana-Champaign.

Goldman, Steven M. (1980). "Consistent Plans." *Review of Economic Studies,* 47, April, 533–537.

Granger, Clive, and Harold Uhlig (1990). "Reasonable Extreme-Bounds Analysis." *Journal of Econometrics,* 44, 159–170.

Greenwood, Jeremy, and Zvi Hercowitz (1991). "The Allocation of Capital and Time over the Business Cycle." *Journal of Political Economy,* 99, December, 1188–1214.

Greenwood, Jeremy, and Boyan Jovanovic (1990). "Financial Development, Growth, and the Distribution of Income." *Journal of Political Economy,* 98, October, 1076–1107.

Greenwood, Michael J. (1975). "Research on Internal Migration in the United States: A Survey." *Journal of Economic Literature,* 13, June, 397–433.

Griliches, Zvi (1957). "Hybrid Corn: An Exploration in the Economics of Technological Change." *Econometrica,* 25, October, 501–522.

Griliches, Zvi (1964). "Research Expenditures, Education, and the Aggregate Agricultural Production Function." *American Economic Review,* 54, December, 961–974.

Griliches, Zvi (1973). "Research Expenditures and Growth Accounting." In B. R. Williams, ed., *Science and Technology in Economic Growth.* New York: Macmillan.

Griliches, Zvi (1979). "Issues in Assessing the Contribution of Research and Development to Productivity Growth." *Bell Journal of Economics,* 10(1), 92–116.

Griliches, Zvi (1988). "Productivity Puzzles and R&D: Another Explanation." *Journal of Economic Perspectives,* 2, Fall, 9–21.

Griliches, Zvi (1997). "The Simon Kuznets Memorial Lecture." Unpublished, Harvard University, October.

Griliches, Zvi, and Frank Lichtenberg (1984). "R&D and Productivity Growth at the Industry Level: Is There Still a Relationship." In Zvi Griliches, ed., *R&D, Patents, and Productivity.* Chicago: University of Chicago Press.

Grossman, Gene M., and Elhanan Helpman (1991). *Innovation and Growth in the Global Economy.* Cambridge, MA: MIT Press.

Gulhati, Ravi, and Raj Nallari (1990). "Successful Stabilization and Recovery in Mauritius." EDI Development Policy Case Series, Analytical Case Studies, no. 5. Washington, DC: World Bank.

Halkin, Hubert (1974). "Necessary Conditions for Optimal Control Problems with Infinite Horizons." *Econometrica,* 42, March, 267–272.

Hansen, Gary D., and Edward C. Prescott (2002). "Malthus to Solow." *American Economic Review,* 92, September, 1205–1217.

Harrod, Roy F. (1939). "An Essay in Dynamic Theory." *Economic Journal,* 49, June, 14–33.

Harrod, Roy F. (1942). *Toward a Dynamic Economics: Some Recent Developments of Economic Theory and their Application to Policy.* London: Macmillan.

Hart, Peter E. (1995). "Galtonian Regression Across Countries and the Convergence of Productivity." *Oxford Bulletin of Economics and Statistics,* 57, August, 287–293.

Hatton, Timothy J., and Jeffrey G. Williamson (1994). "What Drove the Mass Migrations from Europe in the Late Nineteenth Century?" *Population and Development Review,* 20, September, 1–27.

Hayashi, Fumio (1982). "Tobin's Marginal q and Average q: A Neoclassical Interpretation." *Econometrica,* 50, January, 213–224.

Heckman, James J. (1976). "A Life-Cycle Model of Earnings, Learning, and Consumption." *Journal of Political Economy,* 84, August, Part 2, S11–S44.

Henderson, J. Vernon (1988). *Urban Development: Theory, Fact, and Illusion.* Oxford: Oxford University Press.

Heston, Alan, Robert Summers, and Bettina Aten (2002). *Penn World Table Version 6.1.* Center for International Comparisons at the University of Pennsylvania (CICUP), October.

Hicks, John (1932). *The Theory of Wages.* London: Macmillan.

Hirshleifer, Jack (1987). *Economic Behavior in Adversity.* Chicago: University of Chicago Press.

Hossain, Akhtar (2000). "Convergence of Per Capita Output Levels Across Regions of Bangladesh, 1982–97." IMF working paper.

Hsieh, Chang-Tai (2002). "What Explains the Industrial Revolution in East Asia? Evidence from the Factor Markets." *American Economic Review,* 92, June, 502–526.

Inada, Ken-Ichi (1963). "On a Two-Sector Model of Economic Growth: Comments and a Generalization." *Review of Economic Studies,* 30, June, 119–127.

International Currency Analysis (1991). *World Currency Yearbook, 1988–89.* Brooklyn, NY.

International Monetary Fund (1991). *International Financial Statistics Yearbook,* Washington, DC, International Monetary Fund.

Jaumotte, Florence (1999). "Technological Catch-up and the Growth Process." Unpublished, Harvard University, November.

Jeffreys, Harold (1961). *Theory of Probability,* 3rd ed. Oxford: Oxford University Press.

Jones, Charles I. (1995). "R&D-Based Models of Economic Growth." *Journal of Political Economy,* 103, August, 759–784.

Jones, Charles I. (1999). "Growth: With or Without Scale Effects." *American Economic Review,* 89, May, 139–144.

Jones, Charles I. (2001). "Was an Industrial Revolution Inevitable? Economic Growth over the Very Long Run." *Advances in Economics,* 1(2), Article 1.

Jones, Larry E., and Rodolfo E. Manuelli (1990). "A Convex Model of Equilibrium Growth: Theory and Policy Implications." *Journal of Political Economy,* 98, October, 1008–1038.

Jorgenson, Dale W., Frank M. Gollop, and Barbara M. Fraumeni (1987). *Productivity and U.S. Economic Growth.* Cambridge, MA: Harvard University Press.

Jorgenson, Dale W., and Zvi Griliches (1967). "The Explanation of Productivity Change." *Review of Economic Studies,* 34, July, 249–280.

Jorgenson, Dale, and Eric Yip (2001). "Whatever Happened to Productivity Growth?" In E. R. Dean, M. J. Harper, and C. Hulten, eds., *New Developments in Productivity Analysis,* 205–246. Chicago: University of Chicago Press.

Jovanovic, Boyan, and Saul Lach (1991). "The Diffusion of Technological Inequality among Nations." Unpublished, New York University.

Jovanovic, Boyan, and Yaw Nyarko (1996). "Learning by Doing and the Choice of Technology." *Econometrica,* 64, November, 1299–1310.

Judd, Kenneth L. (1985). "On the Performance of Patents." *Econometrica,* 53, May, 567–585.

Judson, Ruth (1998). "Economic Growth and Investment in Education: How Allocation Matters." *Journal of Economic Growth,* 3, December, 337–359.

Kaldor, Nicholas (1963). "Capital Accumulation and Economic Growth." In Friedrich A. Lutz and Douglas C. Hague, eds., *Proceedings of a Conference Held by the International Economics Association.* London: Macmillan.

Kamien, Morton I., and Nancy L. Schwartz (1991). *Dynamic Optimization, The Calculus of Variations and Optimal Control in Economics and Management,* 2nd ed. Amsterdam: North Holland.

Kendrick, John W. (1961). *Productivity Trends in the United States.* Princeton, NJ: Princeton University Press.

Kendrick, John W. (1976). *The Formation and Stocks of Total Capital.* New York: Columbia University Press.

Kimball, Miles S. (1987). "Making Sense of Two-Sided Altruism." *Journal of Monetary Economics,* 20, September, 301–326.

King, Robert G., and Ross Levine (1993). "Finance, Entrepreneurship, and Growth: Theory and Evidence." *Journal of Monetary Economics,* December, 513–542.

King, Robert G., Charles I. Plosser, and Sergio Rebelo (1988a). "Production, Growth and Business Cycles: I. The Basic Neoclassical Model." *Journal of Monetary Economics,* 21, 2/3 (March/May), 195–232.

King, Robert G., Charles I. Plosser, and Sergio Rebelo (1988b). "Production, Growth and Business Cycles: II. New Directions." *Journal of Monetary Economics,* 21, March/May, 309–341.

King, Robert G., and Sergio Rebelo (1993). "Transitional Dynamics and Economic Growth in the Neoclassical Model." *American Economic Review,* 83, September, 908–931.

Knack, Stephen, and Philip Keefer (1995). "Institutions and Economic Performance: Cross-Country Tests Using Alternative Institutional Measures." *Economics and Politics,* 7, 207–228.

Knight, Frank H. (1944). "Diminishing Returns from Investment." *Journal of Political Economy,* 52, March, 26–47.

Koopmans, Tjalling C. (1960). "Stationary Ordinal Utility and Impatience." *Econometrica,* 28, April, 287–309.

Koopmans, Tjalling C. (1965). "On the Concept of Optimal Economic Growth." In *The Econometric Approach to Development Planning.* Amsterdam: North Holland, 1965.

Kremer, Michael (1993). "Population Growth and Technological Change: One Million B.C. to 1990." *Quarterly Journal of Economics,* 108, August, 681–716.

Kremer, Michael, and James Thomson (1998). "Why Isn't Convergence Instantaneous? Young Workers, Old Workers, and Gradual Adjustment." *Journal of Economic Growth,* 3, March, 5–28.

Krugman, Paul (1979). "A Model of Innovation, Technology Transfer, and the World Distribution of Income." *Journal of Political Economy,* 87, April, 253–266.

Krugman, Paul (1991). "History Versus Expectations." *Quarterly Journal of Economics,* 106, May, 651–667.

Kuhn, Harold W., and Albert W. Tucker (1951). "Nonlinear Programming." In J. Neyman, ed., *Proceedings of the Second Berkeley Symposium on Mathematical Statistics and Probability,* 481–492. Berkeley: University of California Press.

Kurz, Mordecai (1968). "The General Instability of a Class of Competitive Growth Processes." *Review of Economic Studies,* 35, April, 155–174.

Kuznets, Simon (1961). "Economic Growth and the Contribution of Agriculture: Notes on Measurement." *International Journal of Agrarian Affairs,* 3, April, 56–75.

Kuznets, Simon (1973). "Modern Economic Growth: Findings and Reflections." *American Economic Review,* 63, June, 247–258.

Kuznets, Simon (1981). "Modern Economic Growth and the Less Developed Countries." *Conference on Experiences and Lessons of Economic Development in Taiwan.* Taipei: Institute of Economics, Academia Sinica.

Kydland, Finn E., and Edward C. Prescott (1982). "Time to Build and Aggregate Fluctuations." *Econometrica,* 50, November, 1345–1370.

Laibson, David (1994). "Self-Control and Saving." Unpublished, Harvard University, May.

Laibson, David (1996). "Hyperbolic Discount Functions, Undersaving, and Savings Policy." National Bureau of Economic Research, working paper no. 5635, June.

Laibson, David (1997a). "Golden Eggs and Hyperbolic Discounting." *Quarterly Journal of Economics,* 112, May, 443–477.

Laibson, David (1997b). "Hyperbolic Discount Functions and Time Preference Heterogeneity." Unpublished, Harvard University, March.

La Porta, Rafael, Florencio Lopez-de-Silanes, Andrei Shleifer, and Robert W. Vishny (1998). "Law and Finance." *Journal of Political Economy,* 106, December, 1113–1155.

Leamer, Edward E. (1978). *Specification Searches.* New York: John Wiley and Sons.

Leamer, Edward E. (1983). "Let's Take the Con Out of Econometrics." *American Economic Review,* 73, March, 31–43.

Leamer, Edward E. (1985). "Sensitivity Analysis Would Help." *American Economic Review,* 75, June, 308–313.

Leontief, Wassily (1941). *The Structure of the American Economy, 1919–1929.* Cambridge, MA: Harvard University Press.

Levine, Ross, and David Renelt (1992). "A Sensitivity Analysis of Cross-Country Growth Regressions." *American Economic Review,* 82, September, 942–963.

Lewis, William Arthur (1954). "Economic Development with Unlimited Supplies of Labor." *Manchester School of Economics and Social Studies,* 22, May, 139–191.

Loewenstein, George, and Drazen Prelec (1992). "Anomalies in Intertemporal Choice: Evidence and an Interpretation." *Quarterly Journal of Economics,* 107, May, 573–598.

Lucas, Robert E., Jr. (1988). "On the Mechanics of Economic Development." *Journal of Monetary Economics,* 22, July, 3–42.

Lucas, Robert E. (2002). "The Industrial Revolution: Past and Future." In *Lectures in Economic Growth.* Cambridge, Mass.: Harvard University Press.

Maddison, Angus (1982). *Phases of Capitalist Development.* Oxford: Oxford University Press.

Maddison, Angus (1989). *The World Economy in the Twentieth Century.* Paris: OECD.

Maddison, Angus (1991). *Dynamic Forces in Capitalist Development.* Oxford: Oxford University Press.

Maddison, Angus (1992). "A Long-Run Perspective on Saving." *Scandinavian Journal of Economics,* 94, 2, 181–196.

Magalhaes, Andre, Geoffrey Hewings, and Carlos Roberto Azzoni (2000). "Spatial Dependence and Regional Convergence in Brazil." Mimeograph, University of Illinois at Urbana-Champaign.

Malthus, Thomas R. (1798). *An Essay on the Principle of Population.* London: W. Pickering, 1986.

Mangasarian, O. L. (1966). "Sufficient Conditions for the Optimal Control of Nonlinear Systems." *SIAM Journal of Control,* 4, February, 139–152.

Mankiw, N. Gregory, David Romer, and David N. Weil (1992). "A Contribution to the Empirics of Economic Growth." *Quarterly Journal of Economics,* 107, May, 407–437.

Mansfield, Edwin (1965). "Rates of Return from Industrial R&D." *American Economic Review,* 55, March, 310–322.

Mansfield, Edwin (1985). "How Rapidly Does New Industrial Technology Leak Out?" *Journal of Industrial Economics,* 34, December, 217–223.

Mansfield, Edwin, Mark Schwartz, and Samuel Wagner (1981). "Imitation Costs and Patents: An Empirical Study." *Economic Journal,* 91, December, 907–918.

Mas-Colell, Andreu, and Assaf Razin (1973). "A Model of Intersectoral Migration and Growth." *Oxford Economic Papers,* 25, March, 72–79.

Matsuyama, Kiminori (1991). "Increasing Returns, Industrialization, and the Indeterminacy of Equilibrium." *Quarterly Journal of Economics,* 106, May, 617–650.

Mauro, Paolo (1995). "Corruption and Growth." *Quarterly Journal of Economics,* 110, August, 681–712.

McCallum, Bennett T. (1984). "Are Bond-Financed Deficits Inflationary? A Ricardian Analysis." *Journal of Political Economy,* 92, February, 123–135.

McCallum, Bennett T. (1989). "Real Business Cycle Models." In Robert J. Barro, ed., *Modern Business Cycle Theory.* Cambridge, MA: Harvard University Press.

Michel, Philippe (1982). "On the Transversality Condition in Infinite Horizon Optimal Problems." *Econometrica,* 50, July, 975–985.

Minasian, Jora R. (1962). "The Economics of Research and Development." In Richard R. Nelson, ed., *The Rate and Direction of Inventive Activity,* NBER Special Conference Series. Princeton, NJ: Princeton University Press.

Mino, Kazuo (1996). "Analysis of a Two-Sector Model of Endogenous Growth with Capital Income Taxation." *International Economic Review,* 37, February, 227–251.

Molle, Willem, Bas Van Holst, and Hans Smits (1980). *Regional Disparity and Economic Development in the European Community.* Westmead, England: Saxon House.

Mulligan, Casey B. (1993). "On Intergenerational Altruism, Fertility, and the Persistence of Economic Status." Ph.D. dissertation, University of Chicago.

Mulligan, Casey B., and Xavier Sala-i-Martin (1991). "A Note on the Time-Elimination Method for Solving Recursive Economic Models." National Bureau of Economic Research Technical Working Paper no. 116, November.

Mulligan, Casey B., and Xavier Sala-i-Martin (1993). "Transitional Dynamics in Two-Sector Models of Endogenous Growth." *Quarterly Journal of Economics,* 108, August, 737–773.

Murphy, Kevin M., Andrei Shleifer, and Robert W. Vishny (1989). "Industrialization and the Big Push." *Quarterly Journal of Economics,* 106, May, 503–530.

Murphy, Kevin M., and Finis Welch (1990). "Empirical Age-Earnings Profiles." *Journal of Labor Economics,* 8, April, 202–229.

Nelson, Richard R., and Edmund S. Phelps (1966). "Investment in Humans, Technological Diffusion, and Economic Growth." *American Economic Review,* 56, May, 69–75.

Ohyama, Michihiro, and Ronald W. Jones (1993). "Technology Choice, Overtaking and Comparative Advantage." Unpublished, University of Rochester, December.

O'Leary, Eoin (2000). "Convergence of Living Standards Across Irish Regions: The Role of Demography and Productivity: 1960–1996." Mimeograph, University College Cork.

Peretto, Pietro (1998). "Technological Change and Population Growth." *Journal of Economic Growth,* 3, December, 283–311.

Persson, Joakim (1997). "Convergence across the Swedish counties, 1911–1993." *European Economic Review,* 41, December, 1835–1852.

Petrakos, George, and Yannis Saratsis (2000). "Regional Inequalities in Greece." *Papers in Regional Science,* 79, 57–74.

Phelps, Edmund S. (1962). "The New View of Investment: A Neoclassical Analysis." *Quarterly Journal of Economics,* 76, November, 548–567.

Phelps, Edmund S. (1966). *Golden Rules of Economic Growth.* New York: Norton.

Phelps, Edmund S., and Robert A. Pollak (1968). "On Second-Best National Saving and Game-Equilibrium Growth." *Review of Economic Studies,* 35, April, 185–199.

Pitchford, John D. (1977). *Applications of Control Theory to Economic Analysis.* Amsterdam: North Holland.

Pollak, Robert A. (1968). "Consistent Planning." *Review of Economic Studies,* 35, April, 201–208.

Pontryagin, Lev S., et al. (1962). *The Mathematical Theory of Optimal Processes.* New York: Interscience Publishers.

Quah, Danny (1993). "Galton's Fallacy and Tests of the Convergence Hypothesis." *Scandinavian Journal of Economics,* 95, 4, 427–443.

Quah, Danny (1996). "Twin Peaks: Growth and Convergence in Models of Distribution Dynamics." *Economic Journal,* 106, July, 1045–1055.

Raftery, Adrian E., David Madigan, and Jennifer A. Hoeting (1997). "Bayesian Model Averaging for Linear Regression Models." *Journal of the American Statistical Association,* 92, 179–191.

Ramsey, Frank (1928). "A Mathematical Theory of Saving." *Economic Journal,* 38, December, 543–559.

Rapping, Leonard (1965). "Learning and World War II Production Functions." *Review of Economics and Statistics,* 47, February, 81–86.

Rebelo, Sergio (1991). "Long-Run Policy Analysis and Long-Run Growth." *Journal of Political Economy,* 99, June, 500–521.

Reinganum, Jennifer F. (1989). "The Timing of Innovation: Research, Development, and Diffusion." In Richard Schmalensee and Robert D. Willig, eds., *Handbook of Industrial Organization,* vol. 1. New York: North Holland.

Ricardo, David (1817). *On the Principles of Political Economy and Taxation.* Cambridge: Cambridge University Press, 1951.

Rivera-Batiz, Luis A., and Paul M. Romer (1991). "Economic Integration and Endogenous Growth." *Quarterly Journal of Economics,* 106, May, 531–555.

Roback, Jennifer (1982). "Wages, Rents, and the Quality of Life." *Journal of Political Economy,* 90, December, 1257–1278.

Robinson, Joan (1938). "The Classification of Inventions." *Review of Economic Studies,* 5, February, 139–142.

Romer, Paul M. (1986). "Increasing Returns and Long-Run Growth." *Journal of Political Economy,* 94, October, 1002–1037.

Romer, Paul M. (1987). "Growth Based on Increasing Returns Due to Specialization." *American Economic Review,* 77, May, 56–62.

Romer, Paul M. (1990). "Endogenous Technological Change." *Journal of Political Economy,* 98, October, part II, S71–S102.

Romer, Paul M. (1992). "Two Strategies for Economic Development: Using Ideas and Producing Ideas." In World Bank, *Annual Conference on Economic Development,* Washington, DC.

Romer, Paul M. (1993). "Idea Gaps and Object Gaps in Economic Development." *Journal of Monetary Economics,* 32, December, 543–573.

Rybczynski, T. M. (1955). "Factor Endowments and Relative Commodity Prices." *Economica,* 22, November, 336–341.

Saint-Paul, Gilles (1992). "Fiscal Policy in an Endogenous Growth Model." *Quarterly Journal of Economics,* 107, November, 1243–1259.

Sala-i-Martin, Xavier (1990). "On Growth and States." Unpublished Ph.D. dissertation, Harvard University.

Sala-i-Martin, Xavier (1997a). "I Just Ran Four Million Regressions." National Bureau of Economic Research working paper no. 6252, November.

Sala-i-Martin, Xavier (1997b). "I Just Ran Two Million Regressions." *American Economic Review,* 87, December, 178–183.

Sala-i-Martin, Xavier (2003a). "The World Distribution of Income, 1970–2000." Unpublished, Columbia University.

Sala-i-Martin, Xavier (2003b). "Estimating Consumption Poverty and the World Distribution of Consumption, 1970–2000." Unpublished, Columbia University.

Sala-i-Martin, Xavier, Gernot Doppelhofer, and Ronald Miller (2003). "Determinants of Long-Term Growth: A Bayesian Averaging of Classical Estimates (BACE) Approach." Unpublished, Columbia University.

Samuelson, Paul A. (1954). "The Pure Theory of Public Expenditure." *Review of Economics and Statistics,* 36, November, 387–389.

Samuelson, Paul A. (1958). "An Exact Consumption-Loan Model of Interest with or without the Social Contrivance of Money." *Journal of Political Economy,* 66, December, 467–482.

Sanchez-Robles, Blanca, and Jose Villaverde (2001). "Polarizacion, Convergencia y Movilidad entre las provincias espanolas, 1955–1997." *Revista Asturiana de Economia,* May, 259–270.

Schmookler, Jacob (1966). *Invention and Economic Growth.* Cambridge, MA: Harvard University Press.

Schultz, T. Paul (1989). "Returns to Women's Education." PHRWD Background Paper 89/001, World Bank, Population, Health, and Nutrition Department, Washington, DC.

Schumpeter, Joseph A. (1934). *The Theory of Economic Development.* Cambridge, MA: Harvard University Press.

Schwarz, Gideon (1978). "Estimating the Dimension of a Model." *The Annals of Statistics,* 6, 461–464.

Searle, Allan D. (1946). "Productivity Changes in Selected Wartime Shipbuilding Programs." *Monthly Labor Review.*

Segerstrom, Paul S. (1991). "Innovation, Imitation, and Economic Growth." *Journal of Political Economy,* 99, August, 807–827.

Segerstrom, Paul S. (1998). "Endogenous Growth Without Scale Effects." *American Economic Review,* 88, December, 1290–1310.

Shell, Karl (1967). "A Model of Inventive Activity and Capital Accumulation." In Karl Shell, ed., *Essays on the Theory of Optimal Economic Growth,* 67–85. Cambridge, MA: MIT Press.

Sheshinski, Eytan (1967). "Optimal Accumulation with Learning by Doing." In Karl Shell, ed., *Essays on the Theory of Optimal Economic Growth,* 31–52. Cambridge, MA: MIT Press.

Shioji, Etruso (1997). "It's Still 2%: Evidence on Convergence from 116 Years of the US States Panel Data." Working Paper Universitat Pompeu Fabra.

Sidrauski, Miguel (1967). "Rational Choice and Patterns of Growth in a Monetary Economy." *American Economic Review,* 57, May, 534–544.

Smith, Adam (1776). *An Inquiry into the Nature and Causes of the Wealth of Nations.* New York: Random House, 1937.

Solow, Robert M. (1956). "A Contribution to the Theory of Economic Growth." *Quarterly Journal of Economics,* 70, February, 65–94.

Solow, Robert M. (1957). "Technical Change and the Aggregate Production Function." *Review of Economics and Statistics,* 39, August, 312–320.

Solow, Robert M. (1969). "Investment and Technical Change." In Kenneth J. Arrow et al., eds., *Mathematical Methods in the Social Sciences.* Palo Alto, CA: Stanford University Press.

Spence, Michael (1976). "Product Selection, Fixed Costs, and Monopolistic Competition." *Review of Economic Studies,* 43, June, 217–235.

Srinivasan, T. N. (1964). "Optimal Savings in a Two-Sector Model of Growth." *Econometrica,* 32, July, 358–373.

Stiglitz, Joseph E. (1969). "Distribution of Income and Wealth among Individuals." *Econometrica,* 37, July, 382–397.

Stone, Richard (1954). "Linear Expenditure Systems and Demand Analysis: An Application to the Pattern of British Demand." *Economic Journal,* 64, September, 511–527.

Streissler, Erich (1979). "Growth Models as Diffusion Processes: II." *Kyklos,* 32, 3, 571–586.

Strotz, Robert H. (1956). "Myopia and Inconsistency in Dynamic Utility Maximization." *Review of Economic Studies,* 23, 165–180.

Summers, Lawrence H. (1981). "Taxation and Corporate Investment: A q-Theory Approach." *Brookings Papers on Economic Activity,* no. 1, 67–127.

Summers, Robert, and Alan Heston (1991). "The Penn World Table (Mark 5): An Expanded Set of International Comparisons, 1950–1988." *Quarterly Journal of Economics,* 106, May, 327–368.

Swan, Trevor W. (1956). "Economic Growth and Capital Accumulation." *Economic Record,* 32, November, 334–361.

Teece, David J. (1977). "Technological Transfer by Multinational Firms: The Resource Cost of Transferring Technological Know-How." *Economic Journal,* 87, June, 242–261.

Temple, Jonathan (1999). "The New Growth Evidence." *Journal of Economic Literature,* 37, March, 112–156.

Temple, Robert (1986). *The Genius of China.* New York: Simon and Schuster.

Terleckyj, Nestor E. (1958). "Factors Underlying Productivity: Some Empirical Observations." *Journal of the American Statistical Association,* 53, June.

Thaler, Richard (1981). "Some Empirical Evidence on Dynamic Inconsistency." *Economics Letters,* 8, 201–207.

Thompson, Earl A. (1976). "Taxation and National Defense." *Journal of Political Economy,* 82, August, 755–782.

Thörnqvist, Leo (1936). "The Bank of Finland's Consumption Price Index." *Bank of Finland Monthly Bulletin,* no. 10, 1–8.

U.S. Department of Commerce, Bureau of the Census (1975). *Historical Statistics of the United States, Colonial Times to 1970.* Washington, DC: U.S. Government Printing Office.

U.S. Department of Commerce, Bureau of the Economic Analysis (2002). *State Personal Income, 1929–87.* Washington, DC: U.S. Government Printing Office.

U.S. Department of Commerce, Bureau of the Census (1990). *Statistical Abstract of the United States.* Washington, DC: U.S. Government Printing Office.

Utrera, Gaston Ezequiel, and Javier Adolfo Koroch (1998). "Convergencia: Evidencia empirica para las provincias argentinas (1953–1994)." In *Anales de la XXXIII Reunión Anual de la Asociación Argentina de Economi Politica,* November.

Uzawa, Hirofumi (1961). "Neutral Inventions and the Stability of Growth Equilibrium." *Review of Economic Studies,* 28, February, 117–124.

Uzawa, Hirofumi (1964). "Optimal Growth in a Two-Sector Model of Capital Accumulation." *Review of Economic Studies,* 31 (January), 1–24.

Uzawa, Hirofumi (1965). "Optimal Technical Change in an Aggregative Model of Economic Growth." *International Economic Review,* 6, January, 18–31.

Uzawa, Hirofumi (1968). "Time Preference, the Consumption Function, and Optimum Asset Holdings." In J. N. Wolfe, ed., *Value, Capital, and Growth.* Chicago, Aldine.

Ventura, Jaume (1997). "Growth and Interdependence." *Quarterly Journal of Economics,* 112, February, 57–84.

Von Furstenberg, George M. (1977). "Corporate Investment: Does Market Valuation Matter in the Aggregate?" *Brookings Papers on Economic Activity,* no. 2, 347–397.

Von Neumann, John (1937). "Über ein Ökonomisches Gleichungssystem und eine Verallgemeinerung des Brouwerschen." *Ergebnisse eines Mathematische Kolloquiums,* 8, translated by Karl Menger as "A Model of General Equilibrium," *Review of Economic Studies* (1945), 13, 1–9.

Wahl, Jenny Bourne (1985). "Fertility in America: Historical Patterns and Wealth Effects on the Quantity and Quality of Children." Ph.D. dissertation, University of Chicago.

Weil, Philippe (1987). "Love Thy Children: Reflections on the Barro Debt Neutrality Theorem." *Journal of Monetary Economics,* 19, May, 377–391.

Weil, Philippe (1989). "Overlapping Families of Infinitely Lived Agents." *Journal of Public Economics,* 38, March, 183–198.

Weitzman, Martin L. (1973). "Duality Theory for Infinite Horizon Convex Models." *Management Science,* 19, 783–789.

Woodberry, Robert D. (2002). "The Shadow of Empire: Church-State Relations, Colonial Policy, and Democracy in Postcolonial Societies." Unpublished, University of North Carolina, November.

World Bank (1990). *World Development Report, 1990.* Washington, DC: World Bank.

Wright, Theodore P. (1936). "Factors Affecting the Cost of Airplanes." *Journal of the Aeronautical Sciences,* 3, 122–128.

Xie, Danyang (1992). "Three Essays on Economic Growth and Development." Ph.D. dissertation, University of Chicago.

Yaari, Menahem E. (1965). "Uncertain Lifetime, Life Insurance, and the Theory of the Consumer." *Review of Economic Studies,* 32, April, 137–150.

Yao, Yudong, and Melvyn Weeks (2000). "Provincial Income Convergence in China, 1953–1997: A Panel Data Approach." Mimeograph, University of Cambridge.

York, Jeremy C., David Madigan, I. Ivar Heuch, and Rolv Terje Lie (1995). "Estimating a Proportion of Birth Defects by Double Sampling: A Bayesian Approach Incorporating Covariates and Model Uncertainty." *Applied Statistics,* 44, 227–242.

Young, Allyn (1928). "Increasing Returns and Economic Progress." *Economic Journal,* 38, December, 527–542.

Young, Alwyn (1989). "Hong Kong and the Art of Landing on One's Feet: A Case Study of a Structurally Flexible Economy." Ph.D. dissertation, Fletcher School, Tufts University, May.

Young, Alwyn (1992). "A Tale of Two Cities: Factor Accumulation and Technical Change in Hong Kong and Singapore." *NBER Macroeconomics Annual, 1992,* 13–54. Cambridge, MA: MIT Press.

Young, Alwyn (1993). "Invention and Bounded Learning by Doing." *Journal of Political Economy,* 101, June, 443–472.

Young, Alwyn (1995). "The Tyranny of Numbers: Confronting the Statistical Realities of the East Asian Growth Experience." *Quarterly Journal of Economics,* 110, August, 641–680.

Young, Alwyn (1998). "Growth Without Scale Effects." *Journal of Political Economy,* 106, February, 41–63.

Index

Abel, Andrew, 160n, 202
Absolute convergence, in Solow-Swan model, 45–46, 65
Acemoglu, Daron, 20, 53, 288n, 519
Ades, Alberto F., 497
Adjustment costs for investment
for human versus physical capital, 173–177, 246–247
in Ramsey model, 152–160
accumulation of human capital, 173–177
behavior of firms, 152–155
equilibrium for closed economy with fixed saving rate, 159–160
equilibrium with given interest rate, 155–159
Africa. *See also specific African nations*
GDP growth in, 3, 4–5
income distribution in, 10–11
Age structure, GDP growth and, 539
Aggregate quality index, 329–331
Aghion, Philippe, 20, 63, 317, 319n, 322n, 332, 333n, 342n
Ainslie, George W., 122n
AK model, 63–66
determinants of growth rate, 210–211
equilibrium, 207–208
household behavior, 205–206
phase diagram, 209–210
transitional dynamics, 66–68, 208–209
Alesina, Alberto, 540n
Altruism, 179–183, 198–200
Annuities, in overlapping generations model (OLG), 179–180, 180n
Argentina, long-term GDP data, 565
Arnold, Lutz, 251n
Arrow, Kenneth J., 18, 19, 65n, 68, 135, 213, 445
Asher, H., 213
Asset income, taxes on, 146–147
Aten, Bettina, 1n, 2, 6n, 22, 23n, 511n, 512, 560
Australia
domestic investment/saving in, 15
GDP growth in, 13
long-term GDP data, 561
Austria, long-term GDP data, 561
Azzoni, Carlos Roberto, 483

Bagwell, Kyle, 86n
Balanced growth path, 34n
Bangladesh, long-term GDP data, 564
Barrett, David B., 540n
Barro, Robert J., 12–13, 14, 19n, 50n, 86n, 122, 131–132, 141, 166n, 171n, 173, 198, 220, 223, 236, 314, 351, 389, 391, 408–411, 415n, 423, 462, 466n, 471, 474, 479, 484, 516, 521
Basu, Susanto, 443n
Baumol, William J., 14, 462
Bayesian Averaging of Classical Estimates (BACE), 543–547, 559
Becker, Gary S., 408–411, 413, 413n, 415n, 422n, 424n
Behrman, Jere R., 408
Belgium, long-term GDP data, 561
Benhabib, Jess, 269n, 422n
Bequests, 179–183, 198–200
Bernheim, B. Douglas, 86n
β convergence
concept of, 14, 462–463
across European regions, 479–482
across Japanese prefectures, 474–478
in panel data with fixed effects, 495–496
quantitative measure of, 56–59
across U.S. states, 466–472
Bhalla, Surjit S., 6n
Births, in overlapping-generations model (OLG), 412
Black Death, imbalance effect in Europe, 245–246
Blanchard, Olivier, 88n, 137n, 155n, 158, 160n, 178–180, 185, 190, 191n, 202, 203, 235, 393, 395
Bloom, Nicholas, 20, 342n
Blundell, Richard, 20, 342n
Boldrin, Michele, 269n
Bollen, Kenneth A., 528
Bond, Eric, 247n, 266n, 267n
Borjas, George J., 390, 391
Borts, George H., 462
Botswana, GDP growth in, 4
Bowman, Larry W., 350
Brainard, William C., 155
Brain drain, 391–392. *See also* Migration of labor
Braun, Juan, 389, 393, 398–407, 429, 494
Braun model of migration and growth, 398–407
decision to migrate, 401–403
imperfect capital mobility, 406–407
model setup, 399–400
steady state, 403–405
transitional dynamics, 403–405
world economy dynamics, 406
Brazil, long-term GDP data, 565
Bresnahan, Tim, 451
Brezis, Elise, 335n, 375, 376
Broad output, growth rate in two-sector model, 261–262
Brock, William A., 141
Bronars, Stephen G., 390, 391

Caballe, Jordi, 279
Caballero, Ricardo J., 364n
Canada
domestic investment/saving in, 15
GDP growth in, 13
growth accounting for, 439

Canada (cont.)
  long-term GDP data, 561
  R&D outlays versus GDP, 301
  stability of factor shares, 12
Cannon, Edmund S., 213n
Canova, Fabio, 495
Capital. *See also* Human capital; Investment; Physical capital
  in *AK* model, 207–208
  golden rule of capital accumulation, 34–37, 100n, 101n, 196–197
  in growth accounting, 434, 436
  in Ramsey model, 162–163, 183–184
  in Solow-Swan model, 23–24, 25–26, 30–31, 59–61
Capital-saving technological progress, 52
Caselli, Francesco, 19n, 119, 121, 373, 495
Cashin, Paul, 482–483
Cass, David, 18–19, 85
Cass-Koopmans neoclassical growth model, 18–19
Chamley, Christophe, 269n
Chenery, Hollis B., 68
Children
  bequests to, 198–200
  child-rearing costs in overlapping-generations model (OLG), 412–413, 421
Chile, long-term GDP data, 565
China
  economic development in, 350
  GDP growth in, 4
  income distribution in, 7, 8
  long-term GDP data, 564
Chiswick, Barry., 390
Christensen, Laurits R., 12, 438, 440n
Chua, Hak B., 71, 372n
Closed economy. *See* Neoclassical theory; Ramsey model; Solow-Swan model
Coase, Ronald W., 342
Cobb, Charles S., 29n
Cobb-Douglas production function, 67, 74
  capital/output ratio, 118
  capital share in, 39
  described, 29–30
  in one-sector models of endogenous growth, 217–218, 226–229
  origins of, 17
  savings rate in, 49, 107, 109
  technological progress, 43–44
Coe, David T., 452–453
Cohen, Daniel, 166, 166n, 202
Coleman, Wilbur John, 373
Collins, Susan M., 172
Colombia, long-term GDP data, 565
Conditional convergence, in Solow-Swan model, 14, 46–50, 65
Congestion model, in one-sector-models of endogenous growth, 223–225
Connolly, Michelle, 349n
Constant-elasticity-of-substitution (CES) production functions, 68–71, 80–81, 171n, 230–232
Constant intertemporal elasticity of substitution (CIES), 91
Constant returns to scale, 27, 28, 33
Constant terms, GDP growth and, 533–534
Consumer utility. *See also* Household utility
  imitators in follower country, 357
  in neoclassical theory, 16–17, 18
  in Schumpeterian models of quality ladders, 328–329
Consumption function
  as function of wealth, 181–183
  in Ramsey model, 93–94, 103–104, 120, 146, 164–165
  in Uzawa-Lucas model, 257–258
Control variables, 227, 518–520
Convergence across economies
  β convergence
    concept of, 14, 462–463
    across European regions, 479–482
    across Japanese prefectures, 474–478
    in panel data with fixed effects, 495–496
    quantitative measure of, 56–59
    across U.S. states, 466–472
  migration of labor and, 492–496
  in Ramsey model
    convergence coefficient, 114
    speeds of convergence, 111–118, 167
  σ convergence
    concept of, 462–465
    across European regions, 482
    across Japanese prefectures, 478
    across U.S. states, 473–474
  in Solow-Swan model, 44–51
    absolute convergence, 45–46, 65
    conditional convergence, 14, 46–50, 65
    convergence coefficient, 57, 59, 78
    dispersion of per capita income, 50–51
    migration of labor, 388–392
    properties, 78
    quantitative measure of speed of, 56–61
  in technology diffusion, 359–363
Coulombe, Serge, 482
Cournot-Nash equilibrium, 125n, 127n, 333–334
Credit market constraint, 165–177, 188–189
Cummings, Dianne, 12, 438, 440n
Cumulative distribution functions (CDFs), 9n
Cyprus, GDP growth in, 4

David, Paul A., 451
Deaths
  imbalance effect and, 245–246

nature of, 179
in overlapping-generations model (OLG), 179–183, 198–200, 412
Debt, in Ramsey model, 88–89, 92
constraint on international credit, 165–177
DeLong, J. Bradford, 14, 462
Democracy, GDP growth and, 528–529, 538
Democratic Republic of Congo, GDP growth in, 3, 4
Denison, Edward F., 12, 58, 433, 437
Denmark, long-term GDP data, 561
Depreciation curve, in Solow-Swan model, 38–40, 386–387
Development modifier, 214
Devleeschauwer, Arnaud, 540n
Diamond, Peter, 178, 185, 190
Diffusion of technology. *See* Technology diffusion
Dinopoulos, Elias, 332
Dixit, Avinash K., 285–286, 286n, 317
Dolado, Juan, 390
Domar, Evsey D., 17, 71, 73–74
Doppelhofer, Gernot, 541, 543n, 543–544, 547–556
Dougherty, Christopher, 12
Douglas, Paul H., 29n
Dowrick, Steve, 462
Duczynski, Petr, 173
Durlauf, Steven N., 543n
Dynamic inefficiency, golden rule of capital accumulation and, 36–37, 196–197

East Asia
GDP growth in, 3–4, 23
growth accounting for countries in, 438–441, 443–444, 459–460
income distribution in, 10–11
stability of factor shares, 12
Easterlin, Richard A., 462, 497
Easterly, William, 82, 372n, 519n, 540n
Economic growth. *See also* Growth models
empirical regularities of, 12–16
history of modern growth theory, 16–21
importance of, 1–6
Education
GDP growth and, 524, 537
in two-sector models of endogenous growth
in model with two sectors of production, 247–251
Uzawa-Lucas model, 251–268
Effective labor, 54–55, 95
Elias, Victor J., 12, 440n, 441
Emigration. *See* Migration of labor
Endogenous growth models, 19–20, 61–77
constant-elasticity-of-substitution (CES) production functions, 68–71, 80–81, 171n, 230–232
dissatisfaction with neoclassical theory, 61–63, 77–78
Leontief production function, 71–74
one-sector models, 205–235
AK model, 63–66, 205–211
constant-elasticity-of-substitution (CES) form, 230–232
with learning by doing and knowledge spillovers, 212–220
with physical and human capital, 211–212, 240–247
with poverty traps, 74–77
public services and, 220–225
transitional dynamics and, 66–68, 208–209, 226–232, 271–274
and Schumpeterian models of quality ladders, 329–331
Solow-Swan model (*see* Solow-Swan model)
two-sector models, 239–282
conditions for endogenous growth, 268–271
described, 247–251
with reversed factor intensities, 267–268, 280–282
Uzawa-Lucas model, 251–268, 274–279
Equilibrium
in *AK* model, 207–208
Cournot-Nash, 125n, 127n, 333–334
in one-sector models of endogenous growth, 216
in overlapping generations model (OLG), 193–200
in Ramsey model, 96, 97–98, 155–160, 164–177, 193–200
in Solow-Swan model, 33
technological progress and, 295–297
Esquivel, Gerardo, 495
Essentiality of inputs, 28, 77–78
Ethier, Wilfred J., 285–286, 286n
Euler equation, 62, 90–91, 144n, 210
Europe. *See also specific countries*
convergence across regions, 479–482
β convergence, 479–482
σ convergence, 482
income distribution in, 11–12
labor migration across regions, 490–492
regional data sets, 500–506
Exogenous savings rates. *See* Solow-Swan model

Factor share stability, 12
Faig, Miguel, 279
Family budget constraint, in overlapping-generations model (OLG), 414
Farmer, Roger E. A., 269n
Feenstra, Robert C., 437n
Felicity function, 87
Fertility choice, 407–421
overlapping-generations model (OLG), 408–421
births, 412
child-rearing costs, 412–413, 421

Fertility choice (cont.)
deaths, 412
family budget constraint, 414
optimization conditions, 414–416
steady state, 416–421
transitional dynamics, 197–198, 416–421
utility function, 412
Fertility rate, 16, 525
Finland, long-term GDP data, 561
Firm utility. *See also* Prices
in *AK* model, 206
in overlapping generations model (OLG), 192
profit and, 32–33, 96, 212, 215, 221
in Ramsey model, 94–96, 152–155, 192
in Schumpeterian models of quality ladders, 346
taxes on firms' earnings, 146–147
technological progress and, 285–295
Fischer, Stanley, 88n, 141
Fishburn, Peter C., 121n
Fisher, I., 17, 121
Follower country in technology diffusion, 352–363
consumers, 357
dynamic path and convergence, 359–363
imitating firms, 353–357
cost of imitation, 353–355
free-entry condition, 356–357
optimal pricing, once good copied, 355–356
implications for growth rates, 370–373
producers of final output, 352–353
steady-state growth and, 357–358
welfare considerations, 376–379
Foreign investment. *See also* Investment
technology diffusion and, 368–370
France
domestic investment/saving in, 15
growth accounting for, 439
long-term GDP data, 562
number of R&D scientists and engineers, 310
R&D outlays versus GDP, 301
stability of factor shares, 12
Frankel, Marvin, 212–214, 213n, 219
Fraumeni, Barbara M., 12, 58, 60, 437
Free-entry condition
for imitators in follower country, 356–357
for research (R&D) sector, 293–295, 302, 326–328

Gallup, John L., 538, 540
Galor, Oded, 74, 74n, 408n, 413n
Gastil, Raymond D., 528
GDP. *See* Per capita gross domestic product (GDP)
Geary, Robert C., 178
Germany
growth accounting for, 439
imbalance effect post-World War II, 244
long-term GDP data, 562
number of R&D scientists and engineers, 310
R&D outlays versus GDP, 301
stability of factor shares, 12
in switchovers of technological leadership, 376
Gezici, Ferhan, 483
Glaeser, Edward L., 497
GNP (gross national product), gap between GDP and, 172–173
Golden rule of capital accumulation, 34–37, 100n, 101n, 196–197
Goldman, Steven M., 122
Gollop, Frank M., 12, 58, 60, 437
Goria, Alessandra, 390
Government. *See also* Taxes
in one-sector models of endogenous growth, 220–225
congestion model, 223–225
poverty trap, 75–77
public-goods model, 220–223
purchases
GDP growth and, 525–526, 539
in one-sector models of endogenous growth, 222–223
in Ramsey model extension, 147–152
in Ramsey model extension, 143–152
effects of government purchases, 147–152
effects of tax rates, 146–147
modifications of basic framework, 143–146
technological change and subsidies, 299–300, 309
Greenwood, Jeremy, 422n, 539
Greenwood, Michael J., 391
Griffith, Rachel, 20, 342n
Griliches, Zvi, 212–214, 354, 433, 437, 438, 442, 443n, 445, 446, 449–453, 450n, 453
Gross domestic product (GDP). *See* Per capita gross domestic product (GDP)
Grossman, Gene M., 20, 286, 310n, 319n, 344, 344n, 349n
Gross national product (GNP), gap between GDP and, 172–173
Growth accounting, 433–460. *See also* Economic growth; Growth models; Growth rates
dual approach to, 435, 442–444
problems with, 444–450
increasing-returns model with spillovers, 445–447
multiple types of factors, 449–450
taxes, 447–448
sources of growth versus, 457–460
standard primal approach to, 433–442
capital share, 434, 436
labor share, 434, 436
qualities of inputs, 437–438
regression-based estimates of TFP growth, 441–442

results from, 438–441
setup, 433–435
TFP growth and research and development (R&D), 450–456
quality-ladders models, 454–456
varieties models, 451–454
Growth models. *See also* Economic growth; Endogenous growth models; Growth accounting; Technological progress; Technology diffusion
with consumer optimization (*see* Ramsey model)
neoclassical, 18
Growth rates, 521–566. *See also* Economic growth; Growth accounting; Growth models
empirical analysis, 515–520
control variables, 518–520
environmental variables, 518–520
state variables, 517
of follower country in technology diffusion, 370–373
long-term data on GDP, 13–16, 23, 559–566
losers and winners, 1960-2000, 511–515
for models with expanding variety of products, 297, 451–454
regression results, 521–541
additional explanatory variables, 535–541
basic regression, 521–534
tests of stability of coefficients, 534–535
robustness of growth, 541–559
Bayesian Averaging of Classical Estimates (BACE), 543–547, 559
Levine and Renelt model for measuring, 542–543
robustness analysis, 556–559
Sala-i-Martin, Doppelhofer, and Miller model for measuring, 547–556
Gulhati, Ravi, 350

Hansen, Gary D., 408n
Harris, Christopher, 322n, 342n
Harrod, Roy F., 17, 52, 71, 73–74
Harrod-Domar controversy, 71, 73–74
Hart, Peter E., 51
Hatton, Timothy J., 389, 391
Health, GDP growth and, 537–538
Heckman, James J., 424n
Helpman, Elhanan, 20, 286, 310n, 319n, 344, 344n, 349n, 452–453
Henderson, J. Vernon, 487
Hercowitz, Zvi, 422n
Heston, Alan, 1n, 2, 6n, 22, 23n, 511n, 512, 532n, 560
Heuch, I. Ivar, 544
Hewings, Geoffrey, 483
Hicks, John, 52
Hirshleifer, Jack, 246
Hoeting, Jennifer A., 544
Homogeneity of degree one in K and L, 27, 28
Hong Kong
economic development in, 350
GDP growth in, 4
growth accounting for, 440, 443, 459–460
stability of factor shares, 12
Hossain, Akhtar, 483
Household utility. *See also* Consumer utility
in *AK* model, 205–206
labor/leisure choice, 422–428
in overlapping-generations model (OLG), 190–192, 412, 414–416
in Ramsey model, 16–17, 86–94
first-order conditions, 89–94
heterogeneity, 118–121
model setup, 86–89
technological progress and, 295
Howitt, Peter, 20, 63, 317, 319n, 322n, 332, 333n, 342n
Hsieh, Chang-Tai, 442, 443
Human capital. *See also* Education; Labor supply; Migration of labor
adjustment costs for accumulation, 173–177, 246–247
growth rate in two-sector model, 258–250
knowledge and, 23–24, 212–220
mobility of, 171–173, 406–407
in one-sector models of endogenous growth, 211–212, 240–247
basic setup, 240–242
constraint of nonnegative gross investment, 242–247
physical capital versus, 168–175, 241–242
in Ramsey model, 117, 118, 166–167, 168–177
in Solow-Swan model, 59–61

Ichino, Andrea, 390
Imbalance effect, 244–247
Immigration. *See* Migration of labor
Inada, Ken-Ichi, 27n
Inada conditions, 27, 29, 72, 95, 233
Income distribution
convergence and dispersion of per capita income, 50–51
world, 6–12
India
domestic investment/saving in, 15
GDP growth in, 1
income distribution in, 7
long-term GDP data, 564
Indonesia
GDP growth in, 4
long-term GDP data, 564
Inflation rate, GDP growth and, 532–533

Innovation. *See also* Research and development (R&D); Technological progress; Technology diffusion
behavior of imitators in follower country, 352–363, 370–373, 376–379
behavior of innovators in leading country, 351–352
classification of inventions, 51–53
research by sector leader, 333–338, 346–347
switchovers of technological leadership, 333–334, 373–376
Insurance, in overlapping generations model (OLG), 179–180
Intellectual property rights, technology diffusion and, 368–370
Intensive form, 28
of Cobb-Douglas function, 29–30
in Uzawa-Lucas model, 267–268, 280–282
Interest rates
in Ramsey model, 88–89, 94, 129, 155–159, 168, 181
in Solow-Swan model, 40–41
Intergenerational transfer, 179–183, 198–200
Intermediate goods. *See also* Schumpeterian models of quality ladders
for producers of final output, 285–289
subsidies to purchase, 299–300, 309
International credit constraint, 165–177, 188–189
International openness, GDP growth and, 529–530
Investment. *See also* Adjustment costs for investment; Capital; Human capital; Physical capital
foreign, technology diffusion and, 368–370
GDP growth and, 531–532
in one-sector models of endogenous growth
Investment tax credit, 217, 218
transitional dynamics with inequality restrictions, 271–274
Involuntary unemployment, 88
Irreversible investment, in Ramsey model, 134–135
Italy
growth accounting for, 439
long-term GDP data, 562
R&D outlays versus GDP, 301
stability of factor shares, 12

Jaffe, Adam B., 364n
Japan
convergence across prefectures, 474–478
β convergence, 474–478
σ convergence, 478
domestic investment/saving in, 15
GDP growth in, 1–2, 4
growth accounting for, 439
imbalance effect post-World War II, 244
income distribution in, 7
labor migration across prefectures, 486–490
long-term GDP data, 562
number of R&D scientists and engineers, 310
R&D outlays versus GDP, 301
regional data sets, 506–509
stability of factor shares, 12
in switchovers of technological leadership, 376
Jaumotte, Florence, 372, 373
Jefferson, Thomas, 24n, 290
Jeffreys, Harold, 544
Johnson, Simon, 519
Jones, Charles I., 20, 297, 301, 305n, 310, 408, 412
Jones, Larry E., 66, 226
Jones, Ronald W., 375, 382
Jorgenson, Dale W., 12, 58, 60, 433, 437, 438, 440n, 442, 443n, 449–450
Jovanovic, Boyan, 349n, 364n, 375, 539
Judd, Kenneth L., 306n
Judson, Ruth, 118

Kaldor, Nicholas, 12–14, 118, 169
Keefer, Philip, 526
Kendrick, John W., 248, 433
Kimball, Miles S., 199
King, Robert G., 116, 423–424, 539
Knack, Stephen, 526
Knight, Frank K., 16, 20, 63n
Knowledge
in Solow-Swan model, 23–24
spillovers, in one-sector models of endogenous growth, 212–220
Koopmans, Tjalling C., 18, 19, 85, 87n, 121n
Koroch, Javier Adolfo, 483
Kremer, Michael, 159n, 177, 219, 297
Krugman, Paul, 269n, 335n, 349n, 375, 376, 381
Kurlat, Sergio, 540n
Kurz, Mordecai, 66n, 135
Kuznets, Simon, 12n, 450
Kydland, Finn E., 293

Labor-saving technological progress, 52, 53–56
Labor supply, 383–407. *See also* Human capital; Migration of labor; Population growth; Wage rates
in growth accounting, 434, 436
labor/leisure choice, 422–428
in Ramsey model, 86, 393–398
in Solow-Swan model, 23–24, 26, 31–33, 53–56, 78–80, 383, 384–392
Lach, Saul, 349n, 364n
Laibson, David, 122, 123, 127, 127n, 129–131
La Porta, Rafael, 540
Latin America. *See also specific countries*
GDP growth in, 2–3, 4, 5–6
growth accounting for countries in, 438–441
income distribution in, 10–11

Leamer, Edward E., 542n, 544
Leapfrogging, in switchovers of technological leadership, 333–334, 373–376
Learning by doing, in one-sector models of endogenous growth, 212–220
Lee, Frank C., 482
Lee, Jong-Wha, 408, 516
Lefort, Fernando, 495
Leisure, labor/leisure choice, 422–428
Leontief, Wassily, 71
Leontief production function, 71–74
Levine, Ross, 372n, 539, 542n, 542–543, 547n
Lewis, William Arthur, 74n
Lichtenberg, Frank, 453
Lie, Rolv Terje, 544
Life expectancy, GDP growth and, 524–525, 537–538
Life insurance, in overlapping generations model (OLG), 179–180
Loans, in Ramsey model, 88–89, 92
 constraint on international credit, 165–177
Loayza, Norman, 483
Loewenstein, George, 122n, 128n
Long run, 33–34
Lopez-de-Silanes, Florencio, 540
Lucas, Robert E., Jr., 19, 212–214, 219, 239, 251, 267, 270, 283, 408n, 445, 446
Luxembourg, GDP growth in, 1, 3

McCallum, Bennett T., 141, 293
McPherson, Isaac, 24n, 290
Maddison, Angus, 1n, 12, 13, 15, 58, 118, 559–566
Madigan, David, 544
Magalhaes, Andre, 483
Malthus, Thomas R., 16, 17, 20, 407, 407n
Mankiw, N. Gregory, 14, 60, 78, 166n, 171n, 521
Mansfield, Edwin, 354, 355, 364n, 450n
Manuelli, Rodolfo E., 66, 226
Marcet, Albert, 495
Marginal product of capital, in one-sector models of endogenous growth, 215, 218, 221–222, 224
Markets. *See also* Monopoly power
 in Solow-Swan model, 31–33
Markusen, James R., 437n
Mas-Colell, Andreu, 428
Matsuyama, Kiminori, 269n, 273n
Mauritius, economic development in, 350
Mauro, Paolo, 538n
Mexico
 economic development in, 350
 GDP growth in, 1
 long-term GDP data, 565
Middle East and North Africa (MENA), income distribution in, 10–11
Migration of labor, 383–407
 Braun model, 398–407
 convergence across economies and, 492–496
 across European regions, 490–492
 across Japanese prefectures, 486–490
 Ramsey model, 393–398
 Solow-Swan model, 383, 384–392
 to urban areas, 450
 across U.S. states, 483–486
Miller, Ronald, 541, 543–544, 547–556
Minasian, Jora R., 450n
Minhas, Bagicha S., 68
Mino, Kazuo, 247n, 267n
Modified golden rule, 101n
Molle, Willem, 500, 506
Monopoly power
 erosion of, in models with expanding variety of products, 305–310
 in research and development (R&D) process, 290–292, 322–324, 336–338
 in Schumpeterian models of quality ladders
  duration of monopoly position, 324–325, 345–346
  interactions between sector leader and outsiders, 333–336
  sector leader as monopoly researcher, 336–338
Mulligan, Casey B., 114, 177n, 260, 268
Murphy, Kevin M., 74n, 185–186, 413n

Nallari, Raj, 350
Negative dividends, 153n
Nelson, Richard R., 349n, 355, 373
Neoclassical production function, 17, 26–31
 characteristics, 27–29
 Cobb-Douglas example of (*see* Cobb-Douglas production function)
 essentiality of inputs, 77–78
Neoclassical theory, 16–21. *See also* Ramsey model; Solow-Swan model
 AK model, 63–66
 consumer optimization in, 16–17, 18
 diffusion of technology, 20
 dissatisfaction with, 61–63
 neoclassical production function, 17, 26–31, 77–78
 population growth, 16, 20–21
 problems with, 18
 technological progress and, 18–20
Netherlands
 growth accounting for, 439
 long-term GDP data, 562
 stability of factor shares, 12
Neutral technological progress, 52–53
Nguyen, Duc Tho, 462
Nonrival goods, 24, 24n
Norway, long-term GDP data, 562
Nyarko, Yaw, 375

OECD. *See* Organization for Economic Cooperation and Development (OECD)
Ohyama, Michihiro, 375, 382
O'Leary, Eoin, 483
One-sector models of endogenous growth, 205–235
  AK model, 63–66, 205–211
  constant-elasticity-of-substitution (CES) form, 230–232
  with learning by doing and knowledge spillovers, 212–220
    Cobb-Douglas example, 217–218
    equilibrium, 216
    Pareto nonoptimality, 216–217
    policy implications, 216–217
    scale effects, 218–220
    technology component, 212–215
  with physical and human capital, 211–212, 240–247
  public services and, 220–225
    congestion model, 223–225
    poverty trap, 75–77
    public-goods model, 220–223
  and Schumpeterian models of quality ladders, 329–331
  transitional dynamics and, 66–68, 208–209, 226–232, 271–274
Open economy, Ramsey model extension, 161–167, 168–189
  economic growth with finite horizons, 179–189
  model setup, 161–162
  small economy capital stock and output, 162–163
  small economy consumption and assets, 163–164
  variations in preference parameters, 177–178
  world economy, 164–177
Organization for Economic Cooperation and Development (OECD)
  convergence of GDP across economies, 46
  GDP growth in, 2–6
  growth accounting for countries in, 438–441
  number of R&D scientists and engineers, 310
  R&D outlays versus GDP, 301
Output per worker, in *AK* model, 207–208
Overlapping-generations model (OLG), 178, 179, 186–189, 190–200, 408–421
  births, 412
  child-rearing costs, 412–413, 421
  in continuous time, 411–421
  deaths, 412
  equilibrium in, 193–200
  family budget constraint, 414
  firms in, 192
  golden rule of capital accumulation, 196–197
  households in, 190–192, 412, 414–416
  optimization conditions, 414–416
  population growth, 179, 194, 412
  savings rate, 193, 196–197
  steady state, 194–195, 416–421
  transitional dynamics, 197–198, 416–421
  utility function, 412
Oversaving
  in overlapping-generations model (OLG), 196–197
  in Solow-Swan model, 101

Pakistan
  GDP growth in, 1, 4
  long-term GDP data, 564
Pareto optimality
  nature of, 98–99
  in one-sector models of endogenous growth, 211, 216–217, 222, 224–225
  in Ramsey model, 98–99, 150–151
  in Schumpeterian models of quality ladders, 339–342
  technological progress and, 297–300
    subsidies to final product, 300
    subsidies to purchases of intermediate goods, 299–300
    subsidies to research, 300
  in technology diffusion, 377–379
Park, Won Am, 172
Patents, as proxy for learning, 213
Per capita gross domestic product (GDP). *See also* Economic growth; Growth accounting; Growth models; Growth rates
  basic regression of growth, 521–534
    initial per capita GDP, 521–523
    tests of stability of coefficients, 534–535
    variables measured, 521–534, 535–541
  convergence across economies, 44–51. *See also* Convergence across economies
  gap between GNP and, 172–173
  growth of, 1–6, 13–15, 210–211, 219, 223
  long-term data on GDP, 13–16, 23, 559–566
  robustness of growth, 541–559
    Bayesian Averaging of Classical Estimates (BACE), 543–547, 559
    Levine and Renelt model for measuring, 542–543
    robustness analysis, 556–559
    Sala-i-Martin, Doppelhofer, and Miller model for measuring, 547–556
  world, 6–12
Peretto, Pietro, 305n
Perpetual-inventory method, 436
Persson, Joakim, 482–483
Peru, long-term GDP data, 565
Petrakos, George, 483
Phelps, Edmund S., 35, 80, 125n, 127, 349n, 355, 373

Philippines
GDP growth in, 1
long-term GDP data, 564
Physical capital
adjustment costs for accumulation, 246–247
growth rate in two-sector model, 258–250
human capital versus, 168–175, 241–242
in one-sector models of endogenous growth, 211–212, 240–247
basic setup, 240–242
constraint of nonnegative gross investment, 242–247
in Ramsey model, 117, 118, 166–167, 168–173
in Solow-Swan model, 59–61
Plosser, Charles I., 423–424
Poland, GDP growth in, 1
Policy
and Ramsey model, 105–106
and Solow-Swan model, 41–43
and Uzawa-Lucas model, 256–257
Pollak, Robert A., 122, 124n, 125n, 127
Population growth. *See also* Fertility choice
labor/leisure choice, 422–428
in neoclassical theory, 16, 20–21
in overlapping generations model (OLG), 179, 194, 412
in Ramsey model, 129–130
in Solow-Swan model, 26, 42
Posterior inclusion probability, 547
Poverty, world income distribution and, 6–12
Poverty line
defined, 6–7, 9n
world, 6–12
Poverty traps
defined, 74
growth models with, 74–77
Prelec, Drazen, 122n, 128n
Prescott, Edward C., 293, 408n
Present-value factor, in Ramsey model, 93–94
Prices. *See also* Monopoly power
optimal
for imitating firms, 355–356
for invention, 290–292, 322–324
shadow price, 92, 249–250
in Solow-Swan model, 40–41
Producers of final output
behavior of imitators in follower country, 352–353
levels of quality in production technology, 319–321, 343–345
subsidies to final product, 300
technological progress and, 285–289, 300
Production functions
AK function, 63–66, 67
capital-augmenting, 52–53
Cobb-Douglas (*see* Cobb-Douglas production function)
constant-elasticity-of-substitution (CES), 68–71, 80–81, 171n, 230–232
Leontief, 71–74
neoclassical, 17, 26–31, 77–78
Productivity slowdown, 13, 438–441
Profit
in one-sector models of endogenous growth, 212, 215, 221
in Ramsey model, 96
in Solow-Swan model, 32–33
Public goods
nonrival goods versus, 24n
in one-sector-models of endogenous growth, 220–223

Quah, Danny T., 51, 77, 249n, 543n
Quality. *See* Schumpeterian models of quality ladders

Raftery, Adrian E., 544
Ramsey, Frank, 16–18, 85, 87n, 121–122, 122n, 132
Ramsey model, 85–139, 143–200
adjustment costs for investment, 152–160
behavior of firms, 152–155
equilibrium for closed economy with fixed saving rate, 159–160
equilibrium with given interest rate, 155–159
alternative environments for, 98–99
commitment
degree of commitment, 132
results under commitment, 123–124
results without commitment under log utility, 124–129
equilibrium in, 96, 97–98, 155–160, 164–177, 193–200
finite-horizon version, 179–189
closed economy, 183–186
open economy, 186–189
firm utility, 94–96, 152–155, 192
government in, 143–152
effects of government purchases, 147–152
effects of tax rates, 146–147
modifications of basic framework, 143–146
household utility, 16–17, 86–94
first-order conditions, 89–94
heterogeneity, 118–121
model setup, 86–89
irreversible investment, 134–135
with labor migration, 393–398
model setup, 393
optimization conditions, 394–395
steady state, 395–398
transitional dynamics, 395–398

Ramsey model (cont.)
labor supply in, 86, 393–398
log-linearization, 111–113, 132–134
open-economy model, 161–167, 168–189
economic growth with finite horizons, 179–189
model setup, 161–162
small economy capital stock and output, 162–163
small economy consumption and assets, 163–164
variations in preference parameters, 177–178
world economy with constraint on international credit, 165–177
world equilibrium, 164–165
savings rate in, 103–104, 106–110, 135–139, 159–160, 185–186
steady state in, 95, 99–102, 111–113, 120–121, 124–125, 184, 187–189, 395–398
time-preference rates, 121–134
results under commitment, 123–124
results without commitment under log utility, 124–129
zero rate of time preference, 121
transitional dynamics, 102–121
convergence, 111–118, 167
decline in economy, 137–139
household heterogeneity, 118–121
migration of labor, 395–398
paths of capital stock and output, 110–111
phase diagram, 103–104
policy functions, 105–106
population growth, 129–130
results under isoelastic utility, 130–131
savings rate behavior, 85, 106–110, 135–139
technological progress, 129–130
transversality condition, 90, 91–92, 97–98, 101, 103–105, 135–136
Rapping, Leonard, 213
Rational-expectations revolution, 19
Razin, Assaf, 428
Rebelo, Sergio, 19, 116, 247, 423–424, 424n, 519n
Reciprocal of the elasticity of intertemporal substitution, 90–91
Regional data sets, 461–509
convergence across economies, 462–483
β convergence, 14, 462–463, 466–472, 474–478, 479–482, 495–496
measurement error, 472–473
σ convergence, 462–465, 473–474, 478, 482
European regions
convergence across economies, 479–482
description of data sets, 500–506
migration of labor across, 490–492
Japanese prefectures
convergence across economies, 474–478
description of data sets, 506–509
migration of labor across, 486–490
long-term data on GDP, 559–566
migration of labor, 483–492
other regions, convergence across economies, 482–483
U.S. states
convergence across economies, 466–474
description of data sets, 497–500
migration of labor across, 483–486
Reinganum, Jennifer F., 309, 313, 325n
Renelt, David, 542n, 542–543, 547n
Replication argument, 27
Research and development (R&D), 20, 289–295, 321–328. *See also* Technological progress; Technology diffusion
classification of inventions, 51–53
costs of R&D, 300–305
rising costs, 303–305
scale effects in, 300–302
decision to devote resources to invention, 289, 321–326
decision to enter R&D business, 292–295, 321–322
duration of monopoly position, 324–325, 345–346
free-entry condition, 293–295, 302, 326–328
growth accounting and, 450–456
quality-ladders models, 454–456
varieties models, 451–454
optimal price determination of invention, 290–292, 322–324
sector leader as researcher, 333–338, 346–347
interaction between leader and outsiders, 333–336
leader as monopoly researcher, 336–338
subsidies to research, 300
TFP (total factor productivity) growth and, 450–456
Rhee, Changyong, 155n, 158
Ricardo, David, 16, 17
Rivera-Batiz, Luis A., 293n
Roback, Jennifer, 487
Robinson, James A., 519
Robustness of growth, 541–559
Bayesian Averaging of Classical Estimates (BACE) of, 543–547, 559
Levine and Renelt model for measuring, 542–543
robustness analysis, 556–559
"strong" variables that become "weak," 556–558
"weak" variables that become "strong," 558–559
Sala-i-Martin, Doppelhofer, and Miller model for measuring, 547–556
Rogerson, Richard, 422n
Romer, David, 14, 60, 78, 521
Romer, Paul M., 18–19, 20, 63, 65n, 212–214, 237, 285–286, 293n, 310n, 310–313, 350, 445, 446

Romer's model of technological change, 212–214, 310–313
Rubinstein, Ariel, 121n
Rule of law, GDP growth and, 526–528, 538
Rustichini, Aldo, 269n
Rybzczynski, T. M., 201
Ryder, Harl E., 74

Sachs, Jeffrey D., 166, 166n, 202, 538, 540
Sahay, Ratna, 482–483
Saint-Paul, Gilles, 235
Sala-i-Martin, Xavier, 6n, 7, 7n, 8, 9, 9n, 10, 11, 14, 50n, 78, 114, 166n, 171n, 173, 223, 236, 260, 268, 314, 351, 389, 391, 462, 466n, 471, 474, 479, 484, 541, 543–544, 546n, 547–556
Samuelson, Paul A., 178, 190
Sanchez-Robles, Blanca, 483
Santos, Manuel S., 279
Saratsis, Yannis, 483
Savings rate, 15–16
in overlapping-generations model (OLG), 193, 196–197
oversaving, 101, 196–197
in Ramsey model, 103–104, 106–110, 135–139, 159–160, 185–186
in Solow-Swan model, 25, 38–40, 41–42, 44, 49, 85, 97, 101, 109
in transitional dynamics, 85
in Uzawa-Lucas model, 263–264
Scale effects
constant returns to scale versus, 27, 28, 33
in one-sector models of endogenous growth, 218–220, 223
in Schumpeterian models of quality ladders, 331–332
in technological progress, 297, 300–302
Schmookler, Jacob, 213
Schultz, T. Paul, 408
Schumpeter, Joseph A., 16, 317
Schumpeterian models of quality ladders, 317–347
growth accounting, 454–456
innovation by the leader, 333–338, 346–347
levels of quality in production technology, 319–321, 343–345
market value of firms, 346
model components, 319–332
aggregate quality index, 329–331
consumers, 328–329
producers of final output, 319–321, 343–345
research sector, 321–328
scale effects, 331–332
model setup, 317–319
monopoly power
duration of monopoly position, 324–325, 345–346
interactions between sector leader and outsiders, 333–336
sector leader as monopoly researcher, 336–338
Pareto optimality, 339–342
Schwartz, Mark, 354, 355, 364n
Searle, Allan D., 213
Segerstrom, Paul S., 305n, 349n
Shadow price
of human capital, 249–250
nature of, 92
Shell, Karl, 19n
Sheshinski, Eytan, 18, 19, 213
Shioji, Etruso, 496
Shleifer, Andrei, 74n, 540
Short run, 33–34
Sidrauski, Miguel, 88n, 141
σ convergence
concept of, 462–465
across European regions, 482
across Japanese prefectures, 478
across U.S. states, 473–474
Singapore
economic development in, 350
growth accounting for, 440, 444, 459–460
stability of factor shares, 12
Smit, Hans, 500, 506
Smith, Adam, 16
Social planner. *See* Pareto optimality
Solow, Robert M., 17, 25, 30, 52–53, 68, 80, 433–435, 437
Solow residual, 434–435, 452–454
Solow-Swan model, 23–61
basic structure, 17, 23–26
Cobb-Douglas production function examples, 29–30, 43–44, 49
convergence across economies, 44–51
absolute convergence, 45–46, 65
conditional convergence, 14, 46–50, 65
convergence coefficient, 57, 59, 78
dispersion of per capita income, 50–51
migration of labor, 383, 388–392
properties, 78
quantitative measure of speed of, 56–61
dynamic inefficiency, 36–37
extended model with physical and human capital, 59–61
fundamental equation, 30–31, 37–38, 44
golden rule of capital accumulation, 34–37
input prices during transition, 40–41
with labor migration, 383, 384–392
convergence, 388–392
migration rate, 385–387
model setup, 384–385

Solow-Swan model (cont.)
steady state, 387–388
transitional dynamics, 388–392
labor supply in, 23–24, 26, 31–33, 53–56, 78–80, 383, 384–392
markets in, 31–33
neoclassical model of, 26–30
Cobb-Douglas example, 29–30
neoclassical production function, 26–31, 77–78
policy experiments, 41–43
steady state, 33–34, 34n, 43–44, 387–388
with technological progress, 23–24, 43, 51–56
capital-augmenting, 52–53
classification of inventions, 51–53
labor-augmenting, 53–56, 78–80
transitional dynamics
behavior of input prices during transition, 40–41
with labor migration, 388–392
nature of, 37–40
South Korea
domestic investment/saving in, 15
GDP growth in, 4
growth accounting for, 440, 443, 459–460
long-term GDP data, 564
stability of factor shares, 12
Speed of convergence, 56–61, 111–118, 167. *See also* β convergence
Spence, Michael, 285–286, 286n, 317
Spillovers
in increasing-returns model of growth, 445–449
in one-sector models of endogenous growth, 212–220
Srinivasan, T. N., 248n, 265
State variables, 227, 256, 517
Steady state
defined, 33–34
and migration in models of economic growth, 387–388, 395–398, 403–405
in overlapping-generations model (OLG), 194–195, 416–421
in Ramsey model, 95, 99–102, 111–113, 120–121, 124–125, 184, 187–189, 395–398
in Solow-Swan model, 33–34, 34n, 43–44, 387–388
in technology diffusion, 357–358, 364–368
in two-sector models of endogenous growth, Uzawa-Lucas model, 252–253
Stein, Jerome L., 462
Stiglitz, Joseph E., 119n, 285–286, 286n, 317
Stone, Richard, 178
Strotz, Robert H., 122
Structural transformation, 12n
Subsidies
to final product, 300
to purchase intermediate goods, 299–300, 309
to research, 300
Substitution
constant-elasticity-of-substitution production functions, 68–71, 80–81, 171n, 230–232
constant intertemporal elasticity of substitution (CIES), 91
reciprocal of the elasticity of intertemporal substitution, 90–91
Summers, Lawrence H., 155n, 158
Summers, Robert, 1n, 2, 6n, 22, 23n, 511n, 512, 532n, 560
Swan, Trevor W., 17, 25, 30
Sweden, long-term GDP data, 563
Switzerland
GDP growth in, 2
long-term GDP data, 562

Taiwan
GDP growth in, 1, 4
growth accounting for, 440, 459–460
long-term GDP data, 564
stability of factor shares, 12
Tamura, Robert, 413n
Tanzania, GDP growth in, 2, 3, 4
Taxes
in growth accounting, 447–448
in one-sector models of endogenous growth
capital income taxes, 222
consumption taxes, 221
labor taxes, 221
in Ramsey model extension, 143–147
distortionary tax rates, 147–152
effects of tax rates, 146–147
Technological progress. *See also* Research and development (R&D); Technology diffusion
behavior of imitators in follower country, 352–363
consumers, 357
dynamic path and convergence, 359–363
imitating firms, 353–357
implications for growth rates in follower countries, 370–373
producers of final output, 352–353
steady-state growth, 357–358
welfare considerations, 376–379
behavior of innovators in leading country, 351–352
constant (slowly rising) costs of imitation, 353–355, 363–364
as exogenous, 61–63
foreign investment and, 368–370
intellectual property rights and, 368–370
leapfrogging in, 333–334, 373–376
models with expanding variety of products, 285–313
baseline model with variety of products, 285–305

competition and, 305–310
determinants of growth rate, 297
erosion of monopoly power, 305–310
general equilibrium in, 295–296
growth accounting, 451–454
households in, 295
Pareto optimality, 297–300
producers of final output in, 285–289
R&D costs, 300–305
research firms in, 289–295
Romer's model, 212–214, 310–313
scale effects, 300–302
in neoclassical theory, 18–20
in one-sector models of endogenous growth, 212–215
in Ramsey model, 129–130
Schumpeterian models of quality ladders, 317–347
duration of monopoly position, 324–325, 345–346
growth accounting, 454–456
innovation by the leader, 333–338, 346–347
intermediates of quality grades, 343–345
market value of firms, 346
model components, 319–332
model sketch, 317–319
Pareto optimality, 339–342
in Solow-Swan model, 23–24, 43, 51–56
capital-augmenting, 52–53
classification of inventions, 51–53
labor-augmenting, 53–56, 78–80
steady state for, 364–368
determination of, 364–365
imitators in follower country, 357–358
transitional dynamics in, 365–368
switchovers of technological leadership, 333–334, 373–376
transitional dynamics for, 359–363, 365–368
Technology diffusion, 20, 349–379. *See also* Research and development (R&D).
Teece, David J., 355, 368n
Temple, Jonathan, 543n
Temple, Robert, 376n
Terleckyj, Nestor E., 450n
Terms of trade, GDP growth and, 530–531
TFP (total factor productivity) growth, 434–435. *See also* Growth accounting
dual approach to growth accounting, 435, 442–444
regression-based estimates of, 441–442
research and development (R&D) and, 450–456
standard primal approach to growth accounting, 433–442
Thailand
GDP growth in, 4
long-term GDP data, 565
Thaler, Richard, 122n
Thompson, Peter, 332
Thomsen, James, 159n, 177
Time-elimination method, 114
Time-preference rates in Ramsey model, 121–134
results under commitment, 123–124
results without commitment under log utility, 124–129
zero rate of time preference, 121
Tobin, James, 155
Total factor productivity (TFP) growth. *See* TFP (total factor productivity) growth
Trajtenberg, Manuel, 451
Transitional dynamics
defined, 33–34
and migration in models of economic growth, 388–392, 395–398, 403–405
nature of, 37–40
in one-sector models of endogenous growth, 216, 226–232
AK model, 66–68, 208–209
inequality restrictions on gross investment, 271–274
in overlapping-generations model (OLG), 197–198, 416–421
in Ramsey model, 102–121
convergence, 111–118, 167
decline in economy, 137–139
household heterogeneity, 118–121
migration of labor, 395–398
paths of capital stock and output, 110–111
phase diagram, 102–104
policy function, 105–106
population growth, 129–130
results under isoelastic utility, 130–131
savings rate in, 85, 106–110, 135–139
technological progress, 129–130
transversality condition, 90, 91–92, 97–98, 101, 103–105, 135–136
in Solow-Swan model
behavior of input prices during transition, 40–41
endogenous growth models, 66–68
migration of labor, 388–392
for technology diffusion, 359–363, 365–368
in two-sector models of endogenous growth, Uzawa-Lucas model, 253–256
Transversality condition
importance of, 104–105
in Ramsey model, 90, 91–92, 97–98, 101, 103–105, 135–136
Trejo, Stephen J., 390, 390n, 391
Tsiddon, Daniel, 335n, 375, 376
Turkey, GDP growth in, 4
Two-sector models of endogenous growth, 239–282
conditions for endogenous growth, 268–271
described, 247–251

Two-sector models of endogenous growth (cont.)
 Uzawa-Lucas model, 251–268
  basic framework, 251–252
  generalized version, 266–267
  inequality restrictions on gross investment, 264–266
  policy functions, 256–257
  with reversed factor intensities, 267–268, 280–282
  saving rate, 263–264
  solution, 274–279
  steady-state analysis, 252–253
  transitional behavior of growth rates, 257–263
  transitional dynamics, 253–256

Unemployment, involuntary, 88
United Kingdom
 domestic investment/saving in, 15
 growth accounting for, 439
 long-term GDP data, 562
 number of R&D scientists and engineers, 310
 R&D outlays versus GDP, 301
 stability of factor shares, 12–13
 in switchovers of technological leadership, 376
United States
 convergence across economies, 466–474
  β convergence, 466–472
  measurement error, 472–473
  σ convergence, 473–474
 domestic investment/saving in, 15
 GDP growth in, 1, 4, 13
 growth accounting for, 439, 443
 income distribution in, 7
 labor migration across states, 483–486
 long-term GDP data, 562
 number of R&D scientists and engineers, 310
 R&D outlays versus GDP, 301
 regional data sets, 497–500
 stability of factor shares, 12
 in switchovers of technological leadership, 376
USSR, former, income distribution in, 7
Utrera, Gaston Ezequiel, 483
Uzawa, Hirofumi, 19, 177, 239, 248n, 251, 265, 267, 270
Uzawa-Lucas model, 251–268
 basic framework, 251–252
 generalized version, 266–267
 inequality restrictions on gross investment, 264–266
 policy functions, 256–257
 with reversed intensities, 267–268, 280–282
 saving rate, 263–264
 solution, 274–279
 steady-state analysis, 252–253
 transitional behavior of growth rates, 257–263
 transitional dynamics, 253–256

Van Holst, Bas, 500, 506
Ventura, Jaume, 19n, 119, 121, 201, 248n
Vickers, John, 322n, 342n
Villaverde, Jose, 483
Vishny, Robert W., 74n, 540
Von Furstenberg, George M., 155n
Von Neumann, John, 63n

Wacziarg, Romain, 540n
Wage rates. *See also* Labor supply; Migration of labor
 in *AK* model, 206
 in Ramsey model, 88, 180–182, 185
 in Solow-Swan model, 40–41
 taxes on wages, 146
Wagner, Samuel, 354, 355, 364n
Wahl, Jenny Bourne, 408
Wang, Ping, 247n, 266n, 267n
Wealth. *See also* Income distribution
 consumption function as function of, 181–183
 in Schumpeterian models of quality ladders, 346
Weeks, Melvyn, 483
Weil, David N., 14, 60, 78, 408n, 413n, 521
Weil, Philippe, 183, 199, 393, 395
Welch, Finis, 185–186
Welfare, technology diffusion implications, 376–379
Williamson, Jeffrey G., 389, 391
Woodberry, Robert D., 519–520
World economy
 convergence across regions of world, 482–483
 cross-country growth in. *See* Growth rates
 equilibrium in Ramsey model extension, 164–177
 income distribution, 6–12
 migration of labor in, 383–407
  Braun model, 398–407
  Ramsey model, 393–398
  Solow-Swan model, 383, 384–392
 steady state, 187
Wright, Randall, 422n
Wright, Theodore P., 213

Xie, Danyang, 269n

Yaari, Menahem E., 179–180
Yao, Yudong, 483
Yip, C. K., 247n, 266n, 267n, 440n
York, Jeremy C., 544
Young, Allwyn, 12, 13, 16, 332, 350, 376n, 440n, 441, 443

Zaire. *See* Democratic Republic of Congo
Zeira, Joseph, 74n